What's Wrong?

What's Wrong?

Applied Ethicists and
Their Critics

SECOND EDITION

David Boonin
University of Colorado at Boulder

Graham Oddie
University of Colorado at Boulder

New York   Oxford
OXFORD UNIVERSITY PRESS
2010

Oxford University Press, Inc., publishes works that further Oxford University's
objective of excellence in research, scholarship, and education.

Oxford New York
Auckland   Cape Town   Dar es Salaam   Hong Kong   Karachi
Kuala Lumpur   Madrid   Melbourne   Mexico City   Nairobi
New Delhi   Shanghai   Taipei   Toronto

With offices in
Argentina   Austria   Brazil   Chile   Czech Republic   France   Greece
Guatemala   Hungary   Italy   Japan   Poland   Portugal   Singapore
South Korea   Switzerland   Thailand   Turkey   Ukraine   Vietnam

Published by Oxford University Press, Inc.
198 Madison Avenue, New York, New York 10016
http://www.oup.com

Oxford is a registered trademark of Oxford University Press

Library of Congress Cataloging-in-Publication Data

What's wrong?: applied ethicists and their critics/[edited by] David Boonin, Graham Oddie.
   p. cm.
   Includes bibliographical references and index.
   ISBN 978-0-19-533780-8
   1. Applied ethics—Textbooks. I. Boonin, David. II. Oddie, Graham, 1954–
   BJ1031.B66 2010
   170—dc22   2008035080

Printed in the United States of America
on acid-free paper

CONTENTS

ACKNOWLEDGMENTS

The editors wish to thank Julie van Camp, Kenneth Henly, Lawrence Pasternak, and Russ Shafer-Landau for their useful suggestions and to express particular gratitude to Ben Eggleston for his especially careful and probing comments and criticisms.

What's Wrong?

INTRODUCTION

What's Wrong with Arguing?

1 The Importance of Being Argumentative

The word *philosophy* derives from the Greek words *philein*, meaning "to love," and *sophia*, meaning "wisdom." Philosophy is therefore often defined as the love of wisdom. But if one examines the actual practice of people who call themselves philosophers, this common definition might well seem mistaken. The behavior of such people suggests that philosophy is not so much the love of wisdom as the love of argument. Philosophers are people who love to argue.

Ethics is that branch of philosophy concerned with both the content and the nature of morality, and applied ethics is that branch of ethics that concerns itself with practical moral questions. Is abortion morally permissible? Is it wrong to hunt animals for sport or to slaughter them for food? What, if anything, do children owe their parents? Should human cloning be permitted? Applied ethicists are people who love to argue about these sorts of questions.

That applied ethicists are people who love to argue about practical moral questions should be clear from even a quick look at almost any anthology in the field. Such works typically contain articles in which philosophers examine a particular moral controversy and make a point of not simply taking a stand on it but of attempting to offer an argument in defense of a position on the issue, or an argument against some rival position. Typically, in presenting an argument, a philosopher will identify some plausible claims from which to argue and then provide reasoning to show that if those claims are true, then a certain position on the issue must be the right one, or some rival position must be wrong. The claims from which philosophers argue we call the "premises" of their argument. The claim for which they argue we call the "conclusion" of their argument. Although philosophers do not always explicitly identify the premises and conclusion of each argument, those elements are present in every argument nonetheless. This much should be clear from reading any good piece of work in applied ethics or from perusing any anthology in the field.

But philosophers are not simply people who love to argue. They are people who love to argue with one another, to engage in a dialogue, discussing the merits and demerits of a single line of argument. When one person offers an argument in defense of abortion, say, and another

1

counters with a different argument against abortion, the two are arguing about abortion, but they are not arguing with each other in the way that is characteristic of philosophers. In order for them to be arguing with each other as philosophers do, one of them must offer an argument in defense of a particular conclusion about abortion, and the other must then offer, not a second argument in defense of a different conclusion about abortion, but rather an argument about the first argument about abortion. For people to argue with each other is for them to participate in a shared dialogue about a single argument, to work together to clarify that argument's content and structure, to probe its strengths and weaknesses, to discuss its merits, to uncover its implications, and to debate whether or not it should be accepted or rejected. This, above all else, is what philosophers do. And this is the most important thing that philosophers do.

That philosophers love not simply to argue but to argue with each other should be clear to anyone who has ever spent time in a room with more than one philosopher (and sometimes even one philosopher is enough!). It should be especially clear to anyone who has ever attended a convention of the American Philosophical Association. Almost every paper presented at that convention is immediately followed by a second, shorter paper that directly addresses the argument made in the first paper, typically by making some criticism of it. The author of the first paper will then typically respond to the commentator's criticisms, and toward the end of the discussion, members of the audience will raise additional questions and offer yet more comments as a way of advancing the dialogue still further. In addition, many of the featured papers at such conventions are themselves attempts to comment on arguments proposed in still earlier papers. The titles of papers that philosophers present to address other philosophers' arguments are routinely filled with such phrases as "a reply to" this philosopher, "a response to" that one, and "why" a third philosopher "is wrong."

Someone unfamiliar with the habits of philosophers would be likely to walk away from such a scene wondering what the point was of all of the bickering. Isn't it a foolish waste of time and energy to argue endlessly about pressing practical problems, problems for which we need good solutions to act on right now? And isn't foolishness the very opposite of the wisdom that philosophers are traditionally supposed to love?

This reaction to the seemingly endless arguments and counterarguments generated by philosophers is understandable, but it is mistaken. For philosophers do not argue merely for the sake of arguing (even though one might be forgiven for sometimes thinking that they do!). Arguing, the true philosopher understands, is not an end in itself. Rather, philosophers argue because they are interested in determining whether or not a particular view is more or less reasonable than its rivals. A reason for adopting a moral view can be best formulated as an argument in defense of that view. To evaluate the reasonableness of a moral view is thus to evaluate the reasons in favor of adopting that view, which in turn is to evaluate the arguments that people have found persuasive for embracing the view. Argumentation is thus valuable because evaluating reasons is valuable. The wise person would surely want to avoid unreasonable, inconsistent, or poorly thought out moral views. So, argument is valuable precisely because it is our best tool, indeed our only tool, for attaining a consistent and reasonable moral outlook. In addition, by arguing with others who recognize the value of reason and argument, we are much more likely to discover both the weaknesses and strengths of our arguments than we would be if we simply contemplated our own arguments in isolation from others. For creatures such as we are, then, the love of arguing with others who love to argue is an indispensable asset in the pursuit of wisdom. Wisdom may be our ultimate goal, but we make progress toward it only by engaging in honest and open argument.

2   THE STRUCTURE OF THIS ANTHOLOGY

Arguing with each other is thus an essential feature of what it is to practice philosophy in general and applied ethics in particular. This much is clear to those who work in the field, but this crucial aspect of the discipline is all too often rendered invisible to students who learn about philosophy in the classroom. For example, virtually every anthology used in applied ethics courses includes philosophers presenting a variety of arguments on a single *issue,* but virtually none is devoted to philosophers presenting a variety of analyses of a single *argument.* Philosophers in most such anthologies argue, but they do not argue with one another.

To present philosophers arguing with one another about important questions in applied ethics is the central purpose of this book. To accomplish this, we have organized each chapter of the book not simply around a particular moral issue but around a particular moral argument—an argument that has been developed in an attempt to help resolve a particular moral issue and that has been recognized as sufficiently important to merit the critical attention of other philosophers. This central argument is contained in what we refer to as the "featured article," the article that initiates and is the focal point of the set of readings for each chapter. The featured article is then followed by one or more critical-response pieces. The vast majority of these pieces are direct responses to the featured article in question, but even those that are not still address the argument (or arguments) contained in the featured article. By studying the featured article along with the critical response or responses to it, the reader will develop a clearer and more thorough understanding of some of the important ways in which the argument contained in the featured article can be subjected to critical scrutiny.

In addition, each chapter in this anthology is preceded by an editor's introduction. These introductions clarify the thesis defended in the featured article, outline the structure of the argument presented in defense of that thesis, and help the reader to think clearly and specifically about just how the critical-response pieces relate to the original argument. A typical introduction to a chapter will help the reader to think about how the argument contained in the featured article can be stated clearly and explicitly by representing it as a set of premises leading to a conclusion. The introduction will go on to explain how the critical-response pieces can then be understood as criticisms of that particular argument, thereby helping the reader to see clearly and specifically just how the critical-response pieces relate to the original argument. Finally, for those who wish to "follow the trail" of the argument still further, many of the chapters conclude with suggestions for further reading, including additional articles written in response to the featured article and, whenever possible, subsequent works by the authors of the featured articles in which they attempt to address some of the objections that have been raised against their original pieces.

3   ARGUMENTS IN GENERAL

The best way to learn about philosophical argumentation is simply to engage in it. Thus, the best way to learn from this volume is not simply to read the articles it contains, but to discuss them critically with others who have also read them (and even with those who have not). Before jumping into the fray by looking in detail at a particular moral controversy, however, it may be useful to consider a few features of moral argument in general and a few kinds of moral argument in particular. Doing so is the principal goal of the remainder of this introduction.

3.1 What Arguments Are

It is important to begin by being very clear about just what it means to offer an argument in defense of a conclusion. A person might be opposed to a particular practice because the very thought of that practice makes him upset, for example, or disgusted. But basing one's opposition to a practice on the experience of such feelings is not the same as basing it on an argument. As we have noted already, an argument always involves a conclusion, the thesis that is being argued for or supported. The claims that are used to support the conclusion are the premises. The premises are supposed to entail the conclusion. The argument will constitute a reason for adopting the conclusion if two things are true: First, the premises are all plausible, and second, they really do jointly entail the conclusion. Any argument can thus be subjected to two different kinds of criticism. The first kind of criticism attacks the plausibility of one or more of the premises. The second kind attacks the claim that the premises entail the conclusion.

3.2 Evaluating Entailment Claims

What does it mean for some premises to entail a conclusion? It may help to begin with a simple single-premise example, where P is shorthand for "premise" and C for "conclusion" (a convention we apply throughout this book). A line is drawn to separate the premise or premises from the conclusion.

P   Any action that results in the death of a person is morally wrong.

C   Abortion is morally wrong.

One might criticize this argument, of course, by taking issue with the premise itself. It does not take much imagination, after all, to come up with at least a few cases in which an act resulted in the death of a person but in which we nonetheless believe that the act was not morally wrong. But even before we consider the question of whether or not we should accept the argument's premise, we might well wonder if the premise would be enough to justify the conclusion, even if the premise turned out to be true. We might wonder, in short, whether or not the premise really entailed the conclusion. The idea of entailment that we would employ in such a case, and the sense of entailment that is most relevant to our purposes here, runs as follows: For C to follow from P, the truth of P would have to guarantee the truth of C. Anyone who accepted P but rejected C would be implicitly endorsing incompatible claims. If P entailed C, anyone who accepted P would thereby be rationally obliged to accept C as well.

Is that the case with this argument? Grant, for the moment, that the premise is correct. Imagine, that is, that P really does articulate a correct moral principle. Granting that P is correct, can you think of any way in which the conclusion might still be incorrect? If you can, then that shows that even if you accept P, you are not thereby rationally obliged to accept C as well. So, to show that C does not follow from P, all you have to do is describe one possible way in which the premise might be correct while the conclusion is nevertheless incorrect.

Here is one slightly artificial way. First, note that a human embryo, for example, might be aborted—that is to say, expelled from the womb—as the result of human intervention, but that it might also abort spontaneously, without any human action precipitating the expulsion. In the case of a spontaneous abortion, the embryo is aborted, but the abortion was not an action. And it might well not be the result of any action at all. For example, it might have been an expulsion triggered by a genetic defect in the embryo itself. In such a case, no action is performed to bring the abortion about. So, even granted the correctness of P, if no action is performed, then no wrong action is performed. Accepting P does not, therefore, make it obligatory to accept C. And thus, as a result, there is no entailment between P and C. The argument is logically invalid, and this is so regardless of whether or not we ought to accept the argument's premise.

The kind of case we have just outlined is called a "counterexample" to the validity of an argument. A counterexample is a case in which the premise or premises of an argument are true but the conclusion of the argument is nonetheless false. One might suspect that this particular counterexample involves some kind of trick. After all, one might insist, anyone who seriously advanced the argument in question would have been thinking only of the class of induced abortions, abortions that are brought about by an intentional human act. That is, they would have been tacitly assuming that the term *abortion* as it appears in C does not embrace all cases of abortion and, in particular, does not embrace cases of spontaneous abortion. However, even if this is what a proponent of the argument was assuming, it is nonetheless a defect of the argument that it fails to make this assumption explicit. In argumentation, it is important to make explicit what one has in mind and not leave it to your opponent to fill in the gaps. After all, the whole point of making your argument public, whether through speaking or writing, is to communicate to another what you have in mind. Good argumentation avoids ambiguities where ambiguities might be important to the validity of the argument.

Let us eliminate somewhat contrived counterexamples by agreeing to mean by "abortion" the intentional act of expelling an embryo or fetus from the womb. We will save the word *miscarriage* for spontaneous abortions. Even if we do agree to use words in this way, there are other, less artificial counterexamples that count against the validity of this argument. For example, many people deny that a human fetus—or at least a human fetus at relatively early stages of gestation—is a person. It is a potential person, they might concede, but not yet an actual person. Suppose they are right about this. Then, it would turn out that some (or many, or all) abortions do not result in the death of a person at all, even though they do result in the death of a human embryo or fetus. You yourself might not agree with this position. You might firmly believe that every human fetus is a person from the moment of conception onward. But even if you do believe this, you will still have to acknowledge that the premises of the argument presented earlier do not explicitly say this. It would be invalid to move from the claim that bringing about the death of a person is wrong to the conclusion that bringing about the death of a human fetus is wrong without relying on a further claim that all human fetuses are persons. Without this additional premise, the earlier argument is, once again, shown to be invalid. Granting the premise that any action that results in the death of a person is wrong does not, in and of itself, rationally oblige one to accept the conclusion that abortion is wrong. And that is just to say that P does not entail C.

3.3 Evaluating Premises

The sample argument we used in the previous section is a poor one, not just because the conclusion does not follow from the premise, but also because the premise itself is clearly defective. Hardly anyone would be willing to grant that it is a correct moral principle. For a start, hardly anyone thinks that it is always and everywhere wrong to kill a person, no matter what the circumstances. For example, most people consider killing in self-defense to be morally permissible. Also, most people think that it would have been morally permissible, indeed, morally praiseworthy, to have killed Hitler at various stages of his career. But even if one thought that it was always and everywhere wrong to kill someone, P might still be false. For we can make a distinction between intentionally doing something that leads directly to the death of a person (say, deliberately and intentionally administering a lethal dose of poison to your son) and doing something that unintentionally happens to bring about a person's death (say, accidentally administering a dose of lethal poison to your son believing it to be his daily dose of vitamins). Now, a case of accidentally poisoning someone might be a morally wrong action under certain conditions—you might have been negligent, or careless, for example—but not under others. We can certainly imagine cases in which bringing about a person's death would not be morally wrong but rather a genuine and forgivable accident, one that happens to produce a terrible unintended consequence. The premise of our sample argument is thus implausible.

We have said, "hardly anyone thinks that it is always and everywhere wrong to kill a person, no matter what the circumstances." It does not follow from the fact that most people think that something is morally permissible, however, that it actually is morally permissible. People can get things wrong in moral matters just as they can in factual matters. Most people in the United States in the eighteenth century, for example, thought that slavery was permissible; but that fact didn't make slavery permissible. This should be clear for the following reason. A minority of people can clearly endorse immoral practices. And those practices hardly become more moral if the minority recruits further adherents to its immoral point of view. Moreover, since there is nothing morally magical about the figure 50 percent, when an immoral minority manages to recruit more than half of a given population, its immoral outlook does not thereby become magically transformed into a moral one. The fact that a majority of people hold a particular moral view, therefore, does not guarantee that that moral view is the correct one.

So, it might well be asked, why do we bother citing the fact that most people believe there are circumstances in which it is permissible to kill a person? If this fact does not in itself entail that there actually are circumstances in which it is permissible to kill a person, of what possible value can it be in a critical analysis of the simple argument we have been looking at here?

The answer to this question is perhaps best framed in terms of a particular debate taking place between a particular pair of people. So, suppose that Pam and Dan are having an argument about the simple one-premise argument noted earlier. And suppose that in the course of this argument, Dan endorses the principle that any action that results in the death of a person is morally wrong. Pam decides to challenge Dan by citing the case of a nonnegligent, forgivable accident that results in someone's death. In citing this case, Pam is assuming that Dan will agree with her that there was nothing morally wrong about the person who accidentally killed someone. If Dan does agree with Pam about this case, then if he wants to be rational he will have to give up his principle, because his judgment on the case is inconsistent with an endorsement of that principle. To be rational, one must have consistent beliefs. If, on the other hand, Dan disagrees with Pam about the case, then Pam will have to find another case on which she and Dan do agree and use that other case as a means of forcing Dan to abandon his commitment to the general principle. In order for two people to argue profitably with each other they have to appeal to at least some cases and judgments on which they both agree.

If they agree on absolutely nothing (and that is highly unlikely), then it will be virtually impossible for them to engage in a profitable philosophical exchange. So, the point of saying "hardly anyone thinks such and such" is to emphasize the enormous size of the class of people who will make a certain moral judgment on a particular case and who will thus have to take the case seriously. If their considered judgment on that case is inconsistent with a principle they endorse, then, if they want to be rational participants in their quest for wisdom, they will have to give up the principle in question. The more people who agree about a particular case, therefore, the more powerful that case will be as a means of advancing public debate over a particular argument.

This first argument we examined, of course, was a very simple one. A somewhat more complex version of an argument against abortion might be represented in the following multipremise manner (where P1 is short for "premise 1" and so on).

P1   Abortion kills a fetus or an embryo.
P2   A fetus or an embryo is an innocent human being.
P3   Killing an innocent human being is murder.
P4   Murder is morally wrong.
_____
C   Abortion is morally wrong.

Although the authors of the various articles in this anthology rarely present their views using precisely this explicit format (P1, P2, etc.), their arguments can always be reconstructed in this more formal manner. The introductions to most of the featured articles in this text provide suggestions about how to go about developing such reconstructions.

Reconstructing an argument in this illustrative premise-and-conclusion format is useful, in part because it can help one visualize the overall structure of an author's reasoning. In the case of the argument against abortion outlined earlier, for example, the reconstruction helps to make explicit the manner in which the argument attempts to show that abortion is wrong by subsuming it under a broader class of actions that is generally recognized to be wrong—the killing of innocent human beings. But representing arguments in this formal manner is also important as a means of thinking clearly about the various ways in which an argument might be productively criticized.

The preceding argument, for example, is indeed valid. The premises really do jointly entail the conclusion. To see this, note that P1 and P2 together entail that abortion is the killing of an innocent human being. Together with P3, this entails that abortion is murder. That abortion is murder, together with P4, entails that abortion is morally wrong, the conclusion. If the premises are all true, then the conclusion is also true. So, in looking for possible ways to criticize this argument, we will not waste time trying to construct a counterexample to the validity of the argument (although it might be an informative exercise to do so).

The fact that this argument is valid does not mean that its conclusion is true. A valid argument may have a false premise, and if it does have a false premise, then it does not provide a good reason for endorsing its conclusion. Any good criticism of this argument will therefore have to take issue with one or more of the premises. Breaking the argument down into a series of clear, specific premises like this enables us to see more clearly that objecting to some of the assumptions made by the argument will be relatively less promising than objecting to others. In the argument under consideration here, for example, one premise that looks fairly unassailable is P4: the claim that murder is morally wrong. Indeed, by "murder" we generally mean "a wrongful killing of a person." So P4 comes very close to being not only true, but true by definition, and therefore there is not much to be gained by spending time on that premise.

Someone who thought this argument is defective might therefore instead turn his or her attention to P3, the claim that killing an innocent human being is murder. Is the killing of an innocent human being always and everywhere a case of murder, a wrongful killing? Is anyone who kills an innocent human being a murderer? Suppose someone has suffered severe and irreparable brain damage in an automobile accident, has gone into an irreversible coma, and is being kept alive on a heart-lung machine. To switch the machine off would be to do something intentionally to cause that person to die—in other words, to kill him. Let us also suppose that this comatose person is innocent (that is, prior to his accident, he had not, for example, done anything to deserve the death penalty). He is also a human being. Is it a case of murder to turn off the heart-lung machine? This case may be controversial, as we will see in chapter 2, on euthanasia, but most of us would judge it not to be a case of murder. Those who judged the case in this manner would then find that this was a reason to reject the argument's third premise.

Perhaps you think that switching the machine off is not really killing the patient. You might think that it is merely letting him die, and you might think that letting-die is sometimes morally permissible. This is a controversial issue, which we will also address (again in chapter 2). But in the meantime, think about this: Imagine that you are the person on the heart-lung machine and that, unlike the man in the preceding story, you are conscious. Imagine also that if someone unplugs your machine you will die. An intruder, someone who happens to be an enemy of yours, climbs in the hospital window and pulls out the plug in order to ensure your death. Would that not be a case of killing? And if that is a case of killing, why is the earlier case not also a killing?

Of course, when we are asked to imagine cases involving the killing of human beings, we typically imagine cases of murder. When we think of the killing of human beings, we are generally not thinking of unusual human beings, such as irreversibly comatose patients. So, we might initially be inclined to assent to P3 uncritically, until we are presented with an unusual case such as the one involving the intruder. But when we initially think of the killing of human beings, we do not think about other, nonstandard cases of human beings, such as a newly fertilized ovum or a four-week-old fetus. We tend to assent to general moral principles on the basis of typical, rather than atypical, cases. And so the extension of a principle from these typical cases (killing people like you or me) to atypical cases (killing irreparably brain-damaged and irreversibly comatose people or killing embryos and fetuses) might turn out to be unjustified. In such cases, what initially seems to be a plausible and acceptable premise turns out, upon reflection, to represent an unwarranted generalization.

Sometimes adherents to a general principle such as that contained in P3 will try to rescue that principle from the apparent force of such potential counterexamples by reinterpreting a key term in the principle. For example, they might say, "My agreeing that it isn't wrong to turn off the life-support machine for the irreversibly comatose guy is not a violation of the principle I'm defending because the irreversibly comatose guy isn't a real human being anymore. And since he isn't a human being, in my sense of the term, it doesn't matter if I agree with you that killing him is not murder. The general moral principle I support in P3 does not say that all killings are murder, just that all killings of innocent human beings are. And since I don't think this guy is a human being, the fact that killing him is not murder can't count as a counterexample to my general principle."

The problem with this line of defense is that it appears to make use of one sense of the term *human being* to protect the general moral principle from these counterexamples while making use of quite another sense of the term in order to apply the principle to, say, the killing of human embryos. If we retain a broad conception of *human being*—an organism of a particular biological species, *Homo sapiens*—then both the human embryo and the irreversibly comatose patient count as human beings. That much they both have in common with a fully grown, fully functioning, noncomatose human. If it is wrong to kill human beings in that broad biological sense, then, of course, it is wrong to kill any one of the three, and the argument succeeds. But on the broad conception of what is meant by the term *human being*, as we have seen, it is not at all clear that the principle in P3 is correct. Once we agree that it is not wrong to turn off the life-support machine on the permanently comatose patient, then it is not always wrong to kill innocent human beings in the broad sense. To maintain adherence to P3, we would have to employ a narrower conception of human being, one that excludes the being on the life-support machine. But then we as yet have no reason to accept that it does not also exclude the newly fertilized egg, or embryo or fetus as well, in which case P2 cannot be maintained. So whatever meaning of *human being* we choose, at least one of the two premises we are looking at here will prove to be unacceptable. Whenever an argument contains the same term in two different premises—as in the case of the preceding argument, which contains the term *human being* in both P2 and P3—the argument's validity depends crucially on the term's being used to mean precisely the same thing in both premises. If, as in this example, it turns out that P2 is true in one sense of the term and P3 is true in another sense of the term but that there is no one sense in which both P2 and P3 are true, then the argument must be rejected. This problem is commonly referred to as "equivocation," and readers should be alert to the possibility of equivocations lurking in many of the arguments contained in this work.

4   ARGUMENTS IN PARTICULAR

While the notion of logical entailment applies across the board to arguments whatever their form, arguments come in a great variety of shapes and sizes. We cannot provide an exhaustive discussion here of all existing argument forms or of all the critical strategies most promising for evaluating each one of them. However, it is worth examining in some detail a few particularly important and fundamental argument structures that recur at a number of points in this anthology.

4.1 Arguments from Analogy

Arguments from analogy are among the most common kind of argument found in applied ethics. Careful readers will notice the important role that arguments from analogy play in many of the featured articles in this collection, including those in chapters 2, 5, 10, 13, 14, 15, 18, 21, 22, and 27, as well as in many of the response pieces to these and other articles.

4.1.1 *Understanding Arguments from Analogy*

An argument from analogy attempts to justify our accepting a moral assessment of a particular practice by comparing it with a second practice about which most people are already in agreement. Such an argument can be represented more formally (the argument is cashed out here in terms of a practice's being wrong, although everything that is said here would apply equally to cases involving a practice's being permissible, obligatory, bad, good, etc.) as follows:

P1   Practice 1 is wrong.
P2   Practice 2 is morally analogous to (morally on a par with) practice 1.

C   Practice 2 is wrong.

In the article "Famine, Affluence, and Morality," for example, which serves as the featured article in chapter 5, Peter Singer appeals to an analogy between refraining from donating money to a famine-relief effort and refraining from wading into a shallow pond to rescue a small child who will otherwise drown. Virtually everyone would agree that it would be morally wrong not to wade in and save the child, especially in the case where doing so posed no risk of harm to the rescuer and resulted only in his getting his clothes dirty. Singer's argument suggests that the two cases are morally analogous because in each case one person can prevent something very bad from happening to another at only a trivial cost to himself. But if we agree that it would be wrong not to save the child in the shallow-pond case, and if we also agree that the shallow-pond case is morally analogous to the famine-relief case, then Singer's quite strong conclusion seems to follow: that when people refrain from sending money to famine-relief efforts, they behave in a manner that is positively and seriously immoral. This argument in defense of the moral obligation to contribute to famine-relief efforts can be represented as follows:

P1   Refraining from saving the child in the shallow-pond case is wrong.
P2   Refraining from saving the child in the shallow-pond case is morally on a par with refraining from sending money to famine relief.

C   Refraining from sending money to famine relief is wrong.

Reasoning by analogy is one of the most important argumentative tools that moral philosophers have available to them. When used effectively, it can help to resolve a controversial issue by framing it in terms of a less controversial one. A large number of the readings that follow make use of appeals to such analogies. Readers should keep a sharp eye out for these throughout this anthology.

When examining an argument from analogy, it is important to understand as clearly as possible precisely what the argument is meant to establish and precisely why the analogy is supposed to help to establish it. In the case of Singer's argument, for example, one would first have to clarify the argument's thesis: Is it simply that it is a good thing to give money to famine relief, or that it is positively wrong not to give? One would then need to focus in some detail on the analogy itself: What exactly is involved in the story Singer tells? Why does he think it is relevantly analogous to the famine-relief case? And why is he so confident that we will share his assessment of it? When all of these questions can be answered, one can reasonably say that one has a fair and accurate understanding of the argument itself.

4.1.2 Criticizing Arguments from Analogy

After one has attained a clear grasp of an argument, the next step is to subject that argument to critical scrutiny. Since arguments from analogy can almost always be expressed in the simple two-premise format used earlier, there are typically two options available to the argument's critics: They can challenge the assessment of the example offered by the argument's author, or they can accept the assessment of the example but deny that it is relevantly analogous to the problem the argument is designed to resolve. Using Singer's argument, for example, the critic could either maintain that it would not be wrong to let the child in the shallow pond drown or agree that doing so would be wrong but deny that this is relevantly analogous to the case of declining to contribute money to famine-relief efforts. Since most of the analogies to which the arguments in this text appeal involve cases about which most people seem to agree (most people do, for example, seem to agree that it would be wrong not to save the child in Singer's shallow-pond case), the more promising strategy in developing a thoughtful, critical response to such arguments will typically involve trying to identify a disanalogy between the example the author appeals to and the issue with which he or she compares it.

In order to be successful in identifying a disanalogy, the critic of an argument from analogy must establish two things: that there is a difference between the two cases and that the difference is a morally relevant one. Merely identifying a difference is not, in and of itself, sufficient to undermine an argument from analogy. Suppose, for example, that a critic of Singer's argument pointed out that the child drowning in the shallow pond was wet, while the children dying of hunger were dry. This would, indeed, identify a difference between the two cases. Being wet is not the same thing as being dry. But since the difference between a wet child dying and a dry child dying does not seem to be morally relevant, this difference would fail to undermine Singer's argument. If there are no other differences between the two cases—differences that do seem to be morally relevant—then Singer would be justified in maintaining that if it is wrong not to help in one case, then it is (equally) wrong not to help in the other.

In the case of the difference between wet and dry, it is fairly clear and uncontroversial that the difference is not in itself a morally relevant one. But there are other kinds of differences that might be pointed to about which things might not be so clear. For example, a critic of Singer's argument might point out that in one case the child is very near us while in the other the child is very far, or that one child is a member of our community and the other is not, or that the help one can offer in one case is direct and in the other indirect, and so on. An excellent first step in critiquing an argument from analogy is to try to come up with a list of as many differences between the two cases as possible. But once we have found differences between the two cases, how do we decide if the differences are relevant ones?

4.1.3 The Technique of Variant Cases

One useful procedure involves the appeal to what are often referred to as "variant cases." To illustrate this technique let us focus on the simple case of the wet/dry difference as an objection to Singer's shallow-pond argument. (What is said here will apply equally to many other objections to Singer's argument and to many objections to many other arguments from analogy.) So suppose that you were genuinely uncertain about whether or not to treat the difference between wet and dry as a morally relevant one. The technique of variant cases would tell you to begin by constructing a case that is just like the shallow-pond case but that has been altered to correct for the wet/dry variable. What is required, then, is a case in which we have a child who is about to die, as is in the shallow-pond story, but who is dry, as would be the situation in the famine-relief case. And, ideally, we want a case that is in every other respect just like the original shallow-pond case. In this way, we can ensure that we are focusing clearly and precisely on the exact question at hand: Is the wet/dry difference itself a morally relevant one? There are many possible scenarios that might be imagined here. Readers will become more adept at case construction the more they encounter such arguments, but as an illustration of the technique, we will provide one possibility here. Suppose that the child who is drowning is drowning in quicksand rather than in water, so that although he is drowning, he is not getting wet. You know that you are easily tall and strong enough to wade into the quicksand in order to rescue him without any risk of harm to yourself, although doing so will cause you to get your clothes dirty, just as it would in the original version of the shallow-pond case.

After you have arrived at a suitable variant case—such as the case of the child drowning in quicksand—the technique of variant cases adds a second step: Consider the variant case and ask if your intuitive reaction to it is any different from what it was to the original case. Do you think that it would be okay to let the (dry) child drown in the variant case, for example, even though you thought that it would be wrong to let the (wet) child drown in the original case? Or do you find the prospect of letting the (dry) child drown just as wrong as you did in the original version of the story when the child was wet? Finally, assuming that you can give a fairly definitive answer to this question, the technique permits you to draw a conclusion about the merits of the objection under consideration. If the change from the original case to a suitably constructed variant case makes no difference to your moral assessment of the case, then this is evidence that the difference between the two cases (wet versus dry in this instance) is not a morally relevant one; if the change from the original case to a suitably constructed variant case does make a difference to your assessment, then this counts as some evidence that the difference between the two is a morally relevant one. If the change from wet drowning child to dry drowning child did not make any difference to your intuition about whether it is wrong not to prevent the child from drowning, for example, this would be a good reason to deny that the difference between wet and dry is a morally relevant one. But if in the case of some other, more promising objection, you found that the change from the original case to the variant case did make a difference to your intuitive reaction to the case, this would count as good evidence that you had succeeded in identifying a cogent objection to the original argument.

Critically assessing an argument from analogy will not always be as simple and tidy as this discussion may suggest. There are many kinds of differences, which can be combined in various ways, and people's intuitions are not always as clear or as forceful as they would likely be in the simple case we have just focused on. When you encounter an argument from analogy, we suggest that you begin your critical deliberations about it by looking for disanalogies and then trying to use variant cases as one (though not necessarily the only) way to test their merits. Though not always effective, such an approach is often an excellent strategy to try.

4.2 Bare-Difference Arguments

The strategy of using variant cases to test for moral relevance when criticizing an argument from analogy is an instance of a somewhat more general argumentative technique, one that has been dubbed the "method of bare differences." This method is closely related to the technique of variant cases but has much wider application. It can be used not simply as a device for critically responding to an argument but also as a method for generating an argument on its own. It therefore merits attention as a form of argument in its own right.

4.2.1 Understanding Bare-Difference Arguments

Consider, as an example, the debate over the moral permissibility of euthanasia. When suffering from very painful, debilitating, and probably incurable diseases, some people come to regard death as a welcome release. In such cases life can often be prolonged—that is, doing so is technically possible—but, generally speaking, most people do not believe that it ought to be prolonged. What most people seem to believe is that it is sometimes morally permissible to allow a person to die in such circumstances, or, put the other way around, that it is not morally obligatory to continue to keep them alive. Sometimes, however, a person in such a situation wants more than simply that others stop keeping him alive, and it is this something more that tends to generate controversy. What he wants, in such cases, is that others take active steps to end his life and his suffering, rather than simply to stop the treatment that will ensure that he dies a slower (and often more painful) death later. That is to say, he wants others to bring about a more rapid death. He wants them to kill him. This further request generates controversy because many people who believe that it is morally permissible to continue to allow a person to die in such circumstances maintain that it would nonetheless be morally impermissible to kill him under the same circumstances, while many others maintain that it would be permissible not only to let such a person die but also to carry out his request to kill him.

This important debate is often carried out in terms of the distinction between active and passive euthanasia. The word *euthanasia* is derived from the Greek phrase for "a good death." A person's death can be a good one when it is better for him than the only available alternative, that is, continuing to live under intolerable circumstances. And this "good death" can come about in one of two ways. "Active euthanasia" refers to the practice of killing a person under such circumstances. "Passive euthanasia" refers to the practice of letting a person die under such circumstances by withholding treatment that would be necessary for him to go on living. The debate over euthanasia, therefore, is a debate about whether or not active euthanasia is worse than passive euthanasia.

Why should it be the case—as many people believe—that active euthanasia is always and everywhere wrong while passive euthanasia is sometimes permissible and perhaps even obligatory? Presumably, the central idea behind such a position is this: Deliberately killing a person is bad, much worse than merely letting a person die. Even when death is good for the person who dies, and even when the person who dies wants to die, killing is itself so bad a thing that its badness outweighs whatever good or desired effects it brings about. On this account, active euthanasia is always and everywhere morally wrong (since active euthanasia involves killing a person), while passive euthanasia may sometimes be morally justified (since passive euthanasia involves "merely" letting someone die). In order for this position to be acceptable, therefore, it must be the case that killing is worse—indeed, much worse—than letting die.

How could we find out whether there really is such a morally important difference between killing and letting die? One way to do this would be to look at pairs of cases other than those involving suffering and terminally ill patients, pairs of cases that also differ only with respect to the distinction between killing and letting die, and then to see if the difference between killing and letting die seems to make a (big enough) moral difference in those cases. The basic idea is as follows: If killing really is much worse, in itself, than letting die, then it would entail that—given any pair of cases, one of which is a killing and the other of which is a letting-die, that differ only this one respect—the case of the killing must be much worse than the case of the letting-die. Pairs of cases that differ in only one respect are called "barely different cases." And the principle articulated here suggests a potentially powerful argumentative strategy that may be constructed from them: We can test the relative moral weight of killing and letting die by considering various pairs of cases that differ only in this one respect.

In the featured article in chapter 2, for example, James Rachels applies precisely this technique. Indeed, Rachels's article made the technique of the bare-difference argument famous. Rachels considers a pair of stories that differ in only one respect—one is a killing, and the other is a letting-die. (In this respect they resemble a pair of variant cases.) But Rachels's pair of barely different cases is quite unrelated to the euthanasia issue. (In this Rachels's strategy differs from the technique of variant cases, which produces barely different pairs of cases analogous to the case at hand.) Rachels considers two people, Smith and Jones, each of whom stands to gain an inheritance from the death of his rich six-year-old cousin. Each plans to drown his cousin in a bathtub and to make the death look like an accident. Smith does precisely this. Jones, however, comes into the bathroom to find that his cousin is already drowning from a genuine accident (having slipped on the soap and hit his head on the side of the tub). Jones could easily save his cousin, but instead he stands idly by, prepared to shove his cousin's head back underwater if he happens to surface. Much to Jones's delight, he does not need to do this. After thrashing about a bit, Jones's cousin dies without Jones having to kill him. While Smith kills his cousin, Jones merely lets his cousin die. And this is apparently the only difference between the two cases. Everything else that might be morally relevant is the same in both cases. This is what makes the Smith and Jones pair of cases a set of "bare-difference" cases.

Now, is the Smith case worse than the Jones case? If you judge that it is not worse, that they are morally on a par, then it seems that you cannot affirm that killing is worse, in itself, than letting die. Of course, no one wants to say that letting die is, in itself, worse than killing, so the only alternative left seems to be that killing and letting die are on an equal footing and that it is other features of such cases that determine both their badness and their wrongness.

Rachels's argument can be reconstructed in a number of different ways. Let us consider here a simple two-premise version:

P1 The Smith case is a case of killing, and the Jones case is exactly like the Smith case in every respect except that it is a case of letting die.
P2 The Smith case is morally on a par with the Jones case.

C Killing is, in itself, morally on a par with letting die.

The general form of this argument is something like this:

P1 Case A has feature P, and case B is exactly like case A except that it has feature Q rather than feature P.
P2 Case A is morally on a par with case B.

C P is, in itself, morally on a par with Q.

In chapter 2 we will see exactly how Rachels goes on to argue from his application of these strategies to the permissibility of active euthanasia. What is important at this point, however, is not to decide whether or not we agree with Rachels's position but to ensure that we are clear about the nature and structure of the kind of argument he offers in its defense. First, we must be clear what the conclusion of the argument is supposed to be. Rachels is not saying that every killing is morally equivalent to every letting-die. He concedes that, as it happens, most cases of killing are probably worse than most cases of letting someone die. However, most cases of killing differ from most cases of letting die in many other ways, not just in the fact that one involves bringing about a preventable death and the other involves allowing a preventable death to occur. Most killing/letting-die pairs are not barely different. Most killings, for example, are violent affairs; most are done without the consent of the one killed; most cause considerable harm both to the one killed and to his loved ones; most are done with the intention of harming the person killed; and so on. Many, perhaps most, cases of letting die do not have these features. Rachels's point is that it is the badness of these other nasty features of killings that makes most cases of killing worse than most cases of letting die. Those other features may frequently, but do not necessarily, accompany killing. Furthermore, a letting-die might have those bad features, whereas a killing might lack them, and in that case the letting-die may well be much worse than the killing.

Second, we must be clear about the grounds for the validity of the argument. Indeed, as it stands it might not be at all clear that the argument is valid. What exactly establishes the connection between the premises and the conclusion? Why should the fact that killing does not make the Smith case worse than the Jones case mean that killing is not in itself worse than letting die? Perhaps a bad feature, such as its being a killing, will make a difference in some cases but not in others. Maybe it does not make a difference for the worse in the Smith case, but it does make a difference for the worse in the case of euthanasia. An answer to this question lies in a feature that moral reasons share with reasons in general, a feature that is often called their *universalizability*. Suppose someone objects to a certain practice—for example, the practice of sending children of different races to different schools and giving the schools with white children more resources than the schools with black children. One objection to such a practice might be that it is racist, that it involves assigning resources to schools on the basis of racial characteristics. Another might be that it is simply not fair because it gives some children more resources than other, equally deserving children. Note that these are two different reasons for rejecting the practice. We can imagine an arrangement that is not racist but is still unfair (mixed-race schools with differential resource allocations) and cases that may be racist although they do not distribute resources to children unequally (racially segregated schools with the same funding formula, for example). Now, if the fact that a practice is racist is a good reason to reject it, then it is an equally good reason for rejecting any other practice that involves racism to the same degree. If racism is bad, then it cannot count against some racist practices while not counting against other racist practices. For example, one cannot consistently object to the racism that currently favors black farmers over white farmers in Zimbabwe, say, without similarly objecting to the racism that used to favor white farmers over black farmers in Zimbabwe (and vice versa). If racism is an evil, it is an evil wherever and whenever it crops up. And that is what it means to say that racism is itself a bad thing. The basic principle that guarantees the validity of the bare-difference strategy is thus captured in the old adage: What's sauce for the goose is sauce for the gander. As long as one accepts this principle, the inference made by bare-difference arguments should seem well grounded.

4.2.2 Criticizing Bare-Difference Arguments

As we have formalized both the bare-difference strategy of argumentation in general and Rachels's application of it in particular, such arguments can be conceived of in terms of a conclusion that follows from two distinct premises. Assuming, therefore, that the two premises do, in fact, entail the conclusion, a critic of any particular bare-difference argument has two options available to him: He can attack the first premise or he can attack the second.

The first premise of any bare-difference argument involves the construction of two cases that are supposed to differ in only one respect. The first thing to do is to determine if this is true for the case at hand, or if there might be other respects in which they differ, respects that might at first lie hidden and that might be doing some moral work. That is to say, in any bare-difference argument, one might argue that cases presented as being only barely different are not barely different after all and that there is a further difference that has gone unnoticed and is morally relevant. A good example of this sort of strategy can be found in the article by Winston Nesbitt, reprinted as part of chapter 2 in which he criticizes Rachels's Smith/Jones pair on precisely these grounds. (Roy W. Perrett, in his critique of Nesbitt's argument, then attempts to come to the defense of Rachels's original argument.)

The second premise of any bare-difference argument endorses a certain judgment on the cases that the argument presents: the claim that the two cases are morally equivalent. But a critic of a particular bare-difference argument might attempt to reject this claim as well. In the case of Rachels's argument, for example, he might maintain that the Smith case (the killing) really is worse than the Jones case (the letting-die). If most people have an initial intuitive reaction in favor of the claim that P2 is true, it will do the critic of the argument little good simply to insist that P2 is false. An argument that simply boils down to a competing set of conflicting assertions is barely an argument at all. But there might be more subtle ways for a critic of P2 of a particular bare-difference argument to attempt to press his case. Such a critic might point out, for example, that P2 embodies a very precise claim—that the two cases are morally on a par—and he might therefore maintain that we are really not in a position to affirm such a precise judgment even though we may not detect any difference in our response to the cases. Maybe we are inclined to judge that they are exactly equivalent morally simply because they are both so bad that we do not really notice the relatively small additional badness involved in the killing. (*Relatively* small does not mean it is *small*; it is just small relative to the enormous evil involved in both cases.)

Still other, more general objections to the bare-difference argument strategy have been suggested by other writers. Readers who are interested in pursuing this question further should consult the suggested readings listed at the conclusion of chapter 2. In the meantime, however, we will assume that enough has been said about bare-difference arguments here to make their most basic features clear and will therefore turn next to a third kind of argument structure.

4.3 Arguments from Inference to the Best Explanation

A third argument structure that merits preliminary consideration involves an application of what is often referred to as an "inference to the best explanation." This kind of argument attempts to resolve a controversial issue not by comparing it with a single uncontroversial case, as arguments from analogy do, or by focusing exclusively on one pair of cases, as bare-difference arguments do, but rather by extracting a general lesson from a variety of uncontroversial cases and then applying this general lesson to a controversial case.

4.3.1 Understanding Arguments from Inference to the Best Explanation

Arguments from inference to the best explanation are generally somewhat complex. It may therefore help to begin by making a few general comments about them and going through an example or two of how they have most effectively been used before trying to make explicit their overall structure in a more general and formal manner. So, to begin with, it may be useful to note that arguments from inference to the best explanation are, in an important respect, similar to the more simple argument from analogy structure that we discussed in section 4.1. Both kinds of argument begin with our intuitive assessments of relatively clear and uncontroversial cases, and both try to work from them to reach a resolution of a more controversial case. But while an argument from analogy tries to move directly from our response to a single uncontroversial case (like the child drowning in the shallow pond) to a conclusion about a more controversial case (like the children starving in distant countries), arguments from inference to the best explanation begin with a variety of cases and try to make use of all of them in reaching their conclusion.

While arguments from analogy can therefore typically be represented in a simple two-step structure, arguments from inference to the best explanation can more readily be understood as consisting of three distinct steps: In step 1, the argument identifies a set of cases about which most people will have the same sort of general reaction. The argument, for example, might begin with a set of cases about which most people would agree that all of the acts in the set are morally wrong. In step 2, the argument then attempts to provide the best explanation of the intuitive judgments that most people will have about the particular cases. If all of the acts identified in step 1 really are wrong, for example, what would best account for this? What do all of the acts have in common that would most plausibly explain why they all are wrong? Typically, the result of this step in the argument will be the identification of some sort of general moral principle. If the wrongful acts in question have all been found to possess a certain property, for example, and if their possession of this property seems to provide the best explanation of why the acts are wrong, then the second step of the argument might conclude with a principle maintaining that if an act has that property, then the act is wrong. Finally, once some sort of general explanation of the uncontroversial particular cases has been identified, step 3 of the argument takes that explanation and applies it to the more controversial case. If, for example, the controversial case turns out to have the same property that made the acts in the uncontroversial cases wrong, then the best explanation of why they are wrong will imply that it is wrong in the controversial case as well. If, on the other hand, the controversial case turns out to be different from the uncontroversial cases in this respect, then the fact that the acts are wrong in the uncontroversial cases will fail to justify the claim that the act in the controversial case is wrong, too.

This initial presentation of the manner in which arguments from inference to the best explanation proceed is admittedly somewhat abstract. Before moving on to provide a more formal and general representation of the argument structure as a whole, then, it may be useful to look briefly at a few specific, concrete examples. In his article "Why Abortion Is Immoral," which serves as one of two featured articles about abortion in chapter 3, Don Marquis attempts to show that it is seriously immoral to kill the typical human fetus by starting with other cases where it is clearly wrong to kill and then arguing that the best explanation of why it is wrong to kill in the other cases applies to the case of the fetus as well. People on both sides of the abortion debate agree that it would be wrong to kill you or me, for example, and that it would be wrong to kill an unloved hermit or an adult in a temporary coma. He goes on to claim that the best explanation of why it is wrong to kill people in these cases is that a particular moral principle is true. The principle is that it is wrong to kill individuals who have futures that are relevantly like our futures. Marquis dubs this having a "future-like-ours." He then claims that this moral principle, in turn, entails that killing a typical human fetus is also wrong, because a fetus, according to Marquis, also has a future-like-ours. Similarly, in the article "The Case for Animal Rights" (chapter 4), Tom Regan uses inference to the best explanation to develop his argument about the moral status of at least some nonhuman animals. He begins with a set of cases of killing about which people on both sides of the animal-rights debate generally agree—that it is wrong, for example, to kill a severely retarded or severely brain-damaged (but not permanently comatose) human being. He argues that the best explanation for our judgments on these cases is that it is wrong to kill individuals who have a certain set of mental capacities that make them, in Regan's terminology, a "subject of a life." He then uses this principle to argue that killing some nonhuman animals, namely those who are also subjects of a life, is also wrong.

With the examples of Marquis and Regan in mind, we can begin to develop a general picture of the overall structure of arguments from inference to the best explanation by starting with an outline of how the arguments work in the particular case of arguments about the wrongness of killing. In order to do this, it may help to picture the argument as a whole as the result of combining two smaller, simpler sub-arguments. The first sub-argument moves from a set of particular and uncontroversial cases to a more general principle that best explains them; the second sub-argument applies that general principle to the more controversial particular case that is in dispute. In the case of the particular arguments of people like Marquis and Regan, the first sub-argument can be represented as follows:

Sub-Argument 1

P1   Killing is wrong in cases A, B, C, D, and E.
P2   The best explanation for the fact that killing is wrong in cases A, B, C, D, and E is that principle M is true.
P3   It is reasonable to believe the best explanation of a given set of facts.

C   It is reasonable to believe that principle M is true.

The second sub-argument can then be pictured as an argument that builds on the result of the first. Since the result of the first sub-argument is that it is reasonable to believe that principle M is true, the second begins by simply assuming that principle M is, indeed, true and then proceeds to apply this general principle to the specific controversial case at issue. The second sub-argument can thus be represented as follows:

Sub-Argument 2

P1   Principle M is true.
P2   If principle M is true, then killing is also wrong in the controversial case F.

C   Killing is wrong in the controversial case F.

The result of combining these two sub-arguments is therefore an overall argument for the claim that it is wrong to kill in the controversial case (the typical human fetus, in the case of Marquis's argument, a number of nonhuman animals in the case of Regan's argument).

Finally, with this more detailed understanding of these particular examples in mind, we can arrive at a more general and formal representation of arguments from inference to the best explanation as a whole. This model will be useful in analyzing some of the arguments in this book that make use of this argument structure but that are not concerned with the ethics of killing in particular (a nice example of this is the argument defended by Hugh LaFollette in chapter 14; there he tries to show that the best explanation of why we license such activities as driving cars and practicing medicine entails that we should also license the activity of raising children). To do this, we can begin by adopting a few abbreviations.

So consider a controversy that involves some particular kind of action. Call the kind of action "K" for "kind" (killing in the case of Marquis and Regan, requiring a license in the case of LaFollette). Suppose that we have a controversial case—call it "C" for "controversial"—in which people disagree about whether or not doing K is wrong (killing a fetus or a cow in the case of Marquis and Regan, requiring a parenting license in the case of LaFollette). Suppose also that there is a wide range of uncontroversial cases that also involves doing actions of kind K but about which people on both sides of the debate over doing K in the controversial case C generally agree (that it is wrong to kill a temporarily comatose adult or a mentally impaired adult in the case of Marquis and Regan, that it is wrong for the State to fail to require people to get a license in order to drive or practice medicine in the case of LaFollette). Call the uncontroversial cases "U1," "U2," "U3," and so on, for "uncontroversial." And, finally, suppose that there is a moral principle (call it "M" for "moral") that best explains the judgments that most people make about the uncontroversial cases. In that case, we can represent the general structure of arguments from inference to the best explanation as follows (we give a version in which the argument is about something being wrong rather than right and in which the argument begins with four uncontroversial cases in particular, but nothing hangs on these particular details):

Sub-Argument 1

    P1 It is wrong to do K in cases U1, U2, U3, and U4.
    P2 The best explanation for the fact that doing K is wrong in cases U1, U2, U3, and U4 is that principle M is true.
    P3 It is reasonable to believe the best explanation of a given set of facts.

    C   It is reasonable to believe that principle M is true.

Sub-Argument 2

    P1 Principle M is true.
    P2 If principle M is true, then doing K is wrong in case C.

    C   Doing K is wrong in case C.

The result of combining these two sub-arguments is therefore an overall argument for the claim that doing K is wrong in case C.

4.3.2 Criticizing Arguments from Inference to the Best Explanation

When examining an argument from inference to the best explanation, one must begin by understanding as clearly as possible the nature of the argument itself, beginning with the argument's conclusion and then working through its various premises: Is Marquis's argument, for example, meant to apply to abortion in every context? Is Regan's argument supposed to apply to all species of animals? In some cases, the answers may be fairly clear from the texts; in other cases, one may merely have to note levels of unclarity. What, specifically, is involved in the relatively uncontroversial cases to which the arguments appeal? Here, for example, one would have to take care to note that Marquis's case is about a person in a temporary coma rather than a permanent one and that Regan's cases involving brain-damaged people do not involve people who have lost consciousness. Next, what does the author take to be the best explanation of the judgments that we generally accept in the uncontroversial cases? That is, what is it about what all these cases are said to have in common that explains our judgments on them? What exactly is meant by a "future-like-ours" or a "subject of a life"? What is the basis for saying that the various cases have such properties in common? Why does the author think that their having such properties in common serves as an effective explanation of the wrongness of the actions in question? And, finally, why does the author think that this explanation helps to resolve the controversial case on which he is focusing? Why, in the end, does Marquis think that the best account of the wrongness of killing in general applies to human fetuses? Why does Regan think that it applies to (at least some) nonhuman animals?

After one has answered these essentially clarificatory questions, one is again in a position to move on to a more critical examination. As in the case of arguments from analogy and bare-difference arguments, arguments from inference to the best explanation vary considerably from case to case. However, it may be useful to keep in mind a few generalizations as you work your way through some of the readings that follow.

To begin with, there are three general options for confronting any argument from inference to the best explanation. You can: (1) disagree with the judgments about the core cases to which the argument appeals (e.g., say that it is okay to kill someone if she is in a temporary coma, in the case of Marquis's argument); (2) agree with the judgments about the core cases but argue that the author's moral principle fails to provide a satisfactory explanation of them (e.g., deny that what Marquis calls his "future-like-ours" principle is an acceptable moral principle or that it accurately captures our shared judgments); or (3) agree that the author's moral principle provides a satisfactory explanation of the core cases but deny that it has the implication that the author claims it has (e.g., deny that the future-like-ours principle implies that killing a human fetus is wrong, perhaps because fetuses do not have a future-like-ours).

The first option is, generally speaking, the least promising. Just as most arguments from analogy are constructed from cases that most people agree about, so most arguments from inference to the best explanation are constructed from sets of cases that most people agree about (most people, for example, do agree that it is wrong to kill people who are temporarily comatose and that the state should require people to get a license before they can drive). This is not to say that one should accept the foundations of such arguments blindly; indeed, you should always begin by checking to see if you have the kind of intuitive reactions that the author presumes you to have. Rather, it is simply to emphasize that if one agrees with the author's assessment of the core cases, this is only the beginning of one's critical options.

In many instances, much of the sustained critical discussion of an argument from inference to the best explanation will revolve around the second option. Here the key question is: Has the author really given a compelling account of our judgments in the core cases about which we generally share the same moral judgments? Such a discussion may end up going in many different directions, but a few suggestions may help to get things started.

First, why does the author think that his explanation is the best? If the principle is claimed to be simple, what is so simple about it? And why is simplicity so important? If it is claimed to be accurate, why, precisely, does he think it generates the right answers in the uncontroversial cases? If the claim is that the principle picks out properties that seem genuinely to be morally relevant properties, why, specifically, are we supposed to agree that the properties are salient in this way? If there are other features of the explanation that the author appeals to, what are they, and why does he think they make his principle a powerful one?

Second, there are two distinct ways in which a principle might run into trouble with particular cases. One way it can run into trouble is that it may fail to get the answer right in one of the cases it aims to address. Some people, for example, may argue that the moral principle that Regan appeals to cannot successfully account for the wrongness of killing in all of the cases of brain-damaged human beings where they think it would be wrong to kill. And some may think this is true of Marquis's argument as well. The other way a principle can run into trouble is that it may get the answer right in the core cases it addresses but then fail in a further case. Some people have argued, for example, that Marquis's future-like-ours principle gets the right results in the uncontroversial cases of killing that he argues from but that it then gets it wrong in an additional case: that of killing sperm or eggs (see the critical response by Alastair Norcross near the end of the first half of chapter 3 for an example of this kind of argument).

Finally, there is the third option. On this approach, one accepts the judgments of the particular cases that the author begins with and also accepts the general principle that the author provides to account for those judgments but then denies that the general principle supports his particular conclusion. In one of the critical responses to Marquis's article, for example, Peter K. McInerney argues that the human fetus does not yet have the future-like-ours property that Marquis appeals to in explaining the wrongness of killing. And in one of the critical responses we provide to Regan's article, R. G. Frey argues that nonhuman animals lack some of the properties that Regan says are required in order for one to be a subject of a life. If one can make a case for such a response, then one can reject a given author's specific conclusion about the controversial case without having to argue against his general explanation of the core cases about which most people agree. As with the case of arguments from analogy, what has been said here should be taken only as a suggestion and not as a foolproof technique or blueprint for how to initiate and organize an exhaustive critical discussion. Still, these are good ways to begin working through the articles in this anthology that have such a structure.

4.4 Arguments by Process of Elimination

While many of the arguments in this anthology are constructive in ways such as those we have identified and explained, others are essentially destructive. They provide not so much a positive argument for the claim that, say, X is not wrong, as they do a negative argument against other arguments that have been made for the claim that X is wrong.

4.4.1 Understanding Arguments by Process of Elimination

Simply showing that one argument for a particular conclusion is a bad argument does little to demonstrate that the conclusion itself is false. The argument "four is my favorite number, therefore two plus two equals four," for example, is a bad argument for the conclusion that two plus two equals four, but this does not mean that two plus two does not equal four or that there are not other, much better reasons for believing that two plus two equals four. The fact that there exists one bad argument for a given conclusion does not mean that there might not be other, better arguments for it. But if you can show that all of the seemingly plausible arguments for a given conclusion are bad arguments, this can at the least establish a much stronger presumption against the conclusion. In order to do this, such arguments must eliminate not just one argument, but a number of arguments. The manner in which those arguments proceed is thus typically referred to as an "argument by process of elimination."

In his article "Charges Against Prostitution" (chapter 10), for example, Lars O. Ericsson offers a defense of prostitution by trying to show that the various charges that have been raised against prostitution can be successfully overcome. And further examples of arguments that utilize the process of elimination can be found in featured articles throughout this work, including those in chapters 8 and 20.

4.4.2 Criticizing Arguments by Process of Elimination

Argument by process of elimination is not fully distinct from the other kinds of arguments we discuss in this introduction. In attempting to rebut some of the arguments that have been made against prostitution, for example, Ericsson appeals to a variety of analogies comparing prostitution with other professions, so that a complete critical analysis of his position will in the end involve a good deal of the very kind of thinking we discussed in the context of arguments from analogy in section 4.1. Once one has determined that a particular writer is proceeding by means of an argument by process of elimination, one must keep in mind that arguments by process of elimination can fail in one of two distinct ways: They can fail to eliminate one of the arguments they attempt to address, and they can fail to notice a further argument that should have been addressed. Some readers may feel that Ericsson's attempt to overcome what he calls the "feminist charge" against prostitution is unsuccessful, for example (as do two of the critical-response pieces we provide after Ericsson's article, those by Carole Pateman and Laurie Shrage), but others may feel that prostitution is wrong for reasons that Ericsson has not really confronted in the first place (as Karen Green does, for example, in a final response to Ericsson's article).

4.5 Arguments by Reduction to Absurdity

Often known by its Latin label *reductio ad absurdum,* meaning "reduction to absurdity," and frequently by the abbreviation *reductio,* this strikingly simple and effective argumentation strategy is popular in mathematical demonstrations; philosophers are fond of it as well. The basic idea is nicely described in the label. In order to establish that a certain assumption is false we may derive an absurdity from the claim. Any assumption that implies something absurd is itself absurd, and so we can reject the assumption.

4.5.1 Understanding Reductio

The clearest instance of an absurdity is an explicit contradiction. A contradiction is a claim of the form:

B is true and B is not true.

Let us abbreviate "B is not true" to "not-B" and abbreviate "B is true" and "B is not true" to (B and not-B). Now, a claim of (B and not-B) cannot be true whatever claim B is. Whether B is true or false, the conjunction (B and not-B) contains at least one false claim, and so the whole conjunction is false. (B and not-B) is thus absurd because it cannot possibly be true, whatever way the world happens to be.

Now, suppose that claim A logically entails a conjunction of the form (B and not-B). Then it follows from the notion of entailment, and the fact that (B and not-B) cannot be true, that A also cannot be true. A, like (B and not-B), is also absurd. So we might lay out the general form of a reductio as follows:

P1   If A were true, then B and not-B would both have to be true.
P2   B and not-B cannot both be true.

C   A cannot be true.

Sometimes a reductio will use a consequence B of some assumption or theory that, while not actually contradictory, is wildly implausible or known to conflict with known facts. This is a weaker notion of an absurdity than a contradiction, but many arguments that philosophers call reductio use such consequences. If claim A entails a wildly implausible claim B, then A must also be wildly implausible. So, we might summarize the form of such an argument thus:

P1   A entails B.
P2   B is wildly implausible.

C   A is wildly implausible.

Examples of reductio can be found in many of the selections. In chapter 4, Alan White, for example, uses a reductio against Regan's claim that nonhuman animals can be the subject of rights. In chapter 7, James S. Stramel uses a reductio against Mohr's argument for the claim that it is wrong not to "out" closeted homosexuals. In chapter 13, David Boonin uses a reductio against Jordan's argument for the claim that the state should not recognize same-sex marriages. And many other examples can be found among many of the remaining featured articles and critical-response pieces.

4.5.2 Criticizing a Reductio

We have two kinds of reductio. The first kind involves the claim that some theory has as a consequence an explicit contradiction. The second kind involves the claim that some theory entails a wildly implausible consequence. Let us deal with these in this order.

Note first that there is no disputing the absurdity of a claim of the form (B and not-B). Further, if A entails (B and not-B), then A, too, is absurd in the same sense—it cannot possibly be true. So, the only way of criticizing the first kind of reductio is to show that the first premise of the reductio is false. That is to say, one must show that A really does not lead to a contradiction after all. So, either A does not entail B, or else A does not entail not-B, the negation of B.

Now consider the reductio that involves a consequence that while not logically contradictory is held to be wildly implausible. Here we can also attack the first premise: the supposed entailment relation between A and the supposedly absurd consequence. But, in addition, the second premise of the reductio (that B is wildly implausible) might also be challenged. Many claims that people once thought to be wildly implausible (that the Earth moves, that mass is energy, that slavery is wrong) have turned out to be true after all. So, while it is never a mistake to think that an explicit contradiction is absurd, it might be a mistake to think that the consequence of our theory really is wildly implausible. Maybe the reasons we had for thinking B implausible are themselves defective. Maybe it only seems wildly implausible, but we can explain why it seems that way even if it is true. These are all possible ways to defeat the force of the second kind of reductio argument.

5 APPLIED ETHICS AND ETHICAL THEORY

We have now completed our discussion of some of the main ways in which philosophers develop and critically evaluate arguments when they think about particular topics in applied ethics like abortion, euthanasia, and animal rights. In doing all of this, we have said nothing about the subject of ethical theory, that branch of philosophy that concerns itself with more fundamental questions about the nature of the right and the good and that seeks to justify the adoption of more general rules or principles of morality that are meant to be valid across a much broader range of cases. This might seem to be a curious omission. If applied ethics is simply ethics applied, after all, then it would seem that one would have to start by first deciding which general ethical theory to select before one could then attempt to resolve some particular controversy within applied ethics by applying the selected ethical theory to it. And, indeed, some philosophers do seem to picture the relationship between ethics and applied ethics in roughly this way.

We believe, however, that this view of things is importantly misleading and that it results in a failure to appreciate what is most distinctive, and most distinctively valuable, about the enterprise of applied ethics. While a little bit of familiarity with ethical theory can sometimes be useful as preparation for reading and thinking about issues in applied ethics, and while we will therefore provide a bit of background about ethical theory here for just that reason, much of what is most important within the domain of applied ethics takes place in a way that does not presuppose a commitment to, or even an understanding of, any of the particular theories that philosophers argue about when they argue about ethical questions at a more general level. Indeed, at its very best, work in applied ethics holds out the promise that we might come to a reasonable resolution of some of the particular social controversies that divide us without first having to solve the more general sorts of problems that ethical theorists concern themselves with. And since it seems unlikely that a broad consensus about these more general theoretical questions is going to emerge anytime soon, this makes this aspect of the enterprise of applied ethics all the more important to understand and appreciate.

5.1 Ethical Theories

Ethical theories strive to provide us with a general principle or formula for determining the right thing to do and to uncover a fundamental, theoretical explanation of why it is the right thing to do.

5.1.1 Consequentialism

Of the three kinds of ethical theories that are currently the most popular among moral philosophers, it is perhaps easiest to begin with the kind of ethical theory known as *conse-*

quentialism. And to understand consequentialism, in turn, it is perhaps easiest to begin by understanding the distinction between the right and the good. As philosophers use such terms, at least, "good" and "bad" are evaluations that we make of states of affairs, while "right" and "wrong" are evaluations that we make of actions. We might say that it was good that it rained and that the rain helped the crops to grow or bad that there was a drought and that the drought caused the crops to fail, for example, but we would not say that the rain was right or that the drought was wrong.

With this understanding of the distinction between the right and the good in mind, we can define consequentialism as the view that the right is determined exclusively in terms of the good. In order to figure out the right thing to do, that is, one first evaluates the various possible states of affairs that might result from one's choices and then ranks the choices themselves according to the amount of goodness that each choice can reasonably be expected to produce. A choice is the right one to make to the extent that choosing it is more likely to result in better consequences than any available alternative. When put in this very general way, consequentialism is a very general thesis about morality, and some details need to be filled in before it can generate the kind of specific guidance for action that ethical theories aspire to provide. For one thing, people might differ quite sharply about what makes one state of affairs better than another. The most familiar version of consequentialism identifies the good with happiness, or utility. One state of affairs is better than another, on this account, if it contains more total happiness. The version of consequentialism that endorses this view of the good is called *utilitarianism.* But other people might identify other properties with the good. Perhaps one state of affairs is better than another if it contains more equality, for example, or more peace, or more of people getting what they deserve (where good people deserve to flourish and wicked people deserve to suffer). Perhaps the good is to be identified with some still further property or some combination of properties. All of these views can be incorporated into the consequentialist framework by maintaining that, whatever it is that makes one state of affairs better than another, the right choice to make is the one that can most reasonably be expected to bring about the best state of affairs so understood.

A second matter that requires more specificity at this point concerns the choices that are supposed to be made in terms of promoting the good: What, exactly, are we supposed to be choosing? The most straightforward answer to this question is that we are supposed to be choosing what actions to perform. On this formulation of consequentialism, one should always choose to act in such a way that one's act can reasonably be expected to produce more good overall than any available alternative act. This version of consequentialism is known as *act-consequentialism.* If this approach is combined with the view that the good is to be identified with happiness or utility, the result is that one should always choose to act in such a way that one's act can reasonably be expected to produce more happiness or utility overall than any available alternative act. This is *act-utilitarianism.* Other consequentialists have given other answers to the question about what choice we are supposed to evaluate in terms of its good consequences. Some have said that we should choose to follow those rules the following of which will produce the best consequences and then make our acts conform to the rules themselves rather than make our acts conform directly to judgments about the good. This is known as *rule-consequentialism,* and still further answers to this question in terms of things like motives or character traits or institutions can result in still further versions of consequentialism. When the various accounts of the good are combined with the various accounts of what is to be chosen in terms of the good, the result is that there can be many kinds of consequentialism. But what all have in common is the fundamental conviction that by starting with the good and then thinking of the right exclusively in terms of it, we can see what the right thing to do is and why it is the right thing to do.

5.1.2 Deontology

A second common ethical theory can most easily be described by the way in which it stands in opposition to consequentialism. This theory, which is usually referred to as *deontology,* maintains that the right is *not* determined exclusively in terms of the good. At one extreme, a deontologist might deny that consequences have anything to do with morality at all. At the other, a deontological theory might allow that consequences are vitally important, just so long as it adds that they are not the only thing that matters morally. Either way, what makes an ethical theory a deontological one on this analysis is the conviction that there is at least something else besides the consequences of one's act that goes into determining the rightness of the act.

The most familiar way of putting this kind of view is in terms of the language of rights. Suppose, to take the kind of example that is commonly deployed in this context, that either five innocent people will soon die or a sixth innocent person will soon die. All else being equal (they are all the same age, have the same number of friends who will miss them if they die, and so on), it should seem clear that the state of affairs in which the five innocent people die is much worse than the state of affairs in which only the one innocent person dies. If the goodness or badness of the consequences that result from our choices are the only considerations that are morally relevant, as the consequentialist approach to ethical theory would have it, then it should also seem clear that the right thing to do is to bring it about that the one innocent person dies rather than that the five innocent people die. If all six people will soon die unless they are taken to a hospital, for example, and if because of their current location you can either drive the first five to the hospital or drive only the sixth to the hospital, then the right thing for you to do would be to drive the first five to the hospital.

But now suppose that either the first five will soon die or the sixth will soon die for a very different reason: The first five people will soon die if they do not receive needed organ transplants, and the sixth person, who is perfectly healthy, will soon die if you kill him in order to remove his organs to save the first five. From a consequentialist point of view, this second version of the story does not seem to be relevantly different from the first. In both versions of the story, either five will die or one will die, and in both versions of the story, the state of affairs in which five die is much worse than the state of affairs in which only one dies. If this is enough to make it right to save the five by driving them to the hospital in the first version of the story, then it is enough to make it right to save the five by killing the sixth and removing his organs in the second version of the story. While a consequentialist ethical theory would therefore seem committed to treating the two cases as being morally on a par, a deontological theory would insist that they are crucially different. The sixth innocent person in the first version of the story does not have a right to your assistance if your saving him will prevent you from saving the five others. But the sixth innocent person in the second version of the story does have a right not to be killed by you, even if your refraining from killing him will prevent you from saving the five others. In both cases, things will be better if you bring it about that only one innocent person dies rather than five, but while morality permits you to bring about the better result in the first version of the story, it does not permit you to bring about the better result in the second. Morality, on this account, is about more than just the results of your actions. It is also about acting in accordance with certain constraints that limit your permissible options even if these constraints sometimes forbid you from making the world contain as much that is good as it could contain. The denial of the existence of such constraints is characteristic of a consequentialist ethical theory; the insistence on the existence of such constraints is characteristic of a deontological ethical theory.

5.1.3 Contractarianism

A third kind of ethical theory that merits attention here is *contractarianism* or *contractualism* (some people use these terms to mean somewhat different things, but we will use them here interchangeably). Unlike consequentialism and deontology, contractarianism is not so much a specific kind of moral principle as a kind of decision procedure for generating such moral principles. More specifically, contractarianism understands moral principles to be those principles that would be agreed to by rational agents trying to achieve a consensus about rules to govern their conduct while making their decision under a specified set of conditions. Different contractarian theorists have different ideas about just what, precisely, the conditions governing the choice situation should be, and so, as with consequentialism and deontology, there are different versions of contractarianism.

A simple version of contractarianism would accept the results of such agreement where the conditions in question are the conditions of the world as it actually is. If a convention emerges to the effect that when you buy a meal in a restaurant, you should leave a tip for the waitperson, for example, then the fact that people seem to have tacitly agreed to this rule in the world as it is could count as a reason for concluding that you should, in fact, leave a tip when you buy a meal in a restaurant. This view, however, can come dangerously close to the view that morality is just whatever people say it is. And for this reason, most contractarians incline toward the view that the conditions required to make an agreement on moral principles legitimate are more abstract and hypothetical. In one prominent version of this kind of theory, for example, the moral principles that we should act on are those that we would choose to govern our behavior if we attempted to reach agreement on what rules would best promote our own interests while choosing in the absence of specific information about ourselves such as our race, sex, religious beliefs, and so forth. If I know that I am a member of a racial majority, to take one instance of the sort of reasoning that leads some people to accept this view, then it may well seem to be in my interest to support a rule that allows members of the racial majority to oppress members of a racial minority. But if, when deciding which rules to endorse, I am not able to discern my racial identity, I will be deterred from adopting such a rule by the prospect that it might turn out to be used against me. By making the conditions under which the selection of principles takes place more fair, on this account, one ensures that the results of the selection process will themselves be fair.

5.2 The Relationship Between Ethical Theory and Applied Ethics

This very brief overview of the three main kinds of ethical theory represented in the contemporary philosophical literature is, of course, extremely superficial. There is much more that would need to be said about the content of any one version of any of these theories and much more that would need to be said about the reasons that could be given for endorsing any of them. And there are, in addition, a number of other ethical theories that would deserve to be mentioned as well. But enough has nonetheless been said here for our purposes, and enough has surely been said to prompt an obvious question: What, if anything, does all of this have to do with applied ethics?

5.2.1 When Ethical Theory Helps

In some cases, the answer to this question may turn out to be "a fair amount." Regan's argument for animal rights, for example, which we discussed in the context of arguments from inference to the best explanation in section 4.3, is at its foundation an argument against consequentialism and contractarianism and in favor of deontology. Regan argues, that is, that a rights-based ethical theory does a better job of accounting for our obligations to other people than do its rival theories, and he then argues that the best account of why we have the rights that we have entails that at least some nonhuman animals have rights, too. In this kind of case, at least, it is probably helpful to know something in advance about the basic distinctions between and motivations behind the most common ethical theories in the contemporary philosophical literature.

More typically, however, the answer to this question will be "relatively little." Familiarity with the three main kinds of moral theory may prove somewhat helpful in sorting out the different parts of an article, but it will play no real role in understanding or evaluating the arguments the article contains. In its report on the ethics of human cloning, for example, which serves as the featured article of chapter 23, the President's Council on Bioethics offers a number of distinct arguments against the practice of attempting to clone human beings in order to bring new people into existence. One of its principal arguments appeals to the claim that, because of the significant risks of birth defects that would be involved, doing so would be unjust to the people who would be created by the process. Some of its other arguments set aside this concern with the safety of the procedure and instead appeal to the claim that reproductive human cloning would have a variety of negative consequences for families in particular and for society in general. Because the council's report contains a variety of distinct arguments often presented one right after another, it is important to be able to keep track of which point in a given part of the article goes with which argument. Noting that the first kind of argument against cloning is a deontological argument while the second kind of argument is a consequentialist one may help to do this, and so familiarity with the basic differences between the different kinds of ethical theory may help to organize one's reading of the report. But none of the council's arguments appeals directly to any of these sorts of ethical theories, and so familiarity with such theories is not really important to understanding and evaluating the merits of the arguments themselves.

5.2.2 When Ethical Theory Doesn't Help

In a large number of cases, moreover, the answer to the question of what ethical theory has to do with applied ethics will, in effect, be "nothing at all." This is because in a large number of cases, the arguments that philosophers offer when they are working on problems in applied ethics are grounded in assumptions that most people, regardless of their theoretical orientation, are unlikely to deny. Recall, for example, Hugh LaFollette's argument for licensing parents, which was briefly explained in section 4.3 as an instance of an argument from inference to the best explanation. That argument begins with the uncontroversial claim that the State should require people to get a license in order to engage in such activities as driving a car and practicing medicine and then initiates the process of identifying the best explanation of why this is so by pointing to the fact that these activities are potentially harmful to other people. Adherents of different ethical theories are likely to give different explanations of *why* the fact that an activity is potentially harmful to others counts in favor of its being licensed. A consequentialist might point to the terrible harms that would arise if just anyone who wanted to was allowed to get behind the wheel of a car; a deontologist might argue that people have a right not to be exposed to significant risks of harm and that licensing is justified as a means of protecting that right; a contractarian might argue that rational contractors would prefer the security provided by the licensing system to the risk of doing without it, and so on. But while these different ethical theories would provide different answers to the question of *why* the potential harm to others generated by an activity counts in favor of licensing that activity, they would all agree *that* the potential harm counts in its favor. And for the purposes of understanding and evaluating LaFollette's argument, agreeing to this is all that really matters. If we agree that the potential harmfulness of an activity is relevant in the way that LaFollette claims it to be, after all, we will then be in a position to consider the fact that raising children exposes them to risks of significant harm as well. We will be able to understand and evaluate LaFollette's argument, that is, without having to understand or evaluate any of the ethical theories that might be used to provide support for its foundational assumptions. As long as the foundational assumptions are accepted for one reason or another (or for no reason at all, if they simply seem to be obviously correct), it won't really matter why they are accepted. And in this respect, at least, LaFollette's argument is the rule rather than the exception when it comes to understanding how applied ethics is actually practiced. This anthology as a whole contains a large number of instances in which a philosopher asks the reader to consider a particular case and then to make a judgment about it. And in virtually every one of these instances, most people will make the particular judgment that the philosopher is counting on them to make regardless of their views (if any) about the more general matters that ethical theory concerns itself with. For the most part, then, knowledge of ethical theory will not be relevant to understanding or evaluating the arguments that are contained in this book.

Indeed, we would go as far as to say that a familiarity with ethical theory can sometimes do more harm than good when one is attempting to understand and evaluate an argument in applied ethics. Return once more, for example, to that drowning child in the shallow pond that Peter Singer appeals to in making his case for the claim that it is morally wrong not to contribute money to famine-relief efforts (see section 4.1 earlier on arguments from analogy). Singer assumes that virtually everyone will agree that it would be wrong not to save the child in the pond. If leaving the child in the pond to die turns out to be relevantly similar to refraining from sending money to famine-relief organizations, then this will make for a very powerful argument in defense of Singer's position. Now, a reader who is ignorant of arguments about ethical theory will simply accept that it is wrong not to save the child in the pond and move on to the more important questions: What are the differences between the pond case and the famine-relief case, and what sorts of reasons might be given for thinking that these differences are morally relevant? But a reader who knows something about ethical theory might instead be tempted to pause and worry about which ethical theory Singer thinks shows that it would be wrong not to save the child in the pond in the first place. As he has made clear in many of his other writings, Singer himself is a utilitarian. And so the reader who attempts to understand Singer's argument about famine relief in particular through the lens of moral theory in general may well come to the conclusion that we are supposed to save the child in the pond because the total amount of utility created by saving the child is greater than the total amount of utility created by not saving him. Such a reader might also think that there are good reasons to reject utilitarianism as an ethical theory and therefore conclude that there are good reasons to reject Singer's famine-relief argument as a result.

But this would be a great mistake. It is true that Singer is a utilitarian. And it is true that the shallow-pond argument is Singer's argument. But it is not true that the shallow-pond argument is a utilitarian argument. Utilitarians will, of course, agree that it would be wrong not to save the child who is drowning in the shallow pond. But so will virtually everyone else. Since Singer's assessment of the shallow-pond case does not depend on accepting utilitarianism as an ethical theory, raising an objection against utilitarianism as an ethical theory will do nothing to generate an objection to the shallow-pond argument itself. Readers who are unfamiliar with ethical theory will not be tempted to make this serious mistake. But readers who are familiar with ethical theory may well be. For this reason, a familiarity with ethical theory can at times be a handicap rather than an advantage when one is attempting to understand and evaluate an argument in applied ethics. And for this reason, although we acknowledge that the brief overview of ethical theory that we have provided here may prove useful at some points in working one's way through the material that follows, we urge readers to keep in mind that applied ethics, as a whole, is a far more autonomous discipline than its name might seem to imply. Considerations of ethical theory may at times be used to inform or illuminate issues in applied ethics, and thoughts that arise in the process of critically assessing arguments in applied ethics may well lead to ideas that can be used to develop and critically assess positions in ethical theory. But thinking carefully and critically about ethical theory itself will have to be the subject of another book.

6 CONCLUSION

There are many ways in which the readings in this anthology can fruitfully be analyzed and discussed. Readers should take the specific suggestions we have offered in this introduction not as a substitute for applying their own critical thinking but rather as a first step toward thinking critically about the readings on their own.

PART 1

What's Wrong with Killing?

One of the oldest and most familiar moral principles runs as follows: "Thou shall not kill." Virtually everyone recognizes an element of truth to this ancient edict. The deliberate murder of an innocent human being is almost universally treated as among the most serious of moral transgressions. At the same time, virtually no one truly accepts this principle in its unqualified form. A gardener, for example, might kill hundreds of weeds in tending to a garden. A doctor might kill millions of cancer cells in treating her patients. Consumers buy special cleaners aimed at killing mold and mildew, wash their hands with soaps specifically designed to kill bacteria, and buy their pets special collars that promise to kill ticks and fleas. While killing is therefore taken to be seriously immoral in some contexts, it is not taken to be the least bit immoral in many others.

There is little debate among moral philosophers about whether or not killing is wrong in these extreme cases. Virtually all would agree that it would be wrong for me to kill you, for example, but not wrong for me to kill the mold and mildew in my bathroom. In between these two extremes, however, lies an important range of cases that is much more difficult to resolve and, as a result, much more controversial. Part 1 of this book is devoted to such cases. We begin with two cases that involve killing adult human beings in certain specific sorts of circumstances. In chapter 1, we start with the question of whether it is morally permissible to kill enemy noncombatants in wartime and, if not, whether this is compatible with the view that it is morally permissible to kill enemy combatants. We move on, in chapter 2, to the issue of euthanasia: the killing of people who are suffering from terminal, debilitating, or very painful illnesses. We then turn to two further cases that also involve killing but do not involve adult human beings: the subject of killing at the very early stages of human life—is abortion morally permissible (chapter 3)?—and the issue of killing at the mature stages of some forms of nonhuman life—hunting deer for sport, for example, or killing cows in order to eat them (chapter 4). In all of these cases, those who are opposed to a particular form of killing try to justify their opposition to it by trying to show that it is relevantly similar to killing innocent adult human beings, while those who support a particular form of killing attempt to justify their support of it by trying to show that it differs from such cases in morally relevant respects. The investigation into the morality of killing in these controversial cases, that is, typically involves, at least in part, an investigation into the morality of killing in uncontroversial cases as well. Finally, in chapter 5, we turn to a question that is distinct from but closely related to the issue of killing: the question of whether, in the context of global famine-relief efforts, it is wrong to refrain from helping to prevent people from dying prematurely. Here, too, although the issue involves refraining from saving rather than actively killing, the question largely comes down to whether or not the morality of the controversial case under consideration can be successfully illuminated by appealing to other cases about which most people already agree.

1

Is Killing in War Wrong?

Fullinwider and His Critics

In a notorious incident during the Vietnam War, American soldiers attacked the village of My Lai, expecting to confront enemy combatants. Instead they found themselves confronting unarmed villagers. As described here (on a PBS Web site), many of the villagers were killed.

> As the "search and destroy" mission unfolded, it soon degenerated into the massacre of over 300 apparently unarmed civilians including women, children, and the elderly. (Lieutenant) Calley ordered his men to enter the village firing, though there had been no report of opposing fire. According to eyewitness reports offered after the event, several old men were bayoneted, praying women and children were shot in the back of the head, and at least one girl was raped and then killed. For his part, Calley was said to have rounded up a group of the villagers, ordered them into a ditch, and mowed them down in a fury of machine gun fire. (http://www.pbs.org/wgbh/amex/vietnam/trenches/my_lai.html)

War might seem a strange domain in which to begin examining the morality of killing. After all, killing is the business of war. Soldiers are decorated for doing it. But even in war we recognize strong moral differences. Killing enemy combatants on the battlefield is widely regarded not only as morally permissible but also as morally commendable. But killing enemy noncombatants is nearly as widely condemned. What justifies this difference in moral judgment on the killing of enemy combatants and the killing of enemy noncombatants? In order for it to be justified, there must be some morally significant difference between a combatant and a noncombatant, and that difference must be sufficient to make it permissible to kill one but not the other. What is that difference?

In the featured article in this chapter, Robert K. Fullinwider begins by considering one traditional and influential answer to this question, an answer that appeals to the principle that to intentionally kill an innocent human being is seriously morally wrong. According to this answer, noncombatants, even enemy noncombatants, are innocent human beings. Thus, it is seriously morally wrong to kill enemy noncombatants. Enemy combatants, however, are not innocent in the way that noncombatants are, so it may be permissible, or even obligatory, to kill them.

Fullinwider notes that lying behind this justification is something like a principle of punishment: It is morally permissible to kill someone if and only if he has done something to *deserve* death as some sort of *punishment.* If combatants are not innocent, they are guilty of something, and presumably what they are guilty of is intentionally prosecuting a war against your country. Noncombatants are not guilty of this.

Fullinwider argues that this justification rests on a pair of dubious claims. A very reluctant conscripted combatant, one who serves in the army only under threat of punishment, may be much less responsible for the prosecution of the war than, say, an influential and enthusiastic noncombatant. Fullinwider nevertheless goes on to defend the traditional view—that whereas combatants may be killed, noncombatants may not. But he thinks that the difference rests on considerations that have to do with *self-defense,* not on considerations that have to do with *guilt, desert,* or *punishment.*

Fullinwider begins with a short story (involving the ubiquitous Smith and Jones, a pair who seem to be perennially involved in morally messy situations):

> Jones is walking down a street. Smith steps from behind the corner of a nearby building and begins to fire a gun at Jones, with the appearance of deliberate intent to kill Jones. Surrounded by buildings, Jones is afforded no means of escape. Jones, who is carrying a gun himself, shoots at Smith and kills him.

Fullinwider claims that, in killing Smith, Jones is justified by the principle of self-defense: That is, it is morally permissible to kill someone whose actions put your life directly and immediately in mortal danger if that is what is necessary to end the threat. Further, the facts as stated alone constitute a sufficient justification for Jones's killing of Smith. Now Fullinwider adds some further details to the story, details that he claims do not undermine the permissibility of Jones's killing of Smith. (In fact he considers three different additions; we will consider just one of them here.)

> . . . suppose Smith, through heavy gambling losses, is in debt to the mob for $100,000. The mobsters propose to Smith that if he will kill Jones (a crusading district attorney, say), they will forgive his debt. Unable to pay the debt, and knowing what will happen to him if he fails to pay it, Smith seeks out Jones and begins firing.

Fullinwider claims, plausibly, that this additional information does not undermine the permissibility of Jones's killing of Smith. The principle of self-defense still endows Jones with the moral permission to kill. Furthermore, it licenses *only* the killing of Smith.

> . . . suppose the mobsters were parked across the street to observe Smith. After killing Smith, Jones could not turn his gun on them (assuming they were unarmed). No matter how causally implicated the . . . mobsters were in Smith's assault on Jones, in the situation it was only Smith who was the agent of immediate threat to Jones; the . . . mobsters were not posing a direct and immediate danger. From the point of view of justifiably killing in self-defense, they are not justifiably liable to be killed by Jones; they are immune.

Fullinwider is clearly drawing an analogy between Smith and the enemy combatants on the one hand and the unarmed mobsters and enemy noncombatants who support the war on the other.

In his response to Fullinwider, Lawrence A. Alexander begins by elaborating on Fullinwider's story, and he draws some further analogies to argue for his claim that noncombatants may be killed in self-defense. Furthermore, he goes on to argue that sometimes when one has to choose between killing combatants and certain noncombatants, one is morally obliged to kill the noncombatants rather than the combatants.

QUESTIONS FOR CONSIDERATION

In thinking about this issue, consider the following questions.

- What version of the principle of self-defense does each of our two authors use? Is there some other version that might be superior to both?
- Is the principle of self-defense (in any of the versions you are considering) actually true? Try to think of a possible case in which Jones poses an immediate threat to Smith through no fault of Jones, where Smith can avert the threat that Jones poses only by killing Jones but where it does not seem immediately obvious that Smith is entitled to kill Jones.
- Does the principle of self-defense entitle Smith to kill a whole host of Joneses who collectively pose a threat to Smith through no fault of their own?
- What actually is an enemy combatant? Is an army cook, for example, a combatant? Does it make a difference whether the cook is an enlisted soldier or a contract laborer? If the cook is an enemy combatant, is the truck driver who delivers oatmeal (for the soldiers' breakfast) also a combatant? If not, why is he any different from the cook? Both, after all, help to keep the combatants combat ready. But if so, what is the difference between the truck driver and the soldiers' wives (or husbands) and girlfriends (or boyfriends)?

FURTHER READING

Buchanan, Allen. "Institutionalizing the Just War." *Philosophy and Public Affairs* 34, no. 1 (Winter 2006): 2–38.

Johnson, James Turner. "The Just War Idea: The State of the Question." *Social Philosophy and Policy* 23, no. 1 (Winter 2006): 167–95.

MacKinnon, C. "Crimes of War, Crimes of Peace," in *On Human Rights,* ed. S. Shute and S. Hurley (New York: Basic Books), 1993: 83–109.

McMahan, Jeff. "On the Moral Equality of Combatants." *Journal of Political Philosophy* 14, no. 4 (December 2006): 377–93.

McPherson, Lionel K. "Innocence and Responsibility in War." *Canadian Journal of Philosophy* 34, no. 4 (December 2005): 485–586.

Nagel, T. "War and Massacre." *Philosophy and Public Affairs* 1, no. 2 (1971): 123–44.

Walzer, Michael. *Just and Unjust Wars.* New York: Basic Books, 1977.

ROBERT K. FULLINWIDER

War and Innocence

I

In a war, is it morally permissible intentionally to kill noncombatants? Elizabeth Anscombe and Paul Ramsey argue that noncombatants may not be intentionally killed.[1] We are obligated to refrain from such killing because it is murder; and it is murder because noncombatants are innocent.

George Mavrodes questions the grounds for asserting that in war noncombatants are "innocent" and combatants are "guilty." If immunity of noncombatants from killing is to be established this way, he says, then we must find a "sense of 'innocence' such that all noncombatants are innocent and all combatants are guilty," and "this sense must be morally relevant." Mavrodes fears, however, that immunity theorists such as Anscombe and Ramsey are actually using "innocent" and "noncombatant" synonymously. He believes that the sense of "innocence" used in their arguments has no moral content.[2]

Mavrodes' main argument is this. There are noncombatants who may enthusiastically endorse and support the war their nation is waging, while there are combatants who may be under arms unhappily and unwillingly, who may not support the war but are unable to resist conscription. It is odd to claim that the enthusiastically supportive noncombatant is innocent and the reluctant conscript guilty. "Is it not clear," Mavrodes asks, "that 'innocence,' as used here, leaves out entirely all morally relevant considerations . . . ?"[3]

Anscombe and Ramsey both invite this sort of counterargument by the way they defend their immunity thesis. Anscombe implies that the thesis is rooted in the Principle of Punishment: no man is to be punished except for his own crime.[4] Ramsey, too,

employs the model of the criminal in defending the thesis.[5] But, from the point of view of punishment, it is odd, if not perverse, to view the enthusiastically supportive noncombatant as innocent and the reluctant combatant as guilty. Mavrodes, in my judgment, is right in believing this defense fails to establish the immunity of noncombatants from intentional killing.

Mavrodes believes that the obligation not to kill noncombatants intentionally can rest only on a convention among nations. Such an obligation, if it exists, is at best contingent, conditioned as it is on the existence of such a convention in force. Anscombe and Ramsey believe the obligation to refrain from intentionally killing noncombatants is noncontingent. It is not convention-dependent.[6]

In this paper I shall briefly sketch an argument for the immunity of noncombatants which avoids Mavrodes' criticisms. It will establish that in warfare there is a morally relevant distinction between noncombatants and combatants which prohibits the intentional killing of the former at the same time as it justifies the intentional killing of the latter. My argument will appeal to a nonconventional principle, and thus the obligation deriving from the principle will not be convention-dependent (or anyway not wholly so). I will then go on to show that even if certain considerations undercut drawing the line of immunity between combatants and noncombatants, a weaker version of the immunity thesis is still viable.

II

To set the scene, first consider an example. Jones is walking down a street. Smith steps from behind

From Robert K. Fullinwider, "War and Innocence," *Philosophy and Public Affairs* 5, no. 1 (Autumn 1975): 90–97. Some notes have been deleted. Reprinted by permission of Princeton University Press.

the corner of a nearby building and begins to fire a gun at Jones, with the appearance of deliberate intent to kill Jones. Surrounded by buildings, Jones is afforded no means of escape. Jones, who is carrying a gun himself, shoots at Smith and kills him.

Jones is morally justified in killing Smith by the Principle of Self-Defense. Smith's actions put Jones' life directly and immediately in mortal jeopardy, and Jones' killing Smith was necessary to end that threat. From the point of view of self-defense, these facts about Smith's actions are the *only* relevant ones. The moral justification of the killing rests on them alone given the legitimacy of self-defense.

But let me now sketch in some possible background circumstances to Smith's assault on Jones. Suppose Smith's wife, spurned by Jones when she made advances toward him, tells Smith she has been raped by Jones. Furious, and egged on by his wife, Smith seeks out Jones and begins firing. Or, suppose Smith, through heavy gambling losses, is in debt to the mob for $100,000. The mobsters propose to Smith that if he will kill Jones (a crusading district attorney, say), they will forgive his debt. Unable to pay the debt, and knowing what will happen to him if he fails to pay it, Smith seeks out Jones and begins firing. Or, suppose the mobsters kidnap Smith's children and threaten to kill them unless he kills Jones. Driven by the threat, Smith seeks out Jones and begins firing.

None of this background information alters the situation from the point of view of self-defense. Whatever prompted Smith to fire at Jones, the justification for Jones' killing Smith lies solely in the fact that Smith was the direct and immediate agent of a threat against Jones' life. From the point of view of self-defense, this fact justifies Jones in killing Smith— and *only* Smith.

Again, suppose that Smith's wife was standing across the street egging Smith on as he fired at Jones. Jones, though he justifiably shot Smith in self-defense, could not justifiably turn his gun on the wife in self-defense. Or suppose the mobsters were parked across the street to observe Smith. After killing Smith, Jones could not turn his gun on them (assuming they were unarmed). No matter how causally implicated the wife or the mobsters were in

Smith's assault on Jones, in the situation it was only Smith who was the agent of immediate threat to Jones; the wife and the mobsters were not posing a direct and immediate danger. From the point of view of justifiably killing in self-defense, they are not justifiably liable to be killed by Jones; they are immune.

There is a point of view from which these background features I have drawn in become morally relevant, namely the point of view of retribution or punishment. Smith's wife and the mobsters would be viewed as morally culpable for their contribution to Smith's assault on Jones' life. They ought to be punished. Perhaps Jones might be justified in taking his own retribution, and killing the wife or mobsters in revenge; but even if he is justified in killing them in retribution, he still cannot justify killing them on the grounds of self-defense.

In these cases of killing and attempted killing there are two points of view: the point of view of self-defense and the point of view of punishment. Some considerations that become morally relevant from the second point of view in justifying killing are not relevant from the first point of view. We use the notions of guilt and innocence almost always in connection with the second point of view, the perspective of punishment. From that point of view, Smith's wife and the mobsters are as guilty as Smith. In the instance where the mobsters cause Smith to act under duress, perhaps they are more guilty.

If we were to speak of innocence and guilt as categories applying in cases of self-defense, then for the purpose of justifiably killing in self-defense and from that point of view we would say that Smith alone was guilty (justifiably liable to killing) and his wife and the mobsters were innocent (not justifiably liable to killing), though all are guilty from the point of view of punishment.

It should be obvious now how my argument for the immunity thesis is going to run. The moral relevance of the distinction in war between combatants and noncombatants will be derived from the Principle of Self-Defense. Because we most commonly speak of innocence in connection with crime and punishment and because we also speak of innocent victims of war, Anscombe and Ramsey have been led to defend the innocents in war by appeal to the wrong model. For these same reasons, Mavrodes has failed to see an alternative to his conventionalism.

III

I shall now sketch an argument for the moral immunity of noncombatants from intentional killing.

The question at hand is the killing in war and its justifiability. Why is any killing at all justified? I claim that a nation may justifiably kill in self-defense. From the point of view of self-defense, only those are justifiably liable to be killed who pose the immediate and direct jeopardy. In the case of war, it is nations' armed forces which are the agents of the jeopardy. In a war, the armed forces of nation A stand to opponent nation B as Smith stood to Jones. It is against them that B may defend itself by the use of force. The active combatants, their arms, ammunition, war machines and facilities, are the legitimate targets of intentional destruction.

Though A's civilian population may support its war against B and contribute to it in various ways, they stand to B as Smith's wife or the mobsters stood to Jones. For the purpose of justifiably killing in self-defense and from that point of view, the civilian population is morally immune—it is "innocent." To intentionally kill noncombatants is to kill beyond the scope of self-defense. It is to kill unjustifiably from the point of view of self-defense.

This, in brief, is my argument. It provides for drawing a line between combatants and noncombatants, and prohibits intentionally killing the latter. This is just where the immunity theorists want to draw the line of prohibition. Furthermore, they see the prohibition as "natural," not convention-dependent. My argument supports them in this. The distinction between combatants and noncombatants derives from the operation of the Principle of Self-Defense. Our obligation not to kill noncombatants stems from our obligation not to kill without justification; and the Principle of Self-Defense justifies killing only combatants. Since both the obligation to not kill without justification and the Principle of Self-

Defense are "natural" rather than conventional, the moral immunity of noncombatants does not rest (solely) upon the existence of appropriate conventions among nations.

IV

From the point of view of killing in self-defense in war, Mavrodes' reluctant conscript is "guilty" (justifiably liable to killing), and his noncombatant partisan is "innocent" (not justifiably liable to killing). To say that the reluctant conscript is guilty and the noncombatant partisan is innocent is to stand the matter on its head, claims Mavrodes. So it is—from the point of view of punishment. This, I have urged, is not the fundamentally governing point of view when it comes to justifying killing in war. The innocence of the noncombatant seems inexplicable to Mavrodes because he takes up the wrong point of view for evaluating killing in war. He is, of course, encouraged to take up this view by Anscombe's and Ramsey's own arguments in defense of the innocence of noncombatants. Viewing killing in war from this evaluative standpoint, and finding it incapable of explaining the prohibition against killing combatants, Mavrodes turns to conventionalism.

Might it not be contended against my defense of the immunity thesis that the point of view of self-defense is not the sole governing point of view when it comes to killing in war? Nations, it might be argued, exist in a state of nature, and thus possess the right to exact their own punishments on transgressors. Thus, in war, justifying deliberate killing may be done by appeal to both the Principle of Self-Defense *and* the Principle of Punishment. Finally, to the extent that retribution justifies some of the killing in war, it will justify killing some noncombatants.

I have two answers to this challenge. The first answer preserves the strong immunity thesis, but it requires an assumption of fact which may, theoretically, not obtain. The second answer, dropping the assumption, requires me to weaken the immunity thesis.

For purposes of argument, I will concede that nations have the right to exact their own punishment in war. Even so, the Principle of Punishment justifies punishing *only* the *morally guilty* (culpable from the point of view of punishment), not the *morally innocent* (innocent from the point of view of punishment). Techniques of warfare—combat, bombing, shelling, burning—are too indiscriminate in their destruction to serve as legitimate instruments of punishment. They cannot be used discriminatingly between the morally guilty and the morally innocent. It is not justified by the Principle of Punishment intentionally to kill the morally innocent. If a nation claims punitive rights in war, it must adopt mechanisms of punishment which will discriminate between those who deserve punishment and those who do not. Bombing, shelling, and other such techniques kill guilty and innocent alike. Consequently, if we wish to justify killing during war by the means of war, the only applicable perspective is self-defense.[7]

If, however, contrary to the facts, there were some perfectly discriminating techniques of warfare, then, since I have conceded the right of nations to exact their own punishment, I see no argument against a nation legitimately taking up both points of view in its prosecution of a war. Some of the justified killing will be justified by self-defense, some by merited punishment. This would require a weakening of the immunity thesis, since the Principle of Punishment would justify some intentional killing of noncombatants, namely those that were morally guilty. Nevertheless, a version of the immunity thesis can be preserved: some line prohibiting intentional killing would still be mandated. The Principle of Self-Defense will justify intentionally killing combatants, even the morally innocent among them. The Principle of Punishment will justify killing (if this is proportional to the crime) the morally guilty noncombatant. But neither principle will sanction or permit the intentional killing of the morally innocent noncombatant, many of whom will be found in any nation at war. There will thus be a line of immunity required to be drawn around a certain class in war, the class of morally innocent noncombatants. We shall be morally obliged to refrain from intentionally killing members of this class, and this moral obligation will not disappear in the absence of any particular convention among nations.

Because of the indiscriminate nature of modern techniques of destruction, I see two reasons why the line of immunity is to be maintained between combatants and noncombatants. First, if nations recognize the Principle of Punishment, they may nevertheless be required to refrain from attempting to use it as a justification for killing because they shall not be able to meet the discrimination requirement. Second, nations may find it collectively beneficial to agree to forgo the exercise of their punishment rights during war (the exercise of which is morally ruled out anyway). They might thus, as Mavrodes suggests, adopt conventions confirming the line of immunity during warfare between combatant and noncombatant. To this extent, Mavrodes' conventionalism has support. The obligation not to kill noncombatants may be partly conventional; but if my arguments have been correct, it is not wholly so.

NOTES

1. Elizabeth Anscombe, "War and Murder," in *War and Morality,* ed. Richard Wasserstrom (Belmont, Ca., 1970); Paul Ramsey, *The Last War* (New York, 1968). See also John C. Ford, "The Morality of Obliteration Bombing," in *War and Morality.*

2. George I. Mavrodes, "Conventions and the Morality of War," *Philosophy & Public Affairs* 4, no. 2 (Winter 1975): 121, 123.

3. Mavrodes, pp. 122–123.

4. Anscombe, p. 49; Mavrodes, pp. 120, 123.

5. Ramsey, p. 144; Mavrodes, p. 123.

6. For Mavrodes' definition of convention-dependent obligation, see p. 126 of his article.

7. The Principle of Self-Defense also requires discrimination—between combatants and noncombatants. Since usually combatants are in uniform, with weapons, on battlefields, instruments of war can be used in a way which (roughly) avoids the death of noncombatants. However, instruments which cannot be used in a discriminating way, and whose use entails extensive noncombatant casualties (e.g. hydrogen bombs), are ruled out for use even in self-defense. See Richard Wasserstrom, "On the Morality of War: A Preliminary Inquiry," in *War and Morality,* pp. 100–101. (See also pp. 89 ff. where Wasserstrom discusses the justification of self-defense; and pp. 94–96, where he discusses the meaning of innocence in war.)

Critic

LAWRENCE A. ALEXANDER

Self-Defense and the Killing of Noncombatants
A Reply to Fullinwider

In a recent article[1] Robert Fullinwider argued that the distinction between combatants and noncombatants is morally relevant (in a sense unrelated to the existence of a specific convention among nations)[2] to the question of who among the enemy may be intentionally killed by a nation acting in self-defense. He concedes that the distinction is not based on the relative moral guilt or innocence of the two groups in connection with the prosecution of the war, recognizing that many combatants might be morally innocent (for example, reluctant conscripts) and many noncombatants morally guilty (for example, the governmental officials who launched the war). Moreover, he admits that guilt or innocence is relevant to the question of who should be punished by the defending nation. However, says Fullinwider, punishment of the guilty is not the only justification for intentional killing in war. Under the Principle of Self-Defense, innocent combatants, but not innocent noncombatants, may also justifiably be killed.

I do not intend to deny the widely held view that morally innocent persons may be intentionally killed in self-defense (although I believe a case can be made against it).[3] Rather, I intend to show that the permissibility of killing innocents in self-defense does not, as Fullinwider maintains, justify the moral distinction between combatants and noncombatants.

The heart of Fullinwider's argument is the following passage:

... [S]uppose Smith, through heavy gambling losses, is in debt to the mob for $100,000. The mobsters propose to Smith that if he will kill Jones (a crusading district attorney, say), they will forgive his debt. Unable to pay the debt, and knowing what will happen to him if he fails to pay it, Smith seeks out Jones and begins firing. Or, suppose the mobsters kidnap Smith's children and threaten to kill them unless he kills Jones. Driven by the threat, Smith seeks out Jones and begins firing.

None of this background information alters the situation from the point of view of self-defense. Whatever prompted Smith to fire at Jones, the justification for Jones' killing Smith lies solely in the fact that Smith was the direct and immediate agent of a threat against Jones' life. From the point of view of self-defense, this fact justifies Jones in killing Smith—and *only* Smith.

Again ... suppose the mobsters were parked across the street to observe Smith. After killing Smith, Jones could not turn his gun on them (assuming they were unarmed). No matter how causally implicated ... the mobsters were in Smith's assault on Jones, in the situation it was only Smith who was the agent of immediate threat to Jones; ... the mobsters were not posing a direct and immediate danger. From the point of view of justifiably killing in self-defense, they are not justifiably liable to be killed by Jones; they are immune.[4]

Fullinwider is correct that *after* killing Smith, Jones may not invoke the Principle of Self-Defense to then turn and kill the mobsters. *The threat to his life has been removed.* At most the mobsters may be

---

From Lawrence A. Alexander, "Self-Defense and the Killing of Noncombatants: A Reply to Fullinwider," *Philosophy and Public Affairs* 5, no. 4 (Summer 1976): 408–15. Some notes have been deleted. Reprinted by permission of Princeton University Press.

punished for their guilt in instigating the attempted murder.

However, Fullinwider's hypothetical is inapposite when we are discussing whether noncombatants along with combatants may be killed in an on-going war. Surely no one has contended that after surrender, the point analogous to the killing of Smith by Jones, innocent noncombatants may still be killed in self-defense. (Indeed, no one has contended as much for innocent combatants either.) Fullinwider has constructed a straw man.

Let us amend Fullinwider's hypothetical to make it relevant to the issue he is addressing. Suppose the situation is the same except that Jones has not yet killed Smith. May Jones invoke the Principle of Self-Defense to kill the mobsters instead of Smith if by doing so he will cause Smith to relent? Of course he may. If the mobsters had a gun trained on Smith and had ordered him to kill Jones, and he were about to comply, Jones not only could, but should, kill the mobsters rather than Smith if killing them would be no riskier than killing Smith and would remove the threat to Jones by removing Smith's motive for killing him. Jones should kill the mobsters in such a situation even if the mobsters could not kill Jones directly (say, because the range of their guns was sufficient to reach Smith but not Jones, who carried a longer-range gun). From the standpoint of the Principle of Self-Defense, both the mobsters and Smith are necessary causes of the danger to Jones because killing either the mobsters or Smith removes the danger. Jones should, therefore, kill the ones who are morally guilty, not the one who is morally innocent. Such an interpretation of the Principle of Self-Defense is consistent with its application in the law, and any interpretation that permitted only the killing of Smith would be morally perverse.

Indeed, it would be morally perverse to limit Jones' right of self-defense to the killing of Smith, even where the mobsters have not threatened Smith's life. Suppose the chief mobster has merely offered Smith money. The mobster, unarmed, is across the street from Smith and Jones, so that if Jones kills the mobster, Smith will realize that he will not get paid for killing Jones. Jones should be able to kill the mobster instead of Smith if the mobster is morally as guilty or guiltier than Smith (who might have been driven to the wall financially).

What I propose as the correct formulation of the Principle of Self-Defense is that X (a person or persons) may be killed in self-defense, regardless of X's moral innocence, if the defender perceives (reasonably) that: (1) there exists the requisite threshold level of danger or greater; (2) killing X will reduce that danger; (3) more desirable courses of action, such as killing fewer or guiltier persons, or not killing at all, will not eliminate condition (1); and (4) more desirable courses of action will not reduce the danger as much as killing X.

In war, many noncombatants, guilty and innocent, are threats to the defending nation. Many of them are greater threats than many combatants. A combatant at a camp miles behind the lines is often less a threat than a noncombatant delivering arms and ammunition to combatants at the front. Indeed, the combatants at the front individually will quite likely be less of a threat than the noncombatant supplier. In such a case the Principle of Self-Defense would demand that the noncombatant be killed in preference to the combatants, especially if he is no less guilty than they. Consider, also, two alternative courses of action in fighting a hypothetical unjust aggressor: (1) killing millions of enemy soldiers, most of whom are morally innocent (indeed, many are children); or (2) killing a handful of noncombatant enemy leaders, all of whom are morally innocent because of insanity. If either course would end the war, the latter would have to be preferred. Similarly, if one madman is about to deliver bombs to a thousand other madmen, who in turn will throw them, the Principle of Self-Defense demands that we end the danger by killing the former if we are going to be forced to kill in self-defense in any event.

Fullinwider's error could have resulted from assuming that one whose activity or existence is a remote cause (in terms of space, time, or intervening mechanisms or acts) of a threat to another's life is immune from being killed in self-defense, even though he is a necessary or sufficient cause of that threat. In the domestic context, causal remoteness will usually mean that the threat is insufficient to permit killing in self-defense. For in the domestic context, the more remote the cause of the threat, the more likely it is that factors such as the intervention of the police will prevent the harm from occurring, thus obviating the need to kill the cause of the threat. In the context of international warfare, remoteness, although relevant to the degree of the threat, is less significant, for there is less reason to assume that other factors short of killing will intervene and prevent the threat's materializing.

Although causal remoteness is relevant to the questions of whether a threat exists and whether a person is a necessary or sufficient cause of it, it is irrelevant to the right of self-defense once the threat, the necessary or sufficient causal relation, and the lack of superior alternatives to remove the threat are posited. Moreover, even if causal remoteness were the source of immunity from being killed in self-defense, it would not be the source of an immunity for noncombatants vis-à-vis combatants. As the example of the noncombatants front-line supplier and the rear guard combatants illustrates, some combatants are at any time more remote threats than some noncombatants. Fullinwider could, of course, respond that killing rear guard combatants is not consistent with the Principle of Self-Defense, or, what amounts to the same thing, that only front-line combatants are truly combatants. I do not take him to be making such a claim, which would be an indictment of widely accepted norms of warfare.

There is one other possible source of Fullinwider's error. He may hold the view that one is immune from being killed in self-defense if any further choice of a human agent is necessary for the harm to materialize. This view, he might believe, leads to the conclusion that only those who are sufficiently likely themselves to pull triggers (the infantry, but not the top generals, the ordnance personnel) or release bombs (the bombardiers, but not the pilots or navigators) may be killed. Although this view would not necessarily result in a distinction between combatants and noncombatants, because the likelihood of being killed in the future by one who is presently a noncombatant may exceed both the threshold required for self-defense and also the likelihood of being killed by particular combatants, it deserves a short comment. One cannot hold the view forbidding intervention before

the last choice necessary for the harm as an absolute and at the same time accept the Principle of Self-Defense. Most acts sanctioned by the Principle of Self-Defense occur at a point when at least one choice still remains before someone is actually harmed—that is, they occur when the aggressor can still choose to cease his aggression. The fact that further choices are necessary to bring about the harm affects the likelihood of that harm's materializing; and the greater the number of choices required, the less likely it is that the harm will result. Under the Principle of Self-Defense, however, only the likelihood of harm, not the number of choices required to bring it about, is directly relevant.

In some of the hypotheticals I have used, only one choice is required for the harm to result. The mobsters, if they are out of range of Smith's hearing, cannot through any choice affect, in the short run, the likelihood of Smith's killing Jones. Only Smith can.

In other hypotheticals, more than one choice is required. Either the noncombatant munitions supplier or the combatants could through their choices reduce or eliminate the danger. Both must choose to aid the war effort to create the danger.

Whether one or more choices is required, however, is morally irrelevant (so long as the threshold probability of danger has been reached) and in any event is irrelevant to the combatant-noncombatant distinction. Suppose the noncombatant supplier is driving a truck full of munitions under the watchful eyes of his armed countrymen. If he attempts to turn the truck around, he will be stopped, and someone else will drive it. At that point only the choices of those whose hands are on the triggers, not the choice of the supplier, can be considered necessary or sufficient to bring about the harm to the defending nation. The supplier is in a situation analogous to that of a pilot of a bomber which also carries a bombardier. Once the bomber is over the target, no further choice *by the pilot* (at least no choice which would not lead to his death anyway) is necessary or sufficient to cause the bombing to commence. No one who accepts the Principle of Self-Defense could argue that the plane may not be shot down because the bombardier still has a choice to make and might decide not to release the bombs. And I cannot imagine that anyone would argue that the Principle of Self-Defense permits killing *only* the bombardier, not the pilot, where the most effective means of preventing the bombing is shooting down the plane (which, let us suppose, presents a far greater risk of death to the pilot than to the bombardier). But if the pilot, normally thought of as a combatant, may be killed in self-defense, so may the supplier, a noncombatant, perhaps by bombing the truck in order to blow up the munitions.

Finally, if noncombatants (say, children) were involuntarily harnessed with bombs and pushed down a slippery slope towards the troops of the defending nation, the bombs to be released automatically once the children were halfway down the slope, *no* further choice would be necessary to bring about the threatened harm. If the bombs could not be safely shot and detonated once they were released, self-defense would permit shooting the bombs before they were released and blowing up them and their noncombatant carriers, just as it would permit such an act if the carriers were morally innocent conscripted soldiers.

It is apparent, therefore, that neither the number of choices required to bring about the harm nor combatant-noncombatant status is morally relevant to the right to kill in self-defense.

In summary, punishment requires guilt, but guilt, even relative guilt, does not mark the distinction between combatants and noncombatants. On the other hand, the right to kill in self-defense requires only that the person killed be a necessary or sufficient cause of a danger, not that he be morally guilty. Again, however, being a cause of danger does not mark the distinction between combatants and noncombatants. Moreover, noncombatants are not necessarily more remote causes of danger than are combatants; nor is the danger noncombatants pose necessarily more dependent upon further choices than is the danger posed by combatants. Finally, neither causal remoteness nor the necessity of further choices is per se relevant to the Principle of Self-Defense. I conclude, therefore, that the intentional killing of innocent noncombatants is not necessarily immoral if one accepts the Principle of Self-Defense.

Notes

1. Robert K. Fullinwider, "War and Innocence," *Philosophy & Public Affairs* 5, no. 1 (Fall 1975): 90.

2. See George I. Mavrodes, "Conventions and the Morality of War," *Philosophy & Public Affairs* 4, no. 2 (Winter 1975): 121, 126.

3. The formulation I shall give of the principle that allows the killing of innocent persons in self-defense can, for example, logically be extended to cover acts of terrorism, atomic bombings of cities, etc.

4. Fullinwider, "War and Innocence," pp. 92–93.

2

Is Euthanasia Wrong?

Rachels and His Critics

Imagine that you have been diagnosed with cancer, that it has spread to your vital organs, including your brain, and that it is fairly certain that your death is just a matter of days, or, at most, weeks away. Your remaining time is going to be extremely painful, and rather undignified, and you have no desire to live through it at all. You have come to regard your own death not as the ultimate evil but rather as a welcome release from intolerable suffering, suffering that infuses your entire being. You would prefer that someone take active steps to end your life rather than simply allow an indifferent Nature to take its dreadfully slow and humiliating course. You have asked me, in particular, to give you a dose of some drug powerful enough to bring about your quick and painless death now. Would it be wrong for me to do this?

Many people think that it would, in fact, be morally wrong for me to kill you in such circumstances. Now suppose that in addition to all of this, as often happens with bedridden patients, you contract pneumonia. The pneumonia could easily be cured with antibiotics, but if left untreated it will bring about your death—probably a quicker and far less unpleasant death than the one that otherwise awaits you. And suppose that you therefore ask that you not be given the antibiotics. In a case like this, many people think that it would be morally permissible for me to withhold the antibiotics. In other words, they think it would be morally permissible for me to let you die an easily preventable death.

Killing a terminally ill patient who wants to die, and whose death would be a blessing for him, is a case of active euthanasia. Allowing a terminally ill patient, who wants to die, to die, one whose death would be a blessing for her but whose imminent death is preventable, is a case of passive euthanasia. Many people think that passive euthanasia can sometimes be morally permissible, whereas active euthanasia is always morally impermissible. Their reason for endorsing this moral difference is that they think that killing someone is morally worse, in itself, than letting someone die.

In the featured article on the subject in this chapter, James Rachels argues that one cannot rationally maintain this pair of judgments. Killing, Rachels claims, is morally equivalent to letting die. Let us call this the "equivalence thesis." Rachels argues for the equivalence thesis by means of a bare-difference argument. (Indeed, it was Rachels who coined the term "bare-difference argument" in connection with this very issue.) As noted in the Introduction (see section 4.2), the strategy is this: We are interested in what features make a moral difference and whether they make a difference for the better or for the worse. A good-making feature should, *other things being equal,* make a situation better, and a bad-making feature should, *other things being equal,* make a situation worse. If killing is morally worse, in itself, than letting die, then a case of killing should be worse than a case of letting die, provided other things are equal.

Suppose you take a pair of cases, case A and case B, where case A is a killing and case B is a letting-die, and suppose that case A, say, is morally on a par with case B. Does that mean that killing is not worse than letting die? No. This comparison of cases might not be enough, because case A might differ from case B in *other* ways, and one or more of those other features might make up for the moral difference between killing and letting die. In order to know that the killing/letting die difference does not make a moral difference, you have to eliminate any other differences that might make a moral difference. Suppose, then, that the *only* difference between case A and case B is that case A is a killing and case B is a letting-die, and it turns out that case A is morally on a par with case B. Then killing is not worse than letting die, and given the plausible assumption that killing is not better, in itself, than letting die, it seems to follow that killing and letting die are morally on a par.

Rachels considers two stories that apparently differ in only this one respect: One is a killing, and the other is a letting-die. Smith kills his six-year-old cousin in order to gain a large inheritance. Jones lets his six-year-old cousin die (when he could easily prevent it) in order to gain a large inheritance. Is the Smith case worse than the Jones case? If your answer is no, then, Rachels argues, killing must be morally on a par with letting die. And if this is so, then it seems impossible to maintain that passive euthanasia is morally permissible while active euthanasia is not.

In his contribution to this debate, Winston Nesbitt accepts the bare-difference strategy itself. And he does not take issue with Rachels's judgment on the cases of Smith and Jones. But he rejects Rachels's conclusion, and so he is obliged to take issue with the claim that these cases differ only in this respect: that one is a killing and the other is a letting-die. And that is precisely what he does. Nesbitt argues that there is a crucial further difference between the two cases, a difference that is itself morally relevant. In addition, he argues that if one removed this crucial difference and constructed a modified Jones story, then our judgments would actually undermine the equivalence thesis that Rachels endorses.

Roy W. Perrett responds directly to Nesbitt's criticism. He argues that Nesbitt has changed the subject by shifting from moral evaluation of the respective *acts* to moral evaluation of the respective *agents.* Further, Perrett goes on to argue that Nesbitt is wrong to claim that he has identified a morally relevant difference between Rachels's two cases.

QUESTIONS FOR CONSIDERATION

• What, according to Nesbitt, is the morally relevant difference between the cases of Smith and Jones?

• There are certain kinds of differences between the two cases that even Rachels would not deny. For example, Jones is a different person from Smith. Jones's cousin dies at a moment different from that at which Smith's cousin dies. The drownings take place in different bathtubs and so on. Are any of these differences morally relevant? Can you show that they are morally irrelevant by means of bare-difference arguments?

- Take the issue of timing. Can you construct two cases that differ only with respect to the time of occurrence: same location, same participants, same mental states, in the same order? What can you conclude about timing from a consideration of two such cases?
- Nesbitt offers a modified version of Rachels's story. What, if anything, does Nesbitt's modified version of the story tell us? Does it tell us that the only thing that matters in the evaluation of character is intention?
- Perrett maintains that Nesbitt misconstrues the structure of a bare-difference argument. What is his reason for this? Is he right?

FURTHER READING

Gennaro, Rocco J. "The Relevance of Intentions in Morality and Euthanasia." *International Philosophical Quarterly* 36, no. 2 (June 1996): 217–27.

Haslett, D. W. "Moral Taxonomy and Rachels' Thesis." *Public Affairs Quarterly* 10, no. 4 (1996): 291–306.

Hopkins, Patrick D. "Why Does Removing Machines Count as Passive Euthanasia?" *Hastings Center Report* 27, no. 3 (May–June 1997): 29–37.

Kagan, S. "The Additive Fallacy." *Ethics* 99, no. 1 (1988): 5–31.

Oddie, G. "Killing and Letting-Die: From Bare Differences to Clear Differences." *Philosophical Studies* 88 (1997): 267–87.

Steinbock, Bonnie, and Alastair Norcross, eds. *Killing and Letting Die*. 2nd ed. (New York: Fordham University Press), 1994.

JAMES RACHELS

Active and Passive Euthanasia

The distinction between active and passive euthanasia is thought to be crucial for medical ethics. The idea is that it is permissible, at least in some cases, to withhold treatment and allow a patient to die, but it is never permissible to take any direct action designed to kill the patient. This doctrine seems to be accepted by most doctors, and it is endorsed in a statement adopted by the House of Delegates of the American Medical Association on December 4, 1973:

The intentional termination of the life of one human being by another—mercy killing—is contrary to that for which the medical profession stands and is contrary to the policy of the American Medical Association.

The cessation of the employment of extraordinary means to prolong the life of the body when there is irrefutable evidence that biological death is imminent is the decision of the patient and/or his immediate family. The advice and judgment of the physician should be freely available to the patient and/or his immediate family.

However, a strong case can be made against this doctrine. In what follows I will set out some of the rele-

Reprinted by permission of *The New England Journal of Medicine* 292 (January 9, 1975): 78–80.

vant arguments, and urge doctors to reconsider their views on this matter.

To begin with a familiar type of situation, a patient who is dying of incurable cancer of the throat is in terrible pain, which can no longer be satisfactorily alleviated. He is certain to die within a few days, even if present treatment is continued, but he does not want to go on living for those days since the pain is unbearable. So he asks the doctor for an end to it, and his family joins in the request.

Suppose the doctor agrees to withhold treatment, as the conventional doctrine says he may. The justification for his doing so is that the patient is in terrible agony, and since he is going to die anyway, it would he wrong to prolong his suffering needlessly. But now notice this. If one simply withholds treatment, it may take the patient longer to die, and so he may suffer more than he would if more direct action were taken and a lethal injection given. This fact provides strong reason for thinking that, once the initial decision not to prolong his agony has been made active euthanasia is actually preferable to passive euthanasia, rather than the reverse. To say otherwise is to endorse the option that leads to more suffering rather than less, and is contrary to the humanitarian impulse that prompts the decision not to prolong his life in the first place.

Part of my point is that the process of being "allowed to die" can be relatively slow and painful, whereas being given a lethal injection is relatively quick and painless. Let me give a different sort of example. In the United States about one in 600 babies is born with Down's syndrome. Most of these babies are otherwise healthy—that is, with only the usual pediatric care, they will proceed to an otherwise normal infancy. Some, however, are born with congenital defects such as intestinal obstructions that require operations if they are to live. Sometimes, the parents and the doctor will decide not to operate, and let the infant die. Anthony Shaw describes what happens then:

> . . . When surgery is denied the doctor must try to keep the infant from suffering while natural forces sap the baby's life away. As a surgeon whose natural inclination is to use the scalpel to fight off death, standing by and watching a salvageable baby die is the most emotionally

exhausting experience I know. It is easy at a conference, in a theoretical discussion, to decide that such infants should be allowed to die. It is altogether different to stand by in the nursery and watch as dehydration and infection wither a tiny being over hours and days. This is a terrible ordeal for me and the hospital staff—much more so than for the parents who never set foot in the nursery.

I can understand why some people are opposed to all euthanasia, and insist that such infants must be allowed to live. I think I can also understand why other people favor destroying these babies quickly and painlessly. But why should anyone favor letting "dehydration and infection wither a tiny being over hours and days?" The doctrine that says that a baby may be allowed to dehydrate and wither, but may not be given an injection that would end its life without suffering, seems so patently cruel as to require no further refutation. The strong language is not intended to offend, but only to put the point in the clearest possible way.

My second argument is that the conventional doctrine leads to decisions concerning life and death made on irrelevant grounds.

Consider again the case of the infants with Down's syndrome who need operations for congenital defects unrelated to the syndrome to live. Sometimes, there is no operation, and the baby dies, but when there is no such defect, the baby lives on. Now, an operation such as that to remove an intestinal obstruction is not prohibitively difficult. The reason why such operations are not performed in these cases is, clearly, that the child has Down's syndrome and the parents and doctor judge that because of that fact it is better for the child to die.

But notice that this situation is absurd, no matter what view one takes of the lives and potentials of such babies. If the life of such an infant is worth preserving, what does it matter if it needs a simple operation? Or, if one thinks it better that such a baby should not live on, what difference does it make that it happens to have an unobstructed intestinal tract? In either case, the matter of life and death is being decided on irrelevant grounds. It is the Down's syndrome, and not the intestines, that is the issue. The matter should be decided, if at all, on that basis, and not be allowed to depend on the essentially irrelevant question of whether the intestinal tract is blocked.

What makes this situation possible, of course, is the idea that when there is an intestinal blockage, one can "let the baby die," but when there is no such defect there is nothing that can be done, for one must not "kill" it. The fact that this idea leads to such results as deciding life or death on irrelevant grounds is another good reason why the doctrine should be rejected.

One reason why so many people think that there is an important moral difference between active and passive euthanasia is that they think killing someone is morally worse than letting someone die. But is it? Is killing, in itself, worse than letting die? To investigate this issue, two cases may be considered that are exactly alike except that one involves killing whereas the other involves letting someone die. Then, it can be asked whether this difference makes any difference to the moral assessments. It is important that the cases be exactly alike, except for this one difference, since otherwise one cannot be confident that it is this difference and not some other that accounts for any variation in the assessments of the two cases. So, let us consider this pair of cases:

In the first, Smith stands to gain a large inheritance if anything should happen to his six-year-old cousin. One evening while the child is taking his bath, Smith sneaks into the bathroom and drowns the child, and then arranges things so that it will look like an accident.

In the second, Jones also stands to gain if anything should happen to his six-year-old cousin. Like Smith, Jones sneaks in planning to drown the child in his bath. However, just as he enters the bathroom, Jones sees the child slip and hit his head, and fall face down in the water. Jones is delighted; he stands by, ready to push the child's head back under if it is necessary, but it is not necessary. With only a little thrashing about, the child drowns all by himself, "accidentally," as Jones watches and does nothing.

Now Smith killed the child, whereas Jones "merely" let the child die. That is the only difference between them. Did either man behave better, from a moral point of view? If the difference between killing and letting die were in itself a morally important matter, one should say that Jones's behavior was less reprehensible than Smith's. But does one really want to say that? I think not. In the first place, both men acted from the same motive, personal gain, and both had exactly the same end in view when they acted. It may be inferred from Smith's conduct that he is a bad man, although that judgment may be withdrawn or modified if certain further facts are learned about him—for example, that he is mentally deranged. But would not the very same thing be inferred about Jones from his conduct? And would not the same further considerations also be relevant to any modification of this judgment? Moreover, suppose Jones pleaded, in his own defense, "After all, I didn't do anything except just stand there and watch the child drown. I didn't kill him; I only let him die." Again, if letting die were in itself less bad than killing, this defense should have at least some weight. But it does not. Such a "defense" can only be regarded as a grotesque perversion of moral reasoning. Morally speaking, it is no defense at all.

Now, it may be pointed out, quite properly, that the cases of euthanasia with which doctors are concerned are not like this at all. They do not involve personal gain or the destruction of normal healthy children. Doctors are concerned only with cases in which the patient's life is of no further use to him, or in which the patient's life has become or will soon become a terrible burden. However, the point is the same in these cases: the bare difference between killing and letting die does not, in itself, make a moral difference. If a doctor lets a patient die, for humane reasons, he is in the same moral position as if he had given the patient a lethal injection for humane reasons. If his decision was wrong—if, for example, the patient's illness was in fact curable—the decision would be equally regrettable no matter which method was used to carry it out. And if the doctor's decision was the right one, the method used is not in itself important.

The AMA policy statement isolates the crucial issue very well; the crucial issue is "the intentional termination of the life of one human being by another." But after identifying this issue, and forbidding "mercy killing," the statement goes on to deny that the cessation of treatment is the intentional termination of a life. This is where the mistake comes in, for what is the cessation of treatment, in these circumstances, if it is not "the intentional termination of the life of one human being by another?" Of course it is exactly that, and if it were not, there would be no point to it.

Many people will find this judgment hard to accept. One reason, I think, is that it is very easy to conflate the question of whether killing is, in itself worse than letting die, with the very different question of whether most actual cases of killing are more reprehensible than most actual cases of letting die. Most actual cases of killing are clearly terrible (think, for example, of all the murders reported in the newspapers), and one hears of such crises every day. On the other hand, one hardly ever hears of a case of letting die, except for the actions of doctors who are motivated by humanitarian reasons. So one learns to think of killing in a much worse light than of letting die. But this does not mean that there is something about killing that makes it in itself worse than letting die, for it is not the bare difference between killing and letting die that makes the difference in these cases. Rather, the other factors—the murderer's motive of personal gain, for example, contrasted with the doctor's humanitarian motivation—account for different reactions to the different cases.

I have argued that killing is not in itself any worse than letting die; if my contention is right, it follows that active euthanasia is not any worse than passive euthanasia. What arguments can be given on the other side? The most common, I believe, is the following:

> The important difference between active and passive euthanasia is that, in passive euthanasia, the doctor does not do anything to bring about the patient's death. The doctor does nothing, and the patient dies of whatever ills already afflict him. In active euthanasia, however, the doctor does something to bring about the patient's death: he kills him. The doctor who gives the patient with cancer a lethal injection has himself caused his patient's death; whereas if he merely ceases treatment, the cancer is the cause of the death.

A number of points need to be made here. The first is that it is not exactly correct to say that in passive euthanasia the doctor does nothing, for he does do one thing that is very important: he lets the patient die. "Letting someone die" is certainly different, in some respects, from other types of action—mainly in that it is a kind of action that one may perform by way of not performing certain other actions. For example, one may let a patient die by way of not giving medication, just as one may insult someone by way of not shaking his hand. But for any purpose of moral assessment, it is a type of action nonetheless. The decision to let a patient die is subject to moral appraisal in the same way that a decision to kill him would be subject to moral appraisal: it may be assessed as wise or unwise, compassionate or sadistic, right or wrong. If a doctor deliberately let a patient die who was suffering from a routinely curable illness, the doctor would certainly be to blame for what he had done, just as he would be to blame if he had needlessly killed the patient. Charges against him would then be appropriate. If so, it would be no defense at all for him to insist that he didn't "do anything." He would have done something very serious indeed, for he let his patient die.

Fixing the cause of death may be very important from a legal point of view, for it may determine whether criminal charges are brought against the doctor. But I do not think that this notion can be used to show a moral difference between active and passive euthanasia. The reason why it is considered bad to be the cause of someone's death is that death is regarded as a great evil—and so it is. However, if it has been decided that euthanasia—even passive euthanasia—is desirable in a given case, it has also been decided that in this instance death is no greater an evil than the patient's continued existence. And if this is true, the usual reason for not wanting to be the cause of someone's death simply does not apply.

Finally, doctors may think that all of this is only of academic interest—the sort of thing that philosophers may worry about but that has no practical bearing on their own work. After all, doctors must be concerned about the legal consequences of what they do, and active euthanasia is clearly forbidden by the law. But even so, doctors should also be concerned with the fact that the law is forcing upon them a moral doctrine that may well be indefensible, and has a considerable effect on their practices. Of course, most doctors are not now in the position of being coerced in this matter, for they do not regard themselves as merely going along with what the law requires. Rather, in statements such as the AMA policy statement that I have quoted, they are endorsing this doctrine as a central point of medical ethics. In that statement, active euthanasia is condemned not merely as illegal but as "contrary to that for which the medical profession stands," whereas passive euthanasia is approved. However, the preceding considerations suggest that there is really no moral difference between the two, considered in themselves (there may be important moral differences in some cases in their *consequences,* but, as I pointed out, these differences may make active euthanasia, and not passive euthanasia, the morally preferable option). So, whereas doctors may have to discriminate between active and passive euthanasia to satisfy the law, they should not do any more than that. In particular, they should not give the distinction any added authority and weight by writing it into official statements of medical ethics.

Critics

WINSTON NESBITT

Is Killing No Worse Than Letting Die?

I want in this paper to consider a kind of argument sometimes produced against the thesis that it is worse to kill someone (that is, to deliberately take action that results in another's death) than merely to allow someone to die (that is, deliberately to fail to take steps which were available and which would have saved another's life). Let us, for brevity's sake, refer to this as the "difference thesis," since it implies that there is a moral difference between killing and letting die. . . .

2

It might seem at first glance a simple matter to show at least that common moral intuitions favour the difference thesis. Compare, . . . the case in which I push someone who I know cannot swim into a river, thereby killing her, with that in which I come across someone drowning and fail to rescue her, although I am able to do so, thereby letting her die. Wouldn't most of us agree that my behaviour is morally worse in the first case?

However, it would be generally agreed by those involved in the debate that nothing of importance for our issue, not even concerning common opinion, can be learned through considering such an example. . . . [W]ithout being told any more about the cases mentioned, we are inclined to assume that there are other morally relevant differences between them, because there usually would be. We assume, for

Winston Nesbitt, "Is Killing No Worse Than Letting Die?" *Journal of Applied Philosophy* 12, no. 1 (1995): 101–5. Notes have been deleted. Reprinted by permission of Blackwell Publishing Ltd.

example, some malicious motive in the case of killing, but perhaps only fear or indifference in the case of failing to save. James Rachels and Michael Tooley, both of whom argue against the difference thesis, make similar points.[1] . . . Tooley, for example, notes that as well as differences in motives, there are also certain other morally relevant differences between typical acts of killing and typical acts of failing to save which may make us judge them differently. Typically, saving someone requires more effort than refraining from killing someone. Again, an act of killing necessarily results in someone's death, but an act of failing to save does not—someone else may come to the rescue. Factors such as these, it is suggested, may account for our tendency to judge failure to save (i.e., letting die) less harshly than killing. Tooley concludes that if one wishes to appeal to intuitions here, "one must be careful to confine one's attention to pairs of cases that do not differ in these, or other significant respects."[2]

Accordingly, efforts are made by opponents of the difference thesis to produce pairs of cases which do not differ in morally significant respects (other than in one being a case of killing while the other is a case of letting die or failing to save). In fact, at least the major part of the case mounted by Rachels and Tooley against the difference thesis consists of the production of such examples. It is suggested that when we compare a case of killing with one which differs from it *only* in being a case of letting die, we will agree that either agent is as culpable as the other; and this is then taken to show that any inclination we ordinarily have to think killing worse than letting die is attributable to our tending, illegitimately, to think of typical cases of killing and of letting die, which differ in other morally relevant respects. I want now to examine the kind of example usually produced in these contexts.

3

I will begin with the examples produced by James Rachels in the article mentioned earlier, which is fast becoming one of the most frequently reprinted articles in the area. Although the article has been the subject of a good deal of discussion, as far as I know the points

which I will make concerning it have not been previously made. Rachels asks us to compare the following two cases. The first is that of Smith, who will gain a large inheritance should his six-year-old nephew die. With this in mind, Smith one evening sneaks into the bathroom where his nephew is taking a bath, and drowns him. The other case, that of Jones, is identical, except that as Jones is about to drown his nephew, the child slips, hits his head, and falls, face down and unconscious, into the bath water. Jones, delighted at his good fortune, watches as his nephew drowns.

Rachels assumes that we will readily agree that Smith, who kills his nephew, is no worse, morally speaking, than Jones, who merely lets his nephew die. Do we really want to say, he asks, that either behaves better from the moral point of view than the other? It would, he suggests, be a "grotesque perversion of moral reasoning" for Jones to argue, "After all, I didn't do anything except just stand and watch the child drown. I didn't kill him; I only let him die." Yet, Rachels says, if letting die were in itself less bad than killing, this defence would carry some weight.

There is little doubt that Rachels is correct in taking it that we will agree that Smith behaves no worse in his examples than does Jones. Before we are persuaded by this that killing someone is in itself morally no worse than letting someone die, though, we need to consider the examples more closely. We concede that Jones, who merely let his nephew die, is just as reprehensible as Smith, who killed his nephew. Let us ask, however, just what is the ground of our judgement of the agent in each case. In the case of Smith, this seems to be adequately captured by saying that Smith drowned his nephew for motives of personal gain. But can we say that the grounds on which we judge Jones to be reprehensible, and just as reprehensible as Smith, are that he let his nephew drown for motives of personal gain? I suggest not—for this neglects to mention a crucial fact about Jones, namely that he was fully prepared to kill his nephew, and would have done so had it proved necessary. It would be generally accepted, I think, quite independently of the present debate, that someone who is fully prepared to perform a reprehensible action, in the expectation of certain circumstances, but does not do so because the expected circumstances do not eventuate, is just as reprehensible as someone who actually performs that action in those circumstances. Now this alone is sufficient to account for our judging Jones as harshly as Smith. He was fully prepared to do what Smith did, and would have done so if circumstances had not turned out differently from those in Smith's case. Thus, though we may agree that he is just as reprehensible as Smith, this cannot be taken as showing that his letting his nephew die is as reprehensible as Smith's killing his nephew—for we would have judged him just as harshly, given what he was prepared to do, even if he had not let his nephew die. To make this clear, suppose that we modify Jones' story along the following lines—as before, he sneaks into the bathroom while his nephew is bathing, with the intention of drowning the child in his bath. This time, however, just before he can seize the child, *he* slips and hits his head on the bath, knocking himself unconscious. By the time he regains consciousness, the child, unaware of his intentions, has called his parents, and the opportunity is gone. Here, Jones neither kills his nephew *nor* lets him die—yet I think it would be agreed that given his preparedness to kill the child for personal gain, he is as reprehensible as Smith.

The examples produced by Michael Tooley, . . . suffer the same defect as those produced by Rachels. Tooley asks us to consider the following pair of scenarios, as it happens also featuring Smith and Jones. In the first, Jones is about to shoot Smith when he sees that Smith will be killed by a bomb unless Jones warns him, as he easily can. Jones does not warn him, and he is killed by the bomb—i.e., Jones lets Smith die. In the other, Jones wants Smith dead, and shoots him—i.e., he kills Smith.

Tooley elsewhere produces this further example: two sons are looking forward to the death of their wealthy father, and decide independently to poison him. One puts poison in his father's whiskey, and is discovered doing so by the other, who was just about to do the same. The latter then allows his father to drink the poisoned whiskey, and refrains from giving him the antidote, which he happens to possess.

Tooley is confident that we will agree that in each pair of cases, the agent who kills is morally no worse than the one who lets die. It will be clear, however, that his examples are open to criticisms parallel to those just produced against Rachels. To take first the case where Jones is saved the trouble of killing Smith by the fortunate circumstance of a bomb's being about to explode near the latter: it is true that we judge Jones to be just as reprehensible as if he had killed Smith, but since he was fully prepared to kill him had he not been saved the trouble by the bomb, we would make the same judgement even if he had neither killed Smith nor let him die (even if, say, no bomb had been present, but Smith suffered a massive and timely heart attack). As for the example of the like-minded sons, here too the son who didn't kill was prepared to do so, and given this, would be as reprehensible as the other even if he had not let his father die (if, say, he did not happen to possess the antidote, and so was powerless to save him).

Let us try to spell out more clearly just where the examples produced by Rachels and Tooley fail. What both writers overlook is that what determines whether someone is reprehensible or not is not simply what he in fact does, but what he is prepared to do, perhaps as revealed by what he in fact does. Thus, while Rachels is correct in taking it that we will be inclined to judge Smith and Jones in his examples equally harshly, this is not surprising, since both are judged reprehensible for precisely the same reason, namely that they were fully prepared to kill for motives of personal gain. The same, of course, is true of Tooley's examples. In each example he gives of an agent who lets another die, the agent is fully prepared to kill (though in the event, he is spared the necessity). In their efforts to ensure that the members of each pair of cases they produce do not differ in any morally relevant respect (except that one is a case of killing and the other of letting die), Rachels and Tooley make them *too* similar—not only do Rachels' Smith and Jones, for example, have identical motives, but both are guilty of the same moral offence.

4

Given the foregoing account of the failings of the examples produced by Rachels and Tooley, what modifications do they require if they are to be legitimately used to gauge our attitudes towards killing and letting die, respectively? Let us again concentrate on

Rachels' examples. Clearly, if his argument is to avoid the defect pointed out, we must stipulate that though Jones was prepared to let his nephew die once he saw that this would happen unless he intervened, he was not prepared to kill the child. The story will now go something like this: Jones stands to gain considerably from his nephew's death, as before, but he is not prepared to kill him for this reason. However, he happens to be on hand when his nephew slips, hits his head, and falls face down in the bath. Remembering that he will profit from the child's death, he allows him to drown. We need, however, to make a further stipulation, regarding the explanation of Jones's not being prepared to kill his nephew. It cannot be that he fears untoward consequences for himself, such as detection and punishment, or that he is too lazy to choose such an active course, or that the idea simply had not occurred to him. I think it would be common ground in the debate that if the only explanation of his not being prepared to kill his nephew was one of these kinds, he would be morally no better than Smith, who differed only in being more daring, or more energetic, whether or not fate then happened to offer him the opportunity to let his nephew die instead. In that case, we must suppose that the reason Jones is prepared to let his nephew die, but not to kill him, is a moral one—not intervening to save the child, he holds, is one thing, but actually bringing about his death is another, and altogether beyond the pale.

I suggest, then, that the case with which we must compare that of Smith is this: Jones happens to be on hand when his nephew slips, hits his head, and falls unconscious into his bath water. It is clear to Jones that the child will drown if he does not intervene. He remembers that the child's death would be greatly to his advantage, and does not intervene. Though he is prepared to let the child die however, and in fact does so, he would not have been prepared to kill him, because, as he might put it, wicked though he is, he draws the line at killing for gain.

I am not entirely sure what the general opinion would be here as to the relative reprehensibility of Smith and Jones. I can only report my own, which is

that Smith's behaviour is indeed morally worse than that of Jones. What I do want to insist on, however, is that, for the reasons I have given, we cannot take our reactions to the examples provided by Rachels and Tooley as an indication of our intuitions concerning the relative heinousness of killing and of letting die.

So far, we have restricted ourselves to discussion of common intuitions on our question, and made no attempt to argue for any particular answer. I will conclude by pointing out that, given the fairly common view that the raison d'être of morality is to make it possible for people to live together in reasonable peace and security, it is not difficult to provide a rationale for the intuition that in our modified version of Rachels' examples, Jones is less reprehensible than Smith. For it is clearly preferable to have Jones-like persons around rather than Smith-like ones. We are not threatened by the former—such a person will not save me if my life should be in danger, but in this he is no more dangerous than an incapacitated person, or for that matter, a rock or tree (in fact he may be better, for he *might* save me as long as he doesn't think he will profit from my death). Smith-like persons, however, *are* a threat—if such a person should come to believe that she will benefit sufficiently from my death, then not only must I expect no help from her if my life happens to be in danger, but I must fear positive attempts on my life. In that case, given the view mentioned of the point of morality, people prepared to behave as Smith does are clearly of greater concern from the moral point of view than those prepared only to behave as Jones does; which is to say that killing is indeed morally worse than letting die.

NOTES

1. James Rachels (1979) Active and passive euthanasia in James Rachels (ed.), *Moral Problems* (NY, Harper and Row), pp. 490–497; Michael Tooley (1983) *Abortion and Infanticide* (Oxford, Clarendon Press), pp. 187–188.

2. Tooley, op. cit., p. 189.

Roy W. Perrett

Killing, Letting Die, and the Bare Difference Argument

I

In company with many other philosophers, I believe that there is no intrinsic moral difference between killing and letting die. That is, there is no difference that depends solely on the distinction between an act and an omission. I shall call this (following James Rachels) the Equivalence Thesis. I also believe that we can reasonably establish this thesis by appeal to what Rachels calls the Bare Difference Argument. The form of this argument involves considering two imaginary cases in which there are no morally relevant differences present, save the bare difference that one is a case of killing and one a case of letting die. But in the pair of cases under consideration this bare difference makes no moral difference. Hence it cannot be that the bare difference between killing and letting die is in itself a morally important difference.

Winston Nesbitt has recently argued that the Bare Difference Argument fails because "the examples produced typically possess a feature which makes their use in this context illegitimate, and that when modified to remove this feature, they provide support for the view which they were designed to undermine". I shall argue that Nesbitt misunderstands the logic of the Bare Difference Argument and that accordingly his objections to the Equivalence Thesis are mistaken. . . .

III

Nesbitt . . . claims that (i) Rachels' two cases . . . are not in fact exactly similar in all morally relevant respects save that one is a case of killing and one a case of letting die; and (ii) if we modify the two cases so as to remove the extra morally relevant feature, the modified cases instead support the *denial* of the Equivalence Thesis.

It is not that Nesbitt disagrees with Rachels' claim that we should judge that Smith behaves no worse than Jones. However, he believes this should not lead us to embrace the Equivalence Thesis, for there is a crucial, morally relevant feature that is ignored in Rachels' treatment of the two cases:

> Let us ask . . . just what is the ground of our judgement of the agent in each case. In the case of Smith, this seems to be adequately captured by saying that Smith drowned his [cousin] for motives of personal gain. But can we say that the grounds on which we judge Jones to be reprehensible, and just as reprehensible as Smith, are that he let his [cousin] drown for motives of personal gain? I suggest not—for this neglects to mention a crucial fact about Jones, namely that he was fully prepared to kill his [cousin], and would have done so had it proved necessary.

Nesbitt goes on to claim that the following moral principle is generally accepted: "someone who is fully prepared to perform a reprehensible action, in the expectation of certain circumstances, but does not do so because the expected circumstances do not eventuate, is just as reprehensible as someone who actually performs that action in those circumstances." From this he concludes that our condemnation of Jones's action as morally equivalent to Smith's derives not from the moral equivalence of killing and letting die, but from Jones's violation of the above principle.

To bring this out Nesbitt suggests we modify the original Jones story along the following lines:

From Roy W. Perrett, "Killing, Letting Die and the Bare Difference Argument," *Bioethics* 10, no. 2 (1996): 131–39. Some notes and some parts of the text have been deleted. Reprinted by permission of Blackwell Publishing Ltd.

...as before, he sneaks into the bathroom while his [cousin] is bathing, with the intention of drowning the child in his bath. This time, however, just before he can seize the child, *he* slips and hits his head on the bath, knocking himself unconscious. By the time he regains consciousness, the child, unaware of his intentions, has called his parents, and the opportunity is gone. Here Jones neither kills his [cousin] *nor* lets him die—yet I think it would be agreed that given his preparedness to kill the child for personal gain, he is as reprehensible as Smith.[1]

IV

So far as I can see, all of this argumentation is a complete ignoratio elenchi and badly misconstrues the logical structure of the Bare Difference Argument. First, note that in Nesbitt's modified case we are now concerned with *agent* evaluation ("Jones is as morally reprehensible as Smith"), not the *act* evaluation relevant to determining whether there is an intrinsic moral difference between *acts* of killing and letting die (i.e. whether the Equivalence Thesis is true). Secondly, in fact many would dispute that Jones now is as morally reprehensible as Smith, given the way things turned out in Nesbitt's example (this is the problem of moral luck). Thirdly, and most importantly, it is clear that Rachels' original Smith and Jones stories can easily accommodate the supposed moral significance of Jones's willingness to kill the boy if a strategy of letting die proves insufficient to achieve his ends. For insofar as this willingness is morally significant, we can assume it constant in both of Rachels' cases. That is, it is true of Jones (as Rachels makes explicit) that he intends to kill his cousin if the option of letting him die is not feasible. But presumably exactly the same is true of Smith: he also intends to kill his cousin if the option of letting die is not feasible. True, Rachels does not make this explicit about Smith (though perhaps he thought it implicit). However, we can easily stipulate that this is indeed true of Smith, in which case both Smith's and Jones's actions are exactly alike with respect to this supposedly morally relevant intention. Thus the only difference between their actions that now remains is that one is an act of killing and one is an act of letting

die. But if we then agree we should still judge the actions of Smith and Jones to be morally equivalent (as presumably Nesbitt does), we must conclude that the bare difference between killing and letting die cannot be in itself a morally relevant difference.

Having thus misunderstood the point of the examples Rachels (and others) offer in support of the Bare Difference Argument, Nesbitt goes on to suggest that we need to modify their examples to avoid the defect he (mis)perceives himself to have uncovered. In the Jones case the story should now go something like the following (call this "the modified-Jones case"):

> Jones happens to be on hand when his [cousin] slips, hits his head, and falls unconscious into his bath water. It is clear to Jones that the child will drown if he does not intervene. He remembers that the child's death would be greatly to his advantage, and does not intervene. Though he is prepared to let the child die however, and in fact does so, he would not have been prepared to kill him, because, as he might put it, wicked though he is, he draws the line at killing for gain.

Nesbitt reports that when he compares the cases of Smith and modified-Jones he judges that Smith's behaviour is indeed morally worse than modified-Jones's. Whether or not we agree with this judgement is, of course, irrelevant to the central issue here: i.e. the soundness of the Bare Difference Argument. The Argument requires that the two cases invoked are alike in all morally relevant respects, save that one is a case of killing and one is a case of letting die. If we suppose with Nesbitt that an intention to kill the boy if letting die is not a feasible option is itself a morally relevant feature which is not present in both cases, then the original case of Smith and the case of modified-Jones obviously cannot be paired in a Bare Difference Argument. This is because they do not share, as the Argument's structure requires, all morally relevant features save that one is a case of killing and one a case of letting die. But this does not show the Bare Difference Argument fails, only that *this* pair of cases cannot be used to mount such an argument. On the other hand, Rachels' original pair of cases do satisfy this logical requirement on the Bare Difference Argument (provided we assume both Smith and Jones are willing to kill the boy if letting die is not a feasible option). Moreover we do judge the actions of Smith and Jones in *those* circumstances to be morally equivalent, notwithstanding that one is an act of killing and one is an act of letting die. Thus that bare difference in itself makes no moral difference.

Note further that in order to flesh out his (irrelevant) modified-Jones case Nesbitt thinks we need to say more about why his Jones is unwilling to kill the boy:

> It cannot be that he fears untoward consequences for himself, such as detection and punishment, or that he is too lazy to choose such an active course, or that the idea simply had not occurred to him. I think it would be common ground in the debate that if the only explanation of his not being prepared to kill his [cousin] was one of these kinds, he would be morally no better than Smith, who differed only in being more daring, or more energetic, whether or not fate then happened to offer him the opportunity to let his [cousin] die instead. In that case, we must suppose that the reason Jones is prepared to let his [cousin] die, but not to kill him, is a moral one—not intervening to save the child, he holds, is one thing, but actually bringing about his death is another, and altogether beyond the pale.

Once again, Nesbitt confuses the issue by sliding from *act* evaluation to *agent* evaluation. The real issue here is not whether modified-Jones is or is not morally better than Smith, or even whether agents who perform acts of letting die are generally morally better or worse than those who perform acts of killing. The real issue, the issue the Bare Difference Argument directly addresses, is whether the bare difference between an act of killing and an act of letting die in itself makes a moral difference. Rachels' original pair of cases show that this bare difference does not in itself make a moral difference. For (provided we make the tiny modification I suggested) those two cases do share all morally relevant properties, save that one is a case of killing and one a case of letting die. Yet we judge the two *acts* involved to be morally equivalent. Hence the Equivalence Thesis is true.

Of course, it is unsurprising that Nesbitt's own modified-Jones case fails to support the Equivalence Thesis if paired with the Smith case. In the first place we have already seen that he stipulates that the two

cases no longer share all morally relevant features save that one is a killing and one a letting die. Hence it is trivially impossible for that pair of cases to satisfy the demands of the logical structure of the Bare Difference Argument. In the second place he insists that not only is modified-Jones (unlike Smith) not prepared to kill the boy, but that Jones's reluctance to do so is based on a *moral* reason: viz. that while killing the boy is morally wrong, letting him die is not. This latter stipulation, however, admits of both weak and strong construals. Construed weakly it is just the stipulation that modified-Jones's reluctance to kill the boy is based on his moral belief (mistaken or otherwise) that killing is morally wrong. Construed strongly the stipulation is that Jones's reluctance is based on his (correct) moral belief that killing is morally wrong. But this strong construal of what it is for Jones to act on a moral reason would assume the truth of precisely what is in dispute, namely whether the bare difference between killing and letting die is a morally relevant difference. In other words, on the strong construal introducing the modified-Jones case begs the very question such cases are being invoked to settle. If Nesbitt intends the strong rather than the weak construal, then it is no wonder the modified-Jones case lends no support to the Equivalence Thesis when the case is stipulated in a way that presupposes the falsity of that thesis.

I conclude, then, that the Bare Difference Argument is indeed sound and that the Equivalence Thesis is true. The pair of cases Rachels offers do support this conclusion since (with a tiny modification I consider already implicit in Rachels' argument) we have two cases alike in all morally relevant respects, save that one is a case of killing and one a case of letting die. But the *acts* Smith and Jones perform are morally equivalent. Hence the bare difference that one of those acts is a killing and one a letting die is not in itself a morally relevant difference. In other words, the Bare Difference Argument does reasonably establish the Equivalence Thesis: there is no intrinsic moral difference between acts of killing and acts of letting die. Of course, there may be *extrinsic* factors which make various particular cases of killing worse than various particular cases of letting die (or vice versa). But this is not just because some of these cases are killings and some are cases of letting die.

It is perhaps worth saying a little more about this last point, for surely much of the resistance to the Equivalence Thesis that one so frequently encounters is generated by a confusion about this feature of it. It is perfectly consistent to affirm the Equivalence Thesis and also to concede that, in some cases, it may be permissible to let die but not to kill, while in other cases it may be permissible to kill but not to let die. All that is required is that, in such cases, it is some feature other than the bare difference between killing and letting die that makes the moral difference. These other, extrinsic features are often present and do justify differential moral judgements. For instance, it is clearly morally worse to kill an elderly relative without her consent in order to inherit her money than it is to allow her to die of pneumonia at her request from a desire to relieve her sufferings from terminal cancer. But it is the *extrinsic* factors here (permission, motive) that are morally relevant, not the mere fact that one is a killing and one a letting die. And the presence or absence of these same extrinsic features can also on occasion make it morally worse to let die than to kill. For instance, it is plausibly morally worse to let an elderly relative die of pneumonia without her consent in order to inherit her money than it is to kill her at her own request from a desire to relieve her sufferings from terminal cancer. What the Equivalence Thesis tells us is just that the bare difference between killing and letting die is not in itself a morally significant difference, not that every case of killing is morally equivalent to every case of letting die. However, if there is a moral difference, it is due to extrinsic features of the cases; there is no *intrinsic* moral difference between killing and letting die. And the Bare Difference Argument demonstrates that this is so.

NOTE

1. I have changed Nesbitt's references to a "nephew" to a "cousin" throughout to make it consistent with the cases as described in the version from Rachels I cited earlier. (It is also a "cousin" in the original paper by Rachels that Nesbitt cites.)

3

Is Abortion Wrong?

Marquis and His Critics

The moral problem of abortion is really two distinct moral problems. The first problem concerns the moral status of the human fetus, and the second concerns the moral significance of the relationship between the fetus and the pregnant woman whose body the fetus inhabits. Critics of abortion typically respond to the first problem by maintaining that the fetus has the same right to life that you or I have, that killing a typical human fetus is morally on a par with killing a typical adult human being. They then respond to the second problem by maintaining that a pregnant woman's right to control her own body is not strong enough to outweigh this consideration. Defenders of abortion typically respond to this position by attempting to show either that the human fetus does not really have this high moral standing in the first place or that, if it does, the woman's interest in ending an unwanted pregnancy is strong enough to outweigh it. The standard argument about the moral permissibility of abortion, therefore, can be construed in terms of a simple argument with two premises and a conclusion that follows directly from them:

P1   A human fetus has the same right to life as an adult human being.
P2   If a human fetus has the same right to life as an adult human being, then abortion is morally impermissible.

C   Abortion is morally impermissible.

The critic of abortion maintains that both of these premises are true, and the defender of abortion maintains that at least one of them is false.

This chapter is organized around two featured articles, each of which focuses exclusively on one of these two key premises. In "Why Abortion Is Immoral," Don Marquis provides what many philosophers believe to be the most powerful argument in defense of P1. And in "A Defense of Abortion," Judith Jarvis Thomson defends what has become the most famous (or, perhaps, infamous) argument against P2. In arguing for P1, Marquis simply assumes that P2 is true, and in arguing against P2, Thomson assumes, at least for the sake of the argument, that P1 is true. So although Marquis and Thomson represent diametrically opposing views on the morality of abortion, their arguments do not directly address each other and must therefore be investigated separately.

Marquis's argument in defense of the rights of the human fetus (or, at least, of what he refers to as the "standard" or typical human fetus) has the logical structure that we refer to in the Introduction as "inference to the best explanation" (see section 4.3). He begins, that is, by looking at cases of killing about which virtually everyone agrees, regardless of their stance on abortion. We all agree, for example, that it is immoral to kill a typical (innocent) adult human being, and we agree that this is so even if the human being in question is an unloved hermit, a suicidal teenager, or a temporarily comatose adult. Marquis then asks what account of the wrongness of killing in general would do the best job of explaining the wrongness of killing in these uncontroversial cases. The moral principle that he defends in response to this question appeals fundamentally to the claim that in all of these cases, the individual who is killed is deprived of what Marquis refers to as a "future-like-ours": the set of experiences that constitutes her personal future and that she would otherwise have been able to enjoy had she not been killed. Finally, Marquis argues that the "future-like-ours" principle that best accounts for the wrongness of killing in the uncontroversial cases entails that killing is also wrong in the case of the typical human fetus. The result, then, is that starting from judgments that virtually everyone on both sides of the abortion debate already accepts, the argument leads to the conclusion that it is seriously immoral to kill the typical human fetus.

Marquis's argument is among the most prominent in the literature on abortion. It is also, perhaps not surprisingly, one of the arguments for which the most commentary has been generated. In the excerpted critical responses following Marquis's article, three philosophers offer three distinct strategies for attempting to rebut Marquis's future-like-ours argument. In the first reading, Gerald H. Paske argues that Marquis has misidentified the property that renders killing wrong in the cases in which it is uncontroversially wrong. Rather than appealing to facts about the victims' futures in such cases, as Marquis's future-like-ours principle requires us to do, Paske suggests that a more satisfying account of the wrongness of killing them focuses exclusively on facts about their *present* condition, facts that, Paske argues, turn out not to apply in the case of the human fetus.

Alastair Norcross, in the second response piece, also argues against Marquis's future-like-ours explanation of the wrongness of killing. But Norcross's strategy is very different. Rather than arguing that Marquis's principle provides an unsatisfactory account of the wrongness of killing in the cases where killing is clearly wrong, as Paske does, Norcross argues that the principle is unacceptable because it has implications in further cases that render the principle unacceptable. This is to employ the method of argument by reductio ad absurdum that we discussed in section 4.5 of the Introduction. More specifically, Norcross argues that Marquis's account of the wrongness of killing has the unacceptable implication that contraception is morally on a par with killing an adult human being. Marquis briefly attempts to fend off this objection to his argument in section V of his article, but Norcross argues that he is ultimately unsuccessful in this attempt.

Finally, Peter K. McInerney raises a challenge to a different part of Marquis's argument. Even if we accept the moral principle that Paske and Norcross argue against in different ways, McInerney argues that the principle itself does not really entail that killing a typical human fetus is wrong. Although it is true that the fetus will eventually develop into an adult human being, McInerney maintains that this fact does not suffice to establish that a future-like-ours is something that the fetus already has and that Marquis's principle applies to the fetus only if the fetus does already have it. If the future experiences of the future adult that the fetus will later develop into are not psychologically connected to the current fetus in certain important respects, McInerney argues, then they are not yet future experiences of the fetus. And if they are not yet future experiences of the fetus, then the fetus cannot be deprived of them by being killed. If McInerney is right, then even if Marquis's argument can overcome the objections to it raised by Paske and Norcross, it will still fail to support the conclusion that it is prima facie seriously immoral to kill a standard human fetus.

Questions for Consideration

In thinking critically about the exchange between Marquis and his critics, it may be useful to keep some of the following questions in mind.

• Is Paske right in thinking that our current properties account for the wrongness of killing us better than facts about our futures do? What current properties, in particular, are important in trying to answer this question?

• What advantages does Marquis's account of the wrongness of killing have over Paske's? What advantages does Paske's have over Marquis's?

• Is Norcross right in thinking that Marquis has failed to overcome the contraception objection? How does Marquis try to rebut that objection in section V of his article? Where, specifically, does Norcross think Marquis goes wrong? Is there a way that Marquis could modify his position to overcome the objection without losing his ability to defend his antiabortion conclusion?

• Why does McInerney believe that the fetus does not yet have a future-like-ours? Are his reasons convincing?

• Based on the kinds of examples that Marquis gives in response to other possible accounts of the wrongness of killing, how might he try to respond to McInerney's central contention?

Further Reading

Card, Robert. "Two Puzzles for Marquis's Conservative View on Abortion." *Bioethics* 20, no. 5 (September 2006): 264–77.

Cudd, Ann E. "Sensationalized Philosophy: A Reply to Marquis's 'Why Abortion Is Immoral.'" *Journal of Philosophy* 87, no. 5 (1990): 262–64.

Daniels, Charles B. "Having a Future." *Dialogue* 31 (2003): 661–65.

Gelfand, Scott D. "Marquis: A Defense of Abortion?" *Bioethics* 15, no. 2 (April 2001): 135–45.

Marquis, Don. "A Future Like Ours and the Concept of Person: A Reply to McInerney and Paske," in *The Abortion Controversy: 25 Years After Roe v. Wade,* ed. Louis Pojman and Francis J. Beckwith (Belmont, Calif.: Wadsworth, 1998), pp. 372–85.

———. "Shirley's 'Marquis' Argument Against Abortion.'" *Southwest Philosophy Review* 6, no. 2 (1995): 263–65.

Shirley, Edward S. "Marquis' Argument Against Abortion: A Critique." *Southwest Philosophy Review* 6, no. 1 (1995): 79–89.

Sinnott-Armstrong, Walter. "You Can't Lose What You Ain't Never Had: A Reply to Marquis on Abortion." *Philosophical Studies* 96, no. 1 (1999): 59–72.

Stretton, Dean. "The Deprivation Argument Against Abortion." *Bioethics* 18, no. 2 (April 2004): 144–80.

DON MARQUIS

Why Abortion Is Immoral

The view that abortion is, with rare exceptions, seriously immoral has received little support in the recent philosophical literature. No doubt most philosophers affiliated with secular institutions of higher education believe that the anti-abortion position is either a symptom of irrational religious dogma or a conclusion generated by seriously confused philosophical argument. The purpose of this essay is to undermine this general belief. This essay sets out an argument that purports to show, as well as any argument in ethics can show, that abortion is, except possibly in rare cases, seriously immoral, that it is in the same moral category as killing an innocent adult human being.

The argument is based on a major assumption. Many of the most insightful and careful writers on the ethics of abortion—such as Joel Feinberg, Michael Tooley, Mary Anne Warren, H. Tristram Engelhardt, Jr., L. W. Sumner, John T. Noonan, Jr., and Philip Devine[1]—believe that whether or not abortion is morally permissible stands or falls on whether or not a fetus is the sort of being whose life it is seriously wrong to end. The argument of this essay will assume, but not argue, that they are correct.

Also, this essay will neglect issues of great importance to a complete ethics of abortion. Some anti-abortionists will allow that certain abortions, such as abortion before implantation or abortion when the life of a woman is threatened by a pregnancy or abortion after rape, may be morally permissible. This essay will not explore the casuistry of these hard cases. The purpose of this essay is to develop a general argument for the claim that the overwhelming majority of deliberate abortions are seriously immoral.

I

. . . [A] necessary condition of resolving the abortion controversy is a more theoretical account of the wrongness of killing. After all, if we merely believe, but do not understand, why killing adult human beings such as ourselves is wrong, how could we conceivably show that abortion is either immoral or permissible?

II

In order to develop such an account, we can start from the following unproblematic assumption concerning our own case: it is wrong to kill *us*. Why is it wrong? Some answers can be easily eliminated. It might be said that what makes killing us wrong is that a killing brutalizes the one who kills. But the brutalization consists of being inured to the performance of an act that is hideously immoral; hence, the brutalization does not explain the immorality. It might be said that what makes killing us wrong is the great loss others would experience due to our absence. Although such hubris is understandable, such an explanation does not account for the wrongness of killing hermits, or those whose lives are relatively independent and whose friends find it easy to make new friends.

A more obvious answer is better. What primarily makes killing wrong is neither its effect on the murderer nor its effect on the victim's friends and relatives, but its effect on the victim. The loss of one's life is one of the greatest losses one can suffer. The loss of one's life deprives one of all the experiences, activities, projects, and enjoyments that would otherwise

From Don Marquis, "Why Abortion Is Immoral," *Journal of Philosophy* 86, no. 4 (1989): 183–202. Some notes and some text have been deleted. Reprinted by permission of *The Journal of Philosophy*.

have constituted one's future. Therefore, killing someone is wrong, primarily because the killing inflicts (one of) the greatest possible losses on the victim. To describe this as the loss of life can be misleading, however. The change in my biological state does not by itself make killing me wrong. The effect of the loss of my biological life is the loss to me of all those activities, projects, experiences, and enjoyments which would otherwise have constituted my future personal life. These activities, projects, experiences, and enjoyments are either valuable for their own sakes or are means to something else that is valuable for its own sake. Some parts of my future are not valued by me now, but will come to be valued by me as I grow older and as my values and capacities change. When I am killed, I am deprived both of what I now value which would have been part of my future personal life, but also what I would come to value. Therefore, when I die, I am deprived of all of the value of my future. Inflicting this loss on me is ultimately what makes killing me wrong. This being the case, it would seem that what makes killing *any* adult human being prima facie seriously wrong is the loss of his or her future.[2]

How should this rudimentary theory of the wrongness of killing be evaluated? It cannot be faulted for deriving an "ought" from an "is," for it does not. The analysis assumes that killing me (or you, reader) is prima facie seriously wrong. The point of the analysis is to establish which natural property ultimately explains the wrongness of the killing, given that it is wrong. A natural property will ultimately explain the wrongness of killing, only if (1) the explanation fits with our intuitions about the matter and (2) there is no other natural property that provides the basis for a better explanation of the wrongness of killing. This analysis rests on the intuition that what makes killing a particular human or animal wrong is what it does to that particular human or animal. What makes killing wrong is some natural effect or other of the killing. Some would deny this. For instance, a divine-command theorist in ethics would deny it. Surely this denial is, however, one of those features of divine-command theory which renders it so implausible.

The claim that what makes killing wrong is the loss of the victim's future is directly supported by two considerations. In the first place, this theory explains why we regard killing as one of the worst of crimes. Killing is especially wrong, because it deprives the victim of more than perhaps any other crime. In the second place, people with AIDS or cancer who know they are dying believe, of course, that dying is a very bad thing for them. They believe that the loss of a future to them that they would otherwise have experienced is what makes their premature death a very bad thing for them. A better theory of the wrongness of killing would require a different natural property associated with killing which better fits with the attitudes of the dying. What could it be?

The view that what makes killing wrong is the loss to the victim of the value of the victim's future gains additional support when some of its implications are examined. In the first place, it is incompatible with the view that it is wrong to kill only beings who are biologically human. It is possible that there exists a different species from another planet whose members have a future like ours. Since having a future like that is what makes killing someone wrong, this theory entails that it would be wrong to kill members of such a species. Hence, this theory is opposed to the claim that only life that is biologically human has great moral worth, a claim which many anti-abortionists have seemed to adopt. This opposition, which this theory has in common with personhood theories, seems to be a merit of the theory.

In the second place, the claim that the loss of one's future is the wrong-making feature of one's being killed entails the possibility that the futures of some actual nonhuman mammals on our own planet are sufficiently like ours that it is seriously wrong to kill them also. Whether some animals do have the same right to life as human beings depends on adding to the account of the wrongness of killing some additional account of just what it is about my future or the futures of other adult human beings which makes it wrong to kill us. No such additional account will be offered in this essay. Undoubtedly, the provision of such an account would be a very difficult matter. Undoubtedly, any such account would be quite controversial. Hence, it surely should not reflect badly on this sketch of an elementary theory of the wrongness of killing that it is indeterminate with respect to some very difficult issues regarding animal rights.

In the third place, the claim that the loss of one's future is the wrong-making feature of one's being killed does not entail, as sanctity of human life theories do, that active euthanasia is wrong. Persons who are severely and incurably ill, who face a future of pain and despair, and who wish to die will not have suffered a loss if they are killed. It is, strictly speaking, the value of a human's future which makes killing wrong in this theory. This being so, killing does not necessarily wrong some persons who are sick and dying. Of course, there may be other reasons for a prohibition of active euthanasia, but that is another matter. Sanctity-of-human-life theories seem to hold that active euthanasia is seriously wrong even in an individual case where there seems to be good reason for it independently of public policy considerations. This consequence is most implausible, and it is a plus for the claim that the loss of a future of value is what makes killing wrong that it does not share this consequence.

In the fourth place, the account of the wrongness of killing defended in this essay does straightforwardly entail that it is prima facie seriously wrong to kill children and infants, for we do presume that they have futures of value. Since we do believe that it is wrong to kill defenseless little babies, it is important that a theory of the wrongness of killing easily account for this. Personhood theories of the wrongness of killing, on the other hand, cannot straightforwardly account for the wrongness of killing infants and young children.[3] Hence, such theories must add special ad hoc accounts of the wrongness of killing the young. The plausibility of such ad hoc theories seems to be a function of how desperately one wants such theories to work. The claim that the primary wrong-making feature of a killing is the loss to the victim of the value of its future accounts for the wrongness of killing young children and infants directly; it makes the wrongness of such acts as obvious as we actually think it is. This is a further merit of this theory. Accordingly, it seems that this value of a future-like-ours theory of the wrongness of killing shares strengths of both sanctity-of-life and personhood accounts while avoiding weaknesses of both. In addition, it meshes with a central intuition concerning what makes killing wrong.

The claim that the primary wrong-making feature of a killing is the loss to the victim of the value of its future has obvious consequences for the ethics of abortion. The future of a standard fetus includes a set of experiences, projects, activities, and such which are identical with the futures of adult human beings and are identical with the futures of young children. Since the reason that is sufficient to explain why it is wrong to kill human beings after the time of birth is a reason that also applies to fetuses, it follows that abortion is prima facie seriously morally wrong.

This argument does not rely on the invalid inference that, since it is wrong to kill persons, it is wrong to kill potential persons also. The category that is morally central to this analysis is the category of having a valuable future like ours; it is not the category of personhood. The argument to the conclusion that abortion is prima facie seriously morally wrong proceeded independently of the notion of person or potential person or any equivalent. Someone may wish to start with this analysis in terms of the value of a human future, conclude that abortion is, except perhaps in rare circumstances, seriously morally wrong, infer that fetuses have the right to life, and then call fetuses "persons" as a result of their having the right to life. Clearly, in this case, the category of person is being used to state the *conclusion* of the analysis rather than to generate the *argument* of the analysis.

The structure of this anti-abortion argument can be both illuminated and defended by comparing it to what appears to be the best argument for the wrongness of the wanton infliction of pain on animals. This latter argument is based on the assumption that it is prima facie wrong to inflict pain on me (or you, reader). What is the natural property associated with the infliction of pain which makes such infliction wrong? The obvious answer seems to be that the infliction of pain causes suffering and that suffering is a misfortune. The suffering caused by the infliction of pain is what makes the wanton infliction of pain on me wrong. The wanton infliction of pain on other adult humans causes suffering. The wanton infliction of pain on animals causes suffering. Since causing suffering is what makes the wanton infliction of pain wrong and since the wanton infliction of pain on animals causes suffering, it follows that the wanton infliction of pain on animals is wrong.

This argument for the wrongness of the wanton infliction of pain on animals shares a number of structural features with the argument for the serious prima facie wrongness of abortion. Both arguments start with an obvious assumption concerning what it is wrong to do to me (or you, reader). Both then look for the characteristic or the consequence of the wrong action which makes the action wrong. Both recognize that the wrong-making feature of these immoral actions is a property of actions sometimes directed at individuals other than postnatal human beings. If the structure of the argument for the wrongness of the wanton infliction of pain on animals is sound, then the structure of the argument for the prima facie serious wrongness of abortion is also sound, for the structure of the two arguments is the same. The structure common to both is the key to the explanation of how the wrongness of abortion can be demonstrated without recourse to the category of person. In neither argument is that category crucial.

This defense of an argument for the wrongness of abortion in terms of a structurally similar argument for the wrongness of the wanton infliction of pain on animals succeeds only if the account regarding animals is the correct account. Is it? In the first place, it seems plausible. In the second place, its major competition is Kant's account. Kant believed that we do not have direct duties to animals at all, because they are not persons. Hence, Kant had to explain and justify the wrongness of inflicting pain on animals on the grounds that "he who is hard in his dealings with animals becomes hard also in his dealing with men."[4] The problem with Kant's account is that there seems to be no reason for accepting this latter claim unless Kant's account is rejected. If the alternative to Kant's account is accepted, then it is easy to understand why someone who is indifferent to inflicting pain on animals is also indifferent to inflicting pain on humans, for one is indifferent to what makes inflicting pain wrong in both cases. But, if Kant's account is accepted, there is no intelligible reason why one who is hard in his dealings with ani-

mals (or crabgrass or stones) should also be hard in his dealings with men. After all, men are persons: animals are no more persons than crabgrass or stones. Persons are Kant's crucial moral category. Why, in short, should a Kantian accept the basic claim in Kant's argument?

Hence, Kant's argument for the wrongness of inflicting pain on animals rests on a claim that, in a world of Kantian moral agents, is demonstrably false. Therefore, the alternative analysis, being more plausible anyway, should be accepted. Since this alternative analysis has the same structure as the anti-abortion argument being defended here, we have further support for the argument for the immorality of abortion being defended in this essay.

Of course, this value of a future-like-ours argument, if sound, shows only that abortion is prima facie wrong, not that it is wrong in any and all circumstances. Since the loss of the future to a standard fetus, if killed, is, however, at least as great a loss as the loss of the future to a standard adult human being who is killed, abortion, like ordinary killing, could be justified only by the most compelling reasons. The loss of one's life is almost the greatest misfortune that can happen to one. Presumably abortion could be justified in some circumstances, only if the loss consequent on failing to abort would be at least as great. Accordingly, morally permissible abortions will be rare indeed unless, perhaps, they occur so early in pregnancy that a fetus is not yet definitely an individual. Hence, this argument should be taken as showing that abortion is presumptively very seriously wrong, where the presumption is very strong—as strong as the presumption that killing another adult human being is wrong.

III

How complete an account of the wrongness of killing does the value of a future-like-ours account have to be in order that the wrongness of abortion is a consequence? This account does not have to be an account of the necessary conditions for the wrongness of killing. Some persons in nursing homes may lack valuable human futures, yet it may be wrong to kill them for other reasons. Furthermore, this account does not obviously have to be the sole reason killing is wrong where the victim did have a valuable future. This analysis claims only that, for any killing where the victim did have a valuable future like ours, having that future by itself is sufficient to create the strong presumption that the killing is seriously wrong.

One way to overturn the value of a future-like-ours argument would be to find some account of the wrongness of killing which is at least as intelligible and which has different implications for the ethics of abortion. Two rival accounts possess at least some degree of plausibility. One account is based on the obvious fact that people value the experience of living and wish for that valuable experience to continue. Therefore, it might be said, what makes killing wrong is the discontinuation of that experience for the victim. Let us call this the *discontinuation account.*[5] Another rival account is based upon the obvious fact that people strongly desire to continue to live. This suggests that what makes killing us so wrong is that it interferes with the fulfillment of a strong and fundamental desire, the fulfillment of which is necessary for the fulfillment of any other desires we might have. Let us call this the *desire account.*[6]

Consider first the desire account as a rival account of the ethics of killing which would provide the basis for rejecting the anti-abortion position. Such an account will have to be stronger than the value of a future-like-ours account of the wrongness of abortion if it is to do the job expected of it. To entail the wrongness of abortion, the value of a future-like-ours account has only to provide a sufficient, but not a necessary, condition for the wrongness of killing. The desire account, on the other hand, must provide us also with a necessary condition for the wrongness of killing in order to generate a pro-choice conclusion on abortion. The reason for this is that presumably the argument from the desire account moves from the claim that what makes killing wrong is interference with a very strong desire to the claim that abortion is not wrong because the fetus lacks a strong desire to live. Obviously, this inference fails if someone's having the desire to live is not a necessary condition of its being wrong to kill that individual.

One problem with the desire account is that we do regard it as seriously wrong to kill persons who have little desire to live or who have no desire to live or, indeed, have a desire not to live. We believe it is seriously wrong to kill the unconscious, the sleeping, those who are tired of life, and those who are suicidal. The value-of-a-human-future account renders standard morality intelligible in these cases; these cases appear to be incompatible with the desire account.

The desire account is subject to a deeper difficulty. We desire life, because we value the goods of this life. The goodness of life is not secondary to our desire for it. If this were not so, the pain of one's own premature death could be done away with merely by an appropriate alteration in the configuration of one's desires. This is absurd. Hence, it would seem that it is the loss of the goods of one's future, not the interference with the fulfillment of a strong desire to live, which accounts ultimately for the wrongness of killing.

It is worth noting that, if the desire account is modified so that it does not provide a necessary, but only a sufficient, condition for the wrongness of killing, the desire account is compatible with the value of a future-like-ours account. The combined accounts will yield an anti-abortion ethic. This suggests that one can retain what is intuitively plausible about the desire account without a challenge to the basic argument of this paper.

It is also worth noting that, if future desires have moral force in a modified desire account of the wrongness of killing, one can find support for an anti-abortion ethic even in the absence of a value of a future-like-ours account. If one decides that a morally relevant property, the possession of which is sufficient to make it wrong to kill some individual, is the desire at some future time to live—one might decide to justify one's refusal to kill suicidal teenagers on these grounds, for example—then, since typical fetuses will have the desire in the future to live, it is wrong to kill typical fetuses. Accordingly, it does not seem that a desire account of the wrongness of killing can provide a justification of a pro-choice ethic of abortion which is nearly as adequate as the value of a human-future justification of an anti-abortion ethic.

The discontinuation account looks more promising as an account of the wrongness of killing. It seems just as intelligible as the value of a future-like-ours account, but it does not justify an anti-abortion position. Obviously, if it is the continuation of one's activities, experiences, and projects, the loss of which makes killing wrong, then it is not wrong to kill fetuses for that reason, for fetuses do not have experiences, activities, and projects to be continued or discontinued. Accordingly, the discontinuation account does not have the anti-abortion consequences that the value of a future-like-ours account has. Yet, it seems as intelligible as the value of a future-like-ours account, for when we think of what would be wrong with our being killed, it does seem as if it is the discontinuation of what makes our lives worthwhile which makes killing us wrong.

Is the discontinuation account just as good an account as the value of a future-like-ours account? The discontinuation account will not be adequate at all, if it does not refer to the *value* of the experience that may be discontinued. One does not want the discontinuation account to make it wrong to kill a patient who begs for death and who is in severe pain that cannot be relieved short of killing. (I leave open the question of whether it is wrong for other reasons.) Accordingly, the discontinuation account must be more than a bare discontinuation account. It must make some reference to the positive value of the patient's experiences. But, by the same token, the value of a future-like-ours account cannot be a bare future account either. Just having a future surely does not itself rule out killing the above patient. This account must make some reference to the value of the patient's future experiences and projects also. Hence, both accounts involve the value of experiences, projects, and activities. So far we still have symmetry between the accounts.

The symmetry fades, however, when we focus on the time period of the value of the experiences, etc., which has moral consequences. Although both accounts leave open the possibility that the patient in our example may be killed, this possibility is left open only in virtue of the utterly bleak future for the patient. It makes no difference whether the patient's immediate past contains intolerable pain, or consists in being in a coma (which we can imagine is a situation of indifference), or consists in a life of value. If the patient's future is a future of value, we want our account to make it wrong to kill the patient. If the patient's future is intolerable, whatever his or her immediate past, we want our account to allow killing the patient. Obviously, then, it is the value of that patient's future which is doing the work in rendering the morality of killing the patient intelligible.

This being the case, it seems clear that whether one has immediate past experiences or not does no work in the explanation of what makes killing wrong. The addition the discontinuation account makes to the value of a human future account is otiose. Its addition to the value-of-a-future account plays no role at all in rendering intelligible the wrongness of killing. Therefore, it can be discarded with the discontinuation account of which it is a part.

IV

The analysis of the previous section suggests that alternative general accounts of the wrongness of killing are either inadequate or unsuccessful in getting around the anti-abortion consequences of the value of a future-like-ours argument. A different strategy for avoiding these anti-abortion consequences involves limiting the scope of the value of a future argument. More precisely, the strategy involves arguing that fetuses lack a property that is essential for the value-of-a-future argument (or for any anti-abortion argument) to apply to them.

One move of this sort is based upon the claim that a necessary condition of one's future being valuable is that one values it. Value implies a valuer. Given this one might argue that, since fetuses cannot value their futures, their futures are not valuable to them. Hence, it does not seriously wrong them deliberately to end their lives.

This move fails, however, because of some ambiguities. Let us assume that something cannot be of value unless it is valued by someone. This does not entail that my life is of no value unless it is valued by me. I may think, in a period of despair, that my future is of no worth whatsoever, but I may be wrong because others rightly see value—even great value—in it. Furthermore, my future can be valuable to me even if I do not value it. This is the case when a young person attempts suicide, but is rescued and goes on to significant human achievements. Such young people's futures are ultimately valuable to them, even though such futures do not seem to be valuable to them at the moment of attempted suicide. A fetus's future can be valuable to it in the same way. Accordingly, this attempt to limit the anti-abortion argument fails.

Another similar attempt to reject the anti-abortion position is based on Tooley's claim that an entity cannot possess the right to life unless it has the capacity to desire its continued existence. It follows that, since fetuses lack the conceptual capacity to desire to continue to live, they lack the right to life. Accordingly, Tooley concludes that abortion cannot be seriously prima facie wrong (op. cit., pp. 46–7).

What could be the evidence for Tooley's basic claim? Tooley once argued that individuals have a prima facie right to what they desire and that the lack of the capacity to desire something undercuts the basis of one's right to it (op. cit., pp. 44–5). This argument plainly will not succeed in the context of the analysis of this essay, however, since the point here is to establish the fetus's right to life on other grounds. Tooley's argument assumes that the right to life cannot be established in general on some basis other than the desire for life. This position was considered and rejected in the preceding section of this paper.

One might attempt to defend Tooley's basic claim on the grounds that, because a fetus cannot apprehend continued life as a benefit, its continued life cannot be a benefit or cannot be something it has a right to or cannot be something that is in its interest. This might be defended in terms of the general proposition that, if an individual is literally incapable of caring about or taking an interest in some X, then one does not have a right to X or X is not a benefit or X is not something that is in one's interest.[7]

Each member of this family of claims seems to be open to objections. As John C. Stevens[8] has pointed out, one may have a right to be treated with a certain medical procedure (because of a health insurance policy one has purchased), even though one cannot conceive of the nature of the procedure. And, as Tooley himself has pointed out, persons who have been indoctrinated, or drugged, or rendered temporarily unconscious may be literally incapable of caring about or taking an interest in something that is in their interest or is something to which they have a right, or is something that benefits them. Hence, the Tooley claim that would restrict the scope of the value of a future-like-ours argument is undermined by counterexamples.[9]

Finally, Paul Bassen[10] has argued that, even though the prospects of an embryo might seem to be a basis for the wrongness of abortion, an embryo cannot be a victim and therefore cannot be wronged. An embryo cannot be a victim, he says, because it lacks sentience. His central argument for this seems to be that, even though plants and the permanently unconscious are alive, they clearly cannot be victims. What is the explanation of this? Bassen claims that the explanation is that their lives consist of mere metabolism and mere metabolism is not enough to ground victimizability. Mentation is required.

The problem with this attempt to establish the absence of victimizability is that both plants and the permanently unconscious clearly lack what Bassen calls "prospects" or what I have called "a future life like ours." Hence, it is surely open to one to argue that the real reason we believe plants and the permanently unconscious cannot be victims is that killing them cannot deprive them of a future life like ours; the real reason is not their absence of present mentation.

Bassen recognizes that his view is subject to this difficulty, and he recognizes that the case of children seems to support this difficulty, for "much of what we do for children is based on prospects." He argues, however, that, in the case of children and in other such cases, "potentiality comes into play only where victimizability has been secured on other grounds" (ibid., p. 333).

Bassen's defense of his view is patently question-begging, since what is adequate to secure victimizability is exactly what is at issue. His examples do not support his own view against the thesis of this essay.

Of course, embryos can be victims: when their lives are deliberately terminated, they are deprived of their futures of value, their prospects. This makes them victims, for it directly wrongs them.

The seeming plausibility of Bassen's view stems from the fact that paradigmatic cases of imagining someone as a victim involve empathy, and empathy requires mentation of the victim. The victims of flood, famine, rape, or child abuse are all persons with whom we can empathize. That empathy seems to be part of seeing them as victims.[11]

In spite of the strength of these examples, the attractive intuition that a situation in which there is victimization requires the possibility of empathy is subject to counterexamples. Consider a case that Bassen himself offers: "Posthumous obliteration of an author's work constitutes a misfortune for him only if he had wished his work to endure" (op. cit., p. 318). The conditions Bassen wishes to impose upon the possibility of being victimized here seem far too strong. Perhaps this author, due to his unrealistic standards of excellence and his low self-esteem, regarded his work as unworthy of survival, even though it possessed genuine literary merit. Destruction of such work would surely victimize its author. In such a case, empathy with the victim concerning the loss is clearly impossible.

Of course, Bassen does not make the possibility of empathy a necessary condition of victimizability; he requires only mentation. Hence, on Bassen's actual view, this author, as I have described him, can be a victim. The problem is that the basic intuition that renders Bassen's view plausible is missing in the author's case. In order to attempt to avoid counterexamples, Bassen has made his thesis too weak to be supported by the intuitions that suggested it.

Even so, the mentation requirement on victimizability is still subject to counterexamples. Suppose a severe accident renders me totally unconscious for a month, after which I recover. Surely killing me while I am unconscious victimizes me, even though I am incapable of mentation during that time. It follows that Bassen's thesis fails. Apparently, attempts to restrict the value of a future-like-ours argument so that fetuses do not fall within its scope do not succeed.

V

In this essay, it has been argued that the correct ethic of the wrongness of killing can be extended to fetal life and used to show that there is a strong presumption that any abortion is morally impermissible. If the ethic of killing adopted here entails, however, that contraception is also seriously immoral, then there would appear to be a difficulty with the analysis of this essay.

But this analysis does not entail that contraception is wrong. Of course, contraception prevents the actualization of a possible future of value. Hence, it follows from the claim that futures of value should be maximized that contraception is prima facie immoral. This obligation to maximize does not exist, however; furthermore, nothing in the ethics of killing in this paper entails that it does. The ethics of killing in this essay would entail that contraception is wrong only if something were denied a human future of value by contraception. Nothing at all is denied such a future by contraception, however.

Candidates for a subject of harm by contraception fall into four categories: (1) some sperm or other, (2) some ovum or other, (3) a sperm and an ovum separately, and (4) a sperm and an ovum together. Assigning the harm to some sperm is utterly arbitrary, for no reason can be given for making a sperm the subject of harm rather than an ovum. Assigning the harm to some ovum is utterly arbitrary, for no reason can be given for making an ovum the subject of harm rather than a sperm. One might attempt to avoid these problems by insisting that contraception deprives both the sperm and the ovum separately of a valuable future like ours. On this alternative, too many futures are lost. Contraception was supposed to be wrong, because it deprived us of one future of value, not two. One might attempt to avoid this problem by holding that contraception deprives the combination of sperm and ovum of a valuable future like ours. But here the definite article misleads. At the time of contraception, there are hundreds of millions of sperm, one (released) ovum and millions of possible combinations of all of these. There is no actual combination at all. Is the subject of the loss to be a merely possible combination? Which one?

This alternative does not yield an actual subject of harm either. Accordingly, the immorality of contraception is not entailed by the loss of a future-like-ours argument simply because there is no nonarbitrarily identifiable subject of the loss in the case of contraception.

VI

The purpose of this essay has been to set out an argument for the serious presumptive wrongness of abortion subject to the assumption that the moral permissibility of abortion stands or falls on the moral status of the fetus. Since a fetus possesses a property, the possession of which in adult human beings is sufficient to make killing an adult human being wrong, abortion is wrong. This way of dealing with the problem of abortion seems superior to other approaches to the ethics of abortion, because it rests on an ethics of killing which is close to self-evident, because the crucial morally relevant property clearly applies to fetuses, and because the argument avoids the usual equivocations on "human life," "human being," or "person." The argument rests neither on religious claims nor on Papal dogma. It is not subject to the objection of "speciesism." Its soundness is compatible with the moral permissibility of euthanasia and contraception. It deals with our intuitions concerning young children.

Finally, this analysis can be viewed as resolving a standard problem—indeed, *the* standard problem—concerning the ethics of abortion. Clearly, it is wrong to kill adult human beings. Clearly, it is not wrong to end the life of some arbitrarily chosen single human cell. Fetuses seem to be like arbitrarily chosen human cells in some respects and like adult humans in other respects. The problem of the ethics of abortion is the problem of determining the fetal property that settles this moral controversy. The thesis of this essay is that the problem of the ethics of abortion, so understood, is solvable.

NOTES

1. Feinberg, "Abortion," in *Matters of Life and Death: New Introductory Essays in Moral Philosophy,* Tom Regan, ed. (New York: Random House, 1986), pp. 256–293; Tooley, "Abortion and Infanticide," *Philosophy and Public Affairs,* ii, 1 (1972): 37–65, Tooley, *Abortion and Infanticide* (New York: Oxford, 1984); Warren, "On the Moral and Legal Status of Abortion," *The Monist,* 1.vii, 1 (1973): 43–61; Engelhardt, "The Ontology of Abortion," *Ethics,* 1.xxxiv, 3 (1974): 217–234; Sumner, *Abortion and Moral Theory* (Princeton: University Press, 1981); Noonan, "An Almost Absolute Value in History," in *The Morality of Abortion: Legal and Historical Perspectives,* Noonan, ed. (Cambridge: Harvard, 1970); and Devine, *The Ethics of Homicide* (Ithaca: Cornell, 1978).

2. I have been most influenced on this matter by Jonathan Glover, *Causing Death and Saving Lives* (New York: Penguin, 1977), ch. 3; and Robert Young, "What Is So Wrong with Killing People?" *Philosophy,* 1.iv, 210 (1979): 515–528.

3. Feinberg, Tooley, Warren, and Engelhardt have all dealt with this problem.

4. "Duties to Animals and Spirits," in *Lectures on Ethics,* Louis Infeld, trans. (New York: Harper, 1963), p. 239.

5. I am indebted to Jack Bricke for raising this objection.

6. Presumably a preference utilitarian would press such an objection. Tooley once suggested that his account has such a theoretical underpinning. See his "Abortion and Infanticide," pp. 44–5.

7. Donald VanDeVeer seems to think this is self-evident. See his "Whither Baby Doe?" in *Matters of Life and Death,* p. 233.

8. "Must the Bearer of a Right Have the Concept of That to Which He Has a Right?" *Ethics,* xcv, 1 (1984): 68–74.

9. See Tooley again in "Abortion and Infanticide," pp. 47–49.

10. "Present Sakes and Future Prospects: The Status of Early Abortion," *Philosophy and Public Affairs,* xi, 4 (1982): 322–326.

11. Note carefully the reasons he gives on the bottom of p. 316.

GERALD H. PASKE

Abortion and the Neo-Natal Right to Life
A Critique of Marquis's Futurist Argument

In an influential but misleadingly entitled paper, Don Marquis has presented a serious challenge to the pro-choice position.[1] Although the paper is entitled "Why Abortion Is Immoral," Marquis's argument actually allows for abortions of severely mentally defective fetuses. Marquis, thus, is on the conservative end of the prochoice spectrum.

Marquis's challenge remains serious, however, because his argument, if sound, would show that from conception onward all abortions of normal fetuses are seriously immoral. Marquis's argument is based on the following three claims: (1) Personhood is an inadequate foundation for the right to life. (2) The right to life is based on having a future-like-ours. (3) Normal fetuses have a future-like-ours and, hence, normal fetuses have a right to life. Marquis also claims that the personhood concept provides an inadequate basis for the right to life of infants and children, and he takes this to constitute an additional serious challenge to the standard prochoice position.

I shall argue (a) that Marquis's own position presupposes the concept of personhood, (b) that having a future-like-ours is neither a sufficient nor a necessary condition for having a right to life, and (c) that given the concept of personhood, neonates, infants, and children have a right to life.

Marquis summarizes his argument as follows:

In order to develop (my) account, we can start from the following unproblematic assumption concerning our own case: It is wrong to kill *us*. . . . The loss of one's life is one of the greatest losses one can suffer. The loss of one's life deprives one of all the experiences, activities, projects, and enjoyments that would otherwise have constituted one's future. . . . To describe this as the loss of life can be misleading, however. The change in my biological state does not by itself make killing me wrong. The effect of the loss of my biological life is the loss to me of all those activities, projects, experiences, and enjoyments that would otherwise have constituted my future personal life. . . . Therefore, when I die I am deprived of all of the value of my future. Inflicting this loss on me is ultimately what makes killing me wrong. This being the case, it would seem that what makes killing *any* adult human being prima facie seriously wrong is the loss of his or her future. [189–90]

Marquis applies this "deprivation argument" to the abortion issue as follows:

The claim that the primary wrong-making feature of a killing is the loss to the victim of the value of its future has obvious consequences for the ethics of abortion. The future of a standard fetus includes a set of experiences, projects, activities, and such that are identical with the futures of adult human beings and are identical with the

From Gerald H. Paske. "Abortion and the Neo-Natal Right to Life: A Critique of Marquis's Futurist Argument," in *The Abortion Controversy: 25 Years After Roe. v. Wade: A Reader,* 2nd. ed., ed. Louis P. Pojman and Francis J. Beckwith (Belmont, CA: Wadsworth, 1998), pp. 361–71.

futures of young children. Since the reason that is sufficient to explain why it is wrong to kill human beings after the time of birth is a reason that also applies to fetuses, it follows that abortion is prima facie seriously morally wrong. [192]

While granting the appeal of Marquis's argument, I shall nevertheless attack it at its foundation: the claim that having a future-like-ours is a sufficient condition for a right to life. Since Marquis's positive argument is entwined with his negative claims about personhood, I shall begin with the concept of personhood.

Marquis is correct when he offers the "unproblematic assumption" that "it is wrong to kill *us*." But though the assumption is unproblematic, it requires explication. Indeed, if we are to avoid "human chauvinism" and "species bias," this unproblematic assumption must be explicated. Why is it that a future-like-ours is the one that counts and not—say—the future of a pig or a cow? The answer lies in the concept of personhood.

The concept of personhood is both complex and controversial. I will discuss it in some detail later, but first I shall appeal to intuitions. Given the popularity of the television show *Star Trek* and of the movie *E.T.,* most of us are comfortable with the notion of nonhuman rational beings and it is easy to ascribe a right to life to such beings. We do so because, no matter how much they differ physically, their mental lives are very similar to ours. Intuitively, then, personhood is that set of mental characteristics which hypothetical nonhuman rational beings share with humans, but which neither they nor humans share with pigs and cows. It is this personhood which makes a future-like-ours possible and it is, hence, personhood which underlies Marquis's right to life. This becomes quite clear when one examines Marquis's defense of his own position. He offers the following as points in support of his thesis:

In the first place, (my theory) is incompatible with the view that it is wrong to kill only human beings who are biologically human. . . . In the second place, the claim that the loss of one's future is the wrong-making feature of one's being killed entails the possibility that the futures of some actual nonhuman mammals on our own planet are sufficiently like ours that it is seriously wrong to kill them also. . . . In the third place, the claim that the loss of one's future is the wrong-making feature of one's being killed does not entail . . . that active euthanasia is wrong. [190–191]

Since Marquis offers these points in support of his thesis, one assumes that these points are more basic than the thesis itself. But, in response to his first point, if we ask what differentiates those nonhumans who have a right to life from those nonhumans who lack such a right, the answer is clear. Those nonhumans who have a right to life are persons, as are we, and those nonhumans who lack a right to life also lack personhood. With regard to Marquis's second point, the nonhuman mammals on our own planet that have something like a future-like-ours are the higher apes, and they come closest to being persons. And finally, what could justify active euthanasia except that the human *person* is either gone (comatose) or overwhelmed by excruciating pain?

Despite the fact that the Marquis thesis presupposes personhood, Marquis explicitly rejects the personhood criterion when he says that those who accept the personhood criteria are "left with the problem of explaining why *psychological* characteristics should make a *moral* difference." Insofar as this is offered as an argument it commits the *ad ignorantiam* fallacy. One is tempted, therefore, to offer the *ad hominem* response that Marquis has exactly the same problem with regard to explaining why human futures are more important than other futures. But I will not base my case on fallacies. Rather, I will provide an explanation of why certain psychological characteristics make a moral difference.

It is a basic moral principle that harming sentient life requires justification. It is also an empirical fact that different kinds of harm can be done to various forms of sentient life depending on the nature of their consciousness. For example, you can cause a snake physical pain, but you cannot cause it psychological pain by insulting it. Persons can grasp and use many concepts that cannot be understood by nonpersons. Such concepts can generate attitudes and expectations that can be frustrated. Since such frustrations constitute an emotional harm, persons can be harmed in ways that nonpersons cannot. Some of these harms are the most serious that can be done to humans. Thus, what is special about human or person consciousness is that persons are capable of experiencing *conceptually based emotions.*

Conceptually based emotions are feeling states that can be experienced only if one is capable of understanding a variety of quite abstract concepts. Some examples of conceptually based emotions are the feelings of moral guilt, regret, indignation, hope, and pride. We can feel moral guilt only if we have a concept of moral wrong. We can feel indignant only if we have a concept of justice and fairness. We can feel hope only if we can foresee a variety of possible futures.

The conceptually based emotions are the basis of the demand that human beings be treated differently from other animals. For example, the desire to be an autonomous individual is a desire that can be had only by persons, and thus it is only persons whose autonomy can be violated. Also, there is nothing wrong with taking a cat's kittens away from her because, after a brief period, the cat will not and cannot miss the kittens. This is because she has no significant sense of self, nor does she have any prolonged memory of her kittens. If she were able to look forward to raising her kittens, to anticipate eventual grandkittens, and to feel a lifelong despair over the loss of her kittens, then to take her kittens from her would be immoral. But then she would be a person, a cat-person to be sure, but a person nonetheless.

Persons, and only persons, can conceptualize a distant future in which they are a participant. Only persons can anticipate and deliberately shape their own future. Only persons can desire and possess the freedom to shape their own self, their own life, their own future. Only persons can have their long-term plans frustrated by their untimely death. One aspect of the seriousness of death for a person is the loss of an anticipated, intended, longed-for future. No non-person can be harmed in this way. It is the loss of this sort of a future that constitutes a common—but not a universal—harm arising from death. Thus, the harm constituted by the loss of *our* future presupposes that we are persons. This, in brief, is the expla-nation of why psychological states have moral importance.

But, for a person, what is an even more serious loss than the loss of a possible future is the loss of the actual, existent person. It is this immediate loss of personhood which constitutes the basic harm in killing. It is this loss that makes the murder of persons even on their deathbeds a serious harm. One more minute of being a living person is of great value—even if that minute is an innocuous one—and taking that minute is a great harm. The loss of a future increases the harm of a killing, but the primary harm of a killing is the loss of the life of the person. This is a serious harm even when the person has no future.

It might be replied that even if one's future amounts to no more than one more minute, it is nevertheless the loss of that minute, and not the loss of personhood, that constitutes the harm. This reply is certainly plausible, but it gets its plausibility from confusing two distinct harms that result from murder: the loss of one's personhood and the loss of one's future. If, as the reply suggests, the loss of one's future is the only harm, then the badness of the murder under discussion would arise from the harm done by the loss of the last minute of life. But surely, the difference between a life of—say—89 years and a life of 89 years and one minute, given that the minute is an innocuous one, is not sufficient to account for the serious wrongness of a deathbed murder.

Were we to derive the wrongness of a murder solely from the loss of one's future, the degree of wrongness would vary inversely with life expectancy. Murdering the elderly would be less wrong than murdering the young. While such a consequence might be appealing to some, it goes against legal practice and, I believe, it goes against moral intuition. Thus, if all murders, *qua* murder, are equally bad, it is the loss of personhood that accounts for the intrinsic wrongness of murder, and it is the failure to recognize this that constitutes the basic error involved in Marquis's deprivation thesis. However, this error is both understandable and alluring.

Having a future-like-ours and being a person are conceptually independent but empirically related properties. All persons, insofar as they retain their personhood, have a future-like-ours. Thus, whenever a person is killed, there is the simultaneous destruction of a future-like-ours. This empirical entwining of personhood and having a future-like-ours makes it difficult to ascertain whether it is the loss of personhood, the loss of a future-like-ours, or the loss of both that constitutes the definitive harm done by the killing of a person.

However, consider a situation where, because of limited resources, one must choose between saving the life of a 9-year-old and saving the life of an 89-year-old. The differences in their expected futures (as well as their pasts) is surely relevant with regard to who should be saved. Surely one ought to save the child. This indicates that the value of a future-like-ours can vary in degree, one parameter being the expected length of the specific future-like-ours. It is this that makes premature death sadder than death at the end of a normal life-span.

Contrast the difference between premature and "normal" death with the difference between the murders of a 9-year-old and an 89-year-old. It is *not* the case that one murder is less wrong than the other. Both are equally wrong *qua* murder. The murders are equally wrong even though the murder of the 9-year-old causes a greater loss of a future-like-ours than does the murder of an 89-year-old. The degree of loss, the degree of harm, is not relevant to the wrongness of the murder per se. Rather, it is the destruction of personhood that makes all murders, *qua* murder, equally wrong.

Given that we can detach the harm of the loss of personhood from the harm of the loss of a future-like-ours, we can now consider the importance of the loss of a future-like-ours when the entity undergoing the loss has not attained personhood.

Imagine that a kitten is injected with a serum that will have no significant effect on the kitten for nine months but that will, after nine months, instantaneously cause the kitten to become a person and hence, to have both a present and a future-like-ours. Suppose further that an antidote to the serum is available. Would it be morally permissible to give the antidote before the kitten becomes a person? More important, would there be any moral difference between giving the antidote before the kitten becomes

a person and giving the antidote after the kitten becomes a person (assuming that the antidote will then return the kitten to a normal cat state)? Giving the antidote before the acquisition of personhood changes the biological state of the kitten, but giving the antidote after the acquisition of personhood destroys an existing person. Marquis, presumably, would have to conclude that the antidote should never be given. I, on the other hand, believe that the antidote could be given before the kitten becomes a person, but not after.

Perhaps this difference merely reduces to a difference in intuitions, but I think not. It is appropriate to ask what underlies the different intuitions. Marquis and I agree that—for normal adult humans—the loss of a future-like-ours is a tragic loss. But—for normal adult humans—such a loss is simultaneous with the loss of personhood. That is, it is the simultaneous loss of personhood that underlies the tragedy of the loss of a future.

Insofar as this is correct, and insofar as killing a dying patient against their conscious will is wrong, having a future-like-ours is not a necessary condition for having a right to life. Furthermore, insofar as giving our hypothetical kitten the antidote before it becomes a person is morally permissible, having a future-like-ours is not a sufficient condition for having a right to life. What is a sufficient condition for having a right to life is *being* a person. What is wrong with killing us is not the destruction of a future but the destruction of a person.

Marquis recognizes this possibility and he discusses it under the rubric of the "discontinuation account" of the wrongness of killing. This account, he says, seems just as intelligible as the value of a future-like-ours account, but, since it does not justify an anti-abortion position, Marquis feels compelled to argue against it. His argument is as follows:

> The discontinuation account will not be adequate at all, if it does not refer to the *value of* the experience that may be discontinued. One does not want the discontinuation account to make it wrong to kill a patient who begs for death and who is in severe pain that cannot be relieved short of killing. . . . If the patient's future is a future of value, we want our account to make it wrong to kill the patient. If the patient's future is intolerable, whatever his or her immediate past, we want our

account to allow killing the patient. Obviously, then, it is the value of that patient's future that is doing the work in rendering the morality of killing the patient intelligible.

This being the case, it seems clear that whether one has immediate past experiences or not does no work in the explanation of what makes killing wrong. The addition the discontinuation account makes to the value of a human future account is otiose. Its addition to the value-of-a-future account plays no role at all in rendering intelligible the wrongness of killing. [197]

Contrary to Marquis, what the discontinuation account is asserting is that the immediate existence of a person has great value. It is significant that in his purported refutation of this account Marquis refers to both the past and future of a person, but says absolutely nothing about the value of the instantaneous present. Thus he says: "If the patient's future is intolerable, whatever his or her immediate past, we want our account to allow killing the patient." But this is surely a mistake. Even if one is faced with a future life of intolerable pain, one ought not be killed *now*. If possible, euthanasia should be postponed until one's life *is* intolerable. Ideally, euthanasia should not be performed merely because one's life will become intolerable in the future.

In summary, Marquis's deprivation thesis acquires some initial plausibility because a full explanation of all the harms involved in a killing usually must refer to the future, for the loss of a future is *usually* part of the harm. But even if one has no (significant) future, killing one is still wrong. It is the immediate death of a person, the immediate snuffing out of personhood, that constitutes the evil of killing. The loss of a valuable future, when it accompanies the loss of personhood, is a significant *additional* loss. But it is not the loss of the future that is crucial vis-à-vis the killing. What is crucial is the loss of personhood.

The personhood account of the wrongness of killing, explicated by the concept of the conceptually based emotions, can explain the wrongness of killing, including the killing of persons who have no significant future. It is therefore superior to the future-like-ours account. However, the personhood account is still vulnerable to Marquis's claim that it cannot ade-

quately account for the right to life of neonates. This is so, he argues, because neonates are not persons and hence would have no right to life.

Marquis's argument is unsound. His argument rests on the false assumption that a neonatal right to life must arise from the same source that generates an adult right to life. But there are many types of right. Human, or more accurately *person* rights are those rights that each person has by virtue of being a person. Social rights are those rights that are fundamental to the well functioning of a morally acceptable society. The right to life (of persons) is a human or person right. The right to—say—property is a social right. Both types of rights can be important enough to justify sacrificing one's life in their defense.

All persons have a right to life as a result of being persons. But other entities might also have a right to life, a social right to life. Indeed, I shall argue that neonates should have a social right to life. This is not a right that springs *de novo* into existence. It is rather a right that grows out of a specific fetal right, the right to care (to be cared for).

The recognition that the right to care is an increasing, dynamic right makes possible a rational defense of the widespread intuition that late abortions require more justification than early abortions. In addition, the right to care accounts for and is compatible with the equally widespread intuition that some moral significance should be attributed to conception since it is at conception that each of us as a unique biological entity first came into being.

The right to care has four sources that can be divided into two groups: those *intrinsic* to the developing entity and those that relate the entity to others, the *relational* sources. The intrinsic sources are genetic humanness and potentiality of personhood. The relational sources are both the degree to which the fetus is cared about and whether or not a decision has been made to allow it to develop.

Genetic humanness is instantaneously present at conception, and the potentiality for personhood (for normal fetuses) is generated at conception also. This is what underlies the intuition that conception is a morally significant point. Nevertheless, conception is not sufficient to generate a right to life. Conception is the beginning of a biological entity that, after extensive development, may result in the beginnings of a person, but the beginning of personhood is better thought of as occurring when sentience begins and not with mere biological existence.

The concept of brain death is relevant to this point. Brain death clearly indicates that mere genetic humanness does not generate a right to life. Indeed, biologically alive genetic human beings are humanly dead if lacking the possibility of consciousness. Brain dead individuals are biologically living human organisms, but since they permanently lack consciousness they are not living *persons*. They are biological living organisms that, because they have been persons, are now dead people.

Of course the brain dead not only lack consciousness, they also lack the potential for consciousness and, hence, are crucially different from fetuses. It is the fact that most human fetuses are potential persons that generates a minimal right to care at conception. This right is generated as follows: First, we are human and, hence, have both a right and an obligation to treat human entities in a special way even if those entities are not persons. In a sense this is species bias, but if it is thought of on the analogy of a family—the human family—it is quite plausible. If the right to care is kept within legitimate bounds, the species bias that underlies it is quite reasonable. We may legitimately treat the members of our own family in special ways so long as our doing so does not violate the rights of other entities. Family members have claims on one another that others do not. So too with the human family. Exactly what claims our family members have on us, and what responsibilities we have toward them, is a subject for another paper. Nevertheless, if human beings exist whose conceptual abilities are no more than those of a cat, we should not treat them just as we treat cats. They are one of ours, and on that basis we may and ought to treat them as one of ours. We ought to care for them.

The role of *potentiality*, though significant, is minimal. It is significant enough so that the loss of the entity is at least unfortunate, but since a potential person is not a person, its loss is not equivalent to the loss of a person. The loss of an early fetus is less sad than the loss of a more developed fetus because more of the potential becomes actualized as time passes. But at no stage is the fetus a person, and hence its loss is never the equivalent of the loss of a person. The two intrinsic properties of fetuses, therefore, generate a minimal right to care. This right can be strengthened by the relational properties of the fetus.

This first relational property is that of being cared about. Reflection dispels any doubt that merely caring about something can give it value. If we think of a family heirloom we can recognize that the objective value of the heirloom can be quite small compared with the subjective value family members attach to it. This difference in value does not mean that the family members do not know the heirloom's objective value. Its value to the family, however, grows out of the history of the object, a history that they as family members share. This subjective value transcends the mere objective value of the object.

A conceptus, like an heirloom, can acquire a great deal of relational value depending on the response to it by others, primarily its biological progenitors. If the biological progenitors want to have a child the relational value of the fetus can be enormous. Yet this relational value is contingent on the attitude of the biological progenitors. If the pregnancy is not wanted, then the conceptus gains no relational value from this source.

The second source of relational value is possible only in situations where abortions are legally permissible. In such cases, the continuation of a pregnancy is a matter of choice and the decision to continue the pregnancy increases the responsibility of the woman and thereby increases the right to care of the fetus. If a woman decides to continue her pregnancy even though she does not really want a child, that decision nevertheless increases her responsibility towards the fetus. If she decides to continue the pregnancy, the fetus will (most likely) become a person. Hence the woman's support for the continuation of the pregnancy increases the fetal right to care since the well-being of the person-to-be depends on the care given to the fetus. If you allow a process that will result in a person to continue, you acquire some responsibility toward that future person and, hence, for the fetus which will become that person. The woman's decision to continue the pregnancy gives the fetus an additional degree of the right to care. She cannot morally continue the pregnancy and neglect the fetus. If she decides to remain pregnant, she has an obligation to take care of herself for the good of the fetus, and the fetus has a right to such care.

The right to care increases throughout the pregnancy because the woman's voluntary assumption of responsibility increases the longer she continues the pregnancy and the potentiality of the fetus becomes more actualized. Thus late term abortions are justifiable only to prevent the death of or serious harm to the woman. Since this final "threat" ends with birth, the neonate has a full (social) right to life.

In conclusion, personhood is the primary source of the right to life. Until a human passes through the fetal and neonatal stages and develops personhood its rights depend on the other four sources of rights. Those sources generate a range of rights beginning with a minimal and easily defeasible right to care during the early stages of the pregnancy, through an increasingly significant right to care, and culminating in a full social right to life for neonates.

NOTE

1. [Don Marquis, "Why Abortion Is Immoral," *Journal of Philosophy*, 86, no. 4 (April 1989): 183–202.]

ALASTAIR NORCROSS

Killing, Abortion, and Contraception
A Reply to Marquis

Don Marquis, in "Why Abortion Is Immoral,"[1] argues that "abortion is, except possibly in rare cases, seriously immoral, that it is in the same moral category as killing an innocent human being" (183). His argument for this is that abortions share with killings the central feature that makes them wrong. "Killing someone is wrong, primarily because the killing inflicts (one of) the greatest possible losses on the victim . . . the loss . . . of all those activities, projects, experiences, and enjoyment which would otherwise have constituted [the victim's] future personal life" (189). Marquis argues that, since fetuses have futures that include a set of "experiences, projects, activities and such which are identical with the futures of adult human beings," it follows that abortion is "prima facie seriously morally wrong" (192). Marquis answers several possible objections to his account. In this paper, I shall discuss the one objection to which his answer is clearly inadequate. I shall claim not only that his answer is inadequate, but that an adequate answer is not available to him, and thus that his account fails to support the claim that the overwhelming majority of abortions are seriously immoral.

I

Marquis admits that, if his account of the wrongness of killing and of abortion entails that contraception is also seriously immoral, "then there would appear to be a

---

Alastair Norcross, "Killing, Abortion, and Contraception: A Reply to Marquis," *Journal of Philosophy* 87, no. 5 (1990): 268–77. Reprinted by permission of the *Journal of Philosophy*.

difficulty with the analysis of [the] essay" (201). He claims that his analysis would entail that contraception is wrong "only if something were denied a human future of value by contraception. Nothing at all is denied such a future by contraception, however" (201). Marquis considers and rejects four candidates for the role of subject of harm by contraception: (1) some sperm or other, (2) some ovum or other, (3) a sperm and an ovum separately, (4) a sperm and an ovum together. I shall concentrate on his treatment of (4), since I think it is clearly the most promising candidate.

Marquis offers the following argument in response to the suggestion that contraception deprives the combination of sperm and ovum of a valuable future-like-ours:

> At the time of contraception, there are hundreds of millions of sperm, one (released) ovum and millions of possible combinations of all of these. There is no actual combination at all. Is the subject of the loss to be a merely possible combination? Which one? This alternative does not yield an actual subject of harm either. Accordingly, the immorality of contraception is not entailed by the loss of a future-like-ours argument simply because there is no nonarbitrarily identifiable subject of the loss in the case of contraception. (202)

I do not think it is clear from this passage what Marquis is claiming. It is all we get by way of argument against candidate (4), however, so we will have to work with it. I take it that Marquis does not mean that we could never tell which combination of sperm and ovum is the subject of loss in the case of successful contraception. I do not see how such an epistemic difficulty could rescue contraception from the charge of wrongdoing that Marquis's account levels against abortion. Consider the following two scenarios: (i) London is struck by a series of freak accidents involving power plants, which result in the deaths of almost everyone within a twenty-mile radius of Whitehall. The Prime Minister, Mrs. Butcher, is informed that there are a handful of survivors. She orders the army to round up the survivors, make a record of their names, and kill them. (ii) In response to the same information as in the previous example, Mrs. Butcher orders a hydrogen bomb to be detonated in London, thereby eliminating the possibility

of discovering who survived the initial accidents. I hope it is clear that at least part of what is morally wrong with Mrs. Butcher's actions in each case is that some people are killed who would otherwise have lived. It makes no difference that in case (ii) it is impossible to tell which people were killed by the nuclear explosion.

It might be objected that contraception differs crucially from my example (ii) in that one cannot say of every use of contraception that it prevents conception. In most cases pregnancy would not have resulted anyway. One response to this would be to modify (ii) so that Mrs. Butcher is only told that there is a small but significant possibility that there are survivors. More importantly, though, I think it would be small comfort to the proponent of the moral acceptability of contraception to be told that contraception is morally permissible in all those cases in which it does not actually prevent conception. The intuition that contraception is morally permissible is the intuition that it is permissible even, or perhaps especially, in those cases in which it fulfills its purpose.

Perhaps Marquis is not simply making an epistemic claim when he says that there is no nonarbitrarily identifiable subject of loss in the case of contraception. When he says that there are millions of possible combinations of sperm and ovum, but no actual combination, perhaps he means that there is no fact of the matter as to which sperm, if any, would have fertilized the ovum. It may be that the behavior of sperm is not strictly deterministic. Does this distinguish contraception from abortion and killing?

Consider the following scenario: two prisoners of conscience, Smith and Jones, are slated for execution in a small totalitarian republic. The president, Shrub, troubled by the effect of an Amnesty International campaign on his public image, decides to spare one of the prisoners. He cannot make up his mind whose life to spare, so he devises the following apparatus: Smith and Jones are placed in separate cells, each with air vents leading to a cannister of poison gas, which is set to release its contents at noon. A computer is programmed to select a three-digit number at random at one second before noon. If the number is even or zero, the computer will close the air vent in Smith's cell; if the number is odd, the computer will close the air vent in Jones's cell. The random-number selection process is truly indeterministic. The vice-president of the republic, Fowl, does not approve of Shrub bowing to liberal pressure. Fowl unplugs the computer at one minute before noon. The gas is released at noon, and both Smith and Jones die. I hope it is clear that Fowl has done something bad in this example. Two people have died instead of one. It is also clear that there is no fact of the matter as to which prisoner has been deprived of a valuable future by Fowl's actions. I do not think that the moral status of Fowl's action would change if the number of condemned prisoners was increased, but the number to be saved was kept at one. Even if Fowl's action makes it the case that a million and one die, instead of a million, he would have been responsible for the occurrence of one more death than would otherwise have occurred. In both of these cases, it seems that there is no nonarbitrarily identifiable subject of the loss of a valuable future. In both of these cases, Fowl's action is morally on a par with killing one person.

Let us return to the two-person case. We might still want to say that Fowl has harmed both Smith and Jones. We might say that the harm consists in lowering, from fifty percent to zero, their chances of surviving. (Indeed, given uncertainty about the length and quality of anyone's life, we should probably give a similar account of the harm involved in killing anyone.) If we increase the numbers, we can still say that Fowl has harmed all the prisoners. In the case of a million and one prisoners, Fowl has reduced each of their chances of survival from just under one ten thousandth of one percent to zero. However we describe the immorality of Fowl's action, it is clear that what he does is wrong for precisely the same reason as a standard killing is wrong. Either Fowl harms all the prisoners, or the lack of a nonarbitrarily identifiable subject of loss does not provide a morally relevant distinction between this case and a standard case of killing.

The similarities between contraception and the example discussed above are clear in terms of the loss of a valuable future. Either contraception harms all the combinations of sperm and ovum, or the lack of a nonarbitrarily identifiable subject of loss does not provide a morally relevant distinction between contraception and abortion.

<h1 style="text-align:center">II</h1>

It might be claimed that there is a significant difference between the case of contraception and my poison-gas examples. In the poison-gas example, all the candidates for subject of the loss of a valuable future were things, people, in fact. In the case of contraception, the candidates I have been considering—combinations of sperm and ovum—are nonstarters, not because there is no nonarbitrarily identifiable subject of loss, but because a combination of sperm and ovum cannot be a subject of anything, because "it" is not a thing.[2] I do not know whether Marquis would be prepared to make this claim, but it is worth considering on its own merits.

It might be instructive at this point to consider what could be meant by "a combination of sperm and ovum." What has to be the case for such a thing to exist? It might be natural to assume that, for such a thing to exist, a sperm and an ovum would have to be combined. What would have to be the case for a sperm and ovum to be combined? Perhaps a sperm and an ovum would have had to have joined to form a zygote. Marquis might be taken to be espousing this reading of "a combination of sperm and ovum" when he claims that there is no actual combination at the time of contraception. If this is his position, then he is, of course, right to say that there is no actual combination at the time of contraception (in the case of those forms of contraception which prevent a zygote from being formed, that is; it is an interesting question what Marquis would say about those forms of contraception which prevent the zygote from developing). If this is his position, though, why should we agree that his four categories of candidates for subject of harm are exhaustive? Why can we not say that the subject of harm is the mereological sum of a sperm and an ovum? Indeed, this is what I understand "a combination of sperm and ovum" to mean. So what is the response to the claim that a combination of sperm and ovum, understood as a mereological sum, is not a thing?

Perhaps the most obvious answer to the charge that a combination of sperm and ovum is not a thing is simply to deny it. I am inclined to pursue this option. To the extent that I am prepared to admit that a zygote or a fetus is a thing, I would claim that a combination of sperm and ovum is also a thing.

Let us assume, for the sake of argument, that a combination of a sperm and an ovum is not a thing. In that case, either the sperm and ovum, taken separately, *are* things, or neither is (I cannot imagine a plausible metaphysic that would classify one as a thing, but not the other). Consider the former alternative first. If both the sperm and the ovum are things, but the combination of the two is not, why can we not say that contraception harms both, because it deprives each one of the valuable future it would have had as a result of causal interaction with the other? This would appear to be Marquis's candidate (3), "a sperm and an ovum separately." Marquis rejects (3), because, "on this alternative, too many futures are lost. Contraception was supposed to be wrong, because it deprived us of one future of value, not two" (201). The obvious reply to this is that, on the assumption that a sperm and an ovum are both things, there *is* only one future lost as a result of contraception. It is the *same* future for both the sperm and the ovum. It is a shared future. Consider the possibility of human fusion. Imagine that it is possible for two people to fuse physically, so that a single person results, who has, among other things, some of the memories of both of the original people.[3] Imagine further that two people, Smith and Jones, will die, if they do not fuse with each other. Hector, an enemy of both Smith and Jones, knows of their predicament and of their plan to fuse. He locks them in adjoining rooms and waits until their anguished cries die out before gloating over their dead bodies. Given that Smith and Jones would have fused, if Hector had not locked the connecting door, it seems that Hector has deprived both Smith and Jones of a valuable future—the same valuable future. It might be objected that Hector has not deprived Smith and Jones of a valuable future, because they would have ceased to exist after they had fused, and a third person would have come into existence.[4] In this case, Hector has simply prevented the existence of something with a valuable future. I do not think that such a distinction could possibly ground a judgment that Hector has not behaved at least as badly as if he had killed one person, who would otherwise have lived. However we describe Hector's action, it is clear that what he has done is morally on a par with killing. Could anyone honestly insist that it would be permissible for Hector to shoot Smith and Jones as they are running toward each other, about to fuse, but impermissible for him to shoot the person who results from the fusion a few seconds later?

III

The case of contraception, it might be argued, differs from my fusion example, because the sperm and the ovum are not things themselves. Before conception, goes the claim, there is just some stuff—fundamental particles or metaphysical simples or whatever—arranged in such a way that we are inclined to say that there is a sperm and an ovum. At conception, or thereabouts, all this stuff interacts in such a way that a thing comes into existence. This may seem like a drowning metaphysician clutching at straws, but I do not think that this, even if it is a good account of what there is, will ground a moral distinction between contraception and abortion.

Let us say, what is perhaps natural, that, in order to deprive something of a valuable future, that thing must at some time exist. So let us define an intransitive verb, "to deprave" (not to be confused with the transitive verb "to deprave"): to deprave is to act in such a way that some stuff, which would otherwise have interacted in such a way that a thing with a valuable future would have resulted, does not so interact. There would seem to be pairs of cases of contraception and abortion such that the contraception is a case of depraving, and the abortion is a case of depriving something of a valuable future. Some pairs of a depraving and a depriving differ only in that the hostile environment created by the contraceptive/abortifacient has the desired effect on the stuff before a thing comes into existence, in the case of the depraving, but on the thing after it has come into existence, in the case of the depriving. If there is a moral difference between a depraving and a depriving, it must be grounded in the fact that there is just some stuff that would otherwise have resulted in the existence of a thing, in the case of a depraving, but there actually *is* a thing, in the case of a depriving.

If we are to defend Marquis's position on the morality of abortion and contraception by appealing to the distinction between depriving and depraving, we must investigate further the category of "thing," which is at the heart of the distinction. It might be instructive to remind ourselves of Marquis's treatment of the anti-abortionist's attempt to base an argument on the category "human being":

> If "human being" is taken to be a biological category, then the anti-abortionist is left with the problem of explaining why a merely biological category should make a moral difference. Why, it is asked, is it any more reasonable to base a moral conclusion on the number of chromosomes in one's cells than on the color of one's skin? If "human being," on the other hand, is taken to be a moral category, then the claim that the fetus is a human being cannot be taken to be a premise in the anti-abortion argument, for it is precisely what needs to be established. (186)

A similar argument can be used against an attempt to distinguish morally between contraception and abortion by appealing to the category "thing." Consider a case of depraving and a case of depriving something of a valuable future, which differ as little as is consistent with the former being definitely a case of depraving and the latter being definitely a case of depriving (the category of "thing" might have vague boundaries). In each case, there is some stuff that is affected by the contraceptive/abortifacient. In the latter case, but not in the former, there is also a thing that is the result of the interaction of the stuff. How might we establish that there is a thing in the latter case, but not in the former? If Marquis's position is to be defended, whatever makes the difference between thing and nothing must be definable without help from moral judgments on abortion and contraception, because those judgments are supposed to arise out of the difference between thing and no-thing. The most

likely option would be to appeal to biological facts about the arrangement and interaction of the stuff in each case. But if our explanation of the difference between thing and no-thing depends simply on biological facts, it seems that we will still have to argue that the difference between a depraving and a depriving is morally significant.

I V

Marquis might object at this point that he does not have to argue that the difference between a depriving and a depraving is morally significant, because it is just obvious that there is a morally important difference between depriving a thing of its potentialities and preventing it from coming about that there is a thing with potentialities. It is difficult to know what to say to this, except to point out that it is far from obvious to me. Perhaps we could point out that a similar line of defense could be used by the pro-abortionists who argue that fetuses (at least in the early stages) cannot be victims. It is just obvious, we might claim, that an early fetus cannot be a victim, because it lacks sentience. Alternatively, we might claim that it is just obvious that there is a morally significant difference between depriving a sentient victim of a valuable future, on the one hand, and depriving a presentient victim of a valuable future, on the other. Of course, we might also claim that it is obvious that there is a morally significant difference between depriving something that has not been born yet of a valuable future and depriving something that has been born of a similar future. We might disagree with Marquis's claim that the central wrong-making feature of a killing is that it deprives something of a valuable future. On the one hand, we might claim instead that the central wrong-making feature of a killing is that it deprives a certain specified sort of something of a valuable future. On the other hand, we might claim that the central wrong-making feature of a killing is what a depriving and a depraving have in common. I have tried to show that the distinction between thing and no-thing is no more morally significant than the distinction between sentient thing and presentient thing. Of course, one can always claim that a particular intuition is just rock-bottom. But if that is Marquis's claim about the distinction between thing and no-thing, then I would claim that he has given no arguments against abortion that would appeal to any of those who do not share his intuitions. My argument is not, however, that we should simply pick whichever distinction we feel most strongly about, and then base our position around that; at least not with respect to the question of what is bad about depriving something of a valuable future. I would claim that a consideration of the various distinctions—between postnatal and prenatal thing, between sentient and presentient thing, between thing and no-thing—should lead us to reject the claim that any of them makes a moral difference with respect to what is bad about depriving something of a valuable future (and, of course, what is bad about preventing it from coming about that there is a thing with a valuable future).

V

Another approach to the question of whether we should imbue the distinction between thing and no-thing with moral significance would be to ask why it is bad to deprive something of a valuable future. As far as I can see, there are two broad approaches that can be taken to answer this question (other than simply insisting that it *is* bad). On the one hand, we could claim that it is bad to deprive something of a valuable future, because it is bad, other things being equal, to prevent the occurrence of the valuable experiences and the like that constitute a valuable future. I hope it is clear why this approach will militate against drawing a morally significant line between depraving and depriving. On the other hand, we could claim that it is bad to deprive something of a valuable future, because the victim is, in some sense, entitled to her valuable future. We might say that she has a right to her valuable future. This would seem to allow us to draw a line between depraving and depriving. Depriving something of a valuable future violates certain rights of that thing. A depraving, on the other hand, involves no violations of rights, because there is no victim. The right to life, though,

is far from unproblematic. Why does anything have a right to a valuable future, as opposed to, say, a very bad future, or no future at all? Why does this fetus have a right to the future that would ensue if I do not perform the abortion, rather than the future that would ensue if I do?[5] We cannot answer that question with an appeal to the supposed immorality of performing an abortion, since it is that very immorality that we are seeking to establish by appeal to the right to a valuable future. How, in general, can we explain why something has a right to the good aspects of its future, but not to the bad ones? Perhaps we could appeal to the goodness of such good aspects obtaining (goodness, that is, that is not dependent on the claim that the possessor of such a future has a right to those good aspects). If my right to a valuable future is grounded in the value of the occurrence of those experiences and the like that constitute such a future, however, the very same grounding will apply to the immorality of a depraving.

Perhaps it could be argued that my right to a certain sort of future is not restricted to a valuable future. In fact, I have a right to all the unpleasantness that might be in my future, too. It is a common feature of rights that they can be waived, and so I am taken to have waived my rights to the unpleasant aspects of my future. Thus, it is not true to say of a doctor, who has deprived me of much pain and suffering, that she has violated my rights. If we take this line, it is very hard to see what is being claimed as the content of something's right to a future. If my right is not restricted to valuable aspects of my future, just what do I have a right to? I presume the claim is not that I have a right to my *actual* future, because, if that were the case, no actual behavior that affected me could violate such a right. Perhaps the content of my right varies, according to the situation I am in. Perhaps, in general, I have a right to whatever future would ensue, if the agent who might act so as to affect me does not so act. But this clearly will not do. If an agent's action will affect me, then his not performing the action will also affect me, since my future will be different from how it would otherwise have been.

Perhaps we will have to postulate a distinction between *doing* and *allowing*, and claim that I have a right to the future that would have ensued, if the agent had not done the thing in question. Quite apart from the difficulty of drawing a distinction between doing and allowing (or anything remotely resembling such a distinction), and the much greater difficulty, if not impossibility, of establishing that such a distinction can bear any moral weight, this distinction does not accord with our normal intuitions about rights. Any version of the doing/allowing distinction will have to place the neglect of a newborn baby, so that it starves to death, on the side of allowing. But it would be a strange position indeed that condemned abortion as the violation of the fetus's right to a valuable future, but did not render the same judgment about allowing a new-born to starve to death. Perhaps Marquis could claim that a thing that might have a valuable future just does have a right to a valuable future, and that is all there is to it. I would claim that, if we are disinclined to accept such a right as a basic intuition and seek some grounding for the right, we will have a hard time finding grounding for such a right which will not also ground the immorality of contraception.

VI

I have attempted to give reasons why we should be, at the very least, uncomfortable with allowing moral weight to the distinction between thing and nothing, and thus the distinction between abortion and contraception. Lest I be taken to be arguing against contraception (and, indeed, sexual abstinence), I should add that I do not consider the deprivation of a valuable future to be the only, or even the central, wrong-making feature of a standard killing. Thus, although what is bad about depriving someone of a valuable future is shared by abortion, regular use of contraception, and sexual abstinence, there are many morally significant factors that distinguish standard killings from abortions, and abortions from contraception. But they are the subject of another paper.[6]

I have argued in this paper that Marquis fails to distinguish morally between contraception and abortion. I have also argued that an attempt to distinguish between contraception and abortion by appeal to a parsimonious ontology does not provide a morally relevant distinction. I conclude that Marquis is unable to distinguish morally between contraception and abortion without appealing to morally relevant features other than what he calls the "wrong-making feature of one's being killed." I conjecture that any appeal to morally relevant features sufficient to ground a moral distinction between abortion and contraception will also ground a moral distinction between abortion and standard cases of killing.

NOTES

1. Don Marquis, "Why Abortion Is Immoral," *Journal of Philosophy* LXXXVI, 4 (April 1989): 183–202.

2. This argument was suggested to me by Frances Howard.

3. It might be objected that one cannot have a memory of, say, doing *x*, if one did not, oneself, do *x*. So, to say that the resulting person has some of the memories of both original persons might entail that the resulting person *is* both original persons. My argument does not require any such claim, so it is acceptable to modify the story so that it is merely claimed that the resulting person *seems* to have some of the memories of both original persons.

4. It is important to note that, for Marquis, the central wrong-making feature of killing is that it deprives the victim of those valuable experiences which she would otherwise have had. A killing of someone who was about to die is not, therefore, morally bad, or at least does not share the central wrong-making feature of killings of people who would otherwise have lived long happy lives.

5. It might sound strange to talk of the future that would ensue for the fetus if I perform an abortion. The fetus, it would seem, will have no future if I perform an abortion. I think it is clear, however, that the option of nonexistence for a fetus, or an adult human being, can be compared with other possible futures. It is also clear that nonexistence is preferable to some futures, futures filled with unmitigated pain and misery, for example. If we ask what sort of a future a fetus (or any other being) has a right to, it would be strange to exclude nonexistence from the options being considered.

6. Although I do not wish to wade into this topic here, I shall say that I consider the main weakness of Marquis's account of the wrongness of a standard killing to be that it does not take into consideration the full range of consequences of such an act.

PETER K. MCINERNEY

Does a Fetus Already Have a Future-Like-Ours?

Some of the most interesting and underexplored issues in philosophy are those of how human beings are in time. A person's relationship to her future is very complex, particularly if time passes, as we commonsensically believe that it does. In "Why Abortion Is Immoral," Don Marquis[1] argues that what makes killing a person wrong is that it deprives the person of her future. He concludes that abortion is wrong because it deprives the fetus of a "future-like-ours." The line of argument is clear.

> The future of a standard fetus includes a set of experiences, projects, activities, and such which are identical with the futures of adult human beings and are identical with the futures of young children. Since the reason that is sufficient to explain why it is wrong to kill human beings after the time of birth is a reason that also applies to fetuses, it follows that abortion is prima facie seriously morally wrong. (192)

The unexamined premise in the argument is that a fetus *already* has a future-like-ours of which it can be deprived.[2] For the argument to be convincing, it is necessary that a fetus *at its time* "possess" or be related to a future-like-ours in a way that allows the transfer from the wrongness of killing us persons to the wrongness of killing fetuses.

Fetuses are very different from normal adult humans. The connections between a fetus at an earlier time and a person (or person stage) at a significantly later time are very different from the connections between the person stages at different times which compose one person. Philosophical investigations of personal identity through time have revealed the complexity of the biological and psychological connections between the earlier and later stages of one person. These significant differences invalidate the claim that a fetus has a personal future in the same way that a normal adult human has a personal future.

The differences between a person's relationship to her future and a fetus's relationship to its future are striking even when the passage of time is ignored. In B-series time (a time that is composed entirely of earlier and later temporal locations with their occupants), an earlier person stage has many relations with later person stages which make these later person stages be "her future." The most widely considered relations in contemporary discussions of personal identity are those of memory, continuity of character, and intention-to-action.[3] Memory relations are from later person stages to earlier person stages. The later person stages are able to remember the experiences of the earlier person stages or there is an overlapping chain of such memory connections (memory continuity). The relation of continuity of character is that in which later person stages either have a character similar to the earlier person stages or are different in ways that are explicable by the operation of normal causes.[4] The relation of intention-to-action is that between an earlier intention and a later action that carries out that intention. Normal adult humans have all sorts of plans and projects for their short- and long-term futures which take time to implement.

There are other relations that connect earlier and later person stages. Some of the "mental processing" that ordinarily goes on in normal humans, such as forming generalizations from repeated observations or "digesting" an emotionally charged experience, takes a significant amount of time and so can be considered to include relations between person stages. In addition, there are all of the neurophysiological relations that underlie the ordinary continuation of mental life in persons. That a person has pretty much

Peter K. McInerney, "Does a Fetus Already Have a Future-Like-Ours?" *Journal of Philosophy* 87, no. 5 (1990): 264–68. Reprinted by permission of the *Journal of Philosophy*.

the same beliefs, wants, skills, and habits that she had 30 minutes (or 30 days) earlier depends upon a similarity of neurophysiological conditions between the earlier and later person stages.

Most of these relations to later person stages exist even when the earlier person is asleep or temporarily unconscious. Even intentions to perform later actions might be considered to continue through periods of unconsciousness. Since a temporarily unconscious person is still strongly related to her future, to kill her while she is unconscious is to deprive her of her future.

Young infants do not have all of the psychological complexity that adult persons have. Nevertheless, young infants are commonsensically understood to have perceptions, beliefs, desires, and emotions (whether or not the experimental data confirms this) and to learn from experience. For this reason, the neurophysiological states and processes of young infants can be understood to underlie something like the ordinary continuation of mental life in persons. A good case can be made that young infants are related in some (though not all) ways to a personal future.

The situation of a fetus at an early stage of development is very different.[5] A fetus at an early stage of development has neither a mental life of feelings, beliefs, and desires nor a developed brain and nervous system. There are none of the main relations with a personal future which exist in persons. Although there is some biological continuity between them so that there is a sense in which the later person stages "are the future" of the fetus, the fetus is so little connected to the later personal life that it can not be deprived of that personal life. At its time the fetus does not already "possess" that future personal life in the way that a normal adult human already "possesses" his future personal life.

Our commonsense views about time and entities in time involve a past that is fixed and determinate, a future that includes alternative possibilities whose actualization may be affected by action, and a process of what is future becoming present and past. In a time of this sort, how an entity "has a future" is more complex because when some temporal part (stage) of the entity is present, there is not a fixed and fully determinate future to which that entity can now be related. With respect to persons, a present person stage is not now related to a specific determinate later person stage that will become present. A person's future includes a branching range of possibilities (including his death) from which only one life course can become present. The branching of possibilities is such that most outcomes can become present only if certain earlier possibilities have become present. The actualization of one possibility makes available those later possibilities which presuppose it. This is particularly pronounced for the acquisition of skills, abilities, and capacities, which open up new ranges of possibilities that would otherwise not be available.

Many factors external to the person affect which of the person's possibilities become present. A normal adult human has only limited control over which of his possibilities become present. This control which a person exercises and attempts to exercise over his future is the most important connection that now exists with a specifically personal future. This control also depends upon the person's wants, skills, abilities, and capacities. The person wants various things for his future (including wanting himself to act) and exercises his powers to affect what happens.

A fetus is separated from a personal future by many "layers" of possibility. The possibilities that are available to a person or even to a young infant are not now available to the fetus. Only if the fetus develops in the right ways (favorable possibilities become present) will it acquire the capacities that make available the infant's possibilities. A great deal of favorable development would be necessary before the fetus could control its future in the way that persons do. The fetus does not now have a personal future.

Marquis has succeeded in formulating an important feature of people's opposition to abortion: the notion that abortion "cuts off" the fetus's future. A close examination of what it is "to have a future" reveals that at its time a fetus does not have a personal future of which it can be deprived. A living human cell that might be stimulated to develop into a clone of a person does not now have a personal future. A fetus similarly has only the potentiality to develop a personal future. For this reason, killing a fetus is morally very different from killing a normal adult human.

NOTES

1. *Journal of Philosophy,* LXXXVI, 4 (April 1989): 183–202.

2. "Since a fetus possesses a property, the possession of which in adult human beings is sufficient to make killing an adult human being wrong, abortion is wrong" (202).

3. See Derek Parfit, *Reasons and Persons* (New York: Oxford, 1984), pp. 205–7.

4. See *Reasons and Persons,* p. 207, for a brief discussion of "normal causes."

5. As the fetus develops, it becomes more similar to a young infant, and so progressively acquires more of a relationship to a personal future.

Thomson and Her Critics

Marquis's argument is aimed at establishing what we referred to earlier as "P1" of the standard argument against abortion, the claim that the fetus has the same right to life that you or I have. Let us now suppose that Marquis is correct about this. The claim that the fetus has this important right to life will serve to establish that abortion is impermissible only if what we referred to earlier as "P2" of the standard argument is also accepted, the claim that if the fetus has this right to life, then abortion is morally impermissible. Most people on both sides of the abortion debate tend to assume that this is true. As a result, the debate over the morality of abortion tends to focus largely, if not exclusively, on the moral status of the fetus. But in her seminal 1971 article "A Defense of Abortion," Judith Jarvis Thomson argues that this widely accepted assumption is false. Even if the fetus is granted to be a person with the same right to life as any other human being, she argues, abortion is still morally permissible.

Thomson's article touches on a number of distinct points, but her argument is, at its core, what we refer to in the Introduction to this volume as an "argument from analogy" (see section 4.1). Specifically, Thomson compares the situation of a woman burdened by an unwanted pregnancy with you in the following hypothetical scenario:

You wake up in the morning and find yourself back to back in bed with an unconscious violinist. A famous unconscious violinist. He has been found to have a fatal kidney ailment, and the Society of Music Lovers has canvassed all the available medical records and found that you alone have the right blood type to help. They have therefore kidnapped you, and last night the violinist's circulatory system was plugged into yours, so that your kidneys can be used to extract poisons from his blood as well as your own. The director of the hospital now tells you, "Look, we're sorry the Society of Music Lovers did this to you—we would never have permitted it if we had known. But still, they did it, and the violinist is now plugged into you. To unplug you would be to kill him. But never mind, it's only for nine months. By then he will have recovered from his ailment, and can safely be unplugged from you.

Thomson takes it that you will agree that, morally speaking, you have the right to unplug yourself from the famous unconscious violinist in this story, even though this means that he will die. This is not because she thinks your right to control your body is more important than the violinist's right to life, although Thomson has often mistakenly been interpreted in this way. Rather, Thomson's central contention is that it would be permissible for you to unplug yourself in this situation because doing so would not violate the violinist's right to life in the first place. He has a right to life, that is, but this does not mean that he has a right to be kept alive. By unplugging yourself from the violinist, you refrain from making a considerable sacrifice in order to keep him alive, and on Thomson's account at least, this is something that you are morally permitted to do. The crucial lesson of Thomson's violinist story, then, is that (according to her) the right to life does not include or entail the right to life support. But, Thomson then argues, if this is true in the case of the relationship between you and the violinist, why should it not also be true in the case of the relationship between a pregnant woman and the fetus she does not wish to carry to term? Even if we assume that the fetus has a right to life, that is, Thomson claims that it does not have the right to be kept alive by the pregnant woman. And, if this is so, then abortion may prove to be morally permissible even if the fetus does have the same right to life as a typical adult human being.

Although there is more to Thomson's article than this one analogy (readers should be particularly alert to the analogy involving a burglar coming into an open window), most of Thomson's critics have focused their responses on it. And since the vast majority of Thomson's readers seem to agree with her that you do have the moral right to unplug yourself from the violinist, virtually every critical response to Thomson's argument has turned on attempting to identify a morally relevant difference between the violinist scenario and the unwanted pregnancy scenario. Thomson's article has been called the most widely reprinted essay in contemporary philosophy, and it is certainly among the most widely discussed. The two response pieces that follow it in this anthology, therefore, should be taken only as a representative sampling of the many objections that have been raised against Thomson's argument. Readers are encouraged to consult some of the suggested further readings for still more objections worthy of discussion.

Baruch Brody's response piece, "Thomson on Abortion," is important for its clear and forceful statement of two potentially powerful objections: that Thomson's argument neglects the importance of the distinction between killing someone and letting someone die and the importance of the distinction between voluntary and involuntary actions. In both instances, Brody argues that the distinction in question can be used to undermine Thomson's analogy. Francis J. Beckwith's piece, "Arguments from Bodily Rights: A Critical Analysis," an excerpt of which follows Brody's, is valuable for the number and diversity of objections Beckwith is able to defend in a clear and concise manner. Beckwith raises too many points for us to summarize here—readers are urged to work at seeing how many distinct criticisms Beckwith ultimately has to offer—but, at the very least, one should consider the force of his claims that Thomson's argument overlooks the special obligations we can have to our own family members and that it is in various ways inconsistent with a certain kind of feminist stance.

QUESTIONS FOR CONSIDERATION

In thinking about the various objections raised against Thomson's article in both of the critical-response pieces reprinted here, readers will find it useful to consider applying the technique of variant cases discussed in section 4.1.3 of the Introduction. For any particular disanalogy that a critic of Thomson's offers, begin by considering why the difference is supposed to be morally relevant. Test the claim that the difference is relevant by modifying Thomson's violinist scenario so that it is more like the unwanted pregnancy scenario with respect to the particular factor identified by Thomson's critic.

  • How, for example, could Thomson's story be changed so that your being plugged into the violinist was the result of a voluntary act of yours rather than the result of being kidnapped? Would this change make the case more like the case of a typical unwanted pregnancy? How, if it all, does this change in the story change your intuitions about the case? What does this imply about the soundness of Thomson's argument?

  • How could Thomson's story be changed so that your unplugging yourself from the violinist is clearly a case of killing him rather than a case of letting him die? Would this change make the case more like the case of a typical abortion? How, if it all, does this change in the story change your intuitions about the case? What does this imply about the soundness of Thomson's argument?

  • What other differences might a critic point to between Thomson's original story and the case of abortion in typical cases? How could her story be changed to take these further differences into account? How, if at all, do these further changes in the story change your intuitions about the case? What does this imply about the soundness of Thomson's argument?

  • Later in the article, Thomson presents a further analogy involving a burglar and an open window. What is the point of this additional example? Does the example make her point effectively? If not, how might the burglar example be modified to make it more compelling?

FURTHER READING

Boonin, David. *A Defense of Abortion.* Cambridge: Cambridge University Press, 2002, Chapter 4.

Davis, Michael. "Foetuses, Famous Violinists and the Right to Continued Aid." *Philosophical Quarterly* 33 (1983): 259–78.

Finnis, John. "The Rights and Wrongs of Abortion: A Reply to Judith Thomson." *Philosophy and Public Affairs* 2 (1973): 117–45.

Fischer, John. "Abortion and Self-Determination." *Journal of Social Philosophy* 22, no. 2 (1991): 5–13.

Hall, Timothy. "Abortion, the Right to Life, and Dependence." *Social Theory and Practice* 31, no. 3 (July 2005): 405–29.

Hershenov, David B. "Abortions and Distortions: An Analysis of Morally Irrelevant Factors in Thomson's Violinist Thought Experiment." *Social Theory and Practice* 27, no. 1 (January 2001): 129–48.

Meyers, Christopher. "Maintaining the Violinist: A Mother's Obligations to the Fetus She Decides to Keep." *Journal of Social Philosophy* 23, no. 2 (1992): 52–64.

Pavlischek, Keith J. "Abortion Logic and Paternal Responsibility: One More Look at Judith Thomson's 'A Defense of Abortion.'" *Public Affairs Quarterly* 7, no. 4 (1993): 341–61.

Stone, Jim. "Abortion and the Control of Human Bodies." *Journal of Value Inquiry* 17 (1983): 77–85.

Thomson, Judith. "Rights and Deaths." *Philosophy and Public Affairs* 2 (1973): 146–59.

JUDITH JARVIS THOMSON

A Defense of Abortion

Most opposition to abortion relies on the premise that the fetus is a human being, a person, from the moment of conception. The premise is argued for, but, as I think, not well. Take, for example, the most common argument. We are asked to notice that the development of a human being from conception through birth into childhood is continuous; then it is said that to draw a line, to choose a point in this development and say "before this point the thing is not a person, after this point it is a person" is to make an arbitrary choice, a choice for which in the nature of things no good reason can be given. It is concluded that the fetus is, or anyway that we had better say it is, a person from the moment of conception. But this conclusion does not follow. Similar things might be said about the development of an acorn into an oak tree, and it does not follow that acorns are oak trees, or that we had better say they are. Arguments of this form are sometimes called "slippery slope arguments"—the phrase is perhaps self-explanatory—and it is dismaying that opponents of abortion rely on them so heavily and uncritically.

I am inclined to agree, however, that the prospects for "drawing a line" in the development of the fetus look dim. I am inclined to think also that we shall probably have to agree that the fetus has already become a human person well before birth. Indeed, it comes as a surprise when one first learns how early in its life it begins to acquire human characteristics. By the tenth week, for example, it already has a face, arms and legs, fingers and toes; it has internal organs, and brain activity is detectable. On the other hand, I think that the premise is false, that the fetus is not a person from the moment of conception. A newly fertilized ovum, a newly implanted clump of cells, is no more a person than an acorn is an oak tree. But I shall not discuss any of this. For it seems to me to be of great interest to ask what happens if, for the sake of argument, we allow the premise. How, precisely, are we supposed to get from there to the conclusion that abortion is morally impermissible? Opponents of abortion commonly spend most of their time establishing that the fetus is a person, and hardly any time explaining the step from there to the impermissibility of abortion. Perhaps they think the step too simple and obvious to require much comment. Or perhaps instead they are simply being economical in argument. Many of those who defend abortion rely on the premise that the fetus is not a person, but only a bit of tissue that will become a person at birth; and why pay out more arguments than you have to? Whatever the explanation, I suggest that the step they take is neither easy nor obvious, that it calls for closer examination than it is commonly given, and that when we do give it this closer examination we shall feel inclined to reject it.

I propose, then, that we grant that the fetus is a person from the moment of conception. How does the argument go from here? Something like this, I take it. Every person has a right to life. So the fetus has a right to life. No doubt the mother has a right to decide what shall happen in and to her body; everyone would grant that. But surely a person's right to life is stronger and more stringent than the mother's right to decide what happens in and to her body, and so outweighs it. So the fetus may not be killed; an abortion may not be performed.

It sounds plausible. But now let me ask you to imagine this. You wake up in the morning and find yourself back to back in bed with an unconscious violinist. A famous unconscious violinist. He has been found to have a fatal kidney ailment, and the Society of Music Lovers has canvassed all the available medical records and found that you alone have the right

Judith Jarvis Thomson, "A Defense of Abortion," *Philosophy and Public Affairs* 1, no. 1 (Fall 1971): 47–66. Some notes have been deleted. Reprinted by permission of Princeton University Press.

blood type to help. They have therefore kidnapped you, and last night the violinist's circulatory system was plugged into yours, so that your kidneys can be used to extract poisons from his blood as well as your own. The director of the hospital now tells you, "Look, we're sorry the Society of Music Lovers did this to you—we would never have permitted it if we had known. But still, they did it, and the violinist now is plugged into you. To unplug you would be to kill him. But never mind, it's only for nine months. By then he will have recovered from his ailment, and can safely be unplugged from you." Is it morally incumbent on you to accede to this situation? No doubt it would be very nice of you if you did, a great kindness. But do you *have* to accede to it? What if it were not nine months, but nine years? Or longer still? What if the director of the hospital says, "Tough luck, I agree, but you've now got to stay in bed, with the violinist plugged into you, for the rest of your life. Because remember this. All persons have a right to life, and violinists are persons. Granted you have a right to decide what happens in and to your body, but a person's right to life outweighs your right to decide what happens in and to your body. So you cannot ever be unplugged from him." I imagine you would regard this as outrageous, which suggests that something really is wrong with that plausible-sounding argument I mentioned a moment ago.

In this case, of course, you were kidnapped; you didn't volunteer for the operation that plugged the violinist into your kidneys. Can those who oppose abortion on the ground I mentioned make an exception for a pregnancy due to rape? Certainly. They can say that persons have a right to life only if they didn't come into existence because of rape; or they can say that all persons have a right to life, but that some have less of a right to life than others, in particular, that those who came into existence because of rape have less. But these statements have a rather unpleasant sound. Surely the question of whether you have a right to life at all, or how much of it you have, shouldn't turn on the question of whether or not you are the product of a rape. And in fact the people who oppose abortion on the ground I mentioned do not make this distinction, and hence do not make an exception in case of rape.

Nor do they make an exception for a case in which the mother has to spend the nine months of her pregnancy in bed. They would agree that would be a great pity, and hard on the mother; but all the same, all persons have a right to life, the fetus is a person, and so on. I suspect, in fact, that they would not make an exception for a case in which, miraculously enough, the pregnancy went on for nine years, or even the rest of the mother's life.

Some won't even make an exception for a case in which continuation of the pregnancy is likely to shorten the mother's life; they regard abortion as impermissible even to save the mother's life. Such cases are nowadays very rare, and many opponents of abortion do not accept this extreme view. All the same, it is a good place to begin: a number of points of interest come out in respect to it.

1. Let us call the view that abortion is impermissible even to save the mother's life "the extreme view." I want to suggest first that it does not issue from the argument I mentioned earlier without the addition of some fairly powerful premises. Suppose a woman has become pregnant, and now learns that she has a cardiac condition such that she will die if she carries the baby to term. What may be done for her? The fetus, being a person, has a right to life, but as the mother is a person too, so has she a right to life. Presumably they have an equal right to life. How is it supposed to come out that an abortion may not be performed? If mother and child have an equal right to life, shouldn't we perhaps flip a coin? Or should we add to the mother's right to life her right to decide what happens in and to her body, which everybody seems to be ready to grant—the sum of her rights now outweighing the fetus' right to life?

The most familiar argument here is the following. We are told that performing the abortion would be directly killing[1] the child, whereas doing nothing would not be killing the mother, but only letting her die. Moreover, in killing the child, one would be killing an innocent person, for the child has committed no crime, and is not aiming at his mother's death. And then there are a variety of ways in which this might be continued. (1) But as directly killing an innocent person is always and absolutely impermissible, an abortion may not be performed. Or, (2) as directly killing an innocent person is murder, and murder is always and absolutely impermissible, an abortion may not be performed Or, (3) as one's duty to refrain from directly killing an innocent person is more stringent than one's duty to keep a person from dying, an abortion may not be performed. Or, (4) if one's only options are directly killing an innocent person or letting a person die, one must prefer letting the person die, and thus an abortion may not be performed.[2]

Some people seem to have thought that these are not further premises which must be added if the conclusion is to be reached, but that they follow from the very fact that an innocent person has a right to life. But this seems to me to be a mistake, and perhaps the simplest way to show this is to bring out that while we must certainly grant that innocent persons have a right to life, the theses in (1) through (4) are all false. Take (2), for example. If directly killing an innocent person is murder, and thus is impermissible, then the mother's directly killing the innocent person inside her is murder, and thus is impermissible. But it cannot seriously be thought to be murder if the mother performs an abortion on herself to save her life. It cannot seriously be said that she *must* refrain, that she *must* sit passively by and wait for her death. Let us look again at the case of you and the violinist. There you are, in bed with the violinist, and the director of the hospital says to you, "It's all most distressing, and I deeply sympathize, but you see this is putting an additional strain on your kidneys, and you'll be dead within the month. But you *have* to stay where you are all the same. Because unplugging you would be directly killing an innocent violinist, and that's murder, and that's impermissible." If anything in the world is true, it is that you do not commit murder, you do not do what is impermissible, if you reach around to your back and unplug yourself from that violinist to save your life.

The main focus of attention in writings on abortion has been on what a third party may or may not do in answer to a request from a woman for an abortion. This is in a way understandable. Things being as they are, there isn't much a woman can safely do to abort herself. So the question asked is what a third party may do, and what the mother may do, if it is

mentioned at all, is deduced, almost as an afterthought, from what it is concluded that third parties may do. But it seems to me that to treat the matter in this way is to refuse to grant to the mother that very status of person which is so firmly insisted on for the fetus. For we cannot simply read off what a person may do from what a third party may do. Suppose you find yourself trapped in a tiny house with a growing child. I mean a very tiny house, and a rapidly growing child—you are already up against the wall of the house and in a few minutes you'll be crushed to death. The child on the other hand won't be crushed to death; if nothing is done to stop him from growing he'll be hurt, but in the end he'll simply burst open the house and walk out a free man. Now I could well understand it if a bystander were to say, "There's nothing we can do for you. We cannot choose between your life and his, we cannot be the ones to decide who is to live, we cannot intervene." But it cannot be concluded that you too can do nothing, that you cannot attack it to save your life. However innocent the child may be, you do not have to wait passively while it crushes you to death. Perhaps a pregnant woman is vaguely felt to have the status of house, to which we don't allow the right of self-defense. But if the woman houses the child, it should be remembered that she is a person who houses it.

I should perhaps stop to say explicitly that I am not claiming that people have a right to do anything whatever to save their lives. I think, rather, that there are drastic limits to the right of self-defense. If someone threatens you with death unless you torture someone else to death, I think you have not the right, even to save your life, to do so. But the case under consideration here is very different. In our case there are only two people involved, one whose life is threatened, and one who threatens it. Both are innocent: the one who is threatened is not threatened because of any fault, the one who threatens does not threaten because of any fault. For this reason we may feel that we bystanders cannot intervene. But the person threatened can.

In sum, a woman surely can defend her life against the threat to it posed by the unborn child, even if doing so involves its death. And this shows not merely that the theses in (1) through (4) are false; it shows also that the extreme view of abortion is false, and so we need not canvass any other possible ways of arriving at it from the argument I mentioned at the outset.

2. The extreme view could of course be weakened to say that while abortion is permissible to save the mother's life, it may not be performed by a third party, but only by the mother herself. But this cannot be right either. For what we have to keep in mind is that the mother and the unborn child are not like two tenants in a small house which has, by an unfortunate mistake, been rented to both: the mother *owns* the house. The fact that she does adds to the offensiveness of deducing that the mother can do nothing from the supposition that third parties can do nothing. But it does more than this: it casts a bright light on the supposition that third parties can do nothing. Certainly it lets us see that a third party who says "I cannot choose between you" is fooling himself if he thinks this is impartiality. If Jones has found and fastened on a certain coat, which he needs to keep him from freezing, but which Smith also needs to keep him from freezing, then it is not impartiality that says "I cannot choose between you" when Smith owns the coat. Women have said again and again "This body is *my* body!" and they have reason to feel angry, reason to feel that it has been like shouting into the wind. Smith, after all, is hardly likely to bless us if we say to him, "Of course it's your coat, anybody would grant that it is. But no one may choose between you and Jones who is to have it."

We should really ask what it is that says "no one may choose" in the face of the fact that the body that houses the child is the mother's body. It may be simply a failure to appreciate this fact. But it may be something more interesting, namely the sense that one has a right to refuse to lay hands on people, even where it would be just and fair to do so, even where justice seems to require that somebody do so. Thus justice might call for somebody to get Smith's coat back from Jones, and yet you have a right to refuse to be the one to lay hands on Jones, a right to refuse to do physical violence to him. This, I think, must be granted. But then what should be said is not "no one may choose," but only "*I* cannot choose," and indeed not even this, but "*I* will not *act*," leaving it open that

somebody else can or should, and in particular that anyone in a position of authority, with the job of securing people's rights, both can and should. So this is no difficulty. I have not been arguing that any given third party must accede to the mother's request that he perform an abortion to save her life, but only that he may.

I suppose that in some views of human life the mother's body is only on loan to her, the loan not being one which gives her any prior claim to it. One who held this view might well think it impartiality to say "I cannot choose." But I shall simply ignore this possibility. My own view is that if a human being has any just, prior claim to anything at all, he has a just, prior claim to his own body. And perhaps this needn't be argued for here anyway, since, as I mentioned, the arguments against abortion we are looking at do grant that the woman has a right to decide what happens in and to her body.

But although they do grant it, I have tried to show that they do not take seriously what is done in granting it. I suggest the same thing will reappear even more clearly when we turn away from cases in which the mother's life is at stake, and attend, as I propose we now do, to the vastly more common cases in which a woman wants an abortion for some less weighty reason than preserving her own life.

3. Where the mother's life is not at stake, the argument I mentioned at the outset seems to have a much stronger pull. "Everyone has a right to life, so the unborn person has a right to life." And isn't the child's right to life weightier than anything other than the mother's own right to life, which she might put forward as ground for an abortion?

This argument treats the right to life as if it were unproblematic. It is not, and this seems to me to be precisely the source of the mistake.

For we should now, at long last, ask what it comes to, to have a right to life. In some views having a right to life includes having a right to be given at least the bare minimum one needs for continued life. But suppose that what in fact *is* the bare minimum a man needs for continued life is something he has no right at all to be given? If I am sick unto death, and the only thing that will save my life is the touch of Henry Fonda's cool hand on my fevered brow, then all the same, I have no right to be given the touch of Henry Fonda's cool hand on my fevered brow. It would be frightfully nice of him to fly in from the West Coast to provide it. It would be less nice, though no doubt well meant, if my friends flew out to the West Coast and carried Henry Fonda back with them. But I have no right at all against anybody that he should do this for me. Or again, to return to the story I told earlier, the fact that for continued life that violinist needs the continued use of your kidneys does not establish that he has a right to be given the continued use of your kidneys. He certainly has no right against you that *you* should give him continued use of your kidneys. For nobody has any right to use your kidneys unless you give him such a right; and nobody has the right against you that you shall give him this right—if you do allow him to go on using your kidneys, this is a kindness on your part, and not something he can claim from you as his due. Nor has he any right against anybody else that *they* should give him continued use of your kidneys. Certainly he had no right against the Society of Music Lovers that they should plug him into you in the first place. And if you now start to unplug yourself, having learned that you will otherwise have to spend nine years in bed with him, there is nobody in the world who must try to prevent you, in order to see to it that he is given something he has a right to be given.

Some people are rather stricter about the right to life. In their view, it does not include the right to be given anything, but amounts to, and only to, the right not to be killed by anybody. But here a related difficulty arises. If everybody is to refrain from killing that violinist, then everybody must refrain from doing a great many different sorts of things. Everybody must refrain from slitting his throat, everybody must refrain from shooting him—and everybody must refrain from unplugging you from him. But does he have a right against everybody that they shall refrain from unplugging you from him? To refrain from doing this is to allow him to continue to use your kidneys. It could be argued that he has a right against us that *we* should allow him to continue to use your kidneys. That is, while he had no right against us that we should give him the use of your kidneys, it might be argued that he anyway has a right

against us that we shall not now intervene and deprive him of the use of your kidneys. I shall come back to third-party interventions later. But certainly the violinist has no right against you that *you* shall allow him to continue to use your kidneys. As I said, if you do allow him to use them, it is a kindness on your part, and not something you owe him.

The difficulty I point to here is not peculiar to the right to life. It reappears in connection with all the other natural rights; and it is something which an adequate account of rights must deal with. For present purposes it is enough just to draw attention to it. But I would stress that I am not arguing that people do not have a right to life—quite to the contrary, it seems to me that the primary control we must place on the acceptability of an account of rights is that it should turn out in that account to be a truth that all persons have a right to life. I am arguing only that having a right to life does not guarantee having either a right to be given the use of or a right to be allowed continued use of another person's body—even if one needs it for life itself. So the right to life will not serve the opponents of abortion in the very simple and clear way in which they seem to have thought it would.

4. There is another way to bring out the difficulty. In the most ordinary sort of case, to deprive someone of what he has a right to is to treat him unjustly. Suppose a boy and his small brother are jointly given a box of chocolates for Christmas. If the older boy takes the box and refuses to give his brother any of the chocolates, he is unjust to him, for the brother has been given a right to half of them. But suppose that, having learned that otherwise it means nine years in bed with that violinist, you unplug yourself from him. You surely are not being unjust to him, for you gave him no right to use your kidneys, and no one else can have given him any such right. But we have to notice that in unplugging yourself, you are killing him; and violinists, like everybody else, have a right to life, and thus in the view we were considering just now, the right not to be killed. So here you do what he supposedly has a right you shall not do, but you do not act unjustly to him in doing it.

The emendation which may be made at this point is this: the right to life consists not in the right not to be killed, but rather in the right not to be killed unjustly. This runs a risk of circularity, but never mind: it would enable us to square the fact that the violinist has a right to life with the fact that you do not act unjustly toward him in unplugging yourself, thereby killing him. For if you do not kill him unjustly, you do not violate his right to life, and so it is no wonder you do him no injustice.

But if this emendation is accepted, the gap in the argument against abortion stares us plainly in the face: it is by no means enough to show that the fetus is a person, and to remind us that all persons have a right to life—we need to be shown also that killing the fetus violates its right to life, i.e., that abortion is unjust killing. And is it?

I suppose we may take it as a datum that in a case of pregnancy due to rape the mother has not given the unborn person a right to the use of her body for food and shelter. Indeed, in what pregnancy could it be supposed that the mother has given the unborn person such a right? It is not as if there were unborn persons drifting about the world, to whom a woman who wants a child says "I invite you in."

But it might be argued that there are other ways one can have acquired a right to the use of another person's body than by having been invited to use it by that person. Suppose a woman voluntarily indulges in intercourse, knowing of the chance it will issue in pregnancy, and then she does become pregnant; is she not in part responsible for the presence, in fact the very existence, of the unborn person inside her? No doubt she did not invite it in. But doesn't her partial responsibility for its being there itself give it a right to the use of her body? If so, then her aborting it would be more like the boy's taking away the chocolates, and less like your unplugging yourself from the violinist—doing so would be depriving it of what it does have a right to, and thus would be doing it an injustice.

And then, too, it might be asked whether or not she can kill it even to save her own life: If she voluntarily called it into existence, how can she now kill it, even in self-defense?

The first thing to be said about this is that it is something new. Opponents of abortion have been so concerned to make out the independence of the fetus, in order to establish that it has a right to life, just as its mother does, that they have tended to overlook the possible support they might gain from making out that the fetus is *dependent* on the mother, in order to establish that she has a special kind of responsibility for it, a responsibility that gives it rights against her which are not possessed by any independent person—such as an ailing violinist who is a stranger to her.

On the other hand, this argument would give the unborn person a right to its mother's body only if her pregnancy resulted from a voluntary act, undertaken in full knowledge of the chance a pregnancy might result from it. It would leave out entirely the unborn person whose existence is due to rape. Pending the availability of some further argument, then, we would be left with the conclusion that unborn persons whose existence is due to rape have no right to the use of their mothers' bodies, and thus that aborting them is not depriving them of anything they have a right to and hence is not unjust killing.

And we should also notice that it is not at all plain that this argument really does go even as far as it purports to. For there are cases and cases, and the details make a difference. If the room is stuffy, and I therefore open a window to air it, and a burglar climbs in, it would be absurd to say, "Ah, now he can stay, she's given him a right to the use of her house—for she is partially responsible for his presence there, having voluntarily done what enabled him to get in, in full knowledge that there are such things as burglars, and that burglars burgle." It would be still more absurd to say this if I had had bars installed outside my windows, precisely to prevent burglars from getting in, and a burglar got in only because of a defect in the bars. It remains equally absurd if we imagine it is not a burglar who climbs in, but an innocent person who blunders or falls in. Again, suppose it were like this: people-seeds drift about in the air like pollen, and if you open your windows, one may drift in and take root in your carpets or upholstery. You don't want children, so you fix up your windows with fine mesh screens, the very best you can buy. As can happen, however, and on very, very rare occasions does happen, one of the screens is defective; and a seed drifts in and takes root. Does the person-plant who now develops have a right to the use of your house? Surely not—despite the fact that you voluntarily opened your windows, you knowingly kept carpets and upholstered furniture, and you knew that screens were sometimes defective. Someone may argue that you are responsible for its rooting, that it does have a right to your house, because after all you *could* have lived out your life with bare floors and furniture, or with sealed windows and doors. But this won't do—for by the same token anyone can avoid a pregnancy due to rape by having a hysterectomy, or anyway by never leaving home without a (reliable!) army.

It seems to me that the argument we are looking at can establish at most that there are *some* cases in which the unborn person has a right to the use of its mother's body, and therefore *some* cases in which abortion is unjust killing. There is room for much discussion and argument as to precisely which, if any. But I think we should sidestep this issue and leave it open, for at any rate the argument certainly does not establish that all abortion is unjust killing.

5. There is room for yet another argument here, however. We surely must all grant that there may be cases in which it would be morally indecent to detach a person from your body at the cost of his life. Suppose you learn that what the violinist needs is not nine years of your life, but only one hour: all you need do to save his life is to spend one hour in that bed with him. Suppose also that letting him use your kidneys for that one hour would not affect your health in the slightest. Admittedly you were kidnapped. Admittedly you did not give anyone permission to plug him into you. Nevertheless it seems to me plain you *ought* to allow him to use your kidneys for that hour—it would be indecent to refuse.

Again, suppose pregnancy lasted only an hour, and constituted no threat to life or health. And suppose that a woman becomes pregnant as a result of rape. Admittedly she did not voluntarily do anything to bring about the existence of a child. Admittedly she did nothing at all which would give the unborn person a right to the use of her body. All the same it might well be said, as in the newly emended violinist story, that she *ought* to allow it to remain for that hour—that it would be indecent in her to refuse.

Now some people are inclined to use the term "right" in such a way that it follows from the fact that you ought to allow a person to use your body for the hour he needs, that he has a right to use your body for the hour he needs, even though he has not been given that right by any person or act. They may say that it follows also that if you refuse, you act unjustly toward him. This use of the term is perhaps so common that it cannot be called wrong; nevertheless it seems to me to be an unfortunate loosening of what we would do better to keep a tight rein on. Suppose that box of chocolates I mentioned earlier had not been given to both boys jointly, but was given only to the older boy. There he sits, stolidly eating his way through the box, his small brother watching enviously. Here we are likely to say "You ought not to be so mean. You ought to give your brother some of those chocolates." My own view is that it just does not follow from the truth of this that the brother has any right to any of the chocolates. If the boy refuses to give his brother any, he is greedy, stingy, callous—but not unjust. I suppose that the people I have in mind will say it does follow that the brother has a right to some of the chocolates, and thus that the boy does act unjustly if he refuses to give his brother any. But the effect of saying this is to obscure what we should keep distinct, namely the difference between the boy's refusal in this case and the boy's refusal in the earlier case, in which the box was given to both boys jointly, and in which the small brother thus had what was from any point of view clear title to half.

A further objection to so using the term "right" that from the fact that A ought to do a thing for B, it follows that B has a right against A that A do it for him, is that it is going to make the question of whether or not a man has a right to a thing turn on how easy it is to provide him with it; and this seems not merely unfortunate, but morally unacceptable. Take the case of Henry Fonda again. I said earlier that I had no right to the touch of his cool hand on my fevered brow, even though I needed it to save my life. I said it would be frightfully nice of him to fly in from the West Coast to provide me with it, but that I had no right against him that he should do so. But suppose he isn't on the West Coast. Suppose he has only to walk across the room, place a hand briefly on my brow—and lo, my life is saved. Then surely he ought to do it, it would be indecent to refuse. Is it to be said "Ah, well, it follows that in this case she has a right to the touch of his hand on her brow, and so it would be an injustice in him to refuse"? So that I have a right to it when it is easy for him to provide it, though no right when it's hard? It's rather a shocking idea that anyone's rights should fade away and disappear as it gets harder and harder to accord them to him.

So my own view is that even though you ought to let the violinist use your kidneys for the one hour he needs, we should not conclude that he has a right to do so—we should say that if you refuse, you are, like the boy who owns all the chocolates and will give none away, self-centered and callous, indecent in fact, but not unjust. And similarly, that even supposing a case in which a woman pregnant due to rape ought to allow the unborn person to use her body for the hour he needs, we should not conclude that he has a right to do so; we should conclude that she is self-centered, callous, indecent, but not unjust, if she refuses. The complaints are no less grave; they are just different. However, there is no need to insist on this point. If anyone does wish to deduce "he has a right" from "you ought," then all the same he must surely grant that there are cases in which it is not morally required of you that you allow that violinist to use your kidneys, and in which he does not have a right to use them, and in which you do not do him an injustice if you refuse. And so also for mother and unborn child. Except in such cases as the unborn person has a right to demand it—and we were leaving open the possibility that there may be such cases—nobody is morally *required* to make large sacrifices, of health, of all other interests and concerns, of all other duties and commitments, for nine years, or even for nine months, in order to keep another person alive.

6. We have in fact to distinguish between two kinds of Samaritan: the Good Samaritan and what we might call the Minimally Decent Samaritan. The story of the Good Samaritan, you will remember, goes like this:

> A certain man went down from Jerusalem to Jericho, and fell among thieves, which stripped him of his raiment, and wounded him, and departed, leaving him half dead.

> And by chance there came down a certain priest that way; and when he saw him, he passed by on the other side.

> And likewise a Levite, when he was at the place, came and looked on him, and passed by on the other side.

> But a certain Samaritan, as he journeyed, came where he was; and when he saw him he had compassion on him.

> And went to him, and bound up his wounds, pouring in oil and wine, and set him on his own beast, and brought him to an inn, and took care of him.

> And on the morrow, when he departed, he took out two pence, and gave them to the host, and said unto him, "Take care of him; and whatsoever thou spendest more, when I come again, I will repay thee." (Luke 10:30–35)

The Good Samaritan went out of his way, at some cost to himself, to help one in need of it. We are not told what the options were, that is, whether or not the priest and the Levite could have helped by doing less than the Good Samaritan did, but assuming they could have, then the fact they did nothing at all shows they were not even Minimally Decent Samaritans, not because they were not Samaritans, but because they were not even minimally decent.

These things are a matter of degree, of course, but there is a difference, and it comes out perhaps most clearly in the story of Kitty Genovese, who, as you will remember, was murdered while thirty-eight people watched or listened, and did nothing at all to help her. A Good Samaritan would have rushed out to give direct assistance against the murderer. Or perhaps we had better allow that it would have been a Splendid Samaritan who did this, on the ground that it would have involved a risk of death for himself. But the thirty-eight not only did not do this, they did not even trouble to pick up a phone to call the police. Minimally Decent Samaritanism would call for doing at least that, and their not having done it was monstrous.

After telling the story of the Good Samaritan, Jesus said "Go, and do thou likewise." Perhaps he meant that we are morally required to act as the Good Samaritan did. Perhaps he was urging people to do more than is morally required of them. At all events it seems plain that it was not morally required of any of the thirty-eight that he rush out to give direct assistance at the risk of his own life, and that it is not morally required of anyone that he give long stretches of his life—nine years or nine months—to sustaining the life of a person who has no special right (we were leaving open the possibility of this) to demand it.

Indeed, with one rather striking class of exceptions, no one in any country in the world is *legally* required to do anywhere near as much as this for anyone else. The class of exceptions is obvious. My main concern here is not the state of the law in respect to abortion, but it is worth drawing attention to the fact that in no state in this country is any man compelled by law to be even a Minimally Decent Samaritan to any person; there is no law under which charges could be brought against the thirty-eight who stood by while Kitty Genovese died. By contrast, in most states in this country women are compelled by law to be not merely Minimally Decent Samaritans, but Good Samaritans to unborn persons inside them. This doesn't by itself settle anything one way or the other, because it may well be argued that there should be laws in this country—as there are in many European countries—compelling at least Minimally Decent Samaritanism. But it does show that there is a gross injustice in the existing state of the law. And it shows also that the groups currently working against liberalization of abortion laws, in fact working toward having it declared unconstitutional for a state to permit abortion, had better start working for the adoption of Good Samaritan laws generally, or earn the charge that they are acting in bad faith.

I should think, myself, that Minimally Decent Samaritan laws would be one thing, Good Samaritan laws quite another, and in fact highly improper. But we are not here concerned with the law. What we should ask is not whether anybody should be compelled by law to be a Good Samaritan, but whether we must accede to a situation in which somebody is being compelled—by nature, perhaps—to be a Good Samaritan. We have, in other words, to look now at third-party interventions. I have been arguing that no person is morally required to make large sacrifices to sustain the life of another who has no right to demand them, and this even where the sacrifices do not include life itself; we are not morally required to be Good Samaritans or anyway Very Good Samaritans to one another. But what if a man cannot extricate himself from such a situation? What if he appeals to us to extricate him? It seems to me plain that there are cases in which we can, cases in which a Good Samaritan would extricate him. There you are, you were kidnapped, and nine years in bed with that violinist lie ahead of you. You have your own life to lead. You are sorry, but you simply cannot see giving up so much of your life to the sustaining of his. You cannot extricate yourself, and ask us to do so. I should have thought that—in light of his having no right to the use of your body—it was obvious that we do not have to accede to your being forced to give up so much. We can do what you ask. There is no injustice to the violinist in our doing so.

7. Following the lead of the opponents of abortion, I have throughout been speaking of the fetus merely as a person, and what I have been asking is whether or not the argument we began with, which proceeds only from the fetus' being a person, really does establish its conclusion. I have argued that it does not.

But of course there are arguments and arguments, and it may be said that I have simply fastened on the wrong one. It may be said that what is important is not merely the fact that the fetus is a person, but that it is a person for whom the woman has a special kind of responsibility issuing from the fact that she is its mother. And it might be argued that all my analogies are therefore irrelevant—for you do not have that special kind of responsibility for that violinist, Henry Fonda does not have that special kind of responsibility for me. And our attention might be drawn to the fact that men and women both *are* compelled by law to provide support for their children.

I have in effect dealt (briefly) with this argument in section 4 above; but a (still briefer) recapitulation now may be in order. Surely we do not have any such "special responsibility" for a person unless we have assumed it, explicitly or implicitly. If a set of parents do not try to prevent pregnancy, do not obtain an abortion, and then at the time of birth of the child do not put it out for adoption, but rather take it home with them, then they have assumed responsibility for it, they have given it rights, and they cannot *now* withdraw support from it at the cost of its life because they now find it difficult to go on providing for it. But if they have taken all reasonable precautions against having a child, they do not simply by virtue of their biological relationship to the child who comes into existence have a special responsibility for it. They may wish to assume responsibility for it, or they may not wish to. And I am suggesting that if assuming responsibility for it would require large sacrifices, then they may refuse. A Good Samaritan would not refuse—or anyway, a Splendid Samaritan, if the sacrifices that had to be made were enormous. But then so would a Good Samaritan assume responsibility for that violinist; so would Henry Fonda, if he is a Good Samaritan, fly in from the West Coast and assume responsibility for me.

8. My argument will be found unsatisfactory on two counts by many of those who want to regard abortion as morally permissible. First, while I do argue that abortion is not impermissible, I do not argue that it is always permissible. There may well be cases in which carrying the child to term requires only Minimally Decent Samaritanism of the mother, and this is a standard we must not fall below. I am inclined to think it a merit of my account precisely that it does *not* give a general yes or a general no. It allows for and supports our sense that, for example, a sick and desperately frightened fourteen-year-old schoolgirl, pregnant due to rape, may *of course* choose abortion, and that any law which rules this out is an insane law. And it also allows for and supports our sense that in other cases resort to abortion is even positively indecent. It would be indecent in the woman to request an abortion, and indecent in a doctor to perform it, if she is in her seventh month, and wants the abortion just to avoid the nuisance of postponing a trip abroad. The very fact that the arguments I have been drawing attention to treat all cases of abortion, or even all cases of abortion in which the mother's life is not at stake, as morally on a par ought to have made them suspect at the outset.

Secondly, while I am arguing for the permissibility of abortion in some cases, I am not arguing for the right to secure the death of the unborn child. It is easy to confuse these two things in that up to a certain point in the life of the fetus it is not able to survive outside the mother's body; hence removing it from her body guarantees its death. But they are importantly different. I have argued that you are not morally required to spend nine months in bed, sustaining the life of that violinist; but to say this is by no means to say that if, when you unplug yourself, there is a miracle and he survives, you then have a right to turn round and slit his throat. You may detach yourself even if this costs him his life; you have no right to be guaranteed his death, by some other means, if unplugging yourself does not kill him. There are some people who will feel dissatisfied by this feature of my argument. A woman may be utterly devastated by the thought of a child, a bit of herself, put out for adoption and never seen or heard of again. She may therefore want not merely that the child be detached from her, but more, that it die. Some opponents of abortion are inclined to regard this as beneath contempt—thereby showing insensitivity to what is surely a powerful source of despair. All the same, I agree that the desire for the child's death is not one which anybody may gratify, should it turn out to be possible to detach the child alive.

At this place, however, it should be remembered that we have only been pretending throughout that the fetus is a human being from the moment of conception. A very early abortion is surely not the killing of a person, and so is not dealt with by anything I have said here.

Notes

1. The term "direct" in the arguments I refer to is a technical one. Roughly, what is meant by "direct killing" is either killing as an end in itself, or killing as a means to some end, for example, the end of saving someone else's life. . . .

2. The thesis in (4) is in an interesting way weaker than those in (1), (2), and (3): they rule out abortion even in cases in which both mother *and* child will die if the abortion is not performed. By contrast, one who held the view expressed in (4) could consistently say that one needn't prefer letting two persons die to killing one.

Critics

Baruch Brody

Thomson on Abortion

There is a familiar argument that purports to show that it is always wrong for an expectant woman to have an abortion. It runs as follows: (1) from the moment of conception, a foetus is a human being with the same rights to life as any other human being; (2) it is always wrong to take (directly) the life of an innocent human being; (3) therefore, it is always wrong to have an abortion. Judith Jarvis Thomson, in her recent article, criticized the above argument by challenging (2). More importantly, she argued that (at least in most cases) a woman has the right to secure an abortion even if (1) is true, although there are cases in which it would be positively indecent to exercise this right. It seems to me, however, that her discussions of these points, as interesting as they are, are not entirely convincing. I would like in this note to explain why.

I

Professor Thomson unfortunately offers as her counterexample to (2) her very problematic account of the violinist, a case to which we will return below. There are, however, far more straightforward cases that show that (2) is false. One such case—another will be discussed briefly at the end of this note—is the one in which Y is about to shoot X and X can save his life only by taking Y's life. We would certainly want to say that, as part of his right of self-defense, X has the right to take Y's life, and he has that right even if Y is a perfectly innocent child. So the right of self-defense includes in some cases the taking of innocent lives, (2) is false, and the above argument against abortion collapses.

This point raises important theoretical issues and it is therefore worth elaborating upon. In a normal case of self-defense, the following three factors seem to be involved: (a) the continued existence of Y poses a threat to the life of X, a threat that can be met only by the taking of Y's life; (b) Y is unjustly attempting to take X's life; (c) Y is responsible for his attempt to take X's life and is therefore guilty of attempting to take X's life. There is, moreover, a very plausible argument that would seem to suggest that all three of these factors must be involved if X is to be justified in taking Y's life in self-defense. It runs as follows: Why is X justified in killing Y? Isn't it Y's guilt for his attempt to take X's life together with the threat that Y's continued existence poses for X's life that justifies X's killing Y? Or, to put it another way, Y's guilt makes X's life take precedence over Y's. But if this is the justification for taking a life in self-defense, then conditions (a), (b), and (c) must be satisfied. If (a) is not satisfied, then Y's living is no threat to X, and if (b) and (c) are not satisfied, then there is no relevant guilt on Y's part that makes X's life take precedence over his.

What our example of the child shows is that this plausible argument will not do. Even if conditions (a) and (b), but not (c), are satisfied, X has the right to take Y's life in self-defense. This means that the above justification is not the justification for acts of self-defense. And this raises two fundamental and interrelated questions: What is the justification for taking a life in self-defense, and what conditions are required for an act of

Baruch Brody, "Thomson on Abortion," *Philosophy and Public Affairs* 1, no. 3 (Spring 1972): 335–40. Notes have been deleted. Reprinted by permission of Princeton University Press.

self-defense to be justified? The answers to these questions are not clear. One thing is, however, certain. X is not justified in taking Y's life merely because condition (a) is satisfied, and the justification for acts of self-defense is not simply that one has the right to do anything one has to in order to save one's life. After all, if Z threatens to, and will, kill X unless X kills Y, then Y's continued existence poses a threat to the life of X that can only be met by the taking of Y's life. Nevertheless, X is not therefore justified in killing Y. We would understand X's killing Y, and we might even excuse the action, but he would certainly have killed Y unjustly.

All of this has great relevance to the problem of abortion. While our discussion has shown that Professor Thomson is right in claiming that step (2) of the standard argument against abortion is mistaken, it also casts considerable doubt upon a standard argument for abortion. It is often argued that, no matter what status we ascribe to the foetus, the woman has, as part of her right of self-defense, the right to abort the foetus if the continuation of the pregnancy threatens her life. Now the foetus certainly does not satisfy condition (c), but that, as we have seen, is not required for the woman's being able to destroy it in self-defense. However, the foetus is not even attempting to take her life, and it therefore doesn't even satisfy condition (b). This must therefore cast doubt upon the claim that, no matter what the status of the foetus, abortions can sometimes be justified on grounds of self-defense.

II

Assuming that the foetus is human and that one should look at an abortion as a standard case of self-defense, we have seen that even when the foetus' continued existence poses a threat to the life of the woman, she probably has no right, as an act of self-defense, to an abortion. How then does Professor Thomson defend her claim that even if (1) is true the woman (at least in most cases) has the right to have an abortion, whether or not her life is threatened and whether or not she has consented to the act of intercourse in which the foetus is conceived? At one point, she makes the following strange suggestion: "In our case there are only two people involved, one whose life is threatened and one who

threatens it. Both are innocent: the one who is threatened is not threatened because of any fault, the one who threatens does not threaten because of any fault. For this reason we may feel that we bystanders cannot intervene. But the person threatened can." But surely this description is equally applicable to the following case. X and Y are adrift in a lifeboat. Y has a disease which he can survive but which will kill X if he contracts it, and the only way X can avoid that is by killing Y and pushing him overboard. Surely, X has no right to do this. So there must be some other reason why the woman has, if she does, the right to abort the foetus.

There is, however, an important difference between our lifeboat case and an abortion, one that leads us to the heart of Professor Thomson's argument. In the case we envisaged, both X and Y had equal right to be in the lifeboat; but the woman's body is hers, not the foetus', and she has first rights to its use. This is why the woman has a right to an abortion if her life is threatened (and even if it is not). Professor Thomson summarizes this argument, which she illustrates by her violinist example, as follows: "I am arguing only that having a right to life does not guarantee having either a right to be given the use of or a right to be allowed continued use of another person's body—even if one needs it for life itself."

One part of this claim is clearly correct. I have no duty to X to save X's life by giving him the use of my body (or my life savings, my wife, etc.) and X has no right, even to save his life, to any of those things. Thus, if a foetus were conceived in a test tube and would die unless it were implanted in a woman's body, that foetus has no right to any woman's body. But all of this is irrelevant to the abortion issue, for what is at stake there is something else, the right of the woman to kill X to get back the sole use of her body, and that is an entirely different matter.

This point can also be put as follows: we must distinguish the taking of X's life from the saving of X's life, even if we assume that one has a duty not to do the former and to do the latter. Now that second duty, if it exists at all, is much weaker than the first duty; many things will relieve us of it which will not relieve us of the first one. Thus, I am certainly relieved of my duty to save X's life by the fact that fulfilling it means a loss of my life savings. It may be noble for me to save X's life at the cost of everything I have, but I certainly have no duty to do that. And the same thing is true in cases in which I can save X's life by giving him use of my body for an extended period of time. However, I am not relieved of my duty not to take X's life by the fact that fulfilling it means the loss of everything I have and not even by the mere fact that fulfilling it means the loss of my life. As the original example of Y threatening X shows, something more is required before rights like self-defense become applicable. A fortiori, it would seem that I am not relieved of my duty not to take X's life by the fact that its fulfillment means that some other person, who is innocently occupying it, continues to use my body. I cannot see, then, how the woman's right to her body gives her a right to take the life of the foetus.

Perhaps we are missing the point of Professor Thomson's argument. Could we perhaps view her argument as follows: consider the case (and only the case) in which the foetus threatens the life of the woman. Then don't we have a choice between saving the woman and saving the foetus, and doesn't the woman come first because it is her body? I think, once more, that there is a point to such a claim. When one has a choice between using all or part of a woman's body to save her or the foetus, the fact that it is her body gives her precedence. But that is not the choice in the case of an abortion. There one chooses between saving the woman by taking the life of the foetus and not taking the life of the foetus, thereby failing to save the woman. Given that choice, as we have seen, her rights to her body have no revelance.

I conclude, therefore, that Professor Thomson has not established the truth of her claims about abortion, primarily because she has not attended to the distinction between our duty to save X's life and our duty not to take it. Once one attends to that distinction, it would seem that if (1) is true, it is wrong to perform an abortion even to save the life of the woman.

III

What has been said above might seem to suggest that if (1) is true, then it is always wrong for a woman to secure an abortion. I think that this suggestion is a mistake, and I should like, in this final section, to propose that there is at least one case in which, even if (1) is true, the woman has the right to secure an abortion.

The general principle about the taking of human lives that lies behind this case is rather complicated. It can best be stated as follows: it is permissible for X to take Y's life in order to save his own life if Y is going to die anyway in a relatively short time, taking Y's life is the only way to save X's life, and either (i) taking X's life (or doing anything else) will not save Y's life or (ii) there is a way to save Y's life but it has been determined by a fair random method that X's life should be saved rather than Y's. The rationale for this principle is that, in such a case, there is everything to gain by X's taking Y's life and nothing to lose. After all, both X and Y will die soon anyway if nothing is done, so Y loses nothing by X's killing him. Moreover, there is a reason why X should be saved rather than Y; either Y's life cannot be saved or X won over Y in a fair random choice.

It should be noted that this is not a principle of self-defense, for in some of the cases that it covers Y is in no way attempting to take X's life and is doing no action that leads to X's death. It should also be noted that this principle has nothing to do with the objectionable principles that would allow one to save several lives by taking a single innocent life. All such maximization-of-lives-saved principles, but not our principle, fall prey to the same objection that destroys all standard maximization-of-happiness principles, viz., that they fail to insure that no one will be treated unjustly when we maximize the quantity in question.

If we apply this principle to the question of abortion, we see that an abortion would be justified if, were the abortion not performed, both the woman and foetus would die soon, and if we either cannot save the foetus or have determined by a fair random procedure that it is the woman that should be saved.

One important point should be noted about this argument. It makes no appeal to any special fact about the foetus, the woman, or their relation. It depends solely upon a general principle about the taking of some human lives to save others. It is for just this reason that there can be no doubt about its conclusion being perfectly compatible with the claim that the foetus is just another human being.

FRANCIS J. BECKWITH

Arguments from Bodily Rights

A Critical Analysis

There are at least nine problems with Thomson's argument. These problems can be put into three categories: ethical, legal, and ideological.

ETHICAL PROBLEMS WITH THOMSON'S ARGUMENT

1. *Thomson assumes volunteerism.* By using the story as a paradigm for all relationships, thus implying that moral obligations must be voluntarily accepted to have moral force, Thomson mistakenly infers that all true moral obligations to one's offspring are voluntary. But consider the following story. Suppose a couple has a sexual encounter that is fully protected by several forms of birth control short of surgical abortion (condom, the Pill, IUD), but nevertheless results in conception. Instead of getting an abortion, the mother of the conceptus decides to bring it to term, although the father is unaware of this decision. After the birth of the child, the mother pleads with the father for child support. Because he refuses, she takes legal action. Although he took every precaution to avoid fatherhood, thus showing that he did not wish to accept such a status, according to nearly all child-support laws in the United States, he would still be obligated to pay support *precisely because* of his relationship to this child. . . .

But this obligatory relationship is not based strictly on biology, for this would make sperm donors morally responsible for children conceived by their seed. Rather, the father's responsibility for his offspring stems from the fact that he engaged in an act, sexual intercourse, that he fully realized could result in the creation of another human being, although he

took every precaution to avoid such a result. This is not an unusual way to frame moral obligations, for we hold drunk people whose driving results in manslaughter responsible for their actions, even if they did not intend to kill someone prior to becoming intoxicated. Such special obligations, although not directly undertaken voluntarily, are necessary in any civilized culture to preserve the rights of the vulnerable, the weak, and the young, who can offer very little in exchange for the rights bestowed on them by the strong, the powerful, and the postuterine in Thomson's moral universe of the social contract. Thus, Thomson is wrong, in addition to ignoring the *natural* relationship between sexual intercourse and human reproduction,[1] when she claims that if a couple has "taken all reasonable precautions against having a child, they do not by virtue of their biological relationship to the child who comes into existence have a special responsibility for it." "Surely we do not have any such 'special responsibility' for a person unless we have assumed it, explicitly or implicitly." Hence, instead of providing reasons for rejecting any special responsibilities for one's offspring, Thomson simply dismisses the concept altogether.

2. *Thomson's argument is fatal to family morality.* It follows from the first criticism that Thomson's volunteerism is fatal to family morality, which has as one of its central beliefs that an individual has special and filial obligations to his offspring and family that he does not have to other persons. Although Thomson might not consider such a fatality as being all that terrible because she might accept the feminist dogma that the traditional family is "oppressive" to women, a great number of ordinary men and women, who have

From Francis J. Beckwith, "Arguments from Bodily Rights: A Critical Analysis" in *The Abortion Controversy: 25 Years After Roe v. Wade: A Reader,* 2nd ed., ed. Louis P. Pojman and Francis J. Beckwith (Belmont, Calif.: Wadsworth, 1998), pp. 132–50. Some text and notes have been deleted. Reprinted by permission of Baker Book House Company.

found joy, happiness, and love in family life, find Thomson's volunteerism to be counterintuitive. Christina Sommers has come to a similar conclusion:

> For it [the volunteerist thesis] means that there is no such thing as filial duty per se, no such thing as the special duty of mother to child, and generally no such thing as morality of special family or kinship relations. All of which is contrary to what people think. For most people think that we do owe special debts to our parents even though we have not voluntarily assumed our obligations to them. Most people think that what we owe to our children does not have its origin in any voluntary undertaking, explicit or implicit, that we have made to them. And "preanalytically," many people believe that we owe special consideration to our siblings even at times when we may not *feel* very friendly to them . . . The idea that to be committed to an individual is to have made a voluntarily implicit or explicit commitment to that individual is generally fatal to family morality. For it looks upon the network of felt obligation and expectation that binds family members as a sociological phenomenon that is without presumptive moral force. The social critics who hold this view of family obligation usually are aware that promoting it in public policy must further the disintegration of the traditional family as an institution. But whether they deplore the disintegration or welcome it, they are bound in principle to abet it.[2]

3. *A case can be made that the unborn does have a prima facie right to her mother's body.* Assuming that there is such a thing as a special filial obligation, a principle that does not have to be voluntarily accepted to have moral force, it is not obvious that the unborn entity in ordinary circumstances (that is, with the exception of when the mother's life is in significant danger) does not have a natural prima facie claim to her mother's body. There are several reasons to suppose that the unborn entity does have such a natural claim.

a. Unlike Thomson's violinist, who is artificially attached to another person to save his life and is therefore not naturally dependent on any particular human being, the unborn entity is a human being who by her very nature is dependent on her mother, for this is how human beings are at this stage of their development.

b. This period of a human being's natural development occurs in the womb. This is the journey that we all must take and is a necessary condition for any human being's postuterine existence. And this fact alone brings out the most glaring difference between the violinist and the unborn: The womb is the unborn's natural environment whereas being artificially hooked up to a stranger is not the natural environment for the violinist. It would seem, then, that the unborn has a prima facie natural claim on her mother's body.

c. This same entity, when she becomes a newborn, has a natural claim on her parents to care for her, regardless of whether her parents wanted her (see the story of the irresponsible father). This is why we prosecute child abusers, people who throw their babies in trash cans, and parents who abandon their children. Although it should not be ignored that pregnancy and childbirth entail certain emotional, physical, and financial sacrifices by the pregnant woman, these sacrifices are also endemic of parenthood in general (which ordinarily lasts much longer than nine months) and do not seem to justify the execution of troublesome infants and younger children whose existence entails a natural claim to certain financial and bodily goods that are under the ownership of their parents. If the unborn entity is fully human, as Thomson is willing to grant, why should the unborn's natural prima facie claim to her parents' goods differ before birth? Of course, a court will not force a parent to donate a kidney to her dying offspring, but this sort of dependence on the parent's body is highly unusual and is not part of the ordinary obligations associated with the natural process of human development, just as in the case of the violinist's artificial dependency on the reluctant music lover.

As Stephen D. Schwarz points out: "So, the very thing that makes it plausible to say that the person in bed with the violinist has no duty to sustain him; namely, that he is a stranger unnaturally hooked up to him, is precisely what is absent in the case of the mother and her child." That is to say, the mother "does have an obligation to take care of her child, to sustain her, to protect her, and especially, to let her live in the only place where she can now be protected, nourished, and allowed to grow, namely the womb."[3]

If Thomson responds to this argument by saying that birth is the threshold at which parents become fully responsible, then she has begged the question, for her argument was supposed to show us why there is no parental responsibility before birth. That is to say, Thomson cannot appeal to birth as the decisive moment at which parents become responsible to prove that birth is the time at which parents become responsible.

It is evident that Thomson's violinist illustration undermines the deep natural bond between mother and child by making it seem no different from that between two strangers artificially hooked up to each other so that one can "steal" the service of the other's kidneys. Never has something so human, so natural, so beautiful, and so wonderfully demanding of our human creativity and love been reduced to such a brutal caricature.

I am not saying that the unborn entity has an absolute natural claim to her mother's body, but simply that she has a prima facie natural claim. For one can easily imagine a situation in which this natural claim is outweighed by other important prima facie values, such as when a pregnancy significantly endangers the mother's life. Since the continuation of such a pregnancy would most likely entail the death of both mother and child, and since it is better that one human should live rather than two die, terminating such a pregnancy via abortion is morally justified.

Someone may respond to the three criticisms by agreeing that Thomson's illustration may not apply in cases of ordinary sexual intercourse, but only in cases in which pregnancy results from rape or incest, although it should be noted that Thomson herself does not press this argument. She writes, "Surely the question of whether you have a right to life at all, or how much of it you have, shouldn't turn on the question of whether or not you are the product of rape."

But those who do press the rape argument may choose to argue in the following way: Just as the sperm donor is not responsible for how his sperm is used or what results from its use (for example, it might be stolen, or an unmarried woman might purchase it, inseminate herself, and give birth to a child), the raped woman, who did not voluntarily engage in intercourse cannot be held responsible for the unborn human who is living inside her.

But there is a problem with this analogy: The sperm donor's relinquishing of responsibility does not result in the death of a human person. The following story should help illustrate the differences and similarities between these two cases.

Suppose that the sperm donated by the sperm donor was stolen by an unscrupulous physician and inseminated into a woman. Although he is not morally responsible for the child that results from such an insemination, the donor is nevertheless forced by an unjust court to pay a large monthly sum for child support, a sum so large that it may drive him into serious debt, maybe even bankruptcy. This would be similar to the woman who became pregnant as a result of rape. She was unjustly violated and is supporting a human being against her will at an emotional and financial cost. Is it morally right for the sperm donor to kill the child he is supporting to allegedly right the wrong that has been committed against him? Not at all, because such an act would be murder. Now if we assume, as does Thomson, that the raped woman is carrying a being who is fully human (or "a person"), her killing of the unborn entity by abortion, except if the pregnancy has a strong possibility of endangering her life, would be as unjust as the sperm donor killing the child he is unjustly forced to support. As the victimized man can rightly refuse to pay the child support, the raped woman can rightly refuse to bring up her child after the pregnancy has come to term. She can choose to put the child up for adoption. But in both cases, the killing of child is not morally justified. Although neither the sperm donor nor the rape victim might have the same special obligation to their biological offspring as does the couple who voluntarily engaged in intercourse with no direct intention to produce a child, it seems that the more general obligation not to directly kill another human person does apply.

4. *Thomson ignores the fact that abortion is indeed killing and not merely the withholding of treatment.* Thomson makes an excellent point: Namely, there are times when withholding or withdrawing medical treatment is morally justified. For instance, I am not morally obligated to donate my kidney to Fred, my

next-door neighbor, simply because he needs a kidney to live. In other words, I am not obligated to risk my life so that Fred can live a few years longer. Fred should not expect that of me. If, however, I donate one of my kidneys to Fred, I will have acted above and beyond the call of duty because I will have performed a supererogatory moral act. But this case is not analogous to pregnancy and abortion.

Levin argues that there is an essential difference between abortion and the unplugging of the violinist. In the case of the violinist (as well as my relationship to Fred's welfare), "the person who withdraws [or withholds] his assistance is not completely responsible for the dependency on him of the person who is about to die, while the mother *is* completely responsible for the dependency of her fetus on her. When one is completely responsible for dependence, refusal to continue to aid is indeed killing." For example, "if a woman brings a newborn home from the hospital, puts it in its crib and refuses to feed it until it has starved to death, it would be absurd to say that she simply refused to assist it and had done nothing for which she should be criminally liable."[4] In other words, just as the withholding of food kills the child after birth, in the case of abortion, the abortion kills the child. In neither case is there any ailment from which the child suffers and for which highly invasive medical treatment, with the cooperation of another's bodily organs, is necessary to cure this ailment and save the child's life.

Or consider the following case, which can be applied to the case of pregnancy resulting from rape or incest. Suppose a person returns home after work to find a baby at his doorstep. Suppose that no one else is able to take care of the child, but this person has only to take care of the child for nine months (after that time a couple will adopt the child). Imagine that this person, because of the child's presence, will have some bouts with morning sickness, water retention, and other minor ailments. If we assume with Thomson that the unborn child is as much a person as you or I, would "withholding treatment" from this child and its subsequent death be justified on the basis that the homeowner was only "withholding treatment" of a child he did not ask for to benefit himself? Is any person, born or unborn,

obligated to sacrifice his life because his death would benefit another person? Consequently, there is no doubt that such "withholding" of treatment (and it seems totally false to call ordinary shelter and sustenance "treatment") is indeed murder. . . .

IDEOLOGICAL PROBLEMS WITH THE USE OF THOMSON'S ARGUMENT

There are at least three ideological problems in the use of Thomson's argument by others. The latter two problems are usually found in the books, speeches, articles, or papers of those in the feminist or abortion-rights movements who sometimes uncritically use Thomson's argument or ones similar to it. In fact, Thomson might agree with most or all of the following critique.

1. *Inconsistent use of the burden of pregnancy.* Thomson has to paint pregnancy in the most horrific of terms to make her argument seem plausible. Dr. Bernard Nathanson, an obstetrician/gynecologist and former abortion provider, objects "strenuously to Thomson's portrayal of pregnancy as a ninemonth involuntary imprisonment in bed. This casts an unfair and wrongheaded prejudice against the consideration of the state of pregnancy and skews the argument." Nathanson points out that "pregnancy is not a 'sickness.' Few pregnant women are bedridden and many, emotionally and physically, have never felt better. For these it is a stimulating experience, even for mothers who originally did not 'want' to be pregnant." Unlike the person who is plugged into Thomson's violinist, "alpha [the unborn entity] does not hurt the mother by being 'plugged in' . . . except in the case of well-defined medical indications." And "in those few cases where pregnancy is a medical penalty, it is a penalty lasting nine months."[5]

Compare and contrast Thomson's portrayal of pregnancy with the fact that researchers have recently discovered that many people believe that a pregnant woman cannot work as effectively as a nonpregnant woman who is employed to do the same job in the same work place. This has upset a number of feminists, and rightfully so. They argue that a pregnant woman is not incapacitated or ill, but can work just as effectively as a nonpregnant woman.[6] But why then do feminists who use Thomson's argument argue, when it comes to abortion, that pregnancy is similar to being bedridden and hooked up to a violinist for nine months? When it comes to equality in the workplace (with which I agree with the feminists), there is no problem. But in the case of morally justifying abortion rights, pregnancy is painted in the most horrific of terms. Although not logically fatal to the abortion-rights position, this sort of double-mindedness is not conducive to good moral reasoning.

2. *The libertarian principles underlying Thomson's case are inconsistent with the State-mandated agenda of radical feminism.* If Thomson's illustration works at all, it works contrary to the statist principles of radical feminism (of course, a libertarian feminist need not be fazed by this objection). Levin points out that "while appeal to an absolute right to the disposition of one's body coheres well with other strongly libertarian positions (laissez-faire in the marketplace, parental autonomy in education of their children, freedom of private association), this appeal is most commonly made by feminists who are antilibertarian on just about every other issue." For example, "feminists who advocate state-mandated quotas, state-mandated comparable worth pay scales, the censorship of 'sexist' textbooks in the public schools, laws against 'sexually harassing speech' and legal limitations on private association excluding homosexuals, will go on to advocate abortion on the basis of an absolute libertarianism at odds with every one of those policies."[7] Although this criticism is ad hominem, as was the previous one, it underscores the important political fact that many abortion-rights advocates are more than willing to hold and earnestly defend contrary principles for the sake of legally mandating their ideological agenda.

This sort of inconsistency is evident in abortion-rights activity throughout the United States. In the state of Nevada, those who supported an abortion-rights referendum in November of 1990 told the voting public that they wanted to "get the government off of our backs and out of the bedrooms." But when the state legislature met in January these same abortion-rights supporters, under the auspices of the Nevada Women's Lobby, proposed legislation that asked for the taxpayers of the state to fund school-based sex clinics (which will refer teenage girls to abortion services and are euphemistically called health clinics) and assorted other programs. Forgetting that many of us keep our wallets in our back pockets and place them in the evening on our dressers in our bedrooms, the members of the Nevada Women's Lobby did not hesitate to do in January what they vehemently opposed in November: to get the government on our backs and *in* our bedrooms. The libertarians of November became the social engineers of March.

3. *Thomson's argument implies a macho view of bodily control, a view inconsistent with true feminism.* Some have pointed out that Thomson's argument or the reasoning behind it is actually quite antifeminist.[8] In response to a similar argument from a woman's right to control her own body, one feminist publication asks, "What kind of control are we talking about? A control that allows for violence against another human being is a macho, oppressive kind of control. Women rightly object when others try to have that kind of control over them, and the movement for women's rights asserts the moral right of women to be free from the control of others." After all, "abortion involves violence against a small, weak and dependent child. It is macho control, the very kind the feminist movement most eloquently opposes in other contexts."[9]

Celia Wolf-Devine observes that "abortion has something . . . in common with the behavior eco-feminists and pacifist feminists take to be characteristically masculine; it shows a willingness to use violence in order to take control. The fetus is destroyed by being pulled apart by suction, cut in pieces, or poisoned." Wolf-Devine goes on to point out that "in terms of social thought . . . it is the masculine models which are most frequently employed in thinking about abortion. If masculine thought is naturally hierarchical and oriented toward power and control, then the interests of the fetus (who has no power) would naturally be suppressed in favor of the interests of the mother. But to the extent that feminist social thought is egalitarian, the question must be raised of why the mother's interests should prevail over the child's ... Feminist thought about abortion has ... been deeply pervaded by the individualism which they so ardently criticize."[10]

NOTES

1. The lengths to which Thomson will go to deny the natural relationship between sex, reproduction, and filial obligations is evident in her use of the following analogy: "If the room is stuffy, and I therefore open a window to air it, and a burglar climbs in, it would be absurd to say. 'Ah, now he can stay, she's given him a right to use her house—for she is partially responsible for his presence there, having voluntarily done what enabled him to get in, in full knowledge that there are such things as burglars, and that burglars burgle.'" Because there is no natural dependency between burglar and homeowner, as there is between child and parent, Thomson's analogy is way off the mark. Burglars don't belong in other people's homes; whereas preborn children belong in no other place except their mother's wombs.

2. Christina Hoff Sommers, "Philosophers Against the Family," in *Person to Person,* ed. Hugh LaFollette and George Graham (Philadelphia: Temple University Press, 1989). [Reprinted in chapter 12 of this volume.] this volume, chapter 12.

3. Stephen D. Schwarz, *The Moral Question of Abortion.* Chicago: Loyola University Press, 1990, 118.

4. Michael Levin, *Feminism and Freedom.* New Brunswick, N.J.: Transaction, 1987, 288–289.

5. Bernard Nathanson, M.D., *Aborting America.* New York: Doubleday, 1979, 220.

6. Michelle Healy "At Work: Maternity Bias," *USA Today* (30 July 1990): 1A. Conducted by researcher Hal Gruental of State University of New York, Albany, this survey found that 41 percent of those interviewed (133 women and 122 men at eight businesses in the Northeast) "said they think pregnancy hurts a woman's job performance."

7. Michael Levin, review of *Life in the Balance* by Robert Weinberg, *Constitutional Commentary* 3 (Summer 1986): 507–508.

8. Although not dealing exclusively with Thomson's argument, Celia Wolf-Devine's article is quite helpful: "Abortion and the 'Feminine Voice,'" *Public Affairs Quarterly* 3 (July 1989): 181–197. See also Doris Gordon, "Abortion and Thomson's Violinist," a paper published by Libertarians for Life, 1991 (13424 Hathaway Drive, Wheaton, Md. 20906; 301-460-4041); Janet Smith, "Abortion as a Feminist Concern," in *The Zero People,* ed. Jeffe Lane Hensley, Ann Arbor, Mich.: Servant, 1983, 77–95; and John T. Wilcox, "Nature as Demonic in Thomson's Defense of Abortion," *The New Scholasticism* 63 (Autumn 1989): 463–484.

9. N.a., *Sound Advice for all Prolife Activists and Candidates Who Wish to Include a Concern for Women's Rights in Their Prolife Advocacy: Feminists for Life Debate Handbook.* Kansas City, Mo.: Feminists for Life of America, n.d., 15–16.

10. Wolf-Devine, "Abortion," 86, 87.

4

Is Killing Nonhuman Animals Wrong?

Regan and His Critics

One of the most important public developments within the area of applied ethics that concerns the morality of killing in the last few decades has been the rise of the animal-rights movement, a movement that opposes, among other things, the killing of nonhuman animals for sport, for food, and for science. Tom Regan's 1983 book *The Case for Animal Rights* is widely recognized as the most philosophically powerful defense of this animal-rights position. In his 1985 essay of the same title, reprinted in its entirety as the featured article in this chapter, Regan provides a summary version of the core argument of that book.

The overall structure of Regan's argument in his essay is, like that of Marquis's argument in defense of the rights of the human fetus, one of inference to the best explanation (see section 4.3 of the Introduction). Like Marquis, Regan begins by identifying a set of moral beliefs that he assumes most people, regardless of their views on the issue at hand, are likely to share. In the case of Regan's argument, these include beliefs about what morality permits us to do to one another and, more specifically, what it permits us to do to those human beings whose mental lives are considerably less developed than those of typical human beings. Such people are often referred to as "marginal humans." They include severely retarded or brain-damaged adults, for example. Again like Marquis, Regan then proceeds by attempting to uncover the general moral theory that best accounts for these commonly held beliefs. In the course of his discussion, he considers a variety of views, but perhaps most important are what he refers to as the *contractarian view,* the *utilitarian view,* and the *rights view* (see section 5.1 of the Introduction). Regan argues that the contractarian view must be rejected because it fails to account for our duties to the very young and severely retarded; the utilitarian view must be rejected because it fails to account for our duties not to harm one another merely to produce beneficial consequences; and the rights view succeeds where both of these alternatives fail. He argues, in short, that the rights view in general should be accepted on the grounds that it "surpasses all other theories in the degree to which it illuminates and explains the foundation of our duties to one another—the domain of human morality." Finally, once again like Marquis, Regan turns to the question of what the general theory that he has defended implies about the particular case with which he is concerned. Having defended the claim that human beings have important moral rights, that is, he turns to the question of what this implies about the moral standing of nonhuman animals. Here Regan argues that attributing rights to all human beings while withholding them from at least some nonhuman animals would be morally arbitrary. If we attribute rights to a severely brain-damaged human being despite the fact that he is not rational, for example, then we cannot consistently appeal to the claim that a cow is not rational as a basis for denying the cow rights. The best account of why we have the rights we have, Regan therefore concludes, rests on the claim that each of us is what he calls an "experiencing subject of a life, a conscious creature having an individual welfare that has importance to us whatever our usefulness to others." Regan describes this notion in a bit more detail and maintains that it applies as well to the sorts of nonhuman animals with which his work is concerned. If we have these important moral rights, Regan concludes, then so do they.

Regan's argument for animal rights is complex, and his conclusion is controversial. Because of the former, his argument can be attacked from a number of directions. Because of the latter, it has been. The four excerpts that follow Regan's essay help to represent the great variety of distinct strategies that critics have followed in arguing against Regan's essay and against his book. In the first piece, Jan Narveson argues that Regan has failed to justify his rejection of the contractarian approach to morality as an alternative to the rights view. At a general level, Narveson argues that the moral principles we have the best reason to adopt are those whose adoption makes us better off. Applied more specifically to the case of animals, Narveson then argues that such an approach can justify a minimal set of restrictions on our treatment of (at least some) nonhuman animals while stopping well short of adopting the various sorts of rights-based prohibitions that Regan defends. At the same time, Narveson argues—again, contrary to Regan—that the contractarian approach can overcome the argument from marginal cases and explain why we have much stronger duties to, say, a severely retarded child than to a nonhuman animal possessing comparable mental capacities.

In the years since Regan's essay and book were first published, perhaps the most frequent and most prominent critic of Regan's position has been R. G. Frey. In the excerpts from two different works of his that appear following Narveson's, Frey develops two very different kinds of objections to Regan's position. In the first, Frey argues that because animals do not possess language, they lack beliefs; that because they lack beliefs, they lack desires; and that because they lack desires, they fail to have interests in the sense that is relevant to their having moral rights. In the second, Frey responds specifically to the use Regan makes of cases involving so-called marginal humans, arguing that Regan is unsuccessful. In particular, Frey rejects Regan's insistence that all human beings have the same moral value. Finally, in a short excerpt from his book *Rights,* Alan White presents a brief argument that amounts to a reductio ad absurdum objection aimed directly at Regan's conclusion (see section 4.5 of the Introduction). White claims that whether or not a particular subject is "logically capable of having a right" depends upon whether or not it is the kind of subject about which it makes sense to use, in White's words, "the full language of rights." Further, White maintains that since animals cannot, for example, claim, assert, or waive rights, they are not the kinds of things that can have rights in the first place. Only a person can have rights, on White's account, and thus Regan's conclusion is not true because it cannot be true.

QUESTIONS FOR CONSIDERATION

The debate between Regan and his critics ultimately touches on a wide variety of potentially difficult issues; it would be impossible to summarize all of them here. As a good start, however, readers may find it useful to consider the following questions.

• First, how successful is Narveson's attempt to defend contractarian moral theory from Regan's attack? Does he succeed in showing that contractarianism can give a credible account of our duties to one another?

• If Narveson is successful, does he also succeed in showing that such an account can give us at least some duties with respect to animals without giving us what he would regard as too many?

• Second, how credible is Regan's claim that at least some nonhuman animals are what he calls a "subject of a life"? Is Regan naively anthropomorphizing when he pictures animals as having the requisite mental abilities? Or is Frey simply refusing to acknowledge that such animals may be fairly sophisticated? What kinds of considerations could help us to answer such questions given that we cannot literally look into their minds?

• Third, how powerful is the argument from "marginal" cases? Is Regan right that we must admit that some animals have much greater moral standing than has been thought? Or should we agree with Frey that perhaps some human beings have less moral standing than has been thought?

• Is Regan right that marginal humans and nonhuman animals with comparable mental capacities must morally speaking stand or fall together? And, if he is right, should they stand, or fall?

• Finally, is White right to maintain that animals can't have rights because they don't participate in the "full language of rights" in other ways? Is Regan's position even coherent?

FURTHER READING

Carruthers, Peter. *The Animals Issue: Moral Theory in Practice*. Cambridge: Cambridge University Press, 1992.

DeGrazia, David. *Taking Animals Seriously: Mental Life and Moral Status*. Cambridge: Cambridge University Press, 1996.

Machan, Tibor. "Do Animals Have Rights?" *Public Affairs Quarterly* 5 (1991): 163–73.

Paske, Gerald. "Why Animals Have No Right to Life: A Response to Regan." *Australasian Journal of Philosophy* 66 (1988): 498–511.

Pojman, Louis. "Do Animal Rights Entail Moral Nihilism?" *Public Affairs Quarterly* 7, no. 2 (1993): 165–85.

Regan, Tom. *The Case for Animal Rights*. Berkeley: University of California Press, 1983.

Rollin, Bernard E. *Animal Rights and Human Morality*. Buffalo, N.Y.: Prometheus Books, 1992.

Tom Regan

The Case for Animal Rights

I regard myself as an advocate of animal rights—as a part of the animal rights movement. That movement, as I conceive it, is committed to a number of goals, including:

- the total abolition of the use of animals in science;
- the total dissolution of commercial animal agriculture;
- the total elimination of commercial and sport hunting and trapping.

There are, I know, people who profess to believe in animal rights but do not avow these goals. Factory farming, they say, is wrong—it violates animals' rights—but traditional animal agriculture is all right. Toxicity tests of cosmetics on animals violates their rights, but important medical research—cancer research, for example—does not. The clubbing of baby seals is abhorrent, but not the harvesting of adult seals. I used to think I understood this reasoning. Not any more. You don't change unjust institutions by tidying them up.

What's wrong—fundamentally wrong—with the way animals are treated isn't the details that vary from case to case. It's the whole system. The forlornness of the veal calf is pathetic, heart wrenching; the pulsing pain of the chimp with electrodes planted deep in her brain is repulsive; the slow, tortuous death of the racoon caught in the leg-hold trap is agonizing. But what is wrong isn't the pain, isn't the suffering, isn't the deprivation. These compound what's wrong. Sometimes—often—they make it much, much worse. But they are not the fundamental wrong.

The fundamental wrong is the system that allows us to view animals as *our resources,* here for *us*—to be eaten, or surgically manipulated, or exploited for sport or money. Once we accept this view of animals—as our resources—the rest is as predictable as it is regrettable. Why worry about their loneliness, their pain, their death? Since animals exist for us, to benefit us in one way or another, what harms them really doesn't matter—or matters only if it starts to bother us, makes us feel a trifle uneasy when we eat our veal escalope, for example. So, yes, let us get veal calves out of solitary confinement, give them more space, a little straw, a few companions. But let us keep our veal escalope.

But a little straw, more space and a few companions won't eliminate—won't even touch—the basic wrong that attaches to our viewing and treating these animals as our resources. A veal calf killed to be eaten after living in close confinement is viewed and treated in this way: but so, too, is another who is raised (as they say) "more humanely." To right the wrong of our treatment of farm animals requires more than making rearing methods "more humane"; it requires the total dissolution of commercial animal agriculture.

How we do this, whether we do it or, as in the case of animals in science, whether and how we abolish their use—these are to a large extent political questions. People must change their beliefs before they change their habits. Enough people, especially those elected to public office, must believe in change—must want it—before we will have laws that protect the rights of animals. This process of change is very complicated, very demanding, very exhausting, calling for the efforts of many hands in education, publicity, political organization and activity, down to the licking of envelopes and stamps. As a trained and practising philosopher, the sort of contribution I can make is limited but, I like to think, important. The currency of philosophy is ideas—their meaning and rational

Tom Regan, "The Case for Animal Rights," in *In Defense of Animals,* ed. Peter Singer (New York: Blackwell Publishers, 1985), pp. 13–26. Reprinted by permission of Blackwell Publishing Ltd.

foundation—not the nuts and bolts of the legislative process, say, or the mechanics of community organization. That's what I have been exploring over the past ten years or so in my essays and talks and, most recently, in my book, *The Case for Animal Rights.* I believe the major conclusions I reach in the book are true because they are supported by the weight of the best arguments. I believe the idea of animal rights has reason, not just emotion, on its side.

In the space I have at my disposal here I can only sketch, in the barest outline, some of the main features of the book. It's main themes—and we should not be surprised by this—involve asking and answering deep, foundational moral questions about what morality is, how it should be understood and what is the best moral theory, all considered. I hope I can convey something of the shape I think this theory takes. The attempt to do this will be (to use a word a friendly critic once used to describe my work) cerebral, perhaps too cerebral. But this is misleading. My feelings about how animals are sometimes treated run just as deep and just as strong as those of my more volatile compatriots. Philosophers do—to use the jargon of the day—have a right side to their brains. If it's the left side we contribute (or mainly should), that's because what talents we have reside there.

How to proceed? We begin by asking how the moral status of animals has been understood by thinkers who deny that animals have rights. Then we test the mettle of their ideas by seeing how well they stand up under the heat of fair criticism. If we start our thinking in this way, we soon find that some people believe that we have no duties directly to animals, that we owe nothing to them, that we can do nothing that wrongs them. Rather, we can do wrong acts that involve animals, and so we have duties regarding them, though none to them. Such views may be called indirect duty views. By way of illustration: suppose your neighbour kicks your dog. Then your neighbour has done something wrong. But not to your dog. The wrong that has been done is a wrong to you. After all, it is wrong to upset people, and your neighbour's kicking your dog upsets you. So you are the one who is wronged, not your dog. Or again: by kicking your dog your neighbour damages your property. And since it is wrong to damage another person's property, your neighbour has done something wrong—to you, of course, not to your dog. Your neighbour no more wrongs your dog than your car would be wronged if the windshield were smashed. Your neighbour's duties involving your dog are indirect duties to you. More generally, all of our duties regarding animals are indirect duties to one another—to humanity.

How could someone try to justify such a view? Someone might say that your dog doesn't feel anything and so isn't hurt by your neighbour's kick, doesn't care about the pain since none is felt, is as unaware of anything as is your windshield. Someone might say this, but no rational person will, since, among other considerations, such a view will commit anyone who holds it to the position that no human being feels pain either—that human beings also don't care about what happens to them. A second possibility is that though both humans and your dog are hurt when kicked, it is only human pain that matters. But, again, no rational person can believe this. Pain is pain wherever it occurs. If your neighbour's causing you pain is wrong because of the pain that is caused, we cannot rationally ignore or dismiss the moral relevance of the pain that your dog feels.

Philosophers who hold indirect duty views—and many still do—have come to understand that they must avoid the two defects just noted: that is, both the view that animals don't feel anything as well as the idea that only human pain can be morally relevant. Among such thinkers the sort of view now favoured is one or other form of what is called *contractarianism.*

Here, very crudely, is the root idea: morality consists of a set of rules that individuals voluntarily agree to abide by, as we do when we sign a contract (hence the name contractarianism). Those who understand and accept the terms of the contract are covered directly; they have rights created and recognized by, and protected in, the contract. And these contractors can also have protection spelled out for others who, though they lack the ability to understand morality and so cannot sign the contract themselves, are loved or cherished by those who can. Thus young children, for example, are unable to sign contracts and lack rights. But they are protected by the contract none the less because of the sentimental interests of others, most notably their parents. So we have, then, duties involving these children, duties regarding them, but no duties to them. Our duties in their case are indirect duties to other human beings, usually their parents.

As for animals, since they cannot understand contracts, they obviously cannot sign; and since they cannot sign, they have no rights. Like children, however, some animals are the objects of the sentimental interest of others. You, for example, love your dog or cat. So those animals that enough people care about (companion animals, whales, baby seals, the American bald eagle), though they lack rights themselves, will be protected because of the sentimental interests of people. I have, then, according to contractarianism, no duty directly to your dog or any other animal, not even the duty not to cause them pain or suffering; my duty not to hurt them is a duty I have to those people who care about what happens to them. As for other animals, where no or little sentimental interest is present—in the case of farm animals, for example, or laboratory rats—what duties we have grow weaker and weaker, perhaps to vanishing point. The pain and death they endure, though real, are not wrong if no one cares about them.

When it comes to the moral status of animals' contractarianism could be a hard view to refute if it were an adequate theoretical approach to the moral status of human beings. It is not adequate in this latter respect, however, which makes the question of its adequacy in the former case, regarding animals, utterly moot. For consider: morality, according to the (crude) contractarian position before us, consists of rules that people agree to abide by. What people? Well, enough to make a difference—enough, that is, *collectively* to have the power to enforce the rules that are drawn up in the contract. That is very well and good for the signatories but not so good for anyone who is not asked to sign. And there is nothing in contractarianism of the sort we are discussing that guarantees or requires that everyone will have a chance to participate equally in framing the rules of morality. The result is that this approach to ethics could sanction the most blatant forms of social, economic, moral and political injustice, ranging from a repres-

sive caste system to systematic racial or sexual discrimination. Might, according to this theory, does make right. Let those who are the victims of injustice suffer as they will. It matters not so long as no one else—no contractor, or too few of them—cares about it. Such a theory takes one's moral breath away . . . as if, for example, there would be nothing wrong with apartheid in South Africa if few white South Africans were upset by it. A theory with so little to recommend it at the level of the ethics of our treatment of our fellow humans cannot have anything more to recommend it when it comes to the ethics of how we treat our fellow animals.

The version of contractarianism just examined is, as I have noted, a crude variety, and in fairness to those of a contractarian persuasion it must be noted that much more refined, subtle and ingenious varieties are possible. For example, John Rawls, in his *A Theory of Justice,* sets forth a version of contractarianism that forces contractors to ignore the accidental features of being a human being—for example, whether one is white or black, male or female, a genius or of modest intellect. Only by ignoring such features, Rawls believes, can we ensure that the principles of justice that contractors would agree upon are not based on bias or prejudice. Despite the improvement a view such as Rawls's represents over the cruder forms of contractarianism, it remains deficient: it systematically denies that we have direct duties to those human beings who do not have a sense of justice—young children, for instance, and many mentally retarded humans. And yet it seems reasonably certain that, were we to torture a young child or a retarded elder, we would be doing something that wronged him or her, not something that would be wrong if (and only if) other humans with a sense of justice were upset. And since this is true in the case of these humans, we cannot rationally deny the same in the case of animals.

Indirect duty views, then, including the best among them, fail to command our rational assent. Whatever ethical theory we should accept rationally, therefore, it must at least recognize that we have some duties directly to animals, just as we have some duties directly to each other. The next two theories I'll sketch attempt to meet this requirement.

The first I call the cruelty-kindness view. Simply stated, this says that we have a direct duty to be kind to animals and a direct duty not to be cruel to them. Despite the familiar, reassuring ring of these ideas, I do not believe that this view offers an adequate theory. To make this clearer, consider kindness. A kind person acts from a certain kind of motive—compassion or concern, for example. And that is a virtue. But there is no guarantee that a kind act is a right act. If I am a generous racist, for example, I will be inclined to act kindly towards members of my own race, favouring their interests above those of others. My kindness would be real and, so far as it goes, good. But I trust it is too obvious to require argument that my kind acts may not be above moral reproach—may, in fact, be positively wrong because rooted in injustice. So kindness, notwithstanding its status as a virtue to be encouraged, simply will not carry the weight of a theory of right action.

Cruelty fares no better. People or their acts are cruel if they display either a lack of sympathy for or, worse, the presence of enjoyment in another's suffering. Cruelty in all its guises is a bad thing, a tragic human failing. But just as a person's being motivated by kindness does not guarantee that he or she does what is right, so the absence of cruelty does not ensure that he or she avoids doing what is wrong. Many people who perform abortions, for example, are not cruel, sadistic people. But that fact alone does not settle the terribly difficult question of the morality of abortion. The case is no different when we examine the ethics of our treatment of animals. So, yes, let us be for kindness and against cruelty. But let us not suppose that being for the one and against the other answers questions about moral right and wrong.

Some people think that the theory we are looking for is utilitarianism. A utilitarian accepts two moral principles. The first is that of equality: everyone's interests count, and similar interests must be counted as having similar weight or importance. White or black, American or Iranian, human or animal—everyone's pain or frustration matter, and matter just as much as the equivalent pain or frustration of anyone else. The second principle a utilitarian accepts is that of utility: do the act that will bring about the best balance between satisfaction and frustration for everyone affected by the outcome.

As a utilitarian, then, here is how I am to approach the task of deciding what I morally ought to do: I must ask who will be affected if I choose to do one thing rather than another, how much each individual will be affected, and where the best results are most likely to lie—which option, in other words, is most likely to bring about the best results, the best balance between satisfaction and frustration. That option, whatever it may be, is the one I ought to choose. That is where my moral duty lies.

The great appeal of utilitarianism rests with its uncompromising *egalitarianism*: everyone's interests count and count as much as the like interests of everyone else. The kind of odious discrimination that some forms of contractarianism can justify—discrimination based on race or sex, for example—seems disallowed in principle by utilitarianism, as is speciesism, systematic discrimination based on species membership.

The equality we find in utilitarianism, however, is not the sort an advocate of animal or human rights should have in mind. Utilitarianism has no room for the equal moral rights of different individuals because it has no room for their equal inherent value or worth. What has value for the utilitarian is the satisfaction of an individual's interests, not the individual whose interests they are. A universe in which you satisfy your desire for water, food and warmth is, other things being equal, better than a universe in which these desires are frustrated. And the same is true in the case of an animal with similar desires. But neither you nor the animal have any value in your own right. Only your feelings do.

Here is an analogy to help make the philosophical point clearer: a cup contains different liquids, sometimes sweet, sometimes bitter, sometimes a mix of the two. What has value are the liquids: the sweeter the better, the bitterer the worse. The cup, the container, has no value. It is what goes into it, not what they go into, that has value. For the utilitarian you and I are like the cup; we have no value as individuals and thus no equal value. What has value is what goes into us, what we serve as receptacles for; our feelings of satisfaction have positive value, our feelings of frustration negative value.

Serious problems arise for utilitarianism when we remind ourselves that it enjoins us to bring about the best consequences. What does this mean? It doesn't mean the best consequences for me alone, or for my family or friends, or any other person taken individually. No, what we must do is, roughly, as follows: we must add up (somehow!) the separate satisfactions and frustrations of everyone likely to be affected by our choice, the satisfactions in one column, the frustrations in the other. We must total each column for each of the options before us. That is what it means to say the theory is aggregative. And then we must choose that option which is most likely to bring about the best balance of totalled satisfactions over totalled frustrations. Whatever act would lead to this outcome is the one we ought morally to perform—it is where our moral duty lies. And that act quite clearly might not be the same one that would bring about the best results for me personally, or for my family or friends, or for a lab animal. The best aggregated consequences for everyone concerned are not necessarily the best for each individual.

That utilitarianism is an aggregative theory—different individuals' satisfactions or frustrations are added, or summed, or totalled—is the key objection to this theory. My Aunt Bea is old, inactive, a cranky, sour person, though not physically ill. She prefers to go on living. She is also rather rich. I could make a fortune if I could get my hands on her money, money she intends to give me in any event, after she dies, but which she refuses to give me now. In order to avoid a huge tax bite, I plan to donate a handsome sum of my profits to a local children's hospital. Many, many children will benefit from my generosity, and much joy will be brought to their parents, relatives and friends. If I don't get the money rather soon, all these ambitions will come to naught. The once-in-a-lifetime opportunity to make a real killing will be gone. Why, then, not kill my Aunt Bea? Oh, of course I *might* get caught. But I'm no fool and, besides, her doctor can be counted on to co-operate (he has an eye for the same investment and I happen to know a good deal about his shady past). The deed can be done . . . professionally, shall we say. There is *very* little chance of getting caught. And as for my conscience being guilt-ridden, I am a resourceful sort of

fellow and will take more than sufficient comfort—as I lie on the beach at Acapulco—in contemplating the joy and health I have brought to so many others.

Suppose Aunt Bea is killed and the rest of the story comes out as told. Would I have done anything wrong? Anything immoral? One would have thought that I had. Not according to utilitarianism. Since what I have done has brought about the best balance between totalled satisfaction and frustration for all those affected by the outcome, my action is not wrong. Indeed, in killing Aunt Bea the physician and I did what duty required.

This same kind of argument can be repeated in all sorts of cases, illustrating, time after time, how the utilitarian's position leads to results that impartial people find morally callous. It *is* wrong to kill my Aunt Bea in the name of bringing about the best results for others. A good end does not justify an evil means. Any adequate moral theory will have to explain why this is so. Utilitarianism fails in this respect and so cannot be the theory we seek.

What to do? Where to begin anew? The place to begin, I think, is with the utilitarian's view of the value of the individual—or, rather, lack of value. In its place, suppose we consider that you and I, for example, do have value as individuals—what we'll call *inherent value*. To say we have such value is to say that we are something more than, something different from, mere receptacles. Moreover, to ensure that we do not pave the way for such injustices as slavery or sexual discrimination, we must believe that all who have inherent value have it equally, regardless of their sex, race, religion, birthplace and so on. Similarly to be discarded as irrelevant are one's talents or skills, intelligence and wealth, personality or pathology, whether one is loved and admired or despised and loathed. The genius and the retarded child, the prince and the pauper, the brain surgeon and the fruit vendor, Mother Teresa and the most unscrupulous used-car salesman—all have inherent value, all possess it equally, and all have an equal right to be treated with respect, to be treated in ways that do not reduce them to the status of things, as if they existed as resources for others. My value as an individual is independent of my usefulness to you. Yours is not dependent on your usefulness to me. For either of us to treat the other in ways that fail to show respect for the other's independent value is to act immorally, to violate the individual's rights.

Some of the rational virtues of this view—what I call the rights view—should be evident. Unlike (crude) contractarianism, for example, the rights view *in principle* denies the moral tolerability of any and all forms of racial, sexual or social discrimination; and unlike utilitarianism, this view *in principle* denies that we can justify good results by using evil means that violate an individual's rights—denies, for example, that it could be moral to kill my Aunt Bea to harvest beneficial consequences for others. That would be to sanction the disrespectful treatment of the individual in the name of the social good, something the rights view will not—categorically will not—ever allow.

The rights view, I believe, is rationally the most satisfactory moral theory. It surpasses all other theories in the degree to which it illuminates and explains the foundation of our duties to one another—the domain of human morality. On this score it has the best reasons, the best arguments, on its side. Of course, if it were possible to show that only human beings are included within its scope, then a person like myself, who believes in animal rights, would be obliged to look elsewhere.

But attempts to limit its scope to humans only can be shown to be rationally defective. Animals, it is true, lack many of the abilities humans possess. They can't read, do higher mathematics, build a bookcase or make baba ghanoush. Neither can many human beings, however, and yet we don't (and shouldn't) say that they (these humans) therefore have less inherent value, less of a right to be treated with respect, than do others. It is the *similarities* between those human beings who most clearly, most non-controversially have such value (the people reading this, for example), not our differences, that matter most. And the really crucial, the basic similarity is simply this: we are each of us the experiencing subject of a life, a conscious creature having an individual welfare that has importance to us whatever our usefulness to others. We want and prefer things, believe and feel things, recall and expect things. And all these dimensions of our life, including our pleasure and pain, our enjoyment and suffering, our satis-

faction and frustration, our continued existence or our untimely death—all make a difference to the quality of our life as lived, as experienced, by us as individuals. As the same is true of those animals that concern us (the ones that are eaten and trapped, for example), they too must be viewed as the experiencing subjects of a life, with inherent value of their own.

Some there are who resist the idea that animals have inherent value. "Only humans have such value," they profess. How might this narrow view be defended? Shall we say that only humans have the requisite intelligence, or autonomy, or reason? But there are many, many humans who fail to meet these standards and yet are reasonably viewed as having value above and beyond their usefulness to others. Shall we claim that only humans belong to the right species, the species Homo sapiens? But this is blatant speciesism. Will it be said, then, that all—and only—humans have immortal souls? Then our opponents have their work cut out for them. I am myself not ill-disposed to the proposition that there are immortal souls. Personally, I profoundly hope I have one. But I would not want to rest my position on a controversial ethical issue on the even more controversial question about who or what has an immortal soul. That is to dig one's hole deeper, not to climb out. Rationally, it is better to resolve moral issues without making more controversial assumptions than are needed. The question of who has inherent value is such a question, one that is resolved more rationally without the introduction of the idea of immortal souls than by its use.

Well, perhaps some will say that animals have some inherent value, only less than we have. Once again, however, attempts to defend this view can be shown to lack rational justification. What could be the basis of our having more inherent value than animals? Their lack of reason, or autonomy, or intellect? Only if we are willing to make the same judgement in the case of humans who are similarly deficient. But it is not true that such humans—the retarded child, for example, or the mentally deranged—have less inherent value than you or I. Neither, then, can we rationally sustain the view that animals like them in being the experiencing subjects of a life have less inherent value. *All* who have inherent value have it *equally,* whether they be human animals or not.

Inherent value, then, belongs equally to those who are the experiencing subjects of a life. Whether it belongs to others—to rocks and rivers, trees and glaciers, for example—we do not know and may never know. But neither do we need to know, if we are to make the case for animal rights. We do not need to know, for example, how many people are eligible to vote in the next presidential election before we can know whether I am. Similarly, we do not need to know how many individuals have inherent value before we can know that some do. When it comes to the case for animal rights, then, what we need to know is whether the animals that, in our culture, are routinely eaten, hunted and used in our laboratories, for example, are like us in being subjects of a life. And we do know this. We do know that many—literally, billions and billions—of these animals are the subjects of a life in the sense explained and so have inherent value if we do. And since, in order to arrive at the best theory of our duties to one another, we must recognize our equal inherent value as individuals, reason—not sentiment, not emotion—reason compels us to recognize the equal inherent value of these animals and, with this, their equal right to be treated with respect.

That, *very* roughly, is the shape and feel of the case for animal rights. Most of the details of the supporting argument are missing. They are to be found in the book to which I alluded earlier. Here, the details go begging, and I must, in closing, limit myself to four final points.

The first is how the theory that underlies the case for animal rights shows that the animal rights movement is a part of, not antagonistic to, the human rights movement. The theory that rationally grounds the rights of animals also grounds the rights of humans. Thus those involved in the animal rights movement are partners in the struggle to secure respect for human rights—the rights of women, for example, or minorities, or workers. The animal rights movement is cut from the same moral cloth as these.

Second, having set out the broad outlines of the rights view, I can now say why its implications for farming and science, among other fields, are both clear and uncompromising. In the case of the use of animals in science, the rights view is categorically abolitionist. Lab animals are not our tasters; we are not their kings. Because these animals are treated routinely, systematically as if their value were reducible to their usefulness to others, they are routinely, systematically treated with a lack of respect, and thus are their rights routinely, systematically violated. This is just as true when they are used in trivial, duplicative, unnecessary or unwise research as it is when they are used in studies that hold out real promise of human benefits. We can't justify harming or killing a human being (my Aunt Bea, for example) just for these sorts of reason. Neither can we do so even in the case of so lowly a creature as a laboratory rat. It is not just refinement or reduction that is called for, not just larger, cleaner cages, not just more generous use of anaesthetic or the elimination of multiple surgery, not just tidying up the system. It is complete replacement. The best we can do when it comes to using animals in science is—not to use them. That is where our duty lies, according to the rights view.

As for commercial animal agriculture, the rights view takes a similar abolitionist position. The fundamental moral wrong here is not that animals are kept in stressful close confinement or in isolation, or that their pain and suffering, their needs and preferences are ignored or discounted. All these *are* wrong, of course, but they are not the fundamental wrong. They are symptoms and effects of the deeper, systematic wrong that allows these animals to be viewed and treated as lacking independent value, as resources for us—as, indeed, a renewable resource. Giving farm animals more space, more natural environments, more companions does not right the fundamental wrong, any more than giving lab animals more anaesthesia or bigger, cleaner cages would right the fundamental wrong in their case. Nothing less than the total dissolution of commercial animal agriculture will do this, just as, for similar reasons I won't develop at length here, morality requires nothing less than the total elimination of hunting and trapping for commercial and sporting ends. The rights view's implications, then, as I have said, are clear and uncompromising.

My last two points are about philosophy, my profession. It is, most obviously, no substitute for political action. The words I have written here and in other places by themselves don't change a thing. It is what we do with the thoughts that the words express—our acts, our deeds—that changes things. All that philosophy can do, and all I have attempted, is to offer a vision of what our deeds should aim at. And the why. But not the how.

Finally, I am reminded of my thoughtful critic, the one I mentioned earlier, who chastised me for being too cerebral. Well, cerebral I have been: indirect duty views, utilitarianism, contractarianism—hardly the stuff deep passions are made of. I am also reminded, however, of the image another friend once set before me—the image of the ballerina as expressive of disciplined passion. Long hours of sweat and toil, of loneliness and practice, of doubt and fatigue: those are the discipline of her craft. But the passion is there too, the fierce drive to excel, to speak through her body, to do it right, to pierce our minds. That is the image of philosophy I would leave with you, not "too cerebral"

but *disciplined passion.* Of the discipline enough has been seen. As for the passion: there are times, and these not infrequent, when tears come to my eyes when I see, or read, or hear of the wretched plight of animals in the hands of humans. Their pain, their suffering, their loneliness, their innocence, their death. Anger. Rage. Pity. Sorrow. Disgust. The whole creation groans under the weight of the evil we humans visit upon these mute, powerless creatures. It *is* our hearts, not just our heads, that call for an end to it all, that demand of us that we overcome, for them, the habits and forces behind their systematic oppression. All great movements, it is written, go through three stages: ridicule, discussion, adoption. It is the realization of this third stage, adoption, that requires both our passion and our discipline, our hearts and our heads. The fate of animals is in our hands. God grant we are equal to the task.

Critics

JAN NARVESON

On a Case for Animal Rights

. . . [W]hy should the fact that a certain being would feel pain if I were to perform action x constitute a reason why I should refrain from x?

One evident possibility is that I dislike pain—not only my own, but that of others. But unfortunately, not everyone is constituted that way. They may care little or nothing for the pains of others as such. And what do we say to those people? They may not be impressed by the answer that their view of the matter is morally below par. They'd like to know why it's wrong to inflict pain on other creatures, apart from the fact that Tom Regan and quite a few other people have a unique and apparently inexplicable intuition that it is.

I am assuming, of course, that something's being wrong either constitutes or at least implies that

From Jan Narveson, "On a Case for Animal Rights," *The Monist* 70, no. 1 (January 1987): 31–49. Some notes and some parts of the text deleted. Reprinted by permission of the *Monist.*

there is a reason for not doing it. And I am also assuming that for an agent, A, to "have a reason" for not doing x is for it to be the case that among A's values is a negative value attached to x or to something connected with x. What might this be, however, if our information thus far is only that x would cause pain to individual D, where D is not one of the individuals A has any particular interest in or affection for? (Whether D is a human or, say, a dog, is thus far unspecified.)

Suppose we add that D also registers the information that it was A who *did* x. Will this matter? Again, not necessarily. So let us add that D also is able to react to the information in various ways. Perhaps, for instance, that D is able to give A a reproachful look. This might indeed help. A could be sensitive to reproaches, even if they come from a nonmember of Homo sapiens. A might, for that matter, care more about such reproaches from D than from E, who is a member of that species. (It's unusual, but it's quite possible. One has seen it happen!)

If we add still another item, viz., that D is able to react to x by tearing A to shreds, we can well imagine that A will sit up and take notice. But what kind of notice? Avoiding D, shooting D, trying to make friends with D, are all possibilities. But we don't as yet have the particular set of information which will surely supply A with a reason for adopting a *moral* aversion to doing x. When do we have that?

To answer this question, we need two things: first, a reasonably clear characterization of what constitutes having a "moral" aversion to something, as distinct from any other sort of aversion one might have; and second, a characterization of the sort of facts or circumstances which would constitute good reasons for A to adopt such an aversion.

There is a good deal of confusion about the first one. By this I do not mean either that people in general or philosophers in particular are greatly confused about it, but rather, that their various uses of this segment of our vocabulary is confusing. I shall adopt some of the main features of common usage, but I don't suppose that any single analysis would capture all of those that are frequently associated with these terms. I shall seize on these: A morality is a set of prescriptions—requirements, prohibitions,

recommendations, rules—with the following features: (1) Overridingness, (2) Universal application, (3) Internalization, (4) Interpersonal Reinforcement; and (5) Decentralization, or Informality.

Brief explications: (1) Overridingness: A moral rule is *meant to* overrule contrary inclinations or interests, as such. "But I didn't feel like it," or "it wasn't in my interest" cannot be an acceptable justification for doing what morality forbids. (2) Moral rules apply to everyone, or at any rate, everyone in the relevant group whose morality it purports to be. We will assume for present purposes that we are considering rules meant to apply to every moral agent. (3) Part of the idea of a moral rule is that A will apply it to A: e.g., by making A feel uncomfortable for breaking it. An individual, A, is immoral if A does what a (true) moral rule requires, even if A can "get away with" it. Persons disposed to do those things under those circumstances are necessarily to be rated immoral; they lack the degree of internalization that is aimed at, and essential if the system is to work. And (4) people are *not* to "let people get away with it" if they can do something about it (at least, without appreciable cost or risk to themselves). Everybody is to "enforce" morality, especially by the relevant verbal means, just as everyone is subject to its rules. (5) Decentralization: Finally, morality is not a system imposed by force of declared law from without. Everyone is to enforce it, and no central authority can alter its content by fiat. This characterization, it should be noted, does not include the philosophically fancier properties favored by many theorists. A morality could, on this analysis, be clannish, biased, or full of what seem to us arbitrary distinctions without ceasing to be a morality. It could, logically: but if we are addressing ourselves to the question what morality *ought* to be as distinct from what it merely is in this or that group, then we can readily find strong internal reasons why a rationally acceptable morality would not have any of those characteristics. The reason is that morality is informal, and to be universally inculcated and enforced, including self-enforced. But rational individuals will not accept as restrictions on themselves and will not assist in the informal reinforcement of restrictions on behavior that is contrary to reason, restrictions they see no reason to submit to and to induce all others to submit to. Now there are lots of imaginable rules that would be very much in the interest of Group A to advocate and self-apply, but very much contrary to the interest of another group, B, to do so: aristocratic moralities, master/slave moralities, or moralities in which some group's religion is to be enforced on all, and so on. Such rules are non-starters for general morality, although they certainly could be elements in the more restricted morality of some particular group.

Will anything pass all these rquirements? Morality, I have said, is to override individual inclinations and even interests. But how can an individual have a rational interest in overriding his or her own inclinations and interests? The answer is now well known.[1] There are plenty of acts with the interesting property that an individual, A, will want to do them, but they will only be in A's interest *provided that others don't*. However, the others will be in the same boat. And if all act as they wish, all will be worse off than if all were to agree to act in certain ways. A necessary part of making it worth A's while to act on R is that A can reasonably expect that all others will too (and vice versa). Under these circumstances, there will be a temptation for any individual to cheat; but there will be a strong inducement for others not to let him cheat, and everyone knows both of these things. It is, then, in their interest to adopt collective rules overriding any particular interest. Such rules will be components of a rational morality.

But if some individuals are only patients and not agents, then no such schema can apply. It will not necessarily be in the interests of others to adopt and assist in the reinforcement of rules requiring agents to have regard for patients as such. Many will, of course, be interested in many patients, and it will indeed be in everyone's interest to have rules which enable *such* patients to be free from harm and perhaps to share in certain benefits. But rules benefiting patients simply as such, or calling upon everyone to refrain from harming them simply as such, have no fundamental appeal. The fact, for instance, that if I were a pig, I would want pigs (or at least that one) to be treated well is of no interest, so far as it goes. I'm not a pig, and never will be; and the pig himself has no rational clout. He is not able to address himself to the question of what he can do to make life difficult for us if we don't cater to his needs, or of how much better he could make it for us if we do. If we want something out of the pig, and treating the pig well is necessary for getting it, then we shall have reason to treat him well. If we don't, however, or if it isn't, then why should we go to the trouble?

Thus, consider the idea of "relevant" differences and similarities. Is the fact that individual A and individual B are identical in some respect in which they have an interest a good enough reason for having a moral rule which calls upon everyone to treat them alike? It is *not*. Only if they are alike in some respect which there is antecedent reason to insist upon everyone's paying attention to will the identity of their cases in other respects have any weight as such.

It certainly could be that owing to some feature of human psychology, we will have a sympathetic involvement with individuals having certain experiences, quite irrespective of the capacity of those individuals to do anything about it or to enter into arrangements whereby we will do something about it. (Such, very nearly, is the case with human adults in relation to human children.) Or it could be that if agents characterically treat certain sorts of patients in certain ways, that will induce a habit or a cast of mind likely to work ill for other agents in future. But we would need facts to support those claims; they can't be taken to be true a priori; any more than can the claim that humans, *qua* human, take a sympathetic interest in other humans or in rational beings generally.

This characterization of reasons and of morality sets the stakes for establishing that some principle belongs to general human morality very high. Does it set them too high? If we are busy trying to shore up Reganian intuitions, it certainly does, so far as I can see. The suggestion that we, as rational beings, should forego the many benefits available from extensive animal experimentation, not to mention those to be got from eating meat, merely because those benefits are got at considerable cost to the animals themselves is one that looks to have no chance of passing muster.

As it happens, intuition here seems to be on my side, not Regan's. For one who professes so much respect for our ordinary intuitions, he is surely pressing a most unintuitive program. To most humans, it is surely just obvious that we do no wrong in raising animals for their meat, chickens for their eggs, and so on, even though those animals suffer and die as a result. However, there is also the belief that we shouldn't be cruel to animals, and the belief that it is wrong to mistreat or take the lives of human infants and idiots. Indeed, it is perhaps not going too far to suggest that the "argument from marginal cases," as I once called it, is the main intuition-based argument in Regan's armoury. The argument has it that some humans to whom we are inclined to extend the benefits of morality are less qualified for them (on "our" normal view of what qualifies one for the benefits of morality) than are some animals. Yet there is some overlap between the human and some animal species in respects we are currently inclined to ask people to have moral regard for. How, then, can we maintain this disparity?

At this point, many people would simply invoke the fact that the one set of individuals are human and the other are not as quite relevant enough, all by itself. Species membership is, undoubtedly, *a* characteristic; it does, undoubtedly, distinguish the two sets of cases; and ordinary people's morality does pay heed to it. Nor can they be accused of any purely logical incoherence or contradiction in the process. Were we to accept appeals to intuition as of fundamental significance to moral theory, we could stop right here, simply denying Regan's case outright.

But I, for one, am disinclined to do this. I agree with him that "speciesism" looks a poor candidate for moral relevance. There are various reasons one might give for this. But the best way to show it would be to come up with a list of the characteristics of individuals that *are* relevant to morality and then point out that membership in a particular species isn't on the list. This requires that we have a good theory of morality handy. But I claim to have such a theory (or, more modestly, a start at one): moral relevance is established when it is shown that there is good reason for moral agents to have a principle in which the characteristic in question figures signifi-

cantly, i.e., that distinguishes the way we should behave toward individuals having it and those lacking it. And that good reason is provided by showing that there is good reason to think that moral agents will be better off having such a principle than they would not having one. This in turn requires that we find an interest on the part of all such agents, an interest commonly shared and such that there is an individual/collective contrast of the kind depicted above. And I take it as obvious that there is no such fact about the property of being a member of any species, simply as such.

Humans are interested creatures, and formidable in their ability to pursue their interests, including in the means by which they do so the use of force, lethal and otherwise. Some moral theories would put a proscription on the use of force for any such purposes other than that of defending persons against the initial use of force by others. Whether or not that can be made out, it is clear that we have a great and enduring interest in not having force used against ourselves. The "social contract," as we may refer to the general articles of morality on the conception being pressed here, will doubtless be very negative on the use of force for other than defensive purposes. But then, there is the question what "defensive purposes" will include. Consider people inclined to use force to defend their ways of life, where such ways include extensive cultural involvements with many other people. Do they come properly within the scope of such principles? And what about the case where some moral agents identify strongly, in comparable ways, with a group of individuals which are not moral agents: animals, for instance? Take the sacred cows of the Hindus, for example. There are many good reasons for not having their attitude. But while we are in India, will we not respect the customs of the Hindus even though we find them not only strange but perhaps downright irrational? And so, on the present conception, we should.

Similarly, we have good reason to place restrictions on the treatment of some particular animals, such as household pets. People who have no special feelings about animals in general may well develop intense affection for certain particular ones, and these they can, in current circumstances, buy or otherwise appropriate and take under their care. The rest of us are then to treat those animals with due respect. But there is a special problem about persons, such as the members of Greenpeace, who propose to identify with the higher animals *generally,* claiming that animals are members of oppressed groups, comparable to minority groups of humans in various countries. Those people may be inclined to press their claims by force (and sometimes have done do, recently.) Groups might attempt to proselytize elsewhere by force, as did the Moors in the 7th–9th Centuries, giving their victims the choice between subscribing to the Koran or losing their heads. But it must surely be obvious that the members of such groups have no moral leg to stand on, if a morality applicable to moral agents generally is our aim. The only principle that will pass muster among rational agents is an agreement to disagree about such matters: which means, a proscription on the use of force as a means of promoting assent to doctrines lacking the support of fact ascertainable by publicly confirmable procedures.

And such, I suggest, is substantially the current situation in regard to "animal rights." Such commitments to animals, given current knowledge, is comparable to (though not, of course, an actual case of) religious belief. In particular, it is comparable to the moral content of such beliefs, in a different sense of the term *moral* from that employed here. In this sense of the term, a morality is what Mill called a "theory of life": a doctrine about what makes a life a good life, a life worth living in preference to other possible types of life. Those, like Regan, who think to extend the protections of ordinary morality to individuals lacking the usual claims to it, find it intolerable to contemplate, say, the eating of meat when those who "supply" it are defenseless creatures lacking the sophisticated cognitive equipment of persons. Their case, from the point of view of the rest of us, may be accounted a personal one: how, they put it to us, can we *live with* ourselves if we continue to treat some feeling beings badly when we would object strongly to such treatment in the case of others (such as ourselves)?

A fair number of peope do feel like Regan in these respects, and certainly the rest of us, especially if we wish to engage in friendly dealings with them, will wish to consider how much deference to their views we should pay. And this, in turn, seems to me not a matter on which a very definite uniform rule is required. Some vegetarians would be discomfited greatly if their dinner companions in restaurants ordered meat dishes; some nonvegetarians would as a matter of course refrain from ordering such dishes when in company with vegetarians; and so on. But it is clear, I think, that our deference need not extend to taking up vegetarianism ourselves, nor to supporting legislative changes that would deprive everyone of the right to employ animals for laboratory experiments or as sources of food—any more than it need extend to the making of animal sacrifices out of deference to the many religious groups which insist on such practices.

Apart from the case of special sympathizers, as we may refer to the current supporters of rights for animals, we may also point to considerations that underwrite, I think, a claim to public-interest status on the part of some animals. One is ecological. We have come to appreciate that there are interconnections among various elements of our biological environment which make it imprudent to hunt wantonly, for instance. And there is a general sense of curiosity, an intellectual interest, in the continued existence of different species of animals. There is, I think, no special claim by, say, would-be hunters on the members of any hunted species strong enough to outweigh this enduring interest. If the hunters have their way, humankind in general may be deprived of *any* further contact with the species that would succumb to their uninhibited pursuit of that interest (and hunter-kind is deprived of all future quarries of that species). But as Regan rightly observes, this interest is not at all equivalent to a moral claim for the rights of individual members of any of those species. He thinks, for instance, that we would not be justified in killing some innocent animals in order that others may flourish, as an interest in species survival could possibly do. That interest is, for example, quite compatible with controlled hunting, which ensures both that the species will flourish and that individual members of it will on frequent occasions be, in Regan's view, murdered. Or we might engage in involuntary artificial insemination, which Regan might object to as comparable to rape! Thus public interest arguments give some support to protections of animals of various kinds and degrees; but nothing like the sweeping restrictions imposed by Regan's principles.

Let us, finally, return to the Argument from Marginal Cases. The view that emerges from the Contractarian theory of morality must, of course, classify those humans who are so far below the standard for our species as to be unable to communicate effectively or react in a rational way to the actions of the rest of us as not inherently qualified for basic rights. Such individuals are, necessarily, wards of someone, since they cannot care for themselves. Why, then, should we be as concerned for their well-being as we mostly are? Why not allow people to hunt *them*? Or what about infants? All of these are important cases—though it is well to remember that they are also cases concerning which there has been tremendous variation in approved treatment in the de facto moralities of different ages and cultures Exposure of unpromising infants, for instance, was routine in many cultures. Nevertheless, I wish to stand my ground, despite the criticisms advanced by Regan in *The Case for Animal Rights*. The question of how to treat such cases is to be answered by reference to two strongly supporting sets of considerations. First, that essentially every subnormal or infant human individual is the offspring, and often the sibling, of persons who take a close sympathetic interest in its welfare; and second, that there simply is no appreciable general interest in treating such individuals adversely.[2] If we compare the case here with that of animals, we find, of course, a striking contrast. Various animals have much to offer us which motivates impositions on them: the culinary interest, of course, but also that in furs, etc. Apart from the special case of medical experimentation, there is no comparable systematic interest in marginal humans. And there is one special "interest" that properly rates special negative attention: viz., that of cruelty for its own sake. An interest in seeing animals suffer is psychologically very comparable to an interest in seeing people suffer: indeed, since humans are much more capable of expressing their pains than animals, one

would expect sadists to prefer human victims—and experience, to my limited knowledge, bears this out. There is certainly a public interest in exterminating attitudes such as that. Thus the standard attitude toward animals, which is that they are not to be wantonly misused, though they certainly can be used for human purposes in ways that will undoubtedly be uncomfortable or fatal to them, has some basis in commonsense psychology.

But there is no need to defend in detail prevailing attitudes in our culture. Why should there be? We are, I take it, trying to find a rational basis for giving animals a particular moral status, one that is compelling and conceptually coherent with our case for moral rights of humans. Cases of overlap—the "marginal cases," as I call them—are grey areas. There is an overwhelming case for not classifying these cases identically with normal humans, and there is a good case for generally regarding the higher animals as eligible for minimally decent treatment. And since there is strong support, arising from the special attachments to other individual humans that marginal humans have but animals lack, for cultivating a general attitude of care for those cases, we arrive at the reasonable conclusion that marginal humans are, in general, to be given an intermediate status. *Given* is the crucial term here. Marginals are not, so to speak, charter members of the moral club; normal adults are. (Children are still a distinct special case, for children are our only source of future adults, and our duties to them stem overwhelmingly from that special consideration, and not from their current repertoire of psychological attributes.)

CONCLUSION

The de facto morality of any particular time and place is bound to be the product of many factors, some of them quite independent of reason. Philosophical critics who, like Regan, wish to invoke the aid of "intuition," face the formidable task of discerning beneath the surface of the welter of received moral views which of them are due to philosophically respectable causes and which not. They don't come stamped with "Genuine" and "Culturally Biased" labels—especially in view of the fact that the very notion of a bias is itself a part of the conceptual package we are trying to scrutinize. So too, as I have tried to make clear above, is the notion of consistency: rarely do we get an out-and-out case of two principles one of which is the negation or the contrary of the other. Instead, we get groups of cases that are similar in some respects and dissimilar in others, leaving us to decide whether the similarities are what matter, thus leaving us with conflicting judgments stemming from intuited principles telling us to treat them differently, or the dissimilarities, thus leaving those judgments nonconflicting after all. Such is the nature of a terrain ripe for philosophical theorizing. But to propose to avail oneself of the fact that something is intuited as a recourse for theoretical validation is to leave oneself open to the charge that a different selection of those intuitions would have left one with a wholly differing but equally well-grounded theory. In the view of this writer, the only solution to this problem is to jettison appeals to intuition for those purposes. What we must do is to hold that an intuition is just that: an unanalyzed sense, hunch, or feeling, *that* a certain finding is the right one, without quite knowing why. The job of the theorist is then to find out the "why." But if we take the hunch as itself a legitimate part of the explanation, muddle is the almost inevitable result. Or, if one came from a particular cultural milieu happening to be possessed of an exceptionally articulate and coherent set of intuitions (as did, apparently, Oxbridge philosophers of the first decade of this century), one will come up with a beautiful theory the total groundlessness of which is singularly unapt to be noticed by one's fellow theorists from that same culture—and singularly unlikely to persuade anybody else.

Regan, in *Animal Rights,* takes on the job of disavowing very substantial parts of our received morality—he is not far from being a starry-eyed radical by current standards. His weapons on behalf of this rather revolutionary project consist of a judicious selection of (1) logic, (2) intuitions taken from the very set of received beliefs from which he is so considerably dissenting, and (3) higher-level, "meta-ethical" intuitions got from the standard practice of recent Anglo-American philosophy. Those eager for something new to feel guilty about will be impressed. The rest will not. I side with the latter, personally. And philosophically, I should like to know why we should accept the particular selection Regan has come up with on behalf of his rather unintuitive results, rather than another selection which would not at all support those results. Until we have compelling argument for that selection, this writer, at any rate, will continue to eat meat in good conscience.

NOTE

1. David Gauthier's impressive new book, *Morals by Agreement* (New York: Oxford University Press, 1986) is the major source now, but see also, for instance, Kurt Baier's "Justification in Ethics," in J. Roland Pennock and John W. Chapman, eds., *Justification* (NOMOS XXIII, New York University Press, 1985), or the author's "Contractarian Ethics," in R. G. Frey, ed., *Utility and Rights* (Minneapolis, MN: University of Minnesota Press, 1984).

R. G. FREY

Why Animals Lack Beliefs and Desires

Do animals . . . have interests in the . . . sense of having wants which can be satisfied or left unsatisfied? In this sense, of course, it appears that tractors do not have interests; for though being well-oiled may be conducive to tractors being good of their kind, tractors do not *have an interest* in being well-oiled, since they cannot *want* to be well-oiled, cannot, in fact, have any wants whatever. But farmers can have wants, and they certainly have an interest in their tractors being well-oiled.

What, then, about animals? Can they have wants? By "wants" I understand a term that encompasses both needs and desires, and it is these that I shall consider.

If to ask whether animals can have wants is to ask whether they can have needs, then certainly animals have wants. A dog can need water. But *this* cannot be the sense of "want" on which having interests will depend, since it does not exclude things from the class of want-holders. Just as dogs need water in order to function normally, so tractors need oil in order to function normally; and just as dogs will die unless their need for water is satisfied, so trees and grass and a wide variety of plants and shrubs will die unless their need for water is satisfied. Though we should not give the fact undue weight, someone who in ordinary discourse says "The tractor wants oiling" certainly means the tractor needs oiling, if it is not to fall away from those standards which make tractors good of their kind. Dogs, too, need water, if they are not to fall away from the standards which make them good of their kind. It is perhaps worth emphasizing, moreover, as the cases of the tractor, trees, grass, etc., show, that needs do not require the presence either of consciousness or of knowledge of the lack which makes up the need. If, in sum, we are to agree that tractors, trees, grass, etc., do not have wants, and, therefore, interests, it cannot be the case that wants are to be construed as needs.

This, then, leaves desires, and the question of whether animals can have wants as desires. I may as well say at once that I do not think animals can have desires. My reasons for thinking this turn largely upon my doubts that animals can have beliefs, and my doubts in this regard turn partially, though in large part, upon the view that having beliefs is not compatible with the absence of language and linguistic ability. I realize that the claim that animals cannot have desires is a controversial one; but I think the case to be made in support of it, complex though it is, is persuasive. . . .

Suppose I am a collector of rare books and desire to own a Gutenberg Bible: my desire to own this volume is to be traced to my belief that I do not now own such a work and that my rare book collection is deficient in this regard. By "to be traced" here, what I mean is this: if someone were to ask *how* my belief that my book collection lacks a Gutenberg Bible is connected with my desire to own such a Bible, what better or more direct repy could be given than that, without this belief, I would not have this desire? For if I believed that my rare book collection *did* contain a Gutenberg Bible and so was complete in this sense, then I would not desire a Gutenberg Bible in order to make up what I now believe to be a notable deficiency in my collection. (Of course, I might desire to own more than one such Bible, but this contingency is not what is at issure here.)

Now what is it that I believe? I believe that my collection lacks a Gutenberg Bible; that is, I believe that the sentence "My collection lacks a Gutenberg Bible" is true. In constructions of the form "I believe that . . . ," what follows upon the "that" is a declarative sentence; and *what* I believe is that that sentence is true. The same is the case with constructions of the form "He believes that . . .": what follows upon the "that" is a declarative sentence, and what the "he" in question believes is that that sentence is true. The difficulty in the case of

---

From R. G. Frey, "Rights, Interests, Desires, and Beliefs," *American Philosophical Quarterly* 16 (July 1979): 233–39. Notes and some parts of text deleted. Reprinted by permission of North American Philosophical Publications.

animals should be apparent: if someone were to say, e.g., "The cat believes that the door is locked," then that person is holding, as I see it, that the cat holds the declarative sentence "The door is locked" to be true; and I can see no reason whatever for crediting the cat or any other creature which lacks language, including human infants, with entertaining declarative sentences and holding certain declarative sentences to be true.

Importantly, nothing whatever in this account is affected by changing the example, in order to rid it of sophisticated concepts like "door" and "locked," which in any event may be thought beyond cats, and to put in their place more rudimentary concepts. For the essence of this account is not about the relative sophistication of this or that concept but rather about the relationship between believing something and entertaining and regarding as true certain declarative sentences. If what is believed is that a certain declarative sentence is true, then no creature which lacks language can have beliefs; and without beliefs, a creature cannot have desires. And this is the case with animals, or so I suggest; and if I am right, not even in the sense, then, of wants as desires do animals have interests . . .

But is what is believed that a certain declarative sentence is true? I think there are three arguments of sorts that shore up the claim that this *is* what is believed.

First, I do not see how a creature could have the concept of belief without being able to distinguish between true and false beliefs. When I believe that my collection of rare books lacks a Gutenberg Bible, I believe that it is true that my collection lacks a Gutenberg Bible; put another way, I believe that it is false that my collection contains a Gutenberg Bible. I can distinguish, and do distinguish, between the sentences "My collection lacks a Gutenberg Bible" and "My collection contains a Gutenberg Bible," and it is only the former I hold to be true. According to my view, what I believe in this case is that this sentence is true; and sentences are the sorts of things we regard as or hold to be true. As for the cat, and leaving aside now all questions about the relative sophistication of concepts, I do not see how it could have the belief that the door is locked unless it could distinguish this true belief from the false belief that the door is unlocked. But what is true or false are not states of affairs which correspond to or reflect or pertain to these beliefs; states of affairs are not true or false but

either are or are not the case, either do or do not obtain. If, then, one is going to credit cats with beliefs, and cats must be able to distinguish true from false beliefs, and states of affairs are not true or false, then what exactly is it that cats are being credited with distinguishing as true or false? Reflection on this question, I think, forces one to credit cats with language, in order for there to be something that can be true or false in belief; and it is precisely because they lack language that we cannot make this move.

Second, if in order to have the concept of belief a creature must be possessed of the difference between true and false belief, then in order for a creature to be able to distinguish true from false beliefs that creature must—simply must, as I see it—have some awareness of, to put the matter in the most general terms, how language connects with, links up with the world; and I see no reason to credit cats with such an awareness. My belief that my collection lacks a Gutenberg Bible is true if and only if my collection lacks a Gutenberg Bible; that is, the *truth* of this belief cannot be entertained by me without it being the case that I am aware that the truth of the sentence "My collection lacks a Gutenberg Bible" is *at the very least* partially a function of how the world is. However difficult to capture, it is this relationship between language and the world a grasp of which is necessary if a creature is to grasp the difference between true and false belief, a distinction which it must grasp, if it is to possess the concept of belief at all.

Third, I do not see how a creature could have an awareness or grasp of how language connects with, links up with the world, to leave the matter at its most general, unless that creature was itself possessed of language; and cats are not possessed of language. If it were to be suggested, for example, that the sounds that cats make do amount to a language, I should deny it. This matter is far too large and complex to be tackled here; but the general line of argument I should use to support my denial can be sketched in a very few words. Can cats lie? If they cannot, then they cannot assert anything; and if they lack assertion, I do not see how they could possess a language. And I should be strict: I do not suggest that, lacking assertion, cats possess a language in some attenuated or secondary sense; rather, I suggest that, lacking assertion, they do not possess a language *at all*.

R. G. FREY

The Case Against Animal Rights

Regan is convinced that animals have *rights*. Of his rights view, he says that "of course, if it were possible to show that only human beings are included within its scope, then a person like myself, who believes in animal rights, would be obliged to look elsewhere."[1] Presumably, Regan so believes in animal *rights* that any theory whatever that failed to accord them *rights* would, even if it condemned all the practices he condemned and found wrong the maltreatment of animals, be unsatisfactory. It is difficult to know, therefore, how arguments stand that try to weaken his faith in the *rights* of animals. Are they as it were, bound to go awry, a priori? I am unsure exactly how Regan would respond to such questions; that is, I do not know what counts as, indeed, whether anything at all counts as, a challenge to his intuitions on this score. In any event, nothing that follows turns upon Regan's intuition that animals have *rights,* that they are rights-holders; *this* intuition, though I do not share it, is not here at issue.

What *is* at issue is Regan's reliance upon variants of the argument from marginal cases to *support* his claims. In each case, I do not believe these variants do support his claims, do not believe, that is, that appeal to the cases of defective humans does the work on behalf of animals that Regan supposes it does.

First, then, there is Regan's claim of the equal inherent worth of human and animal life:

Well, perhaps some will say that animals have some inherent value, only less than we have. Once again, however, attempts to defend this view can be shown to lack rational justification. What could be the basis of our having more inherent value than animals? Their lack of reason, or autonomy, or intellect? Only if we are willing to make the same judgment in the case of

humans who are similarly deficient. But it is not true that such humans—the retarded child, for example, or the mentally deranged—have less inherent value than you or I.[2]

This affirmation turns entirely upon our agreeing that all human life, however deficient, has the same value; and I, as the reader will know, do not agree. For me, the value of life is a function of its quality, its quality a function of its richness, and its richness a function of its scope or potentiality for enrichment; and the fact is that many humans lead lives of a very much lower quality than ordinary normal lives, lives which lack enrichment and where the potentialities for enrichment are severely truncated or absent. If, then, we confront the fact that not all human life has, not merely the same enrichment, but also the same scope for enrichment, then it follows that not all human life has the same value. (Anyone who thinks that we do not use this argument in order to trade off lives of very low quality would do well to read some of the contributions by health care professionals to many of the contemporary debates in medical ethics over death and dying.) If not all human life has the same value, then Regan's claim of the equal inherent worth of animals collapses; for we do judge some human lives of less value than others.

Second, there is Regan's claim, not of equal inherent worth, but of inherent worth in the first place:

Some there are who resist the idea that animals have inherent value. "Only humans have such value", they profess. How might this narrow view be defended? Shall we say that only humans have the requisite intelligence, or autonomy, or reason? But there are many, many humans who fail to meet these standards and yet

R. G. Frey, "The Case Against Animal Rights," in *Animal Rights and Human Obligations,* 2nd ed., ed. Tom Regan and Peter Singer (Englewood Cliffs, NJ: Prentice-Hall, Inc.), pp. 115–18. Reprinted by permission of R. G. Frey.

are reasonably viewed as having value above and beyond their usefulness to others.[3]

Again, the case of deficient humans is being appealed to, this time to cede animal life inherent value at all. But I do not regard all human life as of equal value; I do not accept that a very severely mentally-enfeebled human or an elderly human fully in the grip of senile dementia or an infant born with only half a brain has a life whose value is equal to that of normal, adult humans. The quality of human life can plummet, to a point where we would not wish *that* life on even our worst enemies; and I see no reason to pretend that a life I would not wish upon even my worst enemies is nevertheless as valuable as the life of any normal, adult human. As the quality of human life falls, trade-offs between it and other things we value become possible; and if this is what one is going to mean by the phrase "usefulness to others," then I see no reason to deny that that label can be applied to me and my views. (But so, too, can it be applied to countless other people. Regan's book is littered with warnings against utilitarianism; but any of the numerous textbooks on medical ethics now on offer will show in, e.g., their sections on death and dying that all kinds of people, utilitarians and non-utilitarians alike, are no longer prepared to concede all human life, irrespective of quality, equal value.) Accordingly, Regan's claim of the inherent worth of animals is compromised; for there are good reasons not to judge deficient human life either of equal value to normal, adult human life or, in extreme cases, even of much value at all.

By lives of not much value at all, I have in mind lives whose quality is so low that they are no longer worth living. I concede the difficulty of determining in many cases when a life is no longer worth living; but in other cases, including cases quite apart from those involving the irreversibly comatose, the matter seems far less problematic. Work recently done in Oxford by Ronald Dworkin on some of the policy implications of the prevalence of Altzheimer's disease leaves me in little doubt that a life wholly and irreversibly in the grip of senile dementia is a life not worth living; and the case of infants born without any brain whatever seems an even clearer instance.

Third, there is Regan's claim that attempts to limit the scope of his rights view to humans come unstuck:

> Animals, it is true, lack many of the abilities humans possess. They can't read, do higher mathematics, build a bookcase or make *baba ghanoush*. Neither can many human beings, however, and yet we don't (and shouldn't) say that they (these humans) therefore have less inherent value, less of a right to be treated with respect, than do others.[4]

Perhaps Regan is right, that a human who cannot build a bookcase does not per se have a less valuable life than other humans; but what about very severely mentally-enfeebled humans or elderly people fully in the grip of senile dementia or infants born without a brain? I think *these* lives have less value than ordinary human life. What is the difference between these cases and the bookcase example? It is that the inability to build a bookcase is unlikely, bizarre circumstances apart, drastically to affect the quality of one's life, whereas severe mental-enfeebledness, senile dementia, and the absence of a brain quite obviously have a seriously negative effect on the quality of life. But one need not go so far afield to find such negative effects: some of the patients in the final stages of AIDS come to the view, I gather, that life is no longer worth living, as first one illness and then another ravages their bodies.

A word on Regan's point about treating deficient humans with respect is necessary. He ties talk of respect in the passage above to some right to respect, without explaining what justifies this linkage; but the real problem is that the use of some right to respect in the present context begs the question. A doctor friend recently described to me the case of a very severely handicapped child who managed to be kept alive to the age of four through a series of eleven operations; the doctor's wife described the case as one of "keeping the child alive long enough for nature to kill it," which nature duly did. How exactly does one show respect to this child? By yet another operation, to extend its life a few weeks longer? It is all well and good to advocate treating deficient humans with respect;

in the absence of some statement in a particular case about what constitutes respect, however, such talk does not come to much. How, for example, does one show respect for an individual with AIDS, who has thought long and hard about suicide and decided to kill himself? By intervening and stopping him? Or by not intervening and permitting him to carry on?

NOTES

1. Tom Regan, "The Case for Animal Rights," in P. Singer (ed.), *In Defence of Animal Rights* (Oxford: Blackwell, 1985), p. 22.
2. Ibid., p. 23.
3. Ibid., p. 22.
4. Ibid., p. 22; italics in original.

ALAN WHITE

Rights

Most discussions about the kinds of things which can possess rights centre on the kinds of capacities either necessary or sufficient for their possible possession, whether it be interests, rationality, sentience, the ability to claim, etc. Advocates of the various capabilities are usually torn between making them so strong, for example rationality or the ability to sue, that they exclude subjects to which they wish to allow rights, whether they be children, the feeble-minded, unborn generations, etc., and making them so weak that they include almost anything, whether they be inanimate objects, artefacts, abstract conceptions etc.

I have tried to show that no criterion couched in terms of substantive characteristics is logically either sufficient or necessary in itself for the possible—or, indeed, the actual—possession of a right. What I would suggest is that such characteristics are at most a mark of a certain type of subject of which the question is whether that type of subject is logically capable of having a right. And the answer to that question depends on whether it is the sort of subject of which it makes sense to use what may be called "the full language of rights."

A right is something which can be said to be exercised, earned, enjoyed, or given, which can be claimed,[1] demanded, asserted, insisted on, secured, waived, or surrendered; there can be a right to do so and so or have such and such done for one, to be in a certain state, to have a certain feeling or adopt a certain attitude. A right is related to and contrasted with a duty, an obligation, a privilege, a power, a liability. A possible possessor of a right is, therefore, whatever can properly be spoken of in such language; that is, whatever can intelligibly, whether truly or falsely, be said to exercise, earn, etc. a right, to have a right to such logically varied things, to have duties, privileges, etc. Furthermore, . . . a necessary condition of something's being capable of having a right to V is that it should be something which logically can V.

In the full language of "a right" only a *person* can logically have a right because only a person can be the subject of such predications. Rights are not the sorts of things of which non-persons can be the subjects, however right it may be to treat them in certain ways. Nor does this, as some contend, exclude infants, children, the feeble-minded, the comatose, the dead, or generations yet unborn.[2] Any of these may be for various reasons empirically unable to fulfil the full role of a right-holder. But so long as they are persons—and it is significant that we think and speak of them as young, feeble-minded, incapacitated, dead, unborn *persons*—they are logically possible subjects of rights to whom the full language of rights can significantly, however falsely, be used. It is a misfortune, not a tautology, that these persons cannot exercise or enjoy, claim, or waive, their rights or do their duty or fulfil their obligations. The law has always linked together the notions of a person and of the bearer of rights, duties, privileges, powers, liberties, liabilities, immunities, etc., so that a change in application of one notion has accompanied a parallel change in application of the other.[3] Thus, at various times in the law, gods, idols, unborn and dead human beings, animals, inanimate things, corporations, and governments, have been treated as persons because they were conceived as possible subjects of such jural relations as rights, duties, etc. who can commit or be the victims of torts and crimes. In Roman law slaves were things, not persons, and, hence, had no rights. The attitudes of various legal systems to the possible rights of an unborn child depend on how far they are regarded as legal persons.[4]

What this legal practice brings out is the importance of using a set of concepts, for example rights, duties, privileges, obligations, etc. together and not isolating one of them, for example rights, so that, as Wittgenstein might put it, the lone concept is only "idling." The concept of a right can, of course, be stretched—as when Trollope, for example talks of a house with certain grandiose features as having "the right" to be called a castle—and debates about the rights of foetuses, animals, works of art, or of nature can become merely terminological. What is important is to ask what job, if any, is being done in such contexts by the notion of "a right" as contrasted with that of "right" when it is isolated from such normal companions as the notions of duty, obligation, power, etc.

Something capable only of sentience or of suffering would not necessarily be capable of exercising, owning, or enjoying a right, much less of claiming, asserting, insisting on, or fighting for its rights or of waiving or relinquishing them. Nor of having obligations, duties, privileges, etc. And though it would be capable of having something done for it or of being in a certain state, it would not necessarily be capable of performing tasks, assuming attitudes, or having emotions. Hence, its possible rights, if any, would be confined to the right to have something done for it, such as to be well treated or protected, or to be in a certain state, such as to be happy or free or to remain alive. Moreover, though sentience or capacity to suffer would be necessary for the possible possession of a right to anything relevant to these, such as a right to protection from suffering—because a right to V implies being logically able to V—they would not be sufficient. The fact that an animal can suffer from growing pains or a man suffer from doubt does not in itself prove that it or he is capable of a right to protection from these.

It is a misunderstanding to object to this distinction between the kinds of things which can have rights and those which cannot on the ground that it constitutes a sort of speciesism. For it is not being argued that it is right to treat one species less considerately than another, but only that one species, that is, a person, can sensibly be said to exercise or waive a right, be under an obligation, have a duty, etc., whereas another cannot, however unable particular members of the former species may be to do so.

Notes

1. The fact that a right can be claimed is no evidence for the mistaken thesis (e.g., Joel Feinberg, "Duties, Rights and Claims." *American Philosophical Quarterly* 64 [1966], pp. 137–44) that a right is a claim.

2. E.g., W. D. Lamont, *The Principles of Moral Judgement* (Oxford, 1946), pp. 83–85.

3. R. Pound, *Jurisprudence* (St. Paul, MN, 1959), IV. ch. 25 and references on p. 191, n. 1.

4. P. D. Lasok, "The Rights of the Unborn" in *Fundamental Rights*, ed. J. W. Bridge, D. Lasok, *et al.* (London, 1973), pp. 18–30; and D. W. Louisell, "Abortion, the Practice of Medicine and the Due Process of Law." *U.C.L.A. Law Review* 16 (1969), 233–54. M. Tooley goes too far in making "is a person" and "has a moral right to life" synonymous. See his "Abortion and infanticide." *Philosophy and Public Affairs* 2 (1972), pp. 37–65.

5

Is Failing to Contribute to Famine Relief Wrong?

Singer and His Critics

There are countries in the world where dying from famine is a commonplace. In affluent countries, such as the United States, there are organizations that are dedicated to famine relief. These organizations can and do save thousands of lives. They could save more lives if we gave them more of our money. Do you have a moral obligation to donate some of your money to famine-relief organizations, and, if so, how much money should you donate? In the featured article of this chapter, Peter Singer raises this question and comes up with a startling answer: Most of us, perhaps all of us, fall seriously short of our moral obligations to the starving. Most people do not contribute money to famine-relief efforts. If you are one of those people, then the conclusion of Singer's argument is that you have behaved in a seriously immoral manner. And even if you have contributed from time to time to famine-relief organizations, even if you have contributed very substantial sums, doubtless you have also spent money on what are, from the perspective of someone who is dying of starvation, relative luxuries—a new CD, a night out at the movies, or a somewhat expensive meal at a restaurant. If Singer's argument is sound, then by failing to spend that money on famine relief, you, too, may well have failed to do what you are morally obliged to do. You may have acted wrongly, and seriously so.

Singer's argument can be understood as arising from three distinct premises. The first makes a claim about the badness of the suffering and death that is caused by starvation. The second makes a claim about the magnitude of the harm that you would incur in preventing some of the suffering and death that is caused by starvation by donating some of your money to a famine-relief organization like Oxfam. The third offers a general moral principle that is meant to govern cases in which you can prevent bad things from happening at some cost to yourself. In its strongest and most unqualified form, the principle maintains that if it is in your power to prevent something bad from happening without sacrificing anything of *comparable moral importance,* then you ought, morally, to do it. In the weaker and somewhat qualified version of the principle that Singer appeals to at one point, the principle instead claims that if it is in your power to prevent something very bad from happening, without sacrificing anything *morally significant,* then you ought, morally, to do it. On either version of the principle, the conclusion that Singer draws is that it is seriously immoral to refrain from contributing money to famine relief. Rather than viewing such acts of assistance as what philosophers refer to as "supererogatory"—acts that go above and beyond the call of duty and that are praiseworthy when done but not objectionable when not done—Singer insists that those who refrain from contributing when they can act in a positively immoral manner. This can be a disturbing claim in itself, and if it is accepted, then it seems to have an even more disturbing implication: that you have to keep giving more and more of your money to famine relief up to the point where you yourself are threatened by death from starvation. That is a radical conclusion indeed. Most people are loath to accept it, and few if any live by it.

If you reject Singer's conclusion, you will have to reject one of his assumptions. The first (that suffering and death are bad) and second (that you will not be seriously harmed by giving some money to an organization like Oxfam) seem fairly unassailable. This means that most of the critical argumentation is likely to involve the moral principle that Singer appeals to. In the Introduction to this anthology, we note that one way of thinking of Singer's argument is as an appeal to an analogy—an analogy between refraining from donating money to a famine-relief organization and refraining from wading into a shallow pond to rescue a small child who will otherwise drown (see section 4.1). Suppose that wading into the shallow pond to save the drowning child will cost you a certain amount of money in terms of cleaning and replacing the clothes that will be ruined. Virtually everyone will agree that it would be morally wrong not to wade in and save the child, given that doing so will pose no risk of harm to the rescuer and will result only in a cost of, say, $200. But then you could also save a starving child in Ethiopia by donating $200 to Oxfam. And if we agree that it would be wrong not to save the child in the shallow-pond case and that the shallow-pond case is morally analogous to the famine-relief case, then Singer's disturbing conclusion seems to follow. When people refrain from sending money to famine-relief efforts they behave in a manner that is seriously immoral.

What is the relation between this argument from analogy and the three-premise argument that preceded it? It is this: Singer's general principle is an attempt to spell out the morally relevant feature that the shallow-pond case and the starving-child case share, the feature that makes them morally on a par. What would explain the judgment that it is wrong to refrain from saving the drowning child in the pond? This is a case in which one can prevent something bad happening without sacrificing anything of comparable moral significance (or indeed, as Singer points at in qualifying his general principle, a case in which one can prevent something very bad from happening without sacrificing anything of any moral significance at all). So maybe that is what explains the moral obligation.

Singer's general principle, then, explains our moral judgment in the shallow-pond case and in closely related cases. But it also delivers the analogous judgment in the starving-child case. What this highlights is that an argument from analogy can often be replaced with an argument from inference to the best explanation. We could begin a criticism of the analogical argument by spelling out differences between the cases, differences that might make a moral difference. For example, you are *near* the boy in the pond, but you are *far* from a child who is dying from starvation in some distant country. Alternatively, there are no other people standing around the pond to save the drowning boy, but there are lots of other people who could save the starving children in distant countries. Singer considers several such differences and argues that each of them is morally irrelevant. For example, how could distance alone make a moral difference to one's obligations? Each of these objections to the analogy, if justified, would also provide objections to the general principle Singer adopts. They point to extra conditions (such as spatial proximity) that would have to be satisfied for one to have the obligation to prevent the very bad thing from happening.

Both of the critical-response pieces that follow attack Singer's general principle (which John Arthur calls the "greater moral evil rule"). Arthur cites what he takes to be obvious counterexamples to the principle. For example, suppose a stranger badly needs a kidney. He will die if he doesn't get one today. As it happens you still have two. What if you could survive on one kidney, albeit at an impaired level of well-being? The greater moral evil rule implies that you are *morally obligated* to donate your kidney to the needy stranger. Are you morally obligated to give away your "spare" kidney to strangers? If not, then it seems that Singer's general principle is false. Arthur does more than point to possible counterexamples to Singer's principle, however. He also goes on to attempt to explain why the principle initially seems plausible, why it applies in the shallow-pond case, and why it fails in the starving-child case.

One obvious difference between the drowning child and the starving child is that the former is *nearby* and the latter is *far away*. Is this difference morally relevant? Singer dismisses this idea rather swiftly: "I do not think I need to say much in defense of the refusal to take proximity and distance into account. The fact that a person is physically near to us . . . does not show that we *ought* to help him rather than another who happens to be further away." The greater moral evil rule reflects this judgment that spatial distance is morally irrelevant in that it makes no mention of physical proximity at all. Michael Slote attempts to explain why we sometimes feel, intuitively, that distance can make a moral difference. However, he derives this explanation from more fundamental considerations. Slote claims that the correct understanding of the nature and role of the virtue of *empathy* explains the intuitive idea that we have a more stringent responsibility to save the boy drowning in the shallow pond than we do to make comparable sacrifices to save people who, we have been told, are dying from starvation. Slote argues that a developed human empathy lies at the basis of moral action. Roughly speaking, an action is wrong if it reflects a deficiency of normal empathy. And it is permissible if it does not reflect a deficiency of normal empathy. To ignore the boy in the pond would be to exhibit a deficiency of normal human empathy and would therefore be wrong. Slote argues that it does not exhibit a deficiency in normal human empathy to say in the case of the distant drowning child, "Well, that's very unfortunate, but I can't spend all my time dwelling on incidents like that." So, according to Slote's virtue theory, it would be wrong to ignore the drowning boy whom you can see but not wrong to ignore some distant drowning boy about whom you know but with whom you have no direct acquaintance.

QUESTIONS FOR CONSIDERATION

In thinking about this issue, first ask yourself what you think about the shallow-pond case.

- Do you agree with Singer that it would be morally wrong to walk away from the drowning boy if it would cost you, say $50, to replace the damaged clothing? What if it would cost you $100? $500? Construct some other possible cases in which you could prevent something very bad from happening to someone else at roughly equivalent costs. Suppose your next-door neighbor needs money to pay for a life-saving operation, money that he doesn't have and that he cannot borrow. But you have more than enough in the bank. Is it your moral responsibility to pay $50 for your neighbor's operation? $100? $500?

• Would it make any difference if your neighbor happened to be on vacation, twelve thousand miles away, when the need for his operation arose?

• Suppose that a needy stranger happens to be visiting your neighbor. Would the fact that he is a stranger (but right next door) make a difference?

• What is an "entitlement," and how does Arthur use this notion to try to undermine Singer's principle?

• How does Slote account for the *apparent* moral significance of physical distance?

• Finally, is Arthur correct in arguing that Singer's general principle is unreasonably demanding? Or can Singer's principle, along with the shallow-pond example, be interpreted in a less demanding way?

• To the extent that Singer provides a qualified and an unqualified version of his general moral principle, what, precisely, is the difference between the two? How important is the difference? Are there cases where the unqualified version would say that it would be wrong not to help but the qualified version would say it would not be wrong? What would such cases look like? Would such cases ultimately support or undermine Singer's position? How?

Further Reading

Kamm, F. M. "Famine Ethics: The Problem of Distance in Morality," in *Singer and His Critics,* ed. Dale Jamieson (Oxford: Blackwell, 1999), pp. 162–208.

Kekes, John. "On the Supposed Obligation to Relieve Famine." *Philosophy* 77, no. 302 (October 2002): 503–17.

Otteson, James R. "Limits on Our Obligation to Give." *Public Affairs Quarterly* 14, no. 3 (2000): 183–203.

Schmidtz, David. "Islands in a Sea of Obligation: Limits of the Duty of Rescue." *Law and Philosophy* 19, no. 6 (November 2000): 683–705.

Unger, Peter K. *Living High and Letting Die: Our Illusion of Innocence.* New York: Oxford University Press, 1996.

Van Wyk, Robert N. "Perspectives on World Hunger and the Extent of Our Positive Duties." *Public Affairs Quarterly* 2 (April 1988): 75–90.

P E T E R   S I N G E R

Famine, Affluence, and Morality

As I write this, in November 1971, people are dying in East Bengal from lack of food, shelter, and medical care. The suffering and death that are occurring there now are not inevitable, not unavoidable in any fatalistic sense of the term. Constant poverty, a cyclone, and a civil war have turned at least nine million people into destitute refugees; nevertheless, it is not beyond the capacity of the richer nations to give enough assistance to reduce any further suffering to very small proportions. The decisions and actions of human beings can prevent this kind of suffering. Unfortunately, human beings have not made the necessary decisions. At the individual level, people have, with very few exceptions, not responded to the situation in any significant way. Generally speaking, people have not given large sums to relief funds; they have not written to their parliamentary representatives demanding increased government assistance; they have not demonstrated in the streets, held symbolic fasts, or done anything else directed toward providing the refugees with the means to satisfy their essential needs. At the government level, no government has given the sort of massive aid that would enable the refugees to survive for more than a few days. Britain, for instance, has given rather more than most countries. It has, to date, given £14,750,000. For comparative purposes, Britain's share of the nonrecoverable development costs of the Anglo-French Concorde project is already in excess of £275,000,000, and on present estimates will reach £440,000,000. The implication is that the British government values a supersonic transport more than thirty times as highly as it values the lives of the nine million refugees. Australia is another country which, on a per capita basis, is well up in the "aid to Bengal" table. Australia's aid, however, amounts to less than one-twelfth of the cost of Sydney's new opera house. The total amount given, from all sources, now stands at about £65,000,000. The estimated cost of keeping the refugees alive for one year is £464,000,000. Most of the refugees have now been in the camps for more than six months. The World Bank has said that India needs a minimum of £300,000,000 in assistance from other countries before the end of the year. It seems obvious that assistance on this scale will not be forth-coming. India will be forced to choose between letting the refugees starve or diverting funds from her own development program, which will mean that more of her own people will starve in the future.[1]

These are the essential facts about the present situation in Bengal. So far as it concerns us here, there is nothing unique about this situation except its magnitude. The Bengal emergency is just the latest and most acute of a series of major emergencies in various parts of the world, arising both from natural and from man-made causes. There are also many parts of the world in which people die from malnutrition and lack of food independent of any special emergency. I take Bengal as my example only because it is the present concern, and because the size of the problem has ensured that it has been given adequate publicity. Neither individuals nor governments can claim to be unaware of what is happening there.

What are the moral implications of a situation like this? In what follows, I shall argue that the way people in relatively affluent countries react to a situation like that in Bengal cannot be justified; indeed, the whole way we look at moral issues—our moral conceptual scheme—needs to be altered, and with it, the way of life that has come to be taken for granted in our society.

In arguing for this conclusion I will not, of course, claim to be morally neutral. I shall, however, try to argue for the moral position that I take, so that

Peter Singer, "Famine, Affluence, and Morality," *Philosophy and Public Affairs* 1, no. 3 (Spring 1972): 229–43. Reprinted by permission of Princeton University Press.

anyone who accepts certain assumptions, to be made explicit, will, I hope, accept my conclusion.

I begin with the assumption that suffering and death from lack of food, shelter, and medical care are bad. I think most people will agree about this, although one may reach the same view by different routes. I shall not argue for this view. People can hold all sorts of eccentric positions, and perhaps from some of them it would not follow that death by starvation is in itself bad. It is difficult, perhaps impossible, to refute such positions, and so for brevity I will henceforth take this assumption as accepted. Those who disagree need read no further.

My next point is this: if it is in our power to prevent something bad from happening, without thereby sacrificing anything of comparable moral importance, we ought, morally, to do it. By "without sacrificing anything of comparable moral importance" I mean without causing anything else comparably bad to happen, or doing something that is wrong in itself, or failing to promote some moral good, comparable in significance to the bad thing that we can prevent. This principle seems almost as uncontroversial as the last one. It requires us only to prevent what is bad, and not to promote what is good, and it requires this of us only when we can do it without sacrificing anything that is, from the moral point of view, comparably important. I could even, as far as the application of my argument to the Bengal emergency is concerned, qualify the point so as to make it: if it is in our power to prevent something very bad from happening, without thereby sacrificing anything morally significant, we ought, morally, to do it. An application of this principle would be as follows: if I am walking past a shallow pond and see a child drowning in it, I ought to wade in and pull the child out. This will mean getting my clothes muddy, but this is insignificant, while the death of the child would presumably be a very bad thing.

The uncontroversial appearance of the principle just stated is deceptive. If it were acted upon, even in its qualified form, our lives, our society, and our world would be fundamentally changed. For the principle takes, firstly, no account of proximity or distance. It makes no moral difference whether the person I can help is a neighbor's child ten yards from me or a Bengali whose name I shall never know, ten thousand miles away. Secondly, the principle makes no distinction between cases in which I am the only person who could possibly do anything and cases in which I am just one among millions in the same position.

I do not think I need to say much in defense of the refusal to take proximity and distance into account. The fact that a person is physically near to us, so that we have personal contact with him, may make it more likely that we *shall* assist him, but this does not show that we *ought* to help him rather than another who happens to be further away. If we accept any principle of impartiality, universalizability, equality, or whatever, we cannot discriminate against someone merely because he is far away from us (or we are far away from him). Admittedly, it is possible that we are in a better position to judge what needs to be done to help a person near to us than one far away, and perhaps also to provide the assistance we judge to be necessary. If this were the case, it would be a reason for helping those near to us first. This may once have been a justification for being more concerned with the poor in one's own town than with famine victims in India. Unfortunately for those who like to keep their moral responsibilities limited, instant communication and swift transportation have changed the situation. From the moral point of view, the development of the world into a "global village" has made an important, though still unrecognized, difference to our moral situation. Expert observers and supervisors, sent out by famine relief organizations or permanently stationed in famine-prone areas, can direct our aid to a refugee in Bengal almost as effectively as we could get it to someone in our own block. There would seem, therefore, to be no possible justification for discriminating on geographical grounds.

There may be a greater need to defend the second implication of my principle—that the fact that there are millions of other people in the same position, in respect to the Bengali refugees, as I am, does not make the situation significantly different from a situation in which I am the only person who can prevent something very bad from occurring. Again, of course, I admit that there is a psychological difference between the cases; one feels less guilty about doing nothing if one can point to others, similarly placed, who have also done nothing. Yet this can make no real difference to our moral obligations.[2] Should I consider that I am less obliged to pull the drowning child out of the pond if on looking around I see other people, no further away than I am, who have also noticed the child but are doing nothing? One has only to ask this question to see the absurdity of the view that numbers lessen obligation. It is a view that is an ideal excuse for inactivity; unfortunately most of the major evils—poverty, overpopulation, pollution—are problems in which everyone is almost equally involved.

The view that numbers do make a difference can be made plausible if stated in this way: if everyone in circumstances like mine gave £5 to the Bengal Relief Fund, there would be enough to provide food, shelter, and medical care for the refugees; there is no reason why I should give more than anyone else in the same circumstances as I am; therefore I have no obligation to give more than £5. Each premise in this argument is true, and the argument looks sound. It may convince us, unless we notice that it is based on a hypothetical premise, although the conclusion is not stated hypothetically. The argument would be sound if the conclusion were: if everyone in circumstances like mine were to give £5, I would have no obligation to give more than £5. If the conclusion were so stated, however, it would be obvious that the argument has no bearing on a situation in which it is not the case that everyone else gives £5. This, of course, is the actual situation. It is more or less certain that not everyone in circumstances like mine will give £5. So there will not be enough to provide the needed food, shelter, and medical care. Therefore by giving more than £5 I will prevent more suffering than I would if I gave just £5.

It might be thought that this argument has an absurd consequence. Since the situation appears to be that very few people are likely to give substantial amounts, it follows that I and everyone else in similar circumstances ought to give as much as possible, that is, at least up to the point at which by giving more one would begin to cause serious suffering for oneself and one's dependents—perhaps even beyond this point to the point of marginal utility, at which by

giving more one would cause oneself and one's dependents as much suffering as one would prevent in Bengal. If everyone does this, however, there will be more than can be used for the benefit of the refugees, and some of the sacrifice will have been unnecessary. Thus, if everyone does what he ought to do, the result will not be as good as it would be if everyone did a little less than he ought to do, or if only some do all that they ought to do.

The paradox here arises only if we assume that the actions in question—sending money to the relief funds—are performed more or less simultaneously, and are also unexpected. For if it is to be expected that everyone is going to contribute something, then clearly each is not obliged to give as much as he would have been obliged to had others not been giving too. And if everyone is not acting more or less simultaneously, then those giving later will know how much more is needed, and will have no obligation to give more than is necessary to reach this amount. To say this is not to deny the principle that people in the same circumstances have the same obligations, but to point out that the fact that others have given, or may be expected to give, is a relevant circumstance: those giving after it has become known that many others are giving and those giving before are not in the same circumstances. So the seemingly absurd consequence of the principle I have put forward can occur only if people are in error about the actual circumstances—that is, if they think they are giving when others are not, but in fact they are giving when others are. The result of everyone doing what he really ought to do cannot be worse than the result of everyone doing less than he ought to do, although the result of everyone doing what he reasonably believes he ought to do could be.

If my argument so far has been sound, neither our distance from a preventable evil nor the number of other people who, in respect to that evil, are in the same situation as we are, lessens our obligation to mitigate or prevent that evil. I shall therefore take as established the principle I asserted earlier. As I have already said, I need to assert it only in its qualified form: if it is in our power to prevent something very bad from happening, without thereby sacrificing anything else morally significant, we ought, morally, to do it.

The outcome of this argument is that our traditional moral categories are upset. The traditional distinction between duty and charity cannot be drawn, or at least, not in the place we normally draw it. Giving money to the Bengal Relief Fund is regarded as an act of charity in our society. The bodies which collect money are known as "charities." These organizations see themselves in this way—if you send them a check, you will be thanked for your "generosity." Because giving money is regarded as an act of charity, it is not thought that there is anything wrong with not giving. The charitable man may be praised, but the man who is not charitable is not condemned. People do not feel in any way ashamed or guilty about spending money on new clothes or a new car instead of giving it to famine relief. (Indeed, the alternative does not occur to them.) This way of looking at the matter cannot be justified. When we buy new clothes not to keep ourselves warm but to look "well-dressed" we are not providing for any important need. We would not be sacrificing anything significant if we were to continue to wear our old clothes, and give the money to famine relief. By doing so, we would be preventing another person from starving. It follows from what I have said earlier that we ought to give money away, rather than spend it on clothes which we do not need to keep us warm. To do so is not charitable, or generous. Nor is it the kind of act which philosophers and theologians have called "supererogatory"—an act which it would be good to do, but not wrong not to do. On the contrary, we ought to give the money away, and it is wrong not to do so.

I am not maintaining that there are no acts which are charitable, or that there are no acts which it would be good to do but not wrong not to do. It may be possible to redraw the distinction between duty and charity in some other place. All I am arguing here is that the present way of drawing the distinction, which makes it an act of charity for a man living at the level of affluence which most people in the "developed nations" enjoy to give money to save someone else from starvation, cannot be supported. It is beyond the scope of my argument to consider whether the distinction should be redrawn or abolished altogether. There would be many other possible ways of drawing the distinction—for instance, one might decide that it is good to make other people as happy as possible, but not wrong not to do so.

Despite the limited nature of the revision in our moral conceptual scheme which I am proposing, the revision would, given the extent of both affluence and famine in the world today, have radical implications. These implications may lead to further objections, distinct from those I have already considered. I shall discuss two of these.

One objection to the position I have taken might be simply that it is too drastic a revision of our moral scheme. People do not ordinarily judge in the way I have suggested they should. Most people reserve their moral condemnation for those who violate some moral norm, such as the norm against taking another person's property. They do not condemn those who indulge in luxury instead of giving to famine relief. But given that I did not set out to present a morally neutral description of the way people make moral judgments, the way people do in fact judge has nothing to do with the validity of my conclusion. My conclusion follows from the principle which I advanced earlier, and unless that principle is rejected, or the arguments shown to be unsound, I think the conclusion must stand, however strange it appears.

It might, nevertheless, be interesting to consider why our society, and most other societies, do judge differently from the way I have suggested they should. In a well-known article, J. O. Urmson suggests that the imperatives of duty, which tell us what we must do, as distinct from what it would be good to do but not wrong not to do, function so as to prohibit behavior that is intolerable if men are to live together in society.[3] This may explain the origin and continued existence of the present division between acts of duty and acts of charity. Moral attitudes are shaped by the needs of society, and no doubt society needs people who will observe the rules that make social existence tolerable. From the point of view of a particular society, it is essential to prevent violations of norms against killing, stealing, and so on. It is quite inessential, however, to help people outside one's own society.

If this is an explanation of our common distinction between duty and supererogation, however, it is not a justification of it. The moral point of view requires us to look beyond the interests of our own society. Previously, as I have already mentioned, this may hardly have been feasible, but it is quite feasible now. From the moral point of view, the prevention of the starvation of millions of people outside our society must be considered at least as pressing as the upholding of property norms within our society.

It has been argued by some writers, among them Sidgwick and Urmson, that we need to have a basic moral code which is not too far beyond the capacities of the ordinary man, for otherwise there will be a general breakdown of compliance with the moral code. Crudely stated, this argument suggests that if we tell people that they ought to refrain from murder and give everything they do not really need to famine relief, they will do neither, whereas if we tell them that they ought to refrain from murder and that it is good to give to famine relief but not wrong not to do so, they will at least refrain from murder. The issue here is: Where should we drawn the line between conduct that is required and conduct that is good although not required, so as to get the best possible result? This would seem to be an empirical question, although a very difficult one. One objection to the Sidgwick-Urmson line of argument is that it takes insufficient account of the effect that moral standards can have on the decisions we make. Given a society in which a wealthy man who gives five percent of his income to famine relief is regarded as most generous, it is not surprising that a proposal that we all ought to give away half our incomes will be thought to be absurdly unrealistic. In a society which held that no man should have more than enough while others have less than they need, such a proposal might seem narrow-minded. What it is possible for a man to do and what he is likely to do are both, I think, very greatly influenced by what people around him are doing and expecting him to do. In any case, the possibility that by spreading the idea that we ought to be doing very much more than we are to relieve famine we shall bring about a general breakdown of moral behavior seems

remote. If the stakes are an end to widespread starvation, it is worth the risk. Finally, it should be emphasized that these considerations are relevant only to the issue of what we should require from others, and not to what we ourselves ought to do.

The second objection to my attack on the present distinction between duty and charity is one which has from time to time been made against utilitarianism. It follows from some forms of utilitarian theory that we all ought, morally, to be working full time to increase the balance of happiness over misery. The position I have taken here would not lead to this conclusion in all circumstances, for if there were no bad occurrences that we could prevent without sacrificing something of comparable moral importance, my argument would have no application. Given the present conditions in many parts of the world, however, it does follow from my argument that we ought, morally, to be working full time to relieve great suffering of the sort that occurs as a result of famine or other disasters. Of course, mitigating circumstances can be adduced—for instance, that if we wear ourselves out through overwork, we shall be less effective than we would otherwise have been. Nevertheless, when all considerations of this sort have been taken into account, the conclusion remains: we ought to be preventing as much suffering as we can without sacrificing something else of comparable moral importance. This conclusion is one which we may be reluctant to face. I cannot see, though, why it should be regarded as a criticism of the position for which I have argued, rather than a criticism of our ordinary standards of behavior. Since most people are self-interested to some degree, very few of us are likely to do everything that we ought to do. It would, however, hardly be honest to take this as evidence that it is not the case that we ought to do it.

It may still be thought that my conclusions are so wildly out of line with what everyone else thinks and has always thought that there must be something wrong with the argument somewhere. In order to show that my conclusions, while certainly contrary to contemporary Western moral standards, would not have seemed so extraordinary at other times and in other places, I would like to quote a passage from a writer not normally thought of as a way-out radical, Thomas Aquinas.

> Now, according to the natural order instituted by divine providence, material goods are provided for the satisfaction of human needs. Therefore the division and appropriation of property, which proceeds from human law, must not hinder the satisfaction of man's necessity from such goods. Equally, whatever a man has in superabundance is owed, of natural right, to the poor for their sustenance. So Ambrosius says, and it is also to be found in the *Decretum Gratiani:* "The bread which you withhold belongs to the hungry; the clothing you shut away, to the naked; and the money you bury in the earth is the redemption and freedom of the penniless."[4]

I now want to consider a number of points, more practical than philosophical, which are relevant to the application of the moral conclusion we have reached. These points challenge not the idea that we ought to be doing all we can to prevent starvation, but the idea that giving away a great deal of money is the best means to this end.

It is sometimes said that overseas aid should be a government responsibility, and that therefore one ought not to give to privately run charities. Giving privately, it is said, allows the government and the noncontributing members of society to escape their responsibilities.

This argument seems to assume that the more people there are who give to privately organized famine relief funds, the less likely it is that the government will take over full responsibility for such aid. This assumption is unsupported, and does not strike me as at all plausible. The opposite view—that if no one gives voluntarily, a government will assume that its citizens are uninterested in famine relief and would not wish to be forced into giving aid—seems more plausible. In any case, unless there were a definite probability that by refusing to give one would be helping to bring about massive government assistance, people who do refuse to make voluntary contributions are refusing to prevent a certain amount of suffering without being able to point to any tangible beneficial consequence of their refusal. So the onus of showing how their refusal will bring about government action is on those who refuse to give.

I do not, of course, want to dispute the contention that governments of affluent nations should be giving many times the amount of genuine, no-strings-attached aid that they are giving now. I agree, too, that giving privately is not enough, and that we ought to be campaigning actively for entirely new standards for both public and private contributions to famine relief. Indeed, I would sympathize with someone who thought that campaigning was more important than giving oneself, although I doubt whether preaching what one does not practice would be very effective. Unfortunately, for many people the idea that "it's the government's responsibility" is a reason for not giving which does not appear to entail any political action either.

Another, more serious reason for not giving to famine relief funds is that until there is effective population control, relieving famine merely postpones starvation. If we save the Bengal refugees now, others, perhaps the children of these refugees, will face starvation in a few years' time. In support of this, one may cite the now well-known facts about the population explosion and the relatively limited scope for expanded production.

This point, like the previous one, is an argument against relieving suffering that is happening now, because of a belief about what might happen in the future; it is unlike the previous point in that very good evidence can be adduced in support of this belief about the future. I will not go into the evidence here. I accept that the earth cannot support indefinitely a population rising at the present rate. This certainly poses a problem for anyone who thinks it important to prevent famine. Again, however, one could accept the argument without drawing the conclusion that it absolves one from any obligation to do anything to prevent famine. The conclusion that should be drawn is that the best means of preventing famine, in the long run, is population control. It would then follow from the position reached earlier that one ought to be doing all one can to promote population control (unless one held that all forms of population control were wrong in themselves, or would have significantly bad consequences). Since there are organizations working specifically for population control, one would then support them rather than more ortho-dox methods of preventing famine.

A third point raised by the conclusion reached ear-lier relates to the question of just how much we all ought to be giving away. One possibility, which has already been mentioned, is that we ought to give until we reach the level of marginal utility—that is, the level at which, by giving more, I would cause as much suf-fering to myself or my dependents as I would relieve by my gift. This would mean, of course, that one would reduce oneself to very near the material circumstances of a Bengali refugee. It will be recalled that earlier I put forward both a strong and a moderate version of the principle of preventing bad occurrences. The strong version, which required us to prevent bad things from happening unless in doing so we would be sacrificing something of comparable moral significance, does seem to require reducing ourselves to the level of mar-ginal utility. I should also say that the strong version seems to me to be the correct one. I proposed the more moderate version—that we should prevent bad occur-rences unless, to do so, we had to sacrifice something morally significant—only in order to show that even on this surely undeniable principle a great change in our way of life is required. On the more moderate principle, it may not follow that we ought to reduce ourselves to the level of marginal utility, for one might hold that to reduce oneself and one's family to this level is to cause something significantly bad to happen. Whether this is so I shall not discuss, since, as I have said, I can see no good reason for holding the moder-ate version of the principle rather than the strong ver-sion. Even if we accepted the principle only in its moderate form, however, it should be clear that we would have to give away enough to ensure that the consumer society, dependent as it is on people spend-ing on trivia rather than giving to famine relief, would slow down and perhaps disappear entirely. There are several reasons why this would be desirable in itself. The value and necessity of economic growth are now being questioned not only by conservationists, but by economists as well.[5] There is no doubt, too, that the consumer society has had a distorting effect on the goals and purposes of its members. Yet looking at the matter purely from the point of view of overseas aid, there must be a limit to the extent to which we should

deliberately slow down our economy; for it might be the case that if we gave away, say, forty percent of our Gross National Product, we would slow down the economy so much that in absolute terms we would be giving less than if we gave twenty-five percent of the much larger GNP that we would have if we limited our contribution to this smaller percentage.

I mention this only as an indication of the sort of factor that one would have to take into account in working out an ideal. Since Western societies gener-ally consider one percent of the GNP an acceptable level for overseas aid, the matter is entirely academic. Nor does it affect the question of how much an indi-vidual should give in a society in which very few are giving substantial amounts.

It is sometimes said, though less often now than it used to be, that philosophers have no special role to play in public affairs, since most public issues depend primarily on an assessment of facts. On questions of fact, it is said, philosophers as such have no special expertise, and so it has been possible to engage in philosophy without committing oneself to any posi-tion on major public issues. No doubt there are some issues of social policy and foreign policy about which it can truly be said that a really expert assessment of the facts is required before taking sides or acting, but the issue of famine is surely not one of these. The facts about the existence of suffering are beyond dis-pute. Nor, I think, is it disputed that we can do some-thing about it, either through orthodox methods of famine relief or through population control or both. This is therefore an issue on which philosophers are competent to take a position. The issue is one which faces everyone who has more money than he needs to support himself and his dependents, or who is in a position to take some sort of political action. These categories must include practically every teacher and student of philosophy in the universities of the Western world. If philosophy is to deal with matters that are relevant to both teachers and students, this is an issue that philosophers should discuss.

Discussion, though, is not enough. What is the point of relating philosophy to public (and personal) affairs if we do not take our conclusions seriously? In this instance, taking our conclusion seriously means acting upon it. The philosopher will not find it any easier than anyone else to alter his attitudes and way of life to the extent that, if I am right, is involved in doing everything that we ought to be doing. At the very least, though, one can make a start. The philosopher who does so will have to sacrifice some of the benefits of the consumer society, but he can find compensation in the satisfaction of a way of life in which theory and practice, if not yet in harmony, are at least coming together.

NOTES

1. There was also a third possibility: that India would go to war to enable the refugees to return to their lands. Since I wrote this paper, India has taken this way out. The situation is no longer that described above, but this does not affect my argument, as the next paragraph indicates.

2. In view of the special sense philosophers often give to the term, I should say that I use "obligation" simply as the abstract noun derived from "ought," so that "I have an obligation to" means no more, and no less, than "I ought to." This usage is in accordance with the definition of "ought" given by the *Shorter Oxford English Dictionary:* "the general verb to express duty or obligation." I do not think any issue of substance hangs on the way the term is used; sentences in which I use "obligation" could all be rewritten, although somewhat clumsily, as sentences in which a clause containing "ought" replaces the term "obligation."

3. J. O. Urmson, "Saints and Heroes," in *Essays in Moral Philosophy,* ed. Abraham I. Melden (Seattle and London, 1958), p. 214. For a related but significantly different view see also Henry Sidgwick, *The Methods of Ethics,* 7th edn. (London, 1907), pp. 220–221, 492–493.

4. *Summa Theologica,* II-II, Question 66, Article 7, in *Aquinas, Selected Political Writings,* ed. A. P. d'Entreves, trans. J. G. Dawson (Oxford, 1948), p. 171.

5. See, for instance, John Kenneth Galbraith, *The New Industrial State* (Boston, 1967); and E. J. Mishan, *The Costs of Economic Growth* (London, 1967).

Critics

JOHN ARTHUR

World Hunger and Moral Obligation
The Case Against Singer

INTRODUCTION

My guess is that everyone who reads these words is wealthy by comparison with the poorest millions of people on our planet. Not only do we have plenty of money for food, clothing, housing, and other neces-

sities, but a fair amount is left over for far less important purchases like phonograph records, fancy clothes, trips, intoxicants, movies, and so on. And what's more we don't usually give a thought to whether or not we ought to spend our money on such luxuries rather than to give it to those who need

Originally published as "Famine Relief and the Ideal Moral Code," in *Applying Ethics,* ed. V. Barry (Belmont, Calif.: Wadsworth, 1981). Reprinted with the permission of the publisher.

it more; we just assume it's ours to do with as we please.

Peter Singer, "Famine, Affluence, and Morality" argues that our assumption is wrong, that we should not buy luxuries when others are in severe need. But [is he] correct? . . .

He first argues that two general moral principles are widely accepted, and then that those principles imply an obligation to eliminate starvation.

The first principle is simply that "suffering and death from lack of food, shelter and medical care are bad." Some may be inclined to think that the mere existence of such an evil in itself places an obligation on others, but that is, of course, the problem which Singer addresses. I take it that he is not begging the question in this obvious way and will argue from the existence of evil to the obligation of others to eliminate it. But how, exactly, does he establish this? The second principle, he thinks, shows the connection, but it is here that controversy arises.

This principle, which I will call the greater moral evil rule, is as follows:

> If it is in our power to prevent something bad from happening, without thereby sacrificing anything of comparable moral importance, we ought, morally, to do it

In other words, people are entitled to keep their earnings only if there is no way for them to prevent a greater evil by giving them away. Providing others with food, clothing, and housing would generally be of more importance than buying luxuries, so the greater moral evil rule now requires substantial redistribution of wealth.

Certainly there are few, if any, of us who live by that rule, although that hardly shows we are *justified* in our way of life; we often fail to live up to our own standards. Why does Singer think our shared morality requires that we follow the greater moral evil rule? What arguments does he give for it?

He begins with an analogy. Suppose you came across a child drowning in a shallow pond. Certainly we feel it would be wrong not to help. Even if saving the child meant we must dirty our clothes, we would emphasize that those clothes are not of comparable significance to the child's life. The greater moral evil rule thus seems a natural way of capturing why we think it would be wrong not to help.

But the argument for the greater moral evil rule is not limited to Singer's claim that it explains our feelings about the drowning child or that it appears "uncontroversial." Moral equality also enters the picture. Besides the Jeffersonian idea that we share certain rights equally, most of us are also attracted to another type of equality, namely that like amounts of suffering (or happiness) are of equal significance, no matter who is experiencing them. I cannot reasonably say that, while my pain is no more severe than yours, I am somehow special and it's more important that mine be alleviated. Objectivity requires us to admit the opposite, that no one has a unique status which warrants such special pleading. So equality demands equal consideration of interests as well as respect for certain rights.

But if we fail to give to famine relief and instead purchase a new car when the old one will do, or buy fancy clothes for a friend when his or her old ones are perfectly good, are we not assuming that the relatively minor enjoyment we or our friends may get is as important as another person's life? And that a form of prejudice; we are acting as if people were not equal in the sense that their interests deserve equal consideration. We are giving special consideration to ourselves or to our group, rather like a racist does. Equal consideration of interests thus leads naturally to the greater moral evil rule.

RIGHTS AND DESERT

Equality, in the sense of giving equal consideration to equally serious needs, is part of our moral code. And so we are led, quite rightly I think, to the conclusion that we should prevent harm to others if in doing so we do not sacrifice anything of comparable moral importance. But there is also another side to the coin, one which Singer ignore[s]. . . . This can be expressed rather awkwardly by the notion of entitlements. These fall into two broad categories, rights and desert. A few examples will show what I mean.

All of us could help others by giving away or allowing others to use our bodies. While your life may be shortened by the loss of a kidney or less enjoyable if lived with only one eye, those costs are probably not comparable to the loss experienced by a person who will die without any kidney or who is totally blind. We can even imagine persons who will actually be harmed in some way by your not granting sexual favors to them. Perhaps the absence of a sexual partner would cause psychological harm or even rape. Now suppose that you can prevent this evil without sacrificing anything of comparable importance. Obviously such relations may not be pleasant, but according to the greater moral evil rule that is not enough; to be justified in refusing, you must show that the unpleasantness you would experience is of equal importance to the harm you are preventing. Otherwise, the rule says you must consent.

If anything is clear, however, it is that our code does not *require* such heroism; you are entitled to keep your second eye and kidney and not bestow sexual favors on anyone who may be harmed without them. The reason for this is often expressed in terms of rights; it's your body, you have a right to it, and that weighs against whatever duty you have to help. To sacrifice a kidney for a stranger is to do more than is required, it's heroic.

Moral rights are normally divided into two categories. Negative rights are rights of noninterference. The right to life, for example, is a right not to be killed. Property rights, the right to privacy, and the right to exercise religious freedom are also negative, requiring only that people leave others alone and not interfere.

Positive rights, however, are rights of recipience. By not putting their children up for adoption, parents give them various positive rights, including rights to be fed, clothed, and housed. If I agree to share in a business venture, my promise creates a right of recipience, so that when I back out of the deal, I've violated your right.

Negative rights also differ from positive in that the former are natural; the ones you have depend on what you are. If lower animals lack rights to life or liberty it is because there is a relevant difference between them and us. But the positive rights you may have are not natural; they arise because others have promised, agreed, or contracted to give you something.

Normally, then, a duty to help a stranger in need is not the result of a right he has. Such a right would be positive, and since no contract or promise was made, no such right exists. An exception to this would be a lifeguard who contracts to watch out for someone's children. The parent whose child drowns would in this case be doubly wronged. First, the lifeguard should not have cruelly or thoughtlessly ignored the child's interests, and second, he ought not to have violated the rights of the parents that he helped. Here, unlike Singer's case, we can say there are rights at stake. Other bystanders also act wrongly by cruelly ignoring the child, but unlike the lifeguard they do not violate anybody's rights. Moral rights are one factor to be weighed, but we also have other obligations; I am not claiming that rights are all we need to consider. That view, like the greater moral evil rule, trades simplicity for accuracy. In fact, our code expects us to help people in need as well as to respect negative and positive rights. But we are also entitled to invoke our own rights as justification for not giving to distant strangers or when the cost to us is substantial, as when we give up an eye or kidney. . . .

Desert is a second form of entitlement. Suppose, for example, an industrious farmer manages through hard work to produce a surplus of food for the winter while a lazy neighbor spends his summer fishing. Must our industrious farmer ignore his hard work and give the surplus away because his neighbor or his family will suffer? What again seems clear is that we have more than one factor to weigh. Not only should we compare the consequences of his keeping it with his giving it away; we also should weigh the fact that one farmer deserves the food, he earned it through his hard work. Perhaps his deserving the product of his labor is outweighed by the greater need of his lazy neighbor, or perhaps it isn't, but being outweighed is in any case not the same as weighing nothing!

Desert can be negative, too. The fact that the Nazi war criminal did what he did means he deserves punishment, that we have a reason to send him to jail. Other considerations, for example the fact that nobody will be deterred by his suffering, or that he is old and harmless, may weigh against punishment and so we may let him go; but again that does not mean he doesn't still deserve to be punished.

Our moral code gives weight to both the greater moral evil principle and entitlements. The former emphasizes equality, claiming that from an objective point of view all comparable suffering, whoever its victim, is equally significant. It encourages us to take an impartial look at all the various effects of our actions; it is thus forward-looking. When we consider matters of entitlement, however, our attention is directed to the past. Whether we have rights to money, property, eyes, or whatever, depends on how we came to possess them. If they were acquired by theft rather than from birth or through gift exchange, then the right is suspect. Desert, like rights, is also backward-looking, emphasizing past effort or past transgressions which now warrant reward or punishment.

Our commonly shared morality thus requires that we ignore neither consequences nor entitlements, neither the future results of our action nor relevant events in the past. It encourages people to help others in need, especially when it's a friend or someone we are close to geographically, and when the cost is not significant. But it also gives weight to rights and desert, so that we are not usually obligated to give to strangers. . . .

But unless we are moral relativists, the mere fact that entitlements are an important part of our moral code does not in itself justify such a role. Singer . . . can perhaps best be seen as a moral reformer advocating the rejection of rules which provide for distribution according to rights and desert. Certainly the fact that in the past our moral code condemned suicide and racial mixing while condoning slavery should not convince us that a more enlightened moral code, one which we would want to support, would take such positions. Rules which define acceptable behavior are continually changing, and we must allow for the replacement of inferior ones.

Why should we not view entitlements as examples of inferior rules we are better off without? What could justify our practice of evaluating actions by looking backward to rights and desert instead of just to their consequences? One answer is that more fundamental values than rights and desert are at stake, namely fairness, justice, and respect. Failure to reward those who earn good grades or promotions is wrong because it's *unfair;* ignoring past guilt shows a lack of regard for *justice;* and failure to respect rights to life, privacy, or religious choice suggests a lack of *respect for other persons.*

Some people may be persuaded by those remarks, feeling that entitlements are now on an acceptably firm foundation. But an advocate of equality may well want to question why fairness, justice, and respect for persons should matter. But since it is no more obvious that preventing suffering matters than that fairness, respect, and justice do, we again seem to have reached an impasse. . . .

The lesson to be learned here is a general one: The moral code it is rational for us to support must be practical; it must actually work. This means, among other things, that it must be able to gain the support of almost everyone.

But the code must be practical in other respects as well. . . . [It] is wrong to ignore the possibilities of altruism, but it is also important that a code not assume people are more unselfish than they are. Rules that would work only for angels are not the ones it is rational to support for humans. Second, an ideal code cannot assume we are more objective than we are; we often tend to rationalize when our own interests are at stake, and a rational person will also keep that in mind when choosing a moral code. Finally, it is not rational to support a code which assumes we have perfect knowledge. We are often mistaken about the consequences of what we do, and a workable code must take that into account as well. . . .

It seems to me, then, that a reasonable code would require people to help when there is no substantial cost to themselves, that is, when what they are sacrificing would not mean *significant* reduction in their own or their families' level of happiness. Since most people's savings accounts and nearly everybody's second kidney are not insignificant, entitlements would in those cases outweigh another's need. But if what is at stake is trivial, as dirtying one's clothes would normally be, then an ideal moral code would not allow rights to override the greater evil that can be prevented. Despite our code's unclear and sometimes schizophrenic posture, it seems to me that these judgments are not that different from our current moral attitudes. We tend to blame people who waste money on trivia when they could help others in need, yet not to expect people to make large sacrifices to distant strangers. An ideal moral code thus might not be a great deal different from our own.

MICHAEL SLOTE

Famine, Affluence, and Empathy

One of the greatest challenges to ordinary moral thinking and to recent moral theory has been the views and arguments advanced by Peter Singer in his classic paper, "Famine, Affluence, and Morality."[1] Philosophers have struggled with and in many cases attempted to refute Singer's conclusion that our moral obligation to relieve hunger or disease in distant parts of the world is just as great as, say, our obligation to save a child drowning in a shallow pool of water right in front of us. But although this debate continues to be very lively, virtue ethics has not joined in the fray. It has simply not taken up the main issue Singer's paper has been thought to raise, the issue of whether the making of substantial sacrifices in order to help those suffering in distant parts of the world is obligatory or (merely) supererogatory. In the present essay, however, I shall attempt to grapple with Singer's ideas from a virtue-ethical perspective. But I shall be making use, not of the tradition of Aristotelian virtue ethics that has occupied so prominent a place in the recent revival of virtue ethics, but of a form of virtue ethics that has its roots in eighteenth-century moral sentimentalism [as espoused by] Francis Hutcheson and David Hume. Let me now say a bit about recent developments within this alternative tradition of virtue ethics and then go on to discuss how such an approach might be able to offer us an answer to the questions Peter Singer raises.

Neither Hume nor Hutcheson focuses on "caring" about others as a motive: their discussions of morality made use, rather, of concepts like benevolence and sympathy. But the ethics of caring recently proposed and developed by Carol Gilligan, Nel Noddings, and others seems very clearly in the moral sentimentalist tradition and is naturally (and typically) also regarded as a form of virtue ethics, since it evaluates human actions by reference to how much (of the inner motive of) caring they express or exhibit.[2] And I regard a virtue ethics of caring as the most promising (and interesting) form of present-day sentimentalism. Speaking very roughly, an ethics of caring holds that an act is morally (all) right if it doesn't exhibit a lack (or the opposite) of caring and wrong if it does. (Brushing your teeth may not evince caring, but the point is that it also doesn't evince, exhibit, or reflect a lack of caring concern about others.)

However, when Noddings originally wrote about caring, she had in mind the kind of caring for others that takes place, so to speak, in intimate or at least face-to-face relationships. Caring *about* the fate of (groups of) people one has merely *heard* about didn't come under the rubric of caring; and since morality does take in our relations with such distant and personally-unknown others, Noddings held that the ethics of caring represented only a limited—though important and previously neglected—part of morality. Others who came later, however, sought to show that caring about people who are distant from us can and should be taken within the purview of the caring approach to ethics (these others include Virginia Held and myself); and nowadays and in recent work Noddings seems to be convinced of the essential rightness of making such an expansionist move on behalf of the ethics of caring.

Therefore, when I speak of acts exhibiting a caring attitude or one inconsistent with caring, the caring I am speaking of includes attitudes toward distant and personally-unknown others, not just attitudes toward people we are acquainted with or love. The term "caring" is thus a placeholder for a description of an overall attitude/motivational state, one that takes in both one's concern for people one knows (intimately) and one's concern for distant others and that embodies some sort of proportionality or balance between these concerns. An ethics of caring will hold that it is virtuous to be more concerned about near and dear than about strangers or those one knows about merely

---

Michael Slote, "Famine, Affluence, and Empathy," is published here with permission of Michael Slote.

by description; but it will also insist that an ideally or virtuously caring individual will be substantially concerned about people who are distant from her (not to mention animals). The question of what constitutes an ideal or morally required proportionality or balance as between these concerns is a complex and difficult one, and our discussion in what follows will constitute an attempt at least partly to deal with it. Certainly, Singer seems to hold that we have as much reason to concern ourselves with distant others as with individuals we are personally intimate with; but there also something morally counterintuitive about this. The idea that we have special (or stronger) moral obligations to those who are near and/or dear to us is both familiar and ethically appealing at a common-sense level. But I hope now to show you how an ethics of caring, which has so far tended merely to *assume* such special obligations on the basis of the intuitive plausibility of such an assumption, can say something at least partly to justify it.

To do so, however, the ethics of caring needs to make use of some notions that play an important role in the thinking of Hume and other eighteenth-century figures, but that have been largely neglected by those seeking to develop a systematic ethics of caring. Hume (especially in his *A Treatise of Human Nature*) holds that our concern for others operates via a mechanism he calls "sympathy," but the notion he is working with (there) is actually closer to our contemporary term "empathy," and the difference or disparity may be partly accounted for by the fact that the latter term didn't enter English till the early twentieth century. So Hume doesn't have the terminology for distinguishing empathy from sympathy, but the phenomenon he calls sympathy seems much closer to what we mean by empathy than by sympathy.

Now these terms are not easy to define, but by "sympathy" I think we mean a kind of favorable attitude toward someone. One feels sympathy for someone in pain, for example, if one feels *for* them (or their pain), wishes they didn't have the pain, wants their pain to end. By "empathy," on the other hand, we mean a state or process in which someone takes on the feelings of another: one empathizes for another who is in pain, if one "feels their pain" (as opposed to feeling *for* their pain). Obviously, a great

deal more could be said about this distinction, but, given the prevalence of these notions in contemporary parlance, I hope the reader will readily follow what I shall be saying about empathy. Hume saw empathy/sympathy as a kind of *contagion* whereby the feelings of one person spread to (cause similar feelings in) another person, but in recent years there has been enormous interest in the subject of empathy on the part of social psychologists, and in that literature the "contagious" aspect of empathy is but one feature of the landscape. Numerous studies of the factors that affect empathy and of how empathy develops have been published, and various psychologists have also offered general accounts of the role empathy plays in human psychology and in human life. But one central aspect of that literature will most concern us here as I suggest a way of developing the ethics of caring further.

Recent work on empathy has to a substantial extent focused on the question whether the development of empathy is necessary to an individual's development of altruistic concern for others—this is called the "empathy-altruism hypothesis." Many (but by no means all) psychologists have seen recent work in the field as supporting the empathy-altruism hypothesis, and this literature is relevant to the present essay at least in part because it is possible to hold that caring works via empathy and that the contours of morally good caring can be specified in relation to how human empathy develops or can be made to develop. I believe that a virtue ethics of caring that grounds caring in human empathy as recently studied by psychologists can provide us with a way of answering Singer's arguments. But before appealing further to this interesting recent psychological literature, let me just briefly say how I came to realize the usefulness of appealing to (developed human) empathy in working out a sentimentalist virtue ethics of caring.

An ethics of caring can easily say that we have a greater obligation to help (born) fellow human beings than to help animals or fetuses, and such a comparative judgment has the kind of intuitive force or plausibility that a virtue ethics of caring might wish to rely on (though I assume that the intuition about born humans and fetuses will operate more weakly or will be undercut altogether in someone with a strong religious conviction that the fetus has an immortal soul). Some years ago, however, I was led in a different direction as a result of having my attention called to an article by Catholic thinker (and U.S. Circuit Court judge) John Noonan, in which (I was told) abortion is criticized, not for failing to respect the rights of the fetus, but for showing a lack of empathy for the fetus. I was absolutely galvanized by hearing about Noonan's article because (for one thing) it immediately occurred to me that the notion or phenomenon of empathy is a double-edged sword, and reading the article itself did nothing to disturb this conclusion. If we believe that empathy has moral force or relevance, then since it is in fact much easier for us to empathize with born humans (even neonates) than with a fetus, we can argue that it is for this reason morally worse to neglect or hurt a born human than to do the same to a fetus or embryo. And this conclusion might end up giving more sustenance to the pro-choice position than to the pro-life view of abortion.

Moreover, it almost as immediately occurred to me that a virtue ethics of caring, rather than rely on our intuitions about our stronger obligations to born humans than to embryos, fetuses, or animals, could explain the intuitions, the differential obligations, by incorporating the idea of empathy. (In thinking thus I was implicitly regarding the empathy-altruism hypothesis as at least somewhat plausible.) Instead of claiming that actions are right or wrong depending on whether they exhibit or reflect what intuition tells us is properly contoured and sufficiently deep caring, one can say that actions are wrong or right depending on whether or not they reflect or exhibit a deficiency of normally or fully empathic caring motivation. It would then, at least other things being equal, be morally worse to prefer a fetus or embryo to a born human being, because such a preference runs counter to the flow of developed human empathy or to caring motivation that is shaped by such empathy. And similar points, arguably, could be made about our moral relations with lower animals.

I believe that the concept or phenomenon of empathy can also help us to formulate a virtue-ethical answer to the questions Singer raises in "Famine, Affluence, and Altruism" (and elsewhere). An ethics of caring expanded and reconfigured so as to hinge on the idea of *developed human empathy* gives us reason to hold, pace Singer, that a failure to save the life of a distant child by making, say, a small contribution to Oxfam is not morally as objectionable or bad as failing to save the life of a child who is drowning right in front of one. We shall see that such a sentimentalist ethics of empathic caring can also allow us to draw other important moral distinctions, and I shall then also speculate briefly on the prospects of such a theory as a general and systematic approach to morality and metaethics.

Recent moral philosophers have written a great deal on the question, raised by Singer's article, of how much we are obligated to spend of our own time, money, or other resources in order to save the lives of people who are personally unknown to us but whom we are in fact in a position to save. But this issue, as I have suggested, rests on the question of whether we are more obligated to help a child drowning before our very eyes than to help any given child whom we know about only indirectly (as part of some labeled group rather than via personal acquaintance). As Singer points out in his article, the most *obvious* difference between the drowning child and a child we can save via contributions to Oxfam is one of spatial distance, and Singer himself hold that sheer distance simply cannot be morally relevant to our obligations to aid (or to how morally bad or objectionable it is *not* to aid). As a result, he concludes that we are just as obligated to give to Oxfam as to save the drowning child, and iterations of this argument lead him to the conclusion that most of us are morally obligated to make enormous sacrifices of our time, money, comfort, etc., in order to help distant (or nearby) others who are much worse off than we are.

However, in recent years Singer's quick dismissal of distance has come to be questioned on the basis of considerations that I want to examine here while, at the same time arguing that empathy in fact gives us a firmer basis than distance for distinguishing the strength of our obligations to the drowning child and our obligations to those we can only help (say) through organizations like Oxfam. Spatial distance and (decreasing) empathy do in fact correlate with one another across a wide range of cases, and that very fact may have helped to obscure the role empathy potentially has in explaining the sorts of distinctions people intuitively, or common-sensically, want to make with regard to the kinds of cases Singer mentions. But before saying anything further about the role of empathy here, it will be useful to say a bit more about the role sheer spatial distance might be thought to play in Singer-like cases.

Some of those who have lately considered the moral relevance of distance have regarded that issue as effectively involving two separate questions: first, whether we intuitively regard distance as making a difference to our obligations and, second, whether different intuitive reactions to third- or first-person cases involving distance would show anything important about (differences in) our actual obligations. In his book *Living High and Letting Die,* for example, Peter Unger considers both these issues and defends a negative answer to both of them.[3] He thinks that our superficial intuitions about cases may not ultimately carry much weight in moral theory of in determining where our obligations really lie. But he also holds that our differing moral intuitions about relevant cases don't track distance so much as (what he calls) salience and conspicuousness.

However, Frances Kamm disagrees with these views. She thinks that (a rather complicated notion of) distance *does* help to explain our differing intuitions about cases and also is relevant to our actual obligations in such cases.[4] Singer asks us to consider the difference between a situation where we can save a child from drowning at small cost to ourselves and one where we can save a distant child from starvation by making a small contribution to a famine relief organization, noting, but also deploring, our initial tendency to think that saving the child is morally more incumbent on us in the former situation than in the latter. But Kamm believes the factor of distance (or proximity) makes a relevant moral difference in/between these two cases, and, in order to rule out other factors that might be thought to be determining our moral judgments in those cases (like whether others are in a position to help), she devises other examples that she believes bring out the intuitive and real moral force of the factor of distance (proximity).

Both Unger's book and Kamm's paper are rich and extremely complicated, and what I have to say here won't go into every nook and cranny of what they say. But I find it interesting and a bit surprising that neither one of them considers the moral importance of our empathic tendencies or capacities. For example, in denying the intuitive or actual moral relevance of distance, Unger comes up with a category of salience/conspicuousness (also with a category of the dramatic or exciting, but I will discuss that a bit later) that he does take to be relevant to our intuitive judgments, but never once considers how what one might easily take to be a related notion—what we can readily or immediately empathize with—might be relevant, or thought to be relevant, here. Similarly, Kamm considers and rejects what Unger says about salience or conspicuousness (she also talks about vividness) in favor of the idea that (complexly understood) distance is relevant to distinguishing between cases like the drowning child and starving examples mentioned earlier, but somehow the subject of empathy never comes up.[5]

But I believe the notion of empathy can help us sort out our intuitive reactions to the kinds of cases Singer, Unger, and Kamm describe better than the explanatory factors they mention, and let me say something about this now. In the familiar drowning examples, someone's danger or plight has a salience, conspicuousness, vividness, and *immediacy* (a term that, for reasons to be mentioned below, I prefer, but that Singer, Unger, and Kamm don't use) that engages normal human empathy (and consequently arouses sympathy and concern) in a way that similar dangers we merely know *about* do not. So if morality is a matter of empathy-based concern or caring for/about people, we can not only explain why a failure to help in the drowning case seems worse to us than a failure to give to famine relief, but also justify that ordinary moral intuition.

The idea that seeing or perceiving makes a difference in arousing or eliciting empathic and altruistic reactions is by no means, however, a new one. Hume makes this essential point (while using the term "sympathy") in the *Treatise;* and Hume also seems to hold that differences in what naturally or normally arouses sympathy/empathy affect the strength of our moral obligations and what virtue calls for.[6] Moreover, there are recent psychological studies of empathy that bear out Hume's earlier observations/speculations. Martin

Hoffman's recent book, *Empathy and Moral Development: Implications for Caring and Justice,* usefully summarizes and reflects upon numerous psychological studies of the development of empathy and its role in creating or sustaining caring/concern for others, and one thing that both Hoffman and the previous studies emphasize is the difference that perceptual immediacy tends to make to the strength of empathic responses.[7] (However, Hoffman is more cautious than Hume is and I want to be about the moral implications of these psychological differences.)

In the light of the present moral emphasis on empathy, then, let's next consider what Kamm and Unger say about various cases. For example, in discussing the salience/conspicuousness that Unger invokes in explaining our (for him misguided) intuitions, Kamm distinguishes subjective and objective salience. Then, focusing on the former, she speaks of the science-fiction case of someone who can see a person suffering overseas with long-distance vision.[8] The suffering would then be salient, conspicuous, or vivid for the individual with the long-distance vision, but Kamm says that it is (intuitively) acceptable for that individual to "turn off" her long-distance vision (and pay no more attention to the fate of the person she has seen than to the fate of distant others she *hasn't* seen). But if she can turn it off, presumably she is also permitted simply to *turn away, avert her gaze;* and that is certainly what the view Kamm defends about the relevance of proximity implies.

However, I don't think this conclusion is in fact morally intuitive, and I believe considerations of empathy help to explain why. Turning away from someone we see (even if only at an extreme distance) seems *worse* than ignoring someone whom one knows about only by description; and assuming, for example, that one has the means instantly to deliver help either to someone whose danger or need one sees through long-distance vision or to someone whose danger or need one merely knows about, most of us, I think, would consider it inhumane to turn away from the person whose plight one saw and then (coldly) decide to give the aid to someone one merely knew about. What is inhumane here arguably has something to do with empathy, with a failure of empathic response to someone whose need one sees. The

immediacy or vividness of such perceived need engages our (normal or fully developed) human empathy more deeply or forcefully than need known only by description, and so a morality that centers around empathy in the way(s) I have been suggesting can explain our moral reactions to Kamm's case here better than Kamm's appeal to (complexly contoured) distance and proximity does, and it is difficult to see how Kamm can use this example to argue successfully against the view that subjective salience or vividness is relevant to our moral intuitions.

Interestingly, Kamm does say that what we see at an overseas distance would exert "psychological pressure" on us to help. But she dismisses that pressure as somehow outside the bounds of our moral intuitions, because she thinks that we lack any intuition that tells us we have more obligation to the person we see than to someone we don't. If, however, and as I have just claimed, we do have such an intuition, then what she terms mere psychological pressure is in fact a moral intuition that her emphasis on distance fails to account for, but that a view based on empathy can.

Kamm then turns to an example of objective salience a la Unger. She imagines that the person with long-distance vision sees a group of people in trouble and that one of the people is wearing a clown-suit and is much more dramatically exhibiting his need for help than the others. Kamm holds that that should make no moral difference to whom one feels one should help, and she uses this example to argue for distance as opposed to objective salience. But a view emphasizing empathy can also (and perhaps more fully) account for our intuitions about this kind of case. The person in danger of drowning or starvation who is in a clown-suit and busy waving his arms or making histrionic gestures may be more visibly obtrusive; but such a person may seem to be faking fear or pain (hamming it up), whereas someone else who is quieter or less demonstrative may bear the marks of suffering or anxiety more genuinely than the person in the clown-suit and for that very reason more strongly engage our empathy. Such a case creates problems for an Ungerian objective-salience account of our moral intuitions, but not for a moral theory that is based in empathy; and I also believe the latter can account for differing intuitive reactions to variants on this kind of case better than a view that stresses distance.

Thus imagine that the person in the clown-suit isn't hamming it up. He and all the others are genuinely writhing in pain, but you notice him first because of his clown-suit and find yourself absolutely riveted on him. Assuming you can help only one of the people in the group, would we find it equally acceptable for you to turn away from the clown-suited man and decide that you might as well help *someone else* in the group, as for you to decide to help him? I think not. I think, again, we would find it lacking in or contrary to normally flowing human empathy, inhumane, for you to turn away from the man instead of helping him *in response to* your vivid recognition of his need. If his need has greater initial immediacy for you, then that, I think, is an intuitively good reason to go with the flow of empathy and help him out, given that one can only help one person in the group. But Kamm's account in terms of distance doesn't allow for this sort of reason. Let us, however, consider a further example.

Unger denies that there is any intuitive or real moral difference between cases where an accident victim one can help is nearby and visible to one and cases where the victim is at some distance and one learns about his plight via Morse code.[9] But Kamm thinks he is mistaken here about our intuitions and claims the difference is due to factors of distance;[10] and while I agree with Kamm that there is a significant difference between such cases, it seems to me more plausible—or perhaps I should say more promising—to explain it in terms of empathy.[11]

We have illustrated the moral force of (considerations relating to) natural human empathy in terms of examples having to do with our moral relations with the fetus (and animals) and have gone on to discuss cases, familiar from the literature that has grown up around Peter Singer's work, that raise issues about our obligations to people whom we see or don't see, or who are near or far from us. The latter kinds of examples all involve dangers or emergencies of one kind or another, but we have yet to consider another sort of danger/emergency case that has often been discussed by philosophers, cases where the issue is

not so much (or cannot so easily be imagined to be) spatial proximity or distance, but rather *temporal* proximity or distance.

I am thinking of the well-known example of miners trapped in a coal-mine (as a result, say, of a cave-in). We typically feel morally impelled to help the miners rather than (at that point) expend an equivalent amount of money to install safety devices in the mines that will save a greater number of lives in the long run. But some have disagreed. Charles Fried discusses this example in his *An Anatomy of Values* and claims that we/society should prefer to install the safety devices and let the miners die. (He gives his argument a rather barbaric twist by saying we should even be willing to convey this decision to the ill-fated miners face-to-face, if that is somehow possible.)[12]

This example, this choice, doesn't turn on a contrast between near and far or between what is perceived and what is not, because we can easily imagine that those who have to choose whom to save are at a distance from the mine and don't know or perceive either the trapped miners or those who might be in danger there in the future. We can well imagine, for example, that *we* are somehow empowered to make the choice, having heard or read reports of the mine cave-in, and I don't think the tendency to prefer saving the presently-trapped miners would then be explainable in terms of an empathy-derived preference for saving those whose dangers we are perceptually aware of rather than those whose dangers we merely know about.

Still, if we have to choose between the presently-trapped miners and those who will be in danger in the future, there is an immediacy to the danger the former are in that does, I think, engage our empathic/sympathetic juices in a way that the danger to the latter does not. Of course, there is also an immediacy to our previous examples of a child drowning and of a clown-suited person whose distress is (immediately) visible to us, but this immediacy, clearly, is perceptual and hinges on issues about the *spatial* distance that direct perception can accommodate. A rather different kind of immediacy is at issue in the miners example, an immediacy having more to do with the present-tense temporal character of the miners' danger—the fact that it is a "clear and present danger"—than with any spatial or spatially-correlated factors. But both kinds of immediacy appeal to our empathy in a way that situations not involving these forms of immediacy tend not to do. (The fact that the word "present" applies both to a time and to a mode of sensory contact seems very apt, given this common appeal to empathy.)

Thus we may not see or hear or personally know the miners who are now trapped, and, because they are thus known to us only as a class or by description, the empathic appeal of their plight—as compared with the plight of those who are going to be in danger later—is different from the empathic (moral) appeal of (dangers to) those we are perceptually aware of. But it is natural to think of both kinds of cases as involving some sort of immediacy, and that may be the best term for describing the (projected?) objective correlate, in certain kinds of situations, of our (subjective or psychological) tendency toward empathy. And the fact that we can use such correlated immediacy and empathy to explain our moral reactions not only in the cases discussed in the Singer literature, but also in the miners case gives further support to what was said above about Singer-type cases and to the general account of morality I have been sketching.[13]

If that account is correct, then what is morally wrong with installing safety devices (as Fried suggests) rather than helping miners who are in clear and present danger is that it exhibits (or reflects or expresses) a deficiency of normal(ly developed) human empathy.[14] But by the same token someone who turns away from someone she sees in order to help someone she merely knows about (as in the kinds of examples Kamm and Unger talk about) will (other things being equal) also exhibit/demonstrate an underdeveloped capacity for empathy and a consequent coldness that we regard as morally questionable. And this sentimentalist (and virtue-ethical) way of approach moral issues also helps to explain why Singer is wrong to think that failures to save via organizations like Oxfam are in the same moral boat (so to speak) as a failure to save a child drowning right in front of one: the former simply doesn't exhibit as great a lack of (normal) human empathy as the latter does or would.

One implication of what I have been saying is that an ethics based on empathy yields a partialist, rather than an impartialist, understanding of morality.

Fried's suggestions about what we should do in the miners case are ethically repugnant or worse, but it is not as if he is advocating a selfish or egoistic indifference to the miners. Rather, he is urging us to see them and everyone else, present or future, in terms of a strictly impartial concern for humans (or sentient beings) generally. If this seems morally inadequate, and if a virtue-ethical sentimentalist approach can make use of the idea of empathy to offer us a promising explanation of why it is inadequate, then we are given reason to see morality (and the world of our moral concern or caring) in a partialist way; and the same partialism likewise conflicts with and tells against the views Peter Singer defends. Indeed, Singer has claimed that partialism has never been given an adequate principled defense;[15] and whether or not this is true, the approach I am taking is intended as offering, or being on the way to offering, such a defense of partialism.

The observant reader may have noticed, however, that I have not so far explicitly argued that Singer is wrong to maintain that we are under a moral obligation to sacrifice a great deal of our time and/or money to help those less fortunate than ourselves. He reaches that conclusion via a lemma that we *have* questioned, namely, the idea that we are as obligated to help distant individuals we don't know as to save a child drowning right in front of us. But it is time for us now to be a little more explicit about the reasons why, on the present approach, we are not obligated to make enormous sacrifices of the kind Singer recommends, but can view such sacrifices, rather, as *supererogatorily* good or praiseworthy.

The social-psychological literature supports, on the whole, the idea that human beings have a substantial capacity for empathy and for altruistic concern(s) based on empathy. Hoffman in particular gives a fascinating and in many ways compelling account of how moral education can lead us in fact toward an empathic concern for (groups of) people we don't know very well or even at all (the people of Bangladesh, the homeless, victims of AIDS).[16] But Hoffman also makes it clear that (he thinks) there are limits to how much empathy for (disadvantaged) groups people can be led to develop. Self-interest (or egocentric desires, fears, hatred, etc.) can often strongly oppose or qualify what we may or might otherwise do out of empathy or empathic concern for others.[17] If so, then our general account will yield the conclusion that we are not morally obligated to sacrifice most of our time and money to help needy others, because a failure to do so doesn't evince an absence of normally or fully developed human empathy. In that case, if it would take someone with an unusually high degree of empathy and empathic concern—a degree of empathy and empathic concern beyond what most people can be led to develop—to be willing to make such a sacrifice, then such sacrifice will be morally supererogatory—morally praiseworthy and/or good but *not* (pace Singer) obligatory.[18]

But even if this is so, it may still be obligatory for individuals like ourselves to make some sort of substantial contribution toward the relief of hunger (or similarly worthy causes). Those who do not may be acting wrongly because they evince a degree of empathic concern that is *less* than what most people can be led to develop. (Hoffman and others say a great deal about how moral education can in fact induce empathy and caring for people we don't know personally.) At the very least, then, even if Singer exaggerates what morality demands of us, it may nonetheless be true that many of us should give a good deal more for the relief of famine or disease around the world than we actually do.

However, in making use of a virtue-ethical moral sentimentalism based on empathic caring in order to argue against Singer's views, I have not considered certain well-known problems that any attempt to revive moral sentimentalism would have to face. Sentimentalism needs to be able to offer a plausible account of deontology (roughly, the moral distinction between doing and allowing, between killing and letting die), and this is something that it has, arguably, never successfully done. It also needs to explain how moral utterances or judgments can be grounded in sentiment rather than in rationality and rational concepts, and there is no doubt that this task represents a very difficult challenge to any attempt to revive moral sentimentalism. There are other difficulties too,[19] but let me at this point, and having noted these problems, simply say that I think that a contemporary sentimentalist ethics of caring is in

fact up to tackling these challenges (something I attempt to do in a forthcoming book entitled *Moral Sentimentalism*). In any case, for present purposes it is enough, I think, to see that and how an ethics of empathic caring can offer us a substantive and intuitively plausible response to the ideas and arguments of Singer's classic paper.

NOTES

1. *Philosophy and Public Affairs* 1, 1972, pp. 229–43.

2. See, e.g., Carol Gilligan, *In a Different Voice: Psychological Theory and Women's Development*, Cambridge: Harvard University Press, 1982; and Nel Noddings, *Caring: A Feminine Approach to Ethics and Moral Education*, Berkeley: University of California Press, 1984. Noddings sees her approach as continuous with eighteenth-century sentimentalism; but the connection has also been frequently mentioned by others.

3. New York: Oxford University Press, 1996.

4. See her "Famine Ethics" in Dale Jamieson, ed., *Singer and His Critics*, Oxford: Basil Blackwell, 1999, pp. 162–208.

5. I don't think Kamm ignores empathy because she thinks it too *subjective*. Unger's salience, as she notes, has a subjective aspect, but can also be viewed in a more objective way as what is or would be salient to a normal observer. But empathy also allows such a distinction, and the view I want to defend focuses on what calls forth (more or less) empathy (or empathy-involving concern) in a human being with a fully developed capacity for empathy.

6. On these points see the *Treatise*, ed., L. A. Selby-Bigge, Oxford: Clarendon Press, 1958, pp. 370, 439, 441, 483f., 488f., 518f.

7. New York: Cambridge University Press, 2000, pp. 209ff.

8. Pp. 182f.

9. Op. cit., esp. p. 36.

10. Op. cit., p. 184.

11. Unger in fact notes (p. 36) that such cases differ with respect to "experiential impact," a notion that ties in with empathy. But he doesn't pay much attention to impact, presumably because he (mistakenly) thinks that it makes no significant difference to our intuitions.

12. Cambridge: Harvard University Press, 1970, pp. 207–27 (esp. p. 226).

13. Interestingly, Hoffman, loc. cit., speaks of empathy as having a "here and now" bias, and the studies he cites make it very clear that our empathy flows more readily not

only in regard to what is visible or perceived, but also in regard to what is current or contemporaneous.

14. Unger (op. cit., pp. 78f.) describes a case in which a meteor has fallen to earth and will explode with disastrous consequences in a densely populated area unless someone immediately steals an "Ejector" machine from its rightful owner and uses it to hurl the meteor to a deserted canyon. He thinks one is permitted to steal and operate the Ejector in such circumstances, but says that the "dramaticness" of the trouble involved here makes no difference to that permission. Yet this example involves just the sort of clear and present danger that we saw in the case of the trapped miners, and if empathy is relevant to morality, then dramaticness (or at least what makes for drama in the case Unger describes, namely, the clear and present danger) may in fact make a difference not only to our intuitions, but to (the strength of) our moral obligations.

15. See Singer's "A Response [to Critics]" in Dale Jamieson, ed., *Singer and His Critics*, Oxford: Basil Blackwell, 1999, p. 308.

16. Hoffman, op. cit., esp. Chapters 3 and 13.

17. See op. cit., esp. Chapters. 2, 8, and 13.

18. A virtue ethics based on empathy can point to the greater ease or naturalness of empathizing with those near and dear to us (with those we know and love) as a basis for arguing that we have especially strong moral reasons to be concerned with such people. But, for simplicity's sake, I am treating the issue of self-interest vs. concern for the unfortunate as if it didn't also involve issues about our obligations to near and dear. Note too that, if what I have been saying is on the right track, the issue of helping needy distant groups will arise (or will arise with greatest force) only when one is not facing any more *immediate* issue of need or danger.

19. For example, one might wonder whether our reliance on empathy would lead us to make *too many* moral distinctions. Thus if people of one race or gender are more empathically sensitive to those of the same race or gender, then the distinctions in our attitudes and behavior that empathy explains may, at least some of them, be morally invidious; and this would represent a serious problem for any attempt to explain morality systematically in terms of empathic caring. I offer a response to such worries in *Moral Sentimentalism.*

PART 2

What's Wrong with Sex?

Some sexual acts generate little moral opposition. Procreative, heterosexual intercourse that takes place within a healthy and loving marriage, for example, is widely taken to be an instance of morally acceptable and even commendable behavior. Other sexual acts are just as clearly recognized to be wrong. The violent rape of a young child is surely an example. But many forms of sexual behavior lie between these two extremes. They are freely engaged in by consenting adults but differ from the case of marital, heterosexual intercourse in ways that many people find morally troubling. Part 2 is devoted to a critical examination of some of these cases. We begin with two issues involving homosexuality. In chapter 6, we look at the question of whether or not homosexual behavior is itself morally objectionable, and in chapter 7, we turn to the question of whether publicly revealing the sexual orientation of people who have attempted to conceal their homosexuality is morally objectionable. In chapter 8, we turn to a controversy that involves the sexual behavior of married people: What, if anything, is wrong with adultery? We then conclude Part 2 by addressing two quite different questions that involve issues of freedom and consent: the question of the moral appropriateness of campus sexual-conduct codes (chapter 9), and the question of whether consenting adults may permissibly engage in acts of prostitution by buying and selling sexual services (chapter 10).

6

Is Homosexuality Wrong?

Levin and His Critics

There is widespread antagonism both to homosexual behavior and to homosexual tendencies, and often along with that antagonism comes a presumption of immorality. It is only relatively recently that laws against homosexual acts have been repealed, and in many countries, and in some states in the United States, those acts are still illegal. Even some of those who support the repeal of those laws think that homosexual acts are immoral. They just think that such acts—like adulterous acts, for example—while immoral, are not the sort of immoral acts that the State should concern itself with discouraging, policing, or punishing. How might one argue for such a view? A popular and rather simple argument is based on the feeling that there is something "unnatural" about homosexual acts and that it is this "unnaturalness" that makes them wrong.

What does it take it for an act to be *natural* or *unnatural?* And why should the *unnatural* be deemed *morally wrong?* Consider eyeglasses, for example. Eyeglasses are not naturally occurring objects, but rather human artifacts manufactured to correct for what are typically naturally occurring problems that people have with their eyesight. So wearing eyeglasses is unnatural. But we do not consider it morally wrong for someone to improve his vision by wearing eyeglasses. By contrast, urinating is clearly a natural act, and most animals in their natural state unabashedly urinate in public, so urinating in public also seems very much a natural act. But despite its apparent naturalness, urinating in public is not highly regarded among human beings, and in at least some circumstances (say, during a lecture) would be regarded as morally improper. So, to the extent that we have a clear idea of what acts are natural, the natural and the moral do not seem to line up. Natural acts can be morally wrong, and unnatural acts can be morally permissible. Perhaps these apparently intuitive judgments of what is natural are false. But if these intuitive judgments are false, then we don't really have a firm grasp of what it takes for something to count as *natural*. Therefore, we really don't know how to tell whether homosexual acts are unnatural or not.

In the featured article in this chapter, Michael Levin offers an argument that has its origin in the same hunch—that homosexual acts are in some morally relevant sense *unnatural*—but his argument develops a number of interesting variations on the simple, intuitive argument.

First, he argues that homosexual acts are *abnormal*. They are abnormal because they involve a *misuse* of bodily parts. The fact that homosexual acts involve a misuse of body parts follows, he claims, from facts about the evolution of those body parts. Second, he argues that misusing bodily parts is very likely to lead to unhappiness. Third, and finally, he argues that because homosexuality is very likely to lead to unhappiness, not only is it imprudent for individuals to indulge in homosexual acts, but it is also wrong for the State to give homosexuality legitimacy by extending to homosexuals the kinds of rights and protections that have been extended to other protected classes. Such legislation is likely to increase the prevalence of homosexuality and hence spread unhappiness.

Timothy F. Murphy criticizes Levin on all three counts. First, he argues that Levin fails to show that the evolutionary origins of sexual behavior have any significant normative force. That our organs evolved in a certain way cannot in itself oblige us to use them in one way rather than another. Thus, saying that a certain use of an organ, given its evolutionary history, is a *misuse* or is *abnormal* does not entail that it is *wrong* in any moral sense. Murphy thus concludes that an activity's being evolutionarily abnormal in Levin's sense has no implications for its wrongness. Second, he attacks Levin's arguments for the supposed greater unhappiness of homosexuals. Finally, Murphy argues that even if it were true that, for various biological reasons, homosexuals had a greater tendency toward unhappiness than heterosexuals, it would not follow that the State should impose extra burdens on people who engage in homosexual activity. Suppose it is a fact that atheists tend to be less happy than theists, for example. Does it follow, then, that the State should discourage atheism by imposing burdens on atheists or that atheists should not enjoy the same rights as theists?

QUESTIONS FOR CONSIDERATION

• Suppose a certain activity was once essential for the survival and reproduction of humanity (say, killing animals and eating their flesh) and that various organs evolved to enable us to do exactly that. Does it follow that it would be wrong for a particular human being to desist from killing animals in order to eat their flesh? Are we morally obliged to be meat eaters? Suppose that although we evolved by eating meat, we no longer needed to eat meat to survive and reproduce (which, as it happens, is the case). Might there not be good moral arguments for becoming vegetarians despite our evolutionary history?

• Suppose an activity had the following feature: that *not everyone* engaged in it played an essential role in our evolution and our survival and that it was essential, for our future survival, that not everyone engage in that activity. (Being completely celibate is clearly an example of this.) Would it follow, then, that *no one* should engage in that activity? (Is it true that *no one* should remain celibate?) If we do not deem it immoral for people to take on a vow of lifelong chastity, what implications does that have for Levin's argument?

• Recently a fad has emerged among those who like piercing their bodies: tongue-splitting. Would tongue-splitting count as a misuse of an organ, according to Levin's theory? Should there be laws discouraging tongue-splitting and body-piercing? Perhaps tongue-splitting, though abnormal, is not a very drastic misuse of an organ. A far more drastic misuse of organs, as reported in the December 2000 issue of *Atlantic Monthly* (C. Elliot, "A New Way to Be Mad"; also available online at http://www. theatlantic.com/issues/2000/12/elliott.htm), involves the following: In January of this year British newspapers began running articles about Robert Smith, a surgeon at Falkirk and District Royal Infirmary in Scotland. Smith had amputated the legs of two patients at their request, and he was planning to carry out a third amputation when the trust that runs his hospital stopped him. These patients were not physically sick. Their legs did not need to be amputated for any medical reason. Nor were they incompetent, according to the psychiatrists who examined them. They simply wanted to have their legs cut off. In fact, both the men whose limbs Smith amputated have declared in public interviews how much happier they are, now that they have finally had their legs removed. Apotemnophilia, or the desire to be an amputee, is a strange and disturbing phenomenon. An apotemnophiliac desires to have one or more of his own healthy limbs amputated and evidently is sometimes able to persuade others to fulfill this desire. Cases are not as uncommon as one might think. Elliot reports several, including that of a seventy-nine-year-old New Yorker who, in May 1998, traveled to Mexico, paid $10,000 for a leg amputation on the black market, and subsequently died of gangrene. Those of us who do not suffer such desires judge them to be perverse, and we feel extremely uncomfortable about Dr. Smith's helping his patients satisfy them. Does Levin's account capture what we think of as abnormal in such desires? And could Murphy's defense of homosexual acts also be used as a defense of apotemnophiliac acts of amputation? If not, why not?

FURTHER READING

Corvino, John. "Homosexuality and the PIB Argument." *Ethics* 115, no. 3 (April 2005): 501–34.

Cuomo, Chris. "Dignity and the Right to Be Lesbian or Gay." *Philosophical Studies* 132, no. 1 (January 2007): 75–85.

Levin, Michael. "Homosexuality, Abnormality, and Civil Rights." *Public Affairs Quarterly* 10, no. 1 (January 1996): 31–48.

Ruse, Michael. "Homosexuality: Right or Wrong?" *Free Inquiry* 13, no. 2. (1993): 35–37.

Salzman, Todd A., and Michael G. Lawler. "New Natural Law Theory and Foundational Sexual Ethical Principles: A Critique and a Proposal." *Heythrop Journal: A Quarterly Review of Philosophy and Theology* 47, no. 2 (April 2006): 182–205.

MICHAEL LEVIN

Why Homosexuality Is Abnormal

1. INTRODUCTION

This paper defends the view that homosexuality is abnormal and hence undesirable—not because it is immoral or sinful, or because it weakens society or hampers evolutionary development, but for a purely mechanical reason. It is a misuse of bodily parts. Clear empirical sense attaches to the idea of *the use* of such bodily parts as genitals, the idea that they are *for*

something, and consequently to the idea of their misuse. I argue on grounds involving natural selection that misuse of bodily parts can with high probability be connected to unhappiness. I regard these matters as prolegomena to such policy issues as the rights of homosexuals, the rights of those desiring not to associate with homosexuals, and legislation concerning homosexuality, issues which I shall not discuss systematically here. However, I do in the last section

From Michael Levin, "Why Homosexuality Is Abnormal," *The Monist* 67 (1984): 251–83. Notes and some parts of text deleted. Reprinted by permission of the Monist.

draw a seemingly evident corollary from my view that homosexuality is abnormal and likely to lead to unhappiness.

I have confined myself to male homosexuality for brevity's sake, but I believe that much of what I say applies *mutatis mutandis* to lesbianism. There may well be significant differences between the two: the data of [4], for example, support the popular idea that sex per se is less important to women and in particular lesbians than it is to men. On the other hand, lesbians are generally denied motherhood, which seems more important to women than is fatherhood—normally denied homosexual males—to men. On this matter, [4] offers no data. Overall, it is reasonable to expect general innate gender differences to explain the major differences between male homosexuals and lesbians.

Despite the publicity currently enjoyed by the claim that one's "sexual preference" is nobody's business but one's own, the intuition that there is something unnatural about homosexuality remains vital. The erect penis fits the vagina, and fits it better than any other natural orifice; penis and vagina seem made for each other. This intuition ultimately derives from, or is another way of capturing, the idea that the penis is not *for* inserting into the anus of another man—that so using the penis is not the way it is *supposed, even intended,* to be used. Such intuitions may appear to rest on an outmoded teleological view of nature, but recent work in the logic of functional ascription shows how they may be explicated, and justified, in suitably naturalistic terms. Such is the burden of Section 2, the particular application to homosexuality coming in Section 3. Furthermore, when we understand the sense in which homosexual acts involve a misuse of genitalia, we will see why such misuse is bad and not to be encouraged. (The case for this constitutes the balance of Section 3.) Clearly, the general idea that homosexuality is a pathological violation of nature's intent is not shunned by scientists. Here is Gadpille:

> The view of cultural relativity seems to be without justification. Cultural judgment is collective human caprice, and whether it accepts or rejects homosexuality is irrelevant. Biological intent . . . is to differentiate male and female both physiologically and psychologically in such a manner as to insure species survival, which can be served only through heterosexual union ([7], 193).

Gadpille refers to homosexuality as "an abiological maladaptation." The novelty of the present paper is to link adaptiveness and normality via the notion of happiness.

But before turning to these issues, I want to make four preliminary remarks. The first concerns the explicitness of my language in the foregoing paragraph and the rest of this paper. Explicit mention of bodily parts and the frank description of sexual acts are necessary to keep the phenomenon under discussion in clear focus. Euphemistic vagary about "sexual orientation" or "the gay lifestyle" encourage one to slide over homosexuality without having to face or even acknowledge what it really is. Such talk encourages one to treat "sexual preference" as if it were akin to preference among flavors of ice cream. Since unusual taste in ice-cream is neither right nor wrong, this usage suggests, why should unusual taste in sex be regarded as objectionable? Opposed to this usage is the unblinkable fact that the sexual preferences in question are such acts as mutual fellation. Is one man's taste for pistachio ice cream really just like another man's taste for fellation? Unwillingness to call this particular spade a spade allows delicacy to award the field by default to the view that homosexuality is normal. Anyway, such delicacy is misplaced in a day when "the love that dare not speak its name" is shouting its name from the rooftops.

My second, related, point concerns the length of the present paper, which has a general and a specific cause. The general cause is that advocates of an unpopular position—as mine is, at least in intellectual circles—assume the burden of proof. My view is the one that needs defending, my presuppositions the ones not widely shared. I would not have entertained so many implausible and digressive objections had not so many competent philosophers urged them on me with great seriousness. Some of these objections even generate a dialectic among themselves. For example, I have to defend my view on two sociobiological fronts—against the view that what is innate is polymorphous sexuality shaped by culture, and against the incompatible view that not only are the details of sexual behavior innate, but homosexuality is one such behavior, and hence "normal."

The third point is this. The chain of intuitions I discussed earlier has other links, links connected to the conclusion that homosexuality is bad. They go something like this: Homosexual acts involve the use of the genitals for what they aren't for, and it is a *bad* or at least *unwise* thing to use a part of your body for what it isn't for. Calling homosexual acts "unnatural" is intended to sum up this entire line of reasoning. "Unnatural" carries disapprobative connotations, and any explication of it should capture this. One can, stipulatively or by observing the ordinary usage of biologists, coin an evaluatively neutral use for "normal," or "proper function," or any cognate thereof. One might for example take the normal use of an organ to be what the organ is used for 95% of the time. But there is a normative dimension to the concept of abnormality that all such explications miss. To have anything to do with our intuitions— even if designed to demonstrate them groundless— an explication of "abnormal" must capture the analytic truth that the abnormality of a practice is a reason for avoiding it. If our ordinary concept of normality turns out to be ill-formed, so that various acts are at worst "abnormal" in some non-evaluative sense, this will simply mean that, as we ordinarily use the expression, *nothing is abnormal.* (Not that anyone really believes this—people who deny that cacophagia or necrophilia are abnormal do so only to maintain the appearance of consistency.)

Fourth, I should mention Steven Goldberg's defense of a position similar to mine ([8]). Goldberg's first approximation to a definition of abnormality runs as follows: behavior is abnormal when it is emitted in circumstances in which it is highly negatively sanctioned. This captures the insight that even if there is nothing *intrinsically* wrong with a bit of behavior, there probably must be something wrong with anyone who persists in doing it when he knows he will be punished. There may be nothing wrong with eating beef per se, but there must be something wrong with a Hindu who invites death by walking the streets of Calcutta eating a hamburger. The trouble with this definition is that as it stands it brands as abnormal a highly-sanctioned behavior done to make a moral point. To exclude such cases Goldberg adds a second clause: person A's doing act B is abnormal if A is caused to do B by conditions one would intuitively judge to be abnormal. This excludes high-minded sacrifices but does include homosexuality if, as Freudians believe, homosexuality results from maternal dominance and paternal indifference, conditions most people regard as abnormal. Goldberg is aware that defining "abnormal" via "abnormal cause" is circular, but he finds the circularity benign. He contends that the definition does capture a definite reality people have in mind when they label homosexuality or necrophilia abnormal, and that anyone who brings the charge of circularity must also take this circularity to prevent us from viewing necrophilia as abnormal. Goldberg assumes that no reasonable person would carry the charge of circularity that far.

Goldberg's analysis is persuasive, and the first clause should be preserved, even if the circular second clause is jettisoned. My own analysis—which I believe to be even clearer than Goldberg's, as well as more formally adequate—is indeed compatible with Goldberg's. It turns out that what Goldberg has correctly analyzed is not what "abnormal" means, but the *evidence* on which ordinary judgements of abnormality are based. That something is abnormal in Goldberg's sense is good evidence that it is abnormal in the central sense I explicate below. I will have occasion to use this lemma.

2. On "Function" and Its Cognates

To bring into relief the point of the idea that homosexuality involves a misuse of bodily parts, I will begin with an uncontroversial case of misuse, a case in which the clarity of our intuitions is not obscured by the conviction that they are untrustworthy. Mr. Jones pulls all his teeth and strings them around his neck because he thinks his teeth look nice as a necklace. He takes pureéd liquids supplemented by intravenous solutions for nourishment. It is surely natural to say that Jones is misusing his teeth, that he is not using them for what they are for, that indeed the way he is using them is incompatible with what they are for. Pedants might argue that Jones's teeth are no longer part of him and hence that he is not misusing any bodily parts. To them I offer Mr. Smith, who likes to play "Old MacDonald" on his teeth. So devoted is he to this amusement, in fact, that he never uses his teeth for chewing—like Jones, he takes nourishment intravenously. Now, not only do we find it perfectly plain that Smith and Jones are misusing their teeth, we predict a dim future for them on purely physiological grounds; we expect the muscles of Jones's jaw that are used for—that *are* for—chewing to lose their tone, and we expect this to affect Jones's gums. Those parts of Jones's digestive tract that are for processing solids will also suffer from disuse. The net result will be deteriorating health and perhaps a shortened life. Nor is this all. Human beings enjoy chewing. Not only has natural selection selected in muscles for chewing and favored creatures with such muscles, it has selected in a tendency to find the use of those muscles reinforcing. Creatures who do not enjoy using such parts of their bodies as deteriorate with disuse, will tend to be selected out. Jones, product of natural selection that he is, descended from creatures who at least tended to enjoy the use of such parts. Competitors who didn't simply had fewer descendants. So we expect Jones sooner or later to experience vague yearnings to chew something, just as we find people who take no exercise to experience a general listlessness. Even waiving for now my apparent reification of the evolutionary process, let me emphasize how little anyone is tempted to say "each to his own" about Jones or to regard Jones's disposition of his teeth as simply a deviation from a statistical norm. This sort of case is my paradigm when discussing homosexuality.

The main obstacle to talk of what a process or organic structure is for is that, literally understood, such talk presupposes an agent who intends that structure or process to be used in a certain way. Talk of function derives its primitive meaning from the human use of artifacts, artifacts being for what purposive agents intend them for. Indeed, there is in this primitive context a natural reason for using some-thing for what it is for: to use it otherwise would frustrate the intention of some purposeful agent. Since it now seems clear that our bodily parts were not emplaced by purposeful agency, it is easy to dismiss talk of what they are for as "theologically" based on a faulty theory of how we came to be built as we are:

> The idea that sex was designed for propagation is a theological argument, but not a scientific one. . . . To speak of the "fit" of penis and vagina as proof of nature's intention for their exclusive union is pure theological reasoning—imposing a meaning or purpose upon a simple, natural phenomenon ([9], 63).

Barash—who elsewhere uses its cognates freely—dismisses "unnatural" as a mere term of abuse: "people with a social or political axe to grind will call what they don't like 'unnatural' and what they do, 'natural' " ([1], 237). Hume long ago put the philosopher's case against the term 'natural' with characteristic succinctness: " 'Tis founded on final Causes; which is a consideration, that appears to me pretty uncertain & unphilosophical. For pray, what is the End of Man? Is he created for Happiness or for Virtue? For this Life or the next? For himself or for his Maker?" ([20], 134).

Until recently, philosophers of science half-countered, half-conceded such doubts by "rationally reconstructing" the locution "structure S is for function F in organism O" as—omitting inessential refinements—"S's doing F in O is necessary for the integrity or prosperity of O". This, the classical analysis, suffers from two weaknesses. First, it quite severs the link stressed earlier between a structure's having a function and the inadvisability of using that structure in a way inconsistent with its function. An organism may not be interested in survival, or prosperity, or the prosperity of some genetically defined group that contains the organism. The classical analysis provides no clue as to why Jones should desist from stringing his teeth on a necklace. It must be supplemented with the premise that survival or fitness are desirable, and however strong the desire to survive may be as a de facto motive, there are too many cogent arguments against survival as a basic norm for this supplement to be plausible.

None of this will disturb proponents of the classical analysis, since their very aim was, in part, to remove the teleological and normative connotations of "function" as unscientific ideas. So what if the classical analysis obstructs the inference from "Jones is not using his teeth for what they are for" to "Jones is misusing his teeth"? That is one of its virtues. However, the more decisive second objection to the classical analysis is the existence of clear counter-examples—counter-examples that turn out, on reflection, to be connected to the first objection. An accidentally incurred heart lesion might be necessary for the heart's pumping blood if it is otherwise diseased; but the lesion is not *for* pumping blood. A patient's heartbeat might be the only way his doctor can diagnose a disease that would be fatal if undiagnosed; but the beat of his heart is not *for* diagnosis. Such cases suggest that the classical analysis pays insufficient attention to how structures come to be in organisms and why they persist in reproductive cohorts. In light of this, a more adequate explication of "S is for F in O" runs:

(i) S conduces to F in O,

(ii) O's being F is necessary for the maintenance of O or O's genetic cohort, and

(iii) (i) and (ii) are part of the causal explanation of the existence or persistence of S in O and member's of O's genetic cohort (see [5], sec. 23; [15]; and esp. [33]).

In rougher and plainer English: an organ is for a given activity if the organ's performing that activity helps its host or organisms suitably related to its host, *and* if this contribution is how the organ got and stays where it is. This disqualifies the fortuitous heart lesion and the symptomatic heartbeat, which did not arise or persist by increasing (inclusive) fitness. This definition also distinguishes what something is for from what it may be *used* for on some occasion. Teeth are for chewing—we have teeth because their use in chewing favored the survival of organisms with teeth—whereas Jones is using his teeth for ornamentation.

Counter-examples to this explication have appeared in the literature, but none administer more than superficial wounds. What if S's being F once was,

but is no longer, necessary? What if, for example, implanting semen in the vagina is no longer necessary for propagation because of artificial insemination? The overall shape of my reply will become clearer only a bit later on, but, roughly speaking, if S is for F in O in my sense, O will find the use of S to F reinforcing. This is the point behind the popular observation that whatever modern society is like, humans still carry a heritage of traits evolved by lower mammals and by their tenure as hunter-gatherers. Anyway, such evolutionary lags tend to be unstable. For example, elaborate but clumsy plumage *for* mating displays would likely disappear from a population of birds whose mating was controlled by human breeders uninterested in bright feathers. After, say, 1000 generations, all surviving structures would be used for what, *per* my definition, they *are* for.

Notice that my definition refers to an organism's "genetic cohort" rather than its species. Dawkins [6] and others have argued that species-selection does not actually occur in nature. Taking the natural unit of replication, the "gene," as whatever bit of chromosome can retain its identity through enough generations to matter, a gene will most fecundly copy itself if either the organism that contains it, or organisms with a good chance of containing it—relatives of the gene's organism—reproduce prolifically. A gene is not helping itself reproduce if it instructs the body housing it to assist unrelated members of that body's species; it helps itself reproduce by instructing the body housing it to assist the organisms that might have reproducible copies of itself. So natural selection selects for "inclusive fitness": for traits that benefit an organism taken together with some group of relatives (see [31], 343). How wide the group should be is a matter of some debate, and will indeed be different for different kinds of organisms. Nor has species-selection lost all its defenders. For this reason, I am using "genetic cohort" to name whatever degree of relatedness turns out to be most appropriate for evolutionary theory.

One might well ask how my analysis of "function" can be what people meant before Darwin was ever heard of, even if people did have some inchoate notion of "minimum chain of emplacement" in mind. Doesn't "function" inherently refer to someone with a purpose—or, if not, what is simply de facto beneficial to organisms? No. What happened, I believe, was that before Darwin people thought that the only way S's aptness for F could cause S's existence was for someone, namely God, to notice that S is apt for F and for this reason choose to put S in O. We now know this is false; we now know of another way S's aptness for F can result in S's implantation—mutational emergence and subsequent natural selection. The core meaning of "function" was always (i)–(iii), the idea that God put organs in organisms being merely a theory about how (iii) was or had to be realized. This theory was so "obvious," however, that it appeared to be part of the meaning of "function" itself. Perhaps in concession to our ancestor's ignorance of causes, "reproductive" ought to replace "genetic" in (iii); beyond that, the present definition does capture what people meant by "function" even before Darwin was ever heard of.

Within a Darwinian setting, the function of bodily parts can be linked to normative notions in a way that imputes no extrinsic direction to evolution. The empirical sense coaxed from "S is for F in O" explains our intuition that, since their efficacy in chewing got them selected in, teeth are for masticating and Jones is preventing his teeth from doing their proper job. To begin, it is clear that "Man has teeth because teeth grind food" cannot mean that the power of teeth to grind food is literally what provided Jones or anyone else with teeth. Causal powers aren't causes, and anyway the causal powers an object would have can hardly be what brings the object into existence. Rather, the presence or persistence of S in O's cohort is better understood in more general evolutionary terms. Genetic mutation brought forth the first S in one of our ancestors. There is a mechanism, the coding of the DNA, that transmits S. Here is where S's causal powers come in. Possession of S aided its first possessor and his cohorts in the struggle for survival, and since S is transmissible, this initial possessor survived to transmit S to his descendants, who, in turn, were better fitted than their S-less competitors to reproduce and transmit S . . . We, the descendants of S's original possessors, possess S as a result of this filtration. And it is just here that a eudaimonistic normative link begins to appear.

Consider this first-approximation guess about one of the mechanisms of natural selection. Imagine for a moment that S is for F in the sense explained, and that exercise of S does not lie wholly within the province of O's autonomic nervous system. It is, loosely speaking, up to O whether to use S, or use S for F. Imagine as well two subpopulations O_1 and O_2. Members of O_1 enjoy using S to F, while members of O_2 do not. Since O_2's do not enjoy using S to F, they will use S to F less frequently than do O_1's. Since S favors the survival of possessors of S precisely because S conduces to F, it is the members of O_1 who are more likely to reproduce themselves and transmit, in addition to S, a desire to use S to F. It is thus likely that present-day O's will enjoy using S to F, because they are more probably descendants of the O_1 than of the O_2. Nature is interested in making its creatures like what is (inclusively) good for them. A creature that does not enjoy using its teeth for chewing uses them less than does a toothed competitor who enjoys chewing. Since the use of teeth for chewing favors the survival of an individual with teeth, and, other things being equal, traits favorable to the survival of individuals favor survival of the relevant cohort, toothed creatures who do not enjoy chewing tend to get selected out. We today are the filtrate of this process, descendants of creatures who liked to chew.

To be sure, the best evolutionary strategy might be a mix of O_1-ness and O_2-ness, so that the filtrate of evolution will be creatures with alleles for enjoying, and alleles for not enjoying, the use of S. Constant use of S might be too much of a good thing. The filtrate would be a population mixing O_1's and O_2's. We will consider in due course whether this model is applicable to homosexuality. But even in its simplified form, the present analysis does suggest that a gene for enjoying the use of S to F would at least tend to spread rapidly through O. It is hard to imagine how the enjoyment of the use of such things as human teeth could not take over, and there seems to be no current benefit associated with the absence of this enjoyment. And here—to return to the main strand of the argument—is why it is advisable to use your organs for what they are for: you will enjoy it. Jones's behavior is ill-advised not only because of the avertible objective consequences of his defanging himself, but because he will feel that something is missing. Similarly, this is why you should exercise. It is not just that muscles are for running. We have already heard the sceptic's reply to that: "So what? Suppose I don't mind being flabby? Suppose I don't give a hang about what will propagate my genetic cohort?" Rather, running is good because nature made sure people like to run. This is, of course, the prudential "good," not the moral "good"—but I disavowed at the outset the doctrine that misuse of bodily parts is *morally* bad, at least in any narrow sense. You ought to run because running was once necessary for catching food: creatures who did not enjoy running, if there ever were any, caught less food and reproduced less frequently than competitors who enjoyed running. These competitors passed on their appetites along with their muscles *to you.* This is not to say that those who suffer the affective consequences of laziness must recognize them as such, or even be able to identify them against their general background feeling-tone. They may not realize they would feel better if they exercised. They may even doubt it. They may have allowed their muscles to deteriorate beyond the point at which satisfying exercise is possible. For all that, evolution has decreed that a life involving regular exercise is on the whole more enjoyable than a life without. The same holds for every activity that is the purpose of an organ.

My loose talk of "enjoyment" can be tightened by appeal to the notion of reinforcement. Psychologists define "R is a reinforcer or reward" as: "R makes more probable the repetition of any behavior R follows." Contrary to a surprisingly wide misconception, this definition allows internal states to be rewards, even unconditioned rewards. We can say that organism O enjoys emitting behavior B without explicitly appealing to O's feeling-tone by saying that O's emission of B puts O in a rewarding internal state. In these terms, my general evolutionary hypothesis holds that nature tends to make rewarding behavior that favors cohort survival, and to make unrewarding behavior that does not. More specifically, it holds that if S is for F, using S to F will be rewarding, while using S for something incompatible with F will be unrewarding. I should add that this standard definition of "reinforcer" does not trivialize the law of effect—the law that the probability of behavior

increases as it is reinforced. What saves the law, in its usual uses, is some antecedent and independent specification of what in fact is reinforcing.

Positing an inherited tendency to find the use of S for F rewarding coheres well with the present evolutionary hypothesis. It may not be clear how so nebulous a state as enjoyment can be transmitted, but prospects for a transmission mechanism are improved by replacing talk of enjoyment with talk of an as-yet unidentified internal state that increases the probability of behavior it follows. Even if the internal state itself is nonphysical, its presence is doubtless correlated with some physical state, and it is easy to imagine DNA instructions for building a nervous system that lapses into the physical correlate of the reinforcing state when some selected behavior is emitted. It is these instructions that transmit "a tendency to enjoy" the behavior. Indeed, its genes would "tell" an organism to emit some bit of behavior by so constructing it that emission of the behavior would be followed by the reinforcing state. It becomes nearly, but not quite fatally, analytic that, if using S to F increases fitness, cohorts or strains that are reinforced by using S to F are more likely to survive, and produce offspring that produce offspring. Finally, construing enjoyment behaviorally renders more natural the idea that one may not know that one's sense of well-being is being impaired by failure to perform certain actions. It is a commonplace that an organism need not be consciously aware of what is reinforcing it, and this holds for internal and external, conditioned and unconditioned rewards. An internal state can be reinforcing even if its subject fails to discriminate it against a general affective background, or to notice its absence.

These speculations are much in the spirit of Barash's, especially if one recalls that by the fitness of an organism Barash means the relative number of copies of that organism's genotype that appear in the next generation:

> Just as we find sugar sweet, we find certain behavior to be sweet as well. This means that, at least in part because of evolution's handiwork, we are inclined to do certain things rather than others, and it should be no surprise that in general our inclinations are those that contribute to our fitness. ([1], 39)

Put this way, it is surprising that anyone denies that evolution can shape behavior, even "social" behavior. We are all sociobiologists. Obviously, physical structures like hearts and earlobes are selected in. But physical structures do things. The line between structure and behavior is further blurred by the heritability of time-dependent phenomena. Stainislaw Ulam reports in his autobiography that John von Neumann's two-year-old grandson, who had never seen his grandfather, had von Neumann's distinctive walk. And who can draw a fixed line between simple patterns of behavior like a characteristic gait, and complex patterns of behavior like altruism? And who will draw a sharp line between either kind of behavior, and physical structure?

3. APPLICATIONS TO HOMOSEXUALITY

The application of this general picture to homosexuality should be obvious. There can be no reasonable doubt that one of the functions of the penis is to introduce semen into the vagina. It does this, and it has been selected in because it does this. (Sexual intercourse itself can probably be explained by the evolutionary value of bisexual reproduction. For $n > 2$, n-sexual reproduction would increase genetic variety at the cost of hardly ever occurring: (see e.g., [3].) The advantages accruing to relatively motile gametes seems to account for the emergence of bisexual reproduction itself.) Nature has consequently made this use of the penis rewarding. It is clear enough that any proto-human males who found unrewarding the insertion of penis into vagina have left no descendants. In particular, proto-human males who enjoyed inserting their penises into each other's anuses have left no descendants. This is why homosexuality is abnormal, and why its abnormality counts prudentially against it. Homosexuality is likely to cause unhappiness because it leaves unfulfilled an innate and innately rewarding desire. And should the reader's environmentalism threaten to get the upper hand, let me remind him again of an unproblematic case. Lack of exercise is bad and even abnormal not only because it is unhealthy but also because one feels poorly without regular exercise. Nature made exercise rewarding because, until recently, we had to exercise to survive. Creatures who found running after game unrewarding were eliminated. Laziness leaves unreaped the rewards nature has planted in exercise, even if the lazy man cannot tell this introspectively. If this is a correct description of the place of exercise in human life, it is by the same token a correct description of the place of heterosexuality.

It hardly needs saying, but perhaps I should say it anyway, that this argument concerns tendencies and probabilities. Generalizations about human affairs being notoriously "true by and large and for the most part" only, saying that homosexuals are bound to be less happy than heterosexuals must be understood as short for "Not coincidentally, a larger proportion of homosexuals will be unhappy than a corresponding selection of the heterosexual population." There are, after all, genuinely jolly fat men. To say that laziness leads to adverse affective consequences means that, because of our evolutionary history, the odds are relatively good that a man who takes no exercise will suffer adverse affective consequences. Obviously, some people will get away with misusing their bodily parts. Thus, when evaluating the empirical evidence that bears on this account, it will be pointless to cite cases of well-adjusted homosexuals. I do not say they are non-existent; my claim is that, of biological necessity, they are rare.

My argument might seem to show at most that heterosexual behavior is (self-) reinforcing, not that homosexuality is self-extinguishing—that homosexuals go without the built-in rewards of heterosexuality, but not that homosexuality has a built-in punishment. This distinction, however, is merely verbal. They are two different ways of saying that homosexuals will find their lives less rewarding than will heterosexuals. Even if some line demarcated happiness from unhappiness absolutely, it would be irrelevant if homosexuals were all happily above the line. It is the comparison with the heterosexual life that is at issue. A lazy man might count as happy by some mythic absolute standard, but he is likely to be less happy than someone otherwise like him who exercises.

Another objection to my argument, or conjectural evolutionary scenario, is that heterosexuality might have been selected in not because it favors survival, but as a by-product of some other inclusively fit structure or behavior. A related suggestion is that what really has been selected in is some blend of dominant heterosexual and recessive homosexual genes. As for the former, it seems extraordinarily unlikely, given how long life has reproduced itself by sexual intercourse, that the apparently self-reinforcing character of heterosexuality is a by-product of some other fitness-enhancing trait. If heterosexual intercourse is not *directly* connected to propagation, what is? Biologists have no trouble determining when bird plumage is there to attract mates, and hence favors survival. It would be astounding if the same could not be said for heterosexual intercourse.

The sophisticate might complain that I am not giving "by-product" hypotheses their due. And indeed at this point sociobiological hypotheses come thick and fast. I will be discussing some others later in this paper, and making some overall observations about sociobiology and homosexuality. Here it is appropriate to examine one hypothesis of the "by-product" school, that of Hutchinson (see [13]). Fact: there can be recessive genes for a trait that inhibits the reproduction of and even kills organisms which exhibit it, but which, when co-occurring with the dominant trait-suppressing allele, give rise to an organism or phenotype more inclusively fit than a comparable organism with two of the dominant alleles. In such cases, the "bad" allele will be passed along in fit heterozygous organisms and its associated trait will occasionally surface. For example, sickle-cell anemia persists because the heterozygote Cc (Non-sickle-cell C, sickle-cell c) confers resistance to malaria. Perhaps a recessive gene predisposing to homosexuality persists in this way. Organisms of genotype Hh—a dominant allele H for heterosexuality, a recessive allele h for homosexuality—might be most fit, and then of course organisms with hh genotype will surface with some regularity.

Without even considering the empirical likelihood of this elegant hypothesis, it is clearly consistent with my chief claim. For as it stands it represents sickle-cell anemia and the perpetuation of the c allele as *unfortunate by-products* of a process that selects in resistance to malaria; and, presumably, the same

would go for homosexuality. For what does it mean to say that sickle-cell anemia is a by-product? Precisely this: had immunity to malaria not been associated with the Cc genotype, the "gene" for malarial immunity would have been selected in anyway; however, had the Cc genotype and hence sickle-cell anemia not been associated with malarial immunity or some other inclusive-fitness-enhancing trait, the c allele would have disappeared. Recurring to our definition of "function," the cause of the persistence of the c allele and the Cc genotype, what that genotype is for, is fending off malaria. Sickle-cell anemia is a maladaptive by-product of the Cc genotype since, had it not been associated with what is in fact the function of the Cc genotype, sickle-cell anemia would have caused the disappearance of the Cc genotype. Nothing, not even the c allele, has sickle-cell anemia as its function. The key question, of course, is whether a maladaptive by-product, so understood, is reinforcing. On the present model, it is not. For suppose sickle-cell anemia could be contracted voluntarily, and there were a gene which (a) made contracting or becoming vulnerable to it reinforcing, but (b) was not connected with malarial immunity. A strain with the tastes this gene confers would soon be selected out. Therefore, surviving humans who get sickle-cell anemia do not find it in any way reinforcing. So the "heterozygote fitness" hypothesis (and the kin-selection hypothesis: see below) predict, consistently with my view, that homosexuality is associated with unhappiness; and, conversely, wide-spread homosexual unhappiness would confirm that homosexuality is a maladaptive by-product.

An important methodological corollary of this discussion is that a trait or tendency may be "in the genes" but still be abnormal. It is normal only if it is in the genes because it itself enhances fitness, not because it is associated with something else that enhances fitness on independent grounds. Sickle-cell anemia is a malfunction of its victims' blood, which was selected in to oxygenate the muscles. A comparable story for homosexuality would involve a gene that instructed its organism to make just a little testosterone. This might have survival value by raising phenotypic verbal sensitivity, and perhaps low testosterone is the only way nature has figured out to secure this inclusively fit trait. Suppose, too, that a disposition to homosexuality was a causal consequence, a by-product, of low testosterone—but not so disadvantageous a by-product that the gene was selected out. Homosexuality would then be a necessary condition for advantageous verbal ability, but it would not follow that homosexuality was selected in because it conduced to verbal ability, or for any other reason. It would not follow that homosexuality is the least reinforcing. Unhappy homosexuals might be the price nature pays for verbal ability, homosexuality being no more a cause of verbal ability than sickle-cell anemia is a cause of malarial resistance.

Talk of what is "in the genes" inevitably provokes the observation that we should not blame homosexuals for their homosexuality if it is "in their genes." True enough. Indeed, since nobody decides what he is going to find sexually arousing, the moral appraisal of sexual object "choice" is entirely absurd. However, so saying is quite consistent with regarding homosexuality as a misfortune, and taking steps—this being within the realm of the will—to minimize its incidence, especially among children. Calling homosexuality involuntary does not place it outside the scope of evaluation. Victims of sickle-cell anemia are not blameworthy, but it is absurd to pretend that there is nothing wrong with them. Homosexual activists are partial to genetic explanations and hostile to Freudian environmentalism in part because they see a genetic cause as exempting homosexuals from blame. But surely people are equally blameless for indelible traits acquired in early childhood. And anyway, a blameless condition may still be worth trying to prevent. (Defenders of homosexuality fear Freud at another level, because his account removes homosexuality from the biological realm altogether and deprives it of whatever legitimacy adheres to what is "in the genes.")

My sociobiological scenario also finds no place for the fashionable remark that homosexuality has become fitness-enhancing in our supposedly overpopulated world. Homosexuality is said to increase our species' chances by easing the population pressure. This observation, however correct, is irrelevant. Even if homosexuality has lately come to favor species survival, this is no part of how homosexuality

is created. Salvation of the human species would be at best a fortuitous by-product of behavior having other causes. It is not easy, moreover, to see how this feature of homosexuality could get it selected in. If homosexuality enhances inclusive fitness precisely because homosexuals don't reproduce, the tendency to homosexuality cannot get selected for by a filtering process when it is passed to the next generation—it doesn't get passed to the next generation at all. The same applies, of course, to any tendency to find homosexuality rewarding.

The whole matter of the survival advantage of homosexuality is in any case beside the point. Our organs have the functions and rewards they do because of the way the world was, and what favored survival, many millions of years ago. *Then,* homosexuality decreased fitness and heterosexuality increased it; an innate tendency to homosexuality would have gotten selected out if anything did. We today have the tendencies transmitted to us by those other ancestors, whether or not the race is going to pay a price for this. That 50 years ago certain self-reinforcing behavior began to threaten the race's future is quite consistent with the behavior remaining self-reinforcing. Similarly, widespread obesity and the patent enjoyment many people experience in gorging themselves just show that our appetites were shaped in conditions of food scarcity under which gorging oneself when one had the chance was good policy. Anyway, the instability created by abundance is, presumably, temporary. If the current abundance continues for 5,000 generations, natural gluttons will almost certainly disappear through early heart disease and unattractiveness to the opposite sex. The ways in which the populous human herd will be trimmed is best left to speculation.

I should also note that nothing I have said shows bisexuality or sheer polymorphous sexuality to be unnatural or self-punishing. One might cite the Greeks to show that only exclusive homosexuality conflicts with our evolved reinforcement mechanism. But in point of fact bisexuality seems to be a quite rare phenomenon—and animals, who receive no cultural conditioning, seem instinctively heterosexual in the vast majority of cases. Clinicians evidently agree that it is possible for a person to be homosexual at one period of his life and heterosexual at another, but not at the same time. Some statistics in [4] confirm this. 18% of the male homosexuals interviewed had been married; while 90% reported having intercourse with their wives during the first year of marriage, 72% reported having homosexual fantasies during intercourse, and 33% reported this "often" ([4], tables 17.1–17.7). So only 4.5% of the sample had "reciprocal" heterosexual intercourse. This coheres well with table 22.4 in [4], which indicates that roughly 95% of male homosexuals in the Bell-Weinberg sample were "exclusively homosexual." But one mustn't move too quickly or dogmatically here. On the face of it, telling its host body "Put your penis in any reasonably small, moist opening" is a sufficiently adaptive gene strategy to ensconce a gene that follows it in the gene pool. A body controlled by such a gene would reproduce itself and hence the gene often enough. The flaw in the plan is that a competitor gene might evolve to tell its body: "Put your penis only in vaginas, i.e., moist openings with a certain feel and which are accompanied by such visual clues as breasts and wide hips." The second gene would reproduce itself even more often and—waiving by-products—would eventually displace the first. But our bisexual gene isn't finished. It might evolve the following strategy: "Body, insert your penis in vaginas most of the time, but insert your penis in male anuses frequently enough to keep other males, who are competing with you for females, occupied." A body with such a gene could keep a harem pregnant. A male who put other males out of commission for n hours by stimulating them to orgasm might himself seem vulnerable to exhausting himself, but he can avoid this by refraining from orgasm during homosexual acts. The fly in *this* ointment is the counter-strategy that purely heterosexual genes could evolve: "Avoid erect penises heading for your anus." If even one such gene appeared in a population of bisexuals it would reproduce itself a little more readily, since it would never waste time spiking the guns of its competitors.

By now we are lost in speculation. There is no way to disprove the existence of a hardy bisexual gene, or to prove that heterosexual counter-measures always evolved. It is *possible,* but not likely and not sug-gested by anything currently known, that a bisexual gene has achieved stable existence in the human gene pool. It is also quite unlikely, on equivalent analytical grounds and the virtual nonexistence of polymorphous animal sexuality in the wild, that males are primed only for an undifferentiated enjoyment of sex that is shaped by culture into heterosexuality.

Utilitarians must take the present evolutionary scenario seriously. The utilitarian attitude toward homosexuality usually runs something like this even if homosexuality is in some sense unnatural, as a matter of brute fact homosexuals take pleasure in sexual contact with members of the same sex. As long as they don't hurt anyone else, homosexuality is as great a good as heterosexuality. But the matter cannot end here. Not even a utilitarian doctor would have words of praise for a degenerative disease that happened to foster a certain kind of pleasure (as sore muscles uniquely conduce to the pleasure of stretching them). A utilitarian doctor would presumably try just as zealously to cure diseases that feel good as less pleasant degenerative diseases. A pleasure causally connected with great distress cannot be treated as just another pleasure to be toted up on the felicific scoreboard. Utilitarians have to reckon with the inevitable consequences of pain-causing pleasure.

Similar remarks apply to the question of whether homosexuality is a "disease." A widely-quoted pronouncement of the American Psychiatric Association runs:

> Surely the time has come for psychiatry to give up the archaic practice of classifying the millions of men and women who accept or prefer homosexual object choices as being, by virtue of that fact alone, mentally ill. The fact that their alternative life-style happens to be out of favor with current cultural conventions must not be a basis in itself for a diagnosis.

Apart from some question-begging turns of phrase, this is right. One's taste for mutual anal intercourse is nothing "in itself" for one's psychiatrist to worry about, any more than a life of indolence is anything "in itself" for one's doctor to worry about. In fact, in itself there is nothing wrong with a broken arm or an occluded artery. The fact that my right ulna is now in two pieces is just a fact of nature, not a "basis for diagnosis." But this condition is a matter for medical science anyway, because it will lead to pain. Permitted to persist, my fracture will provoke increasingly punishing states. So if homosexuality is a reliable sign of present or future misery, it is beside the point that homosexuality is not "by virtue of that fact alone" a mental illness. High rates of drug addiction, divorce and illegitimacy are in themselves no basis for diagnosing social pathology. They support this diagnosis because of what else they signify about a society which exhibits them. Part of the problem here is the presence of germs in paradigm diseases, and the lack of a germ for homosexuality (or psychosis). I myself am fairly sure that a suitably general and germfree definition of "disease" can be extruded from the general notion of "function" exhibited in Section 2, but however that may be, whether homosexuality is a disease is a largely verbal issue. If homosexuality is a self-punishing maladaptation, it hardly matters what it is called.

4. Evidence and Further Clarification

I have argued that homosexuality is "abnormal" in both a descriptive and a normative sense because—for evolutionary reasons—homosexuals are bound to be unhappy. In Kantian terms, I have explained how it is possible for homosexuality to be unnatural even if it violates no cosmic purpose or such purposes as we retrospectively impose on nature. What is the evidence for my view? For one thing, by emphasizing homosexual unhappiness, my view explains a ubiquitous fact in a simple way. The fact is the universally acknowledged unhappiness of homosexuals. Even the staunchest defenders of homosexuality admit that, as of now, homosexuals are not happy. A conspicuous exception to this is [4], which has been widely taken to show that homosexuals can be just as happy as heterosexuals. A look at their statistics tells a different story—an impor-tant matter I have dealt with in some detail in the Appendix.

The usual environmentalist explanation for homosexuals' unhappiness is the misunderstanding, contempt and abuse that society heaps on them. But this not only leaves unexplained why society has this attitude, it sins against parsimony by explaining a nearly universal phenomenon in terms of variable circumstances that have, by coincidence, the same upshot. Parsimony urges that we seek the explanation of homosexual unhappiness in the nature of homosexuality itself, as my explanation does. Having to "stay in the closet" may be a great strain, but it does not account for all the miseries that writers on homosexuality say is the homosexual's lot.

Incorporating unhappiness into the present evolutionary picture also smooths a bothersome ad-hocness in some otherwise appealing analyses of abnormality. Many writers define abnormality as compulsiveness. On this conception, homosexuality is abnormal because it is an autonomy-obstructing compulsion. Such an analysis is obviously open to the question, What if an autonomous homosexual comes along? To that, writers like van den Haag point out that homosexuality is, in fact, highly correlated with compulsiveness. The trouble here is that the definition in question sheds no light on why abnormal, compulsive, traits are such. The present account not only provides a criterion for abnormality, it encapsulates an explanation of *why* behavior abnormal by its lights is indeed compulsive and bound to lead to unhappiness.

One crucial test of my account is its prediction that homosexuals will continue to be unhappy even if people altogether abandon their "prejudice" against homosexuality. This prediction, that homosexuality being unnatural homosexuals will still find their behavior self-punishing, coheres with available evidence. It is consistent with the failure of other oppressed groups, such as American Negroes and European Jews, to become warped in the direction of "cruising," sado-masochism and other practices common in homosexual life (see [19]). It is consistent as well with the admission by even so sympathetic an observer of homosexuality as Rechy ([23]) that the immediate cause of homosexual unhappiness is a taste for promiscuity, anonymous encounters, and humiliation. It is hard to see how such tastes are related to the dim view society takes of them. Such a relation would be plausible only if homosexuals courted multiple anonymous encounters *faute de mieux,* longing all the while to settle down to some sort of domesticity. But, again, Europeans abhorred Jews for centuries, but this did not create in Jews a special weakness for anonymous, promiscuous sex. Whatever drives a man away from women, to be fellated by as many different men as possible, seems independent of what society thinks of such behavior. It is this behavior that occasions misery, and we may expect the misery of homosexuals to continue.

In a 1974 study, Weinberg and Williams ([29]) found no difference in the distress experienced by homosexuals in Denmark and the Netherlands, and in the U.S., where they found public tolerance of homosexuality to be lower. This would confirm rather strikingly that homosexual unhappiness is endogenous, unless one says that Weinberg's and Williams's indices for public tolerance and distress—chiefly homosexuals' self-reports of "unhappiness" and "lack of faith in others"—are unreliable. Such complaints, however, push the social causation theory toward untestability. Weinberg and Williams themselves cleave to the hypothesis that homosexual unhappiness is entirely a reaction to society's attitudes, and suggest that a condition of homosexual happiness is positive endorsement by the surrounding society. It is hard to imagine a more flagrantly *ad hoc* hypothesis. Neither a Catholic living among Protestants nor a copywriter working on the great American novel in his off hours asks more of society than tolerance in order to be happy in his pursuits.

It is interesting to reflect on a natural experiment that has gotten under way in the decade since the Weinberg-Williams study. A remarkable change in public opinion, if not private sentiment, has occurred in America. For whatever reason—the prodding of homosexual activists, the desire not to seem like a fuddy-duddy—various organs of opinion are now hard at work providing a "positive image" for homosexuals. Judges allow homosexuals to adopt their lovers. The Unitarian Church now performs homosexual marriages. Hollywood produces highly sanitized movies like *Making Love* and *Personal Best* about homosexuality. Macmillan strongly urges its authors to show little boys using cosmetics. Homosexuals no

longer fear revealing themselves, as is shown by the prevalence of the "clone look." Certain products run advertising obviously directed at the homosexual market. On the societal reaction theory, there ought to be an enormous rise in homosexual happiness. I know of no systematic study to determine if this is so, but anecdotal evidence suggests it may not be. The homosexual press has been just as strident in denouncing pro-homosexual movies as in denouncing Doris Day movies. Especially virulent venereal diseases have very recently appeared in homosexual communities, evidently spread in epidemic proportions by unabating homosexual promiscuity. One selling point for a presumably serious "gay rights" rally in Washington D.C. was an "all-night disco train" from New York to Washington. What is perhaps most salient is that, even if the changed public mood results in decreased homosexual unhappiness, the question remains of why homosexuals in the recent past, who suffered greatly for being homosexuals, persisted in being homosexuals.

But does not my position also predict—contrary to fact—that any sexual activity not aimed at procreation or at least sexual intercourse leads to unhappiness? First, I am not sure this conclusion is contrary to the facts properly understood. It is universally recognized that, for humans and the higher animals, sex is more than the insertion of the penis into the vagina. Foreplay is necessary to prepare the female and, to a lesser extent, the male. Ethologists have studied the elaborate mating rituals of even relatively simple animals. Sexual intercourse must therefore be understood to include the kisses and caresses that necessarily precede copulation, behaviors that nature has made rewarding. What my view does predict is that exclusive preoccupation with behaviors normally preparatory for intercourse is highly correlated with unhappiness. And, so far as I know, psychologists do agree that such preoccupation or "fixation" with, e.g., cunnilingus, is associated with personality traits independently recognized as disorders. In this sense, sexual intercourse really is virtually necessary for well-being. Only if one is antecedently convinced that "nothing is more natural than anything else" will one confound foreplay as a prelude to intercourse with "foreplay" that leads nowhere at all. One might speculate on the evolutionary advantages of fore-play, at least for humans: by increasing the intensity and complexity of the pleasures of intercourse, it binds the partners more firmly and makes them more fit for child-rearing. In fact, such analyses of sexual perversion as Nagel's ([22]), which correctly focus on the interruption of mutuality as central to perversion, go wrong by ignoring the evolutionary role and built-in rewards of mutuality. They fail to explain why the interruption of mutuality is disturbing.

It should also be clear that my argument permits gradations in abnormality. Behavior is the more abnormal, and the less likely to be rewarding, the more its emission tends to extinguish a genetic cohort that practices it. The less likely a behavior is to get selected out, the less abnormal it is. Those of our ancestors who found certain aspects of fore-play reinforcing might have managed to reproduce themselves sufficiently to implant this strain in us. There might be an equilibrium between intercourse and such not directly reproductive behavior. It is not required that any behavior not directly linked to heterosexual intercourse lead to maximum dissatisfaction. But the existence of these gradations provides no entering wedge for homosexuality. As no behavior is more likely to get selected out than rewarding homosexuality—except perhaps an innate tendency to suicide at the onset of puberty—it is extremely unlikely that homosexuality can now be unconditionally reinforcing in humans to any extent.

Nor does my position predict, again contrary to fact, that celibate priests will be unhappy. My view is compatible with the existence of happy celibates who deny themselves as part of a higher calling which yields compensating satisfactions. Indeed, the very fact that one needs to explain how the priesthood can compensate for the lack of family means that people do regard heterosexual mating as the natural or "inertial" state of human relations. The comparison between priests and homosexuals is in any case inapt. Priests do not simply give up sexual activity without ill-effect; they give it up for a reason. Homosexuals have hardly given up the use of their sexual organs, for a higher calling or anything else. Homosexuals continue to use them, but, unlike priests, they use them for what they are not for.

I have encountered the thought that by my lights female heterosexuality must be abnormal, since according to feminism women have been unhappy down the ages. The datum is questionable, to say the least. Feminists have offered no documentation whatever for this extravagant claim; their evidence is usually the unhappiness of the feminist in question and her circle of friends. Such attempts to prove female discontent in past centuries as [11] are transparently anachronistic projections of contemporary feminist discontent onto inappropriate historical objects. An objection from a similar source runs that my argument, suitably extended, implies the naturalness and hence rewardingness of traditional monogamous marriage. Once again, instead of seeing this as a *reductio,* I am inclined to take the supposed absurdity as a truth that nicely fits my theory. It is not a theoretical contention but an observable fact that women enjoy motherhood, that failure to bear and care for children breeds unhappiness in women, and that the role of "primary caretaker" is much more important for women than men. However, there is no need to be dogmatic. This conception of the family is in extreme disrepute in contemporary America. Many women work and many marriages last less than a decade. Here we have another natural experiment about what people find reinforcing. My view predicts that women will on the whole become unhappier if current trends continue. Let us see. . . .

5. Sociobiology Again

Several sociobiological hypotheses are currently under discussion about the possible function of a "gene for homosexuality," and how this function might have lodged such a gene in the human gene pool. We looked in an earlier section at Hutchinson's "by-product" hypothesis and will return to it. In this section I want to make a general point about current sociobiological speculation and homosexuality, and it will be helpful to examine briefly another hypothesis: "kin selection." This hypothesis stresses that a gene is fit if it copies itself in the next generation, even if not through the organism that houses it. We all recognize the adaptive advantages in a mother's self-sacrifice for her brood; the same holds for a brother's regard for his siblings. So, the hypothesis goes, homosexuality's reproductive costs may be more than balanced by the aid a homosexual gives his close genetic cohort. Homosexuality in one offspring might mean more fecund siblings who have a good chance of carrying the "homosexual gene" (see [31], [32]). Testing this hypothesis would obviously be very difficult, requiring complete data on the relative fecundity of humans with homosexual siblings, nephews, etc., and a detailed and plausible mechanism to explain how an individual's homosexuality contributes to his cohort's fecundity. (Such demographic data would also be pertinent to the Freudian theory, which stresses the overbearing love of the homosexual's mother. A prediction of this theory would seem to be that homosexuality is higher among only children, and decreases as the number of siblings and birth-order increases.) No sociobiologist claims to have such data, and I know of no conjectures about the mechanism. The data of the last section and the appendix suggests that no such mechanism exists because homosexuality serves no inclusively adaptive function.

Where that leaves us is in the following position. Most of the sociobiological speculation about homosexuality known to me—particularly the influential writings of Wilson—simply *assumes* that homosexuality serves a function which accounts for its retention in the human population. Sociobiologists thus see their theoretical task as discovering what this function is. So far as I can tell, they rest this assumption on a single datum: Kinsey's finding that over 10% of the U.S. male population reported itself to be homosexual, by a reasonably strict criterion of homosexuality. Thus Wilson reasons (see [32], 143): given its sheer prevalence, homosexuality must be serving some fitness-enhancing purpose. My central point, in reply, is that there is not a single reason beyond this to think that homosexuality increases fitness or serves any purpose at all. The sociobiological models I've mentioned come into play only if we *already know* that homosexuality enhances fitness.

Kinsey aside, we have no reason to think this, so the sociobiological hypotheses—kin-selection, parental manipulation and superior heterozygote fitness—currently stand as explanations in search of something to explain.

Still, there are the Kinsey data and certain twin studies which suggest some genetic component to homosexuality. What the latter would mean is, precisely, that there can be two males brought up in the same environment such that one becomes a homosexual and the other does not. However, as I noted in an earlier section, a giant chasm separates the existence of a genetic contribution to homosexuality and the existence of a function that homosexuality serves. The point bears amplifying, in terms of the homely example of broken bones. While on the face of it a broken arm seems purely an accident and one wholly caused by environment, at any time a significant proportion of the human race will have broken bones. This might prompt sociologists to think there is a fitness-enhancing gene for broken-bonedness. And in a sense they would be right. People's bones break because, in part, their genes have told the rest of them to hang their muscles on an armature of calcium. Had our genes told the rest of us to make our skeletons out of chrome steel, banging into walls would not break arms. A broken arm is really the result of an environmental cause triggering a genetically determined predisposition.

There is something of truth and something of parody in this account of broken bones. A calcium-based skeleton is adaptively advantageous because calcium is light. But calcium's lightness is inseparable from its softness. The frangibility of bones is genetically coded, but only as a byproduct of an otherwise adaptive process. And it is relatively easy to contrive mechanisms that yield a predisposition to homosexuality in males as a by-product. Low fetal testosterone might be good for organisms. Evolution might never have had to select in genotypes which insure enough testosterone for heterosexuality come what family life may. But this would not mean that homosexuality is for anything or that the gene is for homosexuality, any more than broken arms are for anything. So even a strong form of the kin-selection hypothesis would not mean anything more than a genetic predisposition to homosexuality; the trait thus disposed to need be no more adaptive or reinforcing than the breakability of bones.

6. ON POLICY ISSUES

Homosexuality is intrinsically bad only in a prudential sense. It makes for unhappiness. However, this does not exempt homosexuality from the larger categories of ethics—rights, duties, liabilities. Deontic categories apply to acts which increase or decrease happiness or expose the helpless to the risk of unhappiness.

If homosexuality is unnatural, legislation which raises the odds that a given child will become homosexual raises the odds that he will be unhappy. The only gap in the syllogism is whether legislation which legitimates, endorses or protects homosexuality does increase the chances that a child will become homosexual. If so, such legislation is *prima facie* objectionable. The question is not whether homosexual elementary school teachers will molest their charges. Pro-homosexual legislation might increase the incidence of homosexuality in subtler ways. If it does, and if the protection of children is a fundamental obligation of society, legislation which legitimates homosexuality is a dereliction of duty. I am reluctant to deploy the language of "children's rights," which usually serves as one more excuse to interfere with the prerogatives of parents. But we do have obligations to our children, and one of them is to protect them from harm. If, as some have suggested, children have a right to protection from a religious education, they surely have a right to protection from homosexuality. So protecting them limits somebody else's freedom, but we are often willing to protect quite obscure children's rights at the expense of the freedom of others. There is a movement to ban TV commercials for sugar-coated cereals, to protect children from the relatively trivial harm of tooth decay. Such a ban would restrict the freedom of advertisers, and restrict it even though the last clear chance of avoiding the harm, and thus the responsibility, lies with the parents who control the TV set. I cannot see how one can consistently support such legislation and

also urge homosexual rights, which risk much graver damage to children in exchange for increased freedom for homosexuals. (If homosexual behavior is largely compulsive, it is falsifying the issue to present it as balancing risks to children against the freedom of homosexuals.) The right of a homosexual to work for the Fire Department is not a negligible good. Neither is fostering a legal atmosphere in which as many people as possible grow up heterosexual.

It is commonly asserted that legislation granting homosexuals the privilege or right to be firemen endorses not homosexuality, but an expanded conception of human liberation. It is conjectural how sincerely this can be said in a legal order that forbids employers to hire whom they please and demands hours of paperwork for an interstate shipment of hamburger. But in any case legislation "legalizing homosexuality" cannot be neutral because passing it would have an inexpungeable speech-act dimension. Society cannot grant unaccustomed rights and privileges to homosexuals while remaining neutral about the value of homosexuality. Working from the assumption that society rests on the family and its consequences, the Judaeo-Christian tradition has deemed homosexuality a sin and withheld many privileges from homosexuals. Whether or not such denial was right, for our society to grant these privileges to homosexuals *now* would amount to declaring that it has rethought the matter and decided that homosexuality is not as bad as it had previously supposed. And unless such rethinking is a direct response to new empirical findings about homosexuality, it can only be a revaluing. Someone who suddenly accepts a policy he has previously opposed is open to the same interpretation: he has come to think better of the policy. And if he embraces the policy while knowing that this interpretation will be put on his behavior, and if he knows that others know that he knows they will so interpret it, he is acquiescing in this interpretation. He can be held to have intended, meant, this interpretation. A society that grants privileges to homosexuals while recognizing that, in the light of generally known history, this act can be interpreted as a positive re-evaluation of homosexuality, is signalling that it now thinks homosexuality is all right. Many commentators in the popular press have observed that homosexuals, unlike members of racial minorities, can always "stay in the closet" when applying for jobs. What homosexual rights activists really want, therefore, is not access to jobs but legitimation of their homosexuality. Since this is known, giving them what they want will be seen as conceding their claim to legitimacy. And since legislators know their actions will support this interpretation, and know that their constituencies know they know this, the Gricean effect or symbolic meaning of passing anti-discrimination ordinances is to declare homosexuality legitimate (see [30]).

Legislation permitting frisbees in the park does not imply approval of frisbees for the simple reason that frisbees are new; there is no tradition of banning them from parks. The legislature's action in permitting frisbees is not interpretable, known to be interpretable, and so on, as the reversal of long-standing disapproval. It is because these Gricean conditions are met in the case of abortion that legislation—or rather judicial fiat—permitting abortions and mandating their public funding are widely interpreted as tacit approval. Up to now, society has deemed homosexuality so harmful that restricting it outweighs putative homosexual rights. If society reverses itself, it will in effect be deciding that homosexuality is not as bad as it once thought.

Appendix

The best case for inevitable homosexual unhappiness comes from [4], a study which received much attention when it appeared. As their subtitle suggests, Bell and Weinberg claim to have shown that there is no such thing as homosexuality per se; there are different types of homosexuals, some of whom can be as well-adjusted, on the average, as heterosexuals. Bell and Weinberg admit that demonstrating this was the aim of their study: "We are pleased at the extent to which the aims of our investigation of homosexual men and women have been realized. The tables . . . clearly show that homosexuals are a remarkably diverse group" (217). They always refer to commonly held beliefs about homosexuals as "myths" (15) and "stereotypes" (73), and blame soci-

ety's "homoerotophobia" (188) on the preoccupation of Jews with survival and the Christian Church with sin (149, 195). Working on the principle that a position is seriously weakened if the evidence marshalled by its friends disconfirms it, let us look at the Bell-Weinberg data.

Bell and Weinberg studied 686 San Francisco Bay area male homosexuals (and 293 lesbians, whom I ignore as in the body of the paper). One might question their methods: apart from the nonrandomness of their sample (22), the authors are oddly credulous about their informants' reports. They determined the level of their informants' health, and that of the informants in their heterosexual control group, by simply asking them how their health was (484). Not surprisingly, 87% of the white homosexuals and 91% of the black homosexuals reported that they were in good to excellent health, about the same as for the heterosexuals. But this accords ill with their table 19.2, which shows that 58% of all homosexuals spend 3 or more nights a week out. Common sense agrees with Satchel Paige that the social whirl isn't restful, but in any case the authors use none of the standard objective measures of health—visits to the doctor, use of medication, drugs, average amount of sleep, and the like. This, incidental though it is, warrants scepticism about self-report methodology in a matter like homosexuality.

Of the 206 pages of tables, 3 entries are particularly noteworthy as measures of homosexual unhappiness. The first (337, 339) is that 27% of all homosexuals experience either some or a great deal of regret about being homosexual. Taken with the 24% who experience "very little" regret, this prompts one to ask if only 49% of a random sample of heterosexuals would report no regrets about their heterosexuality. Would 27% of heterosexuals agree or agree strongly that their condition is an emotional disorder? (cf. 339; the control group disappears at this juncture). More strikingly, homosexuals are more than 6 times as likely as heterosexuals to attempt suicide—a criterion of unhappiness independent of the subject's report. The authors try to explain this statistic with an aside to the effect that the suicide rate in San Francisco is very high (211–12), a testimony to their faith in the explanatory power of nonprojectible predicates.

(Perhaps not all philosophers would find this explanation defective. When I asked a well-known social philosopher critical of capital punishment why the murder rate had gone up in states where capital punishment had been abandoned, he said "the crime rate is going up everywhere.") In any case, the heterosexual sample was drawn from the same population, and homosexuals constitute a significant portion of San Francisco's population, so the San Francisco suicide rate is high, in part, because so many homosexuals commit suicide.

Perhaps the most striking trait revealed—or stereotype confirmed—is the extreme impersonality and frequency of homosexual contacts. Roughly speaking, 75% of the respondents reported having had more than 100 sexual partners, and 43% reported having had 500 or more (308). These numbers are not easy to believe. Even taken *cum grano,* they should be compared to the reader's own experience of sex as he tries to imagine what it would be like to move so promiscuously among anonymous encounters—79% of the respondents reported that more than half their partners were strangers. Surely having these many partners is a criterion for maladjustment and compulsivity, a chronic inability to find anyone satisfactory. A harder datum than these numbers is the report that 56% of the respondents usually spend several hours or less with a partner (305); in fact, the authors distinguish "several hours from "all night." Only 2% usually spend as much as a weekend with a partner successfully "cruised." (I interpret this statistic to make it consistent with the amount of "close-coupledness" reported: see below.) Incidentally, the authors say that "the largest numbers of our respondents spent all night with their partners" (77), but this is misleading. 41% of the respondents usually spent all night, and this is the modal number; but, as noted, *most* homosexuals spend considerably less than a whole night with a partner.

What Bell and Weinberg want to emphasize, however, is that their sample tended to cluster around five "types" of homosexual, one of which—the "close-coupled"—seem on the whole to be as well-adjusted as heterosexuals. The finding was duplicated for lesbians. Close-coupled homosexuals are those involved in a sort of marriage, living monogamously

with a partner of the same sex, not cruising, not experiencing any extraordinary amount of "tension" or regret about homosexuality, and displaying much "joy and exuberance in their particular life-style" (231). This, the authors contend, shows that homosexuality "is not necessarily related to pathology" (ibid.).

The existence of close-coupled homosexuals by no means implies that homosexuality is not pathological. As I have noted, there are almost no significant exceptionless generalizations in human affairs. My evolutionary hypothesis implies only that homosexuals are more likely to be unhappy than their heterosexual counterparts. The pertinent questions are, how many "close-coupled" homosexuals are there, and how many homosexuals exhibit "stereotypic" personality disorders? In point of fact, [4] assigns only 67 homosexuals to the "close-coupled" category, less than 10% of the sample. By contrast, 12% fell into the "dysfunctional" category, tormented souls who regret their homosexuality, cruise frequently, and have many sexual partners. An additional 16% were "Asexuals," homosexuals who tend to live alone without lovers or friends, and whose suicide rate is the highest among homosexuals. On the evidence presented, sociopathic homosexuals outnumber well-adjusted ones 2.8 to 1. If one adds to these at least some of the "functionals"—"men and women [who] seem to organize their lives around their sexual experience" (223)—deeply troubled homosexuals outnumber happy ones by at least 3 to 1.

The authors mislead the reader when they say that close-coupled homosexuals are on the average as happy and well-adjusted as heterosexuals. For this is to compare the best-adjusted homosexual subtype with the homogeneous heterosexual control group, and that is special pleading. It would be more appropriate to compare close-coupled homosexuals to happily married men, something Bell and Weinberg admit in passing but for which they offer no statistics. Since a random sample of heterosexuals will include a number of lonely, twisted individuals, the adjustment level of happily "coupled" heterosexuals must be considerably higher than that of the best-adjusted homosexuals. So viewed, monogamous homosexual coupling looks like a vain attempt at marriage—and homosexual cruising looks perhaps like a realization, of sorts, of adolescent male fantasy. "Dysfunctionals and Asexuals have a difficult time of it, but there are certainly equivalent groups among heterosexuals" (231). Certainly. But do such groups make up 28% of all heterosexuals and 41% of all classifiable heterosexuals, as the Dysfunctionals and Asexuals jointly comprise 41% of all classifiable homosexuals in the Bell-Weinberg sample (346, table 13.5)? Moreover, the authors go only so far as to say that close-coupled men "did less cruising" than the homosexual average (132; also see table 13.7, p. 349), leaving the impression that even close-coupled men do sometimes cruise. No quantitative comparisons are offered between such cruising and extra-marital straying for heterosexual males. Table 22.4 shows that 1% of the coupleds cruise at least once a week, but there are no statistics on how many have cruised in, say, the preceding year. Incomplete though it is, this figure should be contrasted with the heterosexual case. It seems unlikely that 1% of the married male readership of this paper had anonymous sexual encounters last week.

Bell and Weinberg's peroration is a textbook example of circular reasoning:

It would appear that homosexual adults who have come to terms with their homosexuality, who do not regret their sexual orientation, and who can function effectively sexually and socially, are no more distressed psychologically than are heterosexual men and women (216).

Obviously, anyone who can "function effectively sexually and socially" will not be especially "distressed psychologically." But even going by the Bell-Weinberg sample drawn from volunteers from the "good scene" (27) of the Bay area, the chances that a homosexual will fall into this category are rather low.

References

[1] Barash, D. *The Whispering Within.* New York: Harper & Row, 1979.

[2] Beach, F. "Cross-Species Comparisons and the Human Heritage." *Archives of Sexual Behavior* 5 (1976): 469–85.

[3] Beadle, G. and M. *The Language of Life.* New York: Anchor, 1967.

[4] Bell, A. and M. Weinberg. *Homosexualities.* New York: Simon and Schuster, 1978.

[5] Bennett, J. *Linguistic Behavior.* Cambridge: Cambridge University Press, 1976.

[6] Dawkins, R. *The Selfish Gene.* Oxford: Oxford University Press, 1976.

[7] Gadpille, W. "Research into the Physiology of Maleness and Femaleness: Its Contribution to the Etiology and Psychodynamics of Homosexuality." *Archives of General Psychiatry* (1972): 193–206.

[8] Goldberg, S. "What is 'Normal'? Logical Aspects of the Question of Homosexual Behavior." *Psychiatry* (1975):

[9] Gould, R. "What We Don't Know about Homosexuality." *New York Times Magazine,* Feb. 24, 1974.

[10] Gary, R. "Sex and Sexual Perversion." *Journal of Philosophy* 74 (1978): 189–99.

[11] Greer, G. *The Obstacle Race.* New York: Farrar, Strauss & Giroux, 1979.

[12] Grice, H. "Utterer's Meaning, Sentence-Meaning, and Word-Meaning." *Foundations of Language* 4 (1968): 1–18.

[13] Hutchinson, G. "A Speculative Consideration of Certain Possible Forms of Sexual Selection in Man." *American Naturalist* 93 (1959): 81–91.

[14] Karlen, A. *Sexuality and Homosexuality: A New View.* New York: Norton, 1967.

[15] Levin, M. "On the Ascription of Functions to Objects." *Philosophy of the Social Sciences* 6 (1976): 227–34.

[16] Levin, M. "'Sexism' is Meaningless." *St. John's Review* XXXIII (1981): 35–40.

[17] Lewis, D. *Convention.* Cambridge, MA: Harvard University Press, 1970.

[18] Masters, W. and V. Johnson. *Homosexuality in Perspective.* Boston, MA: Little, Brown and Company, 1979.

[19] McCracken, S. "Replies to Correspondents." *Commentary,* April 1979.

[20] Mossner, E. *The Life of David Hume,* 1st. ed. New York: Nelson & Sons, 1954.

[21] Nagel, E. "Teleology Revisited." *Journal of Philosophy* 74 (1977): 261–301.

[22] Nagel, T. "Sexual Perversion." *Journal of Philosophy* 66 (1969): 5–17.

[23] Rechy, J. *The Sexual Outlaw.* New York: Grove Press, 1977.

[24] Sagarin, E. "The Good Guys, the Bad Guys, and the Gay Guys." *Contemporary Sociology* (1973): 3–13.

[25] Sagarin, E. and R. Kelley. "The Labelling of Deviance," in W. Grove, ed., *The Labelling of Deviance.* New York: Wiley & Sons, 1975.

[26] Sayre, K. *Cybernetics and the Philosophy of Mind.* Atlantic Highlands, NJ: Humanities Press, 1976.

[27] Schiffer, S. *Meaning.* Oxford: Oxford University Press, 1972.

[28] Singer, P. *Democracy and Disobedience.* Oxford: Oxford University Press, 1968.

[29] Weinberg, M. and C. Williams. *Male Homosexuals: Their Problems and Adaptations.* Oxford: Oxford University Press, 1974.

[30] Will, G. "How Far Out of the Closet?" *Newsweek,* 30 May 1977, p. 92.

[31] Wilson, E. *Sociobiology: The New Synthesis.* Cambridge, MA: Harvard University Press, 1975.

[32] Wilson, E. *On Human Nature.* Cambridge, MA: Harvard University Press, 1978.

[33] Wright, L. "Functions." *Philosophical Review* 82 (1973): 139–68.

Critic

TIMOTHY F. MURPHY

Homosexuality and Nature
Happiness and the Law at Stake

The nature and legitimacy of homosexual behaviour continue to generate considerable controversy. Since 1973, the American Psychiatric Association has formally professed that homosexuality per se is no disease entity, but one may still seek and find practitioners of sexual conversion therapy. While some religious thinkers have become more tolerant of it, others continue to conceptualize homosexuality as a sin of the first order, a sin said to be formally condemned in strong Old and New Testament language. While at present 26 states of the Union do *not* have criminal statutes for private consensual homosexual behaviour, the US Supreme Court recently held that states may criminalize such behaviour if they so choose.

There are many ways used to argue against the moral legitimacy of homosexual behaviour, whether such behaviour is transient or exclusive. Some seek recourse to concepts of sinfulness, disease or crime in order to flesh out objections. Others appeal to the argument that homosexuality, its religious, medical, and criminal implications apart, is a kind of unnatural aberration which undermines its practitioners' prospects for happiness. I will consider this kind of argument here and contend that such an argument fails to establish that homosexuality is any significant abnormality and that neither its purported abnormality nor the unhappiness said to be associated with such behaviour can constitute a basis for criminaliz-

Timothy F. Murphy, "Homosexuality and Nature: Happiness and the Law at Stake," *Journal of Applied Philosophy* 4 (1987): 195–204. Some notes deleted. Reprinted by permission of Blackwell Publishing Ltd.

ing consensual homosexual behaviour or for failing to provide equal protections under the law for homosexuals in the area of public housing, service, jobs, and so on. I consider Michael Levin's "Why homosexuality is abnormal" as paradigmatic of the kind of argument I wish to investigate. Although I confine myself to his specific argument and frequently use its language, my position is applicable *a fortiori* to all similar kinds of positions.

THE ARGUMENT FROM NATURE

Levin says homosexuality is abnormal because it involves a misuse of body parts, that there is "clear empirical sense" of that misuse, and that homosexual behaviour is contrary to the evolutionary adaptive order. Homosexual behaviour is abnormal, he says, because it is not the kind of behaviour which brought us to be the kind of physically constituted persons that we are today. Persons who used their penises for *coitus per anum* presumably left no ancestors. (Levin does not accept sociobiological contentions that homosexuality plays a supporting role in adaptive success.) That there are penises and vaginas today is due to the fact that they *were* used for heterosexual coitus, and hence we can infer that heterosexual coitus is indeed what such organs are for. Levin says: "an organ is for a given activity if the organ's performing that activity helps its host or organisms suitably related to its host, *and* if this contribution is how the organ got and stays where it is." Homosexual behaviour constitutes, according to this line of thought, an abandonment of certain functions on which species survival depended, and that abandonment is said to imply the loss of naturally occurring rewards selected for by adaptive success. This latter point does not mean that there are *no* compensatory pleasures, for just as the obese person will find gustatory rewards in his or her food, the homosexual who misuses his or her body parts can find *some* compensatory sexual rewards. It is just that the wilful overeater or homosexual cannot reap the deepest rewards that nature has provided for in heterosexual usages and achievements.

Despite the effort which Levin takes to show that homosexual behaviour falls outside the behaviour upon which human adaptive success depended, I cannot say that I think this argument is even remotely convincing. Indeed, I believe it to be subject to a damning criticism. Even if it were certainly established that homosexuality was not part of originally adaptive behaviour, I do not see how that conclusion alone could establish the abnormality of homosexuality because there is neither a premise that natural selection has any kind of ultimate normative force nor a premise that human beings are bound to continue to be the kind of things that cosmic accident brought them to be. There is nothing in Levin's argument to sustain a claim that departures from a blind, accidental force of nature, or whatever metaphor of randomness is chosen, must be resisted. Without a logically prior and controlling premise that patterns of adaptive success possess ultimate, normative force, then it seems that human beings are completely at liberty to dispose of their world, their behaviour, and even such things as their anatomy and physiology as they see fit. H. Tristam Engelhardt has made an argument along similar lines: that we human beings may choose our futures and are in no metaphysically binding sense bound to continue being the kind of persons blind determinants of nature have brought us to be. Violations of a random order of nature carry no inherent penalty for there is no ultimate enforcer, or at least none is specified by this argument. Levin believes that he can show the abnormality of homosexuality without having to show that it violates some cosmic principle, by showing its inherent obstacles to adaptive success. But I think it is because no cosmic principle is invoked that we can judge that adaptive success itself is no binding force. The only guide available for human beings in respect of their lives, sexuality, and future is their will and imagination. Should the entire population of the planet choose to become exclusive homosexuals, for example, leaving the business of reproduction to ectogenesis, I cannot think of a reason *derived from nature* why they should not do so.

Levin's argument, and others like it, ignore the prospects of beneficial departures from the naturally adaptive order. His argument assumes that each departure from our adaptive heritage will be unhappy in result. The argument, too, assumes that *all* behaviour of *all* persons must serve the purpose of adaption. Clearly, it is possible that some departures from the adaptive order are possible which do not threaten a species survival as a whole. If a species can survive if only a majority of its members use their organs in a particular fashion, then it may enjoy a surplus of adaptive protection even for those who act in wholly non-procreative fashion. Homosexuality, then, might have served some beneficial advantage (as sociobiology asserts) or it may have been (and this is more important for my argument) no impediment to selective adaptation. If this is so, it is hard to see in what sense homosexuality would have to be reckoned as a natural aberration.

Even if one were to accept Levin's suggestions regarding the abnormality of homosexuality with respect to natural selection, it seems to me that his definition of homosexuality is highly problematic. He defines homosexuality behaviourally, i.e. as something one does with one's body, specifically with one's organs. It is *behaviour* which is said to be unnatural. Since there are, after all, self-identified gay men and lesbians who have never had sexual relations with a member of the same (or opposite) sex, this definition seems ill-advised. By their own lights, adolescents and closeted adults see themselves as homosexual, their sexual continence notwithstanding. How is one to understand the nature of their sexual dispositions if there is no overt behaviour? Is their homoerotic desire itself abnormal? Or is only behaviour abnormal? I believe that homosexuality is better defined as primarily a psychic phenomenon and that specific homosexual behaviour is virtually epiphenomenal, merely a matter of what biology makes possible (this claim would also apply to heterosexuality). Most psychiatric texts follow this approach. If one accepts the condition that homosexuality is primarily a psychic phenomenon, and if one wanted to argue its abnormality along the lines Levin has suggested, it would seem that one would have to argue that homoeroticism is somehow a misuse of the brain! There are arguments, of course, that attempt to show homosexuality as a result of some psychic disrepair, but even though these arguments are themselves the matter of much debate, that debate is only about psychical development, not about uses of the brain. It is hard to imagine that one could show homoeroticism as a misuse of the brain.

Finally, it is to be noted that Levin believes that homosexuality may be intuited as abnormal. He says that such an intuition "remains vital." Yet however profoundly felt and however psychologically convincing intuitions may be, still they can be conceptually shallow and more importantly even dead wrong. That is, the appeal to intuition is by itself no guarantee of the accuracy of the intuition, for presumably one would, for purposes of confirmation, have to check the intuition against some other external criterion of justification. I am hard-pressed to see how this intuition of homosexuality's abnormality is to be made available to others who do not already share it. Indeed, arguments from intuition are like issues said to be self-evident: precious little can be said on their behalf, they are either seen or not. Yet Levin seems to assume that the readers of his essay *already* share the intuition. For example, he apologizes for the allegedly graphic language that he must use in his essay. Of course, only persons who already share a revulsion *at the mere mention* of mutual fellation will find such terms in need of apology. Levin also says at one point that it is hard to believe the high number of sexual partners homosexual men report having. He then transfers this lack of imagination to all his readers; even when these figures, he says, are "taken *cum grano,* they should be compared to the reader's own experience as he tries to imagine what it would be like to move so promiscuously among anonymous encounters." Evidently, Levin believes that no promiscuous heterosexual or homosexual male (or that any female, promiscuous or not) will read this essay, their time being spent, I suppose, entirely on the prowl. It is clear from these examples, and others, that there is no accommodation of persons who do not find the mere mention of fellation an inherent degradation, who do not find a high number of sexual partners psychically repulsive, or who intuit homosexuality as erotic rather than repulsive. This kind of argument presupposes an audience which already shares Levin's conclusions, and I believe fails to show how another person, lacking these conclusions, could ever come to an appropriation of them. However, even if such a move were made, the position would remain open to the standard, incisive criticisms of intuitonistic moral philosophy.

PROSPECTS FOR HAPPINESS

Levin makes a great deal of the supposed link between homosexuality and unhappiness. One may assume that he would reply to my foregoing remarks by admitting that even if it were true that humans are not bound by any ultimate metaphysical sexual directive, then it would still remain true that prudential cautions obtain against homosexuality and that these cautions are sufficient to ground legal measures designed to minimize the occurrence of homosexuality. "Homosexuality," Levin says, "is likely to cause unhappiness because it leaves unfulfilled an innate and innately rewarding desire," a desire supposedly ingrained through millennia of evolutionary selection. One might find some happy homosexuals, but Levin believes that such exceptions are inconsequential and do not disable his argument. He does not say that happy homosexuals are non-existent, only that they are rare and that their lives will be inherently less rewarding than those of heterosexuals. Moreover, "Even if some line demarcated happiness from unhappiness absolutely, it would be irrelevant if homosexuals were all happily above that line. It is the comparison with the heterosexual life that is at issue." The happiest persons are practitioners of heterosexuality, therefore, even if, according to Levin, each and every homosexual was, by his or her own admission, happy. But homosexuals are not even proximately happy, Levin says. According to him, awash in the travails of their own self-punishing promiscuity, present-day homosexuals would like to believe that all their ills are the result of an ill-constructed society, that their unhappiness is merely artifactual and in principle eliminable by the appropriate cultural and political accommodations. Levin suggests that this belief is a self-serving rationalization. Happiness has not followed, he says, the Danish and Dutch abandonment of prejudice against homosexuals. Happiness has not followed the work of various American organs to provide a positive image of homosexuals, judges allowing homosexuals to adopt

their lovers, the Hollywood production of "highly sanitized" movies about homosexuality, publishers urging their authors to show little boys using cosmetics, or advertisers appealing directly to the homosexual market. That there has not been a resultant rise in homosexual happiness is said to be evident from (a) the gay press not liking Hollywood's movies, (b) the appearance of especially virulent diseases in homosexual populations, and (c) gay men needing frivolous enticements to get them to support important political causes on their behalf.

By way of comment on all this, I would first note that Levin has formulated his position in terms that *in principle* do not admit of refutation. He said that in principle, however happy homosexuals may be, they still cannot be as happy as heterosexuals. Of course, it is possible that a claim is unfalsifiable because the claim is indeed true. On the other hand, I think one would do better to see a definitional fiat being asserted here: human happiness, *true* human happiness is said to be coextensive with the happiness of heterosexual behaviour. By definition there is nothing which could falsify this proposition, *not even* the self-asserted happiness of each and every homosexual person. I believe that this claim is no argument, avoiding as it does any potentially falsifying statement, and that it ought to be rejected as untestable rather than accepted as true by definition. As I have urged above, moreover, I do not believe that the accidental contingency of the primacy of heterosexual sexuality requires that all human happiness be sought there or that, perhaps, other kinds of happiness cannot be engineered.

Secondly, the kind of evidence that Levin uses to establish the unhappiness of homosexuals is altogether anecdotal and trivial. That Hollywood continues to make bad movies, even when their subjects are "sanitized" gay men and lesbians, is no evidence that homosexuality per se leads to unhappiness. The existence of viral disease *is* a major concern of gay men, but it is not because they are gay that it is their concern; it is because these viral diseases happen by accident of fate to affect the gay population. Would one want to argue that heterosexuals qua heterosexuals are somehow intrinsically headed for unhappiness as AIDS expands into that population? Moreover, that homosexuals mix business with pleasure is no argument that they are any less serious about their political agenda (let alone unhappier) than others. There is a kind of unfair asymmetry being used here in adducing Levin's evidence. If one uses such issues as he conjures up as evidence of the continuing unhappiness of homosexuals, why couldn't one equally and legitimately use similar evidence against the supposed happiness of heterosexuals? Most wars, for example, are the doing of heterosexuals. Nuclear weapons are their products. Most bad movies are also theirs. Must one infer therefore the continuing unhappiness of heterosexuals and assert prudential cautions against heterosexuality? If Levin's use of anecdotal evidence is acceptable against homosexuals, then it ought to be equally acceptable as an indictment of heterosexuality. Ironically, the case against heterosexuality would probably have to be seen as more damaging.

As for Levin's claims that homosexuals ought to be happier these days than they were in the past, it is probably the case that this is true. Anecdotal evidence may be used here since Levin uses it. The increasing success of gay pride parades ought to be taken as an indicator of some measure of increased homosexual happiness. At the very least persons who participate in them have been freed of the fear of some of the unhappy consequences that could befall them following public identification of their being gay. It is not without significance that in Boston, for example, the 1986 gay pride parade attracted some 25,000–30,000 participants whereas the first parade of 1970 had but 50! Furthermore, the heady increase in the number of gay and lesbian organizations for social, business, and political and support services indicates that homosexuals are not much inclined to wallow in despair over their sexual fate. One could go on in this vein, but I think it is important to consider that a verdict about the happiness of homosexuals would be a one-sided verdict indeed if it were to follow only from the evidence Levin puts forward.

To put specific quarrels about evidence aside, it seems to me that Levin fails almost culpably to imagine what a society would have to be like in order to be free of the oppressive elements which contribute to the putative unhappiness of homosexuals. In order to see the extent to which homosexual unhappiness is caused by social repressions and to what extent it is intrinsic, society would have to be completely free at every significant level of bias against homosexuals. To begin with—let's call this Phase I of the agenda: there should be no gratuitous assumption of heterosexuality in education, politics, advertising, and so on, just as a gender-neutral society would not presume the priority, real and symbolic, of males. For example, in education, texts and films ought to incorporate the experiences of gay men and lesbians. Educational measures should attempt to reduce antihomosexuality in the same ways and to the same extent they educate against racism. In a society reconstructed along these lines, moreover, there would also have to be no right of access or entitlement possessed by a heterosexual that could be denied to a homosexual. *Only* in such a radically restructured society would one be able to see if homosexual unhappiness were immune to social deconstruction. Even if it weren't, one could still argue that homosexuals are not necessarily unhappy but that their happiness requires social protections or accommodations unrequired by heterosexuals. That is, homosexuals might need, as Phase II of the agenda, entitlements which heterosexuals do not in the way, for example, that legally-mandated minority hiring quotas serve other specific populations. Of course, one might want to argue that such entitlements would be anti-democratic and therefore objectionable. This protestation however would not by itself diminish the point being made: that homosexual unhappiness is perhaps adventitious and that the only way of discovering this is to protect homosexuals in their lives, jobs, and interests in ways that are not presently served.

It is unlikely, of course, that the above-described experiment in social reconstruction is in any important sense immediately forthcoming. Nevertheless, that the experiment may be clearly formulated and seen as the definitive test of the social-reaction theory of homosexual unhappiness is sufficient ground to show that Levin's account of the unhappiness of homosexuals is unproved, its adduced evidence merely anecdotal. Even if it were true, I will argue later, since not all human unhappiness is tractable to social interventions, any residual unhappiness that was to survive Phase I and II of our social reformation agenda would still be no evidence against homosexuality.

ISSUES AT LAW

Levin believes that the abnormality of homosexuality and its attendant unhappiness are warrant enough to ground legal enactments against homosexuality and this is a matter of protecting citizens from lives impoverished by the loss of heterosexual rewards. Any legislation therefore that raises the odds that a child will become homosexual ought to be rejected as prima facie objectionable, as a dereliction of the duty of protecting children from the unhappy homosexual selves they might become. The US Supreme Court recently ruled in Bowers v. Hardwick that states may enact, if they choose, statutes proscribing private consensual homosexual behaviour since, according to the opinion, there is nothing in the Constitution making such behaviour a fundamental right. Levin's argument would presumably extend further since private consensual homosexual behaviour is socially invisible and unlikely as such to influence persons to become homosexual. Although he does not specifically mention what kinds of laws ought to be called for, or what kinds of laws ought to be rejected, presumably he means denying homosexuals protections in jobs, housing, foster-parenting, and so on. In short, the law would presumably have to serve the function of rendering homosexuality entirely invisible else there would continue to exist subtle promptings to homosexuality by virtue of degree of acceptance extended to it. Levin says he does not believe that this legal scenario would put any undue burden on any actual homosexual since, unlike members of racial minorities, he or she can always stay in the closet while applying for jobs, housing and the like. Therefore to give homosexuals protections they don't really need would have to be interpreted as a de facto social legitimation of homosexuality. This implied approval might be causally involved in the production of more homosexuals and therefore ought to be rejected.

I do not believe that this argument is convincing. First of all, the "cause" or "causes" of homosexuality are a matter of continuing controversy. There are metaphysical arguments that homosexuality is the result of some cosmic principle of world ordering; Plato's *Symposium* depicts homosexuals (and heterosexuals) as the result of an angry god's punishment. Biological theories hold homosexuality to be the result of some developmental variance or organismal dysfunction. Genetic theories try to locate the origins of homosexuality at the lowest level of biological causality, the gene. The most numerous kinds of theories are psychosocial theories which see homoeroticism as the result of either original psychical constitution or some developmental influences. Even the briefest perusal of the literature of the "cause" of homosexuality leaves one with the conclusion that the "cause" is an essentially disputed concept. There is not even agreement that homosexuality is a reifiable trait (any more than, say, courage) that can be explained by reference to a universally pre-existing set of conditions. This dispute is important to consider since Levin seems to hold, without justification (at least without explanation), a developmental theory of homosexuality, a theory that homosexuals are made not born. This may or may not be true, but it seems wrong-headed to establish legal policy on the basis of one particular speculative theory of the origins of homosexual behaviour. If homosexuality is primarily a function of biological variance, for example, such laws and forbearances that Levin would see as desirable would have no effect whatever on the production of more homosexuals. Even if the law diligently erased all evidence of homosexual behaviour and persons from public view, one could not automatically assume a reduced number of homosexuals or a decrease in homosexual behaviour. I suspect that most persons are homosexual and become homosexual in ways completely immune to the written or enforced statutes of the various states. Children who never hear a word about homosexuality in their youth nevertheless become homosexuals. Children who walk past homosexual clubs and persons in the streets of certain American cities do not thereby automatically become homosexuals. Would it really be the case that there are more homosexuals spawned in West Virginia because there are no laws against private, consensual homosexual behaviour there than in Virginia where there are such laws? The net result of efforts to criminalize and reduce the visibility of homosexuality then would be to impose burdens on those who are perhaps involuntarily homosexual. At the very least, Levin's theory gratuitously supposes a developmental theory of homosexuality, a theory which has its insistent critics. One should also point out that even if some developmental theory of homosexuality were true, it is not necessarily the case that changing statutes would halt the flow of homosexuals since there may be other pathways to homosexuality. It is also the suspicion of many psychologists that homosexual tendencies are established very early on in childhood, in which case one presumes fairly that statutes criminalizing sodomy and lacks of protection in housing on the basis of sexual orientation have little to do with either ingraining or stifling homosexual dispositions.

If the reason that Levin suggests anti-homosexual measures is to contain human unhappiness, then his argument may be turned on its head. If the reason, or part of the reason that homosexuals are unhappy is because of the existence of certain legally permissible discriminations (or what comes to the same thing: fear of such), then it can certainly be suggested that laws ought to be changed in order to protect and enlarge the happiness of homosexuals, whether their homosexuality is elective or involuntary. In the name of their happiness, they ought to be afforded protections under the law, freedom from fear of prosecution for their private consensual behaviour and freedom to occupy jobs as persons they are, not as the persons others would have them be. The law could further protect them by saving them from blackmailers who would expose their homosexuality to employers, landlords, and so on. It is eminently clear that the law could at least enlarge the happiness of gay men and lesbians in these respects even if it cannot vouchsafe them absolute satisfaction in their lives.

Interestingly enough, even if all the unhappiness said to be associated with being homosexual were not eliminated by a dogged social reconstruction that achieved full parity between homosexuality and heterosexuality, it would still not follow that the law ought to be put to the purpose of eliminating homosexuality (assuming it could). Life, sad to say, is in some of its aspects inherently tragic. For example, in some important ways, law or society could never fully compensate the atheist for the lost rewards of religion. Atheism can discover in the world no incentives to conduct, no promise of the eventual recompense for injustices borne, and no guarantee that the heart's desires will be met.[1] Society might provide such consolations as it can, but it is certainly the case that a certain tragedy antagonistic to human happiness is an irreducible element of atheistic thought. That atheism leads to this measure of unhappiness would certainly not be a reason for instituting social and legal barriers to atheism on the theory that children ought to be glowingly happy (if self-deceived) theists rather than unhappy atheists. Human dignity is not automatically overthrown by a position of atheism; the atheist accepts and honours those satisfactions that are within his or her power. That homosexuality too might lead to a certain amount of unhappiness does not thereby overthrow the dignity of homosexual persons. One realizes merely that the law is no unfailing conduit to human happiness.

Levin's conclusions that legal measures ought to be taken to minimize the possibility that children become themselves the sad new recruits of homosexuality therefore cannot stand. I believe, on the contrary, that the law ought to do what it can to protect homosexuals from socially inflicted unhappiness. Levin's point that to decriminalize homosexual behaviour and to provide legal protections for homosexual persons would be seen as social legitimization of homosexuality (and not just tolerance) is correct. But this is no point over which to despair, for this inference is precisely compatible with the underlying metaphysics of gay activism, that homosexuality is no degrading impoverishment of human life. On the contrary, it has an integrity of its own apart from invidious comparisons with heterosexuality. Therefore, lest society be a political enforcer of sexual ideology, homosexuals ought to be afforded equal standing and protections under the law, and this in the name of serving human happiness.

CONCLUSIONS

Levin has argued that homosexuality is a self-punishing maladaption likely to cause unhappiness since homosexuals do not use their organs for what they are for. Human happiness is said to attend that behaviour which follows out the natural paths plotted by evolutionary selection. As homosexuality has not thus far been shown to have contributed (*pace* sociobiology) to the kind of beings we are today, it may be assumed that homosexual behaviour is abnormal. As such behaviour, too, is linked with unhappiness it is to be rejected as both abnormal and unrewarding. The law ought to follow this conclusion through and reject any inducements to homosexuality.

I have argued against this position on a number of grounds. The most important is this: nature is represented here by Levin as without guiding or controlling force. Therefore, as pathways of evolutionary adaptation are themselves only a matter of metaphysical blind accident, nature lacks normative force and human beings are completely at liberty to dipose of the world, their behaviour, and their bodies as they see fit. One could still try to argue against homosexuality on prudential grounds, on grounds that it causes unhappiness, but I have argued that conclusions from claims about unhappiness are inconclusive because it is not clear how much homosexual unhappiness is adventitious and how much intrinsic.

Levin's evidence that such unhappiness is intrinsic is anecdotal evidence of the most unconvincing kind. A complete reconstruction of society such that homosexuality was on a par with heterosexuality would be required in order to distinguish adventitious from intrinsic unhappiness and make the argument conclusive. But even if there were residual unhappiness attaching to homosexuality under socially liberating conditions of this grand experiment, such unhappiness might be likened to the irreducible tragic aspects of atheism. Such an unhappiness is no writ for legal and social measures designed to stem the genesis of either atheists or homosexuals.

On the contrary, rather than using the law as an instrument of enforcing invisibility on homosexuals, the law should, I think, be used to afford what measure of happiness it can. How far the law ought to serve the needs of gay men and lesbians is, of course, a matter of debate. But it seems to follow that at the very least, the law ought to protect gay men and lesbians from unhappiness caused by victimization and social exclusions which it is within the law's power to reject.

NOTE

1. Ernest Nagel (1965) A defense of atheism, in: P. Edwards & A. Pap *A Modern Introduction to Philosophy*, pp. 460–472, rev edn (New York, Free Press).

7

Is "Outing" Homosexuals Wrong?

Mohr and His Critics

"Outing" refers to the practice of publicly revealing the sexual orientation of people who have attempted to conceal their homosexuality. Richard D. Mohr has been called "perhaps its most eloquent and persuasive advocate." His extensive 1992 essay, "The Outing Controversy: Privacy and Dignity in Gay Ethics," helped initiate the philosophical debate on the subject and has served as a focal point for many subsequent discussions of the issue. In "The Case for Outing," which appears in its entirety as the featured article of this chapter, Mohr presents a much briefer, more recent version of his central argument. The critical responses that follow it refer at times to claims made in Mohr's earlier essay, "The Outing Controversy," but the substantive points they raise can all be brought to bear on the essay reprinted here.

Outings are sometimes defended on punitive grounds. If a gay public official has successfully concealed his homosexuality while pursuing a legislative agenda harmful to the interests of homosexuals, for example, then he may be viewed as guilty of hypocrisy and thus deserving of being revealed publicly as homosexual. More often, those who support the practice of outing appeal to a more utilitarian argument, urging that the long-term benefits of outing outweigh its short-term costs and that this fact suffices to render it morally permissible. What is most important about Mohr's argument is that it embraces neither of these approaches. Instead, Mohr appeals to the value of dignity, maintaining that a person who refrains from revealing the sexual orientation of those he knows to be gay is, in effect, guilty of perpetuating the view that there is something reprehensible about homosexuality. Going along with a closeted gay person's decision to remain in the closet, that is, is in Mohr's words, "a commitment to viewing gayness as disgusting, horrible, unspeakably gross, in short, as abjection."

Of course, many people may be willing simply to endorse the view that homosexuality is all of these things. But Mohr's argument is not aimed at such readers, and so, for the purposes of considering the merits of Mohr's argument, we must assume that this view of homosexuality is misguided. Indeed, Mohr's argument is perhaps most forcefully aimed at the reader who is himself or herself openly gay but who respects the privacy of closeted homosexuals by helping them to keep their secret. Many gay people adopt this stance and view the practice of outing as a morally objectionable violation of the privacy of others. But such an attitude, Mohr maintains, amounts to complicity with the enemy.

In his response to Mohr's argument, James S. Stramel raises several concerns, but most of them point to the same general conclusion: that Mohr's argument fails to take into account the various ways in which outing a person can also reinforce the degrading convention of the closet. Outing a closeted homosexual, on this account, causes even worse consequences from the standpoint of dignity than does refraining from outing him. In their article, "Privacy and the Ethics of Outing," David J. Mayo and Martin Gunderson raise two further objections to Mohr's position. The first maintains that choosing to help a gay person remain closeted need not amount to endorsing the view that homosexuality is shameful or undignified. The second maintains that even if helping a gay person remain closeted does perpetuate negative attitudes toward homosexuality, there may still be other morally relevant considerations that outweigh this fact. The result of both of the response pieces, then, is that pressure can be put on Mohr's argument at a number of different points.

QUESTIONS FOR CONSIDERATION

In considering the relative merits of the positions of Mohr and Stramel, it may prove useful to begin by assessing the relative significance of the intention of the person doing the outing, on the one hand, and the beliefs of the general public, on the other.

• Which does Mohr think is more important in assessing the ethics of outing: the intention of the person doing the outing or the general public's attitude toward homosexuality? Which does Stramel think is more important?

• What reasons does Mohr give for his assessment? What reasons does Stramel give for his? Which assessment, if either, seems more reasonable? Does this assessment help or hinder the case for outing?

In addition, one should consider the merits of Stramel's argument about autonomy.

• Does outing a person violate his autonomy, or does it simply exercise the autonomy of the outer?

• Should autonomy include control over one's public identity? Why or why not?

Finally, it is worth considering the merits of Stramel's rape-based objection.

• Is the analogy between the closeted homosexual and the rape victim strong enough for Stramel's purposes? What sorts of differences might there be between the two cases, and do any of those differences suffice to overcome the objection?

• Should Mohr be willing simply to bite the bullet and accept the implication that helping rape victims conceal their status as rape victims is also morally objectionable? Many newspapers, for example, publish the names of crime victims in general but refrain from publishing the names of victims of rape in particular. Is that a praiseworthy policy or an objectionable one?

In turning next to the objections raised by Mayo and Gunderson, one might begin by returning to the question of intention versus public perception.

• What do Mayo and Gunderson claim about the relative significance of intention and perception in this context? What does Mohr claim? Does Mohr have a consistent position about this in his article as a whole? Why or why not?

In addition, one should consider whether Mayo and Gunderson are correct in their objection to the claim that considerations of dignity must morally trump all other considerations.

• Does Mohr's position require him to rely on this seemingly extreme claim, or could he modify it and still reach the conclusion he wishes to reach?

• Can Mohr show that dignity is important enough to justify outing without making it so important that it would justify acts that most people would think unjustified?

FURTHER READING

Broach, Ronald J. "Does Human Dignity Require Outing Homosexuals?" *Journal of Social Philosophy* 29, no. 23 (1998): 2–45.

Halwani, Raja. "Outing and Virtue Ethics." *Journal of Applied Philosophy* 19, no. 2 (2002): 141–54.

McCarthy, Jeremiah. "The Closet and the Ethics of Outing," in *Gay Ethics*, ed. Timothy Murphy (New York: Haworth Press, 1994), pp. 27–45.

Mohr, Richard. "The Outing Controversy: Privacy and Dignity in Gay Ethics," in *Gay Ideas: Outing and Other Controversies* (Boston: Beacon Press, 1992), pp. 11–48.

RICHARD D. MOHR

The Case for Outing

The disclosure on the Internet in July 1996 that Arizona Republican Congressman Jim Kolbe is gay and his public acknowledgment of this fact the next month—just as the national gay news magazine *The Advocate* was going to press with the story—catapulted the issue of outing back into national headlines. Gays outed Kolbe in response to his voting for the insidiously anti-gay Defense of Marriage Act. Gays deemed that the socially liberal Republican was not liberal enough. But two can play that game. In 1994, far-right Congressman Robert Dornan outed fellow-Republican Congressman Steve Gunderson on the floor of the House. Dornan deemed Gunderson too liberal. In both cases, the outing was vindictive—aimed at punishing and incapacitating its target.

Such outings are of dubious political worth. In the November 1996 elections, Kolbe was reelected, Dornan was not. More important, such outings are morally reprehensible. In order for vindictive outing to be effective, the outer counts upon the amassed anti-gay forces in society to strike out against the person outed. Such outing legitimates the use of anti-gay forces as a political tool and, in that very use, strengthens them.

Vindictive outings are not limited to the political realm. In January 1996, gay novelist and wit Armistead Maupin outed comedienne Lily Tomlin in the *Village Voice* for her failure to come out in her role as the narrator for the movie *The Celluloid Closet*, a history of gay cinema. And a number of gay military court cases have resulted from vindictive outings, as when a disgruntled "roommate" outed her Air Force major "girlfriend" to the military police. But such illegitimate, vindictive outings are not the only form of outing. Not all outing points fingers. Not all outing recriminates. Not all outing shouts from soapboxes to stir up the homophobic crowds.

Some outing is simply news—the letting come to light of a person's sexual orientation in relevant contexts. Take 1995's biggest outing story. After twenty-six years of marriage, *Rolling Stone* founder Jann Wenner left his wife and three sons to move into a Manhattan hotel with a former male model who now works as a designer for Calvin Klein. Despite Wenner's and his wife's efforts to have the

Richard Mohr, "The Case for Outing," in *Same Sex: Debating the Ethics, Science, and Culture of Homosexuality,* ed. John Corvino (New York: Rowman & Littlefield, 1997), pp. 281–83. Reprinted by permission of Rowman & Littlefield Publishers, Inc.

story suppressed, it ran anyway—not in the tabloids and tattlers, but in *Newsweek, New York* magazine, *Advertising Age,* the *Boston Herald,* and the *Wall Street Journal.* What made the story particularly newsworthy was that in 1993 Wenner had jumped on the "family values" bandwagon and had begun publishing a yuppie magazine, *Family Life,* to portray the glories of the heterosexual nuclear family. What was missing from this portrait? The editor himself.

The American press is no longer creating "beards" nor assuring silences for would-be closet cases in order to deflect attention away from gay issues and gay lives as though gayness were just too embarrassing to mention. To its credit, the press is gradually abandoning both its past policy of "don't ask, don't tell" when it comes to gayness and its phony belief that to discuss unasked someone's sexual *orientation* (as opposed to his or her sexual acts) is to violate that person's privacy. It is time that gays carry over these trends into their daily lives as well.

People need to let the gayness of individuals come up when it is relevant, rather than along with the shaming social convention of the closet, the demand that every gay person is bound to keep every other gay person's secret secret. For the closet is the site where anti-gay loathing and gay self-loathing mutually reinforce each other. Even people who are out of the closet demean themselves when they maintain other people's closets. For the closet's secret is a dirty little secret that degrades all gay people.

To put the point systematically, living by the convention of the closet—whether one is closeted oneself or not—is a commitment to viewing gayness as disgusting, horrible, unspeakably gross, in short, as abjection. Core cases of abjection are excrement, vomit, pus, and the smells associated with these. It is exactly around just these (only ever half-

acknowledged) abject matters that society sets up rituals requiring that one may neither inquire nor report about them—rituals of the form "don't ask, don't tell." Take, for example, the case of flatulence in a crowded elevator: no one tells; no one asks; everyone acts as though nothing is amiss, and so this behavior reinforces the abject thing's status as loathsome. This daunting effort to repress knowing and acknowledgment requires a blanket of silence to be cast over the abject thing. To tell of the abject is to break a taboo, for names, like scents, are enough to bring the abject back to full consciousness. And to ask about the abject is to be reminded of its constantly recurring, lurking, louring presence just beyond oneself.

The chief problem of the closet as a social institution, then, is not that it promotes hypocrisy, requires lies, sets snares, blames the victim when snared, and causes unhappiness—though it does have all these results. No, the chief problem with the closet is that it treats gays as less than human, less than animal, less even than vegetable—it treats gays as reeking scum, the breath of death.

Therefore, each time a gay person finds the closet morally acceptable for himself or others, he degrades himself as gay and sinks to the level of abjection dictated for gays by the dominant culture. No gay person with sufficient self-respect and dignity can be required to view himself or other gays in this way. In consequence, the openly gay person, in order to live morally, must not play along with the convention of the closet, lest he degrade himself. He must allow gayness to come up in conversations when it is relevant.

Moral outing is simply living in the truth and withdrawing from the social conventions that degrade gay existence.

JAMES S. STRAMEL

Outing, Ethics, and Politics
A Reply to Mohr

In place of more common utilitarian defenses of outing, Mohr claims that by not outing others one knows to be gay, the openly gay person is participating in "the secret of the closet." He thereby degrades himself by "commit[ting] his life to the very values that keep him oppressed" and trades his own dignity for the happiness of the closet case. So, in defense of their dignity and the dignity of all gays, out gays living in the truth may—are even expected to—"out nearly everyone he or she knows to be gay."

If there is a prima facie privacy right against outing, then (as Mohr admits) even dignity-based outing would not be justified; but I also find Mohr's position troubling on its own terms. Outing may diminish gay dignity, both individual and collective, because the public regards homosexuality as bad or immoral and sees outing as punishment. Rather than serving to dismantle antigay attitudes, outing utilizes and reinforces the notion that homosexuality is shameful. Even when conscientiously motivated, the practice can look petty and vindictive.

Perhaps the most repugnant feature of all outing is that it steals from the outee a major opportunity to take control of and assume responsibility for his identity, integrity and dignity—to come out on his own principles. Mohr complains that this argument—"dressed up in the finery of liberal cant"—misunderstands the scope and possible materials of dignity and the complexity of coming out. Shifting attention to the outee, Mohr says the relevant questions are: (1) Can a person, though outed, still have access to enough dignity to be highly dignified? (2) Are conditions such that individuals can achieve a rich life of their own making given the cussedness of their social and material circumstances? (3) Can the outee still have a positive, robust, dignifying relation to his sexual orientation? I agree that the answer to each question is yes. But none of this refutes the claim that outing wrongly diminishes the dignity of the outee.

It is certainly possible to imagine situations in which a failure to identify a person as gay would involve the loss of one's own dignity. But it is simply not plausible to claim that a person who decides not to out another out of respect for her autonomy and dignity necessarily regards homosexuality as shameful or has committed her life to the oppression of gays. Except in unusual circumstances, the threat to my dignity of your closetude—and my leaving you there—is negligible. As Mohr observes, dignity has many sources, and I can still be highly dignified despite forgoing the opportunity to out you. To see this, we can stand Mohr's questions on their heads to inquire whether a gay person can have access to enough dignity to be highly dignified, a rich life of his own making, and a robust dignifying relation to his sexual orientation—all without engaging in outing. Here too, the answer is yes.

Like many other groups, gay people are faced with a situation in which society unfairly and severely stigmatizes them for having a particular characteristic. One's dignity as a given type of person does not require outing every person one knows to share the relevant characteristic. Compare again the situation of gays to that of women who have been raped. Through no fault of their own rape victims are saddled with a status that is not inherently disrespectable, but that often prompts disrespectful treatment. Suppose that Anne was a victim of rape but has been able to rid herself of the shame and stigma rape victims often internalize; she now works actively in rape-prevention programs, counseling women and giving public talks in which she "comes out" as herself a victim of rape. If Anne knows that Brenda was also raped but remains "closeted," how does Anne's failure to out her cause a loss of Anne's dignity?

Mohr grants that outing can diminish the outee's dignity, but he holds that this will rarely outweigh the dignity gained for all gays by outing because the indignity bred by the secret of the closet is so great and pervasive. I think Mohr too readily trades concrete and significant individual harms and indignities for a hypothetical and incremental increase in the abstract quantity of overall dignity.

It is important to realize that objecting to outing does not require defending the closet. Lesbians and gays should certainly be encouraged to come out as a matter of moral virtue. But as long as homosexuality is stigmatized in ways that heterosexuality is not, being publicly gay will be personally dangerous and politically volatile. Except in unusual circumstances, individuals should have the freedom to decide for themselves whether to join the sociopolitical fray, rather than being made political footballs by others professing to know better the proper course for their lives.

There is no one way—certainly no correct way—to be gay, although some gays speak as if there were. What being gay means to a person and whether, when, and to what extent one shall be publicly identified as gay are decisions properly left to the individual. Tyranny takes many forms—wherever a person is victimized by coercive power. Outers, who know well that information is power, commit a tyranny of the few. In doing so, they betray one of gay activism's fundamental values: the right to pursue one's life free from domination and interference by others.

DAVID J. MAYO
MARTIN GUNDERSON

Privacy and the Ethics of Outing

DIGNITY AND THE CLOSET

According to Mohr, the closet is an institution which is so evil and insidious that the moral individual, as a matter of dignity, cannot participate in its existence or continuation. Mohr's non-utilitarian defense of outing involves rich and complex arguments which we cannot treat fully here. Instead, we will isolate several important threads of his defense of outing in order to assess their success.

Mohr agrees with utilitarian critics that the closet is the primary mechanism by which gays and lesbians are oppressed. Moreover, Mohr grants that

From David J. Mayo and Martin Gunderson, "Privacy and the Ethics of Outing," in *Gay Ethics: Outing, Civil Rights, and Sexual Science*, ed. Timothy F. Murphy (New York: The Haworth Press, 1994), pp. 47–65. Some parts of the text have been deleted. Reprinted by permission of the Haworth Press, Inc.

gays within the gay community do generally recognize a code of secrecy regarding sexual orientation. He refers to this code or convention of honoring each other's secrecy as "The Secret.". Indeed, Mohr sees The Secret as "*the* gay social convention . . . the structuring element, the DNA, the constitutive convention of the gay community" (29–30). The closet and The Secret are especially insidious, he thinks, for two reasons. Borrowing from the account offered by Jeremiah McCarthy in this volume, Mohr insists that the closet doesn't merely oppress gays. Through the convention of The Secret, it also recruits them as willing agents of their own oppression. This dual tyranny is possible only so long as they cooperate and respect The Secret. The second reason is that the gay person who respects The Secret "accept[s] insult so that one avoids harm" (31), and in so doing "commits to the view of gays that the convention presupposes: that gays are loathsome and disgusting, to be kept from sight, nauseating if touched or seen, filth always to be flushed away" (33). Mohr views this as "a complete capitulation to the general social belief that the only good gay is a nonexistent one" (30). Any gay respecting The Secret, regarding himself or another, "commit[s] his life to the very values that keep him oppressed" (31). Mohr concludes that *as a matter of dignity* gays must renounce The Secret, neither remaining closeted themselves, nor participating in the closet on behalf of others.

We take exception to two of these claims. The first is that those who respect The Secret not only pay lip service to the values which oppress them but actually share, embrace, and even "commit their lives" to them. While some persons doubtless remain in the closet out of a sense of shame, it simply doesn't follow that *any* gay or lesbian who remains closeted shares or accepts homophobic values. This is true even if one acknowledges he is indirectly contributing to homophobia. Shame is not the only possible motivation for remaining closeted. Concern for either individual welfare or individual rights might also provide such motivation. For instance, a gay man may believe that remaining closeted himself, or not outing a lesbian, will reduce the risk of very real harms in a homophobic world. But even if he believes

a closeted lesbian's fears are irrational and she would be better off if she were out, he may keep The Secret out of obligation, knowing that another had revealed herself to him in light of the convention and expected benefits of The Secret: trusting others to keep her sexual orientation confidential. He *might* even keep The Secret (again for himself or another) out of love or compassion for a homophobic straight. Imagine a gay man who is comfortable with himself, who loves a frail, elderly parent who is of another age and homophobic. In the abstract, it is easy enough to claim that we shouldn't humor others' hateful prejudices. However, there *are* competing values, and it seems either dogmatic or naive to insist in advance that there are *never* circumstances in which competing values should prevail. Mohr quotes Steve Berry approvingly: "The principle is really very simple. Either being gay is OK or it isn't" (37). But for most of us things really *aren't* that simple.

Second, we take issue with Mohr's claim that consideration of dignity alone should dictate the morality of actions, and that happiness (for oneself or others) is irrelevant to the morality of outing. Having grounded his case for outing squarely in considerations of dignity, Mohr is willing to let the utilitarian chips fall where they may: "It is not one's happiness that one is seeking through outing—it is the avoidance of being an instrument of insult to one's own dignity, the avoidance of complicity in one's own degradation" (43). He does acknowledge that many gays remain closeted for economic reasons or even to retain custody of their children, but he finds this morally irrelevant: "the closet case . . . barter[s] away his self-respect, his worthiness for respect, his dignity, for happiness, regard, and non-respectful love . . . accepts insult to avoid harm . . . [and thus] becomes a simulacrum—a deceptive substitute . . . of a person" (31–32). Moreover, the indignity is not confined merely to the closeted person alone. The openly gay person who keeps The Secret for others commits himself "to a similar vision of gay people and so commit[s] him[self] to give up his own dignity for the happiness of the closeted gay person. To do that," Mohr adds, "is the very inversion of the moral life" (33). At one point, Mohr acknowledges "*if* it were the case . . . that the government was shooting gays, I would morally be expected to suspend my dignity temporarily. . . ." But he then goes on to insist that even this would not be a matter of the protection of happiness but done "so that the current and prospective dignity of others is made possible" (34).

We believe Mohr is simply mistaken in holding that dignity simply outweighs all other values here— that "a dignity may outweigh a dignity, as a pleasure or measure of happiness may not" (34). We would hope, moreover, that Mohr would lie not only to save another's life but that he would be willing to do so simply as a matter of compassion, without having to reconstruct it as a matter of dignity. Again, life is not as simple as Steve Berry suggests it is. In any event, it is not simple enough that one can always put dignity first. Life is morally complicated: along with dignity, we believe morality sometimes requires us to take account of both human welfare and individual rights.

8

Is Adultery Wrong?

Wasserstrom and His Critics

According to traditional Western morality, sex is permissible only between a man and a woman who are married to each other. Since the revolution in attitudes toward sex that occurred in the second half of the twentieth century, however, many of the tenets of traditional sexual morality have been called into question. Relatively few people today outside of deeply religious circles pronounce all sex outside monogamous marital relationships immoral. Various relaxations of the traditional view have been widely accepted. Despite this fact, however, attitudes toward *adultery,* in particular, have remained fairly stable throughout these changes.

In the featured article of this chapter, Richard Wasserstrom raises the question of whether adultery really is immoral, and his answer is negative. His strategy, for the most part, is one of process of elimination (see section 4.4 of the Introduction). He considers what he takes to be the plausible arguments *for* the immorality of adultery, that is, and finds each of them wanting. (He does briefly consider arguments *against* the immorality of adultery, but these are largely dependent on his consideration of the arguments for the immorality of adultery.)

To have an *argument* for the immorality of adultery (as opposed, say, to simply viewing its immorality as self-evident), one must appeal to some feature that adultery necessarily possesses and about which there are already some plausible, or at least agreed upon, moral principles. Two features that adultery appears to have and about the morality of which we are generally agreed are promise-breaking and deception. Both promise-breaking and deception are, in themselves, immoral. That is not to say that it is always and everywhere immoral to break a promise or to deceive someone. We can imagine circumstances in which there are strong reasons in favor of promise-breaking that might well outweigh the wrongness of promise-breaking, making it morally permissible, all things considered. However, the more weighty the promise, the stronger the reason will have to be for breaking it. If people who marry promise to abstain from having sex with third parties, that is, and if that is an especially deep and important promise, then the reasons to override that promise would have to be very weighty indeed.

A second argument appeals to the immorality of deception. Since marriage involves the promise to abstain from sex with third parties, those who indulge in extramarital affairs typically try to hide them from their spouses. This typically involves lying and other forms of deception on a fairly large scale. Again, there is at least an implicit agreement that in marrying someone you will not systematically deceive that person about important matters. Wasserstrom develops an additional argument for the idea that adultery necessarily involves deception of *someone*—either the spouse or the partner in adultery. Wasserstrom grants that both promise-breaking and deception are prima facie immoral. But he disputes the truth of a crucial premise of each argument.

Wasserstrom considers a third and quite different kind of argument for the immorality of adultery, one that involves the desirability of maintaining an institution of marriage in which sexual exclusivity is the norm: namely that this best serves the interests of any children who are brought into the world through the sexual relationship. Wasserstrom disputes the validity of this stability argument by constructing a parallel argument that is valid if and only if the stability argument is valid, but which in fact is invalid.

Bonnie Steinbock, in her contribution, reviews both the deception and promise-breaking arguments and agrees with Wasserstrom's conclusion that neither establishes the moral impermissibility of adultery. However, she presents a rather different kind of argument in favor of marital fidelity: that sexual exclusivity and marital fidelity are an ideal. Steinbock's conclusion is thus that, although it is not obligatory for married partners to impose on themselves an obligation to be faithful, if they want to pursue the worthy and reasonable ideal of romantic love, to be romantically in love with their married partner, then they are justified, morally and rationally, in imposing that obligation on themselves.

Don Marquis finds the accounts of the wrongness of adultery in the articles by Wasserstrom and Steinbock to be "inadequate or oversimplified," while nevertheless granting that there is some aspect of truth buried in each. With Wasserstrom, Marquis thinks that the promise-breaking account fails to explain why adultery is typically considered a *serious* wrong. Breaking promises is not always considered as bad as adultery. Further, Marquis argues that Steinbock's account suffers a related defect: It doesn't entail that adultery is *ever* really wrong at all. To fail to adopt a very worthy ideal or to fail to live up to an ideal once adopted is typically not considered morally wrong. Marquis goes on to offer an account of what makes adultery wrong, when it is wrong, and what would make it permissible—an account that he claims captures whatever truth there is in the preceding three accounts.

Marquis contrasts what he calls the "covenant model" of marriage to the "contract model." In the covenant model, two people make *unconditional* promises (of sexual fidelity, among others). They promise to be faithful and stick with each other "for better or for worse, until death do us part." But in the contract model, marriage is a contract involving various *conditional* promises. A contract is an agreement that two or more people enter into and in which they typically promise to do various things for the other party to the contract. But the promises involved in a contract are typically *conditional* upon the other party's fulfilling various conditions. If one party to the contract fails to satisfy those conditions, that can release the other party from a duty to carry out *his or her* conditional promises. Suppose your spouse keeps up her end of the bargain. Then, in the contract model, it would be morally wrong for you to go out and commit adultery. Suppose your spouse does not keep up his end of the bargain. One response to this might be divorce, but that can be extremely difficult or ill-advised. Marquis outlines a series of cases in which a husband fails to fully comply with the implicit conditions on his wife's promise to remain sexually faithful, thereby releasing his wife from that promise and rendering it permissible for her to engage in adultery.

QUESTIONS FOR CONSIDERATION

• It is striking that neither of the first two articles in this chapter considers that the threat of sexually transmitted diseases or the possibility of unwanted pregnancy raises any moral problems. In fact, both Wasserstrom and Steinbock are even dismissive of the moral importance of these. (Note also that both papers were written after contraception became regarded as morally acceptable, reliable, and widespread but before the HIV/AIDS epidemic took hold.) Does the possibility of contracting a life-threatening and highly contagious disease have a bearing on the morality of sexual fidelity? If adultery exposes your marital partner to a chance of acquiring a fatal condition, does that make it wrong? If not, why not?

• Suppose you agree that the risk of infecting your marital partner with a fatal or debilitating illness does make adultery wrong. Does it follow that taking your marital partner on a surprise rock-climbing adventure or a downhill skiing vacation is morally wrong for the same reason? If not, what is the morally relevant difference between these two?

• Is Marquis right that the *contract* model is the preferred model for marriage? Does his argument fail if the correct model for marriage is the *covenant*? What could adjudicate between these two models? Is it just a matter of choice?

• Should those who are getting married make it explicit whether it is a contract or a covenant that they are entering into? (Would marriage vows under the contract model be different from those under a covenant model? In what ways?)

• Are there arguments for preferring the covenant model? Would those who thought of themselves as being in a covenant be more motivated to keep their promises than those who thought of themselves as being in a contract?

• If marriage is a contract, then why do we not regard the contract as simply *voided* once one of the parties to it violates its conditions? That is to say, if each party promises sexual fidelity to the other (conditional upon various provisos), then once one of the parties is adulterous, has not the contract been broken? Is not the marriage literally over? Compare this situation with other contracts with which you are familiar.

• Does the contract account capture what makes adultery wrong? Why, for example, is the discovery of adultery typically so much more painful for the faithful spouse than the discovery of violations of other contracts?

FURTHER READING

Cicovacki, Predrag. "On Love and Fidelity in Marriage." *Journal of Social Philosophy* 24, no. 3 (Winter 1993): 92–104.

Halwani, Raja Fouad. "Virtue Ethics and Adultery." *Journal of Social Philosophy* 29, no. 3 (1998): pp. 5–18.

Martin, Mike W. "Adultery and Fidelity." *Journal of Social Philosophy* 25, no. 3 (Winter 1994): 76–91.

Wreen, Michael. "What's Really Wrong with Adultery?" in *The Philosophy of Sex: Contemporary Readings*, ed. Alan Soble (Savage, Md.: Rowman & Littlefield, 1991): pp. 179–86.

RICHARD WASSERSTROM

Is Adultery Immoral?

Many discussions of the enforcement of morality by the law take as illustrative of the problem under consideration the regulation of various types of sexual behavior by the criminal law. It was, for example, the Wolfenden Report's recommendations concerning homosexuality and prostitution that led Lord Devlin to compose his now famous lecture, "The Enforcement of Morals." And that lecture in turn provoked important philosophical responses from H. L. A. Hart, Ronald Dworkin, and others.

Much, if not all, of the recent philosophical literature on the enforcement of morals appears to take for granted the immorality of the sexual behavior in question. The focus of discussion, at least, is whether such things as homosexuality, prostitution, and adultery ought to be made illegal even if they are immoral, and not whether they are immoral.

I propose in this paper to think about the latter, more neglected topic, that of sexual morality, and to do so in the following fashion. I shall consider just one kind of behavior that is often taken to be a case of sexual immorality—adultery. I am interested in pursuing at least two questions. First, I want to explore the question of in what respects adulterous behavior falls within the domain of morality at all: For this surely is one of the puzzles one encounters when considering the topic of sexual morality. It is often hard to see on what grounds much of the behavior is deemed to be either moral or immoral, for example, private homosexual behavior between consenting adults. I have purposely selected adultery because it seems a more plausible candidate for moral assessment than many other kinds of sexual behavior.

The second question I want to examine is that of what is to be said about adultery, without being especially concerned to stay within the area of morality. I shall endeavor, in other words, to identify and to

assess a number of the major arguments that might be advanced against adultery. I believe that they are the chief arguments that would be given in support of the view that adultery is immoral, but I think they are worth considering even if some of them turn out to be nonmoral arguments and considerations.

A number of the issues involved seem to me to be complicated and difficult. In a number of places I have at best indicated where further philosophical exploration is required without having successfully conducted the exploration myself. The paper may very well be more useful as an illustration of how one might begin to think about the subject of sexual morality than as an elucidation of important truths about the topic.

Before I turn to the arguments themselves there are two preliminary points that require some clarification. Throughout the paper I shall refer to the immorality of such things as breaking a promise, deceiving someone, etc. In a very rough way, I mean by this that there is something morally wrong that is done in doing the action in question. I mean that the action is, in a strong sense, of "prima facie" prima facie wrong or unjustified. I do not mean that it may never be right or justifiable to do the action; just that the fact that it is an action of this description always does count against the rightness of the action. I leave entirely open the question of what it is that makes actions of this kind immoral in this sense of "immoral."

The second preliminary point concerns what is meant or implied by the concept of adultery. I mean by "adultery" any case of extramarital sex, and I want to explore the arguments for and against extramarital sex, undertaken in a variety of morally relevant situations. Someone might claim that the concept of adultery is conceptually connected with the concept

From Richard Wasserstrom, "Is Adultery Immoral?" in *Philosophy and Sex,* ed. Robert Baker and Frederick Elliston, pp. 207–21 (Buffalo, N.Y.: Prometheus Books, 1975). Reprinted by permission of the author.

of immorality, and that to characterize behavior as adulterous is already to characterize it as immoral or unjustified in the sense described above. There may be something to this. Hence the importance of making it clear that I want to talk about extramarital sexual relations. If they are always immoral, this is something that must be shown by argument. If the concept of adultery does in some sense entail or imply immorality, I want to ask whether that connection is a rationally based one. If not all cases of extramarital sex are immoral (again, in the sense described above), then the concept of adultery should either be weakened accordingly or restricted to those classes of extramarital sex for which the predication of immorality is warranted.

One argument for the immorality of adultery might go something like this: what makes adultery immoral is that it involves the breaking of a promise, and what makes adultery seriously wrong is that it involves the breaking of an important promise. For, so the argument might continue, one of the things the two parties promise each other when they get married is that they will abstain from sexual relationships with third persons. Because of this promise both spouses quite reasonably entertain the expectation that the other will behave in conformity with it. Hence, when one of the parties has sexual intercourse with a third person he or she breaks that promise about sexual relationships which was made when the marriage was entered into, and defeats the reasonable expectations of exclusivity entertained by the spouse.

In many cases the immorality involved in breaching the promise relating to extramarital sex may be a good deal more serious than that involved in the breach of other promises. This is so because adherence to this promise may be of much greater importance to the parties than is adherence to many of the other promises given or received by them in their lifetime. The breaking of this promise may be much more hurtful and painful than is typically the case.

Why is this so? To begin with, it may have been difficult for the non-adulterous spouse to have kept the promise. Hence that spouse may feel the unfairness of having restrained himself or herself in the absence of reciprocal restraint having been exercised

by the adulterous spouse. In addition, the spouse may perceive the breaking of the promise as an indication of a kind of indifference on the part of the adulterous spouse. If you really cared about me and my feelings—the spouse might say—you would not have done this to me. And third, and related to the above, the spouse may see the act of sexual intercourse with another as a sign of affection for the other person and as an additional rejection of the non-adulterous spouse as the one who is loved by the adulterous spouse. It is not just that the adulterous spouse does not take the feelings of the spouse sufficiently into account, the adulterous spouse also indicates through the act of adultery affection for someone other than the spouse. I will return to these points later. For the present, it is sufficient to note that a set of arguments can be developed in support of the proposition that certain kinds of adultery are wrong just because they involve the breach of a serious promise which, among other things, leads to the intentional infliction of substantial pain by one spouse upon the other.

Another argument for the immorality of adultery focuses not on the existence of a promise of sexual exclusivity but on the connection between adultery and deception. According to this argument, adultery involves deception. And because deception is wrong, so is adultery.

Although it is certainly not obviously so, I shall simply assume in this paper that deception is always immoral. Thus the crucial issue for my purposes is the asserted connection between extramarital sex and deception. Is it plausible to maintain, as this argument does, that adultery always does involve deception and is on that basis to be condemned?

The most obvious person on whom deceptions might be practiced is the nonparticipating spouse; and the most obvious thing about which the nonparticipating spouse can be deceived is the existence of the adulterous act. One clear case of deception is that of lying. Instead of saying that the afternoon was spent in bed with A, the adulterous spouse asserts that it was spent in the library with B, or on the golf course with C.

There can also be deception even when no lies are told. Suppose, for instance, that a person has sexual intercourse with someone other than his or her spouse and just does not tell the spouse about it. Is that deception? It may not be a case of lying if, for example, the spouse is never asked by the other about the situation. Still, we might say, it is surely deceptive because of the promises that were exchanged at marriage. As we saw earlier, these promises provide a foundation for the reasonable belief that neither spouse will engage in sexual relationships with any other persons. Hence the failure to bring the fact of extramarital sex to the attention of the other spouse deceives that spouse about the present state of the marital relationship.

Adultery, in other words, can involve both active and passive deception. An adulterous spouse may just keep silent or, as is often the fact, the spouse may engage in an increasingly complex way of life devoted to the concealment of the facts from the nonparticipating spouse. Lies, half-truths, clandestine meetings, and the like may become a central feature of the adulterous spouse's existence. These are things that can and do happen, and when they do they make the case against adultery an easy one. Still, neither active nor passive deception is inevitably a feature of an extramarital relationship.

It is possible, though, that a more subtle but pervasive kind of deceptiveness is a feature of adultery. It comes about because of the connection in our culture between sexual intimacy and certain feelings of love and affection. The point can be made indirectly at first by seeing that one way in which we can, in our culture, mark off our close friends from our mere acquaintances is through the kinds of intimacies that we are prepared to share with them. I may, for instance, be willing to reveal my very private thoughts and emotions to my closest friends or to my wife, but to no one else. My sharing of these intimate facts about myself is from one perspective a way of making a gift to those who mean the most to me. Revealing these things and sharing them with those who mean the most to me is one means by which I create, maintain, and confirm those interpersonal relationships that are of most importance to me.

Now in our culture, it might be claimed, sexual intimacy is one of the chief currencies through which gifts of this sort are exchanged. One way to tell someone—particularly someone of the opposite sex—that you have feelings of affection and love for them is by allowing to them or sharing with them sexual behaviors that one doesn't share with the rest of the world. This way of measuring affection was certainly very much a part of the culture in which I matured. It worked something like this. If you were a girl, you showed how much you liked someone by the degree of sexual intimacy you would allow. If you liked a boy only a little, you never did more than kiss—and even the kiss was not very passionate. If you liked the boy a lot and if your feeling was reciprocated, necking, and possibly petting, was permissible. If the attachment was still stronger and you thought it might even become a permanent relationship, the sexual activity was correspondingly more intense and more intimate, although whether it would ever lead to sexual intercourse depended on whether the parties (and particularly the girl) accepted fully the prohibition on non-marital sex. The situation for the boy was related, but not exactly the same. The assumption was that males did not naturally link sex with affection in the way in which females did. However, since women did, males had to take this into account. That is to say, because a woman would permit sexual intimacies only if she had feelings of affection for the male and only if those feelings were reciprocated, the male had to have and express those feelings, too, before sexual intimacies of any sort would occur.

The result was that the importance of a correlation between sexual intimacy and feelings of love and affection was taught by the culture and assimilated by those growing up in the culture. The scale of possible positive feelings toward persons of the other sex ran from casual liking at the one end to the love that was deemed essential to and characteristic of marriage at the other. The scale of possible sexual behavior ran from brief, passionless kissing or hand-holding at the one end to sexual intercourse at the other. And the correlation between the two scales was quite precise. As a result, any act of sexual intimacy carried substantial meaning with it, and no act of sexual intimacy was simply a pleasurable set of bodily sensations. Many such acts were, of course, more pleasurable to the participants because they were a way of saying what the participants feelings were. And sometimes they were less pleasurable for the same reason. The point is, however, that in any event sexual activity was much more than mere bodily enjoyment. It was not like eating a good meal, listening to good music, lying in the sun, or getting a pleasant back rub. It was behavior that meant a great deal concerning one's feelings for persons of the opposite sex in whom one was most interested and with whom one was most involved. It was among the most authoritative ways in which one could communicate to another the nature and degree of one's affection.

If this sketch is even roughly right, then several things become somewhat clearer. To begin with, a possible rationale for many of the rules of conventional sexual morality can be developed. If, for example, sexual intercourse is associated with the kind of affection and commitment to another that is regarded as characteristic of the marriage relationship, then it is natural that sexual intercourse should be thought properly to take place between persons who are married to each other. And if it is thought that this kind of affection and commitment is only to be found within the marriage relationship, then it is not surprising that sexual intercourse should only be thought to be proper within marriage.

Related to what has just been said is the idea that sexual intercourse ought to be restricted to those who are married to each other as a means by which to confirm the very special feelings that the spouses have for each other. Because the culture teaches that sexual intercourse means that the strongest of all feelings for each other are shared by the lovers, it is natural that persons who are married to each other should be able to say this to each other in this way. Revealing and confirming verbally that these feelings are present is one thing that helps to sustain the relationship; engaging in sexual intercourse is another.

In addition, this account would help to provide a framework within which to make sense of the notion that some sex is better than other sex. As I indicated earlier, the fact that sexual intimacy can be meaningful in the sense described tends to make it also the case that sexual intercourse can sometimes be more enjoyable than at other times. On this view, sexual intercourse will typically be more enjoyable where the strong feelings of affection are present than it will be where it is merely "mechanical." This is so in part because people enjoy being loved, especially by those whom they love. Just as we like to hear words of affection, so we like to receive affectionate behavior. And the meaning enhances the independently pleasurable behavior.

More to the point, moreover, an additional rationale for the prohibition on extramarital sex can now be developed. For given this way of viewing the sexual world, extramarital sex will almost always involve deception of a deeper sort. If the adulterous spouse does not in fact have the appropriate feelings of affection for the extramarital partner, then the adulterous spouse is deceiving that person about the presence of such feelings. If, on the other hand, the adulterous spouse does have the corresponding feelings for the extramarital partner but not toward the nonparticipating spouse, the adulterous spouse is very probably deceiving the nonparticipating spouse about the presence of such feelings toward that spouse. Indeed, it might be argued, whenever there is no longer love between the two persons who are married to each other, there is deception just because being married implies both to the participants and to the world that such a bond exists. Deception is inevitable, the argument might conclude, because the feelings of affection that ought to accompany any act of sexual intercourse can only be held toward one other person at any given time in one's life. And if this is so, then the adulterous spouse always deceives either the partner in adultery or the nonparticipating spouse about the existence of such feelings. Thus extramarital sex involves deception of this sort and is for this reason immoral even if no deception vis-à-vis the occurrence of the act of adultery takes place.

What might be said in response to the foregoing arguments? The first thing that might be said is that the account of the connection between sexual intimacy and feelings of affection is inaccurate. Not inaccurate in the sense that no one thinks of things that way, but in the sense that there is substantially more divergence of opinion than that account suggests. For example, the view I have delineated may describe reasonably accurately the concepts of the sexual world in which I grew up, but it does not capture the sexual *weltanschauung* of today's youth at all. Thus, whether or not adultery implies deception in respect to feelings depends very much on the persons who are involved and the way they look at the "meaning" of sexual intimacy.

Second, the argument leaves to be answered the question of whether it is desirable for sexual intimacy to carry the sorts of messages described above. For those persons for whom sex does have these implications, there are special feelings and sensibilities that must be taken into account. But it is another question entirely whether any valuable end—moral or otherwise—is served by investing sexual behavior with such significance. That is something that must be shown and not just assumed. It might, for instance, be the case that substantially more good than harm would come from a kind of demystification of sexual behavior: one that would encourage the enjoyment of sex more for its own sake and one that would reject the centrality both of the association of sex with love and of love with only one other person.

I regard these as two of the more difficult, unresolved issues that our culture faces today in respect to thinking sensibly about the attitudes toward sex and love that we should try to develop in ourselves and in our children. Much of the contemporary literature that advocates sexual liberation of one sort or another embraces one or the other of two different views about the relationship between sex and love.

One view holds that sex should be separated from love and affection. To be sure sex is probably better when the partners genuinely like and enjoy each other. But sex is basically an intensive, exciting sensuous activity that can be enjoyed in a variety of suitable settings with a variety of suitable partners. The situation in respect to sexual pleasure is no different from that of the person who knows and appreciates fine food and who can have a very satisfying meal in any number of good restaurants with any number of congenial companions. One question that must be settled here is whether sex can be so demystified; another, more important question is whether it would be desirable to do so. What would we gain and what might we lose if we all lived in a world in which

an act of sexual intercourse was no more or less significant or enjoyable than having a delicious meal in a nice setting with a good friend? The answer to this question lies beyond the scope of this paper.

The second view seeks to drive the wedge in a different place. It is not the link between sex and love that needs to be broken; rather, on this view, it is the connection between love and exclusivity that ought to be severed. For a number of the reasons already given, it is desirable, so this argument goes, that sexual intimacy continue to be reserved to and shared with only those for whom one has very great affection. The mistake lies in thinking that any "normal" adult will only have those feelings toward one other adult during his or her lifetime—or even at any time in his or her life. It is the concept of adult love, not ideas about sex, that, on this view, needs demystification. What are thought to be both unrealistic and unfortunate are the notions of exclusivity and possessiveness that attach to the dominant conception of love between adults in our and other cultures. Parents of four, five, six, or even ten children can certainly claim and sometimes claim correctly that they love all of their children, that they love them all equally, and that it is simply untrue to their feelings to insist that the numbers involved diminish either the quantity or the quality of their love. If this is an idea that is readily understandable in the case of parents and children, there is no necessary reason why it is an impossible or undesirable ideal in the case of adults. To be sure, there is probably a limit to the number of intimate, "primary" relationships that any person can maintain at any given time without the quality of the relationship being affected. But one adult ought surely be able to love two, three, or even six other adults at any one time without that love being different in kind or degree from that of the traditional, monogomous, lifetime marriage. And as between the individuals in these relationships, whether within a marriage or without, sexual intimacy is fitting and good.

The issues raised by a position such as this one are also surely worth exploring in detail and with care. Is there something to be called "sexual love" which is different from parental love or the nonsexual love of close friends? Is there something about love in general that links it naturally and appropriately with feelings of exclusivity and possession? Or is there something about sexual love, whatever that may be, that makes these feelings especially fitting here? Once again the issues are conceptual, empirical, and normative all at once: What is love? How could it be different? Would it be a good thing or a bad thing if it were different?

Suppose, though, that having delineated these problems we were now to pass them by. Suppose, moreover, we were to be persuaded of the possibility and the desirability of weakening substantially either the links between sex and love or the links between sexual love and exclusivity. Would it not then be the case that adultery could be free from all of the morally objectionable features described so far? To be more specific, let us imagine that a husband and wife have what is today sometimes characterized as an "open marriage." Suppose, that is, that they have agreed in advance that extramarital sex is—under certain circumstances—acceptable behavior for each to engage in. Suppose, that as a result there is no impulse to deceive each other about the occurrence or nature of any such relationships, and that no deception in fact occurs. Suppose, too, that there is no deception in respect to the feelings involved between the adulterous spouse and the extramarital partner. And suppose, finally, that one or the other or both of the spouses then has sexual intercourse in circumstances consistent with these understandings. Under this description, so the agreement might conclude, adultery is simply not immoral. At a minimum, adultery cannot very plausibly be condemned either on the ground that it involves deception or on the ground that it requires the breaking of a promise.

At least two responses are worth considering. One calls attention to the connection between marriage and adultery; the other looks to more instrumental arguments for the immorality of adultery. Both issues deserve further exploration.

One way to deal with the case of the "open marriage" is to question whether the two persons involved are still properly to be described as being married to each other. Part of the meaning of what it is for two persons to be married to each other, so this argument would go, is to have committed oneself to have sexual

relationships only with one's spouse. Of course, it would be added, we know that that commitment is not always honored. We know that persons who are married to each other often do commit adultery. But there is a difference between being willing to make a commitment to marital fidelity, even though one may fail to honor that commitment, and not making the commitment at all. Whatever the relationship may be between the two individuals in the case described above, the absence of any commitment to sexual exclusivity requires the conclusion that their relationship is not a marital one. For a commitment to sexual exclusivity is a necessary although not a sufficient condition for the existence of a marriage.

Although there may be something to this suggestion, as it is stated it is too strong to be acceptable. To begin with, I think it is very doubtful that there are many, if any, *necessary* conditions for marriage; but even if there are, a commitment to sexual exclusivity is not such a condition.

To see that this is so, consider what might be taken to be some of the essential characteristics of a marriage. We might be tempted to propose that the concept of marriage requires the following: a formal ceremony of some sort in which mutual obligations are undertaken between two persons of the opposite sex; the capacity on the part of the persons involved to have sexual intercourse with each other; the willingness to have sexual intercourse only with each other; and feelings of love and affection between the two persons. The problem is that we can imagine relationships that are clearly marital and yet lack one or more of these features. For example, in our own society, it is possible for two persons to be married without going through a formal ceremony, as in the common-law marriages recognized in some jurisdictions. It is also possible for two persons to get married even though one or both lacks the capacity to engage in sexual intercourse. Thus, two very elderly persons who have neither the desire nor the ability to have intercourse can, nonetheless, get married, as can persons whose sexual organs have been injured so that intercourse is not possible. And we certainly know of marriages in which love was not present at the time of the marriage, as, for instance, in marriages of state and marriages of convenience.

Counterexamples not satisfying the condition relating to the abstention from extramarital sex are even more easily produced. We certainly know of societies and cultures in which polygamy and polyandry are practiced, and we have no difficulty in recognizing these relationships as cases of marriages. It might be objected, though, that these are not counterexamples because they are plural marriages rather than marriages in which sex is permitted with someone other than with one of the persons to whom one is married. But we also know of societies in which it is permissible for married persons to have sexual relationships with persons to whom they were not married, for example, temple prostitutes, concubines, and homosexual lovers. And even if we knew of no such societies, the conceptual claim would still, I submit, not be well taken. For suppose all of the other indicia of marriage were present: suppose the two persons were of the opposite sex. Suppose they had the capacity and desire to have intercourse with each other, suppose they participated in a formal ceremony in which they understood themselves voluntarily to be entering into a relationship with each other in which substantial mutual commitments were assumed. If all these conditions were satisfied, we would not be in any doubt about whether or not the two persons were married even though they had not taken on a commitment of sexual exclusivity and even though they had expressly agreed that extramarital sexual intercourse was a permissible behavior for each to engage in.

A commitment to sexual exclusivity is neither a necessary nor a sufficient condition for the existence of a marriage. It does, nonetheless, have this much to do with the nature of marriage: like the other indicia enumerated above, its presence tends to establish the existence of a marriage. Thus, in the absence of a formal ceremony of any sort, an explicit commitment to sexual exclusivity would count in favor of regarding the two persons as married. The conceptual role of the commitment to sexual exclusivity can, perhaps, be brought out through the following example. Suppose we found a tribe which had a practice in which all the other indicia of marriage were present but in which the two parties were *prohibited* ever from having sexual intercourse with each other.

Moreover, suppose that sexual intercourse with others was clearly permitted. In such a case we would, I think, reject the idea that the two were married to each other and we would describe their relationship in other terms, for example, as some kind of formalized, special friendship relation—a kind of heterosexual "blood-brother" bond.

Compare that case with the following. Suppose again that the tribe had a practice in which all of the other indicia of marriage were present, but instead of a prohibition on sexual intercourse between the persons in the relationship there was no rule at all. Sexual intercourse was permissible with the person with whom one had this ceremonial relationship, but it was no more or less permissible than with a number of other persons to whom one was not so related (for instance, all consenting adults of the opposite sex). Although we might be in doubt as to whether we ought to describe the persons as married to each other, we would probably conclude that they were married and that they simply were members of a tribe whose views about sex were quite different from our own.

What all of this shows is that *a prohibition* on sexual intercourse between the two persons involved in a relationship is conceptually incompatible with the claim that the two of them are married. The *permissibility* of intramarital sex is a necessary part of the idea of marriage. But no such incompatibility follows simply from the added permissibility of extra-marital sex.

These arguments do not, of course, exhaust the arguments for the prohibition on extramarital sexual relations. The remaining argument that I wish to consider—as I indicated earlier—is a more instrumental one. It seeks to justify the prohibition by virtue of the role that it plays in the development and maintenance of nuclear families. The argument, or set of arguments, might, I believe, go something like this.

Consider first a farfetched nonsexual example. Suppose a society were organized so that after some suitable age—say, 18, 19, or 20—persons were forbidden to eat anything but bread and water with anyone but their spouse. Persons might still choose in such a society not to get married. Good food just might not be very important to them because they have underdeveloped taste buds. Or good food might be bad for them because there is something wrong with their digestive system. Or good food might be important to them, but they might decide that the enjoyment of good food would get in the way of the attainment of other things that were more important. But most persons would, I think, be led to favor marriage in part because they preferred a richer, more varied, diet to one of bread and water. And they might remain married because the family was the only legitimate setting within which good food was obtainable. If it is important to have society organized so that persons will both get married and stay married, such an arrangement would be well suited to the preservation of the family, and the prohibitions relating to food consumption could be understood as fulfilling that function.

It is obvious that one of the more powerful human desires is the desire for sexual gratification. The desire is a natural one, like hunger and thirst, in the sense that it need not be learned in order to be present within us and operative upon us. But there is in addition much that we do learn about what the act of sexual intercourse is like. Once we experience sexual intercourse ourselves—and in particular once we experience orgasm—we discover that it is among the most intensive, short-term pleasures of the body.

Because this is so, it is easy to see how the prohibition upon extramarital sex helps to hold marriage together. At least during that period of life when the enjoyment of sexual intercourse is one of the desirable bodily pleasures, persons will wish to enjoy those pleasures. If one consequence of being married is that one is prohibited from having sexual intercourse with anyone but one's spouse, then the spouses in a marriage are in a position to provide an important source of pleasure for each other that is unavailable to them elsewhere in the society.

The point emerges still more clearly if this rule of sexual morality is seen as of a piece with the other rules of sexual morality. When this prohibition is coupled, for example, with the prohibition on non-marital sexual intercourse, we are presented with the inducement both to get married and to stay married. For if sexual intercourse is only legitimate within marriage, then persons seeking that gratification which is a feature of sexual intercourse are furnished explicit social directions for its attainment; namely marriage.

Nor, to continue the argument, is it necessary to focus exclusively on the bodily enjoyment that is involved. Orgasm may be a significant part of what there is to sexual intercourse, but it is not the whole of it. We need only recall the earlier discussion of the meaning that sexual intimacy has in our own culture to begin to see some of the more intricate ways in which sexual exclusivity may be connected with the establishment and maintenance of marriage as the primary heterosexual, love relationship. Adultery is wrong, in other words, because a prohibition on extramarital sex is a way to help maintain the institutions of marriage and the nuclear family.

Now I am frankly not sure what we are to say about an argument such as this one. What I am convinced of is that, like the arguments discussed earlier, this one also reveals something of the difficulty and complexity of the issues that are involved. So, what I want now to do—in the brief and final portion of this paper—is to try to delineate with reasonable precision what I take several of the fundamental, unresolved issues to be.

The first is whether this last argument is an argument for the *immorality* of extramarital sexual intercourse. What does seem clear is that there are differences between this argument and the ones considered earlier. The earlier arguments condemned adulterous behavior because it was behavior that involved breaking of a promise, taking unfair advantage, or deceiving another. To the degree to which the prohibition on extramarital sex can be supported by arguments which invoke considerations such as these, there is little question but that violations of the prohibition are properly regarded as immoral. And such a claim could be defended on one or both of two distinct grounds. The first is that things like promise-breaking and deception are just wrong. The second is that adultery involving promisebreaking or deception is wrong because it involves the straightforward infliction of harm on another human being—typically the nonadulterous spouse—who has a strong claim not to have that harm so inflicted.

The argument that connects the prohibition on extramarital sex with the maintenance and preservation of the institution of marriage is an argument for the instrumental value of the prohibition. To some degree this counts, I think, against regarding all violations of the prohibition as obvious cases of immorality. This is so partly because hypothetical imperatives are less clearly within the domain of morality than are categorical ones, and even more because instrumental prohibitions are within the domain of morality only if the end they serve or the way they serve it is itself within the domain of morality.

What this should help us see, I think, is the fact that the argument that connects the prohibition on adultery with the preservation of marriage is at best seriously incomplete. Before we ought to be convinced by it, we ought to have reasons for believing that marriage is a morally desirable and just social institution. And this is not quite as easy or obvious a task as it may seem to be. For the concept of marriage is, as we have seen, both a loosely structured and a complicated one. There may be all sorts of intimate, interpersonal relationships which will resemble but not be identical with the typical marriage relationship presupposed by the traditional sexual morality. There may be a number of distinguishable sexual and loving arrangements which can all legitimately claim to be called *marriages*. The prohibitions of the traditional sexual morality may be effective ways to maintain some marriages and ineffective ways to promote and preserve others. The prohibitions of the traditional sexual morality may make good psychological sense if certain psychological theories are true, and they may be purveyors of immense psychological mischief if other psychological theories are true. The prohibitions of the traditional sexual morality may seem obviously correct if sexual intimacy carries the meaning that the dominant culture has often ascribed to it, and they may seem equally bizarre when sex is viewed through the perspective of the counterculture. Irrespective of whether instrumental arguments of this sort are properly deemed moral arguments, they ought not to fully convince anyone until questions like these are answered.

Critics

Bonnie Steinbock

Adultery

According to a 1980 survey in *Cosmopolitan,* 54 percent of American wives have had extramarital affairs; a study of 100,000 married women by the considerably tamer *Redbook* magazine found that 40 percent of the wives over 40 had been unfaithful. While such surveys are, to some extent, self-selecting—those who do it are more likely to fill out questionnaires about it—sexual mores have clearly changed in recent years. Linda Wolfe, who reported the results of the *Cosmopolitan* survey, suggests that

Bonnie Steinbock, "Adultery," *QQ: Report from the Center for Philosophy and Public Policy* 6, no. 1 (Winter 1986): 12–14.

"this increase in infidelity among married women represents not so much a deviation from traditional standards of fidelity as a break with the old double standard." Studies show that men have always strayed in significant numbers.

Yet 80 percent of "*Cosmo* girls" did not approve of infidelity and wished their own husbands and lovers would be faithful. Eighty-eight percent of respondents to a poll taken in Iowa in 1983 viewed "coveting your neighbor's spouse" as a "major sin." It seems that while almost nobody approves of adultery, men have always done it, and women are catching up.

The increase in female adultery doubtless has to do with recent and radical changes in our attitudes toward sex and sexuality. We no longer feel guilty about enjoying sex; indeed, the capacity for sexual enjoyment is often regarded as a criterion of mental health. When sex itself is no longer intrinsically shameful, restraints on sexual behavior are loosened. In fact, we might question whether the abiding disapproval of infidelity merely gives lip service to an ancient taboo. Is there a rational justification for disapproving of adultery which will carry force with everyone, religious and nonreligious alike?

TRUST AND DECEPTION

Note first that adultery, unlike murder, theft, and lying, is not universally forbidden. Traditional Eskimo culture, for example, regarded sharing one's wife with a visitor as a matter of courtesy. The difference can be explained by looking at the effects of these practices on social cohesiveness. Without rules protecting the lives, persons, and property of its members, no group could long endure. Indeed, rules against killing, assault, lying, and stealing seem fundamental to having a morality at all.

Not so with adultery. For adultery is a *private* matter, essentially concerning only the relationship between husband and wife. It is not essential to morality like these other prohibitions: there are stable societies with genuine moral codes which tolerate extra-marital sex. Although adultery remains a criminal offense in some jurisdictions, it is rarely prosecuted. Surely this is because it is widely regarded as a private matter: in the words of Billie Holiday, "Ain't nobody's business if I do."

However, even if adultery is a private matter, with which the state should not interfere, it is not a morally neutral issue. Our view of adultery is connected to our thoughts and feelings about love and marriage, sex and the family, the value of fidelity, sexual jealousy, and exclusivity. How we think about adultery will affect the quality of our relationships, the way we raise our children, the kind of society we have and want to have. So it is important to consider whether our attitudes toward adultery are justifiable.

Several practical considerations militate against adultery: pregnancy and genital herpes immediately spring to mind. However, unwanted pregnancies are a risk of all sexual intercourse, within or without marriage; venereal disease is a risk of all non-exclusive sex, not just adulterous sex. So these risks do not provide a reason for objecting specifically to adultery. In any event, they offer merely pragmatic, as opposed to moral, objections. If adultery is wrong, it does not become less so because one has been sterilized or inoculated against venereal disease.

Two main reasons support regarding adultery as seriously immoral. One is that adultery is an instance of promise-breaking, on the view that marriage involves, explicitly or implicitly, a promise of sexual fidelity: to forsake all others. That there is this attitude in our culture is clear. Mick Jagger, not noted for sexual puritanism, allegedly refused to marry Jerry Hall, the mother of his baby, because he had no intention of accepting an exclusive sexual relationship. While Jagger's willingness to become an unwed father is hardly mainstream morality, his refusal to marry, knowing that he did not wish to be faithful, respects the idea that *marriage* requires such a commitment. Moreover, the promise of sexual fidelity is regarded as a very serious and important one. To cheat on one's spouse indicates a lack of concern, a willingness to cause pain, and so a lack of love. Finally, one who breaks promises cannot be trusted. And trust is essential to the intimate partnership of marriage, which may be irreparably weakened by its betrayal.

The second reason for regarding adultery as immoral is that it involves deception, for example, lying about one's whereabouts and relations with others. Perhaps a marriage can withstand the occasional lie, but a pattern of lying will have irrevocable consequences for a marriage, if discovered, and probably even if not. Like breaking promises, lying is regarded as a fundamental kind of wrongdoing, a failure to take the one lied to seriously as a moral person entitled to respect.

OPEN MARRIAGE

These two arguments suffice to make most cases of adultery wrong, given the attitudes and expectations of most people. But what if marriage did not involve any promise of sexual fidelity? What if there were no need for deception, because neither partner expected or wanted such fidelity? Objections to "open marriage" cannot focus on promise-breaking and deception, for the expectation of exclusivity is absent. If an open marriage has been freely chosen by both spouses, and not imposed by a dominant on a dependent partner, would such an arrangement be morally acceptable, even desirable?

The attractiveness of extramarital affairs, without dishonesty, disloyalty, or guilt, should not be downplayed. However satisfying sex between married people may be, it cannot have the excitement of a new relationship. ("Not *better*," a friend once said defensively to his wife, attempting to explain his infidelity, "just *different*.") Might we not be better off, our lives fuller and richer, if we allowed ourselves the thrill of new and different sexual encounters?

Perhaps the expectation of sexual exclusivity in marriage stems from emotions which are not admirable: jealousy and possessiveness. That most people experience these feelings is no reason for applauding or institutionalizing them. Independence in marriage is now generally regarded as a good thing: too much "togetherness" is boring and stifling. In a good marriage, the partners can enjoy different

activities, travel apart, and have separate friends. Why draw the line at sexual activity?

The natural response to this question invokes a certain conception of love and sex: sex is an expression of affection and intimacy and so should be reserved for people who love each other. Further, it is assumed that one can and should have such feelings for only one other person at any time. To make love with someone else is to express feelings of affection and intimacy that should be reserved for one's spouse alone.

This rejection of adultery assumes the validity of a particular conception of love and sex, which can be attacked in two ways. We might divorce sex from love and regard sex as a pleasurable activity in its own right, comparable to the enjoyment of a good meal. In his article "Is Adultery Immoral?" Richard Wasserstrom suggests that the linkage of sex with love reflects a belief that unless it is purified by a higher emotion, such as love, sex is intrinsically bad or dirty.

But this is an overly simplistic view of the connection between sex and love. Feelings of love occur between people enjoying sexual intercourse, not out of a sense that sexual pleasure must be purified, but precisely because of the mutual pleasure they give one another. People naturally have feelings of affection for those who make them happy, and sex is a very good way of making someone extraordinarily happy. At the same time, sex is by its nature intimate, involving both physical and psychological exposure. This both requires and creates trust, which is closely allied to feelings of affection and love. This is not to say that sex necessarily requires or leads to love; but a conception of the relation between love and sex that ignores these factors is inadequate and superficial.

Alternatively, one might acknowledge the connection between sex and love, but attack the assumption of exclusivity. If parents can love all their children equally and if adults can have numerous close friends, why should it be impossible to love more than one sexual partner at a time? Perhaps we could learn to love more widely and to accept that a spouse's sexual involvement with another is not a sign of rejection or lack of love.

The logistics of multiple involvement are certainly daunting. Having an affair (as opposed to a roll in the hay) requires time and concentration; it will almost inevitably mean neglecting one's spouse, one's children, one's work. More important, however, exclusivity seems to be an intrinsic part of "true love." Imagine Romeo pouring out his heart to both Juliet *and* Rosalind! In our ideal of romantic love, one chooses to forgo pleasure with other partners in order to have a unique relationship with one's beloved. Such "renunciation" is natural in the first throes of romantic love; it is precisely because this stage does *not* last that we must promise to be faithful through the notoriously unromantic realities of married life.

FIDELITY AS AN IDEAL

On the view I have been defending, genuinely open marriages are not *immoral,* although they deviate from a valued ideal of what marriage should be. While this is not the only ideal, or incumbent on all rational agents, it is a moral view in that it embodies a claim about a good way for people to live. The prohibition of adultery, then, is neither arbitrary nor irrational. However, even if we are justified in accepting the ideal of fidelity, we know that people do not always live up to the ideals they accept and we recognize that some failures to do so are worse than others. We regard a brief affair, occasioned by a prolonged separation, as morally different from installing a mistress.

Further, sexual activity is not necessary for deviation from the ideal of marriage which lies behind the demand for fidelity. As John Heckler observed during his bitter and public divorce from former Health and Human Services Secretary Margaret Heckler, "In marriage, there are two partners. When one person starts contributing far less than the other person to the marriage, that's the original infidelity. You don't need any third party." While this statement was probably a justification of his own infidelities, the point is valid. To abandon one's spouse, whether to a career or to another person, is also a kind of betrayal.

If a man becomes deeply involved emotionally with another woman, it may be little comfort that he is able to assure his wife that "Nothing happened." Sexual infidelity has significance as a sign of a deeper betrayal—falling in love with someone else. It may be objected that we cannot control the way we feel, only the way we behave; that we should not be blamed for falling in love, but only for acting on the feeling. While we may not have direct control over our feelings, however, we are responsible for getting ourselves into situations in which certain feelings naturally arise. "It just happened" is rarely an accurate portrayal of an extramarital love affair.

If there can be betrayal without sex, can there be sex without betrayal? In the novel *Forfeit,* by Dick Francis, the hero is deeply in love with his wife, who was paralyzed by polio in the early days of their marriage. Her great unspoken fear is that he will leave her; instead, he tends to her devotedly. For several years, he forgoes sex, but eventually succumbs to an affair. While his adultery is hardly praiseworthy, it is understandable. He could divorce his wife and marry again, but it is precisely his refusal to abandon her, his continuing love and tender care, that makes us admire him.

People do fall in love with others and out of love with their spouses. Ought they to refrain from making love while still legally tied? I cannot see much, if any, moral value in remaining physically faithful, on principle, to a spouse one no longer loves. This will displease those who regard the wrongness of adultery as a moral absolute, but my account has nothing to do with absolutes and everything to do with what it means to love someone deeply and completely. It is the value of that sort of relationship that makes sexual fidelity an ideal worth the sacrifice.

Neither a mere religiously based taboo, nor a relic of a repressive view of sexuality, the prohibition against adultery expresses a particular conception of married love. It is one we can honor in our own lives and bequeath to our children with confidence in its value as a coherent and rational ideal.

DON MARQUIS

What's Wrong with Adultery?

The ethics of adultery has received surprisingly little attention from philosophers.[1] On the one hand, many believe that the serious wrongness of adultery is utterly uncontroversial. On the other hand, adultery is hardly uncommon. The adulteries of leading politicians have been widely reported. Almost everyone of a certain age has friends who, they know, have committed adultery and who are not bad people. This suggests that the ethics of adultery is more difficult and subtle than often thought.

The subject of this essay is the morality of extramarital sex by persons in typical marriages in our culture. I shall first argue that accounts of the wrongness of adultery in the philosophical literature are inadequate or oversimplified. I shall then propose an account of the wrongness of adultery that, I hope, is superior to, and incorporates the best features of, other accounts. Many may believe this account is excessively permissive. I shall suggest that this thought results from a tension in our concepts of marriage.

I. SOME ACCOUNTS OF THE WRONGNESS OF ADULTERY

Many believe that adultery is wrong because it involves breaking a promise. This, by itself, does not account for the seriousness of the wrong of adultery. This is why Richard Wasserstrom said

> The breaking of this promise may be more hurtful and painful than is typically the case [with other promises]. Why is this so? To begin with ... [the] spouse may feel the unfairness of having restrained himself or herself in the absence of reciprocal restraint having been exercised by the adulterous spouse. In addition, the spouse may perceive the breaking of the

promise as an indication of a kind of indifference on the part of the adulterous spouse ... And third, and related to the above, the spouse may see the act of sexual intercourse with another as a sign of affection for the other person and as an additional rejection of the nonadulterous spouse as the one who is loved by the adulterous spouse ... [Thus] certain kinds of adultery are wrong just because they involve the breach of a serious promise which, among other things, leads to the intentional infliction of substantial pain by one spouse upon the other.[2]

Although Wasserstrom believed that adultery in a standard marriage also typically involves the wrong of deception, evaluation of Wasserstrom's account of the promise-breaking aspect of the wrong is useful. Two main difficulties are apparent. The less serious difficulty concerns his claim that adultery involves the *intentional* infliction of substantial pain. This seems clearly false, for most adulterers attempt to hide their adulteries. If they intended to inflict pain on their spouses, then they would not, of course, hide their adulteries. However, dealing with this difficulty requires only a minimal alteration in Wasserstrom's account. The more serious difficulty is that, on Wasserstrom's account, the promise-breaking is seriously wrong only if the adultery is discovered. This would have the consequence that adulteries that stay hidden—and surely many do—are not seriously wrong for the promise-breaking reason. Almost no one believes this. In particular, persons who discover that their spouses have been committing adultery do not believe this. When the adulteries are discovered, they believe that they were seriously wronged when the adulteries took place. They do not believe that the seriousness of the wrong begins only when adultery is discovered and the emotional pain begins. Wasserstrom's order of explanation is backwards. Someone who discovers her spouse's adultery suffers

---

This paper is published here with the permission of Don Marquis.

because she believes that she *was seriously betrayed;* it is not the case that she believes that the seriousness of the betrayal is due to the fact that she now suffers. The trouble with Wasserstrom's account is that he attempted to account for the seriousness of a deontological wrong in consequentialist terms.

Those who are wedded to consequence-based wrongs might object that, because the adultery might be discovered and because the discovery would cause one's spouse severe pain, the chance that the adultery will cause the spouse severe pain accounts for the serious wrong of breaking this promise. The trouble with this objection is that, from the considerations to which it appeals, it could be replaced with an even better argument for the adulterer's stringent duty to be exceedingly careful to hide his adultery from his spouse.

Michael Wreen's deontological account of the wrong of adultery avoids the difficulty with Wasserstrom's account. His account is quite simple. To be married is to be committed to having sexual intercourse with no one other than one's spouse. Adulterers have a policy of having sexual intercourse with someone other than their spouses. Therefore, adulterers are committed to rules of conduct that are inconsistent. Wreen says that adultery is wrong because it involves what Kant called "a contradiction in conception."[3]

This account has implications that are, to say the least, unacceptable. According to Wreen, "a commitment to sexual exclusivity is a necessary condition for being married."[4] Since an adulterer is not committed to sexual exclusivity, it follows that an adulterer is not married. Since being married is a necessary condition for committing adultery, Wreen's view entails that adultery is logically impossible. It follows that there are no adulterous acts and therefore, no immoral adulterous acts. The contradiction in conception in Wreen's account is not the adulterer's but Wreen's.

What went so terribly wrong? Wreen's claim that a commitment to sexual exclusivity is a necessary condition of being married is a corollary of his belief that open marriage is logically impossible and his view that the concept of open marriage involves an equivocation on the concept of marriage.[5] Although

I disagree, this disagreement is irrelevant to the analysis of this essay because that analysis concerns typical marriages in our culture. In the ceremonies establishing such marriages, couples do commit themselves to sexual exclusivity. (The possibility that the bride or groom might lie complicates matters, but raises issues that would only divert us from the analysis of this essay.) Nevertheless, changing one's mind is not logically impossible. This is what the adulterer does. The contradiction in conception vanishes.

This suggests nothing problematic about Kant's ethics, for Wreen's view is not really Kantian. Kant's "contradiction in conception" requires universalizing a maxim. (I also waive difficult issues concerning the difference between Kantian contradictions in conception and contradictions in the will.) Wreen's contradiction in conception does not essentially involve universalization. Thus, for another reason, Wreen's contradiction in conception is Wreen's, not Kant's.

Wreen might object that the adulterer vowed at his wedding that on no future occasion would he have sex with anyone else. However, he did have sex with someone else on at least one future occasion. This certainly looks like a contradiction. It isn't. There is nothing whatsoever contradictory about my promise that I shall do X at t and my not doing X at t. It may be wrong, of course, to say that and not to do that, but it is not wrong because it is self-contradictory. The ethics of promising is not that easy.

Of course, adultery would be condemned on Kantian grounds if the maxim of the adulterer's action failed Kant's universalization test. Treating this issue well involves complications that would divert us from adultery. Suffice it to say here that it is not at all difficult to imagine *some* circumstances in which one chooses to commit adultery and wills at the same time that everyone similarly situated chooses to commit adultery without a trace of contradiction. Of course, it does not follow that adultery in *any* circumstance passes the Kantian universalization test. Neither Wreen's view, nor any Kantian universalization view, supports the universal wrongness of adultery.

It is safe to conclude that both an account of the serious wrongness of adultery in terms of the consequences of its discovery and a deontological account of the universal wrongness of adultery are unsatisfactory. A virtue ethics account of adultery avoids the difficulties of these other accounts. On such accounts a major good and a major purpose of a marriage is the establishment and the preservation of a loving relationship. Sexual fidelity is a virtue because it promotes this good.[6] Two positive features of this account are that, as compared with Wasserstrom's account, it seems to explain why undiscovered adultery is seriously wrong and, as compared with Wreen's account it does not imply that adultery is always wrong. On a virtue ethics account, adultery is not a vice in a loveless marriage.[7]

Sexual fidelity promotes the good of a loving relationship because sexual infidelity often will lead to, and perhaps already involve, falling in love with someone else. Falling in love with someone else can lead to loving one's spouse less. Loving one's spouse less departs from a, and perhaps the, valued ideal of marriage.[8] This virtue ethics account is based upon the consequences of the actual adultery, even if it remains undiscovered.

The truth of each of the claims on which the virtue ethics account is based is questionable. First of all, departure from a valued ideal of a marriage is not, *by itself,* a wrong-making feature of an action. Many actions, other than adultery, depart from this valued ideal. Some individuals, because of their career commitments, spend more hours at their jobs than would be optimal if their sole goal were a loving relationship with their spouse. Some marriage partners find themselves more tied up in their children's activities than tied to one another. Often hobbies interfere with optimizing a love relationship. A good life has many aspects. Given the limited number of hours in a day, not all aspects can be pursued to an ideal extent. If the virtue ethics account were correct too *many* activities would be wrong.

Second, as the following excerpt from a story in *The New Yorker* shows, falling in love with someone else does not always lead to loving one's spouse less.

Reclining in his EzeeGuy, he would puff a spliff and try to envision life without one or the other of them. He had always loved Gloria: Senegale had stomped into his life with her goofy belief in the divinity of Ethiopia just when he had started to get sour, making him aware of some motivating force in the world besides money. Until Senegale came along he had not known how much he loved Gloria, because falling in love with Senegale reminded him that he had love inside himself to give. So suddenly he also found himself in love with Gloria again.[9]

A third problem is that an extracurricular sexual relationship not involving love would not be wrong on the virtue ethics analysis. Imagine two people who enjoy friendship and a little more at annual professional conferences. Imagine an affair between two people who find each other great in bed, but who cannot, in their wildest dreams, imagine themselves married to each other. A virtue ethics account does not seem to be able to account for the wrongness of such adulteries. Yet, most think that they are wrong. In short, the truth of each of the claims on which the virtue ethics account is based is at least disputable. This is another instance of a common problem with accounts of wrongness based on consequences.

II. ADULTERY AS BREAKING A CONTRACT

In spite of the weaknesses of accounts of the wrongness of adultery found in the literature, at least one aspect of each is correct. Wasserstrom was right: When adultery is wrong, its serious wrongness is based upon breaking a promise. Wreen was right: The wrongness of adultery is deontological. The virtue ethicists are right in at least two ways: The wrongness of adultery is based upon the nature and value of marriage. Adultery is not always wrong. All of these virtues can be found in a contractual account of the wrongness of adultery.

When adultery is wrong it is wrong because it violates a marriage contract. A typical marriage in our culture is a complex arrangement between two friends in which they have pledged to continue their close friendship, to socialize with others, at least sometimes, as a unit, to have a common domicile which they jointly maintain and (generally) to raise a family together. These two people pledge to be fair in making contributions to their common projects. Their commitment is intended to be life long. They pledge to love one another and to find sexual fulfillment through each other and only with each other. These pledges are not made in a spirit of self-sacrifice, but because each of the partners sincerely believes that marriage to the other will enhance her well being.[10] Because of this, the partners are often willing to make major changes in their life trajectories to promote the ends of the marriage.[11]

This account of the marriage contract explains why adultery is wrong when it is wrong. Suppose that your marriage is a good marriage. If so, then adultery is wrong, for you have entered into a contract one of whose terms is sexual exclusivity. Indeed, adultery would be seriously wrong, not because it could be discovered, but because you would be breaking, not only a pledge but, a very solemn and public pledge, and not only such an important pledge, but a pledge on the basis of which your spouse has changed, or has been willing to change, his life plans. Your adultery would be a sign that you do not take the pledge seriously. Your good marriage is a sign that your partner does take the pledge seriously. Your partner has been prepared to alter his[12] life on the assumption that you did take the pledge seriously. Accordingly, adultery is a serious betrayal. Adultery is seriously wrong, not just because it is breaking a promise, or because it is breaking a promise the breaking of which may have serious consequences, but because it is breaking a contractually based, ceremonial, public, and potentially life altering promise.

III. When Adultery Is Morally Permissible

Not all marriages are good. When one's marriage is bad, divorce frequently is the best option. Nevertheless, a divorce often entails a profound upheaval for yourself, for your spouse and for your children. After all, the nature of the marriage contract is such that one often has altered the trajectory of one's life because of an anticipated lifetime commitment. You made this lifetime commitment in the belief that this commitment would promote your own well being. When you begin to realize that your marriage is less than good, you may be left with the altered life trajectory without the justification for the alteration. This can leave a person in a very disadvantageous situation.

Accordingly, you may have good reasons for not getting a divorce even though your marriage is bad in important respects. Perhaps, you believe that the overall good of your marriage for you outweighs the bad.[13] Perhaps you believe that, because there are children or other relatives involved, it would be better for all concerned to continue the marriage. Perhaps, because you have radically altered your life plans on the basis of your marriage vows, divorce would be very disadvantageous to you. Perhaps you believe that you owe your spouse continued care in a continuing marriage. On the assumption that there are good reasons for not abandoning a marriage that is considerably less than good, is adultery ever morally permissible?

The contractual account of the wrongness of adultery can sometimes allow for a justification of adultery. There are two situations in which this is so. In the first, your spouse is committing adultery. In a traditional wedding, your pledge not to have sex with someone other than your spouse was made on the condition that your future spouse not have sex with someone other than you. Since that condition no longer obtains, then since your commitment not to commit adultery was conditional, adultery is not wrong when one's spouse is committing adultery.

It is not the case that a bride promises at her wedding that she will remain sexually faithful to her husband no matter how many other women he sleeps with. Her pledge not to commit adultery appears to be unconditional because she promises not to have sex with anyone else on the condition that her groom will not have sex with anyone else and he has indeed solemnly promised not to have sex with anyone else. Accordingly, her pledge is conditional. It does not follow that the bride has given the least bit of thought to what she is committed to if the condition does not obtain. Thus, it does not follow from this that the wedding pledge is about what it is permissible to do if one's spouse commits adultery. The wedding pledge omits that possibility entirely. Because this is so, one has not pledged not to commit adultery if one's spouse is committing adultery. Since your obligation not to commit adultery is based on your conditional wedding pledge, if your spouse commits adultery, your adultery is not a violation of your wedding vows.

The second situation requires a somewhat more elaborate analysis. One of the major purposes of marriage is a loving and sexually fulfilling relationship. People get married on the assumption that their marriage will fulfill that purpose. A loving and sexual fulfilling relationship is a presupposition of the pledge of sexual fidelity. No rational person, in a typical marriage ceremony, would pledge not to love a third party or not to have sexual relations with a third party if she did not anticipate, and if her soon-to-be spouse did not encourage her to anticipate, that within marriage she would find a sexually fulfilling relationship and a lifetime love partner. Not to love one's partner or not to offer one's partner a sexually fulfilling relationship is to negate the tacit conditions under which the partner's vow not to be sexually unfaithful was made. Brides and grooms get married in order to promote their well being. (If you don't believe this, ask them on their wedding day!) Plainly no one chooses to be married in order to be sexually unfulfilled or to be emotionally lonely. Thus, the only sensible way of understanding the vow of sexual fidelity is, again, as a conditional vow, as a vow conditioned upon one's partner's willingness to uphold his sex and love part of the marriage contract.

If this account of the love and sex aspect of the marriage contract is correct, then adultery can be morally permissible when your spouse does not love you or when your spouse does not offer you a sexual fulfilling relationship. If either of these conditions obtain, then your spouse is not fulfilling his part of the marriage contract in the sex and love department. Your pledge not to commit adultery presupposed that your spouse would fulfill his part of the contract in the sex and love department. He has not fulfilled the conditions that were presuppositions of your vow not to commit adultery. Therefore, adultery in such a situation may be morally permissible, for it is not a violation of the marriage contract at all.

An argument for the moral permissibility of adultery in this general situation can be developed in a slightly different way. You entered into marriage in order to promote your well being. In particular, you entered into the marriage contract in order to promote your well being in the sex and love department. Your spouse is not making it possible for you even minimally to flourish in this department. Therefore, your sexual fidelity is depriving you of important aspects of your well being, aspects of your well-being that it was a point of the marriage to nurture. Therefore, of course, adultery is permissible when your spouse is not satisfying the terms of the agreement in the sex and love department. It is not that the marriage contract explicitly gives you permission to commit adultery if you are not fulfilled in the sex and love department. Rather, the contract is not about your relationship under that condition at all. Therefore, it is not the case that sexual fidelity is a contractual obligation when you are married and your spouse does not offer you minimal fulfillment in the sex or love department.

Consideration of a superficially similar case will illuminate this analysis. Suppose that traveling is a very important part of what makes your life worthwhile. Suppose that your spouse either will not travel with you or, when he does, hates the travel so much that he makes your trip unpleasant for you both. He promised when you wed to make you happy. Has he violated your marriage contract? Does his behavior justify adultery?

Notice that this case differs from the sex or love case in several respects. In the first place, you can fulfill that aspect of your well being that your spouse does not promote by finding another traveling partner. In the second place, adultery will not promote that dimension of your well being of which you are deprived by not traveling. In the third place, there is no agreement, explicit or tacit, in a typical marriage ceremony that your spouse will promote *every* aspect of your well being. Accordingly, in this traveling case, the considerations based on contract and well being which justified adultery in the former case are absent.

Nevertheless, this contractual analysis may permit adultery in a fairly wide range of cases. In marriages in which one partner is interested in sexual relations and the other is not, adultery by the former partner may be morally permissible. In marriages in which one partner is unwilling (or unable) to satisfy sexually the other partner, adultery may be morally permissible. An example of this might be a case in which a wife has orgasms only with cunnilingus and her husband finds such a sexual act repulsive. A marriage in which a husband clearly cares for his job, his hobbies and his buddies, but not his wife is a marriage is which it may be morally permissible for his wife to take a lover.

Even if adultery is morally permissible with respect to contractual considerations, there may be good reasons not to commit adultery. Suppose that your husband discovers the affair, and he divorces you. Given that you have decided that there are good reasons not to get a divorce, such a consideration may be a good reason either not to commit adultery or to be very careful. Suppose that you acquire a sexually transmitted disease that you pass on to your husband. Adultery may be defensible (because it is not ruled out) on the basis of contractual considerations and may still not be in the interests of the parties who might be affected by it. Adultery can be wrong for good consequentialist reasons even if the adultery passes the contractual tests.

Those skeptical of this analysis will note that the deception of one's spouse has not yet played a role in the analysis of the conditions under which adultery is permissible. One might argue that if one is going to commit adultery, then one has an obligation to tell one's spouse, since otherwise the sexual infidelity is deceptive and one has an obligation not to be deceptive.

A good treatment of this issue requires more analysis than is possible in an essay of this length. However, a few rough and ready comments are relevant. There can be powerful reasons for maintaining some families even though the spouses' relationship with one another is dysfunctional in the sex and love department. If this is so, then there are good reasons for not telling one's spouse of one's adultery if one has good reasons for believing that one's spouse would break up one's family if he learned of it. Nevertheless, since adultery by one spouse makes adultery by the other spouse morally permissible, then your adultery

released your spouse from his obligation not to commit adultery. Furthermore, when your relationship with your spouse is dysfunctional in the sex and love department, moral considerations suggest that you intimate to your spouse that he is under no obligation to live an emotionally lonely or sexually dissatisfied life. Finally, if your marriage is such that the adultery of your wife is morally permissible because you are prepared either not to love your wife or not to sexually satisfy her, then if your spouse has a need for love or sex, then the adultery of your spouse is a not unreasonable expectation. You are not justified in believing that your spouse has misled you by not telling you of her adultery.[14]

A virtue of this contractual account of the moral permissibility of adultery is that it is a unitary analysis. Your spouse at your wedding promised to love and sexually to fulfill you and only you. Violation of that pledge is the ground for the moral permissibility of your adultery.

IV. SOME CONCLUDING REMARKS

No doubt many will be disturbed by the thought that the analysis of this essay has rendered far too much adultery morally permissible. The conflict between this intuition and this analysis can be explained. Our culture endorses two different and incompatible concepts of marriage. On the one hand, we think of marriage as a covenant. When we marry, we marry for better or for worse. We arrange our lives and alter our life's plans on the assumption that marriage is a lifetime commitment. Given that one of the purposes of typical marriages is to raise children and given that the rearing of children is a long-term project, there are excellent reasons for thinking of marriage in terms of the concept of covenant.

On the other hand, we also think of marriage as a contract. Contracts are not unconditionally binding. If the other party does not fulfill his part of the bargain, it is not the case that you are obligated to fulfill yours. Contractual obligations are not "for better or for worse." Each person who enters into a typical marriage contract enters into it in order to promote her well being. Contracts can be broken. Someone who is contemplating divorce thinks of her marriage in these terms. If we thought of marriages exclusively as covenants and not as contracts, we would think that divorce is impermissible. But we don't think that way. These two concepts of marriage, when thought through, have incompatible consequences in some situations. When couples recite their marriage vows they, no doubt, are taking for granted both concepts. This explains two things.

Individuals who commit adultery may be taking for granted the contract concept. People who condemn that same adultery may presuppose the covenant concept. This explains our conflicting intuitions concerning the morally permissibility of adultery.

It also explains the need for adultery. Persons who shape their lives in accordance with the covenant concept may find themselves in unhappy marriages. When thinking of what to do, they think in terms of the contract concept. This can lead to adultery if the argument of this essay is close to the mark.

Two restrictions on the conditions under which adultery is permissible deserve mention. First, suppose, not that your spouse does not love you, but that you have fallen out of love with your spouse. Or suppose that you no longer desire to have sexual relations with your spouse. The contract analysis does not permit adultery in these cases. On the assumption that your spouse is willing to uphold his part of the marriage bargain, if you have fallen out of love with your spouse, you have a duty to do what you can do to develop an emotional bond again if you are going to continue in your marriage. If you are no longer interested in sexual relations with your spouse, then you need to do something about this. In these situations the contract analysis underwrites your obligation not to commit adultery. It is worth noting that it is far easier for us to change our own attitudes and behavior than the attitudes of others.

Notice also that if your spouse does not love you or if your spouse does not sexually satisfy you, the reason may be due to something that you can change. If this is so, then you have an obligation to make that change. The marriage contract contains at least an implicit promise that you will be someone your spouse will find both sexually desirable and lovable.

I regard this essay as a stab at some tough issues that have received little sustained systematic thought in the philosophical literature. The account of the moral permissibility of adultery I have offered is surely incomplete in many ways. The difficult issue of the degree to which a marriage must be unsatisfactory in the sex or love department in order for adultery to be morally permissible has not been explored. An individual's culpable failure to learn of her potential spouse's shortcomings before the wedding may override the moral permissibility of her adultery when those shortcomings become apparent. In addition, the conditions that make adultery morally permissible are nearly always matters of personal judgment rather than publicly verifiable states of affairs. This should not detract from the general philosophical interest in this topic.[15]

NOTES

1. An earlier version of this paper was read at the Mountain-Plains Philosophy Conference in October 1999 and at the meeting of the Pacific Division of the American Philosophical Association in Spring 2000. Eva Dadlez, Hugh LaFollette, Don Loeb, Raja Halwani, Lawrence Houlgate, Jenifer Dodd, Ben Eggleston, and Teresa Robertson have provided me with helpful comments. The comments of Ben Eggleston and Teresa Robertson have been especially helpful.

2. Richard Wasserstrom, "Is Adultery Immoral?" from Richard Wasserstrom ed. *Today's Moral Problems* 2nd ed. (New York: Macmillan, 1979) 290.

3. Michael J. Wreen, "What's Really Wrong with Adultery" from *Philosophy of Sex and Love: A Reader* Robert Trevas, Arthur Zucker, Donald Borchert (ed.) (Upper Saddle River, New Jersey: Prentice Hall, 1997) 176–181.

4. Wreen 177.

5. Wreen 178–179.

6. Raja Halwani, "Virtue Ethics and Adultery," *Journal of Social Philosophy* XXIX #3 (Winter, 1998) 5–18; Mike Martin, *Love's Virtues* (Lawrence, Kansas: University Press of Kansas) 1996 Chapter 4, Sexual Fidelity; and Bonnie Steinbock, "Adultery" *Philosophy and Public Policy* 6, #1 (Winter, 1986) 12–14.

7. See Martin, 81–82; Halwani, 14; and Steinbock, 14–15.

8. See Steinbock, 14, Halwani, 13 and Martin, 77.

9. William Melvin Kelley, "Carlyle Tries Polygamy" *The New Yorker* (August 4, 1997) I thank Teresa Robertson for suggesting this passage.

10. There are difficulties in giving an account of one's own well being in a marriage which can be a new unity. See Robert Nozick's discussion in "Love's Bond" from his *The Examined Life* (New York: Simon and Schuster, 1989).

11. This account is drawn from Lyla O'Driscoll's excellent discussion in "On the Nature and Value of Marriage" which first appeared in Mary Vetterling-Bragging, Frederick A. Elliston and Jane English, eds. *Feminism and Philosophy* (Totowa, New Jersey: Littlefield, Adams and Co. 1978) 249–263. This way of looking at the nature of marriage can accommodate deviations from the paradigm in special circumstances.

12. I shall assume that the person contemplating adultery is a woman because (1) I have to choose some singular pronoun and I prefer the traditionally less conventional one and (2) I have, in my own life, had more opportunity to think through this issue from a feminine than from a masculine perspective.

13. Ann Landers' famous question in these circumstances was: "Are you better off with him or without him?"

14. Consider the following passage from Michele Weiner Davis, *The Sex-Starved Marriage,* (New York: Simon and Schuster, 2003) 10–11. "I also urge you to consider the unfairness of the tacit agreement you have had with your spouse so clearly pointed out in Dr. Pat Love's excellent book, *The Truth About Love.* It goes something like this: 'I know you're sexually unhappy. Although I don't plan on doing anything about it, I still expect you to remain faithful.' Can you see what's wrong with this picture?"

15. I surmise, however, that a lack of philosophical interest in this topic may be explained by the fact that most philosophers are either married or in other serious long term relationships. This may make the topic difficult to write about if one's significant other takes an interest in one's philosophical projects.

9

Is Antioch's Sexual Offense Policy Wrong?

Soble and His Critics

Virtually everyone agrees that having sex with someone without that person's consent is morally wrong. But not everyone agrees about just what, precisely, constitutes consent. The result is the controversy surrounding date rape (also called "acquaintance rape"). In response to concerns about this problem, in the fall of 1990 and winter of 1991, students at Antioch College drafted the college's first Sexual Offense Policy. The policy aims to provide rules for determining what does and does not constitute consent for the purposes of sexual behavior by members of the campus community. The eventual implementation of the policy generated a nationwide debate and helped propel the issue of date rape into the forefront of discussions about sexuality on college campuses across the country. Critics of the policy charged that it was vague and paternalistic, while its defenders maintained that it was an effective, if imperfect, remedy for a serious problem. And while in the decade that followed many campuses adopted policies that were comparable with that of Antioch, the Antioch policy has remained a focal point in the debate over how universities should respond to the problem of date rape.

Alan Soble is perhaps the leading philosopher writing on issues involving human sexuality today. In 1997, he published a widely discussed critique of the Antioch policy (i.e., the version of the policy in effect in 1994; revisions to the policy have been made since then). In the featured article in this chapter, Soble explains the basic motivation behind the policy and then raises a number of objections to it. Most importantly, he charges that the policy places insufficient weight on nonverbal forms of consent and significantly weakens the practice of consent itself. To support the first contention, Soble argues that verbal forms of communication are not always unequivocal—"no" sometimes means "maybe," and "yes" sometimes reveals only the lack of will to say "no"—and nonverbal forms of communication are sometimes virtually unambiguous. To support his second contention, he argues that by requiring additional statements of consent at each additional level of intimacy, the policy prevents people from consenting ahead of time to an entire sexual experience and that this renders impossible a certain kind of valuable commitment that people should be able to make to each other.

In her reply to Soble's article, Eva Feder Kittay admits that she, too, was at first skeptical of the Antioch policy. But upon reflection, she now argues, the policy appears to be more sensible than it might at first seem and more reasonable than Soble claims it to be. This is so, in part, Kittay believes, because Soble's explanation of the *content* of the policy is incomplete in a relevant respect. The content allows, she argues, more weight to be given to nonverbal communication than Soble recognizes, at least in some contexts. But, more importantly, Kittay argues that Soble's critique of the Antioch policy overlooks the importance of the *context* of the policy: its having come from, and stayed in place with the approval of, the student body of the college. This is relevant, Kittay argues, in part because it casts the policy's focus on verbal consent in a different light and in part because it suggests that Soble's concern about the policy's impact on long-term relationships is misplaced. As a result, while Soble's analysis maintains that the Antioch policy infringes on student autonomy in various respects, Kittay suggests that the policy ultimately reaffirms it.

QUESTIONS FOR CONSIDERATION

The debate about Antioch's Sexual Offense Policy in particular, and about date rape in general, is complex and highly charged and touches upon a number of issues beyond those dealt with explicitly in these readings. As a way of initiating a critical discussion of the debate that arises from the clash between Soble and Kittay, however, we would suggest at least beginning with the following questions.

• Is Soble right that the policy places insufficient weight on nonverbal forms of consent, or is Kittay right in thinking that it gives them as much weight as they merit?

• Is Soble right in thinking that the policy precludes a valuable kind of commitment, one that involves consenting ahead of time to everything that follows from the initiation of sexual activity, or is Kittay right to have serious reservations about the value of such open-ended forms of consent?

• Is Kittay justified in maintaining that the context of the Antioch policy helps to overcome some of the objections that might initially seem to warrant rejecting it? In particular, in what sense does the fact that students have generally embraced the policy make its focus on verbal consent more reasonable? Does it make it reasonable even for students who opposed the policy? And does it succeed in overcoming Soble's worry about the effect of the policy on the viability of long-term relationships, or is Kittay unjustifiably cynical about the desire that most students have for less stable interactions?

FURTHER READING

Archard, David. "A Nod's as Good as a Wink: Consent, Convention, and Reasonable Belief." *Legal Theory* 3, no. 3 (September 1997): 273–90.

Francis, Leslie P., ed. *Date Rape: Feminism, Philosophy and the Law.* University Park: Penn State University Press, 1996.

McGregor, Joan. "Is It Rape?: On Acquaintance Rape and Taking Women's Consent Seriously." *Law and Philosophy* 25, no. 6 (November 2006): 663–72.

Panichas, George E. "Simple Rape and the Risks of Sex." *Law and Philosophy* 25, no. 6 (2006): 613–61.

ALAN SOBLE

Antioch's "Sexual Offense Policy"
A Philosophical Exploration

She: For the last time, do you love me or don't you?
He: I DON'T!
She: Quit stalling, I want a *direct* answer.
                            —Jane Russell and Fred Astaire[1]

1. "WHEN IN DOUBT, ASK"

Consider this seemingly innocuous moral judgment issued by philosopher Raymond Belliotti:

> "teasing" without the intention to fulfill that which the other can reasonably be expected to think was offered is immoral since it involves the nonfulfillment of that which the other could reasonably be expected as having been agreed upon.[2]

This might be right in the abstract; provocative and lingering flirtatious glances sometimes can reasonably be taken as an invitation to engage in sex; hence brazenly flirting and not fulfilling its meaning, or never intending to fulfill its meaning, is, like failing to honor other promises or invitations, *ceteris paribus* a moral defect—even if not a mortal sin. Abstractions aside, however, how are we to grasp "can *reasonably* be taken as"? A woman's innocent, inquisitive glance might be taken as a sexual invitation by an awfully optimistic fellow, and he and his peers might judge his perception "reasonable." This is the reason Catharine MacKinnon says that to use "reasonable belief as a standard without asking, on a substantive social basis, to whom the belief is reasonable and why—meaning, what conditions make it reasonable—is one-sided: male-sided."[3] Similarly, a man's innocent, inquisitive glance might be taken as a sexual leer by an anxiously sensitive woman, and

she and her peers might judge this perception "reasonable." Belliotti writes as if all were well with "reasonable":

> Although sexual contracts are not as formal or explicit as corporation agreements the rule of thumb should be the concept of reasonable expectation. If a woman smiles at me and agrees to have a drink I cannot reasonably assume . . . that she has agreed to spend the weekend with me.[4]

I suppose not. But why not? We do not now have in our culture a convention, a practice like the display of colored hankies, in which a smile before an accepted drink has that meaning. But nothing intrinsic to the action prevents its having, in the proper circumstances, that very meaning. And an optimistic fellow might say that the *special* sort of smile she, or another he, gave him constituted a sexual invitation. Belliotti continues his example:

> On the other hand if she did agree to share a room and bed with me for the weekend I could reasonably assume that she had agreed to have sexual intercourse.

Not true for many American couples as they travel through foreign lands together. Or maybe in accepting the invitation to share a room or sleeping car she agreed only to snuggle. Cues indicating the presence and kind of sexual interest are fluid; at one time in the recent past, a woman's inviting a man to her apartment or room carried more sexual meaning than it does now—even if that meaning still lingers on college campuses and elsewhere. To forestall such objections, Belliotti offers these instructions:

> If there is any doubt concerning whether or not someone has agreed to perform a certain sexual act with

Alan Soble, "Antioch's 'Sexual Offense Policy': A Philosophical Exploration," *Journal of Social Philosophy* 28, no. 1 (1997): 22–36. Some notes have been deleted. Reprinted by permission of Blackwell Publishing Ltd.

another, I would suggest that the doubting party simply ask the other and make the contract more explicit.... [W]hen in doubt assume nothing until a more explicit overture has been made.[5]

What could be more commonsensically true than this? But it is wrong. The man who thinks it reasonable in a given situation to assume that the woman has agreed to have sex will not have any doubt and so will have no motive to ask more explicitly what she wants. His failure to doubt, or his failure to imagine the bare possibility of doubting, whether the other has consented to engage in sex is brought about by the same factors that determine, for him, the reasonableness of his belief in her consent. It is silly to suggest "*when* in doubt, ask," because the problem is that not enough doubt arises in the first place, i.e., the brief look is taken too readily as reasonable or conclusive evidence of a sexual invitation. A man touches the arm of a woman who briefly glanced at him; she pulls away abruptly; but he is not caused to have doubts about her interest. Even if he does not take her resistance as further evidence of her desire, the reasonableness, for him, of his belief that her earlier glance was intentionally sexual is enough to prevent doubt from taking root when it should—immediately.

2. "'No' Means 'No'"

According to Susan Estrich, a man who engages in sex with a woman on the basis of an unreasonable belief in her consent should be charged with rape; only a genuinely reasonable belief in her consent should exculpate an accused rapist. Estrich wants it to be legally impossible for a man accused of rape to plead that he believed that the woman consented, when that belief was unreasonable, even though *he* thought it was reasonable. Estrich realizes that "reasonable belief" is a difficult notion. Still, she heroically proposes that "the reasonable man in the 1980s should be the one who understands that a woman's word is deserving of respect, whether she is a perfect stranger or his own wife." The reasonable man "is the one who ... understands that 'no means no'."[6] The man pawing the arm of the woman who pulls

abruptly away—the physical equivalent of "no"—had better immediately doubt the quality of his belief in her sexual interest. At the psychological level, this man might not doubt that she is sexually interested in him; Estrich's normative proposal is that he is to be held liable anyway, because he *should* be doubtful. Beyond this crude sort of case, I think Estrich means that, for the reasonable man, a woman's qualified locution ("Please, not tonight, I think I'd rather not"; "I don't know, I just don't feel like it") is not an invitation to continue trying, but "no." Her wish is expressed softly because she is tactful or frightened or because this is the women's language she has learned to speak. For the reasonable man, her "I'm not sure I want to" is either a tactful "no" or a request to back off while she autonomously makes up her own mind.

As congenial as Estrich's proposal is, she muddies the water with a tantalizing piece of logic:

> Many feminists would argue that so long as women are powerless relative to men, viewing a "yes" as a sign of true consent is misguided.... [M]any women who say yes to men they know, whether on dates or on the job, would say no if they could. I have no doubt that women's silence sometimes is the product not of passion and desire but of pressure and fear. Yet if yes may often mean no, at least from a woman's perspective, it does not seem so much to ask men, and the law, to respect the courage of the woman who does say no and to take her at her word.[7]

Estrich's reasoning seems to be: if something as antithetical to "no" as "yes" can mean "no," then surely something as consistent with "no," "no" itself, means "no." This argument has a curious consequence. If "yes" can mean "no," at least from a woman's *own* perspective (the woman who consents for financial reasons but whose heart and desire are not wrapped up in the act; a woman who agrees, but only after a barrage of pleading), then it will be difficult to deny that "no" spoken by some women can mean "maybe" or even "yes." From the perspective of some women, "no" can mean "try harder to convince me" or "show me how manly you are." Charlene Muehlenhard and Lisa Hollabaugh reported in 1988 that some women occasionally say "no" but do not mean it; 39.3 percent of the 610 college women they surveyed at Texas A&M University indicated that they had offered "token resistance" to sex "even though [they] had every intention to and [were] willing to engage in sexual intercourse."[8] Susan Rae Peterson partially explains these findings: "typical sexual involvement includes some resistance on the part of women . . . because they have been taught to do so, or they do not want to appear 'easy' or 'cheap'."[9]

Men cannot always tell when a woman's resistance is real or token, serious or playful; men are, moreover, often insensitive, even callous, as to what a woman does intend to communicate; and, after all, Muehlenhard and Hollabaugh's figure is only 39 percent and not 99 percent. For these reasons, as well as her own, Estrich's proposal is a wise suggestion. Men, and the courts, should always assume, in order to be cognitively, morally, and legally safe, that a woman's "no" means "no"—*even in those cases when it does or might not.* A man who takes "no" as "no" even when he suspects that a woman is testing his masculinity with token resistance is advised by Estrich to risk suffering a loss of sexual pleasure and a possible blow to his ego, in order to secure the greater good, for both him and her, of avoiding rape.

But if men are always to assume that "no" means "no," even though there is a nontrivial chance that it means "keep trying" or "yes," then Estrich, to be consistent, should permit men to assume that a woman's "yes" always means "yes"—even though, on her view, a woman's "yes" sometimes means "no." If, instead, Estrich wants men to sort out when a woman's "yes" really means "yes" and when it does not, in order that he be able to decide whether to take the "yes" at its face value and proceed with sex, she should propose some workable procedure for men to follow. Yet her description of the reasonable man mentions only what his response to "no" should be, and not what his response to "yes" should be. Encouraging women to abandon the token resistance maneuver, to give up saying "no" when they mean "maybe" or "yes," is helpful. But it will not take theorists of sex, or men in the presence of an apparently consenting woman, very far in deciphering when "yes" means "no."

3. The Antioch Policy

I propose that we understand Antioch University's "Sexual Offense Policy" as addressing the issues raised in our discussion of Belliotti and Estrich. The Policy's central provisions are these:[10]

A1. "Consent must be obtained verbally before there is any sexual contact or conduct."
A2. "[O]btaining consent is an on-going process in any sexual interaction."
A3. "If the level of sexual intimacy increases during an interaction . . . the people involved need to express their clear verbal consent before moving to that new level."
A4. "The request for consent must be specific to each act."
A5. "If you have had a particular level of sexual intimacy before with someone, you must still ask each and every time."
A6. "If someone has initially consented but then stops consenting during a sexual interaction, she/he should communicate withdrawal verbally and/or through physical resistance. The other individual(s) must stop immediately."
A7. "Don't ever make any assumptions about consent."

In an ethnically, religiously, economically, socially, and sexually diverse population, there might be no common and comprehensive understanding of what various bits of behavior mean in terms of expressing interest in or consenting to sex. In the absence of rigid conventions or a homogeneous community, a glance, either brief or prolonged, is too indefinite to be relied on to transmit information; an invitation to come to one's room, or sharing a room, or a bed, on a trip might or might not have some settled meaning; clothing and cosmetics in a pluralistic culture are equivocal. (Young men, more so than young women, take tight jeans and the absence of a bra under a top to signal an interest in sex.) Because physical movements and cues of various kinds can be interpreted in widely different ways, sexual activity entered into or carried out on the basis of this sort of (mis)information is liable to violate someone's rights or otherwise be indecent or offensive. Antioch insists that consent to sexual activity be verbal (A1) instead of behavioral.[11] Following this rule will minimize miscommunication and the harms it causes and encourage persons to treat each other with respect as autonomous agents.

Further, bodily movements or behaviors of a sexual sort that occur in the early stages of a possible sexual encounter can also be ambiguous and do not necessarily indicate a willingness to increase the intensity of, or to prolong, the encounter (hence A2, A3). Verbal communication is supposed to prevent misunderstandings rooted in indefinite body language; we should not assume consent on the basis of expressions of desire (lubrication, groans) or failures to resist an embrace (A1). Neither of these bodily phenomena—reacting with sexual arousal to a touch; not moving away when intimately touched—necessarily mean that the touched person welcomes the touch or wants it to continue. There are times when one's body responds with pleasure to a touch but one's mind disagrees with the body's judgment; Antioch's insistence on verbal consent after discussion and deliberation is meant to give the mind the decisive and autonomous say. Similarly, the verbal request for, and the verbal consent to, sexual contact must be not only explicit, but also specific for any sexual act that might occur (A4). Consenting to and then sharing a kiss does not imply consent to any other sexual act; the bodily movements that accompany the sexual arousal created by the kiss do not signal permission to proceed to some other sexual activity not yet discussed.

One provision (A7) is a rebuttal of Belliotti's advice, "when in doubt, ask." Antioch demands, more strictly than this, that the sexual partners entertain *universal* doubt and therefore *always* ask. Doubt about the other's consent must be categorical rather than hypothetical: not Belliotti's "when in doubt, assume nothing," but a Cartesian "doubt!" and "assume nothing!" To be on the cognitive, moral, and legal safe side, to avoid mistakes about desire or intention, always assume "no" unless a clear, verbal, explicit "yes" is forthcoming (A1, A3, A4). Men no longer have to worry about distinguishing a woman's mildly seductive behavior from her "incomplete

rejection strategy," about which men and boys are often confused; in the absence of an explicit "yes" on her part, he is, as demanded by Estrich, to assume a respectful "no." There's still the question of how a man is to know, when obvious consent-negating factors are lacking (e.g., she's had too much alcohol), whether a woman's "yes" truly means "yes." Antioch's solution is to rely on explicit, probing verbal communication that must occur not only before but also during a sexual encounter (A3, A5). The constant dialogue, the "on-going process" (A2) of getting consent in what Lois Pineau calls "communicative sexuality,"[12] is meant to provide the man with an opportunity to assess whether the woman's "yes" means "yes," to give her the opportunity to say a definite even if tactful "no," and to clear up confusions created by her silence or passive acquiescence. At the same time, there is to be no constant badgering—especially not under the rubric of "communicative sexuality"—of a woman by a man in response to her "no." A man's querying whether a woman's "no" really means "no" is to disrespect her "no" and fails to acknowledge her autonomy. It is also to embark on a course that might constitute verbal coercion.

It is illuminating to look at the Antioch policy from the perspective of the sadomasochistic subculture, in particular its use of "safe words." A set of safe words is a language, a common understanding, a convention jointly created (hence a Cartesian foundation) in advance of sex by the partners, to be used during a sexual encounter as a way to say "yes," "more," "no," to convey details about wants and dislikes, without spoiling the erotic mood. Thus the use of safe words attempts to achieve some of the goals of Antioch's policy without the cumbersome apparatus of explicit verbal consent at each level of sexual interaction (A3, A4). And a tactful safe word can gently accomplish an Antiochian withdrawal of consent to sex (A6). But there is a major difference between sadomasochism and Antiochian sex: a sadomasochistic pair want the activities to proceed smoothly, spontaneously, realistically, so one party grants to the other the right to carry on as she wishes, subject to the veto or modifications of safe words, which are to be used sparingly, only when necessary, as a last resort; the couple therefore eschew

Antiochian constant dialogue. In dispensing with the incessant chatter of on-going consent to higher levels of sexual interaction (A2, A3), the sadomasochistic pair violate another provision (A7): consent is assumed throughout the encounter in virtue of the early granting of rights. No such prior consent to sex into an indefinite future is admissible by Antioch (A2, A3, A4).

4. PLEASURE

Does Antioch's policy make sex less exciting? Does it force a couple to slow down, to savor each finger and tooth, when they would rather be overwhelmed by passion? Sarah Crichton criticizes the Antioch policy on the grounds that "it criminalizes the delicious unexpectedness of sex—a hand suddenly moves to here, a mouth to there."[13] But this consideration is not decisive. One goal of the Policy is to decrease the possibility that a person will unexpectedly experience (i.e., without being warned by being asked) something unpleasant that he or she does not want to experience: a mouth sucking on the wrong toe, a finger too rudely rammed in the rectum. The risk of undergoing unwanted acts or sensations is especially great with strangers, and it is in such a context that the requirement that consent be obtained specifically for each act makes the most sense. Sometimes we do not want the unexpected but only the expected, the particular sensations we know, trust, and yearn for. So there is in the Antioch policy a trade off: we lose the pleasure, if any, of the unexpected, but we also avoid the unpleasantness of the unexpected. This is why Crichton's point is not decisive. Perhaps for young people, or for those more generally who do not yet know what they like, verbal consent to specifically described touches or acts might make less sense. But in this case, too, reason exists to insist, for the sake of caution, on such consent.

Julia Reidhead also attempts to rebut the objection that Antioch's policy begets dull sex.[14] She claims that the Policy gives the partners a chance to be creative with language, to play linguistically with a request to touch the breast or "kiss the hollow of your neck" and to "reinvent [sex] privately." But Antioch thinks that sexual language needs to be less, rather than more, private; more specific, not less.[15] Hence Reidhead's praise for Antioch's policy misses its point: common linguistic understandings cannot be assumed in a heterogenous population. To encourage the creative, poetic use of language in framing sexual requests to proceed to a new level of sex is to provoke the misunderstandings the Policy was designed to prevent. Thus, when Reidhead queries, "What woman or man on Antioch's campus, or elsewhere, wouldn't welcome . . . 'May I kiss the hollow of your neck'," her homogenizing "or elsewhere" betrays the insensitivity to cultural and social differences and their linguistic concomitants that Antioch is trying to overcome.

Reidhead defends Antioch also by arguing that vocalizing creatively about sex before we do it is a fine way to mix the pleasures of language with the pleasures of the body. Indeed, the pleasures of talk are themselves sensual. "Antioch's subtle and imaginative mandate is an erotic windfall: an opportunity for undergraduates to discover that wordplay and foreplay can be happily entwined." Reidhead is right that talking about sex can be sexy and arousing, but wrong that this fact is consistent with the Antioch policy and one of its advantages. This cute reading of communication as itself sex almost throws Antioch's procedure into a vicious regress: if no sexual activity is permissible without prior consent (A1), and consent must be spoken, then if a request for sexual activity is constructed to be a sexually arousing locution, it would amount to a sexual act and hence would be impermissible unless it, in turn, had already received specific consent (A1, A4). So Y's consent to nonverbal sexual activity must be preceded by X's request for that activity *and* by X's request to utter that request. Further, to try to get consent for the sexual act of kissing the neck by talking sensually about kissing the neck is to employ the pleasure elicited by one sexual act to bring about the occurrence of another sexual act. But obtaining consent for a sexual act by causing even mild sexual pleasure with a seductive request is to interfere with calm and rational deliberation—as much as a shot or two of whiskey would. This is why Antioch insists (A3) that between any two sexual levels there must be a pause, a sexual gap, that makes space for three things: (1) a thoughtful, verbal act of request, (2) deliberations about whether or not to proceed, and then (3) either consent or denial. A well-timed hiatus respected by both parties provides an obstacle to misreadings; Augustinian bodily perturbations are to be checked while the mind reconsiders.

5. BODY TALK

The body should not be dismissed. When two people in love embrace tightly, eyes glued to the other's eyes, bodies pulsating with pleasure, they often do know (*how,* is the mystery) without explicit verbalization, from the way they touch each other and respond to these touches, that each wants and consents to the sex that is about to occur. Other cases of successful communication—in and out of sexual contexts—are explicit and specific without being verbal. So even if the truth of the particular claim that the mouth can say "no" while the body exclaims an overriding "yes" is debatable, the general idea, that the body sometimes does speak a clear language, seems fine. Maybe this is why Antioch, even though it requires a verbal "yes" for proceeding with sex (A1), allows a nonverbal "no" to be sufficient for *withdrawing* consent (A6); nonverbal behavior can have a clear meaning. Certain voluntary actions, even some impulsive, reflex-like, bodily movements, do mean "no," and about these there should be no mistake, in the same Estrichian way that about the meaning of the simple verbal "no" there should be no mistake. But if such motions can be assumed or demanded to be understood in a pluralistic community—*pulling away when touched means "no"*—then some voluntary behaviors and involuntary bodily movements must reliably signal "yes."

According to the Policy, a verbal "yes" replaces any possible bodily movement or behavior as the one and only reliable sign that proceeding with sexual activity is permissible. If I ask, "may I kiss you?" I may not proceed on the basis of your bodily reply, e.g., you push your mouth out at mine, or groan and open your mouth invitingly, because even though it seems obvious what these behaviors mean ("yes"), I might be making an interpretive mistake: I see your open mouth as presented "invitingly" because I have

with undue optimism deceived myself into thinking that's what you mean. So I must wait for the words, "yes, you may kiss me,"[16] about which interpretive unclarity is not supposed to arise, else the problem Antioch set for itself is unsolvable. The verbal "yes," *after* communicative probing, is Antioch's Cartesian foundation. But can the ambiguities of the verbal be cleared up by language itself? How much communicative probing is *enough?* This question opens up a hermeneutic circle that traps Antioch's policy. Her "yes," repeated several times under the third-degree of communicative sex, can always be probed more for genuineness, if I wanted to *really* make sure. But, losing patience, she shows her "yes" to be genuine when she grabs me. The body reasserts itself.

My continuing to probe her "yes" over and over again, to make sure that her heart and desire are wrapped up in the act to which she is apparently consenting (must I ask her whether her agreement has been engineered for my benefit by "compulsory heterosexuality"?), is a kind of paternalism. Because the robust respect that Antioch's policy fosters for a woman's "no" is offset by the weaker respect it fosters for her "yes," conceiving of the Antioch policy not as attempting to foster respect for the autonomy of the other, but as attempting to prevent acquaintance rape, i.e., harmful behaviors, is more accurate. At best, the relationship between Antioch's policy and autonomy is unclear. One Antioch student, Suzy Martin, defends the Policy by saying that "It made me aware I *have* a voice. I didn't know that before."[17] Coming in the mid-90s from a college-age woman, the kind of person we expect to know better, this remark is astonishing. In effect, she admits that what Antioch is doing for her, at such an advanced age, is what her parents and earlier schooling should have done long ago, to teach her that she has a voice. Thus Antioch is employing an anti-autonomy principle in its treatment of young adults—in loco parentis—that my college generation had fought to eliminate.

6. CONSENT

The Policy lays it down that previous sexual encounters between two people do not relax or change the rules to be followed during their later encounters (A5); the casual sex of one-night stands and that of on-going relationships are governed by the same standards. Nor does a person's sexual biography (reputation) count for anything. No historical facts allow "assumptions about consent" (A7). Indeed, in requiring consent at each different level of a single sexual encounter, Antioch applies the same principle of the irrelevance of history to each sub-act within that encounter. Earlier consent to one sub-act within a single encounter creates no presumption that one may proceed, without repeating the procedure of obtaining explicit and specific consent, to later sub-acts in the same encounter, in the same way that one sexual encounter does not mean that consent can be assumed for later encounters. The history of the relationship, let alone the history of the evening, counts for nothing. The Antioch policy, then, implies that one cannot consent in advance to a whole night of sex, but only to a single atomistic act, one small part of an encounter. Similarly, in denying the relevance of the historical, Antioch makes a Pauline marriage contract impossible.[18] In such a marriage, one consents at the very beginning, in advance, to a whole series of sexual acts that might comprise the rest of one's sexual life; consent to sex is presumed after the exchange of vows and rings; each spouse owns the body and sexual powers of the other; and so marital rape is conceptually impossible, replaced by a notion of fulfilling the "marriage debt." In rejecting the possibility of such an arrangement, even if voluntarily contracted, Antioch cuts back on a traditional power of consent, its ability to apply to an indefinite, open future. For Antioch, consent is short-lived; it dies an easy death, and must always be replaced by a new generation of consents.

Antioch also cuts back on the power of consent by making it not binding: one can withdraw consent at any time during any act or sub-act (A6). Nothing in the Policy indicates that the right to withdraw is limited by the sexual satisfaction or other expectations of one's partner. Any such qualification would also run counter to the Policy's spirit. This is a difference between Antioch's policy and Belliotti's libertarianism, according to which breaking a sexual promise is at least a prima facie moral fault. It is also contrary to

the indissolubility of Pauline marriage. But that Antioch would be indulgent about withdrawing consent makes sense, given Antioch's distrust of the historical. Consenting is an act that occupies a discrete location in place and time; it is a historical event, and that it has occurred is a historical fact; thus consent is itself precisely the kind of thing whose weight Antioch discounts. Consenting to a sexual act does not entail, for Antioch, that one ought to perform the act, and not even that one has a prima facie duty to do so; the act need not take place because the only justification for it to occur is the act of consenting that has already receded into the past and has become a mere piece of impotent history. When consent into the future, given today for tomorrow, is ruled out, so too is consent into the future, now for ten seconds from now. How could consent have the power to legitimize any subsequent sexual act? An air of paradox surrounds the Policy: it makes consent the centerpiece of valid sexual conduct, yet its concept of consent is emaciated. Of course, "unless refusal of consent or withdrawal of consent are real possibilities, we can no longer speak of 'consent' in any genuine sense."[19] But that withdrawing consent must be possible does not entail that we have carte blanche permission to do so. My guess is that Belliotti is right, that withdrawing consent to an act to which one has consented is prima facie wrong. The logical possibility that consent is binding in this way is necessary for taking consent seriously as a legitimizer of sexual activity.

Still, if X has promised a sexual act to Y, but withdraws consent and so reneges, it does *not* follow from libertarianism that Y has a right to compel X into compliance. Nor does it follow from the terms of Pauline marriage, in which the spouses consent to a lifetime of sexual acts. Neither the fact that each person has a duty, the marriage debt, to provide sexual pleasure for the other whenever the other wants it, nor the fact that in such a marriage the one initial act of consent makes rape conceptually impossible, imply that a spurned spouse may rightfully force himself upon the other. Pauline marriage is egalitarian; the wife owns the husband and his ability to perform sexually as much as he owns her capacity to provide pleasure. In patriarchal practice, the man expects sexual access to his wife in exchange for economic support, and even if rape is conceptually impossible he might extract the marriage debt: "if she shows unwillingness or lack of inclination to engage with him in sexual intercourse, he may wish to remind her of the nature of the bargain they struck. The act of rape may serve conveniently as a communicative vehicle for reminding her."[20] Neither violence nor abuse are legitimated by the principles of Pauline marriage; perhaps their possibility explains why Paul admonishes spouses to show "benevolence" to each other (1 Cor. 7:3).[21]

Finally, Antioch's policy also does not permit "metaconsent," or consent about (the necessity of) consent. Consent, in principle, should be able to alter the background presumption, in the relationship between two people, *from* "assume 'no' unless you hear an explicit 'yes'" *to* "assume 'yes' unless you hear an explicit 'no'," or *from* "don't you dare try without an explicit go-ahead" *to* "feel free to try but be prepared for a 'no'." This power of consent is abolished by Antioch's making history irrelevant; consent to prior acts creates no presumption in favor of "yes" tonight (A5). Further, to give consent into the future allows one's partner to make a prohibited assumption (A7). There is no provision in the Policy that empowers a couple to jettison the Policy by free and mutual consent; here is another way Antioch's policy is not designed to foster autonomy. In Pauline marriage, by contrast, one act of consent, the marriage vow, has the power to change presumptions from "no" to an ongoing "yes." Such is the power of consent for Paul, that it both applies to the future and is binding: we make our bed and then lie in it. Antioch's notion of consent has freed us from such stodgy concerns.

NOTES

1. The epigraph to chapter 9 of Susan Haack's *Evidence and Inquiry* (Oxford: Blackwell, 1993), 182. Professor Haack thanks David Stove for supplying it.

2. "A Philosophical Analysis of Sexual Ethics," *Journal of Social Philosophy* 10, no. 3 (1979): 8–11, at 11.

3. *Toward a Feminist Theory of the State* (Cambridge: Harvard University Press, 1989), 183; see 181.

4. "A Philosophical Analysis of Sexual Ethics," 9.

5. Belliotti repeats the "when in doubt, ask" advice in his essay "Sex" (in Peter Singer, ed., *A Companion to Ethics* [Oxford: Blackwell, 1991], 315–26, at 325) and in his treatise *Good Sex: Perspectives on Sexual Ethics* (Lawrence, Kan.: University Press of Kansas, 1993), 106–107. See my "book note" in *Ethics* 105, no. 2 (1995): 447–48.

6. *Real Rape* (Cambridge: Harvard University Press, 1987), 97–98.

7. Ibid., 102.

8. "Do Women Sometimes Say No When They Mean Yes? The Prevalence and Correlates of Token Resistance to Sex," *Journal of Personality and Social Psychology* 54, no. 5 (1988): 872–79.

9. "Coercion and Rape: The State as a Male Protection Racket," in Mary Vetterling-Braggin, Frederick A. Elliston, and Jane English, eds., *Feminism and Philosophy* (Totowa, N.J.: Littlefield, Adams, 1977), 360–71, at 365. See also Muehlenhard and Hollabaugh on the wide variety of reasons women have for carrying out this sometimes "rational" strategy (875, 878).

10. I quote from a copy of the Policy and its introduction sent to me in 1994 by the Office of the President, Antioch University. The numbering of the provisions is my own. The Policy was intended to be gender- and sexual orientation-neutral, allowing the possibility of gay or lesbian acquaintance rape and the rape of a man by a woman.

11. At least seven times in the Policy and its introduction, it is stated that consent to sexual activity must be verbal. Only once does the Policy depart from this formula: "the person with whom sexual contact/conduct is initiated is responsible to express verbally and/or physically her/his willingness or lack of willingness when reasonably possible." Because the bulk of the Policy insists that consent be verbal, I discount this one awkward and *possibly* contradictory sentence. Further, "reasonably" here nearly destroys the power of the Policy to resolve issues *about* reasonableness.

The Policy also says, "If sexual contact . . . is *not* mutually and simultaneously initiated, then the person who initiates sexual contact . . . is responsible for getting the verbal consent of the other individuals(s) involved" (italics added). From the statement that when mutual and simultaneous initiation is absent, verbal consent is required, it does not follow (nor does the Policy ever assert) that when mutual and simultaneous initiation is present, verbal consent can be dispensed with. To claim otherwise—to deny that the Antioch policy always requires verbal consent—is to commit an elementary logical fallacy. (This mistake was made by my commentator at the APA session.) Anyway, if we are to construe the Antioch policy as an interesting and novel approach to the problems we are discussing, we should not read it as asserting that "mutual and simultaneous initiation," cancels the need for verbal consent. The aroused and optimistic person who subjectively has no doubt that the other person is consenting, but is mistaken about that, is a version of the aroused and optimistic person who assumes that his initiation is reciprocated mutually and simultaneously by the other, but is similarly mistaken. Thus the good intentions of the Antioch policy would fall prey to the same psychological and moral delusions that undermined Belliotti's principle, "when in doubt, ask."

12. A man "cannot know, except through the practice of communicative sexuality, whether his partner has any sexual reason for continuing the encounter"—or any other reason for doing so ("Date Rape: A Feminist Analysis," *Law and Philosophy* 8 [1989]: 217–43, at 239). The essays in Leslie Francis's anthology *Date Rape* (University Park: Penn State University Press, 1996) explore both the Antioch policy and Pineau's essay.

13. "Sexual Correctness. Has It Gone Too Far?" in Susan J. Bunting, ed., *Human Sexuality 95/96* (Guilford, Conn.: Dushkin, 1995), 208–211, at 209.

14. "Good Sex" [letter], *The New Yorker* (Jan. 10, 1994), 8.

15. Antioch, however, does very little to make specific the "specific" of A4. Thus the Policy is vulnerable to wisecracks:

[*X* and *Y* sit on a couch, face-to-face.]

X: May I kiss you?

Y: Of course. Go ahead.

[*Y* makes *Y*'s mouth available; *X* slides *X*'s tongue deeply into *Y*'s oral cavity. *Y* pulls sharply away.]

Y: I didn't say you could *French* kiss me!

16. According to the Policy, "Consent must be clear and verbal (i.e., saying: yes, I want to kiss you also)."

17. Jennifer Wolf, "Sex By the Rules," *Glamour* (May 1994), 256–59, 290, at 258.

18. See 1 Cor. 7: [4]The wife hath not power of her own body, but the husband: and likewise also the husband hath not power of his own body, but the wife. [5]Defraud ye not one the other, except it be with consent for a time, that ye may give yourselves to fasting and prayer; and come together again, that Satan tempt you not for your incontinency.

19. Pateman, "Women and Consent," 150.

20. Carolyn Shafer and Marilyn Frye, "Rape and Respect," in Mary Vetterling-Braggin et al., *Feminism and Philosophy*, 333–46, at 342.

21. "It is in fact justly observed that a conjugal act imposed upon one's partner without regard for his or her condition and lawful desires is not a true act of love, and therefore denies an exigency of right moral order in the relationships between husband and wife" (Paul VI, "Humanae Vitae," in Robert Baker and Frederick Elliston, eds., *Philosophy and Sex*, 2nd ed. [Buffalo, N.Y.: Prometheus, 1984], 167–83, at 173).

EVA FEDER KITTAY

AH! My Foolish Heart

A Reply to Alan Soble's "Antioch's 'Sexual Offense Policy':
A Philosophical Exploration"[1]

A sexual code occupies an uneasy position at the intersection of the public and private, the communal and intimate, the codifiable and spontaneous, the articulate and ineffable. And sexual conduct is located at the troubling interface of pleasure and offense; passion and power; freedom and submission; desire as an individual drive and desire as the epiphany of mutuality—the desiring of the other's desire. How do we regulate sexual conduct? How can any code legislate sexual desire or successfully thwart abusive sexuality? Here the wise say that only fools do tread. Since Antioch announced its Sexual Offense Policy, Antioch has, in the eyes of the media and some retro (and not so retro) feminists and academics, worn a dunce cap. Is it well-deserved?

After a clear, and seemingly sympathetic, discussion of the code that includes much of the motivation for the policy, Alan Soble weighs in with the wise. On three grounds: pleasure, body talk, and consent.[2]

Upon first learning of the Sexual Offense Policy, my romantic heart declared this was a silly, foolish code—though my feminist mind urged a more cautious judgment. To have to verbally consent to each level (and just what is a level anyway?) of sexual intimacy? each time? even with a partner with whom one had been intimate many times before? Many of us

lose the capacity of articulate speech at these moments. Are we to be deprived of our hearts' desire since, unlike Molly Bloom, we don't utter an ecstatic "Yes! yes! yes!" at the appropriate moment?

Reading the harrowing accounts of date rapes recounted by Robin Warshaw,[3] I kept wondering if a code such as Antioch's would help in any of these cases. And if it would not, what *was* the point? Being on sabbatical, I was unable to canvas my classes for the student point of view. Fortunately, I had some private college-aged informants, my twenty-year-old son, his girlfriend (whom I questioned separately), and their friends. I also queried colleagues who had discussed the code with their students. There seemed to be a rather interesting response that came up again and again: "The code is silly, but I wouldn't mind it being there. It would be a way of opening up discussion on these issues." Only one young man I spoke to said it would encourage him to only have sex with himself—he always would know that the answer was "yes."

Taking a closer look at the code, I noticed some interesting phrases that are omitted in Alan Soble's summary. In the seven-point discussion of consent, the first point justifies Soble's claim that "verbal 'yes' . . . is Antioch's "Cartesian foundation":[4]

From Eva Feder Kittay, "AH! My Foolish Heart: A Reply to Alan Soble's 'Antioch's "Sexual Offense Policy": A Philosophical Exploration,'" *Journal of Social Philosophy* 28, no. 2 (1997): 153–59. Some notes and some parts of the text have been deleted. Reprinted by permission of Blackwell Publishing Ltd.

1. For the purpose of this policy, "consent" shall be defined as follows: "the act of willingly and verbally agreeing to engage in a specific sexual contact or conduct."[5]

And yet the next point has an antecedent clause that implies that verbal consent is not *always* demanded:

2. If sexual contact and/or conduct is not mutually and simultaneously initiated, then the person who initiates sexual contact/conduct is responsible for getting the verbal consent of the other individual(s) involved.[6]

"*If* sexual contact and/or conduct is *not mutually* and *simultaneously* initiated . . ." So, if my partner and I simultaneously are seized with the desire to kiss, we don't need to say a thing as our mouths spontaneously move toward each other. And if I am as passionately unbuttoning my partner and my partner unbuttons me, we can both remain undisturbed in our inarticulate bliss.

Therefore, contrary to Soble's reading, we are not always obliged to obtain verbal consent, not forced to "mix the pleasures of language with the pleasures of the body"[7] *if* the sex is mutually initiated.

Now consider the fourth point:

4. The person with whom sexual contact/conduct is initiated is responsible to express verbally and/or *physically* his/her willingness or lack of willingness when *reasonably* possible (emphasis mine).[8]

To express verbally *or physically* willingness or unwillingness, when *reasonably* possible. Aha! If the initiator asks, I can respond physically, I don't have to utter "yes" or even moan. And if the noninitiator is in a swoon of delight and tongue-tiedness, the whole sexual encounter can go on with a minimal amount of question and answer. But, if there is any ambiguity at all, the code protects both the noninitiator and the initiator alike by defining responsibilities for each.

Now this begins to sound less absurd. Under the heading of "Body Talk" Soble writes: "According to the policy, a verbal 'yes' replaces all bodily movements as the only reliable sign that proceeding with sex is permissible. If I ask, "may I kiss you?" I may not proceed on the basis of your bodily reply, e.g., you push your mouth out at mine and open it invitingly . . ."[9] A verbal yes may be the only fully *reliable* sign, but it's not at all clear from the passages cited above that the code *proscribes* sex based on such "body talk," or that it construes heeding (affirmative) body talk—in limited and unambiguous circumstances—as sexual offense.

Soble furthermore insists that the verbal "yes" is only a yes after sufficient probing. The probing requirement isn't explicit in the code, but arises from the possibility that women, because of their socialization to be cooperative and nonconfrontational, may say "yes" when they mean "no," Rather than explicitly calling for the sort of probing Soble envisions, the code sets out a clear set of responsibilities for both initiator and noninitiator. The initiator is responsible for obtaining verbal consent; the noninitiator is responsible for responding verbally or physically whenever possible. As Soble points out, this privileges the physical withdrawal over the physical assent since consent is, both by definition and by explicit statement, verbal. But it also opens the window, when there is no ambiguity in the situation for the sexual activity to respond to body talk.

Two things are learned from considering the passages omitted in Soble's summary.

First: there are allowances for the body language so often more in tune with the heightened sexual state than articulate speech. Perhaps this is a contradiction in the policy. Or perhaps the policy only starts to make sense in a context where there is a great deal of discussion that helps to clarify its intent and purpose.

Second: The noninitiator has a responsibility in this interaction, along with the initiator. A young woman socialized in a stereotypical feminine way has a responsibility to work her way out of such constricting socializing influences. If the policy is more educative and preventative than proscriptive and punitive, as it declares itself to be, "The educational aspects of this policy are intended to prevent sexual offenses and ultimately to heighten community awareness,"[10] then this code serves to encourage previously unassertive partners to be more assertive and to encourage overly assertive partners to reign in their overbearing behavior. Rather than undermining autonomy and acting paternalistically in loco parentis, Antioch encourages autonomy in the form of more responsible and responsive sexuality.

These considerations mark a considerable change in my first reaction to the Antioch code. The clincher came when I located Antioch College on a websurfing night and read the home page addressed to prospective students: "Antioch believes it should be a single cohesive community based on principles of democracy and citizenship. . . . Because Antioch students are considered equal members of the community, they participate in major decision-making committees at the College and have responsibility for student organizations and activities on campus." Although many student handbooks read like this, Antioch has always had a very strong tradition of taking such words seriously. As Alan Guskin, President of Antioch at the time the policy was first formulated, writes,[11] and as discussions with Antioch alumnae confirmed,[12] the policy was arrived at through intensive campus discussion among students and faculty. Even more significant, the code is reviewed each year and each year students elect whether to retain it, modify it, or discard it.

This contextualization of the code is, I believe, crucial to evaluating it. If this policy were handed down from on high by the administration to a reluctant student body that had to puzzle its way through the sorts of unclarities and paradoxes Soble highlights, then I would continue to share his skepticism. Likewise, if this policy were to be adopted outside of a specific and close community in which the code serves as a prod to discussing consensual sex, then again, we should be swayed by Soble's arguments. Although there is a sense in which the policy is, as Matthew Silliman declares in the title of an article, "a community experiment in communicative sexuality,"[13] the policy is also a product of an understanding of a *particular* community. How does contextualizing the policy to the Antioch community help?

Consider first the question of pleasure. Those who mutually initiate sex, at all levels, can have pleasure non-interruptus. But when one initiates sex, then a verbal consent is necessary. Can the verbal question and the consent be less intrusive to the romance than it seems at first? Soble says no, because sexy speech (as MacKinnon likes to remind us) is already sex. So either we have a nonsexy way of asking or we have an infinite regress. When I raised this point with the president of the Alum Association, he responded that the permissibility of making the request a part of the sexual encounter is part of the social contract which established the code in the first place. That is to say, in the numerous workshops and discussions around the policy, the permissibility of this initiatory level of sexual contact is established. It forms part of the background condition and is not explicitly stated in the code.[14] Take the Antioch out of "Antioch's Sexual Offense Policy" and you have a different policy. Of course, this understanding of the policy leaves the door open to a lascivious and unwanted sexual invitation of, say, a faculty member to a student. Such a sexual invitation/question has all the power imbalances in place that can, at worst, make refusal difficult, and, at best, be shocking and highly offensive to the more vulnerable party. Such a possibility exposes a limitation of the policy and the need for more than a code to insure fully consensual sex. But it doesn't vitiate the usefulness of the code.[15]

Second, consider the question of "body talk." We have already seen that in the situation in which all partners are mutually initiating at all points in the encounter, they can speak, moan, groan or remain silent—as long as everything is completely clear to both. For the rest of the cases, Soble argues that not only do we have to ask and reply, but the initiator has to probe for a sincere "yes." This, he suggests, is because the Antioch policy does not sufficiently respect the ways in which the body talks, not only in sexual affairs, but in all matters. This argument is premised on a sexual scenario of a "yes" meaning a "no," one common enough. Soble directs us to a Texas A&M study in which 39 percent of college women polled indicated that they have offered token "resistance" when they *intended* to engage in sex.[16] However, within a community that affirms the sexual offense policy in question each year anew, where the policy becomes the prod to open discussion of matters sexual, and where the responsibility for learning to say no when you mean no is understood as part of the educative purpose of the code, the probing is *de trop*. The demand for verbal consent is not about a disregard for body talk (when affirmative) but about setting forth the conditions for a communication sufficiently *unambiguous* to minimize the dangers and harm of date rape. So contextualized, Soble's claim that "the robust respect that Antioch's policy fosters for a woman's 'no' is offset by the weaker respect it fosters for her 'yes'" is false.

Finally let us consider the question of consent. It is true that "Antioch cuts back on a traditional power of consent, its ability to apply to an indefinite, open future."[17] But perhaps that is just right, when it comes to matters of sexual desire. A Pauline marriage, after all, makes marital rape on oxymoron, and any woman who has been raped by her husband will tell you that there is nothing oxymoronic about her trauma. Antioch's policy, however, is not meant to govern long-term relationships or marriages, Pauline or otherwise. In the context of the Antioch College, the code applies to an undergraduate population that does not, in general, have many long-term relationships. Probably most sexual encounters are first-, second-, thirdtime contacts.[18] It is to these transient relations that the policy is directed. In this context it is inappropriate to think that consent applies to "an indefinite, open future." This is not to say that a marriage or long term relation in which one could not make a transition from "assume 'no' unless you get a 'yes'" to "assume 'yes' unless you get a no" would be a sad affair.

Soble, however, raises a more difficult issue with respect to consent. He points out that Antioch cuts back on the power of consent by making it not binding: I agree to have so much sex with you and while halfway through I change my mind and want you to stop. Am I immoral? Is the policy fostering the immorality of the tease in countering the immorality of the rapist? If I agree to a sexual act in bad faith, then I am a tease. But if I agree in good faith, and if in the midst of the experience I find it unpleasant or unexciting and so ask my partner to stop, I am not *teasing* but responding to something important to my own self-respect. To continue sex past the point of my own desiring is to experience myself as a mere object for another's use. "But," says my partner, "you

consented and you are obliged to let me continue." Why doesn't that work? There is a feature of sexuality that is not amenable to a notion of consent. Consent within policies or codes are generally understood through the model of contract: I voluntarily agree to a specified such and such, and you forming your expectations based on the agreement hold me to the contractual terms.

The contractual model, however, is inappropriate in many intimate domains. Consent in these contexts is less an agreement binding into the future that will override itinerant desires than the expression of a willing, wanting, desiring self that seeks fulfillment with and through another. So-called "surrogate mothering" falls into this category. If a birth mother gives up the child she has born as a gift, that is one thing; if she gives it up for payment, that is quite another. A contractual relation demands the action of an agreed-to giving, whether or not the desire to give continues to be present at the moment, past the time the contract is signed. If I promise you a gift and don't deliver on the promise, I will disappoint you, but you will not have a claim on that gift. While you can accuse me of breaking my promise, you cannot make a claim to that gift. The strong sense that surrogacy ought not to be bound to contract in the same way other transactions are arises from the nature of the act as a gift, that is a giving to which we attach a desire to give another satisfaction through our own actions. Sexual contact has a similar nature. If the sexual contact is not desired at *that* moment, then one makes of oneself a sexual object and not a sexual agent. One makes oneself into a thing, and the other who insists on the sexual act makes of the partner a means only, a means to one's own pleasure regardless of the desire of the partner.

Barbara Herman in a fascinating article argues that Kant's view of sexuality is remarkably akin to that of some radical feminists, in particular, Andrea Dworkin and MacKinnon. Kant's resolution to the problem of sexual love, which makes of the other an object of one's own sexual desire without regard to human nature but to sex alone, is marriage:

> The sole condition on which we are free to make use of our sexual desire depends upon the right to dispose over

the person as a whole—over the welfare and happiness and generally over all the circumstances of that person . . . [I obtain these rights over the whole person (and so have the right of sexual use of that person)] only by giving the person the same rights over myself.[19]

But why not say instead: A sexual encounter with another, which has the recognition of the other's desire (and so the other's sexual agency) as a sine qua non, is the sole way in which we can engage in sex without reducing the other to an object—whether in marriage or in a one-night stand. In that case, consent cannot be understood on the contractual model, but on a model of mutual desiring, a desiring which must be alive at each moment. This, I believe, stands behind the model of communicative sex as better sex that is advocated by Lois Pineau.[20] To the extent that the Antioch policy's demand for consent is understood contractually, it will be a limitation of the policy. But if the policy is used as an educative tool, accompanied by discussion about its meaning and intent, then it can serve to instruct and train young persons for sexual encounters that promote mutuality and respect. In so doing, it can foster both good sex and the autonomy of the one who initiates and the one who responds.

Now I have made a full 180-degree turnabout from my first reactions to the policy. Of course, it seems that some things might be lost: That surprise (not yet consented to) touch that thrills beyond measure; the awakening of ardor through a kiss by someone who never before moved you; and doubtless much else. Then again it would also be fun to drive without seatbelts and road signs, and with only a watchful eye. But even with the road signs there are too many car accidents. Best to keep the seatbelts on.

Maybe the policy seen in context is not so foolish after all. And perhaps it teaches me that I do well to listen to my feminist mind before allowing my foolish heart the last word.

NOTES

1. This paper was first delivered as a commentary to Alan Soble's "Antioch's 'Sexual Offense Policy': A Philosophical Exploration," Dec. 1995, at the Eastern Division APA Meetings.

2. Alan Soble, "Antioch's 'Sexual Offense Policy': A Philosophical Exploration," *Journal of Social Philosophy* 28, no. 1 (Spring 1997): 22–36.

3. Robin Warshaw, *I Never Called It Rape: The Ms. Report on Recognizing, Fighting and Surviving Date Rape* (New York: Harper & Row, 1988).

4. Soble, 27.

5. Antioch College, "The Antioch College Sexual Offense Policy," in *Date Rape: Feminism Philosophy, and the Law*, ed. Leslie Francis (University Park, PA: The Pennsylvania University Press, 1992), 140.

6. Antioch, 140.

7. Soble, 28.

8. Antioch, 140.

9. Soble, 29.

10. Antioch, 139.

11. Alan E. Guskin, "The Antioch Response: Sex, You Just Don't Talk About It," in *Date Rape: Feminism Philosophy, and the Law*, 155–66.

12. My discussions included one with Eric Bates, president of Antioch's Alumnae Association.

13. "The Antioch Policy, a Community Experiment in Communicative Sexuality" in *Date Rape: Feminism Philosophy, and the Law*, 167–76.

14. Personal Communication with Eric Bates.

15. There is, however, a clause in the "Consent" discussion which covers situations of intimidation and coercion used for obtaining the verbal consent:

7. If someone verbally agrees to engage in specific contact or conduct, but it is not of her/his own free will due to any of the circumstances stated in (a) through (d) below, then the person initiating shall be considered in violation of this policy if: . . . (d) the person initiating has forced, threatened, coerced, or intimidated the other individual(s) into engaging in sexual contact and/or sexual conduct.

Antioch College, "The Antioch College Sexual Offense Policy," in *Date Rape: Feminism Philosophy, and the Law*, 141.

16. This study is cited in Soble, 24.

17. Soble, 31.

18. This point is emphasized in Guskin, 1996.

19. Kant, *Lectures on Ethics*, p. 167, quoted in Barbara Herman, "Thinking about Kant on Sex and Marriage," in Anthony and Witt, eds., *A Mind of One's Own: Feminist Essays on Reason and Objectivity* (Boulder: Westview Press, 1993, p. 60.

20. Lois Pineau, "Date Rape: A Feminist Analysis," in *Date Rape: Feminism Philosophy, and the Law*, 1–26.

10

Is Prostitution Wrong?

Ericsson and His Critics

Prostitution involves the exchange of money for sexual services. Although it can come in many forms, the standard case of prostitution involves a man paying a woman in exchange for her having sexual intercourse with him. Many people find this practice to be morally objectionable. Prostitution is forbidden by most religious traditions and by the laws of many nations, and even those who believe that criminal laws against prostitution are unjust still often agree that engaging in the practice is nonetheless itself morally objectionable. Although they might believe that it is none of the government's business, they would feel ashamed to work as a prostitute, to hire one, or even to be friendly with or related to one. Surely the view that prostitution is a morally objectionable profession in this sense is a widespread one.

But one can also regard prostitution as simply one further example of a free and voluntary commercial exchange for services provided, one that is good and valuable rather than noxious and objectionable because it provides each party with something that he or she desires. This is the way that Lars O. Ericsson conceives of the practice in his article "Charges Against Prostitution: An Attempt at a Philosophical Assessment," which serves as the featured article for this chapter. It is true, as Ericsson recognizes, that prostitution differs from the provision of other services in that the services a prostitute provides are sexual in nature. But, he maintains, this difference in itself is not morally relevant. If the general provision of nonsexual services on an open market is morally unobjectionable and a good thing, he argues, then there is no reason not to say the same thing about the similar provision of sexual services.

Most people who find prostitution objectionable, of course, would say that it is precisely the sexual nature of the service that the prostitute provides that makes the difference. This, they would say, is what explains why it is perfectly appropriate to pay a psychologist or a physical therapist to help you feel better, for example, but morally inappropriate to pay a prostitute to have sex with you. The critical question therefore becomes: Why, exactly, should the sexual nature of the services provided make a difference? A number of people have given a number of answers to this question, and by attempting to respond to so many of them—what Ericsson calls the various "charges" that have been made against prostitution—his article takes on the strategy that we discussed in section 4.5 of the Introduction to this book as the process of elimination. Ericsson takes it, that is, that prostitution is a good thing unless there is a positive reason to think otherwise and that if he can eliminate all of the reasons for thinking it is not a good thing, we will be left with the conclusion that it is a good thing after all.

As this strategy and the text itself suggest, Ericsson's defense of the morality of prostitution can be attacked from a number of different sides. And, perhaps not surprisingly, it has been. One important line of criticism maintains that Ericsson has failed to rebut what he calls "the feminist charge," that his defense of prostitution does not do full justice to the ways in which the practice may prove inconsistent with feminist values. This criticism is represented here in the critical responses by Carole Pateman and Laurie Shrage, each of whom maintains that Ericsson fails to understand the ways in which prostitution constitutes a form of male domination over women and contributes to the perpetuation of such domination. Sexual services, Pateman argues, are relevantly different from nonsexual services because sexual services are "inseparably connected to the body," which in turn is "integrally connected to conceptions of femininity and masculinity." Similarly, Shrage argues, reducing sex to a commodity provided by women to men according to economic demand "implies general acceptance of principles which perpetuate women's social subordination," including the belief that men are naturally the dominant members of society and that sexual experience "pollutes" women in a way that it does not pollute men. In addition to attempting to support this feminist objection to prostitution, Pateman's critique can also be understood in part as an attack on the assumption that the sale of sexual services can take place on free and equal terms in the way that the sale of many other services can. It is not a simple coincidence that the vast majority of prostitutes are women and the vast majority of customers are men, on this account, and it is not clear that the exchanges that take place between them are perfectly voluntary.

While Pateman and Shrage attack Ericsson's argument from the standpoint of feminist values, Karen Green attacks it from the standpoint of what she calls "the traditional ideal of the family." More specifically, Green's objection can be understood as a response to Ericsson's attempt to overcome what he calls "the sentimentalist charge" against prostitution. Borrowing from the great social and political philosopher John Rawls, Green argues that a just and well-ordered society must preserve the foundations for the development of important moral sentiments such as justice and benevolence. A close connection between sex and love is essential to such development, on Green's account, and since prostitution involves distributing sexual acts according to economic demand rather than according to mutual love, its acceptance amounts to a severing of this connection. A market in sexual services is relevantly different from a market in nonsexual services, on this account, because the survival of important moral sentiments demands that sexual services be connected to mutual love in a way that nonsexual services need not be.

Questions for Consideration

In thinking about Ericsson and his critics, it may be useful to consider the following questions.

• Has Ericsson in fact neglected some important ways in which the feminist charge against prostitution can be developed? If he has not, then what, specifically, has he said in his article that can counter the worries raised by Pateman and Shrage? If he has, then what might a defender of his position say in response to those worries?

• Is Shrage right to think that the patriarchal context in which prostitution takes place poses a problem for the practice of prostitution?

• In what sense is the prostitute acting freely, and in what sense is she acting unfreely? Is her behavior free in the sense that Shrage clearly thinks it is not free?

- Has Green found a way to vindicate the sentimentalist charge against prostitution? Does Green's claim about the importance of the moral sentiments justify objecting to prostitution as socially corrosive, or does Ericsson's discussion of the sentimentalist charge provide a basis for overcoming this objection?

- If the objections raised by Pateman, Shrage, or Green are successful, would they imply that only prostitution is wrong, or would they imply that other professions are wrong as well? What other professions might their objections apply to? Would these implications pose a problem for their arguments? Or would the implications reinforce their arguments?

- What about the other charges against prostitution that Ericsson considers? How might a critic of prostitution respond to his discussion of those charges? And are there still further charges against prostitution that Ericsson seems to neglect entirely?

Further Reading

Anderson, Scott A. "Prostitution and Sexual Autonomy: Making Sense of the Prohibition of Prostitution." *Ethics* 112, no. 4 (July 2002): 748–80.

Davidson, Julia O'Connell. "The Rights and Wrongs of Prostitution." *Hypatia* 17, no. 2 (Spring 2002): 84–98.

Kupfer, Joseph H. "Prostitutes, Musicians, and Self-Respect." *Journal of Social Philosophy* 26, no. 3 (1995): 75–88.

Marshall, S. E. "Bodyshopping: The Case of Prostitution." *Journal of Applied Philosophy* 16, no. 2 (1999): 139–50.

Miriam, Kathy. "Stopping the Traffic in Women: Power, Agency and Abolition in Feminist Debates over Sex-Trafficking." *Journal of Social Philosophy* 36, no. 1 (2005): 1–17.

Primoratz, Igor. "What's Wrong with Prostitution?" *Philosophy* 68, no. 264 (1993): 159–82.

Lars O. Ericsson

Charges Against Prostitution
An Attempt at a Philosophical Assessment

I. A Neglected Philosophical Task

. . . It is the purpose of this paper to undertake a critical assessment of the view that prostitution is an undesirable social phenomenon that ought to be eradicated. I shall do this by examining what seem to me (and to others) the most important and serious charges against prostitution. I shall try to show that mercenary love per se must, upon closer inspection, be acquitted of most of these charges. Instead, I shall argue, the major culprit is the hostile and punitive attitudes which the surrounding hypocritical society

From Lars O. Ericsson, "Charges Against Prostitution: An Attempt at a Philosophical Assessment," *Ethics* 90 (1980): 335–66. Some notes and some parts of the text have been deleted. Reprinted by permission of University of Chicago Press.

adopts toward promiscuous sexual relations in general and prostitution in particular.

II. THE CHARGE FROM CONVENTIONAL MORALITY

By far the most common ground for holding that prostitution is undesirable is that it constitutes a case of sexual immorality. Society and conventional morality condemn it. The law at best barely tolerates it; sometimes, as in most states in the United States, it downright prohibits it. In order to improve prostitution, we must first and foremost improve our attitudes toward it. Contrary to what is usually contended, I shall conclude that prostitution, although not in any way *ultimately* desirable, is still conditionally desirable because of certain ubiquitous and permanent imperfections of actual human societies.

The prostitute, according to the moralist, is a sinful creature who ought to be banned from civilized society. Whoredom is "the great social evil" representing a flagrant defiance of common decency. The harlot is a threat to the family, and she corrupts the young. The engage in prostitution signifies a total loss of character. To choose "the life" is to choose a style of living unworthy of any decent human being. And so on.

There is also a less crude form of moralism, which mixes moral disapproval with a more "compassionate" and "concerned" attitude. The fate of a whore is "a fate worse than death." The hustler is a poor creature who has to debase herself in order to gratify the lusts of immoral men. Prostitution is degrading for all parties involved, but especially for the woman.

It might seem tempting to say that the best thing to do with respect to the moralistic critique is to ignore it. But this is exactly what moral philosophers have been doing for far too long. It appears that many otherwise sophisticated persons more or less consciously adhere to views of a rather unreflectively moralistic kind where prostitution is concerned. More important, to ignore conventional moralism would be philosophically unsatisfactory for the simple reason that the mere fact that an idea is conventional does not constitute a disproof of its validity. Thus, arguments are what we need, not silence.

How are the hostile and punitive attitudes of society toward prostitution to be explained? It seems to be an anthropological fact that sexual institutions are ranked on the basis of their relation to reproduction. Hence, in virtue of its intimate relation to reproduction, the monogamous marriage constitutes the sexual institution in society which is ranked the highest and which receives the strongest support from law and mores. On the other hand, the less a sexual practice has to do with the bearing and rearing of children, the less sanctioned it is. Therefore, when coitus is practiced for pecuniary reasons (the hooker), with pleasure and not procreation in mind (the client), we have a sexual practice that, far from being sanctioned, finds itself at the opposite extreme on the scale of social approval.[1]

Two other factors should be mentioned in this connection. First, wherever descent is reckoned solely through the male line, promiscuity in the female can hardly be approved by society. And the property relations associated with descent of course point in the same direction. Second, our Christian heritage—especially in its Lutheran and Calvinist versions—is both antisexual and antihedonistic. To indulge in sexual activities is bad enough, but to indulge in them for the sheer fun and pleasure of them is a major feat in the art of sin. Moreover, sex is time consuming and as such quite contrary to Protestant morals with respect to work.

An explanation of our antiprostitution attitudes and their probably prehistoric roots must not, however, be confused with a *rationale* for their continuation in our own time. That we understand why the average moralist, who is a predominantly unreflecting upholder of prevailing rules and values, regards prostitution and prostitutes as immoral gives us no good reason to shield those rules and values from criticism, especially if we find, upon reflection, that they are no longer adequate to our present social conditions.

That prostitution neither is nor ever was a threat to reproduction within the nuclear family is too obvious to be worth arguing for. Nor has it ever been a threat to the family itself. People marry and visit whores for quite different reasons. In point of fact, the greatest threat to the family is also the greatest threat to prostitution, namely, complete sexual liberty for both sexes. The conclusion we must draw from this is that neither the value of future generations nor the importance of the family (if it is important) warrants the view that prostitution is bad and undesirable.

It is hardly likely, however, that the moralist would be particularly perturbed by this, for the kernel of his view is rather that to engage in prostitution is *intrinsically* wrong. Both whore and customer (or at least the former) act immorally, according to the moralist, even if neither of them nor anyone else gets hurt. Mercenary love per se is regarded as immoral.

Personally, I must confess that I, upon reflection, am no more able to see that coition for a fee is intrinsically wrong than I am able to see that drunkenness is. There is something fanatic about both of these views which I find utterly repelling. If two adults voluntarily consent to an economic arrangement concerning sexual activity and this activity takes place in private, it seems plainly absurd to maintain that there is something intrinsically wrong with it. In fact, I very much doubt that it is wrong at all. To say that prostitution is intrinsically immoral is in a way to refuse to give any arguments. The moralist simply "senses" or "sees" its immorality. And this terminates rational discussion at the point where it should begin.

III. The Sentimentalist Charge

There is also a common contention that harlotry is undesirable because the relation between whore and customer must by the nature of things be a very poor relation to nonmercenary sex. Poor, not in a moral, but in a nonmoral, sense. Since the majority of the objections under this heading have to do with the quality of the feelings and sentiments involved or with the lack of them, I shall refer to this critique as "the sentimentalist charge."

Sex between two persons who love and care for one another can of course be, and often is, a very good thing. The affection and tenderness which exists between the parties tends to create an atmo-sphere in which the sexual activities can take place in such a way as to be a source of mutual pleasure and satisfaction. Sexual intercourse is here a way of becoming even more intimate in a relation which is already filled with other kinds of intimacies.

Now, according to the sentimentalist, mercenary sex lacks just about all of these qualities. Coitus between prostitute and client is held to be impoverished, cold, and impersonal. The association is regarded as characterized by detachment and emotional noninvolvement. And the whole thing is considered to be a rather sordid and drab affair.

In order to answer this charge, there is no need to romanticize prostitution. Mercenary sex usually *is* of poorer quality compared with sentimental sex between lovers. To deny this would be simply foolish. But does it follow from this that hustling is undesirable? Of course not! That would be like contending that because 1955 Ch. Mouton-Rothschild is a much better wine than ordinary claret, we should condemn the act of drinking the latter.

The sentimentalist's mistake lies in the comparison on which he relies. He contrasts a virtual sexual ideal with prostitutional sex, which necessarily represents an entirely different kind of erotic association and which therefore fulfills quite different social and individual functions. Only a minute share of all sex that takes place deserves to be described as romantic sex love. And if, in defending mercenary sex, we should beware of romanticizing *it*, the same caution holds for the sentimentalist when he is describing nonprostitutional sex. The sex lives of ordinary people often fall miles short of the sentimentalist's ideal. On the other hand, the sexual services performed by harlots are by no means always of such poor quality as we are conditioned to think. And we would most likely think better of them were we able to rid ourselves of the feelings of guilt and remorse that puritanism and conventional morality create in us.

In fact, the comparison between sex love and mercenary lovemaking is both pointless and naive. That lovers have very little need for the services of hustlers is at best a silly argument against prostitution. Most couples are not lovers. A great number of persons do not even have a sexual partner. And not so few individuals will, in any society, always have great difficulties in finding one. What is the point of comparing the ideal sex life of the sentimentalist with the sexual services of prostitutes in the case of someone whose only alternative to the latter is masturbation? Is there any reason to think that mercenary sex must be impersonal, cold, and impoverished compared with autosex?

By this I do not wish to contend that the typical customer is either unattractive, physically or mentally handicapped, or extremely shy. There is abundant empirical evidence showing that the prostitute's customers represent all walks of life and many different types of personalities.[2] That the typical "John" is a male who for some reason cannot find a sexual partner other than a prostitute is just one of the many popular myths about harlotry which empirical studies seem unable to kill. Approximately 75 percent of the customers are married men,[3] most of whom are "respectable" taxpaying citizens.

This brings us to another aspect of the sentimentalist charge. It is not seldom a tacit and insiduous presupposition of the sentimentalist's reasoning that good sex equals intramarital sex, and that bad sex equals extramarital—especially prostitutional—sex. This is just another stereotype, which deserves to be destroyed. Concerning this aspect, Benjamin and Masters make the following comment: "The experience with a prostitute is probably ethically, and may be esthetically, on a higher level than an affectionless intercourse between husband and wife, such as is all too common in our present society."[4] The demarcation line between marital and mercenary sex is not quality but the contrasting nature of the respective legal arrangements. Furthermore, we must not think that the quality—in terms of physical pleasure—of the sex services of prostitutes varies any less than the quality of "regular" sex. The best prostitutional sex available is probably much better from the customer's point of view than average marital sex.

The sentimentalistic critique of the prostitute-customer relationship, however, has also another side to it. This consists in the notion that sex without love or affection—sex "pure and simple"—is "no good." I have already admitted the obvious here—namely, that sex love is a beautiful thing. But this seems to me no reason for embracing the romantic notion that sex without love or mutual affection must be valueless. On the contrary, satisfaction of sexual desires is, qua satisfaction of a basic need, *intrinsically good,* love or no love.

The argument fails to show that prostitution is undesirable. If it shows anthing at all it shows lack of contact with reality. As I pointed out earlier, sex between lovers hardly dominates the scene of human sex quantitatively. Consequently, the argument entails that a major part of the sex that takes place between humans is worthless. And how interesting is this? Even if correct, it does not show that there is something *particularly* or *distinctively* bad about prostitution.

In conclusion, I would like to counter the charge that the prostitute-customer relationship is bad on the ground that it involves the selling of something that is too basic and too elementary in human life to be sold. This is perhaps not a sentimentalist charge proper, but since it seems to be related to it I shall deal with it here.

Common parlance notwithstanding, what the hustler sells is of course not her body or vagina, but sexual *services.* If she actually did sell herself, she would no longer be a prostitute but a sexual slave. I wish to emphasize this simple fact, because the popular misnomer certainly contributes to and maintains our distorted views about prostitution.

But is it not bad enough to sell sexual services? To go to bed with someone just for the sake of money? To perform fellatio on a guy you neither love nor care for? In view of the fact that sex is a fundamental need, is it not wrong that anyone should have to pay to have it satisfied and that anyone should profit from its satisfaction? Is it not a deplorable fact that in the prostitute-customer relationship sexuality is completely alienated from the rest of the personality and reduced to a piece of merchandise?

In reply to these serious charges I would, first, like to confess that I have the greatest sympathy for the idea that the means necessary for the satisfaction of our most basic needs should be free, or at least not beyond the economic means of anyone. We all need food, so food should be available to us. We all need clothes and a roof over our heads, so these things should also be available to us. And since our sexual desires are just as basic, natural, and compelling as our appetite for food, this also holds for them. But I try not to forget that this is, and probably for long time will remain, an *ideal* state of affairs.

Although we live in a society in which we have to pay (often dearly) for the satisfaction of our appetites, including the most basic and natural ones, I still do not regard food vendors and the like with contempt. They fulfill an important function in the imperfect world in which we are destined to live. That we have to pay for the satisfaction of our most basic appetites is no reason for socially stigmatizing those individuals whose profession it is to cater to those appetites. With this, I take it, at least the nonfanatical sentimentalist agrees. But if so, it seems to me inconsistent to hold that prostitution is undesirable on the ground that it involves the selling of something that, ideally, should not be sold but freely given away. Emotional prejudice aside, there is on *this* ground no more reason to despise the sex market and those engaged in it than there is to despise the food market and those engaged in it.

But still, is there not an abyss between selling meat and selling "flesh"? Is there not something private, personal, and intimate about sex that makes it unfit for commercial purposes? Of course, I do not wish to deny that there are great differences between what the butcher does and what the whore does, but at the same time it seems to me clear that the conventional labeling of the former as "respectable" and the latter as "indecent" is not so much the result of these differences as of the influence of cultural, especially religious and sexual, taboos. That the naked human body is "obscene," that genitalia are "offending," that menstrual blood is "unclean," etc., are expressions of taboos which strongly contribute to the often neurotic way in which sex is surrounded with mysteriousness and secrecy. Once we have been able to liberate ourselves from these taboos we will come to realize that we are no more justified in devaluating the prostitute, who, for example, masturbates her customers, than we are in devaluating the assistant nurse, whose job it is to take care of the intimate hygiene of disabled patients. Both help to satisfy important human needs, and both get paid for doing so. That the harlot, in distinction to the nurse, intentionally gives her client pleasure is of course nothing that should be held against her!

As for the charge that in the prostitute-customer relationship sexuality is completely alienated from the rest of the personality—this is no doubt largely true. I fail to see, however, that it constitutes a very serious charge. My reason for this is, once again, that the all-embracing sex act represents an ideal with which it is unfair to compare the prostitute/customer relationship, especially if, as is often the case, such an all-embracing sex act does not constitute a realizable alternative. Moreover, there is no empirical evidence showing that sex between two complete strangers must be of poor quality.

IV. The Paternalistic Charge

It is a well-established fact that the occupational hazards connected with prostitution constitute a serious problem. The prostitute runs the risk of being hurt, physically as well as mentally. On the physical side there is always the risk of getting infected by some venereal disease. Certain forms of urosis are known to be more common among harlots than among women in general. And then there is the risk of assault and battery from customers with sadistic tendencies. On the mental side we encounter such phenomena as depression and neurosis, compulsive behavior, self-degrading and self-destructive impulses, etc.

It is therefore not uncommon to find it argued that prostitution is undesirable because it is not in the best interest of the prostitute to be what she is. It is held that society should, for the prostitutes' own good, try to prevent people from becoming prostitutes and to try to "rehabilitate" those who already are. This type of criticism I shall refer to as "the paternalistic charge."

I shall not consider the question—discussed by Mill, Devlin, Hart, and others—of whether society has the *right* to interfere with a person's liberty for his own good. I shall limit my discussion to the question of whether the fact that the hustler runs the risks that she runs is a good reason for holding that prostitution is undesirable.

A comparison with other fields clearly shows that the fact that a certain job is very hazardous is not regarded as a good reason for the view that the type of job in question is undesirable. Take, for instance, a miner: he runs considerable risks in his job, but we hardly think that this warrants the conclusion that mining should be prohibited. What we do think (or at least ought to think) is that, since the miner is doing a socially valuable job, everything possible should be done to minimize those risks by improving his working conditions by installing various safety devices, introducing shorter working hours, etc. It seems to me, therefore, that in cases like this—and there are many of them—paternalistic considerations carry no weight. The individual is not to be protected from himself (for wanting to take risks) but from certain factors in the environment. It is not the individual who should be changed but the milieu in which he has to place himself in order to be able to follow his occupational inclinations.

Unless the paternalist simply assumes what remains to be proven, namely, that what the prostitute does is of no value to society, a similar argument also applies in the case of prostitution. The individual whore does not need to be protected from herself if her hustling is voluntary in the same sense of "voluntary" as someone's choice of profession may be voluntary. What she does need protection from are detrimental factors in the social environment, especially the hostile, punitive, or condescending attitudes of so-called respectable citizens. It is not the hooker who should be changed, reformed, or rehabilitated but the social milieu in which she works.

The paternalistic charge is not an independent argument against prostitution. It only seems to work because it has already given in to conventional morality. To oppose prostitution by referring to the welfare, good, happiness, needs, or interests of the prostitute may seem very noble and humanitarian; but in reality it serves the status quo by leaving the norms and values of the surrounding society intact, viewing prostitution through the unreflected spectacles of a conservative public opinion, and placing the "blame" exclusively on the individual.

If public opinion accorded prostitutes the same status as, say, social workers, most of the hazards connected with hustling would probably disappear. And those that would remain would not be thought to make hustling undesirable. Society would try to minimize the risks rather than try to rehabilitate and reform those who run them.

The paternalist does not ask himself *why* depressions and neuroses are common among harlots, *why* they display self-degrading and self-destructive tendencies, *why* their behavior often is antisocial, and so on. Yet the answer should be obvious: the principal cause of these psychological and sociological "dysfunctions" is the social anathema attached to their way of life. Make people outcasts and they will behave like outcasts. It is thus the degradation in which the harlot is held, and as a result also often holds herself, that constitutes the greatest danger to her physical and mental health. In addition, as I shall hereafter argue, this constitutes the basis for her being exploited in various ways.

To sum up. The paternalistic charge rests on two assumptions, neither of which is valid. First, it rests on the assumption that society's scorn for whoredom is justified. Second, it rests on the assumption that the hooker is not doing a socially valuable job. From these assumptions together with the fact that harlotry is known to be a hazardous profession the paternalist jumps to the conclusion that prostitution is undesirable and that society should intervene against it for the prostitutes' own good. . . .

VI. THE FEMINIST CHARGE

In this essay I have deliberately desisted from trying to *define* "prostitution." I have simply relied upon the fact that we seem to know pretty well what we mean by this term. My reason for resisting the well-known predilection of philosophers for definitional questions is that ordinary usage seems to me sufficiently precise for my present purposes.[5] In consequence, I have up till now referred to the prostitute as "she" and to the customer as "he." For in ordinary parlance the whore is a woman and her customer a man. I do not think, however, that ordinary usage is such that this is true by definition. I rather suspect that our habit of thinking of the hustler as a *she* and her customer as a *he* simply reflects the empirical fact that most prostitutes are women and most customers men.

I shall in this section discuss a group of arguments in support of the thesis that prostitution is undesirable whose common feature is this fact. Prostitution is held to be undesirable on the ground that it constitutes an extreme instance of the inequality between the sexes. Whoredom is regarded as displaying the male oppression of the female in its most naked form. It is contended that the relation between hooker and "John" is one of object to subject—the prostitute being reified into a mere object, a thing for the male's pleasure, lust, and contempt. The customer-man pays to use the whore-woman and consequently has the upper hand. He is the dominating figure, the master. It is the whore's task to oblige, to satisfy his most "perverse" and secret desires, desires that the male is unable to reveal to his wife or girl friend. Prostitution, it is argued, reduces the woman to a piece of merchandise that anyone who can pay the price may buy. The unequal nature of prostitution is also contended to consist in the fact that it represents a way out of *misère sexuel* only for men. Instead of trying to solve the sexual problems together with his wife, the married man can resort to the services of the hustler; but the married woman lacks the same advantage, since there are not so many male heterosexual prostitutes around. I shall refer to this group of arguments as "the feminist charge."

Like the moralist and the Marxist, the feminist is of the opinion that prostitution can and ought to be eradicated.[6] Some feminists, like the moralist, even want to criminalize prostitution. But unlike the moralist they want to criminalize both whore and customer.

The core of the feminist charge—that prostitution is unequal and disfavors the female sex—deserves to be taken seriously. For social in-equality is a serious matter both morally and politically. And inequalities based on differences with regard to race, color of skin, religious belief, sex, and the like are particularly serious. Thus, if valid, the feminist critique would constitute powerful support for the view that prostitution is undesirable.

Before I proceed to an attempt to counter the feminist charge, I would like to add a few nuancing facts to the prostitute-customer picture outlined at the beginning of this section.[7] No one denies that a majority of prostitutes are women, and no one denies that a majority of customers are men. But it is clear from the evidence that a large portion of the prostitutes, especially in metropolitan areas, are male homosexuals.[8] There is also lesbian prostitution, though this is not (at least not yet) sufficiently widespread to be of any great social importance. And finally, there is male heterosexual prostitution, the prevalence of which is also rather limited. We may sum up by saying that, rather than constituting a dichotomy between the sexes, prostitution has the characteristic that a considerable portion of the prostitutes are men, and a small minority of the customers are women. I mention this because I think that a rational assessment should not be based on an incomplete picture of the phenomenon under assessment and I consider these data to have some relevance with respect to the feminist charge against prostitution.

There are at least two types of inequalities. In the one, the inequality consists in the fact that some *benefit* is withheld from some group or individual. A typical example: only white members of a society are allowed to vote. In the other, the inequality consists in the fact that some *burden* is placed only on some group or individual. A typical example: a feudal society in which peasants and artisans are the only ones who have to pay taxes. We may also distinguish between unequal practices which, like racial discrimination, are best dealt with through a complete *abolition* of them, and unequal practices which, like male franchise, are best dealt with by *modifying* them (in the case of male franchise, by granting the franchise to women). The one type of unequal practice is always and under all conditions undesirable: there is no remedy to the inequality of apartheid but abolition. The other type of unequal practice is also undesirable, but it has the seed of something defensible or valuable in it: the franchise is something good, although the franchise restricted to males is not. Obviously, these two pairs of categories are not mutually exclusive. On the contrary, all combinations of them are possible.

After these preliminaries, we come to the question of how prostitution is to be classified. Is harlotry an unequal practice? And if so, in what precisely does its inequality consist?

If it is conceded that in exchange for his money the customer receives a service—something that at least the sentimentalist seems most reluctant to concede—it could be argued that harlotry is unequal in the sense that some benefit is withheld from or denied women that is not withheld from or denied men. This is perhaps how the argument that hustling represents a way out only for men should be understood. However, if this is what the feminist charge amounts to, two things appear to be eminently clear. The first is that prostitution is unequal in a less serious way than, for instance, male franchise. For in the latter the benefit (opportunity to vote) which is withheld from women is withheld from them in the strong sense that it is not legally possible for the women to vote, while in the former no such legal or formal obstacle stands in their way. In fact, instead of saying that the sex services of prostitutes are withheld or denied women, it would be more appropriate to say that centuries of cultural and social conditioning makes them desist from asking for them. It is after all only recently that women have begun to define their sexuality and require that their sexual needs and desires be recognized. Rowbotham reminds us that "'Nymphomania' was actually used in the 1840s to describe any woman who felt sexual desire, and such women were seen as necessarily abandoned, women of the streets, women of the lower classes."[9] The second point is that if, through prostitution, a benefit is "withheld" the female sex, the best way to deal with this inequality would not be an attempt to stamp out the institution but an attempt to modify it, by making the benefit in question available to both sexes.

Could it be then that the inequality of whoredom consists in the fact that some burden is unequally placed on the two sexes and in disfavor of the female sex? This allegation can be interpreted in several different ways. And I shall in what follows consider those that seem to me the most important.

To begin with, this allegation can be understood in accordance with the view that it is women, and not men, who are in peril of becoming prostitutes. But first of all, this is largely untrue since, as I have argued earlier, a great many prostitutes are men. Moreover, the perils of being a prostitute, although existent today (due to factors discussed in Sec. IV), do not constitute a good reason for abolishing harlotry; rather they constitute a good reason for a social reform that will reduce the perils to a minimum tomorrow.[10]

Another way of interpreting this allegation is to say that prostitution constitutes exploitation of the female sex, since harlots are being exploited by, inter alia, sex capitalists and customers, and a majority of harlots are women. This interpretation of the allegation merits careful study, and I shall therefore in the first instance limit my discussion to the capitalist exploitation of prostitutes.

It is of course true that not all prostitutes can be described as workers in the sex industry. Some are in point of fact more adequately described as small-scale private entrepreneurs. Others are being exploited without being exploited by sex capitalists. Those who can be regarded as workers in the sex industry—the growing number of girls working in sex clubs and similar establishments for instance—are, of course, according to Marxist theory, being exploited in the same sense as any wage worker is exploited. But exploitation in this Marxist sense, although perhaps effective as an argument against wage labor in general, is hardly effective as an argument against prostitution.

There is no doubt, however, that practically all harlots—irrespective of whether they are high-class call girls, cheap streetwalkers, or sex-club performers—are being exploited, economically, in a much more crude sense than that in which an automobile worker at General Motors is being exploited. I am thinking here of the fact that all of them—there are very few exceptions to this—have to pay usury rents in order to be able to operate. Many are literally being plundered by their landlords—sex capitalists who often specialize in letting out rooms, flats, or apartments to people in the racket. Not a few prostitutes also have to pay for "protection" to mafiosi with close connections to organized crime.

What makes all this possible? And what are the implications of the existence of conditions such as these for the question of the alleged undesirability of prostitution? With respect to the first of these questions the answer, it seems to me, is that the major culprit is society's hypocritical attitude toward harlotry and harlots. It is this hypocrisy which creates the prerequisites for the sex-capitalist exploitation of the prostitutes. . . .

A third way of interpreting the charge that prostitution is unequal in the sense that it places a burden on women that it does not place on men is to say that whores are being oppressed, reified, and reduced to a piece of merchandise by their male customers. To begin with the last version of this charge first, I have already pointed out the obvious, namely, that whores do not sell themselves. The individual hooker is not for sale, but her sexual services are. One could therefore with equal lack of propriety say of any person whose job it is to sell a certain service that he, as a result thereof, is reduced to a piece of merchandise. I cannot help suspecting that behind this talk of reduction to a piece of merchandise lies a good portion of contempt for prostitutes and the kind of services they offer for sale.

As for the version according to which the whore is reified—turned into an object, a thing—it can be understood in a similar way as the one just dealt with. But it can also be understood as the view that the customer does not look upon the prostitute as a human being but as "a piece of ass." He is not interested in her as a person. He is exclusively interested in her sexual performance. As far as I can see, this version of the charge collapses into the kind of sentimentalistic critique that I discussed in Section III. Let me just add this: Since when does the fact that we, when visiting a professional, are not interested in him or her as a person, but only in his or her professional performance, constitute a ground for saying that the professional is dehumanized, turned into an object?

The "reification charge" may, however, be understood in still another way. It may be interpreted as saying that the whore is nothing but a means, a mere instrument, for the male customer's ends. This also comes rather close to the sentimentalist charge. Its Kantian character does perhaps deserve a few words of comment, however. First of all, that the customer treats the harlot as a means to his ends is only partly true. The other part of the truth is that the prostitute treats her customer as a means to *her* ends. Thus, the complete truth (if it deserves to be called that) is that prostitute and customer treat *one another* as means rather than as ends.

I have to say, however, that I do not find much substance in this Kantian-inspired talk about means and ends. The kind of relationship that exists between prostitute and customer is one that we find in most service professions. It is simply cultural blindness and sexual taboos that prevent so many of us from seeing this. Moreover, in virtue of the prevalence of this type of relationship—a contractual relation in which services are traded—I suspect that those who talk about the badness of it in the case of prostitute-customer relationship have in fact long before decided that the relationship is bad on some *other*—not declared—ground. The means-ends talk is just a way of rationalizing a preconceived opinion.

I shall conclude this section by considering the charge that harlotry constitutes oppression of the female sex. Prostitution is here regarded as displaying male oppression of the female in its most overt and extreme form. The seriousness of this charge calls, to begin with, for a clarification of the meaning of the word "oppression." If A oppresses B, I take it that B's freedom of choice and action is severely reduced, against his will, as a result of actions undertaken by A against B. In the case of political oppression, for example, A thwarts B's desire to form unions and political parties, prevents B from expressing his political opinions, throws B in jail if he refuses to comply, and so on.

It can hardly be disputed that prostitutes are oppressed in this sense. They would not have chosen to become hustlers if some better alternative had been open to them. They are very much aware of the fact that to be a prostitute is to be socially devalued; to be at the bottom of society. To become a hooker is to make just the reverse of a career. It should be observed, however, that none of this warrants the charge that prostitution means the oppression of the female by the male sex. The oppression just described is not an oppression on the basis of sex, as male franchise would be. The "oppressor" is rather those social conditions—present in practically all known social systems—which offer some individuals (both men and women) no better alternative than hustling.

But perhaps what the charge amounts to is that the male sex's oppression of the female sex consists in the oppression of the whore by her male customer. It certainly happens that customers treat prostitutes in ways which could motivate use of the term "oppression." But this does not mean that this term typically applies to the prostitute-customer relationship. Moreover, harlots usually develop a keen eye for judging people, and that helps them to avoid many of the (latently) dangerous customers. For it is just a myth that their freedom of choice and action is reduced to a point where they have to accept customers indiscriminately. This is not even true of prostitutes in the lowest bracket, and it certainly is not true of girls in the higher ones.

It is not seldom argued from feminist quarters that the liberation of women must start with the liberation of women from exploitation of their sex. Hence the crusade against prostitution, pornography, and the use of beautiful women in commercial advertising, etc. It is argued that women's lib must have as its primary goal the abolition of the (ab)use of the female sex as a commodity. As long as the female sex is up for sale, just like any other commercial object, there can be no true liberation from oppression.

To the reader who has read this far it should be obvious that, at least in part, this type of reasoning rests on or is misguided by such misnomers as "the whore sells her body," "to live by selling oneself," "to buy oneself a piece of ass," etc. So I need not say any more about that. Instead I wish to make a comparison between a typical middle-class housewife in suburbia and her prostitute counterpart, the moderately successful call girl. And I ask, emotional prejudice aside, which of them needs to be "liberated" the most? Both are doing fairly well economically, but while the housewife is totally dependent on her husband, at least economically, the call girl in that respect stands on her own two feet. If she has a pimp, it is she, not he, who is the breadwinner in the family. Is she a traitor to her own sex? If she is (which I doubt), she is no more a traitor to her own sex than her bourgeois counterpart. For, after all, Engels was basically right when he said that the major difference between the two is that the one hires out her body on piecework while the other hires it out once and for all.

All this does not mean that I am unsympathetic toward the aspirations of the feminist movement. It rather means that I disagree with its order of priorities.

Both men and women need to be liberated from the harness of their respective sex roles. But in order to be able to do this, we must liberate ourselves from those mental fossils which prevent us from looking upon sex and sexuality with the same naturalness as upon our cravings for food and drink. And, contrary to popular belief, we may have something to learn from prostitution in this respect, namely, that coition resembles nourishment in that if it can not be obtained in any other way it can always be bought. And bought meals are not always the worst.

VII. The Charge of Commercialization of Society

Very few reflective persons would regard a totally commercialized society as a good society. Most of us think that there are certain areas of life that should be as exempt from commercialism as possible. We tend, for example, to take a dim view of people who use money to substitute true friendship with bought "friends." And we hardly consider it proper to buy moral or political beliefs as we buy beer or toothpaste.

In a previous section (Sec. III) I have already discussed the charge against prostitution that it involves the selling of something that ought not to be sold. Here I shall examine a different but related view, namely, the charge that prostitution contributes to the commercialization of society. The charge is that prostitution strengthens the commercial elements in society and that, by way of example, it encourages a commercialistic life-style.

To make this charge as strong as possible I shall assume that it is not inspired by the kind of puritanical anticommercialism which considers all business as dirty business. I shall regard it as an expression of the view, which I share, that a thoroughly commercialized society represents not a utopia but a dystopia.

It is, in my opinion, a deplorable fact that we are close to a point where almost any social activity presupposes that we act as consumers. And it gets increasingly difficult, especially for the young, to avoid the illusion that the solution to practically every problem in living lies in consumption.

My objection to the present charge against prostitution is, thus, not normative. It is rather of an empirical nature. I do not wish to exclude the possibility that prostitution, through the power of example, to some extent contributes to the commercialization of society. But I do wish to deny that its causal influence in this direction is more than utterly marginal.

First of all, this charge seems difficult to square with the historical fact that most societies which have seen harlotry flourish have been societies that hardly deserve to be described as commercialized. In no society has prostitution been more than a minor commercial and economic phenomenon.

Moreover, if there were a causal connection between prostitution and commercialization, one would expect the latter to be a contributing cause of the former rather than the reverse. For one would possibly expect a society in which practically everything is bought and sold to be more tolerant also to the buying and selling of sexual services.

However that may be, I think we have to look elsewhere for the real causes of the spreading of commerce to new areas of life. The core of any capitalist society is the production of commodities and services for profit. If a capitalist does not have a superior product to sell, if he does not have more effective methods of marketing at his disposal, or if he is otherwise unable to beat competition, he is likely to try to reach his goal—maximum profit—by introducing a new commodity or service. And in many cases this will of course result in a commercialization of previously noncommercial areas.

I have previously denied the Marxist claim that prostitution is based on and falls with capitalism. And what I just said is not inconsistent with this. For, to begin with, mercenary sex is not a capitalist invention. Furthermore, even in modern capitalist societies, most prostitutes work on their own. Unlike, for instance, porno models, they are typically not workers in the sex industry.

In saying this, I am denying something like the opposite of the Marxist claim, namely, that prostitu-

tion is one of the factors that generates a capitalistic commercialization of society. Capitalism is perfectly able to create commercialistic dystopias on its own. It hardly needs the aid of prostitution in the process.

If we want to fight against the increasing commercialization of society, we must fight against its capitalistic roots rather than against such loosely related symptoms of human dissatisfaction as prostitution.

VIII. The Charge of a Disturbed Emotional Life

Most of the emotional problems that often afflict prostitutes can be traced back to the social stigma that we attach to their way of life. If our attitudes to sexuality, promiscuity, and mercenary sex were different—if for example, prostitutes were held in esteem instead of in degradation—I am convinced that they would display very little of the mental disturbances that not seldom haunt them today.

But is it not possible that certain emotional problems would always remain, no matter how the attitudes of the surrounding society changed? Is it not likely, for instance, that even a harlot whose occupation was held in esteem would find her own love life, her feelings for the man she loves, disturbed by her professional activities? Can one have a well-functioning sexual life if sex is what one lives by? Compulsive behavior apart, the sex drive is no more of an insatiable appetite than hunger. Must not, therefore, the repetitious performance of sexual acts always in the end result in nausea or total indifference? And if the prostitute tries to avoid this effect through a complete detachment, not allowing herself to feel anything when with a customer, will she be able to "switch on" her feelings when with her lover?

I must admit that I do not feel certain what to say about this charge, which we may call "the charge of a disturbed emotional life." Since those prostitutes who are active today are victims of our present scornful attitudes, we cannot but speculate what would happen to their emotional lives if those attitudes were changed in a positive direction. I am inclined to think, however, that some prostitutes, even under the best of circumstances, would run the risk of getting emotional problems. But on the other hand, some prostitutes seem capable of preserving their integrity and sensibility even under the adverse conditions of today.

Since we cannot but speculate, no definite conclusions can be drawn. I wish to add, however, that I think that if prostitution were to be reformed in accordance with the suggestions that I am presently about to make, no prostitute would have to continue in the profession, should she (or he) find that she (or he) was not suited for it. . . .

NOTES

1. Here I am indebted to Kingsley Davis (see his "The Sociology of Prostitution," reprinted in *Deviance, Studies in the Process of Stigmatization and Social Reaction,* ed. A. C. Clarke, S. Dinitz, and R. R. Dynes (New York: Oxford University Press, 1975).

2. See Harry Benjamin and R. E. L. Masters, *Prostitution and Morality* (New York: Julian Press, 1964), chap. 6.

3. Ibid.

4. Ibid., p. 208.

5. I should perhaps stress, however, that I use the term "prostitution" in a neutral, descriptive sense, disregarding the ordinary negative value association of the term. In a later section (X) a normative concept 'sound prostitution' will be developed.

6. The empirical part of this opinion will be examined critically in the next section.

7. My major source of information has here as elsewhere been Benjamin and Masters (n. 4 above), esp. chaps. 5, 6, and 10. I have also consulted the reports of Jersild (Jens Jersild, *Boy Prostitution* [Copenhagen: G. E. C. Gad, 1956]) and Butts (W. M. Butts, "Boy Prostitutes of the Metropolis," *Journal of Clinical Psychopathology* [1947], pp. 673–81).

8. A ratio of 60/40 has been mentioned for big city areas like New York and Los Angeles. I do not regard this (or any other) figure as completely reliable, however. The empirical material available does not seem to allow any exact conclusions.

9. Rowbotham, *Women, Resistance, and Revolution* (London: Penguin Press, 1972) p. 66.

10. To those who find this statement a bit too categorical I suggest a quick glance back to Sec. IV).

CAROLE PATEMAN

Defending Prostitution
Charges Against Ericsson

Ericsson's contractarian defense of prostitution[1] extends the liberal ideals of individualism, equality of opportunity, and the free market to sexual life. The real problem with prostitution, Ericsson claims, is the hypocrisy, prejudice, and punitive attitudes that surround it. Once unblinkered, we can see that prostitution is merely one service occupation among others and that, with some reforms, a morally acceptable, or "sound," prostitution could exist. This defense has its appeal at a time when strict control of sexual conduct is again being strenuously advocated. However, Ericsson's argument fails to overcome the general weaknesses of abstract contractarianism, and his claim that he has rebutted the feminist charge against prostitution cannot be granted. The central feminist argument is that prostitution remains morally undesirable, no matter what reforms are made, because it is one of the most graphic examples of men's domination of women.

Ericsson's argument illustrates nicely how liberal contractarianism systematically excludes the patriarchal dimension of our society from philosophical scrutiny. He interprets feminists as arguing that prostitution is "undesirable on the ground that it constitutes an extreme instance of the inequality between the sexes" (p. 348), and he then interprets inequality to be a matter of the distribution of benefits and burdens. It thus appears that a remedy can be found for the withholding of a benefit (access to prostitutes) from women by extending equality of opportunity to buy and sell sexual services on the market to both sexes. Ericsson ignores the fact that men earn a good deal more than women, so the latter would still have a greater incentive to be sellers than buyers (or would be confined to the cheaper end of the market as buyers; Ericsson pays no attention to the different categories of prostitution). Moreover, Ericsson notes that three-quarters of the men who are in the market for prostitutes are married. Any change in attitudes would have to be sufficient to make it acceptable that wives could spend what they save from housekeeping money, or spend part of their own earnings, on prostitutes. Second, Ericsson dismisses as meaningless the charge that prostitution unfairly burdens women because they are oppressed as prostitutes; properly understood, prostitution is an example of a free contract between individuals in the market in which services are exchanged for money. Ericsson's defense does not and cannot confront the feminist objection to prostitution. Feminists do not see prostitution as unacceptable because it distributes benefits and burdens unequally; rather, to use Ericsson's language of inequality, because prostitution is grounded in the inequality of domination and subjection. The problem of domination is both denied by and hidden behind Ericsson's assertion that prostitution is a free contract or an equal exchange.

The most striking feature of Ericsson's defense is that he makes no attempt to substantiate the key claim that prostitution *is* the sale of sexual services. His

From Carole Pateman, "Defending Prostitution: Charges Against Ericsson," *Ethics* 93 (1983); 561–65. Some notes and some parts of the text have been deleted. Reprinted by permission of University of Chicago Press.

assertion relies on the conventional assumption that free wage labor stands at the opposite pole from slavery. The worker freely contracts to sell labor power or services for a specified period, whereas the person of the slave is sold for an unlimited time. Ericsson comments that if a prostitute "actually did sell herself, she would no longer be a prostitute but a sexual slave" (p. 341). More exactly, since she has the civil and juridical status of a free individual in the capitalist market, she would be in a form of subjection that fell short of slavery. Ericsson avoids discussing whether this is indeed the position of the prostitute because he ignores the problems involved in separating the sale of services through contract from the sale of the body and the self. In capitalist societies it appears as if labor power and services are bought and sold on the market, but "labor power" and "services" are abstractions. When workers sell labor power, or professionals sell services to clients (and Ericsson regards some prostitutes as "small scale private entrepreneurs"),[2] neither the labor power nor services can in reality be separated from the person offering them for sale. Unless the "owners" of these abstractions agree to, or are compelled to, use them in certain ways, which means that the "owners" act in a specified manner, there is nothing to be sold. The employer appears to buy labor power; what he actually obtains is the right of command over workers, the right to put their capacities, their bodies, to use as he determines.

Services and labor power are inseparably connected to the body and the body is, in turn, inseparably connected to the sense of self. Ericsson writes of the prostitute as a kind of social worker, but the services of the prostitute are related in a more intimate manner to her body than those of other professionals. Sexual services, that is to say, sex and sexuality, are constitutive of the body in a way in which the counseling skills of the social worker are not (a point illustrated in a backhanded way by the ubiquitous use by men of vulgar terms for female sexual organs to refer to women themselves). Sexuality and the body are, further, integrally connected to conceptions of femininity and masculinity, and all these are constitutive of our individuality, our sense of self-identity. When sex becomes a commodity in the capitalist market so, necessarily, do bodies and selves. The prostitute cannot sell sexual services alone; what she sells is her body. To supply services contracted for, professionals must act in certain ways, or use their bodies; to use the labor power he has bought the employer has command over the worker's capacities and body; to use the prostitute's "services," her purchaser must buy her body and use her body. In prostitution, because of the relation between the commodity being marketed and the body, it is the body that is up for sale.

Critics of marriage have often claimed that wives are no different from prostitutes. Women who marry also contract away their bodies but (in principle) for life rather than for minutes or hours like the prostitute. However, a form of marriage in which the husband gains legal right of sexual use of his wife's body is only one possible form. The conjugal relation is not necessarily one of domination and subjection, and in this it differs from prostitution. Ericsson's defense is about prostitution in capitalist societies; that is, the practice through which women's bodies become commodities in the market which can be bought (contracted for) for sexual use. The questions his defense raises are why there is a demand for this commodity, exactly what the commodity is, and why it is *men* who demand it.

Ericsson cannot admit that the first two questions arise. The third he treats as unproblematic. He stands firmly in the patriarchal tradition which discusses prostitution as a problem about the women who are prostitutes, and our attitudes to them, not a problem about the men who demand to buy them. For Ericsson it is merely a contingent fact that most prostitutes are women and customers men.[3] He claims that the demand for prostitution could never disappear because of some "ubiquitous and permanent imperfections" (p. 337) of human existence arising from the sexual urge. In other words, prostitution is a natural feature of human life. Certainly, sexual impulses are part of our natural constitution as humans, but the sale of "sexual services" as a commodity in the capitalist market cannot be reduced to an expression of our natural biology and physiology. To compare the fulfillment of sexual urges through prostitution to other natural necessities of human survival, to argue from the fact that we need food, so it should be available, to the claim that "our sexual desires are just as basic, natural, and compelling as our appetite for food, [so] this also holds for them" (p. 341), is, to say the least, disingenuous. What counts as "food" varies widely, of course, in different cultures, but, at the most fundamental level of survival there is one obvious difference between sex and other human needs. Without a certain minimum of food, drink, and shelter, people die; but, to my knowledge, no one has yet died from want of sexual release. Moreover, sometimes food and drink are impossible to obtain no matter what people do, but every person has the means to find sexual release at hand.

To treat prostitution as a natural way of satisfying a basic human need, to state that "bought meals are not always the worst" (p. 355), neatly, if vulgarly, obscures the real, social character of contemporary sexual relations. Prostitution is not, as Ericsson claims, the same as "sex without love or mutual affection" (p. 341). The latter is morally acceptable *if* it is the result of mutual physical attraction that is freely expressed by both individuals. The difference between sex without love and prostitution is not the difference between cooking at home and buying food in restaurants; the difference is that between the reciprocal expression of desire and unilateral subjection to sexual acts with the consolation of payment: it is the difference for women between freedom and subjection.

To understand why men (not women) demand prostitutes, and what is demanded, prostitution has to be rescued from Ericsson's abstract contractarianism and placed in the social context of the structure of sexual relations between women and men. Since the revival of the organized feminist movement, moral and political philosophers have begun to turn their attention to sexual life, but their discussions are usually divided into a set of discrete compartments which take for granted that a clear distinction can be drawn between consensual and coercive sexual relationships. However, as an examination of consent and rape makes graphically clear,[4] throughout the whole of sexual life domination, subjection, and enforced submission are confused with consent, free association, and the reciprocal fulfillment of mutual desire. The assertion that prostitution is no more than an example of a free contract between equal individuals in the market is another illustration of the presentation of submission as freedom. Feminists have often argued that what is fundamentally at issue in relations between women and men is not sex but power. But, in the present circumstances of our sexual lives, it is not possible to separate power from sex. The expression of sexuality and what it means to be feminine and a woman, or masculine and a man, is developed within, and intricately bound up with, relations of domination and subordination.

Ericsson remarks that "the best prostitutional sex available is probably much better from the customer's point of view than average marital sex" (p. 340). It is far from obvious that it is either "quality" or the "need" for sex, in the commonsense view of "quality" and "sex," that explains why three-quarters of these customers are husbands. In the "permissive society" there are numerous ways in which men can find sex without payment, in addition to the access that husbands have to wives. But, except in the case of the most brutal husbands, most spouses work out a modus vivendi about all aspects of their lives, including the wife's bodily integrity. Not all husbands exercise to the full their socially and legally recognized right—which is the right of a master. There is, however, another institution which enables all men to affirm themselves as masters. To be able to purchase a body in the market presupposes the existence of masters. Prostitution is the public recognition of men as sexual masters; it puts submission on sale as a commodity in the market. . . .

NOTES

1. L. O. Ericsson, "Charges Against Prostitution: An Attempt at a Philosophical Assessment," *Ethics* 90, no. 3 (1980): 335–66. Page references to this paper are in parentheses in the text.

2. On workers as "petty entrepreneurs," their labor power or services, see R. P. Wolff, "A Critique and Reinterpretation of Marx's Labor Theory of Value," *Philosophy and Public Affairs* 10 (1981): 89–120, esp. 109–11.

3. In cities like Sydney, male homosexual prostitutes are not uncommon. Following Ericsson, I discuss only heterosexual (genitally oriented) prostitution. It is not immediately clear that homosexual prostitution has the same social significance.

4. See my "Women and Consent," *Political Theory* 8 (1980): 149–68.

LAURIE SHRAGE

Should Feminists Oppose Prostitution?

THE SOCIAL MEANING OF PROSTITUTION

Let me begin with a simple analogy. In our society there exists a taboo against eating cats and dogs. Now, suppose a member of our society wishes to engage in the unconventional behavior of ingesting cat or dog meat. In evaluating the moral and political character of this person's behavior, it is somewhat irrelevant whether eating cats and dogs "really" is or isn't healthy, or whether it "really" is or isn't different than eating cows, pigs, and chickens. What is relevant is that, by including cat and dog flesh in one's diet, a person may really make others upset and, therefore, do damage to them as well as to oneself. In short, how actions are widely perceived and interpreted by others, even if wrongly or seemingly irrationally, is crucial to determining their moral status because, though such interpretations may not hold up against some "objective reality," they are part of the "social reality" in which we live.

I am not using this example to argue that unconventional behavior is wrong but, rather, to illustrate the relevance of cultural convention to how our outward behaviors are perceived. Indeed, what is wrong with prostitution is not that it violates deeply entrenched social conventions—ideals of feminine purity, and the noncommoditization of sex—but precisely that it epitomizes other cultural assumptions—beliefs which, reasonable or not, serve to legitimate women's social subordination. In other words, rather than subvert patriarchal ideology, the prostitute's actions, and the industry as a whole, serve to perpetuate this system of values. By contrast, lesbian sex, and egalitarian heterosexual economic and romantic relationships, do not. In short, female prostitution oppresses women, not because some

women who participate in it "suffer in the eyes of society" but because its organized practice testifies to and perpetuates socially hegemonic beliefs which oppress all women in many domains of their lives.

What, then, are some of the beliefs and values which structure the social meaning of the prostitute's business in our culture—principles which are not necessarily consciously held by us but are implicit in our observable behavior and social practice? First, people in our society generally believe that human beings naturally possess, but socially repress, powerful, emotionally destabilizing sexual appetites. Second, we assume that men are naturally suited for dominant social roles. Third, we assume that contact with male genitals in virtually all contexts is damaging and polluting to women. Fourth, we assume that a person's sexual practice renders her or him a particular "kind" of person, for example, "a homosexual," "a bisexual," "a whore," "a virgin," "a pervert," and so on. I will briefly examine the nature of these four assumptions, and then discuss how they determine the social significance and impact of prostitution in our society. Such principles are inscribed in all of a culture's communicative acts and institutions, but my examples will only be drawn from a common body of disciplinary resources: the writings of philosophers and other intellectuals.

The Universal Possession of a Potent Sex Drive

. . . The assumption of a potent "sex drive" is implicit in Lars Ericsson's relatively recent defense of prostitution: "We must liberate ourselves from those mental fossils which prevent us from looking upon sex and sexuality with the same naturalness as upon our cravings for food and drink. And, contrary to popular

From Laurie Shrage, "Should Feminists Oppose Prostitution?" *Ethics* 99 (1989): 347–61. Some notes and some parts of the text have been deleted.

belief, we may have something to learn from prostitution in this respect, namely, that coition resembles nourishment in that if it cannot be obtained in any other way it can always be bought. And bought meals are not always the worst."[1] More explicitly, he argues that the "sex drive" provides a noneconomic, natural basis for explaining the demand for commercial sex.[2] Moreover, he claims that because of the irrational nature of this impulse, prostitution will exist until all persons are granted sexual access upon demand to all other persons.[3] In a society where individuals lack such access to others, but where women are the social equals of men, Ericsson predicts that "the degree of female frustration that exists today . . . will no longer be tolerated, rationalized, or sublimated, but channeled into a demand for, inter alia, mercenary sex."[4] Consequently, Ericsson favors an unregulated sex industry, which can respond spontaneously to these natural human wants. Although Pateman, in her response to Ericsson, does not see the capitalist commoditization of sexuality as physiologically determined, she nevertheless yields to the assumption that "sexual impulses are part of our natural constitution as humans."[5] . . .

By contrast, consider a group of people in New Guinea, called the Dani, as described by Karl Heider: "Especially striking is their five year post-partum sexual abstinence, which is uniformly observed and is not a subject of great concern or stress. This low level of sexuality appears to be a purely cultural phenomenon, not caused by any biological factors."[6] The moral of this anthropological tale is that our high level of sexuality is also "a purely cultural phenomenon," and not the inevitable result of human biology. Though the Dani's disinterest in sex need not lead us to regard our excessive concern as improper, it should lead us to view one of our cultural rationalizations for prostitution as just that—a cultural rationalization.

The "Natural" Dominance of Men

One readily apparent feature of the sex industry in our society is that it caters almost exclusively to a male clientele. Even the relatively small number of male prostitutes at work serve a predominantly male consumer group. Implicit in this particular division of labor, and also the predominant division of labor in other domains of our society, is the cultural principle that men are naturally disposed to dominate in their relations with others. . . .

Sexual Contact Pollutes Women

To say that extensive sexual experience in a woman is not prized in our society is to be guilty of indirectness and understatement. Rather, a history of sexual activity is a negative mark that is used to differentiate kinds of women. Instead of being valued for their experience in sexual matters, women are valued for their "innocence." . . .

The Reification of Sexual Practice

Another belief that determines the social significance of prostitution concerns the relationship between a person's social identity and her or his sexual behavior.[7] For example, we identify a person who has sexual relations with a person of the same gender as a "homosexual," and we regard a woman who has intercourse with multiple sexual partners as being of a particular type—for instance, a "loose woman," "slut," or "prostitute." As critics of our society, we may find these categories too narrow or the values they reflect objectionable. If so, we may refer to women who are sexually promiscuous, or who have sexual relations with other women, as "liberated women," and thereby show a rejection of double (and homophobic) standards of sexual morality. However, what such linguistic iconoclasm generally fails to challenge is that a person's sexual practice makes her a particular "kind" of person.

I will now consider how these cultural convictions and values structure the meaning of prostitution in our society. Our society's tolerance for commercially available sex, legal or not, implies general acceptance of principles which perpetuate women's social subordination. Moreover, by their participation in an industry which exploits the myths of female social inequality and sexual vulnerability, the actions of the prostitute and her clients imply that they accept a set of values and beliefs which assign women to marginal social roles in all our cultural institutions, including marriage and waged employment. Just as an Uncle Tom exploits noxious beliefs about blacks for personal gain, and implies through his actions that blacks can benefit from a system of white supremacy, the prostitute and her clients imply that women can profit economically from patriarchy. Though we should not blame the workers in the sex industry for the social degradation they suffer, as theorists and critics of our society, we should question the existence of such businesses and the social principles implicit in our tolerance for them. . . .

NOTES

1. Lars O. Ericsson, "Charges Against Prostitution: An Attempt at a Philosophical Assessment," *Ethics* 90 (1980): 335–66.

2. Ibid., p. 347.

3. Ibid., pp. 359–60.

4. Ibid., p. 360.

5. Carole Pateman, "Defending Prostitution: Charges Against Ericsson," *Ethics* 93 (1983): 561–65.

6. Karl Heider, "Dani Sexuality: A Low Energy System," *Man* 11 (1976): 188–201.

7. In "Defending Prostitution," Pateman states: "The services of the prostitute are related in a more intimate manner to her body than those of other professionals. Sexual services, that is to say, sex and sexuality, are constitutive of the body in a way in which the counseling skills of the social worker are not. . . . Sexuality and the body are, further, integrally connected to conceptions of femininity and masculinity, and all these are constitutive of our individuality, our sense of self-identity" (p. 562). On my view, while our social identities are determined by our outward sexual practice, this is due to arbitrary, culturally determined conceptual mappings, rather than some universal relationship holding between persons and their bodies.

KAREN GREEN

Prostitution, Exploitation, and Taboo

A simple free market liberalism would have it that the continuing community sentiment that prostitution is morally suspect is merely an archaic taboo.[1] But this observation can be turned on its head. Psychoanalysts suggest that the acquisition of a certain structure of emotional reactions is of a piece with the acquisition of a sense of oneself as a moral being. The sense that certain acts or objects are unclean or taboo is the reverse side of the sense of oneself as a clean or virtuous person. Sex, according to Ericsson, is just a natural instinctual drive like hunger. Yet, in hunter-gatherer societies, where a clan-member's sense of self involves identification with a sacred animal or food, eating of that food is taboo. This should alert us to the possibility that the taboo status of prostitution, in our society, is connected, at a fundamental level, with the psychological processes that result in the development, in a mature individual, of a structure of moral sentiments.

In the third part of *A Theory of Justice* John Rawls argues that his liberal theory of justice generates its own support within society and is hence stable. In arguing this he describes "how human beings in a well-ordered society might acquire a sense of justice and the other moral sentiments." It is the claim of this paper that when we consider the preconditions for the development of a liberal (or any other) sense of justice and the other moral sentiments, we are

From Karen Green, "Prostitution, Exploitation and Taboo," *Philosophy* 64, no. 250 (1989): 525–34. Some notes and some parts of the text have been deleted. Reprinted with the permission of Cambridge University Press.

forced to recognize that these are incompatible with the conclusion that, on liberal grounds, there is nothing morally wrong with prostitution. Such sentiments are necessary in order for liberal societies to be stable and to reproduce themselves, but such sentiments could not be acquired in a society in which prostitution was seriously considered morally on a par with marriage.

The argument depends on accepting, as at least roughly accurate, certain empirical theories about the development of a moral sense. There are a number of controversies in this area. However, for the sake of this argument all that needs to be accepted is that the preconditions for the development of the most basic set of moral sentiments are accurately outlined in the following passage from Rawls:

> . . . when the parents' love of the child is recognized by him on the basis of their evident intentions, the child is assured of his worth as a person. . . . He experiences parental affection as unconditional; they care for his presence and spontaneous acts, and the pleasure they take in him is not dependent upon disciplined performances that contribute to the well-being of others. . . . Gradually he acquires various skills and develops a sense of competence that affirms his self-esteem. It is in the course of this whole process that the child's affection for his parents develops. He connects them with the success and enjoyment that he has in sustaining his world, and with his sense of his own worth. And this brings about his love for them.
> . . . if he does love and trust his parents, then, once he has given in to temptation, he is disposed to share their attitude towards his misdemeanors. He will be inclined to confess his transgression and to seek reconciliation . . . given the nature of the authority situation and the principles of moral psychology connecting the ethical and natural attitudes, love and trust will give rise to feelings of guilt once the parental injunctions are disobeyed.[2]

The relationship between parent and child, that gives rise to a developed moral sense, is quite different from that which holds between mature equals. It is unconditional and in no way based on contract. Parents' love for their children is partly natural but is largely a result of their own childhood experiences and the development of their own moral sentiments. Particularly, the sentiment that parents have a duty to love their offspring, no matter how demanding and self-centred they may be in their earliest years. By a duty to love I mean a duty to provide for the well-being and self-esteem of another without this being conditional on reciprocal benefits. Without such moral sentiments, the preconditions for the development of children into free rational individuals, imbued with a moral sense, would not be met. Self-esteem depends on the prior love of others, and self-esteem and the fear of its loss is the motive force of virtue.

It is at this juncture that the moral significance of the connection between sex and love arises. If parents are to provide the love their children require, they themselves need self-esteem. Sexual love between parents has moral value because, so long as Freud is at least roughly correct, such sexual love replaces in the adult psyche the infantile desire for satisfaction. Loved, the parent experiences a reflection of earlier parental love. Self-esteem is reinforced and the duty to love is less onerous. The picture of the ideal moral relationship between sex and love is that sex, which leads to procreation, should be accompanied by mutual love. The moral value of such love lies in the part it plays in the reproduction of social beings with a moral sense, a capacity to love and a belief in their own self-worth.

These observations show the moral value of the association of sex and love, where procreation is concerned. But, it might be objected, they fail to show that the existence of prostitution threatens this connection. Prostitution does not involve procreation, its existence is quite compatible with the existence of marriages within which the ideal is realized. In a sense, this is quite true. However, it fails to come to grips with the character of the moral judgment that these considerations imply. What is morally disturbing about prostitution is not its immediate consequences. Rather, it is the moral psychology, or structure of moral sentiments, that is intuitively recognized to accompany it. In the healthy psyche the intimacy of sex evokes the intimacy of earlier parental love, one's sexual self is private because it is felt to be closely linked to one's sense of oneself as a unique and lovable being. Exposing this self in an intimate relationship involves the risk of rebuff but also promises reinforcement of one's sense of self-worth. In order to prostitute oneself, these psychic connections have to be broken. Prostitutes deal with this problem in different ways. Some, like a young male prostitute and homeless youth, recently interviewed on ABC TV, feel that no one cares for them. The experience of the impersonality of prostitutional sex reinforces an attitude of worthlessness and moral anomy already well rooted in a sense of parental rejection.[3] Many others split their sexuality and draw the line between intimacy and indifference at a place different from the norm. Characteristically, they refuse to kiss their clients, disassociating vaginal sex from intimacy and retaining the privacy of their affective being by kissing only those who are close to them.[4] Often, such frigidity in a female prostitute's relationship to her clients is accompanied by a contrasting total dependence on the love of a boy-friend or pimp, who is then in a position to manipulate and abuse her.[5] Yet others, who seem to be the most stable and independent, have a reasonably small clientele of 'regulars' and have less need to suppress all connections between sexuality and feelings of affection. Given this, one can see that prostitution is morally suspect because its practice involves the suppression of a structure of moral sentiments which has its moral value in promoting the altruistic behaviour that is necessary if a just society is to reproduce itself.

This argument must not be interpreted as simply a claim that prostitution is immoral because society could not reproduce itself if we all felt and behaved like prostitutes. Society would not reproduce itself if we were all celibate but celibacy is not therefore immoral.[6] The difference between prostitution and celibacy lies in the fact that prostitution is an extreme which implies a moral psychology destructive even in its less extreme forms. The tendency to treat sex as an arena of self-gratification, divorced from love or duties of care, is destructive of family life, even in its milder forms. On the other hand, the capacity to suppress sexual desire, of which celibacy is an extreme form, is taken to be a moral virtue because its exercise is sometimes necessary in order to preserve the integrity of family life.

A critique of prostitution along these lines depends on a partial defence of the traditional ideal of the family. It need not go so far as to abjure all forms of promiscuity, nor fluid or extended families, so long as these are not destructive of the psychic structures that facilitate parental love. It might turn out, for instance, that a measure of early promiscuity facilitates the later development of a stable relationship with spouse and children. But it sees prostitution as immoral because its practice does involve the suppression of these structures. The value of these structures and of the concept of a duty to love one's sexual partner arises, on this view, out of the need to maintain the duty to love one's children. Liberal society would suffer internal collapse if it did not supplement its rational egoism with sufficient rational altruism to ensure the reproduction of rational beings with a sense of justice.

Liberal feminists might object that the constraints of sexual fidelity have always fallen most heavily on women and that this indicates that their primary purpose has been to secure paternity rather than to facilitate parental altruism. But the following thought experiment shows that the situation is not so simple. Suppose that we were to accept that there is absolutely nothing morally wrong with prostitution. In a society that took such a view, free women, unhampered by patriarchal prudery, would, presumably, choose to have whatever sexual relations they desired. Some, who were particularly attractive, or particularly needy, might sell their services, others would have to pay for sex from male prostitutes but most, no doubt, would enter into open-ended relationships based on mutual attraction. This is not too different from the situation that is developing today. But the practical outcome of a situation in which sex relations are seen in terms of self-gratification is that, for children, the bonds of love with one or another parent, and often both, are loosened. Since mothers usually keep and want to keep their children, it is most often fathers who withdraw from the day-to-day attention to their children's physical and emotional well-being. The effect is that the duties of parenthood fall more heavily than ever on women. The point is not that families headed by women are necessarily defective at rearing children with a moral sense. There is little evidence that this is the case. The point is that a liberal society in which mothers contribute the greatest share of parental altruism is one which maintains, in a new form, Rousseau's double standard. Rousseau maintains the sphere of family relations by condemning women to a life of service in the interests of free, rational men. Liberal feminists have rightly objected that freedom must equally be granted to women. The danger is that by forgetting that human beings do not come into the world as rational individuals, endowed with a moral sense, we are in danger of falling into one or other of two unacceptable outcomes. Either, a society in which all relations are based on contracts in a free market and no one recognizes any duty to love. This would be one in which children were left to survive as best they could, whenever the strains of care conflicted too heavily with parental self-interest. Or, a society in which the constraints placed on self-interest by the duty to love one's children fall largely on women. Which would be one in which women would not have the same lib-

erty as men to pursue their other interests. Neither outcome is such that a liberal feminist should happily rest with it. . . .

NOTES

1. Lars Ericsson, "Charges Against Prostitution: An Attempt at a Philosophical Assessment," *Ethics* 90 (1980): 342.

2. John Rawls, *A Theory of Justice* (Oxford University Press 1972), 464–465.

3. Dr Harold Greenwald, *The Elegant Prostitute* (New York: Ballatine Books, 1958), includes a number of cases of prostitutes who express similar sentiments of deprivation.

4. Eileen Mcleod, *Women Working: Prostitution Now* (London and Canberra: Croom Helm, 1982), 38–42.

5. Kate Millett, *The Prostitution Papers* (New York: Ballantine, 1973).

6. I am indebted to Peter Singer for this observation.

PART 3

What's Wrong with the Family?

Many of the questions that moral philosophers are interested in concern the obligations that we have to other people simply as people. My obligation not to commit murder, for example, extends equally to everyone: relative, friend, neighbor, stranger. But some of the most important moral questions that people confront in their everyday lives concern obligations that they have not simply as one human being to another, but rather as one member of a particular family to another member of that family. The goal of Part 3 is to provide a basis for a discussion of these and related questions. We begin with two questions that arise in the context of the traditional family. The first concerns the moral status of the traditional family structure in general (chapter 11), and the second concerns a particular question that often arises within such families: What obligations, if any, do adult children have toward their aging parents (chapter 12)? From here we turn to the controversy over what has become the most widely debated alternative to the traditional family structure: Should the government officially allow and recognize same-sex marriage (chapter 13)? Finally, since the creating and raising of children has been widely recognized as one of the most important parts of family life, we conclude with three questions that are raised by this feature of the family in particular. In chapter 14, we focus on the raising of children and consider the question of whether of whether the State should require people to get a license in order to become parents. In chapter 15, we focus on the creation of children and consider the question of whether the State should permit the practice of commercial surrogate motherhood. And in chapter 16, we focus on the number of children who are born and consider a puzzle that has been raised about the resulting phenomenon of overpopulation.

11

Is the Traditional Family Wrong?

Sommers and Her Critics

In this chapter's featured article, "Philosophers Against the Family," Christina Hoff Sommers explores a set of arguments offered by contemporary philosophers concerning the obligations traditionally associated with familial relations. One obvious common feature of the arguments treated by Sommers is that they draw conclusions that depart radically from "traditional" and "commonsense" morality.

In the first part of her article (sections 2 and 3), Sommers considers what she calls "the direct attack" on the family. She focuses on feminist critiques of family life, and of the traditional differentiation of family roles in particular, and of gendered obligations more generally. The authors she critiques espouse an ideal of *assimilation,* according to which gender differences should not in any way underwrite differences in duties or obligations. Assimilationism is held out as the appropriate alternative to an unacceptable sexism. The trouble, according to Sommers, is that there are two senses of *sexism.* Literally and popularly sexism connotes *unfair* discrimination. But in its extended philosophical sense it simply connotes discrimination, period. Sommers suggests that there are legitimate differences in roles and obligations based on gender, and she endorses sexism in the *philosophical* sense but not in the *literal* sense. Suppose we could eliminate unfair cases of discrimination (say, in the allocation of jobs or salaries) while leaving untouched "the basic institutions that women want and support, i.e., marriage and motherhood." This would be sexism only in the philosophical sense, that of marking certain differences along gender lines. To simply assert that all such discrimination is necessarily unfair or immoral would be to assume what we need to have proved.

An important part of Sommers's defense of gender roles is that women *want* them. By ignoring women's actual wants, on this account, feminists are not only being condescending but also are violating John Stuart Mill's principle to the effect that "there can be no appeal from a majority verdict of those who have experienced two alternatives." That is to say, if a majority of women who have experienced both an assimilationist society and a society based on gender roles prefer the latter, then the latter must be best for them, regardless of the abstract arguments to which feminists appeal.

In the second part of her article (sections 4 and 5), Sommers focuses on "indirect attacks" on the family, all of which she claims stem from a view that "subverts, ignores or denies the special moral relations that characterize the family and are responsible for its functioning." She takes issue with several of the protagonists we have included in this anthology—Thomson on abortion; Wasserstrom on adultery; Jane English on filial obligations—arguing that all of these authors assume the *volunteer theory of obligation,* which she clearly finds wanting.

Claudia Mills, in her contribution, "The Ties That Bind: Duties to Family Members," is ostensibly addressing the issue raised by English in the featured article of the chapter that follows—namely, what children owe their aging parents. However, Mills's goal is really more ambitious than that of determining the extent of one's obligations to one's aging parents. Rather, she aims to lay bare the distinctive nature of family relationships more generally and of the obligations they generate. She addresses arguments put forward by both Sommers, in the featured article of this chapter, and English in the featured article of the following chapter. Mills does not directly challenge Sommers's methodology—that of placing considerable weight on the judgments that most people make about, for example, family relationships. With Sommers (and against English), Mills rejects the volunteer theory of obligations, along with the idea that family obligations can be reduced to the obligations of voluntary friendships. But she also finds Sommers's views of filial duties inadequate.

Mills offers a new account of family relationships and a new argument for their value and hence their binding nature, one based on an analogy with sibling relationships. Mills argues that the analogy between sibling relationships and parent-child relationships is stronger and more illuminating than the analogies offered by English or Sommers. Further, she argues that the duties that one owes to a sibling are more extensive than those that one owes to strangers but different from those that one owes to friends. They are generated by the unique value of being a participant in relationships that she characterizes as both "unchosen" and "unconditional." But the kinds of obligations that one has to one's siblings, and by extension to one's aging parents, are also different and less demanding than what they have traditionally been deemed to be.

Questions for Consideration

In thinking about this chapter, the following questions might prove fruitful.

• Is Sommers right that radical feminists ignore what women really want? Does she provide evidence for her claims about "what women want"? What kind of evidence would suffice? Would a survey do the job? Who would be the appropriate subjects of the survey? Women in the United States? Women in other Western democracies? Women in industrialized countries? All women everywhere? Would such a survey reveal what women *really* want, or would it reveal merely what they have been socialized into believing they want?

• Do people always want what is in their own best interests? What weight should we put on the wants that people actually express as opposed to what might be in their best interests?

• Now consider Sommers's critique of the indirect attack on the family. Are there clear examples of special obligations that people have that they have not voluntarily agreed to? Take the example of a parent's special duties toward his offspring. Can this be explained by some theory other than the volunteer theory?

• Suppose you have offspring even though you didn't voluntarily agree to have them. Suppose, for example, you were the victim of rape and were forced to carry the pregnancy to term. Does your biological parentage of a child conceived during rape make you responsible for that child's welfare?

- Suppose you have deposited a sample of your sperm in a sperm bank, just in case you might need it at some stage. Suppose someone unknown to you steals that sample of your sperm, artificially inseminates herself with it, and brings your child into the world. Do you now have a special duty to care for and feed that child? Does that child have any special duties to you, like taking care of you in your old age? If, in these cases, the person in question has no special duties toward his or her respective family members, what does that suggest about the volunteer theory?
- Is the analogy introduced by Mills—that of sibling relationships and the obligations they entail—an illuminating one? Why does Mills think that we have special duties to our siblings? Why does she think that this model of family obligation can be extended to other family relationships?

FURTHER READING

Almond, Brenda. *The Fragmenting Family*. Oxford: Clarendon Press, 2006.

Friedman, Marilyn. "They Lived Happily Ever After: Sommers on Women and Marriage." *Journal of Social Philosophy* 21 (1990): 57–65.

Okin, Susan. "Feminism, Women's Human Rights, and Cultural Differences." *Hypatia* 13, no. 2 (1998): 32–52.

Vallentyne, Peter. "Equal Opportunity and the Family." *Public Affairs Quarterly* 3 (October 1989): 27–45.

Wolf-Devine, Celia. "Rawlsian and Feminist Critiques of the Traditional Family," in *The Family, Civil Society and the State*, ed. Christopher Wolfe (Lanham, Md.: Rowman & Littlefield, 1998), pp. 51–66.

CHRISTINA HOFF SOMMERS

Philosophers Against the Family

Much of what commonly counts as personal morality is measured by how well we behave within family relationships. We live our moral lives as son or daughter to this mother and that father, as brother or sister to this sister or brother, as father or mother, grandfather, granddaughter to this boy or girl or that man or woman. These relationships and the moral duties defined by them were once popular topics of moral casuistry; but when we turn to the literature of recent moral philosophy, we find little discussion of what it means to be a good son or daughter, a good mother or father, a good husband or wife, a good brother or sister.

Modern ethical theory concentrates on more general topics. Perhaps the majority of us who involve ourselves with ethics accept some version of Kantianism or utilitarianism, yet these mainstream doctrines are better designed for telling us about what we should do as persons in general than about our special duties as parents or children or siblings. We believe, perhaps, that such universal theories can account fully for the morality of special relations. In

From Christina Hoff Sommers, "Philosophers Against the Family," in *Person to Person*, ed. Hugh LaFollette and George Graham (Philadelphia: Temple University Press), pp. 82–105. Some notes and some parts of the text have been deleted.

any case, modern ethics is singularly silent on the bread and butter issues of personal morality in everyday life. However, silence is only part of it. With the exception of marriage itself, family relationships are a biological given. The contemporary philosopher is, on the whole, actively unsympathetic to the idea that we have *any* duties defined by relationships into which we have not voluntarily entered. We do not, after all, choose our parents or siblings. And even if we do choose to have children, this is not the same as choosing, say, our friends. Because the special relationships that constitute the family as a social arrangement are, in this sense, not voluntarily assumed, many moralists feel bound in principle to dismiss them altogether. The practical result is that philosophers are to be found among those who are contributing to an ongoing disintegration of the traditional family. In what follows I shall expose some of the philosophical roots of the current hostility to family morality. My own view that the ethical theses underlying this hostility are bad philosophy will be made evident throughout the discussion.

1. THE MORAL VANTAGE

Social criticism is a heady pastime to which philosophers are professionally addicted. . . .

Much contemporary social criticism is radical in temper. In particular, I shall suggest that the prevailing attitude toward the family is radical and not liberal. And the inability of mainstream ethical theory to come to grips with the special obligations that family members bear to one another contributes to the current disregard of the commonsense morality of the family cave. We find, indeed, that family obligations are criticized and discounted precisely because they do not fit the standard theories of obligation. If I am right, contemporary ethics is at a loss when it comes to dealing with parochial morality; but few have acknowledged this as a defect to be repaired. Instead the common reaction has been: if the family does not fit my model of autonomy, rights, or obligations, then so much the worse for the family.

To illustrate this, I cite without comment recent views on some aspects of family morality.

1. Michael Slote[1] maintains that any child capable of supporting itself is "morally free to opt out of the family situation." To those who say that the child should be expected to help his needy parents for a year or two out of reciprocity or fair play, Slote responds:

The duty of fair play presumably exists only where past benefits are voluntarily accepted . . . and we can hardly suppose that a child has voluntarily accepted his role in family . . . life.[2]

2. Virgina Held[3] wants traditional family roles to be abolished and she recommends that husbands and wives think of themselves as roommates of the same sex in assigning household and parental tasks. (She calls this the "Roommate Test.") To the objection that such a restructuring might injure family life, she replies that similar objections were made when factory workers demanded overtime pay.

3. The late Jane English[4] defended the view that adult children owe their parents no more than they owe their good friends. "[A]fter friendship ends, the duties of friendship end." John Simmons[5] and Jeffrey Blustein[6] also look with suspicion upon the idea that there is a debt of gratitude to the parents for what, in any case, they were duty-bound to do.

4. Where Slote argues for the older child's right to leave, Howard Cohen[7] argues for granting that right to young children who still need parental care. He proposes that every child be assigned a "trusted advisor" or agent. If the child wants to leave his parents, his agent will be charged with finding alternative caretakers for him.

The philosophers I have cited are not atypical in their dismissive attitude to commonsense morality or in their readiness to replace the parochial norms of the family cave with practices that would better approximate the ideals of human rights and equality. A theory of rights and obligations that applies generally to moral agents is, in this way, applied to the family with the predictable result that the family system of special relations and non-contractual special obligations is judged to be grossly unfair to its members.

2. FEMINISM AND THE FAMILY

I have said that the morality of the family has been relatively neglected. The glaring exception to this is, of course, the feminist movement. Although the movement is complex, I am confined primarily to its moral philosophers, of whom the most influential is Simone de Beauvoir. For de Beauvoir, a social arrangement that does not allow all its participants full autonomy is to be condemned. De Beauvoir criticizes the family as an unacceptable arrangement since, for women, marriage and childbearing are essentially incompatible with their subjectivity and freedom:

> The tragedy of marriage is not that it fails to assure woman the promised happiness . . . but that it mutilates her; it dooms her to repetition and routine . . . At twenty or thereabouts mistress of a home, bound permanently to a man, a child in her arms, she stands with her life virtually finished forever.[8]

For de Beauvoir the tragedy goes deeper than marriage. The loss of subjectivity is unavoidable as long as human reproduction requires the woman's womb. De Beauvoir starkly describes the pregnant woman who ought to be a "free individual" as a "stockpile of colloids, an incubator, an egg."[9] And as recently as 1977 she compared childbearing and nurturing to slavery.[10]

It would be a mistake to say that de Beauvoir's criticism of the family is outside the mainstream of Anglo-American philosophy. Her criterion of moral adequacy may be formulated in continental existentialist terms, but its central contention is generally accepted: who would deny that an arrangement that systematically thwarts the freedom and autonomy of the individual is *eo ipso* defective? What is perhaps a bit odd to Anglo-American ears is that de Beauvoir makes such scant appeal to ideals of fairness and equality. For her, it is the loss of autonomy that is decisive.

De Beauvoir is more pessimistic than most feminists she has influenced about the prospects for technological and social solutions. But implicit in her critique is the ideal of a society in which sexual differences are minimal or nonexistent. This ideal is shared by many contemporary feminist philosophers. The views of Richard Wasserstrom, Ann Ferguson, Carol Gould, and Alison Jaggar are representative.

[According to Wasserstrom,] the ideal society is nonsexist and "assimilationist."[11] Social reality is scrutinized for its approximation to this ideal and criticism is directed against all existing norms. Take the custom of having sexually segregated bathrooms: whether this is right or wrong "depends on what the good society would look like in respect to sexual differentiation." The key question in evaluating any law or arrangement in which sex difference figures is: "What would the good or just society make of (it)?"[12]

Thus the supernal light shines on the cave, revealing its moral defects. *There,* in the ideal society, gender in the choice of lover or spouse would be of no more significance than eye color. *There* the family would consist of adults but not necessarily of different sexes and not necessarily in pairs. *There* we find equality ensured by a kind of affirmative action which compensates for disabilities. If women are somewhat weaker than men, or if they are subject to lunar disabilities, then this must be compensated for. (Wasserstrom compares women to persons with congenital defects for whom the good society makes special arrangements.) Such male-dominated sports as wrestling and football will there be eliminated and marriage, as we know it, will not exist. "Bisexuality, not heterosexuality or homosexuality, would be the typical intimate, sexual relationship in the ideal society that was assimilationist in respect to sex."[13]

Other feminist philosophers are equally confident about the need for sweeping change. Ann Ferguson wants a "radical reorganization of child rearing." She recommends communal living and a deemphasis on biological parenting. In the ideal society "[l]ove relationships, and the sexual relationships developing out of them, would be based on the individual meshing-together of androgynous human beings."[14] Carol Gould argues for androgyny and for abolishing legal marriage. She favors single parenting, co-parenting and communal parenting. The only arrangement she opposes emphatically is the traditional one where the mother provides primary care for the children.[15] Alison Jaggar, arguing for a "socialist feminism," wants a society that is both classless and genderless.

She looks to the day of a possible transformation of such biological functions as insemination, lactation, and gestation "so that one woman could inseminate another . . . and . . . fertilized ova could be transplanted into women's or even men's bodies." This idea is partly illustrated in a science fiction story that Jaggar praises in which "neither sex bears children, but both sexes, through hormone treatments, suckle them . . ."[16] To those of us who find this bizarre, Jaggar replies that this betrays the depth of our prejudice in favor of the "natural" family.

Though they differ in detail, the radical feminists hold to a common social ideal that is broadly assimilationist in character and inimical to the traditional family. Sometimes it seems as if the radical feminist simply takes the classical Marxist eschatology of the Communist Manifesto and substitutes "gender" for "class." Indeed, the feminist and the old-fashioned Marxist do have much in common. Both see [society] as politically divided into two warring factions: one oppressing, the other oppressed. Both see the need of raising the consciousness of the oppressed group to its predicament and to the possibility of removing its shackles. Both look forward to the day of a classless or genderless society. Both deny the value and naturalness of tradition. Both believe that people and the institutions they inhabit are as malleable as Silly Putty. And both groups are zealots, paying little attention to the tragic personal costs to be paid for the revolution they wish to bring about. The feminists tell us little about that side of things. To begin with, how will the benighted myriads in the cave who do not wish to "mesh together" with other androgynous beings be reeducated? And how are children to be brought up in the genderless society? Plato took great pains to explain his methods: would the new methods be as thoroughgoing? Unless these questions can be given plausible answers, the supernal attack on the family must always be irresponsible. The appeal to the just society justifies nothing until it can be shown that the radical proposals do not have monstrous consequences. That has not been shown. Indeed, given the perennially dubious state of the social sciences, it is precisely what *cannot* be shown.

Any social arrangement that falls short of the assimilationist ideal is labeled "sexist." It should be noted that this characteristically feminist use of the term "sexist" differs significantly from its popular or literal sense. Literally, and popularly, "sexism" connotes unfair discrimination. But in its extended philosophical use it connotes discrimination, period. Wasserstrom and many feminists trade on the popular pejorative connotations of sexism when they invite us to be antisexist. Most liberals are antisexist in the popular sense. But to be antisexist in the technical, radical philosophical sense is not merely to be opposed to discrimination against women; it is to be *for* what Wasserstrom calls the assimilationist ideal. The antisexist philosopher opposes any social policy that is nonandrogynous, objecting, for example, to legislation that allows for maternity leave. As Alison Jaggar remarks: "We do not, after all, elevate 'prostate leave' into a special right of men."[17] From being liberally opposed to sexism, one may in this way be led insensibly to a radical critique of the family whose ideal is assimilationist and androgynous. For it is very clear that the realization of the androgynous ideal is incompatible with the survival of the family as we know it.

The neological extension of such labels as "sexism," "slavery," and "prostitution" is a feature of radical discourse. The liberal too sometimes calls for radical solutions to social problems. Some institutions are essentially unjust. To "reform" slavery or a totalitarian system of government is to eliminate them. Radicals trade on these extreme practices in characterizing other practices. They may, for example, characterize low wages as "slave" wages and the workers who are paid them as "slave" laborers. Taking these descriptions seriously may start one on the way to treating a free-labor market system as a "slave system" that, in simple justice, must be overthrown and replaced by an alternative system of production. The radical feminist typically explains that, "existentially," women, being treated by men as sex objects, are especially prone to bad faith and false consciousness. Marxist feminists see them as part of an unawakened and oppressed economic class. Clearly we cannot call on a deluded woman to cast off her bonds before we have made her aware of her bondage. So the first task of freeing the slave woman is dispelling the thrall of a false and deceptive consciousness. One must "raise" her consciousness to the "reality" of her situation. (Some feminists acknowledge that it may in fact be too late for many of the women who have fallen too far into the delusions of marriage and motherhood. But the educative process can save many from falling into the marriage and baby trap.)

In this sort of rhetorical climate nothing is what it seems. Prostitution is another term that has been subjected to a radical enlargement. Alison Jaggar believes that a feminist interpretation of the term "prostitution" is badly needed and asks for a "philosophical theory of prostitution." Observing that the average woman dresses for men, marries a man for protection, and so forth, she says: "For contemporary radical feminists, prostitution is the archetypal relationship of women to men."[18]

Of course, the housewife Jaggar has in mind might be offended at the suggestion that she herself is a prostitute, albeit less well paid and less aware of it than the professional street prostitute. To this the radical feminist reply is (quoting Jaggar):

> [I]ndividuals' intentions do not necessarily indicate the true nature of what is going on. Both men and women might be outraged at the description of their candlelit dinner as prostitution, but the radical feminist argues this outrage is due simply to the participants' failure or refusal to perceive the social context in which their dinner date occurs.[19]

Apparently, this failure or refusal to perceive affects most women. Thus we may even suppose that the majority of women who have been treated to a candlelit dinner by a man prefer it to other dining alternatives they have experienced. To say that these preferences are misguided is a hard and condescending doctrine. It would seem that most feminist philosophers are not overly impressed with Mill's principle that there can be no appeal from a majority verdict of those who have experienced two alternatives.

The dismissive feminist attitude to the widespread preferences of women takes its human toll. Most women, for example, prefer to have children and those who have them rarely regret having them. It is no more than sensible, from a utilitarian standpoint, to take note of such widespread preferences and to take it seriously in planning one's own life. But a significant number of women discount this general verdict as benighted, taking more seriously the idea that the reported joys of motherhood are exaggerated and fleeting, if not altogether illusory. These women tell themselves and others that having babies is a trap to be avoided. But for many women childlessness has become a trap of its own, somewhat lonelier than the more conventional traps of marriage and babies. Some come to find their childlessness regrettable; this sort of regret is common to those who flout Mill's reasonable maxim by putting the verdict of ideology over the verdict of human experience.

3. FEMINISTS AGAINST FEMININITY

It is a serious defect of American feminism that it concentrates its zeal on impugning femininity and feminine culture at the expense of the grass roots fight against economic and social injustices to which women are subjected. As we have seen, the radical feminist attitude to the woman who enjoys her femininity is condescending or even contemptuous. Indeed, the contempt for femininity reminds one of misogynist biases in such philosophers as Kant, Rousseau, and Schopenhauer, who believed that femininity was charming but incompatible with full personhood and reasonableness. The feminists deny the charm, but they too accept the verdict that femininity is weakness. It goes without saying that an essential connection between femininity and powerlessness has not been established by *either* party.

By denigrating conventional feminine roles and holding to an assimilationist ideal in social policy, the feminist movement has lost its natural constituency. The actual concerns, beliefs, and aspirations of the majority of women are not taken seriously *except* as illustrations of bad faith, false consciousness, and successful brainwashing. What women actually want is discounted and reinterpreted as to what they (have been led to) *think* they want ("a man," "children"). What most women *enjoy* (male gallantry, candlelit dinners, sexy clothes, makeup) is treated as an obscenity (prostitution).

As the British feminist, Janet Radcliffe Richards, says:

> Most women still dream about beauty, dress, weddings, dashing lovers, domesticity and babies . . . but if feminists seem (as they do) to want to eliminate nearly all of these things—beauty, sex conventions, families and all—for most people that simply means the removal of everything in life which is worth living for.[20]

Radical feminism creates a false dichotomy between sexism and assimilation, as if there were nothing in between. This view ignores completely the middle ground in which a woman can be free of oppression and nevertheless feminine in the sense abhorred by many feminists. For women are simply not waiting to be freed from the particular chains the radical feminists are trying to sunder. The average woman enjoys her femininity. She wants a man, not a roommate. She wants children and the time to care for them. When she enters the work force, she wants fair opportunity and equal treatment. These are the goals that women actually have, and they are not easily attainable. But they will never be furthered by an elitist radical movement that views the actual aspirations of women as the product of a false consciousness. There is room for a liberal feminism that would work for reforms that would give women equal opportunity in the workplace and in politics, but would leave unimpugned the basic institutions that women want and support, i.e., marriage and motherhood. Such a feminism is already in operation in some European countries. But it has been obstructed here in the United States by the ideologues who now hold the seat of power in the feminist movement.[21] . . .

4. THE INDIRECT ATTACK

The philosophers I shall now discuss do not criticize the family directly; in some cases they do not even mention the family. However, each one holds a view that subverts, ignores, or denies the special moral relations that characterize the family and are responsible for its functioning. And if they are right, family morality is a vacuous subject.

Judith Thomson maintains that an abortion may be permissible even if the fetus is deemed a person from the moment of conception,[22] for in that case being pregnant would be like having an adult surgically attached to one's body. And it is arguable that if one finds oneself attached to another person, one has the right to free oneself even if such freedom is obtained at the price of the other person's death by, say, kidney failure. I shall, for purposes of this discussion, refer to the fetus as a prenatal child. I myself do not think the fetus is a person from the moment of conception. Nor does Thomson. But here we are interested in her argument for the proposition that abortion of a prenatal child/person should be permissible.

Many have been repelled by Thomson's comparison of pregnancy to arbitrary attachment. Thomson herself is well aware that the comparison may be bizarre. She says:

> It may be said that what is important is not merely the fact that the fetus is a person, but that it is a person for whom the woman has a special kind of responsibility issuing from the fact that she is its mother.[23]

To this Thomson replies: "Surely we do not have any such 'special responsibility' for a person unless we have assumed it, explicitly or implicitly." If the mother does not try to prevent pregnancy, does not obtain an abortion, but instead gives birth to it and takes it home with her, then, at least implicitly, she has assumed responsibility for it.

One might object that although pregnancy is a state into which many women do not enter voluntarily, it is nevertheless a state in which one has some responsibility to care for the prenatal child. Many pregnant women do feel such a prenatal responsibility, and take measures to assure the prenatal child's survival and future health. But here one must be grateful to Professor Thomson for her clarity. A mother who has not sought pregnancy deliberately bears *no* special responsibility to her prenatal child. For she has neither implicitly nor explicitly taken on the responsibility of caring for it. For example, the act of taking the infant home from the hospital implies voluntary acceptance of such responsibility. By choosing to take it with her, the mother undertakes to care for the infant and no longer has the right to free herself of the burden of motherhood at the cost of the child's life.

The assumption, then, is that there are no non-contractual obligations or special duties defined by the kinship of mother to child. As for social expectations, none are legitimate in the morally binding sense unless they are underpinned by an implicit or explicit contract freely entered into. If this assumption is correct, sociological arrangements and norms have no moral force unless they are voluntarily accepted by the moral agent who is bound by them. I shall call this the "volunteer theory of moral obligation." It is a thesis that is so widely accepted today that Thomson saw no need to argue for it.

Michael Tooley's arguments in defense of infanticide provide another solid example of how a contemporary philosopher sidetracks and ultimately subverts the special relations that bind the family.[24] Tooley holds that being sentient confers the prima facie right not to be treated cruelly, and that possession of those characteristics that make one a person confers the *additional* right to life. Tooley then argues that infants lack these characteristics and so may be painlessly killed. In reaching this conclusion, Tooley's sole consideration is whether the infant intrinsically possesses the relevant "right-to-life-making characteristic" of personality—a consideration that abstracts from any right to care and protection that the infant's relation to its parents confers on it causally and institutionally. For Tooley, as for Thomson, the relations of family or motherhood are morally irrelevant. So it is perhaps not surprising that one finds nothing in the index under "family," "mother," or "father" in Tooley's book on abortion and infanticide.

Howard Cohen is concerned strictly with the rights of persons irrespective of the special relations they may bear to others.[25] Just as Thomson holds that the mother's right to the free unencumbered use of her body is not qualified by any special obligations to her child, so Cohen holds that the child's right to a no-fault divorce from its parents cannot be diminished because of the special relation it bears to them. Where Thomson is concerned with the overriding right of the mother, Cohen is concerned with the

right of the child. Yet all three philosophers agree that the right of a child is not less strong than the right of any adult. Indeed, Thomson compares the unborn child to a fully grown adult and Tooley holds that any person—be it child, adult, or sapient nonhuman—is equal in rights.

Our three philosophers are typical in holding that any moral requirement is either a general duty incumbent on everyone or else a specific obligation voluntarily assumed. Let us call a requirement a *duty* if it devolves on the moral agents whether or not they have voluntarily assumed it. (It is, for example, a duty to refrain from murder.) And let us call a requirement an *obligation* only if it devolves on certain moral agents but not necessarily on all moral agents. (One is, for example, morally obligated to keep a promise.) According to our three philosophers, all duties are general in the sense of being requirements on all moral agents. Any moral requirement that is *specific* to a given moral agent must be grounded in his or her voluntary commitment. Thus, there is no room for any special requirement on a moral agent that has not been assumed voluntarily by that agent. In other words, *there are no special duties*. This is what I am calling the volunteer theory of obligation. According to the voluntaristic thesis, all duties are general and only those who volunteer for them have any obligations toward them.

This thesis underlies Cohen's view that the child can divorce its parents. For it is unnecessary to consider whether the child has any special duties to the parents that could conflict with the exercise of its right to leave them. It underlies Thomson's view that the woman who had not sought pregnancy has no special responsibility to her unborn child and that any such responsibility that she may later have is assumed implicitly by her voluntary act of taking it home with her. In underlies Tooley's psychobiological method for answering the moral question of infanticide by determining the right-making characteristics of personhood: all we need to know about the neonate is whether or not it possesses the psychological characteristics of personhood. If it does, then it has a right to life. If it does not, then it is not a person and thus may be killed painlessly. It is unnecessary to consider the question of whether the child has a special relation to anyone who may have a "special responsibility" to see to the child's survival.

What I am calling the volunteer thesis is a confidently held thesis of many contemporary Anglo-American philosophers. It is easy to see that the thesis is contrary to what Sidgwick called Common Sense. For it means that there is no such thing as filial duty per se, no such thing as the special duty of mother to child, and generally no such thing as a morality of special family or kinship relations. All of which is contrary to what people think. For most people think that we do owe special debts to our parents even though we have not voluntarily assumed our obligations to them. Most people think that what we owe to our own children does not have its origin in any voluntary undertaking, explicit or implicit, that we have made to them. And, "preanalytically," many people believe that we owe special consideration to our siblings even at times when we may not *feel* very friendly to them. But if there are no special duties, then most of these prima facie requirements are misplaced and without moral force, and should be looked upon as archaic survivals to be ignored in assessing our moral obligations.

The idea that to be committed to an individual is to have made a voluntarily implicit or explicit commitment to that individual is generally fatal to family morality. For it looks upon the network of felt obligation and expectation that binds family members as a sociological phenomenon that is without presumptive moral force. The social critics who hold this view of family obligation usually are aware that promoting it in public policy must further the disintegration of the traditional family as an institution. But whether they deplore the disintegration or welcome it, they are bound in principle to abet it.

It may be that so many philosophers have accepted the voluntaristic dogma because of an uncritical use of the model of promises as the paradigm for obligations. If all obligations are like the obligation to keep a promise, then indeed they could not be incumbent on anyone who did not undertake to perform in a specified way. But there is no reason to take promises as paradigmatic of obligation. Indeed, the moral force of the norm of promise-keeping must itself be grounded in a theory of obligations that moral philosophers have yet to work out.

A better defense of the special duties would require considerably more space than I can give it here.[26] However, I believe the defense of special duties is far more plausible than rival theories that reject special duties. My primary objective has been to raise the strong suspicion that the volunteer theory of obligation is a dogma that is very probably wrong and misconceived, a view that is certainly at odds with common opinion.

Once we reject the doctrine that a voluntary act by the person concerned is a necessary condition of special obligation, we are free to respect the common-sense views that attribute moral force to many obligations associated with kinship and other family relationships. We may then accept the family as an institution that defines many special duties but that is nevertheless imperfect in numerous respects. . . .

It should be said that the appeal to common sense or common opinion is not final. For common sense often delivers conflicting verdicts on behavior. But a commonsense verdict is strongly presumptive. For example, there is the common belief that biological mothers have a special responsibility to care for their children, even their unwanted children. One *takes* this as presumptive evidence of an *objective* moral responsibility on the part of the mother. Note that the "verdict" of common sense is not really a verdict at all. Rather, it is evidence of a moral consideration that *must* enter into the final verdict on what to do and how to behave. Thomson ignores common sense when she asserts that the mother of a child, born or unborn, has no special responsibility to it unless she has in some way voluntarily assumed responsibility for it. Now, to say that a pregnant woman may have a moral responsibility to her unborn child does not entail that abortion is impermissible. For there are other commonsense considerations that enter here and other responsibilities that the mother may have (to her other children, to herself) that may conflict and override the responsibility to the fetus. So common sense is often not decisive. One may say that a commonsense opinion is symptomatic of a prima facie duty or liberty, as the case may be. Yet it still remains for the casuist to determine the *weight* of the duty in relation to other moral considerations that also may have the support of common sense.

Politically and morally, lack of respect for common sense fosters illiberalism and elitism. Here we have the radical temper that often advocates actions and policies wildly at odds with common opinion—from infanticide to male lactation, from non-fault divorce on demand for children to the "roommate test" for marital relationships.

5. THE BROKEN FAMILY

In the final section we look at certain of the social consequences of applying radical theory to family obligation. I have suggested that, insofar as moral philosophers have any influence on the course of social history, their influence has recently been in aid of institutional disintegration. I shall now give some indication of how the principled philosophical disrespect for common sense in the area of family morality has weakened the family and how this affects the happiness of its members. Although much of what I say here is fairly well known, it is useful to say it in the context of an essay critical of the radical way of approaching moral philosophy. For there are periods in history when the radical way has great influence.

The most dramatic evidence of the progressive weakening of the family is found in the statistics on divorce. Almost all divorce is painful and most divorce affects children. Although divorce does not end but merely disrupts the life of a child, the life it disrupts is uncontroversially the life of a person who can be wronged directly by the actions of a moral agent. One might, therefore, expect that philosophers who carefully examine the morality of abortion also would carefully examine the moral ground for divorce. But here, too, the contemporary reluctance of philosophers to deal with the special casuistry of family relations is evidenced. For example, there are more articles on euthanasia or on recombinant DNA research than on divorce.

Each year there are another million and a quarter divorces in the United States affecting over one million children. The mother is granted custody in ninety percent of the cases, although legally it is no longer a matter of course. There is very persuasive evidence that children of divorced parents are affected seriously and adversely. Compared with children from intact families, they are referred more often to school psychologists, are more likely to have lower IQ and achievement test scores, are arrested more often, and need more remedial classes.[27] Moreover, these effects show little correlation to economic class. Children in the so-called latency period (between six and twelve) are the most seriously affected. In one study of children in this age group, one-half the subjects showed evidence of a "consolidation into troubled and conflicted depressive behavior patterns."[28] Their behavior patterns included "continuing depression and low self-esteem, combined with frequent school and peer difficulties."

One major cause for the difference between children from broken and intact families is the effective loss of the father. In the *majority* of cases the child has not seen the father within the past year. Only one child in six has seen his or her father in the past week; only 16 percent have seen their fathers in the past month; 15 percent see them once a year; the remaining 52 percent have had no contact at all for the past year. Although 57 percent of college educated fathers see their children at least once a month, their weekly contact is the same as for all other groups (one in six).[29]

It would be difficult to demonstrate that the dismissive attitude of most contemporary moral philosophers to the moral force of kinship ties and conventional family roles has been a serious factor in contributing to the growth in the divorce rate. But that is only because it is so difficult in general to demonstrate how much bread is baked by the dissemination of philosophical ideas. It is surely fair to say that the emphasis on autonomy and equality, when combined with the philosophical denigration of family ties, may have helped to make divorce both easy and respectable, thereby facilitating the rapid change from fault-based to no-fault divorce. If contemporary moralists have not caused the tide of family disintegration, they are avidly riding it. On the other side, it is not difficult to demonstrate that there is very little in recent moral philosophy that could be cited as possibly contributing to *stemming* the tide.

In the past two decades there has been a celebrated resurgence of interest in applied or practical ethics. It would appear, however, that the new enthusiasm for getting down to normative cases does not extend to topics of personal morality defined by family relationships. Accordingly, the children who are being victimized by the breakdown of the family have not benefited from this. Indeed, we find far more concern about the effect of divorce on children from philosophers a generation or two ago when divorce was relatively rare than we find today. Thus, Bertrand Russell writes:

> [H]usband and wife, if they have any love for their children, will so regulate their conduct as to give their children the best chance of a happy and healthy development. This may involve, at times, very considerable self-repression. And it certainly requires that both should realize the superiority of the claims of children to the claims of their own romantic emotions.[30]

And while Russell is not opposed to divorce, he believes that children place great contraints on it.

> . . . parents who divorce each other, except for grave cause, appear to me to be failing their parental duty.[31]

Discerning and sensitive observers of a generation ago did not need masses of statistics to alert them to the effects of divorce on children. Nor did it take a professional philosopher (citing statistics gathered by a professional sociologist) to see that acting to dissolve a family must be evaluated morally primarily in terms of what such action means for the children.

Writing in the *London Daily Express* in 1930, Rebecca West says:

> The divorce of married people with children is nearly always an unspeakable calamity. It is only just being understood . . . how much a child depends for its healthy growth on the presence in the home of both its parents. . . . The point is that if a child is deprived of either its father or its mother it feels that it has been cheated out of a right.[32]

West describes the harmful effects of divorce on children as effects of "a radiating kind, likely to travel down and down through the generations, such as few would care to have on their consciences."

I have quoted West in some fullness because her remarks contrast sharply with what one typically finds in contemporary college texts. In a book called

Living Issues in Ethics, the authors discuss unhappy parents and the moral questions they face in contemplating divorce.

> We believe that staying together for the sake of the children is worse than the feelings and adjustment of separation and divorce.[33]

Further on the authors give what they feel to be a decisive reason for this policy:

> Remaining together in an irreconcilable relationship violates the norm of interpersonal love.

One of the very few philosophers to discuss the question of divorce and its consequences for children is Jeffrey Blustein in his book, *Parents and Children.* Blustein looks with equanimity on the priority of personal commitment to parental responsibility, pointing out that

> The traditional view . . . that the central duties of husband and wife are the . . . duties of parenthood is giving way to a conception of marriage as essentially involving a serious commitment between two individuals as individuals.[34]

Blustein also tells us (without telling us how he knows it) that children whose parents are unhappily married are worse off than if their parents were divorced.

> Indeed it could be argued that precisely on account of the children the parents' unhappy marriage should be dissolved. . . . [35]

The suggestion that parents who are unhappy should get a divorce "for the sake of the children" is *very* contemporary.

To my knowledge, no reliable study has yet been made that compares children of divorced parents to children from intact families whose parents do not get on well together. So I have no way of knowing whether the claims of these authors are true or not. Moreover, because any such study would be compromised by certain arbitrary measures of parental incompatibility, one should probably place little reliance on them. It is, therefore, easy to see that contemporary philosophers are anxious to jump to conclusions that do not render implausible the interesting view that the overriding question in considering divorce is the compatibility of the parents, and that marital ties should be dissolved when they threaten or thwart the personal fulfillment of one or both the marital partners.

These philosophers set aside special duties and replace them with an emphasis on friendship, compatibility, and interpersonal love among family members. However, this has a disintegrative effect. That is to say, if what one owes to members of one's family is largely to be understood in terms of feelings of personal commitment, definite limits are placed on what one owes. For as feelings change, so may one's commitments. The result is a structure of responsibility within the family that is permanently unstable.

I have, in this final section, illustrated the indifference of contemporary philosophers to the family by dwelling on their indifference to the children affected by divorce. Nevertheless, I hope it is clear that nothing I have said is meant to convey that I oppose divorce. I do not. Neither Russell nor West nor any of the sane and compassionate liberal thinkers of the recent past opposed divorce. They simply did not play fast and loose with family mores, did not encourage divorce, and pointed out that moralists must insist that the system of family obligations is only partially severed by a divorce that cuts the marital tie. Morally, as well as legally, the obligations to the children remain as before. Legally, this is still recognized. But in a moral climate where the system of family obligation is given no more weight than can be justified in terms of popular theories of deontic volunteerism, the obligatory ties are too fragile to survive the personal estrangements that result from divorce. It is, therefore, to be expected that parents (especially fathers) will be off and away doing their own thing. And the law is largely helpless.

I have no special solutions to the tragedy of economic impoverishment and social deprivation that results from the weakening of family ties. I believe in the right of divorce and do not even oppose no-fault divorce. I do not know how to get back to the good old days when moral philosophers had the common sense to acknowledge the moral weight of special ties and the courage to condemn those who failed in them—the days when, in consequence, the *climate* of

moral approval and disapproval was quite different from what it is today. I do not know how to make fathers ashamed of their neglect and inadvertent cruelty. What I do know is that moral philosophers should be paying far more attention to the social consequences of their views than they are. It is as concrete as taking care that what one says will not affect adversely the students whom one is addressing. If what students learn from us encourages social disintegration, then we are responsible for the effects this may have on their lives and on the lives of their children. This then is a grave responsibility, even graver than the responsibility we take in being for or against something as serious as euthanasia or capital punishment—since most of our students will never face these questions in a practical way.

I believe then that responsible moral philosophers are liberal or conservative but not radical. They respect human relationships and traditions and the social environment in which they live as much as they respect the natural environment and its ecology. They respect the family. William James saw the rejection of radicalism as central to the pragmatist way of confronting moral questions.

[Experience] has proved that the laws and usages of the land are what yield the maximum of satisfaction. . . . The presumption in cases of conflict must always be in favor of the conventionally recognized good. The philosopher must be a conservative, and in the construction of his casuistic scale must put things most in accordance with the customs of the community on top.[36]

A moral philosophy that does not give proper weight to the customs and opinions of the community is presumptuous in its attitude and pernicious in its consequences. In an important sense it is not a moral philosophy at all. For it is humanly irrelevant.

NOTES

1. Michael Slote, "Obedience and Illusions," in Onora O'Neill and William Ruddick, eds., *Having Children* (New York: Oxford, 1979), p. 320.

2. Slote, p. 230.

3. Virginia Held, "The Obligations of Mothers and Fathers," in Joyce Trebilcot, ed., *Mothering: Essays in*

Feminist Theory (Totowa, NJ: Rowman and Allanheld, 1983), pp. 7–20.

4. Jane English, "What Do Grown Children Owe Their Parents?" in O'Neill and Ruddick, op. cit., pp. 351–56.

5. John Simmons, *Moral Principles and Political Obligation* (Princeton, NJ: Princeton University Press, 1979), p. 162.

6. Jeffrey Blustein, *Parents and Children: The Ethics of the Family* (New York: Oxford, 1982), p. 182.

7. Howard Cohen, *Equal Rights for Children* (Totowa, NJ: Rowman and Littlefield, 1980), p. 66.

8. Simone de Beauvoir, *The Second Sex,* tr. H. M. Parshley (New York: Random House 1952), p. 534.

9. De Beauvoir, p. 553.

10. De Beauvoir, "Talking to De Beauvoir," *Spare Rib* (March 1977), p. 2.

11. Richard Wasserstrom, *Philosophy and Social Issues* (Notre Dame, IN: University of Notre Dame Press, 1980), p. 26.

12. Wasserstrom, p. 23.

13. Wasserstrom, p. 26.

14. Ann Ferguson, "Androgyny as an Ideal for Human Development," in *Feminism and Philosophy,* eds. M. Vetterling-Braggin, F. Elliston and J. English (Totowa, NJ: Rowman and Littlefield, 1977), pp. 45–69.

15. Carol Gould, "Private Rights and Public Virtues: Woman, the Family and Democracy," in *Beyond Domination,* ed. Carol Gould (Totowa, NJ: Rowman and Allanheld, 1983), pp. 3–18.

16. Alison Jaggar, "Human Biology in Feminist Theory: Sexual Equality Reconsidered," in Gould, op. cit., p. 41. Jaggar is serious about the possibility and desirability of what she calls the "transformation of sexuality," which is elaborated in her book *Feminist Politics and Human Nature* (Totowa, NJ: Rowman and Allanheld, 1983), p. 132.

17. Alison Jaggar, "On Sex Equality," in *Sex Equality,* ed. Jane English (Englewood Cliffs, NJ: Prentice-Hall, 1977), p. 102.

18. Alison Jaggar, "Prostitution," in Marilyn Pearsell, ed., *Women and Values: Reading in Recent Feminist Philosophy* (Belmont, CA: Wadsworth, 1986), pp. 108–121.

19. Jaggar, "Prostitution," p. 117.

20. Janet Radcliffe Richards. *The Skeptical Feminist* (Middlesex, England: Penguin Books, 1980), pp. 341–42.

21. See Sylvia Ann Hewlett, *A Lesser Life: The Myth of Woman's Liberation in America* (New York: William Morrow, 1986).

22. Judith Thomson, "A Defense of Abortion," in *Philosophy and Public Affairs,* vol. 1, no. 1, 1972.

23. Thomson, p. 64.

24. Michael Tooley, "Abortion and Infanticide," in *Philosophy and Public Affairs,* vol. 2, no. 1, 1972.

25. Howard Cohen, *Equal Rights for Children,* chs. V and VI.

26. For a defense of the special duties not assumed voluntarily, see Christina Sommers, "Filial Morality," *The Journal of Philosophy,* no. 8, August 1986.

27. Lenore Weitzman, *The Divorce Revolution: The Unexpected Social and Economic Consequences for Women and Children in America* (New York: The Free Press, 1985).

28. A. Skolnick and J. Skolnick, eds., *Family in Transition* (Boston: Little Brown, 1929), p. 452.

29. Weitzman, p. 259.

30. Bertrand Russell, *Marriage and Morals* (New York: Liveright, 1929), p. 236.

31. Russell, p. 238.

32. Rebecca West, *London Daily Express,* 1930

33. R. Nolan and F. Kirkpatrick, eds., *Living Issues in Ethics* (Belmont, CA: Wadsworth, 1983), p. 147.

34. Blustein, *Parents and Children,* p. 230.

35. Blustein, p. 232.

36. William James, "The Moral Philosopher and the Moral Life", in *Essays in Pragmatism* (New York: Hafner, 1948), p. 80.

Critic

CLAUDIA MILLS

The Ties That Bind
Duties to Family Members

"What do grown children owe their parents?" Over two decades ago philosopher Jane English asked this question and came up with the startling answer: nothing [ref. 1]. English joins many contemporary philosophers in rejecting the once-traditional view that grown children owe their parents some kind of fitting repayment for past services rendered. The problem with the traditional view, as argued by many, is, first, that parents have duties to provide fairly significant services to their growing children, and persons do not owe repayment for others' mere performance of duty; second, even where parents go above and beyond duty in their loving and generous rearing of their children, the benefits are bestowed, at least on young children, without their voluntary acceptance and consent, and so, again, fail to generate any obligation of subsequent repayment on their part (*see* ref. 2, pp. 182–183). Moreover, the entire idiom of obligation and repayment, in English's words, "tends to obscure, or even to undermine, the love that is the correct ground of filial obligation" (ref. 1, p. 352).

English's alternative, however—that children strictly "owe" their parents nothing except what flows naturally from whatever love and affection exist between them—also strikes many as problematic. Sommers offers examples of what seem to be clearly delinquent adult children, who simply do not "feel" like sharing their lives with their aging parents, or

providing any emotional or financial support to them, and so do not (ref. 3, pp. 440–441). Sommers points out that we need some talk of obligations in order to fill in the cracks in human relationships where love and affection fail: "The ideal relationship cannot be 'duty-free,' if only because sentimental ties may come unraveled, often leaving one of the parties at a material disadvantage" (ref. 3, pp. 450–451). Sommers proposes as her alternative to English that legitimate duties arise out of special relationships defined by social roles: Being a father or mother, a son or a daughter, "is socially as well as biologically prescriptive; it not only defines what one is; it also defines who one is and what one owes" (ref. 3, p. 447). According to Sommers, "The filial duties of adult children include such things as being grateful, loyal, attentive, respectful and deferential to parents (more so than to strangers)" (ref. 3, p. 447).

Sommers's view is not without troubles of its own. The stress on social roles seems to make family relationships overly conventional and does not distinguish family relationships from any of the myriad other social roles we all occupy. Moreover, some of the duties Sommers proposes (gratitude, deference) echo traditional debt-based views of the source of filial obligation that most of us now reject.

In what follows, I look at the duties of grown children to parents from a somewhat different angle. I begin with English's claim that the "duties" in

Claudia Mills, "Duties to Aging Parents," in Care of the Aged, ed. James M. Humber and Robert F. Almeder (Totowa, N.J.: Humana Press, 2003). Notes have been deleted. Reprinted by permission of Humana Press, Inc.

273

question are merely "duties of friendship," duties situated within and made sense of through an ongoing mutual relationship, but then offer an argument that allows us to establish genuine filial obligations in a way that she is unable to do. I argue that family relationships are importantly different both from friendship (English's analogy) and from other social roles (Sommers's analogy) in their uniquely unchosen and unconditional nature. I suggest that we can shed light on what grown children owe their parents by looking first at a category of family relationships less shadowed by traditional encrustations of debt and gratitude: the relationship of siblings. I claim that we have strong reasons to participate in unconditional, unchosen relationships and corresponding obligations not to deny others the good of participating in such relationships with us. I conclude by trying to say something about exactly what grown children owe their parents: Grown children owe their parents those things that flow from participating together in an unconditional, unchosen relationship, and not (generally) material goods that can be otherwise obtained.

THE NATURE OF FAMILY RELATIONSHIPS

Many philosophers in the past few decades have turned their attention away from moral impartiality toward special relationships: friendship, membership in a community, family ties. I want to advance a claim about what makes family ties special even among other "special" relationships.

For a point of contrast, let us look first at nonfamilial friendship. As English characterizes friendship, certain "obligations" flow from friendship, but these are obligations only in an attenuated sense. What they are is, rather, defining features of friendship itself, features that, were they absent from A's interactions with B, we would say that A and B were not friends at all. So, friends care about each other, take an interest in each other's problems and successes, spend time together, help each other when needed, and so forth. Are these strictly speaking "obligations"? No, but were two people who claimed

to be friends not to do any of these things for each other, we would question their claim to be friends in the first place. To be friends simply *is* to do these kinds of things for each other. We are given, as it were, the following choice: either be friends (and then do these sort of things for each other) or do not be friends (and so do not do such things for each other). The imperatives of friendship are, at bottom, hypothetical. One can escape the so-called obligations of friendship by declining to be a friend.

Families strike me as importantly different. When it comes to families, there is an imperative not only to fulfill whatever obligations are defined and generated by the underlying relationship but also to continue to participate in the relationship itself. We no longer have the same kind of choice: be a friend or walk away. In the case of families, I will argue, walking away is not the same kind of option.

Of course, there are many different kinds of family relationships: that of spouses to each other, of parents to children, of children to parents, and of siblings to siblings. In a liberal, modern society such as ours, which permits the initial choice of spouse and subsequent easy, no-fault, nonstigmatizing divorce, people may seem to marry each other, and to stay married to each other, through choice. The ideal, however, remains one of lasting commitment; in the vows that are still typical of most marriages, the partners to it pledge to remain with each other for better or worse, for richer or poorer, through sickness and health, as long as they both shall live. Few marriages begin with vows to stay together only as long as either party fails to find any other partner more eligible or attractive. Still, there is an undeniable element of choice in the initial mating.

Parents also seem to choose to have children in a way that children do not choose to have parents: I choose to give birth in a way that I did not choose to be born. However, this appearance of genuine, extensive parental choice cannot survive closer scrutiny. Certainly, the choice that I have of my children is much less than the choice that I have of my spouse, or any of my friends.

First, although one may choose to be a parent, to be the parent of some child or other, in the vast majority of cases, one has little or no choice of the identity of the actual child in question. Except in rare cases of adoption of older children with already revealed and well-established personalities, the choice of a child is the choice of a pig in a poke. Gender, appearance, intelligence, talents, and temperament all appear to the parents as an unfolding surprise. Parents of two or more children are invariably astonished at the differences between individuals produced by the same parental genes and reared in the same family environment. We are still far away from the prospect of "designer" children, tailor-made to match parental expectations.

Second, even beyond one's initial lack of choice regarding the actual children to parent, the continuation of the relationship itself does not reflect parental choice to any significant degree, or so I will argue. Now, many philosophers seek to base parental obligations to children on other than bare biological grounds. In their view, I owe this or that to my children not because of the brute biological fact that I begat them (male) or bore them (female), but because I have voluntarily assumed such an obligation. I signaled my willingness to assume it by taking my child home with me from the hospital rather than exercising the option of giving him or her up, via adoption, to someone else to raise. In a society, like ours, that offers safe and legal abortion, the mother at least could have had an abortion and so declined to bring the child into existence in the first place. Thus, by not aborting, she chooses to give birth, and so, unless she surrenders her parental rights and obligations to another, chooses to become a parent, or so runs one common view.

This grounding of parental obligations in parental choice, however, is vulnerable to challenge on several points. What if I give birth and, as it turns out, there happens to be no one else available and willing to adopt my child? Surely, I have some extra responsibility for this child, *my* child, the child to whom I have just given birth, whether I assume it voluntarily or not. And, a more telling point: Suppose I do accept responsibility for some child, either by taking my own biological child home with me after its birth, or by agreeing to become an adoptive parent. What exactly have I committed myself to, in so doing? If we assimilate parenthood to friendship, then the answer

would be that I have committed myself to taking care of the child as long as I feel like doing so; that taking care of a child is constitutive of being a parent, and I continue in the parental relationship as long as I feel like doing so. However, few would be ready to endorse this view of parenthood. If there is a basic choice involved, I submit, it is to take care of the child *forever,* come what may, whether I still want to or not. The choice of a biological parent to give up his or her child for adoption at birth is seldom criticized; the choice of a parent, biological or adoptive, to give up his or her child several years later would be almost uniformly criticized, and I would argue, rightly so. Now, parents may, and often do, subsequently delegate or transfer certain of the responsibilities of parenthood: They hire nannies, arrange for day care, send their children off to public or private schools, and allow other relatives to establish trust funds in their names. However, what (in most cases) they do not delegate or transfer is the relationship itself. They still, through all of these other alterations in their performed duties, remain parents, the persons unconditionally and permanently committed to the love and care of this particular child.

Why is this? Is the answer simply that this is what you promised in that initial act of assuming parental responsibility—to care for the child forever? Why should we understand the promise in such a sweeping and all-encompassing way? Where else in life do we promise such huge things extending over such a long duration of time? Well, as just noted, we promise them in marriage, understood as the foundation of a family, breaking such promises as often as we manage to keep them. Where else? Consent itself is insufficient to establish such deep and enduring duties. For who could ever consent, in an informed way, to such a thing? Whoever could do it?

My answer to the question of how parents end up in long-term committed relationships with their children instead is this. It is a great good to participate in a relationship that is enduring and unconditional. And because it is a great good for a child to be in that kind of relationship and a great harm to the child to be deprived of that kind of relationship, parents acquire an obligation to stick with the relationship, which means to fulfill the tasks that flow from it, through thick and thin. Indeed, as I will explain, it is a great good precisely to participate in a relationship that is importantly *unchosen.* Thus, far from grounding the obligations of parenthood in a recognition of the importance of choice, my argument grounds these obligations in the recognition of the importance of that which is unchosen.

Now, is the great good here to participate in an unconditional and unchosen *relationship,* or to be the recipient of the unconditional *love* which usually—but not invariably—accompanies it? Some parents—only a few, I would speculate—do not love their children, or more properly, for some sad reason of their own history and constitution, cannot. However, most of us do love our children in this way. It is very odd that we do, that we love them before they were born, with no knowledge of a single fact about them except that in some sense they are *ours.* Biological parents love their children in this way; adoptive parents, waiting for the arrival of a child they have never seen from half the world away, love their children in this way. It is a love based on nothing distinctive about the individual in question, nothing at all. One might wonder why we should even value love like this in the first place. I have heard some people devalue God's love in this way: God loves me? Yeah, well, big deal, God loves *everybody.* However, parents do not love everybody. They love this child, these (small number of) children. Why should I care about being loved if the love is not based on any trait or quality of mine, any distinctive feature, any uniqueness, anything that has to do with *me*? Well, love based on my distinctive uniqueness will come; parents do come to dwell lovingly, and sometimes despairingly, on all of their child's individual characteristics. However, the only answer I can come up with here is that it is simply a great good to have some reservoir of love that does not have to be earned and, more important, cannot be forfeited. As Elizabeth Barrett Browning wrote in one of her *Sonnets from the Portuguese,* love based on any particular trait or feature is vulnerable to altering when that trait or feature alters. So Browning writes, "If thou must love me, let it be for naught/Except for love's sake only." Love based on a choice can vary with changes in the features of the beloved that moti-

vated and justified that choice. Unchosen love is, in this way, uniquely secure.

If this—unconditional, unchosen love—is the great good, is there any value to a continuing parental relationship in which such love is not present? I would argue that there is. One certainly cannot have love of this sort in the absence of the relationship, so the relationship at the least is the necessary precondition of the love; and the relationship itself can breed love over time—not love based on appreciation of any set of traits or characteristics, but love based simply on a shared history, of the passage of time in another's company. Minow notes that "duties and feelings interact in complicated ways" and that "feelings themselves can be educated as someone learns about and carries out responsibilities" (ref. 4, p. 267). Far from familiarity breeding contempt, I have found that familiarity breeds fondness, comfort in each other's presence, a quiet "growing accustomed" to the other's face. Sheer continuity, steadfastness over time, is itself a great good in one's life. Of course, I am assuming here that the parents are making a good-faith effort to love the child. I address the question of indifferent, neglectful, or even abusive parents later.

Now, this argument, appealing to the great good of unconditional and unchosen relationships, as I have stated it, is symmetrical between parents and children. While there may be some asymmetry in the choice involved on the part of parents and of children to enter into the relationship (although I have argued that the asymmetry is easily overstated, through overstating the presence of genuine parental choice), the good of being in the relationship itself is a good for all parties to it. As it is a great good for children to participate in such a relationship, so it is a great good for parents to participate in it as well. It may be a greater good for children, simply in that they are developing and forming their sense of their own identity and of their own self-worth, but for all persons, I submit, it is a great good to have at least some relationships in one's life that are unchosen and unconditional. This will lead me to make some speculations about what grown children owe their parents, but first I want to make a detour to look at the relationship of siblings to each other, for this is also an unchosen relationship. We do not choose our brothers and sisters, as we choose our friends. Herein lies the distinctive good offered to us by this relationship, which will shape our expectations of what siblings owe to each other.

BROTHERS AND SISTERS

What, if anything, do grown brothers and sisters owe each other? Do they owe each other more or less than what they owe friends? How are we to understand their relationship and what flows from it? I would approach an answer to this question by saying that there is no way we can even begin to itemize duties of siblings to each other without first looking at the nature of the relationship they share. Again, the distinctive feature of this relationship, in contrast to most friendships, is that it is unchosen and, in some important sense, uncontingent on the merits, affinities, characters, virtues, and accomplishments of the parties to it. Brothers and sisters are simply born, or adopted, into the same family; they do not select each other; they may not even like each other all that well; it may be that if they were not siblings they would have little or nothing to do with each other. However, they are siblings. They are stuck with each other. Each one is a "given" in the other's life.

Now, if we were to follow English's model, we would say that siblings have only such "obligations" to each other as flow from their ongoing feeling of affection toward each other; insofar as they are friends, they should treat each other in the ways constitutive and definitive of friendship—and if they no longer want to be friends, so be it. If we were to follow Sommers's model, we would say that we would need to look at what flows from the social role of "brother" or "sister." However, I maintain that there is a great good in continuing the relationship and engaging in the activities characteristic of it, even in the absence of the appropriate underlying feelings. I would maintain that the social role of "brother" or "sister" is crucially undefined and largely beside the point. My sister is not special to me because we occupy a certain social role vis-à-vis each other.

So what do brothers and sisters owe each other? My claim is that they owe each other simply this: to continue in an ongoing relationship as brothers and sisters. This means sharing each others' lives to some extent—at the minimum, talking occasionally on the telephone or by e-mail, seeing each other sometimes at family gatherings, keeping each other somehow present in each other's lives. How often is often enough? I am not arrogant enough to prescribe that here; it can certainly vary from family to family. Siblings may be more or less "close," and I do not want to argue that closer is always better. However, all things equal, estrangement is always worse.

If this is what brothers and sisters owe each other, it follows that there are two things brothers and sisters do not owe each other. The first is, to put it in its most general terms, anything they can in principle get from somebody else, whether or not they can actually get it from them in the current state of affairs of their life. They owe each other only what they can get from nobody else: that is, the experience of being in an unchosen, unconditional relationship with a brother or sister. In particular, here I mean to exclude financial support. Money one can get from anywhere. In my view, one should get it from one's own efforts; failing that, one should get it from communally provided support for the indigent. What if the latter fails as well? Do I have any special responsibility to help an indigent brother or sister, more than I have to help an indigent stranger? Or an indigent friend? Is blood thicker than water here? My answer on this point is a bit uncertain. Usually, loving brothers and sisters will want to help each other when they can; at the same time, financial entanglements can deform even the most loving relationships. I have known more siblings estranged from each other for financial reasons than for any others. Thus, from my own admittedly anecdotal evidence, I think it is better if brothers and sisters do not depend on each other financially. Here, too, different families may have different expectations for what it means to participate in an ongoing family relationship. However, for the most part, I would continue to say: siblings do not owe each other what they can get from somebody else.

To put this same point another way, Donaldson distinguishes between what he calls "value-intrinsic" and "value-extrinsic" institutions, where an institution is "value intrinsic" to the "extent to which an institution's ends are logically unobtainable without the existence of the institution itself" and an institution is "value extrinsic" to "the extent to which an institution's ends conceivably could be achieved by other means" (ref. 5, p. 36). Recasting his point in the language of relationships rather than institutions, we can say that it is important that siblings give each other goods that are value intrinsic to their relationship, goods which simply cannot be acquired in any other way, and far less important that they give each other goods that are value extrinsic, even if conventional expectations, in a given society, may tie these goods in some way to the relationship. It is the value-intrinsic goods that are at the heart of family relationships. They are what brothers and sisters most fundamentally owe one another: the goods of being in the relationship itself.

The second, related thing that is not owed by siblings to each other, in my view, is sheer preference for one's siblings in giving out some benefit not directly tied to the relationship itself. Such preference has often been taken to be paradigmatic of "special" relationships and in direct challenge to the "impartiality" required by universal morality: to be in a special relationship just is to favor certain others in this way. However, I do not see that special relationships, such as family relationships, require this at all, in any mechanical way, except for the goods that are value intrinsic to that relationship, as discussed earlier. Siblings do not owe each other preference in hiring, for example. In fact, such preference is often (rightly) frowned on as nepotism. I owe my siblings some measure of preference only in how I spend my time, how I invest my affections, how I structure my days, but that is all. Philosophers at this point will want to introduce a range of hypothetical cases: If a trolley runs off the track and strikes both my sister and a stranger, whom do I help first? How serious of an injury to a stranger outweighs my duty to help my sister first? And so on. I am one who believes that in situations of dire emergency, philosophical argumentation runs out and real human emotion appropriately claims us. As Bernard Williams famously argues, in such cases "we just act, as a possibly confused result of the situation we are in. That, I suspect,

is very often an exceedingly good thing" (ref. 6, p. 118). When the trolley strikes, I will run to my sister's side. What I will do next will depend on the details of the situation in which I find myself. More than this I cannot specify in advance.

PARENTS AND CHILDREN

Let us now draw closer to the case at hand—the duties of grown children to their parents—by asking what parents owe their grown children. My answer here is the same as it was in the case of siblings. Parents do not owe their children what they could, and should, get from anyone else: a job, a place to live, money—either during their lives or in an inheritance after their death. In my view, children have no claim whatsoever on any inheritance of their parents' wealth; to the contrary, we would make great strides toward social justice by eliminating the practice of inheritance altogether (ref. 2, Appendix; ref. 7). Instead, our parents owe us only what we can get from parents alone (to the extent that they can provide it): unconditional love, abiding interest in our activities, pride in our accomplishments, worry over our problems, advice based on knowing us longer and better than anyone else, time, companionship—the continuation of the relationship itself.

What, then, do grown children owe their parents? The very same thing. Grown children do not owe their parents a home to live in, or money to live on, or day-to-day health care; nor, contrary to Sommers, do they owe their parents deference and gratitude. They owe them simply continuation in the relationship as their children, sharing their lives, caring about their lives, building an ongoing life together. Nothing more, nothing less.

Now, if we follow English, grown children may *want* to provide their parents with many other additional goods; they may want to offer them a home, pay their bills, and care for them physically when they are no longer able to care for themselves. If we follow Sommers, there may (or may not be) certain social expectations to do such things. However, this, in my view, goes beyond what is entailed simply by the continuation of the relationship itself. I do not see that such additional services are owed to parents by their grown children any more than they are owed to grown children by their parents, or to grown siblings by each other. All that is owed is the relationship itself. Thus, my view is more demanding than English's and less demanding than Sommers's. English seems to *require* essentially nothing, except what is defined by participation in a relationship of a certain kind, whereas I require participation in the relationship itself. Sommers requires whatever is specified by our social understandings of certain roles, whereas I want to reject certain common (although certainly not universally shared) understandings of what grown children owe their parents as unnecessarily burdensome. We do *not* owe our parents services that can easily be provided by others, such as basic physical care or financial support. I think it is a strength of my view that it identifies a plausible and livable middle ground between two untenable extremes.

OBJECTIONS AND REPLIES

Let me now clarify and further defend my view by considering a range of questions and objections that can be raised regarding it.

1. Can we really require people, morally, to be in a relationship when they do not want to? In part, this objection may be a restatement of the earlier question of whether the relationship itself has any real value in the absence of the unconditional love, which is the real good in question. My answer is the same as it was before: that there is some good in the relationship itself, especially if the parties to it make some real effort to cultivate the feelings that should accompany it. Of course, no one is out there enforcing this obligation. There can be laws mandating financial support of parents by children, laws that I would oppose, but no laws requiring children to visit their parents, or call them on their birthdays, let alone laws mandating love. However, I would say that there is an obligation here nonetheless: the obligation not to deny another a great good that one can supply at relatively modest cost to oneself. This obligation is supported by both prudential as well as moral reasons,

for in providing this great good to another, I also provide it to myself.

2. What about dysfunctional, toxic families? What, if anything, do grown children owe parents, or parents owe grown children, or grown siblings owe each other, when the underlying relationship is seriously damaging to at least one of the individuals participating in it? Here, I would say two things. First, mutuality is an important part of the good of family relationships; it is what makes them *relationships* at all. It is hard, if not impossible, for me to have a relationship of a certain kind with you if you do not have a relationship of that kind with me. If a relationship is proving toxic, or too painful, it is fine to sever it; one is not required to sacrifice one's own personhood—one's identity, one's happiness, one's sanity—to provide some good for others, if one even *can* provide this good in such a setting. That said, second, it is worthwhile to try to mend and heal family relationships when possible, as much for one's own sake as for the sake of one's parents or siblings. Reconciliation and forgiveness are great goods in their own right, although, again, they can be purchased at too high a price. However, most people who reach out to parents, children, and siblings who have wronged them, I suspect, are not sorry for having done so.

3. Does my view give undue weight to biological ties? Does it just mask a fetish for the biological? Where, after all, do truly unchosen relationships come from, if not from our biological links to one another? Although I intend for my view to give equal consideration to adoptive and biological families, to families formed in both conventional and unconventional ways, we may have a clearer case of unchosen relationships in the standard, biological case. It is interesting that in one much discussed surrogacy case, when parties were disputing the custody of a child born with a serious disability, biological ties won out over contractual agreements: "when it was proved that the child was certainly biologically theirs, [the Stivers] accepted the child, named him Christopher Ray, and sought help for him" (ref. 8, p. 336). There may be some primacy given to the biological on my view, but I do not think it is excessive, or disturbing. It simply acknowledges, as Smith writes, that "in setting the boundaries of the

composition of families, . . . in all times and places biology is central."

4. Along the same lines, does my view ignore or wrongly deny the extent to which families, at bottom, *are* chosen? As Minow argues, "family" as defined by law is hardly "natural or obvious" but reveals "the political, religious, and social choices embedded in that institution" (ref. 9, p. 250). Minow is, of course, correct that current family law reflects a long and sometimes confused series of societal choices regarding what should and should not be recognized as a family. However, I think that there is more disagreement at the margins than there is at the core. Moreover, even as Minow argues for an expansive definition of family membership, she argues for a stringent attitude toward family obligation. I read this as saying that although we may have some (fairly small degree of) choice regarding who counts as a family member, to recognize another as a family member is to recognize that one stands to another in a relationship where the concept of choice now ceases to apply.

5. This leads me to another, closely related question. Are family relationships indeed as "special" as I have said? Do not many of us have friends who are as close to us as our siblings, who become, in essence, "families of choice"? My answer here is yes, of course we can, but to treat friends as family is precisely to discard the idiom of "choice" in our interactions with them. A family by *choice,* I submit, is not a family at all. To have a friend who becomes a "sister" or a "brother" is to have a friend to whom one recognizes that one is irrevocably committed, committed come what may, from whom it would be inconceivable to walk away.

6. What if one has several brothers and sisters? Can one opt out of a continuing relationship with one's siblings then, or with one's parents, on the grounds that the great good of participating in an unchosen, unconditional relationship is available to them elsewhere? They do not need to be in such a relationship with *me*; they can enjoy it with *them.* In a very large family, family ties may be somewhat attenuated—this was Aristotle's objection to Plato's model of family relationships in *The Republic*—but, generally, it is a great good to have more than one such relationship in

one's life. It is too much to expect any one relationship to provide the entire good available here. (Again, the good in question that I provide to another is equally, on my view, a good for me.) On a similar note, does my view establish obligations to participate in a continuing relationship not only with parents, children, and siblings, but with grandparents, aunts, uncles, cousins, second cousins twice removed? My answer here would be that this may well be so, depending on the particular configuration of the family. Some large, far-flung families have little interaction beyond the nuclear family, but, in others, such relationships may be an important part of one's participation in family life.

7. What does this view imply for relationships with aged parents who have become senile, who can no longer participate in an ongoing mutual relationship? One implication of my view, which some will view as welcome, some as unwelcome, is that the obligation to participate in an ongoing relationship continues only when the relationship itself remains possible. I do not have—cannot have—an obligation to be in a *relationship* with someone who cannot be in a relationship with me. It is one of the tragedies of senility that genuine relationships with other human beings are no longer possible. However, can't I continue to love, unconditionally, someone who is senile and manifest this love to him or her in various ways, even if he or she is not able to recognize it? Yes. Ideally, familial love continues through all alterations, but, again, the relationship that is in many ways the foundation of the love cannot. Heartless as it may seem to say this, I see little point in spending extensive time with someone who does not know me for who I am. To do so is to engage in a pretense that a relationship still continues that, tragically, is gone forever.

8. Do we generally have an obligation to provide others with a great good that they can get nowhere else? Can we generalize beyond the familial case to establish other obligations to provide others with goods of this sort—for example, to donate blood or bone marrow, if I have the only matching type? My answer here is "maybe." However, such cases will be very rare. My principle is not that I have an obligation to provide others with a great good that no one else *will* provide, but only with a great good that no one

else *can* provide—*if* I can provide it at a relatively modest cost to myself, and especially if I can provide it in a way that benefits me as well. In the family-relationship case, I benefit from benefiting you; we both gain equally from continuing in a mutual relationship with each other. In the bone marrow case, the benefit is almost completely one sided, which makes a difference to our assessment of the two cases.

9. This leads me to my final question. How far should we go in maintaining family relationships in our lives? How much do these relationships demand of us? This echoes our earlier discussion: How "close" a relationship is close enough? Here, we need to remember that although family relationships are a great good, in the view proposed here, they are not the only good that life offers to us, not by a long shot. The good of participating in an unchosen, unconditionally loving relationship needs to be balanced against the many other goods that make up a flourishing life: satisfying and meaningful work, spiritual growth, health and fitness, creative expression, and sheer fun. No mechanical guidelines can be offered here.

I have a friend who has done nothing of significance with her life for the past 10 years but take care of her completely senile and demented mother, including a daily battle over flossing her mother's few remaining teeth. I am fairly confident that this is too much—both because my friend has neglected every other good in her life and because her mother is no longer capable of engaging in a real relationship with her. She flosses her mother's teeth every day not as a daughter who has shared a long, complex, and enduring life with her mother, but as a total stranger. Most of us can also come up with cases where it seems that the relationship is valued and nurtured far too little—where months and years go by, without any effort at achieving a genuine connection. However, again, there is no simple algorithm that can give us all our answers here.

Conclusions

I have argued that family relationships are special in that they are, for the most part, unchosen and unconditional. Because it is a great good to participate in such relationships, one has prudential rea-

sons to do so for the sake of oneself and moral reasons to do so for the sake of others; that is, one has some actual obligation to continue in family relationships. However, what one owes adult family members is only continuation in the relationship itself, and provision of the goods internal to that relationship, not any of a wide range of external goods that can be procured in other ways. Grown children, in my view, do not owe their parents financial support, or a home, or nursing services; they do owe them continuation in the relationship itself, insofar as the (nonsenile) parents are capable of participating in it, too. The great good they provide to their parents through doing this is a good that they equally provide to themselves.

References

[1] English, J. (1979) "What Do Grown Children Owe Their Parents?" in *Having Children: Philosophical and Legal Reflections on Parenthood*, O'Neill, O. and Ruddick, W., eds., Oxford University Press, New York.

[2] Blustein, J. (1982) *Parents and Children: The Ethics of the Family*, Oxford University Press, New York.

[3] Sommers, C. H. (1986) "Filial morality." *J. Phil.* 83(8), 439–456.

[4] Minow, M. (1997) "All in the Family and in All Families: Membership, Loving, and Owing," in *Sex, Preference, and Family: Essays on Law and Nature*, Estlund, D. M. and Nussbaum, M. C., eds., Oxford University Press, New York.

[5] Donaldson, T. (1993) "Morally Privileged Relationships," in *Kindred Matters: Rethinking the Philosophy of the Family*, Meyers, D. T., et al., eds., Cornell University Press, Ithaca, NY.

[6] Williams, B. and Smart, J. J. C. (1973) "A Critique of Utilitarianism," in *Utilitarianism: For and Against*, Cambridge University Press, Cambridge.

[7] Haslett, D. W. (1986) "Is Inheritance Justified?" *Phil. Public Affairs* 15(2), 122–155.

[8] Alpern, K. D. (1992) "Parenting Through Contract When No One Wants the Child," in *The Ethics of Reproductive Technology*, Alpern, K. D., ed., Oxford University Press, New York.

[9] Smith, P. (1993) Family Responsibility and the Nature of Obligation, in *Kindred Matters: Rethinking the Philosophy of the Family*, Meyers, D. T., et al., eds., Cornell University Press, Ithaca, NY.

12

Is Neglecting One's Parents Wrong?

English and Her Critics

One of the Ten Commandments, which Moses reportedly received from God on Mount Sinai, is the injunction to "Honor thy father and thy mother that thy days may be long upon the land which the LORD thy God giveth thee" (Exodus 20:12). In ancient Israel, there wasn't very much in the way of Social Security for elderly people, so if a person's days turned out to be long, the honoring by his children would involve a pretty substantial commitment. Many people accept that adult children have serious moral obligations to their aging parents. In the featured article of this chapter, Jane English takes issue with this widespread view. To the question "What do grown children owe their parents?" her shocking reply is "Nothing."

As English notes, the sacrifices that parents make for their children are often appealed to in support of the standard view. The idea seems to be that if one person makes sacrifices to help another, then the recipient of the benefit is thereby obligated to reciprocate by making comparable sacrifices to help the person who benefited him or her. Since parents make very large sacrifices in order to promote their children's well-being, it seems to follow that children owe their aging parents reciprocal sacrifices comparable with those their parents made for them.

This idea has some nice features. For example, it helps to explain why a person who was abandoned at birth by his natural parents owes his natural parents little or nothing. However, if after being abandoned he was saved from death and adopted by some compassionate couple, who went on to make a large contribution to his well-being, then this idea would also help to explain why he may well owe his adoptive parents quite a lot. So this idea explains why mere genetic relations as such do not generate debts, but familial relations, even nongenetic family relations from which one substantially benefits, do generate debts of obligation.

By means of a clever pair of analogies involving neighborly favors, however, English attempts to undermine this traditional view (see section 4.1 of the Introduction for more on arguments from analogy). There are two cases. In the first, a favor is requested, and accepted. Such favors do generate debts—debts of roughly the same order as the original favor. Further, once the favor is repaid by something equivalent, then that particular debt has been "discharged." However, English does not think that this is the right analogy for the parent-child relationship. Rather, her second story, which involves an *unsolicited* favor, is closer.

English claims that if someone makes a *voluntary sacrifice of the unsolicited variety,* then such sacrifices do not generate debts of reciprocal sacrifice. Since children do not ask their parents to bring them into the world and make the substantial sacrifices involved in raising them, the implications of this for filial obligations are quite important.

English goes on to introduce a different justification for filial obligations, one that is based on friendship rather than reciprocity. Friendship is characterized not by a kind of tit-for-tat accounting but rather by mutuality. English suggests this casts a different light on parental sacrifices. They are not favors, which then guarantee that the recipients have reciprocal obligations. Rather, they are best construed as overtures to friendship.

The friendship model explains a range of filial obligations, but only on the condition that parents and their children are friends. It thus suggests that if friendly overtures do not have their intended effect—if parents and children are not friends—then the children owe their parents nothing. Or, rather, they owe them nothing over and above the normal obligations humans have to one another. And that is precisely the radical and interesting conclusion that English advertises in the first sentence of her article. Further, according to English, the duties of friendship cease when the friendship ceases. It follows that children who were once friends with their parents but who have ceased to be friends no longer owe their parents any special filial duties.

Nicholas Dixon also offers a friendship model of filial duties, but he disagrees with this last conclusion of English. Dixon argues that where English goes wrong is in her account of the duties of friendship. He argues that the duties of friendship might persist even when the friendship dies. In doing so, he does raise what is probably the most obvious objection to the friendship model. Suppose we have a pair of model parents who, in bringing up their child, go far beyond what is required of parents, providing their child, at huge cost to themselves, lots of opportunities to develop interests and talents. The child accepts all these advantages and, as a result, flourishes. However, the child remains cold and distant from his parents, never forming any friendly relationship with them at any time. Does the latter fact really release this rather unpleasant child from all special obligations to his benefactors? Is he not guilty of gross ingratitude, and does that not imply that he is failing in some of his obligations?

QUESTIONS FOR CONSIDERATION

In thinking about the issues raised in this chapter after you have read the selections, it might be helpful to go back to the original cases provided by English and reexamine your reactions to them.

• What do you *now* think Max's obligations to Nina are, in the case where she makes the voluntary sacrifice? Does he simply owe her a "thank you," or is there something more required of him?

• If you agree with English that in the neighborly sacrifice case, Max does not have an obligation of reciprocity to Nina since he did not ask Nina to make the sacrifice, is this enough to show that unsolicited sacrifices *never* generate obligations of reciprocity? Can you think of any cases in which a person helps another without that other person's request and in which such an obligation might well arise? What if a person helps you when you are unconscious? Does this mean that you owe that person nothing in return since you did not ask him or her to help you?

• If there are some cases of unsolicited sacrifice that do generate obligations and others that do not, which are more like the case of the child who did not ask his parents to make sacrifices on his behalf? Does this help or hurt English's position?

• Is it *possible* for parents to achieve friendship with their offspring? (Do you count your parents among your set of friends? Would you *like* to count them as friends?)

- What, if anything, does English's argument imply about the obligations that parents have to their children? If children have no obligations to their parents, does it follow that parents have no obligations to their children? If so, is this a problem for English's position? If not, what difference between the two cases might account for this difference?
- Are Dixon's examples of duties to ex-friends plausible? Are they analogous to the duties that children might have to parents they no longer like?
- Does Dixon adequately defuse the objection of the cold, unfriendly child? Does it follow from Dixon's account that you can minimize your obligations to your parents by remaining aloof and indifferent to them? Is it intuitively plausible that the more unpleasant you are to your parents, the less you owe them?

FURTHER READING

Keller, Simon. "Four Theories of Filial Duty." *Philosophical Quarterly* 56, no. 223 (April 2006): 254–74.

Kristjánsson, Kristján. "Parents and Children as Friends." *Journal of Social Philosophy* 37, no. 2 (Summer 2006): 250–65.

Li, Chenyang. "Shifting Perspectives: Filial Morality Revisited." *Philosophy East and West* 47, no. 2 (1997): 211–32.

JANE ENGLISH

What Do Grown Children Owe Their Parents?

What do grown children owe their parents? I will contend that the answer is "nothing." Although I agree that there are many things that children *ought* to do for their parents, I will argue that it is inappropriate and misleading to describe them as things "owed." I will maintain that parents' voluntary sacrifices, rather than creating "debts" to be "repaid," tend to create love or "friendship." The duties of grown children are those of friends and result from love between them and their parents, rather than being things owed in repayment for the parents' earlier sacrifices. Thus, I will oppose those philosophers who use the word "owe" whenever a duty or obligation exists. Although the "debt" metaphor is appropriate in some moral circumstances, my argument is that a love relationship is not such a case.

Misunderstandings about the proper relationship between parents and their grown children have resulted from reliance on the "owing" terminology. For instance, we hear parents complain, "You owe it to us to write home (keep up your piano playing, not adopt a hippie lifestyle), because of all we sacrificed for you (paying for piano lessons, sending you to college)." The child is sometimes even heard to reply, "I didn't ask to be born (to be given piano lessons, to be sent to college)." This inappropriate idiom of ordinary language tends to obscure, or even to undermine, the love that is the correct ground of filial obligation.

Jane English, "What Do Grown Children Owe Their Parents?" in *Having Children,* ed. Onora O'Neill (New York: Oxford University Press, 1979), pp. 174–78. Notes have been deleted. Used by permission of Oxford University Press, Inc.

1. Favors Create Debts

There are some cases, other than literal debts, in which talk of "owing," though metaphorical, is apt. New to the neighborhood, Max barely knows his neighbor, Nina, but he asks her if she will take in his mail while he is gone for a month's vacation. She agrees. If, subsequently, Nina asks Max to do the same for her, it seems that Max has a moral obligation to agree (greater than the one he would have had if Nina had not done the same for him), unless for some reason it would be a burden far out of proportion to the one Nina bore for him. I will call this a *favor*: when A, at B's request, bears some burden for B, then B incurs an obligation to reciprocate. Here the metaphor of Max's "owing" Nina is appropriate. It is not literally a debt, of course, nor can Nina pass this IOU on to heirs, demand payment in the form of Max's taking out her garbage, or sue Max. Nonetheless, since Max ought to perform one act of similar nature and amount of sacrifice in return, the term is suggestive. Once he reciprocates, the debt is "discharged"—that is, their obligations revert to the condition they were in before Max's initial request.

Contrast a situation in which Max simply goes on vacation and, to his surprise, finds upon his return that his neighbor has mowed his grass twice weekly in his absence. This is a voluntary sacrifice rather than a favor, and Max has no duty to reciprocate. It would be nice for him to volunteer to do so, but this would be supererogatory on his part. Rather than a favor, Nina's action is a friendly gesture. As a result, she might expect Max to chat over the back fence, help her catch her straying dog, or something similar—she might expect the development of a friendship. But Max would be chatting (or whatever) out of friendship, rather than in repayment for mown grass. If he did not return her gesture, she might feel rebuffed or miffed, but not unjustly treated or indignant, since Max has not failed to perform a duty. Talk of "owing" would be out of place in this case.

It is sometimes difficult to distinguish between favors and non-favors, because friends tend to do favors for each other, and those who exchange favors tend to become friends. But one test is to ask how Max is motivated. Is it "to be nice to Nina" or "because she did x for me"? Favors are frequently performed by total strangers without any friendship developing. Nevertheless, a temporary obligation is created, even if the chance for repayment never arises. For instance, suppose that Oscar and Matilda, total strangers, are waiting in a long checkout line at the supermarket. Oscar, having forgotten the oregano, asks Matilda to watch his cart for a second. She does. If Matilda now asks Oscar to return the favor while she picks up some tomato sauce, he is obligated to agree. Even if she had not watched his cart, it would be inconsiderate of him to refuse, claiming he was too busy reading the magazines. He may have had a duty to help others, but he would not "owe" it to her. But if she has done the same for him, he incurs an additional obligation to help, and talk of "owing" is apt. It suggests an agreement to perform equal, reciprocal, canceling sacrifices.

2. The Duties of Friendship

The terms "owe" and "repay" are helpful in the case of favors, because the sameness of the amount of sacrifice on the two sides is important; the monetary metaphor suggests equal quantities of sacrifice. But friendship ought to be characterized by *mutuality* rather than reciprocity: friends offer what they can give and accept what they need, without regard for the total amounts of benefits exchanged. And friends are motivated by love rather than by the prospect of repayment. Hence, talk of "owing" is singularly out of place in friendship.

For example, suppose Alfred takes Beatrice out for an expensive dinner and a movie. Beatrice incurs no obligation to "repay" him with a goodnight kiss or a return engagement. If Alfred complains that she "owes" him something, he is operating under the assumption that she should repay a favor, but on the contrary his was a generous gesture done in the hopes of developing a friendship. We hope that he would not want her repayment in the form of sex or attention if this was done to discharge a debt rather than from friendship. Since, if Alfred is prone to reasoning in this way, Beatrice may well decline the invitation or request to pay for her own dinner, his attitude of expecting a "return" on his "investment" could hinder the development of a friendship. Beatrice should return the gesture only if she is motivated by friendship.

Another common misuse of the "owing" idiom occurs when the Smiths have dined at the Joneses' four times, but the Joneses at the Smiths' only once. People often say, "We owe them three dinners." This line of thinking may be appropriate between business acquaintances, but not between friends. After all, the Joneses invited the Smiths not in order to feed them or to be fed in turn, but because of the friendly contact presumably enjoyed by all on such occasions. If the Smiths do not feel friendship toward the Joneses, they can decline future invitations and not invite the Joneses; they owe them nothing. Of course, between friends of equal resources and needs, roughly equal sacrifices (though not necessarily roughly equal dinners) will typically occur. If the sacrifices are highly out of proportion to the resources, the relationship is closer to servility than to friendship.[1]

Another difference between favors and friendship is that after a friendship ends, the duties of friendship end. The party that has sacrificed less owes the other nothing. For instance, suppose Elmer donated a pint of blood that his wife Doris needed during an operation. Years after their divorce, Elmer is in an accident and needs one pint of blood. His new wife, Cora, is also of the same blood type. It seems not only that Doris does not "owe" Elmer blood, but that she should actually refrain from coming forward if Cora has volunteered to donate. To insist on donating not only interferes with the newlyweds' friendship, but it belittles Doris and Elmer's former relationship by suggesting that Elmer gave blood in hopes of favors returned instead of simply out of love for Doris. It is one of the heartrending features of divorce that it attends to quantity in a relationship previously characterized by mutuality. If Cora could not donate, Doris's obligation is the same as that for any former spouse in need of blood; it is not increased by the fact that Elmer similarly aided her. It *is* affected by the degree to which they are still friends, which in turn may (or may not) have been influenced by Elmer's donation.

In short, unlike the debts created by favors, the duties of friendship do not require equal quantities of sacrifice. Performing equal sacrifices does not cancel the duties of friendship, as it does the debts of favors. Unrequested sacrifices do not themselves create debts, but friends have duties regardless of whether they requested or initiated the friendship. Those who perform favors may be motivated by mutual gain, whereas friends should be motivated by affection. These characteristics of the friendship relation are distorted by talk of "owing."

3. PARENTS AND CHILDREN

The relationship between children and their parents should be one of friendship characterized by mutuality rather than one of reciprocal favors. The quantity of parental sacrifice is not relevant in determining what duties the grown child has. The medical assistance grown children ought to offer their ill mothers in old age depends upon the mothers' need, not upon whether they endured a difficult pregnancy, for example. Nor do one's duties to one's parents cease once an equal quantity of sacrifice has been performed, as the phrase "discharging a debt" may lead us to think.

Rather, what children ought to do for their parents (and parents for children) depends upon (1) their respective needs, abilities, and resources and (2) the extent to which there is an ongoing friendship between them. Thus, regardless of the quantity of childhood sacrifices, an able, wealthy child has an obligation to help his needy parents more than does a needy child. To illustrate, suppose sisters Cecile and Dana are equally loved by their parents, even though Cecile was an easy child to care for, seldom ill, while Dana was often sick and caused some trouble as a juvenile delinquent. As adults, Dana is a struggling artist living far away, while Cecile is a wealthy lawyer living nearby. When the parents need visits and financial aid, Cecile has an obligation to bear a higher proportion of these burdens than her sister. This results from her abilities, rather than from the quantities of sacrifice made by the parents earlier.

Sacrifices have an important causal role in creating an ongoing friendship, which may lead us to assume incorrectly that it is the sacrifices that are the source of obligation. That the source is the friendship instead can be seen by examining cases in which the sacrifices occurred but the friendship, for some reason, did not develop or persist. For example, if a woman gives up her newborn child for adoption, and if no feelings of love ever develop on either side, it seems that the grown child does not have an obligation to "repay" her for her sacrifices in pregnancy. For that matter, if the adopted child has an unimpaired love relationship with the adoptive parents, he or she has the same obligations to help them as a natural child would have.

The filial obligations of grown children are a result of friendship, rather than owed for services rendered. Suppose that Vance married Lola despite his parents' strong wish that he marry within their religion, and that as a result, the parents refuse to speak to him again. As the years pass, the parents are unaware of Vance's problems, his accomplishments, the birth of his children. The love that once existed between them, let us suppose, has been completely destroyed by this event and thirty years of desuetude. At this point, it seems, Vance is under no obligation to pay his parents' medical bills in their old age, beyond his general duty to help those in need. An additional, filial obligation would only arise from whatever love he may still feel for them. It would be irrelevant for his parents to argue, "But look how much we sacrificed for you when you were young," for that sacrifice was not a favor but occurred as part of a friendship which existed at the time but is now, we have supposed, defunct. A more appropriate message would be, "We still love you, and we would like to renew our friendship."

I hope this helps to set the question of what children ought to do for their parents in a new light. The parental argument, "You ought to do x because we did y for you," should be replaced by, "We love you and you will be happier if you do x," or "We believe you love us, and anyone who loved us would do x." If the parents' sacrifice had been a favor, the child's reply, "I never asked you to do y for me," would have

been relevant; to the revised parental remarks, this reply is clearly irrelevant. The child can either do x or dispute one of the parents' claims: by showing that a love relationship does not exist, or that love for someone does not motivate doing x, or that he or she will not be happier doing x.

Seen in this light, parental requests for children to write home, visit, and offer them a reasonable amount of emotional and financial support in life's crises are well founded, so long as a friendship still exists. Love for others does call for caring about and caring for them. Some other parental requests, such as for more sweeping changes in the child's lifestyle or life goals, can be seen to be insupportable, once we shift the justification from debts owed to love. The terminology of favors suggests the reasoning, "Since we paid for your college education, you owe it to us to make a career of engineering, rather than becoming a rock musician." This tends to alienate affection even further, since the tuition payments are depicted as investments for a return rather than done from love, as though the child's life goals could be "bought." Basing the argument on love leads to different reasoning patterns. The suppressed premise, "If A loves B, then A follows B's wishes as to A's lifelong career" is simply false. Love does not even dictate that the child adopt the parents' values as to the desirability of alternative life goals. So the parents' strongest available argument here is, "We love you, we are deeply concerned about your happiness, and in the long run you will be happier as an engineer." This makes it clear that an empirical claim is really the subject of the debate.

The function of these examples is to draw out our considered judgments as to the proper relation between parents and their grown children, and to show how poorly they fit the model of favors. What is relevant is the ongoing friendship that exists between parents and children. Although that relationship developed partly as a result of parental sacrifices for the child, the duties that grown children have to their parents result from the friendship rather than from the sacrifices. The idiom of owing favors to one's parents can actually be destructive if it undermines the role of mutuality and leads us to think in terms of quantitative reciprocal favors.

N ICHOLAS D IXON

The Friendship Model of Filial Obligations

To what extent, if any, are grown children obligated to help their parents? In the light of the immense sacrifices made by our parents as they raised us, should we reciprocate when our parents need our material or emotional assistance? According to Jane English, our duties to our parents are grounded in and vary according to the depth of our friendship with them.[1] The goal of this paper is to develop a more defensible version of English's view, which I will call the *friendship model* of filial obligations. I begin with a sketch of English's statement of the model.

I

English rejects the notion that we owe our parents reciprocal sacrifices. The paradigm case of an obligation to return a favour is when the favour was *requested* in the first place. Since no child asks to be born and given the benefits of parental care, the notion of "repayment" seems inappropriate.[2] Another obstacle to filial duties to parents is that, once they had us, our parents were *obligated* to care for us. Their merely doing what was morally required does not seem to generate any reciprocal duties on our part.[3]

The innovation of English's approach is to argue that the question of what we owe our parents, in the light of what they did for us, is poorly formulated. It wrongly casts parental sacrifices as favours that create debts and the obligation to perform reciprocal favours. Such an approach, she argues, cheapens parent-child and other love relationships, which should be characterised instead by voluntary *friendly gestures* given without any expectation of repayment, parental sacrifices should be freely given, instead of being investments made in the hope of a future "return" from grateful children. However, the absence of reciprocal debts "owed" to parents does not exhaust all filial obligations. Friendly gestures are symptomatic of ongoing friendships, and ongoing friendships give rise to duties of friendship. A decent person, that is, will offer help when her friends are in need. Unlike favours, friendships cannot be "paid off"; and, again unlike favours, my duties of friendship depend on my friends' *needs,* and my ability to help, not on whether and how much they have helped me in the past. To the extent that a grown child enjoys an ongoing friendship with her parents, she has the same duties of friendship towards her parents as she would have toward people with whom she has a similar friendship.

Filial obligations, then, are not a repayment for parental sacrifices. Rather, they arise from the friendship that these sacrifices may have played a role in creating. However, argues English, just as duties of friendship in general are contingent on the continuation of the friendship, our special obligations to our parents would dissolve if we were to cease to be friends with our parents.[4]

Nicholas Dixon, "The Friendship Model of Filial Obligations," *Journal of Applied Philosophy* 12, no. 1 (1995): pp. 77–87. Some notes have been deleted. Reprinted by permission of Blackwell Publishing Ltd.

English's account does justice to the intuition that we should help our parents when necessary, at least when we enjoy friendly relations with them. In contrast to the *repayment model* which she criticises, English places our obligations within the appealing context of voluntary, loving friendship with our parents.

II

Because of the voluntary nature of friendship, and the belief that we should do things for our friends freely and willingly, the idea of duties of friendship may sound odd. Indeed, the voluntariness and spontaneity of friendly gestures is one of the most appealing features of friendship. If we were to discover that a friend's kindness were motivated only by a sense of duty, we would begin to question our friendship. I have two responses.

First, the fact that our friends' actions towards us are typically motivated only by spontaneous affection does not preclude the existence of duties of friendship. That duty may coincide with inclination does not diminish its status as duty. Second, while many occasions exist for optional, supererogatory acts of generosity towards our friends, we can easily think of cases in which it is natural to say that we *should* help them. If a close friend is in desperate need of my help, which would cost me negligible effort, wouldn't I be *wrong*, in the light of our long-lasting and ongoing friendship, to refuse? I mean by "duties of friendship" that we ought to help friends in such circumstances. Such duties arise from the particular relationships I have with my friends, and go beyond any general obligation I have to help strangers.

The notion of duties of friendship would also be severely restricted in the hands of libertarians who restrict all obligations to duties of noninterference. If conjoined with a libertarian approach, the friendship model of filial obligations would require only that we refrain from harming our parents. Since I argue that the friendship model creates the obligation to help our parents in some cases, I am assuming both that there *are* duties of friendship, and that moral obligations in general go beyond mere noninterference with others.[5]

I offer the friendship model as both a justification of the view that we do have duties to our parents, and an explanation of the moral basis of these duties. The friendship model casts filial obligations as a special type of obligation or friendship. As in the case of duties of friendship in general, exactly what is required of us by the friendship model of filial duties depends on both the circumstances in each particular case, and on the broader social context. For example, filial duties will be more extensive in a society in which the government provides only minimally for the needs of older people than in a society with extensive welfare programmes for the elderly.

As long as grown children enjoy a friendly relationship with their parents, the friendship model and the more traditional repayment model will usually require similar filial duties.[6] However, in the absence of friendly relations, English's version of the friendship model imposes no filial obligation to help needy parents, since there is no longer any friendship to ground filial duties, no matter how caring the parents were when the children were younger. English's willingness to embrace this consequence of her view opens her up to the criticism that she is endorsing, or at least tolerating, filial ingratitude. If the end of friendship cancels duties of friendship, so the objection goes, then so much the worse for the friendship model of filial duties, since most people believe that we would still have duties to our parents, even if we were no longer friends with them.

I maintain, on the contrary, that an advocate of the friendship model should not insist that the end of friendship with one's parents signals the end of filial obligations. English has failed to realise that duties of friendship can in general outlive friendships, whether between peers or between children and parents. The reason why English has overlooked the "residual duties" that can remain even after the end of friendships is very likely the fact that many friendships are relatively short-lived and superficial, and arguably create few if any residual duties. However, if we turn to peer friendships comparable in duration and depth to child-parent friendships, the notion of residual duties of friendship becomes much more plausible.

Consider, for instance, a stranger and a former long-term, close friend (who voluntarily made immense sacrifices throughout our friendship) who both urgently need a blood transfusion using my rare blood type. Any obligation I have to help is stronger in the case of my former friend than in the case of the stranger. It would require an overzealous commitment to impartiality to ignore the extra moral ties created by our former long-term, close friendship. These ties are not precipitately dissolved by our unfortunate estrangement. The longevity of our friendship, and depth of friendship indicated by the sacrifices my former friend made for me,[7] make this situation analogous to my relationship with my parents. The existence of filial duties even after my friendship with my parents is over can therefore be accounted for by the friendship model, and does not indicate that filial duties have a different basis.

An analogous situation in which a former friendship can exert a moral claim on us today is the practice of forgiving someone "for old times' sake." The key to forgiveness is being able to separate the sin from the sinner, and forgive the wrongdoer while continuing to condemn her action. One way in which this separation is facilitated is when she is a former friend, and we are able to forgive her in the light of our former friendship, even though we still regard her action as wrong.[8]

I suggest that the moral basis of residual duties to former friends is *respect* for our former friendships, our former friends and ourselves. To treat a former close friend as a stranger (e.g., by refusing to give priority to our former friend in the blood transfusion case) is to discount our former friendship, and indirectly devalues both of us, since we both invested part of ourselves in the friendship. When someone is genuinely unconcerned about the end of a romantic relationship, we suspect that she held no strong feelings for her former partner. Similarly, when someone treats a former friend as a stranger as soon as their friendship is over, we start to question the depth of her friendship in the first place. It may then be a psychological truth that the genuine moral concern for another which characterises friendship is inseparable from feeling residual duties of friendship even after friendship ends. Even if we allow the possibility of

the person who genuinely cares about her friends while the friendship lasts, but whose moral concern completely evaporates when friendship ends, such a person exhibits the vice of *inconstancy*. Her concern for her friends seems to be fickle, and we would hesitate to trust her.

Another vice exhibited by the person who treats former friends as strangers is a form of *inauthenticity*: a desire to disown part of herself. It is comparable to the self-made millionaire who refuses any contact with his family or his former friends from the blue-collar neighbourhood in which he grew up. Aside from the disrespect he shows for others, in some sense he is disrespecting himself, by failing to acknowledge the connections between the person he is now and the earlier stages of his life.[9]

Any residual duties of friendship are of course normally far weaker than those we have toward our current friends. Moreover, if the reason for the end of our friendship was unforgivable behaviour on the part of our former friend, our residual duties may diminish to zero.

The moral ties created by decades of parent-child love, which often develops into friendship from the late teens onwards, are surely even stronger than those of all but the deepest long-term friendships. This is why English's claim that the end of friendship necessarily signals the end of filial obligations is unjust. Granted, the children of abusive parents are very unlikely to have established any friendly relations with their parents in the first place, and would have no obligation to help their parents under the friendship model. But in the case of children who enjoyed good relations with their parents into early adulthood, but then became estranged after a disagreement, respect for their former good relations arguably requires that they help their parents, when doing so would be easy, and would produce major benefits for the parents (e.g., providing for life-saving medical treatment.) Such residual duties are of course far weaker than the filial duties of children who currently enjoy good friendships with their parents.

While seeking a formula that would determine the exact extent of filial obligations in various circumstances would be absurd, it is reasonable to regard three factors as central in the case of adult children no longer friendly with their parents: (1) The extent of parental need, and the cost to adult children of meeting it; (2) the depth and duration of their former friendly relations with their parents; and (3) the reason for and the severity of the argument that caused the estrangement. The adult child has to strike a balance between respect for her former good relations with her parents, and, on the other hand, self-respect in the case of parental misbehaviour.[10] Only in the most extreme limiting case will a child whose friendship with her parents is over have no residual duties to her parents.

III

Another criticism of the friendship model is to point out differences between parent-child relationships and typical friendships. The key question to decide is whether these differences invalidate the friendship model, or whether parent-child relationships can naturally be viewed as a special *kind* of friendship.

The sheer weight of sacrifices typically borne by parents in raising their children creates an inequality unlikely to be met by any services which adult children perform for their parents. Friendship might be a relationship only possible between people who are roughly equal. However, it might be said in defence of the friendship model that the inequality of sacrifices is quite natural, given the parents' superior ability to help, and is quite compatible with friendship.[11] We can easily imagine similarly unequal relationships that we would have no hesitation in calling friendships. For instance, a deep friendship can arise between a wheelchair-bound person and the able-bodied person who looks after her. The alleged inequality in such relationships may be only superficial, since the able-bodied person may gain just as much in terms of emotional satisfaction and intellectual stimulation as she gives in physical assistance.

Joseph Kupfer notes two more significant differences between parent-child relationships and peer friendships.[12] First, we will always lack autonomy *with regard to* our parents because of the immense influence they had in forming our character and cre-

ating our identity. Our self-concept, which "includes the history of the unequal relationship with the parent ... limits the degree to which [we] can function autonomously with the parent."[13] An inequality in autonomy will inhibit the formation of an ideal friendship because it will create undue dependence in the less autonomous friend, for whom the more autonomous friend will consequently have less respect.[14] Second, parents and children lack the independence needed for one characteristic of deep friendships: a voluntary union between two *separate* people, who *achieve* a friendship by growing to know and appreciate each other.[15]

While Kupfer concludes that these two differences between typical friendship and parent-child relationships preclude parents and their adult children from becoming "true" or "ideal" friends, he also asserts that "parents and children can enjoy a kind of friendship that is quite worthwhile in its own right."[16] I will argue that Kupfer's discussion makes it natural for us to regard parent-adult child relationships as legitimate friendships, albeit different from peer friendships.

The positive side of adult children's lack of autonomy from their parents is the "mutual identification" that enables parents to share their children's successes. The parents know that they played a key role in making their children the kind of people likely to succeed, a point of which the children are gratefully aware.[17] However, our close peer friends also to a lesser extent, influence who we are. This may explain why our close friends, especially long-standing ones, often delight in our triumphs just as much as our parents do. It also indicates that we experience a similar, though less pronounced, lack of autonomy with regard to our close friends as we do toward our parents. What follows is that the lack of autonomy with regard to our parents that allegedly precludes parent-child relationships from being friendships is also present, to a lesser degree, in peer relationships we have no hesitation in calling friendships. A similar point can be made about the lack of independence between parents and children. A comparable lack of independence will apply between childhood friends who continue their friendship, without our being tempted to deny to their relationship the status of friendship.[18]

The upshot of the discussion of the current section is that even peer friendships can to a lesser extent display the features alleged to disqualify parent-child relationships from the status of friendships. It would be wiser to recognise a multiplicity of types of friendship. Parent-child relationships may involve more dependence than peer friendships, but they are genuine friendships nonetheless.

If one insists that the differences pointed out by Kupfer prevent parent-child relations from being regarded as a type of friendship, only a minor modification of the friendship model will be required. The parent-child relationship described by Kupfer is a long-term, loving, voluntary relationship, and is consequently quite able to generate duties comparable to those of friendship. Just as in the case of friendship, this relationship creates moral ties that can outlive the relationship itself. Exactly what duties are left after the end of the relationship will depend, as in the case of friendship, on the strength of the former relationship and the reason for its dissolution. In other words, all that would be required would be to *rename* the model, since it would retain all the salient features of the friendship model.

IV

A more fundamental objection to the friendship model of filial obligations can be derived from the work of Christina Hoff Sommers.[19] Sommers dubs as *the volunteer theory of obligation* the view that all moral requirements fall into one of two categories: (1) universal duties owed to everyone, and (2) *voluntarily assumed* obligations to particular persons.[20] The friendship model, which makes filial obligations contingent on the voluntary continuation of friendly relations between parents and children, presupposes the volunteer theory. Theories that base moral obligations on the existence of feelings, such as love and affection for one's parents, are named by Sommers as *sentimentalist*.[21]

Sommers presents an account of filial obligation in direct opposition to the volunteer theory of obligation and sentimentalism. In contrast to the friendship model, according to which "there is no such thing as filial duty *per se,*" Sommers points out that "most people think that we do owe special debts to our parents even though we have not voluntarily assumed our obligations to them."[22] Having rejected the "dogmatic" volunteer theory of obligation, "we are free to respect the commonsense views that attribute moral force to many obligations associated with kinship and other family relationships."[23]

Sommers grounds family obligations, including filial obligations, in our family members' negative right to pursue their "noninvasive" interests (i.e., those that do not violate those of other people.) The particular interests in question are their "legitimate expectations" of our performance of actions in accordance with traditional social roles.[24] The reason why my failure to help my parents is wrong, then, is not because I am violating duties of friendship. It is wrong because I am violating their legitimate (in the context of our society's practices) expectation that I will support them in their later years. It would be wrong even if I were not friends with them. Adherents of the volunteer theory of obligation, Sommers continues, make the mistake of taking the deliberate act of promising as the paradigm case of particular moral requirements. They ignore particular obligations, such as filial duties, that arise from social arrangements that may have developed without any voluntary commitment on our part.

Sommers concedes to sentimentalists that adult children who help their parents are often motivated by love and friendship. However, she points out that the *moral ground* of our obligations may be institutional expectations that are independent of our feelings.[25]

Sommers criticises sentimentalism as too flimsy a basis for filial obligations. Feelings of good will toward our parents are fickle, whereas the institutional expectations on which Sommers grounds filial morality guarantee parents the support they deserve[26] Sentimentalism is "ethics without ethos," and has a "disintegrative effect on tradition."[27]

My strategy in responding to Sommers is to sidestep her main argument, by insisting that the friendship model provides a robust account of filial duty without reference to obligations created by institutional expectations. I remain neutral as to the existence of duties based on such expectations.

The very feature of the friendship model which Sommers attacks—i.e., that it makes filial obligations contingent on the *voluntary* establishment of friendship, as opposed to institutional expectations—is actually a strength. Sommers' use of the term "sentimentalism" to refer to theories such as the friendship model misleadingly casts them in a negative light which obscures this strength. It implies that "sentimentalists" base moral obligations on mere feelings, which are understood by her as more or less arbitrary *passions* over which we have minimal control. As applied to the so-called sentimentalist account of friendship, it de-emphasises the voluntariness of friendship, which is instead portrayed as a natural attraction with no moral significance.

In contrast to this caricature of theories of moral obligation that stress feelings and attitudes, friendship involves a *commitment* to our friends' well-being. Both the exercise of altruism, and the moral effort which is sometimes required to maintain and deepen friendships, are moral excellences.[28] The friendship model bases filial obligations on the voluntariness that makes this commitment and these excellences possible.

The extent of our friendship with and affection for our parents is undeniably limited by factors beyond anyone's control: the complex genetic and environmental factors that can sometimes cause a "personality conflict" even between reasonable and good-willed people. However, this should not blind us to the role of *choice* in parent-child relations. Especially as a child's moral awareness develops, and increasingly throughout adulthood, she appreciates the moral effort involved in parent-child relationships. She recognises, for instance, the need for patience in tolerating her parents' sometimes exasperating ways, and for compromise in reconciling her desire for freedom (both as a child and as an adult) with her parents' demands and needs. Perhaps more than all but the closest peer friendships parent-child relationships are *worked on,* usually over many decades. This sketch reveals parent-child friendship to be a far more substantial basis for filial obligations than one would be led to believe by Sommers' characterisation of it as a "sentimentalist" theory.

V

I complete my defence of the friendship model of filial obligations by considering some problem cases. Central to the friendship model is that the extent of filial obligations is determined by the extent of our friendly relations with our parents. Exactly the same holds in the case of peer friendships, where deeper friendships generate more extensive duties of friendship.

I have shown in section II how the friendship model makes more or less considerable demands on adult children, even when they are no longer friends with their parents. Among the few people who would escape filial duties under the model would be those who have *never* enjoyed friendly relations with their parents. Since this is most likely to occur when the parents have been uncaring and even abusive, this consequence of the model seems right.

A more troubling case for the friendship model as developed so far is the person whose parents were exemplary in providing her loving care, yet who fails to establish any kind of loving relationship with them. Should she fail to provide her parents with much needed financial or emotional support, when she could have easily afforded it, many would condemn her ingratitude. Since there is no friendship on which to build obligations, the friendship model seems unable to account for this condemnation.

Distinguishing the supererogatory benefits her parents have given her from those that they were morally obliged to give is important. Providing food, clothing, and shelter to children is a minimal responsibility that accompanies the decision to bring children into the world, and can hardly be said to require gratitude on the part of the children. On the other hand, the love and support which go beyond the call of duty give rise, in the majority of cases, to the friendship relations that are, on this model, the basis of filial duties. The problem case for the friendship model, then, is the cold, ungrateful child who never responds to her loving parents' supererogatory actions by returning their love and by helping them when they are in need.

If her ingratitude upon further consideration should be considered blameless, then the friendship model's failure to condemn her is an advantage, not a weakness. If, on the other hand, it is culpable, I contend that whatever fault she has can be explained without reference to filial morality per se. The same vice of ingratitude, which she exhibits by her failure to thank her parents for their efforts and to offer them much-needed assistance, can also arise in the context of a peer friendship. More pertinently, since in the hypothetical case we are considering there *is* no friendship between the child and parents, the obligations of the cold child to her loving parents are based on the general duty to be grateful after a series of generous acts by an acquaintance or even a stranger.[29] We can thus explain the filial obligations of the cold, ungrateful child in a manner independent of but perfectly consistent with the friendship model. I leave open exactly what the general duty of gratitude requires of the child who has never had a friendship with her parents. Expressions of thanks are morally required, but it isn't clear that any reciprocal services are obligatory in return for unsolicited benefits.

My account of the filial obligations of the cold, ungrateful child in terms of the general duty of gratitude towards any generous person is open to the objection that I am ignoring crucial differences between the cold child's parents, and, on the other hand, acquaintances and strangers. In reality, the objection continues, the cold, ungrateful child has the same filial duties as any child with loving, generous parents. However, this objection begs the question against the friendship model. While the cold, ungrateful child is *biologically and socially* related to her parents in the same way that any child is, from an emotional point of view the cold child's parents *are* acquaintances or even strangers. If my theory is correct filial obligations are based primarily on friendship. And friendship is simply absent in this case.

A more serious objection is that my admission that duties to our parents exist which are not directly explicable by the friendship model shows that the model is at best incomplete. My response is that the fact that the cold child's filial duties are not grounded in friendship reflects her impoverished relationship with her parents, and not any inadequacy in the friendship model. The friendship model is an account of the moral basis of filial duties in the vast majority of cases, where adult children either currently enjoy or have enjoyed some degree of friendship with their parents. It is not refuted by the logical possibility of unlikely deviant cases in which filial obligations are based on the weaker general duty of gratitude that we owe to *anyone* who is extremely generous.

We are now in a position to see a deeper error in the repayment model of filial obligations. It bases all filial duties on the general duty to show gratitude toward generous people. This general duty is the only basis of the filial obligations of the cold, ungrateful child. However, the filial obligations of the vast majority of us have a far more congenial, extensive basis: the friendship which we enjoy or have enjoyed with our parents. The repayment model is an appropriate account of filial obligations only in a deviant, unrepresentative case.

This is not to deny that even those of us who enjoy friendships with our parents should be grateful for the generous things they have done for us. In this respect, we are like the cold child, and any other beneficiary of generous acts. However, the gratitude we should feel is not the basis of our filial duties, which are based instead on our friendship with our parents. Now there may be a contingent link between the amount of sacrifices our parents made and the depth of our friendship, since our gratitude for our parents' generosity may deepen our friendship. If so, the friendship model may forge a contingent link between the amount of sacrifices our parents made and the extent of our filial duties. But the link *is* only contingent. Deep parent-child friendships, and hence extensive filial duties of friendship, can exist even though our parents have not needed to make great sacrifices in raising us. At the other extreme, parents who have made many sacrifices may be cold and emotionally distant, and fail to form a close friendship with their children, whose filial duties will hence be weaker than those of children who enjoy a loving relationship with their parents.[30] A second error that the repayment model makes, then, is basing filial duties on just one of the possible causes of friendship—parents' sacrifices, and their children's subsequent gratitude— instead of on the friendship itself. The friendship model, in contrast, recognises that the moral basis of our duty to help our parents is just that they are or have been our friends, they need help, and we are able to help them.

Is the child's failure to become friends with her parents in the first place, even though the are models of devoted care, morally blameworthy? We would not want to allow people to minimise their filial obligations by deliberately forming only a weak friendship, or none at all, with their parents. However, blaming someone for the failure to develop a friendship with someone else sounds odd, however loving and caring that other person may be. At worst, the unloving child is guilty of the vice of coldness. A more plausible analysis of the rare occasions when a child fails to develop affection for her loving, generous parents is that the child suffers from a personality disorder which prevents certain kinds of intimacy. While her parents may justly claim that they deserve better treatment from their child, her inability to love them is beyond her control, and hence blameless.

The friendship model of filial obligations accounts well for the obligations which are felt by most adult children who are friendly with their parents. It also explains how residual obligations can remain even after their friendship has ended. The main problem case for the friendship model of filial obligations is the child who never forms a friendship with her loving, caring parents. However, while the friendship model is unable to condemn her, and blameworthiness on her part can be explained by her violation of the general duty to show gratitude toward generous people. That the usual ground of filial obligations is absent in her case reflects only her deficient relationship with her parents, and indicates no flaw in the friendship model.

I conclude that my modified version of the friendship model provides a plausible, fair framework for determining the extent of our filial obligations. Like English's original statement of this model, it retains the advantage of stressing the voluntary, loving nature of sacrifices made by both parents and children, instead of regarding filial duties as repayments for services rendered.

NOTES

1. Jane English (1979) What do grown children owe their parents?, originally published in Onora O'Neill and William Ruddick (eds.) *Having Children: Philosophical and Legal Reflections on Parenthood* (New York, Oxford University Press); and reprinted in Christina Sommers and Fred Sommers (eds., 1993) *Vice and Virtue in Everyday Life,* 3rd edition (Fort Worth, Harcourt Brace Jovanovich), pp. 758–65. Page citations for 'What Do Grown Children Owe Their Parents?' will be from *Vice and Virtue in Everyday Life.*

2. English, op. cit., What Do Grown Children Owe Their Parents?, pp. 759–60. See also Michael Slote Obedience and Illusions, in O'Neill and Ruddick, op. cit., *Having Children,* p. 320; and Jeffrey Blustein (1982) *Parents and Children: The Ethics of the Family* (Oxford, Oxford University Press), excerpted in Joshua Halberstam (ed., 1988) *Virtues and Values* (Englewood Cliffs, NJ, Prentice-Hall), p. 197.

3. Blustein, in op. cit., *Virtues and Values,* p. 197.

4. English, op. cit., What Do Grown Children Owe Their Parents?, pp. 761–63.

5. For a defence of the view that the existence of rights between friends is perfectly compatible with friendship, see Michael J. Meyer (1992) Rights between Friends, *Journal of Philosophy,* Vol. LXXXIX, pp. 467–83. My paper depends on the weaker claim that, regardless of whether rights exist in friendships, obligations of friendship exist.

6. The models will diverge when the degree of parent-child friendship does not correspond to the extent of parental sacrifices. In section V, I will argue that these divergences show the superiority of the friendship model.

7. My residual duties to my former friend are not a repayment for the sacrifices he made for me, since this would be a return to the repayment model which I reject. Instead, his sacrifices are relevant to my duties of friendship only insofar as they deepened our friendship. Extensive residual duties may persist after the end of any deep friendship, even if it did not involve any great sacrifices. Respect for our former friendship (see text below for more detail), and not the repayment of moral debts incurred as a result of my former friend's generosity, is the basis of my residual duties to him.

8. See Jeffrie Murphy (1982) Forgiveness and Resentment, *Minnesota Studies in Philosophy,* Vol. VII, *Social and Political Philosophy;* reprinted in op. cit., *Virtues and Values,* p. 131.

9. Michael Meyer has suggested to me that the faults I have been describing can be characterised as a lack of integrity.

10. Cf., again, Murphy's account of forgiveness, op. cit., in which he stresses maintaining self-respect by avoiding forgiveness unless substantial reasons exist for it.

11. [F]riends offer what they can give and accept what they need, without regard for the total amounts of benefits exchanged, English, op. cit., What do Grown Children Owe Their Parents?, p. 761.

12. Joseph Kupfer (1990) Can parents and children be friends?, *American Philosophical Quarterly* 27:1, pp. 15–26.

13. Ibid., p. 17.

14. Ibid., p. 16.

15. Ibid., pp. 20–21.

16. Ibid., p. 15.

17. Ibid., pp. 21–23.

18. Kupfer, ibid., p. 20, note 11, mentions the lack of independence between adult friends who became friends in childhood.

19. Christina Hoff Sommers (1986) Filial morality, *Journal of Philosophy,* pp. 439–56; and Philosophers against the family, reprinted in Sommers and Sommers, op. cit., *Vice and Virtue in Everyday Life,* pp. 804–29.

20. Sommers, Philosophers against the family, p. 820.

21. Sommers, Filial morality, p. 448.

22. Sommers, Philosophers against the family, pp. 820–21. Sommers' assertion that the friendship mode recognises no filial duties per se is a little misleading. While the model treats filial duties as a special type of duty of friendship, it does not preclude recognition of the uniqueness of our duties to our parents.

23. Ibid., p. 822.

24. Sommers, op. cit., Filial morality, pp. 445–48.

25. Ibid., pp. 449–50.

26. Ibid., pp. 450–51.

27. Ibid., p. 455.

28. See Laurence Blum The Morality of Friendship, reprinted in Halberstam, op. cit., *Virtues and Values,* pp. 205–14.

29. In asserting that we have duties of gratitude after unsolicited acts of generosity, I depart from the volunteer theory of obligation, since I concede that there can be particular duties that are not voluntarily assumed. The main ground of duties of gratitude is that respect for generous people requires that we treat them as ends in themselves, and not merely as sources of benefit for us. See Fred R. Berger (1975) "Gratitude," *Ethics* 85:4, pp. 298–309.

30. The view that parental sacrifices do not in themselves create filial duties is supported by English's claim that the child who was adopted as a newborn has no obligation to repay her biological mother for the sacrifices she made to go through with pregnancy. Her only duties toward her birth mother arise from any friendship they may develop. See English, op. cit., What do grown children owe their parents?, p. 763.

13

Is Same-Sex Marriage Wrong?

Jordan and His Critics

In "Is It Wrong to Discriminate on the Basis of Homosexuality?," which serves as the featured article for this chapter, Jeff Jordan attempts to produce an argument against same-sex marriage that makes no assumptions about the morality of homosexuality itself. He does this by appealing to the idea that marriage is a public rather than a private institution, and to the fact that there is widespread public disagreement about the moral status of homosexuality. Because this argument seems to allow him to avoid depending on controversial claims about the moral status of homosexuality, it is potentially among the most powerful arguments against same-sex marriage. After reading Jordan's article but before reading David Boonin's critical-response piece which immediately follows it, readers should consult the following formal summary of Jordan's position:

P1   If (a) there is a public dilemma about X *and* (b) resolution of the dilemma by accommodation is possible *and* (c) there is no overriding reason to prefer resolution of the dilemma by declaration, *then* (d) the state should resolve the public dilemma about X by accommodation.

P2   There is a public dilemma about same-sex marriage.

P3   It is possible for the State to resolve the dilemma by accommodation if it refuses to sanction same-sex marriage (provided that it permits private homosexual acts between consenting adults).

P4   It is not possible for the State to resolve the dilemma by accommodation if it sanctions same-sex marriage (since that amounts to resolving the dilemma by declaration and leaves no room for accommodation).

P5   There is no overriding reason for the State to resolve the dilemma by declaration.

C   The state should refuse to sanction same-sex marriage (provided that it permits private homosexual acts between consenting adults).

This summary will help readers to better understand the argument itself and will prove essential to understanding Boonin's reasons for rejecting it. Boonin's first objection maintains that Jordan's argument is guilty of equivocation (see section 3.3 in the Introduction).

Boonin draws a distinction between there being disagreement about homosexual marriage and there being disagreement about homosexual sexual behavior, and maintains that once this distinction is taken into account, Jordan's argument runs into difficulties. The second objection maintains that Jordan's argument is undermined by a *reductio ad absurdum* objection (see section 4.5 in the Introduction) that Jordan tries, but fails, to overcome—the claim that if the argument succeeds in showing that the State should not sanction same-sex marriage, then it unacceptably implies that the same is true in the case of interracial marriage.

The excerpt from Andrew Sullivan's book, *Virtually Normal,* which follows Boonin's critical response, does not directly refer to Jordan's article. But it is nonetheless clear that Sullivan means to respond to the kind of argument that Jordan's article offers, one that focuses, in Sullivan's words, on "what the allegedly neutral liberal state should do" with respect to same-sex marriage given the understanding that marriage "is not simply a private contract; it is a social and public recognition of a private commitment." While Jordan argues that State neutrality counts as a consideration against instituting same-sex marriage, however, Sullivan argues that it is a crucial consideration in its favor. More specifically, Sullivan argues that marriage, understood as a public institution, is essentially about a certain kind of personal bond between two people and is not in any way essentially about sexual reproduction. But if this is so, Sullivan maintains, then there is no publicly neutral way to justify extending marriage rights to heterosexuals while denying them to homosexuals. To do so would be to treat heterosexuals and homosexuals unequally in a context in which there was no value-neutral justification for doing so.

QUESTIONS FOR CONSIDERATION

In critically evaluating Boonin's critique of Jordan's argument, readers should focus on two distinct sets of questions.

• First, is Boonin correct in claiming that there are two importantly distinct issues involved—one concerning sexual behavior and one concerning marriage—or are the two so closely intertwined that his separating them is unwarranted?

• Second, is Boonin correct in maintaining that Jordan's argument, if successful, would work against mixed-race marriage as well? Or do the differences between the two cases that Jordan identifies suffice to establish that his case against same-sex marriage does not commit him to opposing mixed-race marriage?

Finally, in considering the excerpt from Sullivan's book, it will help to understand exactly how Sullivan's argument can be taken as an attack on what Boonin calls "P5" of Jordan's argument.

• What is Sullivan's overriding reason for resolving the dilemma in favor of those who favor same-sex marriage? What does he mean by human equality in this context, and why does he take it to be so important?

• Is refusing to recognize same-sex marriage denying equal rights to homosexuals? Or is it simply refraining from extending a further and publicly divisive privilege to them?

FURTHER READING

Beckwith, Francis J. "Legal Neutrality and Same-Sex Marriage." *Philosophia Christi* 7, no. 1 (2005): 19–25.

Bradley, Gerard V. "Same-Sex Marriage: Our Final Answer?" *Notre Dame Journal of Law, Ethics and Public Policy* 14, no. 2 (2000): 729–52.

Buccola, Nicholas. "Finding Room for Same-Sex Marriage: Toward a More Inclusive Understanding of a Cultural Institution." *Journal of Social Philosophy* 36, no. 3 (Fall 2005): 331–43.

McDonough, Richard. "Is Same-Sex Marriage an Equal-Rights Issue?" *Public Affairs Quarterly* 19, no. 1 (January 2005): 51–63.

Schaff, Kory. "Equal Protection and Same-Sex Marriage." *Journal of Social Philosophy* 35, no. 1 (Spring 2004): 133–47.

Wedgwood, Ralph. "The Fundamental Argument for Same-Sex Marriage." *Journal of Political Philosophy* 7, no. 3 (1999): 225–42.

Jeff Jordan

Is It Wrong to Discriminate on the Basis of Homosexuality?

Much like the issue of abortion in the early 1970s, the issue of homosexuality has exploded to the forefront of social discussion. Is homosexual sex on a moral par with heterosexual sex? Or is homosexuality in some way morally inferior? Is it wrong to discriminate against homosexuals—to treat homosexuals in less favorable ways than one does heterosexuals? Or is some discrimination against homosexuals morally justified? These questions are the focus of this essay.

In what follows, I argue that there are situations in which it is morally permissible to discriminate against homosexuals because of their homosexuality. That is, there are some morally relevant differences between heterosexuality and homosexuality which, in some instances, permit a difference in treatment. The issue of marriage provides a good example. While it is clear that heterosexual unions merit the state recognition known as marriage, along with all the attendant advantages—spousal insurance coverage, inheritance rights, ready eligibility of adoption— it is far from clear that homosexual couples ought to be accorded that state recognition.

The argument of this essay makes no claim about the moral status of homosexuality per se. Briefly put, it is the argument of this essay that the moral impasse generated by conflicting views concerning homosexuality, and the public policy ramifications of those conflicting views justify the claim that it is morally permissible, in certain circumstances, to discriminate against homosexuals.[1]

1. THE ISSUE

The relevant issue is this: does homosexuality have the same moral status as heterosexuality? Put differently, since there are no occasions in which it is morally permissible to treat heterosexuals unfavorably, whether because they are heterosexual or because of heterosexual acts, are there occasions in which it is morally permissible to treat homosexuals unfavorably, whether because they are homosexuals or because of homosexual acts?

A negative answer to the above can be termed the "parity thesis." The parity thesis contends that *homosexuality has the same moral status as heterosexuality.* If the parity thesis is correct, then it would be immoral to discriminate against homosexuals because of their homosexuality. An affirmative answer can be termed the "difference thesis"

Jeff Jordan, "Is It Wrong to Discriminate on the Basis of Homosexuality?" *Journal of Social Philosophy* 26, no. 1 (1995): 39–52. Reprinted by permission of Blackwell Publishing Ltd.

and contends that there are morally relevant differences between heterosexuality and homosexuality which justify a difference in moral status and treatment between homosexuals and heterosexuals. The difference thesis entails that *there are situations in which it is morally permissible to discriminate against homosexuals.*

It is perhaps needless to point out that the difference thesis follows as long as there is at least one occasion in which it is morally permissible to discriminate against homosexuals. If the parity thesis were true, then on no occasion would a difference in treatment between heterosexuals and homosexuals ever be justified. The difference thesis does not, even if true, justify discriminatory actions on every occasion. Nonetheless, even though the scope of the difference thesis is relatively modest, it is, if true, a significant principle which has not only theoretical import but important practical consequences as well.[2]

A word should be said about the notion of discrimination. To discriminate against *X* means treating *X* in an unfavorable way. The word "discrimination" is not a synonym for "morally unjustifiable treatment." Some discrimination is morally unjustifiable; some is not. For example, we discriminate against convicted felons in that they are disenfranchised. This legal discrimination is morally permissible even though it involves treating one person unfavorably different from how other persons are treated. The difference thesis entails that there are circumstances in which it is morally permissible to discriminate against homosexuals.

2. AN ARGUMENT FOR THE PARITY THESIS

One might suppose that an appeal to a moral right, the right to privacy, perhaps, or the right to liberty, would provide the strongest grounds for the parity thesis. Rights talk, though sometimes helpful, is not very helpful here. If there is reason to think that the right to privacy or the right to liberty encompasses sexuality (which seems plausible enough), it would do so only with regard to private acts and not public acts. Sexual acts performed in public

(whether heterosexual or homosexual) are properly suppressible. It does not take too much imagination to see that the right to be free from offense would soon be offered as a counter consideration by those who find homosexuality morally problematic. Furthermore, how one adjudicates between the competing rights claims is far from clear. Hence, the bald appeal to a right will not, in this case anyway, take one very far.

Perhaps the strongest reason to hold that the parity thesis is true is something like the following:

1. Homosexual acts between consenting adults harm no one. And,
2. respecting persons' privacy and choices in harmless sexual matters maximizes individual freedom. And,
3. individual freedom should be maximized. But,
4. discrimination against homosexuals, because of their homosexuality, diminishes individual freedom since it ignores personal choice and privacy. So,
5. the toleration of homosexuality rather than discriminating against homosexuals is the preferable option since it would maximize individual freedom. Therefore,
6. the parity thesis is more plausible than the difference thesis.

Premise (2) is unimpeachable: if an act is harmless and if there are persons who want to do it and who choose to do it, then it seems clear that respecting the choices of those people would tend to maximize their freedom.[3] Step (3) is also beyond reproach: since freedom is arguably a great good and since there does not appear to be any ceiling on the amount of individual freedom—no "too much of a good thing"—(3) appears to be true.

At first glance, premise (1) seems true enough as long as we recognize that if there is any harm involved in the homosexual acts of consenting adults, it would be harm absorbed by the freely consenting participants. This is true, however, only if the acts in question are done in private. Public acts may involve more than just the willing participants. Persons who have no desire to participate, even if only as spectators, may have no choice if the acts are done in public. A real probability of there being unwilling participants is indicative of the public realm and not the private. However, where one draws the line between private acts and public acts is not always easy to discern, it is clear that different moral standards apply to public acts than to private acts.[4]

If premise (1) is understood to apply only to acts done in private, then it would appear to be true. The same goes for (4): discrimination against homosexuals for acts done in private would result in a diminishing of freedom. So (1)–(4) would lend support to (5) only if we understand (1)–(4) to refer to acts done in private. Hence, (5) must be understood as referring to private acts; and, as a consequence, (6) also must be read as referring only to acts done in private.

With regard to acts which involve only willing adult participants, there may be no morally relevant difference between homosexuality and heterosexuality. In other words, acts done in private. However, acts done in public add a new ingredient to the mix; an ingredient which has moral consequence. Consequently, the argument (1)–(6) fails in supporting the parity thesis. The argument (1)–(6) may show that there are some circumstances in which the moral status of homosexuality and heterosexuality are the same, but it gives us no reason for thinking that this result holds for all circumstances.[5]

3. MORAL IMPASSES AND PUBLIC DILEMMAS

Suppose one person believes that X is morally wrong, while another believes that X is morally permissible. The two people, let's stipulate, are not involved in a semantical quibble; they hold genuinely conflicting beliefs regarding the moral status of X. If the first person is correct, then the second person is wrong; and, of course, if the second person is right, then the first must be wrong. This situation of conflicting claims is what we will call an "impasse." Impasses arise out of moral disputes. Since the conflicting parties in an impasse take contrary views, the conflicting views cannot all be true, nor can they all be false.[6] Moral impasses may

concern matters only of a personal nature, but moral impasses can involve public policy. An impasse is likely to have public policy ramifications if large numbers of people hold the conflicting views, and the conflict involves matters which are fundamental to a person's moral identity (and, hence, from a practical point of view, are probably irresolvable) and it involves acts done in public. Since not every impasse has public policy ramifications, one can mark off "public dilemma" as a special case of moral impasses: those moral impasses that have public policy consequences. Public dilemmas, then, are impasses located in the public square. Since they have public policy ramifications and since they arise from impasses, one side or another of the dispute will have its views implemented as public policy. Because of the public policy ramifications, and also because social order is sometimes threatened by the volatile parties involved in the impasse, the state has a role to play in resolving a public dilemma.

A public dilemma can be actively resolved in two ways.[7] The first is when the government allies itself with one side of the impasse and, by state coercion and sanction, declares that side of the impasse the correct side. The American Civil War was an example of this: the federal government forcibly ended slavery by aligning itself with the Abolitionist side of the impasse.[8] Prohibition is another example. The 18th Amendment and the Volstead Act allied the state with the Temperance side of the impasse. State mandated affirmative action programs provide a modern example of this. This kind of resolution of a public dilemma we can call a "resolution by declaration." The first of the examples cited above indicates that declarations can be morally proper, the right thing to do. The second example, however, indicates that declarations are not always morally proper. The state does not always take the side of the morally correct; nor is it always clear which side is the correct one.

The second way of actively resolving a public dilemma is that of accommodation. An accommodation in this context means resolving the public dilemma in a way that gives as much as possible to all sides of the impasse. A resolution by accommodation involves staking out some middle ground in a dispute and placing public policy in that location. The middle ground location of a resolution via accommodation is a virtue since it entails that there are no absolute victors and no absolute losers. The middle ground is reached in order to resolve the public dilemma in a way which respects the relevant views of the conflicting parties and which maintains social order. The Federal Fair Housing Act and, perhaps, the current status of abortion (legal but with restrictions) provide examples of actual resolutions via accommodation.[9]

In general, governments should be, at least as far as possible, neutral with regard to the disputing parties in a public dilemma. Unless there is some overriding reason why the state should take sides in a public dilemma—the protection of innocent life, or abolishing slavery, for instance—the state should be neutral, because no matter which side of the public dilemma the state takes, the other side will be the recipient of unequal treatment by the state. A state which is partial and takes sides in moral disputes via declaration, when there is no overriding reason why it should, is tyrannical. Overriding reasons involve, typically, the protection of generally recognized rights.[10] In the case of slavery, the right to liberty; in the case of protecting innocent life, the right involved is the negative right to life. If a public dilemma must be actively resolved, the state should do so (in the absence of an overriding reason) via accommodation and not declaration since the latter entails that a sizable number of people would be forced to live under a government which "legitimizes" and does not just tolerate activities which they find immoral. Resolution via declaration is appropriate only if there is an overriding reason for the state to throw its weight behind one side in a public dilemma.

Is moral rightness an overriding reason for a resolution via declaration? What better reason might there be for a resolution by declaration than that it is the right thing to do? Unless one is prepared to endorse a view that is called "legal moralism"—that immorality alone is a sufficient reason for the state to curtail individual liberty—then one had best hold that moral rightness alone is not an overriding reason. Since some immoral acts neither harm nor offend nor violate another's rights, it seems clear enough that too much liberty would be lost if legal moralism were adopted as public policy.[11]

Though we do not have a definite rule for determining *a priori* which moral impasses genuinely con-

stitute public dilemmas, we can proceed via a case by case method. For example, many people hold that cigarette smoking is harmful and, on that basis, is properly suppressible. Others disagree. Is this a public dilemma? Probably not. Whether someone engages in an imprudent action is, as long as it involves no unwilling participants, a private matter and does not, on that account, constitute a public dilemma. What about abortion? Is abortion a public dilemma? Unlike cigarette smoking, abortion is a public dilemma. This is clear from the adamant and even violent contrary positions involved in the impasse. Abortion is an issue which forces itself into the public square. So, it is clear that, even though we lack a rule which filters through moral impasses designating some as public dilemmas, not every impasse constitutes a public dilemma.

4. Conflicting Claims on Homosexuality

The theistic tradition, Judaism and Christianity and Islam, has a clear and deeply entrenched position on homosexual acts: they are prohibited. Now it seems clear enough that if one is going to take seriously the authoritative texts of the respective religions, then one will have to adopt the views of those texts, unless one wishes to engage in a demythologizing of them with the result that one ends up being only a nominal adherent of that tradition.[12] As a consequence, many contemporary theistic adherents of the theistic tradition, in no small part because they can read, hold that homosexual behavior is sinful. Though God loves the homosexual, these folk say, God hates the sinful behavior. To say that act X is a sin entails that X is morally wrong, not necessarily because it is harmful or offensive, but because X violates God's will. So, the claim that homosexuality is sinful entails the claim that it is also morally wrong. And, it is clear, many people adopt the difference thesis just because of their religious views: because the Bible or the Koran holds that homosexuality is wrong, they too hold that view.

Well, what should we make of these observations? We do not, for one thing, have to base our moral conclusions on those views, if for no other reason than not every one is a theist. If one does not adopt the religion based moral view, one must still respect those who do; they cannot just be dismissed out of hand.[13] And, significantly, this situation yields a reason for thinking that the difference thesis is probably true. Because many religious people sincerely believe homosexual acts to be morally wrong and many others believe that homosexual acts are not morally wrong, there results a public dilemma.[14]

The existence of this public dilemma gives us reason for thinking that the difference thesis is true. It is only via the difference thesis and not the parity thesis, that an accommodation can be reached. Here again, the private/public distinction will come into play.

To see this, take as an example the issue of homosexual marriages. A same-sex marriage would be a public matter. For the government to sanction same-sex marriages—to grant the recognition and reciprocal benefits which attach to marriage—would ally the government with one side of the public dilemma and against the adherents of religion-based moralities. This is especially true given that, historically, no government has sanctioned same-sex marriages. The status quo has been no same-sex marriages. If the state were to change its practice now, it would be clear that the state has taken sides in the impasse. Given the history, for a state to sanction a same-sex marriage now would not be a neutral act.

Of course, some would respond here that by not sanctioning same-sex marriages the state is, and historically has been, taking sides to the detriment of homosexuals. There is some truth in this claim. But one must be careful here. The respective resolutions of this issue—whether the state should recognize and sanction same-sex marriages—do not have symmetrical implications. The asymmetry of this issue is a function of the private/public distinction and the fact that marriage is a public matter. If the state sanctions same-sex marriages, then there is no accommodation available. In that event, the religion-based morality proponents are faced with a public, state sanctioned matter which they find seriously immoral. This would be an example of a resolution via declaration. On the other hand, if the state does not sanction same-sex marriages, there is an accommodation available: in the public realm the state sides with the

religion-based moral view, but the state can tolerate private homosexual acts. That is, since homosexual acts are not essentially public acts; they can be, and historically have been, performed in private. The state, by not sanctioning same-sex marriages is acting in the public realm, but it can leave the private realm to personal choice.[15]

5. The Argument from Conflicting Claims

It was suggested in the previous section that the public dilemma concerning homosexuality, and in particular whether states should sanction same-sex marriages, generates an argument in support of the difference thesis. The argument, again using same-sex marriages as the particular case, is as follows:

7. There are conflicting claims regarding whether the state should sanction same-sex marriages. And,
8. this controversy constitutes a public dilemma. And,
9. there is an accommodation possible if the state does not recognize same-sex marriages. And,
10. there is no accommodation possible if the state does sanction same-sex marriages. And,
11. there is no overriding reason for a resolution via declaration. Hence,
12. the state ought not sanction same-sex marriages. And,
13. the state ought to sanction heterosexual marriages. So,
14. there is at least one morally relevant case in which discrimination against homosexuals, because of their homosexuality, is morally permissible. Therefore,
15. the difference thesis is true.

Since proposition (14) is logically equivalent to the difference thesis, then, if (7)–(14) are sound, proposition (15) certainly follows.

Premises (7) and (8) are uncontroversial. Premises (9) and (10) are based on the asymmetry that results from the public nature of marriage. Proposition (11) is based on our earlier analysis of the argument (1)–(6). Since the strongest argument in support of the parity thesis fails, we have reason to think that there is no overriding reason why the state ought to resolve the public dilemma via declaration in favor of same-sex marriages. We have reason, in other words, to think that (11) is true.

Proposition (12) is based on the conjunction of (7)–(11) and the principle that, in the absence of an overriding reason for state intervention via declaration, resolution by accommodation is the preferable route. Proposition (13) is just trivially true. So, given the moral difference mentioned in (12) and (13), proposition (14) logically follows.

6. TWO OBJECTIONS CONSIDERED

The first objection to the argument from conflicting claims would contend that it is unsound because a similar sort of argument would permit discrimination against some practice which, though perhaps controversial at some earlier time, is now widely thought to be morally permissible. Take mixed-race marriages, for example. The opponent of the argument from conflicting claims could argue that a similar argument would warrant prohibition against mixed-race marriages. If it does, we would have good reason to reject (7)–(14) as unsound.

There are three responses to this objection. The first response denies that the issue of mixed-race marriages is in fact a public dilemma. It may have been so at one time, but it does not seem to generate much, if any, controversy today. Hence, the objection is based upon a faulty analogy.

The second response grants for the sake of the argument that the issue of mixed-race marriages generates a public dilemma. But the second response points out that there is a relevant difference between mixed-race marriages and same-sex marriages that allows for a resolution by declaration in the one case but not the other. As evident from the earlier analysis of the argument in support of (1)–(6), there is reason to think that there is no overriding reason for a resolution by declaration in support of the parity thesis. On the other hand, it is a settled matter that state pro-

tection from racial discrimination is a reason sufficient for a resolution via declaration. Hence, the two cases are only apparently similar, and, in reality, they are crucially different. They are quite different because, clearly enough, if mixed-race marriages do generate a public dilemma, the state should use resolution by declaration in support of such marriages. The same cannot be said for same-sex marriages.

One should note that the second response to the objection does not beg the question against the proponent of the parity thesis. Though the second response denies that race and sexuality are strict analogues, it does so for a defensible and independent reason: it is a settled matter that race is not a sufficient reason for disparate treatment; but, as we have seen from the analysis of (1)–(6), there is no overriding reason to think the same about sexuality.[16]

The third response to the first objection is that the grounds of objection differ in the respective cases: one concerns racial identity; the other concerns behavior thought to be morally problematic. A same-sex marriage would involve behavior which many people find morally objectionable; a mixed-race marriage is objectionable to some, not because of the participants' behavior, but because of the racial identity of the participants. It is the race of the marriage partners which some find of primary complaint concerning mixed-race marriages. With same-sex marriages, however, it is the behavior which is primarily objectionable. To see this latter point, one should note that, though promiscuously Puritan in tone, the kind of sexual acts that are likely involved in a same-sex marriage are objectionable to some, regardless of whether done by homosexuals or heterosexuals.[17] So again, there is reason to reject the analogy between same-sex marriages and mixed-race marriages. Racial identity is an immutable trait and a complaint about mixed-race marriages necessarily involves, then, a complaint about an immutable trait. Sexual behavior is not an immutable trait and it is possible to object to same-sex marriages based on the behavior which would be involved in such marriages. Put succinctly, the third response could be formulated as follows: objections to mixed-race marriages necessarily involve objections over status, while objections to same-sex marriages could involve objections over behavior. Therefore, the two cases are not analogues since there is a significant modal difference in the ground of the objection.

The second objection to the argument from conflicting claims can be stated so: if homosexuality is biologically based—if it is inborn[18]—then how can discrimination ever be justified? If it is not a matter of choice, homosexuality is an immutable trait which is, as a consequence, morally permissible. Just as it would be absurd to hold someone morally culpable for being of a certain race, likewise it would be absurd to hold someone morally culpable for being a homosexual. Consequently, according to this objection, the argument from conflicting claims "legitimizes" unjustifiable discrimination.

But this second objection is not cogent, primarily because it ignores an important distinction. No one could plausibly hold that homosexuals act by some sort of biological compulsion. If there is a biological component involved in sexual identity, it would incline but it would not compel. Just because one naturally (without any choice) has certain dispositions, is not in itself a morally cogent reason for acting upon that disposition. Most people are naturally selfish, but it clearly does not follow that selfishness is in any way permissible on that account. Even if it is true that one has a predisposition to do X as a matter of biology and not as a matter of choice, it does not follow that doing X is morally permissible. For example, suppose that pyromania is an inborn predisposition. Just because one has an inborn and, in that sense, natural desire to set fires, one still has to decide whether or not to act on that desire.[19] The reason that the appeal to biology is specious is that it ignores the important distinction between being a homosexual and homosexual acts. One is status; the other is behavior. Even if one has the status naturally, it does not follow that the behavior is morally permissible, nor that others have a duty to tolerate the behavior.

But, while moral permissibility does not necessarily follow if homosexuality should turn out to be biologically based, what does follow is this: in the absence of a good reason to discriminate between homosexuals and heterosexuals, then, assuming that homosexuality is inborn, one ought not discriminate between them. If a certain phenomenon X is natural in the sense of being involuntary and nonpathological, and if there is no good reason to hold that X is morally problematic, then that is reason enough to think that X is morally permissible. In the absence of a good reason to repress X, one should tolerate it since, as per supposition, it is largely nonvoluntary. The argument from conflicting claims, however, provides a good reason which overrides this presumption.

7. A Second Argument for the Difference Thesis

A second argument for the difference thesis, similar to the argument from conflicting claims, is what might be called the "no-exit argument." This argument is based on the principle that:

A. *no just government can coerce a citizen into violating a deeply held moral belief or religious belief.*

Is (A) plausible? It seems to be since the prospect of a citizen being coerced by the state into a practice which she finds profoundly immoral appears to be a clear example of an injustice. Principle (A), conjoined with there being a public dilemma arising over the issue of same-sex marriages, leads to the observation that if the state were to sanction same-sex marriages, then persons who have profound religious or moral objections to such unions would be legally mandated to violate their beliefs since there does not appear to be any feasible "exit right" possible with regard to state sanctioned marriage. An exit right is an exemption from some legally mandated practice, granted to a person or group, the purpose of which is to protect the religious or moral integrity of that person or group. Prominent examples of exit rights include conscientious objection and military service, home-schooling of the young because of some religious concern, and property used for religious purposes being free from taxation.

It is important to note that marriage is a public matter in the sense that, for instance, if one is an employer who provides health care benefits to the spouses of employees, one must provide those benefits to any employee who is married. Since there is no exit right possible in this case, one would be coerced, by force of law, into subsidizing a practice one finds morally or religiously objectionable.[20]

In the absence of an exit right, and if (A) is plausible, then the state cannot morally force persons to violate deeply held beliefs that are moral or religious in nature. In particular, the state morally could not sanction same-sex marriages since this would result in coercing some into violating a deeply held religious conviction.

8. A CONCLUSION

It is important to note that neither the argument from conflicting claims nor the no-exit argument licenses wholesale discrimination against homosexuals. What they do show is that some discrimination against homosexuals, in this case refusal to sanction same-sex marriages, is not only legally permissible but also morally permissible. The discrimination is a way of resolving a public policy dilemma that accommodates, to an extent, each side of the impasse and, further, protects the religious and moral integrity of a good number of people. In short, the arguments show us that there are occasions in which it is morally permissible to discriminate on the basis of homosexuality.[21]

NOTES

1. The terms "homosexuality" and "heterosexuality" are defined as follows. The former is defined as sexual feelings or behavior directed toward individuals of the same sex. The latter, naturally enough, is defined as sexual feelings or behavior directed toward individuals of the opposite sex.

Sometimes the term "gay" is offered as an alternative to "homosexual." Ordinary use of "gay" has it as a synonym of a male homosexual (hence, the common expression, "gays and lesbians"). Given this ordinary usage, the substitution would lead to a confusing equivocation. Since there are female homosexuals, it is best to use "homosexual" to refer to both male and female homosexuals, and reserve "gay" to signify male homosexuals, and "lesbian" for female homosexuals in order to avoid the equivocation.

2. Perhaps we should distinguish the weak difference thesis (permissible discrimination on *some* occasions) from the strong difference thesis (given the relevant moral differences, discrimination on *any* occasion is permissible).

3. This would be true even if the act in question is immoral.

4. The standard answer is, of course, that the line between public and private is based on the notion of harm. Acts which carry a real probability of harming third parties are public acts.

5. For other arguments supporting the moral parity of homosexuality and heterosexuality, see Richard Mohr, *Gays/Justice: A Study of Ethics, Society and Law* (NY: Columbia, 1988); and see Michael Ruse, "The Morality of Homosexuality" in *Philosophy and Sex*, eds. R. Baker & F. Elliston, (Buffalo, NY: Prometheus Books, 1984), pp. 370–390.

6. Perhaps it would be better to term the disputing positions "contradictory" views rather than "contrary" views.

7. Resolutions can also be passive in the sense of the state doing nothing. If the state does nothing to resolve the public dilemma, it stands pat with the status quo, and the public dilemma is resolved gradually by sociological changes (changes in mores and in beliefs).

8. Assuming, plausibly enough, that the disputes over the sovereignty of the Union and concerning states' rights were at bottom disputes about slavery.

9. The Federal Fair Housing Act prohibits discrimination in housing on the basis of race, religion, and sex. But it does not apply to the rental of rooms in single-family houses, or to a building of five units or less if the owner lives in one of the units. See 42 U.S.C. Section 3603.

10. Note that overriding reasons involve *generally recognized* rights. If a right is not widely recognized and the state nonetheless uses coercion to enforce it, there is a considerable risk that the state will be seen by many or even most people as tyrannical.

11. This claim is, perhaps, controversial. For a contrary view see Richard George, *Making Men Moral* (Oxford: Clarendon Press, 1993).

12. See, for example, Leviticus 18:22, 21:3; and Romans 1:22–32; and Koran IV:13

13. For an argument that religiously-based moral views should not be dismissed out of hand, see Stephen Carter, *The Culture of Disbelief: How American Law and Politics Trivialize Religious Devotion* (NY: Basic Books, 1993).

14. Two assumptions are these: that the prohibitions against homosexuality activity are part of the religious

doctrine and not just an extraneous addition; second, that if X is part of one's religious belief or religious doctrine, then it is morally permissible to hold X. Though this latter principle is vague, it is, I think, clear enough for our purposes here (I ignore here any points concerning the rationality of religious belief in general, or in particular cases).

15. This point has implications for the moral legitimacy of sodomy laws. One implication would be this: the private acts of consenting adults should not be criminalized.

16. An *ad hominem* point: If this response begs the question against the proponent of the parity thesis, it does not beg the question any more than the original objection does by presupposing that sexuality is analogous with race.

17. Think of the sodomy laws found in some states which criminalize certain sexual acts, whether performed by heterosexuals or homosexuals.

18. There is some interesting recent research which, though still tentative, strongly suggests that homosexuality is, at least in part, biologically based. See Simon LeVay,

The Sexual Brain (Cambridge, MA: MIT Press, 1993), pp. 120–122; and J.M. Bailey & R.C. Pillard "A Genetic Study of Male Sexual Orientation" *Archives of General Psychiatry* 48 (1991): 1089–1096; and C. Burr, "Homosexuality and Biology" *The Atlantic* 271/3 (March, 1993): 64; and D. Hamer, S. Hu, V. Magnuson, N. Hu, A. Pattatucci, "A Linkage Between DNA Markers on the X Chromosome and Male Sexual Orientation" *Science* 261 (16 July 1993): 321–327; and see the summary of this article by Robert Pool, "Evidence for Homosexuality Gene" *Science* 261 (16 July 1993): 291–292.

19. I do not mean to suggest that homosexuality is morally equivalent or even comparable to pyromania.

20. Is the use of subsidy here inappropriate? It does not seem so since providing health care to spouses, in a society where this is not legally mandatory, seems to be more than part of a salary and is a case of providing supporting funds for a certain end.

21. I thank David Haslett, Kate Rogers, Louis Pojman, and Jim Fieser for helpful and critical comments.

Critics

DAVID BOONIN

Same-Sex Marriage and the Argument from Public Disagreement

. . . Let me begin by raising a question about P2: the claim that there is a public dilemma about same-sex marriage. On the face of it, this might seem to be the clearest and least problematic of all of the premises in Jordan's argument. If anything at all about same-sex marriage is uncontroversial it is the fact that it is

controversial. But what, exactly, does the claim made by P2 mean? Jordan, remember, defines a public dilemma as a special case of a moral impasse, and a moral impasse as a situation in which people "hold genuinely conflicting beliefs regarding the moral status of *x*." The question is: in the case of the public

David Boonin, "Same-Sex Marriage and the Argument from Public Disagreement," *Journal of Social Philosophy* (Fall 1999): 251–59. Notes and some parts of the text have been deleted. Reprinted by permission of Blackwell Publishing Ltd.

dilemma about same-sex marriage, what does the x stand for?

There are two possibilities: it can stand for acts of homosexual behavior, or it can stand for acts of participating in a same-sex marriage. Jordan at one point speaks of "*the* public dilemma concerning homosexuality, and in particular whether states should sanction same-sex marriages" (78, emphasis added), as if there is a single subject of dispute here, but these are in fact two distinct subjects of disagreement. The former concerns the moral permissibility of certain forms of sexual behavior, regardless of whether the people who engage in them are generally heterosexual or homosexual in their orientation. The latter concerns the moral permissibility of granting certain forms of social recognition and public benefits to same-sex couples, regardless of whether or not they engage in such (or any) sexual behavior.

Suppose that the genuinely conflicting beliefs that generate the dilemma referred to in P2 are beliefs regarding the moral status of acts of participating in a same-sex marriage. This seems to be the most natural interpretation, since the dilemma itself is about same-sex marriage and since a dilemma is simply a special case of an impasse, which is itself a case of conflicting beliefs about something. If this is what is meant by P2, then P3 and P4 are false. P3 says that if the state refuses to sanction same-sex marriages, then it resolves the public dilemma by accommodation (provided that it permits private homosexual acts between consenting adults). If we conflate the two distinct questions about private acts and public benefits into one issue, and think of it as "the" dispute over homosexuality, then this seems plausible enough. Each side gets some of what it wants, and neither side gets all of what it wants. But if the conflict is over the permissibility of same-sex *marriage* in particular, as opposed to about the complex cluster of issues relating to homosexuality taken as a whole, then this is no accommodation at all. It is simply a declaration that one side of the debate is entirely correct (those who oppose same-sex marriages) and the other side entirely incorrect (those who support them). It is as if one were to join together the distinct but related debates about whether or not the government should fund the arts and whether or not it should ban violent pornography, announce that

the government will permit violent pornography but will not subsidize it, and declare that "the" debate in question had been settled in a way that accommodates both sides. This would not be a resolution by accommodation of one dilemma, but rather a resolution by declaration of two distinct but related dilemmas.

On this understanding of P2, P4 is also false, for similar but distinct reasons. P4 says that if the state sanctions same-sex marriage, then it resolves the public dilemma by declaration and leaves no room for accommodation. But if the dilemma is over same-sex marriage rather than over same-sex sex, this too is incorrect. If accommodation is reached in controversies such as that over pornography or abortion by permitting but discouraging the controversial practice, then the same would hold here as well. The state could sanction same-sex marriage, but make it more difficult to obtain a same-sex marriage license than to obtain an opposite-sex marriage license. For example, it could require proof that a homosexual couple had been engaged for two years before obtaining a same-sex marriage license, but not require such proof from heterosexual couples, or require extensive premarital counseling, or charge a greater licensing fee. And it could discourage homosexuals from marrying in other ways, such as by taxing married homosexuals at a higher rate (higher than married heterosexuals and/or higher than unmarried homosexuals), or making it more difficult for them to obtain divorces or to adopt children than it is for heterosexual couples.

None of these suggestions will be fully satisfactory to defenders of same-sex marriage, of course. What they demand is marriage for homosexuals that is on an equal footing with marriage for heterosexuals. Nor will any of these proposals be fully satisfactory to opponents of same-sex marriage. What they demand is that there be no such thing as same-sex marriage. But that is precisely the point. If Jordan is correct that dilemmas of this sort should be resolved by accommodation, and if the dilemma is understood to be one over marriage and not over sex, then following a proposal that is fully satisfactory to neither side is exactly what his argument demands that we do. As in other such cases, the state should find a way to allow those who wish to engage in the disputed behavior to engage in it while at the same time expressing society's disapproval or at least lack of approval of the behavior in question.

Suppose, on the other hand, that the genuinely conflicting beliefs that generate the dilemma referred to in P2 are beliefs regarding the moral status of acts of homosexual behavior. This seems to be what Jordan typically has in mind when he introduces his argument. When he supports the contention that there exists a public dilemma that needs some sort of resolution, for example, he cites the fact that "[t]he theistic tradition, Judaism and Christianity and Islam, has a clear and deeply entrenched position on homosexual *acts*: they are prohibited" (77, emphasis added). And he concludes his argument for the claim by saying that "[b]ecause many religious people sincerely believe homosexual *acts* to be morally wrong and many others believe that homosexual *acts* are not morally wrong, there results a public dilemma" (77, emphasis added).

But if the genuinely conflicting beliefs that generate the dilemma referred to in P2 are beliefs regarding the moral status of acts of homosexual behavior, then P3 and P4 are again false, for different but parallel reasons. If the state sanctions same-sex marriage, it does not resolve the conflicting beliefs about the moral permissibility of acts of homosexual behavior in a way that leaves no room for accommodation. For example, the state could recognize both same-sex and opposite-sex marriage and make it illegal to have homosexual intercourse outside of such a relation while legal to have heterosexual intercourse outside of such a relation. This would have the effect of permitting but restricting the form of behavior whose moral status is the subject of genuinely conflicting beliefs. So if the conflicting beliefs referred to in P2 concern the permissibility of acts of homosexual behavior, then P4 is false. Similarly, if the state refuses to sanction same-sex marriage and permits private homosexual acts between consenting adults, it does not resolve the conflicting beliefs about the moral permissibility of acts of homosexual behavior by accommodation. Rather, it simply declares that one side of the conflict is the correct side, namely, the side that believes that such acts are permissible. Doing so thus renders P3 false as well. So either way

that we specify the meaning of the claim made in P2, the argument as a whole proves to be unsound.

A second objection to Jordan's argument takes the form of a reductio ad absurdum: if the state should refuse to sanction same-sex marriage because it is the subject of a moral impasse, then it should also refuse to sanction mixed-race marriage on the same ground. But the claim that the state should refuse to sanction mixed-race marriage is surely intolerable. So, therefore, is Jordan's argument. Jordan provides three responses to this objection, but none of them are satisfactory.

His first response is that unlike the issue of same-sex marriage, the issue of mixed-race marriages "does not seem to generate much, if any, controversy today" (79). On this account, there is no such public dilemma in the first place, and so it does not matter that Jordan's position would justify forbidding mixed-race marriage if there were. This response is unsuccessful for two reasons. First, it is not at all clear that there is no such dilemma about mixed-race marriage. In many communities in the South, at least, there remains substantial opposition to interracial *dating*, let alone interracial marriage. And although such opposition is traditionally associated with white racists, there is a more recent and hardly less heated controversy within the black community in all parts of the country about whether or not black men, in particular, have an obligation to marry black women. Second, and more importantly, even if Jordan is right that there is no longer a moral impasse on this issue, this response makes the impermissibility of laws forbidding mixed-race marriage contingent on this fact. And surely such laws were impermissible even when many racists supported them.

Jordan's second response to the mixed-race objection is to say that even if it does represent a public dilemma, it is one in which there is an overriding reason in favor of resolution by declaration. The reason is that "it is a settled matter that state protection from racial discrimination is a reason sufficient for a resolution via declaration" while the same is not true of protection from discrimination according to sexual orientation (80). This response fails for the simple reason that a law banning mixed-race marriages does not discriminate against people on racial grounds. It says that *every* person, regardless of race, is free to marry anyone else of his or her race, and that *every* person, regardless of race, is prohibited from marrying anyone else of some other race. A white person who falls in love with a black person is adversely affected in just the same way as is black person who falls in love with a white person. And since every black-white couple consists of one black person and one white person, the total number of blacks and whites who are adversely affected in this way is the same. As a result, a law recognizing mixed-race marriage does not protect anyone from racial discrimination that would occur without such a law.

A law forbidding same-sex marriage, it is worth noting, is fundamentally different in this respect. It says that a heterosexual man can marry any member of the sex he is attracted to while a homosexual man can marry any member of the sex he is *not* attracted to, and that a heterosexual man is forbidden to marry any member of the sex that he is not attracted to while a homosexual man is forbidden to marry any member of the sex that he *is* attracted to. This law does discriminate by sexual orientation, since all of the people who are adversely affected by it (at least directly) are homosexuals. And thus a law recognizing same-sex marriage does protect people from discrimination on the basis of sexual orientation that would otherwise occur without such a law. In short, laws banning mixed-race marriage treat people of all races equally while laws banning same-sex marriage do not treat people of all sexual orientations equally. So Jordan has failed to show that there is an overriding reason for the state to resolve the mixed-race marriage issue by declaration that does not also apply to the case of same-sex marriages. Indeed, if anything, he has pointed to an overriding reason to resolve the same-sex marriage issue by declaration that does not apply to the mixed-race marriage issue.

Jordan's final response to the mixed-race marriage objection turns on his attempt to identify a second disanalogy between the two cases: "A same-sex marriage would involve behavior which many people find morally objectionable; a mixed-race marriage is objectionable to some, not because of the participants' behavior, but because of the racial identity of the participants" (80). And since objections based on a person's identity are different from objections based on a person's behavior, it does not follow from the fact that the objection to mixed-race marriage should be overruled by a resolution by declaration that the objection to same-sex marriage should also be overruled in this manner.

This response must be rejected because it rests on a misdescription of the view held by those who object to mixed-race marriage. It is not that they object to the *identity* of the individuals involved. White racists need not have anything against blacks marrying other blacks, and black separatists surely have nothing against white people marrying other whites. It is not the identity of the individuals that they object to, but the act they perform: the act of weakening the purity of the race, or of violating the obligation to put one's own community first. In this sense, they are no different from the antihomosexual people Jordan describes: they say they object not to what homosexuals are, but to what they do.

ANDREW SULLIVAN

Virtually Normal

An Argument About Homosexuality

... Marriage is not simply a private contract; it is a social and public recognition of a private commitment. As such, it is the highest public recognition of personal integrity. Denying it to homosexuals is the most public affront possible to their public equality.

This point may be the hardest for many heterosexuals to accept. Even those tolerant of homosexuals may find this institution so wedded to the notion of heterosexual commitment that to extend it would be to undo its very essence. And there may be religious reasons for resisting this that, within certain traditions, are unanswerable. But I am not here discussing what churches do in their private affairs. I am discussing what the allegedly neutral liberal state should do in public matters. For liberals, the case for homosexual marriage is overwhelming. As a classic public institution, it should be available to any two citizens.

Some might argue that marriage is by definition between a man and a woman; and it is difficult to argue with a definition. But if marriage is articulated beyond this circular fiat, then the argument for its exclusivity to one man and one woman disappears. The center of the public contract is an emotional, financial, and psychological bond between two people; in this respect, heterosexuals and homosexuals are identical. The heterosexuality of marriage is intrinsic only if it is understood to be intrinsically procreative; but that definition has long been abandoned in Western society. No civil marriage license is granted on the condition that the couple bear children; and the marriage is no less legal and no less defensible if it remains childless. In the contemporary West, marriage has become a way in which the state recognizes an emotional commitment by two people to each other for life. And within that definition, there is no public way, if one believes in equal rights under the law, in which it should legally be denied homosexuals.

Of course, no public sanctioning of a contract should be given to people who cannot actually fulfill it. The state rightly, for example, withholds marriage from minors, or from one adult and a minor, since at least one party is unable to understand or live up to the contract. And the state has also rightly barred close family relatives from marriage because familial emotional ties are too strong and powerful to enable a marriage contract to be entered into freely by two autonomous, independent individuals; and because incest poses a uniquely dangerous threat to the trust and responsibility that the family needs to survive. But do homosexuals fall into a similar category? History and experience strongly suggest they don't. Of course, marriage is characterized by a kind of commitment that is rare—and perhaps declining—even among heterosexuals. But it isn't necessary to prove that homosexuals or lesbians are less—or more—able to form long-term relationships than straights for it to be clear that at least *some* are. Moreover, giving these people an equal right to affirm their commitment doesn't reduce the incentive for heterosexuals to do the same. . . .

Excerpted from Andrew Sullivan, *Virtually Normal: An Argument About Homosexuality* (New York: Alfred A. Knopf, 1995). Used by permission of Alfred A. Knopf, a division of Random House, Inc.

14

Is Licensing Parents Wrong?

LaFollette and His Critics

The thesis of Hugh LaFollette's widely discussed article "Licensing Parents" is as simple as it is shocking: Morally speaking, the State should require people to get a license in order to be parents. LaFollette argues both that this claim is true in principle and that it can be implemented in a fair and workable manner in practice. While LaFollette's thesis strikes most people as outrageous, however, the argument that he offers in its defense is grounded in an assumption that most people already accept: that there are many other forms of activity that people should not be permitted to engage in unless they have first secured a license from the state. LaFollette's argument turns on the claim that if we are right in accepting the practice of licensing in these relatively uncontroversial cases, then we should accept the practice of licensing in the much more controversial case of parenting as well.

The structure of LaFollette's argument as a whole is that of inference to the best explanation (see section 4.3 in the Introduction). The argument begins by identifying particular forms of activity about which most people will be in agreement. In the case of driving a car, for example, most people will agree that the state should require people to obtain a license before they are permitted to engage in the activity. After identifying several cases of this sort, the argument then continues by trying to identify the best explanation of *why* licensing is appropriate in the cases where it seems clearly to be appropriate. Looking carefully at what driving has in common with several other such cases, that is, LaFollette attempts to extract a kind of general principle of licensing, one that tells us what properties an activity must have in order for it to be an appropriate subject for state licensing. Some of what is involved here is fairly straightforward. The fact that an activity is potentially harmful to other people, for example, clearly has something to do with whether or not it should be licensed. But LaFollette's analysis also identifies other features that an activity must have in order for it to be legitimately subject to licensing, and these properties together make up his attempt to uncover the best explanation of why licensing is appropriate in the uncontroversial cases. Finally, after claiming to have arrived at the best explanation of why licensing is appropriate in the relatively uncontroversial cases, LaFollette attempts to apply his explanation to the case of parenting. Here, his argument claims that all of the properties that together justify licensing in the case of something like driving a car are, in fact, found, in the case of the activity of raising children. If parenting does have these various properties, and if these various properties do collectively suffice to justify licensing in the other cases, then they suffice to justify licensing in the case of parenting as well. Although LaFollette's conclusion is certainly controversial, then, his claim is that it is grounded in assumptions that most people already accept.

It is not surprising that the proposal that the State license parents has generated a good deal of critical response. In the first critical-response piece reprinted here, Lawrence E. Frisch raises two distinct objections to LaFollette's argument. The first can be construed as an argument against LaFollette's claim to have identified the best explanation of the appropriateness of licensing in those cases in which licensing is uncontroversial. While conceding that LaFollette has successfully identified some of the properties that are required in order for an activity to be subject to licensing, Frisch maintains that LaFollette has neglected a further requirement having to do with the effectiveness of licensing a given activity. Since Frisch believes that parenting does not satisfy this further requirement, he believes that the best explanation of the appropriateness of licensing in the uncontroversial cases does not, in fact, entail that parenting should be licensed. In addition to this objection, Frisch raises a challenge to the claim that parenting should be licensed even on LaFollette's own account of licensing. Although he agrees with LaFollette that parenting is potentially harmful to the children being parented and that being potentially harmful is part of what makes an activity appropriately subject to a licensing requirement, Frisch maintains that one of LaFollette's other requirements for licensing fails to apply to the case of parenting. Thus, even if LaFollette's explanation of licensing in general proves to be superior to Frisch's explanation, Frisch still maintains that LaFollette has failed to justify the conclusion that parenting should be licensed in particular.

In the second critical reading, Pierre Lemieux presents a very different kind of objection to LaFollette's position, one that can best be understood as a slippery-slope argument: If we were to accept LaFollette's proposal, on this account, we would also have to accept a massive increase in the scope and power of government in all sorts of other areas. In particular, adopting the proposal to license parents would move society further in the direction of what Lemieux calls the "Sanitary State": away from the traditional limited-government model, in which the State serves only to protect our rights, and toward a much more paternalistic system, in which the government attempts to satisfy our every want and desire in a way that Lemieux takes it would clearly be objectionable.

QUESTIONS FOR CONSIDERATION

In critically evaluating the debate between LaFollette and Frisch, readers should begin by being clear about precisely where Frisch is attacking LaFollette's argument and then consider ways in which a defender of LaFollette's position might attempt to reply to them.

• What additional property does Frisch think that an activity must have in order for it to be an appropriate subject for a licensing requirement? Why does Frisch think that the activity of parenting does not have this additional property? How might LaFollette respond to this claim? Could he show that we already license other activities that do not have this additional property? Or could he show that parenting really does have it?

• What part of LaFollette's own account of licensing in general does Frisch think fails to support the proposal to license parents? Does LaFollette's article already contain a response to this concern? If not, how might LaFollette attempt to address it? Could the fact that LaFollette is only seeking to weed out the very worst parents, rather than to try to identify the very best parents, help him to do so? Why or why not?

- LaFollette appeals at a few points to our current attitudes toward the practice of adoption. How does he claim that this provides support for his position? Is the support it is said to provide convincing?

In critically assessing the objection that Lemieux aims at LaFollette's position, one should instead focus primarily on the slippery-slope argument that underlies his attack. Lemieux's argument turns on the claim that the licensing proposal would be a significant step in a more statist direction and that this direction would itself be an undesirable one. One should therefore think about whether there are ways that LaFollette could respond to either of these claims.

- Is it true that adopting LaFollette's proposal would lead to the kind of "Sanitary State" Lemieux finds so objectionable? Or would it be, as LaFollette seems to see it, merely a consistent application of the more traditional view that the State should protect the rights of its citizens (in this case, the rights of its young and newborn citizens)?

- Is what matters the intention behind the proposal or the practical consequences of adopting it?

- If LaFollette were forced to concede that his proposal starts us down a slippery slope to a more paternalistic State, might he be able to deny that this counts as an objection to his proposal? How, for example, might he attempt to draw a line that would prevent us from reaching the kind of undesirable society Lemieux seems to fear? Or might he think that we should simply be willing to bite the bullet because the well-being of young children is of such vital importance?

FURTHER READING

Hedman, Carl. "Three Approaches to the Problem of Child Abuse and Neglect." *Journal of Social Philosophy* 31, no. 3 (Fall 2000): 268–85.

LaFollette, Hugh. "A Reply to Frisch." *Philosophy and Public Affairs* 11, no. 2 (1982): 181–83.

Tittle, Peg, ed. *Should Parents Be Licensed?: Debating the Issues.* Amherst: Prometheus Books, 2004.

Westman, Jack C. *Licensing Parents: Can We Prevent Child Abuse and Neglect?* New York: Insight Books, 1994.

HUGH LAFOLLETTE

Licensing Parents

In this essay I shall argue that the state should require all parents to be licensed. My main goal is to demonstrate that the licensing of parents is theoretically desirable, though I shall also argue that a workable and just licensing program actually could be established.

My strategy is simple. After developing the basic rationale for the licensing of parents, I shall consider several objections to the proposal and argue that these objections fail to undermine it. I shall then isolate some striking similarities between this licensing program and our present policies on the adoption of children. If we retain these adoption policies—as we surely should—then, I argue, a general licensing program should also be established. Finally, I shall

Hugh Lafollette, "Licensing Parents," *Philosophy and Public Affairs* 9, no. 2 (1980): 182–97. Reprinted by permission of Princeton University Press.

briefly suggest that the reason many people object to licensing is that they think parents, particularly biological parents, own or have natural sovereignty over their children.

REGULATING POTENTIALLY HARMFUL ACTIVITIES

Our society normally regulates a certain range of activities; it is illegal to perform these activities unless one has received prior permission to do so. We require automobile operators to have licenses. We forbid people from practicing medicine, law, pharmacy, or psychiatry unless they have satisfied certain licensing requirements.

Society's decision to regulate just these activities is not ad hoc. The decision to restrict admission to certain vocations and to forbid some people from driving is based on an eminently plausible, though not often explicitly formulated, rationale. We require drivers to be licensed because driving an auto is an activity which is potentially harmful to others, safe performance of the activity requires a certain competence, and we have a moderately reliable procedure for determining that competence. The potential harm is obvious: incompetent drivers can and do maim and kill people. The best way we have of limiting this harm without sacrificing the benefits of automobile travel is to require that all drivers demonstrate at least minimal competence. We likewise license doctors, lawyers, and psychologists because they perform activities which can harm others. Obviously they must be proficient if they are to perform these activities properly, and we have moderately reliable procedures for determining proficiency.[1] Imagine a world in which everyone could legally drive a car, in which everyone could legally perform surgery, prescribe medications, dispense drugs, or offer legal advice. Such a world would hardly be desirable.

Consequently, any activity that is potentially harmful to others and requires certain demonstrated competence for its safe performance, is subject to regulation—that is, it is theoretically desirable that we regulate it. If we also have a reliable procedure for determining whether someone has the requisite com-

petence, then the action is not only subject to regulation but ought, all things considered, to be regulated.

It is particularly significant that we license these hazardous activities, even though denying a license to someone can severely inconvenience and even harm that person. Furthermore, available competency tests are not 100 percent accurate. Denying someone a driver's license in our society, for example, would inconvenience that person acutely. In effect that person would be prohibited from working, shopping, or visiting in places reachable only by car. Similarly, people denied vocational licenses are inconvenienced, even devastated. We have all heard of individuals who had the "life-long dream" of becoming physicians or lawyers, yet were denied that dream. However, the realization that some people are disappointed or inconvenienced does not diminish our conviction that we must regulate occupations or activities that are potentially dangerous to others. Innocent people must be protected even if it means that others cannot pursue activities they deem highly desirable.

Furthermore, we maintain licensing procedures even though our competency tests are sometimes inaccurate. Some people competent to perform the licensed activity (for example, driving a car) will be unable to demonstrate competence (they freeze up on the driver's test). Others may be incompetent, yet pass the test (they are lucky or certain aspects of competence—for example, the sense of responsibility—are not tested). We recognize clearly—or should recognize clearly—that no test will pick out all and only competent drivers, physicians, lawyers, and so on. Mistakes are inevitable. This does not mean we should forget that innocent people may be harmed by faulty regulatory procedures. In fact, if the procedures are sufficiently faulty, we should cease regulating that activity entirely until more reliable tests are available. I only want to emphasize here that tests need not be perfect. Where moderately reliable tests are available, licensing procedures should be used to protect innocent people from incompetents.[2]

These general criteria for regulatory licensing can certainly be applied to parents. First, parenting is an activity potentially very harmful to children. The potential for harm is apparent: each year more than half a million children are physically abused or neglected by their parents.[3] Many millions more are psychologically abused or neglected—not given love, respect, or a sense of self-worth. The results of this maltreatment are obvious. Abused children bear the physical and psychological scars of maltreatment throughout their lives. Far too often they turn to crime.[4] They are far more likely than others to abuse their own children.[5] Even if these maltreated children never harm anyone, they will probably never be well-adjusted, happy adults. Therefore, parenting clearly satisfies the first criterion of activities subject to regulation.

The second criterion is also incontestably satisfied. A parent must be competent if he is to avoid harming his children; even greater competence is required if he is to do the "job" well. But not everyone has this minimal competence. Many people lack the knowledge needed to rear children adequately. Many others lack the requisite energy, temperament, or stability. Therefore, child-rearing manifestly satisfies both criteria of activities subject to regulation. In fact, I dare say that parenting is a paradigm of such activities since the potential for harm is so great (both in the extent of harm any one person can suffer and in the number of people potentially harmed) and the need for competence is so evident. Consequently, there is good reason to believe that all parents should be licensed. The only ways to avoid this conclusion are to deny the need for licensing *any* potentially harmful activity; to deny that I have identified the standard criteria of activities which should be regulated; to deny that parenting satisfies the standard criteria; to show that even though parenting satisfies the standard criteria there are special reasons why licensing parents is not theoretically desirable; or to show that there is no reliable and just procedure for implementing this program.

While developing my argument for licensing I have already identified the standard criteria for activities that should be regulated, and I have shown that they can properly be applied to parenting. One could deny the legitimacy of regulation by licensing, but in doing so one would condemn not only the regulation of parenting, but also the regulation of drivers, physicians, druggists, and doctors. Furthermore, regulation of hazardous activities appears to be a fundamental task of any stable society.

Thus only two objections remain. In the next section I shall see if there are any special reasons why licensing parents is not theoretically desirable. Then, in the following section, I shall examine several practical objections designed to demonstrate that even if licensing were theoretically desirable, it could not be justly implemented.

THEORETICAL OBJECTIONS TO LICENSING

Licensing is unacceptable, someone might say, since people have a right to have children, just as they have rights to free speech and free religious expression. They do not need a license to speak freely or to worship as they wish. Why? Because they have a right to engage in these activities. Similarly, since people have a right to have children, any attempt to license parents would be unjust.

This is an important objection since many people find it plausible, if not self-evident. However, it is not as convincing as it appears. The specific rights appealed to in this analogy are not without limitations. Both slander and human sacrifice are prohibited by law; both could result from the unrestricted exercise of freedom of speech and freedom of religion. Thus, even if people have these rights, they may sometimes be limited in order to protect innocent people. Consequently, even if people had a right to have children, that right might also be limited in order to protect innocent people, in this case children. Secondly, the phrase "right to have children" is ambiguous; hence, it is important to isolate its most plausible meaning in this context. Two possible interpretations are not credible and can be dismissed summarily. It is implausible to claim either that infertile people have rights to be *given* children or that people have rights to intentionally create children biologically without incurring any subsequent responsibility to them.

A third interpretation, however, is more plausible, particularly when coupled with observations about the degree of intrusion into one's life that the licensing scheme represents. On this interpretation people have a right to rear children if they make good-faith efforts to rear procreated children the best way they see fit. One might defend this claim on the ground that licensing would require too much intrusion into the lives of sincere applicants.

Undoubtedly one should be wary of unnecessary governmental intervention into individuals' lives. In this case, though, the intrusion would not often be substantial, and when it is, it would be warranted. Those granted licenses would face merely minor intervention; only those denied licenses would encounter marked intrusion. This encroachment, however, is a necessary side-effect of licensing parents—just as it is for automobile and vocational licensing. In addition, as I shall argue in more detail later, the degree of intrusion arising from a general licensing program would be no more than, and probably less than, the present (and presumably justifiable) encroachment into the lives of people who apply to adopt children. Furthermore, since some people hold unacceptable views about what is best for children (they think children should be abused regularly), people do not automatically have rights to rear children just because they will rear them in a way they deem appropriate.[6]

Consequently, we come to a somewhat weaker interpretation of this right claim: a person has a right to rear children if he meets certain minimal standards of child rearing. Parents must not abuse or neglect their children and must also provide for the basic needs of the children. This claim of right is certainly more credible than the previously canvassed alternatives, though some people might still reject this claim in situations where exercise of the right would lead to negative consequences, for example, to overpopulation. More to the point, though, this conditional right is compatible with licensing. On this interpretation one has a right to have children only if one is not going to abuse or neglect them. Of course the very purpose if licensing is just to determining whether people *are* going to abuse or neglect their children. If the determination is made that someone will maltreat children, then that person is subject to the limitations of the right to have children and can legitimately be denied a parenting license.

In fact, this conditional way of formulating the right to have children provides a model for formulating all alleged rights to engage in hazardous activ-ities. Consider, for example, the right to drive a car. People do not have an unconditional right to drive, although they do have a right to drive if they are competent. Similarly, people do not have an unconditional right to practice medicine; they have a right only if they are demonstrably competent. Hence, denying a driver's or physician's license to someone who has not demonstrated the requisite competence does not deny that person's rights. Likewise, on this model, denying a parenting license to someone who is not competent does not violate that person's rights.

Of course someone might object that the right is conditional on actually being a person who will abuse or neglect children, whereas my proposal only picks out those we can reasonably predict will abuse children. Hence, this conditional right *would* be incompatible with licensing.

There are two ways to interpret this objection and it is important to distinguish these divergent formulations. First, the objection could be a way of questioning our ability to predict reasonably and accurately whether people would maltreat their own children. This is an important practical objection, but I will defer discussion of it until the next section. Second, this objection could be a way of expressing doubt about the moral propriety of the prior restraint licensing requires. A parental licensing program would deny licenses to applicants judged to be incompetent even though they had never maltreated any children. This practice would be in tension with our normal skepticism about the propriety of prior restraint.

Despite this healthy skepticism, we do sometimes use prior restraint. In extreme circumstances we may hospitalize or imprison people judged insane, even though they are not legally guilty of any crime, simply because we predict they are likely to harm others. More typically, though, prior restraint is used only if the restriction is not terribly onerous and the restricted activity is one which could lead easily to serious harm. Most types of licensing (for example, those for doctors, drivers, and druggists) fall into this latter category. They require prior restraint to prevent serious harm, and generally the restraint is minor—though it is important to remember that some individuals will find it oppressive. The same is true of parental licensing. The purpose of licensing is to prevent serious harm to children. Moreover, the prior restraint required by licensing would not be terribly onerous for many people. Certainly the restraint would be far less extensive than the presumably justifiable prior restraint of, say, insane criminals. Criminals preventively detained and mentally ill people forceably hospitalized are denied most basic liberties, while those denied parental licenses would be denied only that one specific opportunity. They could still vote, work for political candidates, speak on controversial topics, and so on. Doubtless some individuals would find the restraint onerous. But when compared to other types of restraint currently practiced, and when judged in light of the severity of harm maltreated children suffer, the restraint appears *relatively* minor.

Furthermore, we could make certain, as we do with most licensing programs, that individuals denied licenses are given the opportunity to reapply easily and repeatedly for a license. Thus, many people correctly denied licenses (because they are incompetent) would choose (perhaps it would be provided) to take counseling or therapy to improve their chances of passing the next test. On the other hand, most of those mistakenly denied licenses would probably be able to demonstrate in a later test that they would be competent parents.

Consequently, even though one needs to be wary of prior restraint, if the potential for harm is great and the restraint is minor relative to the harm we are trying to prevent—as it would be with parental licensing—then such restraint is justified. This objection, like all the theoretical objections reviewed, has failed.

PRACTICAL OBJECTIONS
TO LICENSING

I shall now consider five practical objections to licensing. Each objection focuses on the problems or difficulties of implementing this proposal. According to these objections, licensing is (or may be) theoretically desirable; nevertheless, it cannot be efficiently and justly implemented.

The first objection is that there may not be, or we may not be able to discover, adequate criteria of "a good parent." We simply do not have the knowledge, and it is unlikely that we could ever obtain the knowledge, that would enable us to distinguish adequate from inadequate parents.

Clearly there is some force to this objection. It is highly improbable that we can formulate criteria that would distinguish precisely between good and less than good parents. There is too much we do not know about child development and adult psychology. My proposal, however, does not demand that we make these fine distinctions. It does not demand that we license only the best parents; rather it is designed to exclude only the very bad ones.[7] This is not just a semantic difference, but a substantive one. Although we do not have infallible criteria for picking out good parents, we undoubtedly can identify bad ones—those who will abuse or neglect their children. Even though we could have a lively debate about the range of freedom a child should be given or the appropriateness of corporal punishment, we do not wonder if a parent who severely beats or neglects a child is adequate. We know that person isn't. Consequently, we do have reliable and useable criteria for determining who is a bad parent; we have the criteria necessary to make a licensing program work.

The second practical objection to licensing is that there is no reliable way to predict who will maltreat their children. Without an accurate predictive test, licensing would be not only unjust, but also a waste of time. Now I recognize that as a philosopher (and not a psychologist, sociologist, or social worker), I am on shaky ground if I make sweeping claims about the present or future abilities of professionals to produce such predictive tests. Nevertheless, there are some relevant observations I can offer.

Initially, we need to be certain that the demands on predictive tests are not unreasonable. For example, it would be improper to require that tests be 100 percent accurate. Procedures for licensing drivers, physicians, lawyers, druggists, etc., plainly are not 100 percent (or anywhere near 100 percent) accurate. Presumably we recognize these deficiencies yet embrace the procedures anyway. Consequently, it would be imprudent to demand considerably more exacting standards for the tests used in licensing parents.

In addition, from what I can piece together, the practical possibilities for constructing a reliable predictive test are not all that gloomy. Since my proposal does not require that we make fine line distinctions between good and less than good parents, but rather that we weed out those who are potentially very bad, we can use existing tests that claim to isolate relevant predictive characteristics—whether a person is violence-prone, easily frustrated, or unduly self-centered. In fact, researchers at Nashville General Hospital have developed a brief interview questionnaire which seems to have significant predictive value. Based on their data, the researchers identified 20 percent of the interviewees as a "risk group"—those having great potential for serious problems. After one year they found "the incidence of major breakdown in parent-child interaction in the risk group was approximately four to five times as great as in the low risk group."[8] We also know that parents who maltreat children often have certain identifiable experiences, for example, most of them were themselves maltreated as children. Consequently, if we combined our information about these parents with certain psychological test results, we would probably be able to predict with reasonable accuracy which people will maltreat their children.

However, my point is not to argue about the precise reliability of present tests. I cannot say emphatically that we now have accurate predictive tests. Nevertheless, even if such tests are not available, we could undoubtedly develop them. For example, we could begin a longitudinal study in which all potential parents would be required to take a specified battery of tests. Then these parents could be "followed" to discover which ones abused or neglected their children. By correlating test scores with information on maltreatment, a usable, accurate test could be fashioned. Therefore, I do not think that the present unavailability of such tests (if they are unavailable) would count against the legitimacy of licensing parents.

The third practical objection is that even if a reliable test for ascertaining who would be an acceptable parent were available, administrators would unintentionally misuse that test. These unintentional mis-

takes would clearly harm innocent individuals. Therefore, so the argument goes, this proposal ought to be scrapped. This objection can be dispensed with fairly easily unless one assumes there is some special reason to believe that more mistakes will be made in administering parenting licenses than in other regulatory activities. No matter how reliable our proceedings are, there will always be mistakes. We may license a physician who, through incompetence, would cause the death of a patient; or we may mistakenly deny a physician's license to someone who would be competent. But the fact that mistakes are made does not and should not lead us to abandon attempts to determine competence. The harm done in these cases could be far worse than the harm of mistakenly denying a person a parenting license. As far as I can tell, there is no reason to believe that more mistakes will be made here than elsewhere.

The fourth proposed practical objection claims that any testing procedure will be intentionally abused. People administering the process will disqualify people they dislike, or people who espouse views they dislike, from rearing children.

The response to this objection is parallel to the response to the previous objection, namely, that there is no reason to believe that the licensing of parents is more likely to be abused than driver's license tests or other regulatory procedures. In addition, individuals can be protected from prejudicial treatment by pursuing appeals available to them. Since the licensing test can be taken on numerous occasions, the likelihood of the applicant's working with different administrative personnel increases and therefore the likelihood decreases that intentional abuse could ultimately stop a qualified person from rearing children. Consequently, since the probability of such abuse is not more than, and may even be less than, the intentional abuse of judicial and other regulatory authority, this objection does not give us any reason to reject the licensing of parents.

The fifth objection is that we could never adequately, reasonably, and fairly enforce such a program. That is, even if we could establish a reasonable and fair way of determining which people would be inadequate parents, it would be difficult, if not impossible, to enforce the program. How would one deal with violators and what could we do with babies so conceived? There are difficult problems here, no doubt, but they are not insurmountable. We might not punish parents at all—we might just remove the children and put them up for adoption. However, even if we are presently uncertain about the precise way to establish a just and effective form of enforcement, I do not see why this should undermine my licensing proposal. If it is important enough to protect children from being maltreated by parents, then surely a reasonable enforcement procedure can be secured. At least we should assume one can be unless someone shows that it cannot.

An Analogy with Adoption

So far I have argued that parents should be licensed. Undoubtedly many readers find this claim extremely radical. It is revealing to notice, however, that this program is not as radical as it seems. Our moral and legal systems already recognize that not everyone is capable of rearing children well. In fact, well-entrenched laws require adoptive parents to be investigated—in much the same ways and for much the same reasons as in the general licensing program advocated here. For example, we do not allow just anyone to adopt a child; nor do we let someone adopt without first estimating the likelihood of the person's being a good parent. In fact, the adoptive process is far more rigorous than the general licensing procedures I envision. Prior to adoption the candidates must first formally apply to adopt a child. The applicants are then subjected to an exacting home study to determine whether they really want to have children and whether they are capable of caring for and rearing them adequately. No one is allowed to adopt a child until the administrators can reasonably predict that the person will be an adequate parent. The results of these procedures are impressive. Despite the trauma children often face before they are finally adopted, they are five times less likely to be abused than children reared by their biological parents.[9]

Nevertheless we recognize, or should recognize, that these demanding procedures exclude some people who would be adequate parents. The selection criteria may be inadequate; the testing procedures may be somewhat unreliable. We may make mistakes. Probably there is some intentional abuse of the system. Adoption procedures intrude directly in the applicants' lives. Yet we continue the present adoption policies because we think it better to mistakenly deny some people the opportunity to adopt than to let just anyone adopt.

Once these features of our adoption policies are clearly identified, it becomes quite apparent that there are striking parallels between the general licensing program I have advocated and our present adoption system. Both programs have the same aim—protecting children. Both have the same drawbacks and are subject to the same abuses. The only obvious dissimilarity is that the adoption requirements are *more* rigorous than those proposed for the general licensing program. Consequently, if we think it is so important to protect adopted children, even though people who want to adopt are less likely than biological parents to maltreat their children, then we should likewise afford the same protection to children reared by their biological parents.

I suspect, though, that many people will think the cases are not analogous. The cases are relevantly different, someone might retort, because biological parents have a natural affection for their children and the strength of this affection makes it unlikely that parents would maltreat their biologically produced children.

Even if it were generally true that parents have special natural affections for their biological offspring, that does not mean that all parents have enough affection to keep them from maltreating their children. This should be apparent given the number of children abused each year by their biological parents. Therefore, even if there is generally such a bond, that does not explain why we should not have licensing procedures to protect children of parents who do not have a sufficiently strong bond. Consequently, if we continue our practice of regulating the adoption of children, and certainly we should, we are rationally compelled to establish a licensing program for all parents.

However, I am not wedded to a strict form of licensing. It may well be that there are alternative ways of regulating parents which would achieve the desired results—the protection of children—without strictly prohibiting nonlicensed people from rearing children. For example, a system of tax incentives for licensed parents, and protective services scrutiny of nonlicensed parents, might adequately protect children. If it would, I would endorse the less drastic measure. My principal concern is to protect children from maltreatment by parents. I begin by advocating the more strict form of licensing since that is the standard method of regulating hazardous activities.

I have argued that all parents should be licensed by the state. This licensing program is attractive, not because state intrusion is inherently judicious and efficacious, but simply because it seems to be the best way to prevent children from being reared by incompetent parents. Nonetheless, even after considering the previous arguments, many people will find the proposal a useless academic exercise, probably silly, and possibly even morally perverse. But why? Why do most of us find this proposal unpalatable, particularly when the arguments supporting it are good and the objections to it are philosophically flimsy?

I suspect the answer is found in a long-held, deeply ingrained attitude toward children, repeatedly reaffirmed in recent court decisions, and present, at least to some degree, in almost all of us. The belief is that parents own, or at least have natural sovereignty over, their children.[10] It does not matter precisely how this belief is described, since on both views parents legitimately exercise extensive and virtually unlimited control over their children. Others can properly interfere with or criticize parental decisions only in unusual and tightly prescribed circumstances—for example, when parents severely and repeatedly abuse their children. In all other cases, the parents reign supreme.

This belief is abhorrent and needs to be supplanted with a more child-centered view. Why? Briefly put, this attitude has adverse effects on children and on the adults these children will become. Parents who hold this view may well maltreat their children. If these parents happen to treat their children well, it is only because they want to, not because they think their children deserve or have a right to good treatment. Moreover, this belief is manifestly at odds with the conviction that parents

should prepare children for life as adults. Children subject to parents who perceive children in this way are likely to be adequately prepared for adulthood. Hence, to prepare children for life as adults and to protect them from maltreatment, this attitude toward children must be dislodged. As I have argued, licensing is a viable way to protect children. Furthermore, it would increase the likelihood that more children will be adequately prepared for life as adults than is now the case.

NOTES

1. "When practice of a profession or calling requires special knowledge or skill and intimately affects public health, morals, order or safety, or general welfare, legislature may prescribe reasonable qualifications for persons desiring to pursue such professions or calling and require them to demonstrate possession of such qualifications by examination on subjects with which such profession or calling has to deal as a condition precedent to right to follow that profession or calling." 50 SE 2nd 735 (1949). Also see 199 US 306, 318 (1905) and 123 US 623, 661 (1887).

2. What counts as a moderately reliable test for these purposes will vary from circumstance to circumstance. For example, if the activity could cause a relatively small amount of harm, yet regulating that activity would place extensive constraints on people regulated, then any tests should be extremely accurate. On the other hand, if the activity could be exceedingly harmful but the constraints on the regulated person are minor, then the test can be considerably less reliable.

3. The statistics on the incidence of child abuse vary. Probably the most recent detailed study (Saad Nagi, *Child Maltreatment in the United States,* Columbia University Press, 1977) suggests that between 400,000 and 1,000,000 children are abused or neglected each year. Other experts claim the incidence is considerably higher.

4. According to the National Committee for the Prevention of Child Abuse, more than 80 percent of incarcerated criminals were, as children, abused by their parents. In addition, a study in the *Journal of the American Medical Association* 168, no. 3: 1755–1758, reported that first-degree murderers from middle-class homes and who have "no history of addiction to drugs, alcoholism, organic disease of the brain, or epilepsy" were frequently found to have been subject to "remorseless physical brutality at the hands of the parents."

5. "A review of the literature points out that abusive parents were raised in the same style that they have recreated in the pattern of rearing children.... An individual who was raised by parents who used physical force to train their children and who grew up in a violent household has had as a role model the use of force and violence as a means of family problem solving." R. J. Gelles, "Child Abuse as Psychopathology—a Sociological Critique and Reformulations," *American Journal of Orthopsychiatry* 43, no. 4 (1973): 618–19.

6. Some people might question if any parents actually believe they should beat their children. However, that does appear to be the sincere view of many abusing parents. See, for example, case descriptions in *A Silent Tragedy* by Peter and Judith DeCourcy (Sherman Oaks, CA.: Alfred Publishing Co., 1973).

7. I suppose I might be for licensing only good parents if I knew there were reasonable criteria and some plausible way of deciding if a potential parent satisfied these criteria. However, since I don't think we have those criteria or that method, nor can I seriously envision that we will discover those criteria and that method, I haven't seriously entertained the stronger proposal.

8. The research gathered by Altemeir was reported by Ray Helfer in "Review of the Concepts and a Sampling of the Research Relating to Screening for the Potential to Abuse and/or Neglect One's Child." Helfer's paper was presented at a workshop sponsored by the National Committee for the Prevention of Child Abuse, 3–6 December 1978.

9. According to a study published by the Child Welfare League of America, at least 51 percent of the adopted children had suffered, prior to adoption, more than minimal emotional deprivation. See A *Follow-up Study of Adoptions: Post Placement Functioning of Adoption Families,* Elizabeth A. Lawder et al., New York 1969.

According to a study by David Gil (*Violence Against Children,* Cambridge: Harvard University Press, 1970) only .4 percent of abused children were abused by adoptive parents. Since at least 2 percent of the children in the United States are adopted (*Encyclopedia of Social Work,* National Association of Social Workers, New York, 1977), that means the rate of abuse by biological parents is five time that of adoptive parents.

10. We can see this belief in a court case chronicled by DeCourcy and DeCourcy in *A Silent Tragedy.* The judge ruled that three children, severely and regularly beaten, burned, and cut by their father, should be placed back with their father since he was only "trying to do what is right." If the court did not adopt this belief would it even be tempted to so excuse such abusive behavior? This attitude also emerges in the all-too-frequent court rulings (see S. Katz, *When Parents Fail,* Boston: Beacon Press, 1971) giving custody of children back to their biological parents even though the parents had abandoned them for years, and even though the children expressed a strong desire to stay with foster parents.

In "The Child, the Law, and the State" (*Children's Rights: Toward the Liberation of the Child,* Leila Berg et al., New York: Praeger Publishers, 1971), Nan Berger persuasively argues that our adoption and foster care laws are comprehensible only if children are regarded as the property of their parents.

Lawrence E. Frisch

On Licentious Licensing
A Reply to Hugh LaFollette

In his essay "Licensing Parents," Hugh LaFollette fails to make a convincing case in large part because he assumes, without stating or proving, that licensing of parents and parenting is analogous to other societal licensing.[1] He comes close to stating this premise in suggesting that "one could deny the legitimacy of regulation by licensing, but in doing so one would condemn not only the regulation of parenting, but also the regulation of drivers, physicians, druggists, and doctors." Regulation of hazardous activities is indeed "a fundamental task of any stable society," and LaFollette has made a convincing case that parenting is an activity of potential hazard. But hazards may differ significantly in their accessibility to regulatory control, and parenting practices present hazards that cannot be significantly modified by current licensing techniques.

Societies undertake licensing, I believe, because there is reason to expect that the licensing process will exert some control over specific risks. These risks may be usefully divided into the following four categories:

1. Risks arising out of ignorance.
2. Risks arising through physical or mental incapacity.
3. Risks arising from willful misconduct.
4. Risks arising through negligence or inability to exert self-control over behavior.

LICENSING AND IGNORANCE

The assessment of knowledge plays a major role in most licensing procedures, and it is reasonable to assume that imposition of this form of licensing protects society against errors committed through ignorance. With licensed drivers on the roads we can anticipate fewer accidents caused by incorrect turns into one-way streets, and with licensed doctors in the operating theater we can reasonably anticipate fewer kidneys inadvertently removed at gallbladder operations. What could we expect if such an assessment were correspondingly extended to parents?

First, and most laudably, we would anticipate the thorough development of a body of parenting knowledge, the training of appropriate teachers of parenting skills, the promulgation of recognized parenting curricula, and certification for mastery of this knowledge. Second, we could hope for a change in prospective parents' appreciation of the difficulties of good and safe parenting. Some might learn enough about children's needs to decide to defer childrearing until they are ready to meet its challenge. However, there is no empirical reason to believe that making *knowledge of parenting* a prime criterion for licensing would reduce the incidence of child abuse, and such a practice risks denying licensure to potentially excellent parents possessing superior intuitive skills but lacking

Lawrence E. Frisch, "On Licentious Licensing: A Reply to Hugh LaFollette," *Philosophy and Public Affairs* 11, no. 2 (1982): 173–80. Reprinted by permission of Princeton University Press.

knowledge of "what the book says" concerning child behavior or development.[2]

PHYSICAL OR MENTAL INCAPACITY

Obviously, licensing procedures should exclude persons whose inherent incapacities make them unsafe practitioners of the activity we are licensing. For example, most states require a vision evaluation and disqualify from licensure a driver whose visual handicap cannot be optically corrected. If we were to pattern a parenting examination after driver's test, we might require a normative degree of vision, hearing, literacy, and physical mobility. Where impairments were severe we might license only with restrictions— for example, a deaf parent could care for an infant only if flashing lights were provided to alert the parent to the baby's crying.

I have no doubt that parental licensing procedures involving an assessment of physical and mental capacity would have some effect on the incidence of child abuse and neglect. However, we believe that it would be a minimal one because of the relatively small contribution made to child maltreatment by parents with physical and mental disabilities. Some handicapped, retarded, or mentally ill parents do abuse or neglect their children, but many manage to rear children at or above the minimum community standard.

WILLFUL MISCONDUCT

I take willful misconduct to mean purposive violations of accepted modes of behavior or performance in which there is no reason to doubt the wrongdoer's ability to act in accord with reasonable and accepted standards. No licensing procedure with which we are familiar would purposefully license persons who habitually engage in willful misconduct. Unfortunately, most persons do not blatantly announce their intention to violate those standards when applying for licensure and hence may be licensed without these intentions being considered. Just as current

licensing of drivers and doctors stipulates forfeiture for wrongdoing, present child-care laws already allow for removal of maltreated children from a harmful environment. Thus licensing parents to prevent willful maltreatment even if it could succeed in this end, offers no *new* protection to abused children.

NEGLIGENT OR UNCONTROLLABLE BEHAVIOR

Many, if not most, traffic violations and mishaps occur because the driver is distracted, preoccupied, or under the influence of alcohol. They result from negligence rather than purposive wrongdoing. I suspect that most cases of child abuse and neglect fall into this category, particularly if we include in it those cases in which a parent, meaning to punish a child, loses control and in anger inflicts serious injury. Social and economic stresses may play an often unanticipated role. It is difficult to imagine a testing situation which duplicates that, for example, of a mother whose husband has just left her and whose baby, after two days of constant crying due to illness, refuses to go to sleep. Licensing has no traditional interest in determining how examinees react under extraordinary stress—other than that of the examination itself—and LaFollette has made no clear argument for striking out in new licensing directions for parents alone.

Licensing as currently practiced cannot, I submit, prevent either willful child maltreatment or maltreatment having its origins in parental behavior beyond ready control. This means quite simply that licensing, despite laudable intentions, cannot prevent most cases of child abuse and neglect.

LAFOLLETTE'S VIEW OF LICENSING

LaFollette is anxious to make sure that parents are competent, just as he is to make sure that his doctor and the driver in the oncoming car are safely capable. He rightly recognizes that we are at risk from incompetent drivers and doctors and, consequently, license their activities. In a leap, or perhaps a lapse, of logic,

LaFollette peremptorily concludes that "the very purpose of licensing is just to determine whether people *are* going to abuse or neglect their children." Thus, without warning, he appears to have shifted the focus of licensing from its traditional purpose of assessing knowledge to the realm of predicting future behavior and confronting issues of negligence and misconduct—areas in which licensing has no historical interest.[3] Clearly, if we can accurately predict that someone will actually abuse a child we can usefully deny a parenting license to that person. There are many other matters in which such divine foreknowledge would be useful, but lacking divinity, we must rely on other methods. LaFollette falls back on statistics. He envisions tests capable of predicting future abusive behavior, while asking us to forgo our own serious doubts about sociologists' ability to prognosticate, because "even if such tests are not available we could undoubtedly develop them." Unlicensable parents can only be "identified" prior to an abusive incident by their mathematical resemblance on psychological or sociological scales to who, at the time the scales were validated, were thought to be guilty of maltreating their children. This is a most unusual approach to licensing, which he justifies by appealing to analogy with traditional licensing procedures. However, it is just wrong to imply that "the very purpose" of, for example, licensing drivers, is to predict which people will have an accident or violate the law. Licensing procedures, as currently employed, are designed to audit present performance, not to predict future practice.

As LaFollette suggests, his statistical prediction paradigm does "provide a model for formulating all alleged rights to engage in hazardous activities." We could (and perhaps should) try to deny driver's licenses to people who statistically resemble past or current violators. This might result in safer roads (if only because there would be fewer licensees), but it is emphatically not current licensing practice. We cannot exclude a class of potential child maltreaters from parenthood without invoking a new and untested theory of predictive licensure. For example, a recent survey of practicing women psychiatrists has revealed that 73 percent of them suffer from significant mental depression at some point during their working careers. If we believe (or could demonstrate) that a depressed psychiatrist potentially lacks judgment or empathy, would we be justified in refusing to license women to practice psychiatry? We could perhaps add other tests to improve predictive ability to, say, 90 percent, but no matter what numbers we supply, our current licensing procedures do not take such predictive measures into consideration in granting or denying the right to practice hazardous activities. Nor should they. As Davis wrote recently in a different context, "this utilitarian mentality, if pushed to its consistent extreme, would require the identification and confinement of people who seemed to pose a high risk of criminal behavior soon after birth."[4]

PRACTICAL ISSUES

Fundamental to LaFollette's licensing scheme is the presumption that we will be able to predict future abusive behavior. "From what I can piece together," he says, "the practical possibilities for constructing a reliable predictive test are not all that gloomy." The world in which we and our children live is so gloomy that admittedly the least glimmer of light looks positively cheerful. However, it does nothing more than constitute assurance. Even if we accept LaFollette's optimism, there remain a number of practical obstacles which seem virtually insurmountable.

What, for instance, do we do about a situation in which one parent passes the licensing test but the other does not? What if testing shows that a given mother is an adequate parent (licensable) unless she lives with a man who abuses her—and then she moves in with such a man? What if she does this after a child is born? Is the child removed forthwith or only after abuse actually occurs? Should licensing examinations be repeated at intervals, or does a single passing score forever qualify one as a parent? By not retesting we would be ignoring the effect that mounting stresses have on people's abilities to cope. However, if we retest, we run the risk of delicensing parents who have never abused or neglected their children. Such a procedure, if it resulted in child removal, would have all the faults of our current foster-care system (multiple home placements for often arbitrary reasons), but might also place loved and wanted children who have never been abused because their parents were ill or ill-humored on their retest days. Accumulating evidence shows that not all children are alike in temperament; in the simplest terms some are "easy" and some are "difficult." It is plausible that some parents could safely care for an easy child but would be likely to abuse a difficult one. Do we remove a difficult child at six months of age because, no matter how they are actually getting on with him, his parents are licensed only to bring up an easy child?

LaFollette has presented us with a cleverly written and provocative argument which fails theoretically. He has mistakenly construed current licensing procedures for other social goods and has proposed licensing parents based on predictions of future behavior. By confusing competence (in the sense used in examining drivers or doctors and pronouncing them fit to license) with good judgment and acceptable response to stressful situations (qualities we at best consider only indirectly in our present licensing procedures), he is suggesting a licensing of parents which goes beyond forms of licensing that society conventionally employs. Furthermore, he appears to be far too sanguine about the practical difficulties such licensing would pose, relying on a naive faith in the ability of sociological technology to succeed against any obstacle if licensing is adopted.

However, the issue LaFollette raises is not silly even if the arguments he advances to support it (as he himself implies) may be. Should we license parents? Something about the question tells us it is an interesting one to ask, and no one has previously asked it with such good-natured verve.[5] "Parenting," he tells us "is an activity potentially very harmful to children . . . abused children bear the physical and psychological scars of maltreatment throughout their lives . . . even if these maltreated children never harm anyone, they will probably never be well-adjusted, happy adults." The freshness (some would say naivete) of LaFollette's approach is that he bases his argument on an implicit human right to be "well-adjusted and happy" as an adult, and he wants to give children claim on that right for their future.

Unlike LaFollette, most child abuse literature does not ask, How can we bring up the best and happiest children? Perhaps in posing this question he should have moved his argument one step further from the conventional and suggested, not that we license parents, but that we closely monitor the performance of families. When an examiner gives a practical driving test, he or she is observing not so much what the driver does, but how the car performs. The driver may be docked for failing to look both ways at an intersection, but most demerits are given for crossing yellow lines, exceeding speed limits, parking ineptly, and failing to stop for school buses. Similarly, if our goal is successful childrearing, perhaps we would do better not to focus on parents, but to look at how their children are developing from early childhood. We could then offer services if deviations in behavior or development are observed, and remove children from their homes not just (or perhaps not at all) because they have been abused, but because their development is faltering despite offered services. Such an approach would not focus on determining whether parents are fit to raise children in general, but only on whether a given child is being raised to a defined community standard in the family in which he or she is living. If we adopted this approach, and like LaFollette's proposal, it is far from modest, our focus could be on promoting the child's development into a "well-adjusted" and fully realized adult.

The practical problems with monitoring families in this way are very great, the likelihood that social agencies can truly improve unsatisfactory families is not very high, and the idea represents an extraordinary and probably unconstitutional intrusion into family privacy. However, if we believe that childbearing is a privilege (or at least a highly qualifiable right) and that children have the claim right to "well-adjusted" adulthood, such family surveillance may offer an alternative rather more reasonable than licensing.

NOTES

1. "Licensing Parents," *Philosophy & Public Affairs*, 9, no. 2 (Winter 1980): 182–97.

2. This observation was made, en passant, in what remains the most comprehensive psychological study of abusive parenting. The authors conducted extended

interviews with sixty families and concluded that "the central issue involved (in child maltreatment) concerns a breakdown in . . . 'mothering'—a disruption of the maternal affectional system." Lack of parenting knowledge was not a factor described in any of these families, although lack of appropriate parenting "intuitions" was pervasive. We might expect to be able to make similar observations about a number of unsafe (but still licensed) drivers: their knowledge base is acceptable but their intuitive skills are wanting. Brandt F. Steele and Carl B. Pollock, "A Psychiatric Study of Parents who Abuse Infants and Small Children," in Ray Helfer and C. Henry Kempe, *The Battered Child,* 2d ed. (Chicago: University of Chicago Press, 1974), pp. 89–135.

3. Excepting forfeiture of the license, earlier noted, in the case of misconduct.

4. David Brion Davis, "The Crime of Reform," *New York Review of Books 27* (26 June 1980):14–18.

5. Christopher Lasch credits both Judge Ben Lindsey and Margaret Mead with proposals to license parents. He suggests that both intended that the middle and upper classes would carry the major burden of childrearing with the poor largely unenfranchised. Neither, it appears, was as concerned with issues of practicality or fairness as LaFollette. For those who find LaFollette's enthusiasm for social engineering distressing, Lasch may prove a healthful antidote. See Lasch's *Haven in a Heartless World* (New York: Basic Books, 1977).

PIERRE LEMIEUX

Parent Licensing

In the Winter 1980 issue of *Philosophy and Public Affairs,* Hugh LaFollette, a philosophy professor at East Tennessee State University, published an article arguing for the need to license parents.[1] The argument is quite straightforward. "We," or "our society," understandably require licensing for automobile operators, physicians, lawyers, pharmacists, psychologists, and psychiatrists, all activities that require a certain competence and are "potentially harmful to others." The two criteria of potential harm and ascertainable competence apply even more to parenting, which is "an activity potentially very harmful to children." Therefore, would-be parents should be forced to demonstrate their competence, obtain a license, and perhaps be trained, before rearing their children, for the same reasons that we strictly regulate the adoption process. "Undoubtedly," LaFollette writes, "one should be wary of unnecessary government intervention in individuals' lives. In this case, though, the intrusion would not often be substantial, and when it is, it would be warranted."

Since it was originally published, this paradigmatic article has been reproduced in more than a dozen books of public policy, ethical philosophy, and "environmental ethics." The proposal has gained disciples in other countries, and these are often more radical than LaFollette himself, who thought that alternative systems could perhaps protect children adequately. "For example," he wrote, "a system of tax incentives for licensed parents, and protective services scrutiny of nonlicensed parents, might adequately protect children." Two Canadian public health specialists argue that "[n]o one should be allowed to raise children until they have finished high school, completed a parenting course, and obtained a licence."[2] A famous British surgeon, Sir Roy Calne, argues that people should have to pass a parenting test and obtain a reproduction license before being allowed to have children.[3]

Pierre Lemieux, "Parent Licensing," *Laissez Faire City Times* 5, no. 19 (May 7, 2001). Reprinted by permission of Pierre Lemieux.

Note how narrow a conception of rights underlies Prof. LaFollette's argument. Prior restraint of the kind involved in licensing is justified "if the restriction is not terribly onerous and the restricted activity is one which could lead easily to serious harm." In this perspective, only a limited number of real rights exist: rights of free speech (which, coincidentally, apply mainly to intellectuals like LaFollette), religious rights, right to vote, and rights of association. Presumably, individuals will associate to talk and worship, for what else is there to do? Even the enumerated rights can be limited to protect third parties. And "rights" to engage in hazardous activities, like parenting, are conditional on meeting minimal standards. Determination of the nature of harm and the cost of restraint, and definition of real and conditional rights, presumably belong to "society."

Also underlying the proposed scheme is an underestimation of the efficiency of free human interactions, combined with an overblown confidence in political and bureaucratic processes. Statists tend to compare imperfect markets with perfect government. In this perspective, LaFollette would certainly agree with the World Bank researchers who recently wrote: "A priori, parents would ideally always be willing and able to protect children from tobacco themselves. If this happened, there would be little need for government to duplicate such efforts . . . Perfect parents, however, are rare."[4]

LaFollette would probably add, in his usual cool way, that the parent licensing system will not be perfect, but just less imperfect than the harmful system of totally private parenting that we now have. This completely neglects the effect of the proposed system on the growth of state power. It is recommended not to laugh at slippery slope arguments when you are actually speeding on a very slippery one.

In evaluating the efficiency of a parent licensing system, we must factor in the impact it will have on the relations between the individual and the state. LaFollette argues that the system "would increase the likelihood that more children will be adequately prepared for life as adults." This is the standard argument for limiting everybody's liberty in the name of manufactured pubic health causes. Under this general umbrella, the goal of protecting children is especially attractive, since the exploited children cannot defend themselves.[5]

Gun control, the war on drugs, the witch-hunt against child pornographers, tobacco prohibitions, are all aspects of the same trend. Indeed, on all such issues, the same politically-correct, public-health crowd is usually on the statist side of the barricades. LaFollette wrote "Licensing Parents" before Jonesboro, Dunblane, and Littleton, and could not grasp the tragic irony of overly-protected children mass-killing their little classmates. The society being created is not exactly what LaFollette envisions for when children will be adults. The point is that, in the eyes of the authorities, they will never be adults.

It is not clear if, in LaFollette's scheme, a license would be required before conceiving a child, or only for keeping and rearing the baby. LaFollette claims that enforcement problems are "not insurmountable." "We might not punish parents at all," he adds, "we might just remove the children and put them up for adoption." Of course, laws are ultimately enforced by armed men, and scenes similar to agents with fully automatic weapons seizing Elian Gonzalez would be repeated. Usually, though, parents would let a social worker "peacefully" take their children away because they know that they have no chance against the SWAT team. So, with a few exceptions, the tyranny would be soft and quiet—tyranny with an invisible hand.

The project of licensing parents is symptomatic of the rise of what we may call the "Sanitary State," large components of which have already been put in place with the apparent consent of the majority. The Sanitary State is the continuation of the Social State, whose mission was to maximize social welfare. The Social State itself followed the Redistributive State, whose official goal was to redistribute income from the rich to the poor, and which conveniently built up its electoral clienteles this way.

The Sanitary State's mission is to keep its subjects healthy, and cure them when their lifestyles do not correspond to public health diktats. It acts within the limits of the rule of law, which now means that there is a law for every situation, and that you are always free to explain yourself before a judge. The tyrant is nice, soft, and relentlessly pursues its wards' happiness. The majority has nothing to fear. The dissenting minority cannot do much, if only because the state has made sure to disarm ordinary citizens for public health reasons.

Unrealistic? The people will never accept this? Let's hope so. But consider what our ancestors would have said if they had been told that the driver's license would become an ID card, that the state would assign citizens unique identifying number that would become necessary for most private transactions (except for the most trivial), that people would need the government's permission to own or carry guns, that they would need to fill in forms when they deposit more than $10,000 in cash, etc.

Welcome to the 21st century.

NOTES

1. Hugh LaFollette, "Licensing Parents," *Philosophy and Public Affairs,* 9, no. 2 (Winter 1980): 182–197.

2. *National Post,* February 22, 1999.

3. *The Observer,* August 7, 1994.

4. Prabhat Jha et al., "The Economic Rationale for Intervention in the Tobacco Market," in *Tobacco Control in Developing Countries,* edited by Prabhat Jha and Frank Chaloupka (Oxford: Oxford University Press, 2000), p. 164.

5. See my "Why I Hate Children," *Laissez Faire City Times,* April 2, 2001; reproduced at http://www.pierrelemieux.org/artchildren.html.

15

Is Commercial Surrogate Motherhood Wrong?

Anderson and Her Critics

Commercial surrogate motherhood is the practice by which a woman is paid to undergo a pregnancy, bring the pregnancy to term, and deliver the resulting child to the party or parties who have contracted for her services. In "Is Women's Labor a Commodity?," the featured article in this chapter, Elizabeth S. Anderson argues that this practice is immoral, and should be illegal, on the grounds that it "constitutes an unconscionable commodification of children and of women's reproductive capacities."

Anderson's argument against commercial surrogate motherhood is a subtle one and difficult to encapsulate fully in a brief introduction. One useful way to think about her strategy, though, is to think of it in terms of an argument from inference to the best explanation (see section 4.3 of the Introduction). Anderson begins by assuming that the practice of slavery is wrong. A good explanation of the wrongness of slavery, she suggests, can be found in the distinction between what she calls two different "modes of valuation": We can value something purely for its usefulness to us, or we can value and respect it, at least in part, for its own sake. People, we all agree, merit the latter form of respect; treating them as commodities to be bought and sold on the open market treats them as if they were of value only for their usefulness. To treat something as a commodity, on this account, is to allow the market to determine how it will be produced, exchanged, and enjoyed. And while this is (or at least may be) an appropriate way to produce and distribute mere *things*, items that are of value only for their usefulness, it is an inappropriate way to govern the treatment of *persons*, beings who merit respect in their own right, independent of their usefulness to others.

If this account of commodification offers the best general explanation of our attitude toward cases in which we believe that the market is an inappropriate mechanism for determining how something should be done, the question then becomes what, if anything, does this imply about the case of commercial surrogate motherhood? Anderson offers two distinct arguments for the claim that it implies that the practice should be rejected. The first argument turns on the claim that commercial surrogate motherhood inappropriately treats the child who is produced as a commodity. In ordinary circumstances, after all, when a woman gives birth to a child, she has (at least partial) parental rights over that child (as well as parental obligations). The child she gives birth to, that is, is *hers*. By means of the contract the woman signs in the case of commercial surrogacy, however, in exchange for a cash payment, she gives up any rights she would otherwise have to the child. This, on Anderson's account, amounts to the woman's selling the child to the party or parties with whom she has contracted. To sell a child is to treat it as a mere commodity; to treat it as a mere commodity is to treat it as if it were of value only for its usefulness to others. And since doing so fails to value the child in the way he or she should be valued, doing so is unacceptable.

Anderson's second argument builds from the same general account of commodification but focuses instead on the value of the surrogate mother herself. Under typical circumstances, Anderson argues, a pregnant woman is treated in a manner that fully respects her own perspective on her pregnancy—her desires, her emotions, her beliefs, and so forth. But in the case of a commercial surrogate mother, Anderson maintains, this is not so. How the pregnant woman is treated is determined by economic forces, by the terms of the contract that the market has produced. The pregnant woman is treated not so much as a person, but rather as an incubation machine, a device for turning out a desired product. In this respect, Anderson maintains that the woman, like the child, is inappropriately treated as a mere commodity. And this provides a second reason to reject the practice of commercial surrogate motherhood.

Anderson's case against commercial surrogate motherhood rests on two claims: that the practice inappropriately commodifies something and that this fact suffices to warrant opposing and prohibiting the practice. A critic of Anderson's position may therefore respond in one of two ways: He can deny that the practice involves inappropriate commodification, or he can maintain that the practice is an acceptable one even if it does involve such commodification. In an excerpt from a longer piece, Richard J. Arneson largely pursues the first strategy. After raising a few general worries about Anderson's account of commodification in general, he responds to her claims about commodification of children and women. With respect to the former, Arneson argues that a market in surrogate motherhood does not entail that the children are being treated as mere property; he offers the example of pets as a case in point. With respect to the latter, Arneson offers a variety of responses to a number of Anderson's points; many of these responses revolve around the claim that the surrogate contract need not ignore or discount the pregnant woman's feelings or experiences because the contract regulates only how she behaves, not how she feels.

Finally, in an excerpt from a longer article, Alan Wertheimer primarily pursues the second strategy. In particular, he complains that Anderson does not put enough weight on the fact that surrogate motherhood contracts are entered into voluntarily. Acts that might be objectionable when done against a person's will may be acceptable when done with her consent, and Wertheimer suggests that commercial surrogate motherhood may be a case of this sort. In addition, he emphasizes the importance of distinguishing between the claim that an act commodifies someone and the claim that it *harms* someone. Being treated as a commodity might often be harmful, he maintains, but it need not always be. And if the woman who undergoes the pregnancy and the child who is born as a result are not harmed in the process (or if they are harmed but are also benefited in ways that outweigh these harms), then the practice of commercial surrogate motherhood might prove acceptable, even if it involves the sort of commodification that Anderson appeals to in arguing against it.

QUESTIONS FOR CONSIDERATION

In thinking critically about the exchange between Anderson and her critics, readers should consider both the question of whether commercial surrogate motherhood commodifies what should not be commodified and the question of whether, if it does, this provides a sufficient basis for opposing the practice.

• Does the practice, as Anderson maintains, treat the child and the woman as mere things to be used? Or, as both Arneson and Wertheimer suggest, can commercial surrogate motherhood be practiced in a manner that adequately respects both mother and child?

• If the practice does involve an inappropriate form of commodification, is this enough to warrant rejecting it, as Anderson's argument seems to require? Or, as Arneson maintains, might the practice have enough additional positive features to outweigh this fact?

• There is a difference between saying that a practice is immoral and saying that it should be illegal. Do Anderson's arguments do a better job of justifying one claim rather than the other? If so, which one is better justified, and why?

• Finally, readers are encouraged to consider whether the critique of commercial surrogate motherhood presented by Anderson might work better in some cases than in others. Might there be some instances in which her critique really is sufficient and others in which it is not? If so, what sorts of cases ought to be permitted, and what sorts of cases ought to be rejected?

FURTHER READING

Ber, Rosalie. "Ethical Issues in Gestational Surrogacy." *Theoretical Medicine and Bioethics: Philosophy of Medical Research and Practice* 21, no. 2 (2000): 153–69.

Davies, Iwan. "Contracts to Bear Children." *Journal of Medical Ethics* 11 (June 1985): 61–4.

Malm, Heidi. "Paid Surrogacy: Arguments and Responses." *Public Affairs Quarterly* 3 (1989): 57–66.

Prokopijevic, Miroslav. "Surrogate Motherhood." *Journal of Applied Philosophy* (October 1990): 169–81.

Tong, Rosemarie. "The Overdue Death of a Feminist Chameleon: Taking a Stand on Surrogacy Arrangements." *Journal of Social Philosophy* 21, nos. 2 and 3 (1990): 40–56.

Trusted, Jennifer. "Gifts of Gametes: Reflections About Surrogacy." *Journal of Applied Philosophy* 3 (March 1986): 123–6.

Winslade, William. "Surrogate Mothers: Private Right or Public Wrong?" *Journal of Medical Ethics* 9 (September 1981): 153–4.

Elizabeth S. Anderson

Is Women's Labor a Commodity?

In the past few years the practice of commercial sur-rogate motherhood has gained notoriety as a method for acquiring children. A commercial surrogate mother is anyone who is paid money to bear a child for other people and terminate her parental rights, so that the others may raise the child as exclusively their own. The growth of commercial surrogacy has raised with new urgency a class of concerns regarding the proper scope of the market. Some critics have objected to commercial surrogacy on the ground that it improperly treats children and women's reproduc-tive capacities as commodities.[1] The prospect of reducing children to consumer durables and women to baby factories surely inspires revulsion. But are there good reasons behind the revulsion? And is this an accurate description of what commercial surro-gacy implies? This article offers a theory about what things are properly regarded as commodities which supports the claim that commercial surrogacy con-stitutes an unconscionable commodification of chil-dren and of women's reproductive capacities.

What Is a Commodity?

The modern market can be characterized in terms of the legal and social norms by which it governs the production, exchange, and enjoyment of commodi-ties. To say that something is properly regarded as a commodity is to claim that the norms of the market are appropriate for regulating its production, ex-change, and enjoyment. To the extent that moral principles or ethical ideals preclude the application of market norms to a good, we may say that the good is not a (proper) commodity.

Why should we object to the application of a mar-ket norm to the production or distribution of a good?

One reason may be that to produce or distribute the good in accordance with the norm is to *fail to value it in an appropriate way*. Consider, for example, a stan-dard Kantian argument against slavery, or the com-modification of persons. Slaves are treated in accordance with the market norm that owners may use commodities to satisfy their own interests with-out regard for the interests of the commodities them-selves. To treat a person without regard for her interests is to fail to respect her. But slaves are per-sons who may not be merely used in this fashion, since as rational beings they possess a dignity which commands respect. In Kantian theory, the problem with slavery is that it treats beings worthy of *respect* as if they were worthy merely of *use*. "Respect" and "use" in this context denote what we may call differ-ent *modes of valuation*. We value things and persons in other ways than by respecting and using them. For example, love, admiration, honor, and appreciation constitute distinct modes of valuation. To value a thing or person in a distinctive way involves treating it in accordance with a particular set of norms. For example, courtesy expresses a mode of valuation we may call "civil respect," which differs from Kantian respect in that it calls for obedience to the rules of eti-quette rather than to the categorical imperative.

Any ideal of human life includes a conception of how different things and persons should be valued. Let us reserve the term "use" to refer to the mode of valua-tion proper to commodities, which follows the market norm of treating things solely in accordance with the owner's nonmoral preferences. Then the Kantian argument against commodifying persons can be gen-eralized to apply to many other cases. It can be argued that many objects which are worthy of a higher mode of valuation than use are not properly regarded as mere commodities. Some current arguments against

From Elizabeth S. Anderson, "Is Women's Labor a Commodity?" *Philosophy and Public Affairs* 19, no. 1. (Winter 1990): 71–92. Some notes and some parts of the text have been deleted. Reprinted by permission of Princeton University Press.

the colorization of classic black-and-white films take this form. Such films have been colorized by their owners in an attempt to enhance their market value by attracting audiences unused to black-and-white cinematography. But some opponents of the practice object that such treatment of the film classics fails to appreciate their aesthetic and historical value. True appreciation of these films would preclude this kind of crass commercial exploitation, which debases their aesthetic qualities in the name of profits. Here the argument rests on the claim that the goods in question are worthy of appreciation, not merely of use.

The ideals which specify how one should value certain things are supported by a conception of human flourishing. Our lives are enriched and elevated by cultivating and exercising the capacity to appreciate art. To fail to do so reflects poorly on ourselves. To fail to value things appropriately is to embody in one's life an inferior conception of human flourishing.

These considerations support a general account of the sorts of things which are appropriately regarded as commodities. Commodities are those things which are properly treated in accordance with the norms of the modern market. We can question the application of market norms to the production, distribution, and enjoyment of a good by appealing to ethical ideals which support arguments that the good should be valued in some other way than use. Arguments of the latter sort claim that to allow certain market norms to govern our treatment of a thing expresses a mode of valuation not worthy of it. If the thing is to be valued appropriately, its production, exchange, and enjoyment must be removed from market norms and embedded in a different set of social relationships.

The Case of Commercial Surrogacy

Let us now consider the practice of commercial surrogate motherhood in the light of this theory of commodities. Surrogate motherhood as a commercial enterprise is based upon contracts involving three parties: the intended father, the broker, and the surrogate mother. The intended father agrees to pay a lawyer to find a suitable surrogate mother and make the requisite medical and legal arrangements for the conception and birth of the child, and for the transfer of legal custody to himself. The surrogate mother agrees to become impregnated with the intended father's sperm, to carry the resulting child to term, and to relinquish her parental rights to it, transferring custody to the father in return for a fee and medical expenses. Both she and her husband (if she has one) agree not to form a parent-child bond with her child and to do everything necessary to effect the transfer of the child to the intended father. At current market prices, the lawyer arranging the contract can expect to gross $15,000 from the contract, while the surrogate mother can expect a $10,000 fee. . . .

I shall argue that commercial surrogacy . . . represents an invasion of the market into a new sphere of conduct, that of specifically women's labor—that is, the labor of carrying children to term in pregnancy. When women's labor is treated as a commodity, the women who perform it are degraded. Furthermore, commercial surrogacy degrades children by reducing their status to that of commodities. Let us consider each of the goods of concern in surrogate motherhood—the child, and women's reproductive labor— to see how the commercialization of parenthood affects people's regard for them.

Children as Commodities

The most fundamental calling of parents to their children is to love them. Children are to be loved and cherished by their parents, not to be used or manipulated by them for merely personal advantage. Parental love can be understood as a passionate, unconditional commitment to nurture one's child, providing it with the care, affection, and guidance it needs to develop its capacities to maturity. This understanding of the way parents should value their children informs our interpretation of parental rights over their children. Parents' rights over their children are trusts, which they must always exercise for the sake of the child. This is not to deny that parents have their own aspirations in raising children. But the child's interests beyond subsistence are not definable independently of the flourishing of the family, which is the object of specifically parental aspirations. The proper exercise of parental rights includes those acts which promote their shared life as a family, which realize the shared interests of the parents and the child.

The norms of parental love carry implications for the ways other people should treat the relationship between parents and their children. If children are to be loved by their parents, then others should not attempt to compromise the integrity of parental love or work to suppress the emotions supporting the bond between parents and their children. If the rights to children should be understood as trusts, then if those rights are lost or relinquished, the duty of those in charge of transferring custody to others is to consult the best interests of the child.

Commercial surrogacy substitutes market norms for some of the norms of parental love. Most importantly, it requires us to understand parental rights no longer as trusts but as things more like property rights—that is, rights of use and disposal over the things owned. For in this practice the natural mother deliberately conceives a child with the intention of giving it up for material advantage. Her renunciation of parental responsibilities is not done for the child's sake, nor for the sake of fulfilling an interest she sabres with the child, but typically for her own sake (and possibly, if "altruism" is a motive, for the intended parents' sakes). She and the couple who pay her to give up her parental rights over her child thus treat her rights as a kind of property right. They thereby treat the child itself as a kind of commodity, which may be properly bought and sold.

Commercial surrogacy insinuates the norms of commerce into the parental relationship in other ways. Whereas parental love is not supposed to be conditioned upon the child having particular characteristics, consumer demand is properly responsive to the characteristics of commodities. So the surrogate industry provides opportunities to adoptive couples to specify the height, I.Q., race, and other attributes of the surrogate mother, in the expectation that these traits will be passed on to the child. Since no industry assigns agents to look after the "interests" of its commodities, no one represents the child's interests in the surrogate industry. The surrogate agency pro-

motes the adoptive parents' interests and not the child's interests where matters of custody are concerned. Finally, as the agent of the adoptive parents, the broker has the task of policing the surrogate (natural) mother's relationship to her child, using persuasion, money, and the threat of a lawsuit to weaken and destroy whatever parental love she may develop for her child.

All of these substitutions of market norms for parental norms represent ways of treating children as commodities which are degrading to them. Degradation occurs when something is treated in accordance with a lower mode of valuation than is proper to it. We value things not just "more" or "less," but in qualitatively higher and lower ways. To love or respect someone is to value her in a higher way than one would if one merely used her. Children are properly loved by their parents and respected by others. Since children are valued as mere use-objects by the mother and the surrogate agency when they are sold to others, and by the adoptive parents when they seek to conform the child's genetic makeup to their own wishes, commercial surrogacy degrades children insofar as it treats them as commodities.

One might argue that since the child is most likely to enter a loving home, no harm comes to it from permitting the natural mother to treat it as property. So the purchase and sale of infants is unobjectionable, at least from the point of view of children's interests. But the sale of an infant has an expressive significance which this argument fails to recognize. By engaging in the transfer of children by sale, all of the parties to the surrogate contract express a set of attitudes toward children which undermine the norms of parental love. They all agree in treating the ties between a natural mother and her children as properly loosened by a monetary incentive. Would it be any wonder if a child born of a surrogacy agreement feared resale by parents who have such an attitude? And a child who knew how anxious her parents were that she have the "right" genetic makeup might fear that her parent's love was contingent upon her expression of these characteristics.

The unsold children of surrogate mothers are also harmed by commercial surrogacy. The children of some surrogate mothers have reported their fears that they may be sold like their half-brother or half-sister, and express a sense of loss at being deprived of a sibling. Furthermore, the widespread acceptance of commercial surrogacy would psychologically threaten all children. For it would change the way children are valued by people (parents and surrogate brokers)—from being loved by their parents and respected by others, to being sometimes used as objects of commercial profit-making.

Proponents of commercial surrogacy have denied that the surrogate industry engages in the sale of children. For it is impossible to sell to someone what is already his own, and the child is already the father's own natural offspring. The payment to the surrogate mother is not for her child, but for her services in carrying it to term. The claim that the parties to the surrogate contract treat children as commodities, however, is based on the way they treat the *mother's* rights over her child. It is irrelevant that the natural father also has some rights over the child; what he pays for is exclusive rights to it. He would not pay her for the "service" of carrying the child to term if she refused to relinquish her parental rights to it. That the mother regards only her labor and not her child as requiring compensation is also irrelevant. No one would argue that the baker does not treat his bread as property just because he sees the income from its sale as compensation for his labor and expenses and not for the bread itself, which he doesn't care to keep.

Defenders of commercial surrogacy have also claimed that it does not differ substantially from other already accepted parental practices. In the institutions of adoption and artificial insemination by donor (AID), it is claimed, we already grant parents the right to dispose of their children. But these practices differ in significant respects from commercial surrogacy. The purpose of adoption is to provide a means for placing children in families when their parents cannot or will not discharge their parental responsibilities. It is not a sphere for the existence of a supposed parental right to dispose of one's children for profit. Even AID does not sanction the sale of fully formed human beings. The semen donor sells only a product of his body, not his child, and does not initiate the act of conception.

Two developments might seem to undermine the claim that commercial surrogacy constitutes a degrading commerce in children. The first is technological: the prospect of transplanting a human embryo into the womb of a genetically unrelated woman. If commercial surrogacy used women only as gestational mothers and not as genetic mothers, and if it was thought that only genetic and not gestational parents could properly claim that a child was "theirs," then the child born of a surrogate mother would not be hers to sell in the first place. The second is a legal development: the establishment of the proposed "consent-intent" definition of parenthood. This would declare the legal parents of a child to be whoever consented to a procedure which leads to its birth, with the intent of assuming parental responsibilities for it. This rule would define away the problem of commerce in children by depriving the surrogate mother of any legal claim to her child at all, even if it was hers both genetically and gestationally.

There are good reasons, however, not to undermine the place of genetic and gestational ties in these ways. Consider first the place of genetic ties. By upholding a system of involuntary (genetic) ties of obligation among people, even when the adults among them prefer to divide their rights and obligations in other ways, we help to secure children's interests in having an assured place in the world, which is more firm than the wills of their parents. Unlike the consent-intent rule, the principle of respecting genetic ties does not make the obligation to care for those whom one has created (intentionally or not) contingent upon an arbitrary desire to do so. It thus provides children with a set of preexisting social sanctions which give them a more secure place in the world. The genetic principle also places children in a far wider network of associations and obligations than the consent-intent rule sanctions. It supports the roles of grandparents and other relatives in the nurturing of children, and provides children with a possible focus of stability and an additional source of claims to care if their parents cannot sustain a well-functioning household.

In the next section I will defend the claims of gestational ties to children. To deny these claims, as commercial surrogacy does, is to deny the significance of reproductive labor to the mother who undergoes it and thereby to dehumanize and degrade the mother herself. Commercial surrogacy would be a corrupt practice even if it did not involve commerce in children.

WOMEN'S LABOR AS A COMMODITY

Commercial surrogacy attempts to transform what is specifically women's labor—the work of bringing forth children into the world—into a commodity. It does so by replacing the parental norms which usually govern the practice of gestating children with the economic norms which govern ordinary production processes. The application of commercial norms to women's labor reduces the surrogate mothers from persons worthy of respect and consideration to objects of mere use.

Respect and consideration are two distinct modes of valuation whose norms are violated by the practices of the surrogate industry. To respect a person is to treat her in accordance with principles she rationally accepts—principles consistent with the protection of her autonomy and her rational interests. To treat a person with consideration is to respond with sensitivity to her and to her emotional relations with others, refraining from manipulating or denigrating these for one's own purposes. Given the understanding of respect as a dispassionate, impersonal regard for people's interests, a different ethical concept—consideration—is needed to capture the engaged and sensitive regard we should have for people's emotional relationships. The failure of consideration on the part of the other parties to the surrogacy contract explains the judgment that the contract is not simply disrespectful of the surrogate mother, but callous as well.

The application of economic norms to the sphere of women's labor violates women's claims to respect and consideration in three ways. First, by requiring the surrogate mother to repress whatever parental love she feels for the child, these norms convert women's labor into a form of alienated labor. Second, by manipulating and denying legitimacy to the surrogate mother's evolving perspective on her own pregnancy, the norms of the market degrade her. Third, by taking advantage of the surrogate mother's noncommercial motivations without offering anything but what the norms of commerce demand in return, these norms leave her open to exploitation. The fact that these problems arise in the attempt to commercialize the labor of bearing children shows that women's labor is not properly regarded as a commodity.

The key to understanding these problems is the normal role of the emotions in noncommercialized pregnancies. Pregnancy is not simply a biological process but also a social practice. Many social expectations and considerations surround women's gestational labor, marking it off as an occasion for the parents to prepare themselves to welcome a new life into their family. For example, obstetricians use ultrasound not simply for diagnostic purposes but also to encourage maternal bonding with the fetus. We can all recognize that it is good, although by no means inevitable, for loving bonds to be established between the mother and her child during this period.

In contrast with these practices, the surrogate industry follows the putting-out system of manufacturing. It provides some of the raw materials of production (the father's sperm) to the surrogate mother, who then engages in production of the child. Although her labor is subject to periodic supervision by her doctors and by the surrogate agency, the agency does not have physical control over the product of her labor as firms using the factory system do. Hence, as in all putting-out systems, the surrogate industry faces the problem of extracting the final product from the mother. This problem is exacerbated by the fact that the social norms surrounding pregnancy are designed to encourage parental love for the child. The surrogate industry addresses this problem by requiring the mother to engage in a form of emotional labor. In the surrogate contract, she agrees not to form or to attempt to form a parent-child relationship with her offspring. Her labor is alienated, because she must divert it from the end which the social practices of pregnancy rightly promote—an emotional bond with her child. The surrogate contract thus replaces a norm of parenthood, that during pregnancy one create a loving attachment to one's child, with a norm of commercial production, that the producer shall not form any special emotional ties to her product.

The demand to deliberately alienate oneself from one's love for one's own child is a demand which can reasonably and decently be made of no one. Unless we were to remake pregnancy into a form of drudgery which is only performed for a wage, there is every reason to expect that many women who do sign a surrogate contract will, despite this fact, form a loving attachment to the child they bear. For this is what the social practices surrounding pregnancy encourage. Treating women's labor as just another kind of commercial production process violates the precious emotional ties which the mother may rightly and properly establish with her "product," the child, and thereby violates her claims to consideration. . . .

The treatment and interpretation of surrogate mothers' grief raises the deepest problems of degradation. Most surrogate mothers experience grief upon giving up their children—in 10 percent of cases, seriously enough to require therapy. Their grief is not compensated by the $10,000 fee they receive. Grief is not an intelligible response to a successful deal, but rather reflects the subject's judgment that she has suffered a grave and personal loss. Since not all cases of grief resolve themselves into cases of regret, it may be that some surrogate mothers do not regard their grief, in retrospect, as reflecting an authentic judgment on their part. But in the circumstances of emotional manipulation which pervade the surrogate industry, it is difficult to determine which interpretation of her grief more truly reflects the perspective of the surrogate mother. By insinuating a trivializing interpretation of her emotional responses to the prospect of losing her child, the surrogate agency may be able to manipulate her into accepting her fate without too much fuss, and may even succeed in substituting its interpretation of her emotions for her own. Since she has already signed a contract to perform emotional labor—to express or repress emotions which are dictated by the interests of the surrogate industry—this might not be a difficult task. A considerate treatment of the mothers' grief, on the other hand, would take the evaluative basis of their grief seriously.

Some defenders of commercial surrogacy demand that the provision for terminating the surrogate mother's parental rights in her child be legally enforceable, so that peace of mind for the adoptive parents can be secured. But the surrogate industry makes no corresponding provision for securing the peace of mind of the surrogate. She is expected to assume the risk of a transformation of her ethical and emotional perspective on herself and her child with the same impersonal detachment with which a futures trader assumes the risk of a fluctuation in the price of pork bellies. By applying the market norms of enforcing contracts to the surrogate mother's case, commercial surrogacy treats a moral transformation as if it were merely an economic change.

The manipulation of the surrogate mother's emotions which is inherent in the surrogate parenting contract also leaves women open to grave forms of exploitation. A kind of exploitation occurs when one party to a transaction is oriented toward the exchange of "gift" values, while the other party operates in accordance with the norms of the market exchange of commodities. Gift values, which include love, gratitude, and appreciation of others, cannot be bought or obtained through piecemeal calculations of individual advantage. Their exchange requires a repudiation of a self-interested attitude, a willingness to give gifts to others without demanding some specific equivalent good in return each time one gives. The surrogate mother often operates according to the norms of gift relationships. The surrogate agency, on the other hand, follows market norms. Its job is to get the best deal for its clients and itself, while leaving the surrogate mother to look after her own interests as best as she can. This situation puts the surrogate agencies in a position to manipulate the surrogate mothers' emotions to gain favorable terms for themselves. For example, agencies screen prospective surrogate mothers for submissiveness, and emphasize to them the importance of the motives of generosity and love. When applicants question some of the terms of the contract, the broker sometimes intimidates them by questioning their character and morality: if they were really generous and loving they would not be so solicitous about their own interests.

Some evidence supports the claim that most surrogate mothers are motivated by emotional needs and vulnerabilities which lead them to view their labor as a form of gift and not a purely commercial exchange. Only 1 percent of applicants to surrogate agencies would become surrogate mothers for money alone; the others have emotional as well as financial reasons for applying. One psychiatrist believes that most, if not all, of the 35 percent of applicants who had had a previous abortion or given up a child for adoption wanted to become surrogate mothers in order to resolve their guilty feelings or deal with their unresolved loss by going through a process of losing a child again. Women who feel that giving up another child is an effective way to punish themselves for past abortions, or a form of therapy for their emotional problems, are not likely to resist manipulation by surrogate brokers.

Many surrogate mothers see pregnancy as a way to feel "adequate," "appreciated," or "special." In other words, these women feel inadequate, unappreciated, or unadmired when they are not pregnant. Lacking the power to achieve some worthwhile status in their own right, they must subordinate themselves to others' definitions of their proper place (as baby factories) in order to get from them the appreciation they need to attain a sense of self-worth. But the sense of self-worth one can attain under such circumstances is precarious and ultimately self-defeating. For example, those who seek gratitude on the part of the adoptive parents and some opportunity to share the joys of seeing their children grow discover all too often that the adoptive parents want nothing to do with them. For while the surrogate mother sees in the arrangement some basis for establishing the personal ties she needs to sustain her emotionally, the adoptive couple sees it as an impersonal commercial contract, one of whose main advantages to them is that all ties between them and the surrogate are ended once the terms of the contract are fulfilled. To them, her presence is a threat to marital unity and a competing object for the child's affections.

These considerations should lead us to question the model of altruism which is held up to women by the surrogacy industry. It is a strange form of altruism which demands such radical self-effacement, alienation from those whom one benefits, and the subordination of one's body, health, and emotional life to the independently defined interests of others. Why should this model of "altruism" be held up

to *women?* True altruism does not involve such subordination, but rather the autonomous and self-confident exercise of skill, talent, and judgment. (Consider the dedicated doctor.) The kind of altruism we see admired in surrogate mothers involves a lack of self-confidence, a feeling that one can be truly worthy only through self-effacement. This model of altruism, far from affirming the freedom and dignity of women, seems all too conveniently designed to keep their sense of self-worth hostage to the interests of a more privileged class.

The primary distortions which arise from treating women's labor as a commodity—the surrogate mother's alienation from loved ones, her degradation, and her exploitation—stem from a common source. This is the failure to acknowledge and treat appropriately the surrogate mother's emotional engagement with her labor. Her labor is alienated, because she must suppress her emotional ties with her own child, and may be manipulated into reinterpreting these ties in a trivializing way. She is degraded, because her independent ethical perspective is denied, or demoted to the status of a cash sum. She is exploited, because her emotional needs and vulnerabilities are not treated as characteristics which call for consideration, but as factors which may be manipulated to encourage her to make a grave self-sacrifice to the broker's and adoptive couple's advantage. These considerations provide strong grounds for sustaining the claims of women's labor to its "product," the child. The attempt to redefine parenthood so as to strip women of parental claims to the children they bear does violence to their emotional engagement with the project of bringing children into the world.

COMMERCIAL SURROGACY, FREEDOM, AND THE LAW

In the light of these ethical objections to commercial surrogacy, what position should the law take on the practice? At the very least, surrogate contracts should not be enforceable. Surrogate mothers should not be forced to relinquish their children if they have formed emotional bonds with them. Any other treatment of women's ties to the children they bear is degrading.

But I think these arguments support the stronger conclusion that commercial surrogate contracts should be illegal, and that surrogate agencies who arrange such contracts should be subject to criminal penalties. Commercial surrogacy constitutes a degrading and harmful traffic in children, violates the dignity of women, and subjects both children and women to a serious risk of exploitation.

NOTE

1. See, for example, Gena Corea, *The Mother Machine* (New York: Harper and Row, 1985), pp. 216, 219; Angela Holder, "Surrogate Motherhood: Babies for Fun and Profit," *Case and Comment* 90 (1985): 3–11: and Margaret Jane Radin, "Market Inalienability," *Harvard Law Review* 100 (June 1987): 1849–1937.

Critics

RICHARD J. ARNESON

Commodification and Commercial Surrogacy

Consider . . . Elizabeth Anderson's view that "to say that something is properly regarded as a commodity is to claim that the norms of the market are appropriate for regulating its production, exchange, and enjoyment."[1] Leaving aside the quibble that there are no "market norms" of enjoyment, I find this assertion ambiguous. It could mean that if something is a *proper commodity*, market norms *alone* are applicable to its production and exchange (call this the "strong sense"), or it could mean that if something is a proper commodity, market norms—perhaps along with other norms—are applicable to its production and exchange (call this the "weak sense"). I doubt that anything is a proper commodity in the strong sense. For instance, it is perfectly appropriate that strawberries are sold on a free and open market *and* properly appreciated for their color, taste, and other aesthetic qualities, some of which are reliably detectable only by strawberry cognoscenti. But from the fact that

non-market norms are properly applicable to a type of good it does not follow that the good is not a proper commodity in the weak sense.

More important is the following: From the premise that from some reasonable standpoint the nature of a good is such that it should not be exchanged on the market it cannot be inferred that the state should remove the good from the sphere of market exchange. For it may be that from other equally reasonable standpoints the good is legitimately the object of market trading. The state cannot simply associate itself with one viewpoint shared by some citizens and denied by others. The state must be able to justify its policies by appeal to principles that offer a reasonable way of adjudicating among conflicting viewpoints in a diverse democracy.

In passing, I note that even if it were agreed that a good deserves to be treated in accordance with its

From Richard J. Arneson, "Commodification and Commercial Surrogacy," *Philosophy and Public Affairs* 21, no. 2 (1992): 132–64. Some notes and some parts of the text have been deleted. Reprinted by permission of Princeton University Press.

worth and that such treatment is not guaranteed by permitting its exchange on the market, it still would not follow that the good should be made market-inalienable. The market may be the best that we can do so far as ensuring appropriately respectful treatment is concerned.

Allowing a class of goods to be distributed by market exchange permits their sale by persons who do not truly appreciate the goods to persons who do not truly appreciate them either. But the existence of a market for a good does not guarantee unappreciative use. That depends on the tastes and resources of potential consumers and producers. Indeed, an unregulated market displays a tendency to place goods in the hands of those who truly appreciate them. I myself have little understanding or appreciation of Elvis Presley memorabilia, and the market effectively prevents unappreciative persons like me from retaining ownership of them. The market price is driven up by those who have the greatest appreciation of these relics. Of course, this tendency for ownership and appreciation to coincide when goods are freely exchangeable is quite weak, in that willingness to pay is limited by ability to pay. To evaluate the market on this score one must compare it with feasible institutional alternatives such as bureaucratic assignment. One must also evaluate nonmarket distribution mechanisms in the same way. The state may attempt to foster the widespread appreciation of great works of art by displaying them in public museums. This method of distribution allows tourists to degrade classic works of art by applying to them utterly inappropriate standards of interior decoration ("Honey, that Delacroix would look swell in our living room next to our pink sofa, against our velvet wallpaper"). This does not mean that it is deplorable for the state to exhibit great art in ways that permit its degradation. Public display at nominal cost to viewers with guards monitoring the viewers might be the best overall means for fostering widespread aesthetically sophisticated appreciation of the art.

In short, even if securing a particular mode of appropriate respect and valuation of a type of good is deemed to be of top priority, it might be that commodification of the good is the best means to this end. But in most cases, where citizens reasonably maintain quite divergent views about the nature of appropriate treatment of a type of good, the state should regulate the production and distribution of the good in a way that respects this diversity, and here tolerance of commodification is often, though not always, the best diversity-respecting mechanism. . . .

COMMERCIAL SURROGACY AND HARMS TO CHILDREN

One set of arguments against commercial surrogacy concerns harms and benefits to children who might be affected by the practice.

According to its detractors, commercial surrogacy substitutes market norms for norms of parental love. This same encroachment of market norms is threatened by proposals to relax the present constraints of adoption law so as to permit expanded market trading between childless couples who want a baby and women who are contemplating bringing a fetus to term and who might be induced to relinquish the child at birth for a price. These intrusions of the market into parental choice are sometimes called "baby-selling."

Notice first of all that the term *baby-selling* in this context is a misnomer. What those who advocate a market in surrogacy and adoption services propose is that the right and obligation to assume parental responsibility for the care of a particular child should be marketable. This may be a good or a bad idea but is not remotely a proposal for baby-selling.

This claim might be challenged by the observation that talk of buying and selling does presuppose that the object of exchange is private property, but this can be a matter of degree. After all, we do speak of "selling pets" even though there are legal and moral limits on what one may do to a pet one "owns." Pets are not privately owned in the same full sense that cars and toothbrushes are. But this observation does not establish the propriety of the label "baby-selling" for the practice of buying and selling parental rights and responsibilities. A parent does not in any sense own her child even if she acquires parental rights and responsibilities by purchase. For any entity, an owner with a property right in that entity has some (perhaps limited) legitimate freedom to dispose of it at will, according to her whim or pleasure, but parents do not have even limited rights to dispose of their children at will. The rights that parents have to control their children's behavior and to make major decisions affecting their lives while they are young are assigned to parents for the sake of their children's welfare and are supposed to be exercised for the good of their children. The point of parental rights is to enable parents to carry out their obligations to care for their children. These parental rights are not property rights, so buying and selling these rights does not equate with buying and selling a child.

Notice also that even the most extreme advocates of a greater role for markets advocate a very restricted market in the right to parent. After all, the normal presumption in favor of free trade does not apply in this case. Normally, if all parties voluntarily agree to an exchange of goods, the presumption is that all parties benefit from the exchange, so unless third parties are harmed, the sale should be permitted. But if the good being exchanged is the right and obligation to be the parent of a particular infant, that very infant cannot be a consenting party to the transaction, so there can be no presumption from the voluntary character of the transaction that it serves the interests of the infant. There is a prima facie case for free trade here only if the market is regulated in such a way as to ensure that the child who is indirectly the object of the transaction is not wrongfully harmed.

WOMEN'S LABOR

Aside from alleged harms to children and alleged harms to all of us that are supposed to flow from the commodification of childbearing, opponents of paid surrogacy point to the intrinsic indignity and perhaps indecency of the practice from the standpoint of the woman who is paid to bear children. Capron and Radin state that we should not permit women to become "paid breeding stock, like farm animals." They further observe, "The role of paid breeder is incompatible with a society in which individuals are valued for themselves and are aided in achieving a full sense of human well-being and potentiality."[2] Why think this? Hardly anyone, to my knowledge, believes that there is anything degrading about surrogacy when motivated

by altruism or other friendly noncommercial aims. There is surely nothing wrong with a woman volunteering to become a surrogate mother for her infertile sister, who will at birth by prior agreement become the child's mother. Nor is there anything necessarily undesirable or unfair in the acceptance of such offers. Why, then, is it wrong, or degrading, or intrinsically harmful to the surrogate, if she is paid for the service?

The answer sometimes offered is that women's labor—the labor of pregnancy and childbearing—is peculiarly intimate and personal, somewhat like making love. Hence performing women's labor for pay is degrading and alienating, so much so that it is reasonable to judge that the person who engages in commercial surrogacy is harming herself, whatever might be her own perspective on this engagement.

This line of argument against commercial surrogacy is matched by a parallel argument against legal tolerance of prostitution. Consider Elizabeth Anderson's views on the baseness of prostitution: "Sexuality as a specifically human, shared good cannot be achieved except through gift exchange; market motives cannot provide it. The failure of reciprocity implied in the sale of sexual services signifies not simply a failure to realize a good, but a degradation of the prostitute, whose sexuality is reduced to the status of a mere service to the customer: sexuality is equated with the lesser good of money."[3]

But, first of all, it is not clear why Anderson thinks that the distinction between freely given sex and prostitution warrants the judgment that prostitution is base and should be forbidden rather than the judgment that prostitution, though good, is less good than freely given sex. The same question would arise if the same claim were made about commercial surrogacy. One could accept what the quotation above asserts—except for the suitability of the label "degradation"—without accepting that the practice should be subject to either moral condemnation or legal prohibition.

One should recognize that the ideal of freely given sex is itself controversial, and, I claim, would remain controversial even after full rational deliberation with full information among the disputants. In a diverse democracy, citizens affirm many different and conflicting conceptions of the good in sexual matters. Given such deep-seated disagreement, an argument for the conclusion that society should adopt a posture of condemnation or prohibition toward some sexual practice must go beyond the appeal to one controversial ideal among others. Again, the same point holds with respect to a train of thought that concludes that commercial surrogacy should be banned.

The argument under review is that women's labor is noble labor and performance of noble labor for pay is degrading, so commercial surrogacy and other forms of paid women's labor should be banned. Besides the difficulties already canvassed, a further problem with this argument is that it does not identify women's labor as unique and in need of unique legal handling. Many kinds of work thought by many of us to be noble labor are nevertheless regarded as appropriately done for money, and no widely held norm in market societies denigrates the performance of noble labor for pay. One wonders why noble women's labor should be treated differently.

This is not to deny that some types of labor are partly insulated from the economic marketplace. By and large, religious sermons are not bought and sold on the market. Rather, a congregation customarily pays a minister who preaches for free to all who come to church at stated times. Churchgoers are expected to donate money to help defray the expenses of the church, but the nonmarket organization of religious services expresses the feelings of churchgoers that sacred matters should be kept somehow distinct from worldly affairs. The point to note here is that what sustains this partial separation of religious life and ordinary business affairs is the devotion of the faithful, not any legal prohibition.

In point of fact, from what we know of women who have volunteered to be commercial surrogates, many are not acting as purely self-interested profit-maximizers, but are moved by mixed motives, including empathy for the infertile couple they hope to help. One commercial surrogate explained her choice in these terms: "I'm not going to cure cancer or become Mother Theresa, but a baby is one thing I can sort of give back, something I can give to someone who couldn't have it any other way."[4] It strikes me that one has to be quite dogmatic to insist a priori that the personal experience of commercial surrogacy that this woman is describing must have been an instance of alienated, degrading labor.

Elizabeth Anderson argues interestingly for the position that I am claiming is dogmatic. She asserts that the commodification of women's labor—the labor of childbearing—violates women's claims to respect and consideration in three ways. First, permitting women's labor to be sold allows the exploitation of the potential surrogate's altruistic motives in seeking a surrogacy arrangement. The woman will be paid less by virtue of her partially altruistic motivation than she would be in its absence. Second, a surrogacy contract necessarily denies legitimacy to the pregnant woman's own evolving perspective on her pregnancy. Third, the contract turns women's labor into alienated labor by requiring the suppression of the feelings of parental love and attachment that the pregnant woman will predictably experience. Call these the failure of reciprocity, denial of perspective, and suppression of feeling problems.

Failure of Reciprocity

The claim is that the commercial surrogate's desire to help the commissioning couple puts her in a position of vulnerability to exploitation. That the potential commercial surrogate is likely to be poor and the commissioning couple well-to-do exacerbates the former's weak bargaining position.

But so long as there is no fraud or misrepresentation, I do not believe that the failure to reciprocate altruism is necessarily wrongful. If a surrogate mother expects lasting emotional ties to the commissioning couple and she is misled about the chances that long-term ties will develop, she is wronged. But it is reasonable to suppose that surrogacy contracts can be regulated to minimize the dangers of such wrong. (One might require that both parties to the contract engage legal counsel, or receive psychological counseling.) But the fact that someone is willing to accept a lower price for provision of a service because she altruistically cares about those who will benefit from the service does not tend to show that the purchase price is unjust. (Notice that if altruists and purely self-interested agents compete for trade, the altruists need not do worse than the egoists. If those who purchase babysitting services are willing to pay more for a babysitter who truly cares for babies [and provided the purchasers can reliably distinguish caring from noncaring babysitters], then the market will compensate caring babysitters more highly than egoistic babysitters.) At any rate, the failure of altruism issue at most raises a question about how to ensure fair pricing of surrogacy services. This concern might motivate setting a minimum price for the service or regulation of some other sort, but not prohibition.

Denial of Perspective

Any contract ties down the future and determines one's future behavior to some extent. That is what contracts are for. Signing a contract for future performance does not deny that one's views might change in the interim. Undergoing a change of one's perspective, however, does not change the terms of the contract. Our interest in having a device for providing mutual assurances of this sort is what motivates the institution of contract.

In this respect the problems that surrogacy contracts can engender are similar to the difficulties that any contract can cause. In particular, the idea that in case of a breach of contract for labor services, specific performance of the contracted-for labor should not be enforced perhaps applies with special force to surrogacy arrangements. There are two instances of changed views of the surrogate mother that raise special concerns. One is that surrogacy contracts might require amniocentesis and stipulate that the surrogate mother is to obtain an abortion if fetal abnormalities are revealed. I take it to be uncontroversial that courts should not require a surrogate to obtain an abortion against her will, regardless of contractual stipulation. For essentially the same reason, the surrogate mother should have the inalienable right to terminate the pregnancy by abortion against the wishes of the commissioning parties and against any contrary terms in the contract.

A second special concern is that the surrogate mother might change her mind during the pregnancy regarding her decision to turn over the baby to the commissioning couple. It is clearly desirable that the law clearly delineate rights and obligations for such scenarios, to minimize the occurrence of bitter lawsuits. The main alternatives appear to be to decide as a matter of public policy either (a) that whatever terms the parties have voluntarily agreed to will be enforced or (b) that the surrogate mother shall retain the right to keep custody of the child she bears until she relinquishes him physically to the commissioning couple after birth. The argument for (b) is that it is hard for a woman to predict how she will feel about relinquishing the child and that if she eventually wishes to retain custody it would be cruel to snatch the child from her arms.

The call between (a) and (b) seems to me close. Sometimes (b) is urged on grounds of consistency with adoption law, which in most jurisdictions does not regard as binding a prebirth agreement to give up a child for adoption. Adoption law forbids offering financial inducement to a pregnant woman or new mother to give up her baby for adoption, and also prohibits acceptance of such offers by parents. I suppose that if the assignment of the child to parents after birth in surrogacy arrangements is held to be legitimately determined by the terms of the contract, adoption law should probably be liberalized somewhat to bring it into alignment with surrogacy law.

Nonetheless, the situation of a pregnant woman considering whether to give up her child for adoption can be distinguished from the situation of a surrogate mother considering whether to breach the contract. First, we can agree that it would be painfully confusing for many prospective parents, who either have deliberately brought about a pregnancy or simply find themselves with a child in prospect, to be faced with a choice between keeping their child and relinquishing the child to others for money. Offering financial inducement to relinquish one's child in this way might sensibly be prohibited in order to prevent such painful confusion. Similarly, if after the onset of pregnancy a woman decides to relinquish custody of her child, she might sensibly be given the inalienable legal right to change her mind at least up to the point at which the child is born and she has physically relinquished it. The commercial surrogacy case is different because the commissioned child would not exist were it not for the contractual arrangement. The initial intention on the part of the surrogate mother is to assist in producing a child for whom others are to assume parental responsibility. Moreover, this child-creating intention has taken the form of a contractual promise. For the same reason, the commissioning couple has a greater legitimate stake in the outcome of a commercial surrogate pregnancy. The deliberate act of the commissioning couple has brought this child into existence. If they keep their part of the bargain and are not reasonably suspected to be unfit parents, they arguably should get custody of the child even if the surrogate has a change of heart, just as a change of heart on the part of the commissioning couple would not release them from their obligation to become the parents of the child born of the surrogacy arrangement. But on the other side there is the hardship to the surrogate. Perhaps the issue should be decided depending on whether the loss stemming from the lessened value of a voidable contract to commissioning couples plus the loss to couples who are disappointed when the surrogate reverses her decision are outweighed by the loss to the surrogates who would have to give up the children they have borne against their will if specific performance of surrogacy contracts is enforced.

Suppression of Feeling

To repeat: The contract does not require the surrogate mother to feel in certain ways, but rather to act in certain ways. The contract might require the surrogate woman to act against her feelings in order to fulfill its terms. To this extent the labor of fulfilling the contract might turn out to be alienated labor. But in a liberal society (whether capitalist or socialist) alienated labor is not forbidden. Citizens should be left free to arrange their work lives in ways that trade off alienated labor against other benefits according to their own notions of acceptable compromises among diverse goals and values. . . .

NOTES

1. Elizabeth A. Anderson, "Is Women's Labor a Commodity?" *Philosophy & Public Affairs* 19, no. 1 (Winter 1990): 72. See also Elizabeth S. Anderson, "The Ethical Limitations of the Market," *Economics and Philosophy* 6 (1990): 179–205.

2. A. M. Capron and M. J. Radin, "Choosing Family Law over Contract Law as a Paradigm for Surrogate Motherhood," *Law, Medicine, and Health Care* 16 (1988): 36.

3. Anderson, "The Ethical Limitations of the Market," p. 188.

4. Barbara Kantrowitz, "Who Keeps Baby M?" *Newsweek,* 19 January 1987, pp. 44–49, as cited in Martha A. Field, *Surrogate Motherhood* (Cambridge, Mass.: Harvard University Press, 1988), p. 20.

ALAN WERTHEIMER

Two Questions About Surrogacy and Exploitation

. . . Elizabeth Anderson says that "a kind of exploitation occurs when one party to a transaction is oriented toward the exchange of 'gift' values, while the other party operates in accordance with the norms of the market."[1] But *incommensurability*, as such, does not take us very far. First, to say that the values exchanged in a transaction are incommensurable does not establish that a market transaction is wrong, at least not without further argument. The permissibility of market transactions does not require that the goods exchanged be commensurable on a single metric. It requires that the parties transact voluntarily

From Alan Wertheimer, "Two Questions About Surrogacy and Exploitation," *Philosophy and Public Affairs* 21, no. 3. (Summer 1992): 211–39. Some notes and some parts of the text have been deleted. Reprinted by permission of Princeton University Press.

and, perhaps, with a (reasonable) belief that the value received is at least as great as the value given. One can and (arguably) should be able to buy or sell a "priceless" painting without claiming that its value is "commensurate" with the money that is paid. Second, even if incommensurability provides a reason for thinking that a transaction is *wrong,* it does not entail that a party's interests are negatively affected by the transaction. So more will have to be said if incommensurability is going to support the claim that surrogacy is exploitative.

Incommensurability aside, it is widely thought that some goods and services are appropriately exchanged for money whereas others are not. On the one hand, automobiles, houses, books, television sets, and at least *some* forms of labor can legitimately be exchanged for money. By contrast, there are some things that should *not* be exchanged for money—citizenship, human beings, criminal justice, marriage rights, exemption from military service, and perhaps other forms of human labor (e.g., sexual and procreational labor). On this view, surrogacy is exploitative not because it comes too cheap, but because it *commodifies* that which should not be commodified.

If procreational labor should not be commodified, does it follow that surrogacy is harmful to the surrogate? It is not clear. It may have been wrong to commodify exemptions from military service during the Civil War, when citizens were allowed to pay $300 to purchase the services of a substitute, but it was hardly harmful to those who *bought* exemptions. And while the commodification of exemptions may have *caused* harm—by injury or death—to the substitutes, it is much less clear that the commodification of exemptions, as such, *constituted* a harm to them. And so we must ask whether the commodification of the surrogate's labor is (1) harmful, (2) harmful *because* it is wrong, or (3) wrong but not harmful (to the surrogate).

It may be thought that the commodification of the surrogate's labor is *psychologically* harmful to her, but the extent to which that is so is an empirical question, and little evidence has been adduced. We might say that the commodification of procreational labor is *objectively* harmful to the surrogate's interests, even if she does not feel harmed. This could occur in two ways.

First, as with nonmoral forms of objective harm, we might say that a woman has an interest in not being commodified, degraded, or treated merely as a means. But to say that a woman may be objectively harmed is one thing; to identify the nature of that harm is another. And it is not quite clear in what ways a woman is thought to be harmed by commodification or degradation, in the absence of the psychological connection.

Second, it might be claimed that a person can lose the respect of others or be degraded in *their* eyes, even if she does not lose *self*-respect or become degraded in her own eyes. So to the extent that a person has an interest in the way she is regarded by others, surrogacy may injure those interests. But that raises at least two points. First, it is not clear that surrogacy actually does have these effects. Second, to the extent that these effects stem solely from the way surrogacy is regarded by the society—as a matter of fact and without separate normative justification—it is not clear that it represents a basis for condemning the practice rather than a basis for condemning society's reaction. Although homosexuality was (or is) a basis for a loss of social respect, this provides no reason to condemn homosexuality.

In any case, even if commodification or degradation constituted objective harms to the surrogate, it cannot show that surrogacy is harmful to the surrogate, all things considered. Surrogacy would produce a *net* harm to the surrogate only if the degree of harm that resulted from commodification or degradation was *greater* than the benefits that she received *from* the compensation.

But there is a second way in which commodification or degradation might be regarded as harmful to the surrogate. It may constitute a *moral* harm, and this in one or both of two ways. First, we may harm someone by violating her *rights,* independent of any other physical, economic, or psychological harm. A trespasser harms the property owner by violating her rights to exclusive use of her property, even though there is no "ordinary" harm to her property. A man harms a woman by fondling her without her consent, even if the touching causes no physical pain or lasting psychological damage. If a woman has a right not to have her labor commodified, then surrogacy is harmful precisely because it is a violation of her rights. The problem here, of course, is that many acts that would constitute a violation of B's rights if done without B's consent are not rights violations if done with B's consent. It is no violation of a person's rights if her property is entered with her consent or if she is fondled with her consent. More generally, we do not treat a person *merely* as a means rather than an end-in-herself if we treat her in a certain way only if she consents to be treated in that way. Thus commodification is no obvious violation of this Kantian maxim if the commodification is consensual—absent some additional argument, for example, that the rights involved are inalienable or that consent given under objectionable background conditions is not sufficiently voluntary.

Note

1. Elizabeth S. Anderson, "Is Women's Labor a Commodity?" *Philosophy & Public Affairs* 19, no. 1 (Winter 1990): 71–92. For a critique of this view, see Richard J. Arneson, "Commodification and Commercial Surrogacy," *Philosophy & Public Affairs* 21, no. 2 (Spring 1992): 132–64.

16

Is Causing Overpopulation Wrong?

Parfit and His Critics

Suppose that you are put in charge of a developing nation. Your sole concern is to increase the happiness of your fellow citizens. Two advisors approach you with conflicting recommendations about how to achieve this goal. The first advisor tells you that the number one obstacle to raising your country's standard of living is overpopulation. He encourages you to slow the country's rate of population growth so that you can increase the average level of happiness of your people. The second advisor admits that if you reduce the rate of population growth, the *average* level of well-being in your country will go up. But, he points out, if you dramatically increase the rate of population growth, the *total* amount of happiness that your country contains will actually be greater. If you aim for a much larger total population, he says, each individual person in the population will not be very happy, but there will be so many barely happy people that the total amount of happiness in the country will be greater than it would be if there were far fewer (though individually happier) people. Look at it this way, the second advisor says. Compare two hypothetical populations, which we can call simply "A" and "B." B has twice as many people as A. Let's say that A has 10 million people and B has 20 million people. The average level of happiness is higher in A than in B, but it is less than twice as high. Let's say that everyone in A has 10 units of happiness while everyone in B has only 7 units. It's true that the average level of happiness is higher in A than in B. The average is 10 units of happiness in A and 7 units of happiness in B, after all, and 10 is greater than 7. But the total amount of happiness is nonetheless higher in B than in A. A would contain 10 million people with 10 units of happiness each for a total of 100 million units of happiness, but B would contain 20 million people with 7 units of happiness each for a total of 140 million units of happiness. Since you care about the happiness of your country, the second advisor concludes, you should want to create more happiness rather than less, and so you should aim for a future in which there are a tremendous number of people, each of whom is just a little happy but who, collectively, will make for a happier country than one with a smaller, though more affluent, population.

If you are like virtually everyone, you will think that the first advisor's suggestion is far more reasonable than the second advisor's. When you care about the happiness of your country, on this account, what you should really care about is the *average* level of well-being of your citizens, not the *total* amount of happiness that the country as a whole contains. You will think it absurd to drive the standard of living in your country down by producing vastly larger numbers of people, and you will think this absurd even if the sum total of all of their individual levels of happiness will be greater than the total produced by a smaller population with a much higher average quality of life. In short, if you are like most people, you will think it is obvious that A would be a morally better choice than B.

Derek Parfit is not like most people. In his 1984 book, *Reasons and Persons,* which is widely regarded as one of the most important works of philosophy of the twentieth century, Parfit presented an argument that seems to prove that A would not be better than B. Indeed, it seems to show that B would be better than A and that, even more incredibly, an even bigger population with an even lower standard of living would be even better still, as long as there were enough people in it. A world Z in which each person's life was just barely better than no life at all would be better than A or B, that is, in which people live quite good lives, as long as there were a sufficiently large number of people in Z to create a higher total amount of happiness than in A or B. Parfit referred to this result as the "Repugnant Conclusion." As the name indicates, Parfit did not really mean to endorse the claim that the conclusion is true. But he did mean to endorse the claim that there is a surprisingly powerful argument that seems to lead unavoidably to it. And in the years since Parfit introduced what he called the "Mere Addition Paradox," the paradox has prompted a wide variety of attempted solutions but no real consensus among philosophers about which approach, if any, is to be preferred in attempting to resolve it.

Parfit's argument, and the many responses that it has provoked, is at times complex and difficult. For this reason, it is rarely included in textbooks that are primarily aimed at introductory-level students. Because of the tremendous importance of the subject, however, as well as the great prominence of Parfit's philosophical work, we have chosen to include a small sampling of the discussion of the Mere Addition Paradox here as a way of at least introducing the reader to this deep and puzzling problem. In the featured article, excerpted from a longer discussion of the subject, Parfit lays out the basic puzzle. Referring to the descriptions and diagrams contained in Parfit's article, readers should focus in particular on three crucial claims that Parfit makes: that what he calls "A+" is at least as good as A, that what he calls "Divided B" is better than A+, and that what he calls "B" is the same as Divided B. If all three of these claims are true, then it seems to follow inescapably that B is better than A. If B is the same as something (Divided B), which is better than something (A+), which is at least as good as A, after all, then B seems clearly to be better than A. But this, in turn, seems to mean that you should aim to increase the total amount of happiness in the country you are in charge of rather than the average amount of happiness, even though this means driving the standard of living down, and this result seems clearly to be unacceptable.

The responses that Parfit's argument has generated are often quite lengthy and sophisticated. In the two response pieces that are very briefly excerpted here, we try to give the reader at least some sense of some of the options that seem to be available in trying to diffuse the force of Parfit's paradox. Both responses attempt to refute the key claim that A+ would be at least as good as A, though they do so in very different ways. In the first response piece, Thomas Hurka points to a few cases in which the "mere addition" of something that is perfectly good in itself can still make things worse than no addition at all. Adding some perfectly good paintings to an art gallery that contains only masterpieces, for example, might make the gallery worse rather than better. In the same sort of way, he suggests, the addition of some lives that are in themselves worth living could be a bad thing by bringing the average level of happiness down even if at the same time their addition made the total level of happiness in a given population go up. In the second response piece, Don Locke suggests a very different reason that might be given for preferring A to A+. Drawing on a version of the kind of contractarian moral theory that we briefly explained in section 4.5.2 of the Introduction to this book, Locke argues that rational contractors, making a choice between A and A+ under suitably appropriate conditions, would select A over A+. If we end up agreeing with Parfit that A+ is at least as good as A, the rest of his argument can seem virtually impossible to resist. Hurka and Locke, then, although in different ways, defend what may prove to be the best strategy available for defeating Parfit's argument and avoiding his Repugnant Conclusion.

Questions for Consideration

In trying to think critically about Parfit's paradox, readers should first focus clearly on the specific steps that lead to it.

- What does Parfit mean by "A" and "A+"? Why does he think that A+ would be at least as good as A? Can you think of any reasons to prefer A to A+?
- What does Parfit mean by "Divided B"? Why does he think that Divided B would be better than A+? Can you think of any reasons to prefer Divided B to A+?
- What does Parfit mean by "B"? Why does he think that B is the same as Divided B? Can you think of any reasons to prefer one to the other?
- What does Parfit mean by the "Repugnant Conclusion"? Why does it seem to follow from the claim that B is better than A? Could there be a way to accept that B is better than A but still reject the Repugnant Conclusion?
- What does Hurka think is the significance of his examples of the art gallery and the boxing career? Are these cases sufficiently like the cases of A and A+? What differences are there? Are these differences relevant?
- Why does Locke think that rational contractors would prefer A to A+? Does this seem to be correct? Does it seem to be relevant to deciding which one really is better? Which would you choose?
- Parfit's argument depends on the assumption that it makes sense to compare different populations and say that some are better than others. Are there any reasons to deny that this makes sense? What would happen to the argument if we simply said that A and B were neither better nor worse than the other?
- In explaining his argument, Parfit at one point makes an analogy between "better than" and "taller than": If person 1 is taller than person 2, who is taller than person 3, then it is clear that person 1 is taller than person 3 because "taller than" is a transitive relation. If the relation holds between 1 and 2 and between 2 and 3, that is, then it holds between 1 and 3. Does it make sense to think of "better than" as transitive in the same way that "taller than" is? Why does Parfit's argument require this assumption? What would we be committed to if we denied it? Would this be a satisfactory way to dissolve Parfit's paradox?
- If we are unable to find an acceptable solution to the paradox, it seems that we will be forced to accept the Repugnant Conclusion. Should we simply go ahead and do that? Is it obvious that the Repugnant Conclusion is so repugnant? Or should we conclude that Parfit has simply proved that it is true? How, if at all, might one go about trying to make the Repugnant Conclusion seem less repugnant?

Further Reading

Chan, Kai M. A. "Intransitivity and Future Generations: Debunking Parfit's Mere Addition Paradox." *Journal of Applied Philosophy* 20, no. 2 (2003): 187–200.

Mulgan, Tim. "Dissolving the Mere Addition Paradox." *American Philosophical Quarterly* 37, no. 4 (October 2000): 359–72.

Parfit, Derek. *Reasons and Persons*. Oxford University Press, 1984.

Rachels, Stuart. "A Set of Solutions to Parfit's Problems." *Noûs* 35, no. 2 (June 2001): 214–38.

Temkin, Larry S. "Intransitivity and the Mere Addition Paradox." *Philosophy and Public Affairs* 16 (Spring 1987): 138–87.

Wolf, Clark. "Social Choice and Normative Population Theory: A Person Affecting Solution to Parfit's Mere Addition Paradox." *Philosophical Studies* 81, nos. 2 and 3 (March 1996): 263–82.

DEREK PARFIT

Overpopulation and the Quality of Life

How many people should there be? Can there be *overpopulation*: too many people living? I shall present a puzzling argument about these questions. . . .

I   QUALITY AND QUANTITY

Consider the outcomes that might be produced, in some part of the world, by two rates of population growth. Suppose that, if there is faster growth, there would later be more people, who would all be worse off. These outcomes are shown in Fig. I. The width of the blocks shows the number of people living; the height shows how well off these people are. Compared with outcome A, outcome B would have twice as many people, who would all be worse off. To avoid irrelevant

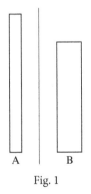

Fig. 1

complications, I assume that in each outcome there would be no inequality: no one would be worse off than anyone else. I also assume that everyone's life would be well worth living.

There are various ways in which, because there would be twice as many people in outcome B, these people might be all worse off than the people in A. There might be worse housing, overcrowded schools, more pollution, less unspoilt countryside, fewer opportunities, and a smaller share per person of various other kinds of resources. I shall say, for short, that in B there is *a lower quality of life*.

Except for the absence of inequality, these two outcomes could be the real alternatives for some country, or mankind, given two rates of population growth over many years. Would one of these outcomes be worse than the other? I do not mean "morally worse" in the sense that applies only to agents and to acts. But one of two outcomes can be worse in another sense that has moral relevance. It would be worse, in this sense, if more people suffer, or die young.

Would it be worse, in this sense, if the outcome was B rather than A? Part of the answer is clear. We would all agree that B would be, in one way, worse than A: it would be bad that everyone would be worse off.

On one view, this is all that matters, and it makes B worse than A. This view is expressed in

The Average Principle: If other things are equal, it is better if people's lives go, on average, better.

The Hedonistic version of this principle substitutes, for "go better," "contain more happiness."[1]

On the other main view about this question, it is good if any extra life is lived, that is worth living. On this view B might be better than A. B would be in one way worse, because everyone would be worse off. But in another way B would be better, because there would be more people living, all of whose lives would be worth living. And the fact that people would be worse off might be less important than—or *outweighed* by—the fact that there would be more people living.

Which of these views should we accept? Could a loss in the *quality* of people's lives be outweighed by a sufficient increase in the *quantity* of worthwhile life lived? If this is so, what are the relative values of quality and quantity? These are the central questions about overpopulation.[2]

The Average Principle implies that only quality matters. At the other extreme is

The Hedonistic Total Principle: If other things are equal, it is better if there is a greater total sum of happiness.

This principle implies that only quantity matters. Its Non-Hedonistic version substitutes, for "happiness," "whatever makes life worth living."

On the Hedonistic Total Principle, B would be better than A because each life in B would be *more than half* as happy as each life in A. Though the people in B would each be less happy than the people in A, they *together* would have more happiness—just as two bottles more than half-full hold more than a bottleful. On the non-Hedonistic version of this principle, B would be better than A because, compared with lives in A, lives in B would be *more than half* as much worth living.

These claims may seem implausibly precise. But lives in B would be more than half as much worth living if, though a move from the level in A to that in B would be a decline in the quality of life, it would take much more than another similarly large decline before people's lives ceased to be worth living. There are many actual cases in which such a claim would be true.[3]

2 THE REPUGNANT CONCLUSION

Consider Fig. 2. On the Total Principle, just as B would be better than A, C would be better than B, D better than C, and so on.

Best of all would be Z. This is an enormous population all of whom have lives that are not much above the level where they would cease to be worth living. A life could be like this either because its ecstasies make its agonies seem just worth enduring, or because it is painless but drab. Let us imagine lives in Z to be of this second kind. There is nothing bad in each of these lives; but there is little happiness, and little else that is good. The people in Z never suffer; but all they have is muzak and potatoes. Though there is little happiness in each life in Z, because there

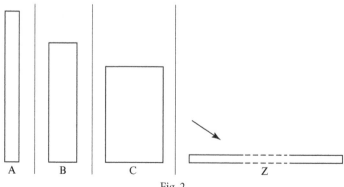

Fig. 2

are so many of these lives Z is the outcome in which there would be the greatest total sum of happiness. Similarly, Z is the outcome in which there would be the greatest quantity of whatever makes life worth living. (The greatest mass of milk might be in a vast heap of bottles each containing only one drop.)

It is worth comparing Z with Nozick's imagined *Utility Monster*. This is someone who would gain more happiness than we would lose whenever he is given any of our resources. Some Utilitarians believe that the Hedonistic Total Principle should be our only moral principle. Nozick claims that, on this Utilitarian theory, it would be best if all our resources were taken away and given to his Utility Monster, since this would produce the greatest total sum of happiness. As he writes, "unacceptably, the theory seems to require that we all be sacrificed in the monster's maw."[4]

How could it be true that, if all mankind's resources were given to Nozick's Monster, this would produce the greatest total sum of happiness? For this to be true, this Monster's life must, compared with other people's lives, be *millions* of times as much worth living. We cannot imagine, even in the dimmest way, what such a life would be like. Nozick's appeal to his Monster is therefore not a good objection to the Total Principle. We cannot test a moral principle by applying it to a case which we cannot even imagine.

Return now to the population in outcome Z. This is another Utility Monster. The difference is that the greater sum of happiness would come from a vast increase, not in the quality of one person's life, but in the number of lives lived. And *this* Utility Monster can be imagined. We can imagine what it would be for someone's life to be barely worth living—containing only muzak and potatoes. And we can imagine what it would be for there to be many people with such lives. In order to imagine Z, we merely have to imagine that there would be *very* many.

We could not in practice face a choice between A and Z. Given the limits to the world's resources, we could not in fact produce the greatest possible sum of happiness, or the greatest amount of whatever makes life worth living, by producing an enormous population whose lives were barely worth living.[5] But this would be merely *technically* impossible. In order to suppose it possible, we merely need to add some assumptions about the nature and availability of resources. We can therefore test our moral principles by applying them to A and Z.[6]

The Total Principle implies that Z would be better than A. More generally, the principle implies

The Repugnant Conclusion: Compared with the existence of very many people—say, ten billion—all of whom have a very high quality of life, there must be some much larger number of people whose existence, if other things are equal, would be *better*, even though these people would have lives that are barely worth living.[7]

As its name suggests, most of us find this conclusion hard to accept. Most of us believe that Z would be much worse than A. To keep this belief, we must reject the Total Principle. We must also reject the broader view that any loss in the quality of life could be outweighed by a sufficient increase in the total quantity of whatever makes life worth living. Unless we reject this view, we cannot avoid the Repugnant Conclusion.

When the stakes are lower, as in the comparison between A and B, most of us believe that B would be worse. We believe that, compared with the existence of ten billion people whose lives are very well worth living, it would be worse if instead there were twice as many people who were all worse off. To keep this belief, we must again reject the Total Principle.

Suppose that we do reject this principle. Unfortunately, this is not enough. As I shall now argue, it is hard to defend the belief that B would be worse than A, and it is also hard to avoid the Repugnant Conclusion.

3 THE MERE ADDITION PARADOX

Consider the alternatives shown in Fig. 3. There is here a new outcome, A+. This differs from A only by the addition of an extra group of people, whose lives are well worth living, though they are worse off than the original group.

The inequality in A+ is *natural*: not the result of any kind of social injustice. Take my waves to show the Atlantic Ocean, and assume that we are considering possible outcomes in some past century, before

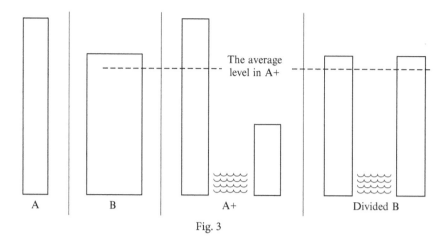

Fig. 3

the Atlantic had been crossed. In A+ there was one group of people living in Europe, Asia, and Africa, and another group, who were worse off, living in the Americas. A is a different possible outcome at this time, in which the Americas were uninhabited. Perhaps the Bering Straits had opened before the land was crossed.

Is A+ worse than A? Note that I am not asking whether it is *better*. If we do not believe that the existence of extra people is in itself good, we shall deny that the extra group in A+ makes A+ better than A. But is A+ *worse* than A? Would it have been better if the extra group had never existed? This is hard to believe. It may seem a bad feature that there is natural inequality in A+—that the extra group are, through no fault of theirs, worse off than the original group. But the inequality in A+ does not seem to justify the view that the extra group should never have existed. Why are they such a blot on the Universe?

You may think that you have no view about whether it would have been better if the extra group had never existed. It may help to consider another outcome: A + Hell. In this outcome the extra group are innocent people who all have lives which are much worse than nothing. They would all kill themselves if they could, but their torturers prevent this. We would all agree that A + Hell *is* worse than A. It would have been better if *this* extra group, as they all passionately wish, had never existed. Since we believe that A + Hell is worse than A, we must be able to compare A+ and A. Unlike the extra group in Hell, the extra people in A+ have lives that are well worth living; and their existence is not bad for anyone. Most of us could not honestly claim to believe that it would have been better if these people had never existed. Most of us would therefore believe that A+ is not worse than A.

Now suppose that, as a result of changes in the environment, A+ turned into Divided B. In both these outcomes the same number of people would exist, so we are not making one of the unfamiliar comparisons which involve different numbers of people in existence. Since the numbers are the same in A+ and Divided B, our ordinary moral principles apply.

On the principles which most of us accept, Divided B would be better than A+. On the Principle of Utility it is better if there is a greater net sum of benefits—a greater sum of benefits minus losses. Divided B would be better than A+ in utilitarian terms, since the benefits to the people who gain would be greater than the losses to the people who lose. On the Principle of Equality it is better if there is less inequality between different people. Divided B would be better than A+ in egalitarian terms, since the benefits would all go to the people who are worse off.

It might be objected that the Principle of Equality does not apply to people who cannot even communicate. But suppose that I know about two such people, one of whom is, through mere bad luck, worse off. Call these people *Poor* and *Rich*. I could either benefit Rich, or give a greater benefit to Poor. Most of us would believe that it would be better if I do the second. And we would believe that this would make the outcome better, not only because I would give Poor a greater benefit, but also because he is worse off than Rich. Most of us would believe this even though Poor and Rich cannot (except through me) communicate.

How could we deny that a change from A+ to Divided B would be a change for the better? We would have to claim that the loss to the best-off people in A+ matters more than the greater gain to the equally numerous worst-off people. This seems to commit us to the *Élitist* view that what matters most is the condition of the best-off people. This is the opposite of Rawls's famous view that what matters most is the condition of the worst-off people.[8] Most of us would reject this Élitist view. Most of us would therefore agree that Divided B would be better than A+.

Suppose finally that the Atlantic is crossed, turning Divided B into B. These two outcomes are clearly equally good. Since Divided B would be better than A+, B must be better than A+.

Let us now combine the conclusions we have reached. Most of us believe both that A+ is not worse than A, and that B is better than A+. These beliefs together imply that B is not worse than A. B cannot be worse than A if it is *better* than something—A+—which is *not worse* than A. In the same way, you cannot be taller than me if you are shorter than someone who is not taller than me. But, as I earlier claimed, most of us also believe that B *is* worse than A. We therefore have three beliefs which are inconsistent, and imply a contradiction. These beliefs imply that B both is and is not worse than A. I call this *the Mere Addition Paradox*.

This is not just a conflict between different moral principles. Suppose that we accept both the Principle of Equality and the Principle of Utility. There can be cases where these principles conflict—where greater equality would reduce the sum of benefits. But such a case does not reveal any inconsistency in our moral view. We would merely have to ask whether, given the details of the case, the gain in equality would be more important than the loss of benefits. We would here be trying to decide what, after considering all the details, we believe would be the better outcome.

In the Mere Addition Paradox, things are different. Most of us here believe, *all things considered*, that B is worse than A, though B is better than A+, which is not worse than A. If we continue to hold these three beliefs, we must conclude that B both is and is not worse than A. But we cannot possibly accept this conclusion, any more than we could accept that you both are and are not taller than me. Since we cannot possibly accept what these three beliefs imply, at least one belief must go.

Which should go? Suppose that we keep our belief that B is better than A+, because we cannot persuade ourselves that what matters most is the condition of the best-off people. Suppose that we also keep our belief that A+ is not worse than A, because we cannot persuade ourselves that it would have been better if the extra group had never existed. We must then reject our belief that B is worse than A. We must conclude that, if these were two possible futures for some society or the world, it would *not* be worse if what comes about is B: twice the population, who are all worse off.

The Mere Addition Paradox does not force us to this conclusion. We can avoid the conclusion if we reject one of our other two beliefs. Some people reject the belief that A+ is not worse than A, because they think that the inequality in A+ is enough to make A+ worse. These people can keep their belief that B is worse than A. Note, however, that we cannot simply claim that A+ must be worse than A, since it is worse than something—B—which is worse than A. We would here be rejecting one of our three inconsistent beliefs simply on the ground that it is not consistent with the other two. This could be said against *each* belief. To avoid the paradox we must believe, without considering the rest of the argument, that A+ is worse than A. We must believe that it was bad in itself that the extra people ever lived, even though these people had lives that were well worth living, and their existence was bad for no one. To the extent that we find this hard to believe, we still face a paradox.

It may be objected: "Your argument involves a kind of trick. When you compare A and A+, you claim that the extra group's existence was bad for no one. But by the time we have moved to B the original group have become worse off. The addition of the extra group *was* bad for the original group."

The argument can be restated. Suppose that A+ was the actual state of the world in some past century. A is a different state of the world which was merely possible. We can ask, "Would A have been better? Would it have been better if the worse-off group had never existed?" As I have said, most of us could not answer Yes. Suppose next that A+ did *not* in fact later change into either Divided B or B. We can ask, "*If* this change had occurred, would it have been a change for the better?" It is hard to answer No. On this version of the argument, the last objection has been met. The better-off group in A+ was not an originally existing group, to which the worse-off group was added. And the existence of the worse-off group was not bad for the better-off group.

It is worth giving another version of the argument. To ensure that there was no social injustice, we assumed that the two groups in A+ did not know of each other's existence. We could assume instead that both these groups live in the same society, and that the people in one group are worse off, not because of social injustice, but because they all have some handicap which cannot be cured. Suppose, for example, that they are deaf. If this is so, would it have been better if these people had never existed? Would this have been better even though these people's lives are worth living, their existence is not bad for anyone, and if they had never existed no one else would have existed in their place? It is hard to believe that these deaf people should never have existed. On this version of the argument, it again seems that A+ is not worse than A.

Suppose next that these deaf people could be cured, at some lesser cost to the other group. This would be like the change from A+ to B. It is again hard to deny that this change would make the outcome better. In this version of the argument, with the groups in one society, we seem again driven to conclude that, since B would be better than A+, which is not worse than A, B cannot be worse than A. . . .

NOTES

1. Of the many economists who appeal to the Average Principle, some make it true by definition. See, for exam-

ple, P. A. Samuelson, *Economics* (New York, 1970), p. 551. Certain writers state this principle so that it covers only the lives that are, at any time, being lived. This makes the principle imply that it would have been better if all but the best-off people had just dropped dead. My versions of the Average Principle do not imply this absurd conclusion. If anyone with a life worth living dies earlier, this causes people's lives to go, on average, worse, and to contain a smaller average sum of happiness.

2. These remarks assume that the quality of life is higher if people's lives go better, and that each life goes better if it contains a greater quantity either of happiness or of whatever else makes life worth living. "Quality" thus means "quantity, per life lived." . . .

3. In what follows I assume, for convenience, that there can be precise differences between the quality of life of different groups. I believe that there could not really be such precise differences. All that my arguments require is that some people can be worse off than others, in morally significant ways, and by more or less.

4. R. Nozick, *Anarchy, State, and Utopia* (Oxford, 1974), p. 41.

5. According to some versions of the widely assumed *Law of Diminishing Marginal Utility*, we could do this. The point can be made most easily in Hedonistic terms. It is assumed that, because resources produce more happiness if they are given to people who are worse off, they would produce most happiness if they are all given to people whose lives are barely worth living. There is here an obvious oversight. Many resources are needed to make each person's life even reach a level where it begins to be worth living. Such resources do not help to produce the greatest possible quantity of happiness, since they are merely being used to raise people to the level where their happiness begins to outweigh their suffering.

6. It may help to give this illustration. Suppose that, as a *Negative Utilitarian*, I believe that all that matters morally is the relief or prevention of suffering. It is pointed out to me that, on my view, it would be best if all life on Earth was painlessly destroyed, since only this would ensure that there would be no more suffering. And suppose I agreed that this would be a very bad outcome. Could I say: "It is true that this very bad outcome would, according to my moral view, be the best outcome. But this is no objection to my view, since we are not in fact able to bring about this outcome"? This would be no defence. On my view, I ought to *regret* our inability to bring about this outcome. Whether my view is plausible cannot depend on what is technically possible. Since this view implies that the destruction of all life on Earth would be the best outcome,

if I firmly believe that this outcome would be very bad, I should reject this view.

7. The phrase "if other things are equal" allows for the possibility that the existence of the larger population might, in some other way, be worse. It might, for instance, involve injustice. What the Repugnant Conclusion claims is that, though the lower quality of life would make Z in one way worse than A, this bad feature could be less important than, or be outweighed by, Z's good feature: the existence of enough extra people whose lives are—even if only barely—worth living.

8. J. Rawls, *A Theory of Justice* (Cambridge, Mass., 1971).

Critics

Thomas Hurka

Value and Population Size

. . . [Suppose] we interpret "well-being" not as happiness but as involving the achievement of some form of human perfection, as Aquinas, Leibniz, and Kant all interpreted it, and as I would want to interpret it as well. When we make judgments involving perfectionist (as opposed to utilitarian) values, we often do object to (at least some) mere additions. Consider, for instance, the judgments we make about careers. Many of us think Muhammad Ali's boxing career, to take a current example, would have been better without those last fights against Larry Holmes and Trevor Berbick. This is not because we think Ali's performances against Holmes and Berbick were by some objective standard bad; we know that, for many other boxers, to do as well as Ali did against these fighters would have marked the pinnacle of their careers. It is rather because we think Ali's performances were so much worse than the performances he produced in his prime that it was bad *for him* to produce them. The Holmes and Berbick fights were mere additions to Ali's boxing career, yet many of us think his career would have been better without them. A similar attitude is present in the judgments many of us make about collections. Consider a collection of 100 exceptionally fine paintings, and then consider the collection which results when it is expanded by the purchase of twenty-five utterly mediocre paintings. If we think the second collection is worse than the first, as I am inclined to myself, then we should not automatically object to a theory which says that, given a world containing 1 billion people leading active, challenging, and autonomous lives, we make that world worse if we add to it 250 million extra people leading mindless, passive, and conditioned lives.

Thomas Hurka, "Value and Population Size," *Ethics,* Vol. 93, No. 3 (April, 1983). Reprinted with the permission of University of Chicago Press.

DON LOCKE

The Parfit Population Problem

... I confess ... that I am not entirely convinced about this paradox. On the one hand it does seem odd that the mere addition of extra lives should make things worse, just because it lowers the average; no matter how happy or successful those extra lives might be. But I can also see a sense in which the A world is better, more nearly perfect, than the A+ world, because everyone in the A world is much better off than many in the A+ World. Hurka illustrates this point by comparing an art gallery containing a limited number of masterpieces with a gallery containing those same masterpieces but in addition some lesser works, albeit works which might be the highspot of many a lesser gallery. Which of these would be the better gallery seems a moot point, but the former does seem more nearly perfect. Or, more excitingly, Hurka contemplates the career of Muhammad Ali, whose last two fights would have been a moment of glory for a lesser boxer, but which in the context of Ali's other fights, only detract from the value of the whole: Ali's career would have been better, more nearly perfect, without those last two fights. Similarly, it might be argued, the A World is more morally perfect, and therefore more morally desirable, than the A+ World. Certainly I know which of the two I would prefer myself, or anyone else, to be in, if I had the choice. Indeed I think that personally I would prefer World A not only if choosing in ignorance of my final position, but even if I knew that in the A+ World I would myself be one of those better off. . . .

Don Locke, "The Parfit Population Problem," *Philosophy*, Vol. 62, No. 240 (April, 1987). Reprinted with the permission of Cambridge University Press.

PART 4

What's Wrong with Race Relations?

Some of the deepest and most divisive debates in contemporary society concern race. While virtually everyone agrees that injustices based on race were committed in the past, for example, sharp disagreement persists about just what, if anything, should be done in response to this fact in the present. Indeed, a growing number of questions relating to race have made their way into the philosophical literature on applied ethics in recent years, and Part 4 is designed to introduce the reader to a variety of them. We introduce the subject of race by focusing on two questions about how we should respond to past injustices. Does the United States government, in particular, have a moral obligation to make reparations to black Americans for the wrongs inflicted as a part of the institution of slavery and its aftermath (chapter 17)? And what, if anything, do the lingering consequences of those earlier injustices imply about the moral status of affirmative action (chapter 18)? From here, we turn to two related but importantly distinct questions about how we should respond to racial hatred: Should colleges and universities have hate speech codes (chapter 19)? And should the State enact hate crime laws (chapter 20)? Finally, Part 4 concludes with two further issues that lie at the intersection of race and the criminal justice system: If capital punishment is administered in a racially imbalanced manner, does this suffice to show that it should be abolished (chapter 21)? And should the State engage in racial profiling in its attempt to thwart criminal activity (chapter 22)?

focusing on two questions about how we should respond to injustices. Does the United

17

Are Reparations for Slavery Wrong?

Horowitz and His Critics

From the beginning of its existence until the Civil War, the United States government permitted and facilitated the practice of slavery on its soil. When slavery was finally abolished, in 1865, the government continued to practice various forms of racial segregation and discrimination for many years after. Millions of Africans and African Americans suffered greatly during those years of slavery, segregation, and discrimination. Virtually everyone now agrees that what the United States government did to Africans and African Americans during this period was terribly wrong. But this does not mean that everyone agrees about what, if anything, should be done about those wrongs now. In particular, while some people believe that the United States now owes reparations to African Americans as a form of compensation for slavery and its aftermath, others believe that this call for reparations is unfounded and unjust. Indeed, putting things this mildly is a great understatement. The current debate over slave reparations is among the most heated and divisive issues in the current debate over race as a whole. Nowhere is this fact more vividly illustrated than in the bitter controversy that surrounded the publication of David Horowitz's now-(in)famous article "Ten Reasons Why Reparations for Blacks Is a Bad Idea for Blacks—and Racist, Too!" In 2001, Horowitz attempted to place that brief article as a paid advertisement in a number of college newspapers. Everywhere it was published, heated discussions followed. Some papers chose to run the ad, others chose not to. In either case, the editors' decisions were praised by some and bitterly criticized by others. In this chapter, we present Horowitz's piece as it appeared in a number of campus newspapers as our featured article, along with a piece written directly in response to it and another that responds to its arguments indirectly.

Horowitz presents his case against slave reparations as a series of ten discrete and unconnected points. However, most of these points can be construed as parts of a larger, single argument, one that takes the form of a criticism of an argument from analogy (see section 4.1 of the Introduction) that Horowitz claims underpins the case for reparations. Horowitz understands the central case in favor of slave reparations to rest on an analogy in which the relationship between the United States government and its present-day African-American citizens is compared to the relationship between a perpetrator of some great injustice and the immediate victims of that injustice (e.g., between Germany and survivors of the Holocaust). In the latter case, most people will agree that it is fair and appropriate that the victims seek compensation from those who wronged them. And by using this analogy, the proponent of reparations, on Horowitz's understanding, hopes that people will come to accept the slave reparations claim as valid as well. Horowitz's "Ten Reasons" can then be largely understood as an attempt to undermine this analogy. This is most explicit in the case of reason 4 but applies as well to reasons 1–3 and reason 6, all of which, in one way or another, attempt to point to problems with the claim that the slave case is suitably analogous to other cases in which a claim of reparations is generally accepted. Reasons 8 and 9 can also be taken as an indirect attack on the analogy, since they argue for the claim that even if there had been a debt the debt has already been paid. Reasons 7 and 10 round out Horowitz's case against reparations by arguing that reparations would have negative consequences for black Americans in particular and for the American people in general.

If Horowitz's article is best understood as an extended criticism of an argument from analogy, then Robert Chrisman and Ernest Allen Jr.'s response to it can best be thought of as an argument by process of elimination (see section 4.4 of the Introduction). One by one, the two authors go through Horowitz's ten reasons and attempt to eliminate each one. Like most arguments that proceed in this manner, Chrisman and Allen's argument is difficult to summarize briefly. Readers are therefore encouraged to attend closely to the points raised under each of the authors' ten headings. This chapter concludes with a short piece by Randall Robinson, author of *The Debt: What America Owes to Blacks* and one of the most prominent proponents of reparations. In "America's Debt to Blacks," Robinson offers a brief restatement of the central argument of his book. Although the article and book were not written as direct responses to Horowitz's "Ten Reasons" in particular, the main point of Robinson's piece can nonetheless be understood in terms of Horowitz's position. Where Horowitz maintains that there is not a close enough connection between present-day African Americans and those who were directly responsible for the injustice of slavery and its aftermath, Robinson argues that the two sides are connected by compelling considerations. The present-day United States government is connected to that of the past because "the life and responsibilities of a nation are not limited to the life spans of its mortal constituents." And present-day African Americans are connected to those who were wronged in the past because each child begins "where its parents left off" and is thus unjustly harmed in those cases where its predecessors were unjustly harmed. Although the harms of slavery and its aftermath were originally inflicted by earlier generations of Americans on earlier generations of Africans and then African Americans, the debt that was generated by their wrongdoing, on this account, is legitimately transferred to the present day because we inherit the debts that our government incurs and because African Americans have inherited the harms that their ancestors were made to suffer.

Questions for Consideration

In thinking critically about the exchange between Horowitz and his critics, it is important to look broadly at all ten of the reasons Horowitz gives and all ten of the reasons Chrisman and Allen provide in response to him. At the same time, it is also important to focus more narrowly on the central question of whether or not the slave reparations case is suitably analogous to other cases in which claims of restitution are generally accepted.

• Is Horowitz correct in insisting that there are too many differences between the cases to allow the argument for reparations to succeed? Or is Robinson correct in maintaining that the apparent differences between the cases can be bridged?

• How does Robinson try to argue that the fact that the government in the past would have owed something shows that the government in the present owes something? Can you think of other cases where a past government act has resulted in a present government obligation? Are these cases relevantly similar to the issue of slave reparations? Why or why not? Would these considerations in the end help to vindicate Horowitz's position or undermine it?

• How does Robinson try to argue that the fact that the immediate victims of slavery and its aftermath would have been owed something shows that the current generation of black Americans is owed something? Can you think of other cases where a harm that was caused to past generations has resulted in harms to some members of the present generation? Are these cases relevantly similar to the issue of slave reparations? Why or why not? Would these considerations in the end help to vindicate Horowitz's position or undermine it?

• Would slave reparations unfairly punish the current generation of Americans, none of whom has ever owned a slave, for the sins of (some of) their predecessors? Or would reparations simply amount to the United States government's finally discharging an obligation that it incurred long ago?

• Finally, readers should stop to consider a question that is not raised in Horowitz's article but that is nonetheless raised by the *existence* of that article. Did the newspapers that accepted Horowitz's advertisement do the right thing, or did those that refused to accept it do the right thing?

Further Reading

Bittker, Boris I. *The Case for Black Reparations*. New York: Random House, 1973.

Boxill, Bernard. "A Lockean Argument for Black Reparations." *Journal of Ethics* 7, no. 1 (2003): 63–91.

Brooks, Roy L. *Atonement and Forgiveness: A New Model for Black Reparations*. Berkeley: University of California Press, 2004.

Horowitz, David. *Uncivil Wars: The Controversy over Reparations for Slavery*. San Francisco: Encounter Books, 2002.

Robinson, Randall. *The Debt: What America Owes to Blacks*. New York: Penguin Putnam, Inc., 2000.

Salzberger, Ronald P., and Mary C. Turck, eds. *Reparations for Slavery: A Reader*. Lanham, Md.: Rowman & Littlefield Publishers, Inc., 2004.

Schedler, George. "Principles for Measuring the Damages of American Slavery." *Public Affairs Quarterly* 16, no. 4 (2002): 377–404.

Winbush, Raymond A., ed. *Should America Pay?: Slavery and the Raging Debate on Reparations*. New York: HarperCollins Publishers, Inc., 2003.

DAVID HOROWITZ

Ten Reasons Why Reparations for Blacks Is a Bad Idea for Blacks—and Racist, Too!

1. There Is No Single Group Clearly Responsible for the Crime of Slavery

Black Africans and Arabs were responsible for enslaving the ancestors of African-Americans. There were 3,000 black slave-owners in the ante-bellum United States. Are reparations to be paid by their descendants too?

2. There Is No One Group That Benefited Exclusively from Its Fruits

The claim for reparations is premised on the false assumption that only whites have benefited from slavery. If slave labor created wealth for Americans, then obviously it has created wealth for black Americans as well, including the descendants of slaves. The GNP of black America is so large that it makes the African-American community the 10th most prosperous "nation" in the world. American blacks on average enjoy per capita incomes in the range of twenty to fifty times that of blacks living in any of the African nations from which they were kidnapped.

3. Only a Tiny Minority of White Americans Ever Owned Slaves, and Others Gave Their Lives to Free Them

Only a tiny minority of Americans ever owned slaves. This is true even for those who lived in the ante-bellum South where only one white in five was a slaveholder. Why should their descendants owe a debt? What about the descendants of the 350,000 Union soldiers who died to free the slaves? They gave their lives. What possible moral principle would ask them to pay (through their descendants) again?

4. America Today Is a Multi-Ethnic Nation and Most Americans Have No Connection (direct or indirect) to Slavery

The two great waves of American immigration occurred after 1880 and then after 1960. What rationale would require Vietnamese boat people, Russian refuseniks, Iranian refugees, and Armenian victims of the Turkish persecution, Jews, Mexicans, Greeks, or Polish, Hungarian, Cambodian and Korean victims of Communism, to pay reparations to American blacks?

5. The Historical Precedents Used to Justify the Reparations Claim Do Not Apply, and the Claim Itself Is Based on Race Not Injury

The historical precedents generally invoked to justify the reparations claim are payments to Jewish survivors of the Holocaust, Japanese-Americans and African-American victims of racial experiments in Tuskegee, or racial outrages in Rosewood and Oklahoma City. But in each case, the recipients of reparations were the direct victims of the injustice or their immediate families. This would be the only case of reparations to people who were not immediately affected and whose sole qualification to receive reparations would be racial. As has already been pointed out, during the slavery era, many blacks were free men or slave-owners themselves, yet the reparations claimants make no distinction between the roles blacks actually played in the injustice itself. Randall Robinson's book on reparations, *The Debt*, which is the manifesto of the reparations movement is pointedly sub-titled *"What America Owes to Blacks."* If this is not racism, what is?

David Horowitz, "Ten Reasons Why Reparations for Blacks Is a Bad Idea for Blacks—and Racist, Too!" Originally posted on frontpagemag.com, January 3, 2001.

6. The Reparations Argument Is Based on the Unfounded Claim That All African-American Descendants of Slaves Suffer from the Economic Consequences of Slavery and Discrimination

No evidence-based attempt has been made to prove that living individuals have been adversely affected by a slave system that was ended over 150 years ago. But there is plenty of evidence the hardships that occurred were hardships that individuals could and did overcome. The black middle-class in America is a prosperous community that is now larger in absolute terms than the black underclass. Does its existence not suggest that economic adversity is the result of failures of individual character rather than the lingering after-effects of racial discrimination and a slave system that ceased to exist well over a century ago? West Indian blacks in America are also descended from slaves but their average incomes are equivalent to the average incomes of whites (and nearly 25% higher than the average incomes of American born blacks). How is it that slavery adversely affected one large group of descendants but not the other? How can government be expected to decide an issue that is so subjective—and yet so critical—to the case?

7. The Reparations Claim Is One More Attempt to Turn African-Americans into Victims. It Sends a Damaging Message to the African-American Community

The renewed sense of grievance—which is what the claim for reparations will inevitably create—is neither a constructive nor a helpful message for black leaders to be sending to their communities and to others. To focus the social passions of African-Americans on what some Americans may have done to their ancestors fifty or a hundred and fifty years ago is to burden them with a crippling sense of victim-hood. How are the millions of refugees from tyranny and genocide who are now living in America going to receive these claims, moreover, except as demands for special treatment, an extravagant new handout that is only necessary because some blacks can't seem to locate the ladder of opportunity within reach of others—many less privileged than themselves?

8. Reparations to African Americans Have Already Been Paid

Since the passage of the Civil Rights Acts and the advent of the Great Society in 1965, trillions of dollars in transfer payments have been made to African-Americans in the form of welfare benefits and racial preferences (in contracts, job placements and educational admissions)—all under the rationale of redressing historic racial grievances. It is said that reparations are necessary to achieve a healing between African-Americans and other Americans. If trillion dollar restitutions and a wholesale rewriting of American law (in order to accommodate racial preferences) for African-Americans is not enough to achieve a "healing," what will?

9. What About the Debt Blacks Owe to America?

Slavery existed for thousands of years before the Atlantic slave trade was born, and in all societies. But in the thousand years of its existence, there never was an anti-slavery movement until white Christians—Englishmen and Americans—created one. If not for the anti-slavery attitudes and military power of white Englishmen and Americans, the slave trade would not have been brought to an end. If not for the sacrifices of white soldiers and a white American president who gave his life to sign the Emancipation Proclamation, blacks in America would still be slaves. If not for the dedication of Americans of all ethnicities and colors to a society based on the principle that all men are created equal, blacks in America would not enjoy the highest standard of living of blacks anywhere in the world, and indeed one of the highest standards of living of any people in the world. They would not enjoy the greatest freedoms and the most thoroughly protected individual rights anywhere. Where is the gratitude of black America and its leaders for those gifts?

10. The Reparations Claim Is a Separatist Idea That Sets African-Americans Against the Nation That Gave Them Freedom

Blacks were here before the *Mayflower.* Who is more American than the descendants of African slaves? For the African-American community to isolate itself even further from America is to embark on a course whose implications are troubling. Yet the African-American community has had a long-running flirtation with separatists, nationalists and the political left, who want African-Americans to be no part of America's social contract. African Americans should reject this temptation.

For all America's faults, African-Americans have an enormous stake in their country and its heritage. It is this heritage that is really under attack by the reparations movement. The reparations claim is one more assault on America, conducted by racial sepa-ratists and the political left. It is an attack not only on white Americans, but on all Americans—especially African-Americans.

America's African-American citizens are the richest and most privileged black people alive—a bounty that is a direct result of the heritage that is under assault. The American idea needs the support of its African-American citizens. But African-Americans also need the support of the American idea. For it is this idea that led to the principles and institutions that have set African-Americans—and all of us—free.

Critics

ROBERT CHRISMAN
ERNEST ALLEN, JR.

Ten Reasons

A Response to David Horowitz

David Horowitz's article, "Ten Reasons Why Reparations for Slavery Is a Bad Idea and Racist Too," recently achieved circulation in a handful of college newspapers throughout the United States as a paid advertisement sponsored by the Center for the Study of Popular Culture. While Horowitz's article pretends to address the issues of reparations, it is not about reparations at all. It is, rather, a well-heeled, coordinated attack on Black Americans which is calculated to elicit division and strife. Horowitz reportedly attempted to place his article in some 50 student newspapers at universities and colleges across the country, and was successful in purchasing space in such newspapers at Brown, Duke, Arizona, UC Berkeley, UC Davis, University of Chicago, and University of Wisconsin, paying an average of $700 per paper. His campaign has succeeded in fomenting outrage, dissension, and grief wherever it has appeared. Unfortunately, both its supporters and its foes too often have categorized the issue as one centering on "free speech." The sale and purchase of advertising space is not a matter of free speech, however, but involves an exchange of commodities. Professor Lewis Gordon of Brown University put it very well, saying

Robert Chrisman and Ernest Allen, Jr., "Ten Reasons: A Response to David Horowitz," *The Black Scholar* 31 (Summer 2001); 49–55. Reprinted by permission of the Black Scholar.

that "what concerned me was that the ad was both hate speech and a solicitation for financial support to develop antiblack ad space. I was concerned that it would embolden white supremacists and antiblack racists." At a March 15 panel held at UC Berkeley, Horowitz also conceded that his paid advertisement did not constitute a free speech issue.

As one examines the text of Horowitz's article, it becomes apparent that it is not a reasoned essay addressed to the topic of reparations: it is, rather, a racist polemic against African Americans and Africans that is neither responsible nor informed, relying heavily upon sophistry and a Hitlerian "Big Lie" technique. To our knowledge, only one of Horowitz's ten "reasons" has been challenged by a black scholar as to source, accuracy, and validity. It is our intention here to briefly rebut his slanders in order to pave the way for an honest and forthright debate on reparations. In these efforts we focus not just on slavery, but also the legacy of slavery which continues to inform institutional as well as individual behavior in the U.S. to this day. Although we recognize that white America still owes a debt to the descendants of slaves, in addressing Horowitz's distortions of history we do not act as advocates for a specific form of reparations.

1. There Is No Single Group Clearly Responsible for the Crime of Slavery

Horowitz's first argument, relativist in structure, can only lead to two conclusions: (1) societies are not responsible for their actions, and (2) since "everyone" was responsible for slavery, no one was responsible. While diverse groups on different continents certainly participated in the trade, the principal responsibility for internationalization of that trade and the institutionalization of slavery in the so-called New World rests with European and American individuals and institutions. The transatlantic slave trade began with the importation of African slaves into Hispaniola by Spain in the early 1500s. Nationals of France, England, Portugal, and the Netherlands, supported by their respective governments and powerful religious institutions, quickly entered the trade and extracted their pieces of silver as well. By conservative estimates, 14 million enslaved Africans survived the horror of the Middle Passage for the purpose of producing wealth for Europeans and Euro-Americans in the New World.

While there is some evidence of blacks owning slaves for profit purposes—most notably the creole caste in Louisiana—the numbers were small. As historian James Oakes noted, "By 1830 there were some 3,775 free black slaveholders across the South. . . . The evidence is overwhelming that the vast majority of black slaveholders were free men who purchased members of their families or who acted out of benevolence" (Oakes, 47–48).

2. There Is No Single Group That Benefited Exclusively from Slavery

Horowitz's second point, which is also a relativist one, seeks to dismiss the argument that white Americans benefited as a group from slavery, contending that the material benefits of slavery could not accrue in an exclusive way to a single group. But such sophistry evades the basic issue: who benefited primarily from slavery? Those who were responsible for the institutionalized enslavement of people of African descent also received the primary benefits from such actions. New England slave traders, merchants, bankers, and insurance companies all profited from the slave trade, which required a wide variety of commodities ranging from sails, chandlery, foodstuffs, and guns, to cloth goods and other items for trading purposes. Both prior to and after the American Revolution, slaveholding was a principal path for white upward mobility in the South. The white native-born as well as immigrant groups such as Germans, Scots-Irish, and the like participated. In 1860, cotton was the country's largest single export. As Eric Williams and C.L.R. James have demonstrated, the free labor provided by slavery was central to the growth of industry in western Europe and the United States; simultaneously, as Walter Rodney has argued, slavery depressed and destabilized the economies of African states. Slaveholders benefited primarily from the institution, of course, and generally in proportion to the number of slaves which they held. But the sharing of the proceeds of slave exploitation spilled across class lines within white communities as well.

As historian John Hope Franklin recently affirmed in a rebuttal to Horowitz's claims:

All whites and no slaves benefited from American slavery. All blacks had no rights that they could claim as their own. All whites, including the vast majority who had no slaves, were not only encouraged but authorized to exercise dominion over all slaves, thereby adding strength to the system of control.

If David Horowitz had read James D. DeBow's "The Interest in Slavery of the Southern Non-slaveholder," he would not have blundered into the fantasy of claiming that no single group benefited from slavery. Planters, did, of course. New York merchants did, of course. Even poor whites benefited from the legal advantage they enjoyed over all blacks as well as from the psychological advantage of having a group beneath them.

The context of the African-American argument for reparations is confined to the practice and consequences of slavery within the United States, from the colonial period on through final abolition and the aftermath, circa 1619–1865. Contrary to Horowitz's assertion, there is no record of institutionalized white enslavement in colonial America. Horowitz is confusing the indenture of white labor, which usually lasted seven years or so during the early colonial period, with enslavement. African slavery was expanded, in fact, to replace the inefficient and unenforceable white indenture system. (Smith)

Seeking to claim that African Americans, too, have benefited from slavery, Horowitz points to the relative prosperity of African Americans in comparison to their counterparts on the African continent. However, his argument that, "the GNP of black America makes the African-American community the 10th most prosperous "nation" in the world is based upon a false analogy. GNP is defined as "the total market value of all the goods and services produced by a nation during a specified period." Black Americans are not a nation and have no GNP. Horowitz confuses disposable income and "consumer power" with the generation of wealth.

3. Only a Tiny Minority of White Americans Ever Owned Slaves, and Others Gave Their Lives to Free Them

Most white union troops were drafted into the union army in a war which the federal government initially defined as a "war to preserve the union." In large

part because they feared that freed slaves would flee the South and "take their jobs" while they themselves were engaged in warfare with Confederate troops, recently drafted white conscripts in New York City and elsewhere rioted during the summer of 1863, taking a heavy toll on black civilian life and property. Too many instances can be cited where white northern troops plundered the personal property of slaves, appropriating their bedding, chickens, pigs, and foodstuffs as they swept through the South. On the other hand, it is certainly true that there also existed principled white commanders and troops who were committed abolitionists.

However, Horowitz's focus on what he mistakenly considers to be the overriding, benevolent aim of white union troops in the Civil War obscures the role that blacks themselves played in their own liberation. African Americans were initially forbidden by the Union to fight in the Civil War, and black leaders such as Frederick Douglass and Martin Delany demanded the right to fight for their freedom. When racist doctrine finally conceded to military necessity, blacks were recruited into the Union Army in 1862 at approximately half the pay of white soldiers—a situation which was partially rectified by an act of Congress in mid-1864. Some 170,000 blacks served in the Civil War, representing nearly one third of the free black population.

By 1860, four million blacks in the U.S. were enslaved; some 500,000 were nominally free. Because of slavery, racist laws, and racist policies, blacks were denied the chance to compete for the opportunities and resources of America that were available to native whites and immigrants: labor opportunities, free enterprise, and land. The promise of "forty acres and a mule" to former slaves was effectively nullified by the actions of President Andrew Johnson. And because the best land offered by the Homestead Act of 1862 and its subsequent revisions quickly fell under the sway of white homesteaders and speculators, most former slaves were unable to take advantage of its provisions.

4. Most Living Americans Have No Connection (Direct or Indirect) to Slavery

As Joseph Anderson, member of the National Council of African American Men, observed, "the arguments for reparations aren't made on the basis of whether every white person directly gained from slavery. The arguments are made on the basis that slavery was institutionalized and protected by law in the United States. As the government is an entity that survives generations, its debts and obligations survive the lifespan of any particular individuals. . . . Governments make restitution to victims as a group or class" (*San Francisco Chronicle,* March 26, 2001, p. A21).

Most Americans today were not alive during World War II. Yet reparations to Japanese Americans for their internment in concentration camps during the war was paid out of current government sources contributed to by contemporary Americans. Passage of time does not negate the responsibility of government in crimes against humanity. Similarly, German corporations are not the "same" corporations that supported the Holocaust; their personnel and policies today belong to generations removed from their earlier criminal behavior. Yet, these corporations are being successfully sued by Jews for their past actions. In the same vein, the U.S. government is not the same government as it was in the pre-Civil War era, yet its debts and obligations from the past are no less relevant today.

5. The Historical Precedents Used to Justify the Reparations Claim Do Not Apply, and the Claim Itself Is Based on Race Not Injury

As noted in our response to "Reason 4," the historical precedents for the reparations claims of African Americans are fully consistent with restitution accorded other historical groups for atrocities committed against them. Second, the injury in question—that of slavery—was inflicted upon a people designated as a race. The descendants of that people—still socially constructed as a race today—continue to suffer the institutional legacies of slavery some one hundred thirty-five years after its demise. To attempt to separate the issue of so-called race from that of injury in this instance is pure sophistry. For example, the criminal (in)justice system today largely continues to operate as it did under slavery—for the protection of white citizens against black "outsiders." Although no longer inscribed in law, this very attitude is implicit to processes of law enforcement, prosecution, and incarceration, guiding the

behavior of police, prosecutors, judges, juries, wardens, and parole boards. Hence, African Americans continue to experience higher rates of incarceration than do whites charged with similar crimes, endure longer sentences for the same classes of crimes perpetrated by whites, and, compared to white inmates, receive far less consideration by parole boards when being considered for release.

Slavery was an institution sanctioned by the highest laws of the land with a degree of support from the Constitution itself. The institution of slavery established the idea and the practice that American democracy was "for whites only." There are many white Americans whose actions (or lack thereof) reveal such sentiments today—witness the response of the media and the general populace to the blatant disfranchisement of African Americans in Florida during the last presidential election. Would such complacency exist if African Americans were considered "real citizens"? And despite the dramatic successes of the Civil Rights movement of the 1950s and 60s, the majority of black Americans do not enjoy the same rights as white Americans in the economic sphere. (We continue this argument in the following section.)

6. The Reparations Argument Is Based on the Unfounded Claim That All African-American Descendants of Slaves Suffer from the Economic Consequences of Slavery and Discrimination

Most blacks suffered and continue to suffer the economic consequences of slavery and its aftermath. As of 1998, median white family income in the U.S. was $49,023; median black family income was $29,404, just 60% of white income. (2001 *New York Times Almanac,* p. 319) Further, the costs of living within the United States far exceed those of African nations. The present poverty level for an American family of four is $17,029. Twenty-three and three-fifths percent (23.6%) of all black families live below the poverty level.

When one examines net financial worth, which reflects, in part, the wealth handed down within families from generation to generation, the figures appear much starker. Recently, sociologists Melvin L. Oliver and Thomas M. Shapiro found that just a little over a decade ago, the net financial worth of white American families with zero or negative net financial worth stood at around 25%; that of Hispanic households at 54%; and that of black American households at almost 61%. (Oliver and Shapiro, p. 87) The inability to accrue net financial worth is also directly related to hiring practices in which black Americans are "last hired" when the economy experiences an upturn, and "first fired" when it falls on hard times.

And as historian John Hope Franklin remarked on the legacy of slavery for black education: "laws enacted by states forbade the teaching of blacks any means of acquiring knowledge-including the alphabet-which is the legacy of disadvantage of educational privatization and discrimination experienced by African Americans in 2001."

Horowitz's comparison of African Americans with Jamaicans is a false analogy, ignoring the different historical contexts of the two populations. The British government ended slavery in Jamaica and its other West Indian territories in 1836, paying West Indian slaveholders $20,000,000 pounds ($100,000,000 U.S. dollars) to free the slaves, and leaving the black Jamaicans, who comprised 90% of that island's population, relatively free. Though still facing racist obstacles, Jamaicans come to the U.S. as voluntary immigrants, with greater opportunity to weigh, choose, and develop their options.

7. The Reparations Claim Is One More Attempt to Turn African-Americans into Victims. It Sends a Damaging Message to the African-American Community

What is a victim? Black people have certainly been victimized, but acknowledgment of that fact is not a case of "playing the victim" but of seeking justice. There is no validity to Horowitz's comparison between black Americans and victims of oppressive regimes who have voluntary immigrated to these shores. Further, many members of those populations, such as Chileans and Salvadorans, direct their energies for redress toward the governments of their own oppressive nations—which is precisely what black Americans are doing. Horowitz's racism is expressed in his contemptuous characterization of reparations as "an extravagant new handout that is only necessary because some blacks can't seem to locate the ladder of opportunity within reach of oth-

ers, many of whom are less privileged than themselves." What Horowitz fails to acknowledge is that racism continues as an ideology and a material force within the U.S., providing blacks with no ladder that reaches the top. The damage lies in the systematic treatment of black people in the U.S., not their claims against those who initiated this damage and their spiritual descendants who continue its perpetuation.

8. Reparations to African Americans Have Already Been Paid

The nearest the U.S. government came to full and permanent restitution of African Americans was the spontaneous redistribution of land brought about by General William Sherman's Field Order 15 in January, 1865, which empowered Union commanders to make land grants and give other material assistance to newly liberated blacks. But that order was rescinded by President Andrew Johnson later in the year. Efforts by Representative Thaddeus Stevens and other radical Republicans to provide the proverbial "40 acres and a mule" which would have carved up huge plantations of the defeated Confederacy into modest land grants for blacks and poor whites never got out of the House of Representatives. The debt has not been paid.

"Welfare benefits and racial preferences" are not reparations. The welfare system was set in place in the 1930s to alleviate the poverty of the Great Depression, and more whites than blacks received welfare. So-called "racial preferences" come not from benevolence but from lawsuits by blacks against white businesses, government agencies, and municipalities which practice racial discrimination.

9. What About the Debt Blacks Owe to America?

Horowitz's assertion that "in the thousand years of slavery's existence, there never was an anti-slavery movement until white Anglo-Saxon Christians created one" only demonstrates his ignorance concerning the formidable efforts of blacks to free themselves. Led by black Toussaint L'Ouverture, the Haitian revolution of 1793 overthrew the French slave system, created the first black republic in the world, and intensified the activities of black and white anti-slavery movements in the U.S. Slave insurrections and conspiracies such as those of Gabriel (1800), Denmark Vesey (1822), and Nat Turner (1831) were potent sources of black resistance; black abolitionists such as Harriet Tubman, Frederick Douglass, Richard Allen, Sojourner Truth, Martin Delany, David Walker, and Henry Highland Garnet waged an incessant struggle against slavery through agencies such as the press, notably Douglass's North Star and its variants, which ran from 1847 to 1863 (blacks, moreover, constituted some 75% of the subscribers to William Lloyd Garrison's Liberator newspaper in its first four years); the Underground Railroad, the Negro Convention Movement, local, state, and national anti-slavery societies, and the slave narrative. Black Americans were in no ways the passive recipients of freedom from anyone, whether viewed from the perspective of black participation in the abolitionist movement, the flight of slaves from plantations and farms during the Civil War, or the enlistment of black troops in the Union army.

The idea of black debt to U.S. society is a rehash of the Christian missionary argument of the 17th and 18th centuries: because Africans were considered heathens, it was therefore legitimate to enslave them and drag them in chains to a Christian nation. Following their partial conversion, their moral and material lot were improved, for which black folk should be eternally grateful. Slave ideologues John Calhoun and George Fitzhugh updated this idea in the 19th century, arguing that blacks were better off under slavery than whites in the North who received wages, due to the paternalism and benevolence of the plantation system which assured perpetual employment, shelter, and board. Please excuse the analogy, but if someone chops off your fingers and then hands them back to you, should you be "grateful" for having received your mangled fingers, or enraged that they were chopped off in the first place?

10. The Reparations Claim Is a Separatist Idea That Sets African-Americans Against the Nation That Gave Them Freedom

Again, Horowitz reverses matters. Blacks are already separated from white America in fundamental matters such as income, family wealth, housing, legal treatment, education, and political representation. Andrew Hacker, for example, has argued the case persuasively in his book *Two Nations*. To ignore such divisions, and then charge those who raise valid claims against society with promoting divisiveness, offers a classic example of "blaming the victim." And we have already refuted the spurious point that African Americans were the passive recipients of benevolent white individuals or institutions which "gave" them freedom.

Too many Americans tend to view history as "something that happened in the past," something that is "over and done," and thus has no bearing upon the present. Especially in the case of slavery, nothing could be further from the truth. As historian John Hope Franklin noted in his response to Horowitz:

> Most living Americans do have a connection with slavery. They have inherited the preferential advantage, if they are white, or the loathsome disadvantage, if they are black; and those positions are virtually as alive today as they were in the 19th century. The pattern of housing, the discrimination in employment, the resistance to equal opportunity in education, the racial, the inequities in the administration of justice, the low expectation of blacks in the discharge of duties assigned to them, the widespread belief that blacks have physical prowess but little intellectual capacities and the widespread opposition to affirmative action, as if that had not been enjoyed by whites for three centuries, all indicate that the vestiges of slavery are still with us.
>
> And as long as there are pro-slavery protagonists among us, hiding behind such absurdities as "we are all in this together" or "it hurts me as much as it hurts you" or "slavery benefited you as much as it benefited me," we will suffer from the inability to confront the tragic legacies of slavery and deal with them in a forthright and constructive manner.
>
> Most important, we must never fall victim to some scheme designed to create a controversy among potential allies in order to divide them and, at the same time, exploit them for its own special purpose.

BIBLIOGRAPHY

2001 *New York Times Almanac* (New York: Penguin Books, 2000).

Richard F. America. *Paying the Social Debt: What White America Owes Black America* (Westport, Conn.: Praeger, 1993).

J. D. B. DeBow. "The Interest in Slavery of the Southern Non-Slaveholder." In *Slavery Defended: The Views of the Old South,* ed. Eric L. McKitrick (Englewood Cliffs, NJ: Prentice-Hall, 1963), 169–77.

Ira Berlin, and others. *Slaves No More: Three Essays on Emancipation and the Civil War* (Cambridge [England]; New York: Cambridge University Press, 1992).

Dalton Conley. *Being Black, Living in the Red: Race, Wealth, and Social Policy in America* (Berkeley: University of California Press, 1999).

LaWanda Cox. "The Promise of Land for the Freedmen." *Mississippi Valley Historical Review* 45 (December 1958): 413–40.

Dudley Taylor Cornish. *The Sable Arm: Black Troops in the Union Army, 1861–1865* (1956; rpt. Lawrence, KS: University Press of Kansas, 1987).

Eric Foner. *Free Soil, Free Labor, Free Men: the Ideology of the Republican Party Before the Civil War* (New York: Oxford University Press, 1970).

John Hope Franklin, and Alfred A. Moss, Jr. *From Slavery to Freedom: A History of African Americans,* 7th ed. (New York: McGraw-Hill, 1994).

Andrew Hacker. *Two Nations: Black and White, Separate, Hostile, Unequal,* rev. ed. (New York: Ballantine Books, 1995).

James Oliver Horton and Lois E. Horton. *In Hope of Liberty: Culture, Community, and Protest Among Northern Free Blacks, 1700–1860* (New York: Oxford University Press, 1997).

James L. Huston. "Property Rights in Slavery and the Coming of the Civil War." *Journal of Southern History* 65 (1999): 249–86.

James Oakes. *The Ruling Race: A History of American Slaveholders* (New York: Vintage Books, 1983).

Melvin L. Oliver, and Thomas M. Shapiro. *Black Wealth/White Wealth: A New Perspective on Racial Inequality* (New York: Routledge, 1995).

Benjamin Quarles. *Black Abolitionists* (New York: Oxford University Press, 1969).

———. *The Negro in the Civil War* (Boston: Little, Brown, 1953).

Walter Rodney. *How Europe Underdeveloped Africa,* rev. ed. (Washington, D.C.: Howard University Press, 1981).

Jack Salzman, David Lionel Smith, and Cornel West, eds. *Encyclopedia of African-American Culture and History,* 5 vols. (New York: Macmillan Library Reference USA: Simon & Schuster Macmillan; London: Simon & Schuster and Prentice Hall International, 1996).

Diana Jean Schemo. "An Ad Provokes Campus Protests and Pushes Limits of Expression." *New York Times,* 21 March 2001, pp. A1, A17.

Abbot Emerson Smith. *Colonists in Bondage; White Servitude and Convict Labor in America, 1607–1776* (Chapel Hill: Pub. for the Institute of Early American History and Culture at Williamsburg, Va., by the University of North Carolina Press, 1947).

Barbara L. Solow and Stanley L. Engerman, eds. *British Capitalism and Caribbean Slavery: The Legacy of Eric Williams* (Cambridge [Cambridgeshire]; New York: Cambridge University Press, 1987).

Eric Williams, *Capitalism & Slavery* (1944; rpt. New York: Russell & Russell, 1961).

RANDALL ROBINSON

America's Debt to Blacks

Well before the birth of our country, Europe and the eventual United States perpetrated a heinous wrong against the peoples of Africa and sustained and benefited from the wrong through the continuing exploitation of Africa's human and material resources. America followed slavery with more than a hundred years of legal racial segregation and discrimination of one variety or another. It was only in 1965, after

Randall Robinson, "America's Debt to Blacks." Reprinted with permission from the March 13, 2000 issue of *The Nation.*

nearly 350 years of legal racial suppression, that the United States enacted the Voting Rights Act. Virtually simultaneously, however, it began to walk away from the social wreckage that centuries of white hegemony had wrought. Our country then began to rub itself with the memory-emptying salve of contemporaneousness. (If the wrong did not just occur, then it did not occur in a way that would render the living responsible.)

But when the black living suffer real and current consequences as a result of wrongs committed by a younger America, then contemporary America must shoulder responsibility for those wrongs until such wrongs have been adequately righted. The life and responsibilities of a nation are not limited to the life spans of its mortal constituents. Federal and state governments were active participants not only in slavery but also in the exclusion and dehumanization of blacks that continued legally up until the passage of key civil rights legislation in the sixties. Black calls for reparations began almost from the moment that slavery officially ended in 1865. However, although our calls far predate those of either the Japanese or the Jews, only the latter two communities have been responded to in a spirit of sober compassion and thoughtful humanity.

In response to our call, individual Americans need not feel defensive or under attack. No one holds any living person responsible for slavery or the later century-plus of legal relegation of blacks to substandard education, exclusion from home ownership via restrictive covenants and redlining, or any of the myriad mechanisms for pushing blacks to the back of the line. Nonetheless, we must all, as a nation, ponder the repercussions of those acts.

There are many ways to begin righting America's massive wrong. But resolving economic and social disparities so long in the making will require great resources (in the form of public initiatives, not personal checks) and decades of national fortitude. Habit is the enemy. Whites and blacks see each other the only way they can remember seeing each other— in a relationship of economic and social inequality. The system, which starts each child where its parents left off, is not fair. This is particularly the case for African-Americans, whose general economic start-

ing points have been rearmost because of slavery and its aftermath. Slaves for two and a half centuries saw not just their freedom taken from them but their labor as well. Were it a line item in today's gross national product report, that value would undoubtedly run into billions of dollars.

America has made an art form by now of grinding its past deeds, no matter how despicable, into mere ephemera. And African-Americans, unfortunately, have accommodated this amnesia all too well. It would behoove African-Americans to remember that history forgets first those who forget themselves. To do what is necessary to accomplish anything approaching psychic and economic parity in the next half-century will require a fundamental shift in America's thinking. Before the country in general can be made to understand, African-Americans themselves must come to understand that this demand is not for charity. It is simply for what they are owed on a debt that is old but compellingly obvious and valid still. (Do not be fooled by individual examples of conspicuous black success. They have closed neither the economic nor the psychic gaps between blacks and whites, and are statistically insignificant.)

The blacks of Rosewood, Florida, and Greenwood, Oklahoma, have successfully brought their case for reparations to national attention. Indeed, in Oklahoma a biracial commission has just concluded that justice demands that reparations be paid to the victims of Oklahoma's Greenwood massacre. Congressman John Conyers has introduced HR 40, a bill "to examine the institution of slavery," subsequent "de jure and de facto discrimination against freed slaves and their descendants," the impact of these forces "on living African -Americans" and to make recommendations to Congress on "appropriate remedies." Passage of this bill is crucial; even the making of a well-reasoned case for broader national restitution will do wonders for the spirits of blacks.

This is a struggle that African-Americans cannot lose, for in the very making of it we will discover, if nothing else, ourselves. And it is a struggle that all Americans must support, as the important first step toward America's having any chance for a new beginning in which all its inhabitants are true co-owners of America's democratic ideals.

18

Is Affirmative Action Wrong?

Himma and His Critics

People who argue about affirmative action tend to occupy a position at one or the other of two extremes. Those who support affirmative action typically don't think that it's just a pretty good idea. They believe that it's a matter of justice. Those who oppose affirmative action usually don't think that it just isn't such a great idea. They claim that it's positively unjust. Critics of affirmative action tend to think it's positively wrong to engage in affirmative action, that is, and defenders of affirmative action tend to think it's positively wrong not to. In the featured article for this chapter, Kenneth Einar Himma defends an argument about affirmative action that is designed to justify a position that falls somewhere in between these two extremes. Affirmative action, on this view, is morally permissible, but it is also nonobligatory. Morally speaking, it is okay for an organization to practice affirmative action, but it is also okay for an organization not to practice affirmative action.

At the heart of Himma's argument is an appeal to the ideal of fairness, and at the heart of his appeal to the ideal of fairness is an analogy (see section 4.1 of the Introduction for more about arguments from analogy). The basic idea behind the analogy is one that has been around since affirmative action programs were introduced in the middle of the 1960s. In 1965, for example, President Lyndon Johnson famously declared that "You do not take a person who, for years, has been hobbled by chains and liberate him, bring him up to the starting line of a race and then say, 'You are free to compete with all others,' and still just believe that you have been completely fair." Himma takes this analogy between affirmative action and runners in a race and refines it, in part making use of more recent research on the effects of institutional discrimination on the aspirations of those it harms. In particular, Himma makes use of studies by the Stanford psychologist Claude M. Steele to support the conclusion that stereotypes about the academic abilities of black and female students result in what Steele calls "academic disidentification." Rather than making high academic achievement an integral part of their self-identity, for example, many black students are led to feel that working hard in school instead amounts to "acting white." This phenomenon gives white and male students an unfair advantage in the competition for academic achievement, and affirmative action, on Himma's account, is therefore justified as a way of ensuring that the final results of the "race" are fair. If we agree that it is fair to adjust the results of a race if one of the runners suffered an unfair disadvantage at the start, that is, and if the case of affirmative action really is suitably analogous to the case of such a race, then we should agree that affirmative action is fair as well.

In her response to Himma's article, Lisa Newton also focuses on the analogy with runners in a race. While Himma maintains that the analogy supports the justice of affirmative action, however, Newton argues that it is ultimately unsuccessful. While she raises a variety of particular concerns about the comparison, readers should be especially careful to note her objections based on the claim that not every black and female student has been disadvantaged in the ways that Himma's argument seems to suggest and that there are many other forms of disadvantage that many other students may have suffered as well. Collectively, Newton maintains, facts such as these can serve to undermine the analogy that Himma constructs and, along with it, his case for the claim that affirmative action is not unjust.

QUESTIONS FOR CONSIDERATION

What are the differences between the analogy about a race that Himma offers in his article and the analogy that President Johnson offers in the speech quoted in the introduction to this chapter? Do the differences help to improve Himma's argument? How?

• What is "academic disidentification"? How does it differ from self-esteem? What role does this distinction play in Himma's argument?

• What differences are there between the case of the running race, on the one hand, and the case of affirmative action, on the other? Do these differences undermine Himma's argument? How might the significance of the differences be evaluated?

• What are the particular objections to the race analogy that Newton identifies? Which seem to be the most compelling? How, if at all, might Himma respond to them?

• Newton objects to Himma's claim that affirmative action is morally permissible. But a critic of Himma's position might also object from the other direction and maintain that it is not only permissible but obligatory as well. How might such a critic object to Himma's argument? Could the analogy of the running race be used to support the stronger claim that affirmative action is obligatory? Why or why not?

FURTHER READING

Beckwith, Francis J., and Todd E. Jones, eds. *Affirmative Action: Social Justice or Reverse Discrimination?* Amherst, N.Y.: Prometheus Books, 1997.

Cahn, Steven M., ed. *Affirmative Action and the University: A Philosophical Inquiry.* Philadelpia: Temple University Press, 1993.

Carter, Stephen L. *Reflections of an Affirmative Action Baby.* New York: Basic Books, 1991.

Eastland, Terry. *Ending Affirmative Action: The Case for Colorblind Justice.* New York: Basic Books, 1997.

Ezorsky, Gertrude. *Racism and Justice: The Case for Affirmative Action.* Ithaca and London: Cornell University Press, 1991.

Himma, Kenneth Einar. "It's the Rationale That Counts: A Reply to Newton." *Journal of Business Ethics* 37 (2002): 407–12.

Sher, George. "Diversity." *Philosophy and Public Affairs* 28, no. 2 (1999): 85–104.

Sowell, Thomas. *Affirmative Action Around the World: An Empirical Study.* New Haven and London: Yale University Press, 2004.

Thomson, Judith Jarvis. "Preferential Hiring." *Philosophy and Public Affairs* 2, no. 4 (1973): 364–84.

KENNETH EINAR HIMMA

Discrimination and Disidentification: The Fair-Start Defense of Affirmative Action

Abstract. The Fair-Start Defense justifies affirmative action preferences as a response to harms caused by race- and sex-based discrimination. Rather than base a justification for preferences on the traditional appeal to self-esteem, I argue they are justified in virtue of the effects institutional discrimination has on the goals and aspirations of its victims. In particular, I argue that institutional discrimination puts women and blacks at an unfair competitive disadvantage by causing academic disidentification. Affirmative action is justified as a means of negating this unfair disadvantage.

According to the Fair-Start Defense (FSD), affirmative action is justified as a response to harms caused by institutional sexism and racism. On this line of defense, institutional discrimination harms the self-esteem of females and blacks and inhibits their academic achievement relative to that of white males. Preferences are justified as a means of ensuring a "fair start" for females and blacks by negating unfair competitive advantages that accrue to white males from such harms.

FSD was initially supported by empirical research, but recent studies seem to refute FSD by showing there is little relationship between self-esteem and academic achievement. Instead of focusing on the effects of discrimination on self-esteem, I argue that preferences are justified as a response to the effects of institutional discrimination on the *aspirations* of women and blacks.[1]

1. DOES AFFIRMATIVE ACTION VIOLATE A RIGHT?

The U.S. experiment with affirmative action began shortly after the Civil Rights Act of 1964 prohibited race- and sex-based discrimination in education and employment when President Johnson required federal contractors to develop "goals and timetables" for employing a workforce that reflects the racial makeup of the community. Subsequently, many colleges and universities attempted to increase minority representation by admitting female and minority applicants over white male applicants with higher test scores.

The first Supreme Court decisions addressing affirmative action accepted its basic rationale. In the land-

Kenneth Einar Himma, "Discrimination and Disidentification: The Fair-Start Defense of Affirmative Action," *Journal of Business Ethics* Vol. 30, No. 3, Springer Publishing (April, 2001).

mark *Bakke* decision, for example, the court held that preferences may be used, when necessary, to achieve a diverse educational environment.[2] Likewise, in the *Fullilove* decision, the court held that the *federal* government may use racial classifications to remedy past discrimination.[3]

More recent decisions, however, suggest increasing discomfort with preferences. In *City of Richmond v. Croson*, the court held that state and local governments may not use racial classifications as a remedial device.[4] Then, in *Adarand Constructors v. Pena*, the court held that affirmative action measures would be evaluated under the difficult "strict scrutiny" standard: to pass constitutional muster, preferences must be necessary to achieve a compelling state interest and narrowly tailored to achieve that interest.[5]

Public opposition to preferences has also emerged, culminating in two successful initiative campaigns to ban race- and sex-based preferences in the public sector. In 1996, California voters passed Proposition 209, which provides that "[t]he state shall not discriminate against, or grant preferential treatment to, any individual or group on the basis of race, sex, color, ethnicity, or national origin in the operation of public employment, public education, or public contracting." Two years later, Washington voters passed Initiative 200, which was modeled after California's Proposition 209.

What typically motivates opposition to affirmative action is a convictioin that race- and sex-based preferences discriminate against white males and deny them positions to which they are morally entitled. On this view, preferences violate two moral principles: (1) every person has a right to be free of discrimination (the Nondiscrimination Principle); and (2) the most qualified applicant for and educational/employment position has a right to the position (the Merit Principle).

Affirmative action defenders often respond by citing the beneficial consequences of affirmative action,[6] but this line of argument implicitly concedes the dispositive point to opponents. As Ronald Dworkin has shown, a right can be outweighed by another right, but never by consequences: "[t]he claim that citizens have a right to free speech . . . impl[ies] that it would be wrong for the Government to stop them from speaking, even when the Government believes that what they will say will cause more harm than good."[7] Thus, if preferences violate a right, they are wrong no matter what their consequences might be.

Nevertheless, the Nondiscrimination and Merit Principles are both problematic. To begin with, there are many morally permissible reasons for hiring other than the most qualified candidate. Suppose two white males, John and Tom, apply for a cashier position. Performance tests show the only difference between them is that Tom completes each transaction a little faster and is hence slightly more qualified. If the most qualified person has a right to the job, it is wrong to hire John. But suppose that during the interview John establishes a better rapport with the employer than Tom. As a result, the employer likes John more—though he also likes Tom quite a bit. Even if the employer has no on-the-job contact with cashiers, she would do no wrong by hiring John.

As a practical matter, employers often choose among *qualified* candidates on the basis of subjective characteristics unrelated to job performance, and there is nothing obviously illegitimate about such practices. In a system of private property, a person may dispose of her property as she sees fit so long as she does not cause unjustifiable harm to others. Thus, other things being equal, a person may sell her property, trade it for services, or give it away outright.

This implies a property owner has considerable freedom to enter into contracts regarding her property. Insofar as such freedom extends to the employment context, a property owner, either directly or indirectly through an agent, has considerable latitude with respect to employment decisions. Of course, there is a strong incentive for an employer to hire the most qualified applicant: in most instances, a business cannot survive unless it offers a quality product at a competitive price. Hiring the best candidate is in the employer's best interest inasmuch as it increases the likelihood of success in the marketplace. But a business owner is not usually morally obligated to do what she can to ensure the competitive quality of her business.[8] To the extent that an owner's property rights entitle her to close the business at will, they would also allow considerable latitude in making hiring decisions.[9] Thus, the most qualified applicant has no right to be hired.[10]

The Nondiscrimination Principle fares no better. The word "discriminate" means "to make a clear distinction; distinguish; differentiate." By definition, then, *every* hiring and admission decision that distinguishes two people involves discrimination. For example, a law firm that hires only law students who graduate *cum laude* discriminates against law students who do not. But notwithstanding that such a policy is "discriminatory," it is justified as a means of ensuring that the firm employs only the most talented, hardest-working attorneys.

One might concede there is no general right of nondiscrimination, but argue there is a right not to be discriminated against on the basis of race and sex.[11] But even this claim is too strong. Discrimination on the basis of a belief that one race or sex is inferior to another is wrong because it violates the moral right to equal respect. When character and abilities are relevant, a person has a right to be judged on *her* character and abilities, and not on a stereotype. Nevertheless, some race- and sex-based discrimination is clearly permissible. It is legitimate for a director to insist that a black character be played by a black performer—even though, strictly speaking, the director's preference involves racial discrimination. It is likewise legitimate to publicly fund an education program that teaches women how to examine themselves for breast cancer.[12]

Whether any type of race- or sex-based discrimination violates a right of some kind, then, seems to depend on the motivation or rationale. What morally distinguishes, for example, a law requiring separate bathrooms in public accommodations for blacks and whites from a law requiring separate bathrooms in public accommodations for men and women has to do with the motivation. The latter law is permissible because its motivation is to protect legitimate privacy interests. The former, though identical in structure to the latter, is impermissible because the only plausible motivation for such a requirement is grounded in racist stereotypes. If this is correct, preferences can be justified by articulating a morally legitimate motivation or rationale.

2. THE FAIR-START DEFENSE OF PREFERENCES

Many theorists attempt to justify race- and sex-based preferences as a response to the psychological effects of discrimination on blacks and women. The general outlines of this approach were first suggested in *Brown v. Board of Education.* In *Brown,* the court struck down race-based segregation in public schools on the ground that it diminishes the self-esteem of black children: "To separate [black children] from others of similar age and qualifications solely because of their race generates a feeling of inferiority as to their status in the community that may affect their hearts and minds in a way unlikely ever to be undone."[13]

The *Brown* court relied on a study by Kenneth Clark in which black and white children were shown two dolls that were identical except for their color. When asked to indicate which doll was better, the vast majority of white and black children chose the white doll.[14] Clark concluded that racism harms black children by causing diminished self-esteem. On the basis of such studies, the *Brown* court struck down school segregation laws on the ground that segregation places black children at a competitive disadvantage by inhibiting their ability to learn:

> Segregation of white and colored children in public schools has a detrimental effect upon the colored children.... [F]or the policy of separating the races is usually interpreted as denoting the inferiority of the negro group. A sense of inferiority affects the motivation of a child to learn. Segregation with the sanction of law, therefore, has a tendency to [inhibit] the educational and mental development of negro children.[15]

A similar argument is often made with respect to the effects of sexism on self-esteem in women. Early on, girls are taught that the traits they are expected to develop are of less value than those boys are expected to develop:

> [I]t is an indisputable *fact* that once a girl develops an understanding of language, it is definitely communicated to her that she is less significant than boys. A girl may have learned of this simply by the absence of strong, autonomous, competent female figures in the male-dominated world of culture and society....

Within her family she may have learned she was insignificant by the way her family listened more attentively during dinner conversation to males than females, or the way her brothers were encouraged to take their ideas and career plans seriously while the girls were told it really didn't matter what they did.[16]

On this line of reasoning, sexism harms girls in the same way racism harms black children: it diminishes the capacity to learn by reducing self-esteem.

Affirmative action defenders conclude that preferences are justified as a morally legitimate response to the harms caused by institutional discrimination to self-esteem. One popular strategy has been to argue that race- and sex-based preferences are justified as a means of compensation.[17] Proponents argue that hiring preferences are *morally required* as compensation for harm to self-esteem caused by institutional discrimination. This argument relies on the following principle of compensatory justice:

(PCJ): One person A is morally obligated to compensate another person B for any harm to B caused by A's culpable conduct.

The problem with PCJ is that the person burdened by the preference is usually *not* individually culpable for the harms caused by institutional racism or sexism to the beneficiary of the preference.[18] In the typical case, one person B receives a preference at the expense of a white male A with no prior contact with B. In such instances, PCJ does not apply because PCJ imputes a duty of compensation only to persons causally responsible for the harms. While A has benefited from discrimination in general and from discrimination against B in particular, PCJ does not impute a duty of compensation to A because A did not cause the harm to B. Indeed, if PCJ is the only relevant principle, A can complain that giving a preference to B at A's expense is wrong because it is *unfair* to exact compensation from A for harms caused *by other persons*.[19]

In contrast to compensation-based justifications, FSD is based on a rationale that does not presuppose individual fault or guilt on the part of white males. To the extent that institutional discrimination causes harm to self-esteem and thereby makes it more difficult for blacks and women to achieve their potential, it

provides white males with an undeserved competitive advantage. Now this is not to say that all, or even most, blacks and women suffer from deficits in self-esteem.[20] Indeed, many blacks and women go on to achieve at a level that is beyond the reach of the vast majority of white males. But it is also true that every successful black person and woman has to confront institutional obstacles that white males do not have to confront.

Thus, on this line of reasoning, every white male has an undeserved competitive advantage in the form of a head start over every black and every woman. Of course, this advantage will often be counterbalanced by other factors. For example, an upper-class black girl will have far better educational opportunities than those of a lower-class white boy. As a result, it is true that an upper-class black female, even in a racist and sexist society, is more likely to achieve her potential than a poor white male. But it is also true that, in such a society, a poor white male receives a head start over a black female because of his race and sex. In such cases, the advantages of whiteness are not enough to overcome the disadvantages of poverty, but it is still true that institutional racism confers upon a poor white child an undeserved competitive advantage over black children.

According to FSD, then, it is not the purpose of affirmative action to *compensate* a person for the competitive disadvantage caused by institutional racism and sexism; rather the purpose is to *negate* the competitive advantages that unfairly accrue to white males as a result of racism and sexism. Here the footrace metaphor comes into play. Suppose a sprinter mistakes a car backfiring for the starter's pistol and begins a fraction of a second before the gun is fired. The runner places second in a field of ten sprinters. Even though the sprinter is not culpable for the false start, it would be unfair to the other runners—including the sprinter who placed first—to allow her to benefit from the head start. For this reason, it is permissible to disqualify the sprinter who got the head start or, if possible, reduce her time by a quantity corresponding to the advantage produced by the head start. According to FSD, it would be unfair to allow white males to benefit from the unfair competitive advantages they accrue as a result of institutional racism and sexism—just as it is would be unfair to allow the sprinter to benefit from her false start. Thus, affirmative action is permissible to negate such advantages.

FSD has a number of significant elements worth noting. First, it does not presuppose that white males are either individually or collectively culpable for institutional discrimination. Second, FSD addresses only one class of injury, namely that which causes a competitive disadvantage of some kind. If injury to self-esteem does not result in competitive disadvantage (as may arguably be true of discrimination against, for example, gay persons), FSD would not justify measures addressing that injury. Third, FSD justifies only those measures that operate to *negate* the competitive disadvantage; it will not justify measures, for example, that seek to *compensate* a person for such harm. Fourth, FSD justifies measures addressing only competitive disadvantages that are *unfair* because caused by a morally wrongful institutional practice. The idea is that the state is obligated to ensure the conditions of a fair start in a competitive market economy.

This last element of FSD has one important advantage over other arguments for affirmative action: it allows the affirmative action supporter to counter the charge that preferences are unfair to white males. For one could plausibly argue that even if a white male does not have a moral *right* violated by preferences, they are nevertheless unfair. If so, preferences can be justified only by considerations strong enough to outweigh this unfairness. And many arguments for preferences are unable to meet this burden. The values associated with encouraging diversity, for example, are not strong enough to outweigh the unfairness of preferences; thus, an argument that justifies preferences solely on the strength of such values is vulnerable to the fairness objection.

In contrast, FSD challenges the idea that granting race- and sex-based preferences necessarily involves unfairness to white males. The fairness objection to affirmative action assumes a preference operates to deprive a white male of something he has earned and hence deserves (even if merit does not give him a *right* to it). FSD counters the objection by denying that the preference deprives him of something he

deserves; for FSD argues that the competitive advantage that accounts for his superior qualifications was itself unfairly conferred and that fairness *requires* a preference to correct that injustice. For this reason, FSD is probably the strongest argument in the affirmative action defender's arsenal.

Nevertheless, it is important not to overstate the strength of FSD: FSD, in and of itself, establishes only that race- and sex-based preferences are morally permissible to negate the unfair competitive advantages accruing from institutional discrimination. This means that a private employer would do no moral wrong, other things being equal, to give a preference to a woman to negate an unfair competitive advantage. But FSD does not, in and of itself, imply the stronger conclusion that a private employer is morally *obligated* to give such preferences. That it is permissible, other things being equal, to take some measure to remedy an instance of unfairness does not imply that it is *obligatory* to do so. A child born to wealthy parents, for example, has many unearned educational opportunities not available to a child born to poor parents. But the unfairness of allowing a wealthy child to benefit from this unearned competitive advantage does not give rise to a moral obligation on the part of the parents to remedy such unfairness to other persons.

Nor does FSD clearly imply that the state should enact a law *requiring* private employers or educational institutions to give race- and sex-based preferences. The problem is that it is not clear that the unfairness of allowing white males to benefit from such advantages justifies the infringement on property rights entailed by a policy requiring preferences. Again, the unfairness of allowing a wealthy child to benefit from the many opportunities available only to such children does not, by itself, justify a *legal* restriction on what the parents can do with their property in the way of educating their child. Thus, respect for property rights, along with FSD, seems to entail that the state should allow, but *not* require, private employers to give preferences.

Most surprisingly, FSD, in and of itself, does not imply that the state itself *should* grant such preferences for employment and educational positions. What distinguishes private employers and educational institutions from public employers and educational institutions is, of course, that public institutions are funded by tax revenues, which are required without the consent of the individual taxpayer. Whereas a shareholder in a private company can opt out of supporting that company if she does not agree with its policies, this is not a genuine option for the taxpayer. If enough taxpayers object to using public money to subsidize race- and sex-based preferences, it might be wrong for the state to do so—even though it is permissible for private employers to grant preferences.[21]

3. FSD and the Concept of Self-Esteem

Recently, the factual claims about self-esteem on which FSD relies have come under attack. To begin with, researchers have noted only a weak statistical correlation between academic achievement and self-esteem. For example, B. C. Hansford and J. A. Hattie reviewed 128 studies and concluded that self-esteem differences account for, at most, 7% of variation in academic achievement among study subjects.[22] Moreover, as Alfie Kohn points out, the most reliable studies indicate the correlation is even weaker:

> [T]he correlation was even lower in studies published more recently; in studies conducted with larger, representative national samples of students; and in studies that used standardized indicators of performance (as opposed to even less reliable measure such as grades). The implication is that the better the research, the less significant the connection it will find between self-esteem and achievement.[23]

There is considerably less evidence showing the existence of a *causal* connection between self-esteem and academic achievement. The mere existence of a correlation between self-esteem and academic achievement does not, of course, imply the existence of a causal relationship between the two.[24] And two comprehensive reviews of the relevant literature conclude there is no evidence that academic perform-ance is causally influenced by self-esteem.[25] Indeed, one influential researcher suggests the relationship between the two variables might be negative: "At times, lack of a sense of worth is a more powerful stimulant to achievement than self-confidence."[26] Thus, the argument concludes, FSD fails as a justification of preferences because it relies on a nonexistent causal relationship between self-esteem and competitive ability.

If this argument is sound, FSD fails as a justification of preferences no matter how much harm institutional racism and sexism cause to the self-esteem of women and blacks. For FSD justifies affirmative action as an attempt to even the playing field by negating unfair competitive advantages. If injury to self-esteem does not engender competitive disadvantage, then FSD cannot justify preferences—no matter how much harm might be caused to well-being. FSD is, by its own terms, limited to restoring competitive equality among blacks, women, and white males.

And damage to self-esteem can have profound effects on well-being. Indeed, according to Nathaniel Branden, there is no more important element to understanding a person's behavior:

> [N]o factor [is] more decisive in [a person's] psychological development and motivation . . . than the estimate he passes on himself. . . . The nature of his self-evaluation has profound effects on a man's thinking processes, emotions, desires, values and goals. To understand a man psychologically, one must understand the nature and degree of his self-esteem, and the standards by which he judges himself.[27]

The reason for this is not difficult to appreciate. Self-esteem is the measure of a person's opinion of her own value and abilities and thus, according to Stanley Coopersmith, entails "personal judgment of worthiness that is expressed in the attitudes the individual holds towards himself."[28] How satisfied a person is with her life clearly depends on how satisfied she is with herself; as Branden puts the point, "[i]n order to seek values, man must consider himself worthy of enjoying them" (PSE 107). Given the obvious importance of self-esteem to psychological well-being,[29] damage to self-esteem constitutes a grave harm.

What determines a person's level of self-esteem, according to William James, is the ratio of successes she experiences relative to her goals.[30] The more successes relative to her goals, the greater her sense of self-esteem; the fewer successes relative to her goals, the lesser her sense of self-esteem. What matters for self-esteem, on this view, is not the total number of achievements; rather, it is the *proportion* of achievements relative to total goals.

Of course, this should not be taken to mean that it is entirely up to the individual to define what aspirations count in determining self-esteem. Self-esteem is essentially connected with a sense of competence and efficacy with respect to the basic aspects of one's life. Accordingly, self-esteem depends on being able to get things done in the world—and there are certain things that presumably matter to every psychologically healthy human being: food, shelter, status, and companionship. Even so, the individual has considerable latitude in deciding what counts in the way of adequate food, what counts in the way of adequate shelter, what counts in the way of social success, and how these values are related to each other. As Coopersmith puts the point, "The term 'success' has a different meaning to each individual. To some it is represented by material rewards, to others by spiritual satisfaction, and to still others by popularity."[31]

For this reason, while self-esteem must obviously be rooted in certain material facts about human needs and desires, people have considerable psychological latitude in determining how to construe, structure, and evaluate those facts in developing the aspirations that shape self-esteem. Accordingly, insofar as self-esteem is a function of the ratio of successes to aspirations, it can be promoted in two ways (subject, of course, to these material constraints). One obvious way is to achieve as many personal aspirations as possible. But, more intriguingly, self-esteem can also be promoted by excluding unsuccessful pursuits from the collection of aspirations that shape self-esteem.

Once we understand what self-esteem amounts to, it is easy to see why there is little relationship between *academic* achievement and self-esteem. A person with high self-esteem may be unmoved by failure in certain pursuits because her aspirations do not include success in those pursuits. For example, there are many more things I cannot do well than things I can: fixing cars, playing sports, making investments, and playing chess to name a few. But my incompetence at these pursuits has no bearing on my self-esteem because they are not among my personal goals. What matters to me is that I have certain intellectual abilities. To find out, for example, that I am not very good at philosophical analysis would be a profound blow to my self-esteem.

We can now explain why there is no significant correlation between academic achievement and self-esteem. A person successful at academic pursuits might be unhappy for any number of reasons unrelated to self-esteem; she might, for example, be clinically depressed. But if a person is successful at academic pursuits but nevertheless lacks self-esteem, it is because she does not regard academic success as an aspiration that shapes her self-concept. If, on the other hand, a person is unsuccessful at academic pursuits but nevertheless maintains high levels of self-esteem, it is for precisely the same reason: she does not regard academic success as an aspirational component of self-esteem. In both cases, academic success is irrelevant with respect to the level of self-esteem because academic pursuits are not highly valued.

While it might be true that institutional discrimination does not impair academic achievement *by reducing self-esteem*, it does so in another way. Claude M. Steele argues that structures of institutional discrimination are grounded in certain stereotypes about the intellectual abilities of women and blacks tht hamper academic achievement by causing "academic disidentification."[32] According to Steele, success in academic pursuits requires a commitment beyond academic self-confidence: "to sustain school success one must be identified with school achievement in the sense of its being a part of one's self-definition, a personal identity to which one is self-evaluatively accountable" (Threat, 613). Thus, a high regard for academic achievement is usually (but not always) a necessary condition of academic success; as Jason Osborne puts it, "students who are more identified with academics should be more motivated to succeed because their self-esteem is directly linked to academic performance."[33]

Steele argues these pervasive stereotypes cause even the most talented women and blacks "to remove the domain [of academic pursuits] as a self-identity, as a basis of self-evaluation" (Threat, 615). On Steele's view, the pressure among women and blacks to disidentify with such pursuits arises because of the fear that academic failure confirms stereotypes about intellectual ability:

> Like anyone, blacks risk devaluation for a particular incompetence, such as a failed test or a flubbed pronunciation. But they further risk that such performances will confirm the broader racial inferiority they are suspected of. Thus, from the first grade through graduate school, blacks have the extra fear that in the eyes of those around them their full humanity could fall with a poor answer or a mistaken stroke of the pen.[34]

In response to such pressure, Steele argues, women and blacks disidentify with academic achievement: "she disidentifies with achievement; she changes her self-conception, her outlook and values, so that achievement is no longer so important to her self-esteem" (Race, 74).[35] Academic disidentification insulates self-esteem from the debilitating effects of academic failure under a stereotype threat by rejecting academic success as a component of self-esteem.

But such protection comes at a high cost because disidentification undermines academic motivation by withdrawing emotional investment from academic pursuits.[36] As a result, women and blacks are more likely to underperform in areas falling within the relevant stereotype. Indeed, standardized test scores consistently overpredict the performance of women and blacks in areas affected by negative stereotypes. Thus, Steele observes:

> [G]iven any level of school preparation (as measured by tests and earlier grades), blacks somehow achieve less in subsequent schooling than whites (that is, have poorer grades, have lower graduation rates, and take longer to graduate), *no matter how strong that preparation is*. Put differently, the same achievement level requires better preparation for blacks than for whites—far better: *among students with a C+ average at the university I just described, the mean American College Testing Program*

(ACT) score for blacks was at the 98th percentile, while for whites it was only at the 34th percentile (Race, 70; emphasis added).

What explains the lower performance is academic disidentification and *not some skill deficit* because the students at each test-score level have comparable skills (Threat, 615).

Steele believes *all* women and blacks, and not just those who perform poorly, disidentify with academic pursuits and thus underperform relative to their potential: "because this anxiety is born of a socialization presumed to influence all members of the stereotyped group, virtually all members of this group are presumed to have this anxiety, to one degree or another" (Threat, 615). The argument here seems to be that since the stereotypes causing the pressure to disidentify are institutional, the effects of those stereotypes must be *universal*.

Nevertheless, the empirical evidence does not clearly support a universal generalization about disidentification, as many blacks and women seem to resist the pressure to disidentify and achieve at high levels. But FSD does not turn on such a strong conclusion. If, as I have argued, what distinguishes permissible from impermissible discrimination has to do with the motivation, then what is needed to justify preferences as a permissible form of discrimination is a morally acceptable motivation that does not involve impermissible stereotypes. Insofar as the motivation for affirmative action preferences is to negate an unfair competitive disadvantage, it involves no impermissible judgments about blacks, females, or white males. To the extent that the disadvantage is widespread among victims of discrimination,[37] the remedial motivation presents a morally plausible rationale for preferences.

In any event, although the claims about self-esteem and achievement presupposed in the last section seem to be false, FSD's basic strategy for justifying affirmative action is sound. According to FSD, it is morally permissible to negate undeserved competitive advantages that are conferred on one class of persons relative to another. The stereotypes supporting institutional sexism and racism encourage women and blacks to underperform relative to their abilities by causing academic disidentification. This confers an unfair head start to white males that may permissibly be negated by affirmative action measures. The use of race- and sex-based preferences, then, constitutes a morally legitimate device for creating the conditions of a fair start.

4. CAN PREFERENCES NEGATE UNFAIR ADVANTAGES?

One might argue that preferences do more harm than good by reinforcing the very stereotypes that ostensibly impede the academic performance of women and blacks; Shelby Steele's formulation of this argument is representative:

> In any workplace, racial preferences . . . make automatic a perception of enhanced competence for the unpreferreds and of questionable competence for the preferreds—the former earned his way, even though others were given preference, while the latter made it by color as much as by competence. Racial preferences implicitly mark whites with an exaggerated superiority just as they mark blacks with an exaggerated inferiority.[38]

Likewise, opponents suggest that preferences reinforce—and may cause—race- and sex-based animosity by creating resentment in the minds of white males.[39] But insofar as FSD is based on a desire to promote the welfare of people unfairly disadvantaged by institutional discrimination, it cannot justify any measure likely to diminish the welfare of such persons.

Nevertheless, if affirmative action reinforces stereotypes and resentment, a recent study suggests preferences are highly effective in accomplishing the legitimizing purpose of negating unfair advantages. Derek Bok and William Bowen tracked the development of more than 8,000 students who entered 28 highly selective colleges in 1976 and 1989.[40] Bok and Bowen found that black students admitted to these colleges with the help of preferences were more likely to graduate than black students at less selective schools (B&B 63).[41] They conclude that "the fact that graduation rates

increase as the selectivity of the college rises and that students of the same academic ability graduate at higher rates when they attend more selective institutions shows that carefully chosen minority students have not suffered from attending colleges heavily populated by white and Asian American classmates with higher standardized scores (B&B 88). Moreover, black students at these institutions are more likely than whites to pursue doctoral or professional degrees (B&B 98).

Preference recipients continue to reap the benefits of affirmative action long after they complete their degrees. Though there remains a gap between white and black earnings, affirmative action has helped to narrow the gap for preference recipients. For example, blacks graduating from these selective universities earn a greater percentage of what their white counterparts earn than blacks attending lesser universities (B&B 123). While whites from these universities are more likely to experience a higher level of job satisfaction than blacks, the gap is much smaller than would be expected if affirmative action had the effects described by Steele. Indeed, blacks are only 18% less likely than whites to report the highest level of job satisfaction (B&B 153). Even more tellingly, blacks are only 7% less likely than whites to report that they are somewhat or very satisfied with life (B&B 181) and are more likely to participate in civic activities (B&B 158). If affirmative action reinforces racial stereotypes and resentment, it is nonetheless successful in negating the unfair advantages that hold back victims of discrimination—which is all FSD requires.[42]

In any event, there is a deeper problem with Steele's view that preferences should be discontinued because of the resentment and stereotypes they cause in white males. Racist and sexist beliefs and sentiments are morally wrong no matter what the cause because they judge a person's character or worth on the basis of sex or skin color.[43] The possibility that preferences may cause or reinforce discriminatory sentiments that are morally wrong cannot outweigh the unfairness of allowing white males to benefit from racism and sexism. No matter how strongly I might want to keep ill-gotten goods, such feelings do not justify allowing me to keep them. To the extent that affirmative action preferences are likely to negate those disadvantages, the possibility that preferences cause racist and sexist sentiments cannot justify abandoning preferences—at least, not unless preferences are replaced with other measures likely to negate those disadvantages.

None of this, however, denies that a preference can harm the intended beneficiary. Charles Krauthammer infers from the high attrition rate of blacks at Berkeley (42% vs. 16% for whites) that affirmative action *harms* promising black students by placing them in universities where they are unlikely to succeed: "these bright black students . . . were perfectly qualified to be successes somewhere else but were instead artificially turned into failures by being admitted to high-pressure campuses, where only students with exceptional academic backgrounds can survive."[44] In such instances, Krauthammer argues, preferences harm the self-esteem of the intended beneficiaries.

While Krauthammer believes *all* affirmative action should be prohibited, the attrition rates at Berkeley support a much weaker conclusion: preferences should not be given to persons who are unable to take advantage of them. In the context of highly competitive endeavors where competence is defined relative to a given population, a preference can harm the very person it is intended to benefit. At Berkeley, preferences were given to individuals who are highly qualified on most threshold measures of competence but not at an institution where competence is defined relative to the very best students. In their zeal to achieve proportionate representation, Berkeley administrators failed to assess accurately the qualifications of some black applicants.

Once the rationale for affirmative action is understood, it becomes clear why society should not give preferences to people who are not likely to benefit from them. Giving a preference to someone who is not in a position to take advantage of it exacerbates, rather than negates, a competitive disadvantage because it causes harm to self-esteem by ensuring failure. Clearly, the concern to negate unfair disadvantages cannot justify doing something that exacerbates those very disadvantages. Indeed, if the rationale for affirmative action is to negate the competitive disadvantages caused by institutional

racism and sexism, it would be wrong to give a preference to someone who cannot benefit from it precisely because doing so would exacerbate that disadvantage.

As Bok and Bowen suggest, recipients of preferences should be carefully chosen to ensure that they meet the minimal requirements to succeed in a given position. For positions where competence is defined by threshold abilities, this will be easy enough. Once the appropriate threshold levels are determined, an exam may be given to determine whether the applicant has the minimum requisite skills. In positions where competence is defined relative to a given population, it will be somewhat harder to assess the necessary skill levels because the characteristics of the relevant population may change from year to year. But this can be done, for example, by determining from year to year the lowest SAT scores positively predicting academic success and taking their average over a period long enough to reflect any existing trends but short enough not to lose those trends in long-term movements. In any case, it is always possible to get a reasonably accurate sense of whether a candidate is likely to benefit from a preference.

In this essay, I have attempted to reconfigure the Fair Start Defense, which attempts to justify affirmative action preferences by an appeal to the psychological effects of institutional racism and sexism. Rather than base a justification for such preferences on the traditional appeal to self-esteem, I have argued they are justified in virtue of the effects institutional discrimination has on the goals and aspirations of its victims. In particular, I have argued that institutional discrimination puts women and blacks at an unfair competitive disadvantage by encouraging academic disidentification. Affirmative action, I conclude, is justified as an attempt to negate this unfair disadvantage.

NOTES

1. A couple of caveats are in order here. First, I do not wish to claim that preferences are *sufficient* to negate the lingering effects of discrimination. The point of

preferences, according to FSD, is to negate an unfair advantage that white males have with respect to admission and hiring decisions. Accordingly, preferences cannot remove further obstacles associated with, for example, high tuition costs; such obstacles require different solutions. Unfortunately, measures that make it easier to afford tuition at a university do not make it easier to be admitted. Insofar as a person faces unfair obstacles to admission resulting from discrimination, preferences are *necessary* to achieve the conditions of a fair start.

Second, while there are many forms of wrongful institutional discrimination, my argument purports to justify only preferences that negate the effects of race-and sex-based discrimination. The reason for this artificially narrow focus is that there is a growing body of social scientific evidence documenting the effects of race- and sex-based discrimination on the academic aspirations of females and blacks. To the extent that other forms of wrongful discrimination cause similar effects, FSD would justify preferences as a means of negating such effects. Unfortunately, I know of no studies addressing the effects of these other forms of discrimination.

2. *Regents of the University of California v. Bakke*, 438 U.S. 265 (1978).

3. *Fullilove v. Klutznick*, 448 U.S. 448 (1980). The court upheld a 10% federal set-aside in public works funding for minority businesses.

4. *City of Richmond v. Croson*, 488 U.S. 469 (1989).

5. *Adarand Constructors, Inc. v. Pena*, 515 U.S. 200 (1995).

6. For example, James Rachels argues that affirmative action increases the number of professional role models for young blacks. James Rachels, "What People Deserve," in John Arthur and William H. Shaw (eds.), *Justice and Economic Distribution* (New York: Prentice Hall, 1978). Derek Bok argues that affirmative action promotes intellectual enrichment by giving black and white students an opportunity to learn about each other. Derek Bok, "The Case for Racial Preference," *The New Republic* 192 (February 4, 1985).

7. See Ronald Dworkin, *Taking Rights Seriously* (Cambridge: Harvard University Press, 1978), p. 190.

8. This is not to deny that employers in some circumstances are obligated to hire the most qualified candidate. Thus, for example, in a publicly held corporation, an employer may have a fiduciary responsibility to stockholders to hire the most qualified candidate. Employers in the health care industry may have a similar obligation to the public. But notice in these cases, the obligation is not owed *to the candidate*.

9. Indeed, on the strength of such considerations, Richard Epstein argues for the repeal of laws prohibiting employment discrimination. Richard A. Epstein, *Forbidden Grounds: The Case Against Employment Discrimination Laws* (Cambridge: Harvard University Press, 1992).

10. Many opponents of race- and sex-based preferences support *other* kinds of preferences. For example, William Blackstone suggests that preferences should be given to economically disadvantaged people regardless of race or sex. See William T. Blackstone, "Reverse Discrimination and Compensatory Justice," *Social Theory and Practice*, vol. 3, no. 3 (Spring 1975). Other opponents support preferences for veterans. But if the most qualified person is morally entitled to the position, then *all* preferences are wrong.

11. See, e.g., Lisa H. Newton, "Reverse Discrimination as Unjustified," *Ethics* 83 (1973), pp. 308–312.

12. In a system of limited health care resources, allocation decisions have to be made efficiently. For this reason, it is permissible to fund AIDS education for people who are in high-risk groups. If this is correct, then it is also permissible to fund education about breast cancer only for persons who are at high risk for it.

13. *Brown v. Board of Education*, 347 U.S. 483 (1954), at 494.

14. K. B. Clark, "Effect of Prejudice and Discrimination on Personality Development" (Midcentury White House Conference on Children and Youth, 1950). These results were replicated decades later. See Daniel Goleman, "Black Child's Self-View Is Still Low, Study Finds," *New York Times*, Aug. 31, 1987, A13.

15. *Brown*, 347 U.S. at 494.

16. Mary Ellen Donovan and Linda Sanford, *Women and Self-Esteem: Understanding and Improving the Way We Think and Feel About Ourselves* (Garden City, NY: Anchor Press, 1984), pp. 40–41.

17. See, e.g., Bernard Boxill, "The Morality of Reparations," *Social Theory and Practice* 2 (Spring 1972); Judith Jarvis Thomson, "Preferential Hiring," *Philosophy & Public Affairs* 2 (Summer 1973); Anne C. Minas, "How Reverse Discrimination Compensates Women," *Ethics* 88 (October 1977).

18. One might counter that white males are *collectively* at fault for such conditions. The collective guilt of white males would justify certain kinds of measures, such as a tax imposed on *all* white males to exact reparations, but not affirmative action preferences because a preference burdens only the white males against whom the preference operates. If the guilt is collective, then the burdens associ-

ated with that guilt should be distributed in a way that reflects its collective nature.

19. Likewise for an argument that attempts to justify preferences as compensation for *benefits* that unfairly accrue to white males as a result of racism and sexism. The duty of one person A to *compensate* another person B extends to only those consequences for which A is individually culpable—and this is so whether the relevant consequence is harm to B or an undeserved benefit to A. Again, in the typical case, B receives a preference at the expense of a white male A with no prior contact with B. A may, of course, benefit from B's diminished self-esteem; but if there is no prior contact between A and B, then it is unlikely that A could have done anything culpable to B that produced that benefit at B's expense.

20. A point that has been made with indignation: "'Oversimplification' and 'primitive modes of analysis' apply as well to the discourse on the psychology of the Black American.... The social scientific literature on Negro identity written between 1936 and 1967 reported that self-hatred and group rejection were typical of Black psychological functioning.... For years thereafter, the conventional wisdom stated that the average Black person suffered from low self-esteem.... [F]ar too simple." See William E. Cross Jr., *Shades of Black: Diversity in African-American Identity* (Philadelphia: Temple University Press, 1991), pp. ix–x.

21. Nevertheless, there is good reason to think a state should give preferences to qualified applicants for educational and employment positions. This issue is beyond the scope of this essay, so I can devote only a few remarks to it here. Insofar as the state uses public resources to confer an unfair competitive advantage on one class of persons, it seems clear that the state is morally obligated to negate that advantage. Consider the justification for veteran preferences given to people drafted into the military. A person who serves in the military must devote considerable energy to learning skills of little value in the private sector. For this reason, someone who does not serve in the military has an unearned competitive advantage over someone who does because the former is better able to devote energy to acquiring commercially valuable skills.

Of course, many people choose to enlist and thus willingly assume whatever competitive disadvantage attends military service; in such cases, one might argue the state has no moral reason to level the playing field. But when the state requires a person to serve in the military, as it did during the draft era, the state should negate the resulting competitive disadvantage. For this reason, the state should take steps to negate any competitive disadvantage

that results from laws supporting institutional racism and sexism.

22. B. C. Hansford and J. A. Hattie, "The Relationship Between Self and Achievement/Performance Measures," *Review of Educational Research*, vol. 52, no. 1 (1982), pp. 123–142.

23. Alfie Kohn, "The Truth About Self-Esteem," *Phi Delta Kappan*, vol. 76, no. 4 (December 1994), pp. 272–283, 285.

24. Nor would it tell us anything about the direction of that relationship. Notice that it might be that a high level of academic performance causes a high level of self-esteem, or it might be that a high level of self-esteem causes a high level of academic performance.

25. See Mary Ann Scheirer and Robert E. Kraut, "Increasing Educational Achievement Via Self-Concept Change," *Review of Educational Research*, vol. 49 (1979); Thomas G. Moeller, "What Research Says About Self-Esteem and Academic Performance," *Educational Digest*, January 1994.

26. Martin Covington, "Self-Esteem and Failure in School," in Andrew Mecca, et al. (eds.), *The Social Importance of Self-Esteem* (Berkeley: University of California Press, 1989), p. 98.

27. Nathaniel Branden, *The Psychology of Self-Esteem* (Los Angeles: Nash Publishing Corp., 1969), p. 103. Hereinafter referred to as PSE.

28. Stanley Coopersmith, *The Antecedents of Self-Esteem* (San Francisco: W. H. Freeman, 1967), p. 5.

29. Indeed, so important is a healthy sense of self-worth to psychological well-being that some researchers characterize self-esteem as a basic human need. See, e.g., Rom Harre, *Personal Being: A Theory for Individual Psychology* (Oxford: Blackwell Publishers, 1983); Abraham H. Maslow, *Motivation and Personality* (New York: Harper & Row, 1954).

30. William James, *Principles of Psychology* (New York: Dover Publications, 1950). Susan Harter puts the point in terms of a discrepancy between a particular aspect of a person's self-concept and the individual's self-rating on that dimension. See Harter, "The Construction and Conservation of the Self," in D. K. Lapsley and F. C. Power (eds.), *Self, Ego, and Identity: Integrative Approaches* (New York: Springer-Verlag, 1988), pp. 42–70.

31. Coopersmith, *The Antecedents of Self-Esteem*, p. 38.

32. Claude M. Steele, "A Threat in the Air: How Stereotypes Shape Intellectual Identity and Performance," *American Psychologist*, vol. 52, no. 6 (1997), pp. 613–629. Henceforth referred to as "Threat."

33. Jason Osborne, "Race and Academic Disidentification," *Journal of Educational Psychology*, vol. 89, no. 4 (1997), p. 728.

34. Claude M. Steele, "Race and the Schooling of Black Americans," *The Atlantic Monthly* (April 1992), pp. 74–75. Hereinafter referred to as "Race." Similarly, Steele points out that "any frustration [the advanced female math student] has at the frontier of her skills could confirm the gender-based limitation alleged in the stereotype, making this frontier, because she is so invested in it, a more threatening place than it is for the nonstereotyped" (Threat, 618).

35. Unfortunately, many young black males regard academic success as involving a "sellout" and an attempt to "be white." It is not that academic success is of low value to self-esteem; rather it is that lack of academic success is of high value to self-esteem. Lack of such success is regarded as evidence of black authenticity expressed through a rejection of the most important values of a white culture that has been built on the oppression of blacks. See, e.g., Signithia Fordham and John Ogbu, "Black Students' School Success: Coping with the Burden of Acting White," *Urban Review*, vol. 18, no. 3 (1986), pp. 176–206.

36. This distinguishes discrimination on the basis of race and sex from other forms of discrimination that may cause psychological injury. Discrimination on the basis of physical attractiveness doubtless causes profound psychological injury, but it is not a likely cause of academic disidentification, which creates a competitive disadvantage by withdrawing emotional energy from the academic pursuits necessary to succeed in professions like law and medicine. Insofar as such discrimination does not result in a psychological injury that diminishes competitive abilities, FSD does not justify corrective measures.

37. Jason Osborne, "Race and Academic Disidentification," note 3, above. See also Jason Osborne, "Academics, Self-Esteem, and Race: A Look at the Underlying Assumptions of the Disidentification Hypothesis," *Personality & Social Psychology Bulletin*, vol. 21, no. 5 (May 1995), pp. 449–455; Brenda Major and Toni Schmader, "Coping with Stigma Through Psychological Disengagement," in Janet K. Swim, et al., *Prejudice: The Target's Perspective* (San Diego: Academic Press, 1998), pp. 219–241; Cynthia Winston, et al., "The Utility of Expectancy/Value and Disidentification Models for Understanding Ethnic Group Differences in Academic Performance and Self-Esteem," *Zeitschrift fuer Paedagogische Psychologie*, vol. 11 (December 1997), pp. 177–186.

38. Shelby Steele, *The Content of Our Character* (New York: St. Martin's Press, 1990), pp. 111–125.

39. See, e.g., Thomas Sowell, "Affirmative Action: A Worldwide Disaster," *Commentary* (December 1989).

40. Derek Bok and William Bowen, *The Shape of the River: Long-Term Consequences of Considering Race in College and University Admissions* (Princeton: Princeton University Press, 1998). Henceforth referred to as B&B.

41. At first glance, this may seem hard to reconcile with Claude Steele's claims about disidentification; after all, one would think that the anxiety levels that produce disidentification as a defense mechanism would be greater in more selective schools than in less. The reverse, however, is more likely true. The anxiety that causes disidentification is related to a fear of confirming racial stereotypes. Black students in more selective schools are less likely to experience anxiety about confirming these stereotypes because students of *all* races are more likely to fail in more selective schools. If all students are more likely to fail, then there is less risk that failure by a black student would be perceived as related to race.

42. In this connection, it is important to realize that what justifies affirmative action, according to FSD, is a concern to negate these unfair disadvantages—and not a concern to eliminate racist and sexist stereotypes.

43. Preferences do not violate this obligation because, properly grounded, they are simply a means of negating unfair advantages that have accrued to the burdened white male and hence make no judgment about the character of either the recipient or the person burdened by the preference. See Section 2, *supra*.

44. See Charles Krauthammer, "Lies, Damn Lies and Racial Statistics," *Time*, vol. 151, no. 15 (April 20, 1998), p. 32. Krauthammer is quoting social theorist Thomas Sowell in this passage.

Critic

Lisa Newton

A Fair Defense of a False Start: A Reply to Kenneth Himma

In his "Discrimination and Disidentification," above, Kenneth Himma argues for a limited permission to prefer candidates for admission to educational opportunities and for employment on the basis of color or gender. With this argument, he steps into the middle of a controversy by now 30 years in the festering, to which at a much earlier date we have contributed.[1] We argued that all such preferences were unjustified, and that seems to disagree with Himma's thesis, hence the invitation to take him on. We do so with great gusto.

Our first task will be to get very clear on just what Himma does say and does not say, so that we do not end up boxing with straw men in our defense. His claim, as we take it, is that the Fair Start Defense (FSD) of Affirmative Action (racial and sexual preference) Programs, as applied to hiring and admissions decisions, can be grounded in the data available for the academic (especially) accomplishments of women and African Americans. The data show no particular correlation between academic achievement and "self-esteem," but do show a correlation between academic achievement and the importance attached to that achievement by the student. For the first reason, the defense of racial integration (and therefore of certain kinds of preferences) in education presented by the Court in *Brown vs. School Board* in 1954, must fail. The Court took judicial notice of the fact that "separate" is inherently unequal since the fact of segregation damages the self-esteem of the black child and therefore makes it

impossible for him to compete on equal terms from that point on. That turns out to be false; there is no correlation between academic achievement and measures of self-esteem.[2] But there is evidence that African Americans and women at least attribute less importance to academic achievement than their peers of a different racial heritage or gender configuration, as Himma points out. Therefore it can be argued that the institutionalized racism and sexism that figure so largely in our nation's recent history have had an adverse effect on the goals and aspirations of blacks and women. From that it can be surmised that they may be expected (if no action is taken) to continue to be under-represented in the advantageous schools and jobs. In the competition for such favored positions, they must start behind the line from which their lighter and more advantaged brothers begin, and therefore it cannot appear to be unjust to allow those preferences which amount to constructing a fair start to the race. Even as, in a footrace in which one runner starts ahead of the gun, it will seem proper to penalize that runner in calculating the prizes, so it seems proper to allow (not compel) employers and admissions committees to take race and gender into consideration in calculating the admissions and employment decisions. That much is claimed, and no more.

In this argument Himma prescinds from all consequentialist considerations. We are not to discuss the advantages of a diversified workplace, we are not to consider what course of action will tend to raise

Lisa Newton, "A Fair Defense of a False Start: A Reply to Kenneth Himma," *Journal of Business Ethics* Vol. 33, No. 2, Springer Publishing (September, 2001).

the collective income of a disadvantaged community, we are not even to worry that the first effect of a racial or gender preference program may be to stigmatize its first beneficiaries, the African Americans and women who are preferred. (Incidentally, it seems that it does not.) For the moment we accept the precision, and place all utilitarian thoughts on the shelf. But let us make it a low shelf, for ultimately, the major argument disposed of, we may wish to return to such considerations.

A few comments seem in order before taking up the argument. First, Himma's claims are modest and plausible, his research is excellent, and his thesis is well argued.[3] We think it fails as a defense, but not for lack of honesty and merit. Second, on the evidence of such honesty, we will not revisit the sources or attempt original research in this reply. We accept the data as given, and disagree, if at all, only in the interpretation placed upon it.

Let's take a closer look at the claim. When the decision-maker (singular or collective) who controls a prize of some sort—a good job or acceptance into the freshman class of a good school, for instance—has reason to believe that of the candidates before him (let us assume the last two candidates), one has suffered a disadvantage such that in the course of their progress to this decision, that one had an extra distance to go, a handicap to overcome, then in that (and only that) case the decision-maker is permitted, out of fairness, to favor that candidate. Note, again, what the claim is not, and does not do.

(1) It is not veiled utilitarianism. We are familiar with the situation in which two persons are in competition for some favored spot (let us assume the last spot), and in which one of the persons seems to have had to struggle harder, or overcome some handicap, to get to that point. It is often reasonable to prefer that person *not* out of justice or some starting-line notion of fairness, but because if that person has the dedication and smarts and guts to overcome the handicap to get here, we can predict with more confidence that that person will succeed in the school or the job. That is a consequentialist argument (a rather good one), and therefore is not what we are talking about. (2) It does not compel research to ensure the correctness of the decision-maker's perception. The decision-maker may be wrong about the handicap, although there is no permission to be irrational about it. As long as he or she honestly and rationally believes there has been such handicap, he or she may in justice prefer the putatively handicapped one. (3) It does not specify some sort of "tie" situation, in which such preference can only be a tie-breaker. (4) It does not compel the preference. The decision-maker is perfectly justified in choosing the other. Therefore (and this is crucially important) the argument can never justify a policy, enforceable at law, demanding preference for such handicapped ones.

We are dealing, then, only with a moral choice and an ethical policy. Is it permissible to do what we can to compensate for the institutionalized prejudices of our society, only by recognizing a marginally superior desert in the person who has had to traverse the greater distance to get to about the same point in the race?

The modesty of the claim, the request, the opportunity, is inherently attractive. What it is not, is just. The answer to the question is no, it is not permissible. We are dealing with academic aspirations only, with females and African Americans only, when the world presents us with starting lines of Byzantine complexity and handicaps as numerous as the sands of the sea. Let us enumerate the problems:

1. The attractive simile is the footrace. Yet by the time any runners in a public footrace get to the starting line, all the selecting has been done to make sure that they are evenly matched. The "fair start" here taken as a model is actually the result of a vigorous (even ruthless) pruning that eliminates all but runners of similar ability and track record. It is the long, painful and sometimes (wholly unknown to the judges) political process that does the heavy lifting of justice. After that, the mechanisms of the start of the race are relatively insignificant. In the real race of real life (swelling organ music) there is no such process, and people arrive on the employment line from so many different preparations that they defy comparison. Handicap relative to what? Discrimination by whom?

2. You can't presume the handicap, or lack of it. We are asked, in the model, to take people of huge variety, and compensate for presumed handicaps of race and gender only. In reality, the handicap may

vary significantly. For instance, let's add obesity to the list. Why would it not surprise us to find that a slim and beautiful girl was preferred to a fat boy in a style-conscious white family, or that an employer instinctively chose a slim African American over an obese Italian American for the clerk's or the salesman's job? On what considerations of justice could we be asked to ignore a condition that is often associated with negative choices, while taking into account other conditions that sometimes, but not always, are associated with societal preference? (We aren't even ashamed, any more, of discriminating against cigarette smokers.) Or take the youth with imperfectly corrected hare-lip, butt of stupid jokes from childhood. On what considerations of justice can we ignore actual evidence of actual prejudice, insult, and assault on aspirations, to favor hypothetical evidence of hypothetical prejudice? Consider some purely anecdotal evidence. Example (1): some years ago a deeply disturbed African American man opened fire on a carload of passengers on the Long Island Rail Road. His lawyers instinctively entered a legal defense of "Black Rage," the maddening frustration of the experience of consistent racial discrimination, which had exploded in this violence, and for which the perpetrator was therefore not entirely to blame. But the history showed that the young man, raised in a society of people of color, had attended favored private schools and enjoyed all other privileges of the elite. While other African Americans surely experience maddening discrimination, *he* had experienced none. The jury was not persuaded by the defense. Example (2): Raised in a wealthy suburb, this author was encouraged in weird intellectual pursuits from an early age by loving if uncomprehending parents, was sent to excellent schools (including Swarthmore College, champion of equality for women since its founding), sailed through graduate school and landed in a rewarding job without noticing any hostile discrimination at all along the way. This was emphatically not the experience of all of our less fortunate sisters in the profession. But on what justification could any preference system favor us in a competition with a man who happened to have the misfortune to be born (say) a middle child in a family? Worse yet, poor?

3. Adding the two points together, we find, should Himma's argument be adopted, a prescription for chaos. Since research is not compelled, the employer is allowed to take into account race and gender for attributing marginally greater desert, if he likes, but if he is conscientious, he may want to take into account other conditions that may limit aspirations in the academic and employment fields. What other conditions might those be? As above, obesity, physical deformity or unattractiveness,[4] childhood abuse, deprivation (physical, cultural or psychological), disfavored national or ethnic group (for awhile no one would hire Indians because they were "too ambitious," and would no doubt cut corners in any job, while Puerto Ricans were assumed to be lazy, loud, and generally inappropriate), disadvantageous position in the family birth order, disfavored socioeconomic origins (not belonging to the right country clubs), disfavored geographical origins, disfavored intonations or accents (for receptionist jobs). . . . But the list can go on forever. We cannot, finally, omit from that list simple genetically conditioned limitations on intellectual ability, ambition, and ability to get along with others. Already, employers are tearing their hair out over the extent to which the Americans with Disabilities Act (ADA) protects the mentally ill in employment situations where they may pose a risk of violence or serious incapacity to get the job done. May we discriminate against the intellectually handicapped in admissions to graduate school?

4. And then we must ask the relationship between desert (reward for overcoming handicaps) and merit. It will be a long time, we suspect, before we pick our basketball team with no regard to athletic ability. We expect that long before that, we will pick our freshman class with no regard to academic ability. But won't that be self-defeating? Our efforts to be "fair" may diminish the value of the prize. This objection is not entirely consequential in force. The effort to make the contest really truly fair and objective may distort the objective of the contest to the point that it is no longer a contest at all, in the sense that it is no longer worth winning (we recall the "Open Admissions" policy of the City University of New York, now abandoned).

In sum, the "competitive" situation of human beings who regard themselves as "in competition" for certain valued societal awards, linked with material success in the society, is infinitely varied and complex, with "starting lines" for the "race" a moving target. People are born with a variety of useful and useless traits (good at word games, lousy at remembering faces and names, strong in athletics, graceless on the dance floor, with a strong resemblance to Uncle Harry), and are chosen or hired for a variety of relevant and irrelevant traits (did well on the SATs, unintentionally insulted the admissions committee member that the dean most dislikes,[5] no good at hockey but fills the Midwest quota, with a strong resemblance to the dean's beloved younger son). We make a footrace fair by rigorous screening of those who may race. Trying to make the race of life fair is beyond the capability of mortals.

So Himma's project, however well argued, fails. Before closing, we would like to fish out of the last pages, and expose to the light, a curious and harmful doctrine that we do not think is essential to his argument, and should be got rid of. "If, as I have argued," he argues, "what distinguishes permissible from impermissible discrimination has to do with the motivation, then what is needed to justify preferences as a permissible form of discrimination is a morally acceptable motivation that does not involve impermissible stereotypes." We submit that secondary discrimination is not justifiable, even though it proceeds from the best motives in the world. Secondary discrimination, as it has been called, is a disposition to make award decisions (for educational slots and jobs, for instance) that are systematically unfavorable to power minorities, not because the decision-maker holds unjustifiably unfavorable stereotypes of those minorities, but because he holds justifiably unfavorable opinions of those among whom the new students or employees will be cast. The woman will not be picked for the job in the garage because "the guys are so crude, you know, they'll make life miserable for her." The African American will not be picked for the elite school because "it's not the boys, it's the boys' parents—he'll be picked on, insulted, and no one will make friends with him, their parents won't let them.

If we put him on a traveling team, he'll be booed. I wouldn't expose a boy to that sort of treatment." The prediction of misery for the woman and the African American may be very well grounded; we think that the conclusion—don't pick them—is entirely wrong. But note that the motivation is entirely innocent.

We conclude where we began: that considerations of fairness cannot justify preferences based on race or gender. Now let's return to that low shelf and look at the consequences of preferences. We have, after all, several societal goals consciously in mind for the selection procedures we use for desired prizes; unless very carefully crafted, preferences interfere with attaining these goals. First, we want the procedures to select the best qualified (whatever that may mean in any given case) for positions in our educational, economic and professional systems. Second, we want the procedures to *appear* to select the best qualified, for we want the gatekeeping mechanisms for the important advantages in the society to model meritarian justice for all other institutions, so that citizens will be encouraged to strive for excellence and merit. Therefore any preference system is *prima facie* unjustifiable as making the system appear to be less than fully directed to hiring the best qualified.

Note that our conclusion does not at all rule out preferences, openly stated, for good utilitarian reasons. There is nothing ethically wrong with deciding that your department, or workplace, would be enhanced by the addition of women or African Americans, and going out and hiring some. (It may be illegal to put that in the ad for the position; so much the worse for the law.) After all, when we decide that our department would be enhanced by the hiring of an Orientalist, we thereby discriminate against medievalists and Wittgensteinians, but not unjustifiably. Similarly, there is nothing wrong with actively recruiting African Americans for our freshman class on grounds that a little diversity in the student population will help all the students. (That, I think, is not illegal.) But current practice in some places—stating solemnly that all candidates will be given equal consideration, while under instructions to hire a woman or the position will be withdrawn—is simply wrong.

In the end, the effect of preferences cannot attain the objective set for them. Almost thirty years ago, we argued that there was no way, even in theory, to compensate the victims of history—the Jews in Egypt, the Untouchables, the prey of Huns, Tartars, Mongols and Vikings, the serfs of the Middle Ages, the Native Americans of North America, the slaughtered Inca and Aztec, the African slaves on all continents, including their own. And from a consequentialist standpoint, the devices engaged in to try to perform long-range cosmic justice do much more harm than good, in stigmatizing those they would benefit, in embittering those who (unoffending themselves) see themselves as being asked to pay the price of the offenses of others, and above all in disrupting generally fair color- and gender-blind procedures, replacing them with political shoving matches and bureaucracies of enforcers of the latest politically correct preference. We have had enough of preferences. Those who have suffered are (mostly) dead. The best we can do for their descendants is to create a scrupulously just society in which we may all be equal citizens.

NOTES

1. Lisa H. Newton: 1973, "Reverse Discrimination as Unjustified," *Ethics* **83**, 308–312.

2. If anything, the assault on self-esteem inherent in sexism (we have no experience with racism) tended to stiffen the resolve of those discriminated against. As long as the prejudice did not actualize in an absolute ban (as in the Jim Crow laws), we were simply told that "in order to be a success in this field, a woman has to be twice as good as a man. Fortunately, that is not difficult." The muscular commitment to hard work and accomplishment that was absolutely required by societal assumptions of inferiority made successes of many of us who otherwise might have happily lingered in mediocrity.

3. We might mention that this is the second time (in almost thirty years!) that "Reverse Discrimination" has been challenged, and the only other challenge was an unfortunate exercise in extravagant claims backed by bad research, requiring us to render the author (philosophically) into very small chunks suitable for Chinese dishes. He has not been heard from since. See our "Corruption of Thought, Word and Deed: Reflections on Affirmative Action and Its Current Defenders," *Contemporary Philosophy* **XIII**(7): 14–16 (January/February 1991). We are delighted, and relieved, that such an exercise is not necessary in this case.

4. There's an organization called "Let's Face It," a support group for the facially disfigured. It's run by a friend of mine who suffered severe facial cancer as a young woman, and knows what facial disfigurement can do to your confidence—and aspirations.

5. That may sound a bit abstruse, but it happened once in our sight and presence. A candidate for a department opening was invited to present a paper to the department, as was the custom. During the question period afterwards, he seriously embarrassed the one member of the department no one else liked. He was hired on the spot.

19

Are Hate Speech Codes Wrong?

Meyers and Her Critics

Hate speech is speech that aims to insult or degrade a person based on that person's membership in some racial, ethnic, religious, or other group. Hate speech codes are policies that prohibit such speech. Hate speech is widely regarded as a problem on college campuses. Are hate speech codes a good solution to this problem? The debate about this difficult question is typically framed in terms of a conflict between two competing kinds of rights. On the one hand, people are generally regarded as having a right to freedom of expression. On the other, people are generally regarded as having a right not to be harmed. Hate speech is a form of expression. But hate speech can also be harmful. When framed in this manner, the debate often proceeds by trying to determine whether hate speech really is a protected form of freedom of expression or whether the harms that people suffer when they are exposed to hate speech are really the kinds of harms that people have a right to be free from. If there really is no right to engage in hate speech in the first place, after all, or if there really is no right to be free from hate speech, then a resolution of the controversy may prove to be fairly straightforward. And if both rights are thought to be genuine, the debate then often turns to the question of which of the rights, if either, is more fundamental or inviolable than the other.

In the featured article for this chapter, Diana Tietjens Meyers attempts to find a way around this standard approach to the problem by offering what she herself characterizes as "an unorthodox proposal." Rather than rejecting the existence of one or the other of these two rights, and rather than ranking one of them ahead of the other, Meyers suggests a way in which colleges could attempt to simultaneously respect both. The key to Meyers's proposal lies in the distinction between saying that a right not to be treated in a certain way generates an obligation in others not to act in that way and saying that a right not to be treated in a certain way generates a right to be compensated if one is treated in that way. If the right not to be exposed to hate speech is construed in the former way, then it will seem to generate an obligation to adopt a hate speech code, which in turn will seem to infringe on the right to freedom of expression. But if the right not to be exposed to hate speech is construed in the latter way, then it need not entail this. Instead, students will be free to engage in hate speech, but students who are harmed by hate speech will nonetheless be empowered to seek compensation for the harms that they incur. In this way, their right not to be harmed by hate speech will also be respected, and thus the controversy over hate speech codes will be resolved in a manner that respects the rights that are involved on both sides.

Meyers offers three distinct arguments in support of this solution in general and in support of her claim that the schools themselves should provide funding to pay for the compensation in particular. One argument appeals to the claim that since colleges benefit from the flourishing of free speech, it is fair that they pay the costs involved in maintaining it; a second appeals to the claim that colleges are partly responsible for the existence of hate speech in the first place, and a third appeals to the claim that it is in the interest of colleges to see to it that students who are harmed by hate speech receive compensation. No one of these three arguments seems to be more central to Meyers's position than the others, and so readers are encouraged to pay careful attention to all three. Meyers then attempts to respond to a few objections to her position, and her responses merit careful attention as well.

In his response to Meyers's article, Thomas W. Peard raises three distinct objections. First, he argues that Meyers has failed to justify the claim that the schools in question should be fully responsible for paying the costs involved in compensating victims of hate speech. Second, he argues that Meyers's proposal would have an objectionable chilling effect on the free exchange of information and ideas. And finally, he argues that the proposal is not practically feasible. Each of these objections, although developed quickly, involves more than one distinct supporting consideration, and so although Peard's response as a whole is relatively brief, it nonetheless contains a large number of points that can be brought to bear in critically evaluating Meyers's position.

QUESTIONS FOR CONSIDERATION

• Is Meyers's proposal to permit hate speech but also to permit victims of hate speech to seek compensation consistent? Are there other forms of behavior that we permit but then treat in this manner?

• What reasons does Meyers give for saying that the schools themselves should incur the costs involved in compensating victims of hate speech? Are these reasons convincing? If the schools should not pay compensation in such cases, who else, if anyone, should?

• Which of Peard's objections seems most compelling? How might Meyers respond to them?

• If Meyers's proposal is rejected, should hate speech simply be prohibited? Or should it be permitted to occur with no compensation to those who are harmed by it? Is there some other sort of compromise position that might be defended?

FURTHER READING

Altman, Andrew. "Liberalism and Campus Hate Speech: A Philosophical Examination." *Ethics* 103, no. 2 (January 1993): 302–17.

Brink, David O. "Millian Principles, Freedom of Expression, and Hate Speech." *Legal Theory* 7, no. 2 (June 2001): 119–57.

Brison, Susan J. "The Autonomy Defense of Free Speech." *Ethics* 108, no. 2 (January 1998): 312–39.

Cox, Philip N. "The Disputation of Hate: Speech Codes, Pluralism, and Academic Freedoms." *Social Theory and Practice* 21, no. 1 (Spring 1995): 113–44.

Shiell, Timothy C. *Campus Hate Speech on Trial.* Lawrence: University Press of Kansas, 1998.

DIANA TIETJENS MEYERS

Rights in Collision: A Non-Punitive, Compensatory Remedy for Abusive Speech

IV. AN UNORTHODOX PROPOSAL

. . . In what follows, I shall confine my comments to the proliferation of discriminatory verbal and pictorial abuse on United States college and university campuses. One reason for narrowing my focus is that concentrating on a single institutional setting makes the problem more tractable. The other is that it is especially important that the problem be solved in this particular setting. The obligation of the university to provide equality of opportunity to all of its students requires that it take measures to create a sanctuary for those students who are vulnerable to discriminatory verbal or pictorial abuse in order to ensure that their ability to learn is not impaired by others' stupidity or malice. Here the right not to be subjected to discriminatory verbal or pictorial abuse is salient. Yet, the mission of the university as a site of inquiry and open dialogue requires that all students and faculty feel free to express their views. Here the right to free speech must be robust. Thus, universities seem to be torn between a pair of equally compelling, yet incompatible moral claims.

By framing these two rights using Hohfeld's technical rights taxonomy, it is possible to dissolve this paradox. It has often been noted that the U.S. Constitution construes free speech not as a claim right correlated with a duty of forbearance, but rather as an immunity correlated with a legislative disability.[1] Censorship is not a crime. But since government bodies lack the power to prohibit free expression, the courts will nullify legislative attempts to restrict speech unduly. Likewise, the right not to be subjected to discriminatory verbal or pictorial abuse need not be construed as a claim right entitling students who are members of socially excluded groups not to hear hate speech and imposing a duty of forbearance spec-

ified in a restrictive speech code. Instead, this right could be construed as a power correlated with the university's liability to that power. Members of historically despised and currently excluded social groups could be empowered to exact compensation from the university upon demonstrating that a fellow member of the university community subjected them to discriminatory verbal or pictorial abuse.[2] On this interpretation, there would be no new restrictions on speech, and yet the right not to be subjected to discriminatory verbal or pictorial abuse would be recognized and respected.

The funds that some states have set up to compensate victims of violent crime provide a precedent for this proposal. However, these funds differ in two major respects from my hate speech compensation scheme. In the case of crime compensation funds, the state prohibits and punishes the conduct for which it compensates victims. Thus, it is in a position to minimize its liability. Likewise, in sexual harassment law, which holds employers responsible for compensating employees who are harassed by supervisory or peer employees, employers are permitted to institute and enforce policies prohibiting harassing behavior. Thus, it may seem unfair to hold universities responsible for compensating victims of discriminatory verbal or pictorial abuse and yet to deny them the right to deter these utterances by establishing and enforcing speech codes.

Of course, it is not true that rejecting speech codes renders universities helpless with respect to discriminatory verbal and pictorial abuse. Universities can establish orientation programs, courses, and workshops that educate students, faculty, and staff about the nature and the harm of discriminatory verbal or pictorial abuse; they can diversify their faculties and student bodies; they can enlist prominent conserva-

Diana Tietjens Meyers, "Rights in Collision: A Non-Punitive, Compensatory Remedy for Abusive Speech." *Law and Philosophy* Vol. 14, No. 2, Springer Publishing (May, 1995).

tive and civil libertarian faculty members and student leaders who claim to abhor hate speech to publicly decry campus incidents; university presidents and deans can vocally condemn hate speech whenever and wherever it occurs. Moreover, unlike crime compensation funds that are statutorily mandated, compensating student victims for violations of the right not to be subjected to discriminatory verbal or pictorial abuse is a moral imperative. I shall leave aside the more complicated, but undeniably important, question of under what circumstances the legislatures or courts should impose this liability on universities. I shall urge only that these educational institutions should assume this responsibility voluntarily.

There are a number of reasons for thinking it proper for universities to accept liability for compensating students whose right not to be subjected to discriminatory verbal or pictorial abuse is violated on campus. Charles Lawrence and Frederick Schauer both question the legitimacy of leaving the victims of harmful speech to shoulder the costs of keeping the marketplace of ideas open.[3] If free speech is a social good, as well as an individual good, it is unfair that members of certain groups are required to bear a disproportionate share of the burdens of free speech by being barred from obtaining compensation for speech that harms them. Yet, requiring those who verbally assault others to pay for the harms they inflict would inhibit and thus constrain free speech. It seems, then, that we must turn to social institutions to defray these costs. Since universities benefit enormously from free speech, it seems especially appropriate that they should do so.

Also, discriminatory verbal or pictorial abuse is not a purely individual wrongdoing. It is substantially aided and abetted by the dominant culture. In the United States, this culture couples official condemnation of racism, sexism, and ethnocentrism (but, notice, not homophobia) with underhanded symbolic inculcation and reinforcement of these very attitudes and the behavior that goes with them.[4] In view of the pervasiveness of these prejudices, and in view of the fact that universities play a vital role in transmitting the dominant culture in which they are encoded, it is fitting that these institutions assume the costs of compensating the victims of discriminatory verbal or pictorial abuse on their own campuses.

Finally, I would point out that it is in the interest of colleges and universities to undertake to compensate students who are victimized by discriminatory verbal or pictorical abuse. Both because it is desirable to distribute the good of education as widely as possible and also because lively and fruitful intellectual debate requires assembling representatives of as many viewpoints as possible, these institutions seek to recruit a diverse student body. Presumably, students from historically despised and currently excluded social groups would find colleges and universities that were committed to respecting their right not to be subjected to discriminatory verbal or pictorial abuse more attractive. If this is so, these institutions would gain a significant advantage in enrolling and retaining students from these groups and thus a significant advantage in achieving one of their principal goals.

V. Non-Ideal Rights Theory in Practice

Turning now to the mechanics of implementing the right not to be subjected to discriminatory verbal or pictorial abuse, I believe that this right calls for innovative methods. The forms of harmful speech and the nature of the harms that speech can cause need to be investigated. Moreover, compensation scales need to be set. It strikes me that universities are unusually well-situated to conduct these inquiries and to implement the power and the liability I have proposed.

One objection that might be lodged against the right not to be subjected to discriminatory verbal or pictorial abuse is that we do not know enough about how speech harms people to identify violations of the right. To some, this may seem like a good reason to confine rights to physical or non-belief-mediated harms—harms that medical science can confidently document and trace to their causes. Compared to our knowledge of physical diseases and injuries, our knowledge of psychological maladies is undeniably in its infancy. But there is a revealing analogy between speech-inflicted harm and environmentally caused harm. Scientists are far from clear about which pesticides and other pollutants endanger human health, and their estimates of what quantities of these chemicals cause serious ailments are very rough. Still, few regard the trial-and-error approach of environmental medicine as a reason to abandon the inquiry or to forgo taking steps to protect public health. There seems to be a consensus (outside agribusiness and the chemical industry, that is) that it is best to prohibit substances and practices that appear to pose a danger, while continuing to do research and revising policy in accordance with the preponderance of the data. University committees charged with implementing the right not to be subjected to discriminatory verbal or pictorial abuse would be in a similar position—examining cases as they arise and doing their best to assess the harm and to devise appropriate remedies. The likelihood that they will occasionally make mistakes does not mean that they should not get to work and start developing a body of findings. Eventually, it may be possible to distill these findings into a cogent system of principles and policies.

Meanwhile, it is necessary to be mindful of the complexities and uncertainties surrounding the right not to be subjected to discriminatory verbal or pictorial abuse in planning for its implementation. Although university committees can undertake preliminary studies to determine what sorts of speech trouble members of socially excluded groups and how these individuals are affected by these utterances, it seems clear that any definition of verbal and pictorial abuse that they formulate is best regarded as provisional. Since these committees will be exploring uncharted territory, it seems unlikely that any committee will be able to anticipate all possible forms of discriminatory verbal or pictorial abuse. Thus, committees created to administer this right will be learning as they go. The experimental nature of this undertaking argues against a punitive interpretation of the right and in favor of my compensatory interpretation, and it also argues against adversarial enforcement procedures and in favor of arbitration procedures.

Interpreting the right not to be subjected to discriminatory verbal or pictorial abuse as mandating a punitive speech code would establish an insuperable presumption in favor of a sharp and narrow defini-

tion of harmful speech and adversarial enforcement procedures. Both the unfairness of meting out punishment when the offense is vaguely defined and the instrumental value of free discussion on campus necessitate minimizing restrictions on speech and maximizing the prerogatives of accused individuals to defend themselves. Yet establishing such a definition would choke off inquiry into the various forms of harmful speech and would almost certainly prove underinclusive. Moreover, the virtue of adversarial proceedings is that they protect the accused, not that they foster inquiry and deepen understanding of vexing social problems.

In contrast, a social compensation scheme of the kind I am proposing does not require a neat and fixed definition of discriminatory verbal or pictorial abuse, nor does it oblige universities to strictly observe disciplinary procedures comparable to those of a fair trial, for no one is being accused of a punishable infraction. Although punishing an innocent individual is a grave injustice, benefiting a person who does not deserve it is a minor mishap as long as no one else is seriously harmed. No terrible moral wrong would be committed if occasionally a student were overcompensated.

The point of the right not to be subjected to discriminatory verbal or pictorial abuse is to protect vulnerable people from a particularly invidious form of harmful speech. Thus, a tenable interpretation of this right will advance three key aims: 1) it will educate people about how speech causes harm; 2) it will make up for harm that is caused by discriminatory verbal or pictorial abuse; and 3) it will deter this harmful speech.

I believe that much harmful speech on campuses stems from ignorance—simple lack of information about different cultures and distorted beliefs transmitted through derogatory stereotypes that are in wide circulation. To reduce the isolation of different social groups and to counteract misinformation about these groups, Lawrence suggests that student victims be compensated by creating minority scholarships or minority faculty lines or by suspending classes and holding teach-ins on racism.[5] I certainly have no objection to the aims underlying Lawrence's proposals, and I would be happy if universities took such measures. However, I think that, whenever possible, the individuals whose rights are violated should be recompensed personally. Thus, I shall offer a compensation scheme that preserves the educational potential of Lawrence's proposal but that gives due recognition to the harm individuals suffer.

A fair compensation scheme will take into account the gravity of the harm and the intent of the speaker. When a speaker unwittingly causes harm and the harm is slight, an apology and a promise to desist seem sufficient as compensation. However, when a speaker deliberately causes harm, or when the harm is severe, material compensation seems necessary, for the sincerity of an apology would be doubtful, and severe injury calls for substantial recompense. In such cases, universities could award victims credit toward the next semester's tuition (or in the case of second-semester seniors a refund on the current tuition bill), and they could tie the amount of credit to the egregiousness of the incident. This remedy seems fitting since it links the compensation to the victim's educational aspirations and contributes to those goals.

This method of compensation can be administered using an arbitration model rather than a legalistic adversarial model. If the right not to be subjected to discriminatory verbal or pictorial abuse is to serve an educational function, it is important to avoid exacerbating hostility and putting the parties on the defensive. When guilt and punishment, on the one hand, or exoneration, on the other, exhausts the possible outcomes for the accused individual, one cannot expect that person to be candid and forthcoming.[6] A compensation scheme that does not penalize the accused individual and that is implemented through arbitration provides a setting for mediation and an opportunity to reach mutual understanding and reconciliation. Student complainants must see these proceedings as an opportunity to learn, as well. As a result of the dialogues such proceedings initiate, a student whom an utterance offended and upset might come to understand the reasonableness and the justifiability of the speech and to regard his or her reaction as excessive. In that case or in cases in which the administrative committee determines that a student should accept this view of the matter, no compensation would be awarded.

In advocating arbitration proceedings, I am not suggesting that universities should accept all claims at face value or that the only issue is how much compensation the alleged victim should receive. On the contrary, to make sure that incidents are not being staged, these claims must be thoroughly investigated, and the testimony of witnesses must be sought. Moreover, I would advise universities to impose fairly onerous penalties when students are found to have lodged fabricated or frivolous complaints. Still, I would expect that some cases will fall in a gray area, and it seems to me that it is better for universities to respond to such cases in a spirit of openness and compromise rather than in a harsh, incredulous spirit that requires students who claim to have been victimized by discriminatory verbal or pictorial abuse to produce incontrovertible proof to support their charges.

I think that flexibility in enforcement, as long as it does not devolve into capriciousness, is both dictated by the typical university's administrative capabilities and also befits the unpredictability and the variety of forms that abusive speech takes. On my compensatory interpretation of the right not to be subjected to discriminatory verbal or pictorial abuse, a somewhat elastic definition of abusive speech that allows for sensitivity to social context and variations in individual temperament is tenable. Since the alternative is to preempt inquiry and to deny justice to many victims of abusive speech, this flexibility constitutes a strong reason to adopt my interpretation.

I suspect that punitive sanctions would martyr many people who violate the right not to be subjected to discriminatory verbal or pictorial abuse, and that this veneration of abusive speakers as heroes of civil liberties would stigmatize their victims. Yet, by itself, answering abusive speech with more speech seems a toothless alternative. If education were as effective as educators would like to believe it is, the incidence of discriminatory verbal and pictorial abuse on campuses should be waning, but it is not. Although my compensation scheme imposes no punishments, it would nevertheless deter discriminatory verbal and pictorial abuse. It would defeat the purposes of malicious speakers, for voicing prejudice would ultimately benefit the very people the bigot wants to hurt. With respect to well-meaning but misguided speakers, using arbitration to implement the right not to be subjected to discriminatory verbal or pictorial abuse incorporates the advantages of the educational approach and strengthens the educational impact by personalizing the process. Tutorials work better than large lecture courses. Finally and most importantly, this interpretation of the right would not leave victims inthe lurch. Whether in the form of an apology and an assurance that the harmful speech will not be repeated or in the form of tuition remission, the victim receives a significant, individuated benefit.

Now, it might be granted that my proposal provides a way for universities to discourage violations of the right not to be subjected to discriminatory verbal or pictorial abuse and to respect victims' rights without encroaching on free inquiry. Still, a critic might regard my proposal as unrealistic and possibly dangerous. First, it might be objected that universities will seek to minimize their liability by accepting only ideologically compatible students. But it seems doubtful that a university that would voluntarily institute the compensation scheme I envisage would secretly reverse its principles and undermine diversity by homogenizing admissions. Moreover, federal law provides further protection for diversity. Discrimination on grounds of race, religion, or sex is illegal at schools that receive public funding. I would add that conservatives who fear that like-minded applicants will be targeted and discriminated against should not concede that bigots can be weeded out by identifying prospective students' conservative political learnings. This stereotype, like all stereotypes, should be resisted.

Second, it might be urged that compensating all the victims whose claims were vindicated would bankrupt universities. If that is true, I would reply that it is all the more urgent for universities to take aggressive measures to implement the right not to be subjected to discriminatory verbal or pictorial abuse. Still, I would also stress that universities need not create lavish funds to compensate victims. Even if budgetary constraints render their compensation awards essentially symbolic, these awards will represent a colossal improvement over the institutional indifference that now prevails on United States campuses. . . .

NOTES

1. David Lyons, "The Correlativity of Rights and Duties," *Noûs* **4** (1970): 50–51; Frederick Schauer, *Free Speech: A Philosophical Inquiry* (Cambridge: Cambridge University Press, 1982), p. 116; Rex Martin, *A System of Rights* (Oxford: Clarendon Press, 1993), p. 30.

2. This right should not be assimilated to the hostile environment theory of discriminatory harassment. Charging an employed or educational institution with maintaining a hostile environment requires demonstrating that a pattern or practice of harassment exists. In contrast, the power I am proposing could be activated by a single incident of discriminatory verbal or pictorial abuse. Often the experience of being a target of hate speech on campus is compounded by similar experiences in childhood and off-campus and by widespread social tolerance of racism, sexism, homophobia, and ethnocentrism. No pattern of abuse need exist on campus for a hate speech incident to be harmful.

Also, one of the reasons for my proposal is that legal remedies are slow in coming and expensive to pursue. Thus, many victims who have a sexual harassment case under the hostile environment theory mandated by the Civil Rights Act do not sue and never obtain any form of relief.

3. Frederick Schauer, "Uncoupling Free Speech," *Columbia Law Review* **92** (1992): 1321–57; Lawrence, "If He Hollers Let Him Go," p. 80.

4. Lawrence, "If He Hollers Let Him Go," p. 68; for an account of culturally normative prejudice, see Meyers, *Subjection and Subjectivity*, pp. 51–56.

5. Lawrence, "If He Hollers Let Him Go," pp. 85–86.

6. Some faculty unions (e.g., the PSC/CUNY) have protested university procedures for addressing sexual harassment complaints on the grounds that these procedures violate due process. Since a finding that someone has committed sexual harassment is grounds for punitive sanctions, it is crucial that universities enforce their sexual harassment regulations in a manner that respects due process. Still, it is clear that these procedural restrictions interfere with the educational function of sexual harassment proceedings since they provide a strong incentive for the accused individual to refuse to cooperate and to deny the charges regardless of the truth. I do not advocate stripping penalties from sexual harassment codes. Nevertheless, I want to point out that the absence of penalties in my interpretation of the right not to be subjected to discriminatory verbal or pictorial abuse eliminates the threat to the accused individual, defuses the conflict between this individual and the complainant, and thus maximizes the chances of fruitful dialogue leading to a mutually satisfactory resolution.

Critic

Thomas W. Peard

Diana Tietjens Meyers's Remedy for Abusive Speech: Objections

In *Rights in Collision: A Non-Punitive, Compensatory Remedy for Abusive Speech,*[1] Diana Tietjens Meyers outlines an admittedly "unorthodox" proposal for compensating victims of abusive speech on college and university campuses. In this paper, I object to her proposal and to its underlying rationale.

In Section I, I describe the remedy Meyers proposes and its grounds. In Section II, I raise the following objections to Meyers's remedy: (i) it unfairly and unjustifiably imposes sole liability on the university for harm caused by hate speech; (ii) it is open to constitutional objections, contrary to one of its principal motivating grounds; (iii) it unnecessarily duplicates existing causes of action and is otherwise infeasible. . . .

I. MEYERS'S PROPOSAL

Meyers holds that universities face a dilemma arising from two seemingly incompatible moral claims. On the one hand, free speech must be robust on university and college campuses. Therefore, even seriously abusive speech should be protected. On the other hand, members of socially excluded groups have a right not to be subjected to discriminatory verbal or pictorial abuse (hereafter "the right not to be subjected to abusive speech"). Meyers views this right as non-universal and basic. For Meyers, a basic right is one that secures agentic capacities.[2] The idea is that the harm inflicted by abusive speech is sufficient to undermine the agentic capacities of hate speech victims, justifying recognition of a basic right not to be subjected to abusive speech.

Meyers believes that this conflict between victim's and speaker's rights gives rise to a dilemma which she endeavors to resolve. To do so, she proposes that the university be liable for damages incurred by victims of abusive speech. Thus she interprets the victim's right not to be subjected to abusive speech as "a power coupled with the university liability to that power."[3] She construes the speaker's right of freedom of speech as an "immunity correlated with a legislative disability" to restrict speech unduly.[4]

These constructions of the speaker's and victim's respective rights purportedly satisfy the competing moral claims of both parties. By virtue of having the right not to be subjected to abusive speech, victims of hate speech have the power to recover damages from the university for harm caused by abusive speech. Because the speaker has the right of freedom of speech, as construed by Meyers, the university may not prohibit the speaker from engaging in abusive speech. The rights of both parties are therefore accommodated, according to Meyers.

II. OBJECTIONS TO MEYERS'S REMEDY

A. Liability of the University

Under Meyers's remedy, the university is *solely* liable for damages to hate speech victims. She claims that the university benefits from free speech and therefore should defray the cost of such speech.[5] However, even

Thomas W. Peard, "Diana Tietjens Meyers's Remedy fo Abusive Speech: Objections," *Law and Philosophy* Vol. 18, No. 1, Springer Publishing (January, 1999).

if A benefits from the exercise of a right, it does not follow that A may be required to pay damages to C caused by B's exercise of the right. Student A may benefit from Professor B's exercise of the right of free speech. But it does not follow that A should be required to pay C's damages that result from B's speech.

In certain cases, universities do bear legal and moral responsibility for harm caused by their members. But that does not justify imposing liability for abusive speech *solely* on the university *in every case*, irrespective of fault. Even if A is vicariously liable for B's acts, it does not follow that A should be *solely* liable for B's actions. A master is vicariously liable for the torts of her servants committed in the course of employment, but that does not preclude liability on the part of the servant, legally or morally.

Meyers also suggests a fault-based rationale for imposing liability on the university. She claims that universities should be held liable because of their role in transmitting the dominant culture, including prejudices against members of oppressed groups. This is speculation. It is just as likely that universities are among the chief proponents of tolerance and the principal critics of the dominant culture.

Finally, the university will have clear conflicts of interest under Meyers's remedy. On the one hand, it should defend the speaker to avoid paying compensation; on the other hand, it should discourage hate speech. Such conflicts frustrate efforts to safeguard *both* interests. Accordingly, Meyers provides no persuasive rationale for holding the university solely liable for abusive speech.

B. Constitutionality of Meyers's Proposal

Meyers claims that noncompensatory speech restrictions that pass constitutional muster would not be broad enough to recognize *all* of the harm caused by verbal or pictorial abuse. She worries that "racist views cloaked in civil language or delivered in the guise of theory, however hurtful their expression may be, could not be prohibited."[6]

However, Meyers's proposal itself is constitutionally suspect. As Melville Nimmer writes:

> Freedom of speech may be abridged by "inhibition as well as prohibition." State action which does not directly curtail speech rights may nevertheless be held invalid if abridgment, although unintended, may "inevitably follow" from such action. Moreover, even if there is not an "inevitable" relationship between given state action and the resulting curtailment of speech, the action may nevertheless be invalid if it constitutes a "discouragement" of speech, or, perhaps, if it eliminates a "basic incentive" to engage in speech.[7]

Under Meyers's broad characterization of abusive speech which includes civil language, the remedy she proposes will have an intolerable chilling effect on the speech of university members. Instructors and students alike will engage in self-censorship to avoid exposing the university to liability. They will further seek to avoid the embarrassment and inconvenience of being hauled before a university tribunal for the purpose of determining whether the university should pay compensation for their conduct. University members will avoid even *protected* speech so as not to *appear* to violate *broad* regulation of hate speech. Self-censorship may even affect course offerings and materials assigned.

A university that adopts Meyers's remedy will presumably require its members to participate in proceedings against the university arising from conduct involving even *civil* speech. Required participation in these proceedings may constitute a penalty for the exercise of free speech and result in impermissible abridgment of free speech through inhibition and discouragement. Meyers's proposal therefore raises significant constitutional concerns for public universities and colleges.

C. Feasibility of Meyers's Proposal

A compelling justification is required for Meyers's proposal that universities incur the potentially enormous expense of paying compensation for the harm caused by hate speech, especially where the proposed form of liability substantially duplicates other causes of action.[8] Universities generally have less expertise and experience in these matters than the judicial system or professional arbitrators and mediators. Under Meyers's scheme, similar determinations must be made as in court proceedings, i.e., liability and damages. Indeed, Meyers urges a thorough investigation of the claims.[9] In some cases, the parties may be entitled to legal counsel. A university's handling of such claims, especially complex ones, is likely to be less efficient and fair than that of the judicial system. Furthermore, the financial repercussions and disruptive effect of Meyers's remedy could significantly hamper the pursuit of other university objectives.

Meyers responds that the costs of her scheme could be controlled through limitations on compensation awarded. She believes that even symbolic compensation would represent an improvement over the "institutional indifference that now prevails on United States campuses."[10]

However, Meyers's suggestion for minimizing compensation awards is problematic for several reasons. First, Meyers thinks that victims have a *moral* right to compensation. Thus, by permitting symbolic awards, Meyers allows the university to violate a moral right where the victim is entitled to damages greater than the symbolic amount. Secondly, Meyers's symbolic compensation scheme is fundamentally unfair: those victims who are seriously harmed are awarded only a fraction of their damages, while those who suffer minimal harm are fully compensated. Thirdly, if the goal of Meyers's remedy is symbolic action reflecting consideration of individuals harmed by hate speech, then this can be achieved in many ways other than through compensation. Meyers herself mentions such measures as condemnation of hate speech by university officials, orientation programs, courses and workshops for the purpose of educating university members about the harms of hate speech, and diversification of faculties and student bodies.[11]

One final practical problem. Meyers states that her compensation scheme "does not require a neat and fixed definition of discriminatory verbal or pictorial abuse."[12] However, failure to make clear what conduct is actionable will not only chill protected speech but can have disastrous practical consequences. Uncertainties will abound with regard to how university members should conduct themselves. Financial planning could be extraordinarily difficult

if the university cannot adequately ascertain the extent of its liability under Meyers's remedy. Meyers's proposal is thus open to multiple theoretical, constitutional and practical objections. . . .

NOTES

1. Diana Tietjens Meyers, "Rights in Collision: A Non-Punitive, Compensatory Remedy for Abusive Speech," *Law and Philosophy* **14** (1995): pp. 203–243.

2. Ibid., p. 215.

3. Ibid., p. 225.

4. Ibid., p. 224.

5. Ibid., p. 227.

6. Ibid., p. 223.

7. Melville B. Nimmer, *Nimmer on Freedom of Speech: A Treatise on the Theory of the First Amendment* (New York: Matthew Bender and Company, 1984), pp. 4–33.

8. There presently exists a cause of action for intentional infliction of emotional distress which has been held to apply to harm resulting from racial epithets. See, e.g., Contreras v. Crown Zellerbach, 88 Wash. 2d 735, 565 P.2d 1173 (1977) (epithets may constitute "outrageous conduct" within the meaning of Restatement (Second) of Torts Section 46), cited in Laurence H. Tribe, *American Constitutional Law*, 2d ed. (Mineola, N.Y.: The Foundation Press, Inc. 1988), p. 838, n. 17. Other claims may also permit recovery, including assault, battery, defamation and claims under constitutional and statutory provisions. See Richard Delgado's discussion of these claims and their applicability to hate speech in "Words that Wound: A Tort Action for Racial Insults, Epithets and Name-Calling," *Harvard Civil Rights-Civil Liberties Law Review* **17** (1982): 133–181 at 150–165. Delgado holds that existing claims fail to provide adequate protection against racial insults and that an independent tort action for such speech is necessary. Delgado's proposed tort action is controversial and open to significant objections. But even if such an action is required, it should be administered through the judicial system, for reasons given below.

9. Meyers, "Rights in Collision," p. 232.

10. Ibid., p. 234.

11. Ibid., p. 226.

12. Ibid., p. 229.

20

Are Hate Crime Laws Wrong?

Wellman and His Critics

Hate crime laws impose increased penalties on criminals who target victims because they are members of a particular group and who target these victims out of animosity toward the group to which the victims belong. Suppose, for example, that two arsonists set out independently to burn down a building and that both do so primarily because they think that watching a building burn to the ground will be fun. The first arsonist selects a building to burn because its design will make it easy to set on fire and its location will make it easy to flee the scene of the crime when he is finished. The second arsonist selects a building to burn because it is a house that is occupied by a black family and he hates black people. Arson, of course, is illegal. And so whatever the penalty is for arson, it will be applied equally to both of these criminals. If there are no hate crime laws on the books in the jurisdiction in which the crimes take place, then both arsonists will likely end up receiving the same sentence, other things being equal (e.g., both have no prior convictions, neither has mitigating circumstances, etc.). But a hate crime law would dictate that the second arsonist would receive a more severe punishment than the first. A hate crime law, in effect, adds an additional penalty when someone commits not just a crime but a hate crime. And the debate about hate crime laws is a debate about the question of whether it is appropriate for the State to do this.

In the featured article for this chapter, Christopher Heath Wellman argues that the answer to this question is "yes." First published in 2006, Wellman's paper represents one of the most recent attempts to justify the controversial practice of adopting hate crime laws. The structure of Wellman's argument involves two distinct applications of the method of process of elimination that was discussed in section 4.4 of the Introduction to this book. In the first part of the article, Wellman begins with the more general question of why the State punishes people for breaking the law in the first place. He identifies six theories of punishment and, for each of them, considers their implications for the more specific question of whether the State should punish people more severely for committing hate crimes in particular. Here, the process of elimination works in the following manner: Consider the various arguments that might be made to show that a particular theory of punishment justifies opposition to hate crime laws, and then eliminate all of them. For each theory of punishment that he considers, that is,

Wellman attempts to show that the theory ultimately supports, rather than opposes, the legitimacy of hate crime laws. In the second part of the article, Wellman then turns to some objections that might be raised against hate crime laws. Here, the process of elimination works in a different way: Consider the various objections that can be raised against such laws, and try to eliminate all of them as well.

Since Wellman's article was published so recently, there do not yet seem to be any critical responses to it available in print. In an article published a few years previously, however, Heidi M. Hurd raised three important objections to hate crime laws, and we reprint an excerpt from that article here as a way of initiating the process of thinking critically about Wellman's position. Hurd begins by identifying three respects in which hate crime laws are different from traditional criminal laws. The three points she raises at the start of her discussion are distinct but related: All point to the idea that hate crime laws ultimately punish people for having a bad character. Hurd then goes on to raise three objections to laws that punish people for bad character in this way: Such laws seem to punish people for what they cannot control; the emotional states that the laws add punishment for in the case of hate crimes are not clearly worse than the emotional states that they do not add punishment for in the case of other kinds of crimes; and the laws violate the liberal ideal of a government that remains neutral about substantive questions about what constitutes the good life.

Questions for Consideration

Since Wellman's argument employs the process of elimination at two different levels, it is important to consider questions that can be raised about it at each level.

• How does each of the six theories of punishment that Wellman identifies attempt to justify the practice of punishment in general? Why is Wellman so confident that, in each case, the theory in question would support the practice of hate crime laws? Which of the theories, if any, might most plausibly be used instead to oppose such laws?

• Are there other justifications for punishment that Wellman does not consider? Might punishment be justified by appealing to the claim that criminals consent to their punishment, for example, or that they forfeit the rights that they violate in their victims? What, if anything, might other theories of punishment imply about hate crime laws?

• How accurate is Hurd's description of hate crime laws? Do they really punish people for having a bad character? Or do they simply punish such people for doing bad actions?

• How might Wellman respond to the three objections that Hurd ultimately presents? Do hate crime laws really punish people for something that is beyond their control? If they do, does this show that such laws are wrong, or are there other cases where the punishments that people receive are in response to things that are similarly beyond their control? Are racially motivated crimes really worse than ordinary crimes? How could we settle such a question? And are hate crime laws ultimately illiberal in the way that Hurd maintains?

Further Reading

Adams, David M. "Punishing Hate and Achieving Equality." *Criminal Justice Ethics* 24, no. 1 (Winter–Spring 2005): 19–30.

Baehr, Amy R. "A Feminist Liberal Approach to *Hate Crime* Legislation." *Journal of Social Philosophy* 34, no. 1 (Spring 2003): 134–52.

Gellman, Susan. "Brother, You Can't Go to Jail for What You're Thinking: Motives, Effects and Hate Crime Laws." *Criminal Justice Ethics* 11, no. 2 (Summer–Fall 1992): 24–28.

Gerstenfeld, Phyllis B. *Hate Crimes: Causes, Controls, and Controversies.* Thousand Oaks, Calif.: Sage Publications, 2004.

Weinstein, James. "First Amendment Challenges to Hate Crime Legislation: Where's the Speech?" *Criminal Justice Ethics* 11, no. 2 (Summer–Fall 1992): 6–19.

CHRISTOPHER HEATH WELLMAN

A Defense of Stiffer Penalties for Hate Crimes

After being beaten, James Byrd Jr., a disabled Black man in Jasper, Texas, was chained to the back of a pick-up truck and dragged to his death.

After being robbed and beaten, Matthew Shepard, a gay student in Wyoming, was tied like a scarecrow to a wooden fence and left to die. He did.

Cases like these have fueled popular support for various measures aimed at educating and deterring those who seek to bolster their self-esteem by dehumanizing others. One prominent suggestion is to impose stiffer punishments for so-called hate or bias crimes. In this essay, I supply a moral defense of this controversial proposal. . . .

TWO PRELIMINARIES

Let us say that one commits a hate crime just in case one selects one's victim at least in part because of an animus toward members of the group to which the victim belongs. A prime example would be if a white person lynched someone because she is black. Notice, however, that it is not enough that a white person lynch a black person; nor is it sufficient that a white person lynch a black person in a society where racist whites sometimes lynch blacks. In order for an offense to qualify as a hate crime, the perpetrator must choose the victim (at least in part) *because* of her membership in the targeted group.

Suppose that Jane punches Juanita in the face in the course of a routine robbery. Imagine also that, on a separate occasion, Jennifer punches Juanita in the face because Jennifer does not like members of the group to which Juanita belongs. According to my characterization of hate crimes, Jennifer's act but not Jane's constitutes a hate crime. The question I address in this essay is whether Jennifer's motivation of group hatred is an aggravating factor that should be taken into account in the sentencing stage. In other words, is it morally permissible to reserve a stiffer criminal punishment for Jennifer than for Jane?

Before I answer this question, I want to emphasize the lack of imagination in asking *only* this question. As important as it is to reflect on how we might best educate and deter those tempted to commit bias crimes, our most important thinking on this subject will not include the criminal law. Rather, it will focus on educational programs designed to raise future generations who will never know the temptation to commit crimes of group hatred. Our preeminent goal must be to move toward a culture in which the remedial question of whether it is permissible to impose stiffer punishments for hate crimes would never arise. Thus, I hope that the lion's share of our thinking on

Christopher Heath Wellman, "A Defense of Stiffer Penalties for Hate Crimes," *Hypatia* Vol. 21, No. 2. Reprinted with the permission of Indiana University Press.

this topic will be directed at education, not punishment. Nonetheless, here I focus narrowly on issues of criminal law because imposing stiffer penalties may be one important element in a package of proposals designed to combat this social ill and because, perhaps more than other measures, the imposition of enhanced penalties incites controversy.

The Case for Enhanced Penalties for Hate Crimes

Whether it is legitimate to enhance penalties for hate crimes presumably depends upon what justifies state punishment in general, but this raises complications because ordinary moral thinking includes a miscellany of intuitions regarding punishment, and none of the traditional theories seems able to accommodate all of them. Thankfully, the limited purposes of this essay do not require us to adjudicate definitively among these rival accounts because proponents of each can make a case for stiffer penalties. With this in mind, I will quickly explain each of the theories and then show why all are compatible with punishing bias criminals more strenuously.[1]

The philosophical literature on punishment is replete with various accounts that defy easy categorization, so any clean taxonomy will necessarily be somewhat arbitrary and insensitive to the subtleties of existing theories. With this disclaimer, I shall divide what I take to be the most prominent options according to their general justifying aims. I label these theories the Retributive, Utilitarian, Moral Education, Expressivist, Restitutive, and Societal Safety-Valve accounts of punishment. Consider each in turn.

According to retributivism, the general justifying aim of punishment is to serve justice: Criminals should be punished, quite apart from whatever consequences might result, simply because they deserve it. Justice demands that people get what they deserve, criminals deserve to be punished, and so we serve justice when we criminally punish wrongdoers. Retributivism is backward looking insofar as its exclusive concern is to ensure that people receive their just deserts for past conduct. In fixing the appropriate punishment, the retributivist will ignore future consequences and mete out a sentence that fits the gravity of the offense.

According to utilitarians, retributivists are wrong to look backward since acts, practices, and institutions are to be morally evaluated in terms of their consequences. Thus, if punishing criminals is morally justified, it is because such a practice produces a better state of affairs. Moreover, since the hard treatment of criminals is among the consequences that must be counted, there is a prima facie case *against* punishment. It is not difficult for a utilitarian to defeat this case, however, because there are also ample benefits. Most notably, because all of us want to avoid punishment, each of us is deterred from behaving criminally. And, because others are similarly deterred, we enjoy a level of security possible only under a system of criminal punishment. Thus, state punishment can be justified on consequentialist grounds despite the pain visited upon those punished, because it allows us to pursue our projects in a way that we could not in its absence.

According to the moral education view, the general justifying aim of punishment is to educate the criminal and, where possible, the general public as well. Underlying this approach is a conviction that criminal behavior emanates from some type of correctable moral failing, and the purpose of punishment is to morally educate offenders so that they (and others) will know better than to behave criminally. Moreover, whereas a simple spanking might be appropriate for a dog, humans have reason and thus are capable of being persuaded not to repeat their errors. As a consequence, when we punish humans, we should set out rationally to persuade them that they ought to behave otherwise. Having done so, we will not have harmed them; rather, we will have benefited them with a moral education. In the end, then, a properly designed penal system will not be so hard to justify because it will be constructed to benefit not only society as a whole, but especially the criminals themselves.

In "The Expressive Function of Punishment," Joel Feinberg argued that a satisfactory definition of punishment must account for its expressive function.

He wrote, "Punishment is a conventional device for the expression of attitudes of resentment and indignation, and of judgments of disapproval and reprobation, on the part either of the punishing authority himself or of those 'in whose name' the punishment is inflicted. Punishment, in short, has a *symbolic significance* largely missing from other kinds of penalties" (1970, 98). Impressed with this insight, some suppose that the general justifying aim of punishment is for society to issue its official pronouncements as to how citizens ought to behave.[2] After all, the state does not merely lock criminals up, it typically does so with a rhetorical flourish that allows a society to express and reinforce its values. In a 1949 memorandum submitted as evidence to the British Royal Commission on Capital Punishment, Lord Justice Denning explained the expressivist position: "The ultimate justification for any punishment is, not that it is a deterrent, but that it is the emphatic denunciation by the community of a crime" (quoted in Lawrence 1999, 163).

According to the restitutive theory of punishment, the ultimate purpose of punishment is to restore the victim. Rather than focus on harming the criminal, advocates of this approach are concerned principally with benefiting the victim. The logic behind this approach is compelling: Criminal behavior involves one person wrongly arrogating herself above another. Thus, crimes leave the criminal unjustly elevated and the victim wrongly degraded. Unlike retributivists (whose chief aim is to harm the criminal so that she no longer enjoys her undeserved, elevated position), restitutivists insist that our concern must be to restore the victim to her rightful, pre-crime position. Punishment is thought to restore the victim by undoing the degradation of the crime. It repairs the victim's position by publicly confirming that the victim has a moral standing that the criminal was wrong to disrespect.

Finally, consider the societal safety-valve theory. As its name suggests, this view takes the general justifying aim of state punishment to be the provision of a safe, institutionally controlled release of destructive animosity and violent ill will. Behind this theory are the twin beliefs that members of society must have some outlet for their thirst for personal revenge and general rage at wrongdoing and that channeling this emotion through the state's legal system is the most effective, peaceful avenue available. If we left it up to individuals to punish those who trespass against them, for instance, many would be frustrated by their inability to apprehend and punish their assailants, while others would let their lust for revenge lead them either to over-punish or, even worse, to punish innocent people. The innocent who were wrongly punished, the guilty who were over-punished, and even the guilty who falsely supposed that they were over-punished would then retaliate in their own bids for revenge. As these considerations reveal, it would not be long before a system of individual punishments deteriorated into a bloody mess. Because state punishment enjoys the moral authority that can come only through impartially adjudicating conflicts, it offers a relatively peaceful safety valve for the passionate resentment against perceived wrongdoers.

In light of this description of the competing accounts, let us consider, in reverse order, whether proponents of each of these approaches could *justify* harsher punishments for hate criminals. As advocates of the societal safety-valve theory emphasize, criminal punishments provide an important outlet for potentially disruptive tensions, especially when the victims have been severely mistreated. Nowhere is this release of societal pressure more important than in cases where divisions within society have led to bias crimes. The stakes are raised so dramatically with hate crimes because, to the extent that members of the target group identify with the victim, each is personally slighted by the crime and thus has much more than an impartial interest in seeing justice done. Thus, whereas only an individual and perhaps her friends and family will be personally invested in an average criminal's penalty, an entire marked group will typically yearn for a hate criminal to receive her just desert. The rioting in Los Angeles following the acquittal of the police officers who brutally beat Rodney King was a striking example of this phenomenon. One did not have to be a black person living in southern California to be outraged by the jury's verdict, but blacks were more than dispassionate enemies of injustice, they were fellow travelers who felt personally degraded by the beating and subsequently insulted by the verdict. Given their understandable investment in the court's decision, the acquittal understandably enraged many blacks.

It would be wrong to pretend that this extreme example is generally representative of what will happen if hate criminals are not given stiffer punishments (even the most heinous case is unlikely to be so combustible in the absence of other aggravating factors), but the Rodney King case does illustrate that hate crimes are lamentably capable of ripping the fabric that binds society's distinct groups.[3] As such, it shows why, if at least one of the functions of criminal punishment is to serve as a peaceful outlet for potentially explosive social pressure, the additional socially disruptive element peculiar to bias crimes explains why we should seek stiffer punishments in these cases.[4]

Turning now to the restitutive view, there are two distinct means of support for more severe punishments. Most obviously, one can claim that a hate crime especially degrades its direct victim, and thus calls for a more strenuous punishment to restore the victim to her *ex ante* position. Although I think it is plausible to suppose that hate crimes are particularly degrading to their primary victims, I will not focus on this claim here.[5] Rather, drawing upon the observations made just above, I suggest that hate crimes require enhanced penalties because, more than other transgressions, hate crimes claim vicarious victims. Each time a person is targeted for assault because of the group to which she belongs, it takes a toll upon everyone in the marked group. This is especially so in a society where members of the group are regularly attacked. Without diminishing the fact that the primary victim is often devastated as no one else could be, I want to stress that others are importantly, if vicariously, made victims because of their identification with the victim and the effect this identification has upon their sense of belonging, and even security, in society. Iris Marion Young's 1990 work on oppression showed why this is so. Regarding violence, she wrote:

> What makes violence a face of oppression is less the particular acts themselves, though these are often utterly horrible, than the social context surrounding them, which makes them possible and even acceptable. What makes violence a phenomenon of social injustice, and not merely an individual moral wrong, is its systemic character, its existence as a social practice. (61–62)

Violence is systemic because it is directed at members of a group simply because they are members of that group. Any woman, for example, has a reason to fear rape. Regardless of what a black man has done to escape the oppressions of marginality or powerlessness, he lives knowing he is subject to attack or harassment. The oppression of violence consists not only in direct victimization, but also in the daily knowledge shared by all members of oppressed groups that they are *liable* to violation, solely on account of their group identity. Just living under such threat of attack on oneself or family or friends deprives the oppressed of freedom and dignity, and needlessly expends their energy (61–62).

Thus, even without asserting that hate crimes are especially damaging to their primary victims, one can cite the real losses of secondary victims to explain why the restoration made necessary by hate crimes is more substantial than that by ordinary crimes. Put simply, hate crimes leave so much pain and degradation in their wake that, in order to restore both the primary and secondary victims, society must employ extraordinary measures to affirm all those who have been degraded. In such circumstances, ordinary criminal censure will not do.

Standing upon the shoulders of the preceding two analyses, one can create a compelling expressivist case for stiffer punishments. To do so, it is important to appreciate that one reason hate crimes are so ghastly and troubling is because of the messages they send. As indicated above, a hate crime can serve as a poignant announcement to all members of the targeted group that they are despised, hunted, and vulnerable. Indeed, part of what attracts hate criminals to these horrific acts is the opportunity to express contempt, not just for the particular victim, but for the entire group to which the victim belongs. Unfortunately, this expression is all too often received loud and clear. Proponents of the expressivist theory of punishment are in a position to recognize that hate crimes send these messages and suggest that the criminal law can be used to counter this message. Think again, for instance, of the reaction to the Rodney King episode. Many blacks interpreted the police brutality as a demonstration of the contempt many whites have for them. Given this message, it was especially important that the police officers who were videotaped committing the assault (and then recorded joking about having enjoyed the beating) be publicly censured and punished by society as a whole. If these officers had been criminally sentenced, this legal condemnation would have gone some way toward showing that, while various individuals may be racist, society as a whole will neither condone nor tolerate racist violence. (On this point, recall Young's insight that it is the likelihood or even acceptability surrounding acts of violence that makes them a manifestation of oppression.) Thus, if the officers had been not only criminally punished but given a more severe sentence for having committed a hate crime, this verdict would have changed the social context surrounding the crime. Such a verdict might have sent a powerful, countervailing message that racist violence is emphatically not accepted. Instead, the acquittal only reinforced the message that America as a society condones violence, as long as it is committed by whites against blacks.[6]

In light of the above, it takes little imagination to see why proponents of the expressivist theory of punishment might favor enhanced punishments. Given that the criminal law is an important expression of a society's values, it follows that we should want more severe penalties for those crimes that we deem to be more serious. As the British Royal Commission on Capital Punishment emphasized: "It is essential that punishments inflicted for grave crimes should adequately reflect the revulsion felt by the great majority of citizens for them" (quoted in Lawrence 1999, 163). And, since we are especially aghast at bias crimes, we should want to express our most solemn condemnation for those who commit these crimes. The most natural way for us to do so, of course, is to impose stiffer penalties for hate crimes. As the foregoing discussion illustrates, this general lesson is particularly important in the case of hate crimes because of the destructive and divisive messages they send. Given the implicit but clear messages of bias crimes, it is all

the more important that society use criminal law to communicate forcefully that the message of hatred not only does not come from all of us, but is a loathsome message which we as a society will not tolerate.

In the section below on retributivism, I contend that hate criminals are morally worse than ordinary criminals. If this is accurate, then clearly the moral education theory of punishment would recommend stiffer punishments for hate criminals. Very simply, the type and extent of moral education one requires depend upon the moral depravity of one's character. Thus, if hate criminals are indeed worse than their counterparts, then it stands to reason that they require a more intense moral education. In other words, just as someone guilty of grand larceny merits more severe punishment than a petty thief, a hate criminal should be punished more than someone guilty of an otherwise comparable, generic crime.

But, while this reasoning supplies a compelling case for enhanced penalties, it is not the most pressing concern moral education theorists should have with hate crimes. As critical as it is that we attend to bias criminals after they have violently acted upon their hatred, it is even more important that we strive to become a society in which no one harbors this bias to begin with. This too is a matter of criminal law because, as education theorists emphasize, the criminal code is an important instrument for morally educating society at large. (It can make an enormous difference, for instance, whether one grows up in a society that outlaws homosexuality or in one that doles out more severe penalties to heterosexists who harass homosexuals.) Since chauvinism and xenophobia are some of the most personally and socially destructive moral vices undermining contemporary society, there are compelling reasons to harness the criminal law's power to shape the general public's values in the campaign against group hatred. In sum, both because hate criminals have revealed themselves to be particularly in need of moral education, and because our criminal code is an educative instrument for society at large, moral education theorists have reason to lobby for enhanced penalties for hate crimes.

The utilitarian case for more strenuous punishments can be mounted on many fronts. In addition to the considerations canvassed above (certainly a utilitarian will want to foster moral education and supply an appropriate societal safety valve, for instance), utilitarians recognize that the optimal punishment is fixed by a number of factors, including the cost of the crime. In short, as the cost of a crime rises, a utilitarian will be more concerned to deter it and will therefore want a more severe punishment. Since hate crimes cause profound social division and unrest, as well as create more pain for a greater number of victims, they are extremely costly. Thus, although a utilitarian might invoke any number of considerations to defend stiffer penalties for hate crimes, one basic and distinctively consequential line of reasoning stands out: the magnified harmfulness of hate crimes gives us reason to attach more severe penalties to those found guilty of committing them.

Finally, because retributivists advocate punishing criminals in accordance with the moral depravity of their offenses, they must establish that hate crimes are worse than their generic counterparts. Corresponding to the two elements of any crime, *actus reus* (bad act) and *mens rea* (guilty mind), there are two ways in which bias crimes and criminals might be morally worse than ordinary ones: if the act is worse or the mind more guilty, then there is a retributive case for stiffer penalties.

The explanation as to why the *actus reus* in a hate crime is particularly bad is straightforward. As outlined above, bias crimes are especially harmful because of the vicarious victims they claim and the psychological distress and social unrest they leave in their wake. And, just as a person who steals one thousand dollars commits a worse act (other things being equal) than someone who steals one hundred, the additional harms involved in bias crimes make the acts worse than they would be otherwise. Clearly, then, proponents of retributivism need cite only the magnified badness of the act in a hate crime to show why bias criminals are especially culpable and thus deserve to be punished more.

If a bias crime's *actus reus* is particularly bad, then a retributivist need not establish that the *mens rea* is any different from that in generic crimes. Because I believe that the mind of a hate criminal is especially

depraved, however, let me suggest how a retributivist might focus on *mens rea* to make the case for enhanced punishment. To most, I suspect that the heightened guilt of the hate criminal's mind seems self-evident. If Ally and Barry both murder someone, for instance, and the only difference between the two is that Ally chooses her victim for monetary gain (suppose she is paid ten thousand dollars to kill someone she has never met) whereas Barry is motivated solely by hatred for the group to which his victim belongs (imagine that Barry kills a Jewish woman he has never met only because she is Jewish), most would agree that Barry's offense is worse. As much as Ally ought to be punished, Barry deserves a stiffer punishment to fit his extreme depravity.

For those who do not share this pretheoretic judgment, let me offer a buttressing explanation. In my view, Barry's murder is made worse by the additional element of invidious discrimination. The wrongness of invidious discrimination is not mysterious; most everyone understands the appeal of Martin Luther King, Jr.'s vision of a time when all will be judged by the content of their character rather than the color of their skin. That one mistreats the person against whom one discriminates explains the commonly held view that making hiring decisions on the basis of the color of an applicant's skin is impermissible. And if selecting employees based upon skin color is wrong, certainly selecting people to criminally dehumanize on that basis is at least equally so.

Perhaps a good way to capture this sentiment is to say that hate crimes are "senseless." Of course, no murder makes sense, but we are liable to lament Barry's act as particularly pointless. As depraved as Ally is for valuing $10,000 more than a person's life, Barry is worse because he regards the act of killing not as a means to some other end, but as an end in itself. He kills simply to indulge his irrational hatred, merely for the satisfaction of killing a Jewish person. Thus, without minimizing our disgust for Ally, there is plenty of room to regard Barry's state of mind as more vicious than Ally's. And, because retributivists assign punishments in accordance with the moral depravity of the criminal, Barry's more reprehensible state of mind explains why he deserves to be punished more strenuously than Ally.

Here, one might protest that hate criminals are not uniquely capable of intrinsically valuing killing: one can imagine a third murderer, Claudia, killing someone out of revenge (perhaps because the person hurt her child, had an affair with her partner, broke her heart, and so on), but it strikes me that Claudia's personal motive makes her mind less guilty than Barry's because of the absence of prejudicial discrimination. Of course, one could imagine a fourth murderer, call her Diane, who kills with neither a personal motive nor group animus. But, someone like Diane, who randomly picks victims for the mere sake of killing, would not be a counterexample because most would readily concede that, if not insane, she is also especially depraved (even if her depravity is distinct from Barry's). In other words, while Diane is admittedly not a hate criminal, few would allege that it would be unjust to punish her more strenuously than typical murderers like Ally and Claudia. In the end, then, it seems as though a retributivist would recommend punishing hate criminals more strenuously because both their *actus reus* and their *mens rea* are worse than their generic criminal counterparts.

As the preceding analysis shows, any of the six theories can help explain the important moral aims that might be realized by punishing hate criminals more severely. If this is right, then we need not choose among the competing justifications for punishment to establish the desirability of imposing stiffer penalties for hate crimes.

POSSIBLE OBJECTIONS

Even if the case in favor of imposing stiffer penalties for hate crimes is strong, it is only prima facie. To determine whether this presumptive case is decisive, we must canvass the arguments against such a measure.

The first objection to meting out harsher punishments for hate crimes is that, like affirmative action, it creates special rights. That is, if people who hate minorities are punished more strenuously for indulging their hatred, then minorities are being given extra protection. Insofar as we construct spe-

cial criminal laws to deter people from satisfying their desires to put down members of a minority group, there is a sense in which we are ascribing special rights to these minorities. But this seems unjust. As terrible as hate crimes are, we should not resort to unjust measures to combat them. Given that we are all equal, minorities have no right to see their enemies punished more, and thus laws that reserve an exalted status for minorities are illegitimate. While it is horrible that some groups have been oppressed, those who voice this objection suggest that the appropriate response is to work diligently to end the oppression, not to add a second wrong in the misguided hope of making things right. Although I have some sympathy for this objection, I remain unconvinced for two reasons. First, I wholeheartedly agree that, other things being equal, we should all have equal rights, but we must bear in mind that other things are emphatically *not* equal. The egalitarian impulse to treat all equally is a noble one, but justice does not require that we treat all cases alike; rather, it demands that we treat *like* cases alike. When there is a morally significant difference between two cases, there is nothing unjust or otherwise inappropriate about responding to these cases differently. (Few object to punishing repeat offenders more severely than first-time offenders, for instance.) Similarly, if only certain minority groups are victimized by hatred, there is nothing wrong with responding to this special, localized problem with a special, localized solution. If not all are terrorized by bias crimes, then there is not necessarily any injustice if not all are protected by hate crime legislation.

Second, and more important, my proposal is not restricted to only minority or oppressed groups. As I characterize them, one commits a hate crime just in case one selects one's victim at least in part because of an animus toward members of the group to which the victim belongs. As a consequence, my view allows anyone to be either guilty or the victim of a hate crime. For instance, the case of *Wisconsin v. Mitchell* involved an event in 1989 when some young black men and boys attacked a young boy because he was white. Several in the group had just seen the movie *Mississippi Burning*, and when the group noticed the boy, one person said: "There goes a white boy; go get him." The group not only got him, they beat him into a four-day coma. Assuming that this account is accurate, the participants in the beating would be guilty of a hate crime.[7] Thus, combining my two points, we see that, while there would be nothing inherently unjust about creating special protections for oppressed groups, my proposal does not do so. Rather, it acknowledges that any one of us might commit a hate crime and that it would be permissible to punish more severely anyone who did.

Perhaps the most obvious and important objection to enhancing penalties for bias crimes is that it violates the moral rights of those punished. The motivation behind this complaint is the quite accurate notion that one does not summarily lose *all* rights against punishment as soon as one commits a crime; one forfeits only one's right against being punished in a manner fitting the crime. Thus, a burglar loses her right against being punished for burglary, but retains her claim against being punished to an extent fitting murder, for instance.

Consider this criticism in terms of Jennifer and Jane, both of whom punched Juanita in the face, but while Jane did so during a routine robbery, Jennifer did so because of a dislike for the group of which Juanita is a member. According to my proposal, Jennifer may be punished more than Jane, but advocates for the present objection question how this could be permissible. After all, Jennifer and Jane committed the same crime: each punched Juanita in the face. Thus, by hypothesis, each is equally morally culpable, each has equally forfeited her right not to be punished, and thus both should be punished alike. If we reserve an especially severe penalty for Jennifer, however, then we violate her right not to be excessively punished. In short, a proponent of this objection will protest that, as useful and tempting as it might be to make an example out of Jennifer, justice prohibits us from treating her merely as a means.

This objection essentially contests the retributive arguments I advanced above. It counters that Jennifer cannot possibly deserve a stiffer punishment than Jane because the two acted identically. One's response to this criticism depends upon the position one takes on contested philosophical issues involving the description and individuation of particular

actions. Specifically, the shape of my answer depends on whether I incorporate intentions into the description of an action or whether I distinguish between the two. This question is well beyond my area of expertise, so I shall not try to convince readers that one option is always and necessarily better than the other. Instead, continuing to use the example of Jennifer and Jane, I suggest that both options leave plenty of room to defend hate crime legislation.

The issue is whether we should describe Jennifer and Jane as having performed the same act, given that they had different intentions. On the one hand, some might insist that their intentions are irrelevant to what act they performed and, insofar as each punched Juanita in the face, both acted identically. The competing view favors incorporating intentions into the very description of an act and suggests that, because Jennifer and Jane had different intentions, they acted differently. If the latter position is correct, then it is not difficult to refute the present objection. Specifically, since Jane's intention was to take Juanita's money, and Jennifer's intention was to assault a member of Juanita's group, the two acted differently: Jane's *act* was one of robbery, whereas Jennifer's *act* was one of group intimidation, and thus there is nothing curious about their deserving different punishments. Given that the two performed different actions, Jennifer has no grounds to insist that she has a right not to be punished more than Jane.

If we presume that an agent's intention is entirely distinct from the act she performs, on the other hand, then it is not so obvious that the present criticism is mistaken. Even if actions are separate from intentions in a manner that implies Jennifer and Jane acted identically, however, there is room to distinguish between the punishment each deserves. This is because once we divorce actions from intentions, we can no longer look solely at an agent's action to determine the appropriate punishment. To see this, imagine an example involving Allison, Barbara, and Carol. Suppose that Allison is a sword swallower who gets along well with Barbara but feuds with Carol. Imagine that Barbara pats Allison on the back. Unfortunately, this friendly gesture is disastrous for Allison because she was swallowing a sword at the time. Suppose further that after

Allison has finally recovered to a point where she can resume her avocation, Carol maliciously pats Allison on the back, again, while she is practicing her routine. Now, if we describe actions without reference to intentions, then it seems reasonable to say that Barbara and Carol acted identically: each patted Allison on the back. However, no one would insist that both deserve the same punishment. After all, Barbara bitterly regrets having unwittingly injured a good friend, whereas Carol secretly revels in the ease with which she was able deliberately to shred an enemy's digestive tract. Even if we admit that Barbara should perhaps be chastised for not exercising more caution, certainly we do not think she deserves to be punished as strenuously as Carol. Thus, if we insist on keeping intentions and actions separate, then there is nothing curious about assigning different punishments to people who commit the same act.[8]

In sum, it is wrong to protest that enhanced punishments violate the rights of hate criminals because, if acts are defined in part by the agents' intentions, then a hate criminal in fact performs a distinctly bad act; and if acts and intentions are to be considered separately, there is nothing unjust about meting out different punishments for people who perform the same bad act.

Let us turn now to the single question regarding hate crime legislation that has received by far the most attention: is it consistent with the United States Constitution to reserve a more strenuous punishment for bias crimes? In part because more qualified people have commented so extensively on this topic, but also because this a descriptive question about what the law is rather than a moral question about what the constitution *ought* to be, I will respond only briefly to this potential objection.

In brief, many critics object that because the First Amendment protects a person's beliefs my proposal would unconstitutionally punish a hate criminal for holding an unpopular belief. In response, the first thing to notice is that my proposal does not suggest punishing someone simply for holding certain beliefs because it requires one first to commit a crime. For instance, if Jack and Jill are equally heterosexist, but only Jack assaults gays, then my proposal recommends that only Jack be punished. Jill should not be

punished despite having identical attitudes about homosexuals.

At this point, a critic might respond that the First Amendment protects freedom of speech as well as freedom of thought, and since Jack's actions against gays can be construed as expressive conduct, it is constitutionally protected. This claim is easily countered, though, because the First Amendment clearly does not protect all potentially expressive activity. Just as the First Amendment does not cover obscenity, defamation, and fighting words, for instance, neither does it protect violent assault, no matter how expressive it might be thought to be.

Here, one might protest that my reasoning is beside the point because the problem is not that Jack is being punished; instead, it is unconstitutional that he is being punished *more severely*. It is unconstitutional that Jack should receive an enhanced penalty when the only reason for this enhancement is that he holds constitutionally protected beliefs. But, as the United States Supreme Court recognized in *Wisconsin v. Mitchell*, there is an important difference between content-based regulations and penalty-enhancement statutes (at 2200). The Court emphasized that, as in other circumstances, there is nothing inappropriate about invoking protected beliefs during sentencing as long as they are relevant to the motive. As David Deitchman has explained:

> Statutes that prohibit activities such as cross burning have been held unconstitutional because they prohibit only particular expressive conduct based on the message conveyed—they are content-based. In contrast, penalty enhancement statutes are not "explicitly directed at expression." Instead, enhancement statutes are "aimed at conduct unprotected by the First Amendment" that is *motivated by* a biased belief. (1994, 406)

A fourth concern about creating special, more strenuous punishments for bias crimes is that doing so sends the message that typical, "garden variety" crimes are not so bad. That is, just as brand name advertising can lead us to undervalue so-called generic equivalents, putting inflated emphasis on hate crimes might cause us to worry less about normal crimes. Even a first-degree murder, for instance, seems less horrific in comparison to an analogous hate crime. Thus, given the importance of sustaining our disgust at all crime, perhaps we should refrain from singling out hate crimes as worthy of special condemnation.

There is some truth to this objection, but it is a truth from which we need not shrink. I concede that ordinary crimes might seem less noxious than hate crimes, but this is unproblematic because these other crimes *are* less horrific. Hate criminals are especially reprehensible, and we need not apologize for being particularly aghast at their crimes. Admittedly, it would be problematic if our heightened reaction to bias crimes made us either less concerned about or, even worse, more inclined to commit more typical crimes, but there is no reason to worry about this. It is standard to make all kinds of discriminations in the criminal law that do not have this affect. The fact that we think worse of murderers has not caused us to be lax with those guilty of manslaughter, for instance, nor has it increased our inclination to commit manslaughter. Similarly, there is plenty of room to insist that hate crimes are particularly bad without thereby denying that other crimes, unmotivated by hate, can also contemptible.[9]

Finally, some might object that my concern with hate crimes is inappropriate because, although there are occasionally abhorrent acts of hatred which transfix our attention, bias crimes are, statistically speaking, relatively insignificant.[10] The *real* problems, an objector of this stripe might suggest, are the more prevalent but less spectacular issues like so-called black-on-black crime. In response, let me emphasize two points. First, even if hate crimes are committed relatively infrequently, their spectacular nature gives them an added moral import. I do not allege that hate crimes are of greater consequence merely because they captivate me; I suggest instead that their spectacular nature is morally relevant insofar as it leaves a deep and painful impression upon members of the targeted group. As I indicated above, bias crimes claim more victims than those who are directly dehumanized and, the more spectacular the crime, the more it will tend to terrorize those who identify with the victim. Second, let me stress that I do not suppose hate crimes to be the only or even the most important problem in contemporary society. But, from the fact that there are other important problems it follows neither that we may not express concern about hate crimes nor that imposing stiffer penalties is imper-

missible. By all means, we should give society's other ills the attention they deserve, but doing so does not make it wrong for us to examine the permissibility and effectiveness of the special solutions necessary to combat the problem of hate crimes.

Like the others, this last objection loses its initial plausibility under scrutiny. And so, while we cannot claim to have considered every possible criticism, it appears that the presumptive case in favor of imposing stiffer penalties for bias crimes is not defeated by any of the standard objections. . . .

REFERENCES

Card, Claudia. 1991. Rape as a terrorist institution. In *Violence, terrorism, and justice*, ed. R. G. Frey and Christopher Morris. Cambridge: Cambridge University Press.

Deitchman, David. 1994. Limits on the right to hate: A look at the Texas Hate Crime Act. *Baylor Law Review* 46: 399–417.

Feinberg, Joel. 1970. The expressive function of punishment. In *Doing and deserving*. Princeton, N.J.: Princeton University Press.

Lawrence, Frederick. 1999. *Punishing hate*. Cambridge, Mass.: Harvard University Press.

Southern Voice. 1999. March 11.

Wisconsin v. Mitchell. 1993. 113 S. Ct. 2194.

Young, Iris Marion. 1990. *Justice and the politics of difference*. Princeton, N.J.: Princeton University Press.

NOTES

1. Rather than demonstrate that all of these theories of punishment are compatible with enhanced penalties for hate crimes, it might be thought preferable to defend my favored theory and then focus exclusively on it. I do not do so here for a number of reasons. First, even if I thought that one of the traditional theories was uniquely satisfactory, I could not hope to defend this judgment conclusively within the confines of a paper focusing on hate crimes. Second, for breadth of argument, it is important to demonstrate that no traditional theory of punishment is inconsistent with imposing stiffer punishments for bias crimes. Finally, my own view is that an adequate theory of punishment will draw upon all six of the accounts canvassed here. In particular, I think each of

the aims the traditional approaches feature is relevant to justifying a state's imposition of the criminal law.

2. I should add that Feinberg never endorses the expressive function as a justification for punishment; he suggests it only as necessary to an adequate definition.

3. One might think police officers deserve stiffer penalties than do ordinary citizens because they violate a special trust by breaking laws they are charged to enforce. I do not deny that police officers may in general deserve more harsh punishments for breaking the law, but this is compatible with my claim that harsher punishments are appropriate for hate crimes.

4. As Russ Shafer-Landau pointed out to me, it does not follow automatically that increased social pressure requires us to enhance the penalty as opposed to, say, stepping up prosecution and convictions. My own view, though, is that the higher stakes make a prima facie case for doing all three.

5. Lawrence argues that bias crimes are particularly psychologically damaging to their victims in *Punishing Hate* (1999, 39–41).

6. Those who doubt the significance of the messages expressed in criminal sentencing would do well to recall the various emotional reactions to O. J. Simpson's acquittal. In addition to the distraught families of the victims, there were remarkably different reactions in the general public, which was split largely along racial lines.

7. We might think it more understandable—and perhaps even more excusable—that members of an oppressed group (blacks in South Africa under apartheid are an obvious example) should commit a hate crime, but this does not make it any less of a hate crime. Thus, even if victims of oppression who strike out in frustration should be punished less than other hate criminals, they should still be punished more than if their action was not a hate crime.

8. Here, one might worry that stiffer penalties for bias crimes punish motivation, not intention. Even if motivation and intention can be neatly distinguished (which seems doubtful), this objection misses the mark because it is common for courts to consider the motivation when sentencing a criminal.

9. Think, for instance, of Ronald Shanabarger. Shanabarger was angry at his fiancée for refusing to cut short her vacation when his father died, so he hatched a plan to marry her, have a child with her, give her enough time to bond with him, and then kill this child—all so that she would know the same loss that he felt when his father died! He executed this plan, killing his seven-month-old son on the eve of Father's Day. Proponents of hate crime legislation are not committed to saying that Shanabarger's behavior was "not that bad." On the contrary, we are right to hold him and his behavior in utter contempt. It is worth noting, however, that Shanabarger's behavior would have been *even worse* if he had carried out such a plan against a woman simply because she was a member of a group against whom he held a prejudice.

10. Steve Rieber raised this question during a very helpful conversation on this subject.

Critic

HEIDI M. HURD

Why Liberals Should Hate "Hate Crime Legislation"

I. THREE DIFFERENCES BETWEEN HATE/BIAS CRIMES AND ALL OTHER CRIMES

... If hate and bias crime legislation construes hate and bias as mens rea requirements, then there are three important differences between hate and bias crimes and virtually all other sorts of crimes with which the criminal law is concerned. And these differences, it seems to me, are both practically and philosophically profound. First, hate/bias crimes are concerned with defendants' motivations for action in a way that no other crimes have ever been concerned. Second, the motivations with which they are concerned are emotional states that attend actions (rather than future states of affairs to which actions are instrumental means). And finally, the emotional states with which these crimes are concerned constitute standing character traits rather than occurrent mental states (such as intentions, purposes, choices, etc.). . . .

If hate/bias crime legislation punishes persons for bad character, as it does if it enhances defendants' punishment for criminal wrongdoing when it is perpetrated because of certain emotions or (dispositional) beliefs, then such legislation is, at least prima facie, morally and politically troubling. In the next section, let us turn to the questions that advocates of hate/bias crime legislation must answer in order to defend the moral and political legitimacy of criminalizing bad character.

II. THE MORAL AND POLITICAL IMPLICATIONS OF CRIMINALIZING VICIOUS CHARACTER TRAITS

If I am right that hate crime legislation punishes persons for bad character, then hate and bias crime statutes have some surprising implications and raise some very important political questions. Let me pose three such questions, and say why the answers that one gives may have profound implications for the future of American criminal law.

A. Can We Choose Our Emotions or Will Our Beliefs?

Most of us are pretty confident that would-be defendants can choose not to rape, steal, and kill. But it seems less clear to what degree people can will away, or choose not to have, particular character traits, and specifically, particular emotions and beliefs. At the moment that a defendant is about to throw a rock through his neighbor's window, we are reasonably sure that he can will to do otherwise; but at that moment, can he will away his hatred of his neighbor as a Jew? Can one simply decide not to be selfish, or greedy, or narcissistic? I suspect that anyone who can is not very selfish, greedy or narcissistic! Can one simply refuse to believe things that one has long been disposed to believe? Surely not by an act of will alone. Certainly one can gather more information about

Heidi M. Hurd, "Why Liberals Should Hate 'Hate Crime Legislation,'" *Law and Philosophy* Vol. 20, No. 2, Springer Publishing (March, 2001).

others so as to make more discriminating, and thus less discriminatory judgments about them. But it is in the nature of bias for one to believe that no further information is required so as to make informed judgments about others. And it is unclear how one could simply will a change in one's epistemic standards.

Persons can, with mixed success, *indirectly* alter aspects of their character by choosing to subject themselves to experiences that promise to be character building. People clearly spend enormous amounts of money in therapy to change themselves for the better. And people can, again with imperfect reliability, alter their characters by repeatedly putting themselves in circumstances that challenge them to behave in ways that, over time, affect their beliefs, emotional reactions, and dispositional responses. For example, someone might not be able to will away his disdain for the poor; but he might be able to rid himself of that disdain by moving to the ghetto and volunteering his time to help those in need, so that over time his disdain fades to pity, and then to admiration for the hardiness required to persevere in poverty.

Perhaps by punishing people particularly harshly when they do bad deeds out of hatred for, or bias against, their victims' race, ethnicity, religion, sexual orientation, etc., we will motivate people to take actions that will indirectly alter, over time, their emotional responses to such characteristics.[1] And perhaps those who do not pursue available avenues for dispositional change deserve punishment for their bad character—not because they chose their character, but because they failed to will actions that might have caused their character to be other than it is.

But while character can be indirectly affected by willed actions, and so is not immutable, one's ability to affect it indirectly is clearly imperfect. And, most importantly, such indirect measures are just that: indirect, and hence, non-immediate. We cannot abandon our emotions and (dispositional) beliefs the way that we can abandon our goals—i.e., simply by choice. Thus, criminal legislation that targets emotions and (dispositional) beliefs targets things that are not fully or readily within defendants' immediate control. And if law ought not to punish us for things that we cannot autonomously affect, then hate and bias crime legislation is suspect for doing just that.

B. Are Hatred and Prejudice Worse Than Other Emotional States That Often Accompany Criminal Actions?

I am in fact quite sympathetic to the view that moral culpability is largely a function of character—of the beliefs that guide us and the emotions that attend our actions (notwithstanding their inelastic nature). But hatred and bias towards particular groups are but two of many culpable dispositions. Are they the worst of the bunch? Are they so rotten as to justify special criminal attention? How does hate compare to greed, jealousy, revenge, sadism, or cowardliness? If hate and bias crimes are going to remain unique among crimes in picking out emotional and dispositional motivations as bases for increased punishment, then it must be possible either (1) to defend the claim that, say, racial hatred or gender bias is morally worse than greed, jealousy, and revenge, or (2) to advance some reason to think that such hatred and bias are uniquely responsive to criminal sanctions in a way that greed, jealousy, and vengeance are not. I think it unlikely that hate crime advocates can sustain either of these arguments, although both may have more promise than some critics have supposed.

It is true that "motives cannot be readily ranked by their degree of culpability,"[2] and this confounds any easy defense of the first claim. One critic suggests that this is because all motivations to assault persons, for example, share a common denominator, i.e., the motive to humiliate, and this makes them all equally culpable.[3] But this explanation is implausible: someone who renders another unconscious so as to pick his pocket is not necessarily subjectively intending to humiliate his victim, and someone who enjoys embarrassing others is clearly not as culpable as someone who enjoys inflicting physical torture on others, even though both may be said to be motivated by a desire to humiliate. Others have suggested, conversely, that the reason that motivations cannot be clearly ranked is because they are so different as to be incommensurable.[4] I find this suggestion equally implausible, not only because the concept of incommensurability is by itself troublesome. If all culpable motivations were incommensurable, there would be no easy cases of comparison. But there clearly are.

A young girl who feels a need to publicly display her affection for her boyfriend (by, say, graffitiing "Sally loves John" on a washroom wall in a manner that constitutes technical destruction of property) is clearly not as culpable as the sadist who seeks to prolong the torture of a child over days.

In my view, the likely reason that motives (goals, emotions, and dispositional beliefs) resist cardinal classifications and even ordinal rankings is that they are highly fact-sensitive. Just as the determination that someone was negligent turns on a detailed appreciation of the circumstances in which she acted and the information reasonably available to her, so the evaluation of someone's motives for action requires an appreciation of the nature and the relative weight of an inevitably complex set of goals, emotions, and (dispositional) beliefs, as well as an overall assessment of the merit of their combination. As such, it appears difficult to say that particular motivations, say racial prejudice or religious hatred, are categorically worse than other motivations, say pedophilia or sadism: as between some persons they probably are; as between others they probably are not.

Those who resort to the second means of defending the unique status of hate and bias crimes must advance reasons to think that racism, sexism, and homophobia can be more readily purged by the criminal law than can other vices. Some might maintain that racism, sexism, and homophobia are learned, while sadism, vengeance, and jealousy are not. They thus might argue that racism, sexism, and homophobia can be unlearned in a way that these other dispositions cannot. Perhaps this is so. Even if one believes that the genesis of group hatred and prejudice is environmental, whereas the genesis of other vices is genetic or otherwise innate, one would need reasons to believe that learned dispositions are less immutable than unlearned ones before criminalizing the former but not the latter. And one would need further proof that racists, sexists, and homophobes will more quickly, effectively, or cheaply unlearn their vices when threatened with enhanced criminal liability, than when educated or coerced in other (non-legal, or at least non-criminal) ways.

If advocates of hate/bias crime legislation are unable to defend either the claim that hate and bias are more culpable than other motivations or the thesis that hate and bias are uniquely susceptible to coercion by criminal penalties, then they have but two avenues of argument available to them. They must either (1) admit and defend the fact that hate/bias crime legislation arbitrarily picks out for extra punishment a set of mental states that are a subset of a larger class of equally vicious states, or (2) convince theorists and legislators to generalize hate/bias crime legislation by radically revising traditional culpability doctrines so as in every case to take into account, and dish out punishment in proportion to, the culpable emotional and (dispositional) belief states that motivated a defendant to commit a criminal deed—from racial bias to jealousy to road rage.

The first line of argument is a dangerous one, for it implies that the criminal law both does not and need not treat like cases alike. Equally culpable defendants who commit equally wrongful acts (for example, one who throws a rock as a result of vengeance and one who throws a rock as a result of racial hatred) can justifiably be punished unequally. While like cases must be judged alike, on pain of irrationality, the argument here is that like cases need not be punished alike. Those who would make such a claim clearly cannot think that equality of treatment is much of a moral value. They must believe that so long as someone is not punished *more than* he deserves, he cannot complain that he is punished more than someone of equal culpability and wrongdoing. The success of such an argument, however, turns on the success with which proponents can defeat the formidable arguments advanced in the vast literature on equality for the proposition that it is a serious injustice to punish equally culpable persons unequally when they have committed equally wrongful deeds.

It might be most tempting, in the end, for advocates of hate and bias crime legislation to argue that the traditional criminal law mens rea concepts ought to be revolutionized in accordance with the model provided by contemporary hate and bias crime statutes. On such an argument, hate and bias crimes ought not to remain unique in punishing the motivations with which defendants act; rather, in all cases, fact-finders ought to assess defendants' motivations (including the emotions attendant upon their actions and the (dispositional) beliefs that might have informed their practical reasoning), and punish defendants proportionate to the viciousness of their character as manifested in their deeds.

This suggestion brings me to the third moral problem that confronts those who advocate hate/bias crime legislation in particular, and criminal legislation that targets emotions and (dispositional) beliefs in general.

C. Should the Criminal Law Punish Persons for Bad Character?

Inasmuch as hate crime legislation ultimately punishes persons for standing traits of character, it is best explained by, and most at home within, what is called a "character theory of the criminal law"—a theory that takes the proper goals of criminal law to be the punishment of vice and the cultivation of virtue. Now these are distinctively *non-liberal* goals.

Political liberals traditionally license the state to enforce the Right, but not the Good. They maintain that the state must limit the use of its power to constructing and protecting a fair framework of cooperation, defined as a system of rights that allows all citizens maximal equal liberty to pursue their own unique conceptions of the good life. Common to contemporary liberalism is the claim that reasonable people do not now agree, and may never be able to agree, on a singular conception of what it means to live a good life. At most, they can agree, in principle, to disagree, and they can agree, in practice, to peaceable institutional means by which to disagree. Inasmuch as state action is both theoretically unjust and practically impotent unless it can command the agreement (if only hypothetically) of reasonable persons, state action is illegitimate if it pursues a particular conception of the good life.[5]

Liberals have long believed that theories that construe certain character traits as virtuous or vicious belong to the province of the Good, rather than the Right. There are several reasons for this. First, it appears that one person's vice is another person's virtue. That is, the vices and virtues of character are not among the things about which reasonable people agree, whatever else they believe. Reasonable people can seemingly disagree over whether persons should experience a love of God, or deep loyalty to friends and family over strangers, or a driving sense of professional ambition, or an exceptionless commitment to keeping promises or telling the truth.

Second, as we have already discussed, vice and virtue appear only indirectly responsive to choice. Out of deference to the fact that persons' liberty to pursue their own conceptions of the good life is chilled by threats of strict liability, liberals typically predicate moral and legal responsibility on matters of choice. Because persons cannot choose their character traits, but can affect them only indirectly and imperfectly, virtues and vices have appeared to liberals to be inappropriate candidates for praise and blame, rewards and punishments.

Third, persons can seemingly peaceably co-exist without settling the question of the sorts of character traits that persons ought to cultivate or suppress. Indeed, until the enactment of hate/bias crimes, our criminal law was testament to the fact that we could meaningfully assess actors' culpability without resolving inevitable disputes over the sorts of traits that people should cultivate. While people no doubt disagree about the relative culpability of acts of spite, jealousy, vengeance, and racism, few have disagreed that purposeful harms are more culpable than harms committed only knowingly; and that harms committed knowingly are more culpable than harms committed recklessly or negligently. Inasmuch as contemporary liberalism is wedded to the view that our peaceable co-existence requires the state to limit its scope to matters upon which we can agree, it is committed to the view that our old ways are better than our new ones—that hate/bias crime legislation exceeds the proper bounds of state action, as would any attempt to radically revise mens rea doctrines so as to use state power to affect people's moral character.[6]

Character theories of the criminal law are most naturally at home with perfectionist political theories. The willingness to use the criminal law to punish people for bad character and to encourage people to cultivate good character is at least closely compatible with, if not required by, the perfectionist directive to use the power of the state to affect individual virtue when possible. Those who advocate the enactment of legislation that punishes racism, sexism, homophobia, and so forth, should thus be wise to align themselves politically with those who view the inculcation of virtue and the elimination of vice as legitimate state goals.

Even still, those who are willing, in principle, to criminalize certain aspects of character must honor what Joseph Raz calls "the morality of freedom." While a political perfectionist, Raz has powerfully insisted that in many instances what is good (virtuous) for persons is a product of what they autonomously chose to do and to believe. Hence, a legislator who seeks to pursue a perfectionist agenda must be careful to preserve a significant arena in which persons can make their own choices about what is good. Inasmuch as many persons come to make virtuous choices only by making a certain number of vicious ones, the state must tolerate a certain number of vices in order to maximize the moral virtues that derive from exercises of liberty.[7]

Thus, not only must those who are willing to criminalize hate and bias meet the challenges of contemporary liberalism generally, but they must be confident that in enacting such legislation, they are not inhibiting the liberty to be bad that is necessary to the cultivation of good. Our long reluctance to prohibit associations that devote themselves to racist, sexist, homophobic, and other intolerant agendas suggests that such associations, while not themselves of moral worth, may be among those unfortunate things that we must tolerate in order to maximize pursuits that are of moral worth. They may contribute to an important marketplace of ideas (if only by revealing how ugly some ideas can be); or they may be such that we must tolerate them on pain of chilling other associations that are of moral worth; or the precedent set by prohibiting them may motivate legislators to prohibit other associations that are in fact quite worthy. Whatever explains our historical commitment to tolerating the non-violent activities of pornographers, anti-Semites, neo-Nazis, the Ku Klux Klan, and other sexist, racist, homophobic, and religiously intolerant groups, may be a good reason for perfectionists to conclude that the vices of group hatred and prejudice are not best repressed by criminalizing them.

In conclusion, if hate and bias have become new conditions of legal culpability, then hate/bias crime legislation has worked important changes in both our criminal law doctrine and our political presuppositions. No longer is character immune from criminal sanctions; no longer are virtue and vice outside the scope of state action. The law now regulates not only what we do, but who we are. Perhaps this is for the better. Perhaps the law is too effective a tool for accomplishing personal improvement to deny its use to those who can show that such evils as racism, sexism, homophobia, and other forms of hatred and bias can be reduced without significant costs to aspects of character that we value. But the burden remains on those who would operate on people's personalities with the state's most powerful instrument to assure us that they will excise only what is diseased.

NOTES

1. I do not embrace a utilitarian theory of punishment, so if this were the point of hate/bias crimes, my objections to them would exceed those articulated in this paper.

2. Alon Harel & Gideon Parchomovsky, "On Hate and Equality," *Yale Law Journal* 109 (1999), pp. 507, 513.

3. See Jeffrie G. Murphy, "Bias Crimes: What Do Haters Deserve?" *Criminal Justice Ethics* 11 (1992), pp. 20, 23.

4. Harel & Parchomovsky, "On Hate and Equality," *supra*, note 5, at p. 513.

5. For the already classic statement of contemporary liberalism, see John Rawls, *Political Liberalism* (New York: Columbia University Press, 1993). For one critique of this political vision, see Heidi M. Hurd, "The Levitation of Liberalism," *Yale Law Journal* 105 (1995), pp. 795–824.

6. Paul Robinson has interestingly argued that if the criminal law does not permit the punishment of bad character as it is expressed in vicious actions, those who are convinced that moral blameworthiness resides primarily in character may eventually force it to permit the punishment of bad character alone. In the interests of preserving an act-oriented system of criminal responsibility, we may do well to permit character-based penalty enhancements. Robinson, "Hate Crimes," *supra*, note 1, at 611.

7. For his defense of the morality of freedom, see Joseph Raz, *The Morality of Freedom* (Oxford: Clarendon Press, 1986), ch.'s 14 & 15.

21

Does Racial Discrimination Make Capital Punishment Wrong?

Nathanson and His Critics

People who oppose capital punishment do so for a variety of reasons. Some believe that every person, even one who commits murder, has a right to life and that capital punishment is wrong because it violates that right. Others concede that the State has the right to execute murderers but believe that considerations of civility or decency should lead it to refuse to exercise that right. And still others argue that the risk of mistakenly executing an innocent person renders the entire enterprise morally unacceptable. On all of these sorts of accounts, capital punishment is an issue about humanity in general and not about race in particular. But there is one kind of argument against capital punishment that puts considerations of race front and center. This is the argument based on the claim that, in the United States at least, the death penalty is administered in a manner that fails to treat white people and black people equally. In the featured article for this chapter, Stephen Nathanson defends this kind of argument as a justification for abolishing capital punishment in the United States.

Nathanson's argument against capital punishment is grounded in the claim that the death penalty has been, and continues to be, administered in an arbitrary manner. More specifically, Nathanson appeals to the claim that the death penalty has been used disproportionately against black people. Black people who kill are more likely to be executed than are white people who kill. Black people who kill white people are the most likely to be executed. White people who kill black people are the least likely to be executed. And these facts, Nathanson claims, suffice to render the practice of capital punishment in the United States morally unacceptable.

At its foundation, Nathanson's position rests on an argument from analogy (see section 4.1 of the Introduction). Setting aside the controversy over the death penalty, that is, Nathanson believes that there are other cases about which most people on both sides of the capital punishment debate will agree: The arbitrary administering of a certain kind of penalty can render its imposition unjust even when the penalty in and of itself seems to be an appropriate one. Early on in the article, for example, Nathanson considers the case of being required to pay a fine for speeding. Most people, presumably, consider this to be a fair and just punishment for that offense. And the mere fact that only some speeders are fined while many other people get away with speeding without getting caught would not seem, in itself, to show that it is wrong to fine those speeders who do get caught. But Nathanson then asks us to consider a case in which tickets are given only to those speeders who have long hair and beards or whose cars have bumper stickers endorsing unpopular political views. In these cases, Nathanson suggests, it could be unjust to fine the drivers even though they were speeding and even though, in general, a fine seems a fair and just punishment for speeding. Similarly, Nathanson later offers an example in which he tells his class that anyone who is caught plagiarizing will fail the course but in which he then fails one plagiarizer and not two others for reasons that do not seem to be clearly relevant. Again, he argues, this case (and others that he presents as well) shows that it can be unjust to impose a penalty on some people, even if the people who receive it deserve it, if the penalty is distributed in an arbitrary and unfair manner. In cases such as these, Nathanson argues, the imposition of a punishment is unjust precisely because it is objectionably discriminatory. Even though the people who receive the punishment were guilty of the offense for which they were punished, it is nonetheless the case that the justice of inflicting punishment on them is affected by the fact that others guilty of the same offense were spared comparable punishments for arbitrary reasons. But if this is so in cases like fining people for speeding and failing them in a course for plagiarizing, the argument concludes, then it is also so in the case of executing people for committing murder.

In his response to Nathanson's article, Ernest van den Haag challenges this argument on several fronts. First, van den Haag raises some questions about the argument's factual basis, the claim that the death penalty has been administered in a racially inequitable manner. Second, and more fundamentally, he argues that even if it is true that black murderers are discriminated against relative to white murderers, this shows only that we should execute more white murderers, not that we should execute fewer black murderers or that we should stop executing murderers altogether. Directly addressing Nathanson's analogies, van den Haag maintains that they fail to establish that the speeders or plagiarizers whom Nathanson describes are unjustly punished. The distribution of punishments may not be just, van den Haag replies, but the punishments of those who deserve them are just nonetheless. While Nathanson argues that it would be better to execute no murderers than to execute some arbitrarily, van den Haag maintains that it is better to ensure that at least some murderers get the punishment they deserve than to ensure that none does.

QUESTIONS FOR CONSIDERATION

In examining the exchange between Nathanson and van den Haag, readers should focus on the issue of the distribution of the death penalty rather than on the question of whether the death penalty in and of itself is justified.

• Is the death penalty administered in as arbitrary a manner as are the punishments in Nathanson's various examples?

• If there are differences between Nathanson's cases and the way that capital punishment is practiced in the United States, are the differences important enough to undermine his argument? Or is the distribution of executions still problematic enough to serve as a foundation for Nathanson's position?

• If Nathanson's analogies are close enough to be acceptable, do they in fact support his conclusion? Which, for example, is more unjust: the teacher who does not fail any of the students who plagiarize (as van den Haag maintains) or the teacher who fails only an arbitrarily selected subset of the students who plagiarize (as Nathanson maintains)?

• Is Nathanson right to think that the injustice of the distribution of punishments can render some punishments of even the guilty unjust? Or is van den Haag right to insist that deserved punishments, even if arbitrarily meted out, are better than no such punishments at all?

• Van den Haag's response to Nathanson involves drawing a distinction between the justice or injustice of individual acts of punishment and the justice or injustice of a given distribution of such acts. How does this distinction help to undermine Nathanson's position? Is the distinction a reasonable one to draw? Or can individual acts of punishment be just only if they are distributed in a just manner?

• The debate between van den Haag and Nathanson threatens to come to a stalemate because they seem to have different reactions to some of the same sets of cases. Are there other cases that might be appealed to that would do a better job of trying to resolve their disagreement?

FURTHER READING

Baird, R. M., and S. E. Rosenbaum, eds. *Punishment and the Death Penalty: The Current Debate.* Buffalo: Prometheus, 1995.

Cholbi, M. "Race, Capital Punishment, and the Cost of Murder." *Philosophical Studies* 127, no. 2 (January 2006): 255–82.

McDermott, Daniel. "A Retributivist Argument Against Capital Punishment." *Journal of Social Philosophy* 32, no. 3 (Fall 2001): 317–33.

STEPHEN NATHANSON

Does It Matter If the Death Penalty Is Arbitrarily Administered?

I

In this article, I will examine the argument that capital punishment ought to be abolished because it has been and will continue to be imposed in an arbitrary manner.

This argument has been central to discussion of capital punishment since the Supreme Court ruling in the 1972 case *Furman v. Georgia*. In a 5-4 decision, the Court ruled that capital punishment as then administered was unconstitutional. Although the Court issued several opinions, the problem of arbitrariness is widely seen as having played a cen-

tral role in the Court's thinking. As Charles Black, Jr., has put it,

> . . . The decisive ground of the 1972 Furman case anti-capital punishment ruling—the ground persuasive to the marginal justices needed for a majority—was that, out of a large number of persons "eligible" in law for the punishment of death, a few were selected as if at random, by no stated (or perhaps statable) criteria, while all the rest suffered the lesser penalty of imprisonment.[1]

Among those justices moved by the arbitrariness issue, some stressed the discriminatory aspects of capital punishment, the tendency of legally irrelevant

Stephen Nathanson, "Does It Matter If the Death Penalty Is Arbitrarily Administered?" *Philosophy and Public Affairs* 14, no. 2 (Spring 1985): 149–64. Some notes have been deleted. Reprinted by permission of Princeton University Press.

factors like race and economic status to determine the severity of sentence, while others emphasized the "freakish" nature of the punishment, the fact that it is imposed on a miniscule percentage of murderers who are not obviously more deserving of death than others.

Although the Supreme Court approved new death penalty laws in *Gregg v. Georgia* (1976), the reasoning of *Furman* was not rejected. Rather, a majority of the Court determined that Georgia's new laws would make arbitrary imposition of the death penalty much less likely. By amending procedures and adding criteria which specify aggravating and mitigating circumstances, Georgia had succeeded in creating a system of "guilded discretion," which the Court accepted in the belief that it was not likely to yield arbitrary results.

The *Gregg* decision has prompted death penalty opponents to attempt to show that "guided discretion" is an illusion. This charge has been supported in various ways. Charles Black has supported it by analyzing both the legal process of decision making in capital cases and the legal criteria for determining who is to be executed. He has argued that, appearances to the contrary, there are no meaningful standards operating in the system. Attacking from an empirical angle, William Bowers and Glenn Pierce have tried to show that even after *Furman* and under new laws, factors like race and geographic location of the trial continue to play a large role and that the criteria which are supposed to guide judgment do not separate those sentenced into meaningfully distinct groups. Perhaps the most shocking conclusion of Bowers and Pierce concerns the large role played by the race of the killer and the victim, as the chances of execution are by far the greatest when blacks kill whites and least when whites kill blacks.[2]

The upshot of both these approaches is that "guided discretion" is not working and, perhaps, cannot work. If this is correct and if the argument from arbitrariness is accepted, then it would appear that a return from *Gregg* to *Furman* is required. That is, the Court should once again condemn capital punishment as unconstitutional.

I have posed these issues in terms of the Supreme Court's deliberations. Nonetheless, for opponents of the death penalty, the freakishness of its imposition and the large role played by race and other irrelevant factors are a moral as well as a legal outrage. For them, there is a fundamental moral injustice in the practice of capital punishment and not just a departure from the highest legal and constitutional standards.

II

The argument from arbitrariness has not, however, been universally accepted, either as a moral or a constitutional argument. Ernest van den Haag, an articulate and longtime defender of the death penalty, has claimed that the Supreme Court was wrong to accept this argument in the first place and thus that the evidence of arbitrariness presented by Black, Bowers and Pierce and others is beside the point. In his words:

> . . . the abolitionist argument from capriciousness, or discretion, or discrimination, would be more persuasive if it were alleged that those selectively executed are not guilty. But the argument merely maintains that some other guilty but more favored persons, or groups, escape the death penalty. This is hardly sufficient for letting anyone else found guilty escape the penalty. On the contrary, that some guilty persons or groups elude it argues for extending the death penalty to them.[3]

Having attacked the appeal to arbitrariness, van den Haag goes on to spell out his own conception of the requirements of justice. He writes:

> Justice requires punishing the guilty—as many of the guilty as possible, even if only some can be punished—and sparing the innocent—as many of the innocent as possible, even if not all are spared. It would surely be wrong to treat everybody with equal injustice in preference to meting out justice at least to some. . . . [I]f the death penalty is morally just, *however discriminatorily applied to only some of the guilty*, it does remain just *in each case* in which it is applied [emphasis added].[4]

Distinguishing sharply between the demands of justice and the demands of equality, van den Haag claims that the justice of individual punishments depends on individual guilt alone and not on whether punishments are equally distributed among the class of guilty persons.

Van den Haag's distinction between the demands of justice and the demands of equality parallels the distinction drawn by Joel Feinberg between "noncomparative" and "comparative" justice.[5] Using Feinberg's terminology, we can express van den Haag's view by saying that he believes that the justice of a particular punishment is a *noncomparative* matter. It depends solely on what a person deserves and not on how others are treated. For van den Haag, then, evidence of arbitrariness and discrimination is irrelevant, so long as those who are executed are indeed guilty and deserve their punishment.

There is no denying the plausibility of van den Haag's case. In many instances, we believe it is legitimate to punish or reward deserving individuals, even though we know that equally deserving persons are unpunished or unrewarded. Consider two cases:

A. A driver is caught speeding, ticketed, and required to pay a fine. We know that the percentage of speeders who are actually punished is extremely small, yet we would probably regard it as a joke if the driver protested that he was being treated unjustly or if someone argued that no one should be fined for speeding unless all speeders were fined.

B. A person performs a heroic act and receives a substantial reward, in addition to the respect and admiration of his fellow citizens. Because he deserves the reward, we think it just that he receive it, even though many equally heroic persons are not treated similarly. That most heroes are unsung is no reason to avoid rewarding this particular heroic individual.

Both of these instances appear to support van den Haag's claim that we should do justice whenever we can in individual cases and that failure to do justice in all cases is no reason to withhold punishment or reward from individuals.

III

Is the argument from arbitrariness completely unfounded then? Should we accept van den Haag's claim that "unequal justice is justice still"?

In response to these questions, I shall argue that van den Haag's case is not as strong as it looks and that the argument from arbitrariness can be vindicated.

As a first step in achieving this, I would like to point out that there are in fact several different arguments from arbitrariness. While some of these arguments appeal to the random and freakish nature of the death penalty, others highlight the discriminatory effects of legally irrelevant factors. Each of these kinds of arbitrariness raises different sorts of moral and legal issues.

For example, though we may acknowledge the impossibility of ticketing all speeding drivers and still favor ticketing some, we will not find every way of determining which speeders are ticketed equally just. Consider the policy of ticketing only those who travel at extremely high speeds, as opposed to that of ticketing every tenth car. Compare these with the policy of giving tickets only to speeders with beards and long hair or to speeders whose cars bear bumper stickers expressing unpopular political views. While I shall not pursue this point in detail, I take it to be obvious that these different selection policies are not all equally just or acceptable.

A second difference between versions of the argument from arbitrariness depends on whether or not it is granted that we can accurately distinguish those who deserve to die from those who do not. As van den Haag presents the argument, it assumes that we are able to make this distinction. Then, the claim is made that from this class of people who deserve to die, only some are selected for execution. The choice of those specific persons from the general class of persons who deserve to die is held to be arbitrary.

Van den Haag neglects a related argument which has been forcefully defended by Charles Black. Black's argument is that the determination of *who* deserves to die—the first step—is itself arbitrary. So his claim is not merely that arbitrary factors determine who among the deserving will be executed. His point is that the determination of who deserves to die is arbitrary. His main argument is that

the official choices—by prosecutors, judges, juries, and governors—that divide those who are to die from those who are to live are on the whole not made, and cannot be made, under standards that are consistently meaningful and clear, but that they are often made, and in the foreseeable future will continue often to be made, under no standards at all or under pseudo-standards without discoverable meaning.[6]

According to Black, even the most conscientious officials could not make principled judgments about desert in these instances, because our laws do not contain clear principles for differentiating those who deserve to die from those who do not. While I shall not try to summarize Black's analysis of the failures of post-*Furman* capital punishment statutes, it is clear that if van den Haag were to meet this argument, he would have to provide his own analysis of these laws in order to show that they do provide clear and meaningful standards. Or, he would have to examine the actual disposition of cases under these laws to show that the results have not been arbitrary. Van den Haag does not attempt to do either of these things. This seems to result from a failure to distinguish (a) the claim that judgments concerning *who deserves to die* are arbitrarily made, from (b) the claim that judgments concerning *who among the deserving shall be executed* are arbitrarily made.

Van den Haag may simply assume that the system does a decent job of distinguishing those who deserve to die from those who do not, and his assumption gains a surface plausibility because of his tendency to oversimplify the nature of the judgments which need to be made. In contrast to Black, who stresses the complexity of the legal process and the complexity of the judgments facing participants in that process, van den Haag is content to say simply that "justice requires punishing the guilty . . . and sparing the innocent." This maxim makes it look as if officials and jurors need only divide people into two neat categories, and if we think of guilt and innocence as *factual* categories, it makes it look as if the only judgment necessary is whether a person did or did not kill another human being.

In fact, the problems are much more complicated than this. Not every person who kills another human being is guilty of the same crime. Some may have committed no crime at all, if their act is judged to be justifiable homicide. Among others, they may have committed first-degree murder, second-degree murder, or some form of manslaughter. Furthermore, even if we limit our attention to those who are convicted of first-degree murder, juries must consider aggravating and mitigating circumstances in order to judge whether someone is guilty enough to deserve the death penalty. It is clear, then, that simply knowing that someone is factually guilty of killing another person is far from sufficient for determining that he deserves to die, and if prosecutors, juries, and judges do not have criteria which enable them to classify those who are guilty in a just and rational way, then their judgments about who deserves to die will necessarily be arbitrary and unprincipled.

Once we appreciate the difficulty and complexity of the judgments which must be made about guilt and desert, it is easier to see how they might be influenced by racial characteristics and other irrelevant factors. The statistics compiled by Bowers and Pierce show that blacks killing whites have the greatest chance of being executed, while whites killing blacks have the least chance of execution. What these findings strongly suggest is that officials and jurors think that the killing of a white by a black is a more serious crime than the killing of a black by a white. Hence, they judge that blacks killing whites *deserve* a more serious punishment than whites killing blacks. Given the bluntness of our ordinary judgments about desert and the complexity of the choices facing jurors and officials, it may not be surprising either that people find it difficult to make the fine discriminations required by law or that such judgments are influenced by deep-seated racial or social attitudes.

Both legal analysis and empirical studies should undermine our confidence that the legal system sorts out those who deserve to die from those who do not in a nonarbitrary manner. If we cannot be confident that those who are executed in fact deserve to die, then we ought not to allow executions to take place at all.

Because van den Haag does not distinguish this argument from other versions of the argument from arbitrariness, he simply neglects it. His omission is serious because this argument is an independent, substantial argument against the death penalty. It can stand even if other versions of the argument from arbitrariness fall.

IV

I would like now to turn to the form of the argument which van den Haag explicitly deals with and to consider whether it is vulnerable to his criticisms. Let us assume that there is a class of people whom we know to be deserving of death. Let us further assume that only some of these people are executed and that the executions are arbitrary in the sense that those executed have not committed worse crimes than those not executed. This is the situation which Justice Stewart described in *Furman*. He wrote:

> These death sentences are cruel and unusual in the same way that being struck by lightning is cruel and unusual. For of all the people convicted of rapes and murders in 1967 and 1968, *many just as reprehensible as these*, the petitioners are among *a capriciously selected random handful* upon whom the sentence of death has in fact been imposed. (emphasis added)[7]

What is crucial here (and different from the argument previously discussed) is the assumption that we can judge the reprehensibility of both the petitioners and others convicted of similar crimes. Stewart does not deny that the petitioners deserve to die, but because other equally deserving people escape the death penalty for no legally respectable reasons, the executions of the petitioners, Stewart thought, would violate the Eighth and Fourteenth Amendments.

This is precisely the argument van den Haag rejected. We can sum up his reasons in the following rhetorical questions: How can it possibly be unjust to punish someone if he deserves the punishment? Why should it matter whether or not others equally deserving are punished?

I have already acknowledged the plausibility of van den Haag's case and offered the examples of the ticketed speeder and the rewarded hero as instances which seem to confirm his view. Nonetheless, I think that van den Haag is profoundly mistaken in thinking that the justice of a reward or punishment depends solely on whether the recipient deserves it.

Consider the following two cases which are structurally similar to A and B (given above) but which elicit different reactions:

C. I tell my class that anyone who plagiarizes will fail the course. Three students plagiarize papers, but only one receives a failing grade. The other two, in describing their motivation, win my sympathy, and I give them passing grades.

D. At my child's birthday party, I offer a prize to the child who can solve a particular puzzle. Three children, including my own, solve the puzzle. I cannot reward them all, so I give the prize to my own child.

In both cases, as in van den Haag's, only some of those deserving a reward or punishment receive it. Unlike cases A and B, however, C and D do not appear to be just, in spite of the fact that the persons rewarded or punished deserve what they get. In these cases, the justice of giving them what they deserve appears to be affected by the treatment of others.

About these cases I am inclined to say the following. The people involved have not been treated justly. It was unjust to fail the single plagiarizer and unjust to reward my child. It would have been better—because more just—to have failed no one than to have failed the single student. It would have been better to have given a prize to no one than to give the prize to my child alone.

The unfairness in both cases appears to result from the fact that the reasons for picking out those rewarded or punished are irrelevant and hence that the choice is arbitrary. If I have a stated policy of failing students who plagiarize, then it is unjust for me to pass students with whom I sympathize. Whether I am sympathetic or not is irrelevant, and I am treating the student whom I do fail unjustly because I am not acting simply on the basis of desert. Rather, I am acting on the basis of desert plus degree of sympathy. Likewise, in the case of the prize, it appears that I am preferring my own child in giving out the reward, even though I announced that receipt of the award would depend only on success in solving the puzzle.

This may be made clearer by varying the plagiarism example. Suppose that in spite of my stated policy of failing anyone who plagiarizes, I am regularly lenient toward students who seem sufficiently repentant. Suppose further that I am regularly more lenient with attractive female students than with others. Or suppose that it is only redheads or wealthy students whom I fail. If such patterns develop, we can see that whether a student fails or not does not depend simply on being caught plagiarizing. Rather, part of the explanation of a particular student's being punished is that he or she is (or is not) an attractive female, redheaded or wealthy. In these instances, I think the plagiarizers who are punished have grounds for complaint, even though they were, by the announced standards, clearly guilty and deserving of punishment.

If this conclusion is correct, then doing justice is more complicated than van den Haag realizes. He asserts that it would be "wrong to treat everybody with equal injustice in preference to meting out justice at least to some." If my assessment of cases C and D is correct, however, it is better that everyone in those instances be treated "unjustly" than that only some get what they deserve. Whether one is treated justly or not depends on how others are treated and not solely on what one deserves.

In fact, van den Haag implicitly concedes this point in an interesting footnote to his essay. In considering the question of whether capital punishment is a superior deterrent, van den Haag mentions that one could test the deterrent power of the death penalty by allowing executions for murders committed on Monday, Wednesday, and Friday, while setting life imprisonment as the maximum penalty for murders committed on other days. In noting the obstacles facing such an experiment, he writes:

> . . . it is not acceptable to our sense of justice that *people guilty of the same crime would get different punishments* and that the difference would be made to depend deliberately on *a factor irrelevant to the nature of the crime* or of the criminal. (emphasis added)[8]

Given his earlier remarks about the argument from arbitrariness, this is a rather extraordinary comment, for van den Haag concedes that the justice of a punishment is not solely determined by what an individual deserves but is also a function of how equally deserving persons are treated in general.

In his case, what he finds offensive is that there is no difference between what the Monday, Wednesday,

Friday murderers deserve and what the Tuesday, Thursday, Saturday, and Sunday murderers deserve. Yet the morally irrelevant factor of date is decisive in determining the severity of the punishment. Van den Haag (quite rightly) cannot swallow this.

Yet van den Haag's example is exactly parallel to the situation described by opponents of the death penalty. For, surely, the race of the criminal or victim, the economic or social status of the criminal or victim, the location of the crime or trial and other such factors are as irrelevant to the gravity of the crime and the appropriate severity of the punishment as is the day of the week on which the crime is committed. It would be as outrageous for the severity of the punishment to depend on these factors as it would be for it to depend on the day of the week on which the crime was committed.

In fact, it is more outrageous that death sentences depend on the former factors because a person can control the day of the week on which he murders in a way in which he cannot control his race or status. Moreover, we are committed to banishing the disabling effects of race and economic status from the law. Using the day of the week as a critical factor is at least not invidiously discriminatory, as it neither favors nor disfavors previously identifiable or disadvantaged groups.

In reply, one might contend that I have overlooked an important feature of van den Haag's example. He rejected the deterrence experiment not merely because the severity of punishment depended on irrelevant factors but also because the irrelevant factors were *deliberately* chosen as the basis of punishment. Perhaps it is the fact that irrelevant factors are deliberately chosen which makes van den Haag condemn the proposed experiment.

This is an important point. It certainly makes matters worse to decide deliberately to base life and death choices on irrelevant considerations. However, even if the decision is not deliberate, it remains a serious injustice if irrelevant considerations play this crucial role. Individuals might not even be aware of the influence of these factors. They might genuinely believe that their judgments are based entirely on relevant considerations. It might require painstaking research to discover the patterns underlying sentencing, but once they are known, citizens and policymakers must take them into consideration. Either the influence of irrelevant factors must be eradicated or, if we determine that this is impossible, we may have to alter our practices more radically.

This reasoning, of course, is just the reasoning identified with the *Furman* case. As Justice Douglas wrote:

A law that stated that anyone making more than $50,000 would be exempt from the death penalty would plainly fall, as would a law that in terms said that blacks, those who never went beyond the fifth grade in school, those who make less than $3,000 a year, or those who were unpopular or unstable should be the only people executed. A law which in the overall view reaches the same result in practice has no more sanctity than a law which in terms provides the same.[9]

The problem, in Douglas's view, was that the system left life and death decisions to the "uncontrolled discretion of judges or juries," leading to the unintended but nonetheless real result that death sentences were based on factors which had nothing to do with the nature of the crime.

What I want to stress here is that the arbitrariness and discrimination need not be purposeful or deliberate. We might discover, as critics allege, that racial prejudice is so deeply rooted in our society that prosecutors, juries, and judges cannot free themselves from prejudice when determing how severe a punishment for a crime should be. Furthermore, we might conclude that these tendencies cannot be eradicated, especially when juries are called upon to make subtle and complex assessments of cases in the light of confusing, semi-technical criteria. Hence, although no one *decides* that race will be a factor, we may *predict* that it will be a factor, and this knowledge must be considered in evaluating policies and institutions.

If factors *as irrelevant as* the day of the crime determine whether people shall live or die and if the influence of these factors is ineradicable, then we must conclude that we cannot provide a just system of punishment and even those who are guilty and deserving of the most severe punishments (like the Monday killers in van den Haag's experiment) will

have a legitimate complaint that they have been treated unjustly.

I conclude, then, that the treatment of *classes* of people is relevant to determining the justice of punishments for *individuals* and van den Haag is wrong to dismiss the second form of the argument from arbitrariness. That argument succeeds in showing that capital punishment is unjust and thus provides a powerful reason for abolishing it.

V

Supporters of the death penalty might concede that serious questions of justice are raised by the influence of arbitrary factors and still deny that this shows that capital punishment ought to be abolished. They could argue that some degree of arbitrariness is present throughout the system of legal punishment, that it is unreasonable to expect our institutions to be perfect, and that acceptance of the argument from arbitrariness would commit us to abolishing all punishment.

In fact, van den Haag makes just these points in his essay. He writes:

The Constitution, though it enjoins us to minimize capriciousness, does not enjoin a standard of unattainable perfection or exclude penalties because that standard has not been attained. . . . I see no more merit in the attempt to persuade the courts to let all capital-crime defendants go free of capital punishment because some have wrongly escaped it than I see in an attempt to persuade the courts to let all burglars go because some have wrongly escaped imprisonment.[10]

It is an important feature of this objection that it could be made even by one who conceded the injustice of arbitrarily administered death sentences. Rather than agreeing that capital punishment should be abolished, however, this objection moves from the premise that the flaws revealed in capital punishment are shared by *all* punishments to the conclusion that we must either (a) reject all punishments (because of the influence of arbitrary factors on them) or (b) reject the idea that arbitrariness provides a sufficient ground for abolishing the death penalty.

Is there a way out of this dilemma for death penalty opponents?

I believe that there is. Opponents of the death penalty may continue to support other punishments, even though their administration also involves arbitrariness. This is not to suggest, of course, that we should be content with arbitrariness or discrimination in the imposition of any punishment.[11] Rather the point is to emphasize that the argument from arbitrariness counts against the death penalty with special force. There are two reasons for this.

First, death is a much more severe punishment than imprisonment. This is universally acknowledged by advocates and opponents of the death penalty alike. It is recognized in the law by the existence of special procedures for capital cases. Death obliterates the person, depriving him or her of life and thereby, among other things, depriving him or her of any further rights of legal appeal, should new facts be discovered or new understandings of the law be reached. In this connection, it is worth recalling that many people were executed and are now dead because they were tried and sentenced under the pre-*Furman* laws which allowed the "uncontrolled discretion of judges and juries."

Second, though death is the most severe punishment in our legal system, it appears to be unnecessary for protecting citizens, while punishments generally are thought to promote our safety and well-being. The contrast between death and other punishments can be brought out by asking two questions. What would happen if we abolished all punishments? And, what would happen if we abolished the death penalty?

Most of us believe that if all punishments were abolished, there would be social chaos, a Hobbesian war of all against all. To do away with punishment entirely would be to do away with the criminal law and the system of constraints which it supports. Hence, even though the system is not a just one, we believe that we must live with it and strive to make it as fair as possible. On the other hand, if we abolish capital punishment, there is reason to believe that nothing will happen. There is simply no compelling evidence that capital punishment prevents murders better than long-term prison sentences. Indeed,

some evidence even suggests that capital punishment increases the number of murders. While I cannot review the various empirical studies of these questions here, I think it can plausibly be asserted that the results of abolishing punishment generally would be disastrous, while the results of abolishing capital punishment are likely to be insignificant.[12]

I conclude then that the argument from arbitrariness has special force against the death penalty because of its extreme severity and its likely uselessness. The arbitrariness of other punishments may be outweighed by their necessity, but the same cannot be said for capital punishment.

VI

In closing, I would like to comment briefly on one other charge made by van den Haag, the charge that the argument from arbitrariness is a "sham" argument because it is not the real reason why people oppose the death penalty. Those who use this argument, van den Haag claims, would oppose capital punishment even if it were not arbitrarily imposed.

At one level, this charge is doubly fallacious. The suggestion of dishonesty introduced by the word "sham" makes the argument into an *ad hominem*. In addition, the charge suggests that there cannot be more than one reason in support of a view. There are many situations in which we offer arguments and yet would not change our view if the argument were refuted, not because the argument is a sham, but because we have additional grounds for what we believe.

Nonetheless, van den Haag's charge may indicate a special difficulty for the argument from arbitrariness, for the argument may well strike people as artificial and legalistic. Somehow, one may feel that it does not deal with the real issues—the wrongness of killing, deterrence, and whether murderers deserve to die.

Part of the problem, I think, is that our ordinary moral thinking involves specific forms of conduct or general rules of personal behavior. The argument from arbitrariness deals with a feature of an *institution*, and thinking about institutions seems to raise difficulties for many people. Believing that an individual murderer deserves to die for a terrible crime, they infer that there ought to be capital punishment, without attending to all of the implications for other individuals which will follow from setting up this practice.

The problem is similar to one that John Stuart Mill highlighted in *On Liberty*. For many people, the fact that an act is wrong is taken to be sufficient ground for its being made illegal. Mill argued against the institutionalization of all moral judgments, and his argument still strikes many people as odd. If the act is wrong, they ask, shouldn't we do everything in our power to stop it? What they fail to appreciate, however, are all of the implications of institutionalizing such judgments.

Likewise, people ask, If so and so deserves to die, shouldn't we empower the state to execute him? The problem, however—or one of many problems—is that institutionalizing this judgment about desert yields a system which makes neither moral nor legal sense. Moreover, it perpetuates and exacerbates the liabilities and disadvantages which unjustly befall many of our fellow citizens. These are genuine and serious problems, and those who have raised them in the context of the capital punishment debate have both exposed troubling facts about the actual workings of the criminal law and illuminated the difficulties of acting justly. Most importantly, they have produced a powerful argument against authorizing the state to use death as a punishment for crime.

NOTES

1. *Capital Punishment: The Inevitability of Caprice and Mistake*, 2d ed. (New York: W. W. Norton & Co., 1981), p. 20.

2. Ibid., passim; W. Bowers and G. Pierce, "Arbitrariness and Discrimination Under Post-*Furman* Capital Statutes," *Crime & Delinquency* 26 (1980): 563–635. Reprinted in *The Death Penalty in America,* 3d ed., ed. Hugo Bedau (New York: Oxford University Press, 1982), pp. 206–24.

3. "The Collapse of the Case Against Capital Punishment," *National Review,* 31 March 1978: 397. A briefer version of this paper appeared in the *Criminal Law Bulletin* 14 (1978): 51–68 and is reprinted in Bedau, pp. 323–33.

4. Ibid.

5. "Noncomparative Justice," in *Rights, Justice, and the Bounds of Liberty: Essays in Social Philosophy* (Princeton, NJ: Princeton University Press, 1980); originally published in the *Philosophical Review* 83 (1974): 297–338.

6. Black, *Capital Punishment,* p. 29.

7. Reprinted in Bedau, pp. 263–64.

8. Van den Haag, "The Collapse of the Case Against Capital Punishment," p. 403, n. 12. (This important footnote does not appear in the shorter version of the paper.)

9. Reprinted in Bedau, pp. 255–56.

10. Van den Haag, "The Collapse of the Case Against Capital Punishment," p. 397.

11. For a discussion of the role of discrimination throughout the criminal justice system and recommendations for reform, see American Friends Service Committee, *Struggle for Justice* (New York: Hill and Wang, 1971).

12. In support of the superior deterrent power of the death penalty, van den Haag cites I. Ehrlich, "The Deterrent Effect of Capital Punishment: A Question of Life and Death," *American Economic Review* 65 (1975): 397–417. Two reviews of the evidence on deterrence, both of which criticize Ehrlich at length, are Hans Zeisel, "The Deterrent Effect of the Death Penalty: Facts v. Faith," and Lawrence Klein et al., "The Deterrent Effect of Capital Punishment: An Assessment of the Evidence." (Both of these articles appear in Bedau.) The thesis that executions increase the number of homicides is defended by W. Bowers and G. Pierce in "Deterrence or Brutalization: What Is the Effect of Executions?," *Crime & Delinquency* 26 (1980): 453–84.

Critic

Ernest Van Den Haag

Refuting Nathanson

Discrimination

... Disagreeing with the Supreme Court, Stephen Nathanson believes that the death penalty still is distributed in an excessively capricious and discriminatory manner. He thinks capital punishment is "unjust" because poor blacks are more likely to be sentenced to death than wealthy whites. Further, blacks who murdered whites are more likely to be executed than those who murdered blacks. This last discrimination has been thrown into relief recently by authors who seem to be under the impression that they have revealed a new form of discrimination against black murderers. They have not. The practice invidiously discriminates against black victims of murder, who are not as fully, or as often, vindicated as white victims are. However, discrimination against a class of victims, although invidious enough, does not amount to discrimination against their victimizers. The discrimination against black victims, the lesser punishment given their murderers, actually favours black murderers, since most black victims are killed by black murderers. Stephen Nathanson and Jeffrey Reiman appear to think that they have captured additional discrimination against black defendants. They are wrong.

Neither the argument from discrimination against black victims, nor the argument from discrimination against black murderers, has any bearing on the guilt of black murderers, or on the punishment they deserve.

Invidious discrimination is never defensible. Yet I do not see wherein it, in Reiman's words, "would consti-tute a separate and powerful argument for abolition," or does make the death penalty "unjust" for those discriminatorily selected to suffer it, as Stephen Nathanson believes.[1] If we grant that some (even all) murderers of blacks, or, some (even all) white and rich murderers, escape the death penalty, how does that reduce the guilt of murderers of whites, or of black and poor murderers, so that they should be spared execution too? Guilt is personal. No murderer becomes less guilty, or less deserving of punishment, because another murderer was punished leniently, or escaped punishment altogether. We should try our best to bring every murderer to justice. But if one got away with murder wherein is that a reason to let anyone else get away? A group of murderers does not become less deserving of punishment because another equally guilty group is not punished, or punished less. We can punish only a very small proportion of all criminals. Unavoidably they are selected accidentally. We should reduce this accidentality as much as possible but we cannot eliminate it.

Equal Injustice and Unequal Justice

Reiman and Nathanson appear to prefer equal injustice—letting all get away with murder if some do—to unequal justice: punishing some guilty offenders according to desert, even if others get away. Equal justice is best, but unattainable. Unequal justice is our lot in this world. It is the only justice we can ever have, for

Ernest Van Den Haag, "Refuting Reiman and Nathanson," *Philosophy & Public Affairs* Vol. 19, No. 2. Reprinted with the permission of Blackwell Publishing.

not all murderers can be apprehended or convicted, or sentenced equally in different courts. We should constantly try to bring every offender to justice. But meanwhile unequal justice is the only justice we have, and certainly better than equal injustice—giving no murderer the punishment his crime deserves.

MORE DISCRIMINATION

Nathanson insists that some arbitrary selections among those equally guilty are not "just." He thinks that selecting only bearded speeders for ticketing, allowing the cleanshaven to escape, is unjust. Yet the punishment of the bearded speeders is not unjust. The escape of the cleanshaven ones is. I never maintained that a discriminatory distribution is just—only that it is irrelevant to the guilt and deserved punishment of those actually guilty.

Nathanson further suggests that it is not just to spare some student plagiarizers punishment for (I suppose) irrelevant reasons, while punishing others. Again the distribution is discriminatory, i.e., unjust. But the punishment of the plagiarizers selected is not. (The non-punishment of the others is.) Nathanson thinks that giving a prize only to one of three deserving children (his own) is unjust. Not to the deserving child. Only to the others, just as it was unjust not to punish the others who deserved it, but not unjust to punish the deserving plagiarizers who were irrelevantly selected.

Nathanson taxes me with inconsistency because in a footnote I wrote that irrelevant discriminations are "not acceptable to our sense of justice." They are not. But I did not say that those who deserved the punishment received, or the reward, were unjustly treated, that is, did not deserve it and should not have received it. Rather those equally situated also should have received it, and the distribution was offensive because they did not. Whenever possible this inequality should be corrected, but certainly not by not distributing the punishment, or the reward at issue, or by not giving it to the deserving. Rather by giving it as well to those who because of discrimination did not get it. (I might have done better to write in my footnote that discriminatory distributions offend our sense of *equal* justice. But neither the Constitution nor I favors replacing justice with equality.)

Nathanson quotes the late Justice Douglas suggesting that a law which deliberately prescribes execution only for the guilty poor, or which has that effect, would be unconstitutional. Perhaps. But the vice would be in exempting the guilty rich; the guilty poor would remain guilty, and deserving of prescribed punishment even if the guilty rich escape legally or otherwise.

Further on Nathanson points out that the inevitable capriciousness in the distribution of punishments (only a very small percentage of offenders are ever punished and the selection unavoidably is morally arbitrary) while no reason to abolish punishment in general, may still be an argument for abolishing capital punishment because of its unique severity, and because we could survive without. We can survive without many things, which is not reason for doing without, if one thinks, as I do, that we survive *better* with. As for the unique severity of the death penalty it is, of course, the reason for imposing it for uniquely heinous crimes. The guilt of those who committed them is not diminished, if they are selected by a lottery from among all those guilty of the crime.

Following Charles Black, Nathanson notes that those executed are not necessarily the worst murderers, since there is no way of selecting these. He is right. It seems quite sufficient, however, that those executed, though not the worst, are bad enough to deserve execution. That others who deserved it even more got away, does not make those executed insufficiently deserving.

Nathanson goes on to insist that "not every person who kills another is guilty of the same crime." True. Wherefore the law makes many distinctions, leaving only a small group of those guilty of homicide eligible for the death penalty. Further, capital punishment is not mandated. The court must decide in each case whether or not to impose it. To impose capital punishment, courts must find that the aggravating circumstances attending the murder outweigh the mitigating ones, both of which must be listed in the law. Nathanson is right in pointing out that the criteria listed in the law are not easy to apply. If they were, we would not need the judgment of the court. That judgment is not easy to make. It may seem too severe, or not severe enough, in some cases, as would mandated penalties. So what else is new?

NOTE

1. Stephen Nathanson, "Does It Matter If the Death Penalty Is Arbitrarily Administered?" *Philosophy & Public Affairs* 14, no. 2. Unless otherwise noted, all further quotations are taken from Nathanson's article.

22

Is Racial Profiling Wrong?

Levin and His Critics

Police in the United States, it is widely believed, tend to stop young black males for questioning more often than they stop young white males. In the wake of the terrorist attacks of September 11, 2001, Immigration and Naturalization Service (INS) officials have taken a far more lively and active interest in young male Arabs from certain Middle Eastern countries than in, say, old white females visiting the United States from Scotland. These are both cases of racial profiling on the part of State officials—using racial characteristics to make decisions about whom to investigate. The question posed in this chapter is whether or not racial profiling is immoral.

In the featured article in this chapter, Michael Levin argues that racial profiling is a kind of discrimination on the basis of race that can be morally justified. Levin's article and some of the rejoinders contain formulations of certain claims about race and crime that many readers may well find deeply offensive. Although it is sometimes difficult to follow this advice, it is important not to be sidetracked by strong emotional reactions (positive or negative) to these claims. The point is to sort out the argumentation and to try to determine whether or not it is any good. If you strongly disagree with Levin's conclusion, then you have a good reason to work out what, if anything, is wrong with his argument.

Levin reports that the frequency of violent crimes committed by young black males is proportionately higher than the frequency of violent crimes committed by other groups. One of the key statistics he cites is that "approximately one black male in four is incarcerated at some time for the commission of a felony, while the incarceration rate for white males is between 2% and 3.5%." Suppose this is true. What follows? Levin considers the following case: "Suppose, jogging alone after dark, you see a young black male ahead of you on the running track, not attired in a jogging outfit and displaying no other information-bearing trait. Based on the statistics given earlier you must set the likelihood of his being a felon at .25." Levin argues that you are justified in concluding that you are at a significant risk of attack and justified in taking appropriate action, such as fleeing. Since it is morally legitimate for an individual to use available information about potential criminal behavior to avoid being a victim of such behavior, in the jogging case, racial profiling by an individual is morally justified. The case for racial profiling by the State is an extension of this argument. According to Levin, the information carried

by racial classification is just like other kinds of information that suggest the likelihood of criminal behavior and that the police routinely make use of in preventing and investigating crimes.

In "Statistical Badness," Laurence Thomas takes issue with Levin's claim that in the jogger case you can legitimately conclude, on the basis of the approaching person's being a black
male, that you have a significant chance of being mugged. Thomas claims that there is a
whole slew of information about the man that you can gather—from his dress, his demeanor,
and so on—that might drastically reduce the likelihood that he is a felon with evil intent.
Suppose he is wearing a tweed jacket and a tie. Doesn't that put him in a different category?
After all, people in tweed jackets and ties (black or white) rarely mug lone joggers.

Louis P. Pojman comes to Levin's defense, pointing out several errors in Thomas's critique. He notes that part of Levin's example was that "the youth was *displaying no other information-bearing trait.*" So Levin is stipulating that all you can tell about the youth is that he is
a young black male. You have no other information (e.g., that he is wearing a tweed coat and
tie or a jogger's outfit) that would enable you to categorize him more precisely.

QUESTIONS FOR CONSIDERATION

Levin's critics concentrate on the plausibility of the first premise of his argument (that racial characteristics carry information relevant to the probability of the imminent commission of a violent crime) or on
Levin's argument for that claim. But perhaps there is more to be said about Levin's second premise as well,
the claim that it is morally legitimate for an individual or the State to use any available information about
potential criminal behavior. Readers are encouraged to critically scrutinize both parts of Levin's position.

• Levin argues that the individual and State cases are sufficiently alike. But are they? The first is a
case of an individual and his right to avoid becoming the victim of a possible crime by fleeing the scene.
The second is a case of the State's claimed right to investigate, detain, and interrogate people on the
basis of probabilistic evidence that they might commit a crime. Are there reasons that might be given
for thinking that these two cases should be treated differently?

• You are relatively powerless and defenseless. The State is neither. Your fleeing a black male you
encounter need not insult or injure anyone (although, of course, it might do so). Being detained by the
police as a suspect inevitably could insult an innocent person. Your treating a black person in a certain
way does not convey any official public attitude toward black people in general, but a police department
policy of racial profiling does seem to convey an official public attitude toward black people in general.
Are these differences important enough to undermine Levin's argument?

• What other differences are there between an individual and the State that might be relevant here?
How might they be used to critique Levin's position?

• Are there constraints on the type of information the State may use in preempting crime? Can you
think of any kinds of information that it might be wrong for the State to use even if using the information had beneficial consequences?

• Might the institutionalization of racial profiling have bad side effects? For example, might it alienate an entire category of people—those singled out on the basis of their skin color—thereby making
them more likely, rather than less likely, to commit violations of the law? Might racial profiling by the
State, therefore, drive up the very crime rate it is intended to diminish?

FURTHER READING

Adler, Jonathan. "Crime Rates by Race and Causal Relevance: A Reply to Levin." *Journal of Social
Philosophy* 24, no. 1 (1993): 176–84.

———. "More on Race and Crime: Levin's Reply." *Journal of Social Philosophy* 25, no. 2 (1994): 105–14.

Cox, Chana Berniker. "On Michael Levin's 'Responses to Race Differences in Crime.'" *Journal of Social Philosophy* 24, no. 1 (1993): 155–62.

Department of Justice. "Fact Sheet: Racial Profiling." http://www.usdoj.gov/opa/pr/2003/June/racial_profiling_fact_sheet.pdf

Harris, David A. *Profiles in Injustice: Why Racial Profiling Cannot Work.* New York: The New Press, 2002.

Levin, Michael. "Reply to Adler, Cox, and Corlett." *Journal of Social Philosophy* 25, no. 1 (1994): 5–19.

———. "Reply to Adler's 'More on Race and Crime: Levin's Reply.'" *Journal of Social Philosophy* 25, no. 2 (1994): 115–18.

Pampel, Fred C. *Racial Profiling.* New York: Facts on File, Inc., 2004.

Michael Levin

Responses to Race Differences in Crime

I

It is widely agreed that young black males are significantly more likely to commit crimes against persons than are members of any other racially identified group. Approximately one black male in four is incarcerated at some time for the commission of a felony, while the incarceration rate for white males is between 2 and 3.5%.[1] Absolutely speaking, blacks commit most of the crime in the US, accounting for half of all arrests for assault and rape and two-thirds of arrests for robbery.[2] (Blacks are in fact proportionally more heavily represented in all categories of felony except those requiring access to large amounts of money, such as stock fraud.[3]) These figures parallel prevalence rates by race according to victims' reports,[4] so they do not represent bias in arrests. Some criminologists use the rule of thumb that a black male is ten times more likely than his white counterpart to be a criminal.[5]

While few people are familiar with these statistics, widespread intuitive a awareness of the reality they report creates the familiar contemporary phenomenon of fear of black crime. The present paper examines some of the philosophical issues about risk assessment and rights of risk avoidance raised by this phenomenon.

Black crime is obviously a problem for both blacks and whites, and most of my remarks will apply equally to black and white apprehension about it. Two considerations should be noted, however, which distinguish them. One is the ability of whites to flee black crime to an extent unavailable to blacks. Blacks, particularly young black males, cannot altogether avoid (other) young black males. It is therefore more pertinent to ask whether whites are entitled to flee black crime than it is to ask the same question of blacks. (Indeed, although black crime might no more threaten blacks than whites if the demographic distribution of the races were made random, such a distribution might—while reducing black exposure to black crime—inequitably increase white exposure.) The second factor is the asymmetry in interracial crime rates. It is commonly known that blacks are

From Michael Levin "Responses to Race Differences in Crime," *Journal of Social Philosophy* 23, no. 1 (1992): 5–29. Some notes and some parts of the text have been deleted. Reprinted by permission of Blackwell Publishing Ltd.

more likely than whites to be crime victims[6] and that their victimizers are more likely to be black than white: in 1987, for instance, 81.7% of aggravated assaults against blacks were committed by blacks, and 13.1% by whites.[7] However, more than 97% of white crime is committed against whites, while one-half to two-thirds of black crime is also committed against whites.[8] Since blacks are 12% of the population, 88% of the victims of black (and white) crime would be expected to be white if victim choice were random. Thus, whites attack blacks at about 1/4 of the rate predicted by random choice, while blacks attack whites at more than 3/5 of the predicted rate. Taking the ratio of these fractions as a measure of preference by race, black preference for white victims is at least 2.4 times that of white preference for black victims. Whether this figure indicates a greater propensity on the part of black criminals to seek white rather than black victims depends on questions of opportunity, but current residential patterns do not seem to present blacks with disproportionately many contacts with whites. The data are thus consistent with a greater preference for white victims on the part of black criminals, and to that extent warrant greater white than black apprehension about black crime.

It is for behavioral scientists to explain black crime, although I pass some methodological remarks below on some proposed explanations. What philosophy can do best is to assess the conflicting epistemic and, especially, moral intuitions such an issue is bound to produce. A system of a priori moral standards would be helpful, but I will not assume any here and I am inclined to doubt any exist.[9] I will confine myself to what I take to be the criteria of rational acceptability already implicit in our commitments on other issues, and noting the application of these criteria in a new, disputed case. (Such applications may of course react back on the initial judgments and commitments until reflection stabilizes at new judgments and commitments.) Indeed, this "our" might well be replaced by "your," with me trying to persuade *you* of something by showing *you* your commitment to it. Whether or not there is some less ad hominem role for reason in ethics is a meaningless question for you the persuadee, since you *endorse* your own standards.

Deducing an individual judgment from principles will *convince* anyone already convinced of the principles, and likewise for extracting principles from antecedently accepted judgments. From within your own moral framework—the perspective you cannot help but take—a deduction from your actual standards is perceived as proof, and a showing of inconsistency with those standards is perceived as refutation. (In my view, moral philosophy can do no more than articulate extant value systems and moral argument is essentially ad hominem, but I can't defend these large theses here and I won't assume them [but see n. 9].)

To be as explicit as possible about ground rules, then, "justified" and its cognates as used here mean "justified modulo general principles and particular judgments I expect the reader to hold with some tenacity"—"ordinary standards," for short.

II

My central claim is that a white (or black) encountering a young black male in isolated circumstances is more warranted in believing himself in danger, and in taking precautions, than when encountering a white in similar circumstances. This differential warrant is both epistemic and moral. Epistemically, one is more justified in believing oneself in danger in the former case, and, absolutely speaking, in believing oneself in some danger in the former but not the latter case. Morally, one is justified in the former case in seeking to escape.

This section discusses the epistemic justification, the next one the moral justification.

The usual rule in statistical decision theory is to reject those hypotheses whose probability falls below .05. If you know that one in four Acme automobiles will break down in traffic, you cannot reject the hypothesis that the Acme you are stepping into will break down. There is a 25% chance it will. The failure of the hypothesis is "too remote to take seriously" only if fewer than 5 Acmes in 100 break down. Common sense is not quantitative, and is rarely called upon to evaluate statistical hypotheses, but it too recognizes fairly low credibility levels above which hypotheses become "likely enough" to be taken seriously. Note that the statistical rule (like common sense) distinguishes non-rejection from acceptance, which is demanded only of those hypotheses whose probability exceeds 95%.

There is nothing magic about .05. Textbook orthodoxy regards statistical hypotheses as never disproved, only shown to be less probable than some arbitrary confidence level—typically .05, but lower when rejection of truth is especially undesirable.[10] Nor does the pragmatist construal of acceptance as action as if a hypothesis were true, and non-rejection as allowance for its possibility when planning, select a natural confidence level. Perhaps the least arbitrary approach when forming expectations is pure Bayesianism, which incorporates a term for every hypothesis with non-zero probability. Rigorous Bayesianism also makes sense of eliminativism, at least about doxastic states. Eliminativism just sounds silly when taken to assert that nobody believes anything, but it is not silly when taken to assert that the binary notion of belief corresponds to nothing in the mind, being merely an abstraction from a Bayesian continuum of degrees of commitment. So there is something to be said for a revisionary theory of belief without confidence levels. Bear in mind, though, that rigorous Bayesianism preserves comparative acceptability judgments. As it should, it remains *more* reasonable to expect an Acme to break down than a Mercedes. Since most of the risk assessment issues raised by black crime are comparative, adopting Bayesianism would make little difference in the present context. In any case, Harman and Goldman have lately criticized Bayesianism on pragmatic, empirical and verific grounds,[11] so we may be stuck with confidence levels after all. In that case, .05 is as good as any.

This standard decision rule applies immediately to black crime. Suppose, jogging alone after dark, you see a young black male ahead of you on the running track, not attired in a jogging outfit and displaying no other information-bearing trait. Based on the statistics cited earlier, you must set the likelihood of his being a felon at .25. Of course, "felon" is a dispositional predicate, so the probability of his being prepared at that moment to attack you will generally be

less than .25. At the same time, circumstances like the one described may raise the conditional probability of his attacking you if he is a felon above .5, in which case the "absolute" probability of danger is still a significant .125 or more. In any event felons are dangerous, so it is rational to take into account the possibility that you are in the presence of one, and irrational not to do so. On the other hand it would be rational to trust a white male under identical circumstances, since the probability of his being a felon is less than .05. Since whatever factors affect the probability of the black attacking you—the isolation, your vulnerability—presumably affect the probability of a white attacking you as well, it remains rational to be more fearful of the black than of the white. Assuming ordinary confidence levels, there will be many occasions on which it is noncomparatively rational to fear the black but not the white, but that conclusion is independent of the rank-ordering by danger.

To be sure, the odds are 3 out of 4 that the approaching black is not a felon. But you do not violate probabilities by acting as if he might be. The odds are 3 out of 4 that the beckoning Acme will hold up in traffic, but you do not violate probabilities by insuring access to other means of transportation. Confused expressions of this statistical intuition should be interpreted charitably. People may *say* "You can't trust Acmes," but what they probably mean is that sufficiently *many* Acmes break down to warrant regarding any one of them with suspicion. By the same token, while (some) people may unthinkingly say "Most blacks are criminals," their aversive behavior reflects the correct probability assessment that a black is likely *enough* to be a criminal for blackness to signify danger.

The black in the park is definitely a felon or definitely not. Ideally, you would base your expectations about him on knowledge of which, just as your expectations about the Acme in front of you would ideally reflect complete knowledge of its characteristics. But you do not know. Relative to your state of knowledge, he is a typical member of a class one fourth of whose members are felons, and the probability to be assigned to a random member of that class being a felon is .25. So doing assumes some version of the principle of indifference, but under conditions which resist its abuse. This probability assignment does not asymmetrically partition the reference class of black males or humans generally, any more than the corresponding inference about Acmes asymmetrically partitions the class of Acmes or automobiles generally. The assignment does not illegitimately conjure knowledge from ignorance, since it does not say anyone *is* a felon. You are indeed reasoning under conditions of ignorance, but when reasoning under conditions of ignorance about the Acme, when it is known only to come from the Acme factory, common sense treats the car *as if* it were randomly chosen.[12] The assignment moves from an "objective" observed relative frequency to a "subjective" credal assessment, but frequencies standardly support subjective assessments despite what may be deep conceptual differences between them; once again, the move is unproblematic in the Acme case. Finally, the assignment obeys the constraints on information-seeking discussed in the post-Gettier literature. Two that might seem to impugn the snap credal decision in the park are: Seek more information when it is available, and, seek more information when judgment from current evidence would be immoral (as when current total evidence appears to condemn a friend). But such obligations may be overridden. Perhaps all Acmes that last 100 hours hold up for five years, but you may reasonably form a snap judgment about the Acme in front of you if you need a car *right now*, or if the salesman won't let you drive it for 100 hours unless you promise to buy expensive options. In general, you need not gather more information before deciding whether p if doing so costs more than error about p. The exemption in the park case would seem to be that you need not do A as a means to deciding whether p if the point of deciding whether p is to help reach a decision about doing A. Your park problem is whether to close the gap between yourself and the black male, but closing the gap is necessary for finding out more. So acting on present knowledge violates no informational constraints.

III

It is natural to treat the justification of private action separately from that of state action, and I do so in the present section. Ideally, discussions of state action should be flagged, in somewhat the way set theorists notationally distinguish theorems requiring the axiom of choice. Trusting such precautions are not necessary, I subsequently treat the two issues in the same breath to avoid stilted exposition.

Private Morality

Precautions against the anonymous black of the last section are also morally justified. Since flight from perceived danger is ordinarily permissible so long as it harms no innocent bystander, you are allowed to turn on your heels. Indeed, the perception of danger is not ordinarily required to be rational. Acrophobes who have wandered onto the observation deck of the Empire State Building are entitled to flee so long as they don't trample anyone on the way down. Anyway, as noted, the perception of danger in the running track case is rational.

It may be objected that, by possibly offending an innocent black, flight does risk harming an innocent. But this harm, should it occur, is (arguably) not imposed by you and is in any case outweighed by the right to safety. Certainly, flight did not cause the innocent black's chagrin in the sense of "cause" appropriate to blameworthiness. Responsibility for harm is ordinarily borne by the author of the original wrong in the chain of events necessitating it, and the events necessitating flight were initiated by other black criminals. The innocent black wouldn't have been offended had you not run away, but you would not have run away were it not for those prior wrongful acts. You flee voluntarily more or less as Aristotle's storm-beset captain voluntarily jettisons his cargo. So responsibility for harm to the innocent black is most naturally assigned to other black criminals, not you. Indeed, the innocent black is epistemically obligated to realize that you are not judging him d*ere*, since you do not know anything about *him*. You are avoiding a statistical possibility he represents.

But even if *you* are responsible for insulting *him*, the expected moral cost incurred by continuing ahead exceeds the expected moral cost imposed by flight. As a first approximation, the expected moral cost of continuing is .25× the evil of assault, while the cost imposed by flight on the black ahead of you is .75× the evil of insult. (Insulting criminals is not an evil.) If assault is more than three times worse than insult, calculations of expected morality favor flight. This calculation overstates the expected evil of continuing ahead since, as noted earlier, a black convicted felon may not intend harm to you, but it *also* overstates the cost of flight, since an innocent black may not notice or care about your running away; he may even be understanding. Because the large moral difference between insult and assault is invariant, more refined estimates of the moral cost of flight and continuing ahead may also be expected to favor flight.

State Action

The right of individuals to use racial classification in preemptively seeking safety would seem to extend to the state.

The state's regular use of other information-bearing traits to prevent serious crime sets a precedent for state use of information supplied by race for the same purpose, in the same manner, and to the same extent. Consider, in particular, suspect profiles and search for probable cause. It is uncontroversial that customs agents may subject violin possessors to special scrutiny if possession of a violin suitable for hiding contraband is known to increase the probability that its possessor is a smuggler. A glimpse of a rifle and a stack of car radios on the back seat of an automobile similarly entitles the highway patrol to search it. The state may "discriminate" on the basis of such traits as possession of a violin and occupancy of a car with a stack of radios, i.e. it may calibrate its treatment of individuals on the basis of these traits even when they do not indicate specific wrongful acts. Indeed, the authorities charged with preventing and detecting crime are *obligated* to use relevant information in screening.

Race is an information-bearing trait. Knowledge of race redistributes probabilities about past and potential commission of crimes. So, unless countervailing considerations can be brought, the state is entitled to use race in screening. The New Jersey Highway Patrol, for instance, reportedly stops young black males in expensive new cars for drug searches. The reasoning behind the violin case covers this practice as well, if most drug couriers are young black males driving expensive cars, and few blacks not involved in drug trafficking or other illicit activity own expensive cars (as the low average income and high unemployment rates of young black males would suggest is the case). Given that the presence of a young black male in an expensive car is a better predictor of drug involvement than that of a young white male, ordinary standards sanction and possibly mandate searches of black males under circumstances in which searching white males would be impermissible. If the race of a driver affects the probability of finding drugs in his vehicle, agents of the state may stop vehicles on the basis of their drivers' skin color, just as state agents may search violin owners at airports if most violins at airports contain contraband and most smugglers use violins.

To repeat, these precedents create (modulo ordinary standards) a *presumption* favoring racial screening, rebuttable by some relevant difference between race and other information-bearing traits. A number of such proposed differences will be reviewed presently. Prior to that review, however, it is well to reinforce the permissibility of racial screening by a systematic argument.

This argument begins with a reminder of what the state is *for*. All currently favored theories of the state assign provision of security as its raison d'etre. Lockeans base the state on protection of antecedent natural rights to property, which includes one's person; Hobbesians base the state on amoral interest in avoiding general war.[13] (Anarchists, who believe the state illegitimate, don't [vacuously] regard any state function as preceding security. Marxists, who expect the state to disappear, evidently regard state-enforced redistribution of property to its rightful owners as a temporary necessity.) Locke and Hobbes are both contractarians, deriving the state from an agreement between individuals to transfer their right of self-defense (Hobbes speaks of a "natural liberty") to some one enforcer. Now, part of that transferred right of self-defense is the use of information to gauge threats to oneself. Traces of this right can be discerned even in civil society, in the right of each individual to preempt clear and present dangers to himself. (If I see someone next to me draw a gun, I may disarm him.) Locke seems to accord each man in the state of nature the right to enforce the rights of another. On this view, although my right to use information in civil society does not extend to my entering a car if I see a stack of radios in the back seat, I presumably did have this right in the state of nature, since I had a right to act against perceived threats to anyone as well as myself. The state's right to preempt both non-specific threats (a man carrying burglar's tools) and threats to unknown targets (the burglar keeping his destination secret) does not emerge from or supervene upon individual rights. I myself am less confident of Locke's general executive right, and would prefer to derive the state's right by existentially generalizing over the individual rights it has received. Individual I_i can transfer only his right to pre-empt threats to I_i, but the state, having acquired the rights to pre-empt threats to $I_1, \ldots I_n$, takes upon itself the right to pre-empt threats to $I_1 \vee \ldots \vee I_n$, and thence threats whose target can be characterized only as "some I_i." However the state's right is derived, we *do* think the police may stop a car with a rifle on the back seat even if they cannot specify who the driver is threatening.

To be sure, the contractarian cannot argue that the state assumes an *obligation* to enforce individual rights by agreeing to do so. Individuals do not transfer their rights to the state by an agreement with *the state*, but by an agreement with each other to form a state. The effect, however, is much the same. The state acquires the rights of the individuals, with the understanding (between individuals) that this creature of their own will enforce those rights. Individuals acquire a right to have their rights enforced by the state, although this right is not against the state. (The salesman's promise that the vacuum cleaner will work gives me a right to a reliable vacuum cleaner, although it is not the vacuum cleaner that owes me proper functioning.) Moreover, since the state needs *agents* to achieve effective existence, these agents—the police—may literally be viewed as promising the rest of society to enforce their rights. So the state, as embodied in its agents, is *obligated* (because it has obligated itself) to provide security. Since what is obligatory is per-

missible, and the right to an end implies a right to otherwise permissible means, the state may use any otherwise permissible means to prevent attacks against individuals. Given the empirical salience of race in the commission of crime, attention to race is, absent some independent countervailing reason, permitted and indeed required by the state's protective function.

It is useful, in pursuing this argument, to follow theorists of the 14th Amendment in distinguishing two rationales for government classification of individuals corresponding to two "levels of scrutiny." (There is also an "intermediate" level of scrutiny, but as the philosophical questions are whether race can survive *any* scrutiny, or the *highest* degree of scrutiny, intermediate scrutiny may be ignored.) A classification is "benign" if, in the language of the Supreme Court's *Metro Broadcasting v FCC* (1990) decision, it "serve[s] important governmental objectives [and is] substantially related to the achievement of those objectives." "Benign" here does not mean "kindly"; it means "not intended to burden any individual or group on the basis of race." In fact, as in *Metro*—where the court permitted preferences for blacks competing for broadcast licenses to serve the state's interest in "diversity in broadcasting"—the US Supreme Court has countenanced benign racial classifications. The argument from Locke and Hobbes is that if the state may identify individuals by race to enhance diversity, it surely may identify individuals by race for its more essential purpose of controlling aggression.

At the same time, however, the Court has held that race is a "suspect" category, that classification by race must be "strictly" scrutinized and permitted only when shown to be necessary for the achievement of a "compelling state interest." (The Court apparently resolves this inconsistency by construing as benign those racial classifications beneficial to blacks, and suspect those racial classifications burdensome to blacks; see below.) Insistence on this more stringent standard will not daunt Hobbes or Locke. Clearly, they say, protecting citizens from attack is a compelling state interest; it is in fact the state's primary function. Crime statistics strongly suggest that race-consciousness can reduce attack, and might well be *necessary* for its adequate control. In all-white states like Utah and Idaho, the rate of death by homicide is about 1 per 100,000, comparable to European rates. In predominantly black areas like Detroit and Washington, D.C., the rate of death by homicide exceeds 70 per 100,000. It is difficult to deny that a greater police readiness to stop and search groups of young black males would decrease the murder rate. Perhaps all crime could be prevented by race-neutrally stationing policemen every fifty feet, but short of turning society into an armed camp, the marked black propensity to violence may be controllable only by attention to factors extensionally equivalent to race.

The court has offered reasons for striking down virtually all race-based classifications burdensome to blacks; its chief reason, as expressed in *Korematsu*, another recent decision, is that such classifications may reflect "racial antagonism [rather than] pressing public necessity." This language suggests that, in the Court's view, such classifications *merely* express racial antagonism, and cannot serve any other purpose. This is at bottom an empirical claim about the motives behind such classifications and their possible uses; in fact, the claim about the malign motive behind racial classifications is in large measure an inference from their presumed inutility. The point of the crime statistics is precisely that special police attention to (say) groups of young black males is not a baseless expression of "racial antagonism." Stopping acts which, as a matter of objective fact young black males are more likely to commit, by perhaps an order of magnitude, is a "pressing public necessity" if anything is.

Mention of these recent Supreme Court decisions is apt to raise the point that the impermissibility of state racial screening has indeed become a "fixed point of moral intuition." As observed, the Court, a reasonable guide to contemporary standards, strictly scrutinizes and by this standard rejects many racial classifications. To be sure, not all stated racial classifications are deemed impermissible by this guide. There are laws (e.g. sec. 8a of the Small Business Administration Act) reserving funds for black-owned businesses and National Science Foundation Fellowships reserved for blacks, and, as also noted, the Supreme Court scrutinizes less closely, and permits, some racial classifications (in the preferential assignment of broadcast licenses to blacks in *Metro*, for instance). What appears to have become a fixed point is the impermissibility of classifications burdening blacks. If this appearance is accurate, then, in conjunction with the methodological resolve of Sec. I, it outweighs the analogies and arguments lately deployed.

Before looking more closely at this appearance, I'll reformulate it less tendentiously. Certainly, the Court prefers to term "benign" those classifications, like *Metro*'s, whose *purpose* is not burdening whites but some other end such as helping the disadvantaged or increasing diversity. But whatever the state's *purpose* when classifying by race (or classifying in any other way, for that matter), some individuals are better off and some worse off than they would have been had the state not so classified. Under some racial classifications permitted by the Court, for example those giving preference to blacks in the acquisition of broadcast companies in *Metro*, whites are worse off than they would have been had the classification been struck down. And here is the point of substance: the Court has *not* been as ready to permit classifications under which blacks would be worse off than otherwise. It is this asymmetry I mean when I speak of the impermissibility of only those classifications burdening blacks. Those who accept the doctrine of "disparate impact"—that any practice which adversely affects blacks is, however intended, prima facie discriminatory—should have no trouble with this terminology.

The distinction registered, let me underscore some important differences between strict scrutiny for racial classifications burdening blacks and such paradigm fixed moral points as the wrongness of lying. First, strict scrutiny is new—less than three decades old—whereas lying seemed as wrong to the Greeks as it does to us. Thirty years is too little time to establish an intuition's fixity. Second, the paradigm fixed points as a class give hope of immediate subsumption under some one sweeping characteristic, such as "maximizing happiness" of "being driven by a universalizable maxim." Strict scrutiny for classifications burdening blacks lacks that same logical lucidity. A related point, or perhaps the same one differently expressed, is that the strict scrutiny rule is complex and asymmetrical in ways that paradigm fixed points are not. Lower levels of scrutiny are permitted for racial classifications benefitting blacks and burdening whites; the intuitive rule against lying recognizes exceptions, but not a large class of lies seemingly similar in principie to the lies it forbids. How can legal classifications burdening blacks be distinguished morally from symmetrical classifications exchanging "black" for "white"? There are reasons commonly cited, of course, but, ironically these reasons generate the deepest difference between strict scrutiny and paradigm fixed points. Unlike the imperative of honesty, the imperative of color-consciousness when and only when not burdensome to blacks is commonly based on a number of contingent and historically limited assumptions, among them: that the state seriously mistreated blacks in the past, that racial classifications burdening blacks reflect wrong and harmful "stereotypes," that such classifications can be motivated only by racial hostility. The wrongness of lying also has its empirical presuppositions, but such as are taken to be *self-evident* and *universal*: that lying destroys trust, that co-operation requires reliance on the words of others, that (a la Wittgenstein and Davidson) universal lying is impossible because the meanings of words are determined by their conditions of use. I am not now denying the factual presuppositions of strict scrutiny or their ability to support strict scrutiny itself, although I will later address "stereotypes," and I earlier suggested that crime statistics allow racial classifications burdening blacks to survive strict scrutiny. I am asserting, rather, that these factual presuppositions do *too much* work. The value of strict scrutiny is not *inherent*, as the value of truth-telling is, but a consequence of more fundamental values (no needless state burdens, no catering to hatred) presumed to apply to a particular sort of racial classification. Classifications burdensome to blacks are thought wrong because blacks were once enslaved, and (moral axiom) slavery is wrong; because such classifications indulge hatred, and the indulgence of hatred is self-evidently wrong and leads to further (self-evident) wrongs.[14] Color consciousness does

not remain immediately and intuitively impermissible when the associated factual assumptions are relaxed, as they may easily be in imagination. Indeed, racial classifications burdening whites are thought more permissible precisely because the parallel factual assumptions are known to be untrue of whites. By contrast, it's more difficult to imagine lying not causing distrust or not destroying communication. The wrongness of lying is integral to the human condition, while the wrongness of racial classifications burdening blacks is not.

In any case, the "fixed point" objection is pertinent only if racial screening in fact is found to fail the Court's strict scrutiny test. At the time this is written, the Court is admittedly unlikely actually to permit measures like those under discussion. But times change. It is conceivable that at some point the Court might find black violence so threatening to public order, and its control so compelling a state interest, as to permit race-conscious measures while maintaining its doctrine that racial classifications are "suspect."

IV

The permissibility of private and especially state race-consciousness in seeking security will draw a number of objections, which I will consider in order of increasing intuitive force. But the burden of proof, as I have noted, rests on the objector. The statistical prevalence of black crime in conjunction with the rest of our ordinary moral beliefs may not force acceptance of race-consciousness, but the precedents cited together with the argument from the purpose of the state create a presumption favoring race-consciousness. Failure to rebut this presumption leaves race-consciousness permissible.

(1) Basing treatment on race is racist.

Much of the force of this objection depends on an ambiguity in "racism." If "racism" means *unjustified* race-consciousness, race-based differentiations need not be racist. In particular, race-based screening is not "racist" if justified by differential crime rates, and calling it "racist" in this sense simply begs the question. On the other hand, if—as it sometimes seems to—"racism" denotes any race-consciousness, racism is not automatically objectionable. Practices "racist" in *this* sense must be evaluated on their own merits. For those who favor them, affirmative action and the casting of white actors as Hamlet are unobjectionable forms of "racism," as the casting of female Ophelias is presumably an acceptable form of "sexism". Race-based screening is indeed "racist" in this sense, but must be evaluated on its merits.[15]

Of course, one might hold that in fact all forms of racism in this *second* sense are wrong, a claim both non-trivial and sweeping enough to bar racial screening. However, the moral objection it mounts to racial screening is not that it uses racial factors, but that all use of racial factors is wrong. Because this is the most penetrating and philosophically interesting objection, I am deferring it to last, as objection (5) below.

(2) Rights precede utility. Rights against screening by race override the possible benefits of screening.

This argument can easily beg the question, since the very issue at hand is the existence of a strong right against screening by race. But I won't press that point very hard at this stage, since the argument implicit in common sense for ordinary (and by extension racial) screening is not utilitarian at all, but "rights maximizing."[16] Maximum protection of rights permits local rights invasion which minimize invasion overall. Rights-maximizers admit the wrongness of detention without specific evidence of wrongdoing, but see such detention as most efficiently protecting citizens' net rights against aggression. Screening is not a matter of preferences vs. rights, but of rights vs. more rights. Criticizing racial screening for favoring *utility* is thus an ignoratio.

The distinction between rights- and preference-maximizing suffices to turn the present objection, but its contribution to the intrinsic plausibility of screening, and thereby racial screening, deserves to be noted. "Utilitarianism of rights," which is deontological in its fashion, takes the more attractive side of the rights-vs.-utility debate and withstands the counterexamples that blow away classical preference-maximizing utilitarianism. (Act-utilitarianism tells you to rescue ten strangers instead of your own child from a burning building; the implications of rule-utilitarianism are less clear. Aggression-minimizing allows you in no uncertain terms to ignore the strangers, since refusal to rescue is not aggression.)

Objection (2) might be modified to an endorsement of an absolute ban on rights violations as against any brand of maximizing. This again begs the question when applied to race, but, again, there are more illuminating replies which concede arguendo a right of indeterminate strength against racial screening. The maximizer might boldly adapt the utilitarian idea that ordinary morality really is maximizing but *appears* Kantian to get us to maximize successfully.[17] The maximizing character of morality is revealed (the maximizer continues) when maximizing is preferred to Kantianism in hard cases—such as probable cause detention. Or, the maximizer may reply more concessively that if ordinary morality is indeed Kantian, the pre-theoretical acceptability of screening shows such measures to be consistent with Kantianism. (The maximizer gladly leaves to the Kantian the job of reconciling Kantianism with screening.) And if screening is consistent with Kantianism, another argument is needed to show that *racial* screening is not.

In connection with the general case for "rights utilitarianism" against side-constraint Kantianism, it is instructive to recall the role of "minimizing" preemption in Nozick's rights-based derivation of the state.[18] A seeming absolutist about the obligation not to aggress, Nozick insists that the state is legitimate only if it can emerge from anarchy without aggression. He easily derives a dominant voluntary protective association, but he cannot get it to achieve an enforcement monopoly, the defining characteristic of the state, without its aggressively imposing its rules on "independents." To permit this imposition, Nozick cites, rather plausibly, the anxiety created in association members by the prospect of independents conducting affairs according to their own rules. This anxiety is deemed great enough to justify the association in imposing *its* rules on the independents, so long as it compensates ex-independents for this imposition by protecting them as well. Nozick's argument thus requires levels of merely potential aggression that justify limited preemptive aggression by the (proto)state, pretty much the principle I take to underlie extent screening practices. (State protection of the other rights of screening detainees realizes the compensation proviso.) Nozick's reluctant appeal to maximizing indicates the extent which maximizing intuitions permeate our conception of permissible state action.

Insofar as Objection (2) mounts a challenge to screening per se, it effectively concedes that racial screening is permissible if screening in general is. Not surprisingly, this Objection proves too sweeping. The impermissibility of race-based measures must rest on specifically racial factors, if on anything. An obvious one is:

(3) Slippery slope.

Once race-based screening is countenanced, where does use of racial criteria stop? Doesn't it grease the slope down to concentration camps?

Drawing the line on uses of race raises no issue of principle. Just as the use of race in screening is governed by general norms governing the traits to be used in screening, permissible uses of race are limited by the norms which govern the use of all classification.

I have already mentioned two principles that may be used to govern state classification, namely substantial relation to an important government objective, and service of a compelling state interest. These principles can be abused, but so can any principles. A bad will could interpret "reasonable" search and seizure to cover anything, yet, recognizing this danger, we permit wiretapping. The philosophical rights-utilitarian, certainly, has a clear standard: a race-conscious policy A is permissible if A maximizes *expected morality*, the sum over world-states W_i of the products $p(W_i)m(A/W_i)$, where $m(A/W)$ is the net respect for rights achieved by following A in W and $p(W)$ is the probability of W holding. Now, if objection (3) is an expression of the worry that the expected morality of race-based action is *always* suboptimal, always less than some race-blind alternative, it becomes a version of objection (5), the wrongness of any use of race whatever. So (3) is best interpreted as referring to possible misuses, particularly by the state, of racial classifications.

It is difficult to respond to the Hitler comparison, since mention of Hitler seems to paralyze thought. (Max Hocutt and George Graham call this ploy "argumentum ad Nazium."[19]) Nazis persecuted an inoffensive population, the Jews, for being too clever and for imagined anti-German conspiracies. The historical situation of blacks in the US is entirely dissimilar. It is a fact, not fantasy, that the murder rate in US cities has increased almost tenfold in the last half century as their black population has increased. Here are real innocent deaths, not hypothetical ones. Ordinary morality would demand that something be done about so large an increase if it were unrelated to race; it seems perverse to do nothing because it involves a factor reminiscent of something of concern to Hitler. Hitler's minions invented the multistage rocket—does this mean NASA should not use them?

To have any bite, objection (3) must explain without hyperbole why race is so amenable to abuse that, unlike abusable factors that are used, it must be ignored. The most familiar such explanation is the reinforcement of racial stereotypes by public or private use of racial factors. I now turn to that worry, but under the more general heading "race is special," which also permits discussion of a number of other important issues. In fact, so many topics arise that this objection merits its own section.

V

(4) Race differs from other screening criteria.
(4i) Causal irrelevance.

Standard probable causes, such as concealed rifles and stacks of car radios, are *causally relevant* to the commission of crime, while skin color is not. A stack of car radios, unlike race, carries information because it *results from* crime. (Car radios are *specific symptoms*; few crimes produce stacks of car radios in the back seat, but most stacks of car radios in the back seat are produced by crime.) The presence of a gun informatively correlates with the occurrence of a crime because both are effects of a common cause, criminal intent. Alternatively, a gun might be thought of as a factor likely to *cause* a crime. But race is not a characteristic cause of crime, or effect of crime, or co-effect with crime of some underlying cause. What is sometimes called the "unfairness" of race-based screening derives in part from this causal irrelevance.

This difference between race and many standard screening criteria is irrelevant to its informational value. Standard criteria are used because they carry information, *whatever* the source of this informativeness. *Why* they carry information is the separate issue of *why* they are criteria. To ask this is not to question, indeed it is to assume, that they are. Even though the rifle carries information due to its causal role, it is the information the rifle carries, not the reason that it carries information, that warrants a search when a rifle is noticed. Concealed weapons redistribute probabilities, and it is the redistributed probabilities that justify the state in stopping a man with a concealed weapon. Citing the causal relations between concealed weapons, criminal intent and crime is necessary to justify the revised probabilities, but it is the probabilities themselves, so long as they *are* justified, that warrant the search. By parity of reasoning, any factor which redistributes probabilities equally reliably is an equally legitimate probable cause. In general, A becomes a sign of B when $p(B/A)$ is high enough. That $P(B/A)$ is often determined by causal relations between A and B fosters confusion between warrant and its (usual) causal basis. It is the magnitude of $p(B/A)$, *whatever* its basis, that warrants an inference from A to B, and would warrant the inference if it held in virtue of unexplained but projectable correlations.

Suppose Borsalinos become popular among drug couriers and almost no one else because most couriers come from the one city where Borsalinos are in fashion. Neither cause nor effect nor co-effect of drug trafficking, Borsalinos at an airport become a reliable sign of involvement in drug traffic. Now, even though it is *accidental* that most drug couriers wear Borsalinos—or "lucky," as the Aristotle of the *Categories* would say—the state would surely be justified in using Borsalinos as a basis for search. Of course, so doing would be irrational if the correlation between headwear and smuggling were expected to break down at any moment. The correlation between race and crime has held for decades, however, long

enough to be considered projectable. It is difficult to imagine smugglers ignoring the conspicuousness of their Borsalinos for decades, but if they did the hat/crime correlation would also be projectable. (Strictly speaking, of course, it is the predicates "wears a Borsalino" and "is black" that are [or are not] projectable.)

(4ii) Race is a biological trait not chosen by its possessors.

People should not be penalized for what they cannot help. In this sense too race-based screening is unfair.

If screening is regarded as a punishment, the major premise is absurd. Were there a killer on the lose with a conspicuous, ineradicable birthmark, monitoring such men would be permissible even though birthmarks are not chosen. It would be absurd to forego knowledge that might turn up a murderer because the murderer can't help providing it. In fact, however, the use of identifying traits is not a penalty. (So we can keep the axiom that people shouldn't be penalized for what they can't help.) The killer will be penalized for murder, not possession of a birthmark. The involuntariness of the tip-off is irrelevant to the need to identify him; by the same token, the involuntariness of race has nothing to do with the propriety of race-based screening. If race cannot be used because it is biological, neither should birthmarks, eye color, or—if there is a genetic predisposition to obesity—weight.

Consider the use of age, typically 16, in licensing drivers. Not only is one's age not chosen and a denial of the right to drive arguably a state burden, but the age criterion produces injustice. There are individuals under 16 mature enough to drive and individuals over 16 who are not. But testing every adolescent for maturity is impossible, and traffic accidents (many of which involve rights-violations) must be minimized, so age is used as a reasonably accurate proxy for physical and psychological maturity. Protecting the innocent from reckless drivers is felt to offset the attendant injustice. To be sure, 15-year-olds eventually become 16-year-olds, but the unalterability of race does not destroy the analogy. There will be mature 15-year-olds who, dying before their 16th birthday, are never licensed. We regard an age proxy as proper despite the inevitability of such injustices. What is more, justice delayed is said to be justice denied, so the injustice of denying an able 15-year-old his license is not cancelled when he gets his license on his 16th birthday. That a biological condition may change is evidently irrelevant to the permissibility of imposing a burden on the basis of that condition before it changes. If mutability still seems crucial in the licensing case, it is well to re-emphasize the immutability of birthmarks and inherited obesity, which the state can use in classifying suspects.

It might be allowed that involuntary tests, including race, may be used to identify perpetrators of known acts, but not merely potential malefactors. That an act's ontological status should determine the traits to be used in identifying perpetrators seems quite ad hoc, but assume it so. This ontological feature of racial screening, as well as the immutability of race, is also found in the use of genetic predictors of aggression, should they be found, to track potential criminals from birth. Thought experiments involving such predictors might seem at first to decide against racial screening, since many people now say they would reject tracking. Yet it is very far from clear that tracking would be widely rejected were it actually, concretely available. Imagine genetic information on file but disregarded, while every year post-conviction tests showed that 10,000 murderers (committing about half the murders in the US annually) had the crime gene. Would tracking still be considered wrong if we could *see* the victims who would not have been murdered had potential criminals been tracked?[20] To intensify the problem, instead of supposing 50% of murders are committed by possessors of a crime gene, suppose that 50%, or 90%, of unsupervised possessors of the crime gene eventually commit murder. Would tracking *still* be considered impermissible because nobody chooses his genes? It seems to me likely that at some point the average person would endorse tracking, and even restrictions on the freedom of carriers. Intuitions about genetic tracking may thus prove to reinforce racial screening.

(4iiia) Racial screening will strengthen stereotypes and mistrust of blacks.

Indeed, since white suspicions are in considerable part responsible for black crime, racial screening unfairly hounds blacks for their reaction to being hounded.

Whether racial screening will cause rights violations comparable to those it prevents, and encourage private acts of injustice as whites become irrationally mistrustful of blacks, is an empirical issue which cannot be decided by quasi-a priori speculation. As my doubts about the incipiency of Nazism might suggest, I am somewhat skeptical about this prediction, and in fact there are reasons for skepticism which also bear on the second part of the objection. The stereotype of black criminality is indeed already strong, but there is no evidence that it depends significantly on any variable other than the black crime rate itself. This point is unnecessary for meeting objection (4iiia) if, as I go on to argue, racial screening is permissible even if it self-fulfillingly predicts black crime. (I eventually argue that the etiological question as a whole is virtually irrelevant.) Nonetheless, many people seem certain that black crime is caused by white attitudes and actions, so that burdening blacks for black criminality impermissibly "burdens the victim." The self-fulfilling stereotype idea thus requires some discussion.

The most apparent shortcoming of this theory is methodological. It is not to be denied that many people privately view blacks as less intelligent, industrious and self-restrained than members of other groups, or that black educational and economic attainment, and obedience to law, conforms to this stereotype. Indeed, denying *either* point surrenders the self-fulfilling prophecy idea, by denying the prophecy or its fulfillment. As is widely recognized, however, the direction of the causal arrows between social phenomena is not self-evident, and in fact explaining stereotyped behavior by expectations quickly runs in a circle. Such an explanation renders inexplicable both the origin of stereotypes themselves and the assignment of particular stereotyped traits to particular groups. Group traits once *in place* may be supposed without circularity to be partly or wholly sustained by the expectations they confirm. But what starts the cycle? Whence the initial expectations? Positing a human propensity to stereotype, if it is just an aspect of the tendency to generalize experience, presupposes the stereotyped behavior. Stereotypes so construed are summaries of antecedently observed—perhaps misinterpreted but nonetheless observed—behavior. Including in the tendency to stereotype a need by the ingroup to ascribe disvalued traits to outgroups, the account favored by Sartre and Bettelheim, still fails to explain the ascription of *particular* traits to *particular* outgroups. If the array of outgroups is initially a *tabula rasa*, observation of which does not constrain ingroup ascriptions, these ascriptions must be supposed to be determined *arbitrarily*. Such a theory cannot explain why blacks are considered financially improvident and Jews canny, for instance, rather than vice-versa. And lacking an account of the choice of permutation among group/trait assignments we have no account of the origin of the feedback process, so no account of group traits *or* stereotypes. (It might also be noted that some racial stereotypes, such as Japanese efficiency and Jewish legal skill, are positive and do not obviously favor a need to feel superior.[21])

Reversing the causal arrow, by taking perceived group/trait correlations as independent variables and stereotypes as the dependent variables, explains stereotypes and leaves the cause of the correlations themselves an open question instead of a cul-de-sac. Such a "paradigm," in addition to permitting inquiry to continue[22] would be consistent with the kernel of empirical truth in most stereotypes.[23] And I think many critics of racial screening would, after some reflection, admit as much. However, as suggested earlier, the black behavior empirically validating stereotypes is itself often attributed to white misdeeds. To distinguish the idea that black crime is caused by the expectation thereof from the idea that black crime is caused by more general forms of racial thinking and acting, it is useful at this point to register objection (4iiib):

(4iiib) Even if stereotypes about black crime reflect rather than cause black criminal behavior, this behavior is a consequence of past racism.

Other information-bearing traits like birthmarks and Borsalinos differ from race because their association with crime was not wrongfully caused. Anyone who

would screen blacks on the basis of race resembles the Potter of the *Rubaiyat* "who threatens he will toss to Hell the luckless Pots he marr'd in making."

Indeed, since racism and poverty are often mentioned in the same breath as the "root causes" of black crime, it is also important to mention objection (4iiic):

(4iiic) Root causes.

Society has a special responsibility to address the causes of black crime, not take it as a given to be handled by standard means.

(4iiic) can be treated in passing because it is an ignoratio. The legitimacy of racial screening and other race-conscious responses to black crime does not require their being the *best* or *only* legitimate responses. So long as race-conscious measures do not conflict with other legitimate measures, the existence of these other measures does not discredit race-consciousness. The root cause of arson may be depressed real estate values, but the urgency of buoying the real estate market does not forbid otherwise acceptable methods for foiling arson. Similarly, if poor education amplifies black crime, the need to improve schools has no bearing on what may be done to control the present criminal tendencies which past poor education has, unfortunately, already produced. Indeed, the very deployment of (4iiic) is special pleading unless measures against crime associated with other ethnic groups (the Mafia, Chinese tongs, Jewish insider trading) are also to be assessed by their attention to root causes, a yardstick seldom applied. Deploying (4iiic) has the further disadvantage of opening the door to "root cause" hypotheses other than white racism, some of which, especially those involving genetic factors, are often deemed offensive. Since disconfirmation of the racism hypothesis would raise the probability of offensive alternatives, I note that inclusion of (4iiic) is a response to insistence on it by many readers.

Recurring to (4iiia-b), I view (4iiib) like (4iiia) as a non sequitur. Race-conscious state measures are permitted even if white racism has caused black crime. However, as with (4iiia), the empirical assumption behind (4iiib) is so often viewed as both obvious and morally dispositive that failure to discuss it might seem to ignore everything important. Once again, then, some remarks, primarily methodological, are in order.

Slavery, and subsequent public and private discrimination against blacks, certainly occurred. However, neither the direction nor even the existence of any causal relation between these actions, contemporary black crime and correlates like poverty immediately follows therefrom. In fact, two morally salient causal distinctions must be observed. The first separates the endogenous/exogenous question—whether the cause(s) of black crime lie(s) within or without the black population—from the fault question. The cause of wrongdoing need not itself be wrongdoing, much as our sense of fitness might prefer it so. Perhaps some environmental factor unrelated to past mistreatment differentially affects blacks. Perhaps some accidental, unintended and unsuspected, byproduct of past wrongs differentially produces black crime. In neither case would whites be responsible for the higher black crime rate—nobody would be—and restraints on race-consciousness imposed by such responsibility would fall away. (It would of course be imperative to remove the environmental factor.) Or, disproportionate black crime might be produced by some non-moral factor within the black population, such as genetically greater average aggressiveness.[24] Since people are not responsible for their genes, neither blacks nor whites would be to blame for black crime in that case either.[25]

The response of dismissing such possibilities as absurd in light of history necessitates the second distinction, between the thesis that white mistreatment has causally contributed to black crime and its correlates, and the thesis that white mistreatment is its sole cause. The causal relevance of state action or white mistreatment generally to some aspect of black crime (or socioeconomic attainment) does not imply that that mistreatment has caused all the discrepancy between black and white crime rates (or other behaviors). Black crime may resemble many social phenomena in being a vector sum; in statistical terms, the question bearing on (4iiib) is the "proportion of variance explained" by white misconduct. If race-conscious responses to crime are held to be illegitimate *because* black crime is the result of racism, such

responses are illegitimate only *to the extent* that black crime is the result of racism. Race-conscious measures regain legitimacy with decreases in the proportion of variance white racism explains. The reasoning behind (4iiib) even seems to admit moral thresholds. If for instance white misdeeds account for 10% of the difference between black and white crime rates, white responsibility might be too slight to restrain race-conscious measures to any extent at all. So white causal contributions to black crime do not by themselves show race-consciousness to be just more of what originally caused black crime, or to "burden the victim" impermissibly.

It may again seem obvious that white misdeeds directly or indirectly explain *all* the variance in crime rates, but a number of writers have begun to question this hypothesis. First, black crime rates in other countries, including all-black countries, are comparable to those in the US.[26] White racism, while still perhaps a sufficient or INUS condition, is thus not necessary for the black crime rate. Second, however, black crime has increased since the passage of the Civil Rights Act in 1964 and the inception of affirmative action in 1965. The racism hypothesis predicts a decrease in black crime with more equitable treatment of blacks, and it is difficult to argue that white racism has increased in the US since 1965.[27] Indeed, most black crime is committed by black males under 25 who have never experienced Jim Crow and have been raised in a society in which preferences for blacks is public policy. The idea that blacks have had insufficient time to recover from slavery and Jim Crow predicts similar crime patterns and recovery times for similarly mistreated groups, but this prediction is also unsustained. One may insist on the uniqueness of the black experience in America, but the Jewish experience worldwide certainly looks comparable. In much of Europe Jews were legally confined to ghettos and forbidden to engage in certain trades. The accepted estimate of the number of Jews killed by the Nazis is 6,000,000; the highest estimate I have seen of the number of blacks lynched in the American South between 1900 and 1954 is 5,000. According to T.E. Reed,[28] at most 400,000 slaves were shipped to America during the slave trade, most of them during the 18th century. If one is assumed to have died for every two who survived, the resultant death rate remains three orders of magnitude smaller than that of the Holocaust.

Turn of the century Jewish immigrants fleeing European anti-Semitism lived in extreme poverty in New York, and Jewish crime of the period supports the poverty/oppression/crime link to some extent. However, while Jewish crime was then high relative to Jewish norms elsewhere, it was not, as is black crime, disproportional to the number of Jews in the overall population.[29] Moreover, Jewish crime was directed primarily against property rather than persons, as is black crime.[30] Finally, even the relative prevalence of Jewish crime subsided by World War II,[31] the period 1900–1939 being about equal in length to that between *Brown* (1954) and the present.

Positing ever more obscure forms of racism to explain away such data yields a theory vulnerable as a whole to the question Hume so devastatingly asks of theism in the *Dialogues*: Is the world as we would expect it to be if all we knew beforehand was that this theory were true? Does the world look as if blacks and whites are equally behaviorally restrained but for white racism? Additional assumptions may reconcile the racism theory with ubiquitously high black crime rates and increases in black crime upon passage of protective legislation, but the theory does not predict these phenomena. The theory becomes "conjecture piled atop hypothesis" without independent support.[32]

But race-conscious safety-seeking measures remain proper even if white racism, or stereotyping, or some combination of the two, is the cause of black crime. So much seems unarguable in the case of "private" safety-seeking. That the black male on the running track is more likely than a white to attack a jogger *because* of the jogger's suspicions, or because his father suffered discrimination, does not diminish the jogger's danger or his right to avoid it. This right might be challenged on grounds of the jogger's obligation to break the vicious cycle, a challenge arising from (4iiia) particularly. However, his obligation to weaken the cycle cannot be greater than his contribution to it, weighted by his chances of weakening it by running ahead, and this is less than the danger of continuing. So the jogger's flight remains "subjec-

tively" permissible and probably objectively permissible as well. A more general obligation not to flee a danger by means which might sustain or increase it, on the other hand, seems not to exist. Even if the burning of fossil fuel has so poisoned my city's air that I must leave immediately or asphyxiate, most people would permit me to escape by car. Despite the appearance of involving a ban on the use of means to avoid evils caused by those very means, both principles actually derive what plausibility they enjoy from the general rule that flight must not injure the innocent. My automotive flight imposes some pollution on others, and my flight from the running path, we are supposing, to some slight extent sustains black crime. Yet the reflexive character of these acts does not enter into their evaluation, which consists entirely in balancing my right to safety against the harm I may impose. (In my own non-philosophical view, continuing to run toward the black man is the cowardly subordination of one's own instinct for survival to a heteronomous fear of violating taboos against "racism.")

State action raises facially additional issues, since the fleeing jogger does not interfere with the black, while a police search does actively burden him. Yet this distinction does no work, since, as observed earlier, the state is usually understood to have acquired a right to use information to intervene preemptively from each individual's right or natural liberty to seek security. If some state intervention is permissible, (4iiia) and (4iiib) purport to show why it cannot be based on race. (4iiia) is the logically more compelling argument, in effect plausibly generalizing the rule against entrapment, namely: Do not punish a wrong caused by that very punitive act. The right to detain does not permit detaining someone for breaking a window in the room in which he is being held for breaking that window, since it is the state that has created the wrong on which it is basing detention. This is why acting on race-based suspicion seems wrong, on the self-fulfilling prophecy model. The cop on the beat is justifiably suspicious of black teenagers, but only because his suspicions dispose them to crime (by lowering their self-esteem or convincing them they have nothing to lose). But this objection loses its force when *specific* self-fulfillment is distinguished from *generic* self-fulfillment. Let us call an expectation-token E specifically self-fulfilling if E creates E-fulfilling conditions, whereas E is *generically* self-fulfilling if other tokens of E's type have created E-fulfilling conditions. The generalized rule against entrapment applies to specifically self-fulfilling suspicions but not to generically self-fulfilling ones. If this black's criminal propensity was not caused by this policeman's present suspicions of him, but only by past suspicions of blacks, possibly including him, this policeman's very suspicions are not responsible for the behavior which justifies them, and the policeman's acting on them does not impose a burden for a wrong created by the act of imposition. Perhaps those other suspicions should not have been harbored, but they *were* harbored and *have* had their effect on the black's character. These suspicions, we are assuming, have made him more likely to commit a crime. As an agent of the state the policeman is obligated to prevent those effects from manifesting themselves as criminal acts. The wrongness of the earlier suspicions bar the policeman from acting on his present ones only if he may never take preventive action in the light of *any* suspicions which are justified by (behavior produced by) some past wrong.

The response that the wrongs which cause black crime were not just any wrongs, but race-conscious wrongs, returns us to (4iiib): race-based measures are impermissible now because the purported need for them was created by past race-based injustice. But the character of those past causes, whatever they are, has turned out to be irrelevant so long as present race-based measures are not the specific causes of the behavior these measures are intended to prevent. Indeed, limited race-conscious screening is not even generically similar to the race-conscious measures said to have caused black crime. Stopping a group of black males because they are especially likely to be carrying guns is not slavery, lynching, separate drinking facilities or segregated schools. Such a measure does not resemble segregation in "reflecting racial antagonism," if this expression means that the measure exists *only* to express racial antagonism, without any further purpose. The crime statistics show such a measure to serve the independently justified purpose of controlling crime. To insist on an analogy between screening and segregation is simply to ignore the empirical fact that race predicts crime, and crime, to an even greater extent, predicts race.

Weakening (4iiib) to the impermissibility of race-based measures now because black crime was caused by *some* (perhaps distinct) unjust race-based measures, leaves it a non sequitur. Crime, like everything else, has causes, some of which are injustices, and the presence of a wrong in the causal chain leading to a crime does not normally constrain state action. It doesn't matter that I plan to steal your car because a swindle in 1950 impoverished my family, so long as my mental capacity is otherwise undiminished. It doesn't matter if the state abetted the swindle by finding the swindler innocent in a fixed trial. The state doesn't care *why* I plan to steal your car. (My theft might acquire some immunity if you had been the swindler and I meant to retaliate, but black criminals give no evidence of harboring retaliatory motives.) Our occasional tendency to think past wrongs mitigate their present effects may be due to a tendency to collapse causal chains—to think that when A causes B and B causes C it is really A that causes C, with B a sort of epiphenomenal intermediary. This fallacy is particularly tempting when A and C are actions and B is the desire which caused C. Because my desire to steal was caused by wrongful action, we think, I am not the real criminal; the real criminal is the agent behind A. That this is sheer confusion is, I trust, obvious.

If in general the presence of wrongs in the causal history of behavior is irrelevant to state treatment of it, it is hard to see how the *racial* character of those wrongs can create relevance. The intuition that it does, the intuition behind (4iiib), is that race-consciousness is special because race-consciousness is what caused all the trouble in the first place. The countervailing intuition is: so what? Suppose the Holocaust turned many Jews into bank robbers. The police see a man with a Mogen David and a concentration-camp mark on his arm eyeing a bank vault. Should they disregard these factors in deciding whether to enhance surveillance because these factors and perhaps the crime being plotted were the result of anti-Semitism? Consider race-consciousness from the perspective of you, the social contractor in the street, attacked by a black male. Imagine a policeman arriving just too late to save you who confides: "I saw the black approach you and suspected he might attack, but I didn't intercede even to the minimal extent of showing myself to discourage him because my belief that he might attack was *race*-based. I would have felt no impulse to intercede had your attacker been white. But I shouldn't act on thoughts I shouldn't think, and I shouldn't think that way. I shouldn't think that way because your attacker's turn to crime was a result of his great-grandfather's enslavement, his father's inferior education and his own constricted opportunities, circumstances based on racial thinking. Doing *anything* because of his race is just the sort of thinking that caused him to attack you." If you retained your composure, you would surely note your personal innocence with respect to your attacker's history. You would insist that segregation was based on factual errors, while his suspicion of the black was based on empirical realities. In signing the social contract, you would continue, you created the office of policeman to prevent such attack. When he agreed to take this office, the constable assumed the enforcement of your right to self-defense and thereby obligated himself to protect you. You would admit to having limited his protective activities—no third degree, perhaps, no unreasonable invasion of privacy, no generalized entrapment. But the information that race predicts crime is untainted, because innocently acquired. Why couldn't the use it? Is it enough that use of that information bears a family resemblance to the thinking of segregationists?

VI

Even those who admit the irrelevance of the "root cause" issue may balk at the use of racial information because

(5) People should be treated as individuals, not as members of groups.

The alleged right of each person to be treated solely on the basis of his own traits rather than the category to which he belongs, particularly his racial category, is the fundamental objection.

I will eventually argue that Objection (5) rests on a confusion about "treating people as individuals," but let me first, dialectically, deny the objection to supporters of affirmative action. I take it as uncontroversial that affirmative action favors individual blacks (and women) solely on the basis of their race (and sex), without attention to the specifically demonstrated claims of any particular black or female beneficiaries. This is clear enough for the most familiar justification of affirmative action, the need to compensate or "remedy" blacks (and women) for the disabilities they now carry as a consequence of wrongs to themselves and their ancestors.[33] The presumption that a black favored over a better-qualified white has suffered from white misdeeds is applied to him not on the basis of his known individual circumstances and history, but on the racial group to which he belongs. Affirmative action entitlements to individuals are thus probability judgments based on empirical generalizations about classes, just as avoidance of an anonymous black is an implicit probability judgment about an individual based on empirical generalizations about classes. A black applying for a job is deemed so *likely* to bear the burdens of discrimination, because a high but unspecified proportion of blacks do, that favoring him now "makes him whole." Even if, the replies to (4iiia–b) notwithstanding, it is insisted that every American black has been harmed by white racism, it must also be admitted, I think, that the extent of the harm cannot be exactly determined in any concrete case. It cannot be shown specifically, for instance, that the less-senior blacks promoted over Brian Weber in the *Weber* case would have been *senior to Brian Weber* had there been no racism. So preference for a particular black over a better-qualified white, since it cannot rest on a showing that that black would have been better qualified than that white absent racism, must rest on the statistical inference that that black *probably* suffered an injury as great as the difference in their qualifications.

Other arguments extant for affirmative action also involve classifying by race. If, for instance, more black role models are needed because there aren't as many inspiring blacks as there would have been absent discrimination, we have not advanced beyond the compensation argument. (Many role-model theorists seem not to realize this.) If on the other hand more black role models are needed because the presence of more blacks in different walks of life is not a requirement of justice but a good thing by some more general criterion, the question shifts to why it is good. "Diversity" might be considered good in itself, like pleasure or acting from universalizable maxims. Whatever the merits of such a view—as a justification of affirmative action it is circular, "diversity" being another name for what affirmative action seeks to achieve[34]—diversity as an end in itself self-evidently requires racial consciousness. Blacks become fungible if the end is proportionality per se, with no black being chosen because of any individual trait (except race). Or, one might justify "diversity" and derivatively affirmative action in terms of some values that blacks can distinctively contribute.[35] In that case, however, unless one is prepared to specify a desirable trait possessed by every black and no white, one must believe certain desirable traits more prevalent in the black population, so that preferring a black over a better-qualified white on the basis of his race is *likely* to inject that trait into a given situation. By contrast, a racial classification may be justified, as in the *Metro* case, as helping the disadvantaged—which once again selects individuals because of presumed correlates of group membership rather than individual traits. (The Federal Communication Commission policy sanctioned in *Metro* did not extend preference to possibly disadvantaged white purchasers, or demand a showing by individual black purchasers that *they* had been disadvantaged.) On its face, the argument that preference-generated diversity will destroy stereotypes is a "distinctive black virtue" argument, since it takes all and only blacks to have the desirable characteristic of 'tending to contribute to the destruction of stereotypes.' But this property itself may involve appeal to a probabilistic assessment, the *likely* effect of a preferred black on stereotypes; more significantly, the thinking that is to be encouraged by affirmative action so justified—that blacks are more talented than might have been supposed—classifies individuals by race.[36]

It appears, then, that affirmative action however defended distributes benefits and burdens on the basis of group membership.[37] (This conclusion should not be surprising.) Proponents of affirmative action therefore cannot consistently deploy individualism—the principle that the distribution of benefits and burdens should never be based upon membership in racial groups—against racial screening, or anything else.[38]

In contrast, a proponent of racial classification in the service of individual security can consistently oppose affirmative action. He may claim that, because assaults are far worse than uncompensated discrimination, the expected morality of screening (the probabilistically weighted value of assaults prevented less the disvalue of detaining innocent blacks) exceeds the expected morality of affirmative action (the probabilistically weighted value of compensating discrimination-induced disabilities less the disvalue of penalizing innocent whites).[39] The burden imposed by affirmative action on possibly innocent whites is heavy, he may say, and the probability of a given white's actually having contributed to a given black's present position not clearly high. As noted, the harm of not compensating discriminatory injury certainly seems less than the harm of an assault. But the harm of an assault is very great and the burden imposed on blacks by race-based measures to prevent it—the inconvenience of search—is lighter than the burden whites are made to bear by affirmative action. A great enough difference between the expected moralities of screening and affirmative action would justify endorsement of screening and rejection of affirmative action. After a time, affirmative action without screening may come to seem intuitively absurd. To be sure, the value of affirmative action can be raised above that of screening by suitable assumptions about the extent of discriminatory injury to blacks, the moral cost of not compensating it, and the harm to innocent blacks of screening. Nor would the screening proponent necessarily reject those assumptions. It is no part of his argument to call affirmative action *unjustified*, or to *deny* the remedial rationale for it. (Nor need he deny any of the other rationales, although he finds it strange that the state may use race-conscious measures thought to be related to subsidiary state goals like diversity, but not race-conscious measures more clearly related to the more fundamental state goal of security.) But even given empirical and normative assumptions favorable to affirmative action, the screening proponent regards it as hypocritical to advocate affirmative action while opposing race-based responses to crime *on the principle that individuals should always be treated solely as Individuals*. The advocate of racial screening, having accepted no such principle, can be accused of no comparable hypocrisy. He accepts race-based classifications rationally related to basic moral goods, chiefly prevention of aggression.

Now, I have been arguing thus far as if there is an acceptable principle of individualism, the only question being who has a right to it. There is in fact no such principle. People are and must always be judged by the classes to which they belong, the traits they share with others. What are called individual or intrinsic traits are simply traits which, given past experience with others possessing those traits, are known to have high predictive value. "Judging" an individual consists largely in anticipating his behavior and personality on the basis of observed correlations between traits he is known to have and further traits he may then be presumed to have. "Natural kind" traits, which seem a distinctively appropriate basis for judgment, are simply traits whose predictive value and role in quasi-laws has made reliance on them second nature.

Both proponents and opponents of race-based classification would probably agree in contrasting a student's high-school grades with his race as, respectively, an "individualistic" and a "group" criterion for college admission. Use of grades, especially, would be thought to illustrate judging a student "on his own merits." But why are grades an *intrinsic* trait, and a permissible basis of judgment? Simply because of the reliable correlation between high school grades and success in college. Simplifying greatly, there is a correlation coefficient of .5 between high school and college grade point averages; i.e. 75% of those with high school g.p.a.'s of 3.5 or above achieve the same g.p.a. in college.[40] College admissions officers favor an applicant with a 3.5 g.p.a. because most other applicants with that same g.p.a. have performed well. Admitting an applicant with high grades, then, is a probabilistic judgment based on the group to which he belongs. Grades are unlike race in reflecting effort

and choice, and thus are susceptible of moral evaluation. So, we feel, students deserve what their grades, but not their race, earn them. But other expressions of effort and choice, such as a student's physique from years of body-building or his splendid collection of beer cans, play no role in admissions' deliberations because they do not predict academic performance.

It is in fact sheer error to look to voluntariness for a way of distinguishing individual from group traits. Many intuitively "individual" traits are acquired as involuntarily as group traits like race. A 5′4″ 125-lb. freshman will be made waterboy rather than linebacker because of his size (as opposed to his race) and we would agree that the coach had judged him on an "individual" trait, his size. But size is largely beyond one's control. And here, too, the coach's basis for judgment is statistical: very few boys that size have ever succeeded as linebacker. There are exceptions, but that is the reasonable expectation—a conclusion dovetailing with that of (4ii) about the irrelevance of the biological character of race.

VII

It would be tempting but misguided to dismiss the cluster of problems I have discussed as "racist." Some of them are significant enough to reach all of social philosophy. While I am fairly confident of the conclusions I've presented here, many problems remain to be explored. We need to determine the limits of race consciousness. If there are race differences in maturation rates[41] would it be permissible to treat blacks as adult offenders at an earlier age than whites? If reinforcement schedules strongly differentiate by race, would different average deterrent effects for the same punishment on the three main racial groups justify race-based punishment schedules? Is a presumed narrowness in the variance of responses to punishment the only reason punishments are not individually tailored *now*? The courts do have discretion in sentencing and in setting bail, with the likely effect on the individual an important determinant of the latter especially. Perhaps the idea of equal treatment under law does not mean that everyone should receive the same punishment for the same crime, but that everyone should receive an equally aversive punishment, a punishment with the same deterrent effect, for the same crime. These questions are as interesting as they are disturbing, and I would hope to see philosophers take them up.

I would also hope these discussions treat black crime for what it is—a difficult, many-sided dilemma like abortion, capital punishment or euthanasia. There is no need to falter in following the argument as if one has stepped onto holy ground.

NOTES

1. "The Black-on-Black Crime Plague," *US News and World Report*, Aug. 22, 1988, p. 54.

2. J. Philippe Rushton, "Race Differences in Behavior: A Review and Evolutionary Analysis," *Personality and Individual Differences* 9, 6 (1988), p. 1016; also see James Q. Wilson and R. J. Herrnstein, *Crime and Human Nature* (Basic Books, New York: 1985), pp. 461–66.

3. Rushton, loc. cit.

4. Rushton, 1016–17; also see Michael J. Hindelang, "Race and Involvement in Common Personal Crime," *American Sociological Review* 4 (February 1978), pp. 100–01.

5. "Marvin E. Wolfgang, a criminologist at the University of Pennsylvania, said that perceptions about who is more likely to commit a crime have some statistical basis. For four violent offenses—homicide, rape, robbery and aggravated assault—the crime rates for blacks are at least 10 times as high as they are by whites." Joseph Berger, *The New York Times News Service*, June 19, 1987.

6. Between 1979 and 1986, 44.3 out of 1,000 blacks, as opposed to 34.5 out of 1,000 whites, were victims of violent crime; *Black Victims*, Special Report, Bureau of Justice Statistics, United States Department of Justice, April 1990, Table 1.

7. National Crime Survey, Department of Justice, telephone interview, June 28, 1990.

8. In 1987, 50.2% of simple assaults by blacks had white victims (National Crime Survey); between 1979 and 1986, 2,416,696 of the 4,088,945 simple assaults committed by blacks were directed against whites (*Black Victims*, Tables 1, 16).

9. See my "Further Reflections on a Philosophical Problem," in Peter Suedfeld, ed., *Torture: Interdisciplinary Perspectives* (Westview, Washington, D.C.: 1990).

10. Thus R. L. Larsen and M. L. Marx: "*in many situations the beginning of reasonable doubt is taken as that critical value that is equalled or exceeded only 5% of the time* (when H_O [the null hypothesis] *is true*" (*Statistics* [Prentice-Hall, Englewood Cliffs, N.J.: 1990], p. 380). Also see e.g. William Feller, *An Introduction to Probability Theory and Its Applications*, vol I, 3rd ed. (Wiley, NY: 1968), p. 189; more typical in its *va sans dire* use of a confidence level of .95 is Dennis Aigner, *Principles of Statistical Decisions Making* (Macmillan, NY: 1968), chapters 5 and 6.

11. Harman stresses the unavailability of epistemic resources for the assignment of precise probabilities; see *Change of View* (MIT Press: Cambridge, Mass., 1986), pp. 22–26. Goldman cites experimental evidence of widespread de facto violations of the probability axioms, and discusses simple neurological models for transforming information into binary yes/no belief "decisions": see *Epistemology and Cognition* (Harvard University Press: Cambridge, Mass., 1986), pp. 90, 324–43. A judicious discussion of whether belief is analytically connected to behavior is F. Dretske, *Knowledge and the Flow of Information* (MIT Press: Cambridge, Mass., 1981), pp. 197ff.

12. To see why, consider arbitrary Acme A. If there are n Acmes, some subset of size $n/4$ are the defectives. There are $n!-(n-n/4)!$ such subsets *if A is assumed to be in 25% of them*. Assuming A to be in any other proportion of $n/4$-tuples of defective Acmes reduces the number of realizations of a 25% distribution of defective Acmes. So, if the distribution of defectives is known to be 25%, the "maximum entropy" distribution is more likely to be realized than any other. This is one approach to what Bayesians call the problem of "informationless priors." For a highly general discussion of this argument, see Roger Rosenkrantz, *Inference, Method and Decision* (Reidel, Dordrecht: 1977), Chapter 2.

13. The Hobbesian state aims at least at security, but is often thought to go farther. For a reconstruction of a libertarian Hobbes, and an attempt to explain why security is a special value, see Michael Levin, "A Hobbesian Minimal State," *Philosophy and Public Affairs* 11 (Fall 1982): 338–53; also J. Ronald Penock, "Correspondence," *Philosophy and Public Affairs* 13, 3 (Summer 1984): 255–62; Levin, "Reply to Pennock," ibid.: 263–67; Christopher Morris, "A Hobbesian Welfare State?," *Dialogue* 27 (1988): 653–63; David Schmidtz, "Contractarianism Without Foundations," *Philosophia* 19, 4 (December 1989): 461–70; Levin, "To the Lighthouse," ibid.: 471–74. Also see Gregory Kavka, *Hobbesian Moral and Political Philosophy* (Princeton, N.J.: Princeton University Press, 1986).

14. See Michael Levin, "Is Racial Discrimination Special?," *Journal of Value Inquiry*, 15 (1981): 225–32. The specialness of past racial discrimination is a theme that recurs in the Objections section of the present paper.

15. It is sometimes argued that "racism" must by definition disadvantage blacks. Since whites occupy a dominant position, race-conscious distinctions by or favoring blacks must therefore proceed from the good desire to create equality, while race-conscious distinctions burdening blacks must proceed from the bad desire to oppress. Whatever else may be said about this refinement of the second sense of "racism," it reinforces the point that the wrongness of race-consciousness depends upon its nature and purpose.

16. The phrase is Nozick's; he contrasts it with a Kantian morality of "side constraints" against doing wrong. See Robert Nozick, *Anarchy State and Utopia* (Basic Books, NY: 1975), pp. 28–33.

17. See "Further Reflections."

18. Op. cit., pp. 78–84, 110–113.

19. Max Hocutt, "Must Relativism Tolerate Evil?," *Philosophical Forum* 17 (Spring 1986): 188–200.

20. Cf. Roger Wertheimher's discussion of visible fetuses in "Understanding the Abortion Problem," in Marshall Cohen, Thomas Nagel and Thomas Scanlon, eds., *The Rights and Wrongs of Abortion* (Princeton University Press, Princeton, N.J.: 1974).

21. The self-fulfilling prophecy theory also fails to explain the cross-cultural robustness of stereotypes. 15th-century Arab slave-owners, with no prior direct or indirect contact with blacks, regarded them as highly sexed, highly rhythmic, and unintelligent. This perception cannot be explained by the servile status of the blacks with whom the Arabs were familiar, since Arabs stereotyped their Jewish slaves as very clever (as did the Romans); see Bernard Lewis, *Race And Slavery In The Middle East* (Oxford University Press: Oxford, 1990).

22. For a discussion of the idea that explanations should never limit further inquiry, see Michael Slote, *Reason and Scepticism* (Humanities, N.Y.: 1970), chapter II. A further methodological defect of the stereotype theory is the non-existence of any detailed, well-confirmed model of the transformation of perceived white mistrust into omnidirectional black aggression. Nor is it clear how such a model could be consistently constructed. Self-hate caused by disdain and mistreatment might explain black-on-black crime, but not black-on-white crime, while black resentment of whites does not easily explain black-on-black crime.

23. Of the theoretical works on prejudice known to me, only William Helmreich's *The Things They Say Behind Your Back* (Doubleday, N.Y.: 1982) attempts to gauge the empirical correctness of stereotypes. Helmreich examines 75 generalizations about Jews, blacks, Italians and other groups, and decides that one-third are true and "about half have a factual basis" (p. 244). Already considerably more than would be predicted by the psychological-needs theory, this number increases upon examination of Helmreich's examples. Many of Helmreich's assessments tend to treat wrongly caused group traits as not really there (calling to mind Russell's definition of a metaphysician as someone who says that something does not exist, and defines evil as the counterexamples). For instance, he discounts the stereotype of black oversensitivity by explaining this oversensitivity as a response to oppression. But a phenomenon cannot simultaneously be explained and denied, since the explanans of an explanation must be true and (at least on the DN model) entail the explanandum.

24. "Population P is genetically more prone to X than population Q" can be taken to mean "P is phenotypically more X than Q in any environment." The weaker definiens "P is phenotypically more X than Q in all likely environments" accommodates the possibility that there are some environments in which P is more X than Q and some in which P is less X. (Any theoretically satisfactory definition should include the proviso that phenotypic X was more adaptive in the environment in which P evolved than that in which Q evolved.) Block and Dworkin ("IQ, Heritability, and Inequality," in N. Block and G. Dworkin, eds., *The IQ Controversy* [Pantheon: New York, 1976]. pp. 479–85), like many authors, emphasize gene/environment interaction vis-a-vis race differences in intelligence, but cite no evidence of environments in which the norms of reaction for black and white genotypes yields similar phenotypes. The point of the well-formedness of both definitions and their rough extensional equivalence is that talk of genotypic differentiation is not impugned by the need for environmental mediation of genotypes.

It might be wondered how blacks can be more prone to aggression than whites, given that the most destructive wars have been waged by Europeans and Asians. One natural answer is a white advantage in organizational ability and technology. Although tribal conflict runs through African history, Africans were unable to form themselves into large armies with any regularity or develop weapons of mass destruction. The crime data is consistent with blacks being on average more *individually* aggressive than whites. Counterfactuals about what blacks would have done had they formed million-man armies runs into cotenability problems, since high levels of individual aggressiveness may impede cooperative enterprises.

25. The degree to which individual black criminals would then be responsible for their crimes is one aspect of the perennial determinism puzzle, which warrants four specific comments here. First, environmental causes are no more in the control of the agents affected than are genetic causes, so if genetic causation diminishes criminal responsibility, so does environmental causation. If genetic causation diminishes responsibility, so does any cause short of noumenal agency. Second, genetic factors diminish the responsibility of black criminals only if a genetic predisposition to race hatred diminishes the responsibility of bigots, an implication many will be reluctant to draw. Third, compatibilists such as the present author distinguish freedom to desire from freedom to act on one's possibly unfree desires. The consequent possibility of free action from desires not freely chosen reconciles genetic determination of high aggressiveness with responsibility for aggressive acts. However—and this fourth comment moves against the trend of the first three—the more refined compatibilism of Frankfort, Davidson, Sen, Davis and myself construes fully free action as action proceeding from desires the agent finds acceptable. (See my *Metaphysics and The Mind-Body Problem* [Oxford University Press: Oxford, 1979], Chapter 7; also Lawrence Davis, *Philosophy of Action* [Prentice-Hall: Englewood Cliffs, N.J.] for a graceful statement of this view.) Since aggressive emotions tend to preclude second-order reflection—indeed reflection of any sort—congenital aggression may well diminish freedom and responsibility.

26. See Rushton, and Herrnstein and Wilson.

27. This point is made in William Junius Wilson, *The Truly Disadvantaged* (University of Chicago Press: Chicago, 1987), pp. 11ff. Wilson explains relative black poverty in terms of the disappearance of manufacturing jobs, but he does not explain why blacks have not adapted to an economy more geared to service and information.

28. T. E. Reed, "Caucasian Genes in American Negroes," *Science* 165 (1969): 762–68.

29. "[A]t no time during the prewar period did Jews have more lawbreakers than their proportion of the population warranted. Rather, Jews were consistently underrepresented among those charged with committing felonies with, on occasion, half as many felony arrests as their numbers allowed. From a purely statistical perspective, Jews did not exceed admissible levels of criminal behavior." Jenna Weissman Joselit, *Our Gang: Jewish Crime and the New York Jewish Community, 1900–1940* (University of Indiana Press: Bloomington, 1983), p. 32.

30. "Close to 80 percent of all felony charges brought against Jews between 1900 and 1915 had to do with the commission of property crimes: burglary, larceny, arson, horse-poisoning, and receiving stolen goods. In contrast, only 12 percent of these arrests related to the commission of a violent crime, such as assault, murder, or rape." Ibid., p. 33.

31. "[F]or New York Jews, crime was a one-generation phenomenon, a social and economic consequence of the immigrant experience." Ibid., pp. 158–59.

32. Another popular explanation of black crime is low self-esteem caused by whites, but the boundary condition in this explanation appears to be a non-fact. In a survey of the literature as of 1966, Audrey Shuey found "at the preschool level there seems to be some evidence of awareness of color differences and a feeling of inferiority associated with dark skin, but at the grade school level and continuing through high school and college there is no consistent evidence of lower self esteem in Negroes; if there is a difference, it would appear to be more likely that Negroes have a *greater sense of personal worth*, rather than the reverse" (*The Testing of Negro Intelligence*, 2nd ed. [Social Science Press: NY, 1966], p. 512; ital. in original). A recent study of adolescent girls by Carol Gilligan indicated, to its author's apparent surprise, that black adolescent females enjoy *higher* self-esteem than white adolescent females. (The survey has not been published at this writing; but see Suzanne Daley, "Little Girls Lose Their Self-Esteem on Way to Adolescence, Study Finds," *The New York Times*, Jan. 9, 1991.) The evidence for low black self-esteem most commonly cited (by, among others, the Supreme Court in *Brown v. Board of Education*) is the experimentally observed preference of American black children for white dolls in the United States. This experiment has been replicated in the all-black Dominican Republic, however, and the reply that racism has eroded the self-esteem even of blacks who have little contact with whites seems ad hoc. It should be remembered that self-esteem reflects one's idea of one's own abilities and, to a decreasing extent with a sharp gradient, those of one's immediate circle. But, as Nozick has perceptively remarked (op. cit., pp. 240–44), ability is comparative; to be good at something is to be better at it than most members of a reference group. Most blacks in racially mixed societies find themselves worse than average at most socially expected cognitive tasks, like reading. Cosmopolitan blacks elsewhere know that their societies have developed none of the technology developed by Europeans and Asians. (Whether good or evil, technology requires traits not displayed by black societies.) *If* contact with whites has lowered black self-esteem, this perceived disparity in achievement is the simplest explanation.

The cause of black crime, then, is likely to be endogenous, but explanations in terms of the values reinforced by black culture are circular. Perhaps young black males are socialized to defy authority, but why does black culture produce this particular value? Even if psychosocial explanation is autonomous in the sense that its characteristic predicates are not coextensive with any finite Boolean functions of biological predicates, as anti-reductivists claim, treating it as absolutely autonomous amounts to treating society or culture as an Unmoved Mover. Any non-circular account of culture, or a specific culture, must eventually appeal to noncultural, presumably biological factors. There is obviously no genetic proneness to commit crime, since crime is socially defined. What you get when you subtract the motion of a hand from an act of forgery is a legal norm. The well-formed empirical hypothesis is that blacks are genetically more prone than whites (see n. 24) to actions which in fact tend to be criminalized in societies with legal codes. Among such actions are those intended to cause physical injury. A readiness on the part of other members of the same social group to "punish" (i.e. negatively reinforce) such behavior is apparently found even in non-human primates (see L. Ellis, "Evolution and the Nonlegal Equivalent of Aggressive Behavior," *Aggressive Behavior* 12 [1987]; 57–71).

Genetic proneness requires a mediating physiological mechanism, and this may be found in the higher average level in black males of serum testosterone, a known facilitator of aggression: see R. Ross et al, "Serum Testosterone Levels in Healthy Young Black and White Men," *Journal of the National Cancer Institute* 76 (1986): 45–48; L. Ellis and H. Nyborg: "Racial Ethnic Variations in Male Testosterone Levels: A Probable Contributor to Group Differences in Health," *Steroids* 57 (February 1992): 1–4. There is some discrepancy between the Ross et al and Ellis-Nyborg estimates of the race difference, which Ellis and Nyborg attribute to age differences in the samples. It could of course be argued that higher black levels of serum testosterone is itself an effect of the stresses of racism, but, according to Ellis and Nyborg, "recent evidence has shown that black men exhibit biochemical responses to stress that are, on average distinct from white men" (Ellis and Nyborg). These differences in response readiness are themselves presumably non-social in origin.

33. "But the remedy is necessarily designed, as all remedies are, to restore the victims of discriminatory conduct to the position they would have occupied in the absence of such conduct," *Milliken v. Bradley* (1974). A clear statement of the compensation argument is George Sher, "Justifying Reverse Discrimination in Employment,"

Philosophy and Public Affairs 4 (Winter 1975). A very recent statement of the same argument is Sterling Harwood, "Fullenwider on Affirmative Action as Compensation," Abstract, *Proceedings of the American Philosophical Association* 64 (February 1991): 68.

34. See Lino Graglia, "The 'Remedy' Rationale For Permitting Otherwise Prohibited Discrimination: How the Court Overcame the Constitution and the 1964 Civil Rights Act," *Suffolk University Law Review* 22, 3 (Fall 1988), p. 581.

35. This maneuver triggers a series of awkward questions. It forces one to ask, first, whether there are any race differences, for, absent race differences, it is hard to see why one black/white ratio in a situation is better than another. But if there are race differences, is discrimination their cause? If these differences are not caused by discrimination—if they are endogenous to the black population—they may explain the very black attainment shortfall usually attributed to white racism and used to justify affirmative action in the first place. And where do these endogenous differences come from? "Culture," we saw, is circular. But if, to avoid calling these differences biological, we recur to discrimination, we must explain how the psychological residue of racism—said to be low self-esteem, mistrust, aggrievement, poor academic attainment—can improve the university or workplace. Anyone basing affirmative action on "diversity" must answer these questions.

36. Appeal to the destruction of stereotypes is self-defeating without the assumption that less-qualified blacks will perform as well as better-qualified whites. This assumption is plausible if the usual selection criteria—grades, scores on standardized tests, and the like—are biased against blacks, but in fact these predictors are as valid for blacks as for whites; see Alexandra K. Wigdor and Wendel R. Garner, eds., *Ability Testing: Uses, Consequences and Controversies* (National Academy Press: Washington, D. C., 1982), vol. I, p. 77.

37. Ronald Dworkin's non-compensatory "utilitarian and ideal" rationale for preference (*Taking Rights Seriously* [Harvard University Press: Cambridge, Mass., 1977], pp. 223–39) parallels the reasoning of *Metro*-like decisions. Since Dworkin apparently cannot conceive a utilitarian basis for discriminating against blacks beyond the "external preferences" of whites for black frustration, he does not see the Pandora's box opened by utilitarian arguments for discriminating against whites. Suppose the presence of more than a threshold number of black children in a classroom impedes the intellectual development of white children. (There is some evidence for this: see Shuey, p. 120.) Here would be a utilitarian argument for school segregation

appealing only to the "personal" preferences of white parents and children for academic success. Black males rape almost as many white females as they do black females, and (proportion of population held constant) rape white females twice as frequently as white males do. (Applying the rates given in *Black Victims* for single offender victimization [Table 16, part 1] to the aggregated number of victimizations [Table 1], black males rape 25,000 white females annually and 26,700 black females; the corresponding numbers for white males are 105,000 and 3,300. Applying the rates for multiple offender victimizations [Table 16, part 2] to any proportion of aggregate victimizations decreases white-on-white rape and increases black-on-white rape.) Given the opportunity for unplanned contact created by residence patterns, these figures indicate a pronounced preference by black rapists for white females. If separating black men from white women would sharply decrease the incidence of rape among white women without raising its incidence among black women correspondingly, the personal preference of white women to avoid rape would be utilitarian grounds for such separation.

38. Strictly speaking, the expected morality $e(A_i)$ of any affirmative action program A_i is $\Sigma_{jk} p(B_{jk}) m(A_i/B_{jk})$, where $p(B_{jk})$ is the probability that black j has been damaged by discrimination to degree k. When B_{jk} is sufficiently near 0, $m(A_i/B_{jk})$ will fall below 0 because of the attendant injustice to whites.

39. A point made by Dworkin; see his "Why Bakke Has No Case," in R. Wasserstrom, ed. *Today's Moral Problems*, 3rd ed. (MacMillan: NY, 1985), pp. 141–42.

40. For more precise data, see Robert Linn, "Ability Testing: Individual Differences, Prediction, and Differential Prediction," in Wigdor and Garner, vol. II, pp. 335–88.

41. For evidence of a relatively accelerated black life cycle, see Rushton, pp. 1012–1013 and references therein.

Critics

Laurence Thomas

Statistical Badness*

If you know that one out of every four Acme cars is defective, then clearly: You really ought, from a rational perspective, to think twice about buying an Acme—certainly an Acme randomly chosen off of the dealer's lot. Of course, if turns out that you are friends with a dazzling mechanic, who first gives the car you chose a thorough going over and the car comes through in shining colors, then buying that particular Acme car suddenly becomes imminently more rational—perhaps even decisively so (given certain assumptions about price and so on.)

It is hardly irrational to buy an Acme that you actually know to be good, the general reputation of Acme cars notwithstanding. But, of course, if all that you have got to go on is the statistical information about the performance of Acme cars in general, then simply buying one off of the lot, without the blessings of a dazzling mechanic, is simply to act somewhat

Laurence Thomas, "Statistical Badness," *Journal of Social Philosophy* 23, no. 1 (1992): 30–41. Reprinted by permission of Blackwell Publishing Ltd.

foolishly. This is so, even if after the fact it could be demonstrated that the Acme you would have purchased would have lasted you for years. (Suppose you remember the serial number on the car (for you have a keen memory for numbers); and two years later you run into a dazzling mechanic who happens to be driving that very car.)

Now, it has seemed to various individuals, Michael Levin among them, that this line of reasoning applies with equal force to fearing any *and all* black American male youths, given the statistics on crimes committed by them. If you are a white alone (with no real self-protection skills, as is true of most people) and you encounter a black jogging in the park, it would be rational for you to take flight and run on account of being afraid of the harm that you might suffer at the hands of the jogger. Hence, it is not racist for you to do so; for presumably a person does not act racist or sexist or whatever if rationality, and only that, is the explanation for her or his behavior (though see the comment in the following paragraph). That the charge of racism does not obtain here is, obviously, what makes all of this particularly interesting. Given the usual assumptions, a white male running from another white male in a similar setting is presumably not being racist, whatever else is true. Silly?—Perhaps. Racist?—No.

Let me hasten to add here that I am well aware that the rationality of behavior is always relative to background assumptions. Normally, it is not rational for an adult to crawl as a means of moving through a hallway; but not so, if the hallway is full of smoke and the only means of escaping a fire. In times past, in an incredible display of *mauvaise foi*, some white owners of restaurants claimed that while they had no objection to serving blacks, doing so would be bad for business, since white customers would no longer patronize the restaurant. The white owners were quite right about serving blacks being bad for their business, given a racist society. Their claim constituted bad faith only because they were usually lying in saying that they, themselves, had no objections to serving blacks. Background assumptions can be morally suspect, as with the restaurant owners, or outright irrational, as is usually the case with fear of heights. The analogy—let us call it the black-car anal-

ogy—can have the force it is intended to have only if (Levin and others who would join him correctly hold that) whites are not irrational or morally suspect in their beliefs about black male youths. For the time being I want to grant that this is so.

Obviously, if the black-car analogy holds it is extremely powerful, indeed. For are you not a racist for taking flight and running even if harming you is the furthest thing from the black jogger's mind (that Acme car would actually have held up), and even though you did not take any extra steps to discern the intentions of the jogger. (Given the statistics on Acme cars, you need not consult a mechanic in order for it to be rational for you not to buy such a car.) In either case, your behavior conforms to the canons of rationality, in dealing with statistical cases.

In response, I can imagine some wanting to find fault with the statistics on crimes committed by black male youth. For instance, suppose either that crimes committed by blacks are more likely to be reported than are crimes committed by whites, or that crimes committed by blacks are more likely to meet with a conviction, or that blacks are not as likely as whites to be charged with a lesser crime. The statistics, then, would be skewed against blacks in favor of whites. Others will no doubt suppose that, owing to the history of slavery and racism in America, a special burden falls upon white people, when it comes to discerning the intentions of blacks. More generally, one may vigorously object to the idea of treating people on the basis of the group to which they belong rather than as individuals. These approaches, especially the first, might very well meet with some success. However, I shall proceed in a different way. It is important to see what does and does not follow even if we proceed by conceding too much because, in truth, things are not as bad as they are made out to be. The more that can be conceded without having to accept the conclusion, the better.

Still, I shall challenge the thesis that the statistics about crimes committed by black male youth can be indiscriminately applied to all black male youths, as is maintained by those who put forth the black-car analogy. I shall also conclude (Section IV) with an example which turns the black-car analogy on its head. For there is a way in which it turns out to be perfectly rational for whites to avoid black male youth; but this is so, not because it is always next to impossible to discern, reasonably and safely, a good black from a bad black, but because, owing to past injustices, whites may very well have ASMI with respect to blacks—that is, acquired social monitoring inadequacy.

I

The black-car analogy breaks down precisely because human beings (including black people) are not cars, and conversely. Cars are not agents; nor, a fortiori, are cars social creatures. Cars have no stake in how they are perceived by people; nor, in particular, do cars do things that bear upon how people perceive them. Whether on the dealer's lot or the street, there are no actions which cars perform (qua agent) which bear upon how they are viewed by persons. Cars do not have themselves painted in hot pink in order to come across to humans as sexy, or in dark blue in order to come across as "cool." Nor do cars insist upon leather interior so that the wealthy will purchase them. Cars do not—because they cannot—posture at all. In the language of contemporary psychology, self-presentational behavior is not just something that cars refrain from doing, it is something that they absolutely cannot do.[1] Cars lack the capacity to either exhibit self-presentational behavior or to monitor it.

By contrast, self-presentational behavior is a part of the human condition, from the tribes in primitive societies to the Queen of England. Such behavior ranges over both attire and bodily language, including posture and acts of decorum. A person's overall self-presentational behavior usually reveals a great deal about the lifestyle to which she or he is accustomed. A person's self-presentational behavior on a specific occasion usually reveals a great deal about the kind of image that the person wants to project at the moment. The latter can be out of step with the former, as when an ordinary citizen of England is invited to be a guest at the Queen's table. And when, on a given occasion, a person's self-presentational behavior is out of character, this can often be detected, especially if a number of social activities must be performed during the occasion. Remember that an important part of self-

presentational behavior is often referred to as comportment, a vague but yet ever so important notion. Two people in the finest of attire may comport themselves differently and revealingly. We suppose, and often correctly, that one is accustomed to be so attired and the other is not. Needless to say, if self-presentational behavior is a deep feature of the human condition, another such feature is that of social monitoring. A gesture, a pause, a moment of hesitation can all be so revealing precisely because human beings have considerable social monitoring skills which are often employed quite effortlessly and unreflectively. Naturally, some modes of self-presentation are culturally bound. (while visiting Paris, I once asked for "une baguette" in an admirable French accent. As I was leaving the bakery the woman asked me what country I was from. Noticing that I was stunned, she remarked "You extended your hands to receive the change." Change is definitely returned on the counter in France! As I said, a slight gesture can be ever so revealing. Interestingly, an unobservant American with a minimal command of the French language might see the French manner of returning change as one more sign that they do not like Americans or of so-called French arrogance. I have hardly denied that the self-presentational behavior of individuals can be misread.)

Suppose, then, that one is walking alone in an isolated area and one encounters a black male youth—call him Lester—coming towards one. Lester is well attired, sporting a tweed coat and a tie. It is late spring, and one can see that this is what he is wearing. According to the black-car analogy, it is reasonable to cross the street or whatever out of fear of being harmed by Lester. This is so simply on account of the fact that he is a black male youth, and the statistics indicate that there is a high probability that a black male youth will harm one.

But surely this is way too fast. To put it mildly, very few white people—in fact, very few people of any group—can report having been robbed or otherwise harmed on the street by a black male youth sporting a tweed coat and tie. As of yet, anyway, it has not been a tactic on the part of black male youth to don traditional attire of respectability as a way of catching people, white or otherwise, off guard. If so, then the statistics do not apply to black male youth across the board, as proponents of the analogy would have us believe. Not only that, there are some rather visible indicators as to whether or not the statistics might apply to the black male youth approaching one. If, nothing else, if the black male youth is dressed like Lester, then it is probably no more likely that he will harm one than if he were white. The point here, of course, is not that only black male youths in tweed coats will refrain from harming individuals traveling alone, or that this attire is the only sort of reliable and visible indicator that a person could have that such a youth will not harm an individual walking alone. The point rather is that it would be unreasonable to fear that a Lester might harm one, notwithstanding the statistics about black male youth, since those statistics most certainly do not include people like him. Hence, it is false that the statistics can be applied indiscriminately to all black male youths.

I have focused on attire because it is one of the most important modes of self-presentational behavior in Western culture, and it is a very important dimension of social monitoring, especially among strangers. (Twenty years ago, foreigners could readily spot an American youth traveling: tennis shoes and jeans. These are the attire of a great many youth nowadays.) We have the saying that "The clothes make the person." If we have nothing else concrete to go on, how a person dresses makes all the difference in the world in terms of our initial thoughts about the person. One could insist that black people are the exception to this saying. But I take it to be obvious that such a move would be just so much nonsense. As I have remarked, very few people can report having been robbed or otherwise harmed on the street by a black male youth sporting a tweed coat. There is every good reason to believe that any such black youth has quite commendable moral and professional aspirations. A sports coat, after all, is markedly different in appearance from a jacket that is an outer-garment, certainly a black leather jacket of the sort that is often associated, rightly or wrongly, with gangs—the jackets that are commonly called motorcycle jackets.

It is already overkill to insist upon both a sports coat and tie. Surely a tie would suffice. For aside from weddings and funerals, a hoodlum, black or white, in a tie has got to be an extremely rare occurrence. But never mind that.

With typical social monitoring, it is quite normal to mark the difference between a white male stranger in a tweed coat and a white male stranger in gang-like garb, and to suppose that an isolated encounter with the former is less likely to be hostile than an isolated encounter with the latter. There is absolutely nothing about black males to suggest that a different judgment is warranted between either a black male in a tweed coat and a black male in gang-like garb or, for that matter, a black male in a tweed coat and a white male in gang-like garb. The latter point cannot be over emphasized. Only racism would have people, black or white, fearing a black male youth in a tweed coat and tie more than a white male youth in boots and a black leather motorcycle jacket, given an isolated encounter with either, or fearing the tweed coat youth as much as they would fear a black with all the mannerisms and appearances of a hoodlum.

II

Let us allow that there is a class of black American male youths, call them black hoodlums, who are disposed to harm others, especially whites, and that, given the statistics, it would be rational to fear for one's safety if while walking alone one encountered a black hoodlum. What I should like to know is: How does it turn out that statistics about blacks male hoodlums apply indiscriminately to all black male youth? One answer is that it is absolutely impossible to distinguish, safely and with confidence, a decent black male youth from a black male hoodlum. But, of course, our story of Lester shows this to be patently false. In some cases, contrary to what is claimed by those who advance the black-car analogy, rudimentary social monitoring skills enable us to distinguish between the two, quite safely and confidently.

As an aside, or perhaps not, does it matter as well where one encounters a black American male youth? In the summer of 1990, an American woman traveling in Israel thought that a black American male, who walked from the guests rooms into the hotel lobby, was about to steal her pocketbook. There were no other blacks around. Was it rational for her to have had that thought? The black American called the woman on her behavior. She retorted that she had once been robbed by a black man in Harlem. He retorted that he had once been called a nigger in Harvard Yard (between Emerson Hall and Widener Library). Her response was: "I am not that kind of person." Well, consider: How many not-so-well-off people, black hoodlums or otherwise, take a holiday in Israel to relieve themselves of the monotony of poverty?

The example is less of an aside than one might have thought because it reveals the absurdity of indiscriminate generalizations, in the face of overwhelming evidence that the generalization does not hold, when it comes to imputing hostile intentions to human beings on account of their ethnicity. Why it is absurd to generalize indiscriminately is irrelevant. (I am the black American male about whom I have just written.)

If I dare say so, Michael Levin's example of a black jogger is quite revealing of rashness of thought on his part. For it is a black that one sees and takes to be a jogger—not simply a black youth running, a difference which makes all the difference in the world. It makes a difference regardless of the person's ethnicity, race, or gender. Anyone walking alone, in a somewhat isolated area, will want to determine just what is the concern of a person running towards him. The person's running will certainly be one very straightforward reason for having some concern. The observation that the person is a jogger provides a perfectly good explanation for the person's running. And notice that whether white or black, or female or male, a stranger who is running will be recognized as a jogger only if she or he is attired in a certain way: shorts, or a sweat suit, tennis shoes, and so on. No one is in the least bit inclined to suppose that a person in business attire or high-heels might be a jogger, regardless of the grace with which they manage to move. (So far, only the fictional character known as Wonder Woman is able gracefully to run in high-heels!) Recall the above remarks about self-presentational behavior. It is not simply a coincidence that no one in business attire or heels might be a jogger. The custom is that joggers wear attire suitable to that activity; and it holds regardless of race, ethnicity, or gender. What is

more, jogging attire being what it is, most joggers are not likely to be carrying any assault weapons on their person; and the jarring of jogging being what it is, most joggers would probably not carry an assault weapon, because they would find it dangerous to themselves to do so, even if they could manage to conceal it. Most joggers have innocent intentions which is precisely why most of us feel a measure of relief when, upon hearing the running of someone behind us, we turn to discover that it is the running of a jogger.

Now, it could very well be that when a black youth is attired as a jogger he is nonetheless likely to act the part of a hoodlum, with a concealed weapon and all. Once more, it could be a strategy to catch people off guard. But, as with a black youth wearing a tweed coat and tie, there is no evidence to support such a view about black youths who are joggers. This should not come as any surprise. Black joggers have not proven to be particularly adept at concealing potent weapons in socks and scanty jogging shorts; and the jarring of jogging is not race specific. Needless to say, it will not do to point to very isolated instances here, since by that line of reasoning there would be no category of people of whom all the world should not be afraid. Thus, once again, we can see that by the most rudimentary social monitoring skills, it is implausible to act as if a black jogger might harm one. As I have observed, then, Levin's example of the black jogger is quite revealing of rashness of thought. No doubt a different author would put the point less delicately.

Pulling the above remarks together in a more structured way, let me explicitly state the difference between a statistic that three out of four Acme cars do not hold up and a statistic that black hoodlums are likely to commit crimes. The first applies to all Acme cars; the second applies only to a particular group of black male youths. Regardless of the percentage of black hoodlums, it is rational to extend the statistic to all black youths only if black hoodlums cannot be reasonably and safely distinguished from other black youths, given a modicum of social monitoring skills and prevailing norms of self-presentational behavior.

To see that this is so, suppose that every so often Acme managers worked on the car assembly line, and that only the serial numbers of cars worked on by managers contain an "M." Suppose, further that, since everyone is especially careful when a manager is working on the line, these are especially durable cars, holding their own against the very best cars among other models in the same class. Now, if one has this information at one's disposal and one spots an Acme M-car in a dealer's showroom—imagine that all serial numbers are imprinted on the dash-board—it would be absurd to refrain from purchasing the car on the grounds that statistically three out of four, or four out of five, or nine out of ten Acme cars do not hold up well; for, ex hypothesi, if it's an Acme M-car, then it will hold up extremely well; and this is precisely what one knows.

To be sure, there may be a thousand and one reasons why one would rather not own an Acme car, even if it's an M-car. Perhaps one wanted a model in a better class, say, a luxury car. Or, perhaps one's reputation for being a person of good taste will be sullied, Acme cars being what they are generally. And it is certainly possible that one's attitude here is, strictly speaking, irrational in the way that fear of flying is. But having a few quirks seems to be a part of the human condition. Just so, the general statistics simply cannot be justifiably invoked as a reason for not buying an Acme M-car, no more than the statistics about airplane accidents can be justifiably invoked as a reason for being afraid of flying. Mutatis mutandis, a statistic about black hoodlums who are disposed to harm others cannot be indiscriminately applied to all black youth when there are perfectly good reasons to believe that it does not apply to all such individuals, and a modicum of social monitoring skills enable us to distinguish, reasonably and safely, blacks who are hoodlums from those who are not.

Now, an irrational and negative attitude about a car model that one does not correct in light of the facts available to one is just that—an incorrect, irrational, and negative attitude towards a particular model of car. Not so with human beings. A mistaken, negative, and irrational attitude about a group of human beings that one does not correct in light of the facts readily available to one constitute a prejudice. What would make anyone think that a statistic specifically about black hoodlums could be justifiably extended to all black youth? Similarly, what would make anyone think that with regard to readily observable appearances and behavior it was next to impossible to dis-

tinguish between black youths who are hoodlums and those who are not, especially in a society which is as mindful of appearances as ours? The latter point cuts in two different directions. One is that we customarily and quite naturally make judgments about strangers on the basis of their appearances; the other is that it is silly to think that the attire of black youths who are not hoodlums will generally resemble that of black youths who are, just as it is equally silly for any black to treat any white as if she or he might be a redneck, a paradigm example of a racist, on the grounds that generally it is rather difficult to distinguish on the basis of attire a redneck from a non-redneck. Most people think that they can readily spot a redneck.

III

It is well known that a statistic about, say, group Alpha of Gammas, claiming that they have property P, can be justifiably extended to all Gammas only if Alpha is representative of all Gammas. It is equally well known that one commits a statistical fallacy if one holds that P applies to all Gammas simply because the population of Alphas is so large that on any given chance encounter a Gamma is more likely to be an Alpha than a non-Alpha. For the truth that the population of Alphas is that large is formally compatible with the population of Gammas being divisible between Alphas and Betas, and that Betas, though few and far between, are readily distinguishable from Alphas.

Consider. Let Gamma stand for the class of Jews, Beta stand for the class of ultra-Orthodox Jews, and Alpha stand for the class of non-Orthodox Jews. The class of non-Orthodox Jews, Alpha, easily dwarfs the class of ultra-Orthodox Jews, Beta. This, however, leads to relatively little confusion as to who is and is not an ultra-Orthodox Jew—who is and is not an Alpha. Ultra-Orthodox Jews—Alphas—are recognizable at a glance; only the most obtuse of persons would have difficulty generally determining who, among Jews, is an ultra-Orthodox Jew, of distinguishing between Alphas and Betas within the class of Gammas. Suppose, then, to take a very silly example, that nine out of ten non-Orthodox Jews dine out six days a week in non-kosher restaurants. It would be very bad reasoning, indeed, to infer from that statistic that nine out of ten ultra-Orthodox Jews dine out six days a week in non-kosher restaurants, since that would surely be false.

So, as I have said, it is false as anything could be that if Alphas are Gammas, and it is true of most Gammas that they have the property P, then it follows, as a matter of logic or, at any rate, rational inference, that all Gammas have the property P, since there may be Betas of whom it is manifestly clear that they do not have the property P. And if it is manifestly clear that they do not have the property P, and if they can be reasonably and safely distinguished from those who do have P, then it cannot be rational to act as if they do have P just because most Gammas do.

When, in discussing a people, a person ignores well-known aspects of statistics while attributing negative behavioral traits to the people at large, one has to wonder about the innocence of the individual's motives. This is not to balk at rational inquiry, and thus at letting the factual chips fall where they may.[2] Rather the issue is about ignoring canons of reasoning, the ignoring of which in other domains would simply not be tolerated. Naturally, a canon of reasoning may itself be challenged, as classical two-valued logic has been challenged by, for instance, Alan Ross Anderson and Nuel D. Belnap.[3] But that is not what is being done by those who use statistics—the black-car analogy, in particular, to show that fear of any and all black youths is rationally justified. Quite the contrary, traditional techniques in statistics are being employed.

Consider an example in a related but different context. Time and time again, there are those who object to affirmative action solely on the grounds that an undesirable minority person might be hired. Whatever one thinks about affirmative action, this is a most peculiar kind of objection to a hiring practice. For there is no hiring practice known to humankind which precludes the possibility of hiring an undesirable person. By the line of reasoning of this objection, there would be no hiring at all. One can be opposed to affirmative action, and yet find this line of reasoning deplorable. What is intriguing, again, is that so many have found this line of reasoning against affirmative action incisive—people who are capable of detecting fallacies rather like a blood-hound is thought to be capable of detecting prey.

The fact that so many competent and able thinkers reason badly in a particular domain cries out for an explanation. This is especially so if the bad reasoning results in attitudes that are harmful to others, in particular, a group of people readily identifiable on the basis of their race, ethnicity, or gender. In the case at hand, the domain in question is black people. As a matter of logic, the explanation need not be racism. Perhaps the very idea of black people has certain mystical properties yet to be discovered which randomly interferes with the thinking of people who reason about blacks. Perhaps this is true when it comes to Jewish people as well, since some quite absurd reasoning about Jews tends to occur. Still, it must be acknowledged that as far as explanations go, racism is a very attractive candidate. For racism is not just a matter of having the belief that a people are inferior, but of having an invested interested in their being inferior.

Surely an objectionable bias is operating against a group Gamma: (i) when negative facts or statistics about Alpha, a sub-group of Gamma, are routinely generalized to all members of Gamma in ways that are obviously at odds with acceptable canons of reasoning, where the canons of reasoning are not themselves being challenged; or (ii) when, contrary to the facts of rudimentary social monitoring skills and prevailing norms of self-presentational behavior, it is denied that Alphas, of whom the negative facts or statistics hold true, can be reasonably and safely distinguished from Gammas who are not Alphas, and thus maintained that it is rational to act as if all Gammas are Alphas; or (iii) when assumptions of confidence which are routinely extended to persons who perform a specified set of tasks are not extended to members of Gammas who likewise perform the exact same tasks. A corollary of (iii) is this: An objectionable bias is operating against Gammas when a mistake made by virtually any member of Gamma counts more heavily against the judgment that Gamma is competent at the task at hand than do like mistakes made by others count against the judgment that they are competent. At the very least, racism is the propensity so to reason with respect to a race or an ethnicity.

Now, it is very much worth noting that in arguing that the black-car analogy fails, I have not argued that each and every black stranger encountered should be judged on an individual basis, where this is understood to mean that no relevant statistical information about the black stranger's intentions are to be employed. This view is no more plausible than is the view that each and every white stranger should be judged on an individual basis. Quite the contrary, what I have argued is that precisely what set of statistical information one employs is rightly a function of the self-presentational mode of the black stranger in question, where the focus has been upon appearances. It does not take the observational genius of an Erving Goffman to see that the facts do not support lumping blacks in jogger attire and blacks in tweed coats together with black hoodlums; accordingly, it has to be wrong to apply the statistics which hold for black hoodlums to either black joggers or blacks wearing tweed jackets. A different set of statistics apply to the former two; and those statistics warrant the conclusion that those blacks are very unlikely to harm one; for as I have noted, it simply has not been a strategy of black hoodlums to don jogging attire or tweed jackets in order to give the appearance of having innocent intentions. It has not by any means been shown that the statistics which hold for black hoodlums hold equally well for black joggers or blacks wearing tweed coats. Of course, things could change; and black hoodlums might very well see wearing suits as a wonderful way to disarm whites. But a view about how we should treat a group of people cannot be based upon a remote possibility. Black strangers should be treated on a group basis just as any other kind of stranger should be. The fallacy lies both in supposing that the only statistics about the behavior of blacks with respect to the intention to harm others, whites especially, which holds for all blacks are the statistics which hold for black hoodlums, and that blacks who are not hoodlums cannot be readily and easily distinguished from those who are, given rudimentary social monitoring skills.

I deny that all blacks, even at a distance, look alike, just as I deny that all whites from afar look alike.

Because I have not objected to treating blacks on a group basis, but only to treating them on the basis of one group, namely that of black hoodlums, the argument which I have presented is not vulnerable to a certain kind of dilemma, which goes something like this (Levin, Section VI):

P1   Affirmative action treats blacks on a group basis, not an individual basis.

P2   If it is wrong to treat blacks on a group basis, in one moral context, it is wrong to do so in another.

C3   Therefore, either affirmative action is unjustified or there is nothing wrong with responding to black strangers on a group basis.

I take it to be obvious that P2 is false, and thus the argument is unsound. Human beings are generally treated as a group in some instances, and on an individual basis in others. Although most people who do not steal treat human beings as a group, since the reasons for not stealing generally apply with equal force to all human beings, I dare say that most people treat close friends on an individual basis.

But even if P2 were true, rendering the argument sound, this argument opposing affirmative action would have no force against the argument which I have presented, since I allow that treating blacks as a group can be perfectly acceptable. What I have objected to is indiscriminately applying negative statistics and facts about a particular group of blacks to all groups of blacks—indeed, to applying any statistics and facts about one group of blacks to all blacks. And if the truth be told, even affirmative action distinguishes between groups of blacks. In universities and colleges, for instance, affirmative action has never meant indiscriminately hiring blacks off of the streets. Only blacks with certain qualifications are to be hired, a truth which holds even if it were true that blacks were being held up to a lower standard than whites; for a lower standard is not no standard at all.

IV

I should like to conclude with a number of remarks that I hope will serve to forestal misunderstanding. Along the way, I shall summarize various points.

It is not my view that treating strangers on the basis of some group is preferable to treating them as individuals. On the other hand, I realize that it is next to impossible not to invoke group categories when assessing strangers. What I have tried to show, however, is that even when we invoke group categories, things are far more complicated than defenders of the black-car analogy have allowed. Specifically, I have argued that the statistical reasoning which the analogy employs is so manifestly flawed that this creates a presumption of bias on the part of those employing the analogy. This is because even if we allow that there are black hoodlums, there is no reason whatsoever to believe either that all blacks are hoodlums or that at least some of the time, blacks who are not hoodlums cannot be reasonably and safely distinguished from those who are, given rudimentary social monitoring skills.

The last claim appealed to what I have called self-presentational behavior. Rather than rehearse those points, I should like to observe that although I focused upon attire for simplicity's sake, attire is but one of many salient features of self-presentational behavior, which human beings are quite adept at monitoring. Body language (a person's posture, gait, manner of gesticulation) is another. We are often able to determine the gender of a person simply on the basis of the manner in which the individual walks. The way in which a person comports himself is crucial to our assessment of him; and no black male youth dressed in a tweed jacket is likely to comport himself in a manner resembling a hoodlum. His gait is most unlikely to have the kind of readily recognizable swagger that is commonly associated with the "bad" black walk.[4] In fact, for any black male youth whose walk does not display this strut, whether in a tweed coat or not, the odds are very high that he is not a hoodlum.

My argument no doubt smacks of elitism. Joggers in immediately recognizable jogging outfits and wearers of sports coats are hardly the only black male youths who can be trusted not to harm others, especially white people. There are thousands upon thousands of black male youth who do not mean anyone any harm. But I have focused upon these two categories as a very swift and demonstrably clear way of securing the point that even if there are hordes of black hoodlums roaming the streets, it would be possible, with the most rudimentary of social monitoring skills, to recognize that some blacks are not black hoodlums and, therefore, that one has no reason to fear such blacks. But it is probably much closer to the truth that the average person has extensive social monitoring skills, as is evidenced by the fact that just about everyone is capable of instantly recognizing flirting behavior, for example; though such behavior is often very subtle in its display: a faint smile; a raised eyebrow. We are so adept at monitoring individuals on the basis of their self-presentational behavior, both attire and body language, that we generally do so easily and rather unreflectively.

Now, it is an unfortunate fact about life in America that (most) blacks are likely to be far more familiar with the non-verbal manner of whites than (most) whites are of blacks. For one thing, owing to the differential in power relations between blacks and whites, with the latter often having power over the former, thus generally making it in the interest of blacks to win favor with whites, it has been considerably more in the interest of blacks to grasp the non-verbal manner of whites than it has been for whites to grasp the non-verbal manner of blacks. Grasping the non-verbal behavior of whites has been very much in the self-interest of blacks. Obviously, this would be true of the interactions of any two groups of people with a substantial power differential between them, including women and men. It is true, for example, of interactions between children who have parents who abuse them. In general, whenever A is dependent upon B for A's well-being, where B is given to harmful behavior towards A, it will be far more in the interest of A—in fact, it will be a coping mechanism on A's part—to be sensitive to what might trigger hostile intentions on the part of B towards A, and to be deft at ways of diffusing B's hostile intentions towards A (whether A and B both range over individuals or both range over groups). Other things being equal, the more skillful an A is in this regard, the less harm A will suffer at the hands of B.[5] This is a particularly telling consideration against the black-car analogy. In the next two paragraphs, I shall illustrate this point with a very fanciful example.

Suppose that a group of five million well-off individuals with a very distinguishable phenotype, out of a population of 25 million, with yet a different very distinguishable phenotype, go into self-imposed isolation for twenty years, each unto her- or himself, never seeing a face for twenty years, with the results being that the five million become completely unable to read facial expressions generally. They cannot be counted upon even to see the difference between a frown and a smile, to say nothing of the difference between a look of concern or distress and a look of anger. A coy look of sexual interest is absolutely lost on them. This loss makes them easy prey for all sorts of social misfits. Clearly, it would be most rational for our former isolationists to avoid just about any meaningful public contact. What must be just as clear, however, is that the rationality of their avoiding public contact would have everything to do with their inadequacies and nothing to do with the shortcomings of Mary Q. Public as such. It is the former isolationists whose social monitoring skills are in need of serious augmentation. And if our former isolationists are beyond hope on this score, what most certainly does not follow is that Mary Q. Public can be held to blame because the poor social monitoring skills of our former isolationists make it next to impossible for them to read facial expressions. Mary Q. Public shoulders no blame even if things are somewhat awkward socially for our former isolationists because of their acquired social monitoring inadequacy (ASMI).

Because our former isolationists were easy prey for all sorts of social misfits, each adopted the strategy of having as little public contact as possible. Of course, while it would be nice if the public made things easy for our former isolationists by declaring isolationist time zones, during which times only isolationist were permitted to walk the streets, it is difficult to imagine that the public has an obligation to create such zones, let alone that the former isolationists have a right to having such zones created by the public. Nor, on account of their ASMI, would the former isolationists be justified in forcing the remaining public to adopt such time zone measures.

The significance of this fanciful example is obvious. Suppose that, owing to racism of the past, (most or a great many) whites have something like ASMI (acquired social monitoring inadequacy) with respect to blacks. This is not at all implausible; for it would seem that, in many cases, the number of social contact hours that most whites have with blacks is far less than the number of hours that they watch blacks

on television, which has certainly presented a very skewed view of blacks who are not well off.[6] Most people, black or otherwise, do not emulate the socioeconomic class of the Huxtables. At any rate, given ASMI with respect to blacks, it may very well be rational for whites to avoid any and all black male youth. But, contrary to what the black-car analogy would have us believe, the problem lies not with the behavior of black male youth, as such, but with a significant inadequacy on the part of whites. This, needless to say, turns the analogy on its head. For the rationality of not buying Acme cars is owing to the fact that serious defects in such cars is widespread—not the fact that some Acme cars have glaring defects but the average buyer is incompetent when it comes to recognizing them.

I realize that I have not shown that (most) whites have ASMI with respect to blacks. I have indicated, though, why the idea is not without considerable plausibility. That whites do have ASMI with respect to blacks is a point masterfully made by Ralph Ellison in his *Invisible Man* when he has the president of a black college scold the callow college student driver for showing the white visitors to the campus far too much. And if, as it seems, Booker T. Washington had every reason to believe that his contemporary whites would hear nothing of integrated schools, as W. E. B. DuBois called for, then it is the card of knowing-whites-better-than-they-know-blacks which he played with his brilliant hand metaphor in his Atlanta Exposition Address, when he declared that the races could be as united as the hand but as separate as the fingers. After all, the concession of separate but equal is better than no concession at all; for separate but equal is vastly superior to separate but unequal. And Washington spoke to an audience that had trouble conceding the first.[7]

In any case, I have said more than enough to make it clear that those, such as Michael Levin, who would advocate rounding up blacks, like so much cattle in the name of protecting defenseless whites from blacks, would do well to examine first whether they are in need of removing the beam from their own eye of social observation. And what a beam it must be if, in an isolated encounter, it is thought rational to fear a black male youth in a sports coat and tie or one jogging in sweat socks and running shorts just because he is black; for as I have shown, nothing else should warrant being afraid of such youth. To see black hoodlums for the undesirables that they are is, perhaps, all well and good. However, to write off all black male youth as black hoodlums is, without a very long and unobvious story, yet to be told, morally unconscionable.

Notes

* This essay is a comment upon Michael Levin's paper, "Responses to Race Differences in Crime," *Journal of Social Philosophy* 23:1 pp. 5–29. All references to Levin, parenthetical or otherwise, will be to this essay by him. I am interested in making a general response to the line of reasoning represented by Levin rather than making a point-by-point, line-by-line rebuttal of Levin's claims.

1. See, e.g., Mark Snyder, "Self-Monitoring Processes," *Advances in Experimental Social Psychology* 12: 85–128.

2. Cf. Arthur A. Jenson's claim that blacks tend to score lover than whites on I.Q. tests. So much energy was spent denying the claim that people gave little thought to what followed or, in this case, did not follow if the claim were true. What did not follow, by any stretch of reasoning is that blacks should have less moral or social standing than whites, since the thesis that blacks on average score lower than whites on average is quite compatible with their being whites who score considerably lover than blacks. And it had not been suggested that whites with low I.Q. scores should have less moral and social standing than other whites. Taking Jenson's results at face value, no doubt there are all sorts of explanations for the difference which block the inference that blacks must be deemed intellectually inferior to whites. And these should certainly be aired. Still, it is of no small significance that a certain kind of conclusion is not forthcoming even if such explanations were not to be found. Jenson paper is "How Much Can We Boost I.Q. and Scholastic Achievement?," *Harvard Educational Review* 39: 1–123.

3. *Entailment: The Logic of Relevance and Necessity* (Princeton University Press, 1975).

4. Michael Argyle, an Englishman writes: "Some cultures have distinctive styles of bodily movement. For example, black Americans walk and move with energy and style, swing and swagger in a rhythmic manner, exhibiting their bodily competence and creativity. There is an ancient stereotype that blacks have rhythm of dance, clapping, and music, though this is probably not innate." See his *Bodily Communication*, 2nd ed. (London: Metheun, 1988), p. 62. For all of his astuteness in observation, it probably did not occur to Argyle that his observations are about a particular kind of black American. The class of black Americans who does not fit the mold Argyle has in mind may very well be small. But a small class is not a nonexistent class. The class of whites who are among the true social elite is very small as well; yet, no one has any difficulty acknowledging its existence.

5. Most illuminatingly, Colin A. Ross has this to say about multiple personality disorder (MPD): "MPD is based not on defect but talent and ability. The patients have used their ability to dissociate to cope with overwhelming childhood trauma, which usually involves both physical and sexual abuse. MPD is a creative and highly effective strategy for preserving the integrity of the organism in the face of chronic catastrophic trauma. The problem with adult MPD is that, like any survival strategy gone wrong, it creates more problems than it solves" (p. 2). See his *Multiple Personality Disorder: Diagnosis, Clinical Features, and Treatment* (New York: John Wiley and Sons, 1989).

6. A person with whom I am very close observes with a certain amusement and wonderment that he watches the young boys, at the orthodox synagogue which he attends, mimicking his speaking gestures, much to the liking of their parents. The person is not sure that words can do justice to the symbolic significance of it all, stereotypes of blacks and Jews being what they are. Although ideologically Judaism is prior to race, the fact remains that these young Jewish boys are admiring a black male—not for his sports prowess or his entertainment fitness, but for his life as an intellectual. Few things will rival the positive impact that this will have upon their future interactions with other blacks.

7. Washington distinguished sharply between whites of extraordinary good will whose vision vas limited by racist ideology and whites whose vision was fueled by racist ideology I believe that, mutatis mutandis, this is a fundamental distinction that noways is often lost on groups who consider themselves oppressed. All oppressors are indiscriminately thrown in the latter camp. The distinction was drawn made by Frederic Douglass himself, a former slave who was a fearless and outspoken black critic of slavery. See *Narrative of the Life of Frederick Douglass: An Autobiography of an American Slave Written by Himself*, ed Benjamin Quarles (Harvard University Press, 1988). Needless to say, acting on the distinction requires that one has excellent social monitoring skills, as one cannot afford to be mistaken too often.

LOUIS P. POJMAN

Race and Crime
A Response to Michael Levin and Laurence Thomas

As I write this essay, the National Institute of Health has just announced the cancellation of its funding for a scholarly conference on genetic causes of criminal behavior.[1] At the same time news reports of increased violence by blacks are a common occurrence. It was recently reported by the *New York Times* that on any given day in 1991 42% of black men in the District of Columbia were enmeshed in the criminal justice system (either in prison, on parole or out on bond). Blacks, representing about 12% of the population account for over 50% of violent crimes. In 1989 Jimmy the Greek was removed from CBS for suggesting that blacks had been bred as athletes and had superior musculature to whites, and Janet Morgan, a black teacher in Malverne, Long Island, was suspended without pay for discussing Jimmy the Greek's thesis in class.[2] Similarly in 1990 Andy Rooney was suspended from CBS's "60 Minutes" for his remarks that the "wrong people" were having children.

Race is a highly charged issue in today's society and discussing racism, racial violence, and affirmative action is more likely to raise one's blood pressure than one's level of understanding. Few philosophical journals will touch the subject, let alone face the problems involved head on. Yet it is precisely philosophers who should be on the cutting edge of such social concerns, sifting through the research, evaluating the epistemic claims, discussing the merits of these ideas dispassionately, and putting matters in their larger philosophical and moral perspective. If philosophers cannot discuss these matters rationally and in good faith, who will?

It is in the light of these larger issues that the exchange between Michael Levin and Laurence Thomas needs to be addressed. First of all, this journal has distinguished itself in taking on a topic which other philosophical journals and academic publishers have been too afraid to touch. The editor and reviewers of the *Journal of Social Philosophy* deserve our praise and admiration for publishing material on such a controversial subject. What then is the issue in this debate. It is whether race should be taken into consideration in evaluating people in certain situations where information about individuals is relevantly limited.

If I understand the debate in these essays, Levin is arguing that if we don't have supplementary information, then it is *sometimes* epistemologically and morally acceptable to engage in statistical racial screening. As far as I can see Thomas accepts this conclusion but accuses Levin of not recognizing the need for whites to overcome ASMI (acquired social monitoring inadequacy) in order to distinguish between black hoodlums and the majority of law-abiding black males.

While Thomas' point is well taken, it needs to be qualified, and does not affect Levin's basic argument. In cases where there is relevant information, we normally should use our social monitoring skills to distinguish varieties of self-presenting behavior. On the face of it, Thomas seems to be assuming that Levin wouldn't accept such a principle. Note here that Thomas misrepresents Levin's initial description. On page 7 Levin describes the case he's concerned with this way:

Suppose, jogging alone after dark, you see a young black male ahead of you on the running track, *not attired in a jogging outfit, and displaying no other information-bearing trait*. Based on the statistics cited earlier, you

Louis P. Pojman, "Race and Crime: A Response to Michael Levin and Laurence Thomas," *Journal of Social Philosophy* 24, no. 1 (1993): 152–54. Reprinted by permission of Blackwell Publishing Ltd.

must set the likelihood of his being a felon at .25 (my emphasis).

But here is how Thomas represents Levin:

> Now, it could very well be that when a black youth is *attired as a jogger* he is nonetheless likely to act the part of a hoodlum, with a concealed weapon and all. Once more, it could be a strategy to catch people off guard. But, as with a black youth wearing a tweed coat and tie, there is no evidence to support such a view about black youths who are joggers. . . . As I have observed, then, Levin's example of the black jogger is quite revealing of rashness of thought. No doubt a different author would put the point less delicately (Thomas, p. 34 my emphasis).

But the rashness, alas, is not in Levin's account, but in Thomas' reading of Levin. Levin never says that the black male is a jogger and says specifically that he is *not attired in a jogging outfit*. Levin says that the youth was *displaying no other information-bearing trait*. Thomas has misread Levin and thus his criticism fails to engage the central argument. On p. 32 he accuses Levin of unqualifiedly "fearing any *and all* black American male youths," of claiming it is rational "to take flight and run on account of being afraid of the harm that you might suffer at the hands of a [black] jogger." On p. 32 he accuses Levin of arguing that it is rational to cross the street "out of fear of being harmed by Lester," a well-attired black male "sporting a tweed coat and a tie."

But all of this misses Levin's point, which is that when "no other information-bearing trait" is available, one is rationally and morally justified in reacting by doing a cost-benefit assessment of the situation and acting on it.

A variety of such situations come to mind. A woman, required to work overtime, is walking home on a poorly lit street in a high crime neighborhood. She sees a male (white or black) and runs away as fast as she can, perhaps hurting his feelings. A black visitor from New York is driving down a lonely Mississippi road (say it's 1960) and sees two pick-up trucks coming his way. Reminded of stories of blacks being accosted and harmed along such roads, he quickly turns the car and drives back to Memphis. In Detroit the school board has proposed all black male high schools because of evidence that such youth will develop better in such a

context. Affirmative Action hiring policies justify treating all blacks as deserving preferential treatment on the basis of the high probability that they have suffered disparate impact by belonging to an oppressed minority. Myrl Duncan writes in her defense of affirmative actions, "Because race was made a "morally relevant" factor for purposes of discriminating against a group, it must be "morally relevant" for purposes of compensation," and Jim Nickel similarly argues that affirmative action can be based solely on group membership for reasons of administrative convenience.[3]

Even Thomas' ASMI principle needs qualification. While we all need to improve our ability to distinguish between self-presenting behavior, we may nonculpably lack the opportunity. For example, a woman brought up in a sheltered environment may fail to understand male sex drives and be unable to distinguish men who are respectful from those who might rape her. Such a woman is in greater danger of being raped because she has a case of ASMI. But, surely, it's not her fault if she gets raped. She's the innocent victim. Likewise, with regard to whites being afraid of black males (or blacks being afraid of whites) the fault may not be the individual's, but that of those members of a race or gender who have caused a statistical probability to obtain. Hence, Thomas' claim that "the problem lies not with the behavior of black male youth, as such, but with a significant inadequacy on the part of whites" (p. 39) is not necessarily so. The principle of overcoming ASMI vis-à-vis a group is a prima facie, not an absolute, duty, which may be overridden for any number of reasons and from which a person may be excused. Normally it is far more evil for violence to be perpetrated on the innocent than for the innocent to fail to discern nonviolence.

NOTES

1. *New York Times* (front page), September 5, 1992.

2. Wayne King, "Jimmy the Greek Had Job Troubles. Now She Does," *New York Times*, December 19, 1989.

3. Myrl Duncan, "The Future of Affirmative Action: A Jurisprudential/Legal Critique" (Harvard Civil Rights-Civil Liberties Law Review 17, 1982).

PART **5**

What's Wrong with the State?

Most of the readings contained in the previous parts of this book focus primarily on questions about individual behavior: whether or not it is wrong for people to have an abortion, eat a hamburger, commit adultery, neglect their parents, and so on. This is as it should be. Most of the problems that applied ethics is concerned with are problems about how individuals should and should not behave. But there is more to ethics than problems concerning individual actions. Moral questions can be raised not just about how individuals should behave but also about how institutions should behave. A few such questions have been treated in some of the earlier parts of this book. Chapter 9, on campus sexual conduct codes, for example, and chapter 19, on campus hate speech codes, both focus on issues involving the moral rights and obligations of one particular kind of institution: colleges and universities. The purpose of Part 5 is to focus in significantly more detail on one particular, and particularly powerful, institution: the State. As with the other areas of applied ethics explored in this volume, some forms of State behavior generate relatively little moral controversy. Virtually everyone agrees that it is appropriate for a government to outlaw murder, for example, and virtually everyone agrees that it is wrong for a government to engage in genocide. But a wide range of cases lies between these extremes. We focus on a few such issues in Part 5. We begin by considering two questions about what the State may permissibly forbid its citizens from doing. Is it morally acceptable for a government to ban reproductive human cloning (chapter 23)? And would it be morally acceptable for the State to prohibit the use of tobacco (chapter 24)? We then turn to two questions about what the state may permissibly do in response to the fact that some people violate its prohibitions. In chapter 25, we consider a challenge to the generally accepted belief that it is morally permissible for the State to punish people for breaking the law. And in chapter 26, we focus on the recent controversy over whether it would be permissible for the State to authorize the use of torture, at least in cases where doing so might be necessary to prevent extremely harmful violations of the law. Finally, we conclude this book with two questions that arise when the State goes beyond its function of dealing with crime and punishment. In chapter 27, we consider the question of whether it is permissible for the State to compel its citizens to pay taxes, as many governments do, as a means of redistributing the wealth among its people. And in chapter 28, we look at the question of what obligations a particular government might have in combating a problem that extends well beyond its national borders: the problem of global warming.

institutions should refuse. A few such questions have been treated in some of the earlier p...

23

Is a Government Ban on Human Cloning Wrong?

The President's Council on Bioethics and Its Critics

Cloning involves the artificial creation of a new animal that is genetically identical to the already existing animal of which it is a clone. Cloning experiments have been carried out in recent years on a variety of nonhuman species, with mixed and widely publicized results. As a consequence, there has been an increasingly heated debate over the moral status of attempting to clone human beings, either as a means of producing embryos that might be used in various forms of biomedical research or as a means of producing new children. In July 2002, the President's Council on Bioethics released its report on this subject, "Human Cloning and Human Dignity: An Ethical Inquiry," in which it concluded that human cloning of both sorts is morally unacceptable and should not be attempted. In the excerpt from chapter 5 of the study, which serves as the featured article for this chapter, the members of the council focus specifically on reproductive cloning, what they refer to as "cloning-to-produce-children."

As might be expected of a report that was prepared and endorsed by a group of people rather than by a single author, the chapter contains a variety of distinct arguments against reproductive cloning rather than a single, self-contained argument. As a rough guide to working one's way through the various considerations that follow, however, it may help to draw a basic distinction between two kinds of arguments that the council ultimately endorses: arguments based on concerns about the safety of the procedure and arguments that are meant to apply even if the procedure could be guaranteed to be perfectly safe. The principal example of the first sort of argument is what might be called the *unethical experimentation argument*. This argument begins with the fact that the cloning of nonhuman animals has often resulted in deformed or stillborn offspring. The argument maintains that since cloning a human being is very likely to produce similar results, it should be rejected as a form of unethical experimentation on the resulting human being, what the council refers to as the "child-to-be." Examples of the second sort of argument would include what might be called the *identity argument* and the *manufacturing argument*. These arguments set aside worries about any technical imperfections that might be involved in cloning and instead ask what it would be like to be the result of a successful cloning procedure or to be the parents involved in such a procedure. The identity argument maintains that reproductive cloning would result in significant psychological harm to the cloned offspring. The council presses this concern by focusing both on the effects that cloning would have on parent-child relationships and on the effects it would have on the self-identity of the child himself. The manufacturing argument objects that cloning amounts to replacing reproduction with manufacturing, in a way that would artificially elevate a parent even further over his or her offspring and dehumanize the resulting child. These considerations do not exhaust the objections to reproductive cloning that are raised by the report, but they may provide a useful way to begin to organize and think about them.

Not every defender of cloning has responded directly to the council's report, and not every response to the report has responded to all of the arguments that the report contains. The literature in defense of the moral acceptability of cloning as a whole, however, does try to grapple with many of the objections to cloning that the council's report most prominently represents. And at least some of these objections are addressed in the critical responses that follow the excerpt from the report. Although David B. Elliott's article was written before the council's report was published, for example, the selection from his article reprinted here can readily be construed as a rebuttal to the council's manufacturing argument. Elliott argues that reproductive cloning need not be construed as manufacturing children in the way that the council understands it to be and that even if it is so construed, the same is true of many noncloning forms of reproduction that are commonly taken to be morally acceptable. And although David B. Hershenov's piece was also written before the council's report was published, much of the article excerpted here responds to the anticloning writings of Leon Kass, and Kass was the chair of the council at the time that the report was produced. Much of what Hershenov writes, in particular, can be taken as an attempted rebuttal to the identity argument that Kass had presented in some of his earlier writings and that later found their way into the council's report. In particular, Hershenov accuses Kass (and, by implication, the council as a whole) of the philosophical sin of overgeneralization: Even though some cases of reproductive cloning would have some of the objectionable features identified by the identity argument, Hershenov argues, other cases would lack those features and so reproductive cloning in those cases would not be objectionable.

QUESTIONS FOR CONSIDERATION

In thinking critically about the council's case against reproductive human cloning, readers should begin by focusing on those of arguments within the report to which Elliott and Hershenov can most readily be understood as responding.

• In what sense does cloning involve "manufacturing" a human being? Is it a strong enough sense to warrant the council's opposition to cloning? Or is Elliott right in thinking that we find such "manufacturing" acceptable in other contexts?

• What are the sources of the council's concerns about what it would be like for a person to be the result of a successful cloning procedure? Is the council right to picture these features as essential features of cloning? Or is Hershenov right to think that they would pose problems only in some cases of cloning but not in others? Could there be enough cases in which reproductive cloning would produce a well-adjusted child to justify the permissibility of the practice as a whole?

It is also important to think critically about points raised by the council that neither of the response pieces directly addresses.

• Is the council right, for example, to think that the risks of producing stillborn or deformed children are great enough to justify opposing the attempt to clone human beings? Or is society entitled to undertake such risks in pursuit of scientific progress?

• Is it better to produce no clone at all than to produce one that has significant birth defects? Why or why not? If a clone were born with a birth defect, would he have a legitimate complaint against the people who created him? Would he have been wronged by being created? Would he have been harmed? Would he have had a right not to have been created in the first place? Would he have been better off having not been created in the first place? Do such comparisons even make sense?

• Finally, readers should keep in mind that the council's report seems to point toward two distinct conclusions: that reproductive cloning is morally wrong and that the federal government should prohibit it.

Do the council's arguments entitle us to draw this second conclusion? Or is there room to agree with the council that cloning is morally wrong but to maintain that it should be legally permitted nonetheless?

FURTHER READING

Childress, James F. "Human Cloning and Human Dignity: The Report of the President's Council on Bioethics." *Hastings Center Report* 33, no. 3 (May–June 2003): 15–18.

Glannon, Walter. "The Ethics of Human Cloning." *Public Affairs Quarterly* 12, no. 3 (1998): 287–305.

Kass, Leon, and James Q. Wilson. *The Ethics of Human Cloning*. Washington, D.C.: American Enterprise Institute, 1998.

Lane, Robert. "Safety, Identity and Consent: A Limited Defense of Reproductive Human Cloning." *Bioethics* 20, no. 3 (June 2006): 125–35.

Levy, Neil, and Mianna Lotz. "Reproductive Cloning and a (Kind of) Genetic Fallacy." *Bioethics* 19, no. 3 (June, 2005): 232–50.

Sparrow, Robert. "Cloning, Parenthood, and Genetic Relatedness." *Bioethics* 20, no. 6 (November 2006): 308–18.

PRESIDENT'S COUNCIL ON BIOETHICS

Human Cloning and Human Dignity: An Ethical Inquiry

THE CASE AGAINST CLONING-TO-PRODUCE-CHILDREN

A. The Ethics of Human Experimentation

...We begin with concerns regarding the safety of the cloning procedure and the health of the participants. We do so for several reasons. First, these concerns are widely, indeed nearly unanimously, shared. Second, they lend themselves readily to familiar modes of ethical analysis—including concerns about harming the innocent, protecting human rights, and ensuring the consent of all research subjects. Finally, if carefully considered, these concerns begin to reveal the important ethical principles that must guide our broader assessment of cloning-to-produce-children. They suggest that human beings, unlike inanimate matter or even animals, are in some way *inviolable*, and therefore challenge us to reflect on what it is *about* human beings that makes them inviolable, and

"Human Cloning and Human Dignity: An Ethical Inquiry," from The President's Council on Bioethics (July, 2002)

whether cloning-to-produce-children threatens these distinctly human goods.

In initiating this analysis, there is perhaps no better place to start than the long-standing international practice of regulating experiments on human subjects. After all, the cloning of a human being, as well as all the research and trials required before such a procedure could be expected to succeed, would constitute experiments on the individuals involved—the egg donor, the birthing mother, and especially the child-to-be. It therefore makes sense to consider the safety and health concerns that arise from cloning-to-produce-children in light of the widely shared ethical principles that govern experimentation on human subjects.

Since the Second World War, various codes for the ethical conduct of human experimentation have been adopted around the world. These codes and regulations were formulated in direct response to serious ethical lapses and violations committed by research scientists against the rights and dignity of individual human beings. Among the most important and widely accepted documents to emerge were the Nuremberg Code of 1947[1] and the Helsinki Declaration of 1964.[2] Influential in the United States is also the Belmont Report, published in 1978 by the National Commission for the Protection of Human Subjects of Biomedical and Behavioral Research.[3]

The Nuremberg Code laid out ten principles for the ethical conduct of experiments, focusing especially on voluntary consent of research subjects, the principle that experiments should be conducted only with the aim of providing a concrete good for society that is unprocurable by other methods, and with the avoidance of physical or mental harm. The Helsinki Declaration stated, among other things, that research should be undertaken only when the prospective benefit clearly outweighs the expected risk, when the research subject has been fully informed of all risks, and when the research-subject population is itself likely to benefit from the results of the experiment.

Finally, the Belmont Report proposed three basic ethical principles that were to guide the treatment of human subjects involved in scientific research.

The first of these is *respect for persons*, which requires researchers to acknowledge the autonomy and individual rights of research subjects and to offer special protection to those with diminished autonomy and capacity. The second principle is *beneficence*. Scientific research must not only refrain from harming those involved but must also be aimed at helping them, or others, in concrete and important ways. The third principle is *justice*, which involves just distribution of potential benefits and harms and fair selection of research subjects. When applied, these general principles lead to both a requirement for informed consent of human research subjects and a requirement for a careful assessment of risks and benefits before proceeding with research. Safety, consent, and the rights of research subjects are thus given the highest priority.

It would be a mistake to view these codes in narrow or procedural terms, when in fact they embody society's profound sense that human beings are not to be treated as experimental guinea pigs for scientific research. Each of the codes was created to address a specific disaster involving research science—whether the experiments conducted by Nazi doctors on concentration camp prisoners, or the Willowbrook scandal in which mentally retarded children were infected with hepatitis, or the Tuskegee scandal in which underprivileged African-American men suffering from syphilis were observed but not treated by medical researchers—and each of the codes was an attempt to defend the inviolability and dignity of all human beings in the face of such threats and abuses. More simply stated, the codes attempt to defend the weak against the strong and to uphold the equal dignity of all human beings. In taking up the application of these codes to the case of cloning-to-produce-children, we would suggest that the proper approach is not simply to discover specific places where human cloning violates this or that stipulation of this or that code, but to grapple with how such cloning offends the spirit of these codes and what they seek to defend.

The ethics of research on human subjects suggest three sorts of problems that would arise in cloning-to-produce-children: (1) problems of safety; (2) a special problem of consent; and (3) problems of exploitation of women and the just distribution of risk. We shall consider each in turn.

1. Problems of Safety

First, cloning-to-produce-children is not now safe. Concerns about the safety of the individuals involved in a cloning procedure are shared by nearly everyone on all sides of the cloning debate. Even most proponents of cloning-to-produce-children generally qualify their support with a caveat about the safety of the procedure. Cloning experiments in other mammals strongly suggest that cloning-to-produce-children is, at least for now, far too risky to attempt.[4] Safety concerns revolve around potential dangers to the cloned child, as well as to the egg donor and the woman who would carry the cloned child to birth.

(a) Risks to the child. Risks to the cloned child-to-be must be taken especially seriously, both because they are most numerous and most serious and because—unlike the risks to the egg donor and birth mother—they cannot be accepted knowingly and freely by the person who will bear them. In animal experiments to date, only a small percentage of implanted clones have resulted in live births, and a substantial portion of those live-born clones have suffered complications that proved fatal fairly quickly. Some serious though nonfatal abnormalities in cloned animals have also been observed, including substantially increased birth-size, liver and brain defects, and lung, kidney, and cardiovascular problems.[5]

Longer-term consequences are of course not known, as the oldest successfully cloned mammal is only six years of age. Medium-term consequences, including premature aging, immune system failure, and sudden unexplained death, have already become apparent in some cloned mammals. Some researchers have also expressed concerns that a donor nucleus from an individual who has lived for some years may have accumulated genetic mutations that—if the nucleus were used in the cloning of a new human life—may predispose the new individual to certain sorts of cancer and other diseases.[6]

(b) Risks to the egg donor and the birth mother. Accompanying the threats to the cloned child's health and well-being are risks to the health of the egg donors. These include risks to her future reproductive health caused by the hormonal treatments required for egg retrieval and general health risks resulting from the necessary superovulation.[7]

Animal studies also suggest the likelihood of health risks to the woman who carries the cloned fetus to term. The animal data suggest that late-term fetal losses and spontaneous abortions occur substantially more often with cloned fetuses than in natural pregnancies. In humans, such late-term fetal losses may lead to substantially increased maternal morbidity and mortality. In addition, animal studies have shown that many pregnancies involving cloned fetuses result in serious complications, including toxemia and excessive fluid accumulation in the uterus, both of which pose risks to the pregnant animal's health.[8] In one prominent cattle cloning study, just under one-third of the pregnant cows died from complications late in pregnancy.[9]

Reflecting on the dangers to birth mothers in animal cloning studies, the National Academy report concluded:

> Results of animal studies suggest that reproductive cloning of humans would similarly pose a high risk to the health of both fetus or infant and mother and lead to associated psychological risks for the mother as a consequence of late spontaneous abortions or the birth of a stillborn child or a child with severe health problems.[10]

(c) An abiding moral concern. Because of these risks, there is widespread agreement that, at least for now, attempts at cloning-to-produce-children would constitute unethical experimentation on human subjects and are therefore impermissible. These safety considerations were alone enough to lead the National Bioethics Advisory Commission in June 1997 to call for a temporary prohibition of human cloning-to-produce-children. Similar concerns, based on almost five more years of animal experimentation, convinced the panel of the National Academy of Sciences in January 2002 that the United States should ban such cloning for at least five years.

Past discussions of this subject have often given the impression that the safety concern is a purely temporary one that can be allayed in the near future, as scientific advances and improvements in technique reduce the risks to an ethically acceptable level. But this impression is mistaken, for considerable safety risks are likely to be enduring, perhaps permanent. If so, there will be abiding ethical difficulties *even with efforts aimed at making human cloning safe*.

The reason is clear: experiments to develop new reproductive technologies are necessarily intergenerational, undertaken to serve the reproductive desires of prospective parents but practiced also and always upon prospective children. Any such experiment unavoidably involves risks to the child-to-be, a being who is both the *product* and also the most vulnerable human *subject* of the research. Exposed to risk during the extremely sensitive life-shaping processes of his or her embryological development, any child-to-be is a singularly vulnerable creature, one maximally deserving of protection against risk of experimental (and other) harm. If experiments to learn how to clone a child are ever to be ethical, the degree of risk to that child-to-be would have to be extremely low, arguably no greater than for children-to-be who are conceived from union of egg and sperm. It is extremely unlikely that this moral burden can be met, not for decades if at all.

In multiple experiments involving six of the mammalian species cloned to date, more than 89 percent of the cloned embryos transferred to recipient females did not come to birth, and many of the live-born cloned animals are or become abnormal.[11] If success means achieving normal and healthy development not just at birth but throughout the life span, there is even less reason for confidence. The oldest cloned mammal (Dolly) is only six years old and has exhibited unusually early arthritis. The reasons for failure in animal cloning are not well understood. Also, no nonhuman primates have been cloned. It will be decades (at least) before we could obtain positive evidence that cloned primates might live a normal healthy (primate) life.

Even a high success rate in animals would not suffice by itself to make human trials morally acceptable. In addition to the usual uncertainties in jumping the gap from animal to human research, cloning is likely to present particularly difficult problems of interspecies difference. Animal experiments have already shown substantial differences in the reproductive success of identical cloning techniques used in different species.[12] If these results represent species-specific differences in, for example, the ease of epigenetic reprogramming and imprinting of the donor DNA, the magnitude of the risks to the child-to-be of the first human cloning experiments would be unknown and potentially large, no matter how much success had been achieved in animals. There can in principle be no direct experimental evidence sufficient for assessing the degree of such risk.

Can a highly reduced risk of deformity, disease, and premature death in animal cloning, coupled with the inherently unpredictable risk of moving from animals to humans, ever be low enough to meet the ethically acceptable standard set by reproduction begun with egg and sperm? The answer, as a matter of necessity, can never be better than "Just possibly." Given the severity of the possible harms involved in human cloning, and given that those harms fall on the very vulnerable child-to-be, such an answer would seem to be enduringly inadequate.

Similar arguments, it is worth noting, were made before the first attempts at human in vitro fertilization. People suggested that it would be unethical experimentation even to try to determine whether IVF could be safely done. And then, of course, IVF was accomplished. Eventually, it became a common procedure, and today the moral argument about its safety seems to many people beside the point. Yet the fact of success in that case does not establish precedent in this one, nor does it mean that the first attempts at IVF were not in fact unethical experiments upon the unborn, despite the fortunate results.

Be this as it may, the case of cloning is genuinely different. With IVF, assisted fertilization of egg by sperm immediately releases a developmental process, linked to the sexual union of the two gametes, that nature has selected over millions of years for the entire mammalian line. But in cloning experiments to produce children, researchers would be transforming a sexual system into an asexual one, a change that requires major and "unnatural" reprogramming of donor DNA if there is to be any chance of success. They are neither enabling nor restoring a natural process, and the alterations involved are such that success in one species cannot be presumed to predict success in another. Moreover, any new somatic mutations in the donor cell's chromosomal DNA would be passed along to the cloned child-to-be and its offspring. Here we can see even more the truly intergenerational character of cloning experimentation, and this should justify placing the highest moral burden of persuasion on those who would like to proceed with efforts to make cloning safe for producing children. (By reminding us of the need to protect the lives and well-being of our children and our children's children, this broader analysis of the safety question points toward larger moral objections to producing cloned children, objections that we shall consider shortly.)

It therefore appears to us that, given the dangers involved and the relatively limited goods to be gained from cloning-to-produce-children, conducting experiments in an effort to make cloning-to-produce-children safer would itself be an unacceptable violation of the norms of the ethics of research. There seems to be no ethical way to try to discover whether cloning-to-produce-children can become safe, now or in the future.

2. A Special Problem of Consent

A further concern relating to the ethics of human research revolves around the question of consent. Consent from the cloned child-to-be is of course impossible to obtain, and because no one consents to his or her own birth, it may be argued that concerns about consent are misplaced when applied to the unborn. But the issue is not so simple. For reasons having to do both with the safety concerns raised above and with the social, psychological, and moral concerns to be addressed below, an attempt to clone a human being would potentially expose a cloned individual-to-be to great risks of harm, quite distinct

from those accompanying other sorts of reproduction. Given the risks, and the fact that consent cannot be obtained, the ethically correct choice may be to avoid the experiment. The fact that those engaged in cloning cannot ask an unconceived child for permission places a burden on the cloners, not on the child. Given that anyone considering creating a cloned child must know that he or she is putting a newly created human life at exceptional risk, the burden on the would-be cloners seems clear: they must make a compelling case why the procedure should not be avoided altogether.

Reflections on the purpose and meaning of seeking consent support this point. Why, after all, does society insist upon consent as an essential principle of the ethics of scientific research? Along with honoring the free will of the subject, we insist on consent to protect the weak and the vulnerable, and in particular to protect them from the powerful. It would therefore be morally questionable, at the very least, to choose to impose potentially grave harm on an individual, especially in the very act of giving that individual life. Giving existence to a human being does not grant one the right to maim or harm that human being in research.

3. Problems of Exploitation of Women and Just Distribution of Risk

Cloning-to-produce-children may also lead to the exploitation of women who would be called upon to donate oocytes. Widespread use of the techniques of cloning-to-produce-children would require large numbers of eggs. Animal models suggest that several hundred eggs may be required before one attempt at cloning can be successful. The required oocytes would have to be donated, and the process of making them available would involve hormonal treatments to induce superovulation. If financial incentives are offered, they might lead poor women especially to place themselves at risk in this way (and might also compromise the voluntariness of their "choice" to make donations). Thus, research on cloning-to-produce-children could impose disproportionate burdens on women, particularly low-income women.

4. Conclusion

These questions of the ethics of research—particularly the issue of physical safety—point clearly to the conclusion that cloning-to-produce-children is unacceptable. In reaching this conclusion, we join the National Bioethics Advisory Commission and the National Academy of Sciences. But we go beyond the findings of those distinguished bodies in also pointing to the dangers that will *always* be inherent in the very process of trying to make cloning-to-produce-children safer. On this ground, we conclude that the problem of safety is not a temporary ethical concern. It is rather an enduring moral concern that might not be surmountable and should thus preclude work toward the development of cloning techniques to produce children. In light of the risks and other ethical concerns raised by this form of human experimentation, *we therefore conclude that cloning-to-produce-children should not be attempted.*

For some people, the discussion of ethical objections to cloning-to-produce-children could end here. Our society's established codes and practices in regard to human experimentation by themselves offer compelling reasons to oppose indefinitely attempts to produce a human child by cloning. But there *is* more to be said.

First, many people who are repelled by or opposed to the prospect of cloning human beings are concerned not simply or primarily because the procedure is unsafe. To the contrary, their objection is to the use of a *perfected* cloning technology and to a society that would embrace or permit the production of cloned children. The ethical objection based on lack of safety is not really an objection to cloning *as such*. Indeed, it may in time become a vanishing objection should people be allowed to proceed—despite insuperable ethical objections such as the ones we have just offered—with experiments to perfect the technique. Should this occur, the ethical assessment of cloning-to-produce-children would need to address itself to the merits (and demerits) of cloning itself, beyond the safety questions tied to the techniques used to produce cloned children. Thus, anticipating the possibility of a perfected and usable technology, it is important to delineate the case against the practice itself.

Moreover, because the Council is considering cloning within a broad context of present and projected techniques that can affect human procreation or alter the genetic makeup of our children, it is important that we consider the full range and depth of ethical issues raised by such efforts.

How should these issues be raised, and within what moral framework? Some, but by no means all, of the deepest moral concerns connected to human cloning could be handled by developing a richer consideration of the ethics of human experimentation. Usually—and regrettably—we apply the ethical principles governing research on human subjects in a utilitarian spirit, weighing benefits versus harms, and moreover using only a very narrow notion of "harm." The calculus that weighs benefits versus harms too often takes stock only of bodily harm or violations of patient autonomy, though some serious efforts have been made in recent years to consider broader issues. In addition, we often hold a rather narrow view of what constitutes "an experiment." Yet cloning-to-produce-children would be a "human experiment" in many senses, and risks of bodily harm and inadequate consent do not exhaust the ways in which cloning might do damage. As we have described, cloning-to-produce-children would be a *biological experiment*—with necessary uncertainties about the safety of the technique and the possibility of physical harm. But it would also be an *experiment in human procreation*—substituting asexual for sexual reproduction and treating children not as gifts but as our self-designed products. It would be an *experiment in human identity*—creating the first human beings to inherit a genetic identity lived in advance by another. It would be an *experiment in genetic choice and design*—producing the first children whose entire genetic makeup was selected in advance. It would be an *experiment in family and social life*—altering the relationships within the family and between the generations, for example, by turning "mothers" into "twin sisters" and "grandparents" into "parents," and by having children asymmetrically linked biologically to only one parent. And it would represent a *social experiment* for the entire society, insofar as the society accepted, even if only as a minority practice, this unprecedented and novel mode of producing our offspring.

By considering these other ways in which cloning would constitute an experiment, we could enlarge our analysis of the ethics of research with human subjects to assess possible *nonbodily* harms of cloning-to-produce-children. But valuable as this effort might be, we have not chosen to proceed in this way. Not all the important issues can be squeezed into the categories of harms and benefits. People can be mistreated or done an injustice whether they know it or not and quite apart from any experienced harm. Important human goods can be traduced, violated, or sacrificed without being registered in anyone's catalogue of harms. The form of bioethical inquiry we are attempting here will make every effort not to truncate the moral meaning of our actions and practices by placing them on the Procrustean bed of utilitarianism. To be sure, the ethical principles governing human research are highly useful in efforts to protect vulnerable individuals against the misconduct or indifference of the powerful. But a different frame of reference is needed to evaluate the human meaning of innovations that may affect the lives and humanity of everyone, vulnerable or not.

Of the arguments developed below, some are supported by most Council Members, while other arguments are shared by only some Members. Even among the arguments they share, different Members find different concerns to be weightier. Yet we all believe that the arguments presented in the sections that follow are worthy of consideration in the course of trying to assess *fully* the ethical issues involved. We have chosen to err on the side of inclusion rather than exclusion of arguments because we acknowledge that concerns now expressed by only a few may turn out in the future to be more important than those now shared by all. Our fuller assessment begins with an attempt to fathom the deepest meaning of human procreation and thus necessarily the meaning of raising children. Our analysis will then move onto questions dealing with the effects of cloning on individuals, family life, and society more generally.

B. The Human Context: Procreation and Child-Rearing

Were it to take place, cloning-to-produce-children would represent a challenge to the nature of human procreation and child-rearing. Cloning is, of course, not only a means of procreation. It is also a technology, a human experiment, and an exercise of freedom, among other things. But cloning would be most unusual, consequential, and most morally important as a new way of bringing children into the world and a new way of viewing their moral significance.

In *Chapter One* we outlined some morally significant features of human procreation and raised questions about how these would be altered by human cloning. We will now attempt to deepen that analysis, and begin with the salient fact that a child *is not made, but begotten*. Procreation is not making but the outgrowth of doing. A man and woman give themselves in love to each other, setting their projects aside in order to do just that. Yet a child results, arriving on its own, mysterious, independent, yet the fruit of the embrace. Even were the child wished for, and consciously so, he or she is the issue of their love, not the product of their wills; the man and woman in no way produce or choose a *particular* child, as they might buy a particular car. Procreation can, of course, be assisted by human ingenuity (as with IVF). In such cases, it may become harder to see the child solely as a gift bestowed upon the parents' mutual self-giving and not to some degree as a product of their parental wills. Nonetheless, because it is still sexual reproduction, the children born with the help of IVF begin—as do all other children—with a certain genetic independence of their parents. They replicate neither their fathers nor their mothers, and this is a salutary reminder to parents of the independence they must one day grant their children and for which it is their duty to prepare them.

Gifts and blessings we learn to accept as gratefully as we can. Products of our wills we try to shape in accord with our desires. Procreation as traditionally understood invites acceptance, rather than reshaping, engineering, or designing the next generation. It invites us to accept limits to our control over the next generation. It invites us even—to put the point most strongly—to think of the child as one who is not simply our own, our possession. Certainly, it invites us to remember that the child does not exist simply for the happiness or fulfillment of the parents.

To be sure, parents do and must try to form and mold their children in various ways as they inure them to the demands of family life, prepare them for adulthood, and initiate them into the human community. But, even then, it is only our sense that these children are not our possessions that makes such parental nurture which always threatens not to nourish but to stifle the child—safe.

This concern can be expressed not only in language about the relation between the generations but also in the language of equality. The things we make are not just like ourselves; they are the products of our wills, and their point and purpose are ours to determine. But a begotten child comes into the world just as its parents once did, and is therefore their equal in dignity and humanity.

The character of sexual procreation shapes the lives of children as well as parents. By giving rise to genetically new individuals, sexual reproduction imbues all human beings with a sense of individual identity and of occupying a place in this world that has never belonged to another. Our novel genetic identity symbolizes and foreshadows the unique, never-to-be-repeated character of each human life. At the same time, our emergence from the union of two individuals, themselves conceived and generated as we were, locates us immediately in a network of relation and natural affection.

Social identity, like genetic identity, is in significant measure tied to these biological facts. Societies around the world have structured social and economic responsibilities around the relationship between the generations established through sexual procreation, and have developed modes of child-rearing, family responsibility, and kinship behavior that revolve around the natural facts of begetting.

There is much more to be said about these matters, and they are vastly more complicated than we have indicated. There are, in addition, cultural differences in the way societies around the world regard the human significance of procreation or the way children are to be regarded and cared for. Yet we have said enough to indicate that the character and nature of human procreation matter deeply. They affect human life in endless subtle ways, and they shape families and communities. A proper regard for the profundity of human procreation (including child-rearing and parent-child relations) is, in our view, indispensable for a full assessment of the ethical implications of cloning-to-produce-children.

C. Identity, Manufacture, Eugenics, Family, and Society

Beyond the matter of procreation itself, we think it important to examine the possible psychological and emotional state of individuals produced by cloning, the well-being of their families, and the likely effects on society of permitting human cloning. These concerns would apply even if cloning-to-produce-children were conducted on a small scale; and they would apply in even the more innocent-seeming cloning scenarios, such as efforts to overcome infertility or to avoid the risk of genetic disease. Admittedly, these matters are necessarily speculative, for empirical evidence is lacking. Nevertheless, the importance of the various goods at stake justifies trying to think matters through in advance.

Keeping in mind our general observations about procreation, we proceed to examine a series of specific ethical issues and objections to cloning human children: (1) problems of identity and individuality; (2) concerns regarding manufacture; (3) the prospect of a new eugenics; (4) troubled family relations; and (5) effects on society.

1. Problems of Identity and Individuality

Cloning-to-produce-children could create serious problems of identity and individuality. This would be especially true if it were used to produce multiple "copies" of any single individual, as in one or another of the seemingly far-fetched futuristic scenarios in which cloning is often presented to the popular imagination. Yet questions of identity and individuality could arise even in small-scale cloning, even in the (supposedly) most innocent of cases, such as the production of a single cloned child within an intact family. Personal identity is, we would emphasize, a complex and subtle psychological phenomenon, shaped ultimately by the interaction of many diverse factors. But it does seem reasonably clear that cloning would at the very least present a unique and possibly disabling challenge to the formation of individual identity.

Cloned children may experience concerns about their distinctive identity not only because each will be genetically essentially identical to another human being, but also because they may resemble in appearance younger versions of the person who is their "father" or "mother." Of course, our genetic makeup does not by itself determine our identities. But our genetic uniqueness is an important source of our sense of who we are and how we regard ourselves. It is an emblem of independence and individuality. It endows us with a sense of life as a never-before-enacted possibility. Knowing and feeling that nobody has previously possessed our particular gift of natural characteristics, we go forward as genetically unique individuals into relatively indeterminate futures.

These new and unique genetic identities are rooted in the natural procreative process. A cloned child, by contrast, is at risk of living out a life overshadowed in important ways by the life of the "original"—general appearance being only the most obvious. Indeed, one of the reasons some people are interested in cloning is that the technique promises to produce in each case a particular individual whose traits and characteristics are already known. And however much or little one's genotype *actually* shapes one's natural capacities, it could mean a great deal to an individual's *experience* of life and the expectations that those who cloned him or her might have. The cloned child may be constantly compared to "the original," and may consciously or unconsciously hold himself or herself up to the genetic twin that came before. If the two individuals turned out to lead similar lives, the cloned person's achievements may be seen as derivative. If, as is perhaps more likely, the cloned person departed from the life of his or her progenitor, this very fact could be a source of constant scrutiny, especially in circumstances in which parents produced their cloned child to become something in particular. Living up to parental hopes and expectations is frequently a burden for children; it could be a far greater burden for a cloned individual. The shadow of the cloned child's "original" might be hard for the child to escape, as would

parental attitudes that sought in the child's very existence to replicate, imitate, or replace the "original."

It may reasonably be argued that genetic individuality is not an indispensable human good, since identical twins share a common genotype and seem not to be harmed by it. But this argument misses the context and environment into which even a single human clone would be born. Identical twins have as progenitors two biological parents and are born together, before either one has developed and shown what his or her potential—natural or otherwise—may be. Each is largely free of the burden of measuring up to or even knowing in advance the genetic traits of the other, because both begin life together and neither is yet known to the world. But a clone is a genetic near-copy of a person who is already living or has already lived. This might constrain the clone's sense of self in ways that differ in kind from the experience of identical twins. Everything about the predecessor—from physical height and facial appearance, balding patterns and inherited diseases, to temperament and native talents, to shape of life and length of days, and even cause of death—will appear before the expectant eyes of the cloned person, always with at least the nagging concern that there, notwithstanding the grace of God, go I. The crucial matter, again, is not simply the truth regarding the extent to which genetic identity actually shapes us—though it surely does shape us to some extent. What matters is the cloned individual's *perception* of the significance of the "precedent life" and the way that perception cramps and limits a sense of self and independence.

2. Concerns Regarding Manufacture

The likely impact of cloning on identity suggests an additional moral and social concern: the transformation of human procreation into human manufacture, of begetting into making. By using the terms "making" and "manufacture" we are not claiming that cloned children would be artifacts made altogether "by hand" or produced in factories. Rather, we are suggesting that they would, like other human "products," be brought into being in accordance with some pre-selected genetic pattern or design, and therefore in some sense "made to order" by their producers or progenitors.

Unlike natural procreation—or even most forms of assisted reproduction—cloning-to-produce-children would set out to create a child with a very particular genotype: namely, that of the somatic cell donor. Cloned children would thus be the first human beings whose entire genetic makeup is selected in advance. True, selection from among existing genotypes is not yet design of new ones. But the principle that would be established by human cloning is both far-reaching and completely novel: parents, with the help of science and technology, may determine in advance the genetic endowment of their children. To this point, parents have the right and the power to decide *whether* to have a child. With cloning, parents acquire the power, and presumably the right, to decide *what kind* of a child to have. Cloning would thus extend the power of one generation over the next—and the power of parents over their offspring—in ways that open the door, unintentionally or not, to a future project of genetic manipulation and genetic control.

Of course, there is no denying that we have already taken steps in the direction of such control. Preimplantation genetic diagnosis of embryos and prenatal diagnosis of fetuses—both now used to prevent the birth of individuals carrying genes for genetic diseases—reflect an only conditional acceptance of the next generation. With regard to *positive* selection for desired traits, some people already engage in the practice of sex selection, another example of conditional acceptance of offspring. But these precedents pale in comparison to the degree of control provided by cloning and, in any case, do not thereby provide a license to proceed with cloning. It is far from clear that it would be wise to proceed still farther in our attempts at control.

The problem with cloning-to-produce-children is not that artificial technique is used to assist reproduction. Neither is it that genes are being manipulated. We raise no objection to the use of the coming genetic technologies to treat individuals with genetic diseases, even in utero—though there would be issues regarding the protection of human subjects in research and the need to find boundaries between

therapy and so-called enhancement (of this, more below). The problem has to do with the control of the entire genotype and the production of children to selected specifications.

Why does this matter? It matters because human dignity is at stake. In natural procreation, two individuals give life to a new human being whose endowments are not shaped deliberately by human will, whose being remains mysterious, and the open-endedness of whose future is ratified and embraced. Parents beget a child who enters the world exactly as they did—as an unmade gift, not as a product. Children born of this process stand equally beside their progenitors as fellow human beings, not beneath them as made objects. In this way, the uncontrolled beginnings of human procreation endow each new generation and each new individual with the dignity and freedom enjoyed by all who came before.

Most present forms of assisted reproduction imitate this natural process. While they do begin to introduce characteristics of manufacture and industrial technique, placing nascent human life for the first time in human hands, they do not control the final outcome. The end served by IVF is still the same as natural reproduction—the birth of a child from the union of gametes from two progenitors. Reproduction with the aid of such techniques still implicitly expresses a willingness to accept as a gift the product of a process we do not control. In IVF children emerge out of the same mysterious process from which their parents came, and are therefore not mere creatures of their parents.

By contrast, cloning-to-produce-children—and the forms of human manufacture it might make more possible in the future—seems quite different. Here, the process begins with a very specific final product in mind and would be tailored to produce that product. Even were cloning to be used solely to remedy infertility, the decision to clone the (sterile) father would be a decision, willy-nilly, that the child-to-be should be the near-twin of his "father." Anyone who would clone merely to ensure a "biologically related child" would be dictating a very specific form of biological relation: genetic virtual identity. In every case of cloning-to-produce-children, scientists or parents would set out to produce specific individuals for particular reasons. The procreative process could come to be seen increasingly as a means of meeting specific ends, and the resulting children would be products of a designed manufacturing process, products over whom we might think it proper to exercise "quality control." Even if, in any given case, we were to continue to think of the cloned child as a gift, *the act itself teaches a different lesson*, as the child becomes the continuation of a parental project. We would learn to receive the next generation less with gratitude and surprise than with control and mastery.

One possible result would be the industrialization and commercialization of human reproduction. Manufactured objects become commodities in the marketplace, and their manufacture comes to be guided by market principles and financial concerns. When the "products" are human beings, the "market" could become a profoundly dehumanizing force. Already there is commerce in egg donation for IVF, with ads offering large sums of money for egg donors with high SAT scores and particular physical features.

The concerns expressed here do not depend on cloning becoming a widespread practice. The introduction of the terms and ideas of production into the realm of human procreation would be troubling regardless of the scale involved; and the adoption of a market mentality in these matters could blind us to the deep moral character of bringing forth new life. Even were cloning children to be rare, the moral harms to a society that accepted it could be serious.

3. Prospect of a New Eugenics

For some of us, cloning-to-produce-children also raises concerns about the prospect of eugenics or, more modestly, about genetic "enhancement." We recognize that the term "eugenics" generally refers to attempts to improve the genetic constitution of a particular political community or of the human race through general policies such as population control, forced sterilization, directed mating, or the like. It does not ordinarily refer to actions of particular individuals attempting to improve the genetic endowment of their own descendants. Yet, although

cloning does not in itself point to public policies by which the state would become involved in directing the development of the human gene pool, this might happen in illiberal regimes, like China, where the government already regulates procreation. And, in liberal societies, cloning-to-produce-children could come to be used privately for individualized eugenic or "enhancement" purposes: in attempts to alter (with the aim of improving) the genetic constitution of one's own descendants—and, indirectly, of future generations.

Some people, in fact, see enhancement as the major purpose of cloning-to-produce-children. Those who favor eugenics and genetic enhancement were once far more open regarding their intentions to enable future generations to enjoy more advantageous genotypes. Toward these ends, they promoted the benefits of cloning: escape from the uncertain lottery of sex, controlled and humanly directed reproduction. In the present debate about cloning-to-produce-children, the case for eugenics and enhancement is not made openly, but it nonetheless remains an important motivation for some advocates. Should cloning-to-produce-children be introduced successfully, and should it turn out that the cloned humans do in fact inherit many of the natural talents of the "originals," some people may become interested in the prospects of using it to produce "enhanced children"—especially if other people's children were receiving comparable advantages.

Cloning can serve the ends of individualized enhancement either by avoiding the genetic defects that may arise when human reproduction is left to chance or by preserving and perpetuating outstanding genetic traits. In the future, if techniques of genetic enhancement through more precise genetic engineering became available, cloning could be useful for perpetuating the enhanced traits and for keeping any "superior" manmade genotype free of the flaws that sexual reproduction might otherwise introduce.

"Private eugenics" does not carry with it the dark implications of state despotism or political control of the gene pool that characterized earlier eugenic proposals and the racist eugenic practices of the twentieth century. Nonetheless, it could prove dangerous to our humanity. Besides the dehumanizing prospects of the turn toward manufacture that such programs of enhancement would require, there is the further difficulty of the lack of standards to guide the choices for "improvement." To this point, biomedical technology has been applied to treating diseases in patients and has been governed, on the whole, by a commonsense view of health and disease. To be sure, there are differing views about how to define "health." And certain cosmetic, performance-enhancing, or hedonistic uses of biomedical techniques have already crossed any plausible boundary between therapy and enhancement, between healing the sick and "improving" our powers. Yet, for the most part, it is by some commonsense views of health that we judge who is in need of medical treatment and what sort of treatment might be most appropriate. Even today's practice of a kind of "negative" eugenics—through prenatal genetic diagnosis and abortion of fetuses with certain genetic abnormalities—is informed by the desire to promote health.

The "positive" eugenics that could receive a great boost from human cloning, especially were it to be coupled with techniques of precise genetic modification, would not seek to restore sick human beings to natural health. Instead, it would seek to alter humanity, based upon subjective or arbitrary ideas of excellence. The effort may be guided by apparently good intentions: to improve the next generation and to enhance the quality of life of our descendants. But in the process of altering human nature, we would be abandoning the standard by which to judge the goodness or the wisdom of the particular aims. We would stand to lose the sense of what is and is not human.

The fear of a new eugenics is not, as is sometimes alleged, a concern born of some irrational fear of the future or the unknown. Neither is it born of hostility to technology or nostalgia for some premodern pseudo-golden age of superior naturalness. It is rather born of the rational recognition that once we move beyond therapy into efforts at enhancement, we are in uncharted waters without a map, without a compass, and without a clear destination that can tell us whether we are making improvements or the reverse. The time-honored and time-tested goods of human life, which we know to be good, would be put in jeopardy for the alleged and unknowable goods of a post-human future.

4. *Troubled Family Relations*

Cloning-to-produce-children could also prove damaging to family relations, despite the best of intentions. We do not assume that cloned children, once produced, would not be accepted, loved, or nurtured by their parents and relatives. On the contrary, we freely admit that, like any child, they might be welcomed into the cloning family. Nevertheless, the cloned child's place in the scheme of family relations might well be uncertain and confused. The usually clear designations of father and brother, mother and sister, would be confounded. A mother could give birth to her own genetic twin, and a father could be genetically virtually identical to his son. The cloned child's relation to his or her grandparents would span one and two generations at once. Every other family relation would be similarly confused. There is, of course, the valid counter-argument that holds that the "mother" could easily be defined as the person who gives birth to the child, regardless of the child's genetic origins, and for social purposes that may serve to eliminate some problems. But because of the special nature of cloning-to-produce-children, difficulties may be expected.

The crucial point is not the absence of the natural biological connections between parents and children. The crucial point is, on the contrary, the presence of a unique, one-sided, and replicative biological connection to only one progenitor. As a result, family relations involving cloning would differ from all existing family arrangements, including those formed through adoption or with the aid of IVF. A great many children, after all, are adopted, and live happy lives in loving families, in the absence of any biological connections with their parents. Children conceived by artificial insemination using donor sperm and by various IVF techniques may have unusual relationships with their genetic parents, or no genetic relationships at all. But all of these existing arrangements attempt in important ways to emulate the model of the natural family (at least in its arrangement of the generations), while cloning runs contrary to that model.

What the exact effects of cloning-to-produce-children might be for families is highly speculative, to be sure, but it is still worth flagging certain troubling possibilities and risks. The fact that the cloned child bears a special tie to only one parent may complicate family dynamics. As the child developed, it could not help but be regarded as specially akin to only one of his or her parents. The sins or failings of the father (or mother), if reappearing in the cloned child, might be blamed on the progenitor, adding to the chances of domestic turmoil. The problems of being and rearing an adolescent could become complicated should the teenage clone of the mother "reappear" as the double of the woman the father once fell in love with. Risks of competition, rivalry, jealousy, and parental tension could become heightened.

Even if the child were cloned from someone who is not a member of the family in which the child is raised, the fact would remain that he or she has been produced in the nearly precise genetic image of another and for some particular reason, with some particular design in mind. Should this become known to the child, as most likely it would, a desire to seek out connection to the "original" could complicate his or her relation to the rearing family, as would living consciously "under the reason" for this extra-familial choice of progenitor. Though many people make light of the importance of biological kinship (compared to the bonds formed through rearing and experienced family life), many adopted children and children conceived by artificial insemination or IVF using donor sperm show by their actions that they do not agree. They make great efforts to locate their "biological parents," even where paternity consists in nothing more than the donation of sperm. Where the progenitor is a genetic near-twin, surely the urge of the cloned child to connect with the unknown "parent" would be still greater.

For all these reasons, the cloning family differs from the "natural family" or the "adoptive family." By breaking through the natural boundaries between generations, cloning could strain the social ties between them.

5. Effects on Society

The hazards and costs of cloning-to-produce-children may not be confined to the direct participants. The rest of society may also be at risk. The impact of human cloning on society at large may be the least appreciated, but among the most important, factors to consider in contemplating the morality of this activity.

Cloning is a human activity affecting not only those who are cloned or those who are clones, but also the entire society that allows or supports such activity. For insofar as the society accepts cloning-to-produce-children, to that extent the society may be said to engage in it. A society that allows dehumanizing practices—especially when given an opportunity to try to prevent them—risks becoming an accomplice in those practices. (The same could be said of a society that allowed even a few of its members to practice incest or polygamy.) Thus the question before us is whether cloning-to-produce-children is an activity that we, as a society, should engage in. In addressing this question, we must reach well beyond the rights of individuals and the difficulties or benefits that cloned children or their families might encounter. We must consider what kind of a society we wish to be, and, in particular, what forms of bringing children into the world we want to encourage and what sorts of relations between the generations we want to preserve.

Cloning-to-produce-children could distort the way we raise and view children, by carrying to full expression many regrettable tendencies already present in our culture. We are already liable to regard children largely as vehicles for our own fulfillment and ambitions. The impulse to create "designer children" is present today—as temptation and social practice. The notion of life as a gift, mysterious and limited, is under siege. Cloning-to-produce-children would carry these tendencies and temptations to an extreme expression. It advances the notion that the child is but an object of our sovereign mastery.

A society that clones human beings thinks about human beings (and especially children) differently than does a society that refuses to do so. It could easily be argued that we have already in myriad ways begun to show signs of regarding our children as projects on which we may work our wills. Further, it could be argued that we have been so desensitized by our earlier steps in this direction that we do not recognize this tendency as a corruption. While some people contend that cloning-to-produce-children would not take us much further down a path we have already been traveling, we would emphasize that the precedent of treating children as projects cuts two ways in the moral argument. Instead of using this precedent to justify taking the next step of cloning, the next step might rather serve as a warning and a mirror in which we may discover reasons to reconsider what we are already doing. Precisely because the stakes are so high, precisely because the new biotechnologies touch not only our bodies and minds but also the very idea of our humanity, we should ask ourselves how we as a society want to approach questions of human dignity and flourishing.

D. Conclusion

Cloning-to-produce-children may represent a forerunner of what will be a growing number of capacities to intervene in and alter the human genetic endowment. No doubt, earlier human actions have produced changes in the human gene pool: to take only one example, the use of insulin to treat diabetics who otherwise would have died before reproducing has increased the genes for diabetes in the population. But different responsibilities accrue when one sets out to make such changes prospectively, directly, and deliberately. To do so without regard for the likelihood of serious unintended and unanticipated consequences would be the height of hubris. Systems of great complexity do not respond well to blunt human intervention, and one can hardly think of a more complex system—both natural and social—than that which surrounds human reproduction and the human genome. Given the enormous importance of what is at stake, we believe that the so-called "precautionary principle" should be our guide in this arena. This principle would suggest that scientists, technologists, and, indeed, all of us should be modest in claiming to understand the many possible consequences of any profound alter-

ation of human procreation, especially where there are not compelling reasons to proceed. Lacking such understanding, no one should take action so drastic as the cloning of a human child. In the absence of the necessary human wisdom, prudence calls upon us to set limits on efforts to control and remake the character of human procreation and human life.

It is not only a matter of prudence. Cloning-to-produce-children would also be an injustice to the cloned child—from the imposition of the chromosomes of someone else, to the intentional deprivation of biological parents, to all of the possible bodily and psychological harms that we have enumerated in this chapter. It is ultimately the claim that the cloned child would be seriously wronged—and not only harmed in body—that would justify government intervention.... Members of the Council are in unanimous agreement that cloning-to-produce-children is not only unsafe but also morally unacceptable and ought not to be attempted.

NOTES

1. Nuremberg Report. *Trials of War Criminals Before the Nuremberg Military Tribunals Under Control Council Law* No. 10, Vol. 2, pp. 181–182. Washington, DC: Government Printing Office, 1949.

2. Helsinki Declaration. 18th World Medical Association General Assembly *Ethical Principles for Medical Research Involving Human Subjects*, adopted in Helsinki, Finland, June 1964, and amended in October 1975, October 1983, September 1989, October 1996, and October 2000.

3. Belmont Report. The National Commission for the Protection of Human Subjects of Biomedical and Behavioral Research. *The Belmont Report: Ethical Principles and Guidelines for the Protection of Human Subjects of Research*. Bethesda, MD: Government Printing Office, 1978.

4. See, for instance, *Chapter Four* of the present report, as well as Chapter 3 of the NAS Report.

5. These issues are discussed in the NAS Report (3-2) as well as in Wilmut, I., Roslin Institute, Scotland. "Application of animal cloning data to human cloning," paper presented at *Workshop: Scientific and Medical Aspects of Human Cloning, National Academy of Sciences*,

Washington, DC, August 7, 2001; and Hill, J., Cornell University. "Placental defects in nuclear transfer (cloned) animals," paper presented at *Workshop: Scientific* and *Medical Aspects of Human Cloning, National Academy of Sciences,* Washington, DC, August 7, 2001.

6. See, for instance, Chapter 3 of the NAS Report, and Kolata, G. "In Cloning, Failure Far Exceeds Success" *New York Times*, December 11, 2001, p. D1.

7. See, for instance, Rimington, M., et al. "Counseling patients undergoing ovarian stimulation about the risks of ovarian hyper-stimulation syndrome." *Human Reproduction*, 14: 2921–2922, 1999; and Wakeley, K., and

E. Grendys. "Reproductive technologies and risk of ovarian cancer." *Current Opinion in Obstetrics and Gynecology*, 12: 43–47, 2000.

8. These issues are discussed in greater detail in Chapter 3 of the NAS Report.

9. Hill J. R., et al. "Clinical and pathologic features of cloned transgenic calves and fetuses (13 case studies)" *Theriogenology* 8: 1451–1465, 1999

10. NAS Report, p. 3–2.

11. NAS Report, Figure 3.

12. See, for instance, the NAS Report, Appendix B, tables 1, 3, and 4.

Critics

DAVID B. ELLIOTT

Uniqueness, Individuality, and Human Cloning

THE MANUFACTURING OBJECTION

When you think about it, cloning a human would be a very simple, and yet enormously efficient way to select for an individual with certain biological features. The other way to do this would be to engage in genetic alchemy—gene therapy as it is now (perhaps euphemistically) called—and try to change that individual's genome. But this technology is nascent, uncertain, risky, complicated, enormously expensive, and to date, not terribly successful. This fact alone seems to be why certain forms of mammalian cloning in domestic animal husbandry have been largely favoured over biotechnology that involves manipulating genomes. You simply find the cow that

you like, and then go about producing "copies" of it. Human cloning would seem directly to involve these same 'manufacturing' or selection opportunities. Indeed, someone might suggest that these capacities are built right into the decision to clone. It is inherently a decision to produce an individual of a certain type, with certain features that we hope are based in his or her genome. This is how Jeremy Rifkin, a popular biotechnology critic, sees the matter. As he puts it: "It's a horrendous crime to make a Xerox of someone . . . [because] you're putting a human into a genetic straitjacket. For the first time, we've taken the principles of industrial design—quality control and predictability—and applied them to a human being." The moral idea here seems to be that in manufactur-

From David Elliott, "Uniqueness, Individuality, and Human Cloning," *Journal of Applied Philosophy* 15, no. 3 (1998): 217–30. Notes and some parts of the text have been deleted. Reprinted by permission of Blackwell Publishing Ltd.

ing people, we devalue them; we treat them as objects to be designed rather than as potential subjects or agents capable of their own making.

There are several familiar problems with this familiar line of argument. First, let us assume that the decision to clone is inherently a manufacturing choice (I will question this assumption in a moment). The problem is that these sorts of choices seem to typify so many choices that people make which, even if they are not conscious choices of this sort, at least have the effect of shaping or selecting the traits of their child. The process, for example, of selecting a partner where children could arrive in the future, while it surely is not (and I would hope it never should be) *merely* a decision to select the traits of one's children, it does in part present an opportunity for just this sort of selection. Additionally, if we really do believe that 'manufacturing' choices are morally objectionable, then it becomes difficult to imagine why people seeking to adopt a child should have to be consulted about the adoption of any particular child once they have expressed a general interest in adoption. The same might hold for a woman seeking to have a child through artificial insemination by donor. It seems rather strong to hold that her moral qualities as a future parent are seriously diminished by any interest in the general features of the donor, or that she would be an ideal parent if she were to accept sperm only if she could know nothing at all about the physical appearance, family medical history, etc., of its donor.

Furthermore, even if it were just false that people really do make many choices that have the effect of trait selection prior to the birth of their children, they certainly do go to considerable trouble to see that their children develop certain traits after they are born. All of this "manufacturing" seems appropriate, however, given certain standard moral assumptions—e.g., when it is at least not harmful to the child, when it does not severely restrict her opportunities to become an autonomous, self-affirming individual or when it is in her interest to have (or avoid) certain characteristics (say, a debilitating disease). The same could be said about pre-conception selection decisions. Many of these decisions could indeed be frivolous, selfish, and so on. But many of them

might be capable of moral defence by showing how they might be important for cultivating the capacities and opportunities for a person's self-development.

What tends to upset many of us about manufacturing decisions, I suspect, is not really that *some* of them might occur in ordinary choices about having a child, but rather that *too many* of them might be present. What might be objectionable, then, is the total quantity of the same sort of choice. Too many manufacturing choices, it might be suggested, push us to the point where we would be treating a (potential) child as an object of his or her parent's desires and goals, rather than a person in his or her own right. Furthermore, being able to determine a person's traits to a very considerable extent might raise concerns about whether that parent is capable of valuing or loving a child unconditionally, or loving him for the person that he might become through self-development. It could also raise questions about whether the potential person would be able adequately to develop her own sense of self and personal agency. In this regard, Joseph Fletcher, another early bioethicist, surely overstated his response to the manufacturing argument when he enthusiastically *celebrates* our potential to manufacture people. "Man," he writes, "is a maker and a selecter [sic] and a designer, and the more rationally contrived and deliberate anything is, the more human it is." Fletcher even goes so far as to claim that laboratory reproduction is "radically human compared to conception by ordinary heterosexual intercourse" because the manufacturing is willed, chosen, purposed, controlled; it is a matter of "choice, and not chance."

Whatever merit there might be in responding to the manufacturing objection by arguing either that manufacturing is a standard decision most parents make or that it is not itself morally objectionable, let us for the moment set both of these suggestions aside. There is another consideration that is, I would suggest, even more decisive. The decision to clone is not *inherently* a choice to manufacture a particular individual in a certain way, even though this consequence may be foreseeable. It can simply be a choice to have a child of one's own in the only way possible. The familiar examples standardly offered in the literature as morally defensible reasons to clone illustrate this point. These examples can usually be classified under two main categories: (1) the prevention (by bypassing) of infertility and (2) the avoidance of genetic disease. Given either one or both of these situations, some cloning technique may be the only way that some people might be able to have children of their own. In these cases, however, the decision to have a child could be only that of having a child of one's own; it need not be a detailed manufacturing decision—a point which seems particularly true with respect to bypassing infertility. This is just the sort of outlook that we might arguably suggest is the ideal outlook that couples having children through sexual reproduction should have. Cloning, of course, does come with biological foreknowledge; one would have a fairly good idea of what the child's genome would be,

and all that this entails. But, again, simply because there is foreknowledge that a duplication of one's genome will be the outcome of one's decision to have a child, it simply does not follow that the decision to have a child involves or entails a determination to have a child for these reasons. Imagine an analogy with a couple where infertility and genetic disease is not a known consideration, but who may know in advance (say due to some established medical condition) that all of their offspring will be female. It is not obvious that their choice to have a child should be regarded as an instance of sexselection. If this is right, then there is simply no reason to regard all instances of cloning as instances of manufacturing humans. Other more general, recognizable, and morally defensible motivations, I would suggest, can be present.

DAVID B. HERSHENOV

An Argument for Limited Human Cloning

I believe a rather useful principle can be found for distinguishing legitimate from illegitimate cases of cloning. After surveying the different types of cases, I will present this principle as a guideline for legislative and institutional policy.

My hope is that this guideline will be received by most of the opponents of cloning as a welcome compromise because it rules out the more repugnant cases while allowing the few that are more appealing. We do not have to accept Leon Kass's claim that "the only safe trench we can dig across the slippery slope . . . is to insist upon the inviolable distinction between animal and human cloning."

. . . If a person clones himself, the clone is actually his younger identical win. Many of the opponents of cloning are repulsed by the prospect of children

being created and raised by siblings rather than their true genetic parents. The bioethicist James Nelson imagines clones seeking out their genetic parents and pursuing a child-parent relationship despite the fact that the child's origins are the result of their older siblings' doing and not the parents who perhaps didn't want any more children. It would be very unfair to place the genetic parent in such a situation. And it would be awful for the cloned child who seeks out but is not welcomed by such a parent.

Along similar lines, Leon Kass writes of how cloning will disrupt traditional roles and duties:

> In the case of self-cloning, the "offspring" is, in addition, one's twin; and so the dreaded result of incest—to be parent of one's sibling—is here brought about deliberately,

From David B. Hershenov, "An Argument for Limited Human Cloning," *Public Affairs Quarterly* 14, no. 3 (July 2000): 245–258. Notes and some parts of the text have been deleted. Reprinted by permission of North American Philosophical Publications.

albeit without any acts of coitus. Moreover, all other relationships will be confounded. What will father, grandfather, aunt, cousin, sister mean? Who will bear what ties and what burdens? What sort of social identity will someone have with one whole side—"father's" or "mother's"—necessarily excluded? It is no answer to say that our society, with its high incidence of divorce, remarriage, adoption, extramarital childbearing and the rest, already confounds lineage and confuses kinship and responsibility for children (and everyone else), unless one also wants to argue that this is, for children, a preferable state of affairs.

Kass also expresses the fear that asexual reproduction will give rise to an increase in the number of single parents as people raise their own clones. Kass complains:

> In the case of cloning, however there is but one "parent." The usually sad situation of the "single parent child" is here deliberately planned, and with a vengeance. . . . asexual reproduction, which produces single parent offspring, is a radical departure from the natural human way.

There is also the worry that the cloned child shall be the responsibility of an older sibling who will lack the devotion to the well-being of the child that parents normally have. Just because those who cloned themselves are genetically identical to their younger siblings, it would be a mistake to think that this means that they will care as much about the clones as most parents do for their children. Siblings have not historically been molded by the same evolutionary pressures as their parents, so they are not endowed with the concern and affection for each other that their parents innately possess toward them.

With a little imagination, the reader could add to this list of unsavory cloning scenarios. . . . I will mention four types of scenarios in which cloning is an appealing option. The first, which I also find the most compelling of the set, would involve couples who have become "infertile as couples" through menopause or abnormality, who then lose their only child—or perhaps all their children. Not only is it extremely distressing for parents to have their children precede them to the grave, but to have the family lineage cease just adds to the pain. I imagine that the number of parents who lose all their children

prior to the birth of any grandchildren is not insignificant. And of course, in times of war or epidemic, this number would sadly escalate. And even if in normal times the numbers are not large, the suffering of those few in such predicaments warrant a sympathetic societal response. However, if such infertile parents were allowed to clone their lost child, this would lessen their grief. And if the child had yet to reach what was deemed a mature age, his consent would not be required. But if the deceased child had reached such an age, then perhaps his consent would have to have been acquired through some process analogous to that for organ donation. Where there is not a record of the mature child's view on his posthumous cloning by his parents, maybe the default position should be the parents can choose to clone their deceased child. In any event, the details need not be worked out here.

Less likely to occur than the premature death of an only child, but still compelling, would be a case where an ill child needs a bone marrow transplant. I am just going to assume that the reader would not think it wrong for the parents to conceive another child through normal sexual procreation in order to save the afflicted one, as long as the parents would also love and cherish this additional child. Now suppose that the parents were infertile because of advanced age or some form of abnormality, such that cloning the ill child would in the absence of an available donor be their only recourse. And even if the couple is fertile, the chances of a genetic tissue match makes cloning the preferable option.

Cloning also appears as a sympathetic solution to a third scenario. This involves parents who are at a high risk for passing on a deadly or debilitating disease. Imagine that before they become aware of this, they conceived a child who fortunately wins the genetic lottery, beating the odds by being born healthy. Another possibility is that they are likely to pass on a disease like hemophilia to male offprsing and thus would like to clone their only daughter. Should this family be condemned to a Chinese-style communist one-child family? This hardly seems fair. Most Americans desire, even feel entitled to, at least a two-child family. Cloning would permit the family plagued by unwelcome genes to still reach an acceptable sized family.

There is a fourth scenario, which is basically a combination of the first and third. This would involve a couple who, after having one child, lose the capacity to produce viable eggs or sperm, yet wants to enlarge their family. Allowing them to clone their only child will enable them to have another child to whom they are *both* genetically related—which would not be the case with a gamete donor or adoption.

I hope that the reader is sympathetic to the plight of those in the four types of cases just surveyed. What is it that these cases have in common that the earlier repugnant cases lacked? The four positive cases all mirror normal procreation. That is, *a new child is being deliberately created and brought into the world by the decision of two willing partners (the parents), from each of whom the child gets half of his or her DNA.* Both normal sexual procreation and the advocated form of cloning meet this criterion. The four types of cases of preferred cloning differ from normal sexual procreation only in that the parents make the decision to *reuse* the DNA they earlier decided to fuse in order to create the first child. But none of the repugnant cases involves the cloning decision being made by the parents of the clone or, if they do have a say in the matter, the practice is distasteful for adults other than the genetic parents of the being cloned are taking possession of the clone, perhaps because they purchased the genetic material from which the clone emerges. What also distinguishes the two categories of cloning is that the favored form involves infertility or, at least, the inability to have healthy babies. We are sympathetic to those who want to do what the vast majority of other couples do: combine their genetic material with a loved one and create a new life.

So our short survey suggests some necessary conditions for cloning: (1) people should not be allowed to clone themselves; (2) people should not take possession of the "product" of a cloning process unless they are the genetic parents of the clone; (3) the genetic parents of the clone should themselves be unable or just unlikely to conceive a healthy child; (4) and both genetic parents should freely enter into the discussion to initiate the cloning process. Combining these necessary conditions, we can formulate the promised principle as the following: *A clone may be created only by a pair of people who, unable to conceive together a healthy offspring in any other way, freely decide to create and rear a child that will receive half of his (or her) genetic material from each of them.*

This principle would make the pair who initiate the cloning the parents of the resulting clone and not older siblings of the clone. Such a "pro-family" and "pro-parent" form of cloning, which relieves the distress of infertility, is probably the only feasible form of cloning given the present political environment. It is this principle that allows us to build a barrier on the slippery slope of cloning. Others might want to avoid the slippery slope by never approaching the cloning hill, but I think they do this without having an argument against the cases of cloning that elicit our sympathy. Their only argument against the relief cloning provides in such cases is that permitting cloning there increases the likelihood of the occurrence of the unattractive cases surveyed above. But I believe it is better to have a well-delineated and principled line upon which to base our policies even if this takes us somewhat down the feared slope—provided that we avoid those areas that are *inherently* wrong, i.e., morally flawed even if we slide no further. The recommended principle does just that. All the distasteful cases fail to involve the genetic parents of the clone freely initiating the process and taking possession of the resulting clone when there is no other safe way for them to have more healthy children. In fact, many of the cases mentioned do not even involve the consent of the clone's parents since the decision is being made by their children to clone themselves and take control of their resulting sibling(s). Not only could people be made into parents without their choosing to become so, but they may not even be aware that they have become parents.

II

So we have seen what property all the distasteful cases lack. But this does not rule out that many of the disagreeable attributes of the repugnant cases are shared by our three more attractive types of scenarios. Fortunately, this is not the case—or, at least, the distasteful features in question are not shared to the same extent by the endorsed types of cases. So we will be able to disarm the opponents of cloning by pointing out to them that their general objections to cloning either do not apply to the cases of cloning championed in this essay, or do so only to a much lesser degree than they envisioned.

Many of the opponents of cloning, such as Kass, are repulsed by the prospect of children being created and raised by siblings rather than genetic parents. We have mentioned the fears of the bioethicist James Nelson who imagines clones seeking out their genetic parents and pursuing a child-parent relationship despite the fact that the child's origins are the result of his or her older sibling's doing and not the parents who perhaps did not want any more children. But given the necessary conditions for cloning that I put forth, these objections are not telling. The only clones made are by infertile parents, or more accurately, those who cannot have healthy children through sexual reproduction. Thus traditional family roles, loyalties, and obligations remain the same.

Nor do we need to share Kass's fear of asexual reproduction giving rise to an increase in the number of single parents as people raise their own clones. We can avoid this because the advocated principle stipulates that only the genetic parents of the possible clone can make the cloning decision. Since people would not be allowed to clone themselves, no child will be raised by a single parent except in the case of an untimely death. And not allowing a person to decide by him- or herself to clone themselves avoids not only the distasteful cases of narcissistic and arrogant cloning surveyed, but frees us from the worry that the cloned child shall be the responsibility of an older sibling who will lack the devotion to the well-being of the child that parents normally have. . . .

24

Is a Government Ban on Tobacco Wrong?

Goodin and His Critics

There is a strong presumption in the liberal political tradition that the State has no business passing *paternalistic laws*—laws that forbid knowledgeable and consenting adults from engaging in activities simply because those activities pose a significant risk of harm to the adult engaging in it. And this is presumably because we value *autonomy*, or *freedom*. The idea is that it is the State's business to protect each person's sphere of freedom both from intrusions by the State itself and by others. Laws curtailing the freedom of children, who cannot be assumed to be engaging in the activity with full knowledge of the risks involved, may be justified. But comparable laws for adults are not. In his famous essay *On Liberty*, the nineteenth-century philosopher John Stuart Mill gave expression to this view in what has become the most cited paragraph on this topic:

> The only purpose for which power can be rightfully exercised over any member of a civilized community, against his will, is to prevent harm to others. His own good, either physical or moral, is not a sufficient warrant. He cannot rightfully be compelled to do or forbear because it will be better for him to do so, because it will make him happier, because, in the opinions of others, to do so would be wise, or even right. . . . The only part of the conduct of any one, for which he is amenable to society, is that which concerns others. In the part which merely concerns himself, his independence is, of right, absolute. Over himself, over his own body and mind, the individual is sovereign.

Parents are sometimes justified in preventing their children from doing things that they know would harm the children. This is paternalism, but it is a justified paternalism. Mill's point is that the State cannot legitimately treat its adult members paternalistically. Call this *Mill's antipaternalistic principle*: The State may not prevent a knowledgeable adult from voluntarily engaging in an activity simply on the grounds that it poses a risk of harm to himself. The question in this chapter is whether antismoking laws violate this principle.

In the featured article excerpted in this section, Robert Goodin agrees with Mill's antipaternalistic principle but argues that the State is nevertheless justified in controlling the supply and consumption of tobacco by discouraging its use and even making it illegal. Goodin argues that the conditions under which Mill's principle applies (the knowledge condition and the voluntariness condition) both fail to hold in the case of tobacco.

Goodin has a second argument for State control of tobacco, one that extends to all addictive substances. Goodin claims that being addicted is, in and of itself, a very bad state for anyone to be in or to get into. Being addicted to something is *intrinsically* bad. The reason that being addicted is bad is that being free, or autonomous, is *good*. According to Mill's principle, the State must protect, not undermine, such autonomy. Now, if addiction compromises autonomy, then the State has a legitimate role in discouraging people from becoming addicted in the first place. And it can do this by controlling the supply and consumption of addictive substances such as nicotine, heroin, morphine, and alcohol.

In his response to Goodin, Daniel Shapiro challenges Goodin's first argument for State intervention. He disputes the information presented by Goodin to support the claim that smokers have severe cognitive defects as well as the claim that nicotine is so addictive that, once addicted to it, a smoker cannot be said to be smoking voluntarily anymore. In Graham Oddie's article "Addiction and the Value of Freedom," Oddie investigates Goodin's second argument. He first gives an analysis of addiction and then goes on to ask what has to be assumed about the value of freedom to justify the view that being addicted is *intrinsically* bad—that is to say, bad *in itself*, independent of any of the bad consequences a particular addiction might induce. His analysis makes extensive use of the method of bare differences explained in section 4.2 of the Introduction.

Questions for Consideration

• Consider activities that pose a risk of harm to the person engaging in them: not wearing a seat belt or motorcycle (or bike or ski) helmet, drinking alcohol, smoking marijuana, injecting heroin, rock climbing, listening to loud rock music, skiing, playing rugby, viewing pornography. Some of these are the subjects of State regulation and others are not. Is there a principled difference between those that are and those that are not?

• Does Mill's principle entail that the State has no business regulating any of these activities? What should we say about the bad effects that some of these activities have on third parties? (For example, those who do not wear seat belts and are then involved in an accident are more likely to use up hospital beds that would otherwise be free. They also put their loved ones at risk of distress and unhappiness. Is this what legitimates a mandatory seat-belt law? If so, is there any reasonable analogy with smoking and rock climbing?)

• Under what circumstances is it legitimate for the State to regulate an addictive substance? What about addictive *activities* that are not substance related? For example, many hold that a large amount of exercise can be addictive for reasons that are physiologically connected to the addictiveness of substances—the production of pleasure-inducing endorphins in the brain. If exercising over many hours turns out to be addictive in this way, should the State regulate it?

• What do you think is the value of freedom? Is freedom valuable because free people more often get what they want? Or is freedom valuable for reasons having nothing to do with the consequences of having it?

• If the satisfaction of desires is what is really valuable, then what about satisfying the addict's desires? Why should the addict's desires be singled out for special censure?

• Is Goodin's account of addiction—"being defined in terms of a desire to quit coupled with an inability to quit"—correct? Can someone who is addicted have no desire to quit? Would it nevertheless always be better if he did?

FURTHER READING

Gideon, Yaffe. "Recent Work on Addiction and Responsible Agency." *Philosophy and Public Affairs* 30, no. 2 (2001): 178–221.

Goodin, Robert E. *No Smoking: The Ethical Issues.* Chicago: University of Chicago Press, 1989.

Hansson, Sven Ove. "Extended Antipaternalism." *Journal of Medical Ethics* 31, no. 2 (February 2005): 97–100.

Levy, Neil. "Autonomy and Addiction." *Canadian Journal of Philosophy* 36, no. 3 (September 2006): 427–48.

Sloan, Frank A., V. Kerry Smith, and Donald H. Taylor, Jr. *The Smoking Puzzle: Information, Risk Perception, and Choice.* Cambridge, Mass.: Harvard University Press, 2003.

ROBERT GOODIN

No Smoking

The first and most obvious reason we may have for wanting to restrict smoking is to prevent harms that would be done to smokers themselves by their smoking. . . .

Of course, Mill and his followers would query whether "his own good, either physical or moral" is ever "sufficient warrant" for coercively interfering with a person's own behavior. But they would be the first to concede that it might be, if the behavior is not fully voluntary. If it is autonomy that we are trying to protect in opposing paternalistic legislation in general, then the same values that lead us to oppose such legislation in general will lead us to welcome it in those particular cases where what we are being protected from is something that would deprive us of the capacity for autonomous choice. Evidence of the addictiveness of nicotine, surveyed in section 2.2, suggests that even advocates of personal autonomy ought to favor smoking restrictions on those grounds. . . .

2.1 WHAT ARE THE RISKS?

Folk wisdom has long held tobacco smoking to be unhealthy. During the first outbreak of the smoking epidemic in the seventeenth century, the authorities tried to outlaw it on grounds of public health (Harrison 1986, p. 555). From the earliest days of our own century, cigarettes have been popularly known as "coffin nails," everyone's grandmother warned that they would stunt your growth, and so on.

Proper medical evidence scientifically supporting such suspicions began mushrooming in the 1950s and culminated in the justly famous reports of the Royal College of Physicians of 1962 and of the U.S. surgeon general two years later. The subsequent scientific literature on smoking and health—now numbering over 50,000 studies (U.S. Department of Health and Human Services [DHHS] 1986, p. vii)—has merely served to reinforce those earlier fears. . . .

Excerpted from Robert Goodin, *No Smoking: The Ethical Issues* (Chicago: University of Chicago Press, 1989). Reprinted by permission of University of Chicago Press.

In a way, though, further reading is not really necessary. The basic findings are familiar enough already. Smoking leads to cancer (especially of the lung and respiratory tract, but also of the pancreas and bladder) and to cardiovascular diseases (particularly coronary heart disease, but also peripheral vascular disease) and is the major cause of chronic obstructive lung disease.

If the basic findings are familiar, the magnitude of the effects can still shock. To say that smoking is responsible for more than 350,000 deaths per year in the United States is to say that about 15 percent of all deaths in the United States are smoking-related (U.S. DHHS 1986, pp. vii, 5–6). Put in more personal terms, "about a quarter of the young men who smoke a pack a day or so of cigarettes are killed before their time by smoking"; and "on average . . . [they] have lost ten to fifteen years of life" (Peto 1980, p. 45).

Another way of putting the point is in terms of age-adjusted mortality rates. Of course, the older you are the more likely you are to die over the course of the next year. But factoring out age considerations, the point remains that at any given age smokers are 68 percent more likely to die over the course of the next year than are nonsmokers; and age-adjusted mortality rates for heavy smokers are about double that. In terms of such age-adjusted mortality rates, a moderate smoker's chances of dying from lung cancer are 10.8 times greater than a nonsmoker's; of bronchitis or emphysema, 6.1 times greater; of cancer of the larynx, 5.4 times greater; or oral cancer, 4.1 times greater; of cancer of the esophagus, 3.4 times greater; of coronary artery disease or other heart diseases, 1.7 times greater; and so on down the list (U.S. DHEW 1964, p. 29). . . .

The evidence underlying these medical conclusions is largely epidemiological in character. They rest on analysis of statistical aggregates rather than on analysis of the aetiology of particular cases. What these studies show is simply that, in the population as a whole, smokers contract those various diseases many times more often than nonsmokers; and heavy smokers contract them much more often than light smokers. These differential rates of illness are much too large to be put down to mere chance. They seem to vary, in lagged fashion, with changes in the aggregate consumption of tobacco over time. And so on. . . .

Statistical purists and tobacco apologists will nonetheless insist that the case is still "not proven" because the findings are "merely statistical" (R. J. Reynolds 1986; Burch 1978; Eysenck 1980, 1986). It pays to consider carefully what other causal paths are being contemplated when they say that. In an early letter to the *British Medical Journal,* the distinguished statistician and geneticist, Sir Ronald Fisher, identified two alternative possibilities. One is that we have the causal arrow backward and that incipient cancer is what causes people to smoke rather than vice versa. So far as I can tell, nobody has taken this possibility sufficiently seriously to investigate it properly.

The other, more worrying possibility is multicolinearity. That is simply to say that there might be some common cause that leads both to smoking and to cancer, thus rendering any apparent connection between the two wholly spurious. The textbook example of multicolinearity is that the price of rum in Havana correlates tightly with the wages of Boston preachers—not because the holy men drink up all their extra wages, thus driving up the price of rum, but, rather, because changes in the state of the world economy drive up both prices and wages. Something similar may be going on in the link between smoking and cancer, Fisher fears.

There are, of course, a great many confounding factors involved in the relationship between smoking and lung cancer. Most of them (such as social class and workplace exposure to carcinogens) can be controlled statistically; and when they are, the relationship between smoking and cancer still remains significant. The most worrying possibilities are ones that are hard to control statistically. Primary among them is the possibility that an individual's genetic constitution causes both his smoking and his cancer, either directly or indirectly, through its influence on personality.

The best test of this "genetic constitutional hypothesis" would come through a comparison of smoking and lung cancer rates among monozygotic and dizygotic twins. The former share the same genetic constitution; the latter do not, but they do presumably share much the same environment as their fraternal twins. Early studies suggested that the former were indeed significantly more alike—both in their smoking behavior and in their cancer history—than the latter.

That finding lent credence to the hypothesis that there is no direct link between people's smoking and their lung cancer but, rather, that there is some third factor (their genes) that causes both. Those early studies were beset by a number of methodological problems, however (U.S. DHEW 1964, p. 190; Slade et al. 1986–87). The findings of the latest and most thorough analysis of the most comprehensive collection of twin data—the Swedish Twin Register—"speak strongly against this [genetic] constitutional hypothesis" (Cederlof, Friberg, and Lundman 1977, p. 115). . . .

Certainly carcinogens merely "trigger" tumors in those who are genetically predisposed, so not everyone is necessarily at equal risk from smoking. There may even be both "genetic constitutional" and genuinely "causal" factors linking smoking and cancer (Burch 1978). Advocates of curbs on smoking can concede all that without cost. Their case goes through perfectly well, just so long as: a sufficiently large proportion of the population is genetically vulnerable; among them, smoking makes a sufficiently large contribution in causing their cancers; and there is no way, technically or politically, to target truly effective antismoking policies only at those who are genetically at risk. Given the likelihood of each (indeed, of all) of these conditions being satisfied, antismoking policies can nonetheless be defended as important contributions to public health.[1] . . .

2.2 DO SMOKERS VOLUNTARILY ACCEPT THE RISKS?

Given what we know of the health risks from smoking, we may well be tempted to "ban cigarette manufacturers from continuing to manufacture their product on the grounds that we are preventing them from causing illness to others in the same way that we prevent other manufacturers from releasing pollutants into the atmosphere, thereby causing danger to members of the community." That would be to move too quickly, though. For as Dworkin (1972/ 1983, p. 22) goes on to say, "The difference is . . . that in the former but not the latter case the harm is of such a nature that it could be avoided by those individuals affected, if they so chose. The incurring of the harm

requires the active cooperation of the victim. It would be a mistake in theory and hypocritical in practice to assert that our interference in such cases is just like our interference in standard cases of protecting others from harm." . . .

Certainly there is, morally speaking, a world of difference between the harms that others inflict upon you and the harms that you inflict upon yourself. The question is simply whether, in the case of smoking, the active cooperation of the smoker really is such as to constitute voluntary acceptance of the consequent risks of illness and death. The question is decomposable into two further ones. The first, discussed in section 2.2.1, concerns the question of whether smokers know the risks. The second, discussed in section 2.2.2, concerns the question of whether, even if smoking in full knowledge of the risks, they could be said to "accept" the risks in a sense that is fully voluntary.

2.2.1 Do Smokers Know the Risks?

Here we are involved, essentially, with a question of "informed consent." People can be held to have consented only if they knew to what they were supposedly consenting. In the personalized context of medical encounters, this means that each and every person being treated is told, in terms he understands, by the attending physician what the risks of the treatment might be (Gorovitz 1982, chap. 3). For largely anonymous transactions in the market, such personalized standards are inappropriate. Instead, we are forced to infer consent from what people know or should have known (in the standard legal construct, what a "reasonable man" should have been expected to know) about the product. And in the anonymous world of the market, printed warnings necessarily take the place of face-to-face admonitions.

Cigarette manufacturers, in defending against product liability suits, have claimed on both these grounds that smokers should be construed as having consented to whatever risks that they have run. They claim, first, that any "reasonable" person should have known—and that the "ordinary consumer" did indeed know—that smoking was an "inherently dangerous" activity. Their interrogatories (pretrial questions put to the plaintiff before a case comes to trial) constantly seek to establish that plaintiffs had in their youth consorted with people calling cigarettes "coffin nails," and so on.

Of course, claiming that any reasonable person should have known smoking was unhealthy sits uneasily with the same corporations' claims—often in the very same litigation—that there is no evidence that smoking causes cancer, either in general or in the plaintiffs' particular cases. Caught in this inconsistency, one tobacco company recently withdrew any claims as to the plaintiff's negligence, lest it be required to answer interrogatories stating exactly what any "reasonable person" should have known about the dangers of its products.

Cigarette manufacturers have a fallback position here, though. They claim, second, that the printing of government-mandated health warnings on cigarette packets from 1966 onward has constituted further, explicit warning to users of the dangers of the products. The question, recall, is whether consumers were warned of the risks, not who warned them or why. So the fact that the health warnings were required by the Congress rather than printed voluntarily by manufacturers does nothing to undercut their value for this purpose. Indeed, according to the current run of court opinions, that might actually enhance the value of such warnings in deflecting tort liability suits.

Not only are those government health warnings printed on cigarette packets useful in defending companies against claims for harms that were inflicted at some time after 1966, when they first appeared, but tobacco company lawyers defending against product liability suits have even tried to use post-1966 behavior to infer "hypothetical consent" to risks before the warnings were given. As one company attorney argued in *Cipollone v. Liggett Group*, "because Rose Cipollone continued to smoke for at least 15 years while warnings were on every pack she bought, she would have smoked before January 1, 1966, even if the defendants had voluntarily warned her about possible health consequences" (quoted in Mintz 1988). Now, there may be certain circumstances in which hypothetical consent can be a convincing argument—some such logic must be what justifies the physician in cutting open the comatose patient in

the emergency room, for example. This case does not seem to be among them, though. What we have here is more like an amateur boxer mugging you, on the grounds that since you belong to the same boxing club you obviously would have agreed to fight him if he had only asked. It takes actual, not merely hypothetical, consent to defend against a charge of assault and battery. Likewise, I would argue, in the case of the tobacco companies. That the companies should try to run the argument at all is indicative, however, of the hopes that they are pinning on printed warnings to relieve them of legal liability.

In the best of circumstances, warnings—whether from government or grandmother—will only get us so far. There are some risks of which smokers have historically never been warned by either government or grandmother. Among them are things like Buerger's disease, a circulatory condition induced in often quite young people by smoking, that can result in amputation of limbs.[1]

Furthermore, the warnings of both folk wisdom and cigarette packets, in the 1960s and 1970s at least, were desperately nonspecific. A more general question therefore arises: are all-purpose warnings that "X is hazardous to your health," without specifying just how likely X is to cause just what sorts of harms, adequate warning to secure people's informed consent, at all? Certainly the psychological evidence suggests that an explicit, concrete message is a better spur to action than a vague, abstract one (Borgida and Nisbett 1977).

Problems of nonspecific warnings are not peculiar to cigarettes, of course. In principle, they might be as much of a problem with lawn mowers and insecticides. In practice, though, warnings there tend to be stated more strongly: they tend to say that certain bad things *will* happen to you if the product is misused (e.g., you will be poisoned), not just that they *may* (i.e., not just that the product "is dangerous to your health"); they mention death explicitly (often employing the conventional skull-and-crossbones symbol on the label); they suggest specific antidotes; and so on. All those factors make those warnings more successful at what warnings are supposed to do—convey a real sense of the seriousness of the hazard—than do the sorts of milquetoast warnings traditionally carried on cigarette packets.

There is a fair bit of evidence that smokers—especially young smokers—simply do not read what appears inside the surgeon general's boxed warning on cigarette packets and advertisements. One study, for example, monitored eye tracking of adolescents viewing tobacco advertisements and found that almost half of them did not cast eyes on the warning at all; when subsequently asked to identify, from the surgeon general's rotating list of warnings, which it was that appeared in the advertisement they had seen subjects did only slightly better than random. Warnings that are not—and perhaps are designed not to be—read cannot possibly be effective. The evidence suggests that tobacco health warnings fall largely into that category.

As important, cigarette manufacturers take back through their advertising what is given, inside the surgeon general's boxed notice, by way of warnings (White 1988, chap. 6). There are various examples. Admonitions that "smoking is dangerous to your health," when conjoined with pictures of people enjoying dangerous sports (white water rafting, and the like), perversely serve to make smoking more attractive. Warnings that "smoking by pregnant women may result in fetal injury, premature birth, and low birth weight," when conjoined with sexually provocative photos in magazines devoted to casual sex without procreation, again perversely undercut the health message. Perhaps most important of all, advertising that appeals to the rebelliousness of youth in general and young women and young blacks in particular (the "You've come a long way, baby" campaign, e.g.) constitutes a thinly veiled invitation for them to ignore the advice of authorities. Particularly striking, in this connection, was a 1983 billboard campaign in Britain employing the caption, "We're not allowed to tell you anything about Winston cigarettes, so here's a man blowing a raspberry" (Chapman 1986, p. 16). . . .

The point being made here is not that advertising bypasses consumers' capacity to reason, and somehow renders them unfree to choose intelligently whether or not to partake of the product. No one is saying that consumers of tobacco are brainwashed to quite that extent. The central point here is merely that the tobacco companies in effect are giving out—

and, more important, consumers are receiving—conflicting information. The implicit health claims of the advertising imagery conflict with the explicit health warnings, and thus undercut any *volenti* or informed consent defense companies might try to mount on the basis of those warnings (Edell and Gisser 1985).

2.2.2 Is Acceptance of the Risks Fully Voluntary?

Obviously, people cannot voluntarily accept the health risks of smoking if they do not know what they are. Despite tobacco companies' best efforts, though, the great majority of people—smokers included—knows, in broad outline, what health risks smoking entails. In a 1978 Gallup poll, only 24 percent of even heavy smokers claimed that they were unaware of, or did not believe, the evidence that smoking is hazardous to health. That figure might somewhat overstate the extent of their acceptance of the statistics. There are various other false beliefs smokers sometimes employ to qualify their acceptance of those statistics and hence to rationalize their continued smoking (e.g., that the lethal dose is far in excess of what they smoke, however many that may be). Still, we can reasonably suppose that, in some sense or another, well over half of smokers know that what they are doing is unhealthy.

It is worth pausing, at this point, to consider just how we should handle that recalcitrant residual of smokers who deny the evidence. Having smoked thousands of packets containing increasingly stern warnings, and having been exposed to hundreds of column inches of newspaper reporting and several hours of broadcasting about smoking's hazards, they are presumably incorrigible in their false beliefs in this regard. Providing them with still more information is likely to prove pointless. People will say "if they are so bad for you as all that the government would ban cigarettes altogether." Or they will say "the government says that nearly everything is bad for you." Or they will find still some other way of rationalizing the practice.

Ordinarily it is not the business of public policy to prevent people from relying on false inferences from full information which would harm only themselves.

Sometimes, however, it is. One such case comes when the false beliefs would lead to decisions that are "far-reaching, potentially dangerous, and irreversible"—as, for example, with people who believe that when they jump out of a tenth-story window they will float upward.

We are particularly inclined toward intervention when false beliefs with such disastrous results are traceable to familiar, well-understood forms of cognitive defect. There is something deeply offensive—morally, and perhaps legally as well—about the "intentional exploitation of a man's known weaknesses" in these ways.

One such familiar form of cognitive defect is "wishful thinking": smokers believing the practice is safe because they smoke, rather than smoking because they believe it to be safe. There is substantial evidence that smokers believe, groundlessly, that they are less vulnerable to smoking-related diseases (Leventhal, Glynn, and Fleming 1987, p. 3374). More surprising, and more directly to the "wishful thinking" point, is the evidence that smokers came to acquire those beliefs in their own invulnerability, and to "forget" what they previously knew about the dangers of smoking, *after* they took up the habit.

Another cognitive defect is the so-called anchoring fallacy (Kahneman, Slovic, and Tversky 1982). People smoke many times without any (immediately perceptible) bad effects. Naturally, people extrapolate from their own experience. They therefore conclude—quite reasonably, but quite wrongly—that smoking is safe, at least for them.

Yet another phenomenon, sometimes regarded as a cognitive defect, is "time discounting." Sometimes the ill effects of smoking would be felt almost immediately. Tonight's cigarette will make me short of breath when jogging tomorrow morning, for example. To ignore such effects, just on the grounds that they are in the future, is obviously absurd when the "future" in question is so close; it would imply a discount rate of 100 percent per hour, "compounding to an annual rate too large for my calculator," as Schelling (1980, p. 99) sneers. But most of the really serious consequences of smoking are some decades away for most of us. And since young smokers will not suffer the full effects of smoking-related diseases

for some years to come, they may puff away happily now with little regard for the consequences, just so long as they attach relatively little importance to future pains relative to present pleasures in their utility functions. Economists, of course, are inclined to regard a "pure time preference" as a preference like any other, neither rational nor irrational. But reasons can be given for thinking that a lack of due regard for one's own future truly is a form of cognitive defect.

All of these cognitive defects point to relatively weak forms of irrationality, to be sure. In and of themselves, they might not be enough to justify interference with people's liberty, perhaps. When they lead people to take decisions that are far-reaching, potentially life-threatening, and irreversible, though, perhaps intervention would indeed be justifiable.

Interfering with people's choices in such cases is paternalistic, admittedly. But there are many different layers of paternalism. What is involved here is a relatively weak form of paternalism, one that works within the individual's own theory of the good and merely imposes upon him a better means of achieving what after all are only his own ends.[2] It is one thing to stop people who want to commit suicide from doing so, but quite another to stop people who want to live from acting in a way that they falsely believe to be safe. Smokers who deny the health risks fall into that latter, easier category.

The larger and harder question is how to deal with the great majority of smokers who, knowing the risks, continue smoking anyway. Of course, it might be said that they do not *really* know the risks. Although most acknowledge that smoking is "unhealthy," in some vague sense, few know exactly what chances they run of exactly what diseases. In one poll, 49 percent of smokers did not know that smoking causes most cases of lung cancer, 63 percent that it causes most cases of bronchitis, and 85 percent that it causes most cases of emphysema.

Overestimating badly the risks of dying in other more dramatic ways (such as car crashes, etc.), people badly underestimate the relative risks of dying in the more mundane ways associated with smoking. This allows them to rationalize further their smoking behavior as being "not all that dangerous," compared to other things that they are also doing.

Of course, logically it would be perfectly possible for people both to underestimate the extent of a risk and simultaneously to overreact to it. People might suppose the chances of snakebite are slight but live in mortal fear of it nonetheless. Psychologically, however, the reverse seems to happen. People's subjective probability estimates of an event's likelihood increase the more they dread it, and the more "psychologically available" the event therefore is to them (Kahneman, Slovic, and Tversky 1982). Smoking-related diseases, in contrast, tend to be "quiet killers"of which people have little direct or indirect experience, which tend to be underreported in newspapers (typically not even being mentioned in obituary notices) and which act on people one at a time rather than catastrophically killing many people at once. Smoking-related diseases being psychologically less available to people in these ways, they underestimate their frequency dramatically—by a factor of 8, in the case of lung cancer, according to one study (Slovic, Fischhoff, and Lichtenstein 1982, p. 469).[3] ...

It may still be argued that, as long as people had the facts, they can and should be held responsible if they chose not to act upon them when they could have done so. It may be folly for utilitarian policymakers to rely upon people's such imperfect responses to facts for purposes of constructing social welfare functions and framing public policies around them. But there is the separate matter of who ought to be blamed when some self-inflicted harm befalls people. There, arguably, responsibility ought to be on people's own shoulders. Arguably, we ought to stick to that judgment, even if people were "pressured" into smoking by the bullying of aggressive advertising or peer group pressure.

What crucially transforms the "voluntary acceptance" argument is evidence of the addictive nature of cigarette smoking. Of course, saying that smoking is addictive is not to say that all smokers are hooked and none can ever give it up. Clearly, many have done so. By the same token, though, "most narcotics users ... never progress beyond occasional use, and of those who do, approximately 30 percent spontaneously remit" (U.S. DHHS 1988, p. v). Surprisingly enough, studies show that more than 70 percent of American servicemen addicted to heroin in Vietnam gave it up when returning to the United States (Robins 1973; Pollin 1984; Fingarette 1975, pp. 429–31). We nonetheless continue to regard heroin as an addictive drug. The test of addictiveness is not impossibility but rather difficulty of withdrawal.

There is a tendency, in discussing *volenti* or informed consent arguments, to draw too sharp a distinction between "voluntary" and "involuntary acts" and to put the dividing line at the wrong place, at that. The tendency is often to assume that any act that is in the least voluntary—that is in any respect at all, to any extent at all, within the control of the agents themselves—is to be considered fully voluntary for the purposes. If we want to claim that some sort of act was involuntary, we are standardly advised to look for evidence of "somnambulism" or "automatism" or such like. Thus, U.S. Supreme Court justices wanting to argue for more humane treatment of addicts felt obliged to assert that "once [the defendant] had become an addict he was utterly powerless" to refrain from continuing to service his addiction (Fortas 1968, p. 567). That is an implausibly strong claim, given the above evidence.

There is no need to make such a strong claim, though, to vitiate arguments that the conduct was "voluntary" and the harm thus self-incurred. For purposes of excusing criminal conduct, we are prepared to count forms of "duress" that stop well short of rendering all alternative actions literally impossible. It is perfectly possible for bank tellers to let a robber break their arms instead of handing over the money; but no one expects them to do so. A credible threat of serious pain, or perhaps even very gross discomfort, is ordinarily regarded as more than sufficient to constitute duress of the sort that excuses responsibility for otherwise impermissible behavior.

So, too, I would argue should be the case with addiction-induced behavior. The issue is not whether it is literally impossible, but merely whether it is unreasonably costly, for addicts to resist their compulsive desires. If that desire is so strong that even someone with "'normal and reasonable' self-control" (Watson 1977, p. 331) would succumb to it, we have little compunction in saying that the addict's free will was sufficiently impaired that his apparent consent counts for naught.

This is arguably the case with nicotine addiction. To establish a substance as addictive, we require two sorts of evidence. The first is some sort of evidence of "physical need" for the substance among its users. That evidence is widely thought necessary to prove smoking is an addiction, rather than just a "habit" (U.S. DHEW 1964, chaps. 13–14), a psychological dependence, or a matter of mere sociological pressure (Daniels 1985, p. 159)—none of which would undercut, in a way that addictiveness does, claims that the risks of smoking are voluntarily incurred. That physical link has now been established, though. Particular receptors for the active ingredients of tobacco smoke have been discovered in the brain; the physiological sites and mechanisms by which nicotine acts on the brain have now been well mapped, and its tendency to generate compulsive, repetitive behavior in consequence has been well established. Such evidence—summarized in the surgeon general's 1988 report—has been one important factor in leading the World Health Organization ([WHO] 1978) and the American Psychiatric Association ([APA] 1987, sec. 305.1) to classify nicotine as a dependence-inducing drug. (Strictly speaking, the term "addiction" is out of favor in these circles, with "dependence" taking its place; in what follows, I shall continue using the more colloquial term in preference to the more technical one, though.)

None of that evidence proves that it would be literally impossible for smokers to resist the impulse to smoke. Through extraordinary acts of will, they might. Nor does any of that evidence prove that it is literally impossible for them to break their dependence altogether. Many have. Recall, however, that the issue is not one of impossibility but rather of how hard people should have to try before their will is said to be sufficiently impaired that their agreement does not count as genuine consent.

The evidence suggests that nicotine addicts have to try very hard indeed. This is the second crucial fact to establish in proving a substance addictive. Central among the WHO/APA criteria for diagnosing nicotine dependence is the requirement of evidence of "continuous use of tobacco for at least one month with . . . unsuccessful attempts to stop or significantly reduce the amount of tobacco use on a permanent basis" (APA 1987, sec. 305.1).

A vast majority of smokers do indeed find themselves in this position. The surgeon general reports the results of various studies showing that 90 percent of regular smokers have tried to quit (U.S. DHHS 1979, quoted in Pollin 1984). Another 1975 survey found that 84 percent of smokers had attempted to stop, but that only 36 percent of them had succeeded in maintaining their changed behavior for a whole year (Benfari, Ockene, and McIntyre 1982; see, further, Leventhal and Cleary 1980). Interestingly, graphs mapping the "relapse rate"—the percentage of ex-addicts that are back on the drug after a given period of time—are almost identical for nicotine and for heroin (Winsten 1986; U.S. DHHS 1988, p. 314 and chap. 5 more generally).

On the basis of all this evidence, the surgeon general has been led to three "major conclusions" contained in his 1988 report:

1. Cigarettes and other forms of tobacco are addicting.
2. Nicotine is the drug in tobacco that causes addiction.
3. The pharmacologic and behavioral processes that determine tobacco addiction are similar to those that determine addiction to drugs such as heroin and cocaine. [U.S. DHHS 1988, p. 9]

Evidence of smokers trying to stop and failing to do so is rightly regarded as central to the issue of addiction, philosophically as well as diagnostically. Some describe free will in terms of "second-order volitions"—desires about desires—controlling "first-order" ones (Frankfurt 1971). Others talk of free will in terms of a person's "evaluational structure" controlling his "motivational structure"—a person striving to obtain something if and only if he thinks it to be of value (Watson 1975; 1977). Addiction—the absence of free will—is thus a matter of first-order volitions winning out over second-order ones, and surface desires prevailing over the agent's own deeper values. In the case of smoking, trying to stop can be seen as a manifestation of one's second-order volitions, or one's deeper values, and failing to stop as evidence of the triumph of first-order surface desires over them. The same criteria the WHO and APA use to diagnose nicotine dependence also establish the impairment of the smoker's free will, philosophically.

For certain purposes, at least, even the courts now treat nicotine as addictive. Social security benefits are not payable to those claimants whose disabilities were voluntarily self-inflicted. But the courts have held that "smoking can be an involuntary act for some persons," and that those benefits may not therefore be routinely withheld from victims of smoking-related diseases on the grounds that they are suffering from voluntarily self-inflicted injuries.

Various other policy implications also follow from evidence of addictiveness, though. One might be that over-the-counter sales of cigarettes should be banned. If the product is truly addictive, then we have no more reason to respect a person's voluntary choice (however well-informed) to abandon his future volition to an addiction than we have for respecting a person's voluntary choice (however well-informed) to sell himself into slavery I am unsure how far to press this argument, since after all we do permit people to bind their future selves (through contracts, e.g.). But if it is the size of the stakes or the difficulty of breaking out of the bonds that makes the crucial difference, then acquiring a lethal and hard-to-break addiction is much more like a slavery contract than it is like an ordinary commercial commitment.

In any case, addictiveness thus defined makes it far easier to justify interventions that on the surface appear paternalistic. In some sense, they would then not be paternalistic at all. Where people "wish to stop smoking, but do not have the requisite willpower . . . we are not imposing a good on someone who rejects it. We are simply using coercion to enable people to carry out their own goals" (Dworkin 1972/1983, p. 32). . . .

The real force of the addiction findings, in the context of *volenti* or informed-consent arguments, though, is to undercut the claim that there is any *continuing* consent to the risks involved in smoking. There might have been consent in the very first instance—in smoking your first cigarette. But once you were hooked, you lost the capacity to consent in any meaningful sense on a continuing basis. As Hume says, to consent implies the possibility of doing otherwise; and addiction sub-

stantially deprives you of the capacity to do other than continue smoking. So once you have become addicted to nicotine, your subsequent smoking cannot be taken as indicating your consent to the risks.

The most that we can now say with confidence, therefore, is that "cigarette smoking, at least initially, is a voluntary activity," in the words of a leading court case in this area (Brown 1987, p. 627). If there is to be consent at all in this area, it can only be consent in the very first instance, that is, when you first began to smoke. That, in turn, seriously undercuts the extent to which cigarette manufacturers can rely upon *volenti* or informed-consent defenses in product liability litigation and its moral analogues.

It does so in two ways. The first arises from the fact that many of those now dying from tobacco-induced diseases started smoking well before warnings began appearing on packets in 1966 and were hooked by the time those warnings reached them. Their consent to the risks of smoking could only have been based on "common knowledge" and "folk wisdom." That is a short-term problem, though, since that cohort of smokers will eventually die off.

The second and more serious problem is a continuing problem in a way the first is not. A vast majority of smokers began smoking in their early to middle teens. Evidence suggests that "of those teenagers who smoke more than a single cigarette only 15 percent avoid becoming regular dependent smokers" (Russell 1974, p. 255). Studies show that, "of current smokers, about 60 percent began by the very young age of thirteen or fourteen" (Blasi and Monaghan 1986, p. 503), and the great majority—perhaps up to 95 percent—of regular adult smokers are thought to have been addicted before coming of age (Califano 1981, p. 183; Lewit, Coate, and Grossman 1981, p. 547, n. 8; Pollin 1984; Leventhal, Glynn, and Fleming 1987, p. 3373; Davis 1987, p. 730; U.S. DHHS 1988, p. 397).

The crux of the matter, then, is just this: being below the age of consent when they first began smoking, smokers were incapable of meaningfully consenting to the risks in the first instance. Being addicted by the time they reached the age of consent, they were incapable of consenting later, either. . . .

4.3 BAD HABITS AND ADDICTIONS

Many who oppose government regulation of smoking designed to protect smokers from themselves implicitly or explicitly treat it as nothing more than a bad habit. "Assumption of individual responsibility for one's own health" is, in these terms, far preferable to treating "sloth, gluttony, alcoholic overuse, reckless driving, sexual intemperance, and smoking" as "a national, not an individual responsibility" (Knowles 1977, p. 59).

In many ways, these writers have a point. Presumably it is perfectly true that we expect people to alter their own bad habits—or anyway not to complain when harms befall them in consequence of the practice of their own bad habits. After all, they could have altered their ways. Addictions are otherwise. They may, in the very first instance, have been self-induced. Once induced, however, they are not (easily) remediable thereafter, through any simple act of will. Indeed, that is one of the primary criteria used diagnostically to distinguish "drug dependence" from merely "habitual behaviors" (U.S. DHHS 1988, pp. 7–8).

Thus, the habit versus addiction issue can be cast as an issue about responsibility, but it comes out rather differently than "responsibility for self" theorists suppose. People may bear responsibility for their own bad habits and for whatever follows from them. They bear responsibility for having become addicted to drugs. Once addicted, though, they ought no longer be considered responsible for their addiction-driven actions. For that reason, the addiction evidence is crucial in making the case for governmental action on smoking in several respects.[4]

Some theorists—especially economists—might nonetheless resist these conclusions, insisting that the distinction between addictions and mere bad habits is meaningless. Essentially, there are three bases for grounding this distinction. Economists often remain unimpressed by all of them.

The first basis for the addiction-habit distinction has to do with the way in which, with addictive substances, the more you have consumed of them in the past the more you want to consume of them in the future. But that is merely to say that present preferences over those goods are a positive function of past consumption; and, put that way, there is nothing particularly unique about addictive as against all sorts of other goods.[5] One particularly blunt way of putting the point is to say that "there is, of course, a large degree of habituation in all consumption, in the sense that people seek to repeat activities they enjoy. How," economists ask, "is being 'habituated' to cigarettes any different from being habituated to chewing gum, ice cream, television, jogging, or swimming?" (Tollison and Wagner 1988, p. 39; see similarly Schwartz 1989). There is nothing wrong with habituation per se. Some habits are bad; others are good, in the sense that you are better off objectively as well as subjectively for having cultivated them. On that score, economists are absolutely right.

The second basis for a distinction between addiction and habit rests on essentially physiological evidence. Receptors in the brain have now been identified for the pharmacologically active substances in tobacco smoke; and partly on the basis of that discovery the American Psychiatric Association and the World Health Organization have deemed nicotine addictive. Yet, as economists are quick to add, there are presumably "pleasure centers" in the brain that are stimulated by ordinary consumption goods, too. Where, exactly, those centers are and how, exactly, consumption stimulates them we do not yet know in any detail. But there is no reason to believe that the neurochemical processes involved there are radically different than those involved in the relationship between nicotine and its receptors in the brain.

The third and most important basis for the addiction-habit distinction has to do with the addict's wanting to stop but being unable to do so. This is the central element in the APA/WHO diagnostic criteria used to class nicotine as addictive.

Economists critical of the habit-addiction distinction have a quick retort, here too. They say, "There are, of course, many overeaters who claim they want to lose weight but do not," also (Tollison and Wagner 1988, p. 39). They go on to say, "It is clear that many smokers say they would like to stop. . . . And it is equally clear that for most of them, the intensity of that wish is weak, as judged by the observation that they continue to smoke. Should we therefore say that the demand for cigarettes is somehow fraudulent? Perhaps, alternatively, it is the professed desire to stop smoking that is misleading" (Tollison and Wagner 1988, p. 39).

The central point in this economistic attempt to collapse the addiction-habit distinction is the claim that all temptations are resistable and all addictions curable, at a cost. To quote Tollison and Wagner (1988, p. 39) yet again: "We know that people can change their habits if they truly want to. . . . It surely makes less sense to say that those who do not lose weight are habituated to food . . . than to say that some people value losing weight more highly than others, and are thus willing to pay a higher price to overcome their eating "habit." And the same, they would say, is true of smoking: "There are many ex-smokers, so we know that people can stop smoking, just as they can stop overeating, if they are willing to pay the price—that is, if they value more highly the benefits they think they will derive from reducing their eating or from stopping their smoking than they value the continuation of their present eating or smoking practices" (Tollison and Wagner 1988, p. 39).

Thus, to the economist, the pain of withdrawal is just the cost that an addict has to pay for the good of a "clean" life. In that respect, it is formally analogous to the cost that anyone pays (also in terms of pain, or discomfort anyway) in breaking a bad habit. Neither, furthermore, is there any reason to suppose that the cost of breaking the one (breaking a weak addiction, e.g.) would necessarily always exceed that of breaking the other (breaking a long-standing, well-entrenched bad habit, e.g.). If people are not prepared to pay the price of stopping, then they surely must not mind smoking all that much after all. Or so the economist's logic would hold.

What this comes down to is an issue of whether addicts really are subjectively worse off smoking, or not. Their words may suggest that they are, but their actions suggest that they are not; and the latter is what counts most heavily in contemporary micro-economists' crassly behavioral concept of preference. There is no need to follow them in those conceptual rigidities, however. At least sometimes, what a person says is a better indicator of the true state of his

mind than is what he does. Such would clearly be the case if he were physically restrained, in a way that rendered him simply unable to do what he said he wanted to do. We may well question the practical relevance of a preference for doing what he is unable to do. But we could hardly question, in those circumstances, that his true preference is to do as he says; and we would be quite wrong to infer from the fact that he does not do it that he does not really want to do it, after all. Similarly, if a person is physiologically restrained (by a drug dependence, defined inter alia in terms of the state of certain receptors in his brain), we might also say that he was simply unable to do what he truly wants to do, better revealed once again through his statements than through his actions.

If economists insist upon a more behavioral way of putting this point, we can employ a hypothetical-choice formulation: would the people involved have chosen otherwise, if they had it to do over again? If not, then their initial choice can unambiguously be said to have promoted their welfare; if so, it can unambiguously be said to have ill-served it. Where people plainly "regret" previous choices, and would choose differently next time, that is clear enough. In cases of addiction, matters are only a little more complicated. Once addicted, people would choose the same addictive good next time as last; but if given a chance to choose over whether or not to begin consuming the addictive substance in the first place, they would choose not to do so. (That is how "addiction" is here defined and how it is operationalized in the studies demonstrating the addictiveness of nicotine.) Stopping people from becoming addicts by stopping them from beginning to consume tobacco in the first place would thus be justified in terms of their own self-assessed welfare, defined in terms of their own (hypothetical) choices.

Of course, it is highly desirable that people should take charge of their own lives in both respects, breaking bad habits and addictions alike. Of necessity, that must be primarily a task for individuals themselves. But there are some things that governments can do to help—such as making practices people wish to abandon more expensive (through excise taxes) or restricting the number of hours or number of places in which they can engage in them. Such assistance can be justified on the grounds that, far from imposing paternalist policies on people, we are merely helping them enforce rules of their own choosing upon themselves. That rationale works equally well, whether it is a mere bad habit or an actual addiction that is involved.

Whether or not that argument is convincing in showing that smokers themselves would be subjectively better off if prevented from smoking, it is decisive in establishing another even stronger rationale for public policies against smoking. That has not so much to do with protecting present addicts from themselves as it has to do with preventing future addicts from becoming addicted. Addictions are unambiguously bad, from the point of view of the person addicted. Being defined in terms of a desire to quit coupled with an inability to quit, addictions necessarily would make the addict worse-off; and, on the evidence of section 2.2 above, a vast majority of those who do smoke will become addicted in this way. Once they are addicted, they face a high price to pay in overcoming the addiction, and we cannot be absolutely sure whether their health is worth that price to them. But we can be sure that those who are not yet addicted—just like those who already are—would much rather not have to face that choice. If they were to become addicted, they would almost certainly come to wish they had not. On the basis of that hypothetical choice that we can reasonably impute to people not yet addicted, we can justify public policies to prevent them from getting addicted.

The policy implications of a distinction between addictions and mere bad habits, couched in some such terms, are clear. Since habits are not necessarily bad, public policies discouraging them are not necessarily desirable (although it may of course be socially desirable to curtail the practice of those habits in public). Addictions, in contrast, are necessarily bad. Policies discouraging them are therefore always desirable. We might wish to show compassion toward present addicts. But clearly we should do what we can to prevent new addicts. . . .

NOTES

1. Strides are being made in identification of those at especially high risk of lung cancer and cardiac disease in consequence of smoking (Russell 1974, p. 257); but that, in

itself, is not enough to undercut this case for a general anti-smoking campaign.

2. One of a person's ends—continued life—at least. Perhaps the person has other ends ("relaxation," or whatever) that are well served by smoking; and insofar as "people taking risks actually value the direct consequences associated with them . . . it is more difficult to intrude paternalistically" (Daniels 1985, pp. 158, 163). But assuming that smoking is not the only means to the other ends—not the only way to relax, etc.—the intrusion is only minimally difficult to justify.

3. Thus, health education campaigns have begun focusing on the risks of contracting Buerger's disease from smoking, the amputation of limbs being, like snakebites, psychologically more accessible to people (especially teenagers, before they start to smoke) than rotting lungs.

4. Ranging from publicly sponsored smoking-cessation programs to restricting or banning the sale of tobacco (see, generally, U.S. DHHS 1988, esp. chap. 7).

5. One criterion—which even Stigler and Becker (1977) would recognize—is the tendency for an addict's tolerance to grow, the more of the substance he has taken. With ordinary goods (like olives, say) that are "acquired tastes," the more of the good you have consumed in the past the more pleasure you get out of each subsequent unit of consumption. With addictive substances (like heroin, say), this is not true: it takes increasingly large doses to produce the same subjective effects as before, thanks to increasing tolerance. This is a characteristic which nicotine dependence shares with all other addictions, however (Winsten 1986; U.S. DHHS 1988). That this phenomenon "tops out" sooner (at around twenty—or, given 50 percent underreporting of smoking behavior, perhaps thirty—cigarettes a day for most addicts) rather than later (as with heroin) is surely irrelevant for purposes of classifying a substance as addictive.

REFERENCES

American Psychiatric Association (APA). 1987. *Diagnostic and Statistical Manual of Mental Disorders.* 3d ed. Washington, D.C.: APA.

Benfari, Robert C.; Ockene, Judith K.; and McIntyre, Kevin M. 1982. Control of Cigarette-Smoking from a Psychological Perspective. *Annual Review of Public Health* 3: 101–28.

Blasi, Vincent, and Monaghan, Henry Paul. 1986. The First Amendment and Cigarette Advertising. *Journal of the American Medical Association* 256: 502–9.

Borgida, E., and Nisbett, R. E. 1977. The Differential Impact of Abstract vs. Concrete Information on Decisions. *Journal of Applied Social Psychology* 7: 258–71.

Brown, John R. 1987. Opinion of the U.S. Court of Appeals. *Palmer v. Liggett Group, Inc.* 825 F.2d 620 (1st Cir. 1987).

Burch, P. R. J. 1978. Smoking and Lung Cancer: The Problem of Inferring Cause. *Journal of the Royal Statistical Society,* ser. A, 141: 437–58.

Califano, Joseph A., Jr. 1981. *Governing America.* New York: Simon & Schuster.

Cederlof, R.; Friberg, L.; and Lundman, T. 1977. The Interactions of Smoking, Environment and Heredity and Their Implications for Disease Etiology, *Acta Medica Scandinavica,* vol. 612 (suppl. 1).

Chapman, Simon. 1986. *Great Expectorations: Advertising and the Tobacco Industry.* London: Comedia.

Daniels, Norman. 1985. *Just Health Care.* Cambridge: Cambridge University Press.

Davis, Ronald M. 1987. Current Trends in Cigarette Advertising and Marketing. *New England Journal of Medicine* 316: 725–32.

Dworkin, Gerald. 1972. Paternalism. *Monist* 56, no. 1: 64–84. Reprinted in Sartorius, ed., 1983, pp. 19–34.

Edell, Marc Z., and Gisser, Stewart M. 1985. *Cipollone v. Liggett Group, Inc.:* The Application of Theories of Liability in Current Cigarette Litigation. *New York State Journal of Medicine* 85, no. 7: 318–21.

Eysenck, H. J. 1980. *The Causes and Effects of Smoking.* London: Maurice Temple Smith.

Eysenck, H. J. 1986. Smoking and Health. In Tollison, ed., 1986, pp. 17–88.

Fingarette, Herbert. 1975. Addiction and Criminal Responsibility. *Yale Law Journal* 84: 413–44.

Fortas, Abe. 1968. Dissenting Opinion. *Powell v. Texas.* 392 US 514, 554–70.

Frankfurt, Harry G. 1971. Freedom of the Will and the Concept of a Person. *Journal of Philosophy* 68: 5–20.

Gorovitz, Samuel. 1982. *Doctors' Dilemmas.* New York: Oxford University Press.

Harrison, Larry. 1986. Tobacco Battered and the Pipes Shattered: A Note on the Fate of the First British Campaign against Tobacco Smoking. *British Journal of Addiction* 81: 553–58.

Kahneman, D.; Slovic, P.; and Tversky, A., eds. 1982. *Judgment under Uncertainty.* Cambridge: Cambridge University Press.

Knowles, John H. 1977. The Responsibility of the Individual. *Daedalus* 106, no. 1: 57–80.

Leventhal, Howard; Glynn, Kathleen; and Fleming, Raymond. 1987. Is the Smoking Decision an "Informed Choice"? *Journal of the American Medical Association* 257: 3373–76.

Lewit, E. M.; Coate, D.; and Grossman, M. 1981. The Effects of Government Regulation on Teenage Smoking. *Journal of Law and Economics* 24: 545–69.

Mintz, Morton. 1988. Cigarette Trial Breaks New Ground. *Washington Post,* March 27, pp. H1, H8. Reprinted in *Washington Post National Weekly Edition,* April 11, pp. 20–21.

Peto, Richard. 1980. Possible Ways of Explaining to Ordinary People the Quantitative Dangers of Smoking. *Health Education Journal* 39: 45–46.

Pollin, William. 1984. The Role of the Addictive Process as a Key Step in Causation of All Tobacco-related Diseases. *Journal of the American Medical Association* 252: 2874.

R. J. Reynolds Tobacco Co. 1986. The Health Effects of Smoking. A Submission in the Case of *Browner v. R.J. Reynolds* (California Superior Court, County of Contra Costa). Reprinted in *Tobacco Products Litigation Reporter* 1, no. 4: 5.45–56.

Robins, L. 1973. *A Follow-up of Vietnam Drug Users.* Interim Final Report, Special Actions Office for Drug Abuse Prevention. Washington, D.C.: Executive Office of the President.

Russell, M. A. H. 1974. Realistic Goals for Smoking and Health. *Lancet* 7851: 254–58.

Schelling, Thomas C. 1980. The Intimate Contest for Self-Command. *Public Interest* 60:94–118. Reprinted in Schelling 1984a, pp. 57–82.

Slade, J.; Kopelowicz, A.; Hahn, A.; Gill, J.; Kabis, S.; and Vasen, A. 1986–87. An Analysis of R. J. Reynolds' Position Paper on the Health Effects of Smoking. *Tobacco Products Litigation Reporter* 1, no. 8: 5.97– 105; 1, no. 10: 5.115–21; 2, no. 2: 5.11–21.

Slovic, P.; Fischhoff, B.; and Lichtenstein, S. 1982. Fact vs. Fears: Understanding Perceived Risks. In Kahneman, Slovic, and Tversky, eds., 1982, pp. 463–89.

Stigler, George J., and Becker, Gary S. 1977. De Gustibus Non Est Disputandum. *American Economic Review* 67: 76–90.

Tollison, Robert D., and Wagner, Richard E. 1988. *Smoking and the State: Social Costs, Rent Seeking, and Public Policy.* Lexington, Mass.: Lexington Books, D. C. Heath.

U.S. Department of Health, Education and Welfare (U.S. DHEW). 1964. *Smoking and Health.* Report of the Advisory Committee to the Surgeon General of the

Public Health Service. Washington, D.C.: Government Printing Office.

U.S. Department of Health and Human Services. Surgeon General. 1979. *Smoking and Health.* Washington, D.C.: Government Printing Office.

U.S. DHHS. Surgeon General. 1986. *The Health Consequences of Involuntary Smoking.* Washington, D.C.: Government Printing Office.

U.S. DHHS. Surgeon General. 1988. *The Health Consequences of Smoking: Nicotine Addiction.* Washington, D.C.: Government Printing Office.

Watson, Gary. 1975. Free Agency. *Journal of Philosophy* 72: 205–20.

Watson, Gary. 1977. Skepticism about Weakness of Will. *Philosophical Review* 86: 316–39.

White, Larry C. 1988. *Merchants of Death: The American Tobacco Industry.* New York: Beach Tree Books, William Morrow.

Winsten, Jay A., director. 1986. *Nicotine Dependency and Compulsive Tobacco Use.* A Research Status Report, Center for Health Communication, Harvard School of Public Health. Reprinted in *Tobacco Product Liability Reporter* 1, no. 7.

WHO. 1978. *International Classification of Diseases.* 9th ed. Geneva: WHO.

WHO. 1986. *In Point of Fact,* no. 36. Geneva: WHO.

Critics

DANIEL SHAPIRO

Smoking Tobacco
Irrationality, Addiction, and Paternalism

Smoking tobacco (henceforth, "smoking") is a very risky activity: between 18% to 36% of smokers die prematurely, and smokers on average lose three to seven years of life.[1] Nonsmokers also are seriously affected by smoking, by second-hand smoke, but my concern here is not with the harm that smokers do to others, but with the harm that they do to themselves, and whether laws that aim to prevent or strongly discourage the latter harm are justified in the case of adult smokers. It is generally difficult to justify paternalistic laws for sane adults, that is, laws which aim to prevent or strongly discourage those adults from

harming themselves, particularly if their actions are voluntary and they know the risks involved. However, Robert E. Goodin argues in his provocative book *No Smoking*[2] that neither the voluntariness nor the knowledge condition applies to smokers and that accordingly paternalistic laws to prevent or strongly discourage adult smoking can be justified.[3]

First, he maintains that despite the information available about the risks of smoking, smokers falsely and irrationally underestimate the degree to which smoking can be harmful to themselves. Borrowing an argument made by Gerald Dworkin, Goodin says

Daniel Shapiro, "Smoking Tobacco: Irrationality, Addiction, and Paternalism," *Public Affairs Quarterly* 8, no. 2 (1994): 187–203. Reprinted by permission of North American Philosophical Publications.

that while it is ordinarily not the state's business to prevent people from relying on false and irrational inferences when decisions based on these inferences would harm only themselves, it may be the state's business when such inferences lead to decisions that are far-reaching, potentially dangerous and irreversible. The argument is that while paternalism is unjustified when one is imposing a conception of the good upon a person, it is not unjustified, or is a very weak form of paternalism, when one is simply imposing on someone a better means to achieve her ends. Smokers who deny that smoking is dangerous or do not genuinely appreciate the risks of smoking are not people with a different conception of the good than most of us, as the reason they continue to smoke is not due to their valuing health or continued life less than other people, but rather is due to their irrational and false beliefs about the harms of smoking. So a state policy which makes it harder for them to smoke is thus really a policy which is making it easier for them to each their own ends—health and continued life.[4]

Second, following a recent report by the Surgeon General[5] and the American Psychiatric Association, Goodin argues that smokers do not have a bad habit, but are addicts addicted to nicotine. Thus adult smokers do not voluntarily engage in their risky behavior, and laws which aim to prevent adult smoking cannot be condemned as objectionably paternalistic. Goodin uses this line of argument to suggest that we should consider banning over-the-counter sales of cigarettes.[6]

I will call Goodin's first argument the irrationality argument and the second argument the addiction argument. My specific aim is to show that they both fail, and my general aim is to show that only under very limited conditions could arguments of this type succeed. Section I concerns the irrationality argument, and section II concerns the addiction argument.

I. IRRATIONALITY, SMOKING, AND PATERNALISM

I have three aims in this section. First, I shall discuss whether it is true that smokers falsely and irrationally underestimate the risks of smoking.[7] Second, shall discuss whether *if* the kind of irrationality described by Goodin existed, such irrationality would justify paternalist measures to prevent or strongly discourage smoking. And third, I shall discuss under what conditions, if any, the irrationality argument could justify paternalist intervention.

Are Smokers Irrational?

Goodin's claim that smokers falsely and irrationally underestimate the risks of smoking rests on two kinds of evidence. First, he cites a 1981 survey that shows that smokers do not know or deny that smoking causes most cases of lung cancer, emphysema and bronchitis.[8] Second, he argues that smokers engage in various sorts of reasoning errors, the two most important of which are wishful thinking (believing that they won't be vulnerable to smoking-related diseases), and the anchoring fallacy (reasoning that since they have smoked many times without any ill effect that therefore smoking is safe, at least for them).[9]

The survey that Goodin cites, however, does not reveal smokers' assessment of the relevant risks. The beliefs that are most relevant are not beliefs about the percentage of lung cancer or other diseases caused by smoking, but beliefs about the percentage of smokers that die from those diseases. Surveys taken by the economist W. Kip Viscusi show that smokers as well as nonsmokers *overestimate* the risk of smokers dying from lung cancer. The most recent data from the Surgeon General suggests that smokers face a 5 to 12 percentage chance of dying from lung cancer, while the population at large believe it to be 43 percent, and smokers believe it is 37 percent.[10] (The same overestimation occurs with the overall mortality rate from smoking, though the degree of error here is somewhat smaller.)[11] This overestimation can be explained by recent work of psychologists, which shows that people tend to underestimate hidden risks, and overestimate publicized ones.[12] That smoking can cause lung cancer is very highly publicized, far more than other risks, yet such publicity rarely, if ever, provides information about the degree of risk, so it's not surprising that people think that the risk of smokers dying from lung cancer is quite high. Goodin is aware that people overestimate highly publicized risks, but he argues that deaths from lung cancers are not highly publicized; e.g., they are not featured prominently in news reports, and they tend to occur to people one-by-one rather than catastrophically killing a lot of people at one time—which explains why in one survey the frequency of lung cancer deaths was grossly underestimated.[13] However, people's beliefs about the riskiness of an activity is not revealed by their beliefs concerning how many people prematurely die from it, but from their beliefs about the percentage of people that are harmed by it. So the fact that information about the former is not highly publicized and that people accordingly underestimate it is beside the point.

So smokers do not falsely underestimate the risks of smoking.[14] But do they, as Goodin suggested, irrationally assume that the risks won't apply to them or are they instead simply less risk averse than nonsmokers? The evidence is mixed. Viscusi presents evidence which shows that smokers are less risk averse than nonsmokers: the former are more willing to work in riskier jobs, as measured by how much money they would need to feel compensated by a greater chance of accidents on the job.[15] On the other hand, while some of the surveys that Goodin cites as evidence that smokers irrationally assume the risks won't apply to them can be dismissed on the ground that these were surveys of adolescent smokers—as the concern here is with adults—there does remain one survey which presents evidence of this irrationality in adult smokers.[16] However, the fallacies of wishful thinking and anchoring are common to humans in general, not just smokers.[17] Unless there is evidence that smokers engage in these fallacies far more than nonsmokers, the evidence that smokers are less risk-averse remains as a better explanation of smokers' behavior than does the claim that smokers irrationally believe that they are invulnerable.

Goodin's Irrationality Argument

Goodin's claim that smokers falsely and irrationally underestimate the risks of smoking has been badly damaged. But it's worth considering whether if his claim was true the irrationality argument would justify taking measures to prevent or strongly discourage the harms that adult smokers incur. However, before discussing the irrationality argument, let us note one way in which it needs to be changed. The argument says that we are justified in preventing someone from making decisions based on false and irrational beliefs when these beliefs would lead to decisions that are far-reaching, potentially dangerous, and irreversible. However, a decision to smoke (or continue smoking) is not *irreversible,* since, as I shall discuss in section II, significant numbers quit. So that the irrationality argument applies to smoking, I suggest a reinterpretation whereby the argument refers not only to irreversible decisions, but to decisions that are difficult to reverse. Notice that addiction is one, but not the only, reason decisions could be difficult to reverse. Thus my reinterpretation makes the irrationality argument separate from the issue of addiction, which is at it should be. If to apply the irrationality argument we had to first establish a finding of addiction, then the irrationality argument would be parasitic on the addiction argument. However, while Goodin does indicate that the addiction argument is more important than the irrationality argument,[18] he does not believe that the latter is dependent upon the former.

With this reinterpretation out of the way, let us examine whether the argument succeeds. At first glance, it seems plausible: if smokers place the same value on continued life and health as the rest of us, and if they falsely believe that smoking is not that detrimental to those ends, then preventing or discouraging them from smoking can be viewed as merely enabling them to better achieve their ends, rather than imposing ends or a conception of the good upon them. However, smoking is a very important means to a *variety* of ends. Smokers smoke to relax, to concentrate, to handle anxiety, stress and difficult interpersonal situations, as a way of taking a break during the day, as a social lubricant, as a substitute for putting food in their mouths—the list could be extended.[19] *Why* smoking is so important to smokers' lives is an interesting question (I will address it to some extent in section II), but for now the issue is simply *that* it is important. This means that it is false that preventing or discouraging smoking simply enables the smoker to better achieve her ends of increased life and health. If concentrating and smoking are linked, or smoking and relaxing are linked, or smoking and handling anxiety and stress are linked, etc., then preventing or discouraging smoking doesn't just involve preventing or discouraging a potentially life and health-threatening activity, but involves preventing or discouraging other values or activities, such as relaxing, concentrating, etc.

At one point Goodin recognizes this problem, and replies that since smoking is not the *only* means to other ends, legislation which aims at preventing or discouraging smoking is an intrusion which is only minimally difficult to justify.[20] All this response shows, however, is that preventing someone from smoking does not make it *impossible* for her to concentrate, relax, etc., without smoking; but since it would make it *difficult* for her to achieve a variety to ends, it's hard to see how Goodin can say that such a policy is only minimally difficult to justify. We certainly have moved a long way from the original claim, which was that preventing smoking *merely* enabled a person to achieve her ends of continued life and health. Another problem with the reply is that the most plausible explanation or reason why the state would adopt a policy that makes it easier for some people to achieve some ends (in this case, continued life and health) and harder to achieve others (relaxation, concentration, reduction of stress and anxiety, etc.) is that the former are ranked as more important by the state. Now differences between people's conception of the good often depend heavily on how one *ranks* various values, as opposed to merely being disagreements about which values should be in the ranking. Thus one can claim that when the state ranks continued life and health as more important than concentrating, relaxing, etc., it is not imposing a conception of the good upon smokers only if there is good evidence that smokers have the same ranking. But such evidence is lacking, for on the assumption that smokers underestimate the risks of smoking, they are not directly aware that there is a conflict, as things stand now, between the way in which they achieve relaxation, concentration, etc., and their continued life and health.

Another defect of the irrationality argument is that it does not recognize that an explanation for someone's false and irrational beliefs about the risks of a certain activity could be her epistemic attitudes and values, which are certainly part of one's conception of the good life. The way in which I assess and am open to evidence, the value I place on discovering the truth, the degree to which I desire to hold coherent beliefs—all of these are to some degree a function of the kind of person I want to be, of the kind of life I want to lead. If, despite the voluminous evidence of the risks of smoking, some smokers underestimate the risks of smoking (as we've seen, most don't, but right now we are discussing the hypothetical question), a plausible explanation for this could be that they have a very skeptical (or hostile) attitude towards scientific evidence and inquiry, or perhaps they view themselves as "lucky" persons who can defy the odds, or perhaps they take perverse pride in doing what everyone else considers irrational. These are the sort of considerations that indicate that one wishes to be a certain kind of person or that one wishes to lead a certain kind of life. For these kinds of smokers, the irrationality argument fails. When the irrationality that smokers manifest is due to epistemic values that are an important part of their conception of the good, then it will be untrue that making it more difficult for irrational smokers to smoke simply makes it easier for them to achieve their ends.

Of course, it could be that the smokers who falsely and irrationally underestimate the risks of smoking do so not because of a certain self-conception but because they engage in the kind of reasoning errors to which humans are prone, such as the wishful thinking and anchoring fallacy noted earlier. My point is that Goodin assumes that faulty inferences about risks is simply a cognitive mistake, and does not recognize that some forms of irrationality can be important components of the kind of life one wishes to lead.

Why the Irrationality Argument Fails

We can now generalize the arguments made in this section and see under what conditions the irrationality argument can succeed. Succeed, in this context, means: the argument justifies paternalistic laws which aim to prevent or strongly discourage sane adults from engaging in activities the risks of which they systematically underestimate, on the grounds that such laws merely enable them to achieve important ends, e.g., health or continued life, that they do not realize, due to their underestimation of the risk, are placed in serious jeopardy by that activity.

First, the activity the law aims to prevent or strongly discourage must not be one which is a central or important means to a variety of ends or valued activities. If it is such a means, then it is false that preventing or discouraging people from engaging in that activity merely enables them to achieve the ends that they do not realize are in serious jeopardy by engaging in that activity, e.g., health or continued life. For such prevention or discouragement will also make it more difficult for them to achieve the ends or valued activities with which the risky activity is linked.

Second, it must be true that the reason for the underestimation of the risks of the activity has nothing to do with epistemic attitudes and values that are an important part of one's conception of the good or a desire to be a certain kind of person. If the reason for the underestimation of the risk is due to those factors, then preventing or discouraging a person from engaging in the risky activity will involve imposing a conception of the good upon that person rather than merely helping her to achieve her ends.

Third, the decision to engage in the activity must be one which is difficult to reverse, for if it was not difficult, then it wouldn't matter that much, as far as the person's well-being is concerned, whether or not she underestimated the risks of the activity.

Fourth, the argument must be independent of the question of addiction, for if one is addicted to the activity, then one could justify laws preventing adults from engaging in the activity without using the irrationality argument.

Now the problem is this: the first two conditions work against the third condition. If the activity is not central to a variety of ends and one's underestimation of the risk has nothing to do with epistemic attitudes or values which are central to one's life, then the decision to engage in the activity is not difficult to reverse. What would make the activity difficult to reverse is that it is linked with other activities or ends which the person values, or that it is central to the

kind of person one wishes to be or the life one wants to lead, or that one is addicted. But all of these requirements have been ruled out, given the third and fourth conditions listed above. Thus it is doubtful that there are any conditions under which the irrationality argument could succeed.

II. ADDICTION, SMOKING, AND PATERNALISM

The failure of the irrationality argument seems to have no bearing on the addiction argument.[21] Even if smokers do not falsely and irrationally underestimate the risks of smoking, if they are addicted, then they do not voluntarily assume those risks, in which case paternalistic measures to stop or strongly discourage adult smokers from harming themselves would not appear to be objectionable. I shall first discuss Goodin's addiction argument, show why it fails, and then show that the conditions under which the addiction argument can succeed in justifying paternalist intervention for sane adults are very limited indeed.

Goodin's Addiction Argument

By saying that smokers are addicted, Goodin means that after smoking for a while, the desire to do so is so strong that someone with normal and reasonable self-control would succumb to the desire.[22] Accordingly, we should "have little compunction in saying that the addict's free will was sufficiently impaired that his apparent consent counts for naught."[23] Goodin says two pieces of evidence show that (almost) all smokers are addicted. First, there is a physical need to continue smoking: "the physiological sites and mechanisms by which nicotine acts on the brain have now been well mapped, and its tendency to generate compulsive, repetitive behavior in consequence has been well established."[24] Such evidence, says Goodin, is necessary in order to show that smoking is an addiction, not merely a bad habit, a psychological dependency or a matter of mere sociological pressure, "none of which would undercut, in a way that addictiveness does, claims that the risks of smoking are voluntarily incurred."[25] Second, there is much evidence that smokers have to try very hard to stop smoking: Goodin cites a 1979 Department of Health and Human Services study that shows that 90% of regular smokers have tried to quit, as well as a 1975 survey that showed that 84% of smokers have attempted to stop, but only 36% of them have succeeded in maintaining their changed behavior for a whole year.

Thus Goodin's view is that the physiological (or neurophysiological) effects of smoking make withdrawal from nicotine extremely difficult to do; though a person can resist the compulsive desires that cigarette smoking induces, this involves "extraordinary acts of will"[26] that a person with a normal and reasonable amount of self-control will be unable to muster.

No doubt many smokers find it hard to quit. However, Goodin exaggerates the difficulty by using outdated information. As of a few years ago, almost half of adult smokers had successfully quit,[27] and according to the American Cancer Society, over 90% of those have done so on their own without professional treatment.[28] This throws some doubt on Goodin's claim that it takes extraordinary acts of will to resist the desire to smoke, since resisting that desire seems to be close to an ordinary occurrence for many smokers at some point in their lives. But I will not press this point, as my main concern in this section isn't with the level of difficulty of giving up smoking but with refuting Goodin's claim that this difficulty is due to the neurophysiological effects of nicotine.

Before doing that, one modification in Goodin's concept of addiction is necessary. Goodin maintained that to establish that one is addicted to X, one must show that it is difficult to give up X, *and* that one physically needs to continue X. I agree that the difficulty of giving up X is not *sufficient* to establish that one is addicted to X. It could be difficult to give up something for reasons which have nothing to do with addiction or whether one acts voluntarily. E.g., activities or habits which are central or important to one's life can be difficult to give up, yet were we to say that therefore these activities or habits are addictions or that we are compelled to continue these activities

or habits, much of what we do would not be considered voluntary. However, the something else that in addition to the difficulty of giving up X is required to establish that X is an addiction, does not have to be a physical need to continue to do X or evidence of neurophysiological compulsion. Goodin's point in saying that there is a physical need to smoke is to undercut the claim that smokers voluntarily continue to smoke, since one doesn't voluntarily come to physically need something. However, a need does not have to be *physical* in order to undercut a claim of voluntariness: under some circumstances, psychological or other needs could do so as well. If the key element is nonvoluntariness, it seems completely arbitrary to focus just on physical needs.

I suspect the reason Goodin focused on physical needs and ignored psychological needs is that the former don't seem to be the sort of things for which one could ever be held responsible, while this is untrue for at least some kind of psychological needs. This suggests that Goodin's account of the concept of addiction should be modified so that the two key elements are the difficulty in quitting a certain activity because one needs it and the lack of responsibility for needing it. On this revised account, the neurophysiological evidence that Goodin cites would not be *necessary* to establish that one is addicted or that one does not voluntarily engage in or assume the risks of a certain activity, but would be *one kind,* perhaps the best kind, of evidence that shows that one does not voluntarily engage in the activity. In my discussion of Goodin's argument in what follows, it should be kept in mind that the relevance of the issue of the physical or physiological effects of nicotine concerns the larger issue of smokers' responsibility for their behavior.

Why Goodin's Addiction Argument Fails

The success of Goodin's addiction argument requires, first, that the physical or physiological effects of nicotine must actually *explain*, or play a large role in explaining, why many smokers find it difficult to quit, and, second, that this explanation be compatible with the fact that in the last thirty years an increasing percentage of smokers have quit. I shall concentrate mainly on the former, and say a few words about the latter.

Goodin believes that it is obvious that the physiological effects of nicotine explain the difficulty in quitting: recall his statement that it has been "well established" that the sites and mechanisms in the brain for nicotine tend to "generate compulsive, repetitive behavior *in consequence.*" Goodin is referring here to studies summarized in the Surgeon General's 1988 report on nicotine addiction and in the American Psychiatric Association's account of "tobacco dependence disorder." However, if these studies show that the physical need to continue to smoke or the physiological effects of nicotine explain the difficulty in quitting, then the difference between successful and unsuccessful quitters should be due in large part to differences in strength of those needs or effects. But these studies do not show that. What they do show[29] is that smokers who quit smoking in a treatment program have a relapse rate similar to heroin addicts in treatment programs, that smoking produces tolerance, and that quitting smoking produces withdrawal symptoms. The relapse rate of smokers in treatment programs is irrelevant, since smokers in treatment programs are a rather atypical group—as mentioned earlier, over 90% of smokers quit on their own. Nor does tolerance to nicotine explain the difficulty of quitting. Tolerance means that smokers must increase their intake until they achieve the effect that they want, and while this explains why smokers smoke every day to achieve the effect they want—the effects of nicotine are partly lost during sleep—it does not show why smokers would find it difficult to stop wanting to achieve this effect.

This leaves us with the existence of withdrawal symptoms after stopping smoking—the more common ones are cravings for tobacco, impairment of concentration, irritability, anxiety and restlessness, sleep and gastrointestinal disturbances[30]—as the way to establish the explanatory link that Goodin requires. But for withdrawal symptoms to establish that link, two conditions must hold: (1) their severity after initial attempts to quit must provide good evidence of the degree of one's physical need to smoke, and (2) there must be a clear connection between the difficulty in quitting and severity of withdrawal symp-

toms. However, both (1) and (2) are false. As for (1), both the American Psychiatric Association and the Surgeon General's report admit that the problems smokers face after initial attempts to quit are not a reliable indicator of physical dependence on nicotine.[31] The problem is fairly obvious: the terms listed as withdrawal symptoms are almost all psychological in nature, or have a psychological component. So, for example, if smoker A suffers from more severe anxiety than smoker B after they both quit smoking, this could be explained by A having a greater physical need to smoke/being subject to greater neurophysiological compulsion than B or by A having more problems than B in handling anxiety provoking situations without nicotine (i.e., A is more anxious than B.) Only the former fits the model of nicotine addiction, but to support the former we need independent evidence that A and B were equally anxious without the use of nicotine. As for (2), studies which compare successful and unsuccessful quitters do not show any significant correlation[32] between success in quitting and the severity of withdrawal problems or symptoms: withdrawal symptoms usually disappear by the end of a few weeks, but many smokers who relapse after quitting do so after that time period.[33] Furthermore, there is no correlation between success in quitting and the years one smoked or between success in quitting and whether one is a heavy or light smoker.[34]

Notice also that the inability of the nicotine dependence model to explain the success and failure of quitting means that Goodin has no suitable way of explaining the increasing percentage of quitters in the last thirty years. During that time publicity about the risks of smoking has increased, as have the costs of smoking, both monetary (increased excise taxes) and nonmonetary (increased unpopularity of smoking, restrictions on smoking in enclosed areas, etc.), while presumably the physiological effects of nicotine have remained the same. Now decisions that the risks or costs of an activity make that activity no longer worthwhile are the type of decisions for which we generally hold people responsible. Goodin is thus logically committed to arguing that whatever contributory role these decisions played in increasing the percentage of quitters, it was not sufficient to hold those smokers who didn't quit responsible for their continuing to smoke.[35] That is, he must argue that while increasing the costs of and information concerning smoking made it somewhat less difficult to resist the compulsive-nicotine induced desire to smoke than would otherwise be the case, these desires are still difficult enough to resist so that smokers who still smoke cannot be said to do so voluntarily. However, that argument must fail since the claim that it is difficult to stop smoking because of the desires induced by nicotine has already been refuted.

Although I have refuted Goodin's addiction argument, unless I can provide a plausible account of why it is difficult to stop smoking, the suspicion may remain that smokers do not voluntarily continue to smoke or assume the risks of smoking. A point made last section, that smoking is a means to or part of a *variety* of ends, suggests an alterative explanation.

Smokers smoke to relax, to concentrate, to handle anxiety, stress and difficult interpersonal situations, as a way of taking a break during the day, as a social lubricant, etc. Smoking is thus linked with a lot of different situations, moods and emotional states. Furthermore, smoking is well *integrated* into smokers' lives. Though most smokers smoke on a fairly continual basis,[36] smokers aren't, for the most part, prevented from carrying out normal life activities: rather, they weave smoking into those activities. This is partly for social reasons—despite the increasing unpopularity of smoking, one can still use nicotine in more situations than other drugs (e.g., there are no legal prohibitions on smoking and driving or on smoking while walking on public streets)—and perhaps partly for pharmacological reasons—the effects of nicotine are mild and subtle enough that it can be used nondisruptively in many situations. Now because smoking is so well-integrated into smokers' lives, it will be difficult to give up: no central change in people's lives is easily achieved. Since concentrating and smoking are linked, or smoking and relaxing are linked, or smoking and handling stress are linked, etc., then giving up smoking doesn't just involve giving up an unhealthy activity, but involves either giving up relaxing, concentrating, etc., which of course almost no one will do, or learning how to concentrate, handle stress, etc., in a new way, and that is something that may be difficult for many people. In light of this, it would seem to be safe to predict that those who will be more successful at quitting will a) have or develop the skills or strategies to handle stress, anxiety, etc., without nicotine, and/or b) have greater self-confidence that they can handle a major life change such as learning how to concentrate, relax, etc., without the use of tobacco. And this is just what has been found. Concerning (a), there is significant evidence that successful quitters employ a wide variety of strategies for coping with the temptation or urge to smoke. Concerning (b) a recent longitudinal study of people who made New Years' resolutions to quit smoking found that the only characteristic that separated successful quitters (after 2 years) from those that did not succeed was that the former expressed, at the beginning of the period when they had given up smoking, a stronger desire to quit smoking and were more likely to believe that quitting would not be that difficult, which bespeaks a greater self-confidence; while some earlier studies found that successful quitters are more likely to be "internally motivated," that is, believe that their own effort rather than fate, luck or things beyond their control will bring them rewards, and still others found them to be more "secure," both of which again point roughly in the same direction of confidence in one's abilities to bring about a major life-change.[37]

This information would seem to wreck the addiction argument. If whether one quits smoking depends largely not on neurophysiology but on psychological characteristics, character traits, etc.,[38] then the claim that smokers do not voluntarily incur the risks of smoking can only succeed at the very large price of viewing such character traits, characteristics, etc., as something one is not responsible for or something that is not voluntarily incurred. This is a very large price in general, because to make such a move would mean most of what we do we are not responsible for or is not voluntary. It would be a large price for Goodin in particular, since such a move would make bad habits, psychological dependencies and the like undercut claims of voluntariness, something Goodin explicitly rejects.

Why It's Difficult for the Addiction Argument to Succeed

Unlike the irrationality argument, there is no in principle reason why an addiction argument cannot succeed. The problem with the addiction argument is not logical or conceptual, it is empirical: the conditions required for this argument to succeed turn out to be exacting.

The addiction argument is supposed to overcome the strong presumption against paternalist laws for sane adults. This means, first, that one must show not just that the harmful activity in question is difficult to give up but that a clear majority have this difficulty. If only some find it difficult to quit, and thus only some could be construed as addicts, then given the presumption against paternalist laws, it will be very difficult to justify such laws unless the law could somehow prevent or strongly discourage addicts without thereby discouraging or preventing the non-addicts. Second, the presumption against paternalism means that the evidence one uses to show that a clear majority of people are not responsible for their continuing to engage in the activity must avoid implying that people aren't responsible for bad habits, their character flaws and the like, for then much of what we do will be nonvoluntary and accordingly the scope for legitimate paternalist intervention would threaten to become enormous. Third, addiction arguments must explain changes, if any, in the number of people who have quit. If those numbers have increased (as they have in the case of smoking) then to maintain the nonresponsibility criterion one is forced to argue either that the changes were caused by factors one is not responsible for, or that these are due to factors one is responsible for, but that these played a minor role in explaining the increasing quit ratio.

To put matters another way, an addiction argument is most likely to succeed if the majority of people that try to quit, fail, and their failure is relatively invariant to differences in character traits, psychological characteristics, assessment of risks, beliefs about the benefits versus the costs of the risky activity, etc. If this invariance held, then adults who engaged in the risky activity would virtually be trapped, for even if they recognized the risks and costs of the activity, no longer thought the benefits of the activity outweighed the costs or risks, and were the kind of people who could make major life changes, this would turn out to make little difference in helping

them to quit. Thus addiction would be a kind of slavery, as it sometimes is analogized to be. But smoking isn't even remotely like this. About half of smokers who try to quit succeed, and their quitting is indeed significantly dependent on the factors just mentioned, and not on matters for which they could not be held responsible for, such as their neurophysiological reactions to nicotine or whether they can summon extraordinary acts of will.

The failure of smoking to fit the requirements of a successful addiction argument indicates the difficulty with addiction arguments. Smoking is a unique legal activity: in no other case do so many people (25% of the population) throughout much of their lives engage in an activity which produces such dramatic self-regarding harms (smoking is the leading cause of preventable death.)[39] If addiction arguments can't succeed in the case of smoking, they are unlikely to succeed with other legal activities: if those have higher quit rates and produce less severe harms, then addiction arguments can't get off the ground. The issues are more complicated in the case of *illegal* activities which harm the participants, such as the use of illegal drugs, for while most users of these drugs are not addicts, and thus the addiction argument doesn't seem to apply,[40] one would need to know the extent of addiction were these drugs legalized, and that is something I cannot discuss here. My own view is that the evidence shows that legalization would bring at most a modest increase in addiction. If I'm right about this, then the addiction argument cannot justify paternalist intervention to stop or strongly discourage adult drug use. This does not mean that there *couldn't* be drug use or a risky activity which fits the requirements of an addiction argument—i.e., an activity which produced such an overwhelming need or desire to continue that most people could only resist using heroic or extraordinary measures. It's just that it's very unlikely that there is such an activity at present. Nor does it mean that addiction, in the sense defined in this paper, does not exist. To say that addiction arguments fail is not to deny that some sane adults are addicted to certain harmful activities, but to deny that this justifies paternalist laws which aim to prevent people from engaging in those activities.

III. Conclusion

My arguments imply that we should reject any smoking regulation whose purported justification would very likely depend upon the addiction and/or irrationality arguments. Many *present* smoking regulations do not fall into this category. Laws regulating smoking in confined places invoke harm-to-other, not harm-to-self arguments. Warning labels are justified by the principle that one's right to choose to engage in risky activities is conditioned on these being informed choices—though given the public's overestimation of the risks of smoking, there's a strong case for revising the warning label so as to yield more accurate information. Even regulations that aim to decrease the amount of tobacco consumption could, perhaps, be defended on grounds other than the irrationality and addiction arguments—one might argue, for example, that tobacco taxes are justified on the grounds of discouraging *minors* from smoking. However, regulations which prohibit or aim at preventing smoking altogether are a different matter: to support them, one would almost certainly rely on irrationality and/or addiction arguments. In the future such regulations may be seriously considered; indeed, Goodin's proposal to ban over-the-counter sale of cigarettes can be viewed as a step in this direction. The failure of his arguments, and the general problems with the addiction and irrationality argument, strongly suggests we should not take this step.[41]

Notes

1. W. Kip Viscusi, *Smoking: Making the Risky Decision,* (New York: Oxford University Press, 1992), p. 70 and p. 80. Except where noted, all statistics in this paper concern the United States.

2. Robert E. Goodin, *No Smoking: The Ethical Issues* (Chicago: University of Chicago Press, 1989). Henceforth called NS.

3. Henceforth, all references to smoking, smokers, etc., exclude minors.

4. NS, pp. 21–4.

5. United States Department of Health and Human Services, A report of the Surgeon General, *The Health Consequences of Smoking: Nicotine Addiction* (Washington, DC: Government Printing Office, 1988).

6. NS, pp. 25–9.

7. Ibid., pp. 21–4.

8. NS, p. 23. The survey is: The U.S. Federal Trade Commission, Matthew Mayers, Chairman *Staff Report on Cigarette Advertising Investigation* (Washington, DC: Government Printing Office, 1981). Goodin also mentions a survey of British smokers: Alan Marsh, "Smoking and Illness: What Smokers Really Believe," *Health Trends,* 17 (1985), pp. 7–12. This presents some special problems which I discuss in note 14.

9. Ibid., pp. 21–2. On the issue of invulnerability, Goodin cites H.M. Alexander, R. Calcott, and A. J. Dobson, "Cigarette and Drug Use in Children. IV: Factors Associated with Changes in Smoking Behavior," *International Journal of Epidemiology,* vol. 12 (1983), pp. 59–65, and Howard Leventhal, Kathleen Glynn, and Raymond Fleming, "Is the Smoking Decision an 'Informed Choice'?" *Journal of the American Medical Association,* vol. 257 (1987), pp. 3373–376. The study by Alan Marsh, "Smoking and Illness" could also be taken to provide evidence about invulnerability; see note 14. Goodin does not actually cite any studies that show that smokers engage in the anchoring fallacy; he instead cites Daniel Kahneman, Paul Slovic and Amos Tversky, eds., *Judgment Under Uncertainty* (Cambridge: Cambridge University Press, 1982), where it is argued that this is a common reasoning error. Goodin also says that smokers discount the future to an irrational extent, but I leave this aside, since the question of how much concern rationality requires one to have for one's future self is quite controversial.

10. Viscusi, *Smoking: Making the Risky Decision,* pp. 68–9.

11. Ibid., pp. 77–8.

12. See Paul Slovic, Baruch Fischhoff, and Sarah Lichtenstein, "Facts and Fears: Understanding Perceived Risk," in *Judgment Under Uncertainty,* pp. 463–87.

13. NS, pp. 23–4. The survey he cites comes from ibid., p. 469.

14. One possible exception to this claim is the survey by Alan Marsh, "Smoking and Illness" pp. 7–8, which found that 33% of all smokers denied that smoking brought about any increased liability to lung cancer. This seems incompatible with the Viscusi results. However, Marsh also found, p. 9, that when smokers were asked *if* they did get lung cancer (or heart disease or bronchitis) how likely it would be due to smoking, 85% implicated smoking at least to some extent. Marsh notes that this inconsistent data probably means that smokers are aware

that they are gambling but deny that anything bad will happen to them. Thus Marsh's data provides some evidence about smokers' belief in invulnerability, rather than an underestimation of the relevant risks of smoking.

15. Viscusi, *Smoking,* pp. 112–13.

16. See note 14. The survey which includes adults in Alan Marsh, "Smoking and Illness."

17. Slovic et al., "Facts and Fears," in *Judgments Under Uncertainty,* pp. 468–72.

18. NS, p. 25 can be read this way.

19. For a thorough list of reasons why people smoke, see J. Alan Best and A. Ralph Hakstian "A Situation-Specific Model for Smoking Behavior," *Addictive Behaviors* vol. 3 (1978) pp. 79–92.

20. NS, p. 23, footnote 20.

21. However, if those addicted to engaging in a very risky activity *thereby,* because of cognitive dissonance, come to irrationally and falsely underestimate the risks, then, by *modus tollens,* the failure of the irrationality argument would undermine the addiction argument. To avoid this easy refutation of the addiction argument, I shall assume that addicts need not irrationally and falsely underestimate the relevant risks.

22. Goodin at times gives a different account of addiction, whereby it is understood in terms of it being "unreasonably costly for addicts to resist their compulsive desires" (p. 25). This is clearly a mistake. First, voluntariness should not be analyzed in terms of the unreasonable costs of resisting a desire. If someone offers me one hundred times the market price for an item I want very much to sell, it would be unreasonably costly for me to resist my desire to sell that item, but this hardly shows that I didn't voluntarily sell it. Second, it's doubtful Goodin could even hope to show that smokers are addicted on this analysis. Probably the best and least controversial way of showing that the costs of giving up an activity are unreasonable is to show that the costs grossly outweigh the net expected benefits (that is, the net benefits that are expected once the activity is given up). It will be difficult to argue, however, that the costs of giving up smoking grossly outweigh the benefits, for even if the costs of giving up smoking are considerable, so are the benefits: a statistically significantly lowered probability of getting cancer, emphysema, heart disease, etc.

23. NS, pp. 25–6.

24. Ibid., p. 27.

25. Ibid., p. 26.

26. Ibid.

27. United States Department of Health and Human Services, A report of the Surgeon General (Executive Summary), *Reducing the Health Consequences of Smoking: 25 Years of Progress* (Washington DC: Government Printing Office, 1989) pp. i and 11. 44.7% of all adult smokers have successfully quit. Since a small fraction of smokers don't try to quit, about half of smokers that have tried to quit have succeeded.

28. Cited in G. Alan Marlatt, S. Curry, and J. R. Gordon, "A Longitudinal Analysis of Unaided Smoking Cessation," *Journal of Consulting and Clinical Psychology,* vol. 56 (1988), pp. 715–20.

29. For a good summary, see Jay Winsten, director of Center for Health Communication at Harvard Medical School *Research Status Report: Nicotine Dependency and Compulsive Tobacco Use,* reprinted in *Tobacco Product Liability Reporter,* vol. 1 (1986), pp. 5.91–5.95.

30. Ibid.

31. U.S. Department of Health and Human Services, *Nicotine Addiction,* pp. 149, 200, 202, 296.

32. Some studies of *smokers who enter treatment clinics* have shown a correlation between the severity of withdrawal symptoms and the difficulty of quitting. But as already noted, this is a very atypical group, and in any event, other studies of this group have shown no correlation between the severity of withdrawal symptoms and success in quitting. Far more significant is a study by Stanley Schacter that looked at unaided smoking cessation in two complete and self-contained communities (the Psychology Department in Columbia University in 1977 and the entrepreneurial community in Amagansett, Long Island in 1980) and found no correlation whatsoever between the difficulty of withdrawal and success in quitting. See "Recidivism and Self-Cure of Smoking and Obesity," *American Psychologist,* vol. 37 (1982) pp. 436–44. Some studies on smokers in treatment programs are P. Zeidenberg, J. H. Jaffe, M. Kanzler, M. D. Levitt, J. J. Langone, and H. V. Vunakis, "Nicotine: Cotinine Levels in Blood During Cessation of Smoking," *Comprehensive Psychiatry,* vol. 18 (January–February 1977) pp. 93–101; O. Pomerleau, D. Adkins and M. Pertschuk, "Predictors of Outcome and Recidivism in Smoking Cessation Treatment," *Addictive Behaviors,* vol. 3 (1978) pp. 65–70; S. M. Hall, R. I. Herning, J. T. Jones, N. L. Benowitz and P. Jacob III, "Blood Cotinine Levels as Indicators of Smoking Treatment Outcome," *Clinical Pharmacology and Therapeutics,* vol. 35 (June 1984) pp. 810–14; and R. C. Gunn, "Reactions to Withdrawal Symptoms and Success in Smoking Cessation Clinics," *Addictive Behaviors,* vol. 11 (1986) pp. 49–53.

33. On withdrawal symptoms see Winstein, *Nicotine Dependency and Compulsive Tobacco Use* p. 5.92; on relapse time, see Howard Leventhal and Paul D. Cleary,

"The Smoking Problem: A Review of the Research and Theory in Behavioral Risk Modification," *Psychological Bulletin,* vol. 88 (1980) p. 390 and Marlatt et al., "Unaided Smoking Cessation," pp. 715–20.

34. U. S. Department of Health and Human Services, *Nicotine Addiction,* p. 521 and Schacter, "Self-Cure of Smoking and Obesity," p. 439.

35. NS, pp. 29, 53, 99, notices that these factors made it easier to quit, but does not notice that he is committed to arguing that their role is not a major one.

36. Less than 10% of smokers are occasional users (i.e., smoke less than 5 cigarettes a day.) 1988 Surgeon General's Report, *Nicotine Addiction,* pp. 253–4.

37. On smokers being more "secure," see Robert C. Benfari, Judith K. Ockene, and Kevin M. McIntyre "Control of Cigarette Smoking From a Psychological Perspective" *Annual Review of Public Health,* vol. 3 (1982) p. 117. On smokers being "internally motivated," see The U. S. Department of Health and Human Services, a report of The Surgeon General *Smoking and Health* (Washington, DC, The Government Printing Office, 1979), chapter 18, p. 9. The information on coping skills comes from the longitudinal study by Marlatt et al., "Unaided Smoking Cessation," pp. 715–20. Corroboration of Marlatt's findings can be found in Alan Marsh, "Smoking: Habit or Choice?," *Population Trends,* vol. 20 (1984), p. 18.

38. The explanation I have offered does not *ignore* the neurophysiological evidence. As noted earlier, it may be that part of the reason smoking is so easy to integrate into people's lives is because the effects of nicotine on the brain are such that smoking does not impair one's ability to do a variety of everyday activities.

39. U.S. Department of Human Health Services, *Nicotine Addiction,* pp. iii and 566 respectively. Only a small fraction of deaths caused by smoking fall on nonsmokers.

40. Most users of cocaine and heroin—the drugs popularly believed to be the most addictive—do not do so on a continual basis. See Michael Gazzaniga, "The Opium of the People: Crack in Perspective," in *Drug Legalization: For and Against* eds. Rod L. Evans and Irwin M. Berent, (La Salle, IL: Open Court Publishing, 1992), pp. 232–46, Arnold S. Trebach, *The Heroin Solution* (New Haven, CT: Yale University Press, 1982), pp. 3–4, and John Kaplan, *The Hardest Drug* (Chicago: University of Chicago Press, 1983), pp. 32–4.

41. I would like to thank the philosophy department of West Virginia University for their comments on an earlier (October 1990) and different version of this paper. I would also like to thank Michael Gorr, Richard Montgomery and Mark C. Wicclair for written comments on an earlier version.

GRAHAM ODDIE

Addiction and the Value of Freedom

It is widely held that being addicted is a bad thing. Obviously there are circumstances in which the consequences of particular forms of addiction will be of low overall value. It may even be that such circumstances are fairly typical. But the opponents of the use of (for example) addictive substances generally cite the possibility of addiction *itself* as one of the main reasons against use. It is not only against recreational uses of addictive substances that this argument is wielded, but also against their use in the treatment of chronic and acute pain. An important philosophical task here is to clarify the nature of addiction with a view to determining the disvalues of addiction, and to determine, in particular, whether addiction possesses a disvalue *in itself*—that is, whether addiction possesses an *intrinsic* disvalue. If the answer to this question is *no* then being addictive is not itself an argument against use, and each case of addiction will have to be assessed on its merits.

From Graham Oddie, "Addiction and the Value of Freedom," *Bioethics* 7, no. 5 (1993): 373–401. Some notes and some parts of the text have been deleted.

I begin with some cases which highlight the role of the presumption against addiction both in medical practice and in policy decisions. I then give a fairly detailed account of the various conceptual features of addiction which form the basis of the ensuing arguments. I argue that these features generate a *prima facie* argument against addiction—I call it *the argument from bad cases*. But the strength of the argument varies considerably according to the circumstances surrounding particular addictions, and in a clear sense the disvalue of addiction which arises from the possibility of bad cases is *not* intrinsic. Then I turn to the question of whether or not addiction might also possess intrinsic disvalue. I show that any argument for the thesis of the intrinsic disvalue of addiction will turn on the loss of freedom, autonomy, or self-control, which addiction involves—and then I show why such arguments must fail. If this is right then we need to take a hard look at a whole range of attitudes and practices connected with addiction and addictive substances.

I. THREE CASES

Case 1

Ms A is a 76 year old, retired school teacher who lives on her own. She has advanced osteoporosis with collapsed vertebrae and severe pain in her back and neck. She has taken a variety of pain medication over time, but is no longer able to take aspirin or other non-steroidal anti-inflammatory drugs because of gastric bleeding. Her GP would like to prescribe morphine but is warned against doing so by a colleague who has been investigated on a charge of inappropriate prescribing of narcotics. Further, in consulting the medical literature the GP is made aware that caution is advised in opioid prescribing, especially in the elderly, since long-term effects of opioids, including the risk of addiction, are not fully understood.

Case 2

Mr B, a 50 year old male with three dependents, has diabetes mellitus and a three-year history of pain related to diabetic neuropathy. He has been treated with a variety of analgesics without adequate pain control. The pain has become worse over the last 12 months and made it impossible for Mr B to continue in his job as a petrol pump attendant so that he is now receiving a sickness benefit. During this time he was referred to a Pain Clinic and was prescribed an opioid drug for a trial of six weeks. He experienced considerable relief from pain and was able to return to his job on a casual basis. He wants to be able to continue on the opioid drug, and to return to full-time paid employment, but neither his GP nor the specialists at the Pain Clinic are willing to prescribe further opioid medication for him, citing the risk of addiction as their main concern. (There is no history of drug abuse, no evidence of inappropriate drug use during the six week trial, and no suggestion of significant psychological problems.) . . .

Case 3

A nicotine inhaler is a device which enables a person to take nicotine directly into the bloodstream via the lungs, thereby closely reproducing many of the effects which smokers desire. Unlike a nicotine patch, which gradually releases the nicotine into the bloodstream, the inhaler delivers a quick burst of the substance to the brain. However, since the nicotine comes without smoke, tar and harmful carcinogens, it has none of the usual harmful side-effects of smoking. Health professionals in Britain advise against the device being made publicly available. The reason?— it might encourage addiction to nicotine.

These three cases, which are by no means unusual, illustrate a commonly held assumption about addiction—an assumption which not only drives medical decisions in the treatment of chronic and acute pain, but influences many policies governing the availability and handling of addictive substances. This assumption is that something's being addictive is a strong reason, often an overriding one, against its availability and use.

In the first two cases becoming addicted was considered, by the health professionals concerned, to be such a harm in itself that they judged it better for their patients to suffer distressing physiological conditions, together with serious side-effects (like unemployment), rather than allow them to run any risk of them becoming addicted.[1]

[The] practitioners (as in case 1) may well have been responding not to their considered judgement on the cases, so much as to the legal situation. We happen to live in a society in which the taking of addictive substances is tightly constrained by law, and practitioners are subject to heavy legal and professional penalties if they are deemed to have transgressed that law. But this only demonstrates that the law has come to embody the strong presumption against addiction.

Of course neither the law, nor the rest of us, are terribly consistent about addiction. Some addictive substances (like alcohol and tobacco) are readily available in western countries for recreational purposes, while others are not. But even in our thinking about these the presumption against becoming addicted operates selectively, sometimes with seemingly bizarre results, as in the third case. The upshot of the decision on the nicotine inhaler is that while nicotine can be traded and consumed provided it comes traditionally packaged with a host of carcinogens and other substances which are harmful to users and bystanders alike, it is not available in a form in which the only possible undesirable effect is that it is addictive. The reason, I conjecture, is that the nicotine inhaler, unlike the cigarette, sharply focuses our attention on the main motive people have for consuming nicotine (sating their addictive desires) and the presumption against addiction then gains ready application. I suspect people would have a similar reaction to the marketing of a small device which enabled people to take alcohol intravenously.

In this article I am not mainly concerned about the availability of addictive substances in general, although the analysis of addiction and the associated arguments are quite general and important implications can be readily drawn. However, I am concerned about the effect which the presumption against addiction has on the treatment of pain by health professionals. That "the treatment of severe pain in hospitalized patients is regularly and systematically inadequate"[2] is now well documented.[3] That children

suffer particularly badly in this respect seems an unfair twist to the situation.[4] That this systematic undertreatment is driven by the strong presumption against addiction seems undeniable.[5] If the presumption against addiction is not generally justified then an excess of needless preventable suffering has been sanctioned, and continues daily to be sanctioned, by the medical profession.

II. ADDICTION: AN ANALYSIS

Much of the literature on addiction is sceptical about the possibility of giving a unified and coherent treatment of the concept. I am not so pessimistic. Firstly, many of the studies on addiction begin with an interest specifically in drug addiction, and import into the study special features of particular forms of drug taking which are no part of addiction, or even of drug addiction itself (for example, tolerance). Secondly, the fact that the concept has grey edges does not mean that no explication can be successful. To be successful an explication need only give us the right judgements in the *clear-cut* cases. An explication which is successful in those cases is entitled to legislate for the unclear cases. Lastly, there is now a generally accepted criterion of *dependence* which is on the right tracks, but which is not quite fully adequate as an analysis of addiction.

We will begin with the standard account of dependence, endorsed by the World Health Organisation and the American Psychiatric Association. According to this account, a person is dependent upon something to the extent that s/he wants to give it up, tries to give it up, but tends to fail to do so. (And by extension a substance is classified addictive if that is the standard experience amongst most of its users.) This account (which we will dub the WHO/ APA account) certainly helps to distinguish addictions from a host of habits (provided we grant that habits can be broken relatively easily). But the WHO/APA account as it stands is too narrow—and if it is amended in an obvious way it is too wide.

To see that it is too narrow, suppose that there is substance, call it *soma,* which a chemist accidentally manufactures in her laboratory. For some reason she consumes it, it has very pleasant effects, but it is also addictive, and she duly becomes addicted to it. She can make as much of it for herself as she wants, and she does so. She never gives a sample to anybody else, nobody else ever consumes it, and she continues to want to take it, and does so, for the rest of her life. The chemist was (by assumption) addicted to soma, but soma does not possess the WHO/APA property, since nobody who took it (the chemist is the only one) ever actually wanted to stop taking it, and so nobody ever found it difficult or impossible to stop taking it. And since nobody else ever took soma, there are no experiences which are typical of soma-takers. Hence the substance is not, according to the WHO/APA account, addictive.

Of course, the chemist *would have* found it difficult or impossible to stop taking soma *if* she had wanted to. It is this *conditional* feature, rather than the unconditional WHO/APA feature, which undergirds her addiction. The fact that she never wanted to is neither here nor there.

Unfortunately it is not sufficient to modify the definition quite generally along these conditional lines. Suppose we do so amend it, and say that for a person to be addicted to something is tantamount to the following: *if* that person were to want to give it up and tried to do so, she *would* (tend to) backslide. This captures the chemist's soma addiction, but it catches too much besides. On this account it would transpire that most people would be addicted to eating, drinking, and breathing. And, by extension, food, water and air would all be addictive substances.

In what follows I will give a more accurate account of the concept of addiction, one which will explain where the WHO/APA definition gets it right, while correcting it where it goes wrong.

Substance addiction assumes a high profile in our thinking about addiction—perhaps because of the importance of drug addiction in law, and the relative ease with which addictive substances can be legally controlled—and this might easily mislead one into thinking that the objects of addiction are invariably substances. But, firstly, there can be addictions which do not involve material substances, or involve them only indirectly—like addiction to violence, or to exercise or (if advertised treatments to it are genuine) to relationships. Only if all addictions are grounded

in physiological dependence on a substance will they all involve material substances, and even if that is true *in fact* it is no part of the *concept* of addiction. One can easily conceive of addictions which are not substance-related. Secondly even substance addiction is more fruitfully thought of as directed towards an *activity* rather than simply towards a substance. The substance addict does not just want the *substance*. Give him the substance in an impenetrable steel cask and he will be disappointed. What the addict wants is for there to be an appropriate *interaction* between himself and the substance.

What this suggests is that addiction is primarily directed to special kinds of states of affairs, or processes: namely, to *activities* in which the addict himself plays a prominent role.

Clearly addiction to an activity—like taking cocaine, drinking coffee or exercising—involves a disposition for the person to desire that s/he engage in the activity. I maintain that the addiction *is* this disposition. The desires produced by the addiction are not the addiction itself. Call the desires so triggered by the addiction *addictive desires*. The addictive desires need not plague the addict constantly (although they may), but will typically be triggered by characteristic circumstances. (To speak here from experience, a mild addiction to coffee usually triggers desire for coffee drinking only at certain times of the day.)

An addiction is a disposition to trigger desires, but not all such dispositions are addictions. We have to distinguish addictions from a host of other dispositions to desire, and in particular from some dispositions which share many features in common with addiction.

Firstly there are the basic "natural" dispositions to desire food, water, air, sex and other fundamental goods, and (typically) these dispositions are not addictions. They are natural to the extent that they are constitutive of human nature. But they are not distinguished from addictions simply by virtue of being natural. For some of these natural dispositions can *become* addictions, and it is not at all illuminating to characterise the transition as that from a "natural" to an "unnatural" condition.

Secondly there are a host of dispositions to desire which are "unnatural" or perhaps "non-natural" in the sense that they are not constitutive of human nature in general, and these may also either be, or not be, addictions. A person who has a standing disposition to desire listening to Mozart whenever a well-known exponent of Mozart's music is in town, would not necessarily be judged to be addicted to listening to Mozart. Similarly, a person who has a disposition to desire to floss his teeth at bedtime is not necessarily addicted to bedtime flossings. Neither disposition is "natural" in the strict sense (they are not constitutive of human nature) and so the addictive/non-addictive distinction does not coincide with the natural/non-natural distinction.

Clearly the addictive disposition and the associated addictive desires have to have a certain character. Three features of addiction are particularly important for our purposes.

Firstly, both the disposition and the addictive desires it generates must have a certain *resilience:* they are difficult to dislodge. It is important to note that resilience, of both desires and dispositions, is a matter of a degree. But being addicted is also a matter of degree, and I submit that the degree of addiction will be some appropriate function of the degrees of resilience of disposition and resulting desires. What exactly does resilience amount to?

Take the resilience of the disposition first. The resilience of the disposition is part of what distinguishes an addiction from a mere habit. To the extent that a habit is not an addiction it is within the power of the habit-bearer to break it, or override it, should circumstances *require* it. Smoking may be a habit, but if it is an addiction it is not merely a habit. This feature explains why it sounds distinctly odd to say: "I am addicted to smoking, but the addiction is one it is easy for me to throw off. I could cease being an addict at any moment I choose."

But it is not just the disposition which is resilient. An important feature of addictions is that the addictive desires are also resilient in an important sense. It is difficult for the addict to dislodge an addictive desire without the desire being fulfilled. Other desires, like that to floss teeth at bedtime, or to have a large gin and tonic, may be strong without being the products of an addiction. So what does this difficulty involve?

The resilience at issue involves an important normative component. A desire is resilient to the extent that the strength of the desire is *insufficiently sensitive* to considerations of the person's overall interests or of overall value. The resilience of a desire clearly admits of degrees. At one extreme a desire which is not resilient (in this sense) is one which the desirer is capable of overriding *if that is what is required.* The more severe the addiction the more resilient are the addictive desires, the more difficult it is for the desirer to dislodge them or override them when required to do so. At the other extreme, when resilience is *complete,* the desire cannot be voluntarily dislodged without its first being fulfilled, even when fulfilment of the desire is not in the person's best interests, or in the interests of overall value, and the person knows it. Typically the resilience of addictive desires will not be complete. Only in the most intransigent cases of addiction will the addictive desires have that kind of grip on the desirer. But in cases of severe addiction the addictive desires will have a high degree of resilience.

The resilience of addictive desires is what underlies the addict's sense of loss of control. It connects addiction with weakness of the will, and that seems right. Weakness of the will occurs just when a person does not act in accordance with his own best, all-things-considered, judgement (however that is to be analysed). In many of those circumstances in which an addictive desire is stronger than its fulfilment warrants, to act in accordance with the desire will be to display weakness of will.

Resilience of addictive desires is one feature which distinguishes a natural disposition, like the disposition to want to breathe, from an addiction. One reason it is inappropriate to say that one is addicted to breathing is that rarely is fulfilment of the desire to breathe against a person's own best interests.

Resilience of the addictive desires also distinguishes addiction from other resilient dispositions to desire. Contrast an alcoholic's desire for a gin and tonic with a strong desire on the part of a non-alcoholic for the same thing. The alcoholic's and the non-alcoholic's desire might be equally strong. What distinguishes the alcoholic is that he is less likely to be able to act on overriding factors. For example, suppose his child requires medical attention and the delay involved in his having the drink may put the child's health at some risk. The non-alcoholic will typically be able to forego satisfying even a strong desire for a gin and tonic for the child's sake. The strength of his desire can be moderated by other considerations of value. But suppose that the risk to his child's health would not move the desirer to forego his drink. Suppose he (perhaps reluctantly) acknowledges the greater claim of the child, but nevertheless feels driven to have the gin and tonic. In this case his desire is resilient, and so at least bears the marks of addiction. . . .

The third important feature of addictive desires turns on the familiar distinction between desire fulfilment and desire satisfaction. A desire for a state is *fulfilled* if the state desired actually comes about. The desire is *satisfied* if, upon its fulfilment (or belief in its fulfilment), the person feels a characteristic subjective sense of relief at release from the desire. A desire can be fulfilled without being satisfied (like the desire that one's friends mourn one's death); or satisfied without being fulfilled (like the desire that one achieve something significant).

A salient feature of addictive desires is that lack of fulfilment ensures lack of satisfaction. Of course, this lack of satisfaction must be something relatively unpleasant for the addict: relative, that is, to satisfaction of the desire. I will call this property of addictive desires—that lack of fulfilment ensures relative dissatisfaction—the *dissatisfaction* property. . . .

Thus an addiction is a resilient disposition to form resilient desires with the dissatisfaction property. Particular desires other than those that spring from addiction can, of course, be both resilient and have the dissatisfaction property. What is characteristic of addictive desires is that they are brought about by a resilient disposition to generate such desires in a certain range of circumstances.

It is worth noting that all three properties are involved in, and jointly entail, a familiar feature of addiction: withdrawal. Intuitively, someone would not be addicted if withdrawal were not an unpleasant and difficult affair. To withdraw the addict must resist the addictive desires. But, by the resilience of the addictive desires, to resist individual addictive desires will be difficult and, by the dissatisfaction property, unpleasant. Further, by the resilience of the disposition itself, to dislodge the disposition will itself be difficult and hence will tend to take time. These features of withdrawal explain in turn why people who are addicted tend to backslide when they try to withdraw. Hence the account delivers as a consequence the core of truth in the WHO/APA account of dependence.

III. THE ARGUMENT FROM BAD CASES

It should now be evident that there is a rational kernel to the presumption against addiction. By becoming addicted one becomes more or less bound to a disposition to generate desires. *That,* however, is a common enough phenomenon and far from objectionable in itself. By developing a keen interest in one's own career, in music, knowledge, art, sport, a love affair, or in any number of human projects, one may well be binding oneself to such a disposition. What separates addiction from these more common (and presumably acceptable) dispositions are the two properties of resilience and dissatisfaction.

Because of resilience, the addictive desires will be hard to resist even when their fulfilment is not in the addict's best interests. This is because the strength of an addictive desire can be well out of proportion to the importance of its fulfilment. And because of dissatisfaction, if *either* the addict can and does choose to deny an addictive desire, *or* the addictive desire is thwarted by external circumstances, the addict will suffer.

So we have two sorts of *bad cases* for the addict. The first kind of bad case is that in which it is possible for the addictive desires to be fulfilled, but in which it is not the best thing (either for the addict, or perhaps for the world) for the addictive desires to be so fulfilled. When the resilience of the addictive desires becomes complete, and the addict is in a position to fulfil the desire, then she simply has *no choice* but to keep in step with the addiction, even when that is not in her own best interests. But if the addiction is not complete, the addict can overcome the addictive desire only at the cost of dissatisfaction. So by becoming addicted a person may well be engineering for her future self situations in which she cannot win. Either she will be bound to the addiction even when it is not in her own best interests to act on the addictive desires; or, even if she is not so bound, resisting the addictive desire will carry with it dissatisfaction.

The second kind of bad case is that in which external circumstances deny the fulfilment of the addictive desire. Then, of course, the addict will again suffer dissatisfaction.

Thus there is a prima facie case against voluntarily becoming addicted based on conceptual features of addiction: that it generates the possibility of bad cases. Bad cases arise from the fact that denying the addictive desires will be difficult and unpleasant, together with the fact that denying them may be either necessitated by circumstances beyond the addict's control, or in the addict's own best interests.

That is the down-side of addiction in general. But how good is the argument from bad cases? Its strength will clearly depend on local features. More precisely, it will depend on just how likely, and how bad, bad cases are likely to be. In other words, it will depend on how likely it is that the fulfilment of addictive desires will conflict with one's best interests or with overall value, how likely it is that circumstances will make fulfilment impossible, and how much disvalue attaches to lack of fulfilment.

Consider three fairly unproblematic cases: becoming addicted to coffee; becoming addicted to heroin when one would otherwise have a long future and good prospects; becoming addicted to morphine in the last year of a terminal illness.

Many of us elect to become addicted to coffee. Drinking coffee has its modest pleasures, and an addiction to coffee may enhance the pleasure of drinking it. The supply of the substance is fairly well assured, and it is cheap—so to keep feeding the addiction one does not have to forego a lot of other important options. Coffee addicts are usually aware that there might well be a point at which continuing to drink coffee will not be in their own best interests, because of the likelihood of kidney damage, headaches and so forth. But, if the coffee addict is forced to forgo consumption by lack of supply, or chooses to forgo because of countervailing disvalues, the dissatisfaction is not usually so great that it cannot be handled. Withdrawal from caffeine addiction is uncomfortable, but not disastrous. So, not unreasonably, many of us judge the pleasures to be gained from caffeine addiction to be worth the risk. The coffee addict may well be engineering bad cases for his future self, but the risk is small and the disvalues whichever way he chooses in a bad case will not usually be so great.

Heroin addiction, at least for a youngster with otherwise good prospects, is quite a different matter, at least under current conditions. While the pleasures of heroin are much greater than those of coffee, the dissatisfaction which results from the addictive desires being thwarted are much greater. The difficulty of withdrawing from the addiction is considerable. Further, it is an expensive addiction, and so, for all but the very wealthy, the addict must forgo lots of other opportunities to assuage the addictive desires. And because it is both illegal and expensive, the supply is by no means assured, the quality of the substance is difficult to guarantee, and there are obvious risks involved in procuring it. In contemplating activities likely to produce heroin addiction a young person with an otherwise promising future would probably be well advised to turn the offer down. By becoming addicted he will almost certainly be engineering for himself some very bad cases.

Now consider a person with a painful terminal illness, with rather a long time to die: say, one year. To manage the pain effectively large doses of morphine are necesary, and the regularity and sizes of these doses will certainly engender an addiction. Suppose the person does want to live through this final year; that he finds the prospect of enduring the pain of the illness worse than the disvalues of being constantly on morphine; that he will be in a position to monitor and handle the dosages himself eliminating the possibility that he will be dependent on the judgement of others about his need for relief; and that he lives in a stable and fairly wealthy society in which the supply of the drug is well assured for the duration of the illness. Given these conditions he is unlikely to face any future bad cases. It will almost certainly be in his interests throughout his terminal illness to keep taking whatever dosages of morphine are necessary to make the pain tolerable and to assuage his addictive desires. The balance here clearly goes in favour of becoming addicted.

The upshot of this sample of cases is straightforward. The argument from bad cases against addiction can be strong or weak depending on particular circumstances. It depends ultimately on whether addiction is likely to generate bad cases, and just how great the disvalues in such cases will be. In the coffee example the argument is very weak; the bad cases are not so terribly problematic, and not terribly likely. In the morphine example, the argument has no force at all: bad cases are very unlikely, even if the disvalues in such cases may be considerable. In the heroin example the argument carries considerable force: bad cases are both highly likely, given the addict's circumstances, and will involve considerable disvalues. It all depends on the addiction at issue and the circumstances which surround it. The disvalues are thus in a clear sense extrinsic.

IV. FREEDOM AND ADDICTION

Those who largely agree with my analysis of the concept of addiction may still find the foregoing analysis of the values and disvalues of addiction shallow and even question begging. By weighing the consequences of addiction in particular cases I could be accused of assuming that being addicted is not *itself* a disvalue to be weighed in the balance. I have assumed, in other words, that addiction is not itself a morally relevant feature.

Indeed the prima facie argument against addiction in the case of heroin is strong, according to this analysis, partly *because* of the current law against it. It is this law which is largely responsible for the fact that supply is precarious, expensive and dangerous. So according to my analysis heroin addiction is likely to be a bad choice at least partly *because* it is currently illegal. But according to the opponents of the addiction the rationale should presumably be the other way around. It is supposed to be illegal because, heroin being an addictive substance, it is bad to use it.

To counter this line the opponent of addiction will have to maintain that addiction possesses an intrinsic disvalue, that this intrinsic disvalue is considerable, and that in many cases it can be relied upon to outweigh whatever benefits an addiction is supposed to yield.

It is not easy to find explicit advocates of the view that addiction has an intrinsic disvalue. It is clear to me from the literature that that is the most plausible suppressed premise in many of the arguments (where arguments occur at all). But non-philosophers tend not to make a clear distinction between intrinsic and extrinsic disvalue, and philosophers tend to be rather wary of making unequivocal claims about what is of intrinsic value. However, I am grateful to Robert Goodin for as clear and unequivocal statement as one could hope for: "The policy implications for a distinction between addictions and mere bad habits are clear. . . . Since habits are not necessarily bad, public policies discouraging them are not necessarily desirable. *Addictions, in contrast, are necessarily bad. Policies discouraging them are therefore always desirable.*"[6]

What argument could there be that addiction is necessarily bad, that it possesses an intrinsic disvalue, a cost additional to whatever consequential costs becoming addicted might have in a particular circumstance? What have been characterised here as the consequential costs of addiction are closely tied to the essential nature of addiction: the resilience and dissatisfaction properties which make withdrawal difficult and unpleasant. But these costs arise only in bad cases: that is, if the fulfilment of the addictive desires is prevented by external circumstances, or non-fulfilment is in the addict's best interests. If these are consequential disvalues then any intrinsic disvalue attaching to addiction cannot turn *simply* on the likelihood of bad cases.

Goodin doesn't just define an addiction as a harmful habit. He has an argument to support the claim that addiction is necessarily bad, and the argument is valid (the conclusion follows from the assumptions). But unfortunately one of the assumptions is the WHO/APA account of dependence/addiction, which I have shown independently to be inadequate: "Addictions are unambiguously bad, from the point of view of the person addicted. Being defined in terms of a desire to quit coupled with an inability to quit, addictions necessarily would make the addict worse off."[7] Goodin's argument is thus essentially connected with bad cases. He assumes that the addict will always have to face bad cases, because (by the WHO/APA account) the addict is someone who wants to deny some of his addictive desires, but (because he is addicted) finds himself unable to do so. However, as pointed out in section 2, the assumption that an addict will invariably want, at some stage, to quit is unjustified. That is no part of the notion of addiction. And if the addict never wants to quit, and he faces no problem of supply, then he may never face a bad case, and so may never be worse off.

What, apart from bad cases, could support the intrinsic disvalue of addiction? The answer here is fairly obvious: the disvalue must turn on the addict's loss of freedom. A resilient disposition to generate resilient desires will limit a person's freedom: the greater the resilience the more severe the limitation. In the extreme case a complete addict will simply have no choice but to follow the dictates of his addictive desires. Suppose, what is entirely plausible, that freedom has an intrinsic value. Since addiction is *necessarily* in conflict with freedom, it is necessarily in conflict with something of intrinsic value. But that is just what it is for something to possess intrinsic disvalue.

V. A Bare Difference Argument

One way of determining whether or not a certain feature possesses intrinsic value or disvalue is the method of bare difference. Construct two situations which are alike in all respects *except* the feature in question, and then ask whether there is any *value* difference between the two situations. In order to determine whether or not addiction has a disvalue in itself we have to construct two situations in which the only difference is that addiction occurs in one and not in the other.

Suppose that a person, say Ernie, has a chronic medical problem for which there are two different but equally effective remedies: drug A and drug B. Neither remedy yields a permanent cure, but a daily dose of either would make the problem entirely manageable. There is only one difference between the two remedies: drug A (A for addiction) is highly addictive, while drug B is not addictive at all. In order to ensure bare difference, taking drug A must, in the circumstances, have no bad or good consequences for Ernie which are not also associated with taking drug B.

But herein lies a real difficulty for bare difference. As we have seen, withdrawal from addiction necessarily involves relative disvalues. If Ernie became A-addicted failing to take the drug would not only involve the return of his ailment (as would failing to take drug B if that were the treatment he opted for), but it would also involve the relative dissatisfaction of denying an addictive desire. That is an *extra* disvalue not involved in the B-treatment.

What this means is that to ensure bare difference we must build into the story that if Ernie chooses drug A there will be absolutely no chance that he will have to face withdrawal. We must stipulate that the supply of A is completely assured, and that there are no hassles or anxieties associated with treatment A that are not also associated with treatment B.

Provided we build all these factors into the story the argument from bad cases against becoming addicted does not work against drug A, for the story guarantees that Ernie will not face bad cases. The consequences of Ernie's opting for drug A are thus identical to his opting for drug B—apart from the addiction itself, and whatever is directly and necessarily involved in A-addiction. What *is* necessarily involved is a certain loss of freedom.

Two questions arise. Firstly, is there, intuitively, any residual value-difference between the two treatments provided all these conditions are met? Secondly, if the answer to the first question is *yes*, is the value-difference explained by Ernie's loss of freedom consequent upon treatment A?

I suspect that answers to the first question will vary somewhat. On the one hand there really doesn't seem to be much, if anything, to choose between the two treatments. But many people may be inclined to have a preference for treatment B. And a preference for treatment B would suggest that addiction in itself is deemed to possess intrinsic disvalue. However, this does not follow directly, for there may be another rational explanation for the preference. It may be that the judgement that treatment A is less satisfactory than treatment B stems from an unwillingness to accept the very stringent conditions of the story: namely, that there really is *no chance* that, once A-addicted, Ernie will ever have to face withdrawal. After all, how can I, or Ernie, be *sure* about that?

The answer is that *I* can be sure (even if Ernie cannot) because I am the story teller. From my God-like vantage point I simply stipulate it. It's *my* story. However, it would be very unrealistic to suppose that *Ernie,* if he is anything like us, can be sure about that—since none of us has a God's-eye view of the situations in which we find ourselves. And given even a very modest subjective uncertainty about the continued supply of A it would be rational for Ernie to prefer B. A non-zero probability that the supply of A will dry up yields a non-zero probability that Ernie will face bad cases. No matter how small the probability, that will be enough to tip the balance of *expected* value in favour of treatment B. This still holds if the same subjective uncertainty attaches to the possibility of the supply of drug B drying up. This is because, by the resilience and dissatisfaction properties, the possibility of the supply of drug A drying up is worse than the possibility of the supply of drug B drying up.

So Ernie, by virtue of limited knowledge, is justified in *regarding* treatment B as more valuable than treatment A. But this does not show that treatment B *is* more valuable. For Ernie's subjective ranking of the two treatments is based on what we (from our God's-eye view) know to be *false* information: namely that there is some small chance the supply of A will dry up.

What this shows is that for agents, such as ourselves, who have limited knowledge of the future the argument from bad cases will always have to be weighed in deciding what it *seems* best to do. There will always be some subjective probability that, once addicted, a bad case will turn up. But that is only on the side of *estimated* value, not on the side of actual value. (Even in actual cases this will not necessarily be a decisive factor in our estimates of value, because the probability of a bad case might be quite small.)

In Ernie's case, then, the possibility that treatment A is *objectively* worse than treatment B must turn on some feature other than that of the possibility of bad cases. The only difference between the two situations, as I will show, involves a certain loss of freedom.

How is Ernie's freedom impaired by A-addiction? Let us suppose that A is *powerfully* addictive. By taking A *once* Ernie will be completely hooked: he will acquire a *completely* resilient disposition to desire a daily dose (the disposition cannot be thrown off); the addictive desires themselves will also be completely resilient (Ernie will not be able to forego satisfying them whenever it is possible to do so); and it would be extremely unpleasant for Ernie if the desires are denied by external circumstances (dissatisfaction upon non-fulfilment is high). So, once addicted Ernie will be incapable of choosing to kick the addiction or forego the addictive desires. However, to ensure bare difference, no *other* choices of Ernie's will be impaired because, by assumption, we want to rule out other consequential effects. What is the structure of Ernie's choice situation in the two cases?

With treatment A Ernie becomes and remains addicted to A. In particular he cannot choose to revert to the non-addictive state. Consequently he cannot, for example, switch treatments and be just as well off. With treatment B, we may suppose, Ernie has more choice. He could halt the treatment, and then either suffer the ailment, or switch to the alternative treatment. So in case of treatment B Ernie definitely has some extra choices which are denied to him on treatment A. The intuition that even in the case of bare difference his freedom is impaired is born out. But the question remains whether this particular *kind* of freedom is intrinsically valuable.

Let us strengthen the story a little in a way which should not affect the judgement on the value-ranking of the two treatments. Suppose that Ernie's ailment is an incredibly painful one, so that faced with an apparent choice between continuing with the pain on the one hand, and having one or other of the treatments on the other, Ernie cannot do anything but to opt for some treatment or other. He really has no choice between being treated and not being treated. Given this, treatment A will still involve relative loss of freedom. Once hooked on A Ernie *cannot* switch to B. But treatment B does not limit his freedom in this way. If he is taking treatment B he can give it up—but only, by assumption, to switch to A. So as far as choices affected by the two treatments go Ernie's future choice-structure looks like this:

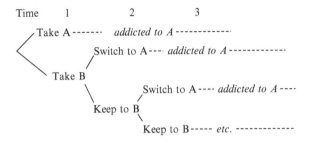

Abstracting from the particular details of the case what this amounts to is the following:

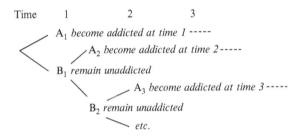

So Ernie's fundamental choice (remember bare difference) is between becoming addicted on the one hand, and remaining unaddicted with the opportunity to so choose again at a later date.

VI. THE VALUE OF FREEDOM: THE STRONG THESIS

In this section I will consider what I call the *strong* thesis about the value of freedom: that intrinsic value attaches merely to the *having* of genuine choices *regardless of whether there are any value differences between those choices*. Assume the strong thesis of the value of freedom. Then at each decision node in the above tree, where Ernie faces the choice between addiction (A_i) and remaining non-addicted (B_i), the latter choice will be more valuable than the former.

This is because opting for addiction involves a loss of future choice, whereas opting for non-addiction does not. The strong thesis thus tells us that having the choice (in this case between addiction and non-addiction) is valuable even if there is no *other* value difference between addiction and non-addiction.

The strong thesis thus yields the required intrinsic disvalue of addiction: but at a cost. For the strong thesis is unattractive. According to the strong thesis it would be more valuable to be able to choose from a range of ten different brands of toothpaste than from a certain subset of that range, say five different brands, *even if there are no value-differences between the brands*. While one might think such choice instrumentally valuable (say, through the effect of competition on quality or price of the end products) it is hard to see why one would consider it intrinsically valuable.

Or again, suppose you go into a travel agent because you have seen advertised a Pacific Island holiday of which you would like to take advantage. When you ask to book for the holiday the travel agent replies:

"We can do better than merely booking you. We can offer you a choice between two different Pacific Island holidays: you can either go to the Pacific Island we advertised, or you can go to another Pacific Island."

"What is the difference between them? What do they each offer?" you ask.

"No real difference at all!" the agent replies, and continues: "In fact we can *guarantee* that they are equally valuable because, although they are distinct islands, they are almost completely indistinguishable. One is the *mirror image* of the other. Apart from that inversion you would never know you were on one rather than the other. But aren't you lucky to have the choice?"

Pehaps these stories and arguments will not change the opinion of a devotee of the intrinsic value of sheer choice. But such a devotee would have to admit that the value involved, even if positive, must be rather small. As such it would hardly be sufficient to swamp the other, instrumental, values and disvalues. For example, suppose that in order to have the choice between a Pacific Island Holiday and its mirror image Island Holiday you had to deal with a slightly boorish and unpleasant travel agent. Would it not be better to deal with the agency which, while it offers only the one island holiday, nevertheless has pleasant and helpful staff?

VII. The Value of Freedom: The Weak Thesis

The examples in section VI undermine the strong thesis of the value of freedom and motivate consideration of a (logically) weaker thesis. What we value in freedom, what it is about being free that makes us significant and valuable beings, is not merely that we have choices which differ in their *content*. Rather, what we value is that our choices make a *value-difference:* that our choices differ in their *value*. The more significantly they differ in their value, the more significant the value of the choice itself. According to this more plausible view of the value of freedom it is not just the sheer number of choices that is valuable. Rather, it is being able to choose between options which differ in value. We don't just value making a *difference* to the world, or to our lives, we value making a *value*-difference. Call this the weak thesis of the value of freedom

Consider Ernie again in the last scenario of section 5. Can we apply the weak thesis of the value of freedom to generate the postulated intrinsic disvalue of addiction? Consider again Ernie's choice situation. By the bare difference postulate A_1 and B_1 differ only over what choices they leave Ernie in the future. A_1 leaves Ernie no choice at all: B_1 leaves Ernie with a choice between A_2 and B_2. So by the weak principle B_1 will be more valuable than A_1 if and only if there is a value-difference between A_2 and B_2. But the *only* difference between A_2 and B_2 is that between being addicted and not being addicted. Hence, *the weak principle delivers the desired result only on the assumption that there is a value difference between being addicted and not being addicted.* The argument thus begs the very question at issue. . . .

Note that there is nothing special about this particular scenario which guarantees the argument will be question-begging. The same conclusion applies equally to *any* case in which the only difference between becoming addicted and remaining unaddicted is that the former does not, and the latter does,

allow the person future choices between becoming addicted and remaining unaddicted. In any such case any argument for the intrinsic disvalue of addiction which appeals to the weak principle of the value of freedom will have to beg the question by assuming that there is such an intrinsic value-difference. This is in no way a criticism of the weak thesis of freedom's intrinsic value. Indeed, it is a thesis which I myself endorse, along with other theses of the value of autonomy. . . .

VIII. Reviewing the Cases

It will be instructive to review the cases I began with in the light of the above discussion. But before doing so let me briefly summarize the main results of this analysis. An addiction is a resilient disposition to generate resilient desires with the dissatisfaction property. That an activity is addictive is the basis of a prima facie argument against indulging in it—an argument from bad cases. But the strength of this argument depends on how likely, and how bad, bad cases are likely to be. Any argument for an additional intrinsic disvalue to addiction, a disvalue which could substantially alter the balance against possible consequential benefits, will have to invoke the value of freedom. But then it will either appeal to an implausibly strong thesis of freedom's value; or, if it settles for a more attractive (and, in my view, *true*) thesis, it will have to beg the question at issue. I conclude that there is no intrinsic disvalue to addiction, and each case of possible addiction will have to be examined for consequential values and disvalues before deciding what should be done.

With regard to the first two cases much of the medical literature suggests, other things being equal, that the risk of becoming addicted to narcotics through their use in the treatment of pain is surprisingly small.[8] However, the *risk* of such treatment could still be large, and hence worthy of taking seriously, if being addicted were a sufficiently bad thing. For the size of a risk is a function not just the *probability* of a bad outcome, but the *badness* of that outcome: a small chance of a very bad outcome may generate a risk worth noting. But quite apart from the magnitude of the chance of becoming addicted, what I have shown is that *the chance of becoming addicted by itself does not constitute a reason for preferring one course of action to another*. Rather, we have to examine the *nature* of the addiction, in particular the likelihood and severity of the bad cases it could generate. In many cases this is enough to substantially shift the burden of proof, *especially* if we place a value on rational autonomy.

Case 1

In itself becoming addicted to the morphine is not bad for Ms A. Provided the health professionals she employs are reliable and trustworthy, she can clearly be confident of keeping up the supply for as long as is required. . . . The known effects of long-term addiction to morphine would appear to be much less undesirable than the effects of her condition. Given that there are no other relevant and unstated factors to the case, and given the presumed value of rational autonomy, Ms A should have the known advantages and disadvantages of prolonged morphine use explained to her and then given the choice.

Case 2

Very similar remarks apply to Mr B's condition. The use of the morphine enabled him to lead a satisfying life. Even if he did become addicted to morphine, the known long-term effects of this seem much less undesirable than the effects of his condition. . . .

Case 3

Whatever one's views of the disvalue of addiction, the nicotine inhaler is clearly far preferable to cigarettes as a means of delivering nicotine to the body. Since both contain nicotine they are equally addictive, but cigarette smoke harbours all manner of additional disvalues. Particularly important here are the disvalues which smoking involves for the surrounding non-smokers—from the moral point of view the inhaler is far superior to the cigarette. But even prudentially it would be wise for a nicotine addict to choose the inhaler. It seems that any defensible justification for

restricting the availability of the inhaler while cigarettes continue to be freely available, must be to do with the *indirect* consequences of its availability. That is to say, to make the inhaler available would be to concede that a substance's being highly addictive (as nicotine is) is not a good reason, in itself, for constraining its availability—and that might encourage people to think that they should have the choice concerning the consumption of *other* addictive substances. And, of course, they might be right about that.

NOTES

1. For an insightful account, by a medical practitioner, of the inter-relations between pain, pain treatment, and concomitant suffering, see Cassel 1982.

2. See Angell 1982.

3. Marks and Sachar 1973 in a much cited study concluded that undertreatment was the *characteristic* treatment. Morgan and Pleet 1983 concluded that ten years later there had been "minimal evidence of improvement and patients with severe pain are still markedly undertreated."

4. For example, see Beyer, De Good, Ashley, and Russell 1983.

5. Consider, for example the following passage in Melzack 1990, p. 19: "Morphine is the safest, most effective analgesic (painkiller) known for constant severe pain, but it is also addictive for some people. *Consequently* it is typically meted out sparingly, if it is given at all." The italics are mine, but the point is clear. It is because of the risk of addiction that it is not used. Or again, in Bakalar and Grinspoon 1984 "The most important justification for strict legal and social control on drugs is dependency or addiction . . . it provides the best reason for saying that the drug user is not free, and that anyone exposed to the drug may lose personal freedom." (p. 35).

6. Goodin 1989, p. 100 (my emphasis).

7. Goodin 1989, p. 99.

8. See Robins, Davis and Nurco 1974, Porter and Hershel 1980, Morgan and Pleet 1983, and Melzack 1990.

REFERENCES

American Psychiatric Association. *Diagnostic and Statistical Manual of Mental Disorders* (3rd edition), Washington DC: American Psychiatric Association, 1987.

Angell, M. "The quality of mercy." *The New England Journal of Medicine* 306 (2), 1982, pp. 98–99.

Bakalar, J.B. and Grinspoon, L. *Drug Control in a Free Society.* Cambridge: Cambridge University Press, 1984.

Beyer, J.E., De Good, D.E. Ashley, L.C. and Russell, G.A. "Patterns of post-operative analgesic use with adults and children following cardiac surgery." *Pain* (17), 1982, pp. 71–81.

Cassel, E.J. "The nature of suffering and the goals of medicine." *The New England Journal of Medicine,* 306 (11), 1982, pp. 639–645.

Goodin, R.E. *No Smoking: The Ethical Issues,* Chicago: The University of Chicago Press, 1989.

Marks, R.M. and Sachar, E.J. "Undertreatment of medical inpatients with narcotic analgesics." *Annals of Internal Medicine,* 78(2), 1973, pp. 173–181.

Melzack, R. "The tragedy of needless pain," *Scientific American,* 262 (2), Feb. 1990, pp. 19–25.

Morgan, J.P. and Pleet, D.L. "Opiophobia in the United States: the undertreatment of severe pain," in Morgan, J.P. and Kagan, D.V. (eds) *Society and Medication: Conflicting Signals for Prescribers and Patients,* D.C. Heath and Company, 1983.

Porter, J. and Herschel, J. "Drug addiction rare in patients treated with narcotics." *New England Journal of Medicine,* 10, Jan 1980, p. 123.

Robins, L.N., Davis, D.H., and Nurco, D.N. "How permanent was Vietnam drug addiction?" *American Journal of Public Health Supplement,* 96, Dec. 1974, pp. 38–43.

World Health Organisation, *International Classification of Diseases* (9th edition), Geneva: World Health Organisation, 1978.

25

Is Legal Punishment Wrong?

Barnett and His Critics

When a government raises a sales tax or builds a highway or summons a person for jury duty, it acts in ways that predictably cause harm to some of its citizens. An increased tax will be costly to some businesses and some consumers; a new highway will cause headaches for those who live close by; and being on a jury will be time consuming and stressful for those who are drafted into serving. In all of these cases, of course, the State does not do what it does *in order to* harm these people. It does what it does in order to bring about a presumably legitimate end while recognizing that some harm will fall upon some of its citizens in the process. The State builds roads in order to facilitate transportation, for example, not in order to give some of its citizens headaches, but building roads will cause some headaches nonetheless. There is one instance, however, in which the State does act with the explicit intention of causing harm to some of its own citizens: when it punishes people for breaking the law. When a criminal is put in prison, for example, he is put there *in order to* make him suffer for his wrongdoing. The harm to the criminal is not merely a foreseen byproduct of the act, in the way that the harm to people living near the highway is merely an unfortunate side effect of the road's being built. Rather, the harm to the criminal is precisely the point of the act of imprisoning him. The State punishes him in order to harm him. This difference between punishment and other government acts renders the moral justification of punishment distinctly problematic. After all, most people would agree that, in general, it would be wrong for the State to intentionally harm some of its own citizens. Why, then, is it morally permissible for the State to intentionally harm some of its citizens merely because they have broken the law? This is the problem of punishment.

The problem of punishment has generated a large number of attempted solutions, most of which fall into two distinct camps: the *deterrence position* and the *retributivist position*. Put briefly, the deterrence position maintains that the State may punish people for breaking the law because doing so will presumably discourage others from breaking the law. The retributivist position maintains that the State may punish people for breaking the law because people who break the law deserve to be punished. In addition, a number of thinkers have argued that punishment can be justified as a form of rehabilitation on the grounds that punishment is actually good for the person being punished (anyone whose parents ever told her "I'm doing this for your own good" will understand the core of this third position). Philosophers who have written on the subject disagree sharply about just *how* the practice of punishment is justified, but virtually all of them agree that it is justified. Randy E. Barnett, however, does not accept that punishment can be justified. In "Restitution: A New Paradigm of Criminal Justice," which serves as the featured article for this chapter, Barnett argues that the State does not, in fact, have the right to punish people for breaking the law. When a person breaks the law, on Barnett's account, the State has the right to compel him to make restitution to his victims (where restitution means restoring them to the level of well-being they rightfully enjoyed prior to the offender's wrongful act), but that is all it may permissibly do. Barnett refers to this position as the theory of *pure restitution*.

This position, as Barnett recognizes, is a radical one. Virtually everyone agrees that restitution should be one part of the criminal justice system, but virtually no one other than Barnett thinks that it should be the only part. Barnett's argument for his extreme position can best be understood as consisting of two parts, each of which proceeds by means of process of elimination (see section 4.5 of the Introduction). In the first part, Barnett considers the attempts that have been made to show that punishment is permissible and tries to show that all of them fail. Even though most people think that one of the three positions—deterrence, retributivist, or rehabilitationist—must be correct, Barnett attempts to establish that all of them have implications that most people will reject. In the second part of his argument, Barnett considers a variety of objections that can be raised directly against the theory of pure restitution itself. Here, he proceeds by process of elimination in a different way: attempting to eliminate the various objections that can be raised against his theory by showing that they all can be overcome. In short, Barnett first attempts to eliminate any reason for believing that punishment can be justified and then attempts to eliminate any reason for rejecting the rejection of punishment.

Since Barnett's argument depends on this two-pronged approach, it is vulnerable to two distinct kinds of criticism. First, a critic could attempt to provide a positive defense of punishment, trying to establish, for example, that Barnett's objections to the deterrence position or the retributivist position can be overcome or providing a still further defense of punishment. Second, a critic could attempt to identify an unacceptable implication of the theory of pure restitution, either by showing that Barnett fails to overcome satisfactorily one of the objections he considers or by raising still further objections to the theory that Barnett does not consider.

In his brief reply to Barnett, Franklin G. Miller offers objections of both of these sorts. In response to Barnett's arguments against the various justifications of punishment, Miller charges that Barnett neglects two further possibilities: the possibility of combining some of the justifications he does consider into a more powerful justification and the possibility of appealing to the condemnatory aspect of punishment, the respect in which the State uses punishment as a means of communicating its disapproval of the offender's behavior. In response to Barnett's attempt to fend off various objections to the pure restitution approach, Miller maintains that the exclusive focus on making restitution to victims leaves the approach unable to handle a variety of cases in which it is not clear just who the victim is or how he should be compensated, especially cases in which no particular individual was harmed or in which the offender attempted to cause harm or risked causing harm but did not, in fact, cause harm.

In two excerpts from a longer piece, Roger Pilon also offers objections of both sorts to Barnett's position. With respect to Barnett's attempt to defend the theory of pure restitution against a variety of objections, Pilon considers cases involving wealthy individuals. He uses these cases to press the objection that restitution alone cannot address the guilty-mind component of criminal acts (that is, the component that distinguishes criminal acts from acts that warrant merely civil lawsuits). And with respect to Barnett's attempt to defeat the various defenses of punishment that have been proposed, Pilon defends a particular version of retributivism in which the offender has forfeited certain rights, which thereby renders him liable not merely to restitution but to punishment.

Finally, two quick points from a longer piece by Stanley S. Kleinberg round out the critical responses to Barnett's proposal (readers interested in pursuing the debate still further should read the pieces by Pilon and Kleinberg in their entirety): First, even crimes that have clear individual victims, such as armed robbery, also victimize other members of society in a way that Barnett's proposal does not seem prepared to accommodate. Second, the system that Barnett envisions would seem to favor not only the wealthy (a point also noted by Pilon) but also, perhaps even more disturbing, the professional criminal. The cumulative effect of the critical responses to Barnett, then, is that many of his readers believe that he has failed to show that punishment is unjustified and that he has failed to show that his proposed alternative is sufficiently plausible.

Questions for Consideration

In thinking about the exchange between Barnett and his critics, readers should focus on the two main sets of argument outlined here.

• Has Barnett succeeded in raising sufficient doubts about the justifiability of punishment, or have his critics succeeded in making a satisfactory case in its defense?

• Can punishment be justified by one of the theories that Barnett discusses or by one he neglects or by some combination of these? Or is Barnett correct to insist that, in the end, none of these considerations can justify the intentional harm of people in response to their having violated the law?

• Has Barnett succeeded in rendering his theory of restitution sufficiently attractive, or have his critics succeeded in demonstrating that it would have unacceptable implications?

• All of Barnett's examples of offenders making restitution involve their making monetary payments to their victims. Are there other ways that offenders could try to restore people to their previous level of well-being? If there are, could the existence of nonmonetary forms of restitution help Barnett to overcome some of the objections to his theory?

Further Reading

Barnett, Randy. "The Justice of Restitution," in *Moral Issues*, ed. Jan Narveson (Toronto and New York: Oxford University Press, 1983), pp. 140–53.

———. "Pursuing Justice in a Free Society: Part One—Power vs. Liberty." *Criminal Justice Ethics* 4, no. 2 (1985): 50–72.

Boonin, David. *The Problem of Punishment*. Cambridge: Cambridge University Press, 2008.

Dagger, Richard. "Restitution: Pure or Punitive?" *Criminal Justice Ethics* 10, no. 2 (Summer–Fall 1991): 29–39.

Ellin, Joseph. "Restitutionism Defended." *The Journal of Value Inquiry* 34 (2000): 299–317.

RANDY E. BARNETT

Restitution

A New Paradigm of Criminal Justice

This paper will analyze the breakdown of our system of criminal justice in terms of what Thomas Kuhn would describe as a crisis of an old paradigm—punishment. I propose that this crisis could be solved by the adoption of a new paradigm of criminal justice—restitution. The approach will be mainly theoretical, though at various points in the discussion the practical implications of the rival paradigms will also be considered. A fundamental contention will be that many, if not most, of our system's ills stem from errors in the underlying paradigm. Any attempt to correct these symptomatic debilities without a reexamination of the theoretical underpinnings is doomed to frustration and failure. Kuhn's theories deal with the problems of science. What made his proposal so startling was its attempt to analogize scientific development to social and political development. Here, I will simply reverse the process by applying Kuhn's framework of scientific change to social, or in this case, legal development.[1]

In the criminal justice system we are witnessing the death throes of an old and cumbersome paradigm, one that has dominated Western thought for more than 900 years. While this paper presents what is hoped to be a viable, though radical alternative, much would be accomplished by simply prompting the reader to reexamine the assumptions underlying the present system. Only if we are willing to look at our old problems in a new light do we stand a chance of solving them. This is our only hope, and our greatest challenge.

THE CRISIS IN THE PARADIGM OF PUNISHMENT

"Political revolutions are inaugurated by a growing sense, often restricted to a segment of the political community, that existing institutions have ceased adequately to meet the problems posed by an environment they have in part created. . . . In both political and scientific development the sense of malfunction that can lead to crisis is prerequisite to revolution."[2] Kuhn's description of the preconditions for scientific and political revolutions could accurately describe the current state of the criminal law. However, simply to recognize the existence of a crisis is not enough. We must look for its causes. The Kuhnian methodology suggests that we critically examine the paradigm of punishment itself.

The problems which the paradigm of punishment is supposed to solve are many and varied. A whole literature on the philosophy of punishment has arisen in an effort to justify or reject the institution of punishment. For our purposes the following definition from the *Encyclopedia of Philosophy* should suffice: "Characteristically punishment is unpleasant. It is inflicted on an offender because of an offense he has committed; it is deliberately imposed, not just the natural consequence of a person's action (like a hangover), and the unpleasantness is *essential* to it, not an accompaniment to some other treatment (like the pain of the dentist's drill)."[3]

Two types of arguments are commonly made in defense of punishment. The first is that punishment is an appropriate means to some justifiable end such as, for example, deterrence of crime. The second type of argument is that punishment is justified as an end in itself. On this view, whatever ill effects it might engender, punishment for its own sake is good.

The first type of argument might be called the *political* justification of punishment, for the end which justifies its use is one which a political order is presumably dedicated to serve: the maintenance of

Randy E. Barnett, "Restitution: A New Paradigm of Criminal Justice," *Ethics* 87, no. 4 (July 1977): 279–301. Some notes have been deleted. Reprinted by permission of University of Chicago Press.

peaceful interactions between individuals and groups in a society. There are at least three ways that deliberate infliction of harm on an offender is said to be politically justified.

1. One motive for punishment, especially capital punishment and imprisonment, is the "intention to deprive offenders of the power of doing future mischief."[4] Although it is true that an offender cannot continue to harm society while incarcerated, a strategy of punishment based on disablement has several drawbacks.

Imprisonment is enormously expensive. This means that a double burden is placed on the innocent who must suffer the crime and, in addition, pay through taxation for the support of the offender and his family if they are forced onto welfare. Also, any benefit of imprisonment is temporary; eventually, most offenders will be released. If their outlook has not improved—and especially if it has worsened—the benefits of incarceration are obviously limited. Finally, when disablement is permanent, as with capital punishment or psychosurgery, it is this very permanence, in light of the possibility of error, which is frightening. For these reasons, "where disablement enters as an element into penal theories, it occupies, as a rule, a subordinate place and is looked upon as an object subsidiary to some other end which is regarded as paramount. . . ."[5]

2. Rehabilitation of a criminal means a change in his mental *habitus* so that he will not offend again. It is unclear whether the so-called treatment model which views criminals as a doctor would view a patient is truly a "retributive" concept. Certainly it does not conform to the above definition characterizing punishment as deliberately and essentially unpleasant. It is an open question whether any end justifies the intentional, forceful manipulation of an individual's thought processes by anyone, much less the state. To say that an otherwise just system has incidentally rehabilitative effects which may be desirable is one thing, but it is quite another to argue that these effects themselves justify the system. The horrors to which such reasoning can lead are obvious from abundant examples in history and contemporary society.[6]

Rehabilitation as a reaction against the punishment paradigm will be considered below, but one aspect is particularly relevant to punishment as defined here. On this view, the visiting of unpleasantness itself will cause the offender to see the error of his ways; by having "justice" done him, the criminal will come to appreciate his error and will change his moral outlook. This end, best labeled "reformation," is speculative at best and counterfactual at worst. On the contrary, "it has been observed that, as a rule . . . ruthless punishments, far from mollifying men's ways, corrupt them and stir them to violence."[7]

3. The final justification to be treated here—deterrence—actually has two aspects. The first is the deterrent effect that past demonstrations of punishment have on the future conduct of others; the second is the effect that threats of future punishment have on the conduct of others. The distinction assumes importance when some advocates argue that future threats lose their deterrent effect when there is a lack of past demonstrations. Past punishment, then, serves as an educational tool. It is a substitute for or reinforcement of threats of future punishment.

As with the goals mentioned above, the empirical question of whether punishment has this effect is a disputed one.[8] I shall not attempt to resolve this question here, but will assume *arguendo* that punishment even as presently administered has some deterrent effect. It is the moral question which is disturbing. Can an argument from deterrence alone "justify" in any sense the infliction of pain on a criminal? It is particularly disquieting that the actual levying of punishment is done not for the criminal himself, but for the educational impact it will have on the community. The criminal act becomes the occasion of, but not the reason for, the punishment. In this way, the actual crime becomes little more than an excuse for punishing.

Surely this distorts the proper functioning of the judicial process. For if deterrence is the end it is unimportant whether the individual actually committed the crime. Since the public's perception of guilt is the prerequisite of the deterrent effect, all that is required for deterrence is that the individual is "proved" to have committed the crime. The actual occurrence would have no relevance except insofar as a truly guilty person is easier to prove guilty. The judicial process becomes, not a truth-seeking device, but solely a means to legitimate the use of force. To treat criminals as means to the ends of others in this way raises serious moral problems. This is not to argue that men may never use others as means but rather to question the use of force against the individual because of the effect such use will have on others. It was this that concerned del Vecchio when he stated that "the human person always bears in himself something sacred, and it is therefore not permissable to treat him merely as a means towards an end ouside of himself."[9]

Finally, deterrence as the ultimate justification of punishment cannot rationally limit its use. It "provides *no* guidance until we're told *how much* commission of it is to be deterred."[10] Since there are always some who commit crimes, one can always argue for more punishment. Robert Nozick points out that there must be criteria by which one decides how much deterrence may be inflicted.[11] One is forced therefore to employ "higher" principles to evaluate the legitimacy of punishment.

It is not my thesis that deterrence, reformation, and disablement are undesirable goals. On the contrary, any criminal justice system should be critically examined to see if it is having these and other beneficial effects. The view advanced here is simply that these utilitarian benefits must be incidental to a just system; they cannot, alone or in combination, justify a criminal justice system. Something more is needed. There is another more antiquated strain of punishment theory which seeks to address this problem. The *moral* justifications of punishment view punishment as an end in itself. This approach has taken many forms.[12] On this view, whatever ill or beneficial results it might have, punishment of lawbreakers is good for its own sake. This proposition can be analyzed on several levels.

The most basic question is the truth of the claim itself. Some have argued that "the alleged absolute justice of repaying evil with evil (maintained by Kant and many other writers) is really an empty sophism. If we go back to the Christian moralists, we find that an evil is to be put right only by doing good."[13] This question is beyond the scope of this treatment. The subject has been extensively dealt with by those more knowledgeable than I.[14] The more relevant question is what such

a view of punishment as a good can be said to imply for a system of criminal justice. Even assuming that it would be good if, in the nature of things, the wicked got their "come-uppance," what behavior does this moral fact justify? Does it justify the victim authoring the punishment of his offender? Does it justify the same action by the victim's family, his friends, his neighbors, the state? If so what punishment should be imposed and who should decide?

It might be argued that the natural punishment for the violation of natural rights is the deserved hatred and scorn of the community, the resultant ostracism, and the existential hell of *being* an evil person. The question then is not whether we have the right to inflict some "harm" or unpleasantness on a morally contemptible person—surely, we do; the question is not whether such a punishment is "good"—arguably, it is. The issue is whether the "virtue of some punishment" justifies the *forceful* imposition of unpleasantness on a *rights violator* as distinguished from the morally imperfect. Any *moral* theory of punishment must recognize and deal with this distinction. Finally, it must be established that the state is the legitimate author of punishment, a proposition which further assumes the moral and legal legitimacy of the state. To raise these issues is not to resolve them, but it would seem that the burden of proof is on those seeking to justify the use of force against the individual. Suffice it to say that I am skeptical of finding any theory which justifies the deliberate, forceful imposition of punishment within or without a system of criminal justice.

The final consideration in dealing with punishment as an end in itself is the possibility that the current crisis in the criminal justice system is in fact a crisis of the paradigm of punishment. While this, if true, does not resolve the philosophical issues, it does cast doubt on the punishment paradigm's vitality as the motive force behind a system of criminal justice. Many advocates of punishment argue that its apparent practical failings exist because we are not punishing enough. All that is needed, they say, is a crackdown on criminals and those victims and witnesses who shun participation in the criminal justice system; the only problem with the paradigm of punishment is that we are not following it.[15] This response fails to consider *why* the system doggedly refuses to punish to the degree required to yield beneficial results and instead punishes in such a way as to yield harmful results. The answer may be that the paradigm of punishment is in eclipse, that the public lacks the requisite will to apply it in anything but the prevailing way.

Punishment, particularly state punishment is the descendant of the tradition which imparts religious and moral authority to the sovereign and, through him, the community. Such an authority is increasingly less credible in a secular world such as ours. Today there is an increasing desire to allow each individual to govern his own life as he sees fit provided he does not violate the rights of others. This desire is exemplified by current attitudes toward drug use, abortion, and pornography. Few argue that these things are good. It is only said that where there is no victim the state or community has no business meddling in the peaceful behavior of its citizens, however morally suspect it may be.[16]

Furthermore, if the paradigm of punishment is in a "crisis period" it is as much because of its practical drawbacks as the uncertainty of its moral status. The infliction of suffering on a criminal tends to cause a general feeling of sympathy for him. There is no rational connection between a term of imprisonment and the harm caused the victim. Since the prison term is supposed to be unpleasant, at least a part of the public comes to see the criminal as a victim, and the lack of rationality also causes the offender to feel victimized. This reaction is magnified by the knowledge that most crimes go unpunished and that even if the offender is caught the judicial process is long, arduous, and far removed from the criminal act. While this is obvious to most, it is perhaps less obvious that the punishment paradigm is largely at fault. The slow, ponderous nature of our system of justice is largely due to a fear of an unjust infliction of punishment on the innocent (or even the guilty). The more awful the sanction, the more elaborate need be the safeguards. The more the system is perceived as arbitrary and unfair, the more incentive there is for defendants and their counsel to thwart the truth-finding process. Acquittal becomes desirable at all costs. As the punitive aspect of a sanction is diminished, so too would be the perceived need for procedural protections.

A system of punishment, furthermore, offers no incentive for the victim to involve himself in the criminal justice process other than to satisfy his feelings of duty or revenge. The victim stands to gain little if at all by the conviction and punishment of the person who caused his loss. This is true even of those systems discussed below which dispense state compensation based on the victim's need. The system of justice itself imposes uncompensated costs by requiring a further loss of time and money by the victim and witnesses and by increasing the perceived risk of retaliation.

Finally, punishment which seeks to change an offender's moral outlook, or at least to scare him, can do nothing to provide him with the skills needed to survive in the outside world. In prison, he learns the advanced state of the criminal arts and vows not to repeat the mistake that led to his capture. The convict emerges better trained and highly motivated to continue a criminal career.

The crisis of the paradigm of punishment has at its roots the collapse of its twin pillars of support: its moral legitimacy and its practical efficacy. As Kaufmann concludes, "the faith in retributive justice is all but dead."[17]

ATTEMPTS TO SALVAGE THE PARADIGM OF PUNISHMENT

"All crises begin with the blurring of a paradigm and the consequent loosening of the rules for normal research."[18] And yet until a new paradigm is presented, authorities will cling to the old one, either ignoring the problem or salvaging the paradigm with ad hoc explanations and solutions. Why are paradigms never rejected outright? Why must there always be a new paradigm before the old one is abandoned? Kuhn does not explicitly discuss this, but R. A. Childs hypothesizes "that, as such, paradigms may serve the function of increasing man's sense of control over some aspect of reality, or some aspect of his own life. If this is so, then we would expect that a straightforward abandonment of a paradigm would threaten that sense of control."[19]

This psychological need for an explanation may in turn explain the many efforts to shore up the paradigm of punishment. The three attempts to be examined next have at their roots a perception of its fundamental errors, and at the same time they highlight three goals of any new paradigm of criminal justice.

1. Proportionate punishment. The king abandoned the composition system[20] for the system of punishment because punishment struck terror in the hearts of the people, and this served to inspire awe for the power of the king and state. But there was no rational connection between the seriousness of the crime and the gravity of the punishment and, therefore, no limit to the severity of punishment. Hideous tortures came to be employed: "But some of the men of the Enlightenment sought to counter the inhumanity of their Christian predecessors with appeals to reason. They thought that retributive justice had a mathematical quality and that murder called for capital punishment in much the same way in which two plus two equals four."[21]

The appeal to proportionality was one of the early attempts to come to grips with deficiencies in the paradigm of punishment. It was doomed to failure, for there is no objective standard by which punishments can be proportioned to fit the crime. Punishment is incommensurate with crime. This solution is purely ad hoc and intuitive. We shall, however, find the *goal* of proportionate sentencing useful in the formation of a new paradigm.

2. Rehabilitation. It was noted earlier that the infliction of punishment tends to focus attention on the plight of the criminal. Possibly for this reason, the next humanitarian trend was to explore the proper treatment of criminals. Punishment failed to reform the criminal, and this led observers to inquire how the situation might be improved. Some felt that the sole end of the penal system was rehabilitation, so attention was turned to modifying the criminal's behavior (an obviously manipulative end). Emphasis was placed on education, job training, and discipline.

Unfortunately, the paradigm of punishment and the political realities of penal administration have all but won out. There is simply no incentive for prison authorities to educate and train. Their job is essentially political. They are judged by their ability to keep the prisoners within the walls and to keep incidents of violence within the prison to a minimum; as a result, discipline is the main concern. Furthermore, since he

is sentenced to a fixed number of years (less time off for good behavior—so-called good time), there is no institutional incentive for the prisoner to improve himself apart from sheer boredom. Productive labor in prison is virtually nonexistent, with only obsolete equipment, if any, available. Except perhaps for license plates and other state needs, the prisoners produce nothing of value; the prisons make no profit and the workers are paid, if at all, far below market wages. They are unable to support themselves or their families. The state, meaning the innocent taxpayer, supports the prisoner, and frequently the families as well via welfare.

Rehabilitation has been a long-time goal of the penal system, but the political nature of government-run prisons and the dominance of the paradigm of punishment has inevitably prevented its achievement. Prisons remain detention centers, all too temporarily preventing crime by physically confining the criminals.

3. Victim compensation. It is natural that the brutalities resulting from the paradigm of punishment would get first attention from humanitarians and that the persons subjected to those practices would be next. Until recently, the victim of crime was the forgotten party. Within the last few years a whole new field has opened up called victimology.[22] With it has come a variety of proposals, justifications, and statutes.[23]

Certain features are common to virtually every compensation proposal: (a) Compensation for crimes would be dispensed by the state from tax revenue. (b) Compensation is "a matter of grace" rather than an assumption by the state of legal responsibility for the criminal loss suffered by the victim. (c) Most proposals allow for aid only on a "need" or "hardship" basis. (d) Most are limited to some sort of crime of violence or the threat of force or violence. (e) None questions the paradigm of punishment.

The goal of these proposals and statutes is laudable. The victim *is* the forgotten man of crime. But the means proposed is the same tired formula: welfare to those in "need." In short, the innocent taxpayer repays the innocent victim (if the victim can prove he "needs" help) while the guilty offender is subjected to the sanction of punishment with all its failings. Like proportionate punishment and rehabilitation, the goal of victim compensation is a recognition of very real problems in our criminal justice system, and at the same time it ignores the source of these problems: our conception of crime as an offense against the state whose proper sanction is punishment. Until a viable, new paradigm is presented, ad hoc solutions like the ones discussed here are all that can be hoped for. And it is a vain hope indeed, for they attack the symptoms while neglecting the causes of the problem. What is needed is a new paradigm.

Outline of a New Paradigm

The idea of restitution is actually quite simple. It views crime as an offense by one individual against the rights of another. The victim has suffered a loss. Justice consists of the culpable offender making good the loss he has caused. It calls for a complete refocusing of our image of crime. Kuhn would call it a "shift of world-view." Where we once saw an offense against society, we now see an offense against an individual victim. In a way, it is a common sense view of crime. *The armed robber did not rob society; he robbed the victim.* His debt, therefore, is not to society; it is to the victim. There are really two types of restitution proposals: a system of "punitive" restitution and a "pure" restitutional system.

1. Punitive restitution. "Since rehabilitation was admitted to the aims of penal law two centuries ago, the number of penological aims has remained virtually constant. Restitution is waiting to come in."[24] Given this view, restitution should merely be added to the paradigm of punishment. Stephen Schafer outlines the proposal: "[Punitive] restitution, like punishment, must always be the subject of judicial consideration. Without exception it must be carried out by personal performance by the wrong-doer, and should even then be equally burdensome and just for all criminals, irrespective of their means, whether they be millionaires or labourers."[25]

There are many ways by which such a goal might be reached. The offender might be forced to compensate the victim by his own work, either in prison or out. If it came out of his pocket or from the sale of

his property this would compensate the victim, but it would not be sufficiently unpleasant for the offender. Another proposal would be that the fines be proportionate to the earning power of the criminal. Thus, "A poor man would pay in days of work, a rich man by an equal number of days' income or salary."[26] Herbert Spencer made a proposal along similar lines in his excellent "Prison-Ethics," which is well worth examining.[27] Murray N. Rothbard and others have proposed a system of "double payments" in cases of criminal behavior.[28] While closer to pure restitution than other proposals, the "double damages" concept preserves a punitive aspect.

Punitive restitution is an attempt to gain the benefits of pure restitution, which will be considered shortly, while retaining the perceived advantages of the paradigm of punishment. Thus, the prisoner is still "sentenced" to some unpleasantness—prison labor or loss of X number of days' income. That the intention is to preserve the "hurt" is indicated by the hesitation to accept an out-of-pocket payment or sale of assets. This is considered too "easy" for the criminal and takes none of his time. The amount of payment is determined not by the *actual harm* but by the *ability of the offender to pay*. Of course, by retaining the paradigm of punishment this proposal involves many of the problems we raised earlier. In this sense it can be considered another attempt to salvage the old paradigm.

2. Pure restitution. "Recompense or restitution is scarcely a punishment as long as it is merely a matter of returning stolen goods or money. . . . The point is not that the offender deserves to suffer; it is rather that the offended party desires compensation."[29] This represents the complete overthrow of the paradigm of punishment. No longer would the deterrence, reformation, disablement, or rehabilitation of the criminal be the guiding principle of the judicial system. The attainment of these goals would be incidental to, and as a result of, reparations paid to the victim. No longer would the criminal deliberately be made to suffer for his mistake. Making good that mistake is all that would be required. What follows is a possible scenario of such a system.

When a crime occurred and a suspect was apprehended, a trial court would attempt to determine his guilt or innocence. If found guilty, the criminal would be sentenced to make restitution to the victim.[30] If a criminal is able to make restitution immediately, he may do so. This would discharge his liability. If he were unable to make restitution, but were found by the court to be trustworthy, he would be permitted to remain at his job (or find a new one) while paying restitution out of his future wages. This would entail a legal claim against future wages. Failure to pay could result in garnishment or a new type of confinement.

If it is found that the criminal is not trustworthy, or that he is unable to gain employment, he would be confined to an employment project.[31] This would be an industrial enterprise, preferably run by a private concern, which would produce actual goods or services. The level of security at each employment project would vary according to the behavior of the offenders. Since the costs would be lower, inmates at a lower-security project would receive higher wages. There is no reason why many workers could not be permitted to live with their families inside or outside the facility, depending, again, on the trustworthiness of the offender. Room and board would be deducted from the wages first, then a certain amount for restitution. Anything over that amount the worker could keep or apply toward further restitution, thus hastening his release. If a worker refused to work, he would be unable to pay for his maintenance, and therefore would not in principle be entitled to it. If he did not make restitution he could not be released. The exact arrangement which would best provide for high productivity, minimal security, and maximum incentive to work and repay the victim cannot be determined in advance. Experience is bound to yield some plans superior to others. In fact, the experimentation has already begun.[32]

While this might be the basic system, all sorts of refinements are conceivable, and certainly many more will be invented as needs arise. A few examples might be illuminating. With such a system of repayment, victim *crime insurance* would be more economically feasible than at present and highly desirable. The cost of awards would be offset by the insurance company's right to restitution in place of the victim (right of subrogation). The insurance company would be better suited to supervise the offender and mark his progress than would the victim. To obtain an earlier recovery, it could be expected to innovate so as to enable the worker to repay more quickly (and, as a result, be released that much sooner). The insurance companies might even underwrite the employment projects themselves as well as related industries which would employ the skilled worker after his release. Any successful effort on their part to reduce crime and recidivism would result in fewer claims and lower premiums. The benefit of this insurance scheme for the victim is immediate compensation, conditional on the victim's continued cooperation with the authorities for the arrest and conviction of the suspect. In addition, the centralization of victim claims would, arguably, lead to efficiencies which would permit the pooling of small claims against a common offender.

Another highly useful refinement would be *direct arbitration* between victim and criminal. This would serve as a sort of healthy substitute for plea bargaining. By allowing the guilty criminal to negotiate a reduced payment in return for a guilty plea, the victim (or his insurance company) would be saved the risk of an adverse finding at trial and any possible additional expense that might result. This would also allow an indigent criminal to substitute personal services for monetary payments if all parties agreed.

Arbitration is argued for by John M. Greacen, deputy director of the National Institute for Law Enforcement and Criminal Justice. He sees the possible advantages of such reform as the " . . . development of more creative dispositions for most criminal cases; for criminal victims the increased use of restitution, the knowledge that their interests were considered in the criminal process; and an increased satisfaction with the outcome; increased awareness in the part of the offender that his crime was committed against another human being, and not against society in general; increased possibility that the criminal process will cause the offender to acknowledge responsibility for his acts."[33] Greacen notes several places where such a system has been tried with great success, most notably Tucson, Arizona, and Columbus, Ohio.[34]

Something analogous to the medieval Irish system of *sureties* might be employed as well.[35] Such a system would allow a concerned person, group, or company to make restitution (provided the offender agrees to this). The worker might then be released in the custody of the surety. If the surety had made restitution, the offender would owe restitution to the surety who might enforce the whole claim or show mercy. Of course, the more violent and unreliable the offender, the more serious and costly the offense, the less likely it would be that anyone would take the risk. But for first offenders, good workers, or others that charitable interests found deserving (or perhaps unjustly convicted) this would provide an avenue of respite.

RESTITUTION AND RIGHTS

These three possible refinements clearly illustrate the flexibility of a restitutional system. It may be less apparent that this flexibility is *inherent* to the restitutional paradigm. Restitution recognizes rights in the victim, and this is a principal source of its strength. The nature and limit of the victim's right to restitution at the same time defines the nature and limit of the criminal liability. In this way, the aggressive action of the criminal creates a *debt* to the victim. The recognition of rights and obligations make possible many innovative arrangements. Subrogation, arbitration, and suretyship are three examples mentioned above. They are possible because this right to compensation[36] is considered the property of the victim and can therefore be delegated, assigned, inherited, or bestowed. One could determine in advance who would acquire the right to any restitution which he himself might be unable to collect.

The natural owner of an unenforced death claim would be an insurance company that had insured the deceased. The suggestion has been made that a person might thus increase his personal safety by insuring with a company well known for tracking down those who injure its policy holders. In fact, the partial purpose of some insurance schemes might be to provide the funds with which to track down the malefactor. The insurance company, having paid the beneficiaries would "stand in their shoes." It would remain possible, of course, to simply assign or devise

the right directly to the beneficiaries, but this would put the burden of enforcement on persons likely to be unsuited to the task.

If one accepts the Lockean trichotomy of property ownership,[37] that is, acquiring property via exchange, gifts, and *homesteading* (mixing one's labor with previously unowned land or objects), the possibility arises that upon a person's wrongful death, in the absence of any heirs or assignees, his right to compensation becomes unowned property. The right could then be claimed (homesteaded) by anyone willing to go to the trouble of catching and prosecuting the criminal. Firms might specialize in this sort of activity, or large insurance companies might make the effort as a kind of "loss leader" for public relations purposes.

This does, however, lead to a potentially serious problem with the restitutional paradigm: what exactly constitutes "restitution"? What is the *standard* by which compensation is to be made? Earlier we asserted that any such problem facing the restitutional paradigm faces civil damage suits as well. The method by which this problem is dealt with in civil cases could be applied to restitution cases. But while this is certainly true, it may be that this problem has not been adequately handled in civil damage suits either.

Restitution in cases of crimes against property is a manageable problem. Modern contract and tort doctrines of restitution are adequate. The difficulty lies in cases of personal injury or death. How can you put a price on life or limb, pain or suffering? Is not any attempt to do so of necessity arbitrary? It must be admitted that a fully satisfactory solution to this problem is lacking, but it should also be stressed that this dilemma, though serious, has little impact on the bulk of our case in favor of a restitutional paradigm. It is possible that no paradigm of criminal justice can solve every problem, yet the restitutional approach remains far superior to the paradigm of punishment or any other conceivable rival.

This difficulty arises because certain property is unique and irreplaceable. As a result, it is impossible to approximate a "market" or "exchange" value expressed in monetary terms. Just as there is no rational relationship between a wrongfully taken life and ten years in prison, there is little relationship between that same life and $20,000. Still, the nature of this possibly insoluble puzzle reveals a restitutional approach theoretically superior to punishment. For it must be acknowledged that a real, tangible loss *has* occurred. The problem is only one of incommensurability. Restitution provides *some* tangible, albeit inadequate, compensation for personal injury. Punishment provides none at all.[38]

It might be objected that to establish some "pay scale" for personal injury is not only somewhat arbitrary but also a disguised reimplementation of punishment. Unable to accept the inevitable consequences of restitutional punishment, the argument continues, I have retreated to a pseudorestitutional award. Such a criticism is unfair. The true test in this instance is one of primacy of intentions. Is the purpose of a system to compensate victims for their losses (and perhaps, as a consequence, punish the criminals), or is its purpose to punish the criminals (and perhaps, as a consequence, compensate the victims for their losses)? The true ends of a criminal justice system will determine its nature. In short, arbitrariness *alone* does not imply a retributive motive. And while arbitrariness remains to some extent a problem for the restitutional paradigm, it is less of a problem for restitution than for punishment, since compensation has *some* rational relationship to damages and costs.

ADVANTAGES OF A RESTITUTIONAL SYSTEM

1. The first and most obvious advantage is the assistance provided to victims of crime. They may have suffered an emotional, physical, or financial loss. Restitution would not change the fact that a possibly traumatic crime has occurred (just as the award of damages does not undo tortious conduct). Restitution, however, would make the resulting loss easier to bear for both victims and their families. At the same time, restitution would avoid a major pitfall of victim compensation/welfare plans: Since it is the criminal who must pay, the possibility of collusion between victim and criminal to collect "damages" from the state would be all but eliminated.

2. The possibility of receiving compensation would encourage victims to report crimes and to appear at trial. This is particularly true if there were a crime insurance scheme which contractually committed the policyholder to testify as a condition for payment, thus rendering unnecessary oppressive and potentially tyrannical subpoenas and contempt citations. Even the actual reporting of the crime to police is likely to be a prerequisite for compensation. Such a requirement in auto theft insurance policies has made car thefts the most fully reported crime in the Unites States. Furthermore, insurance companies which paid the claim would have a strong incentive to see that the criminal was apprehended and convicted. Their pressure and assistance would make the proper functioning of law enforcement officials all the more likely.

3. Psychologist Albert Eglash has long argued that restitution would aid in the rehabilitation of criminals. "Restitution is something an inmate does, not something done for or to him. . . . Being reparative, restitution can alleviate guilt and anxiety, which can otherwise precipitate further offenses."[39] Restitution, says Eglash, is an active effortful role on the part of the offender. It is socially constructive, thereby contributing to the offender's self-esteem. It is related to the offense and may thereby redirect the thoughts which motivated the offense. It is reparative, restorative, and may actually leave the situation better than it was before the crime, both for the criminal and victim.[40]

4. This is a genuinely "self-determinative" sentence.[41] The worker would know that the length of his confinement was in his own hands. The harder he worked, the faster he would make restitution. He would be the master of his fate and would have to face that responsibility. This would encourage useful, productive activity and instill a conception of reward for good behavior and hard work. Compare this with the current probationary system and "indeterminate sentencing" where the decision for release is made by the prison bureaucracy, based only (if fairly administered) on "good behavior"; that is, passive acquiescence to prison discipline. Also, the fact that the worker would be acquiring *marketable* skills rather than more skillful methods of crime should help to reduce the shocking rate of recidivism.

5. The savings to taxpayers would be enormous. No longer would the innocent taxpayer pay for the apprehension and internment of the guilty. The cost of arrest, trial, and internment would be borne by the criminal himself. In addition, since now-idle inmates would become productive workers (able, perhaps, to support their families), the entire economy would benefit from the increase in overall production.[42]

6. Crime would no longer pay. Criminals, particularly shrewd white-collar criminals, would know that they could not dispose of the proceeds of their crime and, if caught, simply serve time. They would have to make full restitution plus enforcement and legal costs, thereby greatly increasing the incentive to prosecute. While this would not eliminate such crime it would make it rougher on certain types of criminals, like bank and corporation officials, who harm many by their acts with a virtual assurance of lenient legal sanctions.[43] It might also encourage such criminals to keep the money around for a while so that, if caught, they could repay more easily. This would make a full recovery more likely.

A restitutional system of justice would benefit the victim, the criminal, and the taxpayer. The humanitarian goals of proportionate punishment, rehabilitation, and victim compensation are dealt with on a *fundamental* level making their achievement more likely. In short, the paradigm of restitution would benefit all but the entrenched penal bureaucracy and enhance justice at the same time. What then is there to stop us from overthrowing the paradigm of punishment and its penal system and putting in its place this more efficient, more humane, and more just system? The proponents of punishment and others have a few powerful counterarguments. It is to these we now turn.

Objections to Restitution

1. Practical criticisms of restitution. It might be objected that "crimes disturb and offend not only those who are directly their victim, but also the whole social order."[44] Because of this, society, that is, individuals other than the victim, deserves some satisfaction from the offender. Restitution, it is argued, will not satisfy the lust for revenge felt by the victim or the "community's sense of justice." This criticism appears to be overdrawn. Today most members of the community are mere spectators of the criminal justice system, and this is largely true even of the victim.[45] One major reform being urged presently is more victim involvement in the criminal justice process.[46] The restitution proposal would necessitate this involvement. And while the public generally takes the view that officials should be tougher on criminals, with "tougher" taken by nearly everyone to mean more severe in punishing, one must view this "social fact" in light of the lack of a known alternative. The real test of public sympathies would be to see which sanction people would choose: incarceration of the criminal for a given number of years or the criminal's being compelled to make restitution to the victim: While the public's choice is not clearly predictable, neither can it be assumed that it would reject restitution.

This brings us to a second practical objection: that monetary sanctions are insufficient deterrents to crime. Again, this is something to be discovered, not something to be assumed. There are a number of reasons to believe that our *current* system of punishment does not adequately deter, and for the reasons discussed earlier an increase in the level of punishment is unlikely. In fact, many have argued that the deterrent value of sanctions has less to do with *severity* than with *certainty*,[47] and the preceding considerations indicate that law enforcement would be more certain under a restitutional system. In the final analysis, however, it is irrelevant to argue that more crimes may be committed if our proposal leaves the victim better off. It must be remembered: *Our goal is not the suppression of crime; it is doing justice to victims.*

A practical consideration which merits considerable future attention is the feasibility of the employment project proposal. A number of questions can be raised. At first blush, it seems naively optimistic to suppose that offenders will be able or willing to work at all, much less earn their keep and pay reparations as well. On the contrary, this argument continues, individuals turn to crime precisely because they lack the skills which the restitutional plan assumes they have. Even if these workers have the skills, but refuse to work, what could be done? Would not the use of force to compel compliance be tantamount to slavery? This criticism results in part from my attempt to sketch an "ideal" restitution system; that is, I have attempted to outline the type toward which every criminal justice system governed by the restitution paradigm should strive. This is not to say that every aspect of the hypothetical system would, upon implementation, function smoothly. Rather, such a system could only operate ideally once the paradigm had been fully accepted and substantially articulated.

With this in mind, one can advance several responses. First, the problem as usually posed assumes the offender to be highly irrational and possibly mentally unbalanced. There is no denying that some segment of the criminal population fits the former description.[48] What this approach neglects, however, is the possibility that many criminals are making rational choices within an irrational and unjust political system. Specifically I refer to the myriad laws and regulations which make it difficult for the unskilled or persons of transitory outlook[49] to find legal employment.[50] I refer also to the laws which deny legality to the types of services which are in particular demand in economically impoverished communities.[51] Is it "irrational" to choose to steal or rob when one is virtually foreclosed from the legal opportunity to do otherwise? Another possibility is that the criminal chooses crime not because of foreclosure, but because he enjoys and obtains satisfaction from a criminal way of life.[52] Though morally repugnant, this is hardly irrational.

Furthermore, it no longer can be denied that contact with the current criminal justice system is itself especially damaging among juveniles.[53] The offenders who are hopelessly committed to criminal behavior are not usually the newcomers to crime but those who have had repeated exposure to the penal system. In Kuhn's words, "Existing institutions have ceased to meet the problems posed by an environment *they have in part created.*"[54] While a restitutionary system might not change these hard-core offenders, it could, by the early implementation of sanctions perceived by the criminal to be just, break the vicious circle which in large part accounts for their existence.

Finally, if offenders could not or would not make restitution, then the logical and just result of their refusal would be confinement until they could or would. Such an outcome would be entirely in their hands. While this "solution" does not suggest who should justly pay for this confinement, the problem is not unique to a restitutionary system. In this and other areas of possible difficulty we must seek guidance from existing pilot programs as well as from the burgeoning research in this area and in victimology in general.

2. Distributionary criticisms of restitution. There remains one criticism of restitution which is the most obvious and the most difficult with which to deal. Simply stated, it takes the following form: "Doesn't this mean that rich people will be able to commit crimes with impunity if they can afford it? Isn't this unfair?" The *practical* aspect of this objection is that whatever deterrent effect restitution payments may have, they will be less for those most able to pay. The *moral* aspect is that whatever retributive or penal effect restitution payments may have they will be less for those who are well off. Some concept of equality of justice underlies both considerations.

Critics of restitution fail to realize that the "cost" of crime will be quite high. In addition to compensation for pain and suffering, the criminal must pay for the cost of his apprehension, the cost of the trial, and the legal expenditures of *both* sides. This should make even an unscrupulous wealthy person think twice about committing a crime. The response to this is that we cannot have it both ways. If the fines would be high enough to bother the rich, then they would be so high that a project worker would have no chance of earning that much and would, therefore, have no incentive to work at all. If, on the other hand, you lower the price of crime by ignoring all its costs, you fail to deter the rich or fully compensate the victim.

This is where the option of arbitration and victim crime insurance becomes of practical importance. If the victim is uninsured, he is unlikely to recover for all costs of a very severe crime from a poor, unskilled criminal, since even in an employment project the criminal might be unable to earn enough. If he had no hope of earning his release, he would have little incentive to work very hard beyond paying for his own maintenance. The victim would end up with less than if he had "settled" the case for the lesser amount which a project worker could reasonably be expected to earn. If, however, the victim had full-coverage criminal insurance, he would recover his damages in full, and the insurance company would absorb any disparity between full compensation and maximal employment project worker's output. This cost would be reflected in premium prices, enabling the insurance company which settled cases at an amount which increased the recovery from the criminal to offer the lowest rates. Eventually a "maximum" feasible fine for project workers would be determined based on these considerations. The "rich," on the other hand, would naturally have to pay in full. This arrangement would solve the practical problem, but it should not be thought of as an imperative of the restitutional paradigm.

The same procedure of varying the payments according to ability to pay would answer the moral considerations as well (that the rich are not hurt enough) and this is the prime motive behind *punitive* restitution proposals. However, we reject the moral consideration outright. The paradigm of restitution calls not for the (equal) hurting of criminals, but for restitution to victims. Any appeal to "inadequate suffering" is a reversion to the paradigm of punishment, and by varying the sanction for crimes of the same magnitude according to the economic status of the offender it reveals its own inequity. *Equality of justice means equal treatment of victims.* It should not matter to the victim if his attacker was rich or poor. His plight is the same regardless. Any reduction of criminal liability because of reduced earning power would be for practical, not moral, reasons.

Equality of justice derives from the fact that the rights of men should be equally enforced and respected. Restitution recognizes a victim's right to compensation for damages from the party responsible. Equality of justice, therefore, calls for equal enforcement of each victim's right to restitution. *Even if necessary or expedient, any lessening of payment to the victim because of the qualities of the criminal is a violation of that victim's rights and an inequality of justice.* Any such expedient settlement is only a recognition that an imperfect world may make possible only imperfect justice. As a practical matter, a restitutional standard gives victims an enormous

incentive to pursue wealthy criminals since they can afford quick, full compensation. Contrast this with the present system where the preference given the wealthy is so prevalent that most victims simply assume that nothing will be done.

The paradigm of restitution, to reiterate, is neither a panacea for crime nor a blueprint for utopia. Panaceas and utopias are not for humankind. We must live in a less than perfect world with less than perfect people. Restitution opens the possibility of an improved and more just society. The old paradigm of punishment, even reformed, simply cannot offer this promise.

OTHER CONSIDERATIONS

Space does not permit a full examination of other less fundamental implications of such a system. I shall briefly consider five.

1. Civil versus criminal liability. If one accepts a restitutionary standard of justice, what sense does it make to distinguish between crime and tort, since both call for payment of damages? For most purposes I think the distinction collapses. Richard Epstein, in a series of brilliant articles, has articulated a theory of strict liability in tort.[55] His view is that since one party has caused another some harm and one of the parties must bear the loss, justice demands that it falls on the party who caused the harm. He argues that intention is only relevant as a "third-stage" argument; that notwithstanding some fault on the part of the plaintiff (a second-stage argument), the defendant intended the harm and is therefore liable.[56] With a restitutional system I see no reason why Epstein's theory of tort liability could not incorporate criminal liability into a single "system of corrective justice that looks to the conduct, broadly defined, of the parties to the case with a view toward the protection of individual liberty and private property."[57]

There would, at least initially, be some differences, however. The calculation of damages under the restitutionary paradigm which includes cost of apprehension, cost of trial, and legal costs of both parties would be higher than tort law allows. A further distinction would be the power of enforcers to confine unreliable offenders to employment projects.

2. Criminal responsibility and competency. Once a criminal sanction is based not on the offender's badness but on the nature and consequences of his acts, Thomas Szasz's proposal that the insanity plea be abolished makes a great deal of sense,[58] as does his argument that "all persons charged with offenses—except those grossly disabled—[are fit to stand trial and] should be tried."[59] On this view, Epstein's concept of fairness *as between the parties* is relevant. A restitution proceeding like a "lawsuit is always a comparative affair. The defendant's victory ensures the plaintiff's [or victim's] defeat.... Why should we prefer the injurer to his victim in a case where one may win and the other lose? ... As a matter of fairness between the parties, the defendant should be required to treat the harms which he has inflicted upon another as though they were inflicted upon himself."[60]

3. Victimless crimes. The effect of restitutional standards on the legality of such crimes as prostitution, gambling, high interest loans, pornography, and drug use is intriguing. There has been no violation of individual rights, and consequently no damages and, therefore, no liability. While some may see this as a drawback, I believe it is a striking advantage of the restitutional standard of justice. So-called victimless crimes would in principle cease to be crimes. As a consequence, criminal elements would be denied a lucrative monopoly, and the price of these services would be drastically reduced. Without this enormous income, organized crime would be far less able to afford the "cost" of its nefarious activities than it is today.

4. Legal positivism. What is true for victimless crimes is true for the philosophy of legal positivism. On the positivist view, whatever the state (following all the correct political procedures) says is law, is law; hence, whatever the state makes a crime is a crime. A restitutional standard would hold the state to enforcing individual rights through the recovery of individual damages.

5. Legal process. Because the sanction for crime would no longer be punitive, the criminal process could explore less formal procedures for dispute settlement. Also, the voice of the victim would be added to the deliberations. One possible reform might be a three-tiered verdict: guilty, not proven, and not guilty. If found "guilty," the offender would pay all the costs mentioned above. If the charges are "not proven," then neither party would pay the other. If found "not guilty," the defendant would be reimbursed by the enforcement agency for his costs and inconvenience. This new interpretation of "not guilty" would reward those defendants who, after putting on a defense, convinced the trier of fact that they were innocent.

These and many other fascinating implications of restitution deserve a more thorough examination. As any new paradigm becomes accepted, it experiences what Kuhn calls a period of "normal research," a period characterized by continuous expansion and perfection of the new paradigm as well as a testing of its limits. The experimentation with restitutionary justice will, however, differ from the trial and error of the recent past since we will be guided by the principle that the purpose of our legal system is not to harm the guilty but to help the innocent—a principle which will above all restore our belief that our overriding commitment is to do justice.

NOTES

1. What immediately follows is a brief outline of Kuhn's theory. Those interested in the *defense* of that theory should refer to his book, *The Structure of Scientific Revolutions*, 2d ed., enl. (Chicago: University of Chicago Press, 1970). A paradigm is an achievement in a particular discipline which defines the legitimate problems and methods of research within that discipline. This achievement is sufficiently unprecedented to attract new adherents away from rival approaches while providing many unsolved questions for these new practitioners to solve. As the paradigm develops and matures, it reveals occasional inabilities to solve new problems and explain new data. As attempts are made to make the facts fit the paradigm, the theoretical apparatus gradually becomes bulky and awkward, like Ptolemaic astronomy. Dissatisfaction with the paradigm begins to grow. Why not simply discard the paradigm and find another which better fits the facts? Unfortunately, this is an arduous process. All the great authorities and teachers were raised with the current paradigm and see the world through it. All the texts and institutions are committed to it. Radical alternatives hold

promise but are so untested as to make wary all but the bold. The establishment is loath to abandon its broad and intricate theory in favor of a new and largely unknown hypothesis. Gradually, however, as the authorities die off and the problems with the old paradigm increase, the "young turks" get a better hearing in both the journals and the classroom. In a remarkably rapid fashion, the old paradigm is discarded for the new. Anyone who still clings to it is now considered to be antiquated or eccentric and is simply read out of the profession. All research centers on the application of the new paradigm. Kuhn characterizes this overthrow of one paradigm by another as a revolution.

2. Ibid., p. 92.

3. Stanley I. Benn, "Punishment," in *The Encyclopedia of Philosophy*, ed. Paul Edwards (New York: Macmillan Publishing Co., 1967), 7:29 (emphasis added).

4. Heinrich Oppenheimer, *The Rationale of Punishment* (London: University of London Press, 1913), p. 255.

5. Ibid.

6. See Thomas Szasz, *Law, Liberty, and Psychiatry* (New York: Macmillan Co., 1963).

7. Giorgio del Vecchio, "The Struggle against Crime," in *The Philosophy of Punishment,* ed. H. B. Acton (London: Macmillan Co., 1969), p. 199.

8. See, e.g., Samuel Yochelson and Stanton E. Samenow, *The Criminal Personality,* vol. 1, *A Profile for Change* (New York: Jason Aronson, Inc., 1976), pp. 411–16.

9. Del Vecchio, p. 199.

10. Robert Nozick, *Anarchy, State, and Utopia* (New York: Basic Books, 1974), p. 61.

11. Ibid., pp. 59–63.

12. For a concise summary, see Oppenheimer, p. 31.

13. Del Vecchio, p. 198.

14. See, e.g., Walter Kaufmann, *Without Guilt and Justice* (New York: Peter H. Wyden, Inc., 1973), esp. chap. 2.

15. See, e.g., "Crime: A Case for More Punishment," *Business Week* (September 15, 1975), pp. 92–97.

16. This problem is examined, though not ultimately resolved, by Edwin M. Schur in his book *Crimes without Victims—Deviant Behavior and Public Policy, Abortion, Homosexuality, and Drug Addiction* (Englewood Cliffs, N.J.: Prentice-Hall, Inc., 1965).

17. Kaufmann, p. 46.

18. Kuhn, p. 82.

19. R. A. Childs, "Liberty and the Paradigm of Statism," in *The Libertarian Alternative,* ed. Tibor Machan (Chicago: Nelson-Hall Co., 1974), p. 505.

20. Composition was the medieval version of a restitutionary system. For a fascinating outline of how such a system operated and how it came to be supplanted by state-authored punishment, see Stephen Schafer, *Compensation and Restitution to Victims of Crime,* 2d ed., enl. (Montclair, N.J.: Patterson Smith Publishing Corp., 1970); Richard E. Laster, "Criminal Restitution: A Survey of Its Past History and an Analysis of Its Present Usefulness," *University of Richmond Law Review* 5 (1970): 71–80; L. T. Hobhouse, *Morals in Evolution* (London: Chapman & Hall, 1951).

21. Kaufmann, p. 45.

22. For a brief definition of "victimology," see Emilo C. Viano, "Victimology: The Study of the Victim," *Victimology* 1 (1976): 1–7. For an extensive collection of papers on various aspects of victimology, see Emilo C. Viano, ed., *Victims and Society* (Washington, D.C.: Visage Press, 1976).

23. For a discussion and list of symposiums, journal articles, and statutes concerning victim compensation, see Steven Schafer, pp. 139–57, and appendix; see also Joe Hudson and Burt Galaway, eds., *Considering the Victim: Readings in Restitution and Victim Compensation* (Springfield, Ill.: Charles C. Thomas, 1975), esp. pp. 361–436.

24. Gerhard O. W. Mueller, "Compensation for Victims of Crime: Thought before Action," *Minnesota Law Review* 50 (1965): 221.

25. Schafer, p. 127.

26. Ibid.

27. Herbert Spencer, "Prison-Ethics," in *Essays: Scientific, Political and Speculative* (New York: D. Appleton & Co., 1907), 3:152–91.

28. Murray N. Rothbard, *Libertarian Forum* 14, no. 1 (January 1972):7–8.

29. Kaufmann, p. 55.

30. The nature of judicial procedure best designed to carry out this task must be determined. For a brief discussion of some relevant considerations, see Laster, pp. 80–98; Burt Galaway and Joe Hudson, "Issues in the Correctional Implementation of Restitution to Victims of Crime," in *Considering the Victim,* pp. 351–60. Also to be dealt with is the proper standard of compensation. At least initially, the problem of how much payment constitutes restitution would be no different than similar considerations in tort law. This will be considered at greater length below.

31. Such a plan (with some significant differences) has been suggested by Kathleen J. Smith in *A Cure for Crime: The Case for the Self-determinate Prison Sentence* (London: Gerald, Duckworth & Co., 1965), pp. 13–29; see also Morris and Linda Tannehill, *The Market for Liberty* (Lansing, Mich.: Privately printed, 1970), pp. 44–108.

32. For a recent summary report, see Burt Galaway, "Restitution as an Integrative Punishment" (paper prepared for the Symposium on Crime and Punishment: Restitution, Retribution, and Law, Harvard Law School, March 1977).

33. John M. Greacen, "Arbitration: A Tool for Criminal Cases?" *Barrister* (Winter 1975), p. 53; see also Galaway and Hudson, pp. 352–55; "Conclusions and Recommendations, International Study Institute on Victimology, Bellagio, Italy, July 1–12, 1975," *Victimology* 1 (1976): 150–51; Ronald Goldfarb, *Jails: The Ultimate Ghetto* (Garden City, N.Y.: Anchor Press/Doubleday, 1976), p. 480.

34. Greacen, p. 53.

35. For a description of the Irish system, see Joseph R. Peden, "Property Rights in Medieval Ireland: Celtic Law versus Church and State" (paper presented at the Symposium on the Origins and Development of Property Rights, University of San Francisco, January 1973); for a theoretical discussion of a similar proposal, see Spencer, pp. 182–86.

36. Or, perhaps more accurately, the compensation itself.

37. For a brief explanation of this concept and several of its possible applications, see Murray N. Rothbard, "Justice and Property Rights," in *Property in a Humane Economy,* ed. Samuel L. Blumenfeld (La Salle, Ill.: Open Court Publishing Co., 1974), pp. 101–22.

38. That the "spiritual" satisfaction which punishment may or may not provide is to be recognized as a legitimate form of "compensation" is a claim retributionists must defend.

39. Albert Eglash, "Creative Restitution: Some Suggestions for Prison Rehabilitation Programs," *American Journal of Correction* 40 (November–December 1958): 20.

40. Ibid.; see also Eglash's "Creative Restitution: A Broader Meaning for an Old Term," *Journal of Criminal Law and Criminology* 48 (1958): 619–22; Burt Galaway and Joe Hudson, "Restitution and Rehabilitation—Some Central Issues," *Crime and Delinquency* 18 (1972): 403–10.

41. Smith, pp. 13–29.

42. An economist who favors restitution on efficiency grounds is Gary S. Becker, although he does not break with the paradigm of punishment. Those interested in a mathematical "cost-benefit" analysis should see his "Crime and Punishment," *Journal of Political Economy* 76 (1968): 169–217.

43. This point is also made by Minocher Jehangirji Sethna in his paper, "Treatment and Atonement for Crime," in *Victims and Society,* p. 538.

44. Del Vecchio, p. 198.

45. William F. McDonald, "Towards a Bicentennial Revolution in Criminal Justice: The Return of the Victim," *American Criminal Law Review* 13 (1976): 659; see also his paper "Notes on the Victim's Role in the Prosecutional and Dispositional Stages of the Criminal Justice Process" (paper presented at the Second International Symposium on Victimology, Boston, September 1976); Jack M. Kress, "The Role of the Victim at Sentencing" (paper presented at the Second International Symposium on Victimology, Boston, September 1976).

46. McDonald, pp. 669–73; Kress, pp. 11–15. Kress specifically analyzes restitution as a means for achieving victim involvement.

47. Yochelson and Samenow, pp. 453–57.

48. For a discussion rejecting the usefulness of the latter description, see Szasz, pp. 91–146; for a recent study verifying Szasz's thesis, see Yochelson and Samenow, esp. pp. 227–35.

49. Edward C. Banfield put forth his controversial theory of time horizon in his book *The Unheavenly City* (Boston: Little, Brown & Co., 1970) and amplified it in *The Unheavenly City Revisited* (Boston: Little, Brown & Co., 1974), and most recently, "Present-orientedness and Crime" (paper prepared for the Symposium on Crime and Punishment: Restitution, Retribution, and Law, Harvard Law School, March 1977). For a critical, but favorable analysis of this approach, see Gerald P. O'Driscoll, Jr., "Professor Banfield on Time Horizon: What Has He Taught Us about Crime?" (paper prepared for the same symposium). A contrary, but ultimately compatible view is presented by Yochelson and Samenow, pp. 369–72.

50. For example, minimum wage laws, and so-called closed-shop union protectionist legislation.

51. For example, laws prohibiting gambling, prostitution, sale of drugs, "jitney" cab services, etc.

52. "It is not the environment that turns a man into a criminal. Rather it is a series of choices that he makes at a very early age. . . . [T]he criminal is not a victim of circumstances" (Yochelson and Samenow, pp. 247, 249). This is in essence the main conclusion of their research. (For a concise summary of their provocative book, see Joseph Boorkin, "The Criminal Personality," *Federal Bar Journal* 35 [1976]: 237–41.) In *The Criminal Personality,* vol. 2, *The Process of Change* (New York: Jason Aronson, Inc., 1977) they relate and examine the methods they have employed to change the criminal thought pattern. Of course, such an approach can itself be subject to abuse.

53. See, e.g., Edwin M. Schur, *Radical Nonintervention, Rethinking the Delinquency Problem* (Englewood Cliffs, N.J.: Prentice-Hall, Inc., 1973).

54. Kuhn, p. 92 (emphasis added).

55. Richard A. Epstein, "A Theory of Strict Liability in Tort," *Journal of Legal Studies* 2 (1973): 151–204.

56. Richard A. Epstein, "Intentional Harms," *Journal of Legal Studies* 3 (1975): 402–8; see also his article "Defenses and Subsequent Pleas in a System of Strict Liability," ibid., 3 (1974): 174–85.

57. Epstein, "Intentional Harms," p. 441.

58. Szasz, pp. 228–30.

59. Ibid., pp. 228–29. "The emphasis here is on gross disability: it should be readily apparent or easily explicable to a group of lay persons, like a jury" (p. 229). But even the qualification of gross disablement might be unjustified (see Yochelson and Samenow, pp. 227–35).

60. Epstein, p. 398. In his article "Crime and Tort: Old Wine in Old Bottles," he takes exactly this approach with the insanity defense in tort law.

Critics

Franklin G. Miller

Restitution and Punishment
A Reply to Barnett

Randy E. Barnett argues in a recent article, "Restitution: A New Paradigm of Criminal Justice,"[1] that traditional modes of punishment for criminal offenses should be abandoned. No longer should offenders be sentenced to prison or ordered to pay a fine to the state. Rather, they should be compelled to compensate their victims for the injuries or damages suffered as a result of the crime. In other words, Barnett proposes to substitute the "paradigm" of restitution for that of punishment.

Barnett rejects punishment on the grounds that none of the standard goals or reasons—deterrence, retribution, and rehabilitation—adequately justifies the practice of punishment. Against the rationale of deterrence, for example, he advances the familiar argument that a system devoted solely to deterrence

would fail to be a system of criminal *justice*. For it would permit or require the "punishing" of the innocent if that would in fact deter crime. Barnett apparently believes that he can refute the paradigm of punishment by pointing out the grave difficulties involved in making deterrence, retribution, or rehabilitation the single overriding goal of a system of criminal justice. But this is mistaken. The argument rests on the dubious assumption that the institution of punishment can be justified, if at all, only by reference to a *single* fundamental rationale.[2] Barnett ignores the complexity of the problem of punishment. In performing a set of different though interconnected functions, a system of criminal justice should pursue a plurality of goals, none of which is allowed free reign. For instance, the goal of deterring

Franklin G. Miller, "Restitution and Punishment: A Reply to Barnett," *Ethics* 88 (1978): 358–60. Reprinted by permission of University of Chicago Press.

crime must be coordinated with the imperative of just allocation of punishment. Although theories of pure deterrence or retribution or rehabilitation are unsatisfactory, a complex theory of punishment, combining deterrent, retributive, rehabilitative, *and* restitutive elements at appropriate points, might offer a satisfactory justification of punishment.

Barnett's argument against punishment is deficient not only because it fails to consider complex theories of punishment. It neglects an important aspect of punishment that bears upon its justification. The act of punishment constitutes symbolic condemnation of the offender for his offense. As such it serves to uphold and enforce collective moral norms violated by the criminal.[3] Before we choose to reject the paradigm of punishment in favor of the paradigm of restitution, we need to consider what might be lost as a result. Could a system of *pure* restitution preserve this condemnatory aspect of punishment? If not, is this something that we should be willing to give up? Even the civil law, dedicated to the purpose of compensating victims for harm intentionally or negligently caused by others, allows for *punitive* damages in some cases.

Barnett's theory of pure restitution raises some practical problems as well. Since the goal of a system of criminal justice should be to compensate victims of crimes rather than to punish offenders, the idea of crime as an offense against society has no place in Barnett's theory: "A restitutional standard would hold the state to enforcing individual rights through the recovery of individual damages."[4] A variety of acts that our legal system regards as criminal could not be accounted for on the premise that the sole purpose of a system of criminal justice is to enforce *individual* rights by requiring restitution. Many crimes do not involve individual victims. Barnett considers it a virtue of his paradigm that "victimless" activities such as prostitution, pornography, gambling, and drug use would not be made criminal.

Fortunately there is no need to broach this difficult issue here, for there are less controversial crimes that cannot be easily adapted to Barnett's theory. (1) Cruelty to animals. Suppose a person, living in the country, delights in capturing wild deer and torturing them. Unless we are willing to consider deer as

individual persons possessing legal rights, there can be no crime in this behavior under Barnett's restitutional paradigm. Moreover, to whom should restitution be paid? (2) Harm to public institutions. The criminal law prohibits tax evasion, bribery, obstruction of justice, and damage to public property. The rights of private persons are not necessarily violated by instances of such conduct. A system of restitution might provide for compensation payable to the state, but this would conflict with the individualistic focus of Barnett's paradigm. (3) Attempts. Attempted crimes may not cause any harm to particular individuals. For example, a terrorist is apprehended planting a bomb in the men's room of an office building. Whose individual rights has the terrorist violated? Restitution to the owner of the building merely for trespass would be far out of proportion to the gravity of the act. (4) Reckless driving and driving under the influence of alcohol. On what grounds could persons be prosecuted for such acts if no tangible harm is caused to others? What restitution would be appropriate? Other cases could be mentioned, but this list suffices to indicate the practical difficulties of Barnett's theory of restitution. If we do not wish to give up such crimes, then we cannot accept a paradigm of pure restitution.

Barnett makes a strong case for the merits of restitution. Punishment as practiced today does have serious defects, some of which might be remedied by provisions for restitution. It remains to be shown, however, that punishment should be abandoned in favor of a new paradigm of restitution.

NOTES

1. Randy E. Barnett, "Restitution: A New Paradigm of Criminal Justice," *Ethics* 87, no. 4 (1977): 279–301.

2. Cf. H. L. A. Hart, *Punishment and Responsibility* (New York: Oxford University Press, 1968), p. 3.

3. For the classical statement of this perspective see Émile Durkheim, *The Division of Labor in Society,* trans. George Simpson (New York: Free Press, 1964), chap. 2. See also Joel Feinberg, "The Expressive Function of Punishment," in *Doing and Deserving* (Princeton, N.J.: Princeton University Press, 1970), pp. 95–118.

4. Barnett, p. 301.

Roger Pilon

Criminal Remedies
Restitution, Punishment, or Both?

...To be sure, Barnett has correctly shifted our focus, for criminal acts of the kind under consideration do involve harms to victims—hence our first concern ought to be to make victims whole again. But is that all they involve? Are we really to treat, by way of remedy, my accidentally hitting you with my automobile and my intentionally hitting you with a club as acts of the same kind? Is the *mens rea* element to be allowed *no* place in the calculation? Even if we include in the compensation due the victim all that Barnett believes we should—special damages, including the costs of apprehension, trial, and legal fees for both sides, and general damages, including pain and suffering (p. 298)—there still remains a crucial element that these considerations do not touch. For thus far the compensation is identical with that ideally due the victim in a simple civil action.

Nowhere are these misgivings and this missing element brought out more sharply—if misleadingly, about which more in a moment—than in cases involving wealthy principals. Barnett considers and then elides but one of the variations, that of the wealthy criminal (p. 297). There is also the case of the wealthy victim and, perhaps of most interest, the case in which both the criminal and the victim are wealthy. However uncommon these three variations may be in the larger world of criminal activity (but perhaps they are not so uncommon), they are of interest because they bring clearly into focus the *mens rea* element omitted from Barnett's account, an element present in *all* criminal transactions but captured most poignantly here. What, really, does the wealthy criminal care about having to compensate his victim? Or the wealthy victim about receiving compensation? If a rich man rapes a rich woman, are we really to suppose that monetary damages will restore the status quo, will satisfy the claims of justice? A wealthy child molester will treat compensation simply as the price of pleasure! And what of the terrorist who murders, knowing that his wealthy backer will settle the account? The reduction of criminal wrongs to civil wrongs, in short, or at least the addressing of criminal wrongs with civil remedies, bespeaks an all too primitive view of what in fact is at issue in the matter of crime.

For all their heuristic value, however, we must not let examples such as these confuse the issue. It is not, as they may have suggested, that the requirement to compensate the victim does not make the criminal suffer if he is wealthy (as it seems to when he is not wealthy), for that would conflate the different purposes of punishment and compensation: thus, raising the compensation to fit the criminal will not only continue to miss the point but will produce this conflation as well. Rather, it is simply that the civil remedy by itself is altogether inadequate in the case of criminal acts. For the element missing from the mere tort but present in the criminal act is the guilty mind. The criminal has not simply harmed you. *He has affronted your dignity.* He has *intentionally* used you, against your will, for his own ends. He cannot simply pay damages as though his action were accidental or unintentional. How would this right the wrong? Using even Barnett's criterion for determining the obligation now owing, how would compensation make the victim whole again? For compensation does not reach the whole of what is involved—it does not reach the *mens rea* element. There is simply no amount of money that will rectify certain kinds of wrongs. The criminal act and the mere tort are of altogether different magnitudes; they are different categories of action, calling for different remedies.

Franklin G. Miller, "Restitution and Punishment: A Reply to Barnett," *Ethics* 88 (1978): 358–60. Reprinted by permission of University of Chicago Press.

Indeed, the criminal act calls not only for compensation but for punishment as well. . . .

We look at the original act to determine what form [. . .] the remedy should take. That act involved a violation of the victim's dignity; the criminal intentionally used the victim for his own ends, and against the victim's will. In so doing, the criminal alienated his own right against being similarly treated by the victim (or by anyone else acting on behalf of the victim), just as the tort-feasor alienates his right to that amount of his property necessary to right the wrongs he has caused. Notice that here, the problem of reflecting in the form of the remedy the mental character of the original act does not arise as it does in torts, for here we have an intentional wrong, capable of being mirrored in the remedy. The original act thus creates a right in the victim (or his surrogate) to use the criminal as he himself was used. Only so will the parties be treated as equals. For only so will the *character* of the original act be reflected in the remedy. Money damages simply do not do this. It is the *using* of one person by another—this affront to the victim's dignity or integrity—that must be captured in the criminal remedy. Thus the victim's treatment of the criminal is equal in character to the treatment he himself suffered. (Again, I leave open the question of what specifically constitutes equal treatment, just as I left open the criterion for measuring tort losses. These questions, especially the latter, involve a theory of value, which is beyond my present scope. . . .

STANLEY S. KLEINBERG

Criminal Justice and Private Enterprise

. . . If we address ourselves only to crimes which undoubtedly have individual victims (e.g., a violent assault on a child in a public park) it is clear that the upset is not confined to the victim and his immediate family. Barnett is aware of this but treats community reaction as "lust for revenge" and thus not to be taken too seriously. But the upset is not identical with a vindictive desire to see the child's assailant suffer. What about the apprehension of parents of other children in the vicinity and the inconvenience caused by the fact that they can no longer safely allow their children to play in the park? Whether they have the right to expect the state to take action against the criminal, supposing that, for example, the child's parents do not wish to involve themselves in legal action, is not in my view a difficult moral issue. All that needs to be claimed against Barnett, however, is that criminals do offend against society, not just against their victims.[1] . . .

Apart from being wealthy, an additional source of advantage for a defendant would lie in being a professional criminal. Barnett says that crime would not pay, but clearly this only applies if the criminal is apprehended. A professional, I suggest, is confident of escaping detection in a certain proportion of his crimes. In case he should be apprehended, he would retain the gains of each crime until he judged that crime no longer to be under active investigation. If his calculations go astray so that it looks as if he may face the possibility of being required to pay more than he has available, he can endeavor to commit some profitable crimes while awaiting trial.

From Stanley S. Kleinberg, "Criminal Justice and Private Enterprise," *Ethics* 90 (1980): 270–82. Some notes and some parts of the text have been deleted. Reprinted by permission of University of Chicago Press.

Alternatively, a fellow professional may be prepared to advance him the money in return for participation in some future crime. I conclude that in Barnett's system wealth and criminal professionalism, especially in combination, would confer a great advantage on any defendant. . . .

NOTE

1. There is not space to discuss Barnett's position on victimless crimes. It should be noted, however, that he appears to favor the legalization of all proscribed victimless acts, including unsuccessful criminal attempts and reckless conduct.

26

Is Issuing Warrants to Torture Wrong?

Dershowitz and His Critics

According to the *Convention against Torture and Other Cruel, Inhuman or Degrading Treatment or Punishment* (1984), to which the United States is a signatory, "No one shall be subjected to torture or to cruel, inhuman or degrading treatment or punishment." In Article 1 of Part 1 of the convention the concept of torture is further clarified:

> For the purposes of this Convention, the term "torture" means any act by which severe pain or suffering, whether physical or mental, is intentionally inflicted on a person for such purposes as obtaining from him or a third person information or a confession, punishing him for an act he or a third person has committed or is suspected of having committed, or intimidating or coercing him or a third person, or for any reason based on discrimination of any kind, when such pain or suffering is inflicted by or at the instigation of or with the consent or acquiescence of a public official or other person acting in an official capacity. (http://www.unhchr.ch/html/menu3/b/h_cat39.htm)

A report in the *British Guardian* on October 27, 2006, states this:

> The use of a form of torture known as waterboarding to gain information is a "no-brainer," the US vice-president, Dick Cheney, told a radio interviewer, it was reported today. Mr. Cheney implied that the technique—a form of simulated drowning—was used on the alleged September 11 mastermind, Khalid Sheikh Mohammed, who is being held at Guantánamo Bay. (http://www.guardian.co.uk/guantanamo/story/0,,1933317,00.html)

However, the vice president was quick to qualify his remarks by effectively disqualifying waterboarding as a form of torture, even though it seems clearly to fall under Article 1 of the convention. Cheney is not alone in thinking like this. Since the September 11, 2001, terrorist attacks on the United States, the use of various "enhanced" interrogation techniques—like simulated drowning—to extract information or confessions from suspected terrorists has come to be seen as necessary to help prevent future terrorist attacks. In its 2007 report on the United States, Amnesty International has this to say under the heading "Torture and other ill-treatment":

> A general lack of accountability for torture and other ill-treatment by US personnel in the "war on terror," including under interrogation techniques authorized by senior administration officials,

continued. . . . Both the UN Committee against Torture and the UN Human Rights Committee expressed concern at the apparent leniency and impunity being enjoyed by US personnel.

. . . A revised Army Field Manual was published in September, reiterating the ban on cruel, inhuman or degrading treatment of any detainee, a position the government had previously held not to apply to "unlawful enemy combatants." The Manual also expressly banned certain techniques during interrogation, including sexual humiliation, use of dogs, hooding, "water-boarding" (simulated drowning), mock executions and deprivation of food and water. The Army Field Manual did not apply to CIA interrogations conducted outside a military-run facility.

In other words, it appears that certain harsh forms of interrogation, long regarded as torture, are illegal, and yet they are clearly being used, tolerated, and even apparently encouraged and endorsed by high-ranking State officials.

In the featured article of this chapter, Alan Dershowitz deplores the hypocrisy of the status quo. Instead of arguing, as one might have expected, that the law against torture should be rigorously policed and enforced, however, he instead argues that a system of "torture warrants" should be instituted, modeled on the institution of search warrants. Dershowitz's argument at first seems to be straightforward, but it is, in fact, quite subtle. Suppose we know or suspect that there is a "ticking bomb" that, if undiscovered, will explode, killing many innocent civilians, perhaps thousands. Moreover, we have in our custody a terrorist, or suspected terrorist, who apparently knows the whereabouts of the ticking bomb but who is disinclined to reveal the information. Many argue that in the ticking-bomb scenario, torture would be morally permissible and so should be made legally permissible. This is not Dershowitz's argument, however. Rather, Dershowitz claims that in these circumstances torture will *in fact* be employed by State officials to gain the information. Further, he argues that *if* torture by State officials in these circumstances is *in fact* going to occur, then it should be carried out in a way that gives the State oversight and makes the torturers accountable. He concludes that the only way to make State officials appropriately accountable is to require that they seek a torture warrant from a judge. The judge would be responsible for making sure that the situation justifies torture—that there really is a significant probability that there is a serious imminent threat and that the person in custody has the information that could avert disaster. This, Dershowitz argues, would actually serve to limit the occurrence of torture and force torturers to publicly justify their actions.

In her response, Elaine Scarry criticizes a number of aspects of Dershowitz's argument. She claims that ticking-bomb scenarios in which torture would actually help avert disaster are so rare and improbable as to be almost impossible. Further, she argues that it would be unnecessary to issue warrants legitimizing torture, even in a genuine ticking-bomb scenario. In such a scenario, a person of courage will torture, if it is absolutely necessary to do so to save thousands, without being granted legal immunity, even at the possible cost of prosecution and imprisonment. Further, a system of torture warrants would not yield greater accountability but rather simply lend legitimacy to torture, which would probably become more widespread.

In Dershowitz's brief reply, he claims that Scarry—like many others—has misunderstood the structure of his argument. He claims that he is not arguing for the moral permissibility of torture even in ticking-bomb cases. Nor is he arguing for the legalization of torture in ticking-bomb cases on the basis of its absolute moral permissibility. He returns to his two premises: that officials will, in fact, employ torture in ticking-bomb scenarios and that, given that they are going to torture in these circumstances, a system of legalized torture warrants should be instituted.

QUESTIONS FOR CONSIDERATION

In thinking about this issue, consider the following questions.

• Dershowitz claims that most people believe torture will be employed in ticking-bomb cases. Do you agree? Is torture morally justified in ticking-bomb cases? Does it make a difference to the argument if it is morally justified? Can there be good reasons for making something that is morally justified nevertheless illegal?

• There is a well-known paradox in the logic of obligation (Chisholm's paradox) that seems to parallel Dershowitz's argument. First let us accept an obvious moral truth A.

A Jones ought not to murder his mother.

Now suppose that the following is, in fact, true:

P1 Jones is going to murder his mother.

The following appears to be a conditional moral truth:

P2 If Jones is going to murder his mother, he ought to murder her painlessly.

From P1 and P2 we can conclude C1 (by the standard logical rule of inference called *modus ponens*):

C1 Jones ought to murder his mother painlessly.

And from this we can conclude:

C2 Jones ought to murder his mother.

However, C2 contradicts A. Somehow we have derived from one conditional moral truth (P1) and one factual truth (P2) a conclusion (C2) that directly contradicts another known moral truth (A).

Now Dershowitz's premises look rather like P1 and P2:

P*1 State officials are going to use torture in ticking-bomb scenarios.
P*2 If State officials are going to use torture in ticking-bomb scenarios, then State officials ought to use torture in ticking-bomb cases by means of warrants.

From P*1 and P*2 we can conclude C*1:

C*1 State officials ought to use torture in ticking-bomb cases by means of warrants.

And from this we can conclude:

C*2 State officials ought to use torture in ticking-bomb cases.

C*2 is incompatible with what many people regard as obvious: (A*) that even in ticking-bomb cases, torture is morally impermissible and should remain legally impermissible. More importantly, Dershowitz claims that his argument does not depend on the claim that torture really should be used in such cases, and yet the apparent parallel between these two arguments seems to suggest that his argument does commit him to that claim.

Are these arguments, in fact, parallel? Is Dershowitz's argument valid if and only if the argument about Jones's painlessly murdering his mother is valid? Is the Jones argument valid? If the Jones argument is valid, then do we have to reject A or reject C1 and C2? If we reject C2, then (since C1 is simply a stipulated factual truth) do we have to reject the conditional moral claim P2? If we reject P2 in the case of murder, should we reject P*2 in the case of torture?

• Scarry seems to be arguing that using torture in the ticking-bomb scenario is morally unacceptable and should remain illegal but is such that one should do it and be "courageous" enough to risk being prosecuted and thrown into prison for doing it. Is this a coherent set of claims?

• Scarry raises the question of the risks of torture. In the bomb-ticking case it is often assumed that we know that the suspect has the information, that we know there is a bomb ticking away, and that we know we can get the relevant information by torturing the suspect. But in real life all of these assumptions would be less than fully known. Does this change the equation?

• The argument for torturing in ticking-bomb cases is that we will be safer if it is allowed. But if torture of suspects is allowed, then you might end up a suspect on false grounds. Does the risk of an ordinary innocent citizen's being tortured if torture is legalized change the risk equation?

• Dershowitz's argument is limited to the use of torture as an interrogation tactic. But might the argument be extended to the use of torture as a form of punishment? If the argument does imply that the State should warrant torture as a form of punishment in some cases, is this a problem for the argument? Twenty lashes with a whip is considered cruel and unusual punishment in the United States, while life in prison is not. But most people would surely prefer the whipping to life in prison. Is our attitude toward corporal punishment justified?

FURTHER READING

Bufacchi, Vittorio, and Jean Maria Arrigo. "Torture, Terrorism and the State: A Refutation of the Ticking-Bomb Argument." *Journal of Applied Philosophy* 23, no. 3 (2006): 355–73.

Curzer, Howard J. "Admirable Immorality, Dirty Hands, Ticking Bombs, and Torturing Innocents." *Southern Journal of Philosophy* 44, no. 1 (Spring 2006): 31–56.

Dershowitz, Alan M. *Why Terrorism Works: Understanding the Threat, Responding to the Challenge.* New Haven: Yale University Press, 2002.

Fiala, Andrew. "A Critique of Exceptions: Torture, Terrorism, and the Lesser Evil Argument." *International Journal of Applied Philosophy* 20, no. 1 (Spring 2006): 127–42.

Kershnar, Stephen. "For Interrogational Torture." *International Journal of Applied Philosophy* 19, no. 2 (Fall 2005): 223–41 (note that this issue contains several other articles on torture).

Miller, Seumas. "Torture." *Stanford Encyclopedia of Philosophy* (http://plato.stanford.edu/entries/torture/), February 7, 2006.

Shue, Henry. "Torture." *Philosophy and Public Affairs* 7, no. 2 (Winter 1978): 124–43.

Steinhoff, Uwe. "Torture—The Case for Dirty Harry and Against Alan Dershowitz." *Journal of Applied Philosophy* 23, no. 3 (2006): 337–53.

Sussman, David. "What's Wrong with Torture?" *Philosophy and Public Affairs* 33 (2005): 1–33.

Waldron, Jeremy. "Torture and Positive Law: Jurisprudence for the White House." *Columbia Law Review* 105, no. 6 (2005): 1681–1750.

Wolfendale, Jessica. "Training Torturers: A Critique of the Ticking Bomb Argument." *Social Theory and Practice* 32, no. 2 (April 2006): 269–87.

ALAN DERSHOWITZ

Tortured Reasoning

... Nonlethal torture is currently being used by the United States in an effort to secure information deemed necessary to prevent acts of terrorism. It is being done below the radar screen, without political accountability, and indeed with plausible deniability. All forms of torture are widespread among nations that have signed treaties prohibiting all torture. The current situation is unacceptable: it tolerates torture without accountability and encourages hypocritical posturing. I would like to see improvement in the current situation by reducing or eliminating torture, while increasing visibility and accountability. I am opposed to torture as a normative matter, but I know it is taking place today and believe that it would certainly be employed if we ever experienced an imminent threat of mass casualty biological, chemical, or nuclear terrorism. If I am correct, then it is important to ask the following question: if torture is being or will be practiced, is it worse to close our eyes to it and tolerate its use by low-level law enforcement officials without accountability, or instead to bring it to the surface by requiring that a warrant of some kind be required as a precondition to the infliction of any type of torture under any circumstances?

That is the important policy question about which I have tried to begin a debate. It is about how a democracy should make difficult choice-of-evil decisions in situations for which there is no good resolution.[1]

... First, a word about how I, a civil libertarian who has devoted much of his life to defending human rights against governmental overreaching, came to advocate this controversial proposal. It began well before September 11, 2001, and it was offered as a way of reducing or eliminating the use of torture in a nation plagued with terrorism.

In the late 1980s I traveled to Israel to conduct research and teach a class at Hebrew University on civil liberties during times of crisis. In the course of my research I learned that the Israeli Security Services (the GSS or Shin Bet) were employing what they euphemistically called "moderate physical pressure" on suspected terrorists to obtain information deemed necessary to prevent future terrorist attacks. The method employed by the security services fell somewhere closer to what many would regard as very rough interrogation (as practiced by the British in Northern Ireland and by the U.S. following September 11, 2001) than to outright torture (as practiced by the French in Algeria and by Egypt, the Philippines, and Jordan). In most cases the suspect would be placed in a dark room with a smelly sack over his head. Loud, unpleasant music or other noise would blare from speakers. The suspect would be seated in an extremely uncomfortable position and then shaken vigorously. Statements that were found to be made under this kind of nonlethal pressure could not—at least in theory—be introduced in any court of law, both because they were involuntarily secured and because they were deemed potentially untrustworthy, at least without corroboration. But they were used as leads in the prevention of terrorist acts. Sometimes the leads proved false; other times they proved true. There is little doubt that some acts of terrorism—which might have killed many civilians—were prevented. There is also little doubt that the cost of saving these lives—measured in terms of basic human rights—was extraordinarily high.

In my classes and public lectures in Israel, I strongly condemned these methods as a violation of core civil liberties and human rights. The response that people gave, across the political spectrum from civil libertarians to law-and-order advocates, was essentially the same: but what about the "ticking bomb" case?

The ticking bomb case refers to variations on a scenario that has been discussed by many philoso-

---

phers, including Michael Walzer, Jean-Paul Sartre, and Jeremy Bentham. The current variation on the classic "ticking bomb case" involves a captured terrorist who refuses to divulge information about the imminent use of weapons of mass destruction, such as a nuclear, chemical, or biological device, that are capable of killing and injuring thousands of civilians.

In Israel, the use of torture to prevent terrorism was not and is not hypothetical; it was and continues to be very real and recurring. I soon discovered that virtually no one in Israel was willing to take the "purist" position against any form of torture or rough interrogation in the ticking bomb case: namely, that the ticking bomb must be permitted to explode and kill dozens, perhaps hundreds, of civilians, even if this disaster could be prevented by subjecting the captured terrorist to nonlethal torture and forcing him to disclose its location. I realized that the extraordinarily rare situation of the hypothetical ticking bomb terrorist was serving as a moral, intellectual, and legal justification for the pervasive *system* of coercive interrogation, which, though not the paradigm of torture, certainly bordered on it. It was then that I decided to challenge this system by directly confronting the ticking bomb case. I presented the following challenge to my Israeli audience: If the reason you permit nonlethal torture is based on the ticking bomb case, why not limit it exclusively to that compelling but rare situation? Moreover, if you believe that nonlethal torture is justifiable in the ticking bomb case, why not require advanced judicial approval—a "torture warrant"? That was the origin of the controversial proposal that has received much attention, largely critical, from the media. Its goal was, and remains, to reduce the use of torture to the smallest amount and degree possible, while creating public accountability for its rare use. I saw it not as a compromise with civil liberties but rather as an effort to maximize civil liberties in the face of a realistic likelihood that torture would, in fact, take place below the radar screen of accountability.

The Israeli government and judiciary rejected my proposal. The response, especially of Israeli judges, was horror at the prospect that they—the robed embodiment of the rule of law—might have to dirty their hands by approving so barbaric a practice in advance and in specific cases. . . .

In 1999 the Supreme Court of Israel confronted the issues raised in the Landau Commission report. The case, in essence, posed the following question. If an arrested terrorist knew the location of a ticking time bomb that was about to explode in a busy intersection but refused to disclose its location, would it be proper to torture the terrorist in order to prevent the bombing and save dozens of lives? The court answered no. As the president of the Supreme Court, Aharon Barak, put it: "Although a democracy must often fight with one hand tied behind its back, it nevertheless has the upper hand." It specifically outlawed many of the nonlethal techniques—"torture lite"—currently being employed by American authorities in their rough interrogations of captured terrorist suspects.

The Supreme Court of Israel left the security services a tiny window of opportunity in extreme cases. Borrowing from the Landau Commission, it cited the traditional common-law defense of necessity, and it left open the possibility that a member of the security service who honestly believed that rough interrogation was the only means available to save lives in imminent danger could raise this defense. This leaves each individual member of the security services in the position of having to guess how a court would ultimately resolve his case. That is unfair to such investigators. It would have been far better, in my view, had the court required any investigator who believed that torture was necessary in order to save lives to apply to a judge, when feasible. The judge would then be in a position either to authorize or refuse to authorize a "torture warrant." Such a procedure would require judges to dirty their hands by authorizing torture warrants or bear the responsibility for failing to do so. Individual interrogators should not have to place their liberty at risk by guessing how a court might ultimately decide a close case. They should be able to get an advance ruling based on the evidence available at the time.

In response to the decision of the Supreme Court of Israel, it was suggested that the Knesset—Israel's parliament—could create a procedure for advance judicial scrutiny, akin to the warrant requirement in the Fourth Amendment to the United States Constitution. It is a traditional role for judges to play, since it is the job of the judiciary to balance the needs for security against the imperatives of liberty. Interrogators from the security service are not trained to strike such a delicate balance. Their mission is single-minded: to prevent terrorism. Similarly, the mission of civil liberties lawyers who oppose torture is single-minded: to vindicate the individual rights of suspected terrorists. It is the role of the court to strike the appropriate balance. The Supreme Court of Israel took a giant step in the direction of striking that balance. But it—or the legislature—should take the further step of requiring the judiciary to assume responsibility in individual cases. The essence of a democracy is placing responsibility for difficult choices in a visible and neutral institution like the judiciary.

Issues of this sort are likely to arise throughout the world, including in the United States, in the aftermath of the World Trade Center disaster. Had law enforcement officials arrested terrorists boarding one of the airplanes and learned that other planes, then airborne, were headed toward unknown occupied buildings, there would have been an understandable incentive to torture those terrorists in order to learn the identity of the buildings and evacuate them. It is easy to imagine similar future scenarios.

Following the terrible events of September 11 and the reported use of rough interrogation techniques— "torture lite"—by American military and civilian officials, I tried to start a debate about the concept of a torture warrant in this country. In proposing some kind of advanced approval for the use of limited force in extreme situations, I deliberately declined to take a position on the normative issue of whether I would personally approve of the use of nonlethal torture against a captured terrorist who refuses to divulge information deemed essential to prevent an avoidable act of mass terrorism, though I did set out the argument in favor of (and against) it. I sought a debate about a different, though related, issue: if torture would, *in fact* be employed by a democratic nation under the circumstances, would the rule of law and principles of accountability require that any use of torture be subject to some kind of judicial (or perhaps executive) oversight (or control)? On this normative issue, I have expressed my views loudly and clearly. My answer, unlike that of the Supreme

Court of Israel, is yes. To elaborate, I have argued that unless a democratic nation is prepared to have a proposed action governed by the rule of law, it should not undertake, or authorize, that action. As a corollary, if it needs to take the proposed action, then it must subject it to the rule of law. Suggesting that an after-the-fact "necessity defense" might be available in extreme cases is not an adequate substitute for explicit advance approval.

The possible case of a ticking bomb terrorist or terrorist with weapons of mass destruction has provided a justification for a persuasive and unregulated use of torture (or other forms of rough interrogation) by American officials, just as it had in Israel. Few are prepared to give up use of that option in really extreme cases. Instead of expressly limiting its use to such a case—and regulating it by procedural controls—many argue that is better to leave it to the "discretion" of law enforcement officials. A sort of "don't ask, don't tell" policy has emerged, enabling our president and attorney general to close their eyes to its use while being able to deny it categorically—the kind of willful blindness condemned by the courts in other contexts. With no limitations, standards, principles, or accountability, the use of such techniques will continue to expand. . . .

Let me once again present my actual views on torture, so that no one can any longer feign confusion about where I stand, though I'm certain the "confusion" will persist among some who are determined to argue that I am a disciple of Torquemada.

I am against torture as a *normative* matter, and I would like to see its use minimized. I believe that at least moderate forms of nonlethal torture are *in fact* being used by the United States and some of its allies today. I think that if we ever confronted an actual case of imminent mass terrorism that could be prevented by the infliction of torture, we would use torture (even lethal torture) and the public would favor its use. Whenever I speak about this subject, I ask my audience for a show of hands on the empirical question "How many of you think that nonlethal torture *would* be used if we were ever confronted with a ticking bomb terrorist case?" Almost no one dissents from the view that torture *would in fact* be used, though there is widespread disagreement about whether it *should* be used. That is also my empirical conclusion. It is either true or false, and time will probably tell. I then present my *conditional norma-tive* position, which is the central point of my chapter on torture.

I pose the issue as follows. If torture is, in fact, being used and/or would, in fact, be used in an actual ticking bomb terrorist case, would it be *normatively* better or worse to have such torture regulated by some kind of warrant, with accountability, recordkeeping, stan-dards and limitations? *This* is an important debate, and *a different one* from the old, abstract Benthamite debate over whether torture can ever be justified. It is not so much about the substantive issue of torture as it is about accountability, visibility, and candor in a democracy that is confronting a choice of evils. For example, William Schulz, the executive director of Amnesty International USA, asks whether I would favor "brutality warrants," "testilying warrants,"[2] and "prisoner rape warrants."[3] Although I strongly oppose brutality, testilying, and prisoner rape, I answered Schulz with "a heuristic yes, if requiring a warrant would subject these horribly brutal activities to judicial control and accountability." In explaining my prefer-ence for a warrant, I wrote the following.

> The purpose of requiring judicial supervision, as the framers of our Fourth Amendment understood better than Schulz does, is to assure accountability and neu-trality. There is another purpose as well: it forces a dem-ocratic country to confront the choice of evils in an open way. My question back to Schulz is do you prefer the current situation in which brutality, testilying, and prisoner rape are rampant, but we close our eyes to these evils?
>
> There is, of course, a downside: legitimating a horri-ble practice that we all want to see ended or minimized. Thus we have a triangular conflict unique to democratic societies: If these horrible practices continue to operate below the radar screen of accountability, there is no legitimation, but there is continuing and ever expand-ing *sub rosa* employment of the practice. If we try to control the practice by demanding some kind of accountability, then we add a degree of legitimation to it while perhaps reducing its frequency and severity. If we do nothing, and a preventable act of nuclear terror-ism occurs, then the public will demand that we con-strain liberty even more. There is no easy answer.

I praise Amnesty for taking the high road—that is its job, because it is not responsible for making hard judg-ments about choices of evil. Responsible government officials are in a somewhat different position. Professors have yet a different responsibility: to provoke debate about issues before they occur and to challenge absolutes.

That is my position. I cannot say it any more clearly.

The strongest argument against my preference for candor and accountability is the claim that it is better for torture—or any other evil practice deemed neces-sary during emergencies—to be left to the low-visi-bility discretion of low-level functionaries than to be legitimated by high-level, accountable decision-mak-ers. Posner makes this argument:

> Dershowitz believes that the occasions for the use of torture should be regularized—by requiring a judicial warrant for the needle treatment, for example. But he overlooks an argument for leaving such things to exec-utive discretion. If rules are promulgated permitting torture in defined circumstances, some officials are bound to want to explore the outer bounds of the rules. Having been regularized, the practice will become reg-ular. Better to leave in place the formal and customary prohibitions, but with the understanding that they will not be enforced in extreme circumstances.

The classic formulation of this argument was offered by Justice Robert Jackson in his dissenting opinion in one of the Japanese detention camp cases:

> Much is said of the danger to liberty from the Army pro-gram for deporting and detaining these citizens of Japanese extraction. But a judicial construction of the due process clause that will sustain this order is a far sub-tler blow to liberty than the promulgation of the order itself. A military order, however unconstitutional, is not apt to last longer than the military emergency. Even dur-ing that period a succeeding commander may revoke it all. But once a judicial opinion rationalizes such an order to show that it conforms to the Constitution, or rather rationalizes the Constitution to show that the Constitution sanctions such an order, the Court for all time has validated the principle of racial discrimination in criminal procedure and of transplanting American citizens. The principle then lies about like a loaded weapon ready for the hand of any authority that can bring forward a plausible claim of an urgent need. Every

repetition imbeds that principle more deeply in our law and thinking and expands it to new purposes. All who observe the work of courts are familiar with what Judge Cardozo described as "the tendency of a principle to expand itself to the limit of its logic." A military commander may overstep the bounds of constitutionality, and it is an incident. But if we review and approve, that passing incident becomes the doctrine of the Constitution. There it has a generative power of its own, and all that it creates will be in its own image.

Experience has not necessarily proved Jackson's fear or Posner's prediction to be well founded. The very fact that the Supreme Court expressly validated the detentions contributed to its condemnation by the verdict of history. Today the Supreme Court's decision in *Korematsu* stands alongside decisions such as *Dred Scott, Plessy v. Ferguson,* and *Buck v. Bell* in the High Court's Hall of Infamy. Though never formally overruled, and even occasionally cited, *Korematsu* serves as a negative precedent—a mistaken ruling not ever to be repeated in future cases. Had the Supreme Court merely allowed the executive decision to stand without judicial review, a far more dangerous precedent might have been established: namely, that executive decisions during times of emergency will escape review by the Supreme Court. That far broader and more dangerous precedent would then lie about "like a loaded weapon" ready to be used by a dictator without fear of judicial review. That comes close to the current situation, in which the administration denies it is acting unlawfully, while aggressively resisting any judicial review of its actions with regard to terrorism.

The *New York Times*, on March 9, 2003, reported on the "pattern" being followed by American interrogators. It includes forcing detainees to stand "naked," with "their hands chained to the ceiling and their feet shackled." Their heads are covered with "black hoods"; they are forced "to stand or kneel in uncomfortable positions in extreme cold or heat," which can quickly vary from "100 to 10 degrees." The detainee is deprived of sleep, "fed very little," exposed to disorienting sounds and lights, and, according to some sources, "manhandled" and "beaten." In one case involving a high-ranking al-Qaeda operative, "pain killers were withheld from Mr. [Abu]

Zubaydah, who was shot several times during his capture."[4]

A Western intelligence official described these tactics as "not quite torture, but about as close as you can get." At least two deaths and seventeen suicide attempts have been attributed to these interrogation tactics

Intelligence officials "have also acknowledged that some suspects have been turned over [by the United States] to security services in countries known to engage in torture."[5] These countries include Egypt, Jordan, the Philippines, Saudi Arabia, and Morocco. Turning captives over to countries for the purpose of having them tortured is in plain violation of the 1984 International Convention against Torture, to which we, and the countries to which we are sending the captives, are signatories.

The *Wall Street Journal* reported that "a U.S. intelligence official" told them that detainees with important information could be treated roughly:

> Among the techniques: making captives wear black hoods, forcing them to stand in painful "stress positions" for a long time and subjecting them to interrogation sessions lasting as long as 20 hours.
>
> U.S. officials overseeing interrogations of captured al-Qaeda forces at Bagram and Guantanamo Bay Naval Base in Cuba can even authorize "a little bit of smacky-face," a U.S. intelligence official says. "Some al-Qaeda just need some extra encouragement," the official says.
>
> "There's a reason why [Mr. Mohammed] isn't going to be near a place where he has Miranda rights or the equivalent of them," the senior federal law-enforcer says. "He won't be someplace like Spain or Germany or France. We're not using this to prosecute him. This is for intelligence. God only knows what they're going to do with him. You go to some other country that'll let us pistol whip this guy." . . .
>
> U.S. authorities have an additional inducement to make Mr. Mohammed talk, even if he shares the suicidal commitment of the Sept. 11 hijackers: The Americans have access to two of his elementary-school-age children, the top law enforcement official says. The children were captured in a September raid that netted one of Mr. Mohammed's top comrades, Ramzi Binalshibh.[6]

There is no doubt that these tactics would be prohibited by the Israeli Supreme Court's decision described earlier, but the U.S. Court of Appeals for the District of Columbia recently ruled that American courts have no power even to review the conditions imposed on detainees in Guantanamo or other interrogation centers outside the United States.[7] That issue is now before the U.S. Supreme Court, despite efforts by the administration to preclude review.

This, then, is the virtue of explicitness. The Supreme Court of Israel was able to confront the issue of torture precisely because it had been openly addressed by the Landau Commission in 1987. This open discussion led to Israel being condemned—including by countries that were doing worse but without acknowledging it. It also led to a judicial decision outlawing the practice. As I demonstrated in *Why Terrorism Works*, it is generally more possible to end a questionable practice when it is done openly rather than covertly.[8]

My own belief is that a warrant requirement, if properly enforced, would probably reduce the frequency, severity, and duration of torture. I cannot see how it could possibly increase it, since a warrant requirement simply imposes an additional level of prior review. As I discussed in *Why Terrorism Works*, here are two examples to demonstrate why I think there would be less torture with a warrant requirement than without one. Recall the case of the alleged national security wiretap being placed on the phones of Martin Luther King by the Kennedy administration in the early 1960s. This was in the days when the attorney general could authorize a national security wiretap without a warrant. Today no judge would issue a warrant in a case as flimsy as that one. When Zaccarias Moussaui was detained after trying to learn how to fly an airplane, without wanting to know much about landing it, the government did not even seek a national security wiretap because its lawyers believed that a judge would not have granted one. If Moussaui's computer could have been searched without a warrant, it almost certainly would have been.

It should be recalled that in the context of searches, the framers of our Fourth Amendment opted for a judicial check on the discretion of the police, by requiring a search warrant in most cases.

The Court has explained the reason for the warrant requirement as follows. "The informed and deliberate determinations of magistrates . . . are to be preferred over the hurried actions of officers."[9] Justice Jackson elaborated:

> The point of the Fourth Amendment, which often is not grasped by zealous officers, is not that it denies law enforcement the support of the usual inferences, which reasonable men draw from evidence. Its protection consists in requiring that those inferences be drawn by a neutral and detached magistrate instead of being judged by the officer engaged in the often-competitive enterprise of ferreting out crime. Any assumption that evidence sufficient to support a magistrate's disinterested determination to issue a search warrant will justify the officers in making a search without a warrant would reduce the Amendment to nullify and leave the peoples' homes secure only in the discretion of police officers.[10]

Although torture is very different from a search, the policies underlying the warrant requirement are relevant to whether there is likely to be more torture or less if the decision were left entirely to field officers, or if a judicial officer had to approve a request for a torture warrant. As Mark Twain once observed, "To a man with a hammer, everything looks like a nail." If the man with the hammer must get judicial approval before he can use it, he will probably use it less often and more carefully.

The major downside of any warrant procedure would be its legitimization of a horrible practice, but in my view it is better to legitimate and control a *specific* practice that will occur than to legitimate a *general* practice of tolerating extralegal actions so long as they operate under the table of scrutiny and beneath the radar screen of accountability. Judge Posner's "pragmatic" approach would be an invitation to widespread (and officially—if surreptitiously—approved) lawlessness in "extreme circumstances." Moreover, the very concept of "extreme circumstances" is subjective and infinitely expandable.

We know that Jordan, which denies that it ever uses torture, has, in fact, tortured the innocent relatives of suspect terrorists. We also know that when we captured Mohammed, we also took into custody his two elementary-school-age children—and let him know that we had them.

There is a difference in principle, as Bentham noted more than two hundred years ago, between torturing the guilty to save the lives of the innocent and torturing innocent people. A system that requires an articulated justification for the use of nonlethal torture and approval by a judge is more likely to honor that principle than a system that relegates these decisions to low-visibility law enforcement agents whose only job is to protect the public from terrorism.

As I pointed out in *Why Terrorism Works,* several important values are pitted against each other in this conflict. The first is the safety and security of a nation's citizens. Under the ticking bomb scenario, this value may argue for the use of torture, if that were the only way to prevent the ticking bomb from exploding and killing large numbers of civilians. The second value is the preservation of civil liberties and human rights. This value requires that we not accept torture as a legitimate part of our legal system. In my debates with two prominent civil libertarians (Floyd Abrams and Harvey Silverglate) both acknowledged that they would want nonlethal torture to be used if it could prevent thousands of deaths, but they did not want torture to be officially recognized by our legal system. As Floyd Abrams put it: "In a democracy sometimes it is necessary to do things off the books and below the radar screen." The former presidential candidate Alan Keyes took the position that although torture might be *necessary* in a given situation, it could never be *right*. He suggested that a president *should* authorize the torturing of a ticking bomb terrorist but that this act should not be legitimated by the courts or incorporated into our legal system. He argued that wrongful and indeed unlawful acts might sometimes be necessary to preserve the nation but that no aura of legitimacy should be placed on these actions by judicial imprimatur. Professor Elshtain makes a similar point. Though she strongly favors the use of nonlethal torture in certain extreme cases, she does not want "a law to cover such cases." Indeed, she characterizes my proposal for a torture warrant as "a stunningly bad idea." She prefers instead to have each individual "grapple with a terrible moral dilemma" rather than to have an open debate and then codify its results.[11] This understandable approach is in conflict with the third important value: namely, open accountability and visibility in a democracy. "Off-the-book actions below the radar screen" are antithetical to the theory and practice of democracy. Citizens cannot approve or disapprove of governmental actions of which they are unaware. We have learned the lesson of history that off-the-book actions can produce terrible consequences. President Nixon's creation of a group of "plumbers" led to Watergate, and President Reagan's authorization of an "off-the-books" foreign policy in Central America led to the Iran-Contra scandal. And these are only the ones we know about!

Perhaps the most extreme example of this hypocritical approach to torture comes—not surprisingly—from the French experience in Algeria. The French army used torture extensively in seeking to prevent terrorism during France's brutal war between 1955 and 1957. An officer who supervised this torture, General Paul Aussaresses, wrote an account of what he had done and seen, including the torture of dozens of Algerians. "The best way to make a terrorist talk when he refused to say what he knew was to torture him," he boasted. Although the book was published decades after the war was over, the general was prosecuted—but not for what he had *done* to the Algerians. Instead, he was prosecuted for *revealing* what he had done and seeking to justify it.[12]

In a democracy governed by a rule of law, we should never want our soldiers or president to take any action that we deem wrong or illegal. A good test of whether an action should or should not be done is whether we are prepared to have it disclosed—perhaps not immediately, but certainly after some time has passed. No legal system operating under the rule of law should ever tolerate an "off-the-books" approach to necessity. Even the defense of necessity must be justified lawfully. The road to tyranny has always been paved with claims of necessity made by those responsible for the security of a nation. Our system of checks and balances requires that all presidential actions, like all legislative or military actions, be consistent with governing law. If it is necessary to torture in the ticking bomb case, then our governing laws must accommodate this practice. If we refuse to change our law to accommodate any particular action, then our government should not take that action.[13] Requiring that a controversial, even immoral, action be made openly and with accountability is one way of minimizing resort to unjustifiable means. . . .

NOTES

1. Dershowitz, Alan M. *Why Terrorism Works: Understanding the Threat, Responding to the Challenge* (New Haven, Conn.: Yale University Press, 2002).

2. "Testilying" is a term coined by New York City police to describe systematic perjury regarding the circumstances that led to a search, seizure, or interrogation.

3. William F. Schulz, "The Torturer's Apprentice: Civil Liberties in a Turbulent Age," *Nation*, May 13, 2002.

4. Raymond Bonner, "Questioning Terror Suspects in a Dark and Surreal World," *New York Times*, March 9, 2003.

5. *New York Times*, March 9, 2003, A1.

6. Jess Bravin and Gary Fields, "How Do Interrogators Make Terrorists Talk?" *Wall Street Journal*, March 3, 2003.

7. *Al Odah v. United States*, 321 F.3d 1134 (2003).

8. *Why Terrorism Works*, 155–160.

9. *U.S. v. Lefkowitz*, 285 U.S. 452, 464 (1932).

10. *Johnson v. U.S.*, 333 U.S. 10, 13–14 (1948).

11. For many, capital punishment is a moral evil that should not be, but is, employed by society. For some it is worse than nonlethal torture. The strongest argument made for it often uses extreme examples: the mass-murdering recidivist who kills while in prison and has the capacity to escape. If killing that individual were somehow deemed necessary, would Elshtein prefer that it be done by an individual state actor, after grappling with his conscience, or as a result of a codification, after democratic processes have been followed?

12. Suzanne Daley, "France Is Seeking a Fine in Trial of Algerian War General," *New York Times*, November, 2001.

13. Indeed, there is already one case in our jurisprudence in which this has already occurred and the courts have considered it. In the 1984 case of *Leon v. Wainwright*, Jean Leon and an accomplice kidnapped a taxi cab driver and held him for ransom. Leon was arrested while trying to collect the ransom but refused to disclose where he was holding the victim. "When he refused to tell them the location, he was set upon by several of the officers . . . they threatened and physically abused him by twisting his arm and choking him until he revealed where [the victim] was being held." Although the appellate court disclaimed any wish to "sanction the use of force and coercion, by police officers," the judges went out of their way to say that this was not the act of "brutal law enforcement agents trying to obtain a confession." "This was instead a group of concerned officers acting in a reasonable manner to obtain information they needed in order to protect another individual from bodily harm or death." Although the court did not find it necessary to invoke the "necessity defense," since no charges were brought against the policemen who tortured the kidnapper, it described the torture as having been "motivated by the immediate *necessity* to find the victim and save his life." *Leon v. Wainwright*, 734 F.2d 770 11th Circuit 1984; emphasis added. If an appellate court would so regard the use of police brutality—torture—in a case involving one kidnap victim, it is not difficult to extrapolate to a situation in which hundreds or thousands of lives might hang in the balance.

Critics

Elaine Scarry*

Five Errors in the Reasoning of Alan Dershowitz

At the center of Alan Dershowitz's recent account of torture is the argument that a hypothetical case can be imagined in which saving a city from a nuclear, chemical, or biological bomb might depend on torturing the terrorist who placed it there or knew where it was hidden. His chapter "Should the Ticking Bomb Terrorist Be Tortured?" is the centerpiece of his book *Why Terrorism Works*, and his essay herein is again structured around the dramatic instance of the ticking bomb, which occurs at the beginning, middle, and end of his argument. He believes that in such a situation it would be permissible to torture if one first obtained a judicial or executive warrant; the prohibition against torture, dissolved by means of the warrant, would continue in place for any act of torture that had not been warranted.

The first error in Alan Dershowitz's argument is that he wrongly addresses us as a population whose members are morally impaired. (It is of course the case that if we disagree with him we are perceived to be deficient: the charge of "hypocrisy" to any who believe the prohibition against torture should remain firmly in place recurs at intervals throughout his two essays; but the problem I wish to identify is more grave and applies to us whether we agree or disagree with him; and I believe it distorts his reasoning about the key questions.) Let us see precisely how this is so.

Introducing an "imaginable" occasion for torture that has no correspondence with the thousands of cases that actually occur has the effect of seeming to change torture to a sanctionable act. As Henry Shu

urges in his essay . . . , the unwavering prohibition against torture must be kept in place; and should the unlikely "imaginable" instance actually ever occur, the torturer would have to rely on convincing a jury of peers that the context for the act was exceptional.

But exposing the defect of the ticking bomb argument requires that we go further. Anyone, we are told, who had the choice between on the one hand torturing and saving-the-city and on the other hand not torturing and not saving-the-city would be likely to choose the first. That may be. But so, too, anyone confronted with the choice between on the one hand saving-the-city and being herself imprisoned, or on the other hand not saving-the-city and not being imprisoned, would almost certainly also choose the first. That is, torturing should be perceived with the same acute aversion with which one's own legal culpability and one's own death are perceived; and while it is possible that a jury would exonerate someone in this situation, it does not follow that any such guarantee should be provided before the fact. Nor should someone enter into the act expecting exoneration after the fact. That one might *have to do* something someday that is wrong does not mean the act has ceased to be "wrong" and "punishable." It is unlikely that any savior of the city would actually be inhibited by the lack of preexisting moral and legal assurances of immunity.

It is a peculiar characteristic of such hypothetical arguments on behalf of torture that the arguer can always "imagine" someone large-spirited enough to overcome (on behalf of a city's population) his aversion to torture, but not so large-spirited that he or she can also accept his or her own legal culpability and punishment.

The first major error in Alan Dershowitz's argument, then, is that he severely midjudges the compatriots to whom, and about whom, he is speaking. He rules out, at the outset, the possibility that if one of us had the chance to save the Earth from the scourge of a nuclear weapon, the person would forfeit his or her liberty or even life to carry out that act. The entire argument is premised on the idea that the population lacks the simple attribute of courage. The act of inflicting torture requires no courage (the aversiveness is wholly borne by someone else), whereas the forfeit of one's future liberty requires that some portion of the severe adversity be endured by the actor himself.

Dershowitz tells us . . . that he repeatedly asks his students and lecture audiences to raise their hands if they believe someone who could stop a nuclear bomb by torturing would do so; he reports that invariably many hands rise in the air. What if he followed that simple experiment with another: "Raise your hand if you believe that someone who saw she had it within her power to save hundreds of thousands of lives would forfeit her own liberty or give her own life?" Will not as many hands go up when this question is posed as when the imaginary opportunity to torture is posed? In fact, many more people (such as soldiers) have shown themselves willing to give their lives to save other human beings than have ever shown themselves willing to perform an act of torture, so it is unclear why any legal impunity needs to be offered to cover the unlikely ticking bomb situation.

The way a person's legal culpability for torture enables him to test the situation in front of him can be seen by noticing not just the final action that is taken but the stations along the way. If I believe I am in the presence of someone who knows where an armed nuclear bomb is ticking away, I must ask myself *how certain* I am that this person actually knows that information. Now the testing ratio comes into play. If I say "I am confident enough that he holds this knowledge that I am willing to torture him," then I ought also to be able to say "I am confident enough that he holds this knowledge that I am willing to forfeit my liberty and possibly my life in order to procure that

knowledge." If I instead find myself saying "Come to think of it, I'm not quite sure enough that I can give up my liberty to it," it is the signal to revise my assessment of confidence that torturing him would produce any knowledge worth having. Performing this test is more accurate (and certainly more rapid) than finding a judge who can issue a warrant, unless we design the warrant situation as one in which any judge who generates the warrant also agrees to go to jail.

In addition to the two defects of the argument on behalf of issuing warrants to permit torture in the ticking bomb situation—first, that it assumes a cowardly population incapable of acting without prior guarantees of immunity, and second, that it eliminates the procedure for testing one's level of confidence—there is a third problem. The ticking bomb scenario is often described as highly improbable. What makes it improbable is not the existence of a ticking bomb (it is entirely possible that a terrorist or a deranged state leader will one day try to use a nuclear bomb, or a chemical or biological weapon capable of killing hundreds of thousands). What instead makes the ticking bomb scenario improbable is the notion that in a world where knowledge is ordinarily so imperfect, we are suddenly granted the omniscience to know that the person in front of us holds this crucial information about the bomb's whereabouts. (Why not just grant us the omniscience to know where the bomb is?)

In the two and a half years since September 11, 2001, five thousand foreign nationals suspected of being terrorists have been detained without access to counsel, only three of whom have ever eventually been charged with terrorism-related acts; two of those three have been acquitted.[1] When we imagine the ticking bomb situation, does our imaginary omniscience enable us to get the information by torturing one person? Or will the numbers more closely resemble the situation of the detainees: we will be certain, and incorrect, 4,999 times that we stand in the presence of someone with the crucial data, and only get it right with the five thousandth prisoner? Will the ticking bomb still be ticking?

Almost all aspects of our post–September 11 world bring us face to face with our lack of omniscience. We have failed, in two and a half years, to find the anthrax murderer, despite the fact that the precisely identified strain of anthrax limits the pool of eligible candidates to a tiny handful of people; this is not like finding a needle in a haystack, it's like finding a needle in a bright red pincushion that contains one needle and nineteen straight pins. We have gone to war against a country that was "known" to have weapons of mass destruction, only to find it had none. We knew our troops would be welcomed as liberators, at least by the Shi'ites, who are now killing our soldiers as the Sunnis hang our civilians from bridges. And yet, despite our overwhelming miscalculation, mismeasurement, and inability to solve mysteries both before and after they happen—or to put it in the fairest light, despite the excruciating difficulty of ever being right—we are asked to entertain the possibility of lifting the unconditional prohibition against torture, and to do so by imagining that one of us will recognize the ticking bomb accomplice the moment we see him.

Oddly, and conversely, torturing a person in order to get information about a ticking bomb is sometimes introduced in situations where the information is already available through means that require inflicting no cruelty. Although Alan Dershowitz usually formulates the ticking bomb license-to-torture as a case in which hundreds of thousands of people stand to die from a nuclear, chemical, or biological weapon, he at one point asks us to imagine that we are back on September 11; and that by capturing and torturing the hijacker on one of the planes we can learn the target of another plane and enable the people in that targeted building to evacuate. But a great deal of information about the plane that eventually hit the Pentagon was known from FAA air controllers, radar images, and a passenger cell phone call placed directly to the Justice Department. For fifty-five minutes before the plane hit the Pentagon, it was clear that American Airlines Flight 77 was highly likely to be one of the hijacked planes, since it was off course, was not answering air controllers, and had turned off its secondary radar; for twenty minutes before it hit the Pentagon, it was certain (because passenger Barbara Olson phoned her husband, Theodore Olson, in the Justice Department) that the plane was under the control of hijackers; for twelve minutes before it hit the Pentagon, an air controller saw it on primary radar headed for Washington; for nine minutes before it hit the Pentagon, a C-130 watched it flying fast and low.[2] We need to wonder why we were not able to use this available information to get people out of the Pentagon and other Washington buildings, rather than supposing that it would have been helpful to torture someone to learn its target.

To summarize, then, the ticking bomb scenario, with warrant as a license to torture, presents us with three major problems: (1) it assumes a population that is (against robust evidence) cowardly and self-regarding—able and willing to torture but unable and unwilling to themselves suffer harm; (2) it assumes a population that is (against robust evidence) omniscient; and (3) by providing legal immunity, it eliminates the felt-aversiveness to cruelty that acts as a way to test one's level of conviction that thousands of lives are at risk and that one is uniquely positioned to act as their savior.

Alan Dershowitz has asked us to put aside our commitment to an unwavering prohibition on torture, to enter into an open debate with him, and to step into that debate by passing through the threshold of the ticking bomb case, a case whose framing assumptions are erroneous. But it may be useful to proceed forward and examine some of his other arguments, for it is apparent that here, too, he presents us with errors both in the substance and the style of the reasoning; and perhaps if the errors are articulated, he will be persuaded to return to his own original position, which (he several times tells us) was until recently a blanket condemnation of torture.

The proposal we are asked to contemplate is one in which a judge or an executive branch officer will issue a warrant licensing the holder of the warrant to torture, and the claim is that the existence of the warrants will, by introducing judicial scrutiny and by providing a documentary record, reduce the number of incidents of torture that take place and increase the accountability of those carrying out such acts.

This is a puzzling claim. We are asked to assume that a judge or executive branch officer, acting under the pressure of a ticking bomb, will be able to discriminate between acceptable and unacceptable cases. Are acceptable cases those that involve weapons of mass destruction (and therefore tens of thousands of deaths) and unacceptable cases those that involve smaller numbers of injuries? Or is some factor other than number of persons the key, as at many moments appears to be the case in Dershowitz's own examples? Dershowitz might fairly complain that we only lack an answer to that question because so far the debate has not really gotten underway, and therefore the practical details of the arrangement have not been worked out.

But there does already exist a solid basis for our skepticism that a warrants system will produce coherent discrimination. The court set up to issue warrants under the Foreign Intelligence Surveillance Act (FISA) has declined only one requested warrant in twenty-five years: the estimated number of warrant requests is twenty-five thousand.[3] If a torture warrant court were based on this model,[4] the incidence of torture would not be likely to decline, nor would the level of accountability increase.

But let us assume that the torture warrant court would, unlike the FISA court, operate with a high level of resistance and would grant only a small number of warrant requests (those providing strong evidence that extreme injury is about to take place very soon, and also providing strong evidence that one specified prisoner holds the key that will enable us to prevent the injury). In other words, let us assume that a coherent principle of discrimination is at work, and now let us see if we can decipher how this will decrease the incidence of torture and increase the level of accountability. Nothing about the results appears to let us reach this conclusion.

Under this new system, the prohibition against torture will dissolve in those cases where the torturer obtains a warrant but will continue in place for any act that has not first been warranted. Of these two groups of persons, the permitted and the prohibited, is it the first group, the second group, or the two groups together that enable us to achieve a level of accountability that surpasses the level available under our longstanding blanket prohibition of torture? Clearly, it cannot be the second group. All acts of torture that are carried out without a warrant (either because the torturers refuse to consult the court, or because they surreptitiously carry out their acts of torture even after their application for warrants have been turned down) will be undocumented—or, more accurately, they will have only the level of documentation that we have today under the blanket prohibition (a point that will be returned to). Is it, instead, the first group that will be accountable? We will, by virtue of the warrant, have a record of the person's actions, the reasons for those actions, the outcome (assuming the warrant holder does not stray from what he or she requested and what the judge granted) and can now request to see concrete evidence of the ticking bomb that was dismantled. But since the torturer has, by means of the warrant, already been released from the usual constraints against torture, in what does his or her accountability consist? Didn't the judicial review, by taking account of his or her proposed actions, release him or her from further accountability? It may be that we can review his or her actions: would this mean we should understand the warrant as a temporary grant of permission that is, upon review, subject to retrospective revocation, at which point the torturer's exemption from punishment would dissolve? Long experience with search warrants suggests the opposite: search warrants, far from facilitating review, historically have tended to close the door on review. In *The Bill of Rights: Creation and Reconstruction*, Akhil Amar describes the way the search warrant has often acted as a shield against the charge of trespass.[5]

The torture warrant system, then, appears to leave us with an unknowable number of illegal instances that cannot be reviewed (that is, cannot be reviewed in any way that is not already available to us under our current blanket prohibition) and a knowable number of legal instances that because they have been warranted are unlikely to be reviewed—even in the way that is currently available to us under the blanket prohibition system. Under the proposed system, our ability to review acts of torture has gotten no better, and actually appears to have gotten worse, than under our present blanket prohibition.

Alan Dershowitz, then, credits the warrant system with a power of documentation and accountability it does not appear to have. Conversely, he undercredits the forms of documentation and accountability that already exist under the present across-the-boards prohibition. He seems to believe that if someone wants the ban on torture to be absolute yet acknowledges that torture occurs, the person must be a hypocrite who pretends to denounce brutality while letting it take place "under the radar." The most baffling moment in his essay comes when he accuses William Schulz, the executive director of Amnesty International USA, of having an insufficient understanding of the purpose of accountability. Because William Schulz opposes warrants for torture, as well as warrants for brutality, testilying, and prisoner rape, Alan Dershowitz asks Schulz: "Do you prefer the current situation in which brutality, testilying and prisoner rape are rampant, but we close our eyes to those evils?"

Does Alan Dershowitz not know, or has he somehow forgotten, that Amnesty International's major work in the world is relentlessly to document instances of torture that have taken place, to make a public record, and through that record, to bring public pressure to bear on stopping the acts of torture even as they are taking place? Torture is itself a ticking bomb (it inflicts grave and widespread physical injury); Amnesty works to stop it, not only before it goes off but often in the very midst of its explosion. The suggestion that Amnesty, because it opposes warrants, prefers that "we close our eyes" is astonishing, given that no group has so steadily required us to keep our eyes on torture. This does not mean that the record is close to complete. Amnesty International continually reminds us that its own records are incomplete, that it can document instances of torture only in countries where Amnesty members are permitted to speak with prisoners. Many other research bodies—newspapers, human rights groups, congressional or U.N investigative groups—also contribute to the widespread commitment, and ability, to document torture.[6]

We encounter, then—in addition to the three major problems earlier summarized in the ticking bomb frame—a fourth and fifth major problem in the proposal for warranting torture. The fourth is that Alan Dershowitz credits the warranting system with a power to provide documentation and accountability that it does not appear to have. The fifth is that his proposal greatly undercredits the forms of documentation and accountability already available to us. These allow us continually to strive for some measure of accountability, while keeping national and international prohibitions on torture fully in place.

Although I have focused here on the framing assumptions and substance of his argument, problems also occur in the form and style of that argument. He often exposes the flaw of a particular idea (e.g., the necessity defense), form of sequencing (e.g. slippery slope), or phrase (e.g., "torture lite")—seeming in each case to repudiate it in unequivocal terms—only to bring that idea, form of sequencing, or phrase back into the service of his own proposal, usually without identifying it by its earlier name or label. The phrase "nonlethal torture," though it literally designates a horrifying set of

practices, is in the context of his essay used as though it meant "moderation," without announcing that cruel linguistic trick in the way "torture lite" openly does. He critiques the "necessity" defense, accurately identifying it as "the most lawless of legal doctrines" and warning us that it is so elastic it can accommodate any person and any position; yet his warrant system gives center stage to the necessity defense, bestows on it a material form, and turns it into a formal procedure. Through this method of repudiating, then using, phrases, forms of sequencing, and ideas, he protects his arguments by giving them deniability. Were we to fault him for relying on the "necessity defense," he would look startled, indignant, and quote back to us the four pages in which he has discredited that defense. Thus we arrive at the climactic moment in his essay where he quotes those who fault him for countenancing the legitimation of torture—quotes them with astonishment, as though he cannot comprehend where on earth such descriptions (straightforward summaries of his view) could possibly have come from.

No one should take Alan Dershowitz lightly (even when face to face with his light, bright spirit). He means business. He intends to open a debate. He intends that debate, in turn, to reopen the law, to alter it, to replace the blanket prohibition on torture with partial legitimacy. He assumes—rightly—that he and those to whom he addresses himself have the power to change law and legal practice. He dedicates his book on the ticking bomb to the "nearly ten thousand students" he has taught over thirty-eight years at Harvard Law School (many of whom now hold legal positions around the country and the world). "You are our future," he tells them. "Preserve it from our enemies."

Let us hope that his former students and all other readers will see the errors in his reasoning and conclude that the best way to preserve the future from "our enemies" is to reaffirm each day the blanket prohibition on torture, and to work with newspapers, human rights groups, and investigative bodies to document and hold those who torture accountable for their acts.

NOTES

*A reader wishing to learn my own view of torture should see the opening chapter of *The Body in Pain*.

An accurate understanding of torture cannot—in my view—be arrived at through the ticking bomb argument, which (quite apart from what any one advocate may intend) opportunistically provides a flexible legal shield whose outcome is a systematic defense of torture.

Why, then, should the ticking bomb argument be answered? In the years following 9/11, the ticking bomb argument has come to seem omnipresent and urgent, not only because of Alan Dershowitz's startling articulations of it but because our own leaders have repeatedly cited imminent nuclear, chemical, or biological threats as reasons for modifying constitutional and international rules on an array of matters (many of which Alan Dershowitz himself would fiercely oppose).

Answers must therefore be given to the ticking bomb argument, even though the arguments (both for and against it) provide a false location for achieving a genuine understanding of torture.

1. David Cole, lecture, Harvard Law School, September 24, 2003.

2. The inability to act on available information is described in more detail in Elaine Scarry, *Who Defended the Country?* ed. Joshua Cohen and Joel Rogers (Boston: Beacon Press, 2003).

3. David Cole, *Enemy Aliens: Double Standards and Constitutional Freedoms in the War on Terrorism* (New York: New Press, 2003), 68; Dan Eggen and Susan Schmidt,

"Secret Court Rebuffs Ashcroft," *Washington Post*, August 23, 2002, 1.

4. Alan Dershowitz does sometime appear to be assuming the warrant court will be, like the FISA court, secret. He at one point speaks of a "special cabinet committee or judicial panel authorized to approve special measures under extraordinary circumstances" (n. 3).

5. Akhil Reed Amar, *The Bill of Rights* (New Haven, Conn.: Yale University Press, 1998), 71–73. Amar writes: "In the end, the Fourth Amendment framers accepted some warrants as necessary but imposed strict limits on these dangerous devices. Warrantless searches did not pose the same threat because those searches would be subject to full and open after-the-fact review in civil trespass cases featuring civil juries" (73).

6. For an example of the documentation of acts of torture (and those who have trained torturers) gathered by multiple research groups, see Timothy Kepner, "Torture 101: The Case Against the United States for Atrocities Committed by School of the Americas Alumni," *Dickinson Journal of International Law* (2001). Kepner assesses the potential liability of the School of Americas in a domestic court, using the Alien Tort Act and the Torture Victim Protection Act of 1991; he takes into consideration complications that arise from the Federal Tort Claims Act, the Combatant Activity Exception, the Foreign Country Exception, and the Political Questions Doctrine.

ALAN DERSHOWITZ

Reply to Scarry

. . . I am especially pleased that Professor Elaine Scarry's essay is included in this collection, because it demonstrates how a very smart person, who has read my essay and my other writing on this issue,[1] persists in confusing my *empirical* descriptions and predictions (that torture *is* being practiced and *will be* practiced by democracies in extreme situations) with my *normative* preference (that torture *should* not be employed and that its use *should* be reduced or eliminated). Here is how Profesor Scarry erroneously

characterizes my view: "He believes that in such a situation [the ticking bomb scenario] *it would be permissible* to torture if one first obtained a judicial or executive warrant." She contrasts my purported normative views with "our commitment to an unwavering prohibition on torture." But my point is precisely that we have no such commitment. In fact, our commitment instead is to "the way of the hypocrites: they declare that they abide by the rule of law, but turn a blind eye to what goes on beneath the surface." If we indeed had an unwavering commitment to prohibiting torture, I never would have begun this debate. It is because I believe that we are moving toward the worst of all possible worlds—a smug, self-satisfied willingness to condemn torture openly, while at the same time encouraging its secret use in extreme cases—that I decided to try to force this issue into the public consciousness.

What would Professor Scarry have us do instead? She would want torture to be used if it could save multiple lives, but she would leave the initial decision to the ex ante decision of "the torturers" and then leaves the post facto decision about whether the torturer did the right thing to "a jury of peers." This is extraordinarily naive, as anyone with any experience in criminal justice will quickly understand. No prosecutor would prosecute and no jury would convict if it *turned out* that the torturer was right, even if the basis on which he acted was weak or bigoted. But some juries might well convict if the torturer turned out to be wrong, even if he or she had a very strong basis on which to act. Our legal (and moral) systems should make accountability turn on a defendant's mens rea (state of mind) at the time he or she acted, not on fortuities beyond his or her control.

An analogy may prove helpful. The former head of counterterrorism, Richard A. Clark, reports that on the morning of September 11, 2001, while several planes that were believed to have been hijacked remained in the air, an excruciatingly difficult decision had to be made: whether "we need to authorize the Air Force to shoot down any aircraft—including a hijacked passenger flight—that looks like it is threatening to attack and cause large-scale death on the ground." Had a passenger jet been shot down, it is certainly possible that a terrible mistake could have been made. Perhaps that plane was not, in fact, being hijacked; or maybe the passengers were in the process of gaining control; or possibly the plane was being hijacked as leverage in negotiations and not to be crashed into a building. It would always be tragic to choose to kill innocent passengers, but it might be necessary in order to prevent even more deaths. Who should make a decision—a tragic choice—of this type and magnitude?

Surely the answer must be: the highest-ranking public official capable of doing so—someone with accountability and responsibility. No one would want to leave it to a low-ranking, anonymous Air Force pilot, without guidance or criteria (unless, of course, there was no time to pass it up to higher authorities). And certainly no one would want the fate of that pilot to be determined by "a jury of peers" after the fact. Tragic choices should be made at the top whenever feasible. And the decision whether to threaten or inflict nonlethal torture in order to prevent a mass terrorist attack is a tragic choice of evils, as is the decision to shoot down a passenger jet and kill hundreds of innocent people.

Professor Scarry also seems willing to rely on the willingness of the torturer to break the law and violate morality in an extreme case: "It is unlikely that any savior of the city would actually be inhibited by the lack of preexisting moral and legal assurances of immunity." But that is precisely the problem: we don't want individual "saviors" to be taking ad hoc, secret, unaccountable decisions whether to inflict torture. An ex ante process would offer some protection against the evils of the current ad hoc system of deniability and unaccountability—admittedly at a cost. The real question, and one Professor Scarry avoids, is whether the cost is worth the benefits. That is the debate I have tried to begin.

Professor Scarry correctly raises the question of whether "a judge or executive branch officer, acting under the pressure of a ticking bomb, will be able to discriminate between acceptable risks." But the alternative that she apparently prefers is to leave such difficult discriminating choices to each low-ranking "savior" who believes there may be a need to torture—and to a jury of peers to decide, on an ad hoc basis, whether he struck the appropriate balance.[2]

At bottom, my argument is not in favor of torture of any sort. It is against all forms of torture without accountability. Let us continue to reaffirm not only our opposition to torture but our opposition to the kind of hypocrisy that loudly denounces torture while discreetly closing our eyes to its increasing use.

The recent disclosure of significant abuses by military intelligence and military police officers in the

Abu Ghraib prison outside of Baghdad demonstrates what happens when high-ranking officials have a "don't ask, don't tell policy" toward the use of extraordinary pressures in interrogation. While our leaders in Washington and our commanders in the field adamantly denied the use of any form of torture—light or otherwise—a subtle message was being conveyed down the chain of command that intelligence and police officials on the ground could do what they had to do to obtain important information. If this had not been perceived by the soldiers as the message from above, there is no way the photographs they took would have been so openly distributed.

When the message is sent in this way—by a wink and nod—no lines are drawn, no guidelines issued, and no accountability accepted. The result was massive abuses by those on the ground, coupled with deniability by those at the top.

How much better it would have been if we required that any resort to extraordinary means—means other than routine interrogation—be authorized in advance by someone in authority and with accountability. If a warrant requirement of some kind had been in place, the low-ranking officers on the ground could not plausibly claim that they had been subtly (or secretly) authorized to do what they did, since the only acceptable form of authorization would be in writing. Nor could the high-ranking officials hide behind plausible deniability, since they would have been required to give the explicit author-

ization. Moreover, since authorization would have to go through the chain of command, limitations would have been imposed on allowable methods. These would not have included the kind of gratuitous humiliation apparently inflicted on these prisoners.

There are of course no guarantees that individual officers would not engage in abuses on their own, even with a warrant requirement. But the current excuse being offered—we had to do what we did to get information—would no longer be available, since there would be an authorized method of securing information in extraordinary cases by the use of extraordinary means. Finally, the requirement of securing advanced written approval would reduce the incidence of abuses, since it would be a rare case in which a high-ranking official, knowing that the record will eventually be made public, would authorize extraordinary methods—and never methods of the kind shown in the Abu Ghraib photographs.

NOTES

1. Professor Scarry characterizes the chapter on torture as "the centerpiece of his book, *Why Terrorism Works*." It is, in fact, a brief illustrative detour (32 pages out of 271) in a book about the broad policy issues surrounding terrorism.

2. The remainder of Professor Scarry's criticisms are fully answered in the body of my essay, and I leave it to the reader to decide who is making the "errors in reasoning."

27

Is Redistributive Taxation Wrong?

Nozick and His Critics

Modern nation-states, without exception, redistribute people's incomes and assets through taxation. Typically they take some money from the rich in order to benefit the poor (for example, Medicaid). And sometimes they take some money from the poor and redistribute it to the relatively wealthy (for example, U.S. farm subsidies). Under what circumstances, if any, is it morally legitimate for the State to take a portion of one person's income or assets and give it to someone else in order to increase the latter's welfare?

In the featured reading in this chapter, an excerpt from his influential book, *Anarchy, State and Utopia*, Robert Nozick argues that *redistributive* taxation is unjust (note that he does not argue that *all* taxation is unjust). If a person legitimately owns a good, Nozick argues, then the State is not entitled to take it from him in order to increase someone else's welfare, even someone who is very much worse off. The State may be entitled to tax him for other purposes, like defense, but it is not entitled to tax him as a means of redistributing wealth.

Nozick first analyzes what it takes to own something. There was a time when nobody owned anything. Now lots of people own lots of things. So somehow, people can *acquire* a property right to something that was not previously owned, and Nozick calls the principles that govern acquisition of previously unowned property "principles of justice in acquisition." Furthermore, once something is owned, ownership can be transferred to others. Ownership can be transferred in ways that are illegitimate (stealing it, for example) and others that are legitimate (buying it at a mutually agreed-upon price, giving it away, etc.). The principles governing the legitimate *transfer* of ownership Nozick calls "principles of justice in transfer." He then characterizes a class of theories of ownership that we will call "pure entitlement" theories. Roughly, you own something legitimately if and only if you acquire it through repeated applications of the two principles of acquisition.

A pure entitlement theory may well be incompatible with what Nozick calls an "end-state principle." One example of an end-state principle is the following version of extreme egalitarianism: The only legitimate distributions of holdings are those in which everyone owns holdings of the same value. Nozick introduces his famous Wilt Chamberlain analogy to both illustrate the difference between these two kinds of theories and to support the pure entitlement theories (for more on arguments from analogy, see section 4.1 of the Introduction). Chamberlain agrees to play basketball for a team provided he gets 25 cents from every ticket sold for every game he plays in. Suppose he becomes very rich in this way, richer than those who paid to see him play. Would some third party be justified in taking back some or all of those earnings and redistributing it among those who had paid to see Chamberlain in an effort to equalize income or wealth? Nozick is suggesting that redistributive taxation is like that.

But suppose that among the spectators at the game there are some people who cannot find work and who have children to feed and clothe and house. Isn't the State justified in taking *some* of Chamberlain's earnings to relieve the suffering of those children? Nozick introduces a second argument to show that the State does not have a right to *any* portion of Chamberlain's earnings for redistributive purposes—not even to help the children of those who are destitute. The basic idea is that people are entitled to the fruits of their own labor. To deprive a worker of some percentage of the fruits of his labor for redistribution to others is to violate the worker's right of self-ownership. It is to force him to work on behalf of others.

Alan H. Goldman also begins with intuitions about what holdings people are entitled to. If someone is entitled to some holding, he is also entitled to give it freely to another—for example, to his children. And if he is free to give it to his children, surely his children are entitled to keep it. However, "people are not entitled to socially contingent advantages that they don't deserve," and "people often don't deserve the monetary advantages they are given, for example, by their parents as children." Suppose a small percentage of the population ends up *inheriting* a large percentage of the total wealth generated in society, while a vast number of the children of those with no accumulated wealth are starving. Are the fabulously wealthy few entitled to retain all their inherited wealth in such circumstances? Goldman asks why we should accept the principles of the pure entitlement theory when those principles lead to conclusions we find clearly unacceptable—for example, the right of a minority of largely undeserving inheritors of wealth to keep that wealth while masses of unlucky poor starve. If a system of acquisition and transfer gives unfair advantages to some over others, on this account, then people can legitimately demand that redistributive taxation be used to moderate the worst outcomes of the rules of acquisition and transfer coupled with the initial undeserved advantages.

QUESTIONS FOR CONSIDERATION

In thinking about these arguments, the following may be useful questions to consider.

• In discussing the principle of justice in acquisition, Nozick spends a good deal of time on the Lockean proviso. John Locke, a seventeenth-century English philosopher, stipulated that one can legitimately acquire unowned resources *provided* one leaves "as much and as good" for others. Are there any resources of that sort left? Clearly, most of the *land* on the planet has now been appropriated. Most of the oil has been claimed by one body or another (states, corporations, individuals, and so on). What kinds of resources could satisfy the Lockean proviso? If the answer is "None," then does it follow that gross inequalities brought about by current acquisitions are unjust?

• Are there any resources that are effectively infinite so that the Lockean proviso always applies to them? Think of nonmaterial items that people sometimes claim ownership over—things such as musical works (or the copyright of musical works), poems, novels, inventions, medical cures, philosophical ideas, and so on. Did Mozart leave "as much and as good" to other composers? Does each successive composer diminish the stock of unowned musical compositions or not? If he does, does that mean he has less of a property right in those works than did the first composers (who more nearly satisfied the Lockean proviso)?

• If you own a resource, are you entitled to dispose of it as you see fit, to give it away to whomever you choose, or to destroy it if you no longer want it, and so on? Suppose you make a lucky break in research on AIDS, discovering a cure for it. Are you entitled to hoard all the revenue you could make on the patent of the cure? Are you entitled to destroy the stocks of the cure that you have made or your current knowledge of how to make it?

• Suppose someone gives you a famous artwork, say Picasso's *Guernica*. Are you, as the new owner, entitled to burn it in your fireplace to heat your living room?

• Suppose Bill Gates decides to buy the remains of the Amazon jungle. Is he entitled to burn it all down to make room for more cattle farms to supply McDonald's with beef for cheap hamburgers, even if it means that the world might run out of sufficient oxygen? (Gates himself, we may imagine, will have built a machine to generate a constant supply of oxygen for himself.) If states made it illegal for Gates to burn down the Amazon jungle in order that others might simply breathe, would that (according to the pure entitlement theory) be a violation of Gates's property rights? Would it be similar to redistributive taxation—taking something belonging to Gates (the jungle's power to generate oxygen) and distributing it among those who don't have enough oxygen to live? Would that be morally wrong?

Further Reading

Kearl, J. R. "Do Entitlements Imply That Taxation Is Theft?" *Philosophy and Public Affairs* 7 (Fall 1977): 74–81.

Michael, Mark A. "Redistributive Taxation, Self-Ownership and the Fruit of Labour." *Journal of Applied Philosophy* 14, no. 2 (1997): 137–46.

Narveson, Jan. "Property Rights: Original Acquisition and Lockean Provisos." *Public Affairs Quarterly* 13, no. 3 (1999): 205–27.

Skillen, Tony. "Active Citizenship as Political Obligation." *Radical Philosophy* no. 58 (1991): 10–13.

Robert Nozick

Distributive Justice

The Entitlement Theory

The subject of justice in holdings consists of three major topics. The first is the *original acquisition of holdings,* the appropriation of unheld things. This includes the issues of how unheld things may come to be held, the process, or processes, by which unheld things may come to be held, the things that may come to be held by these processes, the extent of what comes to be held by a particular process, and so on. We shall refer to the complicated truth about this topic, which we shall not formulate here, as the prin-

Excerpted from Robert Nozick, *Anarchy, State and Utopia* (New York: Basic Books, 1974). Reprinted by permission of Basic Books, a member of Perseus Books, L.L.C.

ciple of justice in acquisition. The second topic concerns the *transfer of holdings* from one person to another. By what processes may a person transfer holdings to another? How may a person acquire a holding from another who holds it? Under this topic come general descriptions of voluntary exchange, and gift and (on the other hand) fraud, as well as reference to particular conventional details fixed upon in a given society. The complicated truth about this subject (with placeholders for conventional details) we shall call the principle of justice in transfer. (And we shall suppose it also includes principles governing how a person may divest himself of a holding, passing it into an unheld state.)

If the world were wholly just, the following inductive definition would exhaustively cover the subject of justice in holdings.

1. A person who acquires a holding in accordance with the principle of justice in acquisition is entitled to that holding.
2. A person who acquires a holding in accordance with the principle of justice in transfer, from someone else entitled to the holding, is entitled to the holding.
3. No one is entitled to a holding except by (repeated) applications of 1 and 2.

The complete principle of distributive justice would say simply that a distribution is just if everyone is entitled to the holdings they possess under the distribution.

A distribution is just if it arises from another just distribution by legitimate means. The legitimate means of moving from one distribution to another are specified by the principle of justice in transfer. The legitimate first "moves" are specified by the principle of justice in acquisition. Whatever arises from a just situation by just steps is itself just. The means of change specified by the principle of justice in transfer preserve justice. As correct rules of inference are truth-preserving, and any conclusion deduced via repeated application of such rules from only true premises is itself true, so the means of transition from one situation to another specified by the principle of justice in transfer are justice-preserving, and any situation actually arising from repeated transitions in

accordance with the principle from a just situation is itself just. The parallel between justice-preserving transformations and truth-preserving transformations illuminates where it fails as well as where it holds. That a conclusion could have been deduced by truth-preserving means from premises that are true suffices to show its truth. That from a just situation a situation *could* have arisen via justice-preserving means does *not* suffice to show its justice. The fact that a thief's victims voluntarily *could* have presented him with gifts does not entitle the thief to his ill-gotten gains. Justice in holdings is historical; it depends upon what actually has happened. We shall return to this point later.

Not all actual situations are generated in accordance with the two principles of justice in holdings: the principle of justice in acquisition and the principle of justice in transfer. Some people steal from others, or defraud them, or enslave them, seizing their product and preventing them from living as they choose, or forcibly exclude others from competing in exchanges. None of these are permissible modes of transition from one situation to another. And some persons acquire holdings by means not sanctioned by the principle of justice in acquisition. The existence of past injustice (previous violations of the first two principles of justice in holdings) raises the third major topic under justice in holdings: the rectification of injustice in holdings. If past injustice has shaped present holdings in various ways, some identifiable and some not, what now, if anything, ought to be done to rectify these injustices? What obligations do the performers of injustice have toward those whose position is worse than it would have been had the injustice not been done? Or, than it would have been had compensation been paid promptly? How, if at all, do things change if the beneficiaries and those made worse off are not the direct parties in the act of injustice, but, for example, their descendants? Is an injustice done to someone whose holding was itself based upon an unrectified injustice? How far back must one go in wiping clean the historical slate of injustices? What may victims of injustice permissibly do in order to rectify the injustices being done to them, including the many injustices done by persons acting through their government? I do not know of a thorough or theoretically sophisticated treatment of such issues. . . .

The general outlines of the theory of justice in holdings are that the holdings of a person are just if he is entitled to them by the principles of justice in acquisition and transfer, or by the principle of rectification of injustice (as specified by the first two principles). If each person's holdings are just, then the total set (distribution) of holdings is just. To turn these general outlines into a specific theory we would have to specify the details of each of the three principles of justice in holdings: the principle of acquisition of holdings, the principle of transfer of holdings, and the principle of rectification of violations of the first two principles. I shall not attempt that task here. (Locke's principle of justice in acquisition is discussed below.)

HISTORICAL PRINCIPLES AND END-RESULT PRINCIPLES

The general outlines of the entitlement theory illuminate the nature and defects of other conceptions of distributive justice. The entitlement theory of justice in distribution is *historical;* whether a distribution is just depends upon how it came about. In contrast, *current time-slice principles* of justice hold that the justice of a distribution is determined by how things are distributed (who has what) as judged by some *structural* principle(s) of just distribution. A utilitarian who judges between any two distributions by seeing which has the greater sum of utility and, if the sums tie, applies some fixed equality criterion to choose the more equal distribution, would hold a current time-slice principle of justice. As would someone who had a fixed schedule of trade-offs between the sum of happiness and equality. According to a current time-slice principle, all that needs to be looked at, in judging the justice of a distribution, is who ends up with what; in comparing any two distributions one need look only at the matrix presenting the distributions. No further information need be fed into a principle of justice. It is a consequence of such principles of justice that any two structurally identical distributions are equally just. (Two distributions are structurally identical if they present the same profile, but perhaps have different persons occupying the particular slots. My having ten and your having five, and my having five and your having ten are structurally identical distributions.) Welfare economics is the theory of current time-slice principles of justice. The subject is conceived as operating on matrices representing only current information about distribution. This, as well as some of the usual conditions (for example, the choice of distribution is invariant under relabeling of columns), guarantees that welfare economics will be a current time-slice theory, with all of its inadequacies.

Most persons do not accept current time-slice principles as constituting the whole story about distributive shares. They think it relevant in assessing the justice of a situation to consider not only the distribution it embodies, but also how that distribution came about. If some persons are in prison for murder or war crimes, we do not say that to assess the justice of the distribution in the society we must look only at what this person has, and that person has, and that person has, . . . at the current time. We think it relevant to ask whether someone did something so that he *deserved* to be punished, deserved to have a lower share. Most will agree to the relevance of further information with regard to punishments and penalties. Consider also desired things. One traditional socialist view is that workers are entitled to the product and full fruits of their labor; they have earned it; a distribution is unjust if it does not give the workers what they are entitled to. Such entitlements are based upon some past history. No socialist holding this view would find it comforting to be told that because the actual distribution A happens to coincide structurally with the one he desires D, A therefore is no less just than D; it differs only in that the "parasitic" owners of capital receive under A what the workers are entitled to under D, and the workers receive under A what the owners are entitled to under D, namely very little. This socialist rightly, in my view, holds onto the notions of earning, producing, entitlement, desert, and so forth, and he rejects current time-slice principles that look only to the structure of the resulting set of holdings. (The set of holdings resulting from what? Isn't it implausible that how holdings are produced and come to exist has no effect at all on who should hold what?) His mistake lies in his view of what entitlements arise out of what sorts of productive processes.

We construe the position we discuss too narrowly by speaking of *current* time-slice principles. Nothing is changed if structural principles operate upon a time sequence of current time-slice profiles and, for example, give someone more now to counterbalance the less he has had earlier. A utilitarian or an egalitarian or any mixture of the two over time will inherit the difficulties of his more myopic comrades. He is not helped by the fact that *some* of the information others consider relevant in assessing a distribution is reflected, unrecoverably, in past matrices. Henceforth, we shall refer to such unhistorical principles of distributive justice, including the current time-slice principles, as *end-result principles* or *end-state principles.*

In contrast to end-result principles of justice, *historical principles* of justice hold that past circumstances or actions of people can create differential entitlements or differential deserts to things. An injustice can be worked by moving from one distribution to another structurally identical one, for the second, in profile the same, may violate people's entitlements or deserts; it may not fit the actual history.

PATTERNING

The entitlement principles of justice in holdings that we have sketched are historical principles of justice. To better understand their precise character, we shall distinguish them from another subclass of the historical principles. Consider, as an example, the principle of distribution according to moral merit. This principle requires that total distributive shares vary directly with moral merit; no person should have a greater share than anyone whose moral merit is greater. (If moral merit could be not merely ordered but measured on an interval or ratio scale, stronger principles could be formulated.) Or consider the principle that results by substituting "usefulness to society" for "moral merit" in the previous principle. Or instead of "distribute according to moral merit," or "distribute according to usefulness to society," we might con-

sider "distribute according to the weighted sum of moral merit, usefulness to society, and need," with the weights of the different dimensions equal. Let us call a principle of distribution *patterned* if it specifies that a distribution is to vary along with some natural dimension, weighted sum of natural dimensions, or lexicographic ordering of natural dimensions. And let us say a distribution is patterned if it accords with some patterned principle. (I speak of natural dimensions, admittedly without a general criterion for them, because for any set of holdings some artificial dimensions can be gimmicked up to vary along with the distribution of the set.) The principle of distribution in accordance with moral merit is a patterned historical principle, which specifies a patterned distribution. "Distribute according to I.Q." is a patterned principle that looks to information not contained in distributional matrices. It is not historical, however, in that it does not look to any past actions creating differential entitlements to evaluate a distribution; it requires only distributional matrices whose columns are labeled by I.Q. scores. The distribution in a society, however, may be composed of such simple patterned distributions, without itself being simply patterned. Different sectors may operate different patterns, or some combination of patterns may operate in different proportions across a society. A distribution composed in this manner, from a small number of patterned distributions, we also shall term "patterned." And we extend the use of "pattern" to include the overall designs put forth by combinations of end-state principles.

Almost every suggested principle of distributive justice is patterned: to each according to his moral merit, or needs, or marginal product, or how hard he tries, or the weighted sum of the foregoing, and so on. The principle of entitlement we have sketched is *not* patterned. . . . The set of holdings that results when some persons receive their marginal products, others win at gambling, others receive a share of their mate's income, others receive gifts from foundations, others receive interest on loans, others receive gifts from admirers, others receive returns on investment, others make for themselves much of what they have, others find things, and so on, will not be patterned. Heavy strands of patterns will run through it; significant portions of the variance in holdings will be accounted for by pattern-variables. If most people most of the time choose to transfer some of their entitlements to others only in exchange for something from them, then a large part of what many people hold will vary with what they held that others wanted. More details are provided by the theory of marginal productivity. But gifts to relatives, charitable donations, bequests to children, and the like, are not best conceived, in the first instance, in this manner. Ignoring the strands of pattern, let us suppose for the moment that a distribution actually arrived at by the operation of the principle of entitlement is random with respect to any pattern. Though the resulting set of holdings will be unpatterned, it will not be incomprehensible, for it can be seen as arising from the operation of a small number of principles. These principles specify how an initial distribution may arise (the principle of acquisition of holdings) and how distributions may be transformed into others (the principle of transfer of holdings). The process whereby the set of holdings is generated will be intelligible, though the set of holdings itself that results from this process will be unpatterned. . . .

How Liberty Upsets Patterns

It is not clear how those holding alternative conceptions of distributive justice can reject the entitlement conception of justice in holdings. For suppose a distribution favored by one of these non-entitlement conceptions is realized. Let us suppose it is your favorite one and let us call this distribution D_1; perhaps everyone has an equal share, perhaps shares vary in accordance with some dimension you treasure. Now suppose that Wilt Chamberlain is greatly in demand by basketball teams, being a great gate attraction. (Also suppose contracts run only for a year, with players being free agents.) He signs the following sort of contract with a team: In each home game, twenty-five cents from the price of each ticket of admission goes to him. (We ignore the question of whether he is "gouging" the owners, letting them look out for themselves.) The season starts, and people cheerfully attend his team's games; they buy their tickets, each time dropping a separate twenty-five cents of their admission price into a special box with Chamberlain's name on it. They are excited about seeing him play; it is worth the total admission price to them. Let us suppose that in one season one million persons attend his home games, and Wilt Chamberlain winds up with $250,000, a much larger sum than the average income and larger even than anyone else has. Is he entitled to this income? Is this new distribution D_2, unjust? If so, why? There is *no* question about whether each of the people was entitled to the control over the resources they held in D_1; because that was the distribution (your favorite) that (for the purposes of argument) we assumed was acceptable. Each of these persons *chose* to give twenty-five cents of their money to Chamberlain. They could have spent it on going to the movies, or on candy bars, or on copies of *Dissent* magazine, or of *Montly Review*. But they all, at least one million of them, converged on giving it to Wilt Chamberlain in exchange for watching him play basketball. If D_1 was a just distribution, and people voluntarily moved from it to D_2, transferring parts of their shares they were given under D_1 (what was it for if not to do something with?), isn't D_2 also just? If the people were entitled to dispose of the resources to which they were entitled (under D_1), didn't this include their being entitled to give it to, or exchange it with, Wilt Chamberlain? Can anyone else complain on grounds of justice? Each other person already has his legitimate share under D_1. Under D_1, there is nothing that anyone has that anyone else has a claim of justice against. After someone transfers something to Wilt Chamberlain, third parties *still* have their legitimate shares; *their* shares are not changed. By what process could such a transfer among two persons give rise to a legitimate claim of distributive justice on a portion of what was transferred, by a third party who had no claim of justice on any holding of the others *before* the transfer? To cut off objections irrelevant here, we might imagine the exchanges occurring in a socialist society, after hours. . . .

The general point illustrated by the Wilt Chamberlain example and the example of the entrepreneur in a socialist society is that no end-state principle or distributional patterned principle of justice can be continuously realized without continuous interference with people's lives. Any favored pattern would be transformed into one unfavored by the principle, by people choosing to act in various ways; for example, by people exchanging goods and services with other people, or giving things to other people, things the transferrers are entitled to under the favored distributional pattern. To maintain a pattern one must either continually interfere to stop people from transferring resources as they wish to, or continually (or periodically) interfere to take from some persons resources that others for some reason chose to transfer to them. (But if some time limit is to be set on how long people may keep resources others voluntarily transfer to them, why let them keep these resources for *any* period of time? Why not have immediate confiscation?) It might be objected that all persons voluntarily will choose to refrain from actions which would upset the pattern. This presupposes unrealistically (1) that all will most want to maintain the pattern (are those who don't, to be "reeducated" or forced to undergo "self-criticism"?), (2) that each can gather enough information about his own actions and the ongoing activities of others to discover which of his actions will upset the pattern, and (3) that diverse and far-flung persons can coordinate their actions to dovetail into the pattern. Compare the manner in which the market is neutral among persons' desires, as it reflects and transmits widely scattered information via prices, and coordinates persons' activities.

REDISTRIBUTION AND PROPERTY RIGHTS

. . . Proponents of patterned principles of distributive justice focus upon criteria for determining who is to receive holdings; they consider the reasons for which someone should have something, and also the total picture of holdings. Whether or not it is better to give than to receive, proponents of patterned principles ignore giving altogether. In considering the distribution of goods, income, and so forth, their theories are theories of recipient justice; they completely ignore any right a person might have to give something to

someone. Even in exchanges where each party is simultaneously giver and recipient, patterned principles of justice focus only upon the recipient role and its supposed rights. Thus discussions tend to focus on whether people (should) have a right to inherit, rather than on whether people (should) have a right to bequeath or on whether persons who have a right to hold also have a right to choose that others hold in their place. I lack a good explanation of why the usual theories of distributive justice are so recipient oriented; ignoring givers and transferrers and their rights is of a piece with ignoring producers and their entitlements. But why is it *all* ignored?

Patterned principles of distributive justice necessitate *re*distributive activities. The likelihood is small that any actual freely-arrived-at set of holdings fits a given pattern; and the likelihood is nil that it will continue to fit the pattern as people exchange and give. From the point of view of an entitlement theory, redistribution is a serious matter indeed, involving, as it does, the violation of people's rights. (An exception is those takings that fall under the principle of the rectification of injustices.) From other points of view, also, it is serious.

Taxation of earnings from labor is on a par with forced labor.[1] Some persons find this claim obviously true: taking the earnings of *n* hours labor is like taking *n* hours from the person; it is like forcing the person to work *n* hours for another's purpose. Others find the claim absurd. But even these, *if* they object to forced labor, would oppose forcing unemployed hippies to work for the benefit of the needy. And they would also object to forcing each person to work five extra hours each week for the benefit of the needy. But a system that takes five hours' wages in taxes does not seem to them like one that forces someone to work five hours, since it offers the person forced a wider range of choice in activities than does taxation in kind with the particular labor specified. (But we can imagine a gradation of systems of forced labor, from one that specifies a particular activity, to one that gives a choice among two activities, to . . . ; and so on up.) Furthermore, people envisage a system with something like a proportional tax on everything above the amount necessary for basic needs. Some think this does not force someone to work extra hours, since there is no fixed number of extra hours he is forced to work, and since he can avoid the tax entirely by earning only enough to cover his basic needs. This is a very uncharacteristic view of forcing for those who *also* think people are forced to do something *whenever* the alternatives they face are considerably worse. However, *neither* view is correct. The fact that others intentionally intervene, in violation of a side constraint against aggression, to threaten force to limit the alternatives, in this case to paying taxes or (presumably the worse alternative) bare subsistence, makes the taxation system one of forced labor and distinguishes it from other cases of limited choices which are not forcings.

The man who chooses to work longer to gain an income more than sufficient for his basic needs prefers some extra goods or services to the leisure and activities he could perform during the possible nonworking hours; whereas the man who chooses not to work the extra time prefers the leisure activities to the extra goods or services he could acquire by working more. Given this, if it would be illegitimate for a tax system to seize some of a man's leisure (forced labor) for the purpose of serving the needy, how can it be legitimate for a tax system to seize some of a man's goods for that purpose? Why should we treat the man whose happiness requires certain material goods or services differently from the man whose preferences and desires make such goods unnecessary for his happiness? Why should the man who prefers seeing a movie (and who has to earn money for a ticket) be open to the required call to aid the needy, while the person who prefers looking at a sunset (and hence need earn no extra money) is not? Indeed, isn't it surprising that redistributionists choose to ignore the man whose pleasures are so easily attainable without extra labor, while adding yet another burden to the poor unfortunate who must work for his pleasures? If anything, one would have expected the reverse. Why is the person with the nonmaterial or nonconsumption desire allowed to proceed unimpeded to his most favored feasible alternative, whereas the man whose pleasures or desires involve material things and who must work for extra money (thereby serving whomever considers his activities valuable enough to pay him) is constrained in what he can realize?

Perhaps there is no difference in principle. And perhaps some think the answer concerns merely administrative convenience. (These questions and issues will not disturb those who think that forced labor to serve the needy or to realize some favored end-state pattern is acceptable.) . . .

What sort of right over others does a legally institutionalized end-state pattern give one? The central core of the notion of a property right in X, relative to which other parts of the notion are to be explained, is the right to determine what shall be done with X; the right to choose which of the constrained set of options concerning X shall be realized or attempted. The constraints are set by other principles or laws operating in the society; in our theory, by the Lockean rights people possess (under the minimal state). My property rights in my knife allow me to leave it where I will, but not in your chest. I may choose which of the acceptable options involving the knife is to be realized. This notion of property helps us to understand why earlier theorists spoke of people as having property in themselves and their labor. They viewed each person as having a right to decide what would become of himself and what he would do, and as having a right to reap the benefits of what he did.

When end-result principles of distributive justice are built into the legal structure of a society, they (as do most patterned principles) give each citizen an enforceable claim to some portion of the total social product; that is, to some portion of the sum total of the individually and jointly made products. This total product is produced by individuals laboring, using means of production others have saved to bring into existence, by people organizing production or creating means to produce new things or things in a new way. It is on this batch of individual activities that patterned distributional principles give each individual an enforceable claim. Each person has a claim to the activities and the products of other persons, independently of whether the other persons enter into particular relationships that give rise to these claims, and independently of whether they voluntarily take these claims upon themselves, in charity or in exchange for something.

Whether it is done through taxation on wages or on wages over a certain amount, or through seizure of profits, or through there being a big *social pot* so that it's not clear what's coming from where and what's going where, patterned principles of distributive justice involve appropriating the actions of other persons. Seizing the results of someone's labor is equivalent to seizing hours from him and directing him to carry on various activities. If people force you to do certain work, or unrewarded work, for a certain period of time, they decide what you are to do and what purposes your work is to serve apart from your decisions. This process whereby they take this decision from you makes them a *part-owner* of you; it gives them a property right in you. Just as having such partial control and power of decision, by right, over an animal or inanimate object would be to have a property right in it.

End-state and most patterned principles of distributive justice institute (partial) ownership by others of people and their actions and labor. These principles involve a shift from the classical liberals' notion of self-ownership to a notion of (partial) property rights in *other* people. . . .

LOCKE'S THEORY OF ACQUISITION

. . . [W]e must introduce an additional bit of complexity into the structure of the entitlement theory. This is best approached by considering Locke's attempt to specify a principle of justice in acquisition. Locke views property rights in an unowned object as originating through someone's mixing his labor with it. This gives rise to many questions. What are the boundaries of what labor is mixed with? If a private astronaut clears a place on Mars, has he mixed his labor with (so that he comes to own) the whole planet, the whole uninhabited universe, or just a particular plot? Which plot does an act bring under ownership? The minimal (possibly disconnected) area such that an act decreases entropy in that area, and not elsewhere? Can virgin land (for the purposes of ecological investigation by high-flying airplane) come under ownership by a Lockean process? Building a fence around a territory presumably would make one the owner of only the fence (and the land immediately underneath it).

Why does mixing one's labor with something make one the owner of it? Perhaps because one owns one's labor, and so one comes to own a previously unowned thing that becomes permeated with what one owns. Ownership seeps over into the rest. But why isn't mixing what I own with what I don't own a way of losing what I own rather than a way of gaining what I don't? If I own a can of tomato juice and spill it in the sea so that its molecules (made radioactive, so I can check this) mingle evenly throughout the sea, do I thereby come to own the sea, or have I foolishly dissipated my tomato juice? Perhaps the idea, instead, is that laboring on something improves it and makes it more valuable; and anyone is entitled to own a thing whose value he has created. (Reinforcing this, perhaps, is the view that laboring is unpleasant. If some people made things effortlessly, as the cartoon characters in *The Yellow Submarine* trail flowers in their wake, would they have lesser claim to their own products whose making didn't *cost* them anything?) Ignore the fact that laboring on something may make it less valuable (spraying pink enamel paint on a piece of driftwood that you have found). Why should one's entitlement extend to the whole object rather than just to the *added value* one's labor has produced? . . . No workable or coherent value-added property scheme has yet been devised, and any such scheme presumably would fall to objections (similar to those) that fell the theory of Henry George.

It will be implausible to view improving an object as giving full ownership to it, if the stock of unowned objects that might be improved is limited. For an object's coming under one person's ownership changes the situation of all others. Whereas previously they were at liberty (in Hohfeld's sense) to use the object, they now no longer are. This change in the situation of others (by removing their liberty to act on a previously unowned object) need not worsen their situation. If I appropriate a grain of sand from Coney Island, no one else may now do as they will with *that* grain of sand. But there are plenty of other grains of sand left for them to do the same with. Or if not grains of sand, then other things. Alternatively, the things I do with the grain of sand I appropriate might improve the position of others, counterbalancing their loss of the liberty to use that grain. The crucial point is whether appropriation of an unowned object worsens the situation of others.

Locke's proviso that there be "enough and as good left in common for others" is meant to ensure that the situation of others is not worsened. (If this proviso is met is there any motivation for his further condition of nonwaste?) It is often said that this proviso once held but now no longer does. But there appears to be an argument for the conclusion that if the proviso no longer holds, then it cannot ever have held so as to yield permanent and inheritable property rights. Consider the first person Z for whom there is not enough and as good left to appropriate. The last person Y to appropriate left Z without his previous liberty to act on an object, and so worsened Z's situation. So Y's appropriation is not allowed under Locke's proviso. Therefore the next to last person X to appropriate left Y in a worse position, for X's act ended permissible appropriation. Therefore X's appropriation wasn't permissible. But then the appropriator two from last, W, ended permissible appropriation and so, since it worsened X's position, W's appropriation wasn't permissible. And so on back to the first person A to appropriate a permanent property right.

This argument, however, proceeds too quickly. Someone may be made worse off by another's appropriation in two ways: first, by losing the opportunity to improve his situation by a particular appropriation or any one; and second, by no longer being able to use freely (without appropriation) what he perviously could. A *stringent* requirement that another not be made worse off by an appropriation would exclude the first way if nothing else counterbalances the diminution in opportunity, as well as the second. A *weaker* requirement would exclude the second way, though not the first. With the weaker requirement, we cannot zip back so quickly from Z to A, as in the above argument; for though person Z can no longer *appropriate,* there may remain some for him to *use* as before. In this case Y's appropriation would not violate the weaker Lockean condition. (With less remaining that people are at liberty to use, users might face more inconvenience, crowding, and so on; in that way the situation of others might be worsened, unless appropriation stopped far short of such a point.) It is arguable that no one legitimately can complain if the

weaker provision is satisfied. However, since this is less clear than in the case of the more stringent proviso, Locke may have intended this stringent proviso by "enough and as good" remaining, and perhaps he meant the non-waste condition to delay the end point from which the argument zips back.

The Proviso

Whether or not Locke's particular theory of appropriation can be spelled out so as to handle various difficulties, I assume that any adequate theory of justice in acquisition will contain a proviso similar to the weaker of the ones we have attributed to Locke. A process normally giving rise to a permanent bequeathable property right in a previously unowned thing will not do so if the position of others no longer at liberty to use the thing is thereby worsened. It is important to specify *this* particular mode of worsening the situation of others, for the proviso does not encompass other modes. It does not include the worsening due to more limited opportunities to appropriate (the first way above, corresponding to the more stringent condition), and it does not include how I "worsen" a seller's position if I appropriate materials to make some of what he is selling, and then enter into competition with him. Someone whose appropriation otherwise would violate the proviso still may appropriate provided he compensates the others so that their situation is not thereby worsened; unless he does compensate these others, his appropriation will violate the proviso of the principle of justice in acquisition and will be an illegitimate one. A theory of appropriation incorporating this Lockean proviso will handle correctly the cases (objections to the theory lacking the proviso) where someone appropriates the total supply of something necessary for life.

A theory which includes this proviso in its principle of justice in acquisition must also contain a more complex principle of justice in transfer. Some reflection of the proviso about appropriation constrains later actions. If my appropriating all of a certain substance violates the Lockean proviso, then so does my appropriating some and purchasing all the rest from others who obtained it without otherwise violating the Lockean proviso. If the proviso excludes someone's appropriating all the drinkable water in the world, it also excludes his purchasing it all. (More weakly, and messily, it may exclude his charging certain prices for some of his supply.) This proviso (almost?) never will come into effect; the more someone acquires of a scarce substance which others want, the higher the price of the rest will go, and the more difficult it will become for him to acquire it all. But still, we can imagine, at least, that something like this occurs: someone makes simultaneous secret bids to the separate owners of a substance, each of whom sells assuming he can easily purchase more from the other owners; or some natural catastrophe destroys all of the supply of something except that in one person's possession. The total supply could not be permissibly appropriated by one person at the beginning. His later acquisition of it all does not show that the original appropriation violated the proviso (even by a reverse argument similar to the one above that tried to zip back from Z to A). Rather, it is the combination of the original appropriation *plus* all the later transfers and actions that violates the Lockean proviso.

Each owner's title to his holding includes the historical shadow of the Lockean proviso on appropriation. This excludes his transferring it into an agglomeration that does violate the Lockean proviso and excludes his using it in a way, in coordination with others or independently of them, so as to violate the proviso by making the situation of others worse than their baseline situation. Once it is known that someone's ownership runs afoul of the Lockean proviso, there are stringent limits on what he may do with (what it is difficult any longer unreservedly to call) "his property." Thus a person may not appropriate the only water hole in a desert and charge what he will. Nor may he charge what he will if he possesses one, and unfortunately it happens that all the water holes in the desert dry up, except for his. This unfortunate circumstance, admittedly no fault of his, brings into operation the Lockean proviso and limits his property rights. Similarly, an owner's property right in the only island in an area does not allow him to order a castaway from a shipwreck off his island as a trespasser, for this would violate the Lockean proviso.

Notice that the theory does not say that owners do have these rights, but that the rights are overridden to avoid some catastrophe. (Overridden rights do not disappear; they leave a trace of a sort absent in the cases under discussion.) There is no such external (and *ad hoc?*) overriding. Considerations internal to the theory of property itself, to its theory of acquisition and appropriation, provide the means for handling such cases. The results, however, may be coextensive with some condition about catastrophe, since the baseline for comparison is so low as compared to the productiveness of a society with private appropriation that the question of the Lockean proviso being violated arises only in the case of catastrophe (or a desert-island situation).

The fact that someone owns the total supply of something necessary for others to stay alive does *not* entail that his (or anyone's) appropriation of anything left some people (immediately or later) in a situation worse than the baseline one. A medical researcher who synthesizes a new substance that effectively treats a certain disease and who refuses to sell except on his terms does not worsen the situation of others by depriving them of whatever he has appropriated. The others easily can possess the same materials he appropriated; the researcher's appropriation or purchase of chemicals didn't make those chemicals scarce in a way so as to violate the Lockean proviso. Nor would someone else's purchasing the total supply of the synthesized substance from the medical researcher. The fact that the medical researcher uses easily available chemicals to synthesize the drug no more violates the Lockean proviso than does the fact that the only surgeon able to perform a particular operation eats easily obtainable food in order to stay alive and to have the energy to work. This shows that the Lockean proviso is not an "end-state principle"; it focuses on a particular way that appropriative actions affect others, and not on the structure of the situation that results.

Intermediate between someone who takes all of the public supply and someone who makes the total supply out of easily obtainable substances is someone who appropriates the total supply of something in a way that does not deprive the others of it. For example, someone finds a new substance in an out-of-the-way place. He discovers that it effectively treats a certain disease and appropriates the total supply. He does not worsen the situation of others; if he did not stumble upon the substance no one else would have, and the others would remain without it. However, as time passes, the likelihood increases that others would have come across the substance; upon this fact might be based a limit to his property right in the substance so that others are not below their baseline position; for example, its bequest might be limited. The theme of someone worsening another's situation by depriving him of something he otherwise would possess may also illuminate the example of patents. An inventor's patent does not deprive others of an object which would not exist if not for the inventor. Yet patents would have this effect on others who independently invent the object. Therefore, these independent inventors, upon whom the burden of proving independent discovery may rest, should not be excluded from utilizing their own invention as they wish (including selling it to others). Furthermore, a known inventor drastically lessens the chances of actual independent invention. For persons who know of an invention usually will not try to reinvent it, and the notion of independent discovery here would be murky at best. Yet we may assume that in the absence of the original invention, sometime later someone else would have come up with it. This suggests placing a time limit on patents,

as a rough rule of thumb to approximate how long it would have taken, in the absence of knowledge of the invention, for independent discovery.

I believe that the free operation of a market system will not actually run afoul of the Lockean proviso. . . . If this is correct, the proviso will not play a very important role in the activities of protective agencies and will not provide a significant opportunity for future state action. Indeed, were it not for the effects of previous *illegitimate* state action, people would not think the possibility of the proviso's being violated as of more interest than any other logical possibility. (Here I make an empirical historical claim; as does someone who disagrees with this.) This completes our indication of the complication in the entitlement theory introduced by the Lockean proviso.

NOTE

1. I am unsure as to whether the arguments I present below show that such taxation merely *is* forced labor; so that "is on a par with" means "is one kind of." Or alternatively, whether the arguments emphasize the great similarities between such taxation and forced labor, to show it is plausible and illuminating to view such taxation in the light of forced labor.

ALAN H. GOLDMAN

The Entitlement Theory of Distributive Justice

According to Robert Nozick,[1] a social distribution is just if it is arrived at through legitimate acquisitions and transfers. Original acquisitions of property will be just if they violate no rights of others, e.g., if the goods are not already owned or claimed and if their appropriation does not leave others in a worse position (other than simply more limited opportunities to appropriate). Thereafter transfers are legitimate when voluntary. We are to measure the legitimacy of a distribution only according to how it came about, i.e., whether property to which owners were entitled was freely transferred or exchanged without violation of rights. Such historical principles are held incompatible in application with what Nozick appropriately terms *end-state principles,* principles that aim at some favored pattern of distribution like equality, maximization of average or mean utility, or the difference principle, since legitimate acquisitions and transfers are unlikely to result in any fixed pattern. If a fixed pattern were accidentally and momentarily achieved, it would immediately be upset by further free exchange, e.g., paying for entertainment when entertainers already have more than allowable under any likely end-state principle. What Nozick clearly has in mind as an embodiment of his just historical principles is the operation of free market exchange, without state controls (other than enforcement of contracts) or forced redistribution. All end-state principles imply that persons can have claims on others' property, but this contradicts the betterentrenched historical principles which imply that persons are entitled to what they acquire through free exchanges.

Why do our moral intuitions rebel at such unhindered operation of a free market economy as sole distributor of advantages? Have we come so far from it only through bureaucratic power-seeking or misguided good intentions? The deepest moral problem with such operation is that it allows or rather forces some to start in life with nothing but economic handicaps and prospects of misery and deprivation, through injustices done to their ancestors or perhaps simply through their stupidity. These factors may be impossible to separate in practice, but in any case we cannot see why children should be held responsible for the sins or omissions of their ancestors, or why they must remain almost inevitably locked within material and cultural deprivation because of their initial environments. Our intuition is that no system could be just which would allow this to an even greater extent than occurs in our present somewhat redistributive society; nor, as I will show, do Nozick's arguments force us from this initial reaction.

Let us analyze the sources of plausibility for the pure entitlement theory—why are certain individuals entitled to their holdings? We want to say first that persons are entitled to what they earn, that they are entitled to those rewards of their socially productive efforts which others are willing to pay. Second, we will admit that they are entitled to what they can freely appropriate even when this does not result in

---

Alan H. Goldman, "The Entitlement Theory of Distributive Justice," *Journal of Philosophy* 73 (1976): 823–35. Reprinted by permission of the *Journal of Philosophy.*

benefits to others, as long as their appropriation does not directly worsen the lot of others (this will have little application in an age when there is little left to legitimately appropriate as opposed to trade for). Third, if persons are entitled to their holdings, they seem entitled to control their further distribution, to spend or give them as they like, e.g., on entertainment or to their children. It seems, finally, that the recipients must then be entitled to the assets if the givers were truly allowed to disburse them as they pleased. The right to give money to your children amounts to no right at all if the money may be confiscated as soon as it is in their hands.

On a deeper level we may ask further whether any more general principles justify these separate intuitions regarding entitlements. Do any moral features of free exchange and the market system which these modes of acquisition and transfer exemplify make that system prima facie morally preferable to alternatives? The principle that comes most readily to mind is maximizing freedom. Of course attempts at utilitarian justification have been made—we might view *The Wealth of Nations* as one—and we could conceive of arguments to the effect that totally free exchange satisfies the difference principle of Rawls. Empirical evidence seems to fall against such arguments, however, although the issue is still debated by economists and congressmen. Nozick would presumably dismiss such justifications for a different reason: he seems to think them inconsistent in that they call for patterns of distribution which must be upset by free exchange. But the principle of maximizing freedom is not an end-state principle that could be applied to current timeslice distributions of other goods in the way principles of welfare can be applied. It might seem rather to call for those historical rules of acquisition and transfer embodied in the unhindered exchange market. It certainly seems that what is morally noteworthy about free exchange is that it is free (not simply that each particular exchange tends to benefit both parties).

The justification of rules of entitlement themselves is relative to some more general conception of good or right which underlies them and, in application, to other moral rules embodying a system of values. It seems that, if principles of free acquisition and trans-fer are indeed to take precedence over all other claims on material property, it must be because we place a higher value on freedom than upon other goods like life (is this possible?), equality, or welfare, and because free exchange alone recognizes a maximum freedom of action for individuals. Nozick, however, objects to talk of maximization of any good as the goal of moral theory, and points out that his is not a maximization-of-freedom theory as utilitarianism is a maximization-of-welfare theory. We are not, for example, permitted to violate the rights of an individual in order to maximize the rights or freedom of others. Rather the underlying moral theory is Kantian in that it treats individuals as inviolable—we may never treat an individual without his consent as a means to the good of others or to any maximization of social good.

Thus the general principle from which Nozick's rules of transfer and acquisition must be seen to follow is the second formulation of Kant's categorical imperative. But if the principles of acquisition and transfer are meant to follow from the rule "Never treat another as a means without his consent," we want to examine more closely whether they do avoid such treatment as distinct from all alternatives. I admit at least the coherency of the distinction between maximizing freedoms or rights and prohibiting their violation in all cases. But it still seems that the Kantian prohibition is a way of expressing the absolute priority of the freedom of individuals over their welfare, for example. In any case we may raise questions at two levels: first, regarding the status of Nozick's principles of acquisition and transfer within the Kantian framework—do they fail to violate the Kantian injunction, and do all redistributive systems do so?; second, must we recognize the priority of individual freedom over all social goods expressed in Kant's principle? (I speak of the Kantian injunction as narrowly interpreted, but will argue that the spirit of Kant's injunction militates against the narrow interpretation Nozick gives it.) In deference to Nozick's refusal to remain too long on this level of moral theory, let us return for a moment to his specific entitlement principles, with these background questions in mind to be answered later.

As pointed out above, we want to say that (1) people are entitled to what they earn through socially productive efforts, and also that (2) they are entitled to spend their own earnings as they like. (Of course we can define "socially productive efforts" so as to build in end-state principles, but since this seems to violate the Kantian injunction and does not allow people to decide what they consider beneficial, I leave it for later.) (2) seems to follow from (1). It follows from (2) that (3) if these people desire to give away their earnings, then those to whom they are given must be entitled to them. The problem with this is that we also want to say that (4) people are not entitled to socially contingent advantages they don't deserve, and (5) people often don't deserve the monetary advantages they are given, for example, by their parents as children. (4) and (5) are clearly incompatible with (3). The fact that an individual has a moral right to what he acquires through effort and has the consequent right to do with those earnings what he wants does not seem to make it less morally arbitrary that one child starts off with all advantages and another with none. The right of the receiver here is totally dependent upon the right of the giver and cannot be independently claimed by him. If, as in traditional theories of distributive justice, we concentrate on the right of the receiver, that is, on (4) and (5), we are likely to limit the range of (3); whereas if, as Nozick does, we direct attention mainly to (1) and (2), we are likely to discount (4) and (5). We can use the first strategy to argue against Nozick that, since the right to give is correlative to the right to receive, it should not be construed more extensively than its counterpart. But of course he can simply reply that, given the correlation between giving and receiving, rights of receiving should not be construed as more limited than rights to give. Is there not some resolution or middle ground here?

First, we might discount the last reply by consideration of certain other analogous limitations on rights. Nozick himself admits that one's right to engage in a cooperative activity is limited by others' rights to do so. My right to hear different political views and thus various speakers on my campus is limited by the fact that some speakers I might want to hear are in jail and hence have no right to travel to speak. Insofar as giving is a relational or cooperative right, we might claim similarly that limitations generally take precedence over extensions from one participant to the other. Free exchanges are clearly to be limited by other rights—I cannot spend money to purchase nerve gas, since this violates others' rights to be free of unnecessary risk. Of course there is a question regarding gifts whether, in addition to not deserving their benefits, the recipients in this case violate others' rights in receiving them, and I will address that question shortly.

Even, however, if we refuse to allow the generalization regarding the precedence of limitations to this case and even if we continue to concentrate upon the right of the giver, i.e., the parent, that right does not seem to imply a right of the receiver to all future benefits accruing to his unequal start. We might, for example, allow the right to receive the total amount of money, but still claim the right to tax future interest or earnings on it for social benefits or remedial institutions. Since the receiver cannot claim his right to the money and its continued earning power with the same moral force as the giver can claim his right to bequeath the initial amount, the receiver cannot complain if later earnings are taxed. Furthermore, given that the receiver's future earning power in general, e.g., the job he gets, is also partially a function of his undeserved unequal start, we might tax in order to equalize somewhat that score as well. It might be objected in behalf of the *giver* that he meant to bequeath not only the capital, but the capital with its future earning power as well as the advantages it bestows, and that the capital is of far less use without these. It is doubtful, however, that a person earns the right to give more than the amount he earns, and in any case we would be taxing only a marginal amount of the future earnings. But the full answer to this awaits discussion of whether the rights of deprived children are violated by the unhindered operation of free transfer. We may admit a certain limitation on the right to give (and control future use) and yet argue that this results not only in a maximization of freedom, but in a satisfaction of Kant's injunction more sympathetic to its spirit.

We should first note an objection of Nozick to a point above, namely that, since future position and earning power are to a large extent determined by undeserved unequal starting position, we can tax these future rewards without legitimate complaint.

He argues that attributing success to initial position denigrates the degree of effort and autonomous choice involved, amounting to an overly deterministic and pessimistic view of human nature. In fact, however, the empirical evidence seems to support such a claim, if we compare the percentage of those who succeed starting with all advantages versus those who succeed starting with economic and cultural deprivation. (We have not yet justified taxing the latter.) Initial advantage constitutes neither a necessary nor a sufficient condition for future success (I assume a barometer for success), but I will stake this much of the argument on the belief that in our present society (and certainly in the society Nozick envisages) it comes statistically close to amounting to both. (In any case why should those with initial disadvantages have to work harder for success?) Second, those who do succeed could feel more certain of this as a reflection of effort or worth, within a system with remedial institutions to make competition more stiff and fair. Such a system, rather than lowering these persons' dignity and sense of achievement, would ensure that their accomplishments were recognized as such rather than regarded as the results of undeserved good fortune. It is true that those who do not succeed within a fair system may feel worse with the recognition that this is non-accidental. But there are other indicators of worth besides monetary success or even social productivity, and in any case we are after fairness, concerned with who is on top and who on bottom and why, not with minimizing the feelings of resentment of those who occupy the lower ranks.

Nozick has a further argument against redistributive taxation independent of these considerations regarding the giver-receiver relation, which will lead directly to our reassessment of the Kantian injunction in its relation to forced redistribution. He claims that such taxation is equivalent to forced labor—to take the results or earnings of someone's labor amounts to making him work a certain amount of time against his will purely for the benefit of others. This is to be equated with the doctrine that some persons (the beneficiaries of redistribution or the state) have property rights in others, and this seems clearly to violate the Kantian rights of those others not to be treated as means for the welfare of those who benefit.

Nozick bolsters the argument further with examples of cases in which individuals have no right to make demands on the free activity of others even when their welfare depends upon such demands. Although Toscanini's orchestra members' welfare depended upon his continuing to conduct, they had no right to demand he not retire.

Once taxation is equated with forced labor, the argument seems to go through. But we must first question this equation more closely and, second, ask whether nonredistributive systems might not involve features plausibly construed as in violation of Kant's principle as well. There is certainly an initial distinction between what we usually picture as forced labor, e.g., chain gangs or Siberian work camps, and taxation even without consent. In the case of taxation a person is still free to work as long as he likes and at the job he chooses. He is simply required to contribute a percentage of earnings, presumably under a certain level of marginal utility to him, to those for whom it has a far greater marginal utility. Thus a demand on the conduct of Toscanini's life, for example, is far different from a demand on a marginal amount of his income.

Perhaps an equally damaging point is that differences in earnings are generally not a function of effort expended or hours worked. They are more often an indirect reflection of the initial undeserved advantages of that individual for obtaining that job. For this reason we can in no way equate redistributive taxation, which takes a portion of those extra earnings to provide for basic needs of those who lack such advantages, with making the individual work longer or harder for their benefit. Nor are the hours a person works very often a function of how much he wants to earn, so that if he doesn't earn as much as he needs in a given week he simply works longer to make up the difference. This may be true for those on the bottom of the economic scale whom redistribution benefits, but certainly almost never for those wealthy enough to lose through equitable social redistribution. Thus the equation of taxation for redistributive purposes with forced labor does not hold up in the face of all these disanalogies. And the claim that taxation involves using a *person* (as opposed to some of the money he acquires) as a means without his consent and therefore violates the second formulation of the categorical imperative would require an extremely stretched interpretation of that principle.

The other assumed side of Nozick's position requires closer scrutiny as well, the question whether an economic system supported partly by those whose wages do not allow decent living, while others are maintained by that system in soft jobs for the acquisition of which they had initial advantages, does not more clearly violate a faithful rendering of the injunction against using persons as means. The ability and freedom to frame a meaningful life plan for oneself, which Nozick sees as underlying the demand to respect the autonomy of the individual, is denied to those who lack conditions that render such plans practicable. But for him this question does not arise, since he views the system of free exchange as based throughout on consent. Admittedly, the consent is often restricted—it may be a choice of working at a particular unpleasant low-paying job or starving. But Nozick points out that not all constraints on actions render them involuntary—the fact that I cannot choose to fly rather than walk to work does not render my choice of walking illusory. His criterion here is that restricted consent is not rendered involuntary unless those actions of others which constitute the restraints violate the rights of the person in question. My working as a professor when I would prefer to sing opera since other more competent baritones have been chosen for that profession still leaves my choice of profession voluntary (even if all other positions are taken?); my working as a professor under threats from avid students is not voluntary since my rights are violated in this case. But to use this criterion to justify a free market system in terms of consent is to beg the question of whether persons' rights are violated by that system.

The central question regarding the application of Kant's principle to the choice among rival social and economic systems is whether it violates the injunction against treating people as means to require or force certain individuals to help others in need by giving up some marginal amount of their earnings. It is clear that we do not violate the principle when we require that individuals not harm others or detract from their welfare in seeking their own satisfaction,

and Nozick holds that the state violates no rights in enforcing this principle. Can the difference between the injunction not to harm others and the demand to help others in need be construed as so great that we violate the fundamental principle of morals in enforcing the second but follow it in enforcing the first? Nozick would presumably claim that the difference in the two cases is that, whereas it is moral to help others in need, no one can claim a right to be helped, and since people can claim rights to their property, we cannot enforce the demand to help in the name of justice—in fact to do so would be to violate the rights of property owners in treating them as means to others' welfare.

It is interesting to note in this context that Kant meant the second formulation of the categorical imperative to be equivalent to the first, the notion of acting under moral rules applied equally to all. It is also interesting that one of Kant's own examples of the application of the first principle involves the command to help others in need, under the claim that no one would will not to be helped when in need himself. A case could be made from this that a society with a set of rules of acquisition and transfer in which some are in need and not helped violates the first formulation of the principle in its rules and hence the second as well; that an economic system in which some prosper partly through the consumption and labor of those who, because of their initial positions (determined by the prior operation of the system), never have human needs filled, embodies rules that treat the latter individuals merely as means. This is equivalent to the claim that such a system embodies rules that could not be willed universally to apply in all conditions or could not be willed by anyone with the possibility of role switches (from a Rawlsian initial position).

It might be replied again that the first formulation of Kant's principle shows only that not helping others in need is immoral, not that the needy have a right to be helped or that this is a question of justice in which the state has a right to interfere. This much could be answered by pointing out that if, when attempting to will universally (playing the role of legislator in a "kingdom of ends"), we place ourselves in the position of someone in need, we undoubtedly not only would want to be helped or to be answered favorably when begging for help, but would want to be able to demand help as a right so that the need for begging with its additional degradation would not arise. We would want not to await the beneficence of others as a hungry dog might do, but to be able to demand satisfaction of basic needs as a right of human beings in virtue of their worth or dignity. If the demand for satisfaction then becomes a right according to Kant's method of generating rules and if the state has the right to enforce rights or prevent their violation, then the state has the right of redistributive taxation, at least for this purpose.[2]

But Nozick has a further two-step argument to show that need does not create a right to the property of others. He first points out that we do not recognize such rights outside a mutual social context—one Robinson Crusoe who is faring very badly does not have a claim to the fruits of another's labor even when the other man is prospering; nor do we recognize claims of all people in the world in need upon our property. The second step consists in a challenge to stipulate what social cooperation adds to this picture in order to create the rights in question. I admit with Nozick that the difference does not lie in the fact that assets somehow become collective when a society is formed, nor in the fact that those on top benefit from social cooperation (since those on bottom are perhaps also better off than Robinson Crusoe). Part of the answer here is that, whereas in the case of Robinson Crusoe differences between their conditions are due to differences in natural assets or labor expended, in the social context of a relatively free market economy, differences are often due to unequal starts determined only by the prior operation of the conventional system itself. If the system had been set up differently, then the differences would not now exist to the same degree; therefore the system is responsible for lessening their effects somewhat.

A deeper answer can again be spelled out in Kantian terms in relation to what it means to enter a single moral community with others or to consider oneself part of such a community. Part of what this means is to recognize the common humanity of others and their moral equality. If this recognition is to be given content as well as form, it means that the rules

one accepts within such a community must not only have equal application to all, but operate for the common good of all. This is expressed by Kant in the demand to place yourself in the position of another, i.e., under a different set of conditions, when attempting to will certain actions or rules, and by Rawls in his banning special advantages in the initial position from which rules are chosen. It means that there must be a presumption within the rules of an equality of conditions arising from common human needs, from which deviations must be justified. That this presumption operates on the level of moral intuition is clear from the fact that, although we feel uncomfortable if persons are treated differently or gain different benefits when no relevant difference between them has been found, we do not feel uncomfortable about treating people the same or giving them equal shares without finding a relevant sameness (other than a common humanity).

Nozick admits that before the operation of specific rules of entitlement or in the absence of satisfaction of those rules by the individuals in question there is a presumption of equal distributive shares of any good to be divided. Yet he claims that when such rules are in operation goods will generally be divided according to them, and equality becomes one type of end-state pattern incompatible with the operation of the rules. But if deviations from equality must be justified in the absence of such rules, it seems that this important presumption must have some consideration in the choice of rules themselves, must act as a constraint upon which principles are chosen. The rules must be justified not only in terms of the freedom to acquire and transfer (and how much of that freedom do those on the bottom have?) but insofar as they recognize a common humanity and consequent presumption of equality of conditions. The freedom to transfer must be weighed against the great inequalities created by it precisely in the name of the moral equality and autonomy of all individuals, so that they may be autonomous and capable of realistically framing meaningful life plans.

Nozick assumes in this last argument that his principles of entitlement apply in the Robinson Crusoe case or in a state of nature, and he cannot see why living in a society changes anything. My view is that no moral principles whatsoever would apply in a truly asocial context—in a real state of nature property would be seized when the opportunity arose, or rather it would make no sense to talk of property. Nozick has not succeeded in deriving a natural right to property, and admits difficulties in Locke's account. When such a right is determined within a social context by the choice of rules of acquisition and transfer, these will be relative to a balancing of moral values within the whole community. And if these are to be moral rules, they must be capable of being chosen by all from a position of equality, or capable of being willed by one who places himself in all possible conditions. These amount to the same constraints and are present in Kant's system, to which Nozick appeals, no less than in Rawls's, the target of his attack.

It might be replied one final time that I still have not done justice to the distinction between maximizing satisfaction of rights and absolutely prohibiting their violation, between an end-state moral system and a system with what Nozick terms "side constraints." Granted that a redistributive system will maximize satisfaction of Kant's principles, given that under it fewer will be in need and more will be able to formulate meaningful life plans, do *we* as members of a moral community or state have the right to interfere with the free activity (spending or saving) of some in order to realize this situation? Do we have a right to force it upon the wealthy? A negative answer would first of all assume that taxation is equivalent to treating others as means, which I questioned above. On a deeper level, I admitted above the intelligibility of the distinction between the two types of moral system, but not the rationality of accepting the "side constraint" type. To refuse to violate the absolute freedom of those who fail to recognize the rights of others arising from basic needs, is to press the distinction between positive and negative duties to an irrational point. It amounts here to a refusal to assume responsibility for an unjust state of affairs when the means to alter it are known. Finally, the abridgment of freedom involved in redistributive taxation is no more a violation of rights than is that involved in the prohibition against stealing, given that the right to the satisfaction of basic needs in an affluent society is as basic as the right to property.

One not inconsistent way in which considerations of equality or equity operate is through the operation of end-state principles in placing constraints on more specific rules of acquisition and transfer. Nozick sometimes writes, however, as if all end-state principles were incompatible with all rules of transfer or exchange which allow a reasonable degree of freedom in those activities. His reasoning here is that any distributive pattern that momentarily satisfied the end-state principle would be upset by any further free exchanges of money for services, for example, exchanges that would no longer leave the participants with the relative assets they had before. Nozick is guilty in this point of a straw-man fallacy, since no serious theory of justice, and certainly not Rawls's, demands a fixed pattern in final or current time-slice distributions, nor does any theory measure the justice of such distributions only according to their approximations to such patterns. If Rawls's difference principle were applied in this way to given patterns of held assets at a single time, it would be trivially equivalent to the demand for complete equality, since the maximization of each possible worst-off group at a single time would require making all equal (or, if we take the maximization of the actual worst-off group, the principle would demand switches whenever applied between worst off and best off at the extremes). It is clearly not meant to be applied in this way, but is intended for use at the level of designing basic institutions for society, when choosing rules of acquisition and transfer, for example, to guide future exchanges and property rights. According to its application at this level, extensive free exchange would undoubtedly be allowed (as it is under the most controlled economies), since such exchanges generally raise utility levels for both parties, worse as well as better off. Thus although basic institutions are to aim at a certain pattern in their design, the principles expressing this are self-defeating when applied to current time-slice distributions. The fact that principles are to apply to institutional design but not to results or instantiations of that design is similar to the familiar distinctions between rule and act utilitarianism, rule and act egoism, etc. Considerations are applied at different levels not necessarily in virtue of some independently discoverable features of the levels (for which Nozick apparently seeks), but for the simpler reason that application at the more general level alone yields results in accord with moral intuitions against which the theory is to be tested.

To return to the relation of free exchange to end-state theories of distributive justice, none of the arguments I have put forward precludes the desirability of this universal institution as it operates within somewhat redistributive systems. No reasonable theory would prevent a person from spending money to see Wilt Chamberlain play basketball (Nozick's example), even though Wilt already has more money than his fans. I have not ruled out allowing a person to spend *all* his money on watching basketball, and am inclined to say that he deserves to starve if he should do so. I question only whether his children deserve to starve as well, whether we are not justified in requiring Chamberlain to give back a portion of his earnings beyond material needs and wants (no more would be required for truly redistributive purposes) to prevent such tragic occurrences.

To summarize: Nozick's principles of free acquisition and transfer rely upon his tacit claim that they alone accord with Kant's injunction to recognize the autonomy of individuals and not to use some as means to others' welfare; but he fails to show either that limited forced redistribution of wealth violates this injunction or that a system in which some prosper partly through the production and collective consumption of those in need does not. His equation of redistributive taxation with forced labor is artificial, and he fails to recognize the implications of entering into a moral community with others. The recognition of the moral equality of others generates a presumption of equality of conditions which constrains the choice of rules of transfer and exchange, and renders consistent and morally necessary in this choice the balancing of freedom with end-state goals like equality or social welfare. Brilliant and provocative philosophizing often occurs at the extremes in philosophical positions, for example, libertarian and egalitarian. It is the less spectacular and easier lot of some of us, having been provoked, to point out occasionally that truth or rightness lie somewhere between.

NOTES

1. *Anarchy, State, and Utopia* (New York: Basic Books, 1974).

2. Kant sees the duty to beneficence as imperfect, which means that (according to him) there is no duty to give specific amounts to specific individuals in need. I am not claiming here that Kant himself recognizes a right of individuals to have specific basic needs satisfied, but only that such a right can plausibly be generated from the Kantian moral point of view (furthermore, that this is more plausible than the attempt to generate an absolute right to property from that fundamental moral viewpoint).

28

Is Ignoring Global Warming Wrong?

Traxler and His Critics

The International Panel on Climate Change—the UN body that shared the 2007 Nobel Peace Prize with former Vice President Al Gore for work on researching and publicizing global warming—recently issued its 2007 assessment report. In the *Summary for Policymakers* (available as a download from its Web site http://www.ipcc.ch/) the panel makes several disturbing claims, among them the following:

> Warming of the climate system is unequivocal, as is now evident from observations of increases in global average air and ocean temperatures, widespread melting of snow and ice, and rising global average sea level. (p. 1)
>
> Most of the observed increase in globally-averaged temperatures since the mid-20th century is *very likely* due to the observed increase in anthropogenic GHG (Green House Gas) concentrations. It is *likely* there has been significant anthropogenic warming over the past 50 years averaged over each continent (except Antarctica). (p. 6)

The report details various likely effects of global warming on the world's ecosystems, food supply, water supply, the prevalence of disease, and the general impact of these on human and animal welfare. What, if any, are our moral obligations in the light of the likely impact of GHG emissions, and how can those obligations best be met?

In the featured article of this chapter, Martino Traxler argues that because warming will impose significant hardships on future generations and because global warming is caused by GHG emissions, the present generation has a moral obligation to limit and control its GHG emissions. This problem has a structure that will be familiar to anyone who has some acquaintance with game theory. It is an instance of the *Tragedy of the Commons*, which itself is an instance of the *Prisoners' Dilemma*. The latter gets its name from the following story. Suppose two suspects have been brought in for questioning in relation to some crime. Each can deny that he played any part in the crime, or each can admit complicity and testify against the other. They are put into separate cells, and the district attorney offers both the following deal. If you don't rat on the other guy, and he doesn't rat on you, you will both be put into prison for two years on some minor charge. But if you rat, and he doesn't, then you will get off scot-free, and he will go to jail for twenty years. On the other hand, if he rats and you don't, then he will get off scot-free, and you will go to jail for twenty years. If you both rat, then you will both go to jail for eighteen years. What is it in your interest to do if you are a suspect and you want to minimize your own prison sentence? You cannot control whether the other guy rats or not. If he rats, then you are better off ratting yourself (eighteen years in jail as opposed to twenty). If he doesn't rat, then you are also better off ratting (you get zero years in jail as opposed to two). So either way you will be better off ratting. But he can reason in exactly the same manner. So he is better off ratting as well. If you both do what maximizes your own interests, then you both will end up in jail for eighteen years. On the other hand, if neither of you had ratted, if neither had done what was in your own individual self-interest, then you both would have been much better off (two years in jail). A prisoners' dilemma arises whenever you find yourself in as situation in which if you and someone else cooperate in some way a relatively good situation will come about. But you each will do better individually if you defect while the other cooperates, and you each will do worse individually if you cooperate while the other defects.

The tragedy of the commons is a prisoners' dilemma writ large. Suppose there is a common resource (e.g., fish in the sea) to which we all have access. Perhaps the fish population is sustainable up to one fish per person per day. So if no one catches more than one fish per day, everyone will eat well. Perhaps there is some spare capacity in the supply. Some people could catch two fish a day without impacting sustainability. If you catch two fish and sell one, then you not only eat well but also have some extra cash in your pocket. However, suppose that if a significant number of people catch two fish per day, overfishing will result, and the resource will eventually be depleted, and you all will go hungry. Each person stands to gain if others do the cooperative thing (limit themselves to one fish per day) while he takes an extra fish. But each person also stands to gain by taking an extra fish even if others are not doing the cooperative thing. If the fish population is going to be depleted anyway, you may as well eat now and pocket the extra cash. So everyone has a reason to overfish, and so everyone, acting in his own individual self-interest, will end up contributing to global hunger.

People in this kind of situation may well have a *moral* obligation to do the cooperative thing (e.g., limit themselves to one fish per day) even though it is in the interests of each to defect (take more than his fair share). Morality here seems to conflict with individual self-interest. In practice, we try to solve these problems by giving people incentives to do the morally right thing. We do this by changing the payoffs for cooperation and defection. For example, we institute a system of fishing quotas and punish those who exceed them. But this, of course, requires an institution with the authority to impose a quota system and the power to punish those who violate it. If the fish population lives in waters that are not under the authority of any governing body, then it is difficult to see how the problem of overfishing can be avoided.

With this background in mind, we can now see how GHG emissions constitute a global tragedy of the commons in which the actors are not individuals but rather nation-states. Each nation-state stands to gain economically by emitting more and more GHGs, regardless of what others do. However, if everyone emits more and more GHGs, global warming will result with all its attendant deleterious effects for all nations. Nations may well have a moral obligation to curb their emissions, but typically nations act in their own interests without regard for moral considerations. And there is no supranational body, no world government, with the authority and the power to align the motivations of nation-states with their moral obligations. Nevertheless, nations sometimes do agree to cooperate in situations like these if they perceive other nations to be carrying out their share of the burdens of cooperation. The Kyoto Treaty was an attempt to get an agreement among nations to bring GHG emissions down. But as is well known, when George W. Bush became the president of the largest GHG emitter in the world—the United States—he refused to sign, on the grounds that the treaty required no sacrifices on the part of developing nations (like China and India) but did require substantial sacrifices on the part of developed nations. He was in effect arguing that the allocation of emissions quotas that the treaty required was not "fair."

Traxler argues that to have a chance at succeeding in reducing GHG emissions, any agreement will have to allocate the burdens of emissions reductions in a way that is perceived to be reasonably fair to all the parties. Only if the allocation of burdens is seen as fair will nations have the motivation to forgo the benefits of exceeding their quotas and be able to bring moral pressure on uncooperative nations to abide by their quota. One apparently fair way of allocating the burden would be to assign a fixed per capita emissions limit on all. But that would mean that nations like the United States (with 5 percent of the world's population emitting about 23 percent of the world's GHGs) would have to make extremely painful adjustments, while those with a relatively low per capita output (like India and China) would have to make few or no adjustments in the short to medium term. Traxler argues that this allocation has no chance of succeeding because the developed nations, which bear all the burdens of adjustment, will perceive it to be unfair. He argues that instead each nation should be required to bear an equal share of the burdens of reduction and that the way to implement this is to require that each nation pay an equal share of the *opportunity costs*. It follows that emission reductions with a very low opportunity cost would be the first to be undertaken (presumably those that involve the production of luxuries) and that those with the highest opportunity cost (presumably those that involve the production of necessities) would be last.

In his response, Stephen Gardiner points out that (as Traxler himself acknowledges) this allocation ignores the past history of GHG emissions and the contribution that the developed nations have made to the existing problem. This will not be perceived as resulting in a fair distribution of burdens by those who played little or no role in the cause of the problem. He also argues that requiring equal opportunity costs of both rich and poor nations alike means that the poor nations may have to make cuts in already low standards of living while the rich merely have to give up various luxuries. That won't be perceived as fair. However, if the measurement of opportunity costs is arranged so that it does not have this consequence, then it will have the consequence that richer nations will have to make very substantial adjustments before poorer nations have to make any adjustments at all. Either way, it will be perceived by one group or another as "unfair."

QUESTIONS FOR CONSIDERATION

• Traxler draws a distinction between the *justice* of various allocations and the *fairness* of those allocations. In what is this distinction grounded? How do just allocations differ from fair allocations? Do you think that (in Traxler's sense) justice or fairness is the more important consideration in allocating burdens? If justice is to be given any weight at all, is Traxler's proposal defensible?

• Is Traxler arguing that his proposal for distributing burdens is the fairest one, and hence the morally right distribution, or is he arguing that it is the distribution that has the best chance of succeeding given current circumstances? Is there any connection between these two claims?

- Traxler argues that nations should share equal burdens as measured by the opportunity costs of forgoing emissions. Why does he think that opportunity costs are not accurately measured by the price of the goods that would be forgone? How should opportunity costs be measured?
- Traxler argues that certain GHG emissions should be exempt from any reduction in any distribution of burdens. What are those? Can you think of circumstances in which those kinds of emissions should be reduced?
- Do some peoples have a right to more GHG emissions than others? For example, do we in the United States have a right to use more energy, per capita, than people in, say, China, in order to maintain our lifestyle? What could endow us with such a right? For example, do those who live in very cold or very hot climates have a right to use more energy than those who live in more temperate climates?
- Gardiner argues that Traxler's proposal would not, in fact, be welcomed as more fair than the Kyoto Treaty by developed countries like the U.S. Why?

FURTHER READING

Caney, Simon. "Cosmopolitan Justice, Rights and Global Climate Change." *Canadian Journal of Law and Jurisprudence* 19, no. 2 (July 2006): 255–78.

DeSombre, Elizabeth R. "Global Warming: More Common Than Tragic." *Ethics and International Affairs* 18, no. 1 (2004): 41–46.

Gardiner, Stephen M. "The Global Warming Tragedy and the Dangerous Illusion of the Kyoto Protocol." *Ethics and International Affairs* 18, no. 1 (2004): 23–39.

———. "The Real Tragedy of the Commons." *Philosophy & Public Affairs* 30 (2001): 387–416.

Shue, Henry. "Environmental Change and the Varieties of Justice," in *Earthly Goods: Environmental Change and Social Justice*, eds. Fen Osler Hampson and Judith Reppy (Ithaca, N.Y.: Cornell University Press, 1996), pp. 9–29.

Singer, Peter. "One Atmosphere," in *One World: The Ethics of Globalization* (New Haven: Yale University Press, 2004), pp. 14–87.

MARTINO TRAXLER

Fair Chore Division for Climate Change

A hitherto neglected way of dividing chores fairly offers the best likelihood of promoting international cooperation in dealing with the problem of global climate change. The largest obstacle to international cooperation in this matter is, arguably, the problem of allocation—how to divide among nations the costs or chores of climate change mitigation and adaptation. The difficulties of this allocation problem are compounded by the absence of an overseeing supra-national authority with the power to police and enforce any agreement that the nations of the world may reach. Allocation according to a fair chore division into equally burdensome shares best promotes international cooperation in the absence of such an overseeing authority. Still, for all

Martino Traxler, "Fair Chore Division for Climate Change," *Social Theory and Practice* Vol. 28, No. 1 (2004). Department of Philosophy, Florida State University.

its practical advantages, this approach to the allocation problem remains morally problematic for neglecting past iniquities and bringing only partial remedy to present and future iniquities arising from climate change.

... I review what I take to be the strongest grounds for our having moral obligations to deal with climate change. Given that it is highly likely that climate change will cause serious distress to large portions of the future human population, all those who can do something about it are under an obligation to deal with this threat to future humanity. Our obligation comes from two sorts of universal moral duties: a duty of non-maleficence—not doing wrongful harm to others—and a duty to assist those who need help in order to avoid harm and suffering. These two universal duties give rise to two distinct strains of moral argument for our having obligations to deal with climate change and they each support different ways of allocating the chores and costs of climate change adaptation or mitigation. Violations of duties of non-maleficence give rise to obligations to compensate for or rectify the maleficence for which one is responsible. Obligations of assistance, instead, fall equally on all who can help those who will otherwise suffer. Because of this, these last obligations are better suited to equitable or fair allocations or chore divisions. Thus there are grounds for resolving the problem of allocation according to two different principles—a principle of responsibility and a principle of equitable or fair allocation.

I evaluate the merits of different approaches to the allocation problem in the second part of the paper. I argue for the practical superiority of a chore division into equally burdensome shares. I then consider the iniquities left unanswered by this approach as well as some difficulties that would arise in implementing this solution to the allocation problem. ...

1. Why Should We Worry About Dealing with Climate Change?

Is the present human population (or a subset thereof) under some moral obligation to do something about the future effects of climate change induced by global warming from anthropogenic greenhouse gas emissions? Yes—on two counts. First, if past and current emissions will harm humans of future generations, then those who made those emissions may be responsible for causing this harm. Those responsible would then bear obligations toward the future potential victims of this harm. The second count does not turn on moral responsibility for what one has done. It rests, instead, on the recognition that we have duties to help others avoid harm, that is, that we have duties not to let harm happen to them, particularly when we can do something about it and they cannot and will not be able to do so.

The stronger argument for saying that at least some of the present generation has a moral duty to deal with predicted climate change is the first, responsibility-based argument: we, the present human generation (or parts thereof), owe assistance to future humans for presently and knowingly violating our duties of non-maleficence toward future human beings. Duties of non-maleficence are duties to not bring about (whether by act or omission) bad results to others, unless our ignorance of doing so is non-culpable. These are duties to not bring about a worsening of the condition of others. Duties of non-maleficence range in moral stringency from the most stringent duties not to bring about physical harm or damage to others to the less stringent duty not to cause mere displeasure to others. The duty not to bring about physical harm or damage to others, I assume, is among our most stringent moral duties. So violating this duty is among the worst things we can do, morally speaking, to future human generations (among others). This means that, other things being equal, when we violate this duty, our subsequent duties to make amends for our violation are also among our most stringent duties. That is why this is the strongest or most compelling moral argument for having duties to deal with climate change from global warming.

This duty of non-maleficence is, moreover, a universal duty, which means that distance, whether spatial or temporal, does not directly affect the stringency of the duty. (Of course, even though this duty of non-maleficence is equally stringent for all, we may have other moral obligations that may counterbalance or outweigh it, so that the all-things-considered stringency of our duty to not harm particular people may be correspondingly weakened.) Rectificatory or compensatory duties arising from a violation of non-maleficence, however, are not universal—they invest only those responsible for the violation.

Thus, in order to establish the existence of obligations from either line of argument sketched above, one must establish that harm will occur from climate changes caused by global warming caused by anthropogenic greenhouse gas emissions, unless something is done. Establishing that much and establishing that we can only be culpably ignorant of these dire predictions are sufficient to establish that we have the weaker or less stringent duties to help future people to avoid this harm. In order to establish the more stringent duty from responsibility we must show that we are morally responsible for violating our duty of non-maleficence. Proving this responsibility, in turn, requires showing that we are inflicting suffering on future generations, that we know that we are doing so, and that we are not otherwise excused for doing so—in particular, that our actions are not excused by our intending to avoid either harm or comparable suffering to ourselves (or to still other intermediate generations). I will assume that these conditions, when persuasively established, are also sufficient to show responsibility for this maleficence.

Are harmful climate changes predicted for future generations? They certainly seem to be. The Intergovernmental Panel on Climate Change (IPCC) has reached a scientific near-consensus for the claim that anthropogenic emissions of greenhouse gases (GHGs) will cause climate change from global warming. The IPCC has also expressed something close to this near-consensus for the claim that this global warming will lead to disruptive, frequently devastating climate changes that are predicted to result in much human distress, including physical harm, unless something (sometimes a great deal) is done beforehand. . . .

Although the conclusion that suffering will ensue is neither certain nor even as highly probable as that some climate changes or other will occur, still, the relatively small measure of uncertainty surrounding the potential for harm from our greenhouse gas emissions does not excuse our present inactivity. For it seems quite clear that we are morally required to prepare for this occurrence at least in proportion to its likelihood. Since that likelihood is great enough, it places us under enough of a moral obligation that we should acknowledge that we ought to act.

On to the next point: are we *aware* that we are inflicting suffering on future generations or is our apparent maleficence excused on grounds of ignorance? This question assumes that ignorance, or non-culpable ignorance anyway, would exonerate us from responsibility for the harm caused by our emissions. This assumption is highly questionable. But even if we assume that non-culpable ignorance exonerates, the conclusions of the IPCC and of other scientific bodies, and the play they have had in the media, should lead us to conclude that what ignorance exists of the possibility of climate change and of its potentially dire consequences can only be considered culpable ignorance—ignorance that does not excuse our responsibility. . . .

We may argue—as scientists and economists, among others, do—about how much future suffering we may be inflicting; but we cannot plausibly argue that we are unaware that we are most likely causing some serious future suffering. So we are not relieved of our responsibility either to help future humans avoid harm, or for our maleficence in causing them harm. . . .

If we are acting maleficently and if we are not excused by our ignorance, then are we morally obligated to act on account of our maleficence? Not necessarily: even if we are responsible for a maleficent result, we may still not violate a duty of non-maleficence when we are properly excused for the resulting maleficence. Are we excused somehow for knowingly inflicting this suffering on future generations? Arguably, not having any choice in the matter would excuse this maleficence. Matters of logical or nomological necessity—of literally not being able to do otherwise—would count as having no choice in the matter and therefore excuse us. Assuming that this is not the case, one may still reasonably argue that certain options among which we can choose are so rationally compelling as to count as excusing or *rationally forced choices*. Rationally forced choices are matters of social or physiological necessity. Social necessity amounts to what a society needs or finds indispensable in order to survive; physiological necessity is a matter of what is needed or indispensable in order for the members of a society to survive (barring illness or age, etc.) or in order for them to live at some minimally acceptable level of health, say, at which they are able to avoid enduring physiological harm or damage. When socially or physiologically necessary options, as rationally compelling options, are maleficent, they are excusably maleficent. Thus those emissions that are rationally compelling or indispensable emissions are excusably maleficent.

These socially or physiologically indispensable emissions—what Henry Shue[1] calls "subsistence emissions"—are excusably maleficent because they present their potential emitters with such a hard choice between avoiding a harm today or avoiding a harm in the future. Where the choice is hard enough to make, either option may be permitted and may excuse us from not opting for the alternative. For where the present harm from not emitting is conspicuous enough, we would be unrealistic, unreasonable, and maybe even irrational to expect present people to allow present harm and suffering to visit them or their kith and kin in order that they might avoid harm to future people far less closely related to them. In these cases, we may with good reason speak of having so strong or so rationally compelling a reason to emit that, in spite of the harm these emissions will cause to (future) others, we are excused for our maleficence. Much like self-defense may excuse the commission of an injury and even a murder, so their necessity for our subsistence may excuse our indispensable current emissions and the resulting future infliction of harm they cause. Subsistence emissions are emissions we cannot reasonably be expected not to make, because they are rationally compelling emissions, and we are excused for making them.

Another way of reaching the same conclusion is to state our duties of non-maleficence as duties not to inflict unnecessary suffering on others. The suffering of others may be unnecessary in at least two ways: it may not be necessary for others to suffer (we could do something to prevent their suffering) or, in the case that interests us here, it may not be necessary *for*

us to inflict suffering on others in order to avoid greater, equal, or probably even some lesser measure of suffering to ourselves. I have proposed that subsistence emissions are rationally compelling emissions because they are socially or physiologically indispensable emissions, that is, roughly, because these emissions are necessary for us to make in order to subsist.

To some, this argument for complete exoneration from responsibility for future harm for currently indispensable emissions may seem excessive. They will argue that even maleficence excused by necessity may still give rise to compensatory or rectificatory obligations on the part of those whose actions harm others, even if their performance of the action is excused. It seems correct to hold those emitting greenhouse gases (especially if they know that they are (most likely) causing harm to others in the future) to be morally obligated to do what they can to minimize the damage caused by their presently indispensable emissions or to make some sort of reparation for the harm they have caused, even when the indispensability of these emissions leaves the emitters no choice but to emit. So it seems that while those rationally compelled to emit gases that are likely to cause damage in the future may be excused for their emissions, they may still, perhaps, owe some compensatory obligations to those who will be harmed in the future.

It seems clear that subsistence emissions present the strongest case for being fully excused. But what about our *dispensable* emissions? What about those emissions without which we would have been less well off, but whose absence would not have brought upon us any such harm as long-term physical or psychological damage or debilitation? Insofar as these emissions are not, strictly-speaking, indispensable or subsistence emissions, their maleficence is not excused.

This conclusion is most obvious for straightforward *luxury emissions*—emissions produced to furnish goods and services that are luxuries. These luxury emissions are expendable or unnecessary, save perhaps for their status-conferring nature. If we reasonably expect (as we do) that these emissions will contribute to inflicting unnecessary suffering, then, excluding ignorance and excusing circumstances (as we do), these emissions are inexcusably maleficent. If they are inexcusably maleficent, then they are the emissions that we have obligations to omit or reduce as a matter of justice.

Of course, much of our emissions (in developed countries) fall somewhere in the middle—between the extremes of luxury and necessity. Should all these in-between emissions be treated the same way? Are only maleficent subsistence emissions excused or are all non-luxury emissions excused? It seems more reasonable to draw the line of excusable maleficence somewhere in between luxury and necessity. Perhaps we should hold that only subsistence and suitably defined near-subsistence emissions are excused on the grounds that they are the only emissions that we are rationally compelled to produce. An argument for drawing the line at near-subsistence emissions runs thus: they are the only emissions allowed by our duty of non-maleficence if it is correct to add that there is a priority to not harming those near or dear to us over not causing similar harm to strangers. Thus we can reasonably draw the line of excusable maleficent emissions at near-subsistence emissions.

An alternative way to settle this question of which maleficent emissions are excused is to hold that emissions become progressively more excusable as we move from inexcusable luxury emissions to fully excused subsistence emissions. One relatively familiar way to add some definition or particulars to this approach would be to suppose that our duties of non-maleficence are based on a fundamental concern to promote the least suffering or harm overall (over time). In this case, we could hold that the only infliction of suffering that is permitted is an infliction that still results in an improvement overall (over time) in this regard. Thus, all and only those emissions made today that avoid more suffering for us than they will produce for others in the future are morally permissible. So, in line with a view expressed by Peter Singer writing about famine relief,[2] we might say that if we were truly non-maleficent, we ought to refrain from all emissions that create more suffering to others in the future than they spare us today. What part of our current emissions is this? I do not know but I'll wager that it is a substantial part of the GHG emissions of developed nations.

The long and short of this excursion into matters of maleficence is that it is likely that a great deal of the world's current greenhouse gas emissions, at least in developed countries, are inexcusably maleficent because they are luxury emissions, or the least indispensable emissions. If emissions are maleficent, then we are morally obligated to refrain from making these emissions. If we emit greenhouse gases maleficently, then we are responsible for the future suffering that they will cause and we are obligated to do what we can to minimize this suffering. Here, then, is the source of our stronger obligation regarding climate change. Here also is the key to determining which emissions are most excusable: those that will avoid harm—subsistence emissions, above all. . . .

The foregoing conclusion—that we, the unexcused maleficent greenhouse gas emitters, ought to worry about the effects of climate change and that it is our collective responsibility to do something about this risk—should come as no great surprise. It is a conclusion that most politicians appear to have accepted, most notably in agreeing to the United Nations Framework Convention on Climate Change, in May 1992. . . .

Politicians of the world, however, have agreed to much less about how to deal with climate change. . . .

By "dealing with climate change" I mean that it is in our power to do some of both of the following:

(1) *mitigate* harmful climate change by reducing our GHG emissions (that is, deal with the cause as the Kyoto Protocol envisions);
(2) *adapt* to predicted harmful climate change caused by global warming (that is, prepare to deal with the effects of climate change). . . .

Several considerations have prevented nations and their political leaders both from actively dealing with climate change—whether by pursuing their Kyoto Protocol goals or by other means—and from even agreeing to act in concert with other nations. First of all, short-term national interests and the interests of national leaders have tempered the dictates of long-term prudence or morality. Emissions reductions are a hard sell for politicians of any stripe because they are costly. Reductions in greenhouse gas emissions generally require reductions in energy consumption, which, in turn, result in reductions in economic activity and in national and per capita earnings, which, almost invariably, make the government itself less popular.

Scientists are also uncertain about the precise changes in weather patterns that we should expect from global warming. More importantly, perhaps, many economists and others disagree about what should be done to adapt to this harm. For all these reasons, some hesitance to commit to action may be justified by caution or by the understandable fear of making technically unnecessary sacrifices. . . .

Moreover and no less importantly, even assuming politicians all were to agree both *that* something needs to be done and *on* what needs to be done, they would still face a typical problem of collective action here—a problem of cooperation before a commons. . . .

A public good is a good to which many have virtually unrestricted access and which they can enjoy, at a negligible cost, regardless of whether or not they contribute to its maintenance. Some public goods, like the starry skies above, are virtually imperishable (on a human time scale). Most of the public goods that we care about, however, including the nighttime visibility of the stars, are perishable. Typically, our enjoyment of a public good reduces in some measure the enjoyment that we or others can subsequently derive from the good. This occurs, for instance, when one's enjoyment of a finite and non-renewable public good involves some, however slight, irreversible diminution of this good. But even renewable public goods are often perishable goods. For instance, their existence may be threatened by over-use. Many public goods require that we, collectively, devote some energies and resources to their renewal. Other public goods may require that we not use them up faster than they can renew themselves.

All such public goods are *commons* when, for each relevant agent with low-cost, virtually free access to the good, the choice of whether to contribute to its maintenance or renewal or the choice to refrain from enjoying the public good has the payoffs of a Prisoners' Dilemma (PD). Choices with the payoffs of a PD are those for which these two conditions hold:

1) it is in the interest of each agent that the public good not be exhausted so that each agent would prefer that everyone contribute to its maintenance (or refrain . . .), that is, that all *cooperate* rather than that no one contribute to it, that is to say, that everyone *defect* or free-ride,

but 2) it is more in the interest of each agent, or rational for each agent, to *defect*, that is, to not contribute to the maintenance of this good (or not refrain . . .), regardless of what others choose to do. (The choice to defect is said to rationally *dominate* the alternative of cooperating.)

The typical fate of a commons is a "tragedy" in which each individual's rational choice to defect brings about a collective setback in the exhaustion or destruction of the public good from which all or many previously could benefit. To name but one sort of example, this tragedy is one we have come close to achieving by overfishing several fish and whale populations.

What is to be done about preserving a commons? In many cases, the maintenance of public goods that are commons can be ensured by altering the payoffs of this choice so that they are no longer the payoffs of a commons. This result can be achieved by altering the payoffs that agents face so as to make it rational for everyone (or for enough agents) to cooperate, that is, to contribute to maintaining the public good in question (or to reduce the use of the good so that it has time to renew itself). An adequate interest in cooperating in the maintenance of a public good may be achieved through the addition of inducements to cooperation, for instance, in the form of monetary rewards. More often, however, it is easier or more effective to employ coercive measures in order to increase either the costs of enjoying the good or the (expected) costs of defection or free-riding (for instance, by means of fines, etc.). Increasing the costs of enjoying the good typically occurs by enforcing restrictions on the enjoyment of the good. . . .

There are important public goods, however, for which neither inducements to cooperation nor coercive restrictions of access are advisable or practically feasible. This happens when, for instance, no overseeing authority can be trusted either to disburse inducements fairly or to properly enforce the sanctions threatened for defection. Such conditions presently obtain among the nations of the world that do not wish to grant international organizations, such as the United Nations, adequate independent enforcement muscle of their own in the form of an army or a police force, or of courts able to impose their own jurisdiction and judgments on states. . . .

The problem of dealing with the likely harmful effects of climate change from global warming presents just such a commons. In this case, the public good is constituted by our current global weather patterns. For, much as we may enjoy maligning the weather we experience, we still prefer it to the globally warmer weather patterns we are collectively bringing about. The costs of maintaining this global public good are whatever it would take for the current and future population of the earth to prevent the changes in these weather patterns or else what it would take to deal with the changes effectively so that the living conditions of those affected populations were not worsened by climate changes. Climate change presents a commons precisely because, on the one hand, it is in each person's or each nation's interest that our climate patterns not be negatively affected by our greenhouse gas emissions while, on the other hand, it is in each person's or nation's interest to let others bear the burdens or costs of preserving this global good.

Thus, even if action against climate change today is thought worthwhile in the long run, its costs are such that each national government would rather see other nations take action while it avoids, as far as possible, making any such costly commitments. . . .

As if these prudential grounds were not enough, nations may also claim moral grounds of justice or fairness for hesitating or refusing to contribute to dealing with climate change. I will discuss these below in considering the question of how the collective chore of dealing with climate change should be divided.

Just how much harm and suffering the damage from climate change causes is, to an important extent, up to us to determine in how we adapt to the predicted effects of climate change. Since we have moral obligations not to harm people, then, insofar as it is in our power not to harm others inexcusably, we have moral obligations to deal with climate change that is so likely to cause harm. This realiza-

tion leads me to rephrase the previous conclusion and hold that we should heed the more sanguine reactions of many economists and conclude that a great deal of the world's current greenhouse gas emissions will prove inexcusably maleficent unless we do enough to deal with their maleficence—by mitigation or otherwise adapting to it. . . .

In the rest of this paper, I assume that the nations of the world can come to some agreement, or perhaps that a majority of its atmospheric scientists can come to some consensus, about what needs to be done to deal with this problem. With this assumption in hand we can ask, "How then should nations divide up this global bill—whatever it turns out to be—for mitigating the effects of climate change and for adapting to its effects?"

2. HOW TO SPLIT THE BILL FOR DEALING WITH CLIMATE CHANGE?

Dealing with the problem of climate change involves abating and adapting. Abatement involves reducing emissions of greenhouse gases; adapting, instead, involves preparing in other ways for those climate changes that we do not expect to get around to abating. Adaptation is a cost, since resources that could have been used otherwise must be put aside or invested in adaptation. Abatement, too, is a cost. Reducing emissions typically involves forgoing those goods whose production involves emissions as a by-product. . . . Similar considerations are true of investments made in the sequestration of carbon dioxide in trees and other plants. Since all measures requiring investments can be divided up among nations, they are all matters for chore division.

If a cap in global emissions is set, then shares of these emissions can be allocated to various countries through a system of permits. This is the so-called allocation problem. Dealing with global warming forces us to confront problems of allocation and problems of chore division. Since both these sorts of problems can be solved according to the same principles, I will deal with them together in what follows.

I group the principal proposals made for the allocation or chore division into two—just proposals and fair proposals. This grouping highlights several differences in the moral concerns that the two sorts of proposals attempt to address. I also argue for the adoption of a fair division into equally burdensome shares because it offers the best prospects of success at promoting international cooperation in mitigation and adaptation. I conclude with some considerations about how to measure burden-someness.

The distinction I adopt between just and fair proposals is, to some degree, a matter of expository convenience. The point of the distinction is to serve as a reminder that some proposals call for allocating according to backward-looking or historical rectificatory principles while other proposals appeal to forward-looking principles for the promotion of well-being. The just principles are mainly principles of rectificatory justice intended to restore an acceptable moral order that past actions had disturbed. In contrast to these just principles stand fair principles of chore division and allocation. These are forward-looking principles. They do not take account of past behavior or of past benefits or losses accrued, rather, they seek to maintain matters at least as morally acceptable as they are found to be at present in the future. In so doing, forward-looking principles of fair division can be faulted for taking the status quo as morally acceptable. . . .

[P]rinciples of fair division are, for the most part, various ways of trying to divide goods or chores as if each party had equal title or claim to a share of the good or chore in question. For this reason, it will be apparent that principles of fair chore division are intuitively better suited, morally speaking, to divisions of collective chores where each has an equally strong prima facie obligation to contribute, such as, for instance, universal moral obligations of assistance with famine relief.

Principles of fair chore division are intuitively less well suited to collective obligations that are crucially shaped by the history of their formation—for instance, obligations stemming from past violations of other duties, such as duties of non-maleficence. These last duties are intuitively better assigned according to responsibility. Yet even if the industrialized nations' obligations to deal with climate change should be, ideally, divided by responsibility, still we have good practical reasons to divide them fairly instead. The main reason for preferring a fair principle of division to a just one has to do with seeking the best solution to the associated problem of collective action or of commons.

2.1. Just (Backward-Looking) Proposals

In matters of climate change, the following proposals for allocation or chore division have garnered most attention: (i) pay or contribute in proportion to the benefits received from the greenhouse gases (GHGs) emitted; (ii) pay or contribute in proportion to the GHGs emitted (in proportion to responsibility); and (iii) pay or contribute on an equal per capita basis. This third proposal belongs to what I am calling "fairness-based proposals," so I deal with it in the next section. Here I argue that although each of the first two "just" principles is admirable in its own way, neither is a serious candidate for an international chore division for lacking the practical advantages of a (fair) division by equal burdensomeness described in the subsequent section. . . .

A. Pay in Proportion to the Benefits Received from the GHGs Emitted

This principle . . . allots shares in proportion to the benefits derived from the emission of GHGs. . . . This principle is intuitively plausible for placing the burdens of dealing with climate change on those who have most benefited from the very cause of this climate change: the greenhouse gases they have emitted.

This principle, however, also has certain disadvantages. It penalizes the least beneficial GHG emissions just as much as it penalizes the most beneficial emissions if one considers only payments in fixed proportion to the benefits derived, regardless of the quantities of gases emitted to derive them. Applying this principle, in short, offers no incentive to emit GHGs efficiently and so to reduce wasteful emitting. The principle can be adjusted to avoid this drawback to the extent that payments are made proportional to the inefficiency of emissions made. But even this revised principle still has the further considerable defect of not taking into account the relative indispensability of these emissions, in the sense discussed above. In fact, we could reach the morally counterintuitive result that, insofar as indispensable or subsistence emissions bring the greatest benefits, they turn out to be the most heavily costed and penalized by this principle. Besides, if we assume that most GHG emissions have benefited humans to some degree or other, then there will be little practical difference between this principle and the next one, which is, perhaps, the most intuitive principle of all regarding the division of costs of dealing with climate change.

B. Pay in Proportion to the GHGs Emitted, or in Proportion to Responsibility

This principle follows the lead of "polluter pays" principles and reflects, to this extent, the intuitive idea that those whose actions cause harm or disturbance are liable to compensate for or rectify the ill done to those who have been affected. In its crudest form—where nations should pay in proportion to their total historical emissions—this principle, like its crude counterpart for paying according to benefits received, would violate the idea that we can only be responsible for what we were not excusably ignorant of. Since the IPCC was formed in 1988 and since it issued its first report in 1990, we should perhaps limit responsibility to emissions after 1990 and hold that the costs of dealing with climate change should be allotted in proportion to a nation's share of the global greenhouse gas emissions since 1990.

In requiring the developed nations to foot most of the bill for dealing with climate change, this principle recognizes their responsibility in causing the problem. To this extent, this principle reflects our intuitive views about what justice demands. This principle may also further reflect the demands of justice in requiring more from those nations that are relatively better off, especially if we think that they have been made better off by their use of the very energy whose production released these greenhouse gases into the atmosphere. This principle retains the defect of not taking account of the relative indispensability

of these emissions. Subsistence and luxury emissions are costed alike. . . .

C. Pay in Proportion to One's Ability to Pay

This principle is not, strictly speaking, a backward-looking principle. It considers the current state of affairs and divides costs accordingly. For this reason it should not be considered in this section. On the other hand, this principle derives much of its moral plausibility as a principle of cost or chore-division from our awareness of how nations came to have their current ability to pay. This ability results, to a great extent, from economic development which, in turn, resulted from or was, at any rate, accompanied by great greenhouse gas emissions. Thus, this principle, although in theory not a backward-looking principle and so not a just principle, according to my classification, is mentioned here because its supporting arguments are clearly those of the first two principles mentioned above. Only when economic development (and accompanying ability to pay) will have become effectively uncoupled from greenhouse gas emissions should this proposal to pay according to ability to pay be taken under consideration on its own merits.

The point of offering this list of just principles is to show the many ways in which one can reason morally to the conclusion that, as a matter of justice, the developed nations should pay for a lion's share of the bill of dealing with climate change. The developed nations caused the problem, they benefited most from these emissions, they most clearly violated the Lockean proviso to the just taking of goods previously held in common, and they, more than other nations, have the means to pay for the costs of dealing with the problem. So they, above all, should pay for most of dealing with climate change. This much, for instance, seems to be reflected in the Kyoto Protocol's approach, which requires emissions stabilization from only developed countries and eastern European countries "undergoing the process of transition to a market economy."

The largest drawback of adopting any of these just principles of chore or cost division is a practical one. As we have seen, dealing with climate change presents the nations of the world with a commons. Each nation is (let us hope) genuinely concerned with this problem, but each nation is also aware that it is in its interest not to contribute or do its share, regardless of what other countries do. Admittedly, describing the problem this way may exaggerate the negative. For instance, international moral pressure is sometimes able to nudge a nation to conform its behavior to internationally promoted standards. But this is not always true and it is less likely to be true when the costs of contributing or conforming are high, particularly when each nation suspects that every other nation is just as keen to defect as it is. This problem of commons is exacerbated by the awareness that there is no overseeing authority capable of altering the situation so as to coerce contributions or to make contributions cost-effective for each country. In short, in the absence of the appropriate international coercive muscle, defection, however unjust it may be, is just too tempting.

Few are ready to speak what they think in these matters. So it is that some have couched their resistance to sticking to the terms of the Kyoto Protocol on the grounds that this Protocol doesn't deal justly or fairly with the problem. The Protocol is said to be unjust because some developing nations (with the People's Republic of China leading the way) may soon be contributing more to this problem than the currently developed countries will. Some projections indicate that the total emissions of developing nations will exceed those of developed countries in about thirty years, unless these developing nations alter their current course of industrial development. So, by parity of reasoning about justice, these developing nations should be prepared to make similar sacrifices, too, even if this means slowing down their short-term economic development.

Even if the projections for emissions on which the previous argument rests are found to be incorrect, still the Kyoto Protocol is unfair, say some, including U.S. President George W. Bush, since it calls for only the developed countries to act. This division of burdens is obviously unfair and contributes to making the treaty "fatally flawed." The apparent unfairness of the Kyoto Protocol should come as no surprise, since the Protocol itself is clearly the result of the recogni-

tion that the developed nations have been the largest contributors to the problem of climate change. This recognition, moreover, had already been stated in the U.N. Framework Convention on Climate Change. All this makes it difficult not to question the merits of using this obvious "unfairness" to justify withdrawing from the Kyoto Protocol talks, as President Bush did in March 2001. . . .

2.2. The Case for a Fair Chore Division

A. Pay or Contribute on an Equal Per Capita Basis

This is surely the simplest proposal based on grounds of fairness. In this approach, the allotted chores or costs of the global collective effort required to deal with the effects of global warming are allotted to nations based on an equal per capita division for all persons on the globe. So, for instance, each human on our planet would be assigned an equal share of the chore of dealing with climate change. This division could result in each person having to cut back on her or his emissions by the same amount, or it could offer each the same alternatives between cutting back emissions or contributing to some Adaptation Fund of the sort described above. Surely this proposal is unfeasible. If each Chinese and each North American were asked to reduce their emissions in the same amount, when per capita emissions are currently ten times higher in the U.S. than in China, this would impose ridiculously unjust or unfair emissions cutbacks.

Alternatively, if humanity on our planet, as a whole, chooses to cap its emissions—to allow itself to emit only a certain amount of greenhouse gases each year—then this approach of equal per capita division would hold that each person across the globe has an equal emissions entitlement. Each nation, presumably, would then have emission entitlements that are the aggregate of its residents' individual entitlements. The great moral attraction of this per capita entitlement approach is its egalitarian result of not making matters still worse for those who are presently emitting the least (on average) and who are worst off economically.

The main disadvantages of this approach are three. First, like all forward-looking principles of fair division, it does not consider the justice of the present inequalities in emissions or consumption levels. Second, it does not take into account the relative need or indispensability of these emissions. In dividing emissions entitlements into equal per capita shares, the populations of developing countries whose current emissions are very low would suddenly find themselves with emissions rights they cannot use while people of developing countries would be undergoing great reductions in their standard of living to comply with their emissions-rights restrictions. Neither scenario is particularly inviting nor has much hope of ever being politically palatable. One importantly palliative solution for emissions rights would be to allow for trading of these emissions rights, once they have been fairly allotted. This solution, if it were workable, would have the advantage of allowing everyone some time to adjust to their new entitlements. On the other hand, it would still require vast redistributions of income as developed countries rushed in to buy emissions rights from developing countries. It is quite likely that the size of these transfers of wealth and the disruptions they would create would be great enough to doom this proposal by themselves. . . .

These last two drawbacks combine to produce the following realization. Although this principle of per capita division is fair in giving the same thing to each, it is fair only in that sense and that sense need not amount to the last word, or what we care about most, in desiring a fair division of chores or of emissions rights.

What an equal per capita chore division fails to achieve is a division that affects each person in the same way or in the same amount. In particular, a per capita division places equal burdens on each person, but it fails to allot equally burdensome chore-shares, and, in matters of chore division, burdensomeness is the consideration that is closest to our hearts so that an equally burdensome division is deemed the fairest chore division.

The principal reason why we dislike chores is that they burden us by requiring our time, effort, or resources, which we feel we could employ more profitably in other ways. In other words, chores burden us because of the opportunity costs they present, that is, as a function of the difference in expected returns between the course of action under consideration and that course of action, from among those open to us, with the best expected returns for us (including doing nothing).

Thus, if we were to divide chores in the way that treats everyone equally in the sense that (I suggest) matters most to them, then we should be dividing the chore into equally burdensome shares. But how do we do this? What are equally burdensome shares? Insofar as it is the opportunity costs that chores present for us that concern us most, an equally burdensome chore division is one in which each contributor is asked to contribute chores with opportunity costs for her, him, or it (a nation) that are the same as are the opportunity costs of the allotted chores for every other contributor to this collective chore. These considerations lead me to propose another principle of chore division—division into equally burdensome shares.

B. Pay or Contribute in Inverse Proportion to Relative Burdensomeness

The idea here is for the whole collective chore of what is to be done to deal with climate change, whether by mitigation or by adaption, to be divided among the nations of the world into shares such that each nation's share presents the same opportunity costs for that nation as every other nation's share presents for it. There are several important details concerning the nature of the opportunity costs in question that I will address in the next part of the paper. For now I accentuate the positive results of this proposal.

This principle of chore division deals effectively with the defects of the other principles. First, it takes account of indispensability by costing in inverse proportion to burdensomeness, that is, to the opportunity costs associated with either reducing emissions or with setting aside resources for adaptation. The same holds true for financial set-asides for adaptation mechanisms. Projects with the lowest or least beneficial returns for a nation present the lowest opportunity costs and they will be the first to be set aside. Projects with the highest beneficial returns for a nation present the highest opportunity costs and will be the last to be required to be set aside.

Which emissions present highest or lowest opportunity costs? The answer depends on how opportunity costs are measured. If current market prices are used to measure these costs, then forgoing luxury emissions may well present the highest opportunity costs. But if any reasonable measure of human welfare is used instead of market prices, then we can expect luxury emissions to have the lowest opportunity costs and so to be the first to be sacrificed. Subsistence emissions, meanwhile, will have the highest opportunity costs and so will be the last ones to be cut. . . .

Also, because this principle of fair division looks at opportunity costs, it promotes efficiency. For, the more efficient a particular use of greenhouse-gas emissions is, the higher are the opportunity costs of reducing these particular emissions. The higher the opportunity costs are, the less expendable these emissions are. In short, the principle of fair division fares at least as well as the other approaches do on these counts.

To clarify, this principle of division by equal burdensomeness would first require countries to act in those ways whose opportunity costs are lowest. This means that so-called "no-regrets" emissions savings are most encouraged (since they don't really cost anyone anything anyway). Which emissions would go next depends on how these opportunity costs are being estimated. If opportunity costs were measured in monetary amounts, as they are ordinarily measured in project evaluations by economic institutions, then the next emissions cuts would be those with the smallest monetary costs. The danger in this case is that subsistence or near-subsistence emissions might well be called for next, before cuts in luxury emissions are called for. The reason for this would be that cuts in luxury emissions may well cost more (monetarily) than would the more needed subsistence or near-subsistence emissions. Thus an approach that is intended to equalize the burdensomeness of dealing with climate change could easily result in a division which would require cuts in subsistence emissions—the most precious emissions to human well-being—before they require cuts in luxury emissions—the least precious emissions to human well-being. For this reason it is clear that the measure of opportunity

costs must not be the standard currently used in the financial cost/benefit analysis; instead, a measure of opportunity costs in terms of human welfare must be adopted.

If, then, opportunity costs were measured in terms of human welfare, rather than in monetary terms, what cuts would occur next? In this case, presumably, nations with substantial luxury emissions will reduce those next because the opportunity costs in terms of human well-being of these cuts would be lowest. Next, countries with quasi-luxury emissions will be required to cut those next, as they have the next best opportunity costs. The idea is to keep requiring cuts in emissions (or savings for adaptation measures) with progressively greater opportunity costs or burdensomeness (in terms of human well-being) until the global chore of dealing with climate change has been completed with every nation being required to make equally burdensome sacrifices. So it should go in each country.

Can the total of what is needed to deal with the problem of climate change be so great that it will require great sacrifices by poor or developing nations? In this division scheme, every country is required to make sacrifices that are equally burdensome. This means that the opportunity costs for each country are supposed to be the same. This, unfortunately, means that, quite possibly, one (developed) country's aggregate opportunity costs from luxury and near-luxury cuts could be equaled in a developing country only if it makes cuts in near-subsistence emissions. What about cuts in subsistence emissions, proper? These should not be called for, because, as I argued above, when emissions and spending are *rationally compelling*, they are morally excused. This is the point at which this principle of fair division meets the two arguments for our having obligations to deal with climate change: no one and no country can be morally required to make cuts to its subsistence emissions. Besides, it makes no sense to attempt to enforce such cuts anyway.

So, for all its attractions, and even when opportunity costs are measured in terms of human well-being rather than in straightforward monetary terms, this scheme for chore division can weigh more heavily on developing countries than on developed countries, because it may require them to make cuts in near-subsistence emissions. . . .

This principle of contribution in inverse proportion to relative burden-someness has three further advantages. First, because it is not backward-looking—because it does not consider past emitting behavior—it avoids allotting responsibility for their past actions to the various parties in question. It thus avoids a predictable occasion for recrimination and ill will to which such judgments would most likely give rise at international negotiations where national contributions would be apportioned. . . .

In practice, requiring an agreement by which to implement a division into justly proportional shares would amount to holding the question of division hostage to reaching a prior international agreement on what constitutes international distributive justice and on how to compensate for this injustice in this fair division. Since I doubt that such an agreement is likely in our lifetime, I conclude that insisting on this requirement would amount to putting off any implementation concerning climate change indefinitely. That would be a shame, I think. Plain equally burdensome chore division, complicated enough as it is, seems greatly preferable if we want to see anything done at all. *Fiat iustitia, pereat mundus*—let justice be done, even if the world perish—just does not seem to be an especially appealing principle for developing countries who stand to be the first and worst victims of climate change. . . .

The second advantage of this principle of fair division is one that it shares with all principles of fair division. It offers to all a point or position by which to measure the fairness and unfairness of resolutions reached in international bargaining sessions from positions of unequal bargaining strength.[3] I doubt that the nations of the world will easily agree to divvy up the costs of dealing with climate change just as this principle of fair division would tell them to. But insofar as this principle serves to indicate to all what is fair in principle (in this sense of fairness), it should help everyone appreciate the unfairness or iniquity of other bargaining outcomes. That is a morally useful measure to have, I think, especially if it can help weaker nations obtain a fairer deal.

Finally, there is a third and most important reason for preferring this kind of principle of division in the version requiring a division into equally burdensome shares. As I mentioned above, dealing with the adverse consequences of global warming presents nations with a commons-type problem of collective action and, under suitable conditions, an equally burdensome chore division holds the promise of giving each nation no stronger reasons to defect from doing its (fair) share than it gives any other nation. This result, in turn, would place the most moral pressure possible on each nation to do its part. This is a precious result in dealing with problems of commons for which enforcement is impractical, unadvisable, or unacceptable.

What are these suitable conditions? (1) that the terms of this fair division can be made public; (2) that cooperation or defection can be monitored and recorded publicly; (3) that each nation be satisfied that this division is truly an equally burdensome one (or as close to a truly equally burdensome one as can be hoped for in practice).

Under these conditions, the broadcasting of the results of an equally burdensome division and the public monitoring of compliance could prove particularly useful in assuring better cooperation whenever nations wish to avoid public embarrassment and where defecting would prove embarrassing. No nation would have a better excuse for defecting than any other nation had, at least not in terms of what it costs to cooperate. So when the burdensomeness is equal, defecting when others cooperate simply indicates ill will or not wanting to do one's fair share. In this manner, this kind of chore division would place the most moral pressure possible on each nation to do its part. This pressure is the pressure that comes from knowing that each nation's interests are being given equal concern and that defecting means treating one's own condition differently in the absence of better prudential (or non-moral) reasons for doing so. This, I think, is a precious result in dealing with problems of commons for which enforcement is unadvisable or unacceptable. It is an important reason for advocating efforts to "crunch numbers" to make public what such a division would look like. . . .

CONCLUSION

How should the "bill" of dealing with climate change be split up among the nations of the world? I have argued that there are strong practical reasons for agreeing to divide this bill or these chores fairly—into equally burdensome shares—even though the evidence for maleficence and so for a just division according to responsibility is very strong. Since a just treatment of this problem can be expected to lead to international defections in the face of a commons, a fair division into equally burdensome shares is the best solution available for ensuring international cooperation in dealing with climate change.

NOTES

1. Henry Shue, "Subsistence Emissions and Luxury Emissions," *Law and Policy* 15 (1993): 39–59.

2. Peter Singer, "Famine, Affluence, and Morality," *Philosophy & Public Affairs* 1 (1972): 229–43.

3. For concern with the problem of bargaining for a fair agreement under conditions of great inequality, see Henry Shue, "Avoidable Necessity: Global Warming, International Fairness, and Alternative Energy," in Ian Shapiro and Judith Wagner DeCew (eds.), *Theory and Practice* (NOMOS XXXVII) (New York: New York University Press, 1995), pp. 239–64.

Critic

STEPHEN GARDINER

Ethics and Global Climate Change

ALLOCATING FUTURE EMISSIONS

. . . Martino Traxler proposes a "fair chore division" which equalizes the marginal costs of those aiming to prevent climate change. Such a proposal, he claims, is politically expedient, in that it (*a*) provides each nation in the global commons with "no stronger reasons to defect from doing its (fair) share than it gives any other nation" and so (*b*) places "the most moral pressure possible on each nation to do its part" (Traxler 2002, p. 129).

Unfortunately, it is not clear that Traxler's proposal achieves the ends he sets for it. First, by itself, *a* does not seem a promising way to escape a traditional commons or prisoner's dilemma situation. What is crucial in such situations is the magnitude of the benefits of defecting relative to those of cooperating; whether the relative benefits are equally large for all players is of much less importance. Second, this implies that *b* must be the crucial claim, but *b* is also dubious in this context. For Traxler explicitly rules out backward-looking considerations on practical grounds. But this

Stephen Gardiner, "Ethics and Global Climate Change," *Ethics* Vol. 114, No. 3 (2004). Reprinted with the permission of University of Chicago Press.

means ignoring the previous emissions of the rich countries, the extent to which those emissions have effectively denied the less developed countries "their share" of fossil-fuel-based development in the future, and the damages which will be disproportionately visited on the less developed countries because of those emissions. So, it is hard to see why the less developed countries will experience "maximum moral pressure" to comply. Third, equal marginal costs approaches are puzzling for a more theoretical reason. In general, equality of marginal welfare approaches suffer from the intuitive defect that they take no account of the overall level of welfare of each individual. Hence, under certain conditions, they might license taking large amounts from the poor (if they are so badly off anyway that changes for the worse make little difference), while leaving the rich relatively untouched (if they are so used to a life of luxury that they suffer greatly from even small losses). Now, Traxler's own approach does not fall into this trap, but this is because he advocates that costs should be measured not in terms of preferences or economic performance but, rather, in terms of subsistence, near subsistence, and luxury emissions. Thus, his view is that the rich countries should have to give up all of their luxury emissions before anyone else need consider giving up subsistence and near-subsistence emissions. But this raises a new concern. For in practice this means that Traxler's equal burdens proposal actually demands massive action from the rich countries before the poor countries are required to do anything at all (if indeed they ever are). And however laudable, or indeed morally right, such a course of action might be, it is hard to see it as securing the politically stable agreement that Traxler craves, or, at least, it is hard to see it as more likely to do so than the alternatives. So, the equal marginal costs approach seems to undercut its own rationale. . . .

CPSIA information can be obtained at www.ICGtesting.com
Printed in the USA
BVOW09s1605130914

366711BV00002B/3/P